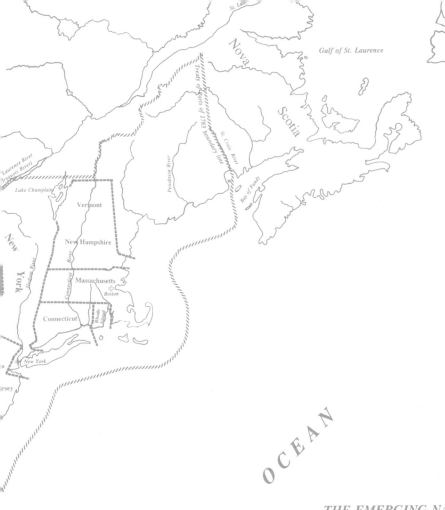

Newfoundland

Gulf of St. Laurence

Nova

Scotia

St. Law.

Treaty of Paris of 1783 boundary line

St. Croix River

Penobscot River

Bay of Fundy

St. Laurence River
(Iroquois River)

Lake Champlain

New

York

Vermont

New Hampshire

Connecticut River

Hudson River

Massachusetts

✠ Boston

Connecticut

Rhode
Island

New York

rsey

OCEAN

THE EMERGING NATION

1783

*United States map showing geographical features as
described in Article II of the Treaty of Paris of 1783—
derived from B. F. Stevens' 1897 Facsimile of "A
Map of the British Colonies of North America . . .
[perpared by] Jno. Mitchell" in 1755. (Source:
Boundary and Claims Commissions and Arbitrations
. . . ls, National Archives, Washington, DC)*

ATLANTIC

E FOR CENTER OF MAP

TE MILES

300   450

The Emerging Nation: A Documentary History
of the
Foreign Relations of the United States
under the
Articles of Confederation, 1780-1789

Mary A. Giunta, Editor-in-Chief and Project Director

J. Dane Hartgrove, Associate Editor

Norman A. Graebner, Peter P. Hill, Lawrence S. Kaplan
Consulting Editors

Richard B. Smith, Project Publication Specialist, 1994

Mary-Jane M. Dowd, Editor and Project Director, 1985-1991

National Historical Publications and Records Commission

1996

The cover illustration is taken from a photograph of the die of the Great Seal of the United States, adopted in 1782 and engraved by Robert Scot of Philadelphia. For further information on the design, adoption, and use of the Great Seal, see Richard S. Patterson and Richardson Dougall, *The Eagle and the Shield: A History of the Great Seal of the United States* (Washington, 1976).

Library of Congress Cataloging-in-Publication Data

The emerging nation: a documentary history of the foreign relations of the United States under the Articles of Confederation, 1780-1789 / Mary A. Giunta, editor in chief; J. Dane Hartgrove, associate editor; Norman A. Graebner, Peter P. Hill, Lawrence S. Kaplan, consulting editors; Richard B. Smith, project publication specialist; Mary-Jane M. Dowd, editor and project director.

1044 pps 150mm x 225mm
Includes bibliographical references and index.
Contents: v. 1. Recognition of independence, 1780-1784 — v. 2. Trials and tribulations, 1780-1785 — v. 3. Toward federal diplomacy, 1780-1789.
ISBN 0-16-048498-7 (vol. 1: alk. paper). — ISBN 0-16-048499-5 (vol. 2: alk. paper). — ISBN 0-16-048500-2 (vol. 3: alk. paper).
1. United States—Foreign relations—1783-1815—Sources. 2. United States—Foreign relations—1775-1783—Sources.
I. Giunta, Mary A. II. Hartgrove, J. Dane. III. Dowd, Mary-Jane M.
E303.E44 1996
327.73'009'033—dc20   96-10279
                                                        CIP

Preface

The Emerging Nation: A Documentary History of the Foreign Relations of the United States under the Articles of Confederation, 1780-1789, traces the battles of John Adams, Benjamin Franklin, John Jay, Thomas Jefferson and others to establish a credible international presence for the United States of America as a new nation.

This is an extraordinary collection of documentary materials brought together from universities, libraries, historical societies, and private organizations, including the National Archives, the Library of Congress, and French, British, and other European repositories. The collection of diplomatic despatches, treaties, private letters, and other documents is an essential record of the formative years of United States diplomacy.

These documents provide teachers and students with a basic reference work. They brim with information and insights valuable to historians, political scientists, government officials, lawyers, and other individuals interested in the development of early United States foreign policy. They provide insight into how a new nation gains diplomatic stature and shapes a foreign policy out of the ashes of war and amidst divergent interests at home and abroad.

The National Historical Publications and Records Commission is proud to present this three-volume documentary record of the beginnings of United States foreign policy.

John W. Carlin
Archivist of the United States
and Chair, National Historical
Publications and Records Commission

General Introduction

> We believe that God has hardened the heart of the
> Pharaoh, so that he cannot let the people go, till the
> first-born of his land are destroyed, 'till the hosts are
> overthrown in the midst of the sea, and till poverty
> and distress like the lice of Egypt shall have covered
> the land.[1]

So declared the first Secretary for Foreign Affairs under the Articles of
Confederation, Robert R. Livingston, in a letter to John Jay as he attacked
King George III's refusal to make peace during the waning days of the
American Revolution. But through diplomatic negotiations peace did come,
a peace that challenged American leaders–John Jay, Benjamin Franklin,
John Adams, Thomas Jefferson, and Livingston, among others–to secure
the new nation, to forge in diplomatic arenas the freedom gained on the
battlefield. In the letters, despatches, and other documents that record their
actions, one can see their struggles to gain recognition from foreign powers,
to negotiate treaties and agreements with other countries, and to protect
the sovereign rights of the United States. One can see their efforts to
defend American claims to western territories in the face of attempts to
define U.S. borders in narrow terms, and one can see the intrigues that
aroused political jealousies and competitive interests among the American
states. In like manner, in letters, despatches, and other documents of their
European counterparts, one can see attempts to maintain authority and to
increase influence in world affairs through diplomatic schemes and
negotiations.

[1] *Robert R. Livingston to John Jay, 9 May 1782, National Archives, RG 360: Papers of
the Continental and Confederation Congresses and the Constitutional Convention, item
79, v. 1, pp. 714-723 (LBkC); M247, reel 105.*

The Emerging Nation: A Documentary History of the Foreign Relations of the United States under the Articles of Confederation, 1780-1789, presents significant historical documents in three volumes. Volume One, *Recognition of Independence*, covers the extensive peace negotiations leading to the Treaty of Paris of 1783; Volume Two, *Trials and Tribulations*, explores the frustrations in diplomacy associated in part with the inability of the government under the Articles to control commerce, to tax the states for needed revenues, and to enforce treaties; Volume Three, *Toward Federal Diplomacy*, reflects continued diplomatic efforts to reach foreign agreements to enhance United States security in the world community while political leaders established a federal union.

It is the goal of the editors of this publication to make available significant documents to serve as a starting point for the study of United States diplomacy for the years 1780 to 1789. The documents begin with John Adams' acceptance of his commission as minister plenipotentiary to negotiate peace with Great Britain, continue with United States efforts to seek treaties and financial aid from European nations, and end with United States diplomatic efforts at the opening of the First Federal Congress.

In order to present the historical richness of as many documents as possible, introductions, headnotes, and annotations have been used judiciously in support of a basic understanding of the events. This editorial philosophy reflects the goal of the editors "to let the documents speak for themselves." As gathered here, they have much to say.

Historical Overview

During the 17th and 18th centuries Great Britain and France engaged in a series of wars as they fiercely competed for territories in India, Africa, the West Indies, and North America. The capstone of these wars in North America came in 1754 when conflict over claims to land and trade west of the Appalachian Mountains by French and British colonials ignited the French and Indian War, 1754-1763, which became a worldwide conflict known as the Seven Years War, 1756-1763. At the close of hostilities, France relinquished to Great Britain its rights to Canada, Acadia, Cape Breton Island, the islands in the St. Lawrence River, and all territories east of the Mississippi River. It gave all French territories west of the Mississippi River and New Orleans to Spain. Although France retained fishing rights off the coast of Newfoundland by the terms of the Treaty of Paris of 1763, the result of defeat was virtual expulsion from the continent. Only Great Britain and Spain held colonies in North America.

But while the French were defeated, they remained undaunted. Some French leaders saw that the British in their victory had sown the seeds of future difficulties. The French presence in North America had made the American colonials dependent on British support. Now that the French presence was removed, the Americans were free to acquire additional territory, rely even more on their own local governing bodies, and in general pursue a more independent course.

Following the signing of the Treaty of Paris of 1763, postwar attempts by Parliament to enforce tighter controls and impose higher taxes on the colonies met with strong resistance. Disputes grew more serious from 1765 to 1775. In April 1775 open warfare erupted with the battles of Lexington and Concord in Massachusetts. In November of that year, the Continental Congress began to search abroad for financial aid and military stores to meet its obligations. A major, albeit clandestine, source was found in France. It was this secret aid that kept America's hopes for nationhood alive during the difficult years of 1775, 1776, and 1777.

America's victory at Saratoga in the fall of 1777 helped to precipitate formal French involvement in the war. France's leadership acted less from a conviction that the United States had demonstrated an ability to maintain its independence by force of arms, than from a concern that the Americans might accept a peace settlement with Great Britain. For its part, the United States was now prepared to ally itself with France, necessity having replaced earlier altruistic plans of minimal relations with foreign powers. American and French diplomats signed treaties of alliance and of amity and commerce on February 6, 1778. Congress ratified the treaties that Spring without substantive debate and proceeded to seek the assistance of other nations.

Spain's entry into the war as France's ally in June 1779 provided Congress with the opportunity to seek another alliance. Congress hoped for Spanish recognition of American independence and material aid in conducting the war. For its part, Spain was ready to provide assistance that might discomfit Great Britain, but regarded the American rebellion as a dangerous example for its own American colonies. In addition, the refusal of the United States to renounce its right to navigate the Mississippi River, or its claims to lands west of the Appalachians, gave Spain reason not to honor American requests. John Jay, who arrived in Spain in January 1780, spent two and a half years in negotiations with small success.

John Adams, who represented the United States in France, 1778-1779, returned to Europe in early 1780 as American commissioner to draw up a treaty of peace and a commercial agreement with Great Britain. Disputes with the Comte de Vergennes, the French Foreign Minister, over the proper timing of an announcement of his mission to London caused Adams to transfer his residence to Holland, where he might establish American credit with one or more of the Dutch banks. After many months filled with frustrations, Adams was successful in obtaining Dutch recognition and financial support in 1782.

Congress also sought aid from Russia. In late 1781, it sent Francis Dana, Adams' secretary, as minister plenipotentiary to the Court of St. Petersburg, with instructions to enroll the United States in the League of Armed Neutrality and to negotiate a treaty of amity and commerce with the Russian monarch. After spending almost two years in the Russian capital, Dana found that Catherine II had no intention of recognizing the United States. Thus his mission was a failure.

Peace negotiations with Great Britain, the most successful effort of United States diplomacy of the period, began in the spring of 1782. Under Lord Shelburne's direction, British representative Richard Oswald contacted Benjamin Franklin in April 1782 to begin talks. The negotiations culminated on November 30, 1782, with the American representatives (Adams, Franklin, Jay, and Henry Laurens) signing the preliminary articles. They agreed to terms without informing the French beforehand, thereby incurring the disapproval of Vergennes, whose own peace efforts were directed towards the negotiation of the European preliminary articles, signed in January 1783. The Anglo-American definitive treaty of peace signed on September 3, 1783, was basically the same as the preliminary treaty. Congress ratified the treaty on January 14, 1784, and Franklin and David Hartley exchanged instruments of ratification in June.

Following the signing of the preliminary treaty, the Anglo-American discussions continued in the hope of producing a commercial agreement in addition to the peace treaty. When Shelburne's ministry fell in February 1783, to be replaced by a Fox-North coalition, Richard Oswald was replaced by David Hartley as the British negotiator in Paris. Charles James Fox and Hartley at first seemed of one mind in their desire to resolve trade matters with the Americans. However, British public opinion quickly hardened against allowing the Americans to enjoy their prewar trade relationship with any part of the Empire. American withdrawal of all restrictions on trade with the former mother country in April 1783 accordingly met with no parallel British response. While American ships were permitted to bring American produce to Great Britain, an Order in Council in July 1783 banned all but small American ships from carrying produce to British possessions in the West Indies. Hartley spent several frustrating and unsuccessful months trying to change the British position on trade with the United States.

Failure to negotiate a trade agreement with Great Britain was but one difficulty in United States trade relations with the leading powers. The

Franco-American treaty of amity and commerce specified most-favored-nation status for each country's trade goods. French goods should therefore have had an advantage over British goods in any competition for American markets. However, French commercial practices made no allowance for credit, and French manufacturers did not adapt their products to the American market. Despite the lack of an Anglo-American commercial agreement, British goods were made available on credit, and with the removal of American trade restrictions, soon commanded a lion's share of sales.

In spite of overwhelming difficulties, Congress sought to negotiate commercial treaties with the other nations of Europe based upon principles of reciprocity. While John Jay, soon to become Secretary for Foreign Affairs, returned to New York in 1784, Thomas Jefferson joined Franklin and Adams that year to participate in the negotiations. These three American commissioners, working together in Paris, notified more than twenty European nations of their readiness to treat, but the response was meager. Franklin had already negotiated a treaty with Sweden, and Adams and Jefferson would complete a treaty with Prussia. Despite preliminary talks with Denmark and Portugal, the commissioners signed no other commercial treaties with European states in the 1780s.

Congress appointed John Adams its minister to Great Britain in February 1785. Adams diligently reported on his reception in London, but soon perceived that the British were disinterested in any commercial arrangements with the United States. His protests regarding Britain's failure to evacuate the Northwest posts, to settle the Northeast boundary in Passamaquoddy Bay, or to provide compensation for slaves removed from the United States, were met by British complaints of American failure to repay British creditors or compensate loyalists for confiscated property. In response, Adams advised Congress to retaliate against British commerce by establishing imposts and prohibitions, emphasizing that the British government otherwise would refuse to resolve its differences with the United States. He also counselled the American States to facilitate strict observance of peace treaty terms.

Jefferson's experience in France was certainly more pleasant than that of Adams, but only slightly more productive. France wished to promote an expansion of Franco-American trade, but without disrupting its economic system or suffering a decline in government revenues. France made L'Orient, Bayonne, Dunkirk, and Marseilles free ports for American trade, but navigation fees charged American ships at these ports eliminated any possibility of profitable commerce. French notions of most-favored-nation status did not extend to certain privileges, such as admission of American whale oil on the same basis as that admitted from the Hanse towns, until

Jefferson pointed out the anomaly. Jefferson also mounted a major effort to persuade the French to make the terms upon which the Farmers General (which collected taxes and duties on various categories of imported goods) purchased tobacco more congenial to American merchants. French officials were generally sympathetic to Jefferson's efforts, but France's antiquated economic system and precarious financial situation prevented a genuine Franco-American commercial rapprochement. The only really bright spot on America's trade horizon was its incipient China trade, which would yield handsome profits while stimulating America's shipbuilding industry and providing experience for future American naval officers.

Another difficulty that confronted the American envoys in Europe was the declaration of war on the United States by the Barbary pirates of North Africa. Congress authorized Adams and Jefferson to appoint agents to negotiate peace treaties with the North African rulers, setting aside $80,000 for use in this effort. The American diplomats sent Thomas Barclay, the U.S. Consul General in France, to handle the Moroccan negotiations. Morocco's ruler promptly released his American captives and signed a peace treaty. However, American efforts to negotiate with Algiers and Tripoli failed to reach a satisfactory conclusion. It is interesting to note that Jefferson favored building a fleet with which to suppress the Barbary corsairs, while Adams advocated raising adequate funds to meet the pirates' demands.

Congress had better success in matters relating to its authority regarding foreign diplomats and consuls in the United States. It refused to extradite a French adventurer calling himself the Chevalier de Longchamps for trial and punishment in France on the demand of the French government for his physical attack on the French Consul General, François Barbé de Marbois, on the principle of extraterritoriality, because the culprit had a valid claim to American citizenship. Longchamps was sentenced in an American court to an appropriate punishment for his crime, and the French government ultimately accepted the logic of the American position.

Congress had equal success in asserting its authority to approve the appointment of foreign consuls to posts in the United States, chiding Richard Soderstrom, the Swedish Consul at Boston, for proceeding to his post and soliciting an exequatur from the Governor of Massachusetts without first receiving congressional approval. When Sir John Temple, the British Consul General, overstepped his authority by approaching Secretary for Foreign Affairs John Jay in behalf of loyalists seeking redress of grievances in accordance with the terms of the definitive treaty of peace, Jay asked Adams to inform the British government that such requests were the province of a diplomat, not a consul.

As Secretary for Foreign Affairs, it fell to Jay to make a second effort to reconcile Spanish-American differences over the western lands and the navigation of the Mississippi. In mid-1785, Don Diego de Gardoqui, Spanish chargé d'affaires, arrived in the United States to negotiate a trade agreement and an arrangement regarding the river. Congress empowered Jay to negotiate, but not to sign any agreement without first submitting it for approval. A year passed, during which Jay allowed himself to be persuaded that a commercial agreement with Spain was worth closing the Mississippi to American navigation for 25 or 30 years. When Jay laid his proposal before Congress in late August 1786, the Eastern and Southern States formed voting blocs for and against it respectively. There would be no agreement with Spain under the Articles of Confederation.

A major theme during the period from 1778 to 1788 was French pressure for a consular convention with the United States to codify the powers, privileges, and immunities each side accorded to the other's consuls. Congress wanted consular officials to confine themselves to matters of navigation and commerce, without according them any extraterritorial qualities. The convention went through several drafts, one of which was signed by Franklin in 1784, but left unratified by Congress. Jefferson, commissioned to negotiate a convention in October 1787, achieved a practical agreement that minimized extraterritorial privileges. It was signed in August 1788, but not ratified by the United States until 1790.

Domestic upheavals in Massachusetts and elsewhere in the mid-1780s, fostered high glee in the reports of the British Consul General, who was convinced that the unrest marked the beginning of the end of the American experiment in self-rule. The British diplomat's view reflected the position of many foreign leaders toward the United States. Though it had succeeded in extricating itself from colonial rule and was, if ever so slowly, emerging as a new nation in the world community, its central government was considered weak and ineffectual. For prominent American leaders, this situation offered potential for change.

The need to strengthen the central government through an overhaul of America's fundamental law was a recurring theme in the correspondence of Jay and Adams, as it was in Madison's missives to Jefferson. For them, only by establishing a government with the power to control commerce, to raise revenues, and to force individual States to comply with federal laws and international agreements would the United States redeem itself in the eyes of Europe. The Constitution that emerged from the convention in Philadelphia in the summer of 1787 would win the general approval of America's principal diplomatic figures, although all would concede the need for a bill of rights.

When John Adams left Europe in 1788, he returned to a country in the throes of debate regarding ratification of the United States Constitution.

Some States were eager to adopt the charter, others were indifferent, and a few were hostile, given the absence of a bill of rights. The authors of the *Federalist Papers* (including John Jay) were quick to point out the advantages of the Constitution for American diplomacy and foreign trade. After much debate, ratification was successful and a new federal government was established.

Positive foreign response evolved over time. The Comte de Moustier, the French minister to the United States, was at first suspicious of the new measure, but by 1789 had come to accept and support it, as had the French Foreign Ministry in Paris, on the premise that a stronger central government in America would ultimately serve French interests. British leaders eventually favored the new Constitution and came to view its adoption as advantageous to their interests. While some feared that a strong federal government would discriminate against British commerce or shipping in retaliation for British restrictions on American trade, they also realized that such a government would be able to enforce compliance with the terms of the 1783 peace treaty regarding recovery of debts and confiscated property.

Of the major European powers, only Spain had reason to regret the adoption of the Constitution. Given increasing immigration from Europe and the shift of population westward beyond the Appalachians, a stronger federal government could only mean increasing pressure on Spanish lands east of the Mississippi and on Spain's control of the mouth of that river. Despite the machinations of Spain's representatives in Louisiana, the Old Southwest, Tennessee, and Kentucky became integral parts of the United States.

The experience gained by the American diplomats under the Articles of Confederation served the nation well when they were elected or appointed to federal positions under the Constitution. Adams became Vice-President of the United States, Jefferson, Secretary of State, and Jay, Chief Justice of the United States. When the federal government began functioning in March of 1789, a period filled with challenges had ended; a new era with the same or similar challenges, but filled with even greater potential, had begun.

Note on Sources

The major source for documents included in this three-volume edition is National Archives Record Group 360: Records of the Continental and Confederation Congresses and the Constitutional Convention. Other significant sources include copies of records from the Public Record Office of Great Britain and the Archives du Ministère des Affaires Etrangères of France relating to the diplomacy of the 1780s in the Manuscripts Division of the Library of Congress; the papers of Richard Oswald, David Hartley, and Lord Shelburne in the William L. Clements Library of the University of Michigan; The Adams Papers in the Massachusetts Historical Society; and the John Jay Papers in the Columbia University Libraries. Additional materials are included from the George Bancroft Papers in the Rare Books and Manuscripts Division of the New York Public Library; the Benjamin Franklin Papers and the Thomas Jefferson Papers at the Library of Congress; and the Benjamin Vaughan Papers in the American Philosophical Society Library. Whenever possible, research has been conducted in modern documentary editions. These include: *The Papers of John Adams, The Papers of Benjamin Franklin, John Jay: The Making of a Revolutionary, Unpublished Papers, 1745-1780, John Jay: The Winning of the Peace, Unpublished Papers, 1780-1784, The Papers of Thomas Jefferson, Lafayette in the Age of the American Revolution, The Papers of James Madison, The Papers of Robert Morris, The Papers of George Washington, Letters of Delegates to Congress, 1774-1789, Documentary History of the First Federal Congress of the United States of America, March 4, 1789-March 3, 1791, The Documentary History of the Ratification of the Constitution,* and *The United States and Russia: The Beginning of Relations, 1765-1815.*

Note on Maps

The maps included in these volumes are extracted from "A Map of the British and French Dominions in North America with the Roads, Distances, Limits, and Extent of the Settlements, Humbly Inscribed to the Right Honourable The Earl of Halifax, And the other Right Honourable The Lords Commissioners for Trade & Plantations, By their Lordships Most Obliged and very humble Servant Jno. Mitchell," annotated "B. F. Stevens's Facsimile of the Red-Line-Map in the British Museum ... 1897" from R.G. 76: Records of Boundary and Claims Commissions and Arbitrations. Additional information was extracted from the maps included in Samuel Flagg Bemis, *The Diplomacy of the American Revolution,* copyright 1935 by The American Historical Association, and from Samuel Flagg Bemis, *Pinckney's Treaty,* copyright 1926 by the Johns Hopkins University Press. National Archives and Records Administration volunteer Dean Aurecchia, formerly a cartographer with the United States government, rendered the FRUAC maps. The American Historical Association and the Johns Hopkins University Press gave permission to use their maps in the preparation of the project maps.

Editorial Methodology

Document selection reflects the establishment of the United States as an independent nation in the world community. Selections are from the official papers of the United States Congress; British, French, and Spanish government records; and unofficial documents, including the papers of individuals who played a prominent role in United States foreign relations during this period. Where appropriate, selected documents, of significant value are included in their entirety. Where only part of a document contains significant diplomatic information, that portion has been excerpted. It was common to prepare multiple copies of letters and documents to defeat the accidents of 18th century travel and foreign interception. Whenever possible the editors have selected the recipient copy or record copy. When other copies have been printed, their selection is reflected in the citation. Headnotes were prepared to bridge documents or to present information necessary to understand the historical context of the documentation. Standard biographical reference works and modern documentary editions, including the *Dictionary of American Biography*, the *Dictionary of National Biography*, the *Biographical Directory of the United States Congress, 1774-1989*, *The Papers of Thomas Jefferson*, *The Diary of John Adams*, *The Papers of John Adams*, *John Jay: The Making of a Revolutionary, Unpublished Papers, 1745-1780*, *John Jay: The Winning of the Peace, Unpublished Papers, 1780-1784*, and *The Papers of Benjamin Franklin*, along with other research sources, were used to identify historical figures.

With few exceptions, documents are in chronological order. To ensure textual accuracy in the preparation of documents for publication, stylistic characteristics, including spelling, capitalization, and punctuation are maintained. Encyphered documents are provided in plain script. Ship names have been placed in italics. Contractions, abbreviations, and diacritical marks are retained as written. Unintelligible text is indicated by asterisks. Crossed-out words have been indicated by canceled text. Crossed-out text which is unintelligible is indicated by asterisks placed in angle brackets. Interlineations and marginalia are placed on the line in the closest approximate position, as indicated by the writer. Significant docketing information is placed at the end of the document. Conjected words and dates are placed in brackets. Contemporary translations are indicated in the source citation at the end of the document. Translations provided by the project staff are indicated at the beginning of the document. Dates written at the end of the document are placed at the beginning. Salutations and closings are included as written but are placed on a continuous line.

Textual Devices and Abbreviations

...	the deletion of a small amount of text completing a sentence or paragraph
. . . . .	the deletion of a larger section of text comprising one or more paragraphs
*******	unintelligible text
< ***** >	unintelligible crossed out text
~~which~~	crossed out text in original
[which]	conjected text
AD	autograph draft
ALS	autograph letter signed
AN	autograph note
APS	American Philosophical Society
C	copy
DS	document signed
f	folio
ff	microfilm frames
FFAA	Archives du Ministère des Affaires Etrangères
HC	copy in hand of Hartley
JCC	printed Journal of the Continental Congress
LBkC	letterbook copy
LC	Library of Congress
LS	letter signed
M23	National Archives Microfilm Publication of the Despatches from the United States Consuls in Algiers, Algeria, 1785-1906
M40	National Archives Microfilm Publication of the Domestic Letters of the Department of State, 1784-1906
M61	National Archives Microfilm Publication of the Foreign Letters of the Continental Congress and the Department of State, 1785-1790
M247	National Archives Microfilm Publication of the Papers of the Continental Congress, 1774-1789
M332	National Archives Microfilm Publication of the Miscellaneous Papers of the Continental Congress, 1774-1789
MHS	Massachusetts Historical Society
NA	National Archives
NSDAR	National Society Daughters of the American Revolution
NYPL	New York Public Library
PCC	Papers of the Continental Congress

List of Presidents of the Congress

· Maps

Parts of the United States Held by British and Spanish Forces, June 1781

The Emerging Nation, 1782

The Emerging Nation, Suggested Boundaries, 1782

The Emerging Nation, 1783

Illustrations

Surrender of the Army of Cornwallis designed by Berbier and engraved by Godefroy. Courtesy of the Library of Congress.

John Adams by John Singleton Copley. Courtesy of Harvard University.

Benjamin Franklin by Joseph Siffred Duplessis. Courtesy of Independence National Historical Park.

John Jay engraved by B.B.E., published by R. Wilkinson, 1783. Courtesy of the Library of Congress.

Charles Gravier, Comte de Vergennes, engraved by Vangelisti. Courtesy of the Library of Congress.

Henry Laurens by John Singleton Copley. Courtesy of the National Portrait Gallery, Smithsonian Institution.

David Hartley, M.P., 1783, by George Romney. Courtesy of Columbia University in the City of New York.

Richard Oswald and Benjamin Franklin Discussing the Treaty of Peace at Paris, drawn by Howard Pyle. Courtesy of the Library of Congress.

The Treaty of Paris by Benjamin West. Courtesy of the Winterthur Museum.

George III by Allan Ramsay. Courtesy of the Colonial Williamsburg Foundation.

Louis XVI by C. C. Bervic. Courtesy of the National Portrait Gallery, Smithsonian Institution.

Robert R. Livingston by Charles Willson Peale. Courtesy of Independence National Historical Park.

Chevalier de la Luzerne by Charles Willson Peale. Courtesy of Independence National Historical Park.

Acknowledgements

In the fall of 1983, the National Archives decided to publish a documentary history of the foreign relations of the United States for the period 1783 to 1789. Later the period was expanded to include the years 1781 and 1782. The project, referred to as FRUS, was based on records in the National Archives. In 1986 the Department of State became a co-sponsor and provided financial assistance in the initial work of document transcription. In the early years of the project, some 6,000 documents were copied from the records of the National Archives. Several National Archives employees were assigned to work on this project. These included Mary-Jane M. Dowd, who served as editor and project director of FRUS, 1985-1991, Alec B. Kirby, and Angie Spicer VanDereedt. Under Ms. Dowd's direction some 2,600 documents from a base of some 6,000 documents primarily from Record Group 360: Papers of the Continental Congress and Confederation Congresses and the Constitutional Convention, were selected and transcribed for inclusion in the FRUS project. Three National Archives volunteers–Renée F. Cooper, Patricia D. Gray, and Mary S. Woods–also worked with Ms. Dowd. Each provided valuable service in document transcription, proofreading, and translation of French-language documents located in the National Archives.

In 1991, the Archivist of the United States placed the project under the administration and sponsorship of the National Historical Publications and Records Commission (NHPRC). NHPRC staff member Mary A. Giunta was appointed project director and editor-in-chief. A revised plan for the project was developed. The plan included an evaluation of the document database and an evaluation of documents located in significant archival and historical collections in the United States and Europe. Based on this plan, several important changes were made. The project name was changed to The Emerging Nation: A Documentary History of the Foreign Relations of the United States under the Articles of Confederation, 1780-1789 (FRUAC) to reflect American attempts under the then operative plan of government to become a separate nation in the world community. Three distinguished historians–Norman A. Graebner, Peter P. Hill and Lawrence S. Kaplan–were invited to join the project as consulting editors. They participated in the selection of documents, wrote introductory essays, and provided essential advice on the work of the project. J. Dane Hartgrove, a diplomatic historian and records specialist of the Office of the National Archives, was assigned to the project staff in 1992 as associate editor. He secured copies of documents located in significant manuscript and archival collections at the Library of Congress, in various repositories outside the Washington, DC, area, and from NHPRC project offices. Through his efforts some 1900 new documents, primarily copies of documents located in foreign repositories, were selected for consideration for inclusion in FRUAC. In addition, Dr. Hartgrove played a significant role in the translation of French-language documents and the preparation of headnotes and annotations. Richard B. Smith, formerly of the staff of the National Archives, served as project publication specialist through most of calendar year 1994. The project benefited greatly from his interest, skills, and labors in scholarly publication. National Archives printing specialist Isabelle V.

Saunders served as coordinator with the Government Printing Office staff in seeing the volumes through publication. Her efforts greatly facilitated the publication of these volumes.

Beginning in 1991, volunteer participation was significantly expanded. FRUAC volunteers transcribed, translated, verified texts, conducted historical research, worked on document databases, located and copied documents in manuscript repositories, located copies of pictures, coded documents for publication, and drew maps. They visited libraries and worked at home and on vacation. Their many hours of labor, their commitment to work on FRUAC, their sharing of their expertise, and their general desire to contribute were simply extraordinary. From student interns to retired individuals, volunteers played an extremely important role in this project. It is accurate to say that the day-to-day work of the project could not have been completed without them. They are: Carol S. Aiken, Patricia A. Alfredson, Dean Aurecchia, Nathanael Cavanaugh, Marjorie Cooper, Renée F. Cooper, Helen G. Cullinan, Mary H. Curzan, Elizabeth Drain Hardin, Yvette M. Fallin, Maria Flesher, Arthur L. Gamson, Sherry S. Harris, Norma S. Hoehndorf, Burt Knauft, Elizabeth S. Lourie, Lisa Mastney, Beatrice B. Meyerson, Betty Moore, Laurent Pion-Goureuau, William F. Reed, Jr., Peter Ringland, Renee Schick, Widajanti Soekarso, and Mary S. Woods. Patricia A. Eames, Coordinator of the NARA volunteer program, identified potential volunteers for the project. Her role deserves recognition.

The following individuals, dedicated to documentary scholarship, made our labors lighter: Paul H. Smith and Gerald W. Gawalt, Letters of Delegates project, Library of Congress Manuscript Division; Barbara Oberg, Jonathan Dull, Ellen Cohn, Karen Duval, and Kate Ohno, the Benjamin Franklin Papers project, Yale University; Ene Sirvet, John Jay Papers project, Columbia University; Elizabeth M. Nuxoll and Mary A. K. Gallagher, Robert Morris Papers project, Queens College, CUNY; C. James Taylor and Peggy J. Clark, Henry Laurens Papers project, University of South Carolina; and Richard A. Ryerson, Celeste Walker, Gregg L. Lint, Joanna M. Revelas, and Anne Decker, The Adams Papers project, Massachusetts Historical Society. It is with particular appreciation that we acknowledge the assistance of Ene Sirvet, Richard A. Ryerson, Kate Ohno, and Anne Decker. They provided document identification and verification of several important items which enhanced document selection of Jay, Franklin, and Adams materials. John P. Kaminski of the Ratification of the Constitution project produced our indexes. His acumen provides the user of these volumes with easy access to the documents. Kenneth R. Bowling, First Federal Congress project, shared his thoughts on the editing of documents, especially government documents of the period.

Members of the staffs of manuscript and archival repositories were most helpful in answering questions, providing copies of materials and arranging for interlibrary loans. These include: Frederick Bauman, Ernest Emrich, Jeffrey Flannery, Charles Kelly, Michael Klein, Kathleen McDonough, Joseph Sullivan, and Mary Wolfskill, Library of Congress Manuscript Division Reading Room; Beth Carroll-Horrocks, Associate Librarian and Manuscripts Librarian, American Philosophical Society Library; Deborah L. Sisum, Deputy Keeper, Catalog of American Portraits, Smithsonian Institution; Catherine H. Grosfils, Editorial Librarian, Audio-Visual Library, Colonial Williamsburg Foundation; Elizabeth Gombosi, Harvard University Art Museum; Shirley A. Mays, Library Technician, Independence National Historical Park Photographic Library; Joanna Britto, Manager, Rights and Reproductions, National Portrait Gallery, Smithsonian Insitution; Jennifer Tolpa, Assistant Reference Librarian, Massachusetts Historical Society; Richard Salvato, Rare Books and Manuscripts Division, New York Public Library; Christine Nelson, Associate Curator of Autograph Manuscripts, Pierpont Morgan Library; Rob Cox and Arlene Shy, William L. Clements Library, University of Michigan; and Grace Eleazer, Manager, Museum Registration, and Jennifer Menson, Registration Assistant, Winterthur Museum. In particular, Dr. Shy provided detailed information on various manuscripts in the Shelburne, Hartley, and Oswald collections.

The volumes include documents from modern documentary editions sponsored by the NHPRC. The following publishers have granted permission to publish a number of documents included in Volume One: The University of Pittsburgh Press, *The Papers of Robert Morris, 1781-1784*, materials from Volume 4: January 11-April 15, 1782, E. James Ferguson, Editor, John Catanzariti, Associate Editor, copyright 1978; Volume 6: July 22-October 31, 1782, John Catanzariti, and E. James Ferguson, Editors, copyright 1784; Princeton University Press, *The Papers of Thomas Jefferson*, Volume 6, 21 May 1781 to 1 March 1784, edited by Julian P. Boyd, copyright 1952; HarperCollins, *John Jay, The Making of A Revolutionary, Unpublished Papers, 1745-1780*, edited by Richard B. Morris, copyright 1975, *John Jay, The Winning of the Peace, Unpublished Papers, 1780-1784*, edited by Richard B. Morris, copyright 1980. We encourage the use of these and other modern documentary editions for a further understanding of history.

Curators, librarians, and directors of several collections and repositories have granted permission to include copies of a number of documents and pictures entrusted to their responsibility and care: Richard A. Ryerson, Editor-in-Chief, The Adams Papers, Massachusetts Historical Society; Beth Carroll-Horrocks, Associate Librarian and Manuscripts Librarian, American Philosophical Society; John C. Dann, Director, William L. Clements Library; Jean Ashton, Director, The Rare Book and Manuscript Library,

Columbia University; Sarah Elliston Weiner, Curator of Art Properties, Low Library, Columbia University; François Renouard, Director of Archives and Documentation, Archives du Ministère des Affaires Etrangères; William A. Moffett, Director of the Library, The Huntington; Stuart M. Frank, The Kendall Whaling Museum; Louis L. Tucker, Director, Massachusetts Historical Society; Georgane F. Love (Mrs. Dale Kelly Love), Historian General, National Society Daughters of the American Revolution; Margaret Heilbrun, Director of the Library and Curator of Manuscripts, New-York Historical Society; Wayne Furman, Director, Office of Special Collections, New York Public Library; Christine Nelson, Associate Curator of Autograph Manuscripts, The Pierpont Morgan Library; Patton Hash, Director, The South Carolina Historical Society; and Nancy M. Shawcross, Curator of Manuscripts, Van Pelt Library, the University of Pennsylvania. Materials from the British Public Record Office are included by permission of the Controller of Her Britannic Majesty's Stationery Office. Materials from the Royal Library, Windsor Castle, are included with the permission of Her Majesty Queen Elizabeth II.

Staff members of the National Archives Library, including Lida H. Churchville, Maryellen Trautman, Jeffrey T. Hartley and David Lake, provided research assistance, filled interlibrary loan requests, and sought elusive identifications or facts. John A. Dwyer, Richard H. Smith, and Robert E. Richardson of the National Archives Cartographic and Architectural Branch provided reference service in the preparation of the FRUAC maps.

Gerald W. George, executive director of the NHPRC, provided significant support for the project. Roger A. Bruns, former deputy executive director of the NHPRC, provided administrative support and assistance. NHPRC staff members Laurette O'Connor, Nancy Taylor Copp, Delores G. Taylor, and Sheneé Turner provided computer and administrative assistance.

Documentary editing is a cooperative endeavor. Each of the above-mentioned individuals, institutions, and organizations deserve full acknowledgment for the role they have played in the publication of these volumes.

Mary A. Giunta
Editor-in-Chief

Volume One: Recognition of Independence

Early American Foreign Relations

The leaders of the American colonies that became the United States served their diplomatic apprenticeship in the relations that existed between their colonial agents and such entities as Parliament, the Board of Trade, and those ministers who dealt with colonial affairs. Some Americans, including Benjamin Franklin and Arthur Lee, the two colonial agents who later served the United States in a diplomatic capacity, were knowledgeable public men long before the Continental Congress presented petitions to the king for the redress of grievances. However difficult the relations between the colonies and their mother country prior to the American Revolution, they were more benevolent than those existing between foreign states in this period. The diplomatic representatives of the fledgling United States had no experience to match that of the foreign statesmen they would encounter.

Eighteenth-century European diplomacy was nothing if not Machiavellian. Benevolence between nations always had its price, and no alliance or dynastic link could stand in the way of the good of the state. Frederick the Great's wresting of Silesia from the Hapsburgs, the first partition of Poland, and Russia's dismemberment of Turkey by the Treaty of Kuchuk-Kanardzhi were but the more flagrant examples of European diplomacy prior to the start of the American Revolution. An example of this type of diplomacy, crucial for the American colonies, followed the Seven Years War.

France had emerged from the war much reduced in her faculties. She had lost Canada to the British, as well as all of Louisiana east of the Mississippi except New Orleans, and had given up her fortifications in India. The French also were obliged to transfer New Orleans and all of Louisiana west of the river to Spain, in order to induce the Spanish to make peace. Bereft of her possessions on the North American continent, France found herself subordinate to Britain in European diplomatic councils. Circumstances thus dictated France's disposition to revenge herself upon Britain, provided this could be done without risk and with relative certainty of success. The outbreak of fighting in the American colonies in 1775 provided just such an opportunity.

Prompted by the reports of secret agents Julien-Alexandre Achard de Bonvouloir[1] and Pierre-Augustin Caron de Beaumarchais,[2] French Foreign Minister Charles Gravier, Comte de Vergennes, had concluded by January 1776 that France should provide the American colonies with arms and munitions under the guise of private commercial transactions. The American rebellion offered France the opportunity to increase her power as that of Great Britain diminished, to extend French trade at British expense, and perhaps to recover certain possessions in North America, such as her pre-1763 fishing grounds. Arthur Lee passed along to Beaumarchais an added incentive: if the American rebellion collapsed, Britons and Americans might seize the French sugar islands out of frustration. Beaumarchais chose to put the argument in practical terms: France could spend a relatively small sum now to ensure confusion to the enemy, or lose vastly more in any future confrontation with a united British Empire.

These arguments won over Louis XVI, and on March 1, Vergennes wrote to the Spanish Foreign Minister, Jerónimo, Marqués de Grimaldi,[3] to ask if Spain would join France in rendering secret aid to the American rebels. Vergennes also submitted a statement regarding this covert assistance to the other principal French ministers, which argued that France and Spain should begin making military preparations for a war with Great Britain while feigning friendship with that power. Secret assistance would go to the American colonies, but there would be no convention with them until their independence had been established. On May 2, 1776, Louis XVI ordered one million livres tournois supplied to the American rebels in the form of munitions through Beaumarchais, masquerading as a private trader under the name of Roderigue Hortalez and Company. Charles III of Spain matched that amount, using the same channel. Before any American diplomatic representative had even set foot in France, the French, moved by considerations of European diplomacy, were preparing to join the American rebels in their war against the British.

With the outbreak of fighting in the spring of 1775, the American colonies had formed non-importation and non-exportation associations in order to secure redress of their grievances. On August 23, the king responded with a proclamation declaring the colonies to be in a state of rebellion. An act of Parliament of December 22, 1775, cut off trade with the colonies, at least in part to prevent the rebels from obtaining munitions.

At the same time, the Continental Congress, through the Articles of Association, was then trying to prevent foreign trade. Opening American ports to foreign ships would be the same as declaring the colonies independent, a step which Congress was not ready to consider until the spring of 1776.

On April 6, 1776, Congress resolved to open trade with all other countries except Great Britain. Three major documents were soon in preparation: a declaration of independence, a model treaty of amity and commerce with other countries, and a framework for governing the American confederation. When independence was declared in early July, plans for an American foreign policy were already well in hand.

Benjamin Franklin had returned to Pennsylvania from England in the spring of 1775 and soon became an active member of the Continental Congress. On November 29, 1775, Congress established a secret committee "for the sole purpose of corresponding with our friends in Great Britain, Ireland, and other parts of the world." The original members of this Secret Committee of Correspondence were Benjamin Franklin and John Dickinson (PA),[4] John Jay (NY), Thomas Johnson (MD),[5] and Benjamin Harrison (VA).[6] The Committee's membership varied, with James Lovell (MA) one of the more active members. From April 17, 1777, it was known as the Committee for Foreign Affairs.

On December 12, 1775, the Committee wrote to Arthur Lee in London, asking him to provide it with information on the attitude of foreign powers toward the colonies. Around this time, Franklin wrote to C.F.W. Dumas at The Hague, requesting him to report on the disposition of the European powers towards the American rebels. On March 3, 1776, the Committee resolved to send Silas Deane, a former member of Congress from Connecticut, to France as its agent.

Meanwhile, Beaumarchais and Arthur Lee were attempting to define the terms of French assistance to the American colonies. The French government had no expectation of reimbursement, but the available correspondence shows Beaumarchais asking for eventual payment in kind, with Lee agreeing to this, but stressing the importance of keeping supplies moving in order to support the war effort. Lee attempted to report this state of affairs to Congress, but his letters were sunk at sea to avoid capture. The verbal report made to Congress by Lee's courier on December 1, 1776, noted that the French would ship £200,000 in armaments and munitions through the Netherlands to certain Caribbean entrepots that fall for transfer to the Americans, but mentioned nothing about payment terms.

Silas Deane arrived in Paris on July 7, 1776, and approached the French about buying military supplies on credit. Vergennes received Deane courteously, and referred him to Beaumarchais regarding the purchase of munitions. Deane and Beaumarchais proceeded to draw up a contract for the sale of munitions by the Hortalez firm to the Americans. The two million livres provided by France and Spain had largely gone to set up the Hortalez operation, but Beaumarchais supplied the rebels with munitions worth many times that amount on credit. In early 1778, Arthur Lee would complain to Congress about Deane's having made a contract to pay for supplies for which France expected no reimbursement.

On July 18, 1776, the committee to draw up a plan of treaties for negotiation with foreign powers, consisting of John Adams, Benjamin Franklin, John Dickinson, Benjamin Harrison, and Robert Morris, submitted its report, which Congress basically adopted on September 17, 1776. The committee's report included a model treaty of amity and commerce, with articles embodying such maritime principles as free ships, free goods, freedom for neutrals to trade between belligerent ports, restricted lists of contraband (not including foodstuffs or naval stores), and considerate treatment of neutral shipping. The model treaty would form the basis for all U.S. trade pacts in the eighteenth century. This Plan of 1776 ran directly counter to Britain's Rule of 1756, which was designed to limit Britain's enemies' reliance on neutral shipping.

The committee had included some articles specifically designed for a treaty with France. The Plan of 1776 did not call for an alliance with France, but did include French protection of American ships and citizens from the Barbary pirates and the right to sail in each other's naval convoys. In case Great Britain declared war on France for befriending the rebels, the United States would not aid France's enemy, but neither would it agree to joint military campaigns or joint peace talks. France was also expected to eschew any conquests of British dominions in North America or the adjacent islands.

On September 24, 1776, Congress adopted instructions for the diplomats who would present this plan to France. These individuals were given a certain narrow latitude for concessions in any talks, and were also advised to make use of the ultimate argument if circumstances should so warrant – if France delayed too long, the United States might be forced to reunite with Great Britain. America's first commissioners to France were Arthur Lee and Silas Deane, to be joined by Franklin, who arrived in France on December 4, 1776.

Communications during wartime being difficult, no word of the diplomatic ruminations of Congress had reached Deane and Lee for some time. Deane had drawn up a draft treaty of alliance with France and Spain, which he presented to Vergennes in his private capacity on November 23, 1776. Shortly after his arrival, Franklin joined Deane and Lee in professing to France and Spain that the United States would not make a separate peace if those powers had to enter the war as the result of signing treaties of amity and commerce with the rebels.[7]

Although they preserved the formalities of diplomatic relations with the British, the French were providing as much surreptitious support to the American rebels as they could. Vergennes received the American commissioners unofficially, and French and Spanish ports remained open to American merchant ships and privateers. In January 1777, Louis XVI granted the American Commissioners a secret loan of two million livres. Arthur Lee, who went to Spain in February 1777 in search of recognition and alliance, was turned back near the border by the Spanish Foreign Minister, but with promises of secret aid. Deane and Franklin renewed the offer of an alliance to the French and the Spanish that spring.

By late July 1777, Vergennes had resolved on a declaration of war, for which he had secured the king's approval. However, France's plans were dependent on those of her ally Spain, and Spain had different priorities from France. For obvious reasons, Spain had no interest in promoting the independence of American colonies. The Spanish had recently reached an accommodation with Britain's ally Portugal, and on February 19, 1777, José de Moñino y Redondo, Conde de Floridablanca, had replaced Grimaldi as Spain's foreign minister. The new minister was more cautious, and also anxious to distance Spain's foreign policy from that of France. He proposed to Vergennes that the two countries guarantee a truce in America, rather than go to war. Spain's indifference to France's plans for war forced Vergennes to postpone his plans for intervention.

News of Burgoyne's surrender at Saratoga (October 17, 1777) reached France on December 3, 1777. Confronted by this disaster, the British changed their policy to one of reconciliation with the American rebels. William Eden,[8] one of the North Ministry's undersecretaries, sent agent Paul Wentworth to sound out Franklin and Deane in December and January regarding peace terms, but the two commissioners refused to go beyond generalities with anyone but an accredited envoy, which Wentworth was not.

Meanwhile, Vergennes moved to forestall any British peace offers by offering the Americans recognition and a commercial treaty on December 17, 1777. His attempt to draw Spain into a triple alliance failed because Floridablanca did not wish to recognize American independence and resented France having approached the Americans without first having consulted Spain. However, Vergennes was determined to prevent an Anglo-American reconciliation, and decided that France would act alone. To prevent the Americans from bowing out of the war and leaving France to face England by herself, he resolved to bind the United States to an alliance. On January 8, 1778, Vergennes informed the American Commissioners that Louis XVI had granted their previous request for such an undertaking.

American and French representatives signed two treaties on February 6, 1778. The Franco-American treaty of amity and commerce followed the American Plan of 1776 in virtually all respects. The treaty of alliance had as its principal aim the achievement of American independence. Both treaties fully coincided with the immediate purposes of the two parties. The French had their ambassador in London inform the British of the treaty of amity and commerce on March 13, after which both countries recalled their diplomatic representatives. On March 20, Louis XVI formally received the American Commissioners at Versailles. France and England did not formally go to war until June 1778, after a naval encounter off Ushant.

The British Parliament enacted legislation repealing all laws which the American colonies had found objectionable since 1763 on March 9, 1778. The North Ministry proposed a peace amounting to home rule within the British Empire, and named the Earl of Carlisle[9] to head a commission that would negotiate a settlement with the Americans. Copies of the pertinent legislation were sent to America before its passage in order to counter the effect of the French treaties, which reached America on May 2, 1778. Congress, which previously had known nothing about the treaties, ratified them two days later, and joyfully received French Minister Conrad-Alexandre Gérard when he arrived in mid-July. The Carlisle Commission was a failure.

France avoided military involvement in the War of the Bavarian Succession, 1778-1779, which would have sapped its strength during the initial stages of its confrontation with Great Britain. Meanwhile,

Vergennes attempted to determine what would induce Spain to enter the war as an ally. Floridablanca fixed upon Gibraltar, which he first tried to obtain from the British as the price of Spain's neutrality. By the end of the year, Spain's ambassador in London had determined that Britain would not give Spain Gibraltar or anything else in return for her neutrality. On April 3, 1779, Spain sent the British an ultimatum couched as an offer of mediation, but in terms deliberately unacceptable to the British. Spain and France signed the Convention of Aranjuez, which called for Spain's entry into the war upon British rejection of the offer, on April 12. By the terms of this convention, the two powers agreed not to make peace until Gibraltar had been restored to Spain and the restrictions imposed in 1763 on French use of the port of Dunkirk removed. Spain refused to allow any reference to France's commitment to obtaining American independence in the convention, a circumstance that established an incompatibility in France's relations with its two allies. Nevertheless, France's principal objective was achieved when Spain declared war on Great Britain on June 21, 1779.

After its initial commitment to assist the American rebels through the Hortalez company, Spain provided military supplies through the firm of Gardoqui and Sons of Bilbao and through Bernardo de Gálvez, the Governor of Louisiana. She also provided small amounts of money to Arthur Lee and John Jay in Europe, and to Oliver Pollock, the American agent in Havana. Spain's intent was to keep the American rebels in the war as a drain upon British resources, not to secure American independence.

Spain's efforts to mediate the conflict had caused Vergennes to ask Congress to define its peace terms and to send a plenipotentiary to Europe with powers to make peace. Congress debated peace terms from March to August 1779. It finally settled upon independence and the establishment of the Mississippi as the country's western boundary (with the line of 31 degrees north latitude along the West Florida border) as its requirements on August 14, and named John Adams to be peace commissioner.

The western boundary of the United States and the right of Americans to navigate the Mississippi were matters of major concern to Spain. Since the Spanish had no diplomatic representative in the United States, Vergennes instructed French Ministers Gérard and Chevalier de la Luzerne to defend Spain's interests. Both French ministers warned Congress that France would not guarantee American boundaries to the west of the Alleghenies.

John Jay, whom Congress named its minister to Spain, had instructions to obtain Spanish recognition of American independence, Spain's adherence to an alliance with France and the United States, confirmation of the western boundaries set forth in American peace terms, Spanish recognition of the right of Americans to navigate the Mississippi, a port of entry in Louisiana, and a subsidy or loan of five million dollars. Jay was destined to more than two years of frustration in Madrid, for Spain saw no reason to acquiesce in any of these American proposals, especially given her military victories in America. Bernardo de Gálvez, Spain's Governor of Louisiana, had great success in capturing British possessions in the Floridas and along the Mississippi. Spain also conducted a campaign in the Bahamas and planned to seize Jamaica, although the siege operations at Gibraltar consumed the bulk of her military resources.

By the fall of 1779, then, the United States had acquired an ally and a co-belligerent, had settled upon peace terms, and had demonstrated its military capacity on the field of battle. Diplomatically speaking, the United States now had appointed ministers plenipotentiary to France, Spain, and the United Provinces of the Netherlands (Benjamin Franklin, John Jay, and Henry Laurens respectively), as well as a peace commissioner (John Adams).

[1] Bonvouloir et Loyauté, Julien-Alexandre Achard de (1749-1783). French agent. A former army officer who had lived in the French colony of St. Domingue in the early 1770s, Bonvouloir was sent to the British colonies in America in 1775 by the Comte de Guines, France's ambassador to Great Britain, to report on the military and political potential of the American rebels. His favorable reports bolstered Vergennes' determination to intervene in the Anglo-American conflict.

[2] Beaumarchais, Pierre-Augustin Caron de (1732-1799). French playwright, adventurer, and government agent. A commoner who married well, Beaumarchais gained entry to French court circles as music teacher of Louis XV's daughters. His business sense made him several fortunes. Author of The Barber of Seville and The Marriage of Figaro. Served as secret agent in Austria and Great Britain. Organized the clandestine shipment of munitions and supplies to the American rebels, 1776-1778. Lost money on an edition of Voltaire's works, 1784-1790, and in selling Dutch muskets to France's revolutionary armies, 1792. Considered an emigré for a time, but returned to France.

[3] Grimaldi, Jerónimo, Marqués de (1720-1786). Spanish political figure. Secretary of State for Foreign Affairs, 1763-1777.

[4] Dickinson, John (1732-1808). Pennsylvania and Delaware lawyer and political figure. Member, Continental Congress, from Pennsylvania, 1774-1776, and from Delaware, 1779. President of Delaware, 1781, and of Pennsylvania, 1782-1785. Member, Constitutional Convention, 1787.

[5] Johnson, Thomas (1732-1819). *Maryland lawyer and political figure. Member, Continental Congress, 1774-1776. Governor of Maryland, 1777-1779. Member, Maryland House of Delegates, 1780, 1786-1787. Chief Judge of the General Court of Maryland, 1790-1791. Associate Justice of the United States Supreme Court, 1791-1793.*

[6] Harrison, Benjamin (1726-1791). *Virginia political figure. Member, Virginia House of Burgesses, 1749-1775. Member, Continental Congress, 1774-1777. Member, Virginia House of Delegates, 1776-1782, 1787-1791; Speaker, 1778-1782, 1785-1786. Governor of Virginia, 1782-1784.*

[7] Arthur Lee subsequently accused Silas Deane of malfeasance involving the funds which France had provided to support the American rebellion. Congress recalled both Deane and Lee after the signing of the treaties with France. Deane was unable to provide a detailed record of his transactions with the French. Although Congress did not censure him, Deane's attitude toward the revolutionary cause changed. He published articles in the loyalist press urging reconciliation with the mother country, then emigrated to Europe, actions that were deplored by his former colleagues in Congress. Lee's accusations also extended to the actions of Benjamin Franklin, whom he castigated for maintaining too cordial relations with the French, at the expense of the true interests of the United States.

[8] Eden, William (1744-1814). *British statesman and diplomat. Member of Parliament, 1774-1793. Member, Carlisle Commission, 1778. Chief secretary to the lord lieutenant of Ireland, 1780-1782. Vice-treasurer of Ireland, April-December 1783. Special envoy to negotiate commercial treaty with France, 1785-1786, and further agreements with France, 1787. Special ambassador to Spain, 1787. Special envoy to the United Provinces of the Netherlands, 1790; ambassador, 1791-1793. From 1793, Lord Auckland. Postmaster general, 1798-1804. President of the board of trade, 1806-1807.*

[9] Carlisle, Frederick Howard, Earl of (1748-1825). *British political figure. Initially a wastrel, man of fashion, and friend of Charles James Fox, Carlisle turned to politics in 1777. He became a member of the privy council, and in April 1778 was named chief of the commission Lord North sent to America to settle the disorders in the colonies, but his powers were insufficient to satisfy American demands. President of the board of trade, 1779-1780. Lord lieutenant of Ireland, 1780-1782. Lord steward of the household, 1782-1783, resigning in protest over the peace terms. Lord privy seal, April-December 1783.*

∞ *Peace is an Object of such vast Importance...* ∞

On August 14, 1779, Congress approved two sets of instructions for John Adams as Peace Commissioner and as Commissioner to negotiate a treaty of commerce with Great Britain. For peace to be established, Great Britain had to agree to treat with the United States as a sovereign, free, and independent nation; had to confirm U.S. independence by the treaty; and had to accept certain boundaries for the new nation. The treaty of commerce would have to be founded on principles of equality and reciprocity; Great Britain would be granted the same trade privileges as France, and would have to recognize the common right of fishing in established waters. With these instructions in hand, Adams was ready to set off for Europe.

John Adams to the President of Congress

Sir[1]   Braintree November 4. 1779

I had, Yesterday, the Honour of your Letter of the twentyeth of October, inclosed with two Commissions, appointing me Minister plenipotentiary, from the United States, to negotiate Peace and Commerce, with Great Britain, together with Instructions for my Government, in the Execution of those Commissions; Copies of Instructions to the Ministers plenipotentiary at Versailles and Madrid, and two Acts of Congress of the fourth and fifteenth of October.

Peace is an Object of such vast Importance; the Interests to be adjusted, in the Negotiations to obtain it, are so complicated and so delicate; and the Difficulty of giving general Satisfaction so great: that I feel myself more distressed at the Prospect of executing the Trust, than at the Thoughts of again quitting my Country and encountering the Dangers of the Seas and of Enemies. Yet when I reflect on the general Voice in my favour, and the high Honour done me by this appointment; I feel the warmest Sentiments of Gratitude to Congress, and make no hesitation to accept it, and devote myself, without Reserve or loss of Time to discharge the Duties of it.

My Success however may depend, in a great degree, on Intelligence and Instructions, that I may receive, from time to time, from Congress, and on the Punctuality, with which Several Articles, in my Instructions may be kept Secret. It shall be my earnest Endeavour, to transmit the most constant and exact Information of whatever may occur, and to conceal those Instructions which depend in any Measure on my Judgment.

I hope I need not suggest to Congress, the Necessity, of communicating to me as early as possible, their Commands from Time to Time, and of keeping all the discretionary Articles an impenetrable Secret: a Suggestion, however, that the Constitution of that Sovereignty, which I have the Honour to represent, might excuse.

As the Frigate has been sometime waiting, I shall embark in Eight or ten days, at farthest. Your Excellency, will be pleased to present my most dutifull Respects to Congress, and accept my Thanks for the polite and obliging manner, in which you have communicated their Commands. I have the Honour to be, with great Esteem and Respect, your Excellencys most obedient, humble Servant   John Adams[2]

National Archives: Record Group 360: Records of the Continental and Confederation Congresses and the Constitutional Convention hereafter cited as NA: PCC, item 84, v. 1, pp. 117-118 (ALS); National Archives Microfilm Publication M247, hereafter cited as M247, reel 111.

[1] Huntington, Samuel (1731-1796). Connecticut lawyer and political figure. Member, Continental Congress, 1776, 1778-1781, 1783; president, September 1779-July 1781. Lieutenant governor of Connecticut, 1785; governor, 1786-1796.

[2] Adams, John (1735-1826). Massachusetts lawyer, political figure, and diplomat. Massachusetts delegate to the First and Second Continental Congresses, 1774-1778. Commissioner to France, 1778-1779; to negotiate peace, 1779-1783; to conclude a commercial treaty with Great Britain, 1779-1781; and to conclude treaties of amity and commerce with European nations, 1783-1786. Minister to the United Provinces of the Netherlands, 1782-1788, and to Great Britain, 1785-1788. Vice President of the United States, 1789-1797. President of the United States, 1797-1801.

Chevalier de la Luzerne to Comte de Vergennes

[Translation]

Nᵒ 22. Quadruplicate.   Philadelphia, 7 January 1780
My Lord[1]

I had no knowledge of the Negotiations that preceded and accompanied our treaties with the United States of America, and it is only since my arrival on this Continent that I learned that the treaty of amity and Commerce made public by Congress contained two articles that were not inserted in the printed copies made public in France and Europe. They are articles 11 and 12. The one relative to the export of Molasses from our Islands assured to the Subjects of the 13 States an exemption from all duties on that commodity, and the other says that every type of merchandise purchased in the 13 States by the King's[2] Subjects for the use of the Islands that furnish Molasses will be equally exempt from all export duties. When our Treaties were brought to America, these two Articles, the insertion of which only Mr. Arthur Lee[3] is said to have wished to oppose, suffered no difficulty, and Congress ratified the Treaty in its entirety without any reservation. The published Prints in the English language thus contain 33 Articles, while those published in the French language contain only 31, and beyond article eleven the numerical order is inverted. But the chief inconvenience of this difference proceeds from the fact that the Americans, when presenting themselves to the Governors of our Islands with the English Print of the treaty, have been exempted from the duty in question, while the French Merchants are still made to pay it. This duty, although not very considerable, gives sufficient advantages to those who are exempt from it to drive that branch of Commerce fully out of the hands of His Majesty's Subjects if they should continue to be treated less favorably than the Americans in this regard.

The goods exported from the 13 States to our Islands are subject to no duty, and the United States have no exemption to accord to French Merchants equivalent to that which they enjoy. It therefore seems that it would not be disadvantageous at the present time to reestablish the duty in their regard, and to consider the French copy of the Treaty as the more authentic. But, My Lord, this indefinite immunity of the Commerce of the Continent of America will probably not last long beyond the duration of the present war, and then our Merchants will be justified in claiming the benefit of Article 12, as the Americans have enjoyed the advantages assured to them by the Eleventh. One can add to this consideration that the Americans have recently invented a process for extracting from Cornstalks a Sugar that for them takes the place of Molasses, and that the only means of arresting the progress of this invention is to hold that of our Islands at the lowest price possible by exempting it from every duty. The Commerce of Europe rejects Molasses, and if the outlet from the Continent of America were closed to it, it would be in large part a complete loss for our Islands. Besides, there would be some inconvenience in reforming two articles that have received all their Sanction, and if it is permitted to have an opinion on this matter, I think it more proper and more useful to allow them to exist. But in any case, it is desirable that the difference that exists in the publication made of these Documents should be eliminated, and that the condition of the Frenchmen who trade in Molasses should not be worse than that of Americans undertaking the same Commerce.

. . . . .

I am with respect, My Lord, Your most humble and most obedient Servant　　　　　　　　　　　　　　　　　Le chr de la luzerne[4]

Received 22 May.

French Foreign Affairs Archives: Political Correspondence, hereafter cited as FFAA: Pol. Corr., United States, hereafter cited as U.S., v.11, f. 511-512vo. (LC transcription).

[1] Vergennes, Charles Gravier, Comte de (1719-1787). French statesman and diplomat. Minister to the Elector of Trier, 1750-1754, also envoy to Hanover, 1752, and to the Elector Palatinate, 1752-1753. Ambassador to the Ottoman Empire, 1755-1768. Ambassador to Sweden, 1771-1774. Secretary of state and minister of foreign affairs, 1774-1787.

[2] Louis XVI (1754-1793). King of France, 1774-1793.

[3] Lee, Arthur (1740-1792). Colonial agent, diplomat, and Virginia political figure. Practiced law in London, 1770-1776. Commissioned agent of Massachusetts, 1770. Appointed correspondent of Congress in London, 1775. With Silas Deane and Benjamin Franklin (whom he subsequently accused of malfeasance), commissioner to France, 1776-1779. Commissioner to Spain, 1777. Returned to America, 1780. Member, Virginia House of Delegates, 1781-1783, 1785-1786. Member, Continental Congress, 1782-1784. Member, U.S. Board of Treasury, 1785-1789.

[4] Luzerne, Anne-César, Chevalier de la (1741-1791). French diplomat. Envoy extraordinary near the Elector of Bavaria, 1776-1778. Minister to the United States, 1779-1784. Ambassador to Great Britain, 1788-1791.

Don Juan de Miralles to Don José de Gálvez

Sir:[1]   Philadelphia. 24 January, 1780.

·   ·   ·   ·   ·

...Congress suffers from a lack of funds with which to meet so many expenses. The value of its money is greatly depreciated, and so far no benefit has been derived from the bills of exchange Congress has resolved to draw on its ministers at the Spanish and French Courts and the person named to negotiate a loan from Holland. No one is willing to take the bills on the terms asked, which are the following: The bills are to be payable six months from the date of issuance, to be negotiated for twenty-five dollars in Continental money for one dollar in species supplied in Europe, and he who accepts the said bills must deposit in the loan fund a proportionate amount of Continental money upon which an interest of six percent per year will be paid, and at the end of three years the principal will be restored to him.

Emissaries and partisans of the enemy are constantly busy in attempts to introduce distrust of Continental money. They have a very injurious effect even among the adherents to the common cause, who allow themselves to be influenced by the opinions of the enemy even though they recognize the fact that they are baseless. When the independence of the United States is recognized and conceded the states will possess the large territories formerly owned by the English Crown and many of its subjects. The sale of those lands to American citizens will produce a sum much greater than the two hundred million paper dollars which have been printed, and with the remainder invested at six percent they will be guaranteed an annual income sufficient to defray the expenses of an even greater Monarchy.

If it happens that the piety of our Benevolent Sovereign and that of His Most Christian Majesty are favourably disposed toward sustaining and assisting the United States with a sum of money in specie, surely the time when they most sorely need it has come. I do not doubt that reciprocation on the part of these states will be proportionate to the benefaction given to them. In any case, the assistance could be discussed and agreed upon here with the Congress by the respective ministers of both Sovereigns in unison and respectively instructed for the purpose. I hope that Your Excellency will be kind enough to pardon me for this suggestion, which is made with sincere desire for the best results.

I pray to God to preserve Your Excellency's very important person the many years which I desire and need, etc.   Juan de Miralles[2]

Library of Congress, hereafter cited as LC: Aileen Moore Topping Collection, 1780, pp. 463-465 (Typescript translation).

[1] *Gálvez, José de, Marqués de la Sonora (1729-1786). Spanish political figure and colonial administrator. Minister of the Indies, 1775-1786.*

[2] *Miralles, Juan de (d. 1780). Havana merchant and slave trader who served as Spain's unofficial representative in the United States, 1778-1780.*

John Jay to Don José de Gálvez

Sir,   Cadis 27[th.] January 1780.

Permit me through your Excellency to have the Honour of representing to his most catholic Majesty, that on the sixth Day of February 1778 – The respective Plenipotentiaries of his most christian Majesty and the United States of America, by whom the Treaties now subsisting between them were concluded did make and subscribe a Secret Article in the Words following Vizt:[1]

"The Most Christian King declares, in consequence of the intimate union which subsists between him and the King of Spain,[2] that in concluding with the United States of America this treaty of amity and commerce, and that of eventual and defensive alliance, his Majesty had intended, and intends to reserve expressly, as he reserves by this present separate and secret act, to his Catholic Majesty, the power of acceding to the said treaties and to participate in their stipulations, at such time as he shall judge proper. It being well understood, nevertheless, that if any of the stipulations of the said treaties are not agreeable to the King of Spain, his Catholic Majesty may propose other conditions analogous to the principal aim of the alliance, and conformable to the rules of equality, reciprocity, and friendship. The deputies of the United States, in the name of their constituents, accept the present declaration to its fullest extent; and the deputy of the said States, who is fully empowered to treat with Spain, promises to sign, on the first requisition of his Catholic Majesty, the act or acts necessary to communicate to him the stipulations of the treaties above written. And the said deputy shall endeavour, in good faith, the adjustment of the points in which the King of Spain may propose any alteration, conformable to the principles of equality, reciprocity, and perfect amity; he the said deputy not doubting but the person or persons, empowered by his Catholic Majesty to treat with the United States, will do the same with regard to any alterations of the same kind, that may be thought necessary by the said Plenipotentiary of the United States."

The Congress willing to manifest their Readiness fully to comply with an Article which they have Reason to believe particularly agreeable to their great and good Ally, and being desirous of establishing perpetual amity and Harmony with a Prince and Nation whom they greatly respect, and with whom various Circumstances lead them to wish for the most cordial and permanent Friendship, have thought proper to request his most catholic Majesty to accede to the said Treaties, and thereby preclude the Necessity of that Measure's originating in the manner specified in the Article. For this Purpose they have done me the Honor to appoint me their Minister Plenipotentiary, and directed me to communicate to his most christian Majesty the Desire of Congress on this Subject and to request his favorable Interposition. They also made it my Duty to give his most Catholic Majesty the fullest assurances of their sincere Disposition to cultivate his Friendship and Confidence, and authorized me, on their Behalf, to enter into such Treaties of Alliance Amity and Commerce, as would become the lasting Foundations of Perpetual Peace to Spain and the United States, and the Source of extensive advantages to both.

Thus commissioned I embarked without Delay on Board the Frigate which had been appointed to carry the Sieur Gerard[3] to France, and sailed with him for that Kingdom, from Pennsylvania on the 26th. Day of October last.

But after having been thirteen Days at Sea the Frigate was dismasted and so greatly injured her Rudder, as to oblige us to alter our Course and Steer for Martinique. We arrived there on the 18th. Day of December last; and sailed from thence on the 28th. Day of the same Month in a french Frigate which was bound to Toulon, but had Orders to touch at this Port for

Intelligence. We arrived here the 22ᵈ Inst. and received Information of recent Events, which rendered the further Prosecution of our Voyage too hazardous to be prudent.

Providence having thus been pleased to bring me directly to Spain, the Respect due to his most catholic Majesty forbids me to postpone communicating to him my Appointment and Arrival; and the same motive will induce me to remain here 'till he shall be pleased to signify to me his Pleasure. For although nothing would afford me more sensible Pleasure, than the Honor of presenting to his Majesty the Dispatches which I am charged by Congress to deliver to him, yet on this as on every other occasion, it shall be my Study to execute the Trust reposed in me, in the manner most pleasing to his Majesty, agreeable to the true Intent and meaning of the Article above mentioned.

And that his most christian Majesty may have the highest Evidence of the Intention and Desire of Congress fully and faithfully to execute this Article, I shall immediately do myself the Honor of communicating the same together with my Appointment and arrival; and I flatter myself that the Request of Congress for his favorable Interposition, will meet with the same friendly Attention, which he has uniformly extended to all their Concerns, and of which I am too sensible not to derive the highest Satisfaction from acknowledging on every Occasion.

Mʳ· Carmichael[4] my Secretary will have the Honor of delivering this Dispatch to your Excellency, as well as of giving every Information in his Power to afford. This Gentleman was a Member of Congress at the Time of his Appointment, and will be able more fully to express the Ardor with which the United States desire to establish a Union with France and Spain on Principles productive of such mutual Attachment and reciprocal Benefits as to secure to each the Blessings of uninterrupted Tranquillity.

I have the Honor to be, with great Consideration and Respect, &c.

John Jay.[5]

P.S. I do myself the Honor of transmitting to your Excellency herewith enclosed a Copy of my Letter to his Excellency the Count De Vergennes.

NA: PCC, item 110, v. 1, pp. 25-29 (LBkC); M247, reel 135; Henry P. Johnston, editor, The Correspondence and Public Papers of John Jay (New York: G.P. Putnam's Sons, 1890-1893), hereafter cited as Johnston, Jay Correspondence, v. 1, pp. 259-263.

[1] The following paragraph is found in Johnston, Jay Correspondence, v.1, p. 260.

[2] Charles III (1716-1788). King of the Two Sicilies (as Charles VII), 1734-1759. King of Spain, 1759-1788.

[3] Gérard, Conrad-Alexandre (1729-1790). French diplomat. As undersecretary of state to Vergennes, he assisted in the treaty negotiations with Franklin, Deane, and Lee in 1777-1778. Minister to the United States, 1778-1779.

⁴ *Carmichael, William (?-1795). Diplomat. Secretary to the American commissioners in France, 1777-1778. Member, Continental Congress, 1778-1779, from Maryland. Secretary of legation to John Jay in Spain, 1780-1782. Chargé d'affaires ad interim in Madrid, 1782-1790; en titre, 1790-1794.*

⁵ *Jay, John (1745-1829). New York lawyer, political figure, and diplomat. Member, Continental Congress, 1774-1777, 1778-1779; president, 1778-1779. Chief justice of the State of New York, May 1777-December 1778. Principal author, New York State constitution. Appointed minister to Spain, September 27, 1779. With John Adams, Benjamin Franklin, and Henry Laurens, commissioner to negotiate peace, 1781-1784. Secretary for Foreign Affairs, 1784-1790. With Alexander Hamilton and James Madison, author of* The Federalist. *Chief Justice of the U.S. Supreme Court, 1789-1795. Minister to Great Britain, 1794-1795. Governor of New York, 1795-1801.*

John Jay's Instructions to William Carmichael

Sir,   Cadis, 27ᵗʰ· Janʸʳ 1780.

You will proceed to Madrid with convenient expedition, and if Mʳ· Gerard, with whom you set out, should travel too very deliberately, I advise you to go on before him; The propriety of this however will depend much on circumstances, and must be determined by your own discretion.

On delivering my Letter to Mʳ· Galvez it would be proper to intimate that I presume it would be more agreeable to him to receive my dispatch from you, who would give him information on many matters about which he might choose to inquire, than in the ordinary modes of conveyance; and it may not be amiss to let him know, that his not receiving notice of our arrival from me by Mʳ· Gerard's Courier, was owing to a mistake between that Gentleman and me. – Treat the French Ambassador with great Attention and Candor, and that degree of confidence only, which prudence and the Alliance between us may prescribe. – In your Conversation with People about the Court, impress them with an Idea of our strong attachment to France, yet so as to avoid permitting them to imbibe an Opinion of our being under the *direction* of any Counsels but our own; The former will induce them to think well of our constancy, and good faith; the latter of our Independence and Self-Respect.

Discover if possible whether the Courts of Madrid and Versailles entertain in any degree the same mutual disgusts, which we are told prevail at present between the two Nations, and be cautious when you tread on that delicate Ground. It would also be useful to know who are the King's Principal Confidents, and the trains leading to each. To treat prudently with any Nation it is essential to know the state of it's revenues. Turn your Attention therefore to this Object, and endeavor to learn whether the public expenditures consume their annual Income; or whether there be any and what Overplus, or deficiency, and the manner in which the former is disposed of, or the latter supplied.

If an opportunity should offer inform yourself as to the regulations of the Press at Madrid, and indeed throughout the Kingdom, and the particular character of the Person at the head of that department.

Endeavor to find some person of adequate Abilities, and knowledge in the two languages, to translate English into Spanish with propriety, and if possible elegance.

I wish also to know which of the Religious Orders, and the Individuals of it are most esteemed, and favoured at Court.

Mention as matter of Intelligence, rather than in the way of Argument the Cruelties of the Enemy, and the Influence of that Conduct on the Passions of the Americans. This will be the more necessary, as it seems we are suspected of retaining our former Attachment to Britain.

In speaking of American Affairs remember to do Justice to Virginia and the Western Country near the Mississippi. Recount their atchievments against the Savages, their growing numbers, extensive Settlements and aversion to Britain for attempting to involve them in the horrors of an Indian War. Let it appear also from your Representations that ages will be necessary to settle those extensive Regions.

Let it be inferred from your conversation that the Expectations of America as to my Reception, and Success, are sanguine; That they have been rendered the more so by the Suggestions of Persons generally supposed to speak from Authority, and that a disappointment would be no less unwelcome than unexpected.

I am persuaded that pains will be taken to delay my receiving a decided answer as to my Reception until the sentiments of France shall be known; Attempts will also be made to suspend the acknowledgment of our Independence on the condition of our acceding to certain Terms of Treaty Do nothing to cherish either of these Ideas, but without being explicit, treat the latter in a manner expressive of Regret and Apprehension, and seem to consider my Reception as a measure which we hoped would be immediately taken, although the Business of the Negotiation might be postponed, until France could have a Opportunity of taking the Steps she might think proper on the Occasion.

You will offer to transmit to me any dispatches which Mr Galvez may think proper to confide to you, or to return with them yourself, if more agreeable to him.

You will be attentive to all other objects of useful Information, such as the Characters, Views, and connexions of important Individuals: The Plan of operations for the next Campaign; Whether any and what secret overtures have been made by Britain to France, or Spain, or by either of them to her, or each other; Whether any of the other Powers have manifested a disposition to take a Part in the War, and whether it is probable that any and which of them will become Mediators for a general peace; and on what plan. If the War should continue it would be advantageous to know whether Spain means to carry on any serious operations for possessing herself of the Floridas and Banks of the Missisipi &c. &c.

Although I have confidence in your prudence, yet permit me to recommend to you, the greatest circumspection. Command yourself under every circumstance: On the one hand avoid being suspected on Servility; and on the other let your temper be always even, and your attention unremitted.

You will oblige me by being very regular, and circumstantial in your correspondence; and commit nothing of a private nature to Paper unless in Cypher.   John Jay

NA: PCC, item 110, v. 1, pp. 33-37 (LBkC); M247, reel 135.

Don Juan de Miralles to Don José de Gálvez

Sir: Philadelphia. 1 February, 1780

The French Minister[1] informed me today that in a letter dated 8 July, 1779, which he received eight days ago by way of Virginia, Monsieur Vergennes has advised him that he considers that I am sufficiently authorized and instructed to negotiate with the Congress affairs of our Court. That the most important points are these three: the granting of free navigation on the Mississippi River to the Americans, the capture of San Agustíne de la Florida and its cession to Spain, and an agreement concerning territorial possessions on the Mississippi. That all must be done with my concurrence.

I told him that I am without any order or instructions, but that without being opposed to whatever steps he thought it prudent to take, I must remind him that the matter of navigation on the Mississippi had been discussed with the Congress earlier by Monsieur Gérard, who influenced by me had opposed that freedom of navigation as contrary to the intentions and interests of His Majesty, and the result had been that it was left to His Majesty to decide whether to concede it or not, and that the instructions which Congress gave to their Minister Plenipotentiary sent to Spain are in accord with that resolution. That Congress previously had offered to capture San Agustín de la Florida and turn it over to Spain, and that recently it has tacitly repeated that offer in its reply to the memorial which I sent to it on

24 November. That as for agreement concerning establishments on the Mississippi, it is thought that the Americans have none there, as those which they took from the English in February of 1778 were recaptured by the English settlers because the Americans did not leave a garrison strong enough to hold them. Only on the Ohio River do the Americans have some settlements.

That in any case I thought it wise to await His Majesty's orders so as to adhere to his Royal intentions, and moreover it was very probable that those matters and any others considered important would be discussed with the Minister John Jay, and I was inclined to await the results, which probably would not be long delayed.

Because my reasons seemed well founded, the French Minister decided to postpone all negotiations concerning these matters. I hope that this will be to His Majesty's Royal pleasure and that Your Excellency will approve.

I pray God to preserve your very important person the many years which I desire and need, etc. Juan de Miralles

LC: *Aileen Moore Topping Collection, 1780, pp. 475-476 (Typescript translation).*
[1] *Luzerne.*

Benjamin Franklin to David Hartley

Dear friend,[1] Passy, feb. 2. 1780.

. . . . .

I have long post poned answering your Letter of the 29th of June. A principal Point in it, on which you seemed to desire my Opinion, was the Conduct you thought America ought to hold in Case her allies should, from Motives of ambition or resentment of former Injuries desire her to continue the War beyond what should be reasonable and consistent with her particular Interests. As often as I took up your Letter in order to answer it, this Suggestion displeas'd me and I laid it down again. I saw no Occasion for discussing such a Question at Present, nor any good End it could serve to discuss it before the Case should happen, which I believe never will happen; and I saw Inconveniencis in discussing it. I wish therefore you had not mentioned it. for the rest, I am as much for peace as ever I was, and as heartily desirous of seeing the War ended, as I was to prevent its Beginning; of which your Ministers know I gave a strong Proof before I left England, when in order to an accommodation, I offer'd at my own Risque *without Orders* for so doing, and without knowing whether I should be own'd in doing it to pay the whole Damage of destroying the tea at Boston provided the Acts made against that Province were repealed. This offer was refused. I still think it would have been wise to have accepted it. If the Congress have therefore entrusted to others rather than to me, the Negociations for Peace, when such shall be set on foot, as has been reported; it is perhaps because they may have heard of a very singular Opinion of mine, that there hardly ever existed such a thing as a bad Peace, or a good War and that I might therefore easily be induc'd to make improper Concessions. But at the same time, they and you may be assured, that I should think the Destruction of our whole Country, and the Extirpation of our whole People, preferable to the Infamy of abandoning our allies.

As neither you nor I are at Present authoriz'd to treat of Peace It seems to Little purpose to make or Consider Propositions relating to it. I have had so many such put into my hands that I am tired of them. I will however give your Proposal of a Ten Years Truce this Answer, that tho' I think a solid Peace made at once, a much better thing; yet if the Truce is practicable and the Peace not, I should be for agreeing to it. At least I see at present no sufficient Reasons for refusing it, provided our allies approv'd of it. But this is merely a private Opinion of mine, which perhaps may be changed by Reasons, that at Present do not offer themselves. This however I am clear in, that with drawing your Troops will be best for you, if you wish a cordial Reconciliation, and that the Truce should produce a Peace. To show that it was not done by compulsion, being required as a Condition of the Truce, they might be withdrawn before hand for various good Reasons. But all this is idle Chat as I am persuaded that there is no Disposition for Peace on your side, and that this War will yet last many Years. I know nothing and believe nothing of any Terms offered by now to Sir H. Clinton.[2]...

. . . . .

Adieu my dear friend and believe me ever, Your most affectionately,

B. Franklin[3]

LC: Benjamin Franklin Papers, microfilm reel 1 (LBkC).

[1] Hartley, David (1732-1813). British political figure and scientist. Friend of Benjamin Franklin. Member of Parliament, 1774-1780, 1782-1784; a consistent supporter of Rockingham. Opposed American war and African slave trade. Plenipotentiary to negotiate definitive Anglo-American peace treaty, 1783.

[2] Clinton, Sir Henry (1738?-1795). British military leader. Knighted, 1777, for his role in the battle of Long Island and the capture of New York, August-September 1776. Commander, British forces in New York, 1777-1778. Appointed commander-in-chief of British forces in North America, 1778. Captured Charlestown, South Carolina, 1780. Resigned his command to General Sir Guy Carleton, May 1782, and returned to England.

[3] Franklin, Benjamin (1706-1790). Printer, author, philanthropist, inventor, diplomat, scientist, and Pennsylvania political figure. Deputy postmaster general for the colonies,

1753-1774. Pennsylvania representative, Albany Congress, 1754. Colonial agent, 1757-1762, 1764-1775. Member, Continental Congress, 1775-1776. With Silas Deane and Arthur Lee, commissioner to negotiate treaties with France, 1776-1778. Minister to France, 1778-1785. With John Adams, John Jay, and Henry Laurens, commissioner to negotiate peace, 1781-1784. With John Adams and Thomas Jefferson, commissioner to negotiate commercial treaties in Europe, 1783-1785. President, Executive Council of Pennsylvania, 1785-1788. Member, Constitutional Convention, 1787.

Comte de Vergennes to Chevalier de la Luzerne

[Translation]

Nᵒ· 4   Versailles, 5 February 1780

I have received, Sir, the despatches that M. Gerard has written to me from Nᵒ· 119 to Nᵒ· 123 as well as those which you have done me the honor of sending me from Nᵒ· 3 to Nᵒ· 11 inclusive.

I regret that you have lacked occasions to write to me since the month of November because we find ourselves uncertain both of the military situation of the Americans and of the dispositions of Congress; and it is of the essence for us to know both in order to make up for the ignorance in which we find ourselves. We suppose that the resolutions passed by Congress at the moment of M. Gerard's departure have not met with any variation, that not only are the Americans constant in their attachment to the alliance, but that they also persist in the decision they have made relative to Spain.

It is in speaking of this double presupposition that the King is occupied with the means of seconding the efforts of the United States in the most efficacious manner during the next campaign, and of placing them in a state to strike the most telling blows at the common enemy. In order to realize this important object, the King is determined to send a squadron with a body of troops to North America; this expedition is now being prepared and will put to sea at the earliest possible moment. The Marquis de la Fayette[1] has our secret, and he is on his way to America to confide it to General Washington.[2] You yourself will comprehend, Sir, that it is infinitely important to us that it be guarded with great care until our troops have landed in America, and I need not recommend that you take all precautions which depend upon you that it not be divulged. It will perhaps be appropriate to take the President of Congress and the patriots on whose discretion you think you can rely into your confidence. We can only resign ourselves entirely to your prudence in this regard: but in case you judge secrecy necessary, you may limit yourself to saying in general that the King is essentially occupied with the means of sending aid in vessels and troops to the Americans for next spring, and that you have cause to believe that you will soon receive precise information on the strength and the particular destination of this aid, as well as on the time when it will be sent. I am not sending you any details on the use which will be made of it, because that will depend on the plan of campaign on which the American general determines, a plan which he will concert with M. de la Fayette, and which that officer will not fail to communicate to you.

The King does not doubt, Sir, that the United States are cognizant of the full value of the immediate assistance that he is going to give them, and that this step augments their attachment to His Majesty and their zeal for the common cause. In recalling these two sentiments to the Americans in case of need, you will neglect nothing to make them cognizant that it is time that they make the greatest efforts not only to halt the progress of the English on the American continent, but also to drive them from it if possible; that circumstances have never been more favorable for accomplishing this task than those in which America will probably find herself in the course of next summer, since from all appearances the English will be obliged to divide their forces, and they will be the weaker party everywhere. If you are asked about the conquest of Canada and of Nova Scotia, you will observe that the United States should not concern themselves with a distant expedition until they become the masters of their own house, and that by adopting another plan, they would expose themselves to expenses from which they would probably not reap the least advantage: this remark joined to the difficulties presented since last year by Gen. Washington will, I hope, cure the United States of the mania for conquering foreign provinces before having conquered and secured their own territory.

I presume, Sir, that Don Juan Mirales will have made known to you the political system that his Court has followed up to now relative to the Americans, that in consequence you know that the Catholic King has still not made known the point of view under which he envisages them, nor the dispositions which he has taken in their regard. I do not know what impression this silence may have made on Congress, but I think that it has not been misled; that it will have interpreted the sentiments of the King of Spain by those of His Majesty, and that it will consequently be led to this supposition, that is to say, that all its resolutions relative to the Court of Madrid have had the basic goal of pleasing him, and of persuading it by dint of condescension and moderation to accede to the treaties subsisting between His Majesty and the United States; such is, Sir, the language it is appropriate for you to maintain when you speak of Spain; unless it is contrary to that which the Court of Madrid may have stipulated to its agent; and in that case you will comply with the instructions of His

Catholic Majesty unless (which I cannot presuppose) their contrariety to yours and to our ties with America leads you to think that it would be more appropriate for you to remain silent.

I saw Mr. Adams several days ago; he seemed to me to be in the best dispositions; but he has given me cause to judge that he does not understand the full nature and object of his commission at all; he believes that he was sent to Europe to treat for peace with England immediately; I hope that M. Gerard is the bearer of his instructions, and that they will convince him that his commission is only a contingent one, and that its fundamental principle is our treaty of alliance.

I am told, Sir, that Mr. Arthur Lee has dared to state in America that I had written him a letter in which I assured him that M. Gerard and M. Holker[3] had orders to take no part in that which concerned him, and that the King's indignation would be the punishment for the transgression of this Law. It is the more necessary to destroy this imposture, which has only been imagined in order to harm the reputation of M. Gerard and to attribute to Mr. Lee a confidence on my part which was long ago destroyed; you would therefore do well, Sir, to declare to the President of Congress that the letter in question never existed, and that far from having disavowed what I wrote to M. Gerard concerning my mistrust of Mr. Lee, on the contrary, I confirmed it to him by telling him the reason for my train of thought in this regard. I repeated the same thing to Mr. Franklin, entreating him to inform Congress, and I do not doubt that this Minister has acquitted himself with exactitude. It is possible that Mr. Lee, in order to foster new deceit, has showed off the gift which he received from the King; but if that is so, you will state without affectation that this gift was given to Mr. Lee only because he signed the treaties of commerce and of alliance, and not in the view of giving to that former commissioner a particular mark of the satisfaction which the King has with his conduct.

I have still not heard anyone speak of Mr. Laurens,[4] and I do not know if he has already arrived in Europe or not: I hope that this former president will not proceed to his destination without having seen me. I confess, Sir, that I know nothing of his mission; it will only serve to embarrass the States General and perhaps to compromise it. I would not suspect him of having views contrary to the alliance, for he has always manifested a patriotism that leaves nothing to be desired.

While crossing the northern part of America, Sir, you encountered some industry and even some manufactories, and you conclude from this that it will not be long before the Americans are in a position to do without the manufactories of Europe, and that speculations which have been made in this regard will soon be actual fact. But I think it may be observed in the first place, that you have probably encountered only domestic manufactories producing objects of daily use, which consequently would not be furnished by Europe; in the second place, that the manufactories which pursue luxury and taste will probably never be firmly established in America, and that if that should ever happen, it would only be when the population can provide support for arts and for agriculture; in the third place, that the commerce which our manufactories offer has never entered into our political calculations; that the King in resolving to support the independence of North America has had in view only the diminution of the excessive power of England and of procuring for himself direct commerce with a country which has such a need, and which furnishes the materials necessary or useful to Europe. Such are the speculations that the King's Council made when it allied itself with the Congress; it has not done and will never do anything else relative to America.

I do not wish to leave you unaware, Sir, that Mr. Franklin having confided to me the embarrassment in which he has found himself as much for meeting the bills of Congress as for making purchases of arms and vestments with which he has been charged, I have procured him an advance by means of a loan of three million livres; this assistance has placed this Minister not only in a position to discharge the bills of Congress, but also to procure what is needed to clothe ten thousand men. I do not doubt that Mr. Franklin has made it his duty to report this service which the circumstances render important, and which Congress has appreciated at its true value.

Vergennes

FFAA: Pol. Corr., U.S., v. 11, f. 47 (LC transcription).

[1] Lafayette, Marie-Joseph-Paul-Yves-Roch Gilbert du Motier, Marquis de (1757-1834). French military officer and statesman. Inspired by the Declaration of Independence, this wealthy young aristocrat sailed for America in April 1777 without his government's approval. Congress commissioned him a major general in the Continental Army on July 31, 1777; he at first served on the staff of General Washington, who virtually adopted him, and later commanded a division of Virginia light troops. He spent the period from January 1779 to April 1780 in France working for American interests, then returned to America to make preparations for the arrival of Rochambeau's expeditionary force. He played an important part in the Yorktown campaign. In December 1781 he returned to France, where he assisted the American commissioners in their negotiations with France and Spain regarding the western boundaries. Later in the 1780s, he worked diligently with Thomas Jefferson to simplify French trade restrictions that prevented a fuller blossoming of Franco-American commerce. During the initial stages of the French Revolution, he helped to convert the Estates General into a National Assembly; introduced the Declaration of the Rights of Man adopted by that body on July 11, 1789; and served as commander of the Paris National Guard, July 1789-October 1791.

[2] Washington, George (1732-1799). Virginia political figure and military leader. Virginia

militia officer, 1752-1758. Member, Virginia House of Burgesses, 1759-1775. Member, Continental Congress, 1774-1775. Commander-in-Chief, Continental Army, 1775-1783. President, Constitutional Convention, 1787. President of the United States, 1789-1797.

[3] *Holker, John (1745-1822). French Consul at Philadelphia and naval agent for American ports, 1778-1780. French Consul General for Pennsylvania, Delaware, New Jersey, and New York, 1780-1781. Business associate of financier Robert Morris, 1781-1784.*

[4] *Laurens, Henry (1724-1792). South Carolina merchant, planter, political figure and diplomat. Member, Continental Congress, 1777-1779; president, November 1777-December 1778. Elected minister to the United Provinces of the Netherlands, October 21, 1779, he did not sail for Europe until August 1780, and was captured at sea. Confined in the Tower of London, October 1780-December 1781. With John Adams, Benjamin Franklin, and John Jay, commissioner to negotiate peace, 1781-1784.*

James Lovell to Samuel Adams

Febr[y.] 8—80[1]

M[r.] Lowell,[2] whose Opinion *has had* weight with me, expressed himself when here against the Delegates communicating to any Individual of the respective Assemblies of their States what they did not think right to deliver officially to the Goverm[t.] – but Laws of Secresy are so imposed at Times in Chesnutt Street that Communications can only go to Colleagues without *glaring* Criminality. I am sure it would be best for the Governm[t.] of every State in the Confederacy to know what we know here. We must cut Throats another Year at least, and we ought to do it vigorously. F & S will persist in strenuous Cooperation for the Purpose of *securing our* Independ[ce.] and *indemnifing themselves.* An armed mediation is not improbable, in which Case the last mediatorial Offers of Spain may be taken up again so that Britain ought not at the End of the next Campaign to hold Possession of any Part of the Territory of the U.S.[s.] Our Enemie do not meet with Countenance in Europe yet, but some Powers there may be *obliged* by *secret* Treaties, on certain Events, to interfere against our Interests, tho' unwillingly; dissagreable Terms of Peace or additional Force against us & our Allies may therefore become a necessary Alternative.

F is extremely desirous that we should put matters upon such a footing in regard to Spain that a *lasting* Alliance may be formed; and hints at 4 Points.

1 a precise & invariable western boundary to the U.S.[s.]
2 The exclusive Navig[n.] of Mississipi to S.
3 The Possess[m.] of the Floridas
4 The Lands on the left or eastern Side of the Miss.

On the first F thinks we should go no farther west than was permitted by the royal Proclam[n] of 1763.

On the 2[d] she thinks we have no Right because we have no Territory situated on the River.

On the third as it is probable S. will conquer the Flor[das] during this war every Cause of Dispute between us & her should be removed.

On the 4th that the Lands lying on the East Side which were prohibited by the Proclamation above named to be settled by the then Provinces are the Property of the K[g] of Engl[d]3 and proper Objects against which Spain may proceed for a *permanent Conquest*. S. conceives that these States have no Rights to those Lands not having *possessed* them nor having a Claim in the Right of the Sovereign whose Gov we have abjured – On the last we shall assuredly differ – the others are all in a fair Train.

. . . . .

Y[r] affect[ly]   James Lovell[4]

. . . . .

The New York Public Library, Astor, Lenox and Tilden Foundations, Rare Books and Manuscripts Division, hereafter cited as NYPL: Samual Adams Papers (ALS).

[1] Adams, Samuel (1722-1803). *Massachusetts political figure. A leading proponent of the revolutionary cause in Massachusetts. Member, Continental Congress, 1774-1781. Lieutenant governor of Massachusetts, 1789-1793, governor, 1794-1797.*

[2] Lowell, John (1743-1802). *Massachusetts political figure and jurist. Member, Massachusetts House of Representatives, 1778, 1780-1782. Member, Continental Congress, 1782. Judge, state court of appeals, 1784-1789. Judge, U.S. district court of Massachusetts, 1789-1801.*

[3] George III, George William Frederick (1738-1820). *King of Great Britain, 1760-1820.*

[4] Lovell, James (1737-1814). *Massachusetts educator and political figure. Member, Continental Congress, 1777-1782; member, committee for foreign affairs.*

Chevalier de la Luzerne to Comte de Vergennes

[Translation]

N[o] 30 Quadruplicate   Philadelphia, 11 February 1780
My Lord

You will have seen in M. Gerard's despatch N[o] 109 the opinion of Congress relative to the boundaries which should separate the possessions of the thirteen United States from those of Spain in the West, and that this assembly has considered them as not being susceptible of any difficulty on account of the clarity of the Charters and the possession of the States which extend to the banks of the Mississippi.

I have reason to believe that the contrary opinion has never been discussed, and it would seem from the subsequent despatches of that Minister that it is without any sort of contradiction that Congress has drafted, according to this principle, Mr. Jay's instructions on this matter. These instructions must have been communicated to you by that minister on his arrival in Europe; you will have seen, my lord, that the United States have no doubt whatsoever concerning their rights to all the lands that extend to the bank of the Mississippi and that they consider them their property, not by virtue of the right of conquest, but in consequence of their Charters. They also believe that they have, relative to Navigation of the Mississippi, the same rights that the Treaty of Paris assured to England, and they think that by offering to be satisfied with commercial Navigation, to renounce navigation with armed Ships, and to conform to all arrangements thought proper to prevent contraband, they submit to Sacrifices which the Court of Madrid would acknowledge by the concession of a port on the Mississippi, and of commercial navigation in the Gulf of Mexico to reach that Port. I was ignorant of the opinion of the Court of Madrid on these important questions when Don Juan Mirales communicated to me the letters by which the Governor of Havana charged him with requesting the Americans to undertake the Conquest of the parts of Louisiana and its dependencies which the English possess. This letter did not say for whose benefit this conquest was to be made, but I presumed that the Spanish intended that it be done for their benefit, and as this circumstance seemed to me diametrically opposed to the instructions with which Mr. Jay was furnished, I took the liberty of explaining to you the state of things in my letter of 17 December, and of asking you for instructions. Your despatch N° 1 contains important explanations on this matter; however, I thought that I should only execute the orders it contains in this regard after having weighed with the greatest attention whether the events that have occurred in the interim did not authorize me to modify them in some measure. Moreover, I thought I should not communicate them to Congress at the same time that I informed it of His Majesty's wishes relative to the reestablishment of the American Army, because I suspected that this last part of my negotiation would meet with difficulties if it were joined to overtures that I presumed would be disagreeable to Congress. While waiting I sounded out several Delegates on the question of the boundaries in the West; I found those from the South and the Center of the firm persuasion that the lands which extend from the Atlantic Ocean to the Mississippi in lines parallel to the Equator belong to them either by virtue of their Charters or by virtue of various acts of possession that they considered supererogatory. These same charters extend the concessions to the west to the Pacific Ocean through regions still unknown, and the States regard as an act of moderation the decision they have made to confine themselves to the boundaries stated in the instructions of which Mr. Jay is the bearer. Some delegates from the Eastern States have announced the same opinion as those from the South, with the difference, however, that they are inclined to think that if Spain were to seize a part of these same countries while they were still in the hands of the English, the right of the Southern States deprived of possession would become difficult to exercise, and that this might result in awkward situations. Moreover, this opinion of a small number of isolated members appeared not to carry any weight against that of a very large majority with respect to rights which they regard as beyond question and against the concessions which have been made for three years by the respective States on both banks of the Ohio and along the left bank of the Mississippi. As for the Floridas, I do not know if any difficulties will arise with regard to the boundaries which the ultimatum assigns them according to the proclamation of the King of England of October 7, 1763, of which I attach here a translation. The Court of Madrid will perhaps wish to give them greater scope in the north beyond the thirty-first degree of latitude; but Congress is of the opinion that His Catholic Majesty finds greater advantage in the present arrangement whereby the Floridas extend under Spanish domination in the northeast up to the St. John's River, whereas the proclamation assigns them the St. Mary's River as the boundary. As for navigation of the Mississippi, it is likely that the United States will submit to the conditions which the Court of Madrid deems it appropriate to set.

The possession of the regions which are on the left of the Mississippi, and of which the English made conquest, is therefore the only matter which may occasion actual difficulties, given the diametrically opposed pretensions of the Spanish and the English. As the instructions given to Mr. Jay contain the wishes and sentiments of Congress in that regard, I have hesitated to put a hand to a task which M. Gerard has only guided to its conclusion through great obstacles; but since on the other hand these instructions are not, with regard to this article, of a nature to satisfy the Court of Madrid, I have resolved, in conformity with your orders, to share my thoughts in confidence with the Spanish Agent in order to concert with him the conduct which I should maintain. He was of the opinion that I should limit myself to general insinuations in order to prepare the United States in advance to receive the unexpected ideas that Mr. Jay will transmit to them. At the same time he would like me to discuss the matter sufficiently with them to be acquainted with their principles, but without presenting those of the Court of Madrid as peremptory and beyond discussion. He also confided to me that he was authorized to open a negotiation for the purchase of the Floridas or the lands in question in case the Americans should be in position to conquer them. I had begun to act in accordance with this plan when an Express sent from Charlestown by General Lincoln[1] brought the news here that the Spanish had crossed the Mississippi, had seized the fort at Natchez, and had taken around nine hundred English prisoners in the posts which are on the left bank of that River. Congress sensed the importance of this diversion and the influence which it could have on the operations of the next Campaign in Georgia, but I noticed that the satisfaction occasioned by this news was mixed with anxiety concerning the intentions of Spain. Some members were moved to say that She made these conquests not to keep them, but to proceed with greater advantage to that of Pensacola, and that she would end by yielding them to the Americans; others express themselves more freely, and I knew that they were proposing to make a motion that Congress request the explanations that it would be in my power to furnish it on this matter. My silence, my lord, might give them reason to believe that I was adopting their opinion. I therefore thought to anticipate this request and put an end to this ferment and to all the explanations that might be given for Spain's conduct by myself setting forth to Congress the principles on which the behavior of this Power is founded. I brought together the Committee appointed to receive my communications and which may not be dissolved until the purpose for which it was appointed is entirely accomplished. I opened the Conference with a speech on the necessity of settling early all the common points between Spain and America, on the affection which the King held for both, on his great desire to destroy all the sources of difficulties which might arise between them, on the conduct and the peaceful intentions of this Power with regard to its neighbors when they kept within the limits of justice and moderation, on its strengths and its resources, on the weight which it could place in the balance, on the influence that its example would have on the other Powers, and on the innumerable advantages that the Americans could draw from their connections with them. I added that the Catholic King had communicated to the King his claims and his expectation on many points which interested him, and that His Majesty had charged me with informing Congress of them. I spoke of the Floridas and of the navigation of the Mississippi as if I were entirely unaware of the tenor of Mr. Jay's instructions. But I had scarcely explained that which concerns the regions situated on the left of the Mississippi when a member of the Committee, a Delegate from North Carolina, an intelligent man committed to the alliance, but ardent, proud, and stubborn, stood up and, on the pretext that he had not understood me, asked me to repeat that part of my speech. I repeated it, and he seemed to listen to it with impatience; behold, he said, all of a sudden the strangest request that we could hear; our Charters, the Treaty of Paris of 1763, the Proclamation of the same year, and finally our Treaty with the King of France are precise. M. Gerard regarded those acts as having formed the basis for some sort of arrangement with Spain; in the state from which I am a delegate, I make myself out to be an owner of land washed by the Mississippi; I know the force and the extent of our Charters and of our rights, and if those of my constituents in the regions in question are not clear and certain, our rights on the Atlantic coasts are equally obscure and doubtful, for they emanate from the same claim; it rests with Spain to undertake the Conquest, and Congress is not safe in Philadelphia; I answered this delegate that I would ask him to examine the question at issue with the same composure as I, to divest himself for the moment of the prejudices that being an interested party might inspire in him, and that he admit that the Charters for the proclamation that he cited might in his eyes have a value that the King of Spain had never recognized; that by the Treaty of Paris, we had ceded to the King of England, and not to the colonies, which could not have taken part in this Treaty, the dependencies of Louisiana to the left of the river; that we had owned them from the time of their discovery until the war of 1756, and that Spain in seizing them today was only exercising the right of conquest; that this right should not be disputed with regard to a power with which she was at war, and which at this moment had forces and garrisons in the contested regions; that I was persuaded that he himself felt he had exaggerated in saying that the actual regions occupied by the 13 States were not theirs in a clearer and more certain manner than the land in question; that he knew better than I the value of an old and uncontested possession, and especially in America, and the unsound nature of a pretention supported by no act of possession; that I respected their charters, but that they were not unaware of the lack of care with which they had been drafted, and that since they were selfcontradictory, since the 13 States were not in agreement on their own respective boundaries, it was not surprising that they clashed at some points with the claims of some other power; that, moreover, I was unaware in what sense he understood that the Treaty of alliance assured them of possession of the lands in question. All the members of Congress appeared to disapprove of their colleague's quick temper, and thanked me for the moderation with which I had answered him, but they told me positively that they were all of the same opinion as he. As for the heart of the question, they desired that we clarify this matter by reading documents that they pointed out to me, and I agreed to this without difficulty. We perused the Charters, whose tenor indeed favors their opinion, and could even give their pretention the most extravagant compass, if they should decide the question. I again confronted them with possession by France before the last war. They answered me that this possession was one of the causes of that same war, that while the kings of England had not had possession nor right at the time of the granting of the Charters, they nevertheless came fully into effect from the moment of the peace of Paris, and when the crown of Great Britain had seen itself invested with these lands, that the Treaty had removed all difficulty, that the peacemakers had considered the Mississippi as a natural boundary, and that it should be agreed that powers that were truly lovers of peace could not wish to change this border.

I insisted and I replied that the misfortunes of the last war had wrested conditions from France and Spain; that they would have been respected if the ambition and the obstinacy of England had not caused them to take up arms again, but that these conditions were null and void, since it was the fault of the English that the war had recommenced, and that Spain could legitimately seize from her enemy all that we had occupied before the war. I added that she wished to resolve this matter in a manner satisfactory to the United States, and that it was to bring this about that I had made these communications to them, that I besought them to read carefully that same proclamation that they had invoked, that they would see there that the King of Great Britain prohibited the governors of the English Colonies from granting concessions beyond the sources of the rivers which run from west to east and flow into the Atlantic Ocean, that it was clear that on this occasion the Watershed had been considered as forming their boundary to the West, and that they were in fact certain and unalterable limits. The members of the committee told me that their archives were full of protestation contrary to that article of the proclamation, that there was a universal discontent in this regard, that moreover by reading it to the end I would see that these same lands had been considered as being within the scope of the respective charters, and that if I saw on the English maps these regions indicated by the designation *Pire Serves*, it is that England had thought that it was natural equity to allow the savages to inhabit a land that belonged to them by the right of first occupancy and of immemorial possession, and which was necessary for their subsistence, that the United States followed the same principles, that they respected the right of the Savages, but that if the latter were disposed to sell their property, the respective States had the exclusive right to buy it, that they had exercised this right on various occasions, and that the banks of the Mississippi were beginning to be populated with a number of colonists from the 13 States, who continually move there. I replied that I regretted seeing the subtleties of civil jurisprudence take the place of the principles of equity and moderation which alone should decide this question, that they were marshalling to their will the same acts they had cited, that they were rejecting what was contrary to them in the proclamation so that they could take advantage of passages that favored their pretensions, that it was proper to treat in the good faith which had up to now characterized their transactions, and that I could assure them that they ought only to be pleased with the moderation of the Court of Spain. Mr. Burke,[2] that same Delegate who had spoken first, answered me that the States were not giving way on this occasion; that their Plenipotentiaries would confide their instructions to you with complete candor; that they would commit their interests in His Majesty, and that they did not doubt that he would act favorably toward them as soon as he learned the State of the situation, that he would even be presumed by the Treaty of Alliance, which in recalling the Treaty of Paris of 1763, sufficiently indicates that His Majesty's opinion was, in contracting with the Americans, that they should be placed in possession of all that before this Treaty, or by virtue of this Treaty, was recognized as belonging to the Crown of Great Britain or to the States heretofore called English Colonies. Articles 5, 6, and 11 of the Treaty were examined and interpreted in every way, but as Minds appeared to me too deeply affected to continue this discussion with the necessary tranquility, and as moreover I had satisfied the wishes of the Spanish agent, I thought I should put an end to the conference by exhorting the Committee not to lose sight of the principles of equity and moderation, which can alone render their alliance desirable, and not to incur the reproach of injustice and greed at the very moment when they are fighting for the purest and most noble cause that can arm a nation. It did not seem to me, My Lord, that my speeches had made a great impression. However, I will not lose any occasion to renew them; but I cannot flatter myself with rectifying the general idea, for this matter has put down deep roots since the peace of 1763. The Court of Spain has taken the most suitable course of resolving these difficulties by seizing in good time the regions in dispute, and it is desirable that it should at the same time consummate some pecuniary arrangements with the interested States; but only their extreme deprivation could lead them to it, and I observe that the various States already assert that it is contrary to the goal and the principles of the Union of the States to alienate to any Foreign Power the Lands comprised in the scope of the Charters, and that if a State were resolved to sell its rights of Sovereignty over a part of the lands of which it is composed, the other States would have the exclusive right to buy them.

I am with Respect, My Lord, your very humble and very obedient Servant   Le chr de la Luzerne

Received 24 May.

FFAA: Pol. Corr., U.S., v. 11, f. 53 (LC transcription).

¹ Lincoln, Benjamin (1733-1810). Massachusetts military leader and political figure. Militia officer, 1755-1777, appointed major general, 1776. Major general, Continental Army, 1777-1781. Surrendered Charlestown, South Carolina, 1780; fought at Yorktown, 1781. Secretary of War, 1781-1783. One of Massachusetts commissioners who treated with the Penobscot Indians regarding land purchases in Maine, 1784 and 1786. Commanded state troops in suppression of Shays' Rebellion, 1787. Lieutenant governor of Massachusetts, 1788-1789. Collector of the Port of Boston, 1789-1809.

² Burke, Thomas (c.1747-1783). North Carolina physician, lawyer and political figure. Member, Continental Congress, 1777-1781. Governor of North Carolina, 1781-1782. Kidnapped by Tories, September 13, 1781, and taken to Charlestown, S.C., as a hostage; escaped; resumed duties as governor, February 1, 1782.

John Adams to the President of Congress

Sir,   Paris, February 15th, 1780.

I have the Honour to inform Congress, that on the ninth of this Month, and not before, I had the good Fortune to arrive in this City, from Ferrol, (where I arrived on the eighth of December,) with Mr· Dana,¹ Mr· Thaxter² and the rest of the Company in tolerable Health, after a Journey of near five hundred Leagues in the dead of Winter, through bad Roads and worse Accommodations of every kind. We lost no Time, more than was indispensable to restore our Health, which was several Times much affected and in great danger Yet we were more than Twice as long in making the Journey by Land, as we had been in crossing the Atlantic Ocean.

The next Morning after our Arrival in Paris Mr· Dana and myself went out to Passy, and spent the Day with his Excellency Dr· Franklin, who did us the Honour the next Day to accompany us to Versailles, where We had the Honour to wait on their Excellencies the Comte De Vergennes, Mr· De Sartine³ and the Comte Maurepas,⁴ with each of whom we had the Honour of a short Conference, upon the State of public Affairs. It is sufficient for me at present to say in general, that I never heard the French Ministry so frank, so explicit and decided, as each of these were, in the Course of this Conversation, in their Declarations to pursue the War with Vigour, and to afford effectual Aid to the United States. I learned with great Satisfaction, that they are sending under Convoy Cloathing and Arms for fifteen thousand Men to America, that seventeen Ships of the Line were already gone to the West Indies under Monsieur De Guichen⁵ and that five or six more at least are to follow, in addition to ten or twelve they have already there.

I asked Permission of the Comte De Vergennes to write to him, on the Subject of my Mission, which he cheerfully and politely agreed to. I have accordingly written to his Excellency, and shall forward Copies of my Letter and of his Answer as soon as it may be safe to do it.

The English are to borrow twelve Millions this Year, and it is said the Loan is filled up. They have thrown a Sop to Ireland, but have not appeased her Rage. They give out exactly such Threats as they did last Year, and every other Year, of terrible Preparations. But Congress knows perfectly well how these Menaces have been accomplished. They will not be more fully executed the next Year than the last — and if France and Spain should throw more of their Force, especially by Sea, into America, the next Year, America will have no essential Injury to fear.

I have learned, since my Arrival at Paris, with the highest pleasure, the Arrival of Mr Gerard, Mr Jay and Mr Carmichael at Cadiz; for whose Safety we had been under very great Apprehensions. I have now very sanguine Hopes that a solid Treaty will soon be concluded with Spain — hopes, which every thing I saw and heard, seemed to favour.

The *Alliance* Frigate, now under the Command of Captain Jones,[6] with Captain Cunningham[7] on board, is arrived at Corunna, where She is to be careened–after which, She is to return to L'Orient, and from thence to go to America, as I am informed by Dr Franklin.

Mr Arthur Lee and Mr Izard[8] are still in Paris, under many Difficulties in procuring a passage home. Mr William Lee[9] is at Brussells. Mr Izard has been to Holland to obtain a passage from thence, but unfortunately missed his Opportunity, and returned disappointed.

I have the Honour to be, with great Respect and Esteem, Sir, your most obedient and most humble Servant   John Adams
Read May 15. –

NA: PCC, item 84, v. 1, pp. 243-245 (LS); M247, reel 111.

[1] *Dana, Francis (1743-1811). Massachusetts political figure and jurist, diplomat. Member, Continental Congress, 1776-1778, 1784-1785. Secretary of legation to John Adams, 1779-1781. Minister-designate to Russia, 1781-1783, but never recognized. Member, Massachusetts supreme court, 1785-1791, chief justice, 1791-1806.*

[2] *Thaxter, John, Jr. (1755-1791). Massachusetts lawyer. First cousin of Abigail Adams. Clerk in the office of the Secretary of Congress, 1778. John Adams' private secretary, November 1779-September 1783. Carried definitive peace treaty to America.*

[3] *Sartine, Antoine-Raymond-Jean-Gualbert-Gabriel de (1729-1801). French government official. Lieutenant general of police, December 1759-May 1774. Minister of the Navy, August 1774-October 1780. Emigrated at the outset of the Revolution.*

[4] *Maurepas, Jérôme Phelypeaux, Comte de (1701-1781). French statesman. Minister of the Navy, 1723-1749. First minister, as minister of state without portfolio, 1774-1781.*

⁵ Guichen, Luc-Urbain du Bouëxic, Comte de (1712-1790). French naval leader. Appointed lieutenant general and assigned to command the fleet at Brest, March 1779. Took squadron from Brest to West Indies, 1780, to replace d'Estaing's squadron; had three indecisive encounters with Rodney's fleet, cooperated with Spanish in convoying troops to Havana before returning to Brest. In June 1781, sailed from Brest to join Spanish fleet for combined operations off Minorca, later lost 15 merchant ships of a large convoy bound for America to British Admiral Kempenfeld. In 1782, his squadron captured 18 British vessels bound for Newfoundland, then joined the Spanish fleet for a fruitless cruise in the Channel.

⁶ Jones, John Paul (1747-1792). Seafarer and naval officer. Commissioned a lieutenant in the Continental Navy, 1775; captain, 1776. Commanded Providence, 1776-1777; Ranger, 1777-1778; Bonhomme Richard, 1779; Alliance, 1780; Ariel, 1781; and America, 1781-1782. After 1783, agent to solicit payment in Europe for prizes taken by his ships. Rear admiral, Russian navy, 1788-1790. Appointed commissioner to ransom prisoners and negotiate peace with Algiers, 1792, but died before he received commission.

⁷ Conyngham, Gustavus (c.1744-1819). American sea captain who held naval commissions from the American representatives in Paris, 1777-1779, as commander of the lugger Surprise and the cutter Revenge, which together captured more than sixty prizes, but initially created diplomatic problems for the French.

⁸ Izard, Ralph (1741/42-1804). South Carolina planter, diplomat, and political figure. Elected commissioner to Tuscany, 7 May 1777, but never received in that capacity. A close associate of Arthur Lee, he attempted to take part in Franco-American diplomatic negotiations, but was rebuffed by Benjamin Franklin, for whom he developed a deep antipathy. Recalled in 1779, he returned to the United States in 1780. Member, Continental Congress, 1782-1783. U.S. Senator, 1789-1795.

⁹ Lee, William (1739-1795). Merchant and diplomat. Brother of Arthur, Richard Henry, and Francis Lightfoot Lee. Commercial agent at Nantes, 1777. Appointed commissioner to Austria and Prussia, 1777, but not recognized by those courts. Negotiated an unauthorized Dutch-American commercial treaty that provided the British with a pretext for declaring war on the United Provinces of the Netherlands in 1780. Recalled in 1779, he remained in Europe until 1783, when he returned to Virginia.

William Carmichael to John Jay

Dear Sir　　　　　　　　　　　　　　　　Madrid, 18th February 1780

I did myself the honor of writing to you by a Courier whom the French Embassador dispatched to Cadiz yesterday morning since which I have been INTRODUCED¹ BY Him TO THEIR EXCELLENCIES THE Marquis de Florida Blanca² and Don Joseph de Galvez. I DELIVER[ED] YOUR LETTER to the LATTER and EXPLAIN[ED] to the FORMER the REASON which INDUCE[D] you [to] ADDRESS the OTHER with which HE APPEAR[ED] PERFECTLY SATISFY[ED]. Don Joseph de Galvez TOLD me HE SHOULD GIVE your LETTER TO THE Marquis de Florida Blanca whose BUSINESS IT WAS TO LAY it BEFORE the

KING and receive his ORDER on the SUBJECT and that EITHER the Marquis OR Himself WOULD be DIRECTED to ANSWER it. I repeated the Substance of your INSTRUCTIONS to me as far as THEY RESPECT Him and was ANSWERED that he would take an OPPORTUNITY of conversing with Me on OUR AFFAIR[S] and would inform me thro the FRENCH EMBASSADOR when it would be CONVENIENT for Him to RECEIVE me. Some COMPLIMENTS passed with respect to the Characters He had RECEIVED of US which it is unnecessary to repeat. The Marquis de Florida Blanca TOLD me that he would LAY your LETTER BEFORE the KING the same night for his consideration. I took this OPPORTUNITY of mentioning the pleasure it would give CONGRESS to hear of your RECEPTION at Madrid from the earnest desire they had to CULTIVATE the KINGS Friendship, that their Expectations were sanguine, having been led to beleive the DISPOSITION of the COURT WAS FAVORABLE by the suggestions of Persons supposed to be well acquainted with its INTENTIONS, that the hopes of the PEOPLE were also great and HINTED that there were several VESSELS about to SAIL FROM Bilboa and the PORT of France BY WHICH you would be happy to COMMUNICATE these NEWS to CONGRESS and to gratify the Expectations of the PEOPLE. He then told me that He had informed the KING of your ARRIVAL at Cadiz altho They had UNDERSTOOD your original DESTINATION was to France. That the KING had ordered Him to receive your OVERTURES and that I was at Liberty to give you this information and after a PAUSE ADDED that on Monday NEXT He hoped to have it in his power to RETURN an ANSWER to your LETTER. You will please to observe that it had not been READ by OTHER when this CONVERSATION PASSED.

He also told me that he would take an opportunity of CONVERSING with me, and would inform me when it would be convenient for Him to SEE me thro the same channel above mentioned. On MONDAY NEXT I GO TO THE Pardo by THEIR APPOINTMENT. HERE I see every day a PERSON whom I beleive to be sent BY THEM to CONVERSE with me altho I appear to know nothing of his CONNECTION with the COURT.

...Your Most Obedient and Most Humble Servant   Wᵐ· Carmichael

Richard B. Morris, editor, John Jay: The Making of a Revolutionary: Unpublished Papers 1745-1780 *(New York: Harper & Row, Pubishers, 1975) hereafter cited as Morris, Jay Papers, v. I, pp. 732-733;* NA: PCC, Miscellaneous Papers, Diplomatic Despatches Received from William Carmichael, *hereafter cited as Misc. Papers, Carmichael Despatches (C); National Archives Microfilm Publication M332, hereafter cited as M332, reel 2.*

¹ *Capitalized text was encyphered in original.*

² *Floridablanca, José Moñino y Redondo, Conde de (1728-1808). Spanish statesman. Chief minister and secretary for foreign affairs, 1776-1792.*

John Adams to the President of Congress

Sir   Paris February 20th 1780.

. . . . .

A report of my Appointment having also been carried to England by the Cartels from Boston, and being spread in Europe by various other Ways, by Passengers by the Committee by French Passengers in the *Sensible*, of whom there were a great Number, who had heard of it, in all Companies in America, and by many private Letters, and the English ministerial Writers having made Use of this, as Evidence of a drooping Spirit in America, in order to favour their Loan of Money, I thought it my best Policy to communicate my Appointment and Powers to the French Court, and ask their Advice, as our good Allies, how to proceed in the present Emergency. I accordingly wrote to his Excellency the Comte de Vergennes, the Letter of the twelfth of February, Copy of which in inclosed, and received his Answer of the fifeenth, Copy of which is inclosed; to which I replied in a Letter of the nineteenth; Copy of which is also inclosed. When I shall have recieved his Excellency's Answer, I shall do myself the Honour to inclose that.

If there is any thing in these Letters of mine, which is not conformable to the Views and Sentiments of Congress, I wish to be instructed in it; or if Congress should not concur in Sentiment with his Excellency the Comte, I shall obey their Orders with the utmost Punctuality & allacrity.

I have ever understood that Congress were first advised to the Measure of appointing a Minister to negotiate Peace, by the French Minister then at Philadelphia, in the Name of the Comte de Vergennes. however this may have been, it cannot be improper, to have some one in Europe, impowered to think and treat of Peace, which some time or other must come.

. . . . .

I have to the Honor to be, with very great Respect, Sir, your most obedient and most humble Servant   John Adams
Rec^d May 15.

NA: PCC, *item 84, v. 1, pp. 267-269 (LS); M247, reel 111.*

Conde de Floridablanca to John Jay

Sir: Pardo, February 28th, 1780.

Having received by the hands of Don Joseph de Galvez the letter which your Excellency sent by Mr. Carmichael, and having communicated the contents to his Majesty, I have it in command to inform you, that his Majesty highly approves the choice, which the American Congress have made of you to the trust mentioned in your letter, as well on account of the high estimation in which his Majesty holds the members who made the choice, as the information he has received of your probity, talents, and abilities. His Majesty also received with pleasure the information of the desire which the Colonies have to form a connexion with Spain, of whose good disposition they have already received strong proofs. Nevertheless, his Majesty thinks it necessary in the first place, that the manner, the forms, and the mutual correspondence should be settled, upon which that Union must be founded, which the United States of America desire to establish with this monarchy. For this purpose there is no obstacle to your Excellency's coming to this Court, in order to explain your intentions and those of Congress, and to hear those of his Majesty, and by that means settling a basis upon which a perfect friendship may be established, and also its extent and consequences.

His Majesty thinks, that until these points are settled, as he hopes they will be, it is not proper for your Excellency to assume a formal character, which must depend on a public acknowledgment and future treaty. But your Excellency may be assured of the sincerity and good dispositions of his Majesty towards the United States, and of his earnest desire to remove every difficulty, for the mutual happiness of them and of this monarchy. This has been intimated to Mr. Carmichael, who can communicate the same to your Excellency, to whom I beg leave to make a tender of my service, being &c.   Count de Florida Blanca

Johnston, Jay Correspondence, v. 1, pp. 273-274.

John Jay to the President of Congress

Sir,   Cadis 3d. March 1780.

Captain Morgan[1] being still here, waiting for a fair wind gives me an opportunity of transmitting to your Excellency a copy of a Letter just come to hand from the Count de Florida Blanca in answer to mine to Mr. Galvez.

Being apprehensive that if present I should probably be amused with verbal answers capable of being explained away if necessary until the two Courts could have time to consult and decide on their measures, I thought it more prudent that my first application should be by Letter rather than in Person.

The answer in question divested of the gloss which its politeness spreads over it, gives us I think to understand that our Independence shall be acknowledged provided we accede to certain terms of Treaty but not otherwise, so that the acknowledgment is not to be made because we are Independent which would be candid and liberal but because of the previous considerations we are to give for it which is consistent with the principle on which nations usually act.

I shall proceed immediately to Madrid. There are many Reasons (hereafter to be explained) which induce me to suspect that France is determined so to manage between us as to make us debtors to their influence and good correspondence with Spain for every concession on her part and to make Spain hold herself obligated to their influence and good correspondence with us for every concession on our Part. Though this may puzzle the business I think it also promotes it.

M͏ʳ· Gerard has often endeavored to persuade me that a certain resolution of Congress would if persisted in ruin the business which however he did not appear much inclined to believe but on the contrary that if every other matter was adjusted you would not part on that point. I assured him that Ground had in my opinion been taken with too much deliberation now to be quitted and that expectations of that kind would certainly deceive those who trusted them. And indeed as affairs are now circumstanced it would in my Opinion be better for America to have no Treaty with Spain than to purchase [one] on such servile terms. There was a time when it might have been proper to have given that Country for their making common cause with us, but that day is now past. Spain is at War with Britain.

I do not like the Cypher in which I write, and shall therefore defer further Particulars till M͏ʳ· Thomson[2] shall receive the one now sent him.

I have the Honor to be with great Respect and Esteem, Your Excellency's Most Obed͏ᵗ· Servant,   John Jay

NA: PCC, item 110, v. 1, pp. 50-52 (LBkC); M247, reel 135.

[1] Not further identified.

[2] Thomson, Charles (1729-1824). Secretary of the Continental Congress, 1774-1789.

Conde de Floridablanca's Questions for John Jay

Pardo 9th. March 1780.

Before entering into a discussion with Mr. Jay or Carmichael jointly or separately on the Subject of the Affairs of the United States of North America, and their mutual Interest with respect to Spain, it is judged indispensable at Madrid, that the Catholic King should be exactly informed of the civil and military State of the American Provinces, and of their resources to continue the present war, not only for the defence of their own liberty, but also with respect to the aid and succours they may be able to afford Spain in its operations in case hereafter this Crown should become the Ally of America. The civil State ought to comprehend. –

1st. – A true Account of the Population, and form of Government of each Province, of the Union, and Resolution of the Inhabitants to continue the War with vigor as long as it is necessary.

2d – Whether there is any powerful party in favor of England, and what consequences are to be apprehended from it; Whether the heads of this party suffer themselves to be seduced by the great promises of the british Government.

3rd – A State of the revenues of these Provinces, and of their ability to contribute to the general Expense; to which may be added, whether they will be able long to support this burthen and even to increase it should it be judged necessary.

4th. – A State of the public debts, and of the particular debts of each State taken collectively or separately, of their resources to lesson them, and the possibility of their being able to support their credit in all the operations of Government in the commerce of their Inhabitants, and above all in the Protection of National Industry.

5th. – By what means, or by what branches of Commerce will the States of America have it in their power to indemnify Spain whenever this power may second the views and operations of the Americans. And particularly the Court wishes to know whether it may be convenient for the said States to furnish Ships of war of the best construction for the Spanish marine, and likewise Timber, and other Articles of the King's Arsenals, the whole without loss of time, and fixing the terms on which they would make an Agreement of this Nature, and who would be commissioned to bring these Vessels and these naval Stores to Spain.

With respect to the Military State of America, it is necessary to be informed 1st. – Of the number and strength of the different bodies of Troops, armed by the Provinces, and of their present Situation in order to judge whether they are sufficient to oppose the Enemy wherever they may go, and particularly in Carolina and Georgia.

Further, it may be expedient to know, the means of augmenting the American Army in case it is necessary, or to keep it always on the same footing notwithstanding its daily losses. In what condition their Clothing and Arms are at present: Whether they are partly in want of those Articles, and how much it would require to remedy those defects.

The Subsistance of an Army being an object of the greatest consequence, The Court desires to know, if proper measures have been taken for that purpose, that it may be ascertained whether it can act every where, if necessary even in the abovementioned provinces, without danger of its being in want of necessaries.

It is highly essential for the provinces of America to keep up a marine to act against the common Enemy and to secure their own possessions during the present War: The Spanish Minister therefore is desirious of knowing its Strength including the armed vessels which belong to Individuals, and by what means it may be augmented, and what Succours will be necessary for that purpose.

The Court of Spain, desirious of Information on these Subjects with all possible frankness, and precision, doth not pretend to dive into matters which Mr. Jay or Carmichael may regard as reserved to themselves. Its only aim is to be acquainted with the present State of the American forces, their resources and ability to continue the War, so that if it was in consideration for new Allies, to supply them with succours of any kind, the former might be able to plan on solid grounds their operations convenient for the common cause, and for the particular advantage of these States without running the risk of being misled by false calculations for want of foresight and proper Information.

NA: PCC, *item 110, v. 1, pp. 90-94 (LBkC); M247, reel 135.*

Don Juan de Miralles to Don José de Gálvez

Sir: Philadelphia. 12 March, 1780.

By an American vessel which recently came to Boston from France the Chevalier de la Luzerne has received official papers from his Court which repeat the instructions about which I informed Your Excellency in my letter of 1 February. By orders written in the month of October he is charged to negotiate with the Congress freedom of navigation on the Mississippi River, conquest by the Americans of San Agustín de la Florida and its cession to

Spain, and an agreement as to possessions on the Mississippi River, but always provided that it be done with my concurrence.

I based my answer to him on the same reasons expressed in my cited letter, inducing him to wait for later orders conforming to the Royal intentions of His Majesty which Your Excellency might be pleased to send me. I added that the motive for speaking about agreement as to possessions on the Mississippi had ceased to exist since His Majesty's armed forces had captured all that territory from the English, that the Americans have no settlements in it and therefore are totally without any right to the slightest claim. Consequently it has been decided not to discuss those points with the Congress at all.

Although reports of the Spanish conquests on the Mississippi River were well received at first, later several members of Congress displayed some displeasure, as have other private citizens who planned to settle there. I have managed to convince them of the absurdity of their ideas, when they did not possess the smallest part of that territory, when they had not been able to hold what they had conquered in February of 1778 nor much less to retake it from the English, because the fortifications which the English had enlarged and the forces they maintained there combined to make it impossible. I believe that the members are aware of these facts, although they may have flattered themselves that they could have in the future mounted efforts great enough to capture that territory and join it to their possessions on the Ohio River, and I think they know that the Spanish conquest deprives them of any basis for claiming freedom of navigation on the Mississippi although that realization is more painful to them.

. . . . . .

This being all I have to report to Your Excellency, I repeat with the greatest respect that I am at your orders, etc.   Juan de Miralles

LC: *Aileen Moore Topping Collection, 1780, pp. 506-507 (Typescript translation).*

Chevalier de la Luzerne to Comte de Vergennes

[Translation]

Nᵒ· 33 Triplicate   Philadelphia, 13 March 1780

My Lord

I have the honor to send you among the attached extracts of public papers, the translation of a passage in the Pennsylvania Gazette of February 23 last. It contains *the details of the operations of His Catholic Majesty's troops on the Mississippi and of the conquest of some five hundred leagues of lands on the west bank of that* river. This news, when it reached M. de Mirales, was placed by his efforts in the public papers, and he did this, in order not to leave the inhabitants of the thirteen States ignorant of the fact that the King, his Master, far from recognizing their claimed rights to these regions, intends, on the contrary, to conquer them for himself and to unite them to his Crown. This publication at first aroused a ferment that was easy to foresee. Various inhabitants of Philadelphia, claiming possession of these same regions, either by virtue of patents acquired from the respective States, or by virtue of their sale by the savages, were the first to speak to me of it. They told me that they feared that the Court of Madrid was not well informed of the state of the question, and that it was not for want of knowing their rights that it had directed its armies against lands included in the respective Charters of the States. A society of merchants called the Indiana Company continued to grant territories, and it had just handed Baron von Steuben[1] a deed giving him 2500 acres of land situated on the Mississippi as a mark of its recognition of the services he has rendered to America. At the same time, an individual opened an office for the piecemeal sale of eight hundred thousand or a million acres of land situated between the right bank of the Ohio and the Mississippi. You will see his announcement in the public papers, and I enclose herewith an Extract of his property contract, which may indicate what lands he considers as belonging to him. He is asking no more than the equivalent of one *sou tournois* Paris measure[2] for the sale of each acre of land. Several members of Congress finally spoke to me of this conquest and told me that they regretted how much the Thirteen States differed in opinion with the Court of Spain concerning this important question, that it was necessary to prevent early the misunderstanding that could result from it, and that the Delegates of the Southern States, who have the most interest therein, proposed to make a motion that Congress take these circumstances into consideration and attend to the measures that such an important affair demands. I induced these delegates to postpone that motion, and I made them understand that there was no danger in delays, but rather in concerning themselves with this affair unseasonably, which risked diverting their attention from a subject that permits no delay, that of the workings of the next campaign; I added that the subject of boundaries with Spain was of such a delicate nature that it was necessary to abstain from dealing with it while minds were still feeling the effects of the agitation caused by the most recent news from New York; that strengthening the union with the Court of Spain was the most importunate task presented to the United States since their alliance with the King; that it was necessary to proceed with extreme circumspection and not to expose themselves to the danger of displeasing that Monarch at the very moment when by a powerful diversion he renders to the United States the most important service they could expect from him. They promised me, My Lord, to suspend this motion until a more opportune time. As for the heart of the question, I have in spite of myself avoided alluding to it, because Don Juan pleaded with me in the most insistent manner to tell all those who spoke to me of it that I was ignorant of the sentiments of the Court of Madrid. I informed him of what had happened, I asked him if he did not think that the moment had arrived to make use of the instructions that you had given me to concert with him, and if he did not think it important to enlighten Congress before its preoccupation put down stronger roots, and that my silence gave him reason to think that we were disposed to adopt its principles. Don Juan answered me that he intended to wait for clarifications of the latest reports he has made to his Court. I pointed out to him that these clarifications had arrived and that Despatch No. 1 with which you have honored me appeared to contain the opinion of his Court on the points concerning which he had asked directions. I spared nothing to make him understand that it was necessary to prevent, by timely, amicable explanations to Congress, deliberations whose issue cannot fail to be contrary to its interests if they are conducted by certain delegates whose ardour and prejudice I know.

M. de Mirales insisted on the rights of His Catholic Majesty, on the absurdity and ridicule which the 13 States manifest in demanding possessions conquered by Spain from the enemy, while they have not the means to liberate their own territory, and he finished by pleading with me, in a manner which does not permit me to raise the matter again, to remain quiet Spectators of any discussions that might arise and to constantly plead the lack of instructions until the orders of the King, his Master, reach him concerning either the latest accounts he has rendered or the communications which you may receive, My Lord, or which his Court may receive from Mr. Jay. He told me frankly that he had no instructions from the Spanish Ministry but a general approval of his conduct up to 30 August last. He also showed me a letter from M. de Galvez containing the promise of being named Minister to the United States when His Catholic Majesty is disposed to appoint one. I could foresee, My Lord, that M. de Mirales, who had made known his hopes to his friends, would see with pain that an affair which interests the King, his Master, so particularly was handled by someone other than himself; his patriotism and the zeal with which he is animated for his country's glory have made him want to enter into some relation of affairs with Congress, but that assembly, while displaying toward him the personal regard due to his character, has declined with extreme care to treat with him other than through me. In the various political, commercial or maritime transactions which have presented themselves, I avoid offending his fastidiousness. I communicate to him with the necessary nuances the affairs in which his Court may take an interest, and for his part he demonstrates a particular confidence in me, but the recent hopes that he has received singularly augment his desire to be received in a public character, and he would like his Court to adopt some form that would facilitate for him the means and the affair which are precisely of a nature not to suffer long delays. Beyond that, My Lord, in deferring to his wishes and by abstaining from treating of it Ministerially with Congress, I thought that I would fulfill the spirit of the instructions that you gave me if I were to converse in private with the delegates, and if I were to make use of the trust which they seem to accord me to rectify their ideas on these questions. I cannot flatter myself with having converted them, but at least I reaped from my conversations the advantage that they no longer regard their principles as being safe from all scrutiny, and that they will be less astonished by the news they will receive from Mr. Jay, and they will be more disposed to adopt the compromises that Minister will propose to them. I am not far from thinking that from now until then the excitement that still reigns will be in great part appeased. I have already made the sole delegate who represents Carolina in Congress understand that although the United States had the right to conquer those regions before Spain seized them from the common Enemy, that Power nonetheless also had the right to conquer them, and that since they are now in its possession, the United States cannot claim them at the same time without offending the Laws of justice and of good neighborliness, and the rules of prudence. This delegate is Mr. Mathews,[3] a man commendable for his probity and his wisdom. May Heaven preserve us, he told me, from even the idea of a dispute with Spain, but you will agree that for having conquered a corner of land close by the mouths of the Mississippi and the Iberville River, this Power is not entitled to say that a Country five hundred leagues in scope has fallen under its power and to claim Sovereignty over it. I have already heard talk of giving reinforcements to Colonel Clarke[4] in order to put him in a condition to conquer on his side, and you see the consequences of this plan. It is to prevent them, I said to Mr. Mathews, that prudence demands that you give spirits time to calm themselves, and that you avoid discussing this question until you have news from Mr. Jay. That delegate answered me that he saw with sadness that Spain was not acting on principles *as liberal* as the King their great Ally, and he added that for many years there had been numerous emigrations of the inhabitants of the 13 States who had been established in these Regions, each in the scope of the respective Charters of their States, that these emigrants had established in good faith that their intention was to remain under the dependency of the English Colony where they were settled, that I knew that this was the way that most of the regions of America had been acquired from one sovereignty rather than from another, and that since the King had recognized by the Treaty of 1778 the right of the States to conquer everything on the continent that belonged to England, it was necessary to regard this occupation accompanied by acts of jurisdiction as equivalent to a conquest, and that the States having the advantage of priority over the Spanish, it was the latter who were disturbing the States in their possessions. I replied that this occupation gave no more rights to the Subjects of the thirteen States than it could have given to France, to Poland, or to Germany if Frenchmen, Germans, or Poles had been established in that part of the former Louisiana since the Treaty of Paris, that they would have become subjects of England, and that by the conquest that Spain had just made, the inhabitants of those regions had come under her dominion.

I am reporting these details to you because they place you in a position to understand the principles upon which the States will base their defense when the question is properly debated, and because the Court of Madrid will be able, if it judges it appropriate, to prepare its responses; if there are some means to satisfy the individuals most particularly interested in this debate by the acquisitions, actual or imagined, that they have made, I think that the respective States, being no longer aroused by their complaints and their solicitations, will show more moderation than at this moment. I have been asked many times how far the pretensions of Spain extend. I have responded that I did not know. If they were to embrace the entire expanse of Eastern Louisiana, it would perhaps be fitting to fix with precision what is understood by that expression, for it was never comprehended in the same sense by us and by the English when we were its possessors.

I am with Respect, My Lord, Your very humble and very obedient servant   Le chr de la luzerne.
Rec. 19 May.

FFAA: Pol. Corr., U.S., v. 11, f. 79 (LC transcription).

[1] Steuben, Friedrich Wilhelm Ludolf Gerhard Augustin, Baron von (1730-1794). Former Prussian general staff officer who served as inspector general of the Continental Army, 1778-1784, with rank of major general.

[2] There were 25 sous in one livre parisis, the livre being equivalent to the modern franc. Luzerne means that land was selling for extremely low prices.

[3] Mathews, John (1744-1802). South Carolina political figure. Member, state house of representatives, 1776-1780; speaker, 1777-1778. Member, Continental Congress, 1778-1781. Governor of South Carolina, 1782-1783.

[4] Clark, George Rogers (1752-1818). Virginia military leader, surveyor. Secured Virginia's commitment to the defense of Kentucky against British-inspired Indian attacks, 1776. Captured Kaskaskia, Cahokia, and Vincennes in the Illinois country, 1778;

recovered Vincennes after its recapture by the British, 1779. Frustrated British efforts to control Kentucky and the Northwest, 1779-1783. With Richard Butler and S.H.Parsons, commissioner to treat with the Indians of the Northwest, who in January 1786 at Ft. McIntosh acknowledged U.S. sovereignty over former British territories.

John Adams to Richard Henry Lee

My dear Sir[1]   Paris Hotel de Valois Rue de Richelieu March 15th 1780.

.   .   .   .   .

The Chevalier de la Luzerne, I have Reason to think from an agreeable Acquaintance with him in the Course of a Passage to America of forty seven days, from some Knowledge of him that I had before and after, is a candid and impartial Man, possessed of no Principles or Views inconsistent with his public Character, and very able to do Service to his Country and ours – the Same of M[r] Marbois[2] – I lament most sincerely the unhappy Contests that preceeded his Arrival, and wish that they may be extinguished, but I know too well the Circumstances to expect that they will.

As to my Negotiations, our Sons or Grandsons have a better Chance of completing them than I have. There is, or at least there was a System of Policy and of military Operations, that if it had been pursued, might have given me Something to do. It is not my fault, nor the fault of America that it was not.

The Fishery and the Navigation of the Missisippi, are Points of such Importance, that your Grandson, when he makes the Peace, I hope will secure them. I am sure, he will omit nothing in his Power to do, for that Purpose.

.   .   .   .   .

I am with great Esteem, Sir, your Friend & humble Servant.

John Adams

American Philosophical Society, hereafter cited as APS: Richard Lee Papers (LS).

[1] *Lee, Richard Henry (1732-1794). Virginia planter and political figure. Brother of Arthur, William, and Francis Lightfoot Lee. Member, Virginia House of Burgesses, 1758-1775. Member, Continental Congress, 1774-1779, 1784-1785; president, 1784. U.S. Senator, 1789-1792.*

[2] *Marbois, François Barbé de (1745-1837). French diplomat and statesman. Secretary of legation in the United States, 1779-1785; chargé des affaires, 1784-1785. Consul at Philadelphia, 1781-1784; consul general at Philadelphia, 1784-1785. Intendant of St. Domingue, 1785-1789.*

William Lee to John Adams

Dr Sir.   Bruxelles, March 17. 1780

I understand that our Enemies have now in contemplation, the offering of some terms to America, which go no farther than a Truce; probably, somewhat similar to the propositions made last year by spain to Great Britain.

Tho' I am not inform'd of the terms of Peace with which you are charged, nor whether your powers are discretionary, I trust you will not think it an intrusion in me to offer my sentiments on such a proposition as a Truce for America, supposing it should be made.

A Truce with America, must of course accompany a Peace in Europe, in that case our Enemies, after recover[g] from their present exhausted state, having their hands clear of European troubles wou'd have their whole strength to employ against America; for I conceive, that with such a prospect before them, there wou'd not be the most distant probability of agreeing on a Peace before the expiration of the Truce.

In America we must keep up a great Military & Naval establishment, to prevent our being taken by surprize, at nearly as great an expence, as we are now at in War, & besides risk the dreadful misfortunes which have almost universally attended standing Armies & a heavy load of debt on the State. I can't suppose it possible that France & Spain wou'd consent to a Truce with America while the War is to continue between G. Britain & them; but if they shou'd, wou'd it be wise in America to accept of a Truce on such terms, & to let our Allies run the hazard of being destroyed, that we may become an easy prey afterwards?

. . . . . .

...Your most Obliged & Obed[t.] Hble Serv[t.]   W. Lee

Massachusetts Historical Society, hereafter cited as MHS: The Adams Papers, microfilm reel 351 (ALS).

Chevalier de la Luzerne to Comte de Vergennes

[Translation]

N[o.] 35. Duplicate.   Philadelphia, 18 March 1780

My Lord

I have received the letter you did me the honor of writing me on 25 September of last Year.

I have gone through the instructions it contains on different subjects so that I can make the proper use of them when the occasion arises. As for that of the right of fishing along the coasts and on the bank of Newfoundland, the public has completely lost sight of it, since it is known that Mr. John Adams is the bearer of the Ultimatum from Congress on that matter. Since the departure of that minister for Europe, I have made inquiries of his friends through a trustworthy person in order to learn his dispositions and theirs in this regard. What I have been able to gather amounts to the following. The day of his departure, Mr. Adams said to someone in whom he had confidence that he hoped to obtain for America the most extensive advantages, but that he must follow the orders of Congress to mind the circumstances in which the ally which had so generously assisted the United States might find itself, and not put their union in peril for the purely secondary interests of two or three of the thirteen States. Moreover, it appears that he communicated to no one the tenor of his powers, and his most intimate friends seem not to know if the fishery is a condition *sine qua non*, or if he is only supposed to adapt to circumstances and abandon this point after having made every effort to procure that advantage for his compatriots. Those persons best accredited in the State of Massachusetts are of the latter opinion, and although the merchants persist in saying there is no point to a peace without the unlimited right to fish, it is presumed they will yield to the majority, which consists of Farmers who earnesty desire peace. The arguments with which you were good enough to provide me cannot help being of great weight when the question is raised in this case. I have declined to say anything publicly in this regard because that would give warning to certain political Sophists who are only waiting for a pretext to invite debate, and I will limit myself to correcting in individual conversations the ideas of persons who present me with a natural occasion to speak with them of it.

I thought, My Lord, I should inform M. de Mirales of the confirmation of the orders you had previously given me relative to lands situated on the eastern bank of the Mississippi which we ceded to England in the last Treaty of peace. That agent persists in this regard in the sentiments I have had the honor of reporting to you. I have always thought that the position the Court of Madrid has taken of making the conquest of it is the most proper to smoothe away the difficulties which I foresee, which will be insurmountable if it wishes to open a negotiation without supporting its claims to an actual possession. The States could doubtless do no better than frankly express their hopes and desires to His Catholic Majesty and leave it to that Monarch's generosity and magnanimity. But I can only think that they are completely determined upon a step that calls for more confidence and unanimity than I see among them. Perhaps they will be disposed to give the King so great a proof of respect and of their opinion of his justice, but they are already showing jealousy and uneasiness with regard to Spain, and since the news of M. de Galves' success at the fort of Natchez has arrived here, I no longer perceive the same zeal for the success of that Power's arms. However, the moderate and the prudent agree that the United States derive the greatest advantages from the resolution which the Catholic King has taken to join his arms with those of the King, and know that it is a strange delusion to think that the thirteen States, which are unable to drive the enemy from their own territory, would be capable of making conquests from him and dispossessing him of these same distant Regions. They have promised me that they will make every effort to see that this opinion prevails and to calm tempers if the matter is taken under deliberation in Congress.

. . . . .

I shall carry out the orders you have given me, My Lord, relative to the obligation in which unforeseen events may place us of guaranteeing the independence of the United States only in the form of a truce with England. I have only spoken of this matter occasionally until now. When the Ultimatum proposed last year by the Court of Madrid to that of London became known here, the anxieties and even discontent I noted were caused by the proposal of the *uti possidetis*[1] much more than by that of a Truce. I have reported to you, My Lord, the manner in which I explained both subjects. I shall take care to give only my own opinion when I find it necessary to explain this affair. I had previously informed Congress, as you instructed me, that you were exploring methods of sending it arms. I have confirmed these hopes, and in conformity with your last instructions, I have added that you still do not know what His Majesty can provide, but that Congress may count on it that nothing will be neglected to satisfy it, insofar as the state of things will permit.

. . . . .

Before leaving this matter, My Lord, I must return to a misunderstanding into which I was led by reading a publication of our treaties made by Congress. The English print contains, as I had the honor of informing you on 7 January last, two articles which are not in the *French* print, and as this English print accompanied the ratifications, I mistakenly concluded from this that Congress had also ratified the two articles in question. I reported to you the inconveniences which have resulted for the merchants of our Islands, but I abstained from making any observation to Congress, not even private insinuations, wishing to receive your orders beforehand. This reserve occasioned the ignorance in which I remained. It was only a few days ago that in perusing the minutes of the journals of Congress for the year 1778, which have just been printed, I found a resolution relative to the suppression of these two articles. Congress has also made it known that these articles should be considered null and void. They were therefore annulled and struck out of the Treaty by mutual consent, but the inconveniences resulting from their publication with regard to commerce in molasses still existed in our Islands during the last year, and French merchants assure me that they were made to pay a duty, moderate in truth, on the export of this commodity, while the American merchants were exempt from it. Thus, My Lord, the observations I had the honor to submit to you in this regard remain valid.

.   .   .   .   .

I am with Respect, My Lord, Your most humble and most Obedient servant.   Le chr de la luzerne.

P.S. A member of the Committee of Foreign Affairs has come to me, My Lord, to communicate the first proofs of the journals of Congress for the month of May 1778. Our Treaties appear in full, except for the secret article. The two revoked articles also appear there. I pointed this out to that delegate, and I added that this was to perpetuate the error that the stipulations of these articles are still in full force. He replied to me that the plenipotentiaries of Congress had exchanged with you, My Lord, a declaration that does away with them, but that neither the original nor a copy of this declaration has reached Congress, and that it was impossible to inform the thirteen States of this repeal in an authentic manner in its absence. He proposed to me that the Treaties be entirely omitted from the publication of the journal for 1778, and to wait for the arrival of your declaration. As soon as it reaches Congress, it will finally be possible to publish the Treaties in a more correct form than they have been up to now, and they will be inserted in the journal on the day the declaration arrives. This proposal seemed appropriate to me, and it will be acted upon. You may either consider it appropriate to send me your declaration to pass along to Congress, or it may reach that body through its minister plenipotentiary. Rec. 19 May.

FFAA: Pol. Corr., U.S., v. 11, f. 87 (LC transcription).
[1] Literally, as you possess.

John Adams to the President of Congress

Sir,   Paris Hotel de Valois Rue de Richelieu March 24th 1780.
   M[r.] Burke's Bill[1] not being as yet public, we are not yet informed of the Extent of it. But as it already appears, that it strikes at the Department of Secretary of State for America, at the Board of Trade, there seems to be

little Reason to doubt that it goes further and strikes at the American Board of Commissioners, at all the American Judges of Admiralty, Governors of Provinces, Secretaries, and Custom House Officers of all Denominations – at least if this should not be found to be a part of the Bill, there are stronger Reasons if possible for abolishing this whole System of Iniquity, together with all the Pensions granted to the Refugees from America, than even for taking away the Board of Trade; and from several late Paragraphs in the Papers, and from M[r.] Fox's[2] severe Observations in the House of Commons upon Governor Hutchinson,[3] calling him in Substance "The Firebrand" that lighted up all the Fire between the two Countries, it seems pretty clear, that it is in Contemplation to take away all these Salaries and Pensions.

If such a Measure should take place, exiled as these persons are from the Country which gave them Birth, but which they most ungratefully have endeavoured to enslave, they will become melancholy Monuments of divine Vengeance against such unnatural and impious Behaviour.

Nevertheless, as these Persons are numerous, and have some Friends in England as well as in America, where they had once much Property, there is a probability, I think, that whenever or wherever Negotiations for Peace may be commenced, they and their Estates now almost universally confiscated, will not be forgotten: but much Pains and Art will be employed to stipulate for them in the Treaty, both a Restoration of their Property, and a Right to return as Citizens of the States to which they formerly belonged. It is very possible, however, that before a Treaty shall be made, or even Negotiations commenced, these Gentlemen will become so unpopular and odious, that the People of England would be pleased with their Sufferings and Punishment: but it is most probably that the Court will not abandon them very easily.

I should therefore be very happy to have the explicit Instructions of Congress upon this Head, whether I am to agree in any Case whatsoever, to an Article which shall admit either of their Return, or the Restoration of their forfeited Estates. There are Sentiments of Humanity and of Forgiveness which plead on one Side; there are Reasons of State and political Motives, among which the danger of admitting such mischievous Persons as Citizens is not the least considerable, which argue on the other. I shall obey the Instructions of Congress with the utmost pleasure, or if for any Reasons they choose to leave it at Discretion, if I should ever have the Opportunity, I shall determine it, without listening to any Passions of my own of Compassion or Resentment, according to my best Judgment of the public Good.

There is another Point of very great Importance, which I am persuaded will be aimed at by the English Ministers, I am sure it will by the People of England, whenever Terms of Peace shall be talked of. For facilitating the Return of Commerce, they will wish to have it stipulated by the Treaty, that the Subjects of Great Britain shall have the Rights of Citizens in America, and the Citizens of the United States the Rights of Subjects in the British Dominions. Some of the Consequences of such an Agreement to them and to Us, are obvious, and very important, but they are so numerous, and it is so difficult to determine, whether the Benefits or Inconveniences prevail, that I should be sorry to have so great a Question left to my determination: if however, contrary to my Inclinations, it should fall to my Lot to decide it, without Instructions, it shall be decided according to my Conscience and the best Lights I have.

I have the Honor to be, with a sincere Attachment, Sir, your most obedient and most humble Servant   John Adams

Receiv^d July 31$^{st:}$ 1780   Read Aug 1.

NA: PCC, item 84, v. 1, pp. 349-351 (LS); M247, reel 111.

[1] Burke, Edmund (1729-1797). British political figure and philosopher. Member of Parliament, 1765-1794, initially as a Rockingham Whig. Favored reconciliation with the American colonies. Later, opponent of the French revolution. In February 1780, Burke introduced resolutions in Parliament designed to eliminate government corruption and its sources, to secure a more independent Parliament, and to bring about economies in government.

[2] Fox, Charles James (1749-1806). British political figure. As member of Parliament, a vocal opponent of Lord North's American policy. Secretary of State for Foreign Affairs in Rockingham's Ministry, April-July 1782, and in a coalition with Lord North, April-December 1783. Thereafter, steadfast opponent of the policies of William Pitt the Younger.

[3] Hutchinson, Thomas (1711-1780). Massachusetts political figure and historian. Governor of Massachusetts Bay Colony, 1770-1774, having before served as chief justice and lieutenant governor, he was a strong supporter of Parliament's right to legislate for the American colonies.

John Adams to the President of Congress

Sir,   Paris March 30$^{th.}$ 1780.

I have the Honor to inclose to Congress Copies of certain Letters which I have had the Honor to write to the Comte de Vergennes, and of others which I have received from him.

. . . . .

I ought to confess to Congress that the Delicacies of the Comte de Vergennes about communicating my Powers, are not perfectly consonant to my manner of thinking; and if I had followed my own Judgment, I should have pursued a bolder Plan; by communicating, immediately after my Arrival, to Lord George Germaine,[1] my full Powers to treat both of Peace and Commerce: but I hope Congress will approve of my communicating first to this Court my Destination, and asking their Advice and then pursuing it, because I think no doubt can be made, that it is my Duty to conduct my Negotiations at present in Concert with our ally, as I have hitherto done.– I have the Honor to be, with perfect Respect, Sir, your most obedient and humble Servant   John Adams

NA: PCC, item 84, v. 1, pp. 381-382 (LS); M247, reel 111.
[1] Germain, Lord George (1716-1785). British military leader and political figure. Colonial secretary, November 1775-March 1782; primarily responsible for the conduct of the American war.

John Adams to the President of Congress

Sir,   Paris April 18th 1780
    It is my Duty to transmit to Congress, as soon as Prudence will admit, every Thing which deserves Consideration, as having either a direct or an indirect tendency to Peace, or even to Negotiation for that important Object. The inclosed Letter,[1] has been transmitted to Paris in such a Channel, that I have Reasons to believe it was particularly intended for my Inspection. It is from a Gentleman, who, to do him Justice, has long expressed an earnest desire for Peace, but who nevertheless, has never yet reflected maturely enough upon the State of America, of Great Britain, and of all Europe, to get into a right Way of thinking concerning the proper Means to his End: Congress will percieve it, from the Letter itself, in which it is obvious enough.
    The first remarkable Sentiment is, "We must, at all Events support our national Honor, by the most vigorous Exertions, without shrinking: but surely, in such a complicated War as this is, if we can make any equitable Offers of a Treaty to any of the Parties, Common Prudence calls upon Us, to use our Endeavors, to unravel by Negotiation, the Combination of Powers now acting against Us." In this Paragraph, I see the manifest Marks of a Mind that has not yet mastered its Subject. True Policy would have omitted every thing in this Letter, which should call up to the Minds of the People, the Ideas of National Honor. Every Man in the World, who is thoroughly acquainted with the Subject, knows, that Great Britain never can obtain a Peace, without a Diminution of her Honor and Dignity. It is impossible without Miracles, and therefore the Englishman who undertakes to plan for Peace, must be convinced of this and take it into his Plan, and

consequently should avoid with the utmost Caution every Word, which should excite these Ideas in the Minds of the People. For People cannot bear the Ideas of national Disgrace. They stir Passions which make them mad.

He should have avoided with equal Solicitude, every Insinuation of a design to unravel by Negotiation, the Combination of Powers, now acting against Great Britain. This Combination, is in fact, much more extensive, much more universal, and formidable, than the Letter writer had any Idea, or Suspicion of. But if it had been no more extensive than France, Spain and America, the Impracticability of unravelling it, ought to have been too obvious and too clear, for the Writer to have thrown out this Sentiment. By it, he proposes by Negotiation to bring those to dishonour themselves, who have certainly no Occasion for it, at the same time that he stimulates others to cherish and preserve their Honor, who have already lost it, and under an absolute Necessity, sooner or later of sacrificing it. By this Means, he only puts the Confederates more upon their Guard, and renders the Attainment of his professed Object, Peace, impossible.

The next Solecism in Politicks, that he commits, is undertaking to vindicate America from the Charge of having sought and formed this Confederacy. America wanted no such Vindication. It is folly to suppose it a Fault, for all Mankind will agree, even his Correspondents themselves, that it was Wisdom and Virtue. Surely another Turn must be given to popular Ideas, before they will be brought to petition for Peace.

Nor do I think, it was prudent in him to hold up, that America had proceeded with Regret and Reluctance to the Treaty. That this is true I know and feel to this very Moment: for, although I had no such Reluctance myself, those Gentlemen with whom I had the Honor to sit in Congress at the time will remember that I had very good Reasons to be sensible that others had. But how well soever he might be informed of the Fact, and from what Source soever he might draw his Information, it was bad Policy in him to hold up, because he ought to have been equally sure, that America has now no Reluctance to the Treaty, nor any Inclination to violate it. He ought not therefore to have held up a Hope of this to the People.

Neither ought he to have flattered the People with Hopes, that America would not form any perpetual Alliance with France, nor that their limited Alliance might be satisfied and discharged. The Alliance already made is limited it is true, to a certain Number of Articles, but not limited in its Duration. It is perpetual, and he had no Grounds to sooth the People with Hopes either that France would give up any of the Articles of the Treaty, or that America would violate them.

He ought also to have avoided his Insinuations, that America has been so much harrassed by the War. This is an Idea too refreshing to the present Passions of the People of England, that instead of tending to dispose them to Peace, it only revives their Hopes of Success, and inflames their Ardour for War. That America has been harrassed by the War, is true, and when was any Nation at War without being so? especially when did any Nation undergo a Revolution in Government and sustain a War at the same time without it? Yet after all America has not been so much harrassed, or distressed, or terrified, or panic struck from the Beginning, as Great Britain has been, several times in the Course of it.

But the most exceptionable Passage of all is this. "It is apparent to all the World, that *France might long ago, have put an End to that part of the War, which has been most distressing to America*, if She had chosen so to do. Let the whole System of France be considered, from the very Beginning, down to the late Retreat from Savannah, and I think it is impossible to put any other Construction upon it, but this, viz, That it has always been the deliberate Intention and Object of France, for purposes of their own, to encourage the Continuation of the War in America, in Hopes of *exhausting the Strength and Resources of this Country, and of depressing the rising Power of America.*"

Upon this Paragraph, I scarcely know what Remarks to make. But after deliberating upon it, as patiently and maturely as I can, I will clearly write my Opinion of it: for my Obligations to Truth, and to my Country are antecedent and superior to all other Ties.

I am clearly and fully of Opinion then, that the Fact is true, that France might have put an End to that part of the War, which has been most distressing to America; and I certainly know that the means were extreamly simple and obvious, and that they were repeatedly proposed and explained and urged to the Ministry; and I should have had a terrible Load of Guilt of Negligence of my Duty upon my Conscience if it had not been done, while I had the Honor of a Commission to this Court. But when the Letter Writer proceeds so far as to say, that it was to *encourage* the Continuance of the War, in order to exhaust the Strength and Resources of Great Britain, I cannot accompany him, much less can I join with him in the Opinion, that it was to *depress the rising Power of America.*

I believe on the contrary, that France has not wished a Continuance of the War, but that She has wished for Peace. The War has been attended, with too much Loss and Danger to France, to suppose that She wished its Continuance, and if She did not wish its Continuance at all, She could not wish it to depress the Power of America.

She could not wish it, in my opinion, for this End, because it is not the means to this End. It has a contrary Tendency. The longer this War is continued in America, the more will Americans become habituated to the

Characters of the Soldier and the Marine. Military Virtues and Talents and Passions will gain Strength, and additional Activity every Year, while the War lasts, and the more these Virtues, Talents and Passions are multiplied, the deeper will the Foundations of American Power be laid, and the more dangerous will it become, to some or other of the Powers of Europe; to France, as likely as to any other, because it will be more likely to be ambitious, enterprising and to aspire at Conquests by Sea and Land.

This Idea however, deserves to be considered, with all the Attention that Americans can give it. Although I am convinced by every Thing I see, and read and hear, that all the Powers of Europe, except perhaps the House of Austria, and I am not very clear in that Exception, rejoice in the American Revolution, and consider the Independence of America as for their Interest and Happiness, in many Points of View, both respecting Commerce and the Ballance of Europe, yet I have many Reasons to think that not one of them, not even Spain nor France, wishes to see America rise very fast to Power. We ought therefore to be cautious how we magnify our Ideas and exaggerate our Expressions of the Generosity and Magnanimity of any of these Powers. Let us treat them with Gratitude, but with Dignity. Let us remember what is due to ourselves and our Posterity, as well as to them. Let us above all Things, avoid as much as possible, entangling ourselves with their Wars or Politicks. Our Business with them, and theirs with Us, is Commerce, not Politicks, much less War. America has been the Sport of European Wars and Politicks long enough.

I think, however, that this Letter Writer, was very much mistaken in his Judgment, when he threw out this Language of his. It could be meant only to excite a Jealousy and a Quarrel between France and America, or rather, to feed the Yorkshire People, and the People of England with a Hope of exciting such a Quarrel. This is not the Way to come at Peace. They will never succeed in such a Plan, and every attempt towards it is false Policy.

The next Mistake, is the Idea of a Reconciliation and foederal Union with America. This must be intended to seperate us from our Allies, which this Gentleman ought, before now, to have known is totally impracticable.

I have very little more Relish for the Notion of a Truce. We are in a safer Way at War. We cannot make a Truce without France. She will never consent that We should make a Truce, unless She makes a Peace: and such Alterations may be made in the Constitution of the Courts of France and Spain, and in the other Courts and political Connections in Europe, before the Expiration of the Term of the Truce, that it would be attended with too much hazard to Us. Neither France nor Spain, nor the other Powers of Europe might, after a Truce, be ready to go to War again: unforeseen Divisions may be excited among ourselves by artful Emissaries from England. We are going on now in the sure and certain Road: if we go out of it, We may be lost.

Upon the whole; I think that this Letter Writer should have stated the true Situation of Europe, of Great Britain, Ireland and America.

From this State, his immediate Conclusion should have been, open Conferences for Peace: make Peace with all the World upon the best Terms you can. – This is the only Chance you have for Salvation.

It must come to this, very soon; otherwise, there will be a total Dissolution of the British Empire.

I have the Honor to be, with greatest Respect and Esteem, Sir, your most obedient and most humble Servant.   John Adams

rec^d Feb 19 81

NA: PCC, item 84, v. 1, pp. 471-478 (LS); M247, reel 111.
  [1] David Hartley to the Chairman of the Committee of the County of York, March 21, 1780 (NA: PCC, item 83, v. 2, pp. 334-341; M247, reel 110).

Don Diego José Navarro to Don Juan de Miralles

My Dear Sir   Havana, 25 April 1780

. . . . .

...according to a proclamation made by the King which I have just received, we are to admit into this port individual traders of the United States who bring produce, but not manufactured goods or articles of trade, to be exchanged for productions of this island or for money. Export and import duties are to be collected from them. Because news of this Royal permission may be useful to some of the inhabitants of those provinces, especially to the tra[d]ers of the Carolinas, who may bring flour, rice, meats, pitch, tar, timber for masts, etc., I am sending the order to you so that you can publicize and spread the news.

I repeat expressions of constant friendship, etc.   Diego José Navarro[1]

LC: Aileen Moore Topping Collection, 1780, pp. 543-545 (Typescript translation).
  [1] Navarro García de Valladares, Diego José (1708-1784). Spanish military officer and colonial administrator. Lieutenant general, 1777. Governor and captain general of Cuba, 1777-1782.

Richard Henry Lee to John Adams

My dear Sir,   Virginia May the 7th 1780

. . . . .

I hope your efforts will not be wanting to secure us the free navigation of Mississippi – I expect much more I own from such efforts than from any other – without this free Navigation our vast back country will be so distressed as to lay the foundation of future wars and dissention from the necessity of having an outlet to market. Our State hath already dispossessed the English of their holds on the river Illinois, we have great numbers of people settled on the Ohio, and we are now taking a post at the mouth of that river at its confluence with Mississippi – all these places being within our Charter limits....I am dear Sir your most affectionate and obedient Servant

Rec^{d.} 19th. Sept^{r.}   Richard Henry Lee

MHS: The Adams Papers, microfilm reel 351 (ALS).

Notes of a Conference between John Jay and Conde de Floridablanca

Aranjues 11th. May 1780.

Mr. Jay having waited on the Count D'Florida Blanca in Consequence of a Message received on the Evening of the 10th. The latter commenced the Conversation by observing that he was sorry that his Ignorance of the English Language prevented him from speaking with that Ease and Frankness, with which he wished to do in his Conferences with Mr. Jay, and which corresponded with his own Disposition and Character.

He observed that he intended to speak on two Points, – The first related to the Letter Mr. Jay had written to him, on the Subject of Bills of Exchange drawn on him by Congress, that being an Affair the most pressing and more immediately necessary to enter upon. He said that the last Year he should have found no Difficulty on that Head, but that at present, although Spain had money, she was in the Situation of Tantalus, who with Water in View could not make use of it – alluding to the Revenue arising from their Possessions in America, which they were not able to draw from thence. That their Expenses, in the Year 1779 had been so great, particularly for the marine, as to oblige them to make large Loans, which they were negotiating at present. He entered into a Summary of those Expenses, and particularized the enormous Expense of supporting thirty five Ships of the Line and Frigates in French Ports. He observed that to do this, they had prepared a very expensive and numerous Convoy at Ferrol and other Ports of Spain, loaded with Provisions, naval Stores, and every other Article necessary for the Squadron before mentioned, which Convoy did not arrive at Brest, until the Day on which the Spanish Fleet sailed from thence. That the Supplies so sent had emptied their Magazines at Cadiz, Ferrol and their other Ports, and had consequently obliged them to buy at enormous Prices the necessary Stores to supply the Fleet under the Admirals Cordova and Gaston on their arrival in the Ports of Spain. That they had been forced to Sell these Stores thus sent to France, and others purchased for the same purpose at Bordeaux, Nantes and elsewhere, at half Price; and added that their Loss on this occasion could scarce be calculated. This joined to the other Expenses and the great Losses they had sustained in their Marine and Commerce, but chiefly in the former and the great Expenses they were at in Consequence thereof, rendered it difficult for the King to do for America what he could have done easily the last Year, and which he declared repeatedly and in the strongest manner it was his intention to do; as might be judged from his Conduct heretofore, touching slightly on the succours sent us from Spain, the Havanna and Louisiana, but dwelling on his Conduct in the Negotiation last Year with great Britain, in which he would on no Account be brought to sacrifice the Interest of America. Such being his Majesty's Disposition and Intentions previous to the War, M^r. Jay might easily judge that he was not less determined at present to support their Interests, whether formally connected with America by Treaty or not. That notwithstanding the Losses and Misfortunes sustained, the Kings Resolution, Courage and Fortitude induced him to continue the War, and therefore they were obliged to incur much Expense in order to fill their Magazines and make the necessary Preparations for this Campaign and the next, yet that it was his Majesty's Intentions to give America all the Assistance in his Power. That it was as much his Inclination as Duty to second these Dispositions, and that he had received the Kings Orders to confer with his Colleagues thereon. He observed however that although he was first Secretary of State; he must first confer with them on this Subject, and from his own personal Inclinations to second the King's Intentions and to serve America, he was desirous of concerting, with M^r. Jay, measures in such a Manner as would prevent him from meeting with opposition from his Colleagues, and therefore he spoke to him not as a Minister but as an Individual. In order to facilitate this, he said it was necessary to make some overtures for a Contract, in Case M^r. Jay was not absolutely empowered to make one, and then he pointed out the object most essential to the Interests of Spain at the present Conjuncture. He said that for their Marine they wanted light Frigates, Cutters, or swift sailing Vessels of that Size. That for Ships of the Line, they could procure them themselves; That if America could furnish them with the former, they might be sent to their Ports in Biscay loaded with Tobacco or other Produce, and, discharging their Cargoes, be left at the Disposition of Spain. He also mentioned Timber for Vessels, but said that was an Article, which was not so immediately necessary, though it might be an Object of Consequence in future. He observed that he mentioned this at present in Order that M^r· Jay might turn his thoughts on this Subject as soon as possible, and that he would in Order to explain himself with more Precision, send him either on Saturday or Sunday next Notes containing his Ideas on this Subject, and adding that he hoped that the one, Vizt Jay, would assist the other, meaning himself, to manage Matters in such a Way as to procure the means of obtaining for America present Aid.

With respect to the Bills of Exchange which might be presented, he said that at the End of the present Year or in the Beginning of the next, he would have it in his Power to advance 25,000, 30,000 or 40,000 Pounds Sterling, and in the mean Time, should these Bills be presented for Payment, he would take such measures as would satisfy the owners of them Vizt. By engaging in the name of his Majesty to pay them, observing that the Kings good Faith and Credit was so well known, that he did not imagine this would be a difficult matter. He also said that in consequence of what M^r· Jay had written with Respect to Clothing for the American Army, it might be in his Power to send Supplies of Cloth, &c. which he would endeavor to do.

M^r· Jay in answer assured him of his high Sense of the Frankness and Candor with which he had been so obliging as to communicate the Kings Intentions and his own Sentiments, and gave him the strongest assurances that he should for his Part with the same Frankness and Candor give him all the Assistance and Information in his Power, to forward his generous Intentions in Favor of his Country, and that he might depend that in doing this, he would neither deceive him in his Information, or mislead him by ill grounded Expectations.

The Count then expressed his Confidence in these assurances, said he had been well informed of the Characters both of M^r· Jay, and M^r· Carmichael (who was present at the Conference) said that he considered them as *Les Hommes honêttes*, and that no Consideration could have prevailed upon him to have treated with Men who did not sustain that Reputation.

The Count then proceeded to the second Point Vizt: with Respect to the Treaty in Contemplation between Spain and America. He began by observing that he now spoke as a Minister, and as such that he would be as candid and frank as he had just been speaking as a private Man; and that it was always his Disposition to be so with those from whom he expected the same Conduct. He then proceeded to Observe, That there was but one obstacle, from which he apprehended any great Difficulty in forming a Treaty with America, and plainly intimated that this arose from the Pretensions of America to the Navigation of the Mississippi. He repeated the Information which the Court had received from Monsieur Miralles, that Congress had at one Time relinquished that Object;– That he also knew from the same Source that afterwards they had made it an essential Point of the Treaty. He expressed his uneasiness on this Subject, and entered largely into the Views of Spain with Respect to the Boundaries. (He mentioned Cape Antonio and Cape   and expressed their Resolution if possible of excluding the English entirely from the Gulf of Mexico.) They wished to fix by a Treaty which he hoped would be perpetual between the two Countries. He spoke amply of the King's anxiety, Resolution and Firmness on this Point, and insinuated a wish that some method might be fallen upon to remove this Obstacle. He observed that the King had received all his Impressions with Respect to the necessity of this measure previous to his being in Place, and appeared to regard it as a point from which his Majesty would never recede, repeating that still however he was disposed to give America all the Aid in his Power, consistent with the Situation of his Affairs, to distress the common Enemy; – That this Point being insisted on, it would be necessary for the Court of Spain to obtain the most accurate knowledge of local Circumstances, with which he supposed M^r· Jay and his Constituents were more fully apprised than his Majestys Ministers could be. That for this Purpose they had already written to the Havanna and Louisiana, in order to obtain all the necessary Information, which he gave Reason to believe they had not yet received. He dwelt on the Necessity of this Information previous to any Treaty, and expressed his own Regret that Ways and Means could not be found to obviate or overcome this Impediment. M^r· Jay here took an Opportunity to mention that many of the States were bounded by that River, and were highly interested in its Navigation, but observed that they were equally inclined to enter into any amicable Regulations, which might prevent any Inconveniences with Respect to Contraband or other Objects which might excite the Uneasiness of Spain. The Count still however appeared to be fully of Opinion that this was an Object that the King had so much at Heart, that he would never relinquish it; adding however that he hoped some middle Way might be hit on which would pave the way to get over this Difficulty and desired M^r· Jay to turn his thoughts and attention to the Subject, in which he assured him he was as well disposed to assist him, as in the means of procuring the Assistance and Succours for America before mentioned; always repeating the Kings favorable Disposition, his inviolable

Regard to his Promises &c.&c. On this Subject he also subjoined that whenever Mr Jay chose to go to Madrid, he desired to have previous Notice of it; for in those Cases he would leave his Sentiments in Writing for him with M^r· Carmichael, or, if he should also, that he would then write to M^r· Jay there, to which he might return an Answer by the the *Parle*, (a Post which goes to and from Madrid) to Aranjues every Twenty four Hours.

M^r· Jay expressed his full Confidence in what the Count had done him the Honor to communicate to him, and assured him of his Satisfaction and Happiness in having the good Fortune to transact a Business so important to both Countries with a Minister so liberal and candid in his manner of thinking and acting.

The Conference ended with much Civility on the one Part, and on the other, and with an Intimation from the Count that he should take an opportunity of having the Pleasure of M^r· Jay's Company at Dinner and of being on that friendly Footing on which he wished to be with him.

What passed in the Course of this Conference needs no Comment, though it calls for Information and Instruction. If Congress remains firm, as I have no Reason to doubt, respecting the Mississippi I think Spain will finally be content with equitable Regulations, and I wish to know whether Congress would consider any Regulations necessary to prevent Contraband, as inconsistent with their Ideas of free Navigation. I wish that as little as possible may be left to my Discretion, and that, as I am determined to adhere strictly to their Sentiments and Directions, I may be favored with them fully and in Season.

The Count De Florida Blanca had upon all occasions treated me with so much Fairness, Candor, and Frankness, that, between the Confidence due to him, and the Footing I was and ought to be on, with the French Ambassador embarrassed me exceedingly, especially as there is little Reason to doubt of their being on Confidential Terms with each other. I was reduced to the necessity therefore either of acting with exquisite Duplicity, a Conduct which I detest as immoral and disapprove as impolitic, or of mentioning my Difficulties to the Count and obtaining his Answer. I preferred the latter....

NA: PCC, item 110, v. 1, p. 132-142 (LBkC); M247, reel 135.

John Adams to Comte de Vergennes

Sir   Paris May 12th· 1780.

I have received the letter which you did me the honor to write me on the 10th· of this month. Althô the writer of the letter, an extract of which

I had the honor to enclose to you, may be right in his conjecture that the British Administration wish to know more than they do at present of my Sentiments upon the great Subject of a pacification, yet I have had too long experience of their principles views and tempers, and I know that they are too well acquainted with mine, for me to expect that they will directly convey any Propositions to me – When we hear them affirm in Parliament that America is upon the point of returning to an Allegiance to the King of England, and that they seriously believe America will return to such an Allegiance: When the Members of opposition, even those who are most inclined to peace, such as Mr Hartley, General Conway[1] &c. discover plainly by their motions and arguments, that their object is a seperate peace with America, in order to be the better able to gratify their revenge against France and Spain, I can have no expectations that they think of applying to me, because I think they must be convinced of this at least that I shall make no seperate peace.

I thank your Excellency however, for your sentiments, that I ought to hear them, in case overtures shou'd be made to me; I shou'd in such a case endeavour to hear them with decency and respect, but it wou'd require much Philosophy to hear with patience such absurd and extravagant propositions as are published in pamphlets and News-papers, and made in Parliament even by the Members of Opposition who profess to be most zealous for peace.

Our Alliance with France is an honor and a security, which have ever been near my heart. After reflecting long upon the geographical situation of the old world and the new; upon the agriculture, commerce, and political relations of both; upon the connections and oppositions among the Nations of the former, and the mutual wants and Interests of both, according to such imperfect lights as I was able to obtain; the result has long since been this, that my Country, in case she shou'd once be compelled to break off from Great Britain, wou'd have more just reasons to depend upon a reciprocity of the good offices of Friendship from France, Spain, and the other Sovereigns who are usually in their System, than upon those in the opposite Scale of the ballance of Power. I have ever thought it therefore a natural Alliance, and contended for it as a rock of Defence. This object pursued in Congress with persevering assiduity, for more than a year, in opposition to other Gentlemen of much greater Name and Abilities than mine, and had at length the satisfaction to find my Countrymen very generally fall into the same sentiment, and the honour to be appointed to draw the first Treaty which was sent to this Court. These Facts have been well known in America even to the Tories, and the utility and importance of this Alliance being known to be deeply imprinted in my mind and heart, I suppose was a principal cause why the present

Trust was confided to me by my Countrymen. These facts, althô they may have been unknown in France, yet having been well known to the Tories in America, I cannot suppose they are ignorant of them at the Court of St James's. I therefore think that neither Administration nor Opposition in England, will ever think of applying to me, untill they are brought into such a situation as shall compell them to sue for peace with all the Powers at War; which to be sure does not appear to be the case at present, nor likely to be, at least before the end of this Campaign, nor then neither, without some notable good fortune on the part of the Allies in the progress of the War. I have the honor to be with the greatest Respect Your Excellency's most obedient and most humble Servant   John Adams

FFAA: Pol. Corr., U.S., v. 12, f. 65-66 (LS); LC accession 13,773, microfilm reel 7.
  [1] Conway, Henry Seymour (1721-1795). British military and political leader. Member of Parliament, 1741-1774, 1775-1784. Advocate of reconciliation with the American colonies. His March 1782 resolution opposing offensive prosecution of the war and opening the door to peace negotiations helped bring down the North Ministry.

John Adams to John Jay

Dear Sir,   Paris May 13th· 1780.

· · · · · ·

The C. de F. Blanca, is agreed to be a Man of Abilities, but somehow or other, there is something in the European Understanding different from those We have been more used to. Men of the greatest abilities, and the most Experience, are with great difficulty brought to See, what appears to Us, as clear as day. It is habit, it is education, prejudice, what You will, but so it is. I can state a very short Argument, that appears to me a demonstration, upon French and Spanish Principles, alone, that it is more for their Interest, to employ their naval force in America than in Europe, yet it is in vain that you state this to a Minister of State, he cannot see it, or feel it, at least in its full force, and until the proper point of Time is past and it is too late. So I think it may be demonstrated, that it is the Interest of France and Spain to furnish America with an handsome Loan of Money, or even to grant them Subsidies, because a Sum of Money thus expended would advance the Common Cause, and even their particular Interests, by enabling the Americans to make greater Exertions, than the same Sums employed any other Way. But it is in vain to reason in this manner, with an European Minister of State. He cannot understand you. It is not within the Compass of those Ideas that he has been accustomed to.

· · · · ·

I am with much Esteem, dear Sir, your Servant   John Adams

Columbia University Libraries: John Jay Papers (LS).

Chevalier de la Luzerne to Comte de Vergennes

[Translation]

Nº 46. 1.   Philadelphia, 14 May 1780
My Lord
    I ask that you be good enough to read the enclosed letter Nº 4 by which I inform M. de Montmorin[1] of some details I thought might interest the Court of Spain. Before he left, M. Gerard was good enough to explain to me various circumstances of which it would be useful for me to have knowledge. He also informed me that the instructions that were sent to M. de Mirales as early as the month of July will have convinced Congress of Spain's friendly dispositions. M. de Mirales, My Lord, never received those instructions, and his Secretary assured me that since his death, nothing has arrived here from the Court of Madrid. All that has arrived is a letter from the month of August 1779 in which M. de Galves informs him that His Catholic Majesty approved of his conduct and was disposed to name him his minister near Congress when he is ready to name one. Congress is now completely convinced that recognition of independence can only be the result of a negotiation with the Court of Madrid, but while it is aware of the points that can satisfy that Court and hasten the admission of Mr. Jay as a public Minister, this Senate is not at all disposed to change the instructions it gave him last October, or at least it wishes to wait for a direct report from him before again taking into consideration the business of the western boundaries.

· · · · ·

Received 2 August   Le che de la luzerne

FFAA: Pol. Corr., U.S., v. 12, f. 29 (LC transcription).
    [1] *Montmorin-Saint-Hérem, Armand-Marc, Comte de (1745-1792). French diplomat and statesman. Ambassador to Spain, 1778-1784. Minister of foreign affairs, 1787-1791. Accused on pro-Austrian sympathies and killed in the massacre of September 1792.*

Chevalier de la Luzerne to Comte de Vergennes

[Translation]

Nᵒ· 48. 1ˢᵗ·   Philadelphia, 19 May 1780

My Lord

. . . . .

A Delegate who is a member of the Committee for Foreign Affairs has informed me of what has passed, My Lord, between you and Mr. John Adams relative to the revealing of his Character and to the explanations which he requested from you concerning his instructions. Congress appears grateful for the Counsels you have given him in this instance and for the action you have taken of presenting him to His Majesty. It is pleased by the great interest you have shown in him, and I think it should confirm the order not to take any step without your consent. As for the instructions of which he himself has been the bearer, based on various notions I have recorded, he is mistaken as to their true sense if he thinks that they authorize him to treat of peace with England, and if he is not convinced to the contrary that all his conduct should be planned with you and have your approbation. I surmise from what I have been told of his Letters that you have corrected his ideas on that point, and since it appears that nothing is pressing there, I have abstained from any insinuation in that regard.

. . . . .

le chr de la luzerne

FFAA: Pol. Corr., U.S., v. 12, f. 30 (LC transcription).

John Jay to the President of Congress

[Madrid, May 26, 1780]

. . . . .

The House of Gardoqui[1] at Bilboa are rich, in favor with the Ministry, and Friends to America. The Navy Board have sent to them for Goods for the use of the Navy, and have remitted to them only an inconsiderable Part of the Sum to which they will amount, desiring the Residue on Credit, and promising speedy Payment. One of the House now here, spoke to me on the Subject – I advised him to compleat the Orders. It is of the utmost Consequence that the Navy Board be punctual in their Remittances – American Credit is not high, and ought to be higher. I am the more anxious on this Subject, as that House is exceedingly well disposed, and a Disappointment would not only be injurious to them, but much more so to us. Perhaps it would be a good Rule if the United States were to contract

Debts only with Government, and never with Individuals abroad.

. . . . .

The Credit given me by Congress on Doctor Franklin is expended; and I am without other means of obtaining Supplies than private Credit, which I am at a Loss to satisfy. To apply to, and be maintained by the Court, is in my Opinion too humiliating to be for the public Good, and as yet I have neither received nor heard of Remittances from America. It would give me Pleasure to know in what manner Congress mean I should be supplied, and whether any measures have been taken for that Purpose.

I am much embarrassed for the means of conveying and receiving Intelligence. Being at a great Distance from the Sea, all my Letters to, and from thence here, must either be conveyed by private Couriers or the public Post – all my Letters by the latter whether in France or Spain are opened. By that conveyance therefore it would not always be proper to write either to Congress, to Doctor Franklin, M^r· Adams or others, with that Freedom which would often be useful and sometimes necessary. The Salary allowed me so far from admitting the Expense of private Couriers is inadequate to the common Purposes for which it was given. This is a delicate Subject, and I wish it was not my Duty to say any thing respecting it. This Place is the dearest in Europe – The Court is never stationary, passing part of the Year in no less than five different Places Vizt. Madrid, Pardo, Aranjues, S^t· Ildefonso, and the Escurial: Hence considerable Expenses arise. I forbear enumerating particulars, my Design being only to mention this matter to Congress, not to press it upon them. I shall always live agreeable to my Circumstances; and if from their being too narrow, Inconveniences result to the pubic, they ought to be informed of it. I hope what I have said will be viewed in this light only – So far as I am personally interested, I am content.

. . . . .

The Family of Galvez is numerous and of Weight. The one on the Mississippi has written favorably of the Americans to his Brothers here, three of whom are in Office. It would be well to cultivate this Disposition whenever opportunities of doing it offer.

. . . . .

The Reports of Dissensions in Congress which prevailed here prior to my arrival, and the Causes to which they were ascribed had filled this Court with apprehensions; and it gives me Pleasure to assure you that the present Appearance of union in Congress, is attended here with very happy Effects.

The People in this Country are in almost total Darkness about us. Scarce any American Publications have reached, nor are they informed of the most recent and important Events in that Country. The Affair of Stoney point, Paulus Hook &c. were never heard of here except perhaps by the great

Officers of State, and they could scarcely believe that the roman Catholic Religion was even tolerated there.

There are violent Prejudices among them against us – many have even serious doubts of our being civilized, and mention a strange Story of a Ship driven into Virginia by Distress about thirty Years ago that was plundered by the Inhabitants, and some of the Crew killed, in a Manner and under Circumstances which, if true, certainly indicate Barbarity. The King and Ministry are warm, yet I have Reason to believe that the Bulk of the Nation is cold towards us, They appear to me to like the English, hate the French, and to have Prejudices against us.

I mention these Things to shew in a stronger Light the necessity of Punctuality in sending me from Time to Time all American Intelligence of Importance; and observing such conduct towards Spaniards in general, as may tend to impress them with more favorable Sentiments of us. There was a little uneasiness among the Mercantile People at Cadis respecting the Capture of some Spanish Vessels by American privateers. I hope the former have had ample Justice done them: It certainly is of great Importance that they should have Reason to be satisfied.

·   ·   ·   ·   ·

John Jay.

·   ·   ·   ·   ·

NA: PCC, item 110, v. 1, pp. 170-177 (LBkC); M247, reel 135.

[1] Gardoqui, House of. Bilbao-based commercial firm of Joseph Gardoqui and Sons, which served as the principal conduit for Spanish aid to the United States.

John Jay to John Adams

Dear Sir   Aranjues, 4 June 1780

·   ·   ·   ·   ·

...This Court Seems to have great Respect for the old adage "festina lente"[1] — at least as applied to our Independence.

The Count D Florida Blanca has hitherto pleased me. I have found in him a Degree of Frankness and Candor which indicates Probity. His reputation for Talents is high. The acknowledgment of Independence is < obstructed >[2] retarded by Delays which in my opinion ought not to affect it. The Influence of that Measure on the Sentiments and Conduct of our Enemy, as well as the neutral Nations, makes it an object very important to the common Cause. I cannot think Its Suspension is < not > necessary to the Adjustment of the Articles of Treaty. They might with equal Facility be settled afterwards. As America is and will be independent in Fact, the being so in name can be of no great Moment to her individualy; but Britain derives Hopes <prejudice> from the Hesitation of Spain, very injurious to the common Cause, and I am a little suprized that the Policy of destroying these Hopes does not appear more evident <is of great consequence. America will never purchase < <such acknowledgement> >[3] it of any Nation by Terms She would not otherwise accede to. Things not Names are objects. >

If the Delay proceeds from Expectation that they may affect the Terms of Treaty, it is not probable that they will be realized. America is to be attached by Candor, Generosity, Confidence and good Offices. A contrary Conduct will not conciliate or persuade. But whatever may be the Cause of the mistakes on these Subjects, I must do them the Justice to say that the general Assurances given me by the Count D F. B. argue a very friendly Disposition in the Court towards us, and I hope Facts will prove them to have been sincere. They certainly must be convinced that the Power of the united States added to that of Britain and under her Direction, would enable her to give Law to the western World, and that Spanish America and the Islands would then be at her mercy. Our Country is at present so well disposed to Spain, and such cordial Enemies to Britain, that it would be a Pity this Disposition should not be cherished. Now is the time for France and Spain to gain the Affections of that extensive Country. Such another opportunity may never offer.

France has acted wisely. I wish similar Counsels may prevail here. Would it not be a little extraordinary if Britain should be before Spain in acknowledging our Independence? If she had any wisdom left she would do it. She may yet have a lucid Interval, tho she has been very long out of her Senses. Spain will be our Neighbour. We both have Territory enough to prevent our coveting each others and I should be happy to see that perfect Amity and cordial Affection established between us, which would ensure perpetual Peace and Harmony to both....

．　　．　　．　　．　　．

I am Dear Sir Your most affectionate Servant   J.J.

．　　．　　．　　．　　．

Morris, *Jay Papers, v. 1, pp. 764-766.*
    [1] *Literally, make haste slowly.*
    [2] *Angle brackets indicate deleted text in edited copy.*
    [3] *Double angle brackets indicate deletions within cancelled text.*

Conde de Floridablanca to John Jay

Aranjues, June 7th 1780.

His Catholic Majesty would be very glad to be able to furnish at the present Crisis funds for the payment of the one hundred thousand Pounds

Sterling proposed to be addressed to Mr Jay, in order to evince the Concern which the King takes in the Prosperity and Relief of the United States of North America, as well as in the personal satisfaction of the above mentioned Gentleman. But the demands of the present War, and the great difficulty there would be to transport hither, the Treasures of the King's Possessions in that part of the world, renders it impracticable to furnish here the said Sum in Specie, as could be wished. Some expedient however may be found to remedy this Inconvenience. For example; If the owners of the Bills of Exchange, would be content with the security, or responsibility of his Catholic Majesty, to pay the Sum already mentioned in the Term of two Years – The King will readily agree to such an arrangement, even if it shall be found necessary to add a moderate Interest– This Security given by such a Sovereign as the King of Spain would induce the owners of those Bills of Exchange, and the Creditors of Congress to consent to a measure so advantageous, and would equally serve to sustain the Credit and good faith of the same Body. Mr Jay therefore is entreated to reflect on the Idea just stated to him, and in Answer to inform us, what measures he thinks suitable to this Scheme, in order that they may be laid before the King, and his Orders taken thereon. If the Expedient in question should be adopted, it will at the same time be necessary to take measures in concert, to reimburse to the King this considerable Sum, as well as others already expended in favor of the United States. The first Idea which offers for reciprocal convenience, is that Congress should engage to build without delay some handsome Frigates, and other smaller Vessels of War, fixing the Price of each, and the time when they will be finished– This Point once settled, it will be proper immediately to take measures to equip these Vessels as fast as they are ready, to point out what Articles it will be necessary to send from Spain for this purpose, and in what Port they will have notice to receive them. After this, it is expedient to be informed, whether the Americans themselves will engage to come to the Ports of Bilboa, St Ander, Ferrol, or Cadiz for the said Articles, which they will find ready, and afterwards transport them in their own Vessels of war or Letters of Marque to America. On this supposition it is conjectured, that it would be easy to find hands enough in America to Man these new built Vessels, which will sail under Spanish Colours. There are certainly among the Subjects of the said United States, many who have made the Voyage, and are acquainted with the usual Route of the Ships of the English East India Company, and who know perfectly well the Ports and Places at which they stop– This fact established, it is proposed to equip in the Ports of the United States four good Frigates, and some other lighter Vessels with the Effects which shall be sent from hence on Account of Spain– This small Squadron, under Spanish Colours, shall be employed to intercept the

Convoys of the said Company by cruising in the proper Latitudes– The measures just pointed out appear to be the most proper to reimburse, in some shape the Expenses already incurred by his Catholic Majesty, and to answer for such security as hath been proposed to be given in this Memoir– It being always understood that a share of the prizes taken from the English by this small Squadron shall be given to the Crews; and even to Congress, in proportion to the Assistance which they shall furnish for the equipment of the Vessel.

A speedy and decisive Answer to all the Points here enumerated is requested, and Mr Jay is too enlightened not to perceive that the common cause is interested therein.

NA: PCC, item 110, v. 1, pp. 205-209 (LBkC); M247, reel 135.

John Jay to Conde de Floridablanca

Sir,   Aranjues June 9th 1780.

· · · · ·

The enlarged Ideas my Constituents entertain of the Power, Wealth and Resources of Spain, are equal to those they have imbibed of the Wisdom and Probity of his Catholic Majesty, and of that noble and generous System of Policy which has induced him to patronise their Cause, and by compleating their Separation from Great Britain, effectually to disarm the latter. Such wise and liberal designs, followed by such great and extensive consequences, would add a bright page to the Annals of a Reign already signalized by important events. It is therefore with deep regret that Congress would receive information, that the Aid they solicit, small when compared with their Ideas of the Resources of Spain, has been rendered impracticable by the Expenses of a War, which on the part of Spain, is of a recent date. Nor will their disappointment be less than their regret, when they find their Credit diminished by the failure of a measure, from the Success of which they expected to raise it....

· · · · ·

With respect to the Plan proposed for the repayment of such Sums as Spain may lend to the United States, Vizt. by the latter furnishing the former with Frigates &c. &c. I beg leave to submit the following Remarks to your Excellency's consideration. In the United States there are Timber, Iron, Masts, Shipwrights, Pitch, Tar, and Turpentine, and Spain can furnish the other Requisites. But neither the Timber, the Iron, the Masts or the other Articles can be procured without Money....

That Excellent Frigates and other Vessels may be built in America cheaper than in Europe I am persuaded. And I know that Congress will cheerfully give every aid in their Power to facilitate the Execution of any Plan of that kind, which his Majesty may adopt, but Sir their necessities will not permit them to supply Money to these purposes, and I should deceive your Excellency with delusive expectations, were I to lead you to think otherwise....

I have the Honor to be, &c.   John Jay.

NA: PCC, item 110, v. 1, pp. 209-219 (LBkC); M247, reel 135.

Chevalier de la Luzerne to Comte de Vergennes

[Translation]

No. 54. Triplicate.   Philadelphia, 11 June 1780.
My Lord

Although the requests of M. de Mirales had imposed silence upon me concerning the affair of the boundaries between Spain and the United States on the Mississippi, I nonetheless thought I should rectify, as far as it depended on me, and in a private manner, the ideas of many Members of Congress on this matter. The arguments which I used were not without some results, and I learn that several delegates were so struck by them that as early as the month of February last they reported them to Congress and recorded them in its secret journals. But as my communications could not be considered as Ministerial, they could not be made the subject of formal deliberations. As soon as I was informed of this report, I tried to discover the impression that it had made on the different delegates. In my conversations with the individuals in question, those from the North have shown themselves tolerably reasonable and have agreed in principle that, the former eastern Louisiana being now in the hands of England, the appurtenances having being ceded in the peace of 1763, Spain had the incontestable right to conquer it. This clear truth is equally recognized by the general Congress, and several Members from the State of New York.

Those from New Jersey, Delaware, and Pennsylvania, little interested in the question, nevertheless value the ultimatum of Congress on this article and think that a decision rendered after the most mature examination can only be reversed upon the most absolute and best proven necessity. Maryland is the State whose sentiments on this matter are the most reasonable and the best articulated. A Delegate from that State, a man who enjoys great influence, does not hesitate to say that not only can Spain make this conquest without any contradiction, but that without having undertaken any engagement with Congress, if today she seized from the English the State of Georgia, which is in their hands, she would have the same rights as England to the preservation of that conquest. Maryland has in truth no immediate interest in this discussion; but the opinion of a member so eminent as is Mr. Jenifer[1] serves at least to prove that the principles of Congress on this matter are not unanimous. Virginia herself today shows less attachment to those whom she has previously supported on this matter; and I have found the Delegates from that State much more moderate than I would have expected. This change is perhaps due to a particular circumstance; it is that the inhabitants of parts of that State who are far from the Seat of Government announce at this moment views of independence and the plan of forming a separate state. This incident and the difficulty of containing these Insurgents make one realize better than all the reasonings the inconvenience of distant and too-farflung possessions and the danger of a dismemberment or dissolution of the State. North Carolina does not appear so favorably disposed. Mr. Burke, an ardent and obstinate man, although also a good Citizen, regards Spain's plans as unjust, contrary to the rights of the Thirteen States, and prejudicial to their happiness and their tranquility, and if Mr. Jay's reports cause Congress to make some alteration in its ultimatum, I quite fear the vehemence of this Delegate. South Carolina also seems to pay homage to the rights of the Spanish to conquer Louisiana. As for Georgia, she has been represented only for a short time, and I have not had occasion to sound out the delegates she has sent here. These general dispositions are not at all close to what they should be for the satisfaction of His Catholic Majesty. However, they are very different from what they appeared to me at the time of my first insinuations, and I am persuaded that if the affair were of a nature to be deliberated upon, the majority would recognize, without hesitation, that Spain incontestably has the right to make the conquest in question. I also have every reason to believe that the notions that Mr. Jay will be in a position to send here will be much better received than they would have been without this preparation. But at the same time I must add that, if it were a question of reforming the ultimatum with which that Minister has been charged, if it were necessary to deliberate on the question of ceding the contested regions to Spain by a preliminary Treaty, this would provoke violent debates that in which the States of the North, although in principles very moderate, would themselves second the States of the South in the hope of being seconded in turn in their pretensions concerning some parts of Canada comprised in their ultimatum, and that it is impossible for me now to predict what will be the result of these discussions. In this state of things, I believe that the Court of Madrid can do no more than to pursue the conquest it has begun and to exercise over the Lands newly subjected to its Dominion all the acts of sovereignty, of Jurisdiction, and of possession that it judges the most appropriate to destroy in the minds of the Americans the chimerical hope they have conceived of conquering them from England, or at least acquiring them by the Treaty of peace.

I am with Respect, My Lord, Your very humble and very obedient servant   Le chr de la luzerne.
Received 1 September.

FFAA: Pol. Corr., U.S., v. 12, f. 74 (LC transcription).
¹ Jenifer, Daniel of St. Thomas (1723-1790). Maryland political figure. Member, Continental Congress, 1779-1781. Member, Constitutional Convention, 1787.

Comte de Vergennes to John Adams

Sir   Versailles 21 June 1780

I have rec^d the letter which you have done me the honour to write to me on the 16 of this Month: and also the extract of the letter addressed to you from Boston dated 26 April.

~~According to~~ From this it appears that the Assembly of Massachusetts has determined to adopt the resolution of Congress fixing the value of the paper money at 40 for one in specie.[1] In reading that resolution I was persuaded that it had no other object than that of restoring the value of the paper money by lessening its quantity, and that in consequence of that operation, the paper not brought in would take its course according to the circumstance that would give it a greater or less degree of credit. What confirmed me in this Opinion was the liberty given to the possessors of the paper money to carry it to the treasury of their state or to keep it in their own possession.

But from the information I have since rec^d and the letter which you have been pleased to communicate to me I have reason to believe that the intention of Congress is to maintain the paper money invariably at the exchange of 40 for 1. and to settle on that footing all the paper money which has been thrown into circulation, in order to reduce insensibly the two hundred millions of dollars for which it is indebted, to five millions

I will not presume, Sir, to criticize upon this Operation, because I have no right to examine or comment upon the internal arrrangements which Congress may consider as just & profitable; and more over I readily agree that there may be some situations so critical as to force the best regulated governments to adopt extraordinary measures to repair their finances & put them in condition to answer the public expences, and, this, I am persuaded, has been the principal reason that induced Congress to depreciate the money which they themselves have emitted.

But while I admit, Sir, that that Assembly might have recourse to the expedient above mentioned in order to remove their load of debt, I am far from agreeing that it is just & agreeable to the ordinary course of things to extend the effect to strangers as well as to citizens of the United States. On the contrary, I think it ought to be confined to Americans and that an exception ought to be made in favour of strangers or at least that some means ought to be devized to indemnify them for the losses they may suffer by the general law.

In order to make you sensible of the truth of this observation I will only remark, Sir, that the Americans alone ought to support the expence which is occasioned by the defence of their liberty; and that they ought to consider the depreciation of their paper money only as an impost which ought to fall upon themselves, as the paper money was at first established only to relieve them from the necessity of paying taxes. I will only add that the french if they are obliged to submit to the ~~depreciation~~ reduction proposed by Congress, will find themselves victims of their zeal and I may say of the rashness with which they exposed themselves in furnishing the Americans with arms, Ammunition & clothing and in a word with all things of the first necessity, of which the Americans at the time stood in need. You will agree with me, Sir, that this is not what the subjects of the King ought to expect; and that after escaping the dangers of the Sea, the vigilance of the English, instead of dreading to see themselves plundered in America, they ought on the contrary to expect the thanks of Congress & of all the Americans & believe that their property will be as secure & sacred in America as in france itself. It was with this persuasion & in a reliance on public faith that they received paper money in exchange for their merchandize & kept that paper with a view to employ it in new speculations of Commerce: The unexpected reduction of this paper overturns all their calculations at the same time that it ruins their fortune. I ask, Sir, if these consequences can induce you to believe, that this Act of Congress is proper to < **** > advance the credit of the U. S., to inspire confidence in their promises to invite the European Nations to run the same risques to which the subjects of his Majesty have exposed themselves ~~to~~

These, Sir, are the principal reflections occasioned by the resolution of Congress of the 18. of March. I thought it my duty to communicate them to you with an entire confidence because you are too enlightened not to feel the force & justice and too much attached to your country not to use all your endeavours to engage it take steps to do justice to the subjects of the King. I will not conceal from you that M^r the Chev^r de la Luzerne has rec^{d.} order to make the strongest representations on this subject and that the King is firmly persuaded that the United States will be forward to give to him on this Occasion a Mark of their Attachment by granting to his Subjects the just Satisfaction which they solicit and expect from the Justice and Wisdom of the United States.

I have the honor to be most sincerely Sir your most humb & obed^{t.} Servant   De Vergennes

NA: PCC, item 84, v. 2, pp. 407-410 (translation); M247, reel 111.

¹ By an act of 18 March 1780, Congress revalued Continental money at $40 paper to $1 specie. By issuing $5 in new paper for every $100 of old paper retired, but printing $10 million, it planned to create $5 million in "income" with which to finance its continuing operations.

John Adams to the President of Congress

Sir   Paris June 26th 1780

The Resolutions of Congress of the 18th. of March respecting the paper bills, appeared first in Europe as recited in the act of the Assembly of Pennsylvania. They were next published in the English News-Papers as taken from a Boston Paper published by the Council, at last the Resolutions appeared in the Journals of Congress.

A great clamour was raised and spread, that the United States had violated their Faith, and had declared themselves Bankrupts, unable to pay more than Two and a half pr. Cent–

A Gentleman soon after called upon me, and told me that the Court were alarmed, and that the Comte De Vergennes would be glad to consult me upon the Subject. I then received a Letter from Boston, acquainting me that the Legislature of Massachusetts had adopted the Plan. Of this letter I sent an Extract immediately to the Comte, and waited on him at Versailles, where I had the honor of a long Conversation with his Excellency on the Subject. He desired me to converse with his first Commis upon the Subject, which I did particularly.

His Excellency told me he had written to me upon the Subject and that I shou'd receive the letter the next Day. On my return from Versailles, I received a letter from Mr. Gerry¹ informing me of the Resolutions to pay the Loan Office Certificates at the value of money at the Time when they issued. I had before told the Comte, that I was persuaded this was a part of the plan. I sent an Extract of this letter also to the Comte without loss of time. The next day I received the Letter from his Excellency, Copy of which and of my Answer are enclosed – Yesterday Mr. Trumbull² of Connecticut, favoured me with the Law of the State, respecting this matter, and an Estimate of the gradual progress of Depreciation. These papers I forthwith transmitted to his Excellency.

I am determined to give my sentiments to His Majesty's Ministers whenever they shall see Cause to ask them; althô it is not within my Department, untill I shall be forbidden by Congress: and to this End, I will go to Court often enough to give them an opportunity to ask them, if they wish to know them.

The Clamour that has been raised, that has been so industriously spread, that I cannot but suspect, that the Motive at Bottom, has either been a wish to have opportunity of continuing the profitable speculations, which artful Men are able to make in a depreciating Currency, or else by spreading a diffidence in American Credit to discourage many from engaging in American Trade, that the profits of it may still continue [to be] confined to a few. I have the honour to be with the greatest respect your Excellency's Most obedient and most humble Servant   John Adams Read Novr. 30. –

NA: PCC, item 84, v. 2, pp. 153-156 (LS); M247, reel 111.
¹ *Gerry, Elbridge (1744-1814). Massachusetts merchant and political figure. Member, Provincial Congress, 1774-1776. Member, Continental Congress, 1776-1780, 1783-1785. Delegate, Constitutional Convention, 1787; opposed ratification of the Constitution. Member, U.S. House of Representatives, 1789-1793. Member, XYZ Mission, 1797-1798. Governor of Massachusetts, 1810-1812. Vice President, 1813-1814.*
² *Trumbull, Jonathan (1710-1785). Connecticut merchant and political figure. Deputy governor and chief justice of the superior court of Connecticut, 1766-1769; governor, 1769-1784.*

Notes of a Conference between John Jay and Conde de Floridablanca

Madrid July the 5th 1780.

M^r. Jay waited on the Count de Florida Blanca agreeable to an appointment, made by the latter to meet at his House at half after eight this Evening.

. . . . .

M^r. Jay mentioned that if it was agreeable to His Excellency to permit M^r. DelCampo,¹ (a confidential Secretary of the Count, who speaks English, and who translated all the Letters to and from the Count) to be present, he should be able to explain his Sentiments more fully and clearly. Though the Count did not object to this proposal, he appeared disinclined to it, and said that with the Assistance of M^r. Carmichael then present, they could understand each other very well. He then proceeded to speak of the Bills of exchange, in the possession of Mes.ⁿˑ Joyce,[2] and seemed to be surprised that that House should be possessed of so many of them. He advised Mʳˑ Jay to be cautious of those Gentlemen, saying, that they were as much English in their Hearts, as the Ministry of that Country – that he had known them long, that he thought their conduct extraordinary in being so urgent for the acceptance of these Bills. Mʳˑ Jay then informed His Excellency that he had paid these Gentlemen a Visit in order to obtain further Time, and that they had consented to wait until Monday next. The Count mentioned a fortnight or three Weeks as necessary in order that he might have an opportunity of seeing the Person he had sent for, and making some arrangements with him. He said that it would be more agreeable to His Majesty to pay these Bills at Cadis, Bilboa, or Amsterdam than here, lamented the precipitancy with which Congress had enterᵈ into this measure, saying that if they had previously addressed the King on the Subject, ways and means might have been found, either to transport from their Possessions in America, Specie for the service of Congress, or to have enabled them to have drawn Bills of Exchange at a shorter Sight which would have prevented the loss of one third of the Money to which Congress had subjected themselves by the terms on which the present Bills were Sold. Mʳˑ Jay assured His Excellency that by Letters he had received from America, from Members of Congress and others, he was informed that the Terms were judged so unfavorable to the Buyer, that the Bills drawn on him sold heavily, from that circumstance solely, and not from any doubt of their Credit, and Payment – This did not however appear to convince his Excellency who spoke much of the deranged State of our Finances, and Credit, of the advantages taken of Congress by Merchants and others, who availed themselves of that circumstance, which he called cruel Extortions, frequently expressing the King's wishes and his own to render America all the Service in their power in this Crisis of their Affairs; but observed that it was impossible to obtain much Money in Europe, while France, England and Spain were making use of every resource to obtain it for the enormous Expenses of the War, and while the Channel through which the European Merchants received Supplies of Specie was stopped Vizt. the arrival of the usual quantity from America – This induced him to mention the arrival at Cadis of 3,000,000 of Piastres, all of which was on Account of the Merchants, and again to dwell on what he had before said of the Possibility of transmitting Specie to the States, from the Spanish Possessions abroad; and of the Effect that this would have in reestablishing the credit of our Money. Mʳˑ Jay observed in reply, that if a Supply of Specie could be sent to America, and His Excellency thought that measure more convenient, and adviseable than Bills, the Congress would in his Opinion readily suspend drawing, on receiving that information, to which the Count answered, that when the Person he had sent for arrived, this matter might be further discussed.

Mr. Jay then proceeded to observe that by Papers which he had transmitted to His Excellency he would see that Congress had adopted a System to redeem and destroy the former emissions, and to emit other Bills to be paid in Europe with Interest in a certain term of Years, and in fully establishing this System it would be probably in their Power, not only to sustain the Credit of their Money, but to contribute in some measure to assist Spain in the way proposed by his Excellency – Vizt. in building of Frigates &c. &c. He added that as his Majesty's Treasure was detained in America, and as much Expense would be incurred by the Armaments employed by Spain there, that Bills on the Havannah in favor of the United States might be more convenient to Spain, and equally contribute to the End proposed – The Count did not seem to disapprove of the Idea, but did not enlarge upon it – He asked Mr. Jay, if America could not furnish Spain with Masts and Ship Timber – Mr. Jay replied that those Articles might be obtained there – The Count then said that he would defer further Remarks on this Head, 'till the Arrival of the Person whom he expected would succeed Mr. Mirailles, and appeared desirous of leaving this Subject, and indeed all other matters relative to American Affairs to be discussed when he came.

...By his whole conversation he endeavoured to shew, how much he interested himself in the Prosperity of our Affairs – more than once desiring Mr. Jay not to be discouraged, for that with Time and Patience all would go well, expatiating on the King's character, his Religious observation of, and adherence to his promises, and his own desire of having Mr. Jay's entire Confidence – Mr. Jay seized this opportunity of assuring him of his full reliance on the King's Justice and honor, and his particular and entire confidence in his Excellency, asserting to him that all his Letters to Congress breathed these Sentiments....

Mr. Jay reminded his Excellency in a delicate manner of the Supplies of Clothing &c. &c which had been promised in a former Conference, and said that if they could be sent in Autumn, they would be essentially useful. The Count assured him that measures would be taken for this purpose, with the Person so often hinted at in the course of the Conference, that probably these Goods would be embarked from Bilbao, as everything was so dear at Cadis. He also once more told Mr. Jay that at all events he might accept the Bills presented by Messieurs Joyce payable at Bilbao – Though he appeared to wish that this measure might be delayed for a fortnight if possible. The Conference ended with compliments and assurances on the one part, and the other – The Count endeavoring to persuade Mr. Jay of His Majesty's desire to assist the States, and Mr. Jay assuring him of his reliance on His Excellency and of the good Effect which such proofs of his Majesty's friendship would have in America at the present Juncture.

In this Conference not a single Nail would drive, Everything was to be postponed 'till the arrival of the Person intended to succeed M^r· Mirailles.

NA: PCC, item 110, v. 1, pp. 236-245 (LBkC); M247, reel 135.

[1] *Campo, Bernardo del. Spanish diplomat. Floridablanca's English-speaking undersecretary. Authorized to treat with John Jay, September 1781-May 1782. Appointed provisional envoy to Great Britain after the conclusion of the preliminary European peace treaty in January 1783, subsequently minister and ambassador to that power into the 1790s. Created marqués in mid-1780s.*

[2] *Messrs. Joyce. Bilbao mercantile house. The name is also given as Joyces, Joyez, and Joyes.*

Committee for Foreign Affairs
to Benjamin Franklin and John Jay

In Committee of Foreign Affairs   Philad^a· 11 July 1780
Sir

Congress having appointed The Honble Henry Laurens to solicit a Loan of Money in The United Provinces of the Low Countries, in Order to facilitate his Success the enclosed Resolution has been passed. We need say Nothing to explain or urge it, except that it is thought a Mark of Attention and Confidence due to those Powers; that their Interest, if the State of Politicks incline them to exert it, will have a good Effect; and that the Want of Money makes the Loan a very capital Object to the United States. You will, we are assured, give M^r· Laurens every Assistance in your Power, and solicit the Countenance of the Court where you reside to forward his Negociations.

Till M^r· Laurens shall arrive, M^r· Adams is commissioned and empowered to undertake that Business, and in case of his Disability, M^r· Dana is in like Manner commissioned and empowered.

We are Sir your very obed^t hble Servts.   James Lovell
                                        Wm. Churchill Houston[1]

Paul H. Smith, ed., Letters of Delegates to Congress, 1774-1789 (Washington, DC: Library of Congress, 1976 —), hereafter cited as Smith, Letters of Delegates, v. 15, pp. 427-428; National Society Daughters of the American Revolution: Americana Collection, Accession No. 2000, Document 47.

[1] *Houston, William Churchill (c.1746-1788). New Jersey attorney and political figure. Member, Continental Congress, 1779-1781, 1784-1785. Member, Annapolis Convention, 1786. Member, Constitutional Convention, 1787.*

John Jay to Benjamin Franklin

Madrid, 17 July 1780.

.   .   .   .   .

The Papers enclosed with this will make known to you the exact State of <our>[1] Affairs <here> at this Court. I have been permitted <already> to accept Bills <drawn> to the amount of between ten and twelve Thousand Dollars and as the Court and particularly the Count D Florida Blanca seems well disposed towards us I hope the unpleasant Measure will terminate well....

From these Papers you will naturally conclude that it is very far from being in my Power to afford Mr. Ross[2] the Aid mentioned in your Letter. On the Contrary I find myself constrained to request the Favor of you to lodge here for Mr. Carmichael and myself a further Credit to enable us to recieve what may be due on Account of Salaries. <I cannot think of endeavoring> We shall otherwise be very soon in a very disagreable Situation. To take up Money from Individuals <for many Reasons> would not be eligible or reputable and it would not be prudent to trouble Government already a little sore about the Bills with further Requisitions at present.

<To you therefore I must recur, and that> I am also obliged to make this Request without being able to give you other assurances <of> respecting the Time of Repayment, than that the proceeds of the first Remittance I may recieve shall be applied to that in Preference to every other Purpose....

.   .   .   .   .

It is necessary you should be informed that the Papers inclosed with this are known to Count Montmorin and therefore are probably no Secrets to his Court. I am on <exceedingly> good Terms with the Count whom I esteem as a Man of abilities and am pleased with as a Friend to our Country. As France had interested herself so deeply in our Cause, had done us <such> essential Benefits, and had been requested to interpose her friendly offices for us here, I could not think of withholding from him all the Confidence which these considerations dictate, especially as <the Resolutions of Congress respecting their Legation here breathed that Spirit, and as> no personal objections forbid it. To have conducted the Negociation with <slyness> finesse, and unnecessary secrecy, and equivocating cunning was irreconcilable with my Principles of Action and with every Idea I have of Wisdom and Policy—in a word France and America are and I hope will always be Allies. It is the Duty of each Party to cultivate mutual Confidence and Cordiality. From my own Part while their Conduct continues fair, firm and friendly, I shall remain thoroughly attached to their Interest and grateful for their Benefit.

. . . . .

I am Dear Sir with very sincere Regard your most obedient Servant

John Jay

. . . . .

Morris: Jay Papers, v. 1, pp. 793-795.

¹ Angle brackets indicate deleted text in edited copy.

² Ross, John (1729-1800). Pennsylvania merchant with commercial houses in Philadelphia and Nantes.

John Adams to Comte de Vergennes

Sir   Paris July 17th. 1780

In your Excellency's letter to me of the Twenty Fourth of February last, I was honored with your opinion in the following Words. Quant au plein pouvoir, que vous autorise à negocier un Traité de Commerce avec la Cour de Londres, Je pense qu'il sera prudent de n'en donner Communication a qui que se soit, et de prendre toutes les precautions possibles pour que le Ministere Anglois n'en ait pas une connoissance prematuré. Vous senterez surement de vous même les motifs que me portent à vous conseiller cette precaution et il seroit superflu que je vous les expasasse.⊛

1st. I shoud have been very happy, if your Excellency had hinted at the Reasons which were then in your Mind, because after reflecting upon this Subject, as maturely as I can, I am not able to collect any Reasons which appear to me sufficient, for concealing the Nature of my powers in their full extent, from the Court of London. On the contrary, many arguments have occurred to me, which seem to shew it to be both the policy of the United States, and my particular Duty to communicate them.

2ª. Your Excellency will recollect that my Commissions empower me to join with the Ministers of the belligerent Powers in making Peace, – to make a Treaty of Commerce with the Ministers of his Britannic Majesty, and to represent the Congress, as their Minister Plenipotentiary, at the Court of London. It seems to me then inconsistent with the design and nature of my appointments to conceal them from the Court of London

3ª. I think also that announcing my Powers to the Court of London, wou'd have a tendency to draw out from them, some proofs of their present designs; and it is always important to discover early the Intentions of the Enemy, that the People may be prepared both with Councils and Forces, to resist them if hostile.

4º· et 5º· The English nation wou'd expect of the Ministers that some answer shou'd be given to me. If it shou'd be an insolent one, as there is too much Cause to expect, it will prepare the minds of the Americans, and of the other belligerent Powers, for what they are to expect, and it will alarm and arouse, if any thing can, the People of England. At this particular time when an Election approaches, it wou'd throw the Ministry into some Embarrassment; for the People of England sigh for Peace.

6º· Another Consideration has weight with me. A great part of Europe, as well as the People of England are amused by the English Ministry, and their Emissaries, with Reports that there is some secret Treaty between France and the United States, by which the former has secured to themselves, exclusive priviledges in some branches of the American Commerce; which misrepresentations as they are at present an obstruction to Peace, wou'd be cleared up by the Communication of my Powers.

7º· There are at present many Persons of Consideration in England, who have long followed the Ministry in the War against America, who begin to see the impracticability of succeeding, and now vote for Peace, and will lay hold of every occurrence that favors its accomplishment

8º· At this moment, under the wild impression that the surrender of Charlestown has made, it might be improper to make the Communication; but upon the News coming of Monsieur de Ternay's[1] arrival, of Don Solano's,[2] or both, or upon the receipt of some Intelligence which may take off a part of this impression, I submit it to your Excellency's Consideration, whether it wou'd not be proper for me to communicate my appointments to Lord George Germain. It seems to be most proper that it shou'd be done, so that the Nation may consider them before the Meeting of Parliament, and that those who are for Peace, may digest their plans accordingly

9º· Notwithstanding the suppression of the late Riots and the consequent temporary Relaxation of the Committees and Associations, the Nation is in a most critical Situation. Those Disturbances were not simply the Effect of Fanaticism and Bigotry but of deep and general discontent and distress among the People, and although Ministry may at present be confident they have suppressed them forever, they will surely find themselves mistaken, if they pursue this War. I know of no measure that will be more likely to encrease the opposition against Administration than communicating my Powers. It will at least show all the World, that the Continuance of the War, and the consequent Ruin of England, is their own fault, not that of the Americans, who are ready to make Peace upon Terms honourable and advantageous to Great Britain.

10º· et 11º· I am the more confirmed in these opinions, by the Communication your Excellency made to me yesterday of the Message sent by the Court of London to the Court of Madrid.[3] I am convinced in my own Mind, that that Message is insidious in the last degree; and that it is intended to answer two Ends only; first to spy out what they can of the political and military plans of Spain, secondly and principally, to amuse France, Spain, and America too, with false Ideas of pacific Inclinations, simply in order to slacken and enervate their preparations for the next Campaign. Sincere intentions of making Peace upon any Terms which France or America can agree to, consistent with subsisting Treaties, I am as sure they have not, as I am of their Existence. Now, I think, there is no way of conteracting this insidious policy, so honourably and so effectually, as by a frank and decent Communication of my full Powers. This will necessitate them to come to an Explanation of their real intentions concerning America; for there, Sir, lies the Obstacle to peace, all other questions wou'd be soon arranged if that was settled.

I hope your Excellency, will pardon the long letters I write you, because it is really a voluminous subject We have in Contemplation, and Mankind in general, are little less interested in it, than our particular Countries

I shall hope for the honor of your Excellency's Answer upon these Subjects, and remain with the greatest Respect and Attachment, Your Excellency's, Most obedient and Most humble Servant   John Adams

---

® With regard to the full power, which authorizes you to negotiate a Treaty of Commerce with the Court of London, I think it will be prudent not to communicate it to anybody whatever, and to take all possible precautions, that the English Ministry may not have a premature knowledge of it. You will surely of yourself feel the motives which induce me to advise you to take this precaution, and it would be needless to explain them.

NA: PCC, item 84, v. 2, pp. 435-439 (LS); M247, reel 111.

[1] Ternay, Charles-Henri d'Arsac, Chevalier de (1723-1780). French naval officer. Captured St. John's, Newfoundland in 1762, but forced to withdraw before the arrival of a British squadron. Appointed governor of the Iles de France and Bourbon, 1771. Commanded the squadron that convoyed Rochambeau's expeditionary force to Rhode Island, 1780.

[2] Solano y Bote, José, Marqués del Socorro (1726-1806). Spanish naval officer and colonial administrator. Governor and captain general of the provinces of Venezuela, 1763-1770, and of Santo Domingo, 1770-1779. Brigadier, 1773. Chief of squadron, 1779. Took part in the expedition of the combined French and Spanish fleets in the English Channel, 1779. Commanded squadron of 12 ships that convoyed an expeditionary force of 12,000 men to Cuba, 1780. Took part in the conquest of the Floridas and the fall of Pensacola. Lieutenant general, 1782. Marqués del Socorro, 1784. Commander of naval forces in the Departments of Cádiz and Ferrol, 1790. Later, captain general of the fleet.

[3] Presumably a reference to a communication relating to the efforts of British intermediaries to negotiate a separate peace with Spain, 1779-1780.

David Hartley to John Adams

Dear Sir   July 17 1780 London
    Enclosed I send you a copy of a conciliatory bill wch I moved in Parliament on the 27th of the last month – You will perceive by the tenor of it that it is drawn up in very general terms, containing a general power to treat, with something like a sketch of a line of negotiation. As the bill was not accepted by the ministers in this Country, I have nothing further to say relating to it. As to my own private Sentiments & endeavours, they allways have been, & ever will be devoted to the restoration of peace, upon honorable terms. I shall be always ready, and most desirous to conspire in any measues wch may lead to that end.
    I am Dear Sir Your most obed^t humble Servant   D Hartley

MHS: *The Adams Papers, microfilm reel 352 (ALS).*

Comte de Vergennes to John Adams

Sir,   Versailles, the 25 July 1780
    I have received the letter which you have done me the honor to write on the 17 of this Month. I have read it with the most serious attention and in order to give you an answer with greater exactness I have placed it <****> in the margin <*****> ~~every article~~ of every paragraph ~~of it~~ which seemed to require observations on my part. You will there see, Sir, that I continue to be of opinion that the time to communicate your plenipotentiary powers to Lord Germaine is not yet come and you will there find the reasons on which I ground my Opinion. I have no doubt you will feel the force of them & that they will determine you to think as I do. But if that should not be the case I pray and ~~even~~ in the name of the King request you to communicate your letter and my answer to the United States and to suspend until you shall receive orders from them all measures with regard to the English Ministry. I shall, on my part, transmit my observations; to America that M de la Luzerne may communicate them to the members of Congress, and I am persuaded that that Assembly will think the opinion of the Ministry of France worthy [of] some attention and that it will not be afraid of neglecting or betraying the interests of the United States by adopting it as a rule of its conduct. I have the honor to be with the greatest sincerity, Sir, y^r· Your most humble & most Obed^t Servt
                                    De Vergennes

M^r· *Adams' letter*
17 July 1780 to
Le Co^t· de Vergennes

Observations on Mr Adams' letter of
17 July 1780 –

I should have been
very happy – to
communicate them

1. The reasons which determined the count de
Vergennes to give Mr Adams that advice are so
plain that they must appear at first view
1. To be solicitious about a treaty of commerce
before peace is established is like being busy
about furnishing a house before the foundation is
laid
2. In the situation, in which America stands at
present with regard to England, to announce to
that power that they have forgotten her system
of tyranny, her cruelties & her perfidy is
discovering too great a degree of weakness or at
least too much good nature and inviting her to
believe that the Americans have an irresistable
predilection for her, and to fortify her in the
opinion she entertains that the American
patriots will submit through weariness or
preponderating influence of the tories. –
3. To propose a treaty of Commerce which must
be founded on confidence and on a Union
equivalent to an alliance at a time when the war
is raging in all its fury, when the court of
London is wishing to ~~destroy~~ ruin, or to
subjugate America, what is it but to give credit
to the opinion which all Europe entertains
~~agreeable~~ conformable to the assertions of the
English Ministers that the United States incline
towards a defection and that they will ~~not~~ be
faithful to their engagements with France only
till < ** > such time as GB shall < ** > furnish
a pretext for breaking them.

2. Your excellency will
recollect that < * >
the court of London

II. A person may be furnished eventually with
plenipotentiary powers without being under a
necessity of publishing them until circumstances
permit him use them. This happens every day.
Mr Adams is charged with three distinct
commissions. 1. To take a share in the future

negotiations for peace. 2 To conclude a treaty of commerce with GB. And 3. To represent the United States at the court of London. It requires no great effort of genius to shew that these three objects cannot be accomplished at the same moment of time, nor the two last cannot serve as an introduction to the first. It is necessary first of all to obtain from England an acknowledgement of the independence of America And that acknowledgement must serve as a foundation for a Treaty of peace. Until this is obtained Mr Adams cannot talk of a treaty of commerce. To propose one while the court of London is flattering itself with the hopes of subduing America and while with that view it is making the most strenuous efforts, would in the view of that court be to propose <****> what was chimerical & would be taking a step which it would hold in derision. The case would be the same were one at this time to talk of a Minister plenipotentiary from the United States appointed to reside at the court of his Britannic Majesty. – The only powers, therefore, which circumstances permit Mr Adams to announce are those which authorise him to take a part in the negotiations for peace. The two other powers can be of no avail until the conclusion of that peace, so that it would be at least, be useless to produce them at present and consequently Mr Adams will not act inconsistent with the design and nature of his appointment by concealing them from the court of London. Although the count de Vergennes is unacquainted with the instructions of Mr Adams, yet he is persuaded that they are conformable to the foregoing reflections, and that they do not direct him to make an immediate communication of his powers relative to a treaty of commerce any more than they order him to make a separate peace with G.B. This opinion is founded on that which the Kings ministry entertain of the wisdom, prudence and fidelity of Congress. –

I think also that . . .

. . . .

. . . to resist them if
hostile.

III. It is to be observed that the English ministry would consider that communication as ridiculous; so that it is deceiving one's self to suppose, that it will engage them to enter into any conference or to say any thing more than what is contained in the resolutions of Parliament, namely that they will listen to the Americans and receive <*****> them into favour when they return to their former allegiance. It *would be* <*****> *needless* [can answer to good purpose][1] to draw from them such an answer, ~~And~~ nor can the United States want such an answer to inform them of the present sentiments of the court of London & much less to prepare ~~by~~ with councils, and arms to resist them. It is astonishing to talk ~~of talk~~ of preparations of councils and arms when the war is raging in all its fury, when it has now lasted six year and England has not yet made the least overture to the Americans, that can authorise them to believe that she would agree to their independence.

The english nation

. . . .

. . . .

sigh for peace

IV. The English ministry would either return no answer; or if they did it would be an insolent one. In case of the latter; why should a man <***> needlessly expose himself to insult & thereby make himself the laughing stock of all the nations who have not yet acknowledged the independence of the United States. But there is reason to believe M^r· A. would receive no Answer. Because the british Ministry will not think themselves bound to return one to a man, who assumes a character which the Court of London must consider as an insult. It should not be forgotten that that court always considers the Americans as rebellious subjects. With such an Opinion, how could Lord Germaine receive a letter from M^r A taking upon himself the character of minister plenipotentiary from the United States of North America? How could that Minister bear the mention of a treaty of Commerce, which can only take place between independent nations? These observations will convince M^r A that France has no occasion for the expedient which he proposes to discover the sentiments & dispositions of the court of London and that we are already perfectly acquainted with what we ought and may expect from it in the present situation of Affairs.

idem . . .

V. The silence or the answer of the English Ministry, let which will happen; will neither alarm nor arouse the people of England. That people, without doubt, desire peace and an accommodation with America. But we find that only some individuals talk of independence and these more from a spirit of opposition than from conviction. There never has been a single motion made in Parliament tending to grant that independence. Yet the people have friends & protectors in parliament. From this M^r A may judge into what embarrassment the announcing his powers would throw the ministry. —

Another consideration . . . . of my powers

V.I. England as well as the rest of Europe are perfectly acquainted with the nature of the engagements which subsist between France & the United States. The King ~~has~~ caused a declaration to be made by this ministry on the 13 of March 1778 that he had not secured to himself any exclusive privilege by the treaty of commerce of the 6 Feb^y· of the same year, and his Majesty has confirmed that declaration in a ~~working piece~~ writing published by his order. So that the plenipotentiary powers of M^r· A can disclose nothing new either to England or to the other powers of Europe, and the false opinion of the court of London in this matter can be no obstacle to a peace. If any such obstacle existed the English Ministry w^d themselves find means to remove it if they were determined to <*> make peace <*> upon that.

There are at present . . . . . its accomplishm^t·

V.II. It is certain that the whole english Nation and even the ministers themselves wish for peace. But it has been observed that there has not been a single motion made in favour of the independence of America. Certainly the plenipotentiary powers of Mʳ A will ~~assuredly~~ not change the present dispositions of the people in that respect and consequently the communication of them that might be made will neither facilitate nor accelerate the conclusion of peace.

At this moment. . . . digest their plans accordingly?

VIII. This is a sensible reflection. It proves that Mʳ A is himself <**> convinced that <*> circumstances which may induce him to conceal his powers. The King's ministry think that such circumstances will continue till the English nation shall shew a disposition to acknowledge the independence of the United States. That acknowledgement will not be facilitated by <***> proposing a treaty of commerce. For the English <**> are at present well persuaded that they will have such a treaty with America when they shall judge it proper. They have besides, as Mʳ A has himself mentioned in his letter of the 19 of Febʸ last, a full knowledge of his commission, so that the communication of his full powers will teach them nothing new in this respect.

Notwithstanding the suppression of . . . . to great Britain

IX. In answer to this paragraph, it may be observed that there is not an englishman who is not persuaded that the United States are disposed to grant the advantages of commerce to their ancient Metropolis; but it would be a very difficult task to persuade an englishman or any thinking being that by granting independence in exchange for these advantages the court of London would make an honorable and advantageous peace. If this was the real sentiment of the people of England why have they, for these six years past, without murmuring, furnished ruinous supplies for subduing America. —

I am the more confirmed . . . . . if that was settled

X. The english ministry either have sincere intentions of making peace or they mean to amuse and penetrate the designs of Spain. In the first case, they will express the conditions on which ~~which~~ they desire to treat They will then be obliged to explain their views and their demands with regard to America. They will assuredly forget nothing which they think will forward peace; and upon agreeing to her independence, their first care will be to demand ~~their being part of~~ equal privileges with France in regard to commerce. On the contrary if the English ministry only means to amuse Spain, to penetrate her designs and to slacken her preparations for war, Mr A. should do the ministry of Madrid the justice to believe that they have sagacity enough to discover their views and have understanding and prudence sufficient to determine on the conduct they ought to pursue.

Idem.

XI. If M^r A is as sure as he is of their existence that the english ministers have no intentions of making peace on terms which France & America can agree to, to what purpose communicate to them at present powers which can ~~only~~ not be made use of until after the peace? How can M^r A persuade himself that the court of London will be seduced by the bait of a treaty of commerce, while ~~they~~ it still manifests an invincible repugnance to acknowledge the independence of America? Whenever it shall be disposed to acknowledge that independence it will <*> of itself propose the conditions on which it will think it proper to grant it, and M^r A may rest assured that it will not forget the article of Commerce. Then will be the proper time for him to produce his plenipotentiary powers. In the mean time it is necessary to pursue measures for ~~laying~~ establishing the foundation of that negotiation, namely the independence of America; And that can only be effected by carrying on the war with vigour & success. —

NA: PCC, item 84, v. 2, pp. 463-468 (translation); M247, reel 111.
[1] Written above line.

Chevalier de la Luzerne to Comte de Vergennes

[Translation]

Nᵒ· 64. Triplicate   Philadelphia, 25 July 1780
My Lord

· · · · ·

Mr. John Adams has written to Congress to inform it of his presentation; he seems to place much value on the distinctions you have procured for him, My Lord, and on the welcome he has received from you; he comments on the English public papers and the rumors of Paris in his letters; he states that he sees little likelihood of soon being in a position to negotiate for peace, and urges his Compatriots to efforts proportionate to ours. Mr. Franklin writes much more rarely. Nothing has been received from Mr. Jay except the instructions he gave his Secretary of legation when sending him from Cadiz to Madrid; they do honor to that ex-president, and show a spirit of conciliation. Mr. Laurens has arrived here, and always seems to me on the point of leaving immediately for Holland. He affects to be dissatisfied with the action of Congress in drawing Letters of Exchange on him for very considerable sums without having given him the funds necessary to discharge them. "My personal credit would have made up the deficiency," said he, "before the invasion of South Carolina, but I have nothing today that could satisfy such a debt, and Congress is putting me in the position of letting its drafts be protested or, if I accept them, of being put in prison upon their maturity." In spite of these sage reflections, he is neverthelesss disposed to leave, and he intends to pass to the North of Scotland in order to arrive directly at his destination without making his way across France. Congress continues to draw upon its Ministers in Europe without my knowing in what manner it intends for these drafts to be discharged, and I have abstained from asking any question in that regard.

· · · · ·

Recd. 12 September.   Le chr de la luzerne

FFAA: Pol. Corr., U.S., v. 13, f. 62 (LC transcription).

Comte de Vergennes to John Adams

Sir,   Versailles 29 July 1780

I have received the Letter which you did me the honor to write on the 27ᵗʰ of this Month. When I took upon myself to give you a mark of my confidence by informing you of the destination of Messʳˢ· de Ternay and

Rochambeau,[1] I did not expect the animadversions which you have thought it your duty to make on a passage of my letter of the 20$^{th.}$ of this Month. To avoid any further discussions of that sort I think it my duty to inform you that M$^{r.}$ Franklin being the sole person who has letters of credence to the king from the United States, it is with him only that I ought and can treat of matters which concern them and particularly of that which is the subject of your observation

Besides, Sir, I ought to observe to you, that the passage in my letter on which you have thought it your duty to consider more particularly relates only to sending the fleet commanded by the chevalier de Ternay and had nothing further in view than to convince you that the King did not stand in need of your solicitations to induce him to interest himself in the affair of the United States

I have the honor to be with the most perfect regard S^r your most humble & most obedient Servant   De Vergennes

NA: PCC, item 84, v. 2, p. 493 (translation); M247, reel 111.

[1] Rochambeau, Jean Baptiste Donatien de Vimeur, Comte de (1725-1807). French military officer. As lieutenant general, commanded French expeditionary force in the United States, 1780-1783. Commandant of Picardy, Calais, and Boulonnais, 1784-1789; Artois added, 1788. Commander in chief, Alsace, 1789. Commander, District of the North, 1790-1792. Made a marshal of France, 1791. Resigned, 1792, in disapproval of revolutionary developments. Imprisoned during the Terror.

Benjamin Franklin to Comte de Vergennes

Sir   Passy Aug$^{t.}$ 3^d 1780,

It was indeed with very great Pleasure that I received and read the Letter your Ex^y did me the honour of writing to me, communicating that of the President of Congress and the Resolutions of that Body relative to the Succours then expected: For the Sentiments therein express'd are so different from the Language held by Mr Adams, in his late letters to your Excellency as to make it clear that it was from his particular Indiscretion alone, and not from any Instructions received by him, that he has given such just Cause of Displeasure; and that it is impossible his Conduct therein Should be approved by his Constituents. I am glad he has not admitted me to any Participation in those Writings, and he has taken the Resolution he Expresses of not Communicating with me or making use of my Intervention in his future Correspondence; a Resolution that I believe he will keep, as he has never yet communicated to me more of his Business in Europe than

I have seen in the News Papers. I live upon terms of Civility with him, not of Intimacy. I shall as you desire lay before Congress the whole Correspondence which you have sent me for that purpose.

With the greastest & most Sincere Respect, I am, Sir, Your Excellency's most obedient and most humble Servant   B Franklin

FFAA: Pol. Corr., U.S., v. 13, f. 230-230 vo. (LC transcription).

Chevalier de la Luzerne to Comte de Vergennes

[Translation]

N⁰ 66. Duplicate.   Philadelphia, 6 August 1780

My Lord

Mr. Izard, previously designated Minister of the 13 States near the Court of Tuscany, has returned here. This Man, known for his honest intentions but also for his always passionate and often violent character, has tried to inspire in Congress the Sentiments with which he is animated and to endow it with his opinion concerning the various American Ministers Plenipotentiary in Europe, but he has found that assembly in the least appropriate dispositions to receive such impressions, and while it has not acquired anything in terms of increased consideration and vigor, it is nevertheless animated by a spirit of decency and of union which has marked it from the outset, and I believe I can assure you that no one will pay any attention to his reports. I have also learned that he censured Doctor Franklin severely for taking you too much into his confidence concerning the dispositions of the thirteen States, that he is of the opinion that that Minister would serve his Country better by inspiring in the Court of France a salutary fear regarding the possibility of a coalition of the English colonies with England; that then our aid would be more efficacious, we would dispatch larger squadrons, and we would be more inclined to grant pecuniary assistance. I thought I should forewarn Congress against such insidious Counsels, and I easily persuaded all those to whom I had the honor to speak of it that the best policy was to exercise Candor and to tell the truth, and that in exaggerating to the King the obstacles and the dangers which independence entails, Congress would expose itself to an effect entirely opposite to its intentions; that I thought that it had nothing to wish from His Majesty; that the help that he gave America was not limited to the troops and the Squadrons he sent there, but that wherever he attacked the enemy, he would create a diversion useful to the confederation, and that Congress knew enough that it was impossible for us to deploy greater efforts. Such is in fact, My Lord, the opinion of this Assembly and that of the people in general, and I can assure you that the complaints and the insinuations of some malcontents will not change it. Mr. John Adams is following a different route, and while he does not approve of all that we are doing, I know, however, that all his letters tend to inspire confidence in his compatriots for France, and to sustain and excite their attachment to independence. I here enclose an Extract from one of his letters published in the Philadelphia gazettes. This minister is asking for instructions on how to draw up, in the event of a peace negotiation with England, articles corresponding to [numbers] nine and fifteen of our Treaty of Commerce, the one relative to fisheries, the other concerning the abolition of the right of Escheat; he observes that, the thirteen Republics and England having broken all the ties that united them, the rigor of the Laws against foreigners must apply between the two nations, and that if they judge it appropriate to temper them, there must be a special stipulation in the Treaty. He also foresees the possibility that England would insist on the indemnification of all the American refugees whose goods have been sequestered, confiscated, or sold, and he asks for instructions on this matter. As the moment to treat concerning these different subjects does not seem very imminent, I have reason to think that Congress will not hasten to send supplementary instructions to Mr. Adams, and if you were to judge it appropriate to send me orders with respect to that latter article or to any other, I would probably have time to execute them.

I do not know, My Lord, whether it is because of reports that have come from Europe that the Delegates from the East have developed concerns regarding a longterm truce. They have impressed upon me how alarming an arrangement of this nature would be to the Thirteen States. I have reassured them by expressing my thoughts in the manner that you stipulated to me earlier; but as I have given them no peremptory assurance in that regard, they have told me that if ever unforeseen and unfortunate events necessitate a Truce instead of a definitive peace, the States of New England would only think it advantageous to the extent that all commerce would be prohibited between Great Britain and its former colonies; otherwise, they added, we would be exposed to all the baneful effects of English corruption, and in the shadow of this truce and of their operations, that nation might regain an influence against which we would not be sufficiently on guard. These delegates think that these sentiments are those of a very great majority of the States.

Congress had earlier resolved to quit Philadelphia at the Beginning of this year. This resolution, taken a little lightly, could not be put into execution, and when the moment of signing arrived, they have limited themselves to resolving to make a plan and to devise a comprehensive arrangement to accommodate Congress and the offices that accompany it, and to put this establishment in some districts far from the major cities of the 13 States.

I am with respect, My Lord, Your very humble and very Obedient Servant   le chr de la luzerne

FFAA: Pol. Corr., U.S., v. 13, f. 95 (LC transcription).

Comte de Vergennes to Chevalier de la Luzerne

[Translation]

Nᵒ· 8   Versailles, 7 August 1780

. . . . .

It seems, Sir, that the operation of Congress concerning paper money is honored in the provinces of the North, but that it meets with contradiction in those of the South and especially in that of Pennsylvania.

. . . . .

I thought you should not be left unaware, Sir, of a discussion I have had on this matter with Mr. Adams. I had been informed that this plenipotentiary did not limit himself to voicing the greatest praise of the operation of Congress, but that he had also expressed himself in a very strong manner as being opposed to the Sentiments of Congress relative to the French and to the alliance. I thought I should assure myself of Mr. Adams' way of thinking, and he himself furnished me the occasion in communicating to me some American letters that spoke of the devaluation of paper money. I therefore wrote him the letter of which you will find a copy enclosed. It brought me a response as ample as it is erroneously reasoned. It gave rise to some observations on my part, and this correspondence was terminated on my part by my letter of 30 June last. I left that of Mr. Adams of the 22nd without response. I have communicated the whole to Mr. Franklin, requesting him to report on it to Congress, and I have reason to think that that Minister will make it his duty to comply with my request. I inform you of these details, Sir, so that you may speak of it confidentially to the President and the principal members of Congress and put them in a position to judge whether Mr. Adams is endowed with a character that renders him appropriate to the important task with which Congress has charged him. As for myself, I anticipate that this plenipotentiary will only incite difficulties and vexations, because he has an inflexibility, a pedantry, an arrogance, and a conceit that renders him incapable of dealing with political subjects, and especially of handling them with the representatives of great powers, who assuredly will not yield either to the tone or to the logic of Mr. Adams. These reflections seem to me to merit the more attention because this plenipotentiary, whether or not he is truly attached to independence, of which I am unaware, seems to me only very feebly attached to the alliance, in connection with which he has spared no effort to take steps that would indicate the ingratitude of the United States, while the contrary Sentiment is the basis of his instructions. Can such an agent be suitable for us? Can he be suitable for the United States?

There is a second subject on which Mr. Adams has been in correspondence with me, i.e., the use to make of his full-powers. I told him from principle my sentiment in that regard with the greatest frankness, for I owed it to him as the plenipotentiary of an allied nation, but my action served only to provide me with new proof of Mr. Adams' teasing disposition and of his extremely feeble attachment to the principles of the alliance, and I have broken with him completely, as you will see by my letter of 25 July. I hope that Mr. Franklin will not fail to address himself to Congress, as I have requested him to do. On your side, you would do well to communicate them to the chief of that assembly, and to invite it on our part to give its representative orders to show a little more regard than he does for the opinion of the King's Counsel, and especially not to take steps relative to the possible commission with which he is charged (if they still wish to leave it in his hands) without having previously consulted the King's ministry, and without having concerted with it all his steps. This precaution seems necessary to us because Mr. Adams' imagination and principles could easily lead him into mistakes, and compromise the alliance and the honor of his nation.

· · · · · ·

Vergennes

FFAA: Pol. Corr., U.S., v. 13, f. 101 (LC transcription).

Benjamin Franklin to the President of Congress

Sir,   Passy, Aug.ᵗ 9. 1780.

· · · · · ·

M.ʳ Adams has given Offence to the Court here by some Sentiments and Expressions contained in several of his Letters written to the Count de Vergennes. I mention this with Reluctance, tho' perhaps it would have been my Duty to acquaint you with such a Circumstance, even were it not required of me by the Minister himself. He has sent me Copies of the

Correspondence, desiring I would communicate them to Congress; and I send them herewith[1]. Mr. Adams did not show me his Letters before he sent them. I have in a former Letter to Mr. Lovell, mentioned some of the Inconveniences that attend the having more than one Minister at the same Court, one of which Inconveniencies is, that they do not always hold the same Language, and that the Impressions made by one and intended for the Service of his Constituents, may be effaced by the Discourse of the other. It is true, that Mr. Adams's proper Business is elsewhere, but the Time not being come for that Business, and having nothing else here wherewith to employ himself, he seems to have endeavour'd supplying what he may suppose my Negociations defective in. He thinks as he tells me himself, that America has been too free in Expressions of Gratitude to France; for that she is more obliged to us than we to her; and that we should shew Spirit in our Applications. I apprehend that he mistakes his Ground, and that this Court is to be treated with Decency & Delicacy. The King, a young and virtuous Prince, has, I am persuaded, a Pleasure in reflecting on the generous Benevolence of the Action, in assisting an oppress'd People, and proposes it as a Part of the Glory of his Reign: I think it right to encrease this Pleasure by our thankful Acknowledgements; and that such an Expression of Gratitude is not only our Duty, but our Interest. A different Conduct seems to me what is not only improper and unbecoming, but what may be hurtful to us. Mr. Adams, on the other Hand, who at the same time means our Welfare and Interest as much as I, or any Man can do, seems to think a little apparent Stoutness and greater air of Independence & Boldness in our Demands, will procure us more ample Assistance. It is for Congress to judge and regulate their Affairs accordingly. M. De Vergennes, who appears much offended, told me yesterday, that he would enter into no further Discussions with Mr. Adams, nor answer any more of his Letters. He is gone to Holland to try, as he told me, whether something might not be done to render us a little less dependent on France. He says the Ideas of this Court & those of the People in America are so totally different, as that it is impossible for any Minister to please both. He ought to know America better than I do, having been there lately; and he may chuse to do what he thinks will best please the People of America: But when I consider the Expressions of Congress in many of their Publick Acts, and particularly in their Letter to the Chev^{r.} de la Luzerne of the 24th of May last, I cannot but imagine that he mistakes the Sentiments of a few for a general Opinion. It is my Intention while I stay here, to procure what Advantages I can for our Country, by endeavouring to please this Court; and I wish I could prevent any thing being said by any of our Countrymen here that may have a contrary Effect, and increase an Opinion lately shewing itself in Paris that we seek a Difference, and with a View of reconciling ourselves to England: – Some of them have of late been very indiscreet in their Conversations.

I received 8. Months after their Date the Instructions of Congress relating to a new Article for guaranteeing the Fisheries. The expected Negociations for a Peace appearing of late more remote, and being too much occupied with other Affairs, I have not hitherto proposed that Article. But I purpose doing it next Week. It appears so reasonable and equitable that I do not foresee any Difficulty. In my next I shall give you an Account of what passes on the Occasion.

. . . . .

Be pleased, Sir, to present my Duty to Congress, & believe me to be, with great Respect, Your Excellency's most obedient and most humble Servant

B. Franklin

read Feb. 19. 1781

. . . . .

NA: PCC, item 82, v. 1, pp. 263-278 (LS); M247, reel 108.
[1] Correspondence not included. See above and PCC, item 84, v. 2.

John Adams to Benjamin Franklin

Sir   Amsterdam August 17. 1780
I never was more amuzed with political Speculations, than Since my Arrival in this country. – Every one has his Prophecy, and every Prophecy is a Paradox. – one Says America will give France the Go By. another that France and Spain, will abandon America. a Third that Spain will forsake France and America. a Fourth that America, has the Interest of all Europe against her. a Fifth that She will become the greatest manufacturing Country, and thus ruin Europe. a Sixth that She will become a great and an ambitious military and naval Power, and consequently terrible to Europe.

In short it Seems as if they had Studied for every Impossibility, and agreed to forestall it, as a probable future Event.

I tell the first, that if the K. of France would release America from her Treaty and England would agree to our Independance, on condition we would make an Alliance offensive and defensive with her, America ought not to accept it and would not, because She will in future have no Security for Peace even with England, but in her Treaty with France. I ask the

Second, whether they think the Connection of America of So little Consequence to France and Spain, that they would lightly give it up? – I ask the third, whether the Family compact added to the Connection with America is a trifling Consideration to Spain? to the fifth that America will not make manufactures enough for her own Consumption, these 1000 years. – to the Sixth that We love Peace and hate War So much, that We can Scarcely keep up an Army necessary to defend ourselves against the greatest of Evils, and to secure our Independance which is the greatest of Blessings; and therefore while We have Land enough to conquer from the Trees, Rocks and wild Beasts We shall never go abroad to trouble other nations.

To the fourth, I Say that their Paradox is like ~~that~~ several others. viz. that Bachus and Ceres did mischief to mankind when they invented Wine and Bread, that Art, Sciences and Civilization have been general Calamities &c.

That upon their Supposition all Europe ought to agree, to bring away the Inhabitants of America, and divide them among the nations of Europe to be maintained as Paupers, leaving America to grow up again, with Trees and Bushes, and to become again the Habitations of Bears and Indians, forbidding all navigation to that quarter of the globe in future. – That Mankind in general, however, are probably of a different opinion, ~~and~~ believing that Columbus as well as Bachus and Ceres did a service to man kind, and that Europe and America will be rich Blessings to each other, the one Supplying a surplus of manufactures, and the other a Surplus of raw materials, the Productions of Agriculture.

It is very plain, however, that Speculation and disputation, can do Us little service. No Facts are believed, but decisive military Conquests: no Arguments are Seriously alluded to in Europe but Force. – it is to be hoped our Country instead of amusing themselves any longer with delusive dreams of Peace, will bend the whole Force of their Minds to < * > augment their Navy, to find out their own Strength and Resources and to depend upon themselves. — I have the Honour to be, with great Respect, your most obedient servant   John Adams

APS: Benjamin Franklin Papers (ALS).

Chevalier de la Luzerne to Comte de Vergennes

[Translation]

N° 74. Duplicate.   Philadelphia, 26 August 1780
My Lord
...The matter was again taken into deliberation,[1] and after debates that

lasted an entire session, it was resolved "that the General-in-Chief will be authorized to act together with the french General against the common Enemy in the manner which he shall judge to be most advantageous to the United States, and to procure their deliverance the most promptly."

A Member from the States of the East, a most ardent promoter of the resolution, labored to make me see how the attendant consequences would be advantageous. "We do not know," he added, "whether the General will in fact take advantage of it to shift the theater of war to enemy territory, but if he judges that the English can be attacked there with advantage, he need not hesitate to do so. The result can only be useful to the Thirteen States. The worst would be to exchange Nova Scotia or any other place conquered by our arms for Georgia or South Carolina at the time of the peace negotiations." I am very far, My Lord, from sharing the opinion of Mr. Samuel Adams in the latter instance. On the contrary, I think that if events in fact provide an occasion for the proposal of that exchange at the time of the future peace, the English would prefer the possession of the provinces of the South, which form an important object reunited with the Floridas, and which could provide assistance to the English Islands and receive it more promptly than the Colonies of the North, while Halifax and Canada can only have distant ties and difficult, slow relations with the Antilles. The province of Canada has in fact become interesting for the commerce of England through its imports and exports. Nova Scotia also merits the attention of that power because of the facilities it obtains for the fisheries and because of the naval resources found there. I nonetheless presume that England would give preference to the Colonies of the South, if the choice were left to her at the end of the war, and that knowing the disquiets, the ambition, and the forces of the States of the South, she would desire an exchange useful in itself, and which at the same time would deliver her from so dangerous a neighbor. I early understood the necessity of anticipating an order of things that runs no less counter to the principles of the confederation and of the alliance than to the interests of Spain. Consequently, I delayed as long as I could, without appearing to do so openly, the alteration that has just been made in the General's powers, but when I saw that he himself was soliciting it, and that this measure was keenly supported by the portion of the Confederation that at that moment was displaying the greatest energy, I did not think I should make a more lengthy opposition. If, counter to all appearance, counter to all the positive assurances given by General Washington to the Delegates of the South, and counter to the opinion which he has many times expressed to me, he should actually propose an expedition against Halifax and Quebec, I think that M. the Count de Rochambeau could furnish me the means to prevent it by saying that his orders and his commission limit him to assisting the 13

States and to seconding the efforts which they make for their own deliverance. I have still not had occasion to make plans with him, but I hope we will have no difficulty in preventing any external operation. If, however, it were only a question of a brief expedition against Halifax to carry off or destroy the magazines or the naval stores, it seems to me that it could brook no difficulty, and that it would be as profitable for us as for the Americans.

. . . . . .

Received 20 October.   le che de la luzerne

FFAA: Pol. Corr., U.S., v. 13, f. 152 (LC transcription).

¹ *Washington wanted his instructions changed in such a manner as to imply that he might attack the British at the greatest possible number of points, but the Southern States, concerned primarily with expelling the British forces from their territory, had brought about rejection of the proposed resolution.*

Notes of Conferences between
John Jay and Comte de Montmorin

St. Ildefonso 27ᵗʰ· August 1780.

Mʳ· Jay waited on the Count de Montmorin this Morning at Nine OClock agreeable to appointment the Day before. The Former commenced the Conversation by observing that in his first Conferences with the Minister of Spain at Aranjuez, The Minister divided the Subject into two parts, and spoke largely on that of the Bills drawn on Mʳ· Jay, and on the Treaty proposed to be entered into between Spain and America: Mʳ· Jay recapitulating the Ministers assurances, relative to the former, and informing the Ambassador that the result of this Conference was a promise of the Minister to send him written notes on both points, a few Days afterwards. That with respect to the Notes relative to the Treaty, Mʳ· Jay had not received them as yet. That on the other Point he had received Notes, which as well as his Answer he had Shown to the Ambassador. That on the 5ᵗʰ· of July he had another Conference with the Minister at Madrid in which he had endeavored to turn the Conversation to the several objects of his business and mission here, but that the Minister postponed the discussion of them until a Person for whom he had sent with a view to succeed Mʳ· Mirailles should arrive, when all the necessary arrangements should be made.... The Ambassador said that he would willingly speak to the Minister, but that he feared, he should not be able to enter fully into the Subject with him until Wednesday, both the Minister and himself having their Time employed on Objects, which at present and for some Time past had engrossed much of their Attention. He then asked Mʳ· Jay, if he had written to Congress, to stop drawing Bills on him. Mr Jay replied, that he could not with propriety give such information to Congress, after the general and repeated assurances made him by the Count de Florida Blanca ever since his arrival here, and particularly the Ministers declaration that he would be able to furnish him with thirty or forty thousand pounds Sterling at the end of the present or commencement of the next Year, and that in the mean time other arrangements might be taken to pay such Bills as might become due after that Period; He added that if the Count had candidly told him that he could not furnish him with Money to pay the Bills, he should then immediately have informed Congress of it, who would have taken of course the proper measures on the Occasion, but that should he now send a true Account of all that had passed between the Count De Florida Blanca and himself thereon, He could not answer for the disagreeable Effects such Intelligence would produce. The Count seemed to think the Spanish Minister would pay the Bills that had been already presented....

. . . . . .

On Wednesday Afternoon the 30$^{th.}$ of August, I waited on the Ambassador to know the result of the Conversation, he had promised to have with the Minister on our Affairs. He did not appear very glad to see me. I asked him whether he had seen the Minister and conversed with him on our Affairs. He said he had seen the Minister, but that as Count D'Estaing[1] was present, he had only some general, and cursory conversation with him and slipping away from that Topic, went on to observe that I would do well to write another Letter to the Minister, mentioning the number of Letters I had already written, my Arrival here, and my desire of a Conference with him. I told the Ambassador that while four Letters on the Subject remained unanswered, it could not be necessary to write a fifth. That these Letters had been written with great Politeness, and circumspection. That the last was written the Day of my arrival at S$^t.$ Ildefonso, That I had also gone to the Ministers House to pay my Respects to him, and on being told that he was Sick, had left a Card, And that notwithstanding these marks of Attention and Respect, I still continued unanswered, and unnoticed. I observed to him further, that this Conduct accorded ill with the Minister's assurances; That unless I had met with more tenderness from the Holders of the Bills, they would have been returned noted for non acceptance. That if such an Event should at last take place after the Repeated promises, and declarations of the Minister, there would of necessity be an End to the Confidence of America in the Court of Spain. He replied that he hoped things would take a more favorable turn, that to his knowledge the Minister had been of late much occupied and perplexed with business, that I ought not to be affected with the Inattention of his conduct; That I should continue to conduct the Business smoothly, having always in view, the Importance of Spain, and remembering that we were as yet only rising States, not firmly established or generally acknowledged &c. and that he would by all means advise me to write the Minister another Letter *praying* an Audience. I answered that the Object of my coming to Spain was to make *Propositions* not *Supplications*, and that I should forbear troubling the Minister with further Letters, 'till he should be more disposed to attend to them – That I considered America as being, and to continue Independent in *fact*, and that her becoming so in *Name*, was of no further Importance than as it concerned the common Cause, in the Success of which all the Parties were interested, and that I did not imagine Congress would agree to purchase from Spain, the acknowledgement of an undeniable fact, at the Price she demanded for it. That I intended to abide Patiently the fate of the Bills, and should transmit to Congress an Account of all matters relative to them. That I should then write the Minister another Letter on the Subject of the Treaty, and if that should be treated with like neglect, or if I should be informed that his Catholic Majesty declined going into that measure, I should then consider my Business at an End, and proceed to take the necessary Measures for returning to America. That I knew my Constituents were sincerely desirous of a Treaty with Spain, and that their Respect for the House of Bourbon, the desire of France signified in the Secret Article, and the favorable Opinion they had imbibed of the Spanish nation, were the strongest Inducements they had to wish it. That the Policy of multiplying Treaties with European nations was with me very questionable, and might be so with others. That for my own part, I was inclined to think it the Interest of America to rest content with the Treaty with France, and by avoiding Alliances with other Nations, remain free from the Influence of their disputes and Politics – That the Situation of the United States, in my Opinion dictated this Policy; That I knew it to be their Interest, and of course their disposition to be at Peace with all the World, and that I knew too, it would be in their power, and I hoped in their Inclination, always to defend themselves. The Ambassador was at astand; after a little Pause, he said, he hoped my Mission would have a more agreeable Issue. He asked me if I was content with the conduct of France – I answered most certainly; for that she was spending her blood, as well as treasure for us; This Answer was too general for him – He renewed the question by asking whether I was content with the Conduct of France relative to our proposed Treaty with Spain – I answered, that as far as it had come to my knowledge, I was. This required an explanation, and I gave it to him by observing that by the Secret Article Spain was at liberty to accede to our Treaty with France whenever she pleased, and with such Alterations as both Parties might agree to – That Congress had appointed me to propose this Accession now, and had authorized me to enter into the necessary discussions and Arguments – That to give their Application the better Prospect of Success, they had directed me to request the favorable Interposition of the King of France with the King of Spain – That I had done it by Letter to Count DeVergennes, who in Answer had assured me of the King's disposition to comply with the Request of Congress; and informed me that Instructions analogous to this disposition should be given to the Ambassador at Madrid – That it gave me pleasure to acknowledge that his Conduct towards me had always been polite and friendly, but that I still remained ignorant whether any, and what progress had been made in the Mediation – He seemed not to have expected this; but observed that all he could do, was to be ready to do me any friendly Office in his Power, for that he did not see how his *Mediation* could be proper except in cases where Points of the Treaty were discussed, and could not be agreed upon. To this I replied that these were only *secondary* Objects of the expected Mediation, and that the *primary* one was to prevail upon the King of Spain to commence the Negotiation, and enter upon these discussions; but that I remained uninformed of what he might have done on that Subject – The Ambassador made no direct reply to these Remarks but again proceeded to repeat his advice that I should try one more Letter to the Minister; – I told him, I had after much consideration made up my mind on that Subject, and that it appeared to me inexpedient to follow his advice in this Instance; and that when he should see the Letters I had already written, he would probably be of the same Opinion. I promised to shew him the Letters the next day, and took my leave. How far the tone of this conversation may be judged to have been prudent, I know not – It was not assumed however but after previous, and mature deliberation....

. . . . . .

NA: PCC, item 110, v. 1, pp. 257-268 (LBkC); M247, reel 135.

¹ D'Estaing, Jean Baptiste Charles Henri Hector (1729-1794). French naval officer. Vice admiral commanding the French fleet of 17 ships of the line that blockaded New York and attempted to capture Newport, 1778. Captured St. Vincent and Grenada, wounded in failed Franco-American effort to capture Savannah, 1779.

Chevalier de la Luzerne to Comte de Vergennes

[Translation]

Nᵒ 75. Duplicate.   Philadelphia, 30 August 1780
My Lord

. . . . . .

I have observed, My Lord, the effects that the motions of Messieurs Hartley, Pownall,[1] and Conway in the Parliament of Great Britain tending to bring about a reconciliation between America and England can have on public opinion. They have been the subject of conversations for some time. They have been examined as to the different meanings they present, but this examination was made with as much indifference as if it were a question of two other Powers at war. It seems that the general opinion is that, if in consequence of these motions or of some other, England again sends peace commissioners to this Continent, it would be necessary to allow them to produce their powers, and if they contain a positive recognition of independence, to take advantage of the concession of this first point to annihilate the portions that England had been able to save in the midst of the United States, but moreover to send the negotiators to the Court of Versailles, where there is an American Minister ready to treat with them in concert with France. If independence had not been recognized prior to the arrival of these Commissioners or Ministers, they would not even be allowed to set foot on the territory of the Thirteen States. Congress has carefully avoided appearing to have paid the least attention to these motions, but the individual sentiments of the members to whom I have spoken conform to those I have just expounded to you.

. . . . .

Received 20 October.   le che de la luzerne

FFAA: Pol. Corr., U.S., v. 13, f. 154 (LC transcription).

[1] *Pownall, Thomas (1722-1805). British colonial official and political figure. Lieutenant governor of New York, 1753-1757. Governor of Massachusetts, 1757-1759. An enthusiastic proponent of the war against the French. Comptroller of the commissariat for the army in Germany, 1762-1763. Opposed efforts to tax the American colonies. Member of Parliament, 1767-1780. Supported North's ministry on home affairs, but consistently favored peace efforts in America.*

Notes of John Jay's Conference with James Gardoqui and Don Bernardo del Campo

September 3-15, 1780

M. Gardoqui[1] began the conversation by assurances of his personal attachment to our cause and country, which gave occasion to mutual and complimentary professions too unimportant to repeat. I told him that the holders of the bills, after having shown me great forbearance and delicacy, were at length perfectly tired; that the house of Casa Mayor had sent their bills after me, but that as I was not to expect the honour of a conference with the Minister until Tuesday evening, at soonest, I had requested time till Wednesday to give my answer. I therefore begged the favour of him to mention this to the Minister, and obtain his directions what I should do. He asked to what amount Congress had resolved to draw. I told him. He observed, that the Court ought previously to have been applied to. In answer to which I recapitulated the reasons before given to the Minister. He dwelt largely on the necessities of the State, and I expatiated on the extensive ideas entertained of Spanish opulence in America. He assured me they were mistaken, and spoke of the difficulties occasioned by the detention of their treasures abroad. He then remarked, that we offered no *consideration* for the money we solicited. I replied, that we offered the same consideration that other nations did who borrowed money, viz., the repayment of the principal with interest. He asked me if we had nothing further to offer, and mentioned ship timber. I said we had ship-timber, but that as it belonged to individuals, the public could not get it otherwise than by purchase, and that it could answer no purpose to borrow money with one hand and instantly repay it with the other, for that a repayment in money, or in ship timber, was the same thing in fact, and differed only in name. Besides, that if Spain wanted timber from America, it would be better, in case he went there, that he should be charged with that business, than that it should be under the direction of Congress, for that public works were always more expensive than private. He agreed in this. He again asked me whether I could think of nothing else to offer. I told him no. Whether there was nothing on the side of the Mississippi that I could offer. I told him nothing that I could think of except land, and that I did not think it would be worth the King's while to buy a hundred thousand pounds worth of land there, considering the immense territories he already possessed. He inquired whether I thought Congress would draw for the whole sum. I answered that it was in my opinion not improbable, for that they would consider the acceptance of ten or twelve thousand dollars as a prelude to further aids, naturally supposing, that if the King afforded us any supplies at all, they would be such as would correspond with his dignity, and not be limited to that little pittance. He desired me to meet him the next day at M. Del Campo's, which I promised to do.

In the evening M. Gardoqui again paid me a visit, and pointedly proposed my offering the navigation of the Mississippi as a consideration for aids. I told him that object could not come in question in a treaty for a loan of one hundred thousand pounds, and Spain should consider, that to render alliances permanent, they should be so formed as to render it the interest of both parties to observe them; that the Americans, almost to a man, believed that God Almighty had made that river a highway for the people of the upper country to go to the sea by; that this country was extensive and fertile; that the General, many officers, and others of distinction and influence in America, were deeply interested in it; that it would rapidly settle, and that the inhabitants would not readily be convinced of the justice of being obliged, either to live without foreign commodities, and lose the surplus of their productions, or be obliged to transport both over rugged mountains and through an immense wilderness, to and from the sea, when they daily saw a fine river flowing before their doors, and offering to save them all that trouble and expense, and that without injury to Spain. He observed, that the present generation would not want this navigation, and that we should leave future ones to manage their own affairs, etc.

The next day, that is, the 4th of September, I met M. Gardoqui at M. Del Campo's. After some unconnected conversation, I observed to M. Del Campo, that as all the papers between the Minister and myself had passed through his hands, it was unnecessary to give him any information, except what related to the present state of the bills drawn upon me, which I proceeded to state in a short, but particular manner. He replied by making several strictures on the impropriety of drawing bills without previous notice and consent. He remarked, that they might with more propriety have been drawn on France, with whom we were allied, and who were richer than they; that the King must first take care of his own people, before he could supply us; that Spain had been brought into the war by our quarrel, but received no advantage from us; that they had been told of our readiness to assist in taking Pensacola, etc., but instead of aids, he had heard of nothing but demands from us; that our situation was represented as being deplorable, and that the enemy talked of the submission of some of the States, and of negotiations being on foot for that purpose.

Whether this style proceeded from natural arrogance, or was intended to affect my temper, I cannot say; in either case, I thought it most prudent to take no notice of it, but proceed calmly and cautiously, and the more so as this was the first time I had ever conversed with this man. I told him in substance, though more at large, that the assurances given Congress of the friendly disposition of Spain by M. Mirales and others had been confided in, and had induced Congress to expect the aids in question. That if this application could be called a demand, it was still the first they had made to my knowledge; that men in arms against the enemies of Spain were serving her as well as themselves, and therefore might without impropriety request her aid; that our separation from Britain was an object important to Spain, and that the success with which we had opposed her whole force for six years showed what the power of both, if under one direction, might be capable of; that I knew nothing of Spain's having been drawn into the war by or for us, and that this was not to be found among the reasons she had alleged for it; that an attack on Pensacola could not be expected to be made by troops actually employed in repelling the enemy's assaults from their own doors, and that the principles of self-defence would not permit or justify it; that Spain had much to expect in future from our commerce, and that we should be able as well as willing to pay our debts; that the tales told of our despondency and submission resulted from the policy of the enemy, not from fact, and I believed no more of their private negotiations between America and Britain than I did of there being private negotiations between Spain and Britain for a separate peace, which the Minister assured me was not the case; that if on the arrival of the bills I had been told plainly that no money could be advanced, further drafts would soon have been prevented; but that a contrary conduct having been adopted, other expectations had been excited; that as to France, she had done, and was still doing much for us, and that her being our ally did not confer propriety upon every request that we could make to her. He still pressed this point, and complained that the greater part of the money heretofore advanced by Spain had been laid out in France. He saw that France was deriving great commercial advantages from us, but that our commerce never would be an object with Spain, because all her productions would find a better market in her own colonies. He desired a note of the bills which had arrived, and then made some reflections on the proposal of a treaty. We agreed perfectly well that mutual interest should be the basis of it, and I added, that the good opinion entertained of the King and nation by America was also a pleasing circumstance. He said, however that might be, America did not seem inclined to gratify Spain in the only point in which she was deeply interested. Here followed much common-place reasoning about the navigation of the Mississippi, of which your Excellency has heretofore heard too much to require a repetition. He spoke also much of the difficulties of Spain as to money matters, saying that their treasures in America could at present be of no use to them, as they had given orders that none should be sent home during the war, even if it continued these ten years; and this was done in order, by stopping the usual current of specie into Europe, to embarrass the measures which Great Britain must take to obtain her necessary supplies....

On the 13th of September, M. Gardoqui delivered me the following verbal message from Count de Florida Blanca: "That the exigencies of the State would not permit his Majesty to provide for the payment of more of the bills drawn upon me than had been already accepted." I expressed my regret that this had not been told me at first, and told him it appeared a little extraordinary that the Minister should employ himself and me three months in making and answering propositions relative to a loan, which it was not in his power to make....

As the Count's message was a verbal one, and might hereafter be denied or explained away as convenience might dictate, I thought it important to establish it, and for that and other reasons which need no explanation, I wrote the Count the following letter.

Sir: St. Ildefonso, September 14, 1780.
The information I received yesterday from your Excellency by M. Gardoqui, has drawn the affair of the bills of exchange to a conclusion. He told me, that the exigencies of the State would not permit his Majesty to provide for the payment of more of those bills than were already accepted, amounting to about fourteen thousand dollars.

As it is important that every nation at war should know exactly the state of their resources, and as America has been induced to consider the friendship of his Catholic Majesty as among the number of hers, I must request the favour of your Excellency, to tell me frankly whether the United States may expect any, and what aids from Spain. The general assurances of amity, which that country has received from this, together with what has passed between your Excellency and myself relative to clothing for our troops, and supplies of specie in America, will I hope be considered as authorizing this question; and the more so, as M. Gardoqui, to whose arrival your Excellency postponed the discussion of these matters, informs me he is not instructed to say any thing to me on these, or indeed any other subjects.

I have the honour to be, etc.,   John Jay.

The next day, the 15th of September, M. Gardoqui delivered to me a paper by way of answer to my letter of yesterday to the Minister. It is in these words :   St. Ildefonso, September 15, 1780.
The following answer has been dictated to me in his Excellency's name by Don Bernardo del Campo, to be delivered to the honorable John Jay.

That it is not his Majesty's intention to stop assisting the States, whenever means can be found to do it, but that it will be impossible to supply them with money in Europe, there being none to spare, for that which ought to have come this year from America, has neither come, nor is it known when it will, and that which would have facilitated a far advanced negotiation is likely to produce no effect, in a great measure, *through the undermining of some persons of rank in France.*

The States not giving timely advice, nor having taking his Majesty's previous consent, he could not arrange his affairs beforehand, in order to assure the acceptance and payment of the bills they have drawn, for which reasons, and that Congress has not to this day given any tokens of a recompense, his Majesty might have just cause of disgust, but notwithstanding he does not, nor will change his ideas, and will always retain those of humanity, friendship, and compassion, that he has had towards the colonies. That consequently, if Mr. Jay or his constituents should find money upon credit, to the sum of one hundred or one hundred and fifty thousand dollars, that his Majesty will be answerable for the said sum, payable in the space of three years; that his Majesty will besides exert all that is possible to assist them with clothing and other things, and, finally, in order that his Majesty may extend his further dispositions, it is precisely necessary that they should give sure and effective tokens of a good correspondence, proposing reciprocal measures of a compensation that may establish a solid friendship and confidence, without reducing it to words and protests of mere compliment.

This being the substance, I would further suggest to Mr. Jay's consideration, that the continuance of assisting the States by answering the sum expressed in a manner much more public than that of paying the money privately, shows plainly the sincerity of his Majesty, although the States have not to this day proposed any equivalent to the assistance already given, and to the expenses occasioned by a war, which had its true origin from them, to all which must be added, (though by the way no credit is given to it,) that there are hints of some understanding between the colonies and England.   James Gardoqui.

It is to be observed, that this paper when first delivered was not signed, and suspecting that this omission might not be accidental, I mentioned it to M. Gardoqui a day or two afterwards. After some hesitation, and doubts of its being necessary, he signed it. I made no remarks at all to M. Gardoqui on any part of this paper except the last article, which I treated with great indignation....

Johnston, *Jay Correspondence*, v. 1, pp. 392-401.
    [1] *Gardoqui, James. Spanish merchant. Brother of Diego Maria de Gardoqui and scion of the Bilbao-based commercial firm of Joseph Gardoqui and Sons. Most Spanish aid to the United States flowed through this house or James Gardoqui's own establishment in Madrid.*

John Jay to the President of Congress

Sir,   S$^{t.}$ Ildefonso 16$^{th.}$ September 1780
    This Letter and several Copies of it are to be sent by the next Post to Bilboa, Cadis, Nantes &c. The object of it is to inform you that it is

necessary immediately to cease drawing Bills upon me for the present.

Your Excellency may soon expect a full Detail of Particulars, You will then receive an Answer to every Question that may be raised upon this Letter.

His Catholic Majesty has been pleased to offer his Responsibility to facilitate a Loan of 150,000 Dollars for us payable in three Years, and to promise us some Clothing. This need not be kept secret.

I have written several Letters to your Excellency, but have received only one from the Committee since I left America. It covered the Resolutions respecting these Bills.

The Philadelphia Bank, the Ladies Subscriptions, and other Indications of union and public Spirit have a fine effect here.

I have the Honor to be, &c.   John Jay

NA: PCC, item 110, v. 1, pp. 189-190 (LBkC); M247, reel 135.

Notes of a Conference between
John Jay and Conde de Floridablanca

S$^{t.}$ Ildefonso, September 23$^{d.}$ 1780.

After the usual civilities, the Count began the Conference by informing M$^{r.}$ Jay that the Court had received Intelligence from the Havannah of Congress having so far complied with the request made them to permit the Exportation of Provisions for use of his Majesty's fleets and Armies there, as to give Licence for shipping three thousand Barrels of Flour, circumstances not admitting of further Supply at that Time. That this business was conducted by M$^{r.}$ Robert Morris[1] in a manner with which he was well pleased; – That Congress had also, in order to promote the Success of the Spanish operations against Pensacola &c. agreed to make a diversion to the Southward, to detach a considerable Body of regular Troops and Militia to South Carolina under General Gates.[2] That His Majesty was well pleased with, and highly sensible of these marks of their friendly disposition, and had directed him to desire M$^{r.}$ Jay to convey his Thanks to them on the occasion.

M$^{r.}$ Jay expressed his Satisfaction at this Intelligence and promised to take the Earliest opportunity of Conveying to Congress the sense His Majesty entertained of their Friendship manifested by these Measures....

． ． ． ． ．

M$^{r.}$ Jay informed his Excellency that the Subjects on which he was desirous of conferring with him arose from the Paper he had received from

Mr Gardoqui the 15th Instant, containing his Excellency's Answer to Mr Jay's Letter of the 14th.

. . . . .

Mr Jay then proceeded to regret that the pleasure he derived from these instances of his Majesty's friendship to the United States, was mingled with pain from being informed by the Above mentioned Paper, that the King conceived he might have just Cause to be disgusted with them.

Because 1st – They had drawn the Bills of Exchange without his previous Consent, and 2d^{dly} – Because they had not given any tokens of a recompense. Mr Jay reminded his Excellency that these Bills were drawn upon himself, and not on Spain, and that although Congress might have hoped for reasons already assigned, to have been enabled to pay them by a Loan from His Majesty, yet that every other usual Measure was left open for that purpose. That an Application to Spain for such a Loan could give no just Cause of Offence, for that if it had not been convenient to her to make it, all that she had to do, was to have told him so, and he was then at liberty to take such measures for procuring it Elsewhere as he might think proper. The Count replied that what Mr Jay observed was true, but that certainly the Bills were drawn with an Expectation of their being paid by Spain, and that this might probably have been done, if previous notice of the measure had been given. That he always intended to have done something towards their payment, but had been prevented by disappointments, and the Exigencies of the State. Mr Jay continued to observe that the second Cause assigned for this disgust Vizt That Congress had given no tokens of a recompense, must have arisen from a mistake. He reminded his Excellency that he had never requested a *donation* from Spain, but that on the Contrary, he had repeatedly offered to pledge the faith of the United States for the Repayment with Interest within a reasonable term after the War, of whatever Sum his Majesty might be so kind as to lend them. To these Remarks the Count said only that Interest for the Money would have been no object with them; That they would gladly have lent it to us without Interest, and repeated his regret at the Disappointment which had prevented them. He appeared rather uneasy and desirous of waving the Subject.

. . . . .

Mr Jay resumed his animadversions on the Paper in question, by observing that it assured him it was necessary "That Congress should give sure and effective tokens of a good Correspondence, proposing reciprocal measures of a compensation &c. In order that his Majesty might extend his further Dispositions towards them" That for his part, he could conceive of no higher tokens which one Nation could give to another of friendship and good will, than their Commissioning and sending a Person for the express purpose of requesting his Majesty to enter into Treaties of Amity and Alliance with them, and that on Terms of Reciprocity of Interest and mutual advantage....

The Count here interrupted M.ʳ Jay by saying that the Interest of France and Spain with respect to America, were so distinct as necessarily to render different Treaties necessary; M.ʳ Jay answered that admitting this to be the case, the Treaty with France might be made the Basis, and they go on *Mutatis Mutandis*.³...

The Count proceeded to say that it would not conduce to the general Pacification to hurry on the Treaty; That finding Congress were not disposed to Cessions without which the King would not make a Treaty, he thought it best by mutual services and acts of Friendship, to continue making way for more condescensions on both sides and not excite Animosities and warmth by discussing Points which the King would never yield. That therefore M.ʳ Jay might take time to write to Congress on the Subject and obtain their Instructions. He said that previous to M.ʳ Jay's or M.ʳ Gerard's arrival at Madrid, M.ʳ Mirailles had informed him that Congress would yield the Navigation of the Mississippi, but that M.ʳ Gerard informed him that Congress had changed their resolution on that Subject; That he had mentioned these Obstacles to M.ʳ Jay and M.ʳ Carmichael, and it was probable that having done this he had neglected or forgot to give M.ʳ Jay the notes in Question. M.ʳ Jay here reminded his Excellency that the Conference between them of the 2ᵈ Day of June last, turned among other Points on these Obstacles and that they had then mutually expressed hopes that Regulations calculated to remove them in a manner satisfactory to both Parties might be adopted, and that the Conferences respecting them was concluded by his Excellency's promising to give M.ʳ Jay Notes of his Sentiments on the proposed Treaty. The Count admitted this, and made several Observations tending to shew the Importance of this object to Spain, and its determination to adhere to it, saying with some degree of warmth, that unless Spain could exclude all Nations from the Gulph of Mexico, they might as well admit all; That the King would never relinquish it; That the Ministry regarded it as the principal Object to be obtained by the War, and *that obtained,* he should be perfectly Easy whether or no Spain procured any other cession, That he considered it as far more important than the acquisition of Gibraltar, and that if they did not get it, it was a matter of Indifference to him whether the English possessed Mobile or not; That he chose always to speak his Sentiments plainly and candidly on those occasions, for which Reason he generally acted differently from other Politicians in always choosing to commit himself to paper, and appealing to the knowledge of the French Ambassador and others who had done business with him for the proofs of this being the principle of his conduct,

He concluded by saying he would give his Sentiments in writing on this Subject to Mr Jay.

Mr Jay made no reply to the Counts remarks on the Navigation, but observing that being little acquainted with the Practice of Politicians he was happy in having to treat with a Minister of his Excellency's principles; He added that there were many Points necessary to be adjusted in order to [complete] a Treaty; That they might proceed to agree upon as many as they could, and with respect to the others he should State them clearly to Congress and attend their further Instructions.

. . . . .

...The Bills drawn on me was considered as a desperate measure, prompted by our Imbecility, and was a bad card to play at a time we were endeavoring to form a Treaty, and when Prudence demanded that the Importance of Spain to us, should not have been brought forward, or placed in such a glaring point of view.

One good consequence however has resulted from it, The Cordiality of Spain has been tried by it. For I know of a certainty that it was in her power easily to have made the Loan we asked. Indeed we shall always be deceived, if we believe that any Nation in the World, has or will have a disinterested Regard for us especially absolute Monarchies, where the temporary views, or passions of the Prince, his Ministers, his Women, or his Favorites, not the Voice of the People, direct the helm of State. Besides from the manner in which the War is carrying on, it would seem as if it was the design of France and Spain that the longest *purse*, not the longest *Sword*, should decide it. Whether such be really their Intention, or how far it may be politic, I cannot pretend to determine. This however is certain that it would be putting the Affair on a hard issue for us. It is also certain that some Respect is due to appearances, and probable Events, and we should be cautious how we spend our Money, our Men, or our public Spirit, uselessly. In my Opinion we should endeavor to be as Independent on the Charity of our friends, as on the mercy of our Enemies. Jacob took advantage even of his Brother's hunger and extorted from him a higher price than the value of the Mississippi for a single Dinner. The way not to be in Esau's condition is to be prepared to meet with Jacob's.

. . . . .

NA: PCC, item 110, v. 1, pp. 290-321 (LBkC); M247, reel 135.

¹ Morris, Robert (1734-1806). Pennsylvania merchant and political figure. Member, Continental Congress, 1775-1778; member, Committee of Secret Correspondence, Committee of Foreign Affairs, Committee of Commerce. Superintendent of Finance, February 1781-November 1784. Established Bank of North America, January 1782. Member, Annapolis Convention, 1786; Constitutional Convention, 1787. Member, U.S. Senate, from Pennsylvania, 1789-1795.

[2] *Gates, Horatio (1727-1806). British-born American military leader. Retired from the British army as a major in 1765, moved to Virginia in 1772. Commissioned a brigadier general in the Continental Army in July 1775, served as Washington's adjutant-general during siege of Boston. Commissioned a major general in May 1776, sent to command troops retreating from Canada. Commanded American forces that defeated Burgoyne at Saratoga, October 1777. Involved in Conway Cabal, which supposedly sought Washington's replacement by Gates, late 1777. Commanded northern and eastern departments, 1778-1779. Placed in command of southern department, June 1780, after Lincoln's surrender of Charlestown; defeated by Cornwallis at Camden, August 16, 1780.*
[3] *Necessary changes having been made.*

Benjamin Franklin to John Jay

Dear Sir,   Passy, Oct. 2. 1780.

...the little success, that has attended your late Applications for Money mortified me exceedingly; and the Storm of Bills which I found coming upon us both has terrified and vexed me to such a Degree, that I have been depriv'd of Sleep, and so much indispos'd by continual anxiety as to be render'd almost incapable of writing.

At length I got over a Reluctance that was almost invincible, and made another Application to the Goverment here for more Money. I drew up and presented [a state of debts and newly-expected demands, and requested][1] its aid to extricate me.

Judging from your Letters that you were not likely to obtain any thing considerable from your Court, I put down, in my Estimate the 25,000 Dollars drawn upon you with the same Sum drawn upon me, as what would probably come to me for Payment. I have now the Pleasure to acquaint you that my Memorial was received in the Kindest and most friendly Manner, & tho' the Court here is not without its Embarrassments, on Account of Money, I was told to make myself easy, for that I should be assisted with what was necessary....

If you are not so fortunate in Spain, continue however the even good Temper you have hitherto manifested. Spain owes us nothing therefore whatever Friendship she shows us in lending Money or furnishing Cloathing, &c. tho' not equal to our Wants & wishes, is however *tant de gagné;*[2] those who have begun to assist us are more likely to continue than to declaine, and we are still so much obliged as their Aids amount to; but I hope and I am confident that Court will be wiser than to take Advantage of our Distress & insist on our making Sacrifices by an Agreement, which the Circumstance of such Distress would hereafter weaken, & the very Proposition can only give disgust at Present. Poor as we are yet as we know we shall be rich, I would rather agree with them to buy at great Price the whole of their Right on the Missisipi than sell a Drop of its Waters. – A Neigbour might as well ask me to sell my Street Door.

. . . . . .

[...I have the honour to be, dear sir, Your most obedient and most humble servant,]   B Franklin

LC: *Benjamin Franklin Papers, microfilm reel 1 (LBkC); Johnston:* Jay Correspondence, *v. 1, pp. 432-434.*
[1] *Bracketed phrases are from Johnston, Jay Correspondence, v. 1, pp. 432, 434.*
[2] *so much gained*

Instructions to John Jay from the Continental Congress

[Philadelphia, 4 October 1780]

Instructions to the Honorable John Jay, Minister plenipotentiary of the United States of America at the Court of Madrid agreed to unanimously in Congress October 4th, 1780.

That the said Minister adhere to his former instructions respecting the right of the United States of America to the free navigation of the river Mississipi into and from the sea, which right if an express acknowledgement of it cannot be obtained from Spain is not by any Stipulations on the part of *America* to be relinquished.

To render the treaty to be concluded between the two nations permanent, nothing can more effectually contribute than a proper attention not only to the present but the future reciprocal interests of the contracting powers. The river Mississipi being the boundary of several States in the union and their citizens while connected with Great Britain and since the revolution having been accustomed to the free use thereof in common with the subjects of Spain and no instance of complaint or dispute having resulted from it, there is no reason to fear that the future mutual use of the river by the subjects of the two Nations actuated by friendly dispositions will occasion any interruption to that harmony, which it is the desire of America as well as of Spain should be perpetual.

That if the unlimited freedom of the navigation of the river Mississipi with a free port or ports below 31 degrees north latitude, accessible to merchant ships cannot be obtained from Spain, the said minister in that case be at Liberty to enter into such equitable regulations as may appear a necessary security against contraband, provided the right of the United States to the free navigation of the river be not relinquished and a free port or ports as above described be stipulated to them.

With respect to the boundary alluded to in his Letter of 26 May last, that the said Minister be and hereby is instructed to adhere strictly to the boundaries of the United States as already fixed by Congress.

Spain having by the treaty of Paris ceded to great Britain all the country to the north eastward of the Mississipi, the people inhabiting these States while connected with Great Britain and also since the revolution have settled themselves at divers places to the westward near the Mississipi, are friendly to the revolution and being citizens of these United States and subject to the laws of those to which they respectively belong, Congress cannot assign them over as subjects to any other power.

That the said minister be farther informed that in case Spain shall eventually be in possession of East and West Florida at the termination of the war it is of the greatest importance to these United States to have the use of the waters running out of Georgia through West Florida into the bay of mexico for the purpose of navigation and that he be instructed to endeavour to obtain the same, subject to such regulations as may be agreed on between the contracting parties, and that as a compensation for this he be and hereby is empowered to guaranty the possessions of the said Floridas to the Crown of Spain.

...By Order of Congress   (signed) Saml. Huntington, Presdt.
                                      (attest) Charles Thomson, Secy.

Richard B. Morris, ed., John Jay: The Winning of the Peace: Unpublished Papers 1780-1784 (New York: Harper & Row, Publishers, 1980), hereafter cited as Morris, Jay Papers, v. 2, pp. 28-30.

John Adams to Charles W. F. Dumas

Sir[1]   Amsterdam Oct.ʳ· 4. 1780

I have just received your favour of the 3ᵈ, and thank you for the early Information of the Arrival of the Courier from the Plenipotentiaries of this Republick, at Petersbourg. I hope that this Republick will agree without delay to the armed Neutrality:[2] but I should be glad to See a Copy of the Dispatches if possible, or at least as exact an Account of their Substance as possible may be. I should be glad also to learn, whether the object of the Congress is Simply to form a Plan for supporting each other, and making a common cause in defence of those Principles only, which the three northern Powers have already adopted, or whether they have, in contemplation, a more extensive regulation of maritime affairs.

I dont See how this congress can have a Peace between the belligerent Powers, for its Object, when the Parties who compose it, have already so positively declared for a Neutrality. I wish with all my Heart, that another Republick had a Minister at the Congress, or at least at the Court of Petersbourg. neither the Cause nor the Country of America are understood in any Part of Europe, which gives Opportunity to the English, to represent things as they choose. *Onesta è sempre la causa di colui che parla Solo.*[3]

I do not expect Peace so soon as next Spring. And I should dread the Interposition of the Congress at Petersbourg in the Business. – They understand not the Subject.– it is impossible they should.– America is not represented there and cannot be heard. – if they should take into Consideration the Affair of Peace, I should be apprehensive of some recommendations to Save the Pride, or what they would call the Dignity of England, which would be more dangerous and pernicious to America, than a continuance of the War. – I do not dread a continuance of War. I should dread a Truce ten times more.

If all the Powers at the Congress at Petersbourg would agree together to acknowledge American Independency or agree to open a free commerce with America, and admit her merchant ships and Vessells of War into their Ports, like those of the other belligerent Powers, this I think would be just. — indeed that perfect Neutrality which they profess, requires it. refusing Admittance to the American Flagg, while they admit that of England, is so far from a Neutrality, that it is taking a decided Part in favour of England, and against one of the belligerent Powers. a Power too, which in Point of Numbers, Wealth, Industry Capacity, military and naval Power, as well as Commerce is quite as respectable, as several of those, which are or will be represented in the Congress, at Petersbourg. I have the Honour to be, with great Esteem, Sir your humble Servant.

· · · · ·

John Adams

MHS: *The Adams Papers,* microfilm reel 102 (LBkC).

[1] *Dumas, Charles William Frederick (1721-1796). Swiss scholar and translator residing at The Hague. American agent in the United Provinces of the Netherlands, 1775-1792; unofficial American chargé d'affaires, 1785-1792. His pro-Patriot, pro-French stance caused him much difficulty during the 1787 Dutch unrest.*

[2] *The League of Armed Neutrality was proclaimed by Empress Catherine II on 29 February 1780. Its initial members, Russia, Denmark, and Sweden, signed a defensive treaty designed to protect neutral shipping in wartime, to which they invited other neutrals to adhere. The doctrine "free ships make free goods," upon which the League was based, appealed to both the United Provinces and the United States.*

[3] *The only man to speak always has the honest cause.*

James Madison's Notes on François Barbé de Marbois' Observations regarding the Spanish–U.S. Boundary

[October 6-16? 1780]

Sketch of the Observations on the boundary between the Spanish Settlements & the United States (by de Marbois)

The King of France though anxious to effect the Triple alliance, yet thinkg. the pretensions on both sides exorbitant, did not chuse to interfere in support of either. But directed his Ministers at Phila. & Madrid to press the importance of mutual concessions. With this view the former represents to Congress the necessity of concentrating the force agst. the common enemy, for want of which the events of the present campaign have proved inadequate to the exertions. The advantages of an alliance are obvious, in case of a negociation for peace. It will be conducted with perfect harmony between the 3 allied powers. The Spaniards will be as much disposed as the french to support the just claims of U. States. They will not threaten to make a peace excluding them if the others shall be satisfied – on pretence that they are tied to France only, and had no motives to exhaust their resources for a people whose ambition prevented a treaty with a power on whom their safety depended....

The necessity of the Alliance being shewn the means of bringing it about are next to be considered, the observations on which are to be taken not as ministerial communications, but the private sentiments of one more impartially attached to the good of both parties, than acquainted with the pretensions of either.

Spain claims the exclusive navigation of the Mississippi; and as much I can guess that part of the continent which lies eastward of the Mississippi & formerly called the Orientalis Louisiana. On this head the following objections were suggested by the Committee to the french minister in Jany. last, when urging the necessity of satisfying Spain.

Obj: 1. The Charters of the Southern States forbid such a cession.

Answer. The transactions of a power with its own subjects [is] not binding on another power unless communicated, acknowledged, and in a case like the present, unless actual possession can be pleaded. were it otherwise perpetual contests wd. prevail among the Southern powers of Europe, as they have most of them granted such [charters at sundry] times to [their subjects.] The charters of the Colonies [interfere with each other,] most of them having disputes not only with their neigh[bours, but with those] at a distance how then can they be a rule for another [power? How will it ap]pear for the States at the time they are requesting of Spain [an acknowledgment of their] independence to apply to the very record which is the proof [of their subjection? Is it] not plain that in such a case, there is no other solid [plea but actual occupation], or at least a former public manifest possission? The King of Spain however will not recur to these arguments: he will only say – those lands have been ceded 18 years ago by france to G.B. (treaty of Paris 63. art. 7) not to the Colonies. If they become the property of any common enemy, I have a full right to make the conquest of and so I do.

Obj: 2. The lands in question [are] necessary to the safety & prosperity of the States.

Ans: This is not certain. The case of Vermont, Kentucke & some Counties in Massachussets, show the danger of such ext[ensiv]e territories. It is in vain to attempt to convince either party that their claims are agst. their interest, as they are the best judges of it. It rests therefore on the respective possibility of making the conquest, and it may be left even to a partial judge to decide on this point.

Obj: 3. Spain would take advantage of the present situation of the United States to Treat with them on unequal principles.

Ans: This is the case in 99 treaties of a 100 – no such inequality – rather on the side of America. Spain will acknowledge her independence and does not need hers to be so. Spain will grant commercial and very likely other advantages and can not expect the same from America. The benefits she is to reap are not of such a positive nature.

Obj: 4. If these demands were granted Spain might think herself entitled to the demand or conquest of Georgia, Penobscot, N. York &c.

Ans: This objection is extravagant & cannnot be seriously made. The most explicit assurances on this point might at any time be obtained.

Obj: 5. Such conduct in Spain neithe[r generous] nor liberal.

Ans: The Spanish Ministry have probably on this said to the French Ambassador *that the conduct of the Americans is neither liberal nor generous.*

Obj: 6. A war even a long war preferable to such conditions.

Ans: A Patient extremely ill might as well say to his Phycician death is better than not to drink spirituous liquors & other things not to be found on the island where he was.

Obj: 7. The Spaniards would hereafter be the sacrifices of their own ambition. No unequal treaty can last long — the injured party will soon or later break it.

Ans: The cautiousness of Spain may be trusted to provide agst. this evil. She may perhaps upon better ground suggest the same danger to the States. They will chuse rather however to confine themselves to their right of conquest upon a country possessed by their Enemy.

Obj: 8. The territory cannot be given up with out the previous consent of the interested States.

Ans: As this argumt. is founded on the charters, if it be valid, it would prove that no treaty would be valid unless it secured to the States [the lands] as far as the South Sea.

In this manner would reason a Minister of the [Court of Spain, and it would seem] no solid objection could be made to it. If any restricti[ons ought to be laid on these princi]ples, they ought to be taken from the actual settlement [of Americans on the territories] claimed by the Spaniards. By settlement is mea[nt, not temporary incursions] of a few troops, but actual occupancy supported [by the exercise of jurisdiction, and] by building of houses, clearing & inhabiting the [land &c., without contradiction. Here an] impartial mediator might find the line to be drawn be[tween the contending parties. But I shall] Confine myself to represent to the friends of this case that[,in missing the present fair opportunity of ob]taining solid & lasting advantages to run after a shadow & a chimerical object, they expose themselves to the everlasting reproaches of their Country.[1]

Smith, Letters of Delegates, v. 16, pp. 154-157.

[1] Madison, James (1751-1836). Virginia political figure. Member, Continental Congress, 1780-1783, 1787-1789. Member, Virginia House of Delegates, 1784-1786. Delegate, Annapolis Convention, 1786, and Constitutional Convention, 1787. With Hamilton and Jay, author of The Federalist, a collection of essays on the United States Constitution. Member, U.S. House of Representatives, 1789-1797. Secretary of State, 1801-1809. President of the United States, 1809-1817.

Benjamin Franklin to John Adams

Sir,   Passy, Oct. 8. 1780

. . . . .

I ought to acquaint you, *a governo*, as the Merchants Say; that M⁺ Le Comte de V. having taken much amiss some Passages in your Letters to him, sent the whole Correspondence to me, requesting that I would transmit it to Congress. I was myself sorry to see those Passages. If they were the Effects merely of Inadvertance, and you do not on Reflection approve of them, perhaps you may think it proper to write something for effacing the Impressions made by them. I do not presume to advise you; but mention it only for your Consideration.

The vessel is not yet gone, which carries the Papers.

With great Regard, I have the honour to be Sir, Your most obedient and most humble Servant.   B. Franklin

MHS: The Adams Papers, microfilm reel 353 (ALS).

Benjamin Franklin to John Adams

Sir,   Passy 20 Oct. 1780.
Understanding that in Case of M^r· Laurens's Absence; you are charged with the Affair of procuring a Loan in Holland, I think it Right to acquaint you, that by a Letter from M^r· Jay of the 12th Inst, from Madrid, we are informed that the King of Spain has been so good as to offer his Guarantee for the Payment of the Interest and Principal of a Loan of Money for the Use of the United States. M^r· Grand[1] thinks that no considerable Use can be made here of that Guarantee, on Account of the considerable Loan Mr Necker[2] is about to make; but that possibly it may have weight in Holland. – Orders will be sent to the Spanish Ambassador[3] here by the next Post respecting this Matter.
I regret much the taking of M^r· Laurens. His Son,[4] I understand sailed a Fortnight after him, for France; but he has not yet arrived.

. . . . .

I have the honour to be with great Respect, Sir, Your Excellency's most obedient & most humble Ser^{t}·   B. Franklin

. . . . .

MHS: The Adams Papers, microfilm reel 353 (LS).

[1] Grand, Ferdinand. Paris banker who handled U.S. accounts.

[2] Necker, Jacques (1732-1804). Swiss banker who served as France's controller general of finance, 1776-1781, 1788-1789, 1789-1790.

[3] Aranda, Pedro Pablo Abarca de Bolea, Conde de (1718-1799). Spanish statesman and diplomat. After distinguished military service, appointed ambassador to Poland. Later served as captain general of Valencia, then of Aragón. President of the Council of Ministers in 1765. Ambassador to France, 1779-1792. President of the Council of Ministers, 1792-1794.

[4] Laurens, John (1754-1782). South Carolina soldier and diplomat, son of Henry Laurens. Initially a volunteer aide on George Washington's staff, he was later commissioned a lieutenant colonel, and fought at Branywine, Germantown, Monmouth, and Charlestown, where he was captured. Paroled and exchanged, he was commissioned envoy extraordinary to France in order, as a soldier, to explain the need for additional military aid. Arriving in France in March 1781, he was successful in sending to America four transports loaded with money and military supplies. Upon his return to the United

States, he rejoined the army and fought at Yorktown. In South Carolina, he took part in the irregular warfare that persisted in that state, and was killed in action on August 27, 1782.

François Barbé de Marbois to Comte de Vergennes

[Translation]

Nº 92. Duplicate.   Philadelphia, 21 October 1780

My Lord

My personal contacts with two of the three members who comprise the Committee named to draft the letter to Mr. Jay have placed me in position to follow their work, and as it is now completed and has received the approval of Congress, I can render you a true account of it. Mr. Madison, charged by his Colleagues with explaining the state of the question concerning the Navigation of the Mississippi and the possession of the lands situated to the left of that River in a particular Memoir, has communicated that writing to me. At first sight it manifests a little too much of the ambitious principles adopted by Virginia, from which he is a Delegate. His insights and his moderation have provided me the means of inspiring in him sentiments more consonant to the circumstances. As this document must be submitted to you, My Lord, and Mr. Jay will be authorized to communicate it to the Court of Spain, I shall not enter into detail on what it contains. I limit myself to informing you that it is destined to sustain the pretentions which the United States are forming to the navigation and the land in dispute, but that he has worked hard to remove all the expressions that might displease His Catholic Majesty. Much effect is expected from the exposition of the advantages which Spain will acquire from allowing Americans the liberty of navigating the Mississippi and from the inconvenience of forcing the inhabitants of Western establishments to obtain supplies of foreign merchandise by way of Canada and the Lakes. This Memoir explains some points of the first instructions. It gives the American Minister a little more latitude than in the past, and from its assurances one has some hope that these somewhat flimsy changes will satisfy the Court of Madrid and remove the difficulties that oppose the conclusion of a Treaty. However, it was considered, My Lord, that it could happen that Spain may persist in her first demands, and in that case, Congress has written Mr. Jay a secret letter by which he is authorized to give way successively concerning the navigation of the Mississippi in common with the Spanish, to consent to all the restrictions and rules proper to calm the disquiets of the Court of Madrid, and finally, if necessary, not to regard this claim to the navigation as an ultimatum. As for the lands in dispute and the boundaries of the thirteen States in the West, if Mr. Jay finds it a complete impossibility to have the matter settled on the basis of his first instructions, he is also authorized not to present them as an ultimatum, but to give way successively in accordance with what the circumstances and his own prudence suggest to him. It is now feared, My Lord, that there is no Minister who, given so vague a pronouncement, could take it upon himself to make Sacrifices as considerable as those Spain will perhaps demand. Nevertheless, Congress has not changed this article because, knowing very imperfectly the views of the Court of Madrid, it is impossible or at least dangerous to fix with precision what it resolves to cede it, and it would be better to leave it to Mr. Jay's prudence. The mobility of Congress and the incertitude of events do not permit conjecture concerning the extent of the sacrifices on which it will determine if Mr. Jay refers this matter back to its decision with more explicit demands on the part of Spain. However, I have sounded out several Delegates on this matter, and if one can draw conclusions from individual opinions passed in private conversations, I think that at the present time Spain should demand of Congress that part of Louisiana which in Dauville's atlas[1] lies between the Mississippi on the West, the Floridas on the South, the Alabama or even the Appalachicola River on the East, and a line drawn on the North from the sources of these Rivers to the juncture of the Ohio and the Mississippi, the thirteen States would consent to make it the Lot of that Power without changing anything in other respects with regard to what was decided a year ago concerning the Floridas. However, some scruples that previously had not come to mind have been conceived with regard to the rights of the savages. It is claimed that it is impossible formally to cede to Spain what they occupy today, because they are in fact the owners of the Soil, inasmuch as they have not been conquered in a legitimate war or sold their Country. In support of these principles has been cited what may pass for proof, the negotiations of 1761 between France and England, and it is inferred therefrom that the Americans cannot cede this land, but can only renounce ever acquiring it in favor of Spain.

When Congress approved the draft of the letter which I have just recounted, My Lord, the Committee proposed to inform you of its contents. This proposal, born of the impartiality which the 13 States remark in all the conduct of His Majesty on the subject of the negotiations with Spain and of the confidence they have in his wisdom and amity, was received with marks of general approbation. A single delegate observed that, the King being the kinsman and the most intimate Ally of Spain, it could be dangerous to make him master of the negotiations and Trustee of a Secret that it appeared should be concealed from Spain with the greatest care. A number of voices were raised against this reflection, and it was resolved with a general satisfaction that the contents of the secret letter would be sent to Mr. Franklin to be communicated to you. I was told that Mr. Jay would also be authorized to inform M. de Montmorin thereof....I am constantly kept in ignorance of Spain's dispositions in this matter, and I limit myself to simple exhortations that if, contrary to the opinion of Congress, these recent resolutions are found insufficient, My Lord, it is absolutely essential that Mr. Jay be persuaded of it and send word to his Constituents, for one of the greatest obstacles that has obstructed the affair just ended has been that Minister's Sentiment that Spain will in the end treat on the basis of his first instructions. It was decided with some difficulty not to join pecuniary demands to these concessions, and many delegates were inclined toward a renunciation that would strongly resemble a Contract of sale, but motives of decency and dignity turned the scale. These recent deliberations have been notable, My Lord, for the calm and moderation which have reigned here. These dispositions and this change in the cessions, which Congress had regarded as peremptory, are principally due to the respect and sincere attachment of the States for His Majesty. Expression of these sentiments has not ceased during the different debates, and one can show no more Confidence than all the Delegations of Congress have shown in him. Memories of the exhortations of M. le Chevalier de La Luzerne have done the rest. The President of Congress said, without entering into any detail, that he thought that an Impartial Power would find the new instructions satisfactory to the Court of Madrid, and that His Majesty's Counsels have greatly contributed to inspire in Congress sentiments of moderation and disinterest. Congress, My Lord, has informed Messieurs Jay and Franklin by the same Ships that carry these. It learned yesterday by a letter from that Minister that the Successor of M. de Mirales will not delay in leaving for this Continent. It is fortunate that this news only arrived after the conclusion of the affair on which I have just reported. It might have been thought necessary to wait for the new Agent before doing anything. Moreover, they are very impatient to see him arrive.

I am with a profound Respect, My Lord, Your very humble and very obedient Servant   Barbé de Marbois

.   .   .   .   .

FFAA: Pol. Corr., U.S., v. 14, f. 29 (LC transcription).

¹ Danville's atlas. The reference is to the untitled general or universal atlas (atlas général) compiled by French geographer Jean-Baptiste Bourguignon d'Anville (1697-1782), which appeared in several editions from 1740 onwards, each edition containing a different number of maps.

John Adams to Baron van der Capellen

Sir[1]   Amsterdam Nov. 20. 1780
. . . . .
The Hour draws nigh, when this Republick is to determine, whether it
will acceed to the armed Neutrality: but let their determination of that
question be as it will, if they do not disavow the Conduct of Amsterdam,
and punish M[r] Van berckel[2] and the Burgomasters, the King of Great
Britain has threatened, and if I am not deceived by his past Conduct, he
will attempt to carry his Threats into Execution. if he declares War, or
which is more probable, commences hostilities without a declaration it will
be on pretence of an Insult and an Injury, committed by beginning a
Correspondence and a Treaty with his Subjects in Rebellion, altho they
were at that Time as compleatly in Possession of an Independence and a
Sovereignty de Facto as England or Holland were.
...with the Utmost Respect, Sir your most ob[t.] Ser[t.]   John Adams

MHS: The Adams Papers, microfilm reel 102 (LBkC).
[1] Capellen tot den Pol, Joan Derk, Baron van der (1741-1784). Dutch political figure.
Philosophical leader of the Patriot party in the United Provinces. Became a member of the
States (assembly) of Overyssel province, 1771. Favored strengthening the Dutch fleet.
Spoke out against granting British request to transfer the Scots Brigade, stationed in the
Netherlands as part of the Anglo-Dutch defensive alliance, to America, 1775, as violation
of Dutch neutrality. Author of the anonymous pamphlet To the People of the
Netherlands (1781), which espoused democratic government and freedom of the press. A
friend of America who proved a faithful adviser to John Adams throughout his stay in the
United Provinces.
[2] Berckel, Engelbert François van (1726-1796). Dutch political figure. Pensionary of
Amsterdam, 1762-1781. Opponent of the Orange party, but not a democrat. Drawn into
negotiations between Amsterdam and the American rebels, 1778, which the States of
Holland and the States General subsequently did not recognize. Served in the States of
Holland, 1782-1784. A leader of the Patriot party at the time of the Prussian invasion in
1787, after which he withdrew from politics.

Comte de Vergennes to John Jay

[Translation]
Mr. Jay   Versailles, 27 November 1780
I received punctually, Sir, the letter that you did me the honor of writing
me the 22nd of November last.
You have too much evidence, Sir, of the interest that the King takes in

the cause of your homeland not to be persuaded that he would have taken into consideration the request you are making, if that had been possible; but the considerable expenses of the war that His Majesty is sustaining, joined to the extraordinary assistance that I have procured and that I continue to procure for Mr. Franklin, put His Majesty beyond the condition to meet the bills that Congress has judged it appropriate to draw upon you. It is with the greatest regret, Sir, that I convey to you a decision not so favorable, and I infinitely wish to find other occasions in which I could convince you of my zeal for the interests of the United States, and of the desire that I have to oblige you personally.   Vergennes

FFAA: Pol. Corr., U.S., v. 14, f. 337 (LC transcription).

John Jay to the President of Congress

Duplicate   Madrid 30 Novr 1780
Sir
                    .   .   .   .   .
    It is proper that your Ex^y should be informed that on the 8$^{th.}$ Inst, I had a Conference with the Minister at the Escurial, in which I rec^d many good *Words* and friendly assurances, but Time only can decide how they will terminate....
    Altho appearances are not very flattering at present, I hope they will in time become more so – Patience Prudence & Perseverance sometimes effect much. It is in my Opinion very important that no Dissatisfaction be expressed in America at the Conduct of Spain. Complaint and Disgust can answer no good Purpose but may be productive of many disagreable Consequences. A cautious Silence is the more necessary as I am confident there are Persons in America who would make a merit of collecting & transmitting the Sentiments of Congress or *members* of Congress on Subjects interesting to the Views and objects of Persons in Power here.
                    .   .   .   .   .
    I have the Honor to be Your Excellency's most obedient & hble Servt
                                                            John Jay

NA: PCC, item 98, pp. 235-238 (ALS); M247, reel 125.

Comte de Vergennes to Chevalier de la Luzerne

[Translation]

N° 10.   Versailles, 4 December 1780

. . . . .

...As for Mr. Franklin, his conduct leaves nothing for Congress to desire. It is as zealous and patriotic as it is wise and circumspect, and you can assure all whom you judge appropriate that the method this plenipotentiary follows is more efficacious than if he made it his business to be importunate in multiplying his demands and then supporting them with threats, to which we would attach neither credence nor value, and which would only serve to make his person disagreeable. You would hardly be impressed, Sir, for the threats would be so much the more superfluous, and supposing, as we do, Congress incapable of having stipulated them, we would attribute them to its representative, who would derive from them no other fruit than the irreparable loss of our confidence.

Moreover, Sir, in order to place Congress in the position of judging that it may expect more from our goodwill than from the importunities of Mr. Franklin, you will confide to it that at the first request of that Minister, I have procured for him a million in order to meet various objectives he had to pay before the end of this year, that I am busy obtaining for him additional aid for the course of next year, and finally that we will in no case lose sight of the interest of the American Cause....

. . . . .

Pursuant to what you wrote me, Sir, Mr. John Adams has requested contingent instructions 1ˢᵗ· on the dispositions of Article 9 of our treaty of commerce; 2ⁿᵈ· on the right of escheat abolished by Article 13 of the same treaty; 3ʳᵈ· on the restoration of American refugees protected by England.

Article 9 says that the Subjects of one of the two contracting parties will abstain from fishing on the coasts and in the roadsteads, harbors, etc. belonging to the other party. This Stipulation is of the greatest clarity and requires no commentary, so far as I am concerned. As for the respective possessions of France and America, they can only be fixed by the future treaty of peace. Therefore, the extent of our fisheries will only be determined as a consequence of that treaty. Perhaps it is Mr. Adams' intention to renew the pretentions that have already been discussed in Congress relative to fishing on the coasts of Newfoundland. But we have never espoused them, as you can satisfy yourself if you will be good enough to re-read the despatches which I addressed to M. Gerard under N°ˢ· 6 and 9, and N° 2 that I had the honor to write to you yourself on 25 September 1779. We persist in the opinion developed in those despatches, and you would do well to conform the insinuations you may be in a position to make to Congress on this matter thereto.

As for the Suppression of the right of escheat, we must have stipulated it, because the right exists in France with regard to all nations, and a formal law is necessary to make it void. We are unaware whether the same right exists in England with regard to all nations, or only with regard to Frenchmen as a form of reprisal. In the first instance, if the Americans form commercial ties with England, it is natural to suppose that they will wish to suppress a right that would inconvenience them, and we have no reason to oppose it. In the second instance, any Stipulation would be superfluous, because it would be without purpose; moreover, Congress will be guided in that regard according to its own lights, and we have no particular view to suggest to it.

The 3rd object of Mr. Adams' requests, to be informed of the restoration to American refugees of their properties, has not been determined at this time. It will basically depend on the circumstances in which peace is made. If they favor England, that power will doubtless wish to protect its adherents, and Congress will have great difficulty in refusing its demands. In the contrary case, the Court of London will be less exacting. Perhaps it would not wish to prolong the war for so secondary an object; thus it is possible that it will yield after having made the demands that decency would seem to require of it in this respect. I think, Sir, that Congress should direct its intentions on the subject in question in accordance with these two hypotheses. The only thing we desire is that the instructions be expressed in a manner not to authorize Mr. Adams to halt the negotiations in case he meets with invincible obstacles, and that he be ordered to conduct himself in accordance with the counsels of His Majesty's Ministry. This precaution seems necessary to me in view of the inflexibility and obstinacy I perceive in Mr. Adams.

You have had, Sir, a talk with a member of Congress on the opinion that our intention will be to propose a longterm truce relative to America, and it seems that the Eastern States have conceived anxieties in this regard. This matter was amply discussed while your predecessor was still in America; it is also a question in the observations which the King made public at the beginning of this year. Our principles have not changed, and he will not change, but it is possible that circumstances will make the law for us, as I expressed it to M. Gerard, and oblige us to allow modifications, but whatever they may be, we will take the necessary measures to guarantee the de facto independence of the United States against all events that can humanly be foreseen. Moreover, Sir, I presume that the true object of the anxieties, which has been concealed from you, is the *status quo*. Nothing could be more vexatious for America in the present state of affairs, and we are completely determined not to stipulate it for the Americans. It will be for them to judge when it is a question of that subject, of the perseverance or the sacrifices which conjunctures require on their part. Moreover, Sir, I desire that you abstain from discussing this delicate matter at the present time, and that if someone should again speak to you of it, you limit yourself to saying that it has in no wise been a question in Europe since the rupture of the negotiations which the Court of Madrid opened at the beginning of 1778.

The opinion that appears to be held in Philadelphia relative to the proposition which England may make to Congress of separate negotiations entirely conforms to the principles of the alliance, and we are persuaded that it will prevail in Congress if the matter is discussed there, because we would never suspect that assembly of wishing to allow itself the slightest step that might tend to separate it from France and thereby to break the ties that have imparted to America the character of a Sovereign State. Such is the text, Sir, in accordance with which you should express yourself on all occasions when there is a question of separate negotiations with Great Britain.

The state of flux in which Congress appears to be presents a very troubling aspect, and if the proper expedients are not immediately found to make it cease, the dissolution of that Body will be the first consequence, and then America will be without strength because it will no longer exist as a point of reconciliation between the various provinces. The means that could prevent so grave an evil most efficaciously would be, as you observe, Sir, an act of general confederation. But can one suppose the Americans frightened enough of the danger of their present situation to think that they will employ that remedy? I confess to you that we wish for it more than we hope for it, because it seems to us that personal interest still has too much control for it to be sacrificed to the public interest. We would learn with much satisfaction that our conjectures are ill-founded.

Moreover, Sir, in the supposition that a general confederation may exist, we presume sufficient insights and wisdom in Congress to think that this Body will not renew the ratification of our treaties. It should regard that given in 1778 as sufficient, for it is effectively so, and fear that in wishing to renew it, it may give rise to much criticism and discussion, and that the malevolent may use the occasion to attack many of the steps which it took prior to the general confederation. I beseech you, Sir, to make use of these reflections when this question arises. It is important to us that they be taken into consideration, because it is important to us not to have treated with a Body that would appear to think that it did not then have sufficient powers to do so.

You have done very well, Sir, in placing yourself in a position to explain to Congress our way of thinking on the drafts that it does not cease to draw on Mr. Franklin, and the manner in which you explained yourself on that subject has merited His Majesty's approbation. The drafts of which you have been informed are just arriving in Europe, and they inconvenience Mr. Franklin the more, inasmuch as they exceed the funds I will be able to procure for him in the course of next year. M. Necker has asked that plenipotentiary for a letter of credit on Congress for the Sum of 400,000 dollars to be furnished in produce or in securities. If that Sum is furnished, Mr. Franklin will be in a condition to meet all the drafts. It is therefore fundamentally important to Congress to accept M. Necker's proposal, and if that body wishes to have funds in France for its various needs, nothing would be easier than for it to procure supplies for our troops, and I do not know how it can be that it has not done as it assured us, considering the tax in kind that it ordered at the beginning of this year.

· · · · · ·

Vergennes

FFAA: Pol. Corr., U.S., v. 14, f. 111 (LC transcription).

Chevalier de la Luzerne to Comte de Vergennes

[Translation]

Nᵒ 102. Quadruplicate.   Philadelphia, 9 December 1780
My Lord

· · · · ·

...The negotiations with Spain also suffer from the absence of an agent instructed in her pretentions and her designs. The one who has replaced M. Mirales is only imperfectly informed of the matter; moreover, Congress affects not to wish to treat with that agent, even on the most indifferent subjects, if not through my mediation. It is even proposed to conceal from him with extreme Care all the resolutions that may relate to navigation of the Mississippi and eastern Louisiana. Congress will follow the same System with regard to M. Gardochi,[1] Don Juan's designated Successor, so that even though I will be informed of the measures that will be taken, I would not be able to communicate them to him so that he could give me his opinion or transmit them to his Court. But in this case, My Lord, the Silence which you have ordered will be my guide, as it has been up to now.

· · · · ·

Received 31 January 1781   le che de la Luzerne

FFAA: Pol. Corr., U.S., v. 14, f. 114 (LC transcription).
[1] *Either James or Diego de Gardoqui; not identified further.*

Virginia Delegates to Thomas Jefferson

Sir[1]   Philadelphia December 13th. 1780
    The complexion of the intelligence received of late from Spain, with the manner of thinking which begins to prevail in Congress with regard to the claims to the navigation of the Mississippi, makes it our duty to apply to our constituents for their precise full and ultimate sense on this point. If Spain should make a relinquishment of the navigation of that river on the part of the United States an indispensable condition of an Alliance with them, and the State of Virginia should adhere to their former determination to insist on the right of navigation, their delegates ought to be so instructed not only for their own satisfaction, but that they may the more effectually obviate arguments drawn from a supposition that the change of circumstances which has taken place since the former instructions were given may have changed the opinion of Virginia with regard to the object of them. If on the other side any such change of opinion should have happened, and it is now the sense of the State that an Alliance with Spain ought to be purchased even at the price of such a cession if it cannot be obtained on better terms it is evidently necessary that we should be authorized to concur in it. It will also be expedient for the Legislature to instruct us in the most explicit terms whether any and what extent of territory on the East side of the Mississippi and within the limits of Virginia, is in any event to be yielded to Spain as the price of an Alliance with her. Lastly it is our earnest wish to know what steps it is the pleasure of our Constituents we should take in case we should be instructed in no event to concede the claims of Virginia either to territory or to the navigation of the abovementioned river and Congress should without their concurrence agree to such concession.

· · · · ·

We have the honor to be with the most perfect respect & esteem Yr. Excelly's Most Obt. & humble servants,   James Madison Junr.
                                                          Theok. Bland[2]

Smith, Letters of Delegates, v. 16, p. 442.
    [1] Jefferson, Thomas (1743-1826). Virginia political figure, diplomat, scientist, architect, and author. Member, Virginia House of Burgesses, 1769-1775. Member, Continental Congress, 1775-1776, 1783-1784. Author, Declaration of Independence. Governor of Virginia, 1779-1781. Author, Notes on the State of Virginia, written at the behest of French Secretary of Legation François Barbé de Marbois. With John Adams and Benjamin Franklin, commissioner to negotiate commercial treaties in Europe, 1784-1786. Minister to France, 1785-1789. U.S. Secretary of State, 1790-1793. Vice President of the United States, 1797-1801. President of the United States, 1801-1809.

² Bland, Theodorick (1742-1790). Virginia physician, military officer. Member, Continental Congress, 1780-1783. Opposed ratification of Federal Constitution. Member, U.S. House of Representatives, 1789-1790.

Chevalier de la Luzerne to Comte de Vergennes

[Translation]

Nᵒ· 104. Quadruplicate.   Philadelphia, 15 December 1780

My Lord

The plan of taking up again the resolutions relative to the negotiation with Spain seems to have failed, despite the part taken by the three States of the South, to give that Power the most extensive Satisfaction, either as to navigation of the Mississippi or as to the boundaries of Louisiana. A delegate from South Carolina told me that Georgia and the two Carolinas had resolved to abandon one hundred thousand arres of land on the left bank of that river, and that the delegations of those states had made the motion for it through one of their Members; there were long debates, in the course of which Delegates from Massachusetts spoke with the greatest force against this measure and claimed that the resolutions on which M. de Marbois had the honor of reporting to you were sufficient. Virginia was equally opposed to the motion, but one of the Virginia Delegates, all the while declaring himself for the negative, added that it was to conform to the orders of his constituents rather than the result of his own opinion, that he thought on the contrary that it was necessary to try by all means appropriate to gain the friendship and protection of Spain, and that he did not think that the preceding measures could entirely fulfill this object. The motion was rejected by a plurality of a single vote. The great argument used is always that Spain has not articulated her demands with regard to Navigation of the Mississipi, and that a cession such as that which the States of the South propose exposes Congress to the risk of giving more than the Court of Madrid desires, or of inducing that Court to extend its claims when it is informed of the readiness of Congress to make this first concession. The obstinacy with which the State of Massachusetts is opposed to it forms so singular a contrast with the opposition of the States of the South that the latter have been struck by it and see no plausible reason to bring it up but the desire to prolong the war and the fear of being abandoned in their turn by the Southern States when it is a question of recovering the Province of Maine and of settling the boundaries with Canada. Moreover, the Committee of Foreign Affairs is principally directed by a Delegate from the State of Massachusetts, and the whole conduct of this negotiation is necessarily restrained by his personal dispositions. Mr. Jay has nevertheless inspired a new confidence in His Catholic Majesty by conveying to Congress that he has informed him of the steps of the English to induce him to make a separate peace, but that that Monarch had at the same time given him positive assurance of treating only on condition that the independence of the Thirteen United States would be assured.

. . . . .

Another subject, My Lord, has filled Congress with intrigues and Cabals; it is the recall of Mr. Franklin, to which the Delegates of Massachusetts are trying by all sorts of means to persuade their Colleagues. That Minister has no declared support here; but the fear that the different parties have of seeing him replaced by a Successor of the contrary party serves to sustain him. The State of Massachusetts, of South Carolina and some individual votes are the only ones that, carried away by Messrs. Izard and Lee, have positively asserted that there is no one who would not be preferable to a Minister who, they say, has, by his nonchalence and the influence that his surroundings have had on him, lost the cause of America in France. Few persons have believed these exaggerations, but the Silence that this Minister observes towards his Constituents persuades them that he is not very much occupied with public affairs, and that it is advisable to have an Envoy extraordinary sent to France charged with soliciting Aid of every kind from His Majesty, with putting before his eyes the causes of the misfortunes of the last Campaign, the plans formed to render it more active next year and to report forthwith to Congress on the Success of his commission. I was informed of this resolution after it had been passed; but before the choice of Congress was fixed. I could not without inconvenience try to deter it from this step; I limited myself to insinuating that it was not the usage to waste the representative character for a commission of this nature, especially at the time when Congress has a Minister near the King, that this Commission could be equally fulfilled by charging the person to whom it should be confided to address himself to you, My Lord, without giving him letters of credence for the King, that this person would be presented to you by Mr. Franklin, and that you would place the requests of Congress before His Majesty's eyes. I thought I might avoid in that way the pomp and glitter of an extraordinary mission, and I thought besides that if His Majesty does not consider it appropriate to comply with all the requests that will be made of him, his refusals would have less inconvenience than if they were made to a man endowed with a considerable character, and that if on the contrary the King accords the graces that will be asked of him, they will only be dearer to Congress if they are more particularly due to you. Colonel Laurence, son of the former President, has been chosen almost unanimously. His attachment to Military Service and the distinguished reputation that he has made therein make him undecided in undertaking this Commission, and he would have liked the choice to fall upon Mr. Hamilton,[1] the confidential aide de camp of General Washington. I have reason to think that the title of Envoy extraordinary will not be changed, but that he will not be given a Letter of credence addressed to the King, but a Letter of recommendation for you, My Lord, and the order to Doctor Franklin to present it to you and to support him in his negotiation.

· · · · ·

Received 31 January 1781   le che de la luzerne

FFAA: Pol. Corr., U.S., v. 14, f. 120 (LC transcription).
  [1] Hamilton, Alexander (1757-1804). New York soldier and political figure. Aide-de-camp to General Washington, 1777-1781. Member, Continental Congress, 1782-1783, 1788. Member, Constitutional Convention, 1787. Author, with John Jay and James Madison, of The Federalist. Secretary of the Treasury, 1789-1795.

The President of Congress to John Jay

Sir,   Philadelphia, 18 December 1780

· · · · ·

Congress, it is probable, will soon establish an Office for foreign Affairs, to be managed by an Officer stiled *Secretary for foreign Affairs*, who will be constantly devoted to the Business of that Department; which it is to be hoped will remedy many Disadvantages we have hitherto laboured under, and give our Ministers at foreign Courts more frequent, better and earlier Intelligence than they have hitherto received from us.

· · · · ·

Necessity obliges me to confide in the Committee for foreign Affairs to give you the needful and more particular Intelligence.

· · · · ·

Sam. Huntington

Morris, Jay Papers, v. 2, pp. 43-44.

The President of Congress to John Adams

Sir,   Philad[a], January 1. 1781

You will receive herewith inclosed, a Commission as Minister plenipotentiary to the united Provinces of the low Countries, with Instructions for your Government on that important Mission, as also a Plan of a Treaty with those States, and likewise a Resolve of Congress relative to the Declaration of the Empress of Russia[1] respecting the Protection of neutral Ships &c.

Proper Letters of Credence on the Subject of your Mission will be forwarded by the next Conveyance, but it is thought inexpedient to delay the present Despatches on that Account.

I have the Honor to be &c&c   Samuel Huntington

NA: PCC, item 15, p. 194 (LBkC); M247, reel 24.

[1] Catherine II (1729-1796), Empress of Russia, 1762-1796, also known as Catherine the Great.

The President of Congress to John Adams

Sir,   Philadª January 10. 1781

Congress consider your Correspondence with the Count de Vergennes on the Subject of communicating your plenipotentiary Powers to the Ministry of Great Britain as flowing from your Zeal & Assiduity in the Service of your Country: but I am directed to inform you that the Opinion given to you by that Minister relative to the Time and Circumstances proper for communicating your Powers and entering upon the Execution of them is well founded.

Congress have no Expectations from the Influence which the People of England may have on the British Councils, whatever may be the Disposition of that Nation or their Magistrates towards these United States: nor are they of Opinion that a Change of Ministers would produce a Change of Measures, they therefore hope you will be very cautious of admitting your Measures to be influenced by Presumptions of such Events or their probable Consequences –

I am Sir &c &c &c   Samuel Huntington

N.B. This Letter was drawn by a Comᵉᵉ of Congress

NA: PCC, item 15, pp. 205-206 (LBkC); M247, reel 24.

Congressional Committee Report and Resolution

Janʸ 10. 1781

. . . . . .

The committee appointed to consider and report a plan for the department of foreign affairs, report

That the extent and rising powers of these United States entitle them to a place among the great potentates of Europe while our political & commercial interests point out the propriety of cultivating with them a friendly correspondence and connection – That to render such an intercourse advantageous the necessity of a competent knowledge of the interests views, relations and systems of those potentates is Obvious – That a knowledge in its nature so comprehensive is only to be acquired by a constant attention to the State of Europe and an unremitted application to the means of acquiring well grounded information – That Congress are moreover called upon to maintain with our Ministers at foreign Courts a regular correspondence and to keep them fully informed of every circumstance and event which regards the public honor, interest and safety – That to answer these essential purposes, the Committee are of opinion that a fixed and permanent Office for the department of foreign affairs ought forthwith to be established as a remedy against the fluctuation the delay and indecision to which the present mode of managing our foreign affairs must be exposed "Whereupon Resolved That an office be forthwith established for the department of foreign affairs to be kept always in the place where Congress shall reside. That there shall be a Secretary for the despatch of the business of the said Office to be stiled "Secretary for foreign Affairs." That it shall be the duty of the said Secretary to keep & preserve all the books & papers belonging to the department of foreign affairs; to receive and report the applications of all foreigners; to correspond with the ministers of the United States at foreign Courts and with the Ministers of foreign powers and other persons for the purposes of obtaining the most extensive & useful information relative to foreign affairs to be laid before Congress when required, also to transmit such communications as Congress shall direct to the Ministers of these United States and others at foreign courts & in foreign Countries. The said Secretary shall have liberty to attend Congress, that he may be better informed of the affairs of the United States and have an opportunity of explaining his reports respecting his department. He shall also be authorised to employ one or if necessary more clerks to assist him in the business of his Office: And the Secretary as well as such clerks shall, before the president of Congress take an Oath of fidelity to the United States and an Oath for the faithful execution of their respective trusts.

NA: PCC, item 5, pp. 469-471 (Journal); M247, reel 19.

∽ The Dutch Situation ∽

The Netherlands had declined considerably since its Golden Age of exploration and trade in the seventeenth century. In the Periwig Age, the Dutch were more concerned with investments than trade. Indeed, a reverence for English bonds would go a long way to prevent negotiation of the first American loan. But the Dutch were also allied to Great Britain by two important treaties. The peace treaty of 1674 contained a very liberal interpretation of contraband of war, which allowed the Dutch to sell naval stores to Britain's enemies. The defensive alliance of 1678 required the Dutch to provide Britain with 6,000 men and 20 warships if the latter were attacked. As the Dutch became weaker, they were less and less inclined to provide the British with the military assistance their alliance required. On the other hand, as the Dutch became weaker, the British were less and less inclined to accept the liberal interpretation of contraband contained in the 1674 treaty.

In the eighteenth century, the Netherlands was known as the United Provinces. Its central governing body, the States General, known as Their High Mightinesses, was heavily dependent upon the actions of the seven provinces. Each of these had its assembly, composed of nobles and city deputies. The assemblies were oligarchical; there were no elections, and most of the Dutch people in effect had no voice in government. Dutch cities were autonomous, and city councils were elected according to a complicated system of indirect representation. The head of state (Stadhouder), the Prince of Orange and Nassau, was linked by dynastic ties to the English royal family. In the 1780s, this was the weak and hesitant Willem V, who depended heavily upon the Duke of Brunswick, commander of the army.

The Stadhouder was nominally in charge of foreign relations through a minister called the Greffier, but the States General could override the Prince's decisions. Its permanent secretary, the Grand Pensionary of Holland, performed functions more like those of a minister of foreign affairs than those of the Greffier. The Stadhouder could block change by controlling the votes of one or more of the conservative rural provinces in the States General, where decisions on major questions had to be unanimous. Provinces on the losing end in such situations could make their feelings known by withholding their quotas of the republic's revenues.

The Dutch had two domestic political groups, the supporters of the Stadhouder, sometimes called the Orangists, and the Patriots. The Orangists were conservative, pro-army, and pro-British. The Patriots consisted of two factions with differing views. These were the aristocrats, who opposed the pro-British patronage evident in the Stadhouder's official appointments, and the liberals or democrats, who opposed the Stadhouder because he was against progressive ideas. The Patriots used Britain's difficulties with her American colonies in their ongoing battles with the Stadhouder, but they were not necessarily pro-American.

On March 20, 1775, even before Lexington and Concord, the States General issued a proclamation prohibiting the export of munitions from Dutch harbors, European or colonial, except by special license. In practice, a tremendous clandestine trade sprang up, over British protest, between the Caribbean free port of St. Eustatius and North America. Still, all Dutch political factions wished to preserve the republic's neutrality, and with it the profitability of Dutch financial institutions and the Dutch carrying trade between belligerents. The last thing any self-respecting Dutchman wanted was to go to war.

The French became belligerents in June 1778, and after some initial confusion proclaimed the doctrine of free ships, free goods with regard to neutral shipping. Realizing that the treaty of 1674 would allow the Dutch to supply the French with all the naval stores they needed, the British offered the Dutch a compromise: Britain would not call upon the United Provinces to fulfill their obligations as an ally under the treaty of 1678 if they agreed to regard naval stores as contraband of war subject to seizure. The Dutch, particularly the maritime interests in Amsterdam, were making huge profits from the trade in naval stores, and refused the compromise.

The French now embarked upon a policy of discriminatory duties against Dutch vessels to force the United Provinces to protect their shipping with convoys. The British hesitated to invoke the terms of the 1678 alliance because they realized that this would precipitate a crisis in the Low Countries from which they could derive no benefit. However, France's policy toward the United Provinces produced a gradual swing toward Dutch naval armament for convoy duty in the provincial assemblies.

Spain's declaration of war (June 21, 1779) proved the deciding blow;

the following day the British ambassador presented a formal demand for Dutch adherence to the 1678 alliance. The demand was repeated on November 26, 1779, after the Dutch failed to reply. In December a British force overpowered a Dutch convoy and took several ships carrying naval stores into port, where they were condemned by prize courts. Britain made a third demand for the Dutch to invoke the 1678 alliance on March 21, 1780; when no response was received, an Order in Council (April 17, 1780) declared all Anglo-Dutch treaties void, and authorized the Royal Navy to treat Dutch ships in the same manner as other neutral vessels.

The States General now opted for unlimited convoys and an adequate naval armament. Technically, this amounted to a diplomatic victory for the French. However, the French and Dutch navies together were unable to provide adequate protection for Dutch shipping, which became fair game for British privateers. A possible alternative for protecting Dutch commerce had emerged from Russia, where on February 28, 1780, Empress Catherine II addressed a Declaration to the Courts of London, Versailles, and Madrid announcing the formation of a league of armed neutrals to protect their commerce in conformity with a set of fixed principles. These principles included the doctrine of free ships, free goods, with naval stores not included in the definition of contraband.

On April 3, 1780, Russia invited the United Provinces to accede to this Armed Neutrality. The Dutch first tried to negotiate a guarantee of their colonial possessions by the League, but this was refused. On November 20, 1780, the States General resolved to join the League without the guarantee, but before Dutch plenipotentiaries could deliver the necessary instrument of ratification to St. Petersburg, Great Britain declared war on the United Provinces (December 20, 1780). To the British, a weak enemy was better than having a major neutral serve as the supplier of naval stores that would increase the maritime strength of two already-strong enemies.

Although the real reason for the declaration of war was the Dutch attempt to join the Armed Neutrality, the British claimed that the United Provinces had concluded a secret treaty with the United States. This assertion was based upon a draft treaty of amity and commerce drawn up in the summer of 1778 by William Lee and Amsterdam merchant Jean de Neufville. Neither man was empowered to undertake such negotiations, and neither party regarded the draft treaty as binding. However, Henry Laurens was carrying a copy when he was captured by the British en route to take up his post as U.S. Minister to the United Provinces. British demands that the States General disavow the draft treaty coincided with *that body's deliberations regarding accession to the Armed Neutrality.*

John Adams to Francis Dana

My dear Sir,   Amsterdam Jany 18, 1781.

. . . . .

    This Nation can hardly yet believe that the English are or will be at War with them. – instead of depending upon themselves they now look up to Russia and the northern Powers. if these should fail them, which I think however they cannot, I know not what would be the Consequence.

    But I shall never get a single Ducat, untill it is decided, whether the neutral Union will support the Republick.– Every Party and Every Man almost is afraid to do the least thing, that England can complain of and make a noise about, least the Blame of involving the Country in War should be thrown upon them. What I shall do I know not. – Congress draws upon me, but I shall have no Resource, but from Dr Franklin to pay a Farthing. if that fails me, I am undone. I wish our Countrymen would assume Courage enough, to augment the Taxes upon themselves, and reduce the needless Expences, so as to do without Succours which are unattainable.

    at least I think nothing will ever be done here, untill a Treaty is concluded, between the two Republicks. – There are a Million Jealousies, about the *Escault*, about Trade with Emperors Dominions, about the Succession of the Empire or rather another Election in the House of Austria &c &c &c. Individuals dare nothing in this Country, untill the Countenance of government is given, nor in any other part of Europe. a Treaty with this Country is so great a Work that it would require Time, and this is said not to be the proper time to talk about it.

    Affectionately yours   John Adams

MHS: The Adams Papers, microfilm reel 102 (LBkC).

Memoir of Comte de Vergennes on the Methods of Concluding a Truce with Great Britain

[Translation]

February 1781.

. . . . .

In summarizing the details into which we have just entered, we find the following propositions:

1st It is up to the King of England, author of the war, to make Sacrifices to obtain peace.

2nd The first of the Sacrifices to make is the independence of North America.

3rd This independence can be assured by a definitive Treaty or by a Truce.

4th The King of England, whatever form may be adopted, may treat directly with the Americans with the intervention of the two Mediating Powers.

5th The Truce will be for many years, such as 20, 25, 30 years, &c. The United States will be treated as independent in fact, and there will be no restriction placed on the exercise of the rights of Sovereignty.

6th It would be desirable that the *Status quo* may be avoided; but in case it cannot, it will be proper to limit it to South Carolina and to Georgia, and to stipulate the evacuation of New-York.

7th The proposal of the Truce cannot be made to Congress by the King, if it must be linked to that of the *Status quo*; but by isolating these two proposals His Majesty can take it upon himself to persuade Congress to subscribe to the Truce if he has the secret assurance that New-York will be excepted.

8th In the event of a Truce, the King will propose to the Americans, if there is need, a new Convention the object of which will be to reassure them against attacks by England after the expiration of the Truce.

We think we should conclude the present memoir with the following remark. It is by necessity and not by choice that the King is making War on Great Britain; His Majesty has made, up to now, the greatest efforts to sustain the weight of it: would he wish to lose the fruit of such expenditures by yielding on the principal subject of the Contest? Such a Sacrifice could only be justified by the greatest reverses and by the impossiblity of repairing them. If it were the fruit of weakness or of inconstancy, it would tarnish forever the glory and the reputation of His Majesty.

England's means are ready to be exhausted; she is without an ally, her forces are inferior to those of the House of Bourbon; in this state of affairs we can ask the King to be magnanimous; but his condescensions should undermine neither his dignity nor his interest.

FFMA: Pol. Corr., U.S., v. 15, f. 269-278 (LC transcription).

Chevalier de la Luzerne to Marquis de Castries

[Translation]

N° 45. 4ᵗʰ·   Philadelphia, 3 February 1781
Monsieur le Marquis[1]

I have the honor to send you a copy of a resolution passed by Congress relative to the navigation of neutrals. That assembly permits all the nations to navigate and trade freely on the coasts of this continent. It places only those restrictions on that Right which are contained in its treaty of commerce and amity with the King, and it appears determined to make that treaty the basis of the engagements it may be in a position to make with the other powers relative to navigation.

· · · · · ·

le chr de la Luzerne

FFAA: Pol Corr., U.S., v. 15, f. 52 (LC transcription).
[1] Castries, Charles-Eugène-Gabriel, Marquis de (1727-1801). French military leader and government official. Minister of the Navy, 1780-1787. Created marshal of France, 1783. Governor of Flanders and Hainaut, 1787-1790. Emigrated 1790, commanded forces opposing the revolutionary army in 1792, supported Louis XVIII in exile.

Benjamin Franklin to Comte de Vergennes

Sir,   Passy, Febʸ 13, 1781.

I have just received from Congress their Letter for the King, which I have the honour of putting herewith into the hands of your Excellency.

I am charged at the same time to "represent in the strongest Terms the unalterable Resolution of the United States to maintain their Liberties and Independence, and inviolably to adhere to the Alliance at every hazard, and in every Event; And that the Misfortunes of the last Campaign, instead of repressing have redoubled their Ardour; That Congress are resolved to employ every Resource in their Power to expel the Enemy from every Part of the United States, by the most vigorous and decisive Cooperation with Marine and other Forces of their illustrious Ally; That they have accordingly called on the several States for a powerful Army and ample Supplies of Provisions; and that the States are disposed effectually to comply with their Requisitions. That if in Aid of their own Exertions, the Court of France can be prevailed on to assume a Naval Superiority in the American Seas; to furnish the Arms, Ammunition and Cloathing specified in the Estimate heretofore transmitted, and to assist with the Loan mentioned in the Letter, they flatter themselves that under the divine

Blessing the War must speedily be terminated with Glory and Advantage to both Nations."

By several Letters to me from intelligent Persons it appears that the great and expensive Exertions of the last Year, by which a Force was assembled capable of facing the Enemy, and which accordingly drew towards New York and lay long near that City, was rendered ineffectual by the Superiority of the Enemy at Sea; and that their Success in Carolina, had been chiefly owing to that Superiority, & to the Want of the necessary Means for furnishing, marching and paying the Expence of Troops sufficient to defend that Province.

The Marquis de la Fayette writes to me that it is impossible to conceive, without seeing it, the Distress the Troops have suffered for want of Cloathing; and the following is a Paragraph of a Letter from General Washington, which I ought not to keep back from your Excellency Viz:

"I doubt not you are so fully informed by Congress of our political and military State, that it would be superfluous to trouble you with any thing relative to either. If I were to speak on Topicks of the kind, it would be to shew, that our present Situation makes one of two Things essential to us, – a *Peace* – or the most vigorous Aid of our Allies, particularly in the Article of *Money* – Of their Disposition to serve us we cannot doubt: Their Generosity will do every thing their Means will permit."

They had in America great Expectations, I know not on what Foundation, that a considerable Supply of Money would be obtain'd from Spain; but that Expectation has failed And the Force of that Nation in those Seas, has been employ'd to reduce small Forts in Florida, without rendring any direct assistance to the United States: And indeed the long Delay of that Court in acceding to the Treaty of Commerce, begins to have the Appearance of its not inclining to have any Connection with us; so that for effectual Friendship, in the present Conjuncture, we can rely on France alone, & in the Continuance of the King's Goodness towards us.

I am grown old. I feel myself much enfeebled by my late long Illness, and it is probable I shall not long have any more Concern in these affairs. I therefore take this Occasion to express my Opinion to your Excellency, that the present Conjuncture is critical; that there is some Danger lest the Congress should lose its Influence over the People, if it is found unable to procure the Aids that are wanted; and that the whole System of the new Government in America may thereby be shaken. That if the English are suffer'd once to recover that Country, such an Opportunity of effectual Separation as the present, may not occur again in the Course of Ages; and that the Possession of those fertile and extensive Regions & that vast Sea Coast, to afford them so broad a Basis for future Greatness by the rapid Growth of their Commerce, and Breed of Seamen and Soldiers, as will enable them to become the Terror of Europe, and to exercise with Impunity that Insolence which is so natural to their Nation, and which will increase enormously with the Increase of their Power.

I am, with great Respect, Your Excellency's &ᶜᵃ   B. Franklin

NA: PCC, item 82, v. 1, pp. 313-317 (C); M247, reel 108.

Instructions to John Jay from the Continental Congress

Sir,   [Philadelphia], 15 February 1781

Congress having since their Instructions to you of the 29th of September 1779 and the 4th of October 1780, relative to the Claim of the United States to the free Navigation of the river Mississippi, and to a free Port or Ports below the 31st Degree of North Latitude, resumed the Consideration of that Subject, and being desirous to manifest to all the World, and particularly to his Catholic Majesty, the Moderation of their Views, the high Value they place on the Friendship of his Catholic Majesty and their Disposition to remove every resonable Obstacle to his Accession to the Alliance subsisting between his most Christian Majesty and these United States, in order to unite the more closely in their Measures and Operations three Powers who have so great an Unity of Interests, and thereby compel the common Enemy to a speedy, just and honorable Peace, have *resolved*, and you are hereby instructed to recede from the Instructions above referred to, so far as they insist on the free Navigation of that Part of the River Mississippi which lies below the 31st Degree of North Latitude, and on a free Port or Ports below the same, provided such Cession shall be unalterably insisted upon by Spain and provided the free Navigation of the said River above the said Degree of North Latitude shall be acknowledged and guaranteed by his Catholic Majesty to the Citizens of the United States in Common with his own Subjects. It is the Order of Congress at the same Time that you exert every possible Effort to obtain from his Catholic Majesty the Use of the River aforesaid with a free Port or Ports below the said 31st Degree of North Latitude, for the Citizens of the United States, under such Regulations and Restrictions only as may be a necessary safe Guard against illicit Commerce.

By order of Congress.   Sam. Huntington, President

Morris, Jay Papers, v. 2, p. 62.

Benjamin Franklin to John Adams

Sir,   Passy, Feb. 22. 1781

.   .   .   .   .

I have lately made a fresh & strong Application for more Money. I have
not yet received a positive Answer. I have, however, two of the Christian
Graces, Faith and Hope: But my Faith is only that of which the Apostle
Speaks, the Evidence of Things not seen. For in Truth I do not see at
present how so many Bills drawn at random on our Ministers in France,
Spain and Holland, are to be paid; nor that any thing but omnipotent
Necessity can excuse the Imprudence of it. — Yet I think the Bills drawn
upon us by the Congress ought at all Risques to be accepted. I shall
accordingly use my best Endeavors to procure Money for their honourable
Discharge against they become due, if you should not in the mean time be
provided; And if those Endeavours fail, I shall be ready to break, run away,
or go to Prison with you, as it shall please God.

.   .   .   .   .

With great Respect, I have the honour to be, Sir, Your most obedient &
most humble Servant   B. Franklin

MHS: *The Adams Papers, microfilm reel 354 (ALS).*

Chevalier de la Luzerne to Comte de Vergennes

[Translation]

N°· 124. Triplicate.   Philadelphia, 2 March 1781
My Lord

.   .   .   .   .

Yesterday the Delegates from Maryland signed the Act of Confederation,
which is finally consummated after three and a half years of delays. The
accomplishment of this work caused a univeral joy, and the people who had
advance knowledge of it seemed disposed to give it all possible efficacy.
Congress celebrated this event with a public repast; the grand flag of the
thirteen States was unfurled, the cannon of the City and those of the Port
made repeated discharges; all the bells rang, and the day ended with
fireworks.

The President wrote to inform me that the confederation was definitively
ratified; I went to make him my compliments, and in the conversation that

I had with him on this subject, he told me that among the Causes that rendered this event important for the Thirteen States and agreeable to the People, the desire to give new force to the alliance was one of the principal ones, and Congress regarded the ties that unite it to the King as more indissoluble, if it is possible, than they have ever been in the past. I weighed whether it was advisable to seize this occasion to make insinuations to Congress touching on a new ratification of the Treaties of Alliance and of Commerce, but it seemed to me that the single Supposition that the preceding one was insufficient would imply that the Powers given by Congress to its Ministers to treat were equally insufficient; I consequently abstained from all observation in this regard; Congress on its part seems to have perceived the inconveniences which a new Sanction of the various acts that emanated from its authority before the accomplishment of the Confederation would have given, and despite the penchant that some Delegates showed for this Step, Congress abstained from it.

The articles of Confederation, fixed at the number of Thirteen on 15 November 1777, are by everyone's consent an incomplete and irregular System of government. They were the work of many enlightened Delegates, but the incompatibility of interest of various States and the necessity of not alarming the people as to the extent of the Powers that their leaders were conferring on themselves, obliged them to make alterations in their plan, all the disadvantages of which are perceived. Changes were often proposed, before the accession of Maryland, that would have been more practical then than today. But they did not take place, and Article 13 declares that the laws of the Confederation "must be inviolably observed by each State, that the union must be perpetual, and that these laws will receive no alteration unless it be decided in Congress and then ratified by the Legislatures of the various States." This last clause postpones any kind of change to a distant time, and one can regard the articles of Confederation as having to subsist invariably until the invaded States are delivered from the enemy and free to deliberate on interior and general affairs. In addition, Congress will take a more regular form; that assembly conformed only very imperfectly to the laws that it prescribed. A few States followed them rigorously. Some were represented only by one Delegate; others were not represented at all, many Members were in office from the commencement of the Confederation, although by Article 5 they cannot serve more than three years in the space of six. Some delegates, contrary to the tenor of the same article, sat in Congress although invested with offices that subordinated them to its authority. These irregularities and several others should be reformed; but the most important change that should result from this event is the nomination of several Ministers charged with directing the various Departments.

This measure is finally decided, but it has not yet been placed in execution. I will have the honor of reporting immediately to you what will happen in that regard.

I am with Respect, My Lord, Your very humble and very obedient servant,   le che de la luzerne

FFAA: Pol. Corr., U. S., v. 15, f. 78 (LC transcription).

Memorial from John Adams to the States General of the United Provinces of the Netherlands

The Hague 8 March 1781.

High and Mighty Lords,

The Subscriber, a Minister Plenipotentiary from the united States of america, has the Honour to lay before your High Mightinesses, as one of the high contracting Parties to the Marine Treaty, lately concluded relative to the Rights of neutral Vessells, a Resolution of Congress of the fifth of October last, concerning the same Subject.

As the American revolution, furnished the occasion of a Reformation in the Maritime Law of nations, of so much importance to a free communication among mankind, by Sea, the Subscriber hopes it may not be thought improper, that the United States should become Parties to it, entitled to its Benefits, and Subject to its Duties. to this end, the Subscriber has the Honour of requesting, that the resolution of Congress may be taken into the consideration of your High Mightinesses, and transmitted to the Courts of Russia, Sweeden and Denmark.

The Subscriber beg leaves to Subjoin, that he should Esteem it, one of the most fortunate Events of his Life, if this proposition should meet with the approbation of your high Mightinesses, and the other Powers who are Parties to the neutral Confederacy, and he should be admitted, as the Instrument of pledging the Faith of the united States, to the observance, of regulations, which do so much Honour to the present Age.

John Adams

NA: PCC, item 101, v. 1, pp. 164-165 (LBkC); M247, reel 127.

Comte de Vergennes to Chevalier de la Luzerne

[Translation]

N⁰· 14.   Versailles, 9 March 1781.

I must reply to you, Sir, concerning several articles enclosed with the despatches that you have done me the honor of writing me from N⁰· 107 to N⁰· 114 inclusive.

The resolution that Congress has passed relative to the principles adopted by the association of neutrals, could not be wiser; I have hastened to send it to Russia, and I am persuaded in advance that it will be agreeable to the Empress. I do not have the same opinion, Sir, with respect to the nomination of Mr. Dana. Catherine II has made it her duty until now to display the greatest impartiality, and this conduct is the result of the hope of that Power to restore peace through its mediation. In this state of affairs, she would not be able to permit herself any action which would indicate on her part the slightest propensity in the Americans' favor, because she would appear suspect to the English, and would run the risk of being excluded by them from the mediation. Thus the nomination of Mr. Dana seems to me at least premature, and I am of the opinion that this Deputy must in no way make use of it at this time; that is at least the counsel that I will give him if he judges it appropriate to consult me, for it seems to me that that is stipulated to him. It would be infinitely disagreeable for Congress, as you have wisely observed, to experience a refusal; its dignity would be wounded thereby, and it is a satisfaction of which it is appropriate to deprive the Court of London. It will suffice to sound out the Court of St. Petersburg when it has revealed its principles concerning the Americans, and so we will not neglect anything to work towards the admission of their plenipotentiary. You will be able to give assurance of this to Congress.

I am sorry to learn, Sir, that all my despatches have not reached you; you will see by the numbers of those that I am sending you today that you are missing several, of which N⁰ˢ· 8 and 10 are relative to Mr. John Adams; they comprise our way of thinking with regard to the conduct, the principles, and the person of this plenipotentiary. I confess to you, Sir, that whatever good opinion I may have of his patriotism, I regret seeing him charged with a task as difficult and as delicate as that of the peacemaking, because he has a rigidity, an arrogance, and an obstinacy that will cause him to foment a thousand unfortunate incidents and to drive his conegotiators to despair. But I sense the impossiblity of making him change his direction, I especially sense the reluctance that Congress would have in making a decision, and the trouble that would result therefrom for Mr.

Adams, thus you will be able to abstain from taking steps to obtain his recall; you will merely be making Congress feel the necessity of prohibiting this plenipotentiary from making any move without the consent of the King, and of letting himself be directed by me or by the person who will take part in the peace negociations in the name of His Majesty. You will neglect nothing, Sir, to have Mr. Adams given instructions such as I have just indicated; that seems to me of the more consequence, for as allies of the United States we must defend their cause and serve as support to their representative, and should we abandon him in unjust or impossible matters, he would hold us out to Congress as weak or even ill-intentioned friends, and there would be established in the sight of the other negotiators an improper contradiction, which would not miss causing a scandal.

It is the more important, Sir, that the instructions in question be promptly expedited, for the time for putting them into effect seems to be not very far off, as you will be able to judge from the following facts.

The English Ministry, in the erroneous belief that it would bring that of Madrid to a separate peace, has sought to enter into a secret negotiation with it: but nothing has come of it until now because the propositions of the Court of Spain have had as their basis the engagements which the King has contracted with the United States. However, the English emissary continues to reside in Madrid, although he is without any hope of fulfilling the object of his mission. In spite of the knowledge that all Europe has of the direct negotiation of which I have just spoken, the Empress of Russia, excited by motives that it would be useless to explain, has invited the King and the Court of London to invoke her mediation; this latter Court, regarding the mediation as formally offered, has accepted it rather eagerly, and has invited the Emperor to participate. As for the King, he has replied, in substance, that he would be delighted to attain peace through the intercession of Catherine II, but that it was not yet in his power to accept the offers of that Princess because he has allies whose consent would be necessary. The Court of Madrid, solicited as we were, has replied for its part that having opened a direct negotiation, it believed it should await the issue of it before having recourse to a mediation.

The Emperor, called upon by the Court of London, as I have just observed, has yielded to the desire of that Court in complying with its invitation, and that Prince has not delayed in informing the King and in offering his co-mediation to him and to the Catholic King at the same time. His Majesty has made almost the same response to this new offer as to that of the Empress of Russia. As for the King of Spain, he has expressed astonishment that the English Ministry was courting mediators while it still pursues a direct negotiation; and he has announced that while the English themselves have not broken off this negotiation, it would be impossible for him to countenance a mediation, which otherwise would be extremely agreeable to him.

These different responses are regarded as an eventual acceptance of mediation, and in fact it will be difficult for us to avoid it; a refusal on our part would seriously wound the dignity of the two powers that have offered it, while we have the greatest interest in treating them with respect. Besides, our demands are so just, so moderate, that we risk nothing by making them in such a tribunal as this may be. We also have no legitimate motive for declining the mediation of the two Courts.

But as I have remarked above, Sir, we have postponed until now our formal acceptance, because of not knowing the intentions of our allies, who are Spain and the United States. We have reason to flatter ourselves that this conduct will be appreciated by Congress, and that it will furnish a new proof of the King's perseverance in the principles of the alliance, and of his scrupulous exactitude in fulfilling its obligations. In informing Congress in confidence of all the facts that I have just set forth, you will point out that it is urgent that Congress communicate to the King the intentions of the United States concerning the proposed mediation, and that it authorize His Majesty to make them known to all the powers that will take part in the peacemaking. I do not doubt, Sir, that Congress is eager to imitate the example of the King in appearing disposed to receive the peace from the hands of the Emperor and of the Empress of Russia; that assembly may count on the justice of these two Sovereigns; besides, it should be persuaded that His Majesty will defend the cause of the United States with the same zeal with which it attends to the interests of His Crown.

I do not speak to you, Sir, of the conditions on which the Americans should make peace, because the discussion of this matter would at least be premature, and because it would give rise to endless deliberations, and that would divert Congress from the present matter, which is the establishment of the mediation. But I think that you would do very well to observe, as from yourself, to the principal members of that assembly that, from all appearances, the Court of London will treat with as much exigence as obstinacy the points which concern America, because it will cost it a great deal, seeing that it is renouncing forever that vast Region, and you will emphasize this thought in order to make Congress feel the necessity of currying the favor of the mediators by putting into their demands (save for independence, which is not susceptible to any modification) all the moderation and all the reserve of which they are capable. In addition, you will point out to the principal members of Congress that it is possible that the difficuty of effecting a definitive peace may cause the mediators to propose a truce, that it is consequently necessary for the plenipotentiary of the United States to be authorized contingently to make known their determination on that subject.

Perhaps you will be asked for your counsel on the part that it is appropriate for Congress to take in this regard: in that case you will respond that you are without instructions on this matter, that consequently you would not have an opinion; this discretion is necessary in the present circumstances, and we will get out of it only as much as the mediating Courts will have asked us, because we will then present their ideas and not our own, and we will in this way avoid reproaches or at least suspicions, if they are not to the liking of the United States. But it is above all important that you inform Congress that, whether they treat of peace or only for a truce, it is necessary to push the war with the greatest vigor, because that will be the most efficacious means of bringing the English to reason and of obtaining honorable conditions. You will also warn the president of Congress that if the offer of mediation from the two imperial Courts takes a decided-enough turn that the King is obliged to explain himself categorically, His Majesty will accept it conditionally for himself and for the United States. This choice will have so many fewer drawbacks that no currently subsisting reason would prevent them from following the King's example in confiding their interests to mediators as wise as they are enlightened, and a refusal might bring about results as unfortunate as they are incalculable.   Vergennes

FFAA: Pol. Corr., U.S., v. 15, f. 90 (LC transcription).

John Adams to the President of Congress

Sir,   Leyden March 19th 1781.

I have received your Excellency's Letter of the first of January, with the Commission and Instructions inclosed. I am very sensible of this fresh Instance of the Confidence of Congress, and shall do every thing in my Power to discharge the Duties of this new Trust: but I am obliged to say, that no Commission that ever was given, required more Patience, Fortitude and Circumspection than this; Virtues which I much fear have not fallen in sufficient Quantities to my Share.

I have experienced, since my Residence in this Republick, a great Change in the external Behaviour of Several Persons of Rank, who upon my first Arrival received me with distinction; but from the moment of the Publication of the Papers taken with Mr. Laurens have been afraid to see me. The Nation has indeed been in a violent Fermentation and Crisis. It is divided in Sentiments. There are Stadthouderians and Republicans: there are Proprietors in English Funds and Persons immediately engaged in

Commerce: there are Enthusiasts for Peace and Alliance with England, and there are Advocates for an Alliance with France, Spain and America, and there are a third Sort, who are for adhering in all things to Russia, Sweeden and Denmark. Some are for acknowledging American Independence, and entering into Treaties of Commerce and Alliance with her; others start at the Idea with horror, as an everlasting Impediment to a return to the Friendship and Alliance with England. Some will not augment the Navy without increasing the Army; others will let the Navy be neglected rather than augment the Army. In this perfect Chaos of Sentiments and Systems, Principles and Interests, it is no wonder there is Languor, a Weakness and Irresolution that is vastly dangerous in the present Circumstances of Affairs. The Danger lies not more in the hostile designs and exertions of the English, than from Seditions and Commotions among the People, which are every day dreaded and expected. If it were not for a Standing Army and Troops posted about in several Cities, it is probable there would have been popular Tumults before now. But everybody that I see appears to me to live in constant Fear of Mobs, and in a great degree of Uncertainty, whether they will rise in favour of War or against it; in favour of England or against it; in favor of the Prince, or of the City of Amsterdam; in favour of America or against it. I have ventured in the midst of these critical Circumstances, pressed as I am to get Money to discharge the Bills of Exchange which Congress have drawn and I have accepted, to open a Loan: but this is looked upon as a very hardy ~~measure~~: and dangerous measure, which nobody but an American would have risqued, and I am obliged to assure Congress, that People are as yet so much afraid of being pointed out by the Mob, or the Soldiery, as Favourers of this Loan, that I have no hopes at all of succeeding for several Months, if ever.

I have been advised to do nothing in Consequence of my Commission to the States at present, for fear of throwing before the People new Objects of Division and Dissention. I have however communicated to their high Mightinesses, and to the Ministers of Russia, Denmark, Sweeden and France the Resolution of Congress of the fifth of October, relative to the principles of the neutral Confederation. The Memorial and Letters I have transmitted to Congress.

Whenever I shall communicate to their high Mightinesses the full Powers of Congress, the Course will be this – they will lie long upon the Table – then taken *ad referendum*, That is sent to the several Provinces, Cities and Bodies of Nobles, who compose the Sovereignty, or as some say the Deputies of the Sovereignty: these will deliberate, and deliberate and deliberate, and probably some will be for and some against making a Treaty, at least it is supposed that Zealand and one or two other Provinces will be against it. But in the mean time, there will be much Communication and

Negotiation among Individuals at least, between this Country and Russia, Sweeden and Denmark upon the Subject; and if it is true, as I am informed in a Letter from M^r· Gerry, that a Minister is appointed to the Court of Petersbourg, as I hope it is, and that the same minister, or some other is impowered to treat with Sweeden and Denmark, it is not impossible, I think it indeed probable, that We may succeed with those four Nations at once; for let me add, there is not in my apprehension the least prospect of a general Peace. England is at her old Game of Seduction and Division, and is labouring under the Pretence of employing the Emperor of Germany and the Empress of Russia in Mediations for Peace, insidiously to embroil all Europe in the War. From Motives of Philanthropy, I hope She will not succeed, unless the same feelings of Humanity should prompt me to wish all Mankind at War with that Nation, for her Humiliation, which is at this time, if ever one was, *Hostis humani Generis.*   John Adams

NA: PCC, *Misc. Papers, Adams Despatches (LS)*; M332, reel 1, ff. 283-285.

Chevalier de la Luzerne to Comte de Vergennes

[Translation]

N^o· 128 Duplicate.   Philadelphia, 20 March 1781
My Lord.

. . . . .

I must, My Lord, present to you with frankness my opinion on the terrors of which Mr. Deane[1] has told you concerning the zeal and the dispositions of the people and the discredit into which Congress has fallen. One and a half years of observation and of the most regular attention gives me the right to oppose my sentiment to his in many regards. Mr. Deane does not think he has reason to be satisfied with Congress; I am far from pronouncing upon the disagreeable discussion of which he and Mr. Lee have been the subjects, but it is a fact unfortunately too true that he was the first to put before the eyes of the public the papers from his trial and that he gave the first impulsion to all the cabals that have since divided Congress and, I could almost say, the thirteen States for almost a year. Congress has lost precious time in considering whether Mr. Deane or Mr. Lee was wrong or right, whether the latter should or should not have been recalled, whether it was advisable or not to leave Mr. Franklin in place. These debates have afflicted all the good citizens, and Congress is itself so humiliated by the Scandal that it has indicated, on this occasion, that it ordered, seven to eight months ago, that all the printed copies of the journal of the year 1779 be suppressed and that it be reprinted without the debates that took place in the course of that dispute. This reprinting is well advanced, but they were not able to destroy all the old copies, which will be a sad monument to the spirit of disunion that has so long prevailed. Mr. Deane, who has not then obtained the satisfaction that he demanded, has carried to Europe sad impressions against Congress, without observing that he is himself the primary cause of all this trouble. Mr. Lee is then come, and has spared neither intrigues nor tricks of all kinds to renew the disorder. He has found partisans in Congress; there was some movement in his favor, there is still some, but he has not been able even to give his party the consistency that it had when Mr. Deane was the opponent. I have been solicited by many persons who would have desired to see me take an active part in the quarrel of these two adversaries, but, in following to the letter the instructions that you have given me, I have held myself apart, and the dispute has abated on its own. I thought however that I should emerge from this inactivity when it was a question of making Mr. Lee Secretary of State in the Department of Foreign Affairs, and I do not doubt that the conduct that I have pursued on this occasion, and which I will have the honor to report to you, has induced him to number me among his enemies. It is equally possible that Mr. Deane is not content with me because I did not want to take any part in his affairs; but I had to try to keep Congress united; and although all party spirit is not entirely banished from it, for a long time there has been less of it than today. It is not only the publicity of this discussion that has struck a blow at the consideration which this Body has enjoyed during the first years of its existence. Public loss of credit has contributed no less to this change. In the beginning Congress had only to produce the funds necessary for the conduct of the war, trust was complete, the confidence and patriotism of the people made up for the power of which their leaders were destitute. The length of the war has deadened these sentiments, the abuse that was made in 1777, in 1778, and in 1779 of the ability of printing money has depreciated it to the point that Congress has perceived the necessity of denying itself this resource, but those by which it can make up the deficiency are necessarily insufficient and slow. These circumstances have contributed to diminish its consideration and its powers. But although it can only, in regard to its constitution and to that of the thirteen States, recover it slowly, I can assure you positively, My Lord, that its dissolution is not to be feared as long as the war lasts. It was not so even before the accession of Maryland to the Confederation, but it has become impossible since the union was accomplished, and I hope that Congress will gradually recover not all its former stability, but at least that which is necessary to keep its armies at the ready, to recruit them, and to treat without difficulty of subjects relative to peace and war.

· · · · ·

le che de la luzerne

FFAA: Pol.Corr., U.S., v. 16, f. 1 (LC transcription).

¹ Deane, Silas (1737-1789). Connecticut lawyer and merchant, diplomat. Member, Continental Congress, 1774-1776. Sent to France to procure military supplies in return for colonial produce, 1776. With the help of Caron de Beaumarchais, dispatched eight shiploads of military supplies, 1777, as well as many European military officers. With Benjamin Franklin and Arthur Lee, appointed a commissioner to France, September 1776. Signed Franco-American treaties of alliance and amity and commerce, February 6, 1778. Accused of financial improprieties by Arthur Lee, he was recalled later that year. Unable to clear his name because of accounting inadequacies, Deane became embittered and wrote letters urging reconciliation with Great Britain that appeared in a New York loyalist newspaper in 1781. He passed the remainder of his life in bankrupt exile.

Chevalier de la Luzerne to Comte de Vergennes

[Translation]

N°· 129. 1ˢᵗ·   Philadelphia, 21 March 1781

My Lord

The taking of all the Vessels which were at St. Eustatius, numbering thirty-nine, has occasioned a general desolation among the merchants who carried on this commerce.¹ It is thought that the city of Philadelphia alone loses thereby two and a half million livres tournois.² However, the loss falls principally on the Quakers and others ill-intentioned, who have not ceased since the commencement of the war to conduct an immense commerce with England by way of the neutral Islands or through Amsterdam. I thought the moment favorable to explain myself in a private manner with several delegates, on the bad policy of those who conducted this commerce, on the indecency and the danger of the continual liaisons that exist between the Americans and the English, on what recently happened to Governor Trumbull's son in London,³ and on the facility with which many Englishmen are tolerated in the Midst of the Continent. They argued the impossibility of breaking off suddenly and without reserve all the ties that united the two nations, ties all the stronger because the colonies had no other connection before the revolution, because all their affairs were in the hands of English merchants, and because the operations of commerce were too complicated for the Firms to be able to be dissolved at once and for commerce to be able to take its direction entirely through other channels; notwithstanding these observations, Congress seems to me disposed to take efficacious measures to prevent St. Croix and St. Thomas from taking the place of St. Eustatius and to place limits on the smuggling done through New York, through the Bermudas, and even directly with England; I had some writings published at the same time that will be joined to this despatch, and it seems to me that they are rather disposed to adopt the ideas that they contain and to oppose more secure barriers than in the past to commercial and other forms of liaisons between the Americans and the English. These dispositions, which I shall not allow to abate, should procure for the Kingdom requests for more considerable merchandise than in the past, and our negotiation of letters of exchange, so ruinous from the one side, will at least have this advantage, that they will facilitate the extraction of merchandise from France for this Continent; but I must here renew an observation of the American merchants. They agree that many of our goods are, for equal quality, less expensive than those from England, but they complain of the slowness of the shipments; their commerce with England was so well organized that a ship was in the process of leaving eight to ten days after its arrival; all Sorts of reasons prevent the same speed from being able to take place in our Ports, and this slowness absorbs a great part of the profits; I am not capable of indicating the remedies that could be brought to bear on it; but if any exist, it is very important to apply them at once, because it seems to me that the sailings for L'Orient and other Ports of the Kingdom will multiply in the course of this year. At this very moment, many merchants whose ships were about to set sail for St. Eustatius or Amsterdam are changing their destinations and sending them to L'Orient or to the Ports of Sweden.

Another subject no less essential than that of the speed of the shipments is the diminution of the risks of the crossing. English goods imported into New York, Bermuda, and St. Eustatius arrive there well convoyed; the merchants, knowing with some certitude at what time these convoys arrive, are in consequence prepared, the insurance is less, and they can sell their goods at a much better profit than the Americans can sell ours. If it were possible that their ships were convoyed at known times, and I were in a position to inform them of it, I do not doubt that they would apply themselves to the commerce of France with more ardor than in the past, and this subject merits all the more attention because a large quantity of merchandise has recently arrived from England in New York and Charlestown.

Permit, My Lord, that the part of this despatch that you have just read be equally addressed to M. the Marquis de Castries. I shall add that the losses suffered by the first French merchants who brought merchandise to this continent four or five years ago have deterred the greater part of the others from applying themselves to this commerce. However, the small number of those who now pursue it have profited from the reverses which the first ones experienced. Instead of abandoning the conduct of their affairs to the Americans, they have correspondents or associates residing in America. The latter know all about the changes in paper money, they are preparing returns for their correspondents and are charged with the sale of cargoes, and in general their affairs are rather solid.

As for those of the King's subjects who have so unfortunately been victims of their haste to enter into relations of commerce with the Americans, I have received up to now only the orders contained in despatch N°· 7 that you have done me the honor to write me; N°· 8 has not yet arrived. I have abstained, as you have prescribed for me, from any ministerial step, but I have not let any occasion escape to represent forcefully how horrible it would be if the only friends the Americans have found in their distress were punished by the ruin of their fortunes for the confidence that they have shown them. I have found no one who was of my opinion. Leaving aside the penury in which Congress finds itself, I confess that I know no way of remedying this state of affairs. It is impossible to determine the quantity of paper that is in the hands of Frenchmen, and if Congress could make a resolution in their favor, it is not doubtful that the principal part of the paper would soon pass into their hands. Besides, it has continually depreciated since the end of 1777, and it is almost impossible to know whether those who received it at different times have saved it or have rid themselves of it, or to determine with precision at what time they received it; it is even known that most of them, after having lost considerably therein, have converted it into loan certificates, in the fear of suffering still more considerable losses. Mr. John Adams appears either of bad faith or very badly informed in the fact of the matter, when he undertakes to prove that our merchants have not lost. It would have been more just if he had limited himself to exposing the impossiblity of according them a redress, and I confess, My Lord, that pained as much as one can be by the losses that our commerce has suffered, I do not see any way to procure compensation for individuals. Nevertheless, I shall execute your orders when I have received them, and while waiting for them, I seize every occasion that presents itself to inculcate in Congress that it is simple justice to direct the commerce of the thirteen States towards France, in order to compensate the nation at least for the losses that a number of individuals have had.

· · · · ·

le chr de la luzerne

FFAA: Pol. Corr., U.S., v. 16, f. 3 (LC transcription).

[1] *British Admiral Sir George Rodney captured the Dutch island of St. Eustatius, together with all 130 ships in its harbor, on February 3, 1781. Presumably, 39 of the 130 vessels were American.*

[2] *Livre tournois.* French monetary unit, equivalent to the modern franc, minted at Tours and consisting of 20 sous. The livre tournois differed from the livre parisis, which was minted at Paris and consisted of 25 sous. The word livre, when referring to British money, means pound sterling.

[3] *Trumbull, John (1756-1843).* Artist. Youngest son of Connecticut Governor Jonathan Trumbull. Continental Army officer, 1775-1777. Went to London to study painting under Benjamin West, 1780. Arrested on November 19, 1780, on suspicion of treason (possibly as a reprisal for the death of Major André) and imprisoned until Charles James Fox and Edmund Burke secured his release. Returned to London to study with West in 1784; began work on Revolutionary War studies in 1786. Private secretary to John Jay, envoy extraordinary to Great Britain, 1794. Painted four Revolutionary War scenes for the Capitol Rotunda, 1817-1824.

John Adams to John Jay

Sir,   Leyden March 28[th.] 1781.

It is so long since I wrote you, that I am almost ashamed to recollect. I have been in this most curious Country, among the most incomprehensible People and under the most Singular Constitution of Government in the World. I have not been able to write You, what could or would be done here, because I was not able to discover, nor did I ever yet find one Man in the Country, who would pretend to say what Course the Republic would take.

At this moment, altho' I think there cannot be a Peace between them and England; yet I dont see a probability of their being in earnest in the War for Some time.

I can tell You one Thing however for certain, that the Conduct of Spain has great Influence here. Her delay in acknowledging our Independence contributes amazingly to the Indecision of the Republic. If Spain had fully entered into the System this Country would soon follow.

I must therefore beg of You to communicate to me as much concerning this Subject, as you are at Liberty to do. All Nations it is to be feared will wait for Spain, and thus prolong the Evils of War to unnecessary lengths. My best Compliments to your Family, and believe me to be, with great Esteem, Sir, your most obedient Servant   John Adams

Columbia University Libraries: John Jay Papers (LS).

John Adams to Benjamin Franklin

Sir,   Leyden April 10ᵗʰ 1781.

. . . . .

I have received advice from Congress of more Bills drawn upon me: when they arrive and are presented, I must write You concerning them and desire You to enable me to discharge them: for I am sorry to be obliged to say, that although I have opened a Loan according to the best Plan I could, and the Plan and the Loan seems to be countenanced by the Public, yet there is little Money obtained – scarcely enough to defray the Expence of Obligations and Stamps; and it is daily more and more clear to me, that We shall never obtain a Loan here; until our Independence is acknowledged by the States: – 'till then every Man seems to be afraid, that his having any thing to do in it, will be made a foundation of a criminal Process or a Provocation to the Resentment of the Mob.

. . . . .

I have the Honour to be, with the greatest Respect, Sir, your most obedient and most humble Servant.   John Adams.

APS: Benjamin Franklin Papers (LS).

Benjamin Franklin to John Jay

Dear Sir,   Passy, April 12. 1781.

. . . . .

I was much pleas'd to learn that you have obtained a Promise for 150,000 Dollars; your Reflection on the Consequence is just. – As this Sum must be used in Payment of the Bills, drawn upon you, and probably no Part of it can be apply'd to your Subsistance, I desire that you would draw upon me for half a Year of your Salaries immediately, at 30 Days Sight; and for the future while I stay here, draw quarterly, until you receive Remittances or can obtain a disponible Grant or Loan. I mention this the first thing in my Letter, to make you as soon as possible easy on that head.

I thank you for sending me Copy of the Resolution relating to the Empress of Russia, tho' I had before received it and it was already communicated to her imperial Majesty, who I am informed is much pleased with it. – Mʳ Dana, lately Secretary to M. Adams, has received a Commission appointing him Minister to that Court. He is on his Way thither incog. & proposes to appear in that Country merely as a Traveller till a proper time may arrive for avowing his Character. So you will please not to mention it. M. Adams has I believe, received a Commission lately to supply the Place of M. Laurens in Holland. I know not whether he has yet declared it. He has some time since opened a Loan there at the House of Neufville[1] for two Millions of Florins about 4 millions of Livres: I have not yet heard with what Success, but hope it will fill.

I have always found M. Grand here, an able & hearty Friend in our Affairs. I am therefore glad that you are becoming better acquainted with his Friend at Madrid, as together they may on many Occasions be more serviceable to us.

. . . . .

Your Express arrived here on Sunday last at 3 o Clock. I communicated your Letter that evening to Mr. Laurens. We agreed in the Necessity of supporting the Credit of Congress by paying the Bills, tho' his Zeal for supplying the Army made him feel a Reluctance in diminishing the 6 Millions of Livres I had lately obtain'd for that Purpose, and which was either to be laid out in Cloathing &c. here or drawn for by General Washington, as you will see by my Letter to Congress. I have myself experienc'd too much of the same distress'd Situation you are in, not to pity you most Sincerely. I have therefore this Day authoris'd Mr. Grand in writing, to pay the Bills of the Marquis d'Yranda[2] that may be drawn to furnish you with the Sum of 142,220 Dollars. I confide that those Drafts will not come but by Degrees as the Occasion calls, from your Acceptances between May and September, my Receipts of money being gradual, and it may be depended on that the Bills will be duly honoured.

Mr. Laurens is worrying the Ministers for more Money & we shall I believe obtain a farther Sum. But the necessary Supplies of military Stores will demand all & more than we shall get; I hope therefore that you will not relax in your Applications for Aids from Spain on Account of the Sums to be furnished you by me, since it will be hardly possible for me to assist you farther. My Grandson[3] will execute with Pleasure your Commissions. Present my respectful Compliments to Mrs. Jay, and believe me ever, with sincere Esteem & Attachment, Dear Sir, &c.   Benjamin Franklin

. . . . .

LC: *Benjamin Franklin Papers, microfilm reel 2, (LBkC).*

[1] *Neufville, Jean de (1729-1796). Dutch merchant. Negotiated Dutch-American commercial treaty with William Lee, 1778, the pretext for Great Britain's declaration of war against the United Provinces, 1780. Emigrated to Boston, 1785, and later settled in Albany, New York.*

[2] *Yranda, Simón de Aragorri y Olavide, Marqués d'. Spanish political figure. Honorary minister of the Council of the Treasury, 1780-1782.*

[3] *Franklin, William Temple (1762-1823). Grandson of Benjamin Franklin, son of William Franklin. Generally known as Temple Franklin, he served as Benjamin Franklin's secretary while the latter was Minister to France, and also as secretary of the American peace commission, 1782-1783.*

John Laurens to Louis XVI, King of France

[Translation]

Paris, 18 April 1781

The Undersigned Special Minister of the United States of America has the honor to represent to His Most Christian Majesty, on the part of Congress, and by its orders, that the crisis is extreme, and that it requires prompt and decisive aid.

The United States claims with confidence the power and the benevolence of their August Ally. They have requested

1st. twenty-five million in the form of a loan

2nd. a permanent Naval Superiority on the coasts of America.

3rd. Materials for clothing, Equipment, tents, armaments, and munitions of war which the States have put before the eyes of the Administration.

The Undersigned, being informed by Monsieur the Comte de Vergennes of the King's intentions with regard to pecuniary aid, hastens to offer, in the name of Congress, the homage of the most ardent gratitude – but at the same time he observes that it is his duty to represent that although this Aid goes to the objective which His Majesty proposes, it is proved that in the state of things that it is insufficient in view of the urgent needs of the Army and of the Administration, its Commitments, and its debts, the exhaustion in which America finds itself, the absolute lack of Resources and of Specie, and the enormity of the outlays necessary to make war with vigour – it is for this reason that the Undersigned urgently prays His Majesty to accord in credit to the United States of America the artillery, armaments, munitions, &c. that will be drawn from His Majesty's arsenals and storehouses, given that a very considerable sum will be absorbed by payment for the clothing and other objects that it is necessary to assemble in France.

. . . . .

The abasement of England, the dismemberment of her Empire, the inestimable advantages of Commerce for France present great interests and merit great efforts – If this occasion is neglected – If too much is left to chance, If time is lost – and if the means be insufficient – the Pride of this nation will no longer know limits, or brakes – and the object will be lacking perhaps forever. – it is very easy to foresee what would be the dire consequences for the French Islands.

. . . . .

John Laurens

FFAA: Pol. Corr., U.S., v. 16, f. 194-196 (LC transcription).

John Adams to Francis Dana

Dear Sir   Leyden April 18th 1781. —

I am at no loss what advice to give you in answer to the questions in your letter of this Day, because they relate to a subject on which I have long reflected, and have formed an opinion as fully as my understanding is capable of– I think then that it is necessary for you to prepare for a Journey to [St. Petersburg] without loss of time; that you travel in the Character of a Gentleman, without any Distinction of public or private, as far as the publication of your appointment already made in France, will admit. –

I shou'd think it altogether improper to communicate your design to [Prince de Gallitzin][1] of travelling to [Petersbourg] as a private Gentleman, secreting from him at the same time, your public Character. It wou'd expose you to something very disagreable. The [ambassador] wou'd ask you, why you asked his advice, when it is well-known that private Gentlemen travel without Molestation in every Country in Europe. Besides the Ambassador, I have reason to believe, wou'd not give you any advice, without Instructions from his Court; and this wou'd require so much time, that the most favourable opportunity which now presents itself, wou'd be lost. And after applying to the [ambassador] and being advised against the Journey, or to postpone it for Instructions from [his court], it wou'd be less respectful to go, than to go now, when the Circumstances of the Times are very favourable. The same reasoning applies equally against writing to [the court] beforehand. The best opportunity wou'd be lost, and the Court wou'd never encourage you to come, untill they had determined to receive you, and you wou'd have no opportunity to assist the Deliberations upon the Subject, by throwing in any light, by answering objections, or explaining the views of Congress. –

. . . . .

The United States of America have nothing dishonorable to propose to any Court or Country. If the wishes of America, which are for the good of all Nations, as they apprehend, are not deemed by such Courts or Nations consistent with their views and interest, of which they are the Supreme Judges, they will candidly say so, and there is no harm done. On the contrary, Congress will be applauded for their Candour, and good Intentions.

You will make your Communication to the French Ambassador of course, according to your Instructions. This method was taken by this Republick in her struggle with Spain; nay it was taken by the Republican Parliament in England, and by Oliver Cromwell.[2] It was taken by Switzerland, and by

Portugal in similar Cases with great Success, why it shou'd be improper now I know not.

· · · · ·

America, my dear Sir, has been too long silent in Europe. Her Cause is that of all Nations and all Men; and it needs nothing but to be explained to be approved. At least these are my sentiments. –

I have reasons in my Mind which were unknown to their Excellencies the Comte de Vergennes, and M^r· Franklin, when you consulted them; Reasons which it is improper for me to explain at present. But the reasons I have given appear to me conclusive. No measure of Congress was ever taken in a more proper Time, or with more Wisdom, in my opinion, than the appointment of a Minister at the Hague and at [St. Petersburg]. The effects of it may not appear in sudden & brilliant success, but the time was exactly chosen, and the happy fruits of it will appear in their Course. –

Altho I shall be personally a Sufferer by your appointment yet I sincerely rejoice in it for the public good.

When our Enemies have formed Alliances with so many Princes in Germany, and so many savage Nations, against us – when they are borrowing so much of the Wealth of Germany, Italy, Holland, Switzerland, to be employed against us, no wise Court or reasonable Man, can blame us for proposing to form Relations with Countries whose Interest it is to befriend us. An excess of Modesty and Reserve is an excess still. It was no dishonor to us to propose a Treaty to France, nor for our Ministers to reside there, more than a Year, without being acknowledged. On the contrary all wise Men applauded the measure, and I am confident the world in general will now approve of an Application to the Maritime Powers, although we shou'd remain without a public reception as long as our Ministers did in France and Spain; nay altho we shou'd be rejected. In this Case, Congress and their Constituents will all be satisfied. They will have neglected no Duty in their power; and the world will then see the power and resources of three or four Millions of virtuous Men, inhabiting a fine Country, when contending for every thing which renders Life worth supporting. The United States will then fix a Medium, establish Taxes for the payment of Interest, acquire the Confidence of her own Capitalists, and borrow Money at Home; and when this is done, they will find Capitalists abroad willing eno^h to venture in their Funds. With ardent Wishes for your health & success, I have the honor to be, Dear Sir, your Excellency's most obedient & most humble Servant   John Adams

NA: PCC, item 89, v. 2, pp. 540-543 (C); M247, reel 117.
    [1] Golitsyn, Prince Dmitrii Alekseevich (1721-1792). Russian diplomat. Minister to the United Provinces of the Netherlands, 1770-1782.

² *Cromwell, Oliver (1599-1658). British military leader and political figure. Protector, 1653-1658.*

Memorial from John Adams to the States General of the United Provinces of the Netherlands

High and mighty Lords,   Leyden 19. April 1781

The Subscriber has the Honour, to propose to your High mightinesses, "that the United States of America, in Congress assembled have lately thought fit, to send him a Commission, with full Powers and Instructions, to confer with your High Mightinesses, concerning a Treaty of Amity and Commerce, an authentic Copy of which he has the Honour to annex to this Memorial.

.   .   .   .   .

It is Submitted to the Consideration of your High Mightinesses, whether, the System of the United States, which was minutely considered and discussed, and unanimously agreed on, in Congress in the Year one thousand Seven hundred and Seventy Six, in planning the Treaty they proposed to France; to form equitable commercial Treaties with all the maritime Powers of Europe, without being governed or monopolized by any: a System which was afterwards approved by the King, and made the Foundation of the Treaties with his Majesty: a System to which the United States have hitherto constantly adhered, and from which they never will depart unless compelled by Some Persons declaring against them, which is not expected; is not the only means of preventing this growing Country, from being an Object of everlasting Jealousies, Rivalries, and Wars, among the nations. if this Idea is just it follows, that it is the Interest of every State in Europe to acknowledge American Independancy, immediately. if such benevolent Policy should be adopted, the new World, will be a proportional Blessing to every Part of the old.

The Subscriber, has the further Honour of informing your High Mightinesses, that the United States of America in Congress assembled impressed with an high Sense of the Wisdom and Magnanimity of your High Mightinesses, and of your inviolable Attachment to the Rights and Liberties of Mankind, and being desirous of cultivating the Friendship of a Nation, eminent for its Wisdom, Justice, and Moderation, have appointed the Subscriber, to be their Minister Plenipotentiary, to reside near you, that he may give you, more particular Assurances of the great Respect, they entertain for your High Mightinesses, beseeching your High Mightinesses to give entire Credit, to every Thing, which their Said Minister Shall deliver, on their Part, especially when he shall assure you of the Sincerity of their Friendship and Regard. The original Letter of Credence, under the Seal of Congress, the Subscriber is ready to deliver to your High Mightinesses, or to Such Person as you Shall direct to receive it. He has also a Similar Letter of Credence, to his most Serene Highness the Prince, Statholder.

All *which* is respectfully Submitted to the Consideration of your High Mightinesses, together with the Propriety of appointing Some Person or Persons, to treat, on the Subject of his Mission, by   John Adams.

MHS: *The Adams Papers, microfilm reel 104 (LBkC)*.

Comte de Vergennes to Chevalier de la Luzerne

[Translation]

Nº 15   Versailles, 19 April 1781

I sent you by my despatch Nº 14 of the 9th of last month, Sir, the details relative to the mediation proposed by the Courts of Vienna and of St. Petersburg; you will have seen therein that our acceptance depends on the concurrence of our allies, and that of Spain of the breaking off of the direct negotiation existing between that Power and Great Britain. Since my written despatch things have changed; the Court of London has recalled the emissary that it was maintaining in Madrid, and the Catholic King, made free by this recall, has accepted the mediation of the two imperial Courts; the King has done the same: but His Majesty, at the example of the King his uncle, has made known to the two mediators, that the mediation can only have force if preliminary bases of negotiation are established. The correctness of this observation has been perceived in advance by the two mediating Courts, and we are awaiting the effect of the communication that they should have made to that of London. The first question that we have proposed is relative to the admission of an American plenipotentiary; by the second we ask on what basis the King of England intends to treat with the United States.

You would do well, Sir, to inform Congress of this state of affairs and to invite it again to accept the mediation on its part and to send promptly to its plenipotentiary instructions that place him possibly in a position to take part in the negotiations. That assembly can judge, by the questions that we have directed to the mediating powers, the principles that govern the King with regard to the United States; you may assure it that His Majesty is invariably resolved not to deviate from them, and that he will not countenance any negotiation until he is given a satisfactory solution to his two requests. This conduct will convince the Americans more and more, I hope, of the fidelity and perseverance with which the King wants to maintain the obligations that he has contracted towards the United States, and it will doubtless persuade them to imitate His Majesty's example, if they have need to perceive that their honor, like their interest, requires that they remain immutably attached to him, and that they place a confidence without reserve in his friendship. I desire the more, Sir, that this confidence be well established, because it is important to us in influencing the conduct of Mr. Adams, and in being authorized to keep him from the mistakes into which his only too ardent imagination, his stubbornness, and his pride will not fail to draw him. You will easily conceive that the negotiations for peace will be bristling with difficulties, that it will probably be necessary in the claims as in the proceedings to smooth out the gradations well for them, and that Mr. Adams, left to himself, far from being successful therein, would only be suited to augment the harshness to which the English plenipotentiaries will only be too inclined.

I have informed you by my despatch N$^{o.}$ 13, Sir, of the resolution that the King has taken in consequence of the pecuniary requests of Congress. The extreme distress in which you have painted the American army for us, joined to the lack of money and credit and especially to the spirit of insurrection that has been manifested among the troops, had caused us to reconsider this matter at the moment when Mr. Laurens arrived in France; His Majesty has crowned his generosity and his magnanimity by consenting to be surety and guarantor of a loan of 10 million livres tournois to be opened in Holland for the benefit of the United States....

Vergennes

FFAA: Pol. Corr., U.S., v. 16, f. 54 (LC transcription).

Comte de Vergennes to Chevalier de la Luzerne

[Translation]

N$^{o.}$ 16.   Versailles, 19 April 1781

My despatch N$^{o.}$ 15 was already sent off, Sir, when I received news concerning the Court of London's manner of thinking with regard to the United States. In order to explain this matter to you fully, I should observe to you that in the office by which that Court accepted the mediation of Russia and invoked that of the Emperor, it declared that it would be prepared to listen to peace *as soon as the league of France with the rebel*

Subjects of England shall have ceased. This arrogant claim has been received on our part with the contempt it merits; we have declared in turn that if it comprises the final will of England, it will be useless to dream of peace, and we have asked that the British Ministry explain itself positively on the two questions that I indicated in my previous despatch. The Court of Vienna has faithfully transmitted our manner of thinking to that of London, and the result of the response which that court has just had communicated to the imperial minister is: that in all points that will be discussed at the future congress, England will conduct itself with much equity and condescension; but that the dependence of the rebel Subjects of America should be pre-established, that this matter should be left to the sole attention of Great Britain. Such is, Sir, the present state of things relative to the next peacemaking: you will easily understand that so long as it exists, there can be no question either of mediation or of peace; you would do well, Sir, to make known to Congress the dispositions manifested by the Court of London: I presume that that assembly will itself make the unfavorable remarks to which they are susceptible, and I hope that they will finish convincing the Americans of the verity that we do not cease to preach to them, i.e.: that it is only with arms in hand and by making the most vigorous efforts that they will wrest from the Court of London the recognition of their independence. But I begin to fear that there are very few Patriots in the country in which you dwell, it seems that each seeks to take advantage at the expense of the public. I have just transmitted to the Court of Vienna, Sir, the judgment that the King has rendered on the British response, and we shall await without impatience the effect which it will produce in England. If it is isolated, it will probably make only the slightest sensation; but I have reason to think that the Ministry of Vienna will accompany it with reflections suitable to make some impression on that of London. Besides, Sir, some failings that are the probabilities for the next establishment of the mediation, I am of the opinion that Congress should occupy itself no less with the instructions to give to its plenipotentiary. If the negotiations are not opened at this moment, it is possible that they will take place in the course of the next campaign: only an unfortunate event would be necessary to render the English more tractable.

Mr. Dana has come to see me, Sir, to communicate to me the commission which Congress has sent him, and to consult me on the conduct which circumstances may require on his part. I showed him that he runs the risk of compromising himself personally, as well as the Dignity of Congress, if he deploys any character in Russia while the Empress has not recognized the independence of the United States, and that that Power has the hope of filling the role of mediator, which requires the most perfect impartiality. Mr. Dana perceived the justice of my reflection, and he told me that he would present himself in Russia as only a simple traveller: that he would allow his commission to be ignored, and that he would carefully avoid speaking of affairs with anyone whatsoever, unless called upon by the Russian ministry. I strongly applauded Mr. Dana's wise resolution, and made him understand that it removed all the difficulties that I had foreseen for his trip. I recommended him to M. le Marquis de Verac[1], and you may be assured that that Minister will give him the best possible reception, and will aid him with pleasure in his designs when he has recourse thereto.

M. de Verac has communicated to the Russia Ministry the resolution of Congress relative to the principles established in the declaration which the Empress of Russia has had delivered to the belligerent powers, and according to what he sends me, the content of that act has brought great pleasure to M. the Comte Panin;[2] that minister proposes to place it under the eyes of the Empress at once, and M. the Marquis de Verac does not doubt that Catherine 2nd. will be flattered by the alacrity of Congress in conforming to her principles and views.

. . . . .

Vergennes

FFAA: Pol. Corr., U.S., v. 16, f. 55 (LC transcription).

[1] Vérac, Charles Olivier de Saint Georges, Marquis de (1743-1828). French diplomat. Minister to Russia, 1780-1783.

[2] Panin, Nikita Ivanovich, Count (1718-1783). Russian diplomat and political figure. One of Empress Catherine II's closest advisers. First Minister of the College of Foreign Affairs, 1764-1783.

John Jay to the President of Congress

Sir,   Madrid, 25th. April 1781.

I have had the honor of receiving your Excellency's Letters of the 6th. and 17th. October last, with the inclosures. They arrived the 30th. Day of January last. There is more than reason to suspect that the French Court were apprized of their Contents before they arrived, and to believe that the Construction of the Treaty by which the Navigation of the Mississippi is supposed to be comprehended in the Guarantee, does not correspond with their Ideas on that Subject. This Court continues pertinaciously to insist on ceding that Navigation, nor will they, as yet, listen to any middle Line. Whether this be their Real motive for declining a Treaty with us at Present, or whether the Bills drawn upon me have inspired an Expectation of profiting by our necessities, or whether they flatter themselves with a future Majority of Congress on that point, or whether they choose by continuing free from Engagements with us, to be better enabled to improve to their advantage the Casualties of the War, are questions which still remain undecided. Indeed the movements of this Court in general when compared with the great Rules of National Policy, applicable to their situation, is so inexplicable, that I should not be surprised if it should appear in future that they had no fixed System whatever.

. . . . .

Whatever we may get from this Court, is clear gain. We have no demands upon, and if we had we are not in Capacity to insist upon them. In my Opinion therefore it is of the utmost Importance to avoid appearances of Discontent, and rather to impress other Nations with an opinion of the Friendship of Spain for us, than otherwise. Indeed I really believe the King means well towards us, and that the Prime Minister is also well disposed; but whether as much can be said of the Minister's confidential and I believe influential Secretary M^r. Del Campo, is by no means a clear Point. It is proper that Congress should know that the Gentleman intended to succeed M^r. Mirailles was recommended by M^r. Del Campo, with whom he has long been on terms of Intimacy and Friendship. I have nevertheless no room to doubt of this Gentleman's attachment to our Cause, though I am inclined to think his Conduct will be conformable in a certain Degree with the Views of his Patron. This ought to remain a Secret. He is still here, although he expects daily to be dispatched.

. . . . .

I have the Honor to be, &c.   John Jay

NA: PCC, item 110, v. 1, pp. 397-409 (C); M247, reel 135.

John Adams to the President of Congress

Sir,   Amsterdam May 7th 1781.

On the fourth of May I did myself the Honour to wait on Peter Van Bleiswick, Esqr, Grand Pensionary of Holland,[1] and presented him a Letter containing a Copy of my Memorial to the States General &^c. His Excellency said that it was necessary for me to go to the President and Secretary of their High Mightinesses, and that it was not customary for foreign Ministers to communicate any thing to the Pensionary of Holland. I told him that I had been advised by the French Ambassador to present Copies to him, and they were only Copies which I had the Honour to offer him. He said he could not recieve them: that I must go to the President: but says he it is proper for me to apprize you, that the President will make a difficulty: or rather will refuse to recieve any Letter or Paper from you, because the State you say you represent is not acknowledged to be a Sovereign State by the Sovereign of this Nation: the President will hear what you have to say to him, make Report of it to their High Mightinesses, and they will transmit it to the several Provinces for the deliberation of the various Members of the Sovereignty. I thanked his Excellency for this Information and departed.

I then waited on the President of their High Mightinesses for the Week the Baron Linde de Hemmen, a Deputy of the Province of Guelderland,[2] to whom I communicated, that I had lately recieved from my Sovereign, the United States of America in Congress assembled, a Commission with full Powers and Instructions to treat with the States General, concerning a Treaty of Amity and Commerce: that I had also recieved a Letter of Credence as Minister Plenipotentiary to their High Mightinesses; and I prayed him to lay before their High Mightinesses either the Originals or a Memorial in which I had done myself the Honour to state all these facts and to inclose them Copies.

The President said that he could not undertake to recieve from me either the Originals, nor any Memorial; because that America was not yet acknowledged as a Sovereign State by the Sovereign of this Country: but that he would make Report to their High Mightinesses of all that I had said to him, and that it would become the Subject of deliberation in the several Provinces: that he thought it a matter of great Importance to the Republick. I answered that I was glad to hear him say that he thought it important: that I thought it was the Interest of the two Republicks to become connected.

I thanked him for his politeness, and retired after having apprized him that I thought in the present Circumstances it would be my duty to make public in Print my Application to their High Mightinesses.

I had prepared Copies of my Memorial &c for the Secretary Mr. Fagel:[3] but as the President had refused to recieve the Originals, I thought it would be inconsistent for the Secretary to recieve Copies, so I omitted the Visit to his Office.

I then waited on the Baron de Ray, the Secretary of the Prince,[4] with a Letter addressed to his most Serene Highness, containing a Memorial informing him of my Credentials to his Court and Copies of the Memorial to their High Mightinesses. The Secretary recieved me politely, recieved the Letter and promised to deliver it to the Stadtholder. He asked me where I lodged: I answered at the Parliament of England, a public House of that name.

Returning to my Lodgings, I heard about two Hours afterwards that the Prince had been to the Assembly of the States General for about half an Hour; and in about another Hour, the Servant of the House where I lodged announced to me the Baron de Ray. I went down to the Door to recieve him, and invited him into my Room: he entered and said that he was charged on the Part of the Prince with his Compliments to me, and to inform me, that as the Independence of my Country was not yet acknowledged by the Sovereign of his, he could not recieve any Letter from me and therefore requested that I would recieve it back, which I did respectfully: The Secretary then <*> politely said he was very much obliged to me for having given him an Opportunity to see my Person and took his Leave.

The President made Report to their High Mightinesses as soon as they assembled, and his Report was ordered to be recorded: whereupon the Deputies of each of the seven Provinces demanded Copies of the Record to be transmitted to the respective Regencies for their deliberation and decision; or in the Technical Language of the Laws of this Country, it was taken *ad referendum* on the same day.

The next morning I waited on the French Ambassador, the Duc de la Vauguion,[5] and acquainted him with all the Steps I had taken. He said he still persisted in his Opinion that the Time was not the most favourable; but as the Measure was taken I might depend upon it he would as an Individual support and promote it to the utmost of his Power.

It would take a large Space to explain all the Reasons and Motives, which I had for choosing the present time in preference to a later: but I think I can demonstrate that every moment's delay would have been attended with danger and inconvenience. All Europe is in a Crisis, and this Ingredient thrown in at this time will have more Effect than at any other. At a future time I may enlarge upon the Subject.

I have the Honor to be, with the greatest Respect, Sir, your most obedient and most humble Servant.   John Adams.

NA: PCC, Misc. Papers, Adams Despatches (C); M332, reel 1, ff. 302-305.

[1] Bleiswijk, Pieter van (1724-1790). Dutch political figure. Grand pensionary of Holland, 1772-1787. Pro-French, sympathetic to America.

[2] Lynden van Hemmen, Frans or Williem, Baron van. Dutch political figure. President of the States General, May 1781.

[3] Fagel, Hendrik (1706-1790). Dutch political figure. Griffier (secretary) of the States General in the 1780s. A strong supporter of the pro-British House of Orange.

[4] Larrey, Thomas Isaac, Baron de. Dutch nobleman. Secretary of the Stadhouder, Willem V, Prince of Orange, 1779-1781.

[5] Vauguyon, Paul-François de Quélen de Stuer de Caussade, Duc de la (1746-1828). French diplomat. Ambassador to the United Provinces of the Netherlands, 1776-1783.

Louis XVI to Congress

[Translation]

Very dear &C   Versailles, 11 May 1781

Mr. Laurens has delivered to us the letter by which you have accredited him near us in order to persuade us to obtain for you additional pecuniary assistance; he will inform you of the interest that we have taken in the description he has given us of your situation, and we flatter ourselves in having acquired new grounds for your attachment and gratitude by the efforts upon which we have resolved in your interest. We have charged the Chevalier de la Luzerne to make them known to you, and we are persuaded that Mr. Laurens, when he appears before you, will hasten to confirm all that our Minister Plenipotentiary will have said to you on our behalf, and especially to render you new assurances of our particuliar affection for the United States.

FFAA: Pol. Corr., U.S., v. 16, f. 256-256vo. (LC transcription).

Comte de Vergennes to Chevalier de la Luzerne

[Translation]

N°· 17.   Versailles, 11 May 1781

I have had the honor, Sir, of warning you by my despatch N°· 15 of the 19th of last month that in addition to the Sums accorded to Congress, the King has resolved to serve as surety for a loan of 10 millions that will be opened in Holland for the benefit of the United States. Orders consequent to these dispositions have been issued: arms, munitions, and clothing are being furnished to Mr. Laurens for a portion of the 6 millions of which the King has made a gift to Congress; and this officer carries a considerable sum away with him. The rest will be paid out successively as there are occasions for it.

As for the loan, M. the Duc de la Vauguyon has been charged with proposing it to the States of Holland; but he is encountering insurmountable obstacles, not only because the Americans are without credit in Holland, but also because the province of Holland fears being compromised, in effect, by lending to the United States. It recognized their independence indirectly, and this step would be contradictory with the obligations that the Republic has contracted with the neutral powers. To put an end to this difficulty, the King has decided to represent himself as the principal borrower, and to remain solely responsible for the Sums furnished. We await the result of this proposition. I think, Sir, that I do not need to describe to you His Majesty's general and beneficent proceedings, and that it will suffice to explain them to the Americans so that they may be imbued with gratitude for them, if they are susceptible to this sentiment, and that they may then make every effort in their power to second those which His Majesty is making to sustain their cause. We flatter ourselves especially, Sir, that Congress not only will not share but that it will highly condemn the discontent that Mr. Laurens shows, and that he will seek to inspire in it. This officer, little familiar with our usages and with the attentions that are due to the ministers of a great power, has formulated many demands not only with importunate entreaties, but even by employing menace: he required of the King that he furnish the Americans arms, clothing, munitions, &c. for upwards of 8 million livres, and that he lend them besides or at least procure for them 25 million. I have done all that depended on me to convince Mr. Laurens that it would be impossible for us to satisfy all these demands, and that the Sums granted, joined to the loan of 10 million, should fully satisfy Congress: but all my efforts have been useless, Mr. Laurens has neglected me greatly since I informed him of the King's decision, and I know that he permits himself the most indiscrete complaints for not having obtained everything that he required. I transmit these details to you, Sir, so that you may be in a position to enlighten Congress, and to prevent it from yielding in the direction of Mr. Laurens. Moreover, Sir, as my intention is not to occasion disagreement for Mr. Laurens, I pray you to use with much discretion all that I am writing to you on this Subject: the only thing that matters to us is to prevent Congress from being ungrateful by not perceiving the full extent of His Majesty's kindnesses. It will be for Mr. Washington to explain the lesson to his aide de camp, and it is in that view that I indicate something of his conduct to M. the Marquis de La Fayette. You will perceive in addition, Sir, that such an effort as we are making cannot be repeated and that it will be quite useless again to repeat acute demands. It will be good that you present it in advance to Congress so as not be put us in the position of making it a refusal, which would distress us but which would be no less indispensable.

M. the Duc de la Vauguyon has just informed me that Mr. Adams' intention was to display the character of Minister near the States-General; that he has done all he could to deter that American from so imprudent a step; but that it was impossible to make him change his mind. My response to the King's Ambassador was that the Advice he had given to Mr. Adams could not be wiser, and that if that plenipotentiary, insisting on not following it, presented his letters of credence to the States-General, he, M. the Duc de la Vauguyon, should take no step to have him received. I cannot persuade myself, Sir, that Mr. Adams acts as he does in consequence of orders from Congress, I suppose on the contrary that it is only a question of his exalted imagination, and from his desire to play a political role: it is in this opinion, Sir, that I pray you to enlighten Congress confidentially on Mr. Adams' step, and to engage that Body to send its plenipotentiary instructions capable of moderating his ardor. It would be very desirable for Congress to stipulate once and for all to all its agents in Europe not to permit any conduct having reference to politics without having consulted us beforehand: we are too interested in the Fate of the United States for our Counsels not to have their dignity and their advantage at heart above all.

The affair of the mediation, Sir, has made no progress since my last despatch, and there is much appearance that the mediators will not soon be in a position to commence their work. The admission of an American plenipotentiary presents the greatest difficulties, and it should be decided in favor of the United States before the mediation can enter into activity. I pray you to observe to the president of Congress, in informing him of these details, that the surest means of removing the difficulty would be that the Americans win decisive advantages over the English during the next campaign.   Vergennes

· · · · ·

FFAA: Pol. Corr., U.S., v. 16, f. 71 (LC transcription).

John Adams to the President of Congress

Duplicate   Amsterdam May 16ᵗʰ· 1781.
Sir,

There has been much said in the public Papers concerning Conferences for Peace, concerning the Mediation of the Emperor of Germany and the Empress of Russia &ᶜ, &ᶜ, &ᶜ

I have never troubled Congress with these Reports, because I have never recieved any official Information or Intimation of any such Negotiation, either from England or France, or any other way. If any such Negotiation has been going on, it has been carefully concealed from me. Perhaps something has been expected from the United States, which was not expected from me.

For my own part, I know from so long Experience, at the first Glance of Reflection, the real designs of the English Government, that it is no Vanity to say they cannot decieve me; if they can the Cabinets of Europe. I have fully known that all their Pretensions about Peace were insidious, and therefore have paid no other Attention to them than to pity the Nations of Europe, who, having not yet experience enough of British Manoeuvres, are still imposed on to their own danger, disgrace and damage.

The British ministry are exhausting all the resources of their Subtilty, if not of their Treasures, to excite jealousies and Divisions among the neutral as well as belligerent Powers. The same Arts precisely that they have practised so many Years to seduce, decieve and divide America, they are now exerting among the Powers of Europe: but the Voice of God and Man is too decidedly against them to permit them much Success.

As to a Loan of Money in this Republick, after having tried every expedient and made every proposition that I could be justified or excused for making I am in absolute despair of obtaining any, until the States General shall have acknowledged our Independence. The Bills already accepted by me are paying off as they become due, by the Orders of his Excellency M^r· Franklin: but he desires me to represent to Congress the danger and inconvenience of drawing before Congress have Information that their Bills can be honoured. I must intreat Congress not to draw upon me, until they know I have Money: at present I have none, ~~but~~ not even for my Subsistence, but what I derive from Paris.

The true Cause of the obstruction of our Credit here is Fear, which can never be removed but by the States General acknowledging our Independence, which perhaps in the Course of twelve months they may do, but I dont expect it sooner.

This Country is indeed in a melancholy Situation – sunk in Ease – devoted to the pursuits of Gain – overshadowed on all sides by more powerful Neighbours: unanimated by a Love of military Glory, or any aspiring Spirit: feeling little Enthusiasm for the public: terrified at the loss of an old Friend, and equally terrified at the prospect of being obliged to form Connections with a new one: incumbered with a complicated and perplexed Constitution: divided among themselves in Interest and Sentiment; They seem afraid of every thing. Success on the part of France, Spain and especially of America raises their Spirits, and advances the good Cause somewhat: but reverses seem to sink them much more.

The War has occasioned such a Stagnation of business and thrown such Numbers of People out of Employment, that I think it is impossible things should remain long in the present insipid State. One System or another will be pursued – one Party or another will prevail – much will depend on the Events of the War. We have one Security, and I fear but one, and that is the domineering Character of the English, who will make Peace with the Republick upon no other Terms than her joining them against all their Enemies in the War, and this I think it is impossible She ever should do.

I have the Honour to be, with greatest Respect, Sir, your most obedient and most humble Servant.   John Adams
Rec^d. 22 Oct^r.

NA: PCC, Misc. Papers, Adams Despatches (LS); M332, reel 1, ff. 306-307.

John Adams to Benjamin Franklin

Sir,   Amsterdam May 23^d 1781.

· · · · ·

I have just recieved from Gottenbourg the inclosed Letters, one to your Excellency[1] and one to M^r. Jay.[2] I recieved both unsealed with a direction to take Copies. I have put my own Seal upon that to your Excellency, and request the favour of You to put yours upon that to M^r. Jay, and to convey it in the safest manner. It contains matter of great Importance, which ought to be carefully concealed from every Eye but yours and M^r. Jays, for which reason I should be cautious of conveying it, even with the despatches of the Spanish ~~Minister~~ Ambassador, especially as there are intimations in M^r. Lovell's Letter of too much Curiosity with regard to M^r. Jay's despatches, and as M^r. Jay himself complains that his Letters opened. I hope this Instruction will remove all the difficulties with Spain, whose Accession to the Treaty would be of great Service to the Reputation of our Cause in every part of Europe.

It seems to me of vast Importance to Us, to obtain an acknowledgment of our Independence from as many other Sovereigns as possible, before any Conferences for Peace shall be opened: because if that Event should take place first, and the Powers at War with Great Britain, their Armies, Navies and People weary of the War and clamouring for Peace, there is no knowing what hard Conditions may be insisted on from Us, nor into what Embarrassments British Arts and Obstinacy may plunge Us.

By the tenth Article of the Treaty of Alliance, the contracting Parties agree to invite or admit other Powers who may have recieved Injuries from Great Britain to accede to that Treaty. If Russia and the Northern Powers, or any of them; should be involved in the War in support of the Dutch, would it not be a proper Opportunity for the Execution of this Article? Or why would it not be proper, now to invite the Dutch?

· · · · ·

I have the honour to be, Sir, your most obedient and most humble Servant.   John Adams.

APS: *Benjamin Franklin Papers (LS)*.

[1] Presumably *Foreign Affairs Committee to Benjamin Franklin, March 9, 1781* (NA: PCC, item 79, v. 1, pp. 278-279; M247, reel 105.

[2] *Foreign Affairs Committee to John Jay, February 20, 1781* (NA: PCC, item 79, v. 1, p. 277; M247, reel 105). This document enclosed the instruction from Congress to Jay of February 15, 1781, which authorized him to give up U.S. claims to navigate the Mississippi through Spanish territory.

The President of Congress to John Jay

Sir,   in Congress Assembled the 28[th.] day of May 1781.

Your letter of the sixth of November last, detailing your proceedings from the twenty sixth of May down to that period, has been received by the United States in Congress Assembled. At the same time was received your letter of the 30th of November with the several papers therein referred to.

It is with pleasure, Sir, I obey the direction of Congress to inform you that throughout the whole course of your negotiations and transactions, in which the utmost address and discernment were often necessary to reconcile the respect due to the dignity of the United States with the urgency of their wants, and the complaisance expected by the Spanish Court, your conduct is intirely approved by them. It is their instruction that you continue to acknowledge on all suitable occasions the grateful impression made on these States by the friendly disposition manifested towards them by his Catholic Majesty and particularly by the proofs given of it in the measures, which he has taken & which it is hoped he will further take for preserving their credit and for aiding them with a supply of Cloathing for their army. You are also authorised & instructed to disavow in the most positive & explicit terms any secret understanding or negotiation between the United States & Great Britain, to assure his Catholic Majesty that such insinuations have no other source than the invidious designs of the Common Enemy, and that as the United States have the highest confidence in the honor and good faith both of his most Christian and of his Catholic Majesty, so it is their inviolable determination to take no step which shall depart in the smallest degree from their engagements with either.

Should the Court of Spain persist in the refusal intimated by its Minister, to accede to the treaty between the United States and his most Christian

Majesty, or to make it the basis of its negotiations with you, the difficulty it is conceived may easily be avoided, by omitting all express reference to that treaty, and at the same time conforming to the principles and tenor of it; and you are accordingly authorised so far to vary the plan of your original instructions. As his most Christian Majesty however may justly expect in a matter which so nearly concerns him and which was brought into contemplation in the treaty he so magnanimously entered into with these States, the strongest marks of attention and Confidence, you will not fail to maintain in the several steps of your negotiation a due communication with his Minister at the Court of Spain, and to include his interests as far as circumstances will warrant.

You are authorized to acquaint his Catholic Majesty that not only entire liberty will be granted, during the war at least to export naval stores for the royal marine, but that every facility will be afforded for that purpose.

. . . . .

By a letter from Mr· Carmichael dated the 22d· of February, and received on the 27th of April last, Congress are informed that you had received despatches from them dated in October. These must have contained their instructions to you to adhere to the claim of the United States to the navigation of the Mississippi. A reconsideration of that subject determined Congress on the fifteenth day of February last to recede from that instruction so far as it insisted on their claim to the navigation of that river below the 31st· degree of North latitude, and to a free port or ports below the same. On the receipt of this latter instruction Congress have little doubt that the great obstacle to your negotiations will be removed, and that you will not only be able without further delay to conclude the proposed alliance with his Catholic Majesty; but that the liberality, and friendly disposition manifested on the part of the United States by such a cession will induce him to afford them some substantial and effectual aid in the Article of money. The loss attending the negotiation of bills of exchange has been severely felt. A supply of specie through the Havannah would be much more convenient & acceptable.   Samuel Huntington

NA: PCC, item 4, pp. 79-85 (Journal); M247, reel 18.

The President of Congress to the States

Sir,   [June 1, 1781]
I am directed to inform you That Congress have received undoubted intelligence both from their Minister at the Court of Versailles, & the

Minister of France in America by order of his Court That the Courts of Vienna & Petersburgh had offered their mediation to the belligerent powers for the re-establishment of peace. That these ~~King of~~ overtures had been eagerly embraced in the part of G. Britain. That France had declined her full acceptation thereof untill the concurrence of her allies ~~had been~~ could be obtained for that purpose, ~~but~~ at the same time observing, that should she again be pressed on this head, she would be obliged to enter into a previous plan of negotiation, conditionally for herself & Allies. That Spain had answered in such manner to the proposals of the mediating powers as to shew her eventual acceptance.

~~Thus are we likely to have obtruded upon us by the intervention of two such formidable powers, the hard necessity of acceedeing to these overtures at a time when these states are in a less eligible situation to enter into negotiations for peace, than at any other period of the War.~~ The intervention of such formidable powers will undoubtedly prove an event the most favourable to these United States if by a great & timely exertion we sufficiently reduce the force of the enemy now operating in our country. But should lanquor & inaction subject us to the contempt of the negotiators all the consequences will be chargeable upon ourselves. This is a conjuncture that calls for the most serious consideration of these states. ~~It is therefore become a question whether we are determined to suport this union upon the true principles of the confederation, by rejecting every idea of a diminution or not. If the first is to obtain, Congress are decided in their opinion that there it not a~~ Congress have not a doubt in their minds but that each State in the Union, ~~but which~~ is determined, to support the Confederacy that has been so solemnly entered into, through every difficulty, & hand it down unimpaired to their posterity. Under these impressions Congress can with confidence call on their Constituents for such exertions ~~of these~~ as are proportionate to the truely critical situation of our affairs. The plan of Operations for the present campaign having been preconcerted on the principle of obliging the enemy to abandon their possessions in every part of these states; therefore an unequivocal complyance with the demands heretofore made by Congress for provisions, men, & money are what < **** > we have *at present* to ask for should these means be expeditiously and punctually, < *** > put into our hands, we have the most pleasing prospect of putting a speedy & happy issue to the ~~present~~ war; by driving the enemy from their present possessions in every part of these states: but at all events, to confine them to the Sea coasts in order to give as little room as possible to the enemy's claim of *uti possidetis*, which will undoubtedly be most strenuously insisted on by them in the course of the negotiation — ~~which~~ a claim, ~~is in case of~~ totally inadmissible on our part. Of course, then, nothing should be left unessayed by these states, to

prevent the embarrassments that such a claim must inevitably produce. ~~It therefore is~~ Of consequence it is become indispensibly necessary, by our *immediate* — & under Providence — sucessful efforts, to place ourselves in such a situation, as to enable our negotiators to speak a firm & decided language, becoming the Characters of the Ministers of Free, Sovereign, & Independent States, <**>. We conclude with observing, that from the foregoing communications <******> we are so thoroughly <*> convinced of the most strenuous exertions of every State in the Union to accomplish the great objects herein pointed out, that Congress, will immediately proceed to ~~take the necessary measures for~~ carry~~ing~~ into full execution ~~such~~ their plans ~~as necessary to be~~ adopted for defeating <**> the ambitious views of our enemy: & be prepared, to accept of peace upon no other terms, <***> than the Independence of the thirteen United States of America in all their parts.   Samuel Huntington
Passed June 1. 1781

NA: PCC, *item 25, v. 1, pp. 209-212 (Draft); M247, reel 32.*

John Adams to Laurent Bérenger

Sir[1]   Amsterdam June 8. 1781
   I have received the Letter which you did me, the Honour, to write me, on the fifth of this month, informing me, that you have received a Letter from ~~His Excellency~~ the Compte de Vergennes, by which ~~he~~ his Excellency directs you to tell me, that the Interests of the United States require my Presence at Paris, and that he should desire that I would go there, as soon as my Affairs in Holland, will permit me.
   I should be extreamly obliged to you, Sir, if you would confide to me the Nature of the Business that requires me at Paris, that I might be able to form some Judgment, whether it is of so much Importance and so pressing as to make it necessary for me to go forthwith
   His Excellency Dr Franklin, and Coll Laurens, have arranged Affairs in such a manner, that the accounts of the *Indian* are to be produced to me and I am to draw Bills to discharge them, so that it would retard the Departure of that interesting Vessell, if I were to go now, and it is of ~~much~~ some Importance to the Publick that I should compleat my dispatches to go to Congress by her; I am also unfortunately involved in a good deal of Business in accepting and discharging Bills of Exchange, a Course of Business which would be put into some Confusion, if I were to go immediately, and the general affairs of Congress in this Republick might

suffer somewhat by my absence. But notwithstanding all, if I were informed that it is any Thing respecting a general Pacification, or an Invitation of this Republick to acceed to the Alliance between France & the United States or any other affair of Sufficient Weight to justify, my quitting this Post immediately I would do it. otherwise, it would, as I humbly conceive, be more for the public Interest that I should wait, untill ~~I can make put.~~ some of the Business that lies upon me here is dispatched, and the rest put into a better order. Let me beg the favour of your Sentiments, Sir. Whenever I go, I must beg the Favour of ~~a passport~~ you to furnish me with a Passport.

I have the Honour to be, with very great Respect, Sir, &c

John Adams

MHS: *The Adams Papers, microfilm reel 104 (LBkC).*

[1] *Bérenger, Laurent. French diplomat. Chargé d'affaires in the United Provinces of the Netherlands, 1781-1783.*

Chevalier de la Luzerne to Comte de Vergennes

[Translation]

N° 147. 1ˢᵗ·   Philadelphia, 11 June 1781

My Lord

Today I have had a long conference with a Committee of Congress charged with communicating to me the most recent resolutions of this Senate relative to the pacification. The Chairman, in permitting me to make a translation of it, told me that Congress desired that I not consider it as an officially communicated copy. The reason for this reticence is that it would consider itself deprived of the right of changing these resolutions, if this copy were given to me under its Sanction. These resolutions, drafted in the form of instructions addressed to the American Plenipotentiary, are conceived in the following manner: 1° You are authorized to concur in the name of the 13 States with His Most Christian Majesty in the acceptance of the mediation proposed by the Empress of Russia and the Emperor of Germany. 2° But you will accede to a Treaty of peace only insofar as: 1° it will effectively assure the independence of the Sovereignty of the 13 States, conforming to the form and to the effect of the treaties subsisting between the said States and His Most Christian Majesty and: 2° insofar as these Treaties will remain in full force and validity. 3° As for the disputed boundaries and other particular subjects, we refer you to your preceding instructions, which will easily indicate to you the desires and the expectation of Congress. Nonetheless we believe it dangerous, in view of our distance from you, to bind you by absolute and peremptory instructions on all other subjects than the two essential points mentioned above (in article 2). You will therefore use your own judgment and prudence to assure the interests of the 13 United States as the circumstances require, and following the Situation of the belligerent Powers and the dispositions of the Mediators. 4° You will make the most sincere and the most confidential communications on all these subjects to the ministers of our generous Ally the King of France; you will undertake nothing in the course of the negotiations for the peace or the truce without their knowledge and their concurrence; you will make them feel how much we rely on the influence of His Majesty for effective assistance in all that is necessary for the present Safety or the future prosperity of the United States of America.

5° If the repugnance of England to recognize our independence formally occasions difficulties in the course of the negociation, you may agree to a truce or make any other concession which does not constitute a substantial attack on the object of our efforts (*as may not affect the substance of what we contend for*),[1] provided that Great Britain is not left in possession of any part of the 13 United States.

After having passed these resolutions, which have cost Congress a Week of deliberations, I asked the Committee for permission to examine them successively and to express my sentiments freely concerning them. "The present affair submitted to the deliberation of Congress," I continued, "is of the greatest importance. It requires a reciprocal and limitless confidence, and I will make use of no detour in telling you that the instructions that you have just communicated to me are incomplete, fulfill their object only imperfectly, and leave Mr. John Adams the master of making peace for this continent or of prolonging the present war at his pleasure. The first and second articles are worthy of Congress' wisdom, and do not appear to me susceptible of any change; as for the third, it leaves it to the judgment and prudence of Mr. John Adams *to moderate the interests of the 13 states and to decide what the circumstances require*. I render justice to his private qualities, but as a public man, what is the character of the minister to whom you entrust this immense power? It is he who mistook the sense of his powers and his instructions in a manner that merited the censure of Congress. It is he who is infatuated with the interests of the Eastern states, to the point of wishing at any price to assure them a right to the fisheries, and who, for this single object, could destroy a negotiation on which depends the happiness and the tranquility of this whole continent. Mr. John Adams, distanced from this Theater of war, having all his relations in

Massachusetts, will receive pressing letters from some friends not to abandon this point or any other of the same nature. He is unaware of the distress of the Southern states, he will envisage no danger in the continuation of the war, and his obstinacy can cause the best-conceived plans to fail. Is it he who will judge whether we have to fear a war on the continent that would force us to leave you to the mercy of your enemies? Is it he who will judge the danger of seeing a peaceful mediator change into an armed mediator? Will you believe that the same man who brusquely distanced himself from my Court, because it was opposed to the steps that Congress itself has disapproved, has the sociability and skill necessary to negotiate directly with the peacemakers, and that he can be left to the impetuosity of his character without a brake?" A member of the Committee observed, My Lord, "that these inconveniences were anticipated by the 4th article," and I examined it with the same Severity as the 3$^{rd.}$ "It is true," I continued, addressing myself to the Chairman, "that Mr. Adams must communicate in the most confidential manner with the French Plenipotentiaries, but this prescribes a conduct for him to which Congress' formulas for peace could not otherwise fail to subject him. Do you think that the mediators or the Powers who have not recognized your independence, or England, which fights to prevent it, will recognize your minister in his public character? Nothing is less probable. They will perhaps consent to see him as the agent of a rebellious people, but if, as I have no doubt, he fulfills with dignity the place that you have confided to him, he will feel the necessity of having to communicate only through your intermediary. The instructions are therefore reduced in this respect to a pure compliment paid by Congress to the Court of Versailles, but suppose that in the course of the negotiations a discussion arises between the Plenipotentiary of the King and that of the United States. Who will be the judge between them? Who can bend the inflexibility of Mr. Adams to reasons that he does not want to perceive? And is it not clear that in this Supposition, that has only too much foundation, there will arise between the allies contradictions as scandalous as they are prejudicial to the 13 United States. If we consulted only our interests, we would make vows that yours would be left entirely at the discretion of your minister, and we would feel that by making the King arbiter of the peace you desire, we were exposing ourselves to the danger of seeing thrown back upon us what it might contain that is disagreeable to some States in case they do not obtain all they desire. It is to expose ourselves to the interpretations that the suspicions of Mr. Adams may suggest to him. It is, in a word, to put in danger that mutual affection of the two nations, of which I doubt not that Congress had at heart piously to preserve the trust, but I have in this instance conjectured the most deplorable thing that could happen to the alliance, and as it a question of giving *your ultimatum*, it seems appropriate to include in it all the concessions that you are disposed to make, without however renouncing the hope of preserving them, and no one can be more disposed than we to procure for you a complete Satisfaction. No sensible person suspects us of preferring the interests of England to yours, of wishing to aggrandize her at your expense, or of wishing to procure the reestablishment of those of her partisans whose possessions you have confiscated without the greatest necessity. If we were reduced to that extremity, it is manifest that we would yield to it only from the impossiblity of doing otherwise. I therefore do not hesitate to tell you that the only way I see to prevent the inconveniences resulting from the particular dispositions of Mr. Adams, is to put him entirely under the direction of the His Majesty's Plenipotentiaries at the peace Conferences, and it is thus that you will preserve the harmony and understanding between the allies that our enemies are so interested in destroying." The Chairman observed that by the letter of these instructions, Mr. Adams could not make peace without our consent. I told him that this was not enough, and that it was appropriate that he be directed to sign if, after a mature examination and a complete confidence, we judged that the circumstances required it, since it was that which had made me say that the instructions were incomplete and that they were in effect limited to giving us the power to prevent without giving us the power to act. We passed to the 5th article, and I would have made no observation on it if only Congress had not fixed the duration of the truce that it consented to conclude. It doubtless intended that this point be left to the prudence of the negotiators, and the Chairman told me that this was in fact the intention of the 13 United States, although the general wish was for a truce of at least ten years. After this general review of instructions, the Committee passed to an examination of my observations, and all the members that comprise it seemed to me to be surprised by them. They proposed to me various alterations, and since there were several delegations to humor, and the instructions it was a question of reformulating had only passed in Congress by the Vote of seven states, we agreed on the form we thought in fact the most proper to win the Votes, and they returned the proposals to Congress. They at first met with some contradictions, but the Chairman having made use of the arguments that I had suggested to him, the proposed change was accepted, and among the 10 States voting, only Massachusetts Bay was against. Its delegates represented how dangerous it was to leave the King entirely master of the Negotiation, that the boundaries, the fisheries, the restitution of goods confiscated from the English and from the ill-disposed, and a number of other points that would present themselves in the course of the negociation were left to the discretion of a Power which, despite his good intentions, might be unaware of how important these different subjects were to the 13 United States. The response to this objection was that in the more than three years that the King had been the ally of the States, he had exhibited a justice, an impartiality, and an affection that permitted no doubt of the interest that His Majesty would take in their behalf at the next peace-making, and that the less the confidence of the 13 States in him was limited, the more he would find himself drawn to defend their interests. These changes and additions definitively decided, a Member of Congress came to tell me that the two first articles are preserved; in the third, the following words *this is why you have the liberty to assure* were substituted for the underscored lines. Then, to denote the necessary connection from the third article to the fourth, and what is explanatory from that which precedes it, it begins with the following transition: *to this end you will make communications.* After the word "concurrence" in the same article Congress added "*and finally you will govern yourself by their advice and their opinion and you will endeavor also in all your conduct to make them feel how much we rely etc.*"

I observed, My Lord, that these alterations seemed appropriate to fulfill the desired goal. I in fact regard the negotiation as now being in His Majesty's hands, save for independence and the Treaties, and I myself applaud these two reservations. I desire that you give your approbation to these measures, which seem to me to fulfill the orders that you have given me on 9 March last. I attribute the promptness with which Congress has yielded to my representations to two principal causes. The first is the absence of Mr. Samuel Adams. I think I have succeeded, by means of my correspondent, in making him known to the most important of his compatriots, and if the present dispositions continue, he will no longer be returned to Congress. The second is the rupture of the League of the New England States and the annihilation of the System that it had proposed for prolongation of the War.[2] It is to General Sullivan[3] alone that I am obligated for it. That delegate has developed in this whole affair as much patriotism as attachment to the alliance, and I think I can reckon that the efforts of this delegate to reestablish that association will be useless as long as he remains in Congress. I even think that it will be advantageous for the alliance to nourish his attachment to us after he has returned to the State of New Hampshire, where he enjoys much influence. He has renounced the project of which mention is made in my despatch N°. 140.

The absence of all the Delegates from the State of New York has been another happy circumstance, seeing that they are still less tractable than the Virginians on the extent of the boundaries that they have thought to fix for Canada in the West. Some delegates are still not satisfied with the measures taken against the obstinacy and the caprice of Mr. John Adams.

It seemed impossible to me to have him recalled, and I have suggested the idea of giving him two Associates. This project has been approved, and the matter has been decided by Congress. However, their choice will meet with great difficulties. Mr. Jay has been designated as one of the two. He is from the State of New York, and so preoccupied with the ideas of his fellow-citizens relative to the boundaries that he has written to Congress that he thinks it would be necessary rather to renounce an alliance with Spain than to accord her the lands that are to the left of the Mississippi. Mr. Carmichael, the Secretary of Legation, is of a contrary opinion.

I am with Respect, My Lord, your very humble and very obedient servant.   le chr de la luzerne
Received 7 August.

FFAA: Pol. Corr., U.S., v. 17, f. 27 (LC transcription).

¹ In English in transcription.

² Presumably a reference to the five States (New Hampshire, Massachusetts, Rhode Island, Connecticut, and New York) which sent representatives to the Hartford Convention of November 1780. The convention discussed ways to increase the size of the Continental Army and to maintain a steady flow of supplies from the states.

³ Sullivan, John (1740-1795). New Hampshire military and political leader. Member, First and Second Continental Congresses, 1774-1775, 1780-1781. Commissioned brigadier general, June 1775, and major general, August 1776. Captured in the Battle of Long Island, August 27, 1776, he was released to carry peace overtures to Congress. Commanded a division in the Continental Army, 1776-1779. Attorney general of New Hampshire, 1782-1786, president (governor), 1786, 1787, and 1789.

Chevalier de la Luzerne to Comte de Vergennes

[Translation]

Nᵒ· 149. 1ˢᵗ·   Philadelphia, 14 June 1781
My Lord.

Congress has been pondering whether it would be advisable for it to name a plenipotentiary other than Mr. Adams; the recall of that Minister appearing subject to great difficulties, it was proposed to give him two co-plenipotentiaries; Mr. Jay was named unanimously, and Mr. Franklin was placed in nomination to be the third. General Sullivan, who had named him, found insurmountable difficulties in having this choice adopted; this Delegate and his party were opposed in their turn to the nomination of Mr. Jefferson, Governor of Virginia, and of Mr. Henry Laurens, who was successively chosen despite the disadvantages and the type of disadvantage there is in naming as a negotiator for peace a Minister who is a prisoner of the enemy. The impossiblity of managing to name any one of these three Candidates persuaded General Sullivan to represent with new fervor the services of Mr. Franklin and the consideration which he enjoys, the injury done him in appointing a Colleague for him, the necessity of mitigating by a mark of shining confidence the bitterness of this first treatment; he observed that having been unjustly treated upon false reports, he merited some sort of satisfaction, and that a zealous servant who had had such a part in the revolution for its whole duration was the most proper to preside at its consummation; after this preamble, he proposed to add these three Candidates to the two already named; objections were made with regard to the expense and the number; as for the first point, it was replied that American plenipotentiaries would always be approved if they were content with a modest and republican manner, that besides the subject was too important for these expenses to be regarded; as for the number, if one examined the diplomatic collections, one would find that the Republic of Holland had had three, four, and five plenipotentiaries at almost all the peace conferences in which it had taken part. The party opposed to Mr. Franklin then proposed to choose the three Candidates in succession, while leaving this Minister for last. General Sullivan saw the trap, and responded that all three should be elected or rejected together. His firmness brought together all the parties, and the three candidates were named at once unanimously, so that the declared enemies of Mr. Franklin were themselves obliged to give him their votes.

Mr. Laurens is better known by Mr. Gerard than by me, My Lord; I have had the honor of reporting to you some circumstances that render him very suspect to me. If the English, informed of his nomination, release him in order to place him in a position to take part in the peacemaking, these suspicions can only acquire a new consistency, and he will merit being attentively watched; I cannot yet speak to you with certainty of Mr. Jefferson, it even seems doubtful that he will accept; it would be very advantageous to have had Mr. Jay and Mr. Franklin added to Mr. Adams. The secretary of Congress having addressed himself to me for drawing up the instruments by which Congress accepts the mediation and the full powers of its Ministers, I have taken care to have inserted that the five plenipotentiaries, some of them, or one of them, in the event that the others are impeded, may treat and conclude conjointly with His Majesty's plenipotentiaries; it seemed to me advantageous in all respects that Mr. Franklin be among the plenipotentiaries....

                                                    le che de la luzerne

Received 7 August.

FFAA: Pol. Corr., U.S., v. 17, f. 37 (LC transcription).

∞   *Early Peace Efforts*   ∞

In a sense, attempts at reconciliation between the mother country and the colonies before Lexington and Concord flowed or merged into attempts to negotiate peace between Great Britain and her rebellious charges, soon to become the independent United States of America. Lord Frederick North's Conciliatory Resolution, passed by Parliament on February 20, 1775, ignored the Continental Congress as a negotiating body. Addressed through the colonial governors to influential men in each colony, it urged such men to work through the colonial assemblies to see that each voted its fair share toward the defense of the empire. If a colony allocated its defense quota and provided adequate funds to support its own officials, it would be exempt from Parliamentary taxation.

News of the Conciliatory Resolution reached America in the spring of 1775. Despite its title, few regarded its terms as even worthy of discussion in the aftermath of the fighting outside Boston. Negotiations which Benjamin Franklin had been conducting with Lord Dartmouth,[1] Secretary of State for the Colonies, fell apart on March 1. America's proto-diplomat, saddened by the recent death of his wife in Philadelphia, set sail for America shortly thereafter.

The Second Continental Congress, which convened on May 10, 1775, lost no time in condemning Lord North's Conciliatory Resolution as no basis for an accommodation. Early in July, the Congress addressed its Olive Branch Petition to the King, asking him to provide some means of negotiation with his "loyal subjects." However, the petition contained no proposals of reconciliation, and was basically a last-ditch attempt to reach a settlement. Many members regarded it as destined for failure.

Arthur Lee and Richard Penn sent the Olive Branch Petition to Lord Dartmouth's office on August 21, 1775. Two days later, a royal proclamation declared that many of the King's subjects in North America were in "open and avowed rebellion," and called upon all loyal subjects to suppress it. Lee and Penn eventually learned that George III would not *officially receive the petition or make any reply to it.* On October 26, in his speech at the opening of Parliament, the King called for vigorous efforts to end the "rebellious war" being waged "for the purpose of establishing an independent empire." The Rockingham and Chatham factions, supported by the Radicals, attacked North's government for resorting to coercion rather than conciliation, but both houses of Parliament pledged their support of a military solution by large majorities.

The men responsible for achieving that solution were brothers – Admiral Lord Richard Howe, commanding the British naval squadron in North American waters, and General William Howe, commanding British land forces in the American theater. The Howes had conciliatory inclinations, but they also had orders to play to win. They could not treat with the Americans until the rebels had surrendered and colonial officials had regained their authority. When peace had come, the Howes could promise the colonists freedom from Parliamentary taxation if they agreed to pay from five to ten percent of the cost of defending the British empire – a slight variation on Lord North's Conciliatory Resolution. They could not make these terms known until all resistance had ceased, a situation that amounted to having no power to negotiate. The Howes could pardon rebels at their discretion, but that was all.

In America, where rebels were patriots, the conviction grew that no reconciliation with the mother country was now possible. On June 7, 1776, Richard Henry Lee of Virginia submitted three resolutions to the Continental Congress. The first asserted that the United States were free and independent, absolved from all allegiance to the British Crown. Congress approved that resolution on July 2, clearing the way for adoption of the Declaration of Independence on July 4, 1776. But Lee's other two resolutions also had momentous consequences. They called for establishing an American confederation and for attempting to secure allies for the new American government in Europe.

Meanwhile, the Howe brothers were assembling their warships and troop transports in the waters of New York harbor. On July 14, they sought to open negotiations with the American commander by sending a letter addressed to "George Washington, Esq. etc. etc." into the city. Washington refused to accept it on the grounds that the missive was improperly addressed. A British officer explained that the "etc., etc." was meant to cover all Washington's titles, but the general declined to accept such facile reasoning or to meet with the Howes. The brothers' powers to pardon but not to negotiate were never put to the test, for Washington had no powers to treat with the British.

On August 22, General Howe began landing troops on Long Island. The American defenses were poorly sited, with the left wing anchored to no natural obstacle. Howe learned of this weakness from local Tories, and used the knowledge to inflict a stunning defeat on the American forces on August 27. Washington managed to withdraw the remaining defenders to Manhattan. Among those captured was General John Sullivan, whom Admiral Howe released to carry an offer of generous peace terms to Congress in Philadelphia.

Congress resolved to permit Admiral Howe to present his proposals, and appointed a committee consisting of Benjamin Franklin, John Adams, and John Rutledge to listen to what he had to say. The committee met with Lord Howe on Staten Island on September 11. To his proposal that they lay down their arms and await British generosity, they replied that they would accept nothing less than independence. It was obvious that the fighting would continue.

Washington shortly evacuated first New York City and then Manhattan Island, again extricating his army from the jaws of the British lion to fight another day. General Howe's forces pursued the American army up the Hudson, then across New Jersey to the Delaware. Washington always kept ahead of the British, pausing occasionally to stand and fight, as at White Plains. In late December and early January, his victories at Trenton and Princeton even forced Howe to undertake a tactical withdrawal from western New Jersey. Elsewhere, Benedict Arnold's[2] delaying tactics on Lake Champlain kept General Guy Carleton from seizing that strategic waterway until too late in the season for a decisive thrust toward Albany, but General Henry Clinton easily captured Newport in early December, providing the British with a protected anchorage for Admiral Howe's warships. During the winter of 1776-1777, the Howes invited Congress to send two or three of its members to visit General Charles Lee,[3] whom they were holding prisoner in New York City, in the hope of reviving efforts at reconciliation. Although Washington favored accepting the offer, Congress decided against it, rightly divining that the Howes had no new proposals to put on the table.

The year 1777 should have seen the triumph of the British cause in America. British armies held the strategic initiative, and British warships effectively controlled American coastal waters from Rhode Island to the Chesapeake Bay. What was lacking was any effective coordination of military endeavors, not to speak of any pretense of peace negotiations.

While one British army under General John Burgoyne seized Ticonderoga and prepared to descend the Hudson, General Howe's forces remained in garrison in New York and New Jersey until late in the summer, then boarded Admiral Howe's ships for a seaborne assault on Philadelphia. The Howe brothers took Philadelphia, and General Howe inflicted defeat after defeat on Washington's army. But that army remained in being, while Burgoyne's force, after detachments had suffered reverses at Bennington and Fort Stanwix, surrendered to a northern patriot army under General Horatio Gates on October 17. A last-minute relief effort from New York by General Henry Clinton failed to affect the outcome of this debacle north of Albany.

On December 10, Lord North, perhaps still reeling from the loss of Burgoyne's army, announced in the House of Commons that his ministry would offer generous peace terms to the Americans. The King balked at granting them independence, but agreed to offer the Americans quite broad freedom within the empire. On February 17, 1778, with the results of Franco-American negotiations suspected but not known to be definite, North asked Parliament to repeal the Townshend duty on tea, the Massachusetts Government Act, and the Prohibitory Act, as well as to renounce power to tax the Americans. Parliament was also asked to authorize sending commissioners to America to treat of peace. In April the commission, headed by the Earl of Carlisle, with William Eden and George Johnstone as its other members and Henry Strachey as its secretary, sailed for America.

Meanwhile, on March 13, the Marquis de Noailles,[4] the French ambassador, informed the King that France had recognized the United States of America. It was now clear to George III and his advisers that they must shortly go to war with France. North and his colleagues quickly realized how vulnerable were the British troops in Philadelphia and the British ships in Delaware Bay to a sudden attack by the French fleet. Secret orders were sent to Clinton, who had replaced William Howe as commander of British troops in America, to evacuate Philadelphia and assume a defensive posture at New York. Clinton was even authorized to withdraw to Halifax if necessary, with Lord Richard Howe's ships covering his retreat.

The Carlisle Commission arrived in Philadelphia to find the preparations for a British evacuation well under way. Its members soon learned that Congress had ratified the treaties of alliance and of amity and commerce with France on May 4. Even before the French treaties came under consideration, Congress had resolved on April 22 that "the United States cannot with propriety hold any conference or treaty with any commissioners on the part of Great Britain, unless they shall, as a preliminary thereto, either withdraw their fleets and armies or else in positive and express terms acknowledge the independence of said States." Congress had nothing to say to the members of the Carlisle Commission, although one of its members, George Johnstone, did make an unsuccessful attempt to bribe certain members of Congress, among them Francis Dana and Robert Morris. Exposure of Johnstone's efforts placed the commission even further under a cloud. The commissioners left Philadelphia with the British forces in late June, just in time to avoid capture by a French squadron under the Comte d'Estaing, which arrived in Delaware Bay on July 8. The Carlisle Commission returned to England late in the year, having accomplished nothing. No further substantive British efforts at reconciliation occurred until 1782.

On February 15, 1780, a Congressional committee submitted a report on minimum American peace demands: independence, certain boundaries, British withdrawal from all U.S. territory, fishing rights, and free navigation of the Mississippi. Congress accepted these demands, except for fishing rights, on August 14, 1780. John Adams had been named commissioner to negotiate peace with England and to draw up a commercial treaty with that power on September 27, 1779, the same day John Jay was named minister to Spain. On June 11, 1781, Congress agreed to have the peace with England negotiated by a committee instead of by Adams alone; Franklin, Jay, Henry Laurens, and Thomas Jefferson joined Adams in this responsibility. On June 15, Congress cut back its minimum peace demands to two: independence and sovereignty, with the five commissioners given discretion on the other points. In deference to their ally, the United States in Congress assembled also instructed the commissioners to act only with "the knowledge and concurrence" of the French and to "ultimately govern yourselves by their advice and opinions." The stage was effectively set for the drama enacted in 1782 and 1783.

---

[1] Dartmouth, William Legge, Earl of (1731-1801). British political figure. President of the board of trade and foreign plantations, 1765-1766 and 1772-1775. Secretary of state for the colonies, 1772-1775. Lord privy seal, 1775-1782. Lord steward of the household, April-December 1783.

[2] Arnold, Benedict (1741-1801). American military officer, traitor, British military officer. Initially a Connecticut merchant and sea captain, he served as joint commander

with Ethan Allen of the force that captured Fort Ticonderoga, May 1775. Led expedition against Quebec by way of Maine, 1775-1776. Constructed a fleet on Lake Champlain to delay British advance from Canada, 1776. Defeated British attack on Connecticut, 1777. Raised siege of Fort Stanwix, led decisive actions by which Gates' army defeated Burgoyne at Saratoga, September-October 1777. Named commander at Philadelphia, June 1778. Conveyed military information to the British, 1779-1780. Attempt to surrender West Point to the enemy foiled, September 1780; fled to British lines. As British general, led expeditions into Virginia and Connecticut, 1781.

[3] Lee, Charles (1731-1782). British military officer, soldier of fortune, American general. Served with the British army in America, 1755-1761, and in Portugal, 1762-1763. Soldier of fortune in Poland. Returned to America, 1773, and settled in Virginia, 1775. Commissioned major general in Continental Army, 1775. Captured in New Jersey, December 1776. Exchanged, 1778. Court-martialed, July-August 1778, for his behavior during the Battle of Monmouth; suspended from the army. Wounded in a duel by Colonel John Laurens, who resented his disrespect for General Washington. Dismissed from the army, January 1780, after writing an insulting letter to Congress.

[4] Noailles, Emmanuel-Marie-Louis, Marquis de (1743-1822). French diplomat. Ambassador to Great Britain, October 1776-March 1778.

Commission of the American Ministers Plenipotentiary for Negotiating a Peace

[June 15, 1781]

The United States of North America in Congress Assembled to all to whom these presents shall come send Greeting.

Whereas these United States from a sincere desire of putting an end to the hostilities between his Most Christian Majesty and those United States on the one part and his britannic majesty on the other, and of terminating the same by a peace founded on such solid and equitable principles as reasonably to promise a permanency of the blessings of tranquillity did heretofore appoint the hon^le. John Adams late a commissioner of the United States of America at the court of Versailles, late delegate in Congress from the state of Massachusetts & chief justice of the said State, their Minister plenipotentiary with full powers general and special to act in that quality to confer treat agree and conclude with a treaty of peace with the ambassadors or plenipotentiaries of his MCM & of his Br: M^r. & those of any other princes or states whom it may might concern, relating to the reestablishment of peace and friendship; And whereas the flames of war have since that time been extended and other nations and states are involved therein; Now know ye that we still continuing earnestly desirous as far as depends upon us to put a stop to the effusion of Christian blood and to convince the powers of Europe that we wish for nothing more ardently than to terminate the war by a safe and honourable peace have thought proper to renew the powers formerly given to the said John Adams and to ~~our~~ join four other persons in commission with him, and having full confidence in the integrity prudence and ability of the hon^ble. Benjamin Franklin our minister plenipotentiary at the Court of Versailles and the hon^ble. John Jay late president of Congress & chief Justice of the state of New York and our Minister plenipotentiary at the Court of Madrid, and the hon^ble. Henry Laurens formerly president of Congress and commissionated & sent as our Agent to the United provinces of the low Countries, and the hon^ble. Thomas Jefferson governor of the Commonwealth of Virginia have nominated constituted and appointed and by these presents do nominate constitute and appoint the said Benjamin Franklin, John Jay, Henry Laurens and Thomas Jefferson in addition to the said John Adams our ministers plenipotentiary giving and granting to ~~these five persons~~ them the said J. Adams &c. or the majority of them or of such of them as may assemble or in case of the death absence, or indisposition or other impediment of the others to any one of them full power and authority general & special conjoinedly & seperately & general & special command to repair ~~go~~ to such place as may be fixed upon for opening Negotiations for peace and there for us and in our name to confer, treat, agree and conclude with the Ambassadors commissioners and plenipotentiaries of the princes and states whom it may concern, vested with equal powers, relating to the establishment of peace and whatsoever shall be agreed and concluded, for us and in our name to sign and thereupon make a treaty or treaties and to transact every thing that may be necessary for compleating securing and strengthening the great work of pacification in as ample form and with the same effect as if we were personally present and acted therein, hereby promising in good faith that we will accept, ratify, fulfil and execute whatever shall be agreed concluded and signed by our said ministers plenipotentiary or a majority of them or of such of them as may assemble or in case of the Death, absence indisposition or other impediment of the others by any one of them and that we will never act nor suffer any person to act contrary to the same in whole or in any part. In witness whereof we have caused these presents to be signed by our president and sealed with his seal. Done at Philadelphia the fifteenth day of June in the year of our Lord 1781 and in the fifth year of our Independence, by the United States in Congress Assembled.

Agreed to June 15. 1781 –

NA: PCC, *item 25, v.1, pp. 425-427 (Draft)*; M247, *reel 32.*

Instructions to the American
Peace Commissioners from Congress

[Philadelphia, June 15, 1781]

Instructions to the hon^{ble.} John Adams, Benj Franklin, John Jay, Henry Laurens and Thomas Jefferson Ministers plenipotentiary in behalf of the United States to negotiate a treaty of Peace.

You are hereby authorised and instructed to concur in behalf of these United States with his Most Christian Majesty in accepting the mediation proposed by the Empress of Russia and the emperor of Germany:

You are to accede to no treaty of peace which shall not be such as may 1st. *effectually secure* the independence and sovereignty of the thirteen states according to the *form and effect of the treaties subsisting between the* said States *and his Most Christian Majesty*; and 2dly. in which the *said treaties shall not be left in their* full force & validity. –

As to *disputed boundaries and* other particulars we refer you to the Instructions given to M^r J Adams dated 14th. August 1779 and 18 Octr. 1780, from which you will easily perceive the desires and expectations of Congress; *but we think it unsafe at this distance to tye you up by* absolute and peremptory directions upon *any other subject than the two* essential articles *above mentioned:* You are therefore *at liberty* to secure the interest of the United States *in such manner as circumstances may direct and as the state of the belligerent and disposition of the mediating powers may require.* For this purpose you are to make the most *candid and confidential communications upon all subjects to the ministers* of our generous ally the King of France, *to undertake nothing in* the negotiations for peace *or truce without their knowledge and concurrence and ultimately* to govern yourselves by *their advice and Opinion* endeavouring in your whole conduct to make *them sensible how much we rely upon his Majesty's influence for effectual support in* every thing that may be necessary to the *present security or* future prosperity of the United States of America.

If a difficulty should arise in the course of the negotiation for peace from the *backwardness of Britain* to make a formal acknowledgment of our independence you are at liberty to agree to *a truce* or to make such *other concessions as may* not affect the *substance of what* we contend for and provided that Great Britain be not *left in possession of any part of* the thirteen United States. –

NA: PCC, item 25, v. 1, pp. 445-446 (Draft); M247, reel 32.

Gouverneur Morris to John Jay

Dear Jay,   Philadelphia, 17 June 1781

Although I beleive myself thoroughly acquainted with you yet I cannot tell whether I ought to congratulate or condole with you ON YOUR LATE APPOINTMENT.[1] Ere this reaches you you will have learnt that you are on the PART OF THIS COUNTRY ONE OF FIVE COMMISSIONERS TO NEGOTIATE for PEACE. So far you are SOMETHING but when you come to find BY YOUR INSTRUCTIONS THAT YOU MUST ULTIMATELY OBEY THE DICTATES OF the FRENCH MINISTER, I am sure there is some thing in your Bosom which will REVOLT AT THE Servility of the SITUATION. To have relaxed on all Sides, to have given up all Things might easily have been expected from those Minds which softened by Wealth and debased by Fear are unable to gain and unworthy to enjoy the Blessings of Freedom. But that the proud should prostitute the very little little DIGNITY THIS POOR COUNTRY was possessed of would be indeed astonishing if we did not know the near Alliance between Pride and Meanness. Men who have too little spirit to demand of their CONSTITUENTS THAT THEY DO THEIR DUTY, who have sufficient Humility to beg a paltry Pittance at the Hands of ANY AND EVERY SOVEREIGN, such men will always be ready to pay the Price which Vanity shall demand from the Vain.

Do I not know you well enough to beleive that you will not ACT in THIS NEW CAPACITY? I think I do and therefore I will express my Concern that you must DECLINE THE HONOR, if that Name can be applied to SUCH OFFICE. DECLINE, however with Decency tho with Dignity. I mean always if no Alteration takes Place which shall be done if I can effectuate it tho I almost despair.

Having declared what I think you will do let me advise what I wish you to do as the only Mode to BE OF CONSEQUENCE when the Affair is TREATED OF in EARNEST. Let Carmichael GO TO THE MEETING. I must be most egregiously mistaken if SPANISH COURT IS DESIRIOUS OF PEACE. MEET THEM FULLY and in APPEARANCE WITH CONFIDENCE. TELL THEM WE are determined to persist untill the last Necessity. STATE OUR PRESENT TERMS, TO COMPREHEND THE CESSION OF THE FLORIDAS AND EVEN OF Jamaica as an ULTIMATUM OF PEACE. THEIR MINISTER at the CONGRESS CAN DELAY, AND DELAY IS every Thing. No other CONGRESS WILL SURRENDER ALL AS THIS has to an ALLY. I am more moved on this Occasion than I ever have been and therefore it is possible I may be mistaken but I think so strong and deep an Impression cannot be false.

... Remember me properly and beleive me yours.

Gouv. Morris[2]

Morris, Jay Papers, v. 2, pp. 86-87.

[1] *Capital letters used to indicate encyphered passages in original document.*

[2] *Morris, Gouverneur (1752-1816). New York lawyer, diplomat, political figure. Member, Continental Congress, from New York, 1778-1779. Assistant to Superintendent of Finance Robert Morris (not a relative), 1781-1785. Delegate, Constitutional Convention, 1787, from Pennsylvania. Minister to France, 1792-1794.*

The President of Congress to John Adams

Sir   Philadelphia June 20: 1781

You will receive herewith enclos[d] a letter address[d] to his most Christian Majesty; with a Copy of the Same for your information.

Also a Commission constituting the four gentlemen therein named in addition to yourself our Ministers for negotiating peace. Also another commission & duplicate Authorizing them to accept of the Mediation of the Emperor of Germany & Empress of Russia, in one of which you will observe the Emperor is first named, & in the other the Empress these are to be made use of as circumstances shall render expedient.

I have also enclos[d] Instructions (in cypher) for your government in addition to those formerly given for negociating peace with Great Brittain.

No additional Instructions to your former are yet given relative to a treaty of Commerce with Great Brittain.

. . . . .

I have the honour to be with perfect Respect your humble Servant—
Sam. Huntington Presid[t]

MHS: The Adams Papers, microfilm reel 355 (ALS).

James Lovell to John Adams

Sir   June 21. 81.

France appears to be most perfectly satisfied with the {present mediators yet presses us}[1] for an Arrangement final of the most {moderate terms. Franklin, Jay, H Laurence & Jefferson are added to you}. You would be made very happy by such an Event being grounded on a Desire to alleviate the Distress of a great {discretion but blush blush} America {consult & ultimately concur in every thing with} The Ministers of his most Christian Majesty, the Independence of the United States according to the Tenor of our Alliance {kept sole ultimatum}. I might have mentioned a Circumstance, not very material in the present Turn of Affairs {all or less or one can conclude as plenipo}. It is a Satisfaction to me and others alike interested that your other {parchments are untouched}. I hope therefore that we may conclude our {haddock safe}. I presume you will be at very little Loss to come at the Clue of this Labyrinth. {Gravier[2] now} persuaded of the absolute Necessity of the most cordial Intercourse between {him & you strongly pressed for orders of that kind} and Suppleness know not where to stop especially when under the Spur of {at least Marbois}. It is needless to turn Well diggers on this Occasion the whole is at the Superficies....

·　·　·　·　·

Affecty JL

MHS: *The Adams Papers, microfilm reel 355* (ALS); *Smith:* Letters of Delegates, *v. 17, pp. 339-340.*

[1] *Words in braces are encyphered in original document.*

[2] *Vergennes.*

Chevalier de la Luzerne to Comte de Vergennes

[Translation]

N°· 150. Duplicate.   Philadelphia, 23 June 1781
My Lord.

I regarded the affair of the instructions of the Plenipotentiairies for the peace as concluded according to the communication that had been given to me about it by the Committee, when I was informed that the delegates of two States were complaining loudly about this measure, that while rendering justice to the conduct of the King and to his impartiality, they observed that never had a state put itself with so much imprudence at the mercy of another. That when the people were informed of these circumstances, there would be a crowd of the ill-disposed who would not fail to say that they confirmed what the English have so often declared to the inhabitants of the 13 States, *that they have only changed masters and that Congress has betrayed them to France.* That the plenipotentiairies would play a sad role in the conferences. That five considerable persons would be sent there to be passive witnesses of our conduct, that we had confused and even false ideas concerning the fisheries, the boundaries, the confiscated goods, &c.; that to entrust to us without restriction the management of the most important transaction and the most august act in which it could take part would wound in an unprecedented manner the dignity of the 13 States and of the Congress which represents them. That this measure had been adopted with a puerile haste, but that it was excusable as long as Mr. Adams had been the Sole Plenipotentiary, because we had had some Subjects of complaints against him, but that it had become superfluous since he had 4 Colleagues. It was added to justify the concerns that were mentioned that we had had much more offensive ones for Congress, when we had proposed to hand over to General Washington the disposition of the Subsidy accorded by the King. I perceived, My Lord, that these discourses made an impression on many very well-intentioned delegates, that they even penetrated to the public, and some members whose good dispositions were well known to me informed me that they viewed with pain the movements that this state of affairs occasioned in the interior of Congress. They told me that a motion had been made and seconded to reconsider the instructions. That right away a great majority, perceiving how much Versatility a change would proclaim and how little delicate it would be to come inform me that Congress had placed new limits on its confidence in the King after having informed me, although indirectly, that it was complete, had immediately proposed an adjournment, and that the motion had not been taken into consideration. These delegates told me that they strongly desired, for the preservation of harmony, that a compromise might be adopted. I evinced the greatest surprise at all these details. I appeared at first persuaded that such motives could not have an influence on the decisions made by Congress, but when I saw that many delegates appeared alarmed at the discontent of some of their Colleagues, I said to the latter, who spoke to me of it, that the confidence of Congress in the friendship of the King should be spontaneous, that I had envisaged the objections of a small number of them as insufficient to persuade the Senate to make alterations in a resolution previously agreed on; but that the Solicitude shown to me by persons whose opinion I knew determined me to press them to regard the communication that had been made to me as void, to reconsider the resolutions taken, and to be persuaded that we did not wish in any way to avail ourselves of a confidence that would not be the result of a mature deliberation or that would not be unanimous among well-intentioned persons. I added that, judging by what was happening at that moment, the powers that many delegates were afraid to place in the hands of the King were not a very desirable thing for us, that one could judge in advance by the disquiet that they manifested that the peace, whatever were the conditions of it, would not satisfy everyone, that many persons, well-intentioned in other respects, erred nevertheless in the idea that they were made by the European Powers and the persuasion that they were all inclined for independence, which is far from being true, and that according to these circumstances, if we consulted our interests more than those of our allies, we should make vows that the American plenipotentiairies have all the powers that some people want to reserve to them. The effect of this language, My Lord, has been to have these resolutions reconsidered and to confirm them, as I firmly hoped....

le che de la luzerne

Received 10 August.

FFAA: Pol. Corr., U.S., v. 17, f. 48 (LC transcription).

Comte de Vergennes to Benjamin Franklin

[Translation]

Mr. Franklin   Versailles, 29 June 1781

I have received, Sir, the letter that you have done me the honor of writing me the 27th of this month, and to which was joined the one Mr. Hartley sent to you. I see that this Englishman wishes to come to France in order to have political conversations with you, and you are welcome to consult with me concerning the response that you have to make him.

You are too enlightened, Sir, not to sense for yourself that peace will never be made or even facilitated with voluntary and unauthorized negotiators, and that in listening to them you risk compromising yourself fruitlessly by furnishing them material for paragraphs in gazettes or for parliamentary declarations. I think therefore, Sir, that you would do very well to evade Mr. Hartley's offer unless he assures you positively that he has a mission on the part of the English Ministry. What is the less probable is that the Court of London first provoked the mediation of the two Imperial Courts, and that it is not sufficiently inconsistent to want to establish a clandestine negotiation with you. If however, contrary to all probability, Mr. Hartley should declare himself acknowledged by the British ministry, I think that you would be able to listen to him without inconvenience, the mediating powers not having yet made any overture or invitation to Congress, and if you receive an affirmative response, I will make no difficulty in sending you the passport that Mr. Hartley asks for.

Vergennes

FFAA: Pol. Corr., U.S., v. 17, f. 233-233vo. (LC transcription).

Comte de Vergennes to Chevalier de la Luzerne

[Translation]

Nᵒ· 19.   Versailles, 30 June 1781

. . . . .

It is an established fact, Sir, that the United States have the greatest interest in maintaining the integrity of their union, and that they would meet with a sensible loss by the separation of any one of the provinces that have taken part therein. The King's manner of thinking in this respect agrees perfectly with that of Congress, and His Majesty, guided by an enlightened policy as much as by his engagements, is well resolved to do all that depends on him in order that the 13 confederated provinces maintain their link without alteration. But it happens only too often that circumstances make the law for the most powerful Sovereigns, and that they force them to modify the best laid plans. We still cannot foresee whether we are in this situation relative to America: but what I can assure you is that our strong and invariable intention is to avoid it as much as it is in our power, and that the King will only change his resolution when he sees the absolute impossibility of arriving at a reasonable peace without some sort of sacrifice. But, Sir, I repeat, this Sacrifice is the order of probabilities; and if it becomes necessary, it will be necessary to be resigned to it: most of the Belgian Provinces had shaken off the Spanish yoke; however, only 7 have preserved their independence.

If the preponderant members of Congress discuss this matter with you, Sir, you will apply yourself to convincing them that the King holds to his obligations through principle as through sentiment, and that his own interest is a guarantee to them of the fidelity with which he is resolved to fulfill them; but you will take care at the same time gradually to familiarize them with the hypotheses that, in coming true, may render some sacrifice indispensable. I understand perfectly, Sir, how painful this insinuation will be for you as for your confidants, and all the difficulty of making sprout in American heads ideas so contradictory to their calculations, and so proper to revolt them at first sight: but your dexterity and your prudence will indicate to you the means of surmounting these obstacles by preparing their minds in advance and without affectation. It is especially good that you make the Americans understand that the war will not be eternal, and that there is a point at which one is obligated to stop in spite of oneself. But you will have the greatest attention to speak only as from yourself, and not to let it be discovered that you are authorized to do so; because in this latter case the Americans would suppose that the King has taken the position in advance of abandoning them, and they would think all lost: His

Majesty is resolved not to propose any sacrifice to them; he thinks he should leave this deplorable concern to the two mediating courts, if ever it becomes necessary: I presume, Sir, that you will have now received the despatches in which I inform you of all that has happened in Europe for the establishment of a mediation, and that you will have taken the necessary steps to inform Congress of it. Things in this respect have not changed face since my last despatch; there have been some preliminary overtures, but they are not yet sufficiently explicit to be regarded as certain bases of peace. I have, however, had Mr. Adams informed, and I hope that he will yield to the invitation I have tendered him of coming at all events to Paris: it may be necessary from one moment to another to see his full powers, and to know at least the principal articles of his instructions.

The accession of Maryland to the general confederation presents all the more advantages, for up to this time Congress, which should be the soul of the United States' operations, was without vigor, without consideration, and without authority; from which resulted a languor and an incoherence that have been the principal cause of the lack of success that the Americans' efforts have had. As Congress has finally acquired the power that the act of confederation assigns to it, we hope that its orders will be more respected than in the past; that it will know how to take advantage of the resources of America, and that it will give to American patriotism a development unknown until now. You have perfectly perceived, Sir, the spirit of the King's policy and of his opinion on the nature of the government of the United States, in supposing that not only do we not fear the union of these same States, but that we even desire it, and His Majesty as well as his Council have strongly applauded the step you have taken to put an end to the Marylanders' irresolution: If we had ever thought that the confederation of the 13 American States could sooner or later have political disadvantages, we would not have favored it: up to now no event, no circumstance has been of a nature to weaken our manner of thinking in this regard.

In addition, Sir, as you very well observe, the completion of the American confederation should have annihilated any idea of partial ratifications; and I presume that from now on there will be less question of it, that Congress itself is above all interested in it having no sequel. You would do well, Sir, to direct your insinuations on this subject towards this point of view, if, counter to every expectation, it should still be brought into question.

· · · · ·

Vergennes

FFAA: Pol. Corr., U.S., v. 17, f. 53 (LC transcription).

John Adams to the President of Congress

Sir   Paris July 11. 1781

I have only time,...to inform Congress that upon Information from the Comte de Vergennes that Questions concerning Peace under the Mediation of the two imperial Courts were in agitation, that required my Presence here, I undertook the Journey, and arrived here last fryday night the sixth of the Month, and have twice waited on the Comte de Vergennes at Versailles, who this day communicated to me, the inclosed Propositions.

These Propositions are made to all the belligerent Powers, by the Courts of Petersbourg and Vienna, in consequence of Some wild Propositions made to them by the Court of London, "that they would undertake the office of Mediators, upon condition that the League as they call it, between France and their Rebel Subjects in America should be dissolved, and these left to make their Terms with Great Britain, after having returned to their Allegiance and Obedience."

France and Spain have prepared, their answers to these Propositions of the Empress and Emperor, and I am desired to give my Answer to the Articles inclosed. it is not in my Power, at this Time to inclose to Congress my Answer, because I have not made it, nor written it; but Congress must See, that nothing can come of this Maneuore, at least for a long time. Thus much I may Say to Congress, that I have no Objection to the Proposition of treating with the English Seperately in the manner proposed, upon a Peace, and a Treaty of Commerce with them, consistent with our Engagements with France and Spain: but that the Armistice never can be agreed to by me. The objections against it are as numerous as they are momentous and decisive. I may say farther, that as there is no judge upon Earth, of a Sovereign Power, but the nation that composes it I can never agree to the Mediation of any Powers, however respectable, untill they have acknowledged our Sovereignty, So Far ~~as to~~ at least as to admit, a Minister Plenipotentiary from the United States, as the Representative of a free and independent Power. After this We might discuss Questions of Peace or Truce with Great Britain, ~~but~~ ~~and~~ without her Acknowledging our Sovereignty, but not before.

I fancy, however that Congress will be applied to for their Sentiments and I shall be ever ready and happy to obey their Instructions, because I have a full Confidence that nothing will be decided by them, but what will be consistent with their Character and dignity.

Peace will only be retarded by Relaxations and Concessions whereas Firmness, Patience and Perseverance, will insure us a good and lasting one, in the End.

The English are obliged to keep up the Talk of Peace to lull their Enemies and to Sustain their Credit. But I hope the People of America, will not be deceived. Nothing will obtain them, real Peace, but Skillfull and Successfull War.

I have the Honour to be, with great respect, your most obedient and humble Servant   John Adams.
Read March 1. 1782

NA: PCC, Misc. Papers, Adams Despatches (ALS); M332, reel 1, ff. 371-374.

John Adams to Comte de Vergennes

Sir,   Paris, July 13th. 1781.
I have the honor to inclose to your Excellency some remarks upon the Articles to serve as a Basis of the Negotiation for the reestablishment of Peace which you did me the honor to communicate to me.- As I am unacquainted, whether you desired my Sentiments upon these Articles merely for your own Government, or with a design to communicate them to the Imperial Courts I should be glad of your Excellencys Advice concerning them. If your Excellency is of opinion there is any thing exceptionable, or which ought to be altered, I should be glad to correct it: or if I have not perceived the Points, or Questions, upon which you desired my opinion, I shall be ready to give any further Answers.- I have the honor to be, with great respect, your Excellencys most obedient and most humble Servant.   J. Adams

Paris July 13th. 1781.

Answer of the Minister Plenipotentiary of the United States of America, to the Articles to serve as a Basis to the Negotiation for the reestablishment of Peace.

Articles to serve as the basis for the negotiation of the restoration of the Peace.

Art. 1.

The United States of America have no objection, provided their Allies have none, to a Treaty with Great Britain, concerning the

Art. 1.

The restoration of the Peace will be negotiated between Great Britain and the American Colonies, but without the reestablishment of Peace in America, or to another concerning the reestablishment of Commerce, between the two Nations, consistent with their obligations to France and Spain; without the Intervention of any of the other belligerent Parties, and even without that of the two Imperial Courts, at least unless their Mediation should be formally demanded and granted upon this object, according to the first Article communicated to me.

Art. 2.

The United States have nothing to say, provided their Allies have not, against the second Article.

intervention of any of the other belligerent Parties, nor of that of the two Imperial Courts unless their mediation on this subject has been formally requested and granted.

Art. 2.

This specific Peace, however, can only be signed conjointly, and at the same time as that of the Powers whose interests will have been negotiated by the Mediating Courts. The two Peaces, on condition that although they may be negotiated separately, one can in no way be concluded without the other, care will be taken continually to inform the mediators of the progress and the status of what concerns Great Britain and the Colonies, so that the mediation is in a position to set a pace for the progress of that entrusted to it by the status of the Negotiation relative to the Colonies, and both the two pacifications, which will have been concluded at the same time, although separately, must be solemnly guaranteed by the Mediating Courts and every other neutral Power whose guarantee the belligerent Parties may consider it appropriate to require.

Art 3.

To the Armistice, and the *status quo*, in the third Article, the United States have very great Objections; which indeed are so numerous and decisive, and at the same time so obvious, as to make it unnecessary to state them in detail.

The Idea of a Truce is not suggested in these Articles; but as it is mentioned in some Observations shewn me by his Excellency the Comte de Vergennes, it may be necessary for me to add, that the United States are so deeply impressed with an Apprehension, that any Truce whatsoever would not fail to be productive of another long and bloody War, at the termination of it, and that a short Truce would be in many ways highly dangerous to them, that it would be with great Reluctance that they should enter into any discussion at all, upon such a subject.

Two express Conditions would be indispensible Preliminaries to their taking into consideration, the subject of a Truce at all. The first is, that their Allies agree, that the Treaties now subsisting remain in full force during and after the Truce, until the final Acknowledgment of their Independence by Great Britain. The second is, the antecedent Removal of the British Land and Naval Armaments from every Part of the United States. Upon these two express Conditions as Preliminaries, if a Truce should be

Art. 3.

In order to render the peace negotiations independent of the always uncertain events of war, which can halt or at least delay their progress, there will be a general Armistice among all the Parties for the space of one year, to run from the ___ of the month of _____ of the present, or for ____ years to run from the ___ of the month of _____ of the year 1782, if it happens that a general peace is not restored in the course of the first term. And for the duration of one or the other of these two terms everything must remain in the state in which it was on the day of the Signing of the present preliminary articles.

proposed for so long a period, or for an indefinite period, requiring so long notice, previous to a renewal of hostilities, as to evince that it is on the part of Great Britain a virtual Relinquishment of the object of the War, and an Expedient only to avoid the mortification of an express Acknowledgment of the Independence and Sovereignty of the United States, they, with the concurrence of their Allies might acceed to it.

It is requisite however to add: First – that the United States cannot consider themselves bound by this declaration, unless it should be agreed to before the opening of another Campaign. Secondly – That it is not in the Power of the Crown of Great Britain, by the Constitution of that Kingdom, or establish any Truce, or even Armistice with the United States, which would not be illusory without the intervention of an Act of Parliament, repealing or suspending all their Statutes, which have any relation to the United States or any of them. Without this, every Officer of the Navy would be bound by the Laws, according to the Maxims of their Constitution, to seize every American Vessel that he should find, whose Papers and Destination should not be found conformable to those Statutes, and every French, Spanish, Dutch or other foreign Vessel, which he should find going to or coming from America;

notwithstanding any Convention that it is in the Power of the Crown to make.

After all: the greatest difficulty does not lie in any thing as yet mentioned. The great question is, in what Character are the Untied States to be considered?

They know themselves to be a free, sovereign and independent State, of right and in fact.

They are considered and acknowledged as such, by France. They cannot be represented in a Congress of Ministers from the several Powers of Europe, whether their Representative is called Ambassador, Minister or Agent, without an Acknowledgement of their Independence, of which the very Admission of a Representative from them is an avowal. Great Britain cannot agree with their Representative upon a Truce, or even an Armistice, without admitting their freedom and Independence.

As there is upon Earth no judge of a sovereign State, but the Nation that composes it, the United States can never consent, that their Independence shall be discussed or called in question by any Sovereign or Sovereigns however respectable, nor can their Interests be made a question in any Congress, in which their Character is not acknowledged and their Minister admitted. If therefore the two Imperial Courts would acknowledge, and lay down as a preliminary, the Sovereignty of the

United States, and admit their Minister to a Congress: after this, a Treaty might be commenced, between the Minister of Great Britain and the Minister of the United States, relative to a Truce, or Peace and Commerce, in the manner proposed, without any express acknowledgment of their Sovereignty by Great Britain, until the treaty should be concluded.

The Sovereigns of Europe have a right to negotiate concerning their own Interests, and to deliberate concerning the question, whether it is consistent with their Dignity and Interests, to acknowledge expressly the Sovereignty of the United States, and to make Treaties with them, by their Ministers in a Congress or otherwise; and America could make no Objection to it: but neither the United States nor France can ever consent, that the Existence of their Sovereignty shall be made a question in such Congress: because, let that Congress determine as it might, their Sovereignty, with submission only to divine Providence, never can, and never will, be given up.

As the british Court, in first suggesting the Idea of a Congress to the Imperial Courts, insisted upon the annihilation of the League, as they were pleased to call it, between France and their Rebel Subjects, as they were pleased again to phrase it, and upon the return of these to their Allegiance and Obedience, as Preliminaries to any Congress or Mediation; there is too much Reason to fear, that the british Ministry have no serious intentions or sincere dispositions for Peace, and that they mean nothing but Amusement. Because, the support of the Sovereignty of the United States was the primary object of the War, on the part of France and America: the destruction of it that of Great Britain. If therefore the Treaty between France and America were annulled, and the Americans returned to the Domination and Monopoly of Great Britain, there would be no need of troubling all Europe with a Congress to make Peace. All points between France, Spain and Great Britain might be easily adjusted among themselves. Surely the Affairs of Great Britain are in no part of the World so triumphant, nor those of any of their Enemies so adverse, as to give this Ministry any serious hopes, that France and America will renounce the object of the War. There must therefore be some other view.

It is not difficult to penetrate the design of the British Ministry upon this, any more than upon many former Occasions. They think that a distrust of them, and a Jealousy, that they would not adhere with good Faith to the Propositions of Reconciliation, which they have made from time to time, were, in the minds of the Americans, the true Cause why these Propositions were not accepted. They now think, that, by prevailing on the two Imperial Courts, and other Courts to warranty to the Americans any similar terms they may propose to them, they shall remove this Obstacle; and by this means, although they know, that no public Authority in America will agree to such Terms, they think they shall be able to represent things in such a light, as to induce many desertions from the American Army, and many Apostates from the American Independence and Alliance. In this way, they would pursue their long practised Arts of seduction, deception and division. In these again, as in so many former Attempts, they would find themselves disappointed, and would make very few Deserters or Apostates. But it is to be hoped, that the Powers of Europe will not give to these superficial Artifices, with which that Ministry have so long destroyed the Repose of the United States, and of the British Dominions at home and abroad, and disturbed the tranquility of Europe, so much Attention as to enable them to continue much longer such Evils to Mankind.

J. Adams

NA: PCC, Misc. Papers, Adams Despatches; M332; reel 1, ff. 375, 384-392.

François Barbé de Marbois to Comte de Vergennes

[Translation]

Nᵒ· 158. 1.   Philadelphia, 14 July 1781
My Lord

. . . . .

Congress is fully prepared to see Colonel Laurens return without having accomplished the principal objects of his mission; This Senate is persuaded that the aid obtained before his arrival by Mr. Franklin is all that is possible for the King to do for his allies. It is not at all to be feared that our refusal will occasion any coolness. Confidence has never been greater than at this moment, and I think I can assure you that the continuation of the System that His Majesty is following with regard to the 13 *States* will only affirm it; there is therefore nothing to fear concerning the dispositions of Congress; but it remains to examine whether their Situation and their needs do not require the continuation of pecuniary assistance in the event the war should continue. The Superintendent told me that with the Aid of several millions of piastres on the part of Spain, he would be caught up towards the middle of next year and spared from making ulterior demands on France. But a letter from Mr. Jay to Congress arrived since I had this conversation with Mr. Morris, and it augurs very little disposition on the part of the Court of Spain to accord Congress the Subsidy or the loan that it appears to expect. This burden will therefore again fall on us, and if the Spanish Ministry persists in its refusals, it will become almost indispensable to come to the Aid of Congress again next year. I have said almost indispensable, My Lord, because if serious grounds make it absolutely impossible for us to assist the Americans with our money, their cause nevertheless will not collapse. They will be without the ability to attack with vigor, but their affairs are currently in such a posture that they will maintain at least a defensive advantage....Mr. Jay, My Lord, has probably not passed to Mr. Franklin the instructions of Congress relative to the negotiation with Spain on which I had the honor to report to you during the month of October last. That minister disapproves of the concessions that Congress has been disposed to make to that Power, and I have reason to think that it is he who up until then impeded that negotiation. Mr. Carmichael is much better disposed and makes every effort to engage his friends in Congress to send Mr. Jay resolutions still more precise than those that he has until now put off executing. In addition, all Mr. Jay's letters speak with affection of gratitude toward France; one of them was secretly communicated to me, one that I think important to make you aware of, because it paints, better than anything I could say, the character of that minister, and because it proves his esteem for Mr. Franklin, and because it can be concluded therefrom that they will act in concert in the future peacemaking. Mr. John Adams and Mr. Jay are far from being on equally good terms.

Congress has never been better disposed toward Mr. Franklin than at this moment. Your commendations, My Lord, have won him those of a very

great majority; it was decided not to accept his resignation, and as long as the delegations are composed as they now are, I am persuaded that he will not be recalled. As for Mr. John Adams, the party of well-intentioned Delegates, persuaded that he could, by means of the powers he always had to the exclusion of the other plenipotentiaries to conclude a treaty of Commerce, impede the negotiations for peace, have made a motion to take those powers away from him, and to put an End to his commission. This motion was strongly opposed, especially by the Delegates from Massachusetts. The Deliberation having been postponed until the following day, a delegate from the South came to discuss this affair with me. He told me that he himself was against the motion because he thought that when "Congress had revoked the powers of Mr. Adams to conclude a Treaty of Commerce, it would have trouble transferring them to the Plenipotentiaries charged with the Negotiation of peace, and that if the English in that state of affairs made a Treaty of Commerce a condition *sine qua non* of peace, the negotiation would be halted for lack of powers." The objection seemed to me to merit attention, My Lord. However, after an attentive consideration of the matter, I said to that Delegate that the instructions sent to the five Plenipotentiaries seemed to me to give them an indefinite latitude, with the exception of two reserved points only, i.e., independence and the alliance. Thus, I continued, even if Congress did not give them specific instructions for a treaty of Commerce, they have, de facto, the Power to introduce some general stipulations on this subject into the Treaty of peace. It seems to me, My Lord, that there are many fewer disadvantages in rendering difficult the conclusion of a Treaty of Commerce between the English and our Allies than in leaving Adams alone charged with this important part of the negotiation, so that he would find himself thereby on the level of the four other Plenipotentiaries and would only have a part still less than you would have desired for him in the whole conduct of this affair; the motion, having again been taken into consideration in a subsequent Session, passed at a majority of eight votes, and Mr. John Adams is no longer charged with the Negotiation of a Treaty of Commerce....   Marbois.
R. 11 September.

FFAA: Pol. Corr., U.S., v. 17, f. 106 (LC transcription).

John Adams to the President of Congress

Triplicate   Paris July 15th. 1781.
Sir,
    I have the honor to inclose a Copy of a Letter to the Comte de

Vergennes, and of certain Articles and their Answers.

The British Court proposed to the Imperial Courts a Congress upon two preliminary Conditions, the Rupture of the Treaty with France, and the Return of America to their Obedience: The two Imperial Courts have since proposed the inclosed Articles. Spain and France have prepared their Answers – England has not answered yet, and no Ministers are yet commissioned or appointed by any Power. – If She accepts the terms, I should not scruple to accept them too, excepting the Armistice and Statu quo: but I mean I should not insist upon a previous explicit Acknowledgment of the Sovereignty of the United States, before I went to Vienna. I see nothing inconsistent with the Character or Dignity of the United States, in their Minister going to Vienna, at the same [time] when Ministers from the other Powers are there, and entering into Treaty with a British Minister, without any Acknowledgment explicitly of our Independence, before the Conclusion of the Treaty. – The very Existence of such a Congress would be of use to our Reputation: but I cannot yet believe that Britain will wave her Preliminaries – She will still insist upon the Dissolution of the Treaty, and upon the Return of the Americans under their Government. This however will do no honor to her Moderation and pacific sentiments, in the opinion of the Powers of Europe.

Something may grow out of these Negotiations in time; but it will probably be several Years before any thing can be done. Americans only can quicken these Negotiations by decisive strokes. – No depredations upon their trade, no conquests of their possessions in the East or West Indies will have any effect upon the English to induce them to make Peace, while they see they have an Army in the United States, and can flatter themselves with the hope of conquering or regaining America; because they think that with America under their Government, they can easily regain whatever they may lose now in any part of the World.

Whereas the total Expulsion or Captivity of their Forces in the United States would extinguish their hopes, and persuade them to Peace, sooner than the loss of every thing else. The belligerent Powers and the Neutral Powers may flatter themselves with the hopes of a Restoration of Peace, but they will all be disappointed, while the English have a Soldier in America. It is amazing to me that France and Spain do not see it, and direct their forces accordingly.

I have the honor to be, with the greatest Respect, Sir, your most obedient and most humble Servant.   J Adams.
Read Oct. 3. –

NA: PCC, Misc. Papers, Adams Despatches (LS); M332, reel 1, ff. 409-411.

Chevalier de la Luzerne to Comte de Vergennes

[Translation]

Nᵒ· 166 2ⁿᵈ·   Philadelphia, 11 August 1781

My Lord.

The choice of a secretary of State for the Department of foreign affairs has occupied Congress for more than a year. From the moment of his arrival, Mr. Lee placed himself in contention, but without success, although he had five votes. This affair having been lately resumed, he renewed his efforts with the most extraordinary activity, he had won four States, and as he declared with an inconceivable assurance to the Delegates from several others that I was very far from placing the least obstacle to his election, there were some who appeared ready to be seduced when the declarations that I made to them apprised them how they should distrust the veracity of that ex-commissioner. I nevertheless feared to see the same maneuvers be renewed without ceasing, and perhaps with more Success, given the continual mobility of the delegations. The only way to be safe against his intrigues was to cause the Congress to make another choice. Mr. Livingston,[1] Chancellor of the State of New York, was the most suitable man in this place, but the cabal of Messrs. Izard and Lee had kept him distant up to the present. Moreover, these Gentlemen had worked hard to consider him as particularly linked with us, and that, in the opinion of some, is a motive for exclusion. Mr. Livingston having been here for several weeks, he confessed to me his desire to be named to that post, and we agreed on the means to employ to bring this about. There were then three Candidates in the running. Congress had not been so numerous for a very long time. There were a dozen States represented by the number of Delegates necessary, and North Carolina alone had only one Delegate, which rendered its vote null. Mr. Livingston at first had five votes, Mr. Lee four, and Mr. Maclorg,[2] a man almost unknown, had three. I would very much have wished not to be obliged to use my influence to gain for Mr. Livingston the two votes that he lacked, and I perceived the disadvantages of appearing in so delicate an affair. A delegate entirely devoted to Mr. Lee suggested that my predilection for the one should be a motive for his exclusion, and that my dislike for the other should make him preferred. I nevertheless determined to undertake the conversion of two States. I proved to them that the choice of Mr. Lee would have really troublesome consequences for the confidence and the good terms that should exist among Allies, and that Mr. Maclorg was only a phantom brought forward by Mr. Lee's Friends themselves in order to prevent Mr. Livingston from having seven votes, and to have the election postponed until a favorable time for their Candidate. Several sessions passed in fruitless endeavors in which an absence, an illness, or some business somehow always prevented the States inclined toward Mr. Livingston from being fully represented. Finally, My Lord, there was a new vote, and the choice of Congress was fixed on him. He had the seven votes of New Hampshire, Rhode Island, New York, New Jersey, Pennsylvania, Maryland, and Georgia; Mr. Lee had three others, and Mr. Maclorg two. I am persuaded, My Lord, that this assembly could not have made a better choice. Mr. Livingston has filled with honor the place of Chancellor of the State of New York, he is familiar with business, he is perfectly informed about that of the United States, he writes well, he speaks with sufficient eloquence, he has much affability of character, he is sufficiently confident, his conduct has been uniform since this revolution, he makes a profession of attachment to the Alliance; and to these good qualities, as a public man, he adds a reputation of great probity as a private one. He is from one of the oldest families in the State of New York, a near relation of Mr. Jay, and his friend; he enjoys a considerable fortune. The esteem which I have for him does not prevent me from telling you that he is reproached with reason for his considerable indolence and for loving his repose above all. The part I had in his election obliges me to the greatest circumspection in his regard, that is the only way of stopping the complaints of his antagonists. I expect hereafter to find the family of Mr. Lee more contrary than in the past, given that the causes they had to spare me no longer exist, and that they cannot be unaware of the steps I have chosen to take against Mr. Arthur Lee. General Sullivan had the largest part in this election. He cannot show more zeal for the Alliance, and to that Delegate are due in great part the useful resolutions that Congress has passed for several months. That which I have just reported, My Lord, is moreover a proof of His Majesty's influence on Congress, and that assembly is in fact in the most desirable of dispositions with regard to the alliance; I hope that they will be lasting, but that Body is subject to too much change for me to be able to answer for that. That affair alone kept General Sullivan here, and this morning he departed for his State. It is a question of giving a constitution to New Hampshire, of arranging the affairs of Vermont, and besides his domestic affairs are very unsettled. I wish very much for his return; he assured me that it would take place before the end of the year; I am unacquainted with his successor.

I am with Respect, My Lord, your very humble and very obedient servant
le chr. de la luzerne.

Received 18 November.

FFAA: Pol. Corr., U.S., v. 18, f. 23 (LC transcription).
[1] Livingston, Robert R. (1746-1813). New York political figure and diplomat. Member,

Continental Congress, 1775-1776, 1779-1780, 1784. Secretary for Foreign Affairs, August 1781-August 1783. Chancellor of New York State, 1777-1801. Minister to France, 1801-1804.

[2] McClurg, James. Surgeon of a Virginia regiment and Surgeon General of Virginia state troops, 1777-1782. Candidate for the post of Secretary for Foreign Affairs, August 1781. Delegate, Constitutional Convention, 1787.

Instructions to John Adams from Congress

Thursday Aug 16. 1781

The report of the committee on the communications of the hon[ble.] the Minister plenipotentiary of France was taken into consideration and thereupon.

Resolved That the Minister plenipotentiary of these United States at the court of Versailles be directed to inform his most Christian Majesty that the tender of his endeavours to accomplish a coalition between the United provinces of the Netherlands and these states hath been received by Congress as a fresh proof of his solicitude for their interests: that previous to the communication of this, his most Christian Majesty's friendly purpose, Congress impressed with the importance of such a connection had confided to M[r] John Adams full powers to enter, on the part of the United States, into a treaty of Amity and Commerce with the United provinces, with a special instruction to conform himself therein to the treaties subsisting between his Most Christian Majesty and the United States; that Congress do, with pleasure, accept his Most Christian Majesty's interposition and will transmit further powers to their Minister at the Hague to form a treaty of alliance between his Most Christian Majesty, the United provinces and the United States having for its object and limited in its duration to, the present war with great Britain; that he will be enjoined to confer on all occasions in the most confidential manner with his Most Christian Majesty's Minister at the Hague; and that provisional authority will also be sent to admit his Catholic Majesty as a party.

Resolved That the Minister plenipotentiary of these United States at the Hague be and he is hereby instructed to propose a treaty of Alliance between his Most Christian Majesty, the United provinces of the Netherlands and the United States of America, having for its object and limited in its duration to, the present war with great Britain and conformed to the treaties subsisting between his Most Christian Majesty and the United States.

That the indispensible conditions of the alliance be that their High Mightinesses the States general of the United Provinces of the Neitherlands shall expressly recognize the sovereignty and independence of the United States of America, absolute and unlimited as well in matters of government as of commerce: that the war with Great Britain shall be made a common cause, each party exerting itself according to its discretion in the most effectual hostility against the common enemy; And that no party shall conclude either truce or peace with Great Britain without the formal consent of the whole first obtained, nor lay down their arms until the sovereignty and independence of these United States shall be formally or tacitly assured by Great Britain in a treaty which shall terminate the war.

That the said Minister be and he hereby is farther instructed to unite the two Republics by no stipulations of offence nor guarantee any possession of the United provinces: – To inform himself from the Minister of these United States at the court of Spain of the progress of his Negotiations at the said Court; and if an Alliance shall have been entered into between his Catholic Majesty and these United States to invite his Catholic Majesty into the alliance herein intended; if no such alliance shall have been formed, to receive his Catholic Majesty, should he manifest a disposition to become a party to the Alliance herein intended, according to the instructions given to the said Minister at the court of Spain. – That in all other matters not repugnant to these instructions the said Minister at the Hague do use his best discretion.

Resolved that the Minister plenipotentiary of these United States at the Hague be and hereby is instructed to confer in the most confidential manner with his Most Christian Majesty's Minister there.

Ordered That the foregoing resolutions be communicated to our Ministers at the courts of Versailles & Madrid, that they may furnish every information and aid in their power to our Minister at the Hague in the accomplishment of this business.

Ordered That a plenipotentiary commission be prepared authorising Mr John Adams to enter into the Alliance aforesaid.

NA: PCC, item 4, pp. 96-100 (Journal); M247, reel 18.

Benjamin Franklin to John Adams

Sir,   Passy Augt. 16 1781.
I have the honour in inform your Excellency that I yesterday received Dispatches from Congress, refusing for the present, the Dismission I had requested, and ordering me upon an Additional Service, that of being join'd with yourself & Messrs. Jay, H Lawrence & T. Jefferson, in Negociations for Peace. I would send you a Copy of the Commission, and of another which

authorizes us to accept of the Mediation of the Emperor, and the Empress of Russia, but that I suppose you may have them in the enclosed Packet. I shall be glad to learn from your Excellency what Steps have already been taken in this important Business.

With great Regard, I have the honour to be, Sir, Your Excellency's most obedient and most humble Servant   B Franklin

MHS: The Adams Papers, microfilm reel 355 (LS).

John Jay to Benjamin Franklin

Dr Sir,   [St. Ildefonso, 20 August 1781]

. . . . .

I cannot forbear considering the approaching Winter as a very critical Season– It is said that Russia & the Emperor have offered their Mediation, & that it will be accepted – It is further said that France wishes for Peace. For my own Part I fear that France has very little to expect from the Friendship of these Mediators, & unless Appearances deceive me every Nation in Europe, except Prussia, wish better to England than to France. It appears to me expedient to delay the Progress of this Mediation, & in the mean time to endeavour strenuously to form a close defensive Alliance between France, Spain, Holland & America – If France & Spain could be prevailed upon to adopt this Idea *speedily*, & heartily I am persuaded that the Dutch might in their present temper, & to obtain certain guaranties, easily be brought into the Measure – Such a quadruple alliance, followed by a vigorous Campaign could give us a Peace worth our Acceptance. As to the present Campaign, I do not expect great things from it – my Expectations from the Expedition against New-York are far from sanguine – It depends on too many Contingencies not to be very uncertain –

I wish to see some great stroke struck, some great plan wisely concerted, and vigorously executed – Had a french Fleet of decided Superiority to the Enemy, been on our Coast early in the spring, & cooperated with General Washington thro' out the Summer, Halifax, New-York & Charlestown would before Winter have changed Masters, & then we should have been ripe for Peace.

As to this Court, I do not apprehend that they are tired of the War, or that they have the least Objection to another Campaign — They want Jamaica, they want Gibraltar, & Mahon would be a trump card in their hands – If their Activity was equal to their Perseverance, & thus possessed the talent of drawing forth & using all their Resources, they would be very formidable – But take Spain as she is – if she could once be prevailed upon to pass the Rubicon, that is, to acknowledge, & engage to support our Independence, she would give Great Britain a mortal wound, and render essential service to the common Cause. How far France views the Matter in the same light, I know not, nor can I clearly comprehend the Policy of the System she seems to hold relative to it.

The Embassador is well attached to the American Cause, and [has] such proper Views of its importance, as well as the Manner of supporting it, that I have often wished him at Versailles – There is nevertheless a sort of mysterious reserve about him upon this Subject, nor am I informed whether any & what Steps have been taken by him and his Court to influence Spain to an Alliance with us – I have however full confidence in the Friendship of France, & the late Aids she has granted to America give us Reason to rely on the king & his principal Ministers.

There is some Reason to hope that this Court begins to think more seriously of a Treaty with us than heretofore – A few Weeks will enable me to judge better of their Views – In Politics I depend upon nothing but facts, and therefore never risque deceiving myself or others by a reliance on Professions which may or may not be sincere.

The Duke of Crillon[1] is still at sea – I am tempted to wish that Expedition had not been undertaken – If it fails, it will do harm, & I see little Prospect of its succeeding.

You are several Letters in my debt, and I wish to know whether one relative to M^r. Vaughan[2] ever reached you.

As I have reason to think this Letter will go unopened to your Hands, I have written with less reserve than usual....

. . . . .

With great & sincere Esteem & Regard I am, Dear Sir, Your most obed^t. Servt.   John Jay

LC: *Benjamin Franklin Papers, v. 6, pp. 26-29 (C); microfilm reel 2.*

[1] *Crillon-Mahon, Louis de Berton des Balbes de Quiers, Duc de (1718-1796). French general who entered the service of Spain in 1762, after distinguished conduct in the War of the Austrian Succession and the Seven Years War. Commanded Spanish and French forces in the capture of Minorca, August 1781-February 1782. Commanded Franco-Spanish army in the siege of Gibraltar, 1782.*

[2] *Vaughan, Benjamin (1751-1835). Political economist. Friend and follower of Lord Shelburne, acquaintance of Benjamin Franklin. Sent to Paris by Shelburne in summer 1782 to assure Franklin that Rockingham's death and Shelburne's accession to power would cause no change in the ministry's intention of recognizing American independence; later conveyed pacific messages from Franklin and John Jay to Shelburne regarding the settlement of American problems as the key to a European peace. Member of Parliament, 1792-1794. Sympathetic to the revolution in France, he took refuge in that country, 1794-1798, after which he emigrated to the United States.*

John Adams to Benjamin Franklin

Sir   Amsterdam August 25th 1781.

Last Evening I recieved your Excellency's Letter of the 16th. of this month, accompanied with a Letter from the President of Congress containing the Commissions You mention.

You desire to know what Steps have already been taken in this business. There has been no Step taken by me, in pursuance of my former Commission, until my late Journey to Paris at the Invitation of the Comte de Vergennes, who communicated to me certain Articles, proposed by the mediating Courts, and desired me to make such Observations upon them as should occur to me. Accordingly I wrote a Number of Letters to his Excellency of the following Dates – July 13th. inclosing an answer to the Articles 16th. 18th. 19th. 21st. – I would readily send you Copies of the Articles and of those Letters, but there are matters in them which had better not be trusted to go so long a Journey, especially as there is no Necessity for it.

The Comte de Vergennes will readily give you Copies of the Articles and of my Letters, which will prevent all risque.

I am very apprehensive that our new Commission will be as useless as my old one. – Congress might very safely I believe permit Us all to go home, if We had no other business, and stay there some Years: at least until every British Soldier in the United States is killed or captivated. Till then Britain will never think of Peace, but for the purposes of Chicanery.

I see in the Papers, that the British Ambassador at Petersbourg has received an Answer from his Court to the Articles. What this Answer is, We may conjecture from the King's Speech. Yet the Empress of Russia has made an Insinuation to their high Mightinesses, which deserves Attention. Perhaps You may have seen it: but lest You should not, I will add a Translation of it, which I sent to Congress in the time of it, not having the original at hand.

. . . . .

I must beg the favour of your Excellency to communicate to me whatever You may learn, which has any Connection with this Negotiation, particulary the French, Spanish and British Answers to the Articles, as soon as You can obtain them. In my Situation, it is not likely I shall obtain any Information of Consequence, but from the French Court. Whatever may come to my Knowledge, I will communicate to You without delay.

If Britain persists in her two Preliminaries, as I presume She does, what will be the Consequence? Will the two Imperial Courts permit this great plan of a Congress at Vienna, which is public and made the common talk of Europe, to become another sublime Bubble, like the armed Neutrality?

In what a light will these mediating Courts appear, after having listened to a Proposition of England, so far as to make Propositions themselves, and to refer to them in many public Acts, if Britain refuses to agree to them? and insists upon such Preliminaries as are at least an Insult to France and America, and a kind of Contempt to the common Sense of all Europe.

Upon my word I am weary of such round about and endless Negotiations, as that of the armed Neutrality and this of the Congress at Vienna. I think the Dutch have at last discovered the only effectual Method of Negotiation, that is by fighting the British Fleets, until every Ship is obliged to answer the Signal for renewing the Battle by the Signal of distress. There is no Room for British Chicanery in this. If I ever did any good since I was born, it was in stirring up the pure Minds of the Dutchmen, and setting the old Batavian Spirit in motion, after having slept so long. Our dear Country will go fast to sleep in full Assurance of having News of Peace by Winter, if not by the first Vessel. Alas! what a disappointment they will meet. I believe I had better go home and wake up our Countrymen out of their Reveries about peace. Congress have done very well to join others in the Commission for Peace. My Talent, if I have one lies in making War: The Grand Segnior will finish the *Proces des trois Rois* sooner than the Congress at Vienna will make Peace, unless the two Imperial Courts act with Dignity and Consistency upon the occasion, and acknowledge American Independency at once, upon Britain's insisting on her two insolent Preliminaries.

I have the honor to be, Sir, your most obedient and most humble Servant   John Adams.

APS: *Benjamin Franklin Papers (LS).*

Chevalier de la Luzerne to Comte de Vergennes

[Translation]

Nᵒ· 175 Duplicate.   Philadelphia, 6 September [1781]
My Lord.

General Washington left yesterday morning with the Comte de Rochambeau for Head of Elk on the Chesapeake. The Bourbon and the Deux Ponts Regiments and Lauzun's Legion set out at daybreak, after having spent two days in Philadelphia. The Soisson and the Kaintonge

Regiments, which arrived here a day later, spent the whole day there yesterday. The Soisson Regiment held a general small-arms drill on the plain of Philadelphia within General Howe's[1] former lines. There were prodigious throngs of people. The President of Congress, who was there with most of the Delegates, received the honors that are rendered to Marshals of France. Everyone admires the smart turnout of these troops, but what contributes even more to destroying irreversibly the prejudices that the English nation has sought to inspire against us, is the admirable discipline that they maintain. It is on one of the longest marches that an army can undertake. There has been no complaint despite the difficulty of making oneself understood and the difference in the customs of the two nations. All the letters that I have received from the States through which the army has passed are replete with praises for the order that it has maintained. The people have noted the joy with which our Soldiers go in search of the Enemy, and it seems to me that the best spirit and the greatest ardor in fact reign in this Division. It showed the most lively impatience to march on the instant when we learned the news of the arrival of the Comte de Grasse.[2] The Generals of the allied army and the officers of the two French Regiments had just sat down at my table at the moment when an express of General Washington brought me the letter of which I have the honor of sending you the translation, and which told me this good news. It was received to acclamations from all the Officers. The inhabitants of Philadelphia, who were informed of it, came immediately in great numbers to evince their joy and to compliment the French troops. The names of the Generals of the Congress, of the French Regiments, and of all the popular persons were repeated and accompanied by the hurrahs of the people. Bells were rung, bonfires were lit on every side, and the King's name resounded in the town throughout the whole evening. The second Division of our troops set out today. This small army has almost no sick, there has been no desertion, and from the time it learned of the arrival of the King's Fleet, it has been disposed to redouble its speed. I think that it will have joined that of the Marquis de la Fayette in eight or ten days.

The English have evacuated Portsmouth, and Lord Cornwallis[3] has concentrated all his defenses in Gloucester and York on the river of that name.

He commands some four thousand five hundred men of the most hardened troops in the world, and those who made war in America with the most constancy and courage. It is henceforth impossible for him to escape by the Chesapeake; he can endeavor to throw himself towards the South by forcing a passage through the corps commanded by M. de la Fayette and that which M. de Grasse has landed and which M. de S^t.

Simon[4] commands, but he does not have the wagons, supplies, and other things necessary to undertake such a march.

Some militiamen are also assembling to encircle him; in a word, his situation is very critical, and his retreat seems to me very difficult. It is therefore probable that he will seek to hold his forts, and that is what all his movements indicate. But there will inevitably be fourteen thousand regular troops assembled against him, and it is permitted to conceive the hope of a complete Success in this instance. I have received at this instant, My Lord, a letter from the Comte de Grasse, who arrived in the Chesapeake on the 30th of August and not the 26th, as the letter sent to General Washington said. Calms have vexed his voyage, he has put ashore his landing force, numbering 3200 men, and he proposes to add to it 1800 men from his Squadron. The Marquis de la Fayette has put the finishing touches to the excellent conduct that he has maintained up to now. He has made all his dispositions in order to wait for General Washington, and seems to understand the disadvantages of a precipitate attack with insufficient forces against an army so well entrenched.

I am with respect, My Lord, Your very humble and very obedient servant

le che. de la luzerne.

Received 18 November 1781.

FFAA: Pol. Corr., U.S., v. 18, f. 67 (LC transcription).

[1] *Howe, Sir William (1729-1814). British general. Brother of Admiral Lord Richard Howe. Arrived in North America with reinforcements for General Thomas Gage, May 1775; commanded the British force in the Battle of Bunker Hill, June 17, 1775. Succeeded Gage in command of British troops in American colonies, October 1775; withdrew from Boston to Halifax, Nova Scotia, March 1776. With his brother, commissioned to treat with the American rebels and to attempt a reconciliation with the American colonies, May 6, 1776; Congress refused to treat on these terms. Captured Long Island (August 1776), New York (September 1776), and Philadelphia (September 1777). Victorious at White Plains (October 28, 1776), Brandywine (September 11, 1777), and Germantown (September 26, 1777). Submitted resignation in October 1777, complaining of not being properly supported at home. Left America, May 24, 1778.*

[2] *Grasse, François Joseph Paul, Comte de (1722-1788). French naval officer. As admiral commanding Atlantic fleet, fought successful fleet action off the Chesapeake on September 5, 1781, thereby assuring Allied victory at Yorktown. Defeated and captured in the Battle of the Saintes on April 12, 1782. Peripherally involved in peace negotiations, 1782.*

[3] *Cornwallis, Charles, Lord (1738-1805). British general. Although a Whig and a friend of Lord Shelburne, he agreed to serve in the American war, winning victories at Brandywine (September 13, 1777), Camden (August 16, 1780), and Guilford Courthouse (March 15, 1781). After effecting a junction with a smaller British force in Virginia, he established himself, on General Henry Clinton's express orders, at Yorktown, where he was forced to surrender on October 19, 1781. Governor-general and commander-in-chief of*

India, 1783-1793, 1805. Viceroy and commander-in-chief of Ireland, 1798-1801. Negotiated Treaty of Amiens, ending European war, November 1801-March 1802.

⁴ Saint-Simon-Montbléru, Claude-Anne de Rouvroy, Marquis de (1743?-1819). French military officer. Commander of the division of 3470 soldiers De Grasse landed in the Chesapeake, September 1781.

Comte de Vergennes to Chevalier de la Luzerne

[Translation]

Nᵒ· 21   Versailles, 7 September 1781

I have received, Sir, the letters that you have done me the honor of writing me from Nᵒ· 147 to Nᵒ· 150 inclusively.

You were right to observe, Sir, that the first instructions of Congress were imperfect: in fact, they put, so to speak, the Fate of the United States at the mercy of the affections and prejudices of the American plenipotentiary, and they left to him full liberty to follow or reject our counsels and advice: it suffices to know the character and the principles of Mr. John Adams in order to perceive how dangerous such extensive powers would be in his hands, and how exposed we would be to disagreeable and even scandalous Scenes. You may judge by these reflections, Sir, that the King is grateful to you for having commented with such force and verity on the draft of the instructions, and for having insisted on the changes that Congress adopted. The instructions as they have been forwarded seemed to us all the more sufficient because the ardor, stubbornness, and inflexibility of Mr. Adams will be tempered by the calm, sagacity, and experience of Mr. Franklin, and that in last analysis the King's opinion will resolve the difficulties.

I see, Sir, that the article relative to this latter subject has encountered contradictions; that it was feared to offend the dignity and even the independence of the United States by placing them at His Majesty's discretion, as some members of Congress have expressed themselves. To dissipate this anxiety, you may assure whomever it concerns that the King, very far from wanting to abuse the influence that he may have on the negotiations of the American plenipotentiaries, will on the contrary only employ it for the greatest advantage of the United States, and that if he does not succeed in procuring for them all the conditions that each of them specifically may desire, the fault will certainly not be his, but that of circumstances, which imperiously dictate the law. To give to the principal personages of Congress a proof of the interest that the King takes in the American cause, you will observe to them what Mr. Adams should already have remarked, that the King, for what concerns him, has deferred the signing of the preliminary articles proposed by the two mediating courts until the admission of the American plenipotentiaries is resolved in a manner fitting to the dignity and to the independence of the United States. What the King does for form he will doubtless also do for substance; he will be as zealous for America, when he thinks he can procure advantages for her, as he will be reserved when circumstances require Sacrifices: we will use with all the more Sobriety and care our ascendancy over the American plenipotentiaries, because all the unfavorable stipulations to which they will be forced to subscribe will be imputed to us without fail, and because the enemies of the alliance will aggravate our alleged strengths in the intention of destroying it, or at least of rendering us very Suspect.

In addition, Sir, you have done perfectly well to have treated with a kind of indifference the Scruples that were raised in relation to the marks of confidence that Congress gives us, and to have consented to the reconsideration of the instructions: as you have very well observed, that confidence should be as spontaneous as it is unlimited, and you may insinuate to the dominant members of Congress that if that Body has, now or in the future, the least regret at having restrained the liberty of its plenipotentiaries too much, the King will see without trouble that he gives them the advantage therein: but you will take care to make it known at the same time, with dexterity, that if Congress takes this stance, it will remain responsible for what happens; I presume that body too wise to expose itself to such a risk.

I think I should refrain, Sir, from discussion of the article concerning the boundaries of the 13 States because besides the fact that this matter is not yet sufficiently clarified, it is entirely subordinated to the events of the war: if the Americans are successful, they will in law and in fact sustain their claims; but if the English maintain themselves on the continent of America, the United States will be forced to drop its illusions.

In the present state of affairs, Congress has taken a wise stance in not determining the boundaries of the United States, and in leaving in this regard some margin to its plenipotentiaries. I said as much about the duration of the Truce, in the event circumstances place us in the necessity of conceding it: the only thing that I have to observe to you in this regard is that we will prolong the term of the Truce as much as we can; we will find our advantage therein as much as the Americans themselves.

As for the *Statu quo*, it would be personally advantageous to us as well as to Spain, because we have made conquests from the common enemy; but it does not in any way enter into our System relative to America, and very far from being disposed to admit it, we have strongly combatted it in our preliminary response to the two Imperial courts. In addition, Sir, the *Statu quo*, like the Truce and even the peace, will depend on events and especially on the efforts of the Americans, and it is impossible to foresee, at present, what will be settled in this regard; this is likewise so of any kind of dismemberment. We have, moreover, some time remaining to discuss all these subjects: we know that the Court of London absolutely refuses to discuss the affairs of America in Vienna; by which means the mediation is still very far from entering into activity. The Americans can judge by these dispositions how far England still is from making peace with them on reasonable conditions, and how much, consequently, they find themselves in the necessity of wresting it from her by force of arms: you cannot, Sir, impress these important verities on Congress too strongly. I return to the Truce.

We have always thought, Sir, that Congress would have repugnance at signing it because it should wish to procure a solid and permanent tranquility for the American people; we have therefore anticipated that the proposal of a truce would occasion discontent and grumbling; that it would give umbrage to Americans with regard to the purity of our views, and that we would encounter great difficulties in making it acceptable. It was to disperse all these obstacles that the King was determined to propose to Congress, if he had the need, the renewal of the alliance with Stipulations relative to that of the war, in the event that it recommenced after the expiration of the Truce. Very happily neither Mr. Gerard nor you have made use of this Expedient, and it will be from now on all the more prudent not to make mention of it whatever the circumstance that may present itself, that in the event that the renewal of the alliance becomes necessary, it will be always more advantageous that it be requested and solicited by the Americans than if we were to offer it to them ourselves. I will add, Sir, that if this war were to end in a longterm truce, there would be very little likelihood that the English would want to recommence the war at its expiration in order to bring into subjection a country to which peace would have given a consistency of forces much more respectable than they are now. These considerations require that you abstain in the future from any insinuation tending to strengthen the already existing ties.

We have learned with much pleasure, Sir, that Mr. Adams will not be the only one charged with the interests of the United States. It is not that we distrust the patriotism of that plenipotentiary, but as he himself admits, he is more suited to polemical discussions than to conciliatory steps. I am certain, as much as one can humanly be, of Mr. Franklin's probity and Wisdom, and it is very desirable that this plenipotentiary have a preponderant influence over his colleagues. I do not know either Mr. Jefferson or Mr. Jay: but they belong to two States that have exorbitant claims, and I fear that the general good strikes them less than the particuliar interest of their respective provinces. As for Mr. Laurens, his nomination has singularly surprised us: it is inconceivable that a man was chosen who is a kind of hostage in the enemy's hands, who is regarded as one of the chiefs of the alleged American rebellion, and who would probably be the first victim of the anger of the English ministers if events permitted them to satisfy it. Whatever, Sir, may be the motives that could have determined the choice of Congress, I am persuaded that it will not have its effect; for I cannot imagine that Mr. Laurens will recover his liberty before the conclusion of the peace; so that I anticipate that this important work will remain in the hands of Messrs. Franklin, Jay, and Adams: I suppose that Mr. Jefferson will not want to leave home for a labor for which he would not receive all the glory.

. . . . . .

Vergennes

FFAA: Pol. Corr., U.S., v. 18, f. 69 (LC transcription).

Francis Dana to John Adams

S.ᵗ Petersbourg Aug 28ᵗʰ· 1781. O.S. [September 8, 1781]

My dear Sir.

It is not thrô want of attention that I have omitted to this time to acquaint you of our arrival in this City. We reached it, after some perils, on the 27ᵗʰ· of Augᶜᵗ N.S. sufficiently fatigued I assure you. For from Leipsic I began to travel day and night, and continued this practise all along the remaining distance. At Berlin we rested, or were rather stopped, nine days by an unfortunate accident of our *voiture's* being overthrown and broken into pieces, between Leipsic & Berlin, the first time I attempted to travel in the night. I there bôt a new one, which was warranted to carry us to S.ᵗ Petersbourg & back again, in the utmost safety. This however failed in essential parts, and required many repairs on the way: Notwithstanding the above accident, I found our advance so slow, thrô the abominable defects of German Posts, that I resolved to risk all again, & persist in travelling in the night; fortunately nothing of the like kind happened to us. We rested afterwards a day or two, at the following places, Dantzick, Konigsberg, Memel, Riga, and Narva, at most of which stages our *voiture* demanded repairs. This gave me an opportunity, perhaps not wholly unprofitable to our Country, to make enquiries into the commerce of these Towns; for they are all of them Ports. On the whole from Amsterdam to this City, we were fifty one days. M.ʳ Jennings[1] gave me all Augᶜᵗ to get in; but for the ~~first~~ accident to my first *voiture*, and some detentions for the repairs of my second, I wou'd have accomplished my journey 12 or 14 days sooner with equal fatigue. After all *you* will not be surprised to learn I am told, in effect, that I am here *too soon–* that the proper time is not yet come. In the name of common sense, I was about to ask you, what this Gentry can mean; but I believe we are at no loss to answer this question. I am promised however in the most flattering terms, every assistance in matters touching the joint or common interests of the two Houses, yet I am told not to expect it in matters that may be injurious to one, without being advantageous to the other. Such frivolous reasons appeared to me to have been assigned to show the time is not yet come, that I have presumed to question them. This I imagine may give offence, when I wou'd not wish to do it. But must an implicit faith but put in all things w$^{h:}$ may come from a certain quarter? Happily all our communications have hitherto been in writing: so that they, whose right it is to judge each of us, may do it understandingly. I am not disappointed in this difference of sentiments upon my main business, yet I am somewhat shocked that I have been here 12 days, since he knew in a proper way, of my being in Town, and have not received the least mark of attention from our *friend*,[2] except what may be contained in civil words only. The reasons of this, we may conjecture, and perhaps we shall not be far from the Truth. I suspect *Ishmael* may have been a little instrumental in this conduct. It cannot be without design, I think. I have candidly, & I believe decently given my own sentiments upon the subject, and told our friend, what measures I intended to pursue, to endeavour at least to come at the end in view. He received my letter on the evening of the 25$^{th.}$ but I have yet had no answer. It was a long one, it is true, & he not understanding English, must have it translated; so that I do not absolutely conclude that he will not answer it. He communicated to me in confidence, what had been communicated to me before in the same way, touching a proposal made, ~~by~~ to speak in plain English, by the Mediators, agreeable to our utmost wishes. He did not tell me, as the other person had done, that the Mediation was rejected on account of that proposition by the Court of London. This I suppose to be the truth, thô not a lisp of it is to be heard yet without doors here. I wish soon to receive a confirmation of it from your hand: when I can make that use of it I now want exceedingly to make of it. I take it to be a matter of great consequence to our Interests, and I build many hopes upon it in aid of my business. It seems to open the real good disposition of those Sovereigns for our Cause. I have made use of an argument of this sort to our friend in my last. Do not withold from me *a moment*, any information which you think can be ~~approved~~ improved to our advantage. Let no supposition that I may be otherwise informed of it, stay your hand. What comes from you, I shall think myself at liberty to make use of, at my discretion. You must have gained informations on your late tour, which will be of importance to me.

. . . .

Your friend & much obliged Humble Servant   Fra Dana
rec^d Decr 14. 1781.

MHS: The Adams Papers, microfilm reel 355 (LS).

¹ Jenings, Edmund (1731-1819). Maryland-born lawyer and gentleman of leisure who spent most of his life in London, but resided in Brussels, 1778-1783. A friend of Arthur and William Lee, he served as a conduit through which John Adams could place pro-American writings in the London press. Adams never doubted his pro-American sentiments, but Henry Laurens accused Jenings of attempting to sow distrust among the American peace commissioners by means of an anonymous letter accusing Adams of misconduct. The authorship of the letter has never been proved.

² Presumably a reference to Charles Olivier de Saint Georges, Marquis de Vérac, French Minister to Russia, 1780-1783.

John Jay to the President of Congress

Sir,   St Ildefonso 20th Septr 1781.

Your Excellency's Favor of the 5th. July last, with the papers therewith enclosed, were delivered to me on the 29th. ult^o. by Major Franks¹ WHOM THE PROCRASTINATION OF THE MINISTER STILL OBLIGES ME TO DETAIN.²

The new commissions, with which Congress have honored me, argue a degree of confidence, which demands my warmest acknowledgements, and which so far as it may be founded on an opinion of my zeal & integrity, they may be assured will not prove misplaced.

At the commencement of the present troubles, I determined to devote myself, during the continuance of them, to the Service of my Country in any station in which she might think proper to place me. THIS RESOLUTION FOR THE FIRST TIME NOW EMBARRASSES ME I KNOW IT TO BE MY DUTY AS A PUBLIC SERVANT TO BE GUIDED BY MY OWN judgeMENT ONLY IN matters referred to MY DISCRETION, & IN OTHER CASES faithFULLY to EXECUTE MY INSTRUCTIONS without questionING THE POLICY OF THEM. BUT THERE is ONE AMONG THOSE WHICH ACCOMPANIES these COMMISSIONS WHICH occasions SENSATIONS I NEVER before EXPERIENCED & INDUCED ME TO WISH MY name HAD BEEN OMITTED.

SO FAR AS personal PRIDE & reluctance TO HUMILIATION MAY RENDER THIS APpointMENT CONTRagreeable I VIEW IT AS A VERY UNimportant circumstance, and should CONGRESS ON ANY occasion THINK IT FOR the PUBLIC GOOD, TO place ME IN A station INFERIOR & SUBORDINATE TO the one I NOW HOLD, THEY WILL find ME READY TO DESCand FROM THE ONE & chearfully UNDERTAKE THE DUTIES of the OTHER. MY AMBITION WILL always be more GRATIFIED IN BEING useful THAN CONSPICUOUS for in my opinion the SOLID DIGNITY OF A MAN <*> depends less on the height or extent of the SPHERE alloted to HIM THAN ON THE MANNER IN WHICH HE MAY FULFILL THE DUTIES OF IT.

But Sir, AS AN AMERICAN, I FEEL AN interest IN THE DIGNITY OF MY COUNTRY WHICH renders it difficult for ME TO RECONCILE MYSELF TO the idea of the Sovereign INDEPENDANT States OF AMERICA SUBMITTING IN THE PERsons of THEIR MINISTERS to be absolutely GOVERNED BY THE ADvice & OPINIONS OF THE SERVANTS OF ANOTHER Sovereign, especially in a case of such national importance.

THAT GRATITUDE & CONFIDENCE ARE DUE TO OUR ALLIES IS NOT TO BE questionED & THAT IT will probably be in the POWER OF FRANCE ALMOST TO dictate the TERMS OF PEACE FOR US is BUT TOO true. THAT SUCH EXTRAordinary extent of CONFIDENCE MAY stimulate OUR ALLIES to the highest efforts of generous friendship in our favor – IS NOT TO BE DENIED and THAT THIS INSTRUCTION receives some appearance of POLICY FROM THIS considerATION MUST BE admitted.

I must nevertheless take the liberty of observing that HOWEVER OUR SITUATION MAY IN THE opinion OF CONGRESS render IT NECESSARY TO RELAX THEIR demands ON EVERY side & EVEN TO DIRECT THEIR COMmissionERS ULTIMATELY TO CONCUR (IF NOthing BETTER COULD BE DONE) IN ANY PEACE OR TRUCE NOT subversive of OUR INDEPENDANCE WHICH FRANCE be determined TO ACCEDE TO YET THAT THIS INstruckTION, BESIDES BREAthing A DEGREE OF COMPLAISANCY NOT quite republican puts it out of the power of YOUR MININISTERS TO IMPROVE those CHANCES & OPPORTUNIties which in the course of human affairs HAPPEN MORE OR less frequently UNTO ALL MEN. NOR IS IT CLEAR THAT AMERICA, THUS casting HERSELF INTO the ARMS OF THE KING OF FRANCE WILL ADVANCE EITHER HER INTEREST, OR REPUTATION WITH THAT OR OTHER nations.

WHAT THE SENTIMENTS OF MY COLLeagues ON THIS OCCASION MAY BE I DO NOT AS YET KNOW, NOR CAN I FORESEE HOW FAR THE NEGOTIATION OF THE ENSUING WINTER MAY CALL FOR THE execution OF THIS COMMISSION. THUS CIRCUMSTANCED AT SUCH A distance from AMERICA IT WOULD NOT BE PROPER TO decline THIS APpointMENT. I WILL thereFORE DO MY BEST endEAVORS TO FULFIL THE expectATIONS OF CONGRESS on this subject– BUT AS FOR MY OWN PART I THINK IT IMprobable that SERIOUS NEGOTIATIONS FOR PEACE WILL SOON TAKE PLACE. I MUST ENtreat CONGRESS TO TAKE AN EARLY opportunity of relieving ME FROM A STATION WHERE IN CHARACTER OF THEIR MINISTER I MUST NECESSARILY recieve (& ALMOST UNDER THE NAME OF opinions) THE DIRECTIONS OF those ON WHOM I REally THINK NO AMERICAN MINISTER OUGHT TO BE dependANT, AND TO WHOM IN LOVE FOR OUR COUNTRY and ZEAL FOR HER

service I AM SURE THAT MY COLLEAGUES & MYSELF ARE AT LEAST EQUAL.
I have the Honor to be with great Respect, Your Excellency's most obed^t
& most h'ble Servant   John Jay

P.S. I HAD AN INTERview LAST EVENING WITH THE MINISTER. NOTHING
WAS PROMISED OR DENIED. A PERSON IS TO BE NAMED ON SUNDAY TO
CONFER IN EARNEST AS IS SAID WITH ME ABOUT THE TREATIES. I DO NOT
DISPAIR, THO HAVING SO MANY BILLS TO PAY & NO MONEY PERPLEXES ME
EXTREAMLY. THE TREASURY OF SPAIN IS VERY LOW. MUCH OF THE MONEY
FOR THEIR EXPENCES THIS WAR, COSTS THEM BETWEEN THIRTY AND FORTY
PER HUNDRED BY BAD & MISmanageMENT and WANT OF CREDIT. THIS
OUGHT NOT TO BE PUBLIC. HIS EXCELLENCY STILL LOOKS AT YOUR SHIPS
ON THE STOCKS BUT I SHALL WITHOUT REFUSING NOT CONSENT TO THEIR
changING MASTERS.

NA: PCC, item 89, pp. 369-375 (ALS and decyphered copy); M247, reel 117.
  ¹ Franks, David Salisbury (c. 1740-1793). Montreal resident who joined Continental
Army in late 1775, subsequently serving in various capacities, including aide-de-camp to
General Benedict Arnold with the rank of lieutenant colonel. After Arnold's defection,
Franks sought and received a court of inquiry, which absolved him of any complicity in
Arnold's treason. Diplomatic courier, 1781-1784. Vice-consul at Marseilles, 1784.
Assistant to Thomas Barclay in Moroccan treaty negotiations, 1786; carried treaty to the
United States, early 1787.
  ² Words in capitals were encyphered in document received by Congress.

Chevalier de la Luzerne to Comte de Vergennes

[Translation]
N°. 182. 1st.   Philadelphia, 27 September 1781
My Lord
    I have sounded out in some individual conversations many Delegates
from the East and the South on the question of a dismemberment of the
United States, of the independence of one part and the submission of the
other. I have added that it was probable that this would be one of the first
subjects that the mediators would take into consideration, however far this
plan may be from the intentions of His Majesty. But as it is within the
range of possiblity, I have tried to render the idea of it less revolting and
more familiar to various delegations; I cannot flatter myself in having
attained the slightest success; obliged to insist in these conversations on the
fidelity of the King to his engagements towards the alliance, this is the sole
part of my insinuations to which I cling, and in spite of the precautions

with which I present the idea of a partial submission, it is rejected with horror and put in the range of impossible things. They were revolted by it at the time when the enemy was master of Georgia and of South Carolina, was traversing North Carolina in the wake of his victories, and was establishing himself in Virginia. At a time when General Greene[1] keeps the English garrisons withdrawn into Charlestown and Savannah, when the Republican Governor is on the point of being reestablished in South Carolina, and when one sees the flower of the English army's troops as prisoners of the allied army, the idea of a partial submission or of a dismemberment of some states is necessarily that which is the most difficult to make sprout in American heads; besides the furor with which the two parties are making war in the south, the murders committed in cold blood, the burnings, pillage, and confiscations, the ignominious torture of some officers from the first American families have carried the hatred for England and its domination to the supreme degree. In a word, My Lord, it was well demonstrated to me that in the present state of affairs, a dismemberment could not be proposed to Congress, and that it would only be suffered after long reverses and immense losses. As for the consequences that might result and the disadvantages of rendering these beautiful lands to Great Britain, I have already had the honor of explaining them to you, and besides you surely know the full importance of it. As for the comparison that could be made of the revolution of the Belgian provinces, I have several times discussed this historical point in conversations indifferent in appearance; they are very far from admitting the least resemblance in this regard, and the delegates with whom I have sometimes conversed have observed on those occasions that of the seventeen provinces that compose the Netherlands, ten were separated early from the union, while the thirteen states remain inviolably united, that reasons of religion had a part in this separation, and that nothing but violence and a very superior force can effect this decision in the United States; that the provinces that treated with Henry IV in 1596 have remained independent and free; they add that the treaties between that Prince and the United Provinces of the Netherlands have never positively guaranteed their independence, and have nothing that approaches the precision of our treaties with the Thirteen United States. I will continue my insinuations when circumstances present themselves, and I will take care to do so with the necessary circumspection, but I confess that nothing up to now permits me to hope for the least Success in it.

. . . . .

le chr de la luzerne.

Received 18 November.

FFAA: Pol. Corr., U.S., v. 18, f. 117 (LC transcription).

¹ *Greene, Nathanael (1742-1786). Military leader. Commanded Rhode Island troops sent to take part in siege of Boston, April-June 1775. Chosen as brigadier general in Continental Army, June 22, 1775; major general, August 9, 1776. Served as quartermaster general, March 2, 1778 - August 3, 1780. Succeeded Horatio Gates in command of the southern department, October 1780. At Guilford Courthouse (March 15, 1781), Hobkirk's Hill (April 26, 1781), and Ninety-Six (June 19, 1781), he lost battles that proved Pyrrhic victories for the British, who in each case subsequently retreated or abandoned their positions. His victory at Eutaw Springs (September 8, 1781) eliminated the last British outpost in South Carolina outside Charlestown, which he besieged until its evacuation in December 1782.*

John Jay to Gouverneur Morris

Dear Morris,   St. Ildefonso, 28 September 1781

My last to you was of the 24th Ult. Triplicates have been sent. I have recieved none from you later than 10 July by Major Franks. Yours of the 2d January and 4 March never reached me. There is Reason to believe that <minister>¹ THE PRIME MINISTER HERE HAS THEM. Tell me what you think of MY LETTER TO <the President> CONGRESS OF THE [—] <Inst.> OF THIS MONTH. Peace does not appear very nigh. THIS COURT AND THAT OF FRANCE DO NOT DRAW perfectly well. Except a JEW, I CAN HEAR OF nothing SO perfectly ODIOUS TO A Spaniard AS A FRENCHMAN. THIS GOVERNMENT HAS little MONEY, LESS WISDOM, NO CREDIT, NOR ANY RIGHT TO IT. <they have Pride without Dignity, Cunning without Policy, Nobility without Honor> I speake with Certainty; WHAT NEW MEN <may> MIGHT DO IS UNCERTAIN. YOUR BILLS HAVE DONE MUCH MISCHIEF. THE KING MEANS WELL BUT KNOWS NOTHING. VATTEL'S LAW OF NATIONS² WHICH I FOUND QUOTED IN a Letter from CONGRESS IS PROHIBITED HERE. <I confide in your Prudence and Secrecy.>

Some of your letters have you say been drowned; do you suppose that none of mine have <shared that> miscarried. You would have given me some interesting Intelligence, if my Letters had been less laconic. Is this like You? This Sentiment, if <it deserves that Name> I may call it so has indeed flowed from your Pen, but I am sure your Heart <had no concern in> did not dictate it. I CONFIDE IN YOUR Prudence AND SECRECY. YOU DESIRE ME TO SAVE YOU THE TROUBLE OF Repetitions, BY MAKING AND IN TURN recieving Communications. THIS PLAN WOULD ONCE HAVE DONE, BUT THAT TIME is passed — FOREVER. I <told> WROTE YOU SO <before the last> IN JUNE 1780, THE LETTER ARRIVED <safe> at PHILADELPHIA, <to my certain knowledge> BUT I NOW FIND YOU HAVE NEVER SEEN IT;

AS IT WAS IN CYPHERS THE INSPECTOR GAINED NO INFORMATION FROM IT.
WHILE WE <continue to> HAVE FULL CONFIDENCE IN EACH OTHER <I
am persuaded that> NEITHER WILL BE DECIEVED. TO GIVE YOU DETAILS
WOULD BE TO WRITE A HISTORY, BUT I WILL TELL YOU PLAINLY THAT
<that Your Secretary[3] is the most decietful, insidious Man I ever met with
in all my Life, and I have met with many. This I think is being confidential
as well as particular. The Time may come when I shall give you more Facts
than you will be pleased with> THAT THIS SAME MAN IS IN MY JUDGMENT,
THE MOST FAITHLESS AND DANGEROUS ONE, THAT I HAVE EVER MET
WITH, IN ALL MY LIFE. THIS IS STRONG LANGUAGE, BUT TWENTY TWO
MONTHS CONSTANT EXPERIENCE ASSURES ME IT IS JUST. IF I COULD HAVE
TRUSTED MY CYPHERS WHEN AT MARTINICO I WOULD FROM THENCE HAVE
<written to you of this Subject> GIVEN YOU A HINT OF HIS SHAMEFUL
DUPLICITY AND UNKIND CONDUCT. TO DO HIM HARM IS NOT MY WISH,
revenge NEVER HAS NOR EVER SHALL, ACTUATE ME, BUT HAPPY SHALL I
BE TO SEE THE DAY WHEN I SHALL <cease to> <and to have any Thing
to do with him> NO MORE BE PLAGUED WITH HIS TRICKS.

THERE IS SOMETHING VERY DISAGREABLE IN THUS MENTIONING
MATTERS OF THIS SORT, especially considering HOW YOU STAND WITH
RESPECT TO BOTH.

I am very much inclined to think that THIS COURT MEANS IF possible TO
DELAY FORMING ANY political Connections WITH US TILL A GENERAL
PEACE, THEREBY AVOIDING <the Loans and Subsidies> ADVANCES OF
MONEY WHICH <in Reality> THEY ARE NOT <in Capacity> VERY ABLE
TO MAKE, <and as well as> A PRECEDENT WHICH MAY ONE DAY BE
TURNED AGAINST THEM BY THEIR OWN COLONIES. < < <they remaining
free from Engage toward Engagements> > toward Engagements to avail
themselves of Contingencies, and> THEY wish also, BY FREEDOM FROM
ENGAGEMENTS, TO BE READY to take Advantage of CIRCUMSTANCES. AS
TO PAROLE Promises OF THE MINISTERS, THEY PASS HERE AS continentAL
DOES WITH YOU.

· · · · ·

...I am very much yours,   J.J.

· · · · ·

Morris, Jay Papers, v. 2, pp. 108-110; PCC, item 89, pp. 369-375; M247, reel 117.

[1] Editorial apparatus use as follows [———] words missing; [inserted or conjectural
reading]; <canceled matter>; < <deletions within canceled matter> >.

[2] Vattel, Emmerich de (1714-1767). Swiss jurist. Author of Le Droit de Gens [The
Law of Nations], 1758. Vattel applied theories of natural law to international relations,
in particular to the commerce of neutrals in wartime.

[3] Presumably William Carmichael.

John Jay to the President of Congress

Sir,   Saint Ildefonso 3ᵈ· Octʳ 1781

. . . . .

In my letter of the 25ᵗʰ· April last; I informed your Excellency that on the 25ᵗʰ March preceding, the Minister sent me word that the money necessary to pay the Bills due in April could not be advanced to me. The constant inconsistency I experienced between the Minister's promises & conduct often surprised, as well as embarrassed me. This last instance appeared to me to be really cruel, for if he had intended to withold the necessary supplies, he ought to have given me notice of it, and not by keeping up my expectations to within a few days before the holders of the Bills were to call upon me for their money (And the Bills of April amounted to 89,083 Dollars) reduce me to such eminent danger of being obliged to protest them – Speaking on this subject with the french Embassador, he intimated that the Court expected I should have made them some further overtures respecting the Mississippi – I told him, I had no authority to make any others than what I had already made – He replied – *That the Minister believed I had* – At that time, I had received no letters public, or private which gave me the least reason to suspect that Congress had passed the resolution of 15ᵗʰ· Febʸ· last, and it was not before the 18ᵗʰ May, that a letter, I then received from Mʳ· Lovel,[1] enabled me to understand *the reason of the Minister's beleif* – I then recalled to mind his frequent assurances of frankness, and of his speaking *without reserve*, often adding that he was *well informed* of our affairs, and had minute information of what was passing at Philadelphia – There can be no doubt but that some copies of the President's letters to me have fallen into his hands, and that he supposed I had received others, though this was not in fact the case –

. . . . .

It was not, as I said before, until the 18 May that Mr. Lovels letter, enclosing a copy of the resolution of Congress of the 15ᵗʰ Feby reached me....

As Mr. Lovel's letter did not appear to be official, nor the copy of the Instruction of 15ᵗʰ Feby authenticated, I was much at a loss to determine how far it was to be considered as a measure finally concluded upon, and this difficulty was increased by another vizᵗ – Whether my having no letter on the subject from the President, was to be imputed to the miscarriage of it, or to a reconsideration of the Instruction in question– for I recollected that resolutions had in some former Instances, been reconsidered, & either altered or repealed a few days after their date; For these reasons, it appeared to me imprudent *immediately* to hazard overtures on the ground of this Instruction.

The next day viz$^{t.}$ 19 May, I thought it expedient to wait upon the Minister, & again renew the subject of our proposed treaty, expecting that if he was acquainted with the contents of my letter, something might drop from him in the course of conversation, which would lead me to judge of what he might or might not know on that subject, and others connected with it.

He received me with more than usual cordiality....I announced to him formally the completion of our confederation by the accession of Maryland and after dwelling on the advantages, which the States & their allies might expect from it, I endeavoured to impress him with an opinion, that a cordial Union between France, Spain, Holland and America, supported by vigorous measures, would soon reduce the Enemy to the necessity of listening to reasonable terms of peace – The Count replied generally that he was *very minutely* informed of the State of our affairs – That the good dispositions of Congress towards Spain, had not as yet been evidenced in a manner the King expected, and that no one advantage had hitherto been proposed by America to Spain, to induce the latter to come into the measures we desired....

To all this I briefly remarked that his Excellency's knowledge of American affairs must convince him, that it was not in their power to give his Majesty other proofs of their attachment than what they had already done – and that if he alluded to the affair of the Mississippi, I could only add one remark to those which I had often made to him on that head viz$^{t.}$ That even if a desire of gratifying his Majesty *should ever* incline Congress to yield to him a point so essential to their Interest, yet it still remained a question whether new delays, and obstacles to a treaty would not arise to postpone it.

The Count smiled – said he always spoke frankly, and that whenever I should announce to him, my having authority to yield that point, I might depend on his being explicit, & candid; but that as matters stood at present, he could say nothing on that head –

He then informed me that M$^{r.}$ Gardoqui[2] would set out for America the beginning of June – He said it might be in my power to furnish some useful hints & observations relative to the objects & conduct of his mission, adding that he reposed full confidence in me, and wished that I would also consider *whether there were any particular reasons which might render it adviseable either to hasten or retard his going.*

. . . . .

As to the Instruction of 15th Feb$^{y.}$ I had every reason to wish that it had been a secret to the Ministry – The Propriety of them is a subject without my province – To give decided Opinions of the views & designs of Courts, always appeared to me hazardous, especially as they often change, and as different men will often draw different conclusions from the same facts – This consideration has constantly induced me to state facts accurately, and minutely to Congress, & leave them to judge for themselves, & be influenced only by their own opinions –

I could not however forbear seeing the danger to which the proviso, contained in that Instruction, exposed me. I have no reason to flatter myself, that more fortunate than others, the propriety and policy of my conduct will not be drawn, at least impliedly, into doubt. If I should, on a persuasion that this cession would be unalterably insisted upon by Spain, yield that point, I am certain that many little half created doubts, and questions would be cast into & cultivated in America – If on the other hand I should be of opinion that this point could be gained, and the Event prove otherwise, it would soon be whispered, what rich supplies, and golden opportunities the United States had lost by my obstinacy –

I permitted my mind to dwell on these considerations, merely that I might by the utmost degree of circumspection, endeavour to render the uprightness and propriety of my conduct as evident as possible –

My only difficulty arose from this single question – Whether I could prudently risque acting on a presumption, either that Spain did not already, or would not soon be acquainted with the contents of this Instruction.

If such a presumption had been admissable, I should without the least hesitation have played the game a little further, keeping this Instruction in my hand as a trump card to prevent a separate peace between Spain & Britain, in case such an event should otherwise prove inevitable – Had Spain been at peace with our enemies, and offered to acknowledge, guarantee and fight for our Independence, provided we would yield them this point (as once seemed to be the case) I should for my own part have no more hesitation about it now, than I had then – But Spain being now at war with Britain, to gain her own objects, she doubtless will prosecute it full as vigorously as if she fought for our objects – There was, and is little reason to suppose that such a cession would render her exertions more vigorous, or her aids to us much more liberal – The effect which an alliance between Spain & America would have on Britain & other Nations would certainly be in our favor, but whether more so than the free Navigation of the Mississippi is less certain – The cession of this navigation will in my opinion render a future war with Spain unavoidable, and I shall look upon my subscribing the one, as fixing the certainty of the other –

. . . . .

But on the other hand, there being abundant circumstantial Evidence to induce a firm persuasion that the Ministry were well acquainted with the

Contents of this Instruction, this Plan would have been idle – The moment they saw that the cession of this Navigation was made to depend on their persevering to insist upon it, it became absurd to suppose that they would cease to persevere. All that remained for me therefore to do was in the next conference to break this subject as decently as possible, and in such a manner as would account for my not having mentioned this Instruction at our last meeting –

On Wednesday Evening 23ᵈ May, I waited upon the Count agreeable to his appointment –

. . . . .

It surprised me a little that he said nothing of the remarks he had desired me to make on Mr. Gardoqui's going to America, especially as he had appointed this meeting for that purpose....

He then resumed the subject of the letter which I expected from Congress – he expressed his regret at its not having arrived; said he was preparing Instructions for Mʳ· Gardoqui who would certainly depart in June, and that until I could give him precise information of the dispositions of Congress, he could not enter into any further conversations on the subject of the proposed treaty. I joined in regretting the miscarriage of my public letter, and the more so as my private ones gave me reason to expect Instructions, which would enable me to comply so far with his Majesty's views, as that I hoped no further delays would intervene to prevent a perfect Union between Spain & the United States – That my Correspondent had given me to understand that Congress viewed the speedy accomplishment of this Union as very important to the common cause, & therefore if Spain would consent forthwith to come into it, in that case they would gratify his Majesty by ceding to him the Navigation of the Mississippi below their territories on reasonable terms –

He replied that he earnestly desired to see all difficulties on this point removed, but that the treaties subsisting between Spain & other Nations, as well as the particular policy & determination of Spain rendered it necessary, that she should possess the exclusive navigation of the Gulph of Mexico. After a variety of other remarks of little importance, he made a very interesting observation, which will help us to account for the delays of the Court – vizᵗ – *That all these affairs could with more facility be adjusted at a general peace than now, for that such a particular and even secret treaty with us, might then be made as would be very convenient to both* – That he nevertheless wished to know exactly the views & Intentions of Congress, but that I must wait for the arrival of my Letters, & that he would in the mean time finish Mʳ· Gardoqui's Instructions, whose going to America, he did not doubt would make a useful Impression on the English Court. I was beginning to reply to what he had said, when he interrupted me, by mentioning his not having time at present to prolong the conference –

Throughout the whole of this conversation the Count appeared much less cordial, than in the preceding one – he seemed to want Self-possession, & to that cause I ascribe his incautiously mentioning the general peace as the most proper Season for completing our political connections....

. . . . .

On the 11ᵗʰ July, having received no answer from the Minister I waited upon him. . . . he then delivered me a number of letters among which was one from his Excellency the President of the 28ᵗʰ May last –

I need not observe that all these letters bore evident marks of Inspection, for that has uniformly been the case with almost every Letter I have received –

I do not recollect to have ever received a letter that gave me more real pleasure. When I considered that almost the whole time since I left America, had afforded me little else than one continued series of painful perplexities and Embarrassments, many of which I neither expected, nor ought to have met with – That I had been engaged in difficult & intricate negotiations, often at a loss to determine where the line of prudence was to be found, & constantly exposed by my particular situation, to the danger of either injuring the dignity and Interest of my country on the one hand, or trespassing on the over-rated respectability and importance of this Court on the other. I say, Sir, That on considering these things, the approbation of Congress gave me most singular and cordial satisfaction –

. . . . .

On September 17, 1781, Jay wrote to Floridablanca requesting another meeting.

Notes of a conference held at Saint Ildefonso on Wednesday Evening the 19 day of September 1781 between his Excellency the Count de Florida Blanca, and Mʳ Jay agreeably to the appointment of the former.

. . . . .

The Count then proceeded to enumerate the various obstacles arising from his ill health, the multiplicity of business which had so long subjected Mʳ Jay to the delays he had hitherto experienced, and which for his part he could not but regret....

. . . . .

...That with respect to the proposed treaty of Alliance, Mʳ Jay must be sensible that the several engagements, which would thereby be rendered necessary between the parties, the matters of boundary, and the navigation of the Mississippi would give occasion to several important articles, which ought to be maturely considered, and well digested – To this end, he wished that Mʳ· Jay would immediately turn his thoughts on these subjects and offer him such a set of propositions, as might become the basis of future conferences between him, & the person whom he expected his Majesty would appoint –

The Count then took occasion to observe that he had long wished Mr Jay had offered him such propositions, but that his Court had as yet received from Congress nothing but good words, & fair assurances, and that tho' his Majesty had given them some little aids, yet that they had discovered no disposition by acts to acknowledge them – M$^{r.}$ Jay reminded his Exc^y of his having at a very early day undertaken to commit to paper the outlines of the proposed treaties, and that the constant expectations of his perfecting it, had restrained M$^{r.}$ Jay from offering any thing of the like nature on the Subject. That he could conceive of nothing in the power of Congress to do, which could more fully evidence their disposition to gratify his Majesty, than their having offered to recede from their claims to the Navigation of the Mississippi; tho' the preservation of it was deemed of the highest importance to their constituents. The Count admitted the propriety of both these observations, & said he hoped that the delays which had so long embarrassed Mr Jay would soon be terminated – ... The Count then pressed Mr Jay again to send him the Paper abovementioned before Sunday, adding that he sincerely wished nothing might be wanting to put the business in a proper train – That for his part, he had the best disposition towards America, as well as personal regard for Mr Jay and, after adding some complimentary expressions relative to the Character of the latter, concluded –

I was a little surprised that the Count should expect to receive from me in the course of three Days, formal propositions on the several points stated in this conference – But it would not have been proper for me to desire further time –

. . . . .

The Propositions alluded to, & sent enclosed in the preceding letter to the Count de Florida Blanca Dated St Ildefonso – 22nd Septr 1781 –

. . . . .

Remarks   Propositions

Ist

There shall forever subsist an inviolable and universal peace and friendship between his Catholic Majesty and the United States & the Subjects & Citizens of both —

II.

That every privilege, exemption, & favor with respect to commerce, Navigation & personal rights, which now are or hereafter may be granted by either to any the most favored Nation, be also granted by them to each other.

III.

That they mutually extend to the Vessels, Merchants, & Inhabitants of each other all that protection which is usual and proper between friendly and allied Nations –

IV.

That the Vessels, merchants, or other Subjects of his Catholic Majesty, and the United States, shall not resort to, or be permitted (except in cases which humanity allows to distress) to enter into any of those Ports or dominions of the other from which the most favored Nation shall be excluded.

V.

That the following Commerce be prohibited and declared contraband between the Subjects of his Catholic Majesty, & the United States — viz. –All such as his Catholic Majesty may think proper to specify.

VI.

The United States shall relinquish to his Catholic Majesty, and in future forbear to use or attempt to use the navigation of the river Mississippi from the thirty first degree of North latitude, that is from the

On this proposition, M$^{r.}$ Jay can offer nothing, but an assurance of his being ready to concur in every reasonable regulation that may be proposed –

The Impressions made upon the United States by the magnanimity of his Majesty's conduct towards them – The assistance they hope to receive from the further exertions of the same magnaminity. The deep wound which an alliance with so great a Monarch would give to the hopes & efforts of the enemy – The strong support it would afford to their Independence, The favorable influence which the example of such a King would have on other Nations, & the many other great and extensive good consequences, which would result at this interesting period from his Majesty's taking so noble & decided a part in their favor, have all conspired in prevailing upon Congress to offer to relinquish in his favor, the enjoyment of this territorial & national priviledge the importance of which to their Constituents can only be estimated by the value they set upon his Majesty's friendship –

By this proposition, the United States offer to forego all the advantages, & conveniences which nature has given to the Country bordering on the upper parts of that river, by ceasing to export their own, & receiving in return the commodities of other Countries by that *only channel* thereby greatly reducing the value of that Country, retarding its Settlement, & diminishing the benefits which the United States would reap from its cultivation –

Mr Jay thinks it his duty frankly to confess that the difficulty of reconciling this measure to the feelings of their

point where it leaves the United States down to the Ocean –

Constituents has appeared to Congress in a serious light, & they now expect to do it, only by placing in the opposite Scale, the gratitude due to his Catholic Majesty, and the great and various advantages which the United States will derive from the acknowledgement, & generous support of ~~our~~ their Independence by the Spanish Monarchy, at a time when the vicissitudes, dangers, & difficulties of a distressing war, with a powerful, obstinate, and vindictive Nation, renders the friendship, and avowed protection of his Catholic Majesty in a very particular manner interesting to them –.

The offer of this proposition therefore, being dictated by these expectations, & this combination of circumstances, must necessarily be limited by the duration of them, & consequently, that if the acceptance of it, should together with the proposed alliance be postponed to a general peace, the United States will cease to consider themselves bound by any propositions or offers, which he may now make in their behalf –

Nor can M^r. Jay omit mentioning the hopes, & expectations of Congress that his Majesty's generosity, and greatness of mind will prompt him to alleviate, as much as possible, the disadvantages to which this proposition subjects the United States, by either granting them a Free Port under certain restrictions in the vicinity, or by such other marks of his liberality & Justice, as may give him additional claims to the affection, & attachment of the United States –.

Nothing on Mr Jay's part shall be wanting to expedite the happy conclusion of this business, by adhering constantly to the dictates of candor, frankness, & unsuspecting confidence –

He is ready to receive the treaty between the United States & his Christian Majesty as a model for this or with such alterations as, founded on the principles of reciprosity may be more agreeable to his Catholic Majesty, it being his earnest desire to arrive at the important objects of his mission in any way his Majesty may be pleased to prefer –

VII.

That his Catholic Majesty shall guarantee to the United States all their respective territories –

VIII.

That the United States shall guarantee to his Catholic Majesty all his dominions in North America –

Lastly –

As the aforegoing propositions appear to Mr Jay the most essential he omits proposing those lesser & subordinate ones which seem to follow of course. He therefore concludes this subject with a *general offer & Proposition* to make & admit all such articles as in the course of this negotiation shall appear conducive to the great objects of the proposed Treaty –

. . . . .

In forming these propositions, it was my determination to leave them so free from disputed, or disputable points, as that no plausible pretexts for delay should arise from the face of them – I am well apprized nevertheless that in the course of the Negotiation, it will be impossible for me to prevent their practicing as much procrastination as they may find convenient – Almost the only hope I have of their seriously doing business, arises from their fearing that the Instruction respecting the Mississippi will be recalled the moment that either any very decided successes on our part in America, may render a treaty with Spain of less importance to us, or a general treaty of peace give us different views & prospects.

. . . . .

I have the Honor to be with great Respect & Esteem, Your Excellency's Most Obedient and very Humble Servant   John Jay

. . . . .

NA: PCC, item 89, v. 2, pp. 379-440 (ALS); M247, reel 117.

[1] Foreign Affairs Committee to John Jay, February 20, 1781, (NA: PCC, item 79, v. 1, p. 277; M247, reel 105).

[2] Gardoqui, Diego Maria de. Spanish diplomat. Chargé d'affaires in the United States, 1785-1789. Ambassador to Sardinia, 1797-1798.

John Adams to Benjamin Franklin

Sir   Amsterdam October 4[th.] 1781.

Since the 25th of August, when I had the honor to write to You, this is the first Time that I have taken a Pen in Hand to write to any body, having been confined and reduced too low to do any kind of business by a nervous Fever.

The new Commission for Peace has been a great Consolation to me, because it removed from the Public all danger of Suffering any Inconvenience, at a Time when for many days together, there were many Chances to one that I should have nothing more to do with Commissions of any Sort. It is still a great Satisfaction to me, because I think it a Measure essentially right, both as it is a greater demonstration of Respect to the Powers, whose Ministers may assemble to make Peace; and as it is better calculated to give satisfaction to the People of America, as the Commissioners are chosen from the most considerable Places in that Country.

It is probable, that the French Court is already informed of the Alteration. Nevertheless, I should think it proper that it should be officially notified to M. Comte de Vergennes, and if you are of the Same Opinion, as You are near, I should be obliged to You, if You would communicate to his Excellency an Authentick Copy of the new Commission.

I should think too that it would be proper to give Some Intimation of it to the Public in the *Gazette* or *Mercure de France*, the two Papers which are published with the Consent of the Court, and if You are of the Same Opinion, upon consulting the Comte de Vergennes, I should be glad to see it done.

Have You any Information concerning Mr Jefferson, whether he has accepted the Trust? whether he has embarked? or ~~whether~~ proposes soon to embark? I Saw a paragraph in a Maryland Paper, which expressed an apprehension that he was taken Prisoner by a Party of Horse in Virginia.

I feel a Strong Curiosity to know the answer of the British Court to the Articles to Serve as a Basis &^{c} – Should be much obliged to your Excellency, for a Copy of it, if to be procured, and for your Opinion, whether there will be a Congress or not.

I have the honor to be with the greatest Respect Sir, your most obedient and most humble Servant

John Adams.

APS: Benjamin Franklin Papers (LS).

Comte de Vergennes to Chevalier de la Luzerne

[Translation]

N° 22   Versailles, 7 October 1781

. . . . .

I do not understand, Sir, why some members of Congress are so tormented in relation to the confidence that the American plenipotentiaries have been ordered to evince to us; they are poorly acquainted with our principles and our fashion of thinking, and they render very little justice to the interest that the King takes in the American cause. Whatever may be the case, Sir, there is a very simple means of calming them, and of putting them at their ease: it is to leave Congress an entire liberty to revoke or to restrain, according to its good pleasure, the instructions of its plenipotentiaries. You should not hesitate to make the declaration of it confidentially to the President of Congress, requesting him to communicate it to that assembly: It will take in consequence such resolution as it judges proper. This conduct on our part will make, I hope, the anti-Gallicans perceive the inconsistency and the irregularity of their desires, and I am persuaded that it will make them blush for their distrust, and convince them of the necessity to swear themselves henceforth to silence.

In discussing this subject with Mr. McKean,[1] you would do well to make him see, as yourself, the difficulties to which the American plenipotentiaries would daily be exposed if they were left to themselves and also to the impetuosity of the representative of the Court of London: I have too good an opinion of the sagacity of this leader of Congress, not to anticipate that he will perceive without difficulty the dangers to which this position would expose the work of peace, and consequently the necessity of leaving the American agents under the direction of an ally who wants above all the liberty and well-being of the United States.

It must be, Sir, that the members of Congress who wish to remove the American cause from our influence have a great depth of confidence in the means of their homeland to procure peace, or that they think they will find great facilities either near the Court of London or near the two mediators: but to convince themselves up to what point they are deceiving themselves, they have only to glance at the various regions of America. There is, so to speak, no province in which the English do not have some sort of establishment, and all the efforts of the Americans up to now could only serve to impede their progress; in such a position, is it proper to be presumptuous, is it permitted to have unreasonable demands, can one hope to question the Law? The fact is that if we do not control circumstances, they will control us; in the first case, we will second with fervor the wishes of the Americans, in the second they as well as we will be forced to make Sacrifices: however much they exalt themselves, whatever claims they form, wishing to maintain the integrity of their territory and of the confederation, to claim the right to fish &c., they will be no less constrained to yield on all these points to obtain those which constitute the essence of their cause, I mean independence.

Moreover, Sir, we desire very ardently that the reflections that I have just made never find their application, that the Success of our arms and of those of the United States render us masters of the conditions of peace: in that case we will be all the more zealous for the advantages of the United States, which is the principal object for which the King is waging an excessively expensive war: but, I repeat, in the event that we are obliged to yield, the Americans will be obliged to be resolved to it as well as we; I think, Sir, that it will be useful gradually to inculcate this moral in them, in order that they be less astonished if circumstances force them to practice it. I perceive that the task is not easy with a nation all of whose notions, even those that it has of its position, are still very inexact: but we place great confidence in our dexterity and in the intimate relations you have with the principal members of Congress.

I have, Sir, nothing to add to my preceding despatches relative to the peacemaking. The mediators have still not communicated to us the response of the Court of London to their preliminary overtures, nor their Sentiment on the observations that we have made on these same overtures. You will judge by this stagnation that the mediation has not yet reached the moment of being put into activity, and that peace is something less than near: the only means of moving towards it would be some decisive event in North America. It remains to be seen whether M. de Grasse will give us proof of it. In addition, Sir, Mr. Franklin has communicated his instructions to me; they conform entirely to what you have sent to me, and they leave us nothing to desire but the favorable moment to fulfill them to the letter. Your reflections on the full power that authorized Mr. Adams to make a treaty of commerce with England could not be more just, and we see with a great deal of pleasure that it has been revoked. It is not that we wished to prevent the Americans from having commercial ties with their former metropolis; but it would have been dangerous to make peace depend on this article, and especially on the point of view under which Mr. Adams would have judged it appropriate to consider it.

I see, Sir, by despatch N⁰· 152 that the province of Massachusetts is striving to return to the question relative to the fisheries, and that it is drawing new arguments from the association of neutrals. I will not take this matter up again here, because I have treated it thoroughly in my despatch N⁰· 2, which I sent you on 25 September 1779. I shall limit myself to observing that the members of Congress who have revived the affair of the fisheries are not well acquainted with the object of the association of neutrals. It has never come into the thought of the powers who have taken part to render commerce and navigation free in all the points of the globe: this claim, if it were realised, would reverse from top to bottom the System that all the nations have followed up to the present on this matter and would likely plunge Europe into the horrors of a long and disastrous war. The neutrals, in associating themselves, have no other goal than to guarantee their flag and their commerce against the arbitrary and tyrannical jurisprudence of Great Britain: it suffices, to be convinced of this verity, to read the convention that they have made; it explains in a clear and precise manner the intentions and the goal of the contracting parties, and all the articles that it includes can have their applications only in time of war. I do not find any that have, even by the most forced interpretation, the least relation to the fisheries in North America. The Fate of these fisheries is determined by solemn treaties: it is not by a convention made between third parties that it can be reversed. I pray you, Sir, to preach this doctrine, which is the only veritable one, when you have occasion to discuss the article of the fisheries with the principal members of Congress.

. . . . .
                                                                    Vergennes

FFAA: Pol. Corr., U.S., v. 19, f. 17 and 16 (LC transcription).

¹ McKean, Thomas (1734-1817). Jurist and political figure. Member, Delaware House of Assembly, 1762-1775; speaker, 1772. Member, Continental Congress, 1774-1776, 1778-1782; president, 1781. Chief justice of Pennsylvania, 1777-1799. Governor of Pennsylvania, 1799-1808.

Benjamin Franklin to John Adams

Passy, Oct. 12. 1781.

Sir,

I received the Letter your Excellency did me the honour of writing to me the 4th. Instant.

I have never known a Peace made, even the most advantageous, that was not censured as inadequate, and the Makers condemned as injudicious or corrupt. *Blessed are the Peace makers*; is I suppose to be understood in the other World: for in this they are frequently *cursed.* Being as yet rather too much attached to this World, I had therefore no Ambition to be concerned in fabricating this Peace: and know not how I came to be put into the Commission. I esteem it however an honour to be joined with you in so important a Business; and if the Execution of it shall happen in my Time, which I hardly expect, shall endeavour to assist in discharging the Duty according to the best of my Judgment.

Immediately on receipt of the Commission & Instructions, I communicated them, as directed, to this Court. The Steps that have been taken in the Mediation were verbally communicated to me, but as yet I have had no Copies given me of the Papers. I ask'd if it was not proper to communicate to the Ministers of the Mediating Powers, the Commission of Congress impowering us to accept their Mediation; and was advised to postpone it a little. I will endeavour on Tuesday next, to obtain for you a Copy of the Answer of the British Court which you desire, and will consult on the Propriety of mentioning our Commission in the Publick Papers.

I have heard nothing of Mr Jefferson. I imagine the Story of his being taken Prisoner is not true. From his original Unwillingness to leave America when I was sent hither, I think his Coming doubtful, unless he had been made acquainted with & consented to the Appointment.

I hope your health is fully established. I doubt not but you have the Advice of skilful Physicians, otherwise I should presume to offer mine, which would be, though you find yourself well, to take a few Doses of Bark, by way of fortifying your Constitution, & preventing a return of your Fever.

With the greatest Respect, I have the honour to be, Sir, Your Excellency's most obedient and most humble Servant

B. Franklin

·   ·   ·   ·   ·

MHS: *The Adams Papers, microfilm reel 355 (LS).*

John Adams to the President of Congress

Sir,   Amsterdam October 15th 1781.

I wish, if it were possible, to communicate to Congress the present State of every Affair, which they have been pleased to confide in any measure to me.

I have received the new Commission for Peace, and the Revocation of my Commission and Instructions of the 27$^{th.}$ of September 1779. To both of these Measures of Congress, as to the Commands of my Sovereign, I shall pay the most exact Attention. The present Commission for Peace is a demonstration of greater respect to the Powers of Europe, and must be more satisfactory to the People of America, than my former one; besides that it guards against Accidents, which in my late sickness I had reason to think may well happen. I am however apprehensive, that this Commission will lie a long time neglected, and as useless as the former one....

. . . . .

Whether under all these Circumstances Congress will think proper to continue me in Europe: whether it will be in their Power to furnish me with the means of Subsistence, as D$^{r.}$ Franklin in his Letter to me thinks I cannot depend upon him, and I have no hopes at all of obtaining any here, I know not, and must submit to their Wisdom. But after all, the state of my health, which I have little Reason to hope will be restored, without a Voyage home, and more Relaxation from Care and Business, than I can have in Europe, makes it very uncertain whether I shall be able to remain here. In short my Prospects both for the public and for myself are so dull, and the Life I am likely to lead in Europe is likely to be so gloomy and melancholy, and of so little use to the public, that I cannot but wish it may suit with the Views of Congress to recall me.

I have the honor to be, with the greatest Respect, Sir, your most obedient and most humble Servant.   John Adams.

NA: PCC, Misc. Papers, *Adams Despatches* (C); M332, reel 1, ff. 412-417.

Comte de Vergennes to Chevalier de la Luzerne

[Translation]

N$^{o.}$ 24.   Versailles, 18 October 1781

. . . . .

Although the United Provinces are at war with Great Britain, I have reason to think that they will not draw nearer to the Americans at this moment for fear of obstructing the peace negotiations thereby: in that they will follow the example of Spain. In spite of that, I continue to think, Sir, that Congress would do very well in any event to have an accredited person in Holland: circumstances may sooner or later enable him to begin a negotiation with the latter and at least to propose paths to some sort of liaison between the two States. But it is important, as I have already observed in my despatch N° 11, that the American plenipotentiary receive his direction from Mr. Franklin, in order to avoid the disparities in the negotiations that Congress is and will be in need of following in Europe. Mr. Adams is certainly the man to do it. I have notions that he is sought out by members of the opposition in England. I cannot say that his Correspondence is very active, but he has received advances, and I am surprised that he does not disclose them to us. Mysteries of this Kind are dangerous. To indulge in secret negotiations is to wish to arouse our distrust, which cannot be the Intention of Congress.

As for Russia, Sir, I persist in thinking that she is not against the independence of America: but the Americans would be greatly deceiving themselves if they imagine that that Power will make the slightest demonstration in their favor: beyond the fact the Catherine II has no reason to hasten the end of the war, that Power is endowed with the role of mediatrice, and with that title it should devote itself to the most scrupulous impartiality. Thus, Sir, whatever may be the principles of the Empress of Russia with respect to the United States, the latter should not expect any salutary effect as long as war lasts. If advantages for the American cause should result therefrom, it will only be when the events of the war have demonstrated to the English the impossiblity of recovering America. Only then will Catherine II be capable of supporting their interests without risk of compromising herself. It is therefore necessary that the Americans act as if Russia does not exist, and that they be persuaded that they themselves must crown their Labors by developing an energy that responds to the efforts that the King is making in their favor. I return often to this matter, because it could not be too greatly impressed upon the Americans, given their penchant for inertia and for a dangerous confidence in the smallest Successes.

We could only learn with the greatest Surprise, Sir, of the effect that the pecuniary assistance that the King has given and procured for them has produced on the Americans; we were persuaded that in procuring for them extraordinary means to subvent their expenditures, we would incline them to develop all their pecuniary resources with a view toward putting an end to their lack of credit within and without, likewise the extreme needs of their army. But since we were mistaken, it is time that we turn from our error, and that we dissipate that of the Americans. You would do well, Sir, if you have not already done so, to announce in the most positive manner to the dominant members of Congress, and to Congress itself if there be need of it, that it will henceforth be impossible for the King to procure new loans for them or to furnish them new pecuniary aid, and that it is absolutely necessary that the Americans provide by themselves for the expenses of the next campaign. You will add that Congress is all the more in need of concerning itself with this subject without any delay, that the loan from Holland, as you have been in a position to demonstrate, is nearly absorbed by the advances that the King has made, and that there will remain little and perhaps nothing at all for the Service of the next year.

. . . . .

Vergennes

FFAA: Pol. Corr., v. 19, f. 35 (LC transcription).

Robert R. Livingston to Benjamin Franklin

Dear Sir.　　　　　　　　　　　　　　　Philadelphia Oct 20. 1781.

Congress having thought it advisable to alter the arrangement of their great Executive Departments and to desolve the Boards and Committees, under whose direction they formerly were, I am to inform you that they have done me the honor to appoint me their Secretary for Foreign affairs. In which Capacity they have made it my duty, as it will always be my inclination, to maintain an intimate and regular correspondence with you....

. . . . .

I need not tell you, Sir, how anxious I shall be to hear from you on every occasion. Nothing Short of the most constant and regular information, will Satisfy the expectations of Congress. We have much to learn and few opportunities of acquiring information. Your Situation enables you, not only to let us know what passes with you, but to extend your enquiries to Courts where we have no Ministers, and of whose Politicks we would not chuse to be ignorant, tho' they may remotely concern us at present. For my own part, I freely confess, that I rely much upon your knowledge and experience, to supply my want of both –

. . . . .

I have the honor to be &c&c　　　　　　　　　Rob R Livingston

NA: PCC, item 79, v. 1., pp. 287-291 (LBkC); M247, reel 105.

Chevalier de la Luzerne to Comte de Vergennes

[Translation]

Nº 189. 3ʳᵈ   Philadelphia, 22 October 1781

My Lord

The President of Congress has just informed me that an Express which he received last Night had brought him the news that Lord Cornwallis surrendered on the 17th. I do not doubt that a frigate has been dispatched to carry this important news to His Majesty; however, as an Express is being sent to Boston, I am profiting thereby to inform you of it. The news is still not as authentic as would be desired: but the Governor of Maryland,[1] who is transmitting to the President of Congress the Letter that he received from M. the Comte de Grasse, is a man worthy of trust. I have the honor of sending you this Letter. M. de Grasse wrote it in French. The Governor of Maryland had it translated, and the Copy enclosed is the English Translation.

On the 19th of this Month, the English fleet, composed of 26 Ships of the Line, 20 Fireships, several frigates, and some 45 transports left Sandy Hook: The Transports placed on board the Ships of the Line some 5000 men of the landing troops and then went back into the port. The enemy fleet set a course for the south, but the Winds having changed, it was driven towards the North: It is not very probable that the English Admiral really had plans to attack the King's fleet; it appears that he only sortied with the intention of showing that he had made every effort to prevent the loss of an army in which was the flower of the English troops.

I am with Respect, My Lord, your very humble and very obedient servant

le chr de la luzerne.

Received 22 January 1782.

FFAA: Pol. Corr., U.S., v. 19, f. 52 (LC transcription).

[1] Lee, Thomas Sim (1745-1819). Maryland planter and political figure. Governor of Maryland, 1779-1782, 1792-1794. Member, Continental Congress, 1783.

Chevalier de la Luzerne to Comte de Vergennes

[Translation]

Nº 191 Duplicate   Philadelphia, 1 November 1781

My Lord.

Congress having elected by ballot, following usage, Mr. Robert Livingston Secretary of the Department of Foreign Affairs, he has just accepted this

post, and after having given his resignation from that of Chancellor of the
State of New York, he has arrived here and he is just entering upon his
duties. I shall henceforth receive through him the communications that
Congress makes to me, and through him will pass those that I make to that
Assembly. It has reserved to itself the right of conferring with me when it
deems it proper, and for my part I may equally ask to confer with the
Committees when the importance of affairs or the circumstances appear to
require it, and in that case it will depend on me to communicate to Mr.
Livingston the Memorials that I have to remit or not to inform him of
them. He is going to put into order the papers of that Department and
introduce an order there that has not existed until now. The Bureaus and
Committees previously charged with this work are now dissolved, and the
Secretary to the Department will henceforth conduct the correspondence
with the Ministers, agents, and Officers of Congress in Europe. I am
enclosing with the original of this despatch, Sir, a letter by which he
informs you of his nomination; he besought me at the same time to assure
you of the efforts that he will make for the continuance of the good
intelligence that exists between the King and the United States, and I
know all too well his attachment to his country and to the principles of the
alliance not to be entirely persuaded of the sincerity of his protestations.

Mr. Livingston enjoys a great reputation; he has experience and
knowledge, but he is entirely a stranger to the type of affairs with which he
has just been charged. His natural talents will perhaps place him on the
level of this work; he is not unaware of the part that I have had in his
election, but it has taken place only by a majority of Seven States, which
was the most appropriate measure, he knows that most of the others were
against him, and he seems up to now to hold himself apart from all
observations to which personal liaisons with me could give rise.

In addition, he is a man of a uniform character, sure and prudent. We
have to fear on his part neither that he may let himself be penetrated by
the English nor that they find the means to influence him. I even reckon
that there will henceforth be more secrecy in the communications that I
have need of making. There is the matter of choosing a Minister of War.
I have reason to think that it will be a man as distant from England as
Messrs. Livingston and Morris, and all the branches of the ministry being
once established in a permanent manner, he may, even after the peace,
follow a sustained System, which we might not have expected from a body
as mobile as Congress, which is subject to continual changes. Mr.
Livingston has added Mr. Du Ponceau[1] to the number of his secretaries; He
is a Frenchman of good family; he was aide-de-camp to an American
General; his Health not permitting him to follow a military Career, I myself
have encouraged him to attach himself to the Minister of Foreign Affairs,

to whom I have recommended him, he has taken the Oath of an officer, and I hope that you will not disapprove that I have applauded the part that he has taken, and for which it was impossible to ask and to await the orders of the Court....   le che de la luzerne.

Received 22 January 1782.

FFAA: Pol. Corr., U.S., v. 19, f. 66 (LC transcription).
[1] *Du Ponceau, Peter Stephen (Pierre-Etienne) (1760-1844). French-born lawyer and man of letters, residing in Philadelphia. A precocious student, largely self-taught, he came to America in 1777 as interpreter and secretary to Baron von Steuben, who obtained him a commission as captain in the Continental Army, in which he served, 1778-1780. Poor health prompted his resignation, after which he became a naturalized citizen, serving as interpreter in the Department of Foreign Affairs, 1781-1783. Member, American Philosophical Society; a philologist, deeply interested in Indian languages and dialects.*

Robert R. Livingston to Chevalier de la Luzerne

Sir,   Philadelphia, 6th. Novr, 1781

Having been honoured with your Letter of the 4th Inst., I remark with pleasure that the mode in which Congress propose to perpetuate the success obtained by the Allied Armies at York, is Such as will, in your Opinion be agreeable to His Most Christian Majesty. As Congress must concur with you in wishing to render this monument of the alliance & of the Military Virtues of the Combined forces, as lasting, (if possible), as the advantages they may reasonably hope to reap from both, they will, without doubt, pay all due Attention to any Ideas you may think proper to suggest relative to the manner of carrying the resolutions of the 28th. of October, into Effect. I shall receive, Sir, with pleasure, & submit to Congress any Communications that you will do me the honor to make on this subject.

I am sorry to find that you Consider the order in which the allied Nations or their sovereigns are placed in the Resolutions, as anyway Exceptionable. This mode of Expression might perhaps be justified by the absolute Equality Established between sovereign Powers, & the common Practice of Independent Nations to recognize no Superior in Acts to be Executed by themselves, within their own Limits; But, Sir, I am So well Satisfied that Congress wish to avoid discussions which must be treated with great delicacy by Nations circumstanced as ours, where Every demand on the one part, not strictly authorized by the Law of Nations, might derogate from the generous protection which we make it our boast to have received, & the denial of just rights on the other, subject us to the imputation of ingratitude, that I think you may Safely rely upon their practice when Some future Occasion shall present, to Evince that the Order in which the Allied Nations are mentioned, did not originate from any Settled rule, & above all, that no want of respect for his Most Christian Majesty dictated the resolution to which you object. Be persuaded, Sir, that regardless as the United States are of form & ceremony, in matters that relate to themselves alone, they will think their endeavour to Support France in the high rank which her Extent, wealth & power have given her, a small return for the wise & generous use She makes of those advantages.

I have the honor to be with the greatest respect & Esteem, Sir, Your most obed & mo⁵· hum serv⁺·   R. R. Livingston

NA: PCC, item 79, v. 2, pp. 21-23 (C); M247, reel 105.

Robert R. Livingston to the Governors
or Presidents of the States

Sir   Philadelphia, 12ᵗʰ· of Novʳ· 1781.

Congress some time since, called upon the different states to make returns of the damage done by the enemy within each of them by the wanton destruction of property, & no measures that I can learn have as yet been taken to ascertain such damage, tho' as your Excʸ· will easily conceive, it may become an important object of inquiry, whenever a treaty shall be set on foot for a general pacification, or be made to answer valuable purposes during the War, by shewing our Vindictive enemy in his true light to the nations of Europe. In this view, I think it my duty to endeavour to collect them, and you will, Sir, I am persuaded, take the necessary measures to send as soon as possible returns from the state over which you preside; – I would wish to have the damages (particularly that to real property) ascertained by the affidavit of people of known characters, & duplicate copies of such affidavits transmitted to my office under the great seal of your state, & if possible accompanied with a short recital of each transaction so that it may at once appear whether the injuries were such as the Laws of War justified, or whether they originated only in the malice & cruelty of a remorseless enemy. Your excellency will oblige me & serve the public by transmitting to me accounts of every occurrence in which the United States are materially interested which may arise within your government, or which you may derive from your Correspondents abroad. I have the honor to be with great respect & esteem &c –

Robert R. Livingston

NA: PCC, item 119, pp. 13-14 (LBkC); M247, reel 139.

Robert R. Livingston to John Adams

Sir   Philadelphia 20 Nov 1781

. . . . .

We find from your Letters as well as from other accounts of the United Provinces that they are divided into powerful parties for and against the War, and we are sorry to see some of the most distinguished names among what you call the Anglomanes. But your Letters leave us in the dark relative to the principles and views of each party, Which is no small inconvenience to us, as we know not how to adapt our Measures to them. It is so important to the due exertion of your Mission to penetrate the views of all parties, without seeming to be connected with either, that I have no doubt you have insinuated yourself into the good graces and Confidence of the leaders, and that you can furnish the information we require; you may be persuaded no ill use will be made of any you give, and that it is expected from you. We learn from Mr Dumas, that you have presented your Credentials to the States General. *We are astonished that you have not written on so important a Subject, and developed the principles that induced you to declare your public Character before the States were disposed to acknowledge it.* There is no doubt from your own prudence and knowledge of the world, that Some peculiarity in your Situation, or that of the Politicks and parties in the United provinces, furnished you with reasons that over balanced the objections to the Measure which arises from the humiliating light in which it places us. Congress would I believe wish to have them explained, and particularly your reasons for printing your Memorial. I may form improper Ideas of the government Interest and policy of the United ~~provinces~~ States but I frankly confess, that I have no hope that they will recognize us as an independent State, and embarrass themselves, in making this wished for Peace, with our affairs. What inducements can we hold out to them? They know that our own Interest will lead us to trade with them, and we do not propose to purchase their alliance by giving them any exclusive advantage in commerce, your business therefore I think lies in a very narrow Compass. "It is to conciliate the affections of the people – to place our cause in the most advantageous light

– to remove the prejudices that Britain may indeavour to excite – to discover the views of different parties, to watch every Motion that leads to Peace between England and the United provinces and to get the Secret aid of Government in procuring a loan, which is almost the only thing wanted to render our affairs respectable at home and abroad. To these objects I am Satisfied you pay the Strictest attention, because I am satisfied no man has more the interest of his Country at heart, or is better acquainted with its wants – as our objects in Holland must be very Similar to those of France, I should suppose it would be prudent for you to keep up the closest connection with the Minister; to advise with him on great leading objects, and to counteract his opinion only upon the most mature deliberation." You were informed before I came into office, that Mr Jay and Doctor Franklin are joined in Commission with you, & have received copies of the instructions that Congress have given their Commissioners, this Whole business being terminated before I came down, I make no observations upon it; least I should not enter fully into the views of Congress, and by that means help to mislead you on so important a subject – I enclose you a resolution discharging the Commission, *for establishing a Commercial Treaty with Britain.* This also being a business of Long Standing, I for the same reason transmit it without any observations there on.

I would recommend it to you to be in your Language, and Conduct, a private Gentleman, this will give you many advantages in making connections that will be lost on your insisting on the assumption of a public Character, and the rather as this Sentiment prevails generally among the members of Congress, tho' for reasons of delicacy with respect to you, I have not chose to ask the Sense of Congress, to Whom it is my Sincere wish, as well as my leading object in the Free Letters I write you; to enable you to render your measures acceptable. A number of your Letters written last Winter and Spring have this Moment come to hand.

This Letter will be sent to Europe by the Marquis de La Fayette, who has obtained leave of absence during the Winter Season. He wishes to correspond with you, and inform his Connections, his understanding and attachment to this Country, he may be very Servicable to you. I would wish you to write as freely to him, as you conceive those Considerations, may render prudent. I have the honor to be Sir, with great Respect and esteem.

Robert R. Livingston

NA: PCC, item 79, v. 1, pp. 309-313 (C); M247, reel 105.

Benjamin Franklin to Thomas Pownall

Dear Sir,   Passy, Nov. 23. 1781

            . . . . .

    I wish most heartily with you that this cursed War was at an End: But I despair of seeing it finish'd in my Time. Your thirsty Nation has not yet drank enough of our Blood. I am authoriz'd to treat of Peace whenever she is dispos'd to it, ~~I can make no Propositions but I did not~~ but I saw Inconveniences in Meeting & Discoursing with you on the Subject, ~~where~~ or with any one not avow'd by ~~the~~ your Ministry; having already experienc'd such, in several Instances. — Mr. Hobart[1] appeared not fully acquainted with your Ideas, and as he could not communicate them, I could make no Judgment of them. My best Wishes attend you, being with the old long-continued Esteem, Dear Sir, Your most obedient & most humble Servant   Benjamin Franklin

LC: *Banjamin Franklin Papers, microfilm reel 7 (LBkC).*
  [1] *Not further identified.*

Robert R. Livingston's Notes of a Meeting with Chevalier de la Luzerne

                               [November 23, 1781]

    The heads of a verbal communication made by the hon[ble:] the Minister of France to the Secretary of foreign Affairs & by him to the United States in Congress assembled on the 23[d.] Nov[r] 1781.

    The Minister of France informed the Secretary of foreign affairs that the count de Vergennes, in a Letter to him of the 7[th:] Nov[r] 1781. assured him that the King of France had rec[d.] with great pleasure an account of M[r.] Adams, Franklin, & Jays appointment to the place of Ministers for the negotiation of peace and after expressing favourable sentiments of them & M[r] Jefferson from his general reputation, adds that they have little reason to hope the assistance of M[r.] Lawrance since the enemy will probably continue his captivity during the war –

    That the King accepted with pleasure the proof which Congress have given him of their confidence when they entrusted to his care the interests of the United States. That he would use his influence & credit for the advantage of his allies whenever a negotiation should render their interests the subject of discussion. – That if he did not obtain for every State all they wished they must attribute the sacrifices he might be compelled to make of his inclinations to the tyrannic rule of necessity That however he had no reason to believe that the events of the campaign would make an unfavourable change in the situation of affairs and that from the present view of them he had no cause to dread a disadvantageous peace.

The Count adds that he presumes Mr Adams has communicated to Congress his majesty's refusal to accede to the terms of the mediation of the imperial courts until they should agree to acknowledge the American plenipotentiaries in the manner most conformable to the dignity of the United States And observes thereon, that if the King was so attentive to a matter of form (tho it might indeed in our present situation be considered as important) then he would not be less tenacious of our more essential interests, which he will be zealous to promote as far as circumstances will allow.

But that if notwithstanding this, Congress, or even a considerable part of its members, should regret the confidence they had placed in his majesty or wish to free their ministers from this restraint, his majesty would not disapprove the measure provided they made their ministers answerable, [(]as in justice they should) in proportion to the powers with which they invested them.

He expresses his satisfaction at the extensive powers with which the Ministers are invested as to the matter of boundary, & the truce, which he says the interests of France as well as of us requires to be as long as possible.

With respect to the statu quo, he says, that tho from the number of their conquests it would be benificial both to France & Spain yet it has not entered into their system so far as it regards America And that his majesty accordingly refused to accede to the plan of negotiation proposed by the mediating powers which held up that Idea.

He exhorts the Minister to recommend to Congress the most vigorous exertions, & to assure them that the expulsion of the enemy from this continent depends in a great measure on the exertion of the United States. That France would be able to afford us very Little assistance. And that Britain so far from discovering any inclination to peace upon reasonable terms <****> <**> had absolutely refused the plan of negotiation proposed by the mediating powers so that arms alone could compel her to it.

He mentions that the King being apprehensive that the capture of the *Marquis La Fayette* might reduce us to some difficulties had ordered her cargo to be replaced immediately And that in consequence of applications from the States of Virginia & Maryland he had ordered a number of arms & military Stores to be shiped to them subject however to the order of Congress. That this & the cargo designed to replace that of the *Marquis De*

Lafayette were to be paid for out of the loan negotiated in Holland which he had reason to think would be compleated.

He expresses a desire that the plan for the appointment of consuls should be digested & adopted as the court of France wished to make it the basis of some commercial arrangements between France & the United States.

Robt R Livingston
Secretary for foreign Affairs

NA: PCC, item 95, v. 2, pp. 47-50 (DS); M247, reel 123.

John Adams to Duc de la Vauguyon

Sir   Amsterdam November 25. 1781

I have the honour to inclose to your Excellency, ~~the fresh~~ a Copy of the fresh Instructions of Congress of the Sixteenth of August last which I received ~~from Congress~~ by the post on the 23^d instant. – I have also received a further Commission, from Congress, with full Powers, to confer treat, agree and conclude with the Person or Persons vested with equal Powers, by his most Christian Majesty, and their high mightinesses the States General of the United Provinces of the Netherlands, of and concerning a Treaty of Alliance, between his most Christian Majesty, the United Provinces of the Netherlands, and the United States of America.

This Measure was apparently concerted between the Congress and the French Minister residing near them, and Seems to be very happily adapted to the present Times, and Circumstances.

I beg Leave to assure your Excellency, that I shall be at all times ready to attend you, at the Hague or elsewhere, to confer with you in the most entire Confidence, respecting this negotiation, and shall take no material Step in it, without your Approbation and Advice.

There are three Ways of proposing this Business to their High Mightinesses. 1. Your Excellency may alone propose it, in the Name of his most Christian Majesty. 2. it may be proposed jointly by the Minister of his Majesty and the Minister of the United States, or it may be proposed, by the Minister of the United States alone and as a Consequence of his former Proposal of a Treaty of Commerce. – I beg leave to submit these three Measures to your Excellencys Consideration and shall very chearfully comply with any, which you may most approve.

I have the Honour to be, with great Respect, Sir, your most &c.

John Adams

MHS: The Adams Papers, microfilm reel 104 (LBkC).

Robert R. Livingston to John Jay

Dear Sir,   Philadelphia, 28 November 1781

. . . . .

Congress are occupied in taking measures for an active campaign and they feel themselves satisfied with every thing both at home and abroad EXCEPT THE RECEPTION YOU MEET WITH. Plain and ingenuous THEMSELVES THEY ARE astonished AT THE FINESSES OF THE COURT, THE CANDID MANNER IN WHICH FRANCE HAS TREATED WITH THEM leading THEM TO EXPECT LIKE CANDOR ELSEWHERE. THEY FEEL PRIDE HURT AT the measures OF SPAIN AND IN SPITE OF ALL THEIR attachment to the MONARCH AND PEOPLE OF THAT COUNTRY THEY begin to talk of ceasing to APPLY WHERE THEY ARE CONSIDERED NOT AS AN INDEPENDENT PEOPLE BUT AS HUMBLE SUPPLICANTS.

Tell me seriously what your opinion [is] about being directed to GO TO PARIS. IF NO LOANS CAN BE OBTAINED, IT NO TREATY CAN BE OPENED, WHY STAY WHERE YOU [ARE] AND experience NOTHING BUT MORTI-FICATION? But this is only mentioned to know your opinion in case it should become a subject of discussion here. Congress have dissolved Mr Adams's powers to make a treaty of commerce with Great Britain and as you know joined you and Mr Franklin and Mr Lawrance in his other commission if England should at length be wise enough to wish for peace.

The Marquis De Lafayette is the bearer of this. He has promised to convey it with safety to you and to correspond with you in such manner as to enable you to avail yourself of the knowledge which he has acquired that may be useful to you. The resolves of which I enclose you a copy shew the sense of Congress on this subject and the confidence which they very justly repose in him. His aid waits for this.... Adieu my Dear Sir. Believe me to be with the highest respect and esteem, Your Most Obedient Humble Servant,   Rob. R. Livingston

Morris, Jay Papers, v. 2, pp. 117-118.

Robert R. Livingston to Charles W. F. Dumas

No 1.   Philadelphia 28 Novr 1781

. . . . .

...The Minute detail into which you go of the facts in which either your government; or ours, are concerned, is highly acceptable to Congress, you will not therefore fail to continue it, and from time to time transmit in addition thereto, such papers and pamphlets as serve to throw light on the Politicks of the United Provinces or that of the Northern powers. Doctor Franklin will defray the expence to which this may put you. Be pleased to subscribe for the Leyden and Amsterdam Gazettes, and transmit them as opportunity offers to me....

...Congress are very Sensible of your attention to their Interest, and wish the Situation of their finances would admit of their rewarding it more liberally, but having retrenched expences of every kind, and reduced the Salaries as low as the Strictest frugality requires, they do not think it expedient at this time, ~~they do not think it expedient~~ to make any additions to that allowed you by Doctor Franklin, which they will direct him to pay regularly. You will be pleased in future to direct your Letters, not to the President, but to me, as the Secretary of the States, for Foreign Affairs, and when you favor us with any thing written in French, or Dutch, to give it in the original Language, this may save you some trouble, and enable us in quoting it, to make use of the original expressions, which you know is often very necessary....

...I am Sir, with great esteem & respect &ᶜ·   Robert R. Livingston

NA: PCC, item 79, v. 1, pp. 314-317 (LBkC); M247, reel 105.

John Adams to the President of Congress

Duplicate   Amsterdam Decʳ· 4ᵗʰ· 1781.
Sir,

I have received those Instructions with which I was honored by Congress on the sixteenth of August, and communicated them forthwith to the French Ambassador, to their High Mightinesses, and to the American Ministers at Versailles and Madrid. The Duke de la Vauguyon was of opinion, that they were very well considered and very well timed, to counteract another Fruit of British Policy, in agreeing to the Mediation of Russia, for a separate Peace with Holland. The British Ministry mean only to aid the Stocks and lull the Dutch.

There is no longer any talk of a Congress at Vienna. The late News of General Washington's Triumphs in Virginia, and of the friendly and effectual Aid of the Comtes De Rochambeau and de Grasse have made a great Impression here, and all over Europe.

I shall punctually observe my Instructions, and consult in perfect Confidence with the Duke de la Vauguion, in the Execution of my late

Commission. A quadruple Alliance for the duration of the War, would probably soon bring it to a Conclusion. But the Dutch are so indolent, so divided, so animated with Party Spirit, and above all so entirely in the Power of their Chief, that it is very certain, that they will take the Proposition ad referendum immediately and then deliberate upon it a long time. This Nation is not blind: it is bound and cannot get loose. There is great Reason to fear, that they will be held inactive until they are wholly ruined. Cornwallis's fate however has somewhat emboldened them, and I have received unexpected Visits of Congratulation from several Persons of Note; and there are Appearances of a growing Interest in favor of an Alliance with France and America. If I were now to make the proposition, I think it would have a great effect. I must however wait for the approbation of the Duke, and he perhaps for Instructions from Versailles, and indeed a little delay will perhaps do no harm, but give Opportunity to prepare the Way. The general Cry at this time in Pamphlets and public Papers is for an immediate Connection with France and America.

. . . . .

I have the Honor to be, with the greatest Respect, Sir, your most obedient and most humble Servant.   J. Adams
Read 13. March 1782.

NA: PCC, item 84, v.3, pp. 422-425 (LS); M247, reel 112.

John Adams to Francis Dana

My dear Sir   Amsterdam Dec.ʳ 14. 1781

. . . . .

We must have Patience, and must humour our Allies as much as possible consistent with our other Duties. I see no near prospect of your being rec.ᵈ, any more than myself, but if, without being rec.ᵈ, we can gain and communicate Information We shall answer a good End. I am at present apparently and I believe really upon good terms with the D. de la V. and the Miffs at Versailles and Passy seem to be wearing away

Let me intreat you to write me as often as possible. Our Country by all Accounts is in great Spirits, Paper Money wholly stopped. every thing conducted in Silver. Trade flourishing, although many Privateers and Merchant Vessells taken. Crops the finest ever known. G. B. has not lost less than 20,000 Men, the last twelve months in America. They will not be able to send 10, but if they could send 20, they would only give oppertunities for more Cornwallizations and Burgoinizations.

With every Sentiment of Affection and Esteem, Your obliged Fri^d &
Sert   no matter for the name.

. . . . .

MHS: *Dana Family Papers* (ALS).

John Jay to John Adams

Sir   Madrid 15 December 1781

. . . .

As to the Progress of my Negotiations here – I can only inform you that
the last offers of America were made so long ago as July last, the Court has
not as yet found it convenient to give me an answer. I could give you a
particular History of Delays, but it would be useless – I could also
communicate to You my Conjectures as to the real Causes of them, but by
the Post it would be improper. In a Word, it is not in my power to write
any thing of Importance, but what I ought not to write by such a
Conveyance, unless in Cypher.

Delay is and has long been the System, & when it will cease, cannot be
divined. Mr Del Campo the Ministers first and confidential Secretary has
been appointed near three Months to confer with me, and yet this
appointment was not announced to me till the last Week. I have not yet
had a Conference with him – he has been sick, and it seems is not yet
sufficiently recovered to do Business, &c.&c.&c.

. . . . .

I have the Honor to be with great Respect & Esteem Your Excellency's
most ob$^{t.}$ & most h'ble Servant   John Jay

MHS: *The Adams Papers, microfilm reel 355* (ALS)

Benjamin Franklin to David Hartley

My Dear Friend,   Passy, Dec. 15, 1781.

I received your favour of September 26, containing your very judicious
proposition of securing the spectators in the opera and play-houses from the
danger of fire. I communicated it where I thought it might be useful. You
will see by the enclosed that the subject has been under consideration here.
Your concern for the security of life, even the lives of your enemies, does
honor to your heart and your humanity. But what are the lives of a few idle

haunters of play-houses compared with the many thousands of worthy men and honest industrious families butchered and destroyed by this devilish war? O! that we could find some happy invention to stop the spreading of the flames, and put an end to so horrid a conflagration! Adieu. I am ever yours most affectionately,   B. Franklin.

William Temple Franklin, editor, Memoirs of the Life and Writings of Benjamin Franklin *(London: R. Bentley, 1833), hereafter cited as WTF, Franklin Memoirs, v. 4, pp. 44-45.*

John Adams to Duc de la Vauguyon

Sir   The Hague Dec.ʳ [19,] 1781
It has been insinuated to me, that the Spanish Ambassador, here, has Instructions from his Court to enter into Negotiation with their High Mightinesses, concerning an Alliance between Spain and the Republick. if this fact has come to your Excellency's Knowledge, and there is no Inconvenience nor Impropriety in communicating it to me, I should be very much obliged to You for the Information, not from Curiosity merely but for my Government in the Steps I may have to take.

By my late Instructions, of which your Excellency has a Copy, I am to inform myself concerning the progress of American Negotiations at the Court of Spain, and if an Alliance shall have been entered into between his Catholic Majesty and the United States, to invite his Catholic Majesty into the Alliance proposed between France, their High Mightinesses and the Congress: if no such Alliance shall have been formed, to recieve his Catholic Majesty, should he manifest a disposition to become a Party &c.

Congress have wisely enjoined it upon me, to confer in the most confidential manner with your Excellency, and I have made it a Law to myself to take no material step in this Negotiation, without your approbation: but my Instructions seem to make it necessary to take some Measures at least to sound the disposition of the Spanish Ambassador. I would therefore beg leave to propose to your Consideration and to request your Opinion, whether You think it adviseable for me to do myself the Honor of making a Visit to the Spanish Ambassador, and communicating to him the substance of my Instructions as far as it relates to the Court of Madrid; or whether it would be better to communicate it by Letter, or whether your Excellency will be so good as to take upon yourself this Communication, and inform me of the result of it.

I am advised here to wait on the President of their High Mightinesses as soon as possible, & demand a categorical Answer to my former Proposition, and then to wait on the Grand Pensionary, and Mʳ· Secretary Fagel, and in turn upon the Pensionaries of all the Cities of Holland, to inform them of the demand made to the President. But I submit it to Consideration whether it will not be expedient to communicate the Project of a tripple or quadruple Alliance; to some confidential members of the States, as to the Pensionaries of Dort, Haerlem and Amsterdam for Example with Permission to them to communicate it, where they shall think it necessary, in order to give more Weight to my demand.

The Court of Great Britain are manifestly availing themselves of the Mediation of Russia in order to amuse this Republick, and restrain it from exerting itself in the War and forming Connections, with the other belligerent Powers, without intending to make Peace with her upon any Conditions which would not be ruinous to her. It is therefore of the last Importance to Holland, as well as of much Consequence to the other belligerent Powers to draw her out of the Snare, which one should think might be now easily done, by a Proposition of a triple or quadruple Alliance.

Tomorrow Morning at ten, I propose to do myself the Honor of waiting on your Excellency, if that Hour is agreable, in order to avail myself more particularly of your Sentiments upon these points. In the mean time, I have the honor to be, with the most perfect Respect & Consideration, Sir, your most obed^t &c.   John Adams

MHS: *The Adams Papers, microfilm reel 104 (LBkC).*

William Carmichael to Robert R. Livingston

No 1 Duplicate   Madrid 20th. Decr 1781
Sir,

. . . . .

Our affairs are in much the same situation they were when I had the honor to forward the letter to the Committee above mentioned. Mr de Campos sickness of which he is but just recovered, is the occasion or pretext for this Delay, his appointment however has been formally announced to Mr Jay by the Minister, & was made at the Time mentioned in my former Letters. It is probable that little will be done in this business until the Court goes to the Pardo the 7th of next month. A Principle of Delicacy perhaps prevents it from seeming at present to precipitate its Conduct in consequence of the Favorable aspect of our affairs since the news of the Capture of Ld Cornwallis and the Victory obtained by General Greene in S. Carolina. But the delay attending the Transaction of the

Smallest Affair in this Country is a sufficient reason to Acc^t for the difficulties which Mr Jay encounters at present without surmising other Motives. On this Subject I speak from the Experience of Almost all the Corps Diplomatic, as well as from the Authority of Individuals who have much business with the Various Branches of Administration –

The news above mentioned was received apparently with great Pleasure by the King & Prince of Asturias,[1] as I was informed the Same day by several of their Officers in waiting. The Public at Large was highly satisfied & has spoken more favorably since of our Allies, than it has Done from the Commencement of the War. The Foreign Ministers were not all so well pleased with this Event – Particularly those of Germany Russia & Denmark – However in general they regard it as a blow which decides the Independance of the States – ...

. . . . .

I have the honor to be with much Respect Your Most Obed$^{t\cdot}$ & Humble Ser^t W$^{m\cdot}$ Carmichael
Read March 18.

NA: PCC, item 88, v.1, p. 179-186 (ALS); M247, reel 116.
    [1] Asturias, Carlos, Prince of (1748-1819). Crown prince of Spain, 1748-1788. As Charles IV, king of Spain, 1788-1808.

Chevalier de la Luzerne to Comte de Vergennes

[Translation]

N$^{o\cdot}$ 205 Triplicate   Philadelphia, 1 January 1782
My Lord.

It was about eight months ago that Mr. Samuel Adams returned to the State of Massachussets. His being so far away contributed not a little to the amelioration of the affairs which that Delegate hindered by his obstinacy and by a poorly-reasoned attachment to the principles of democracy and to a speculative perfection of administration that cannot subsist with the state of war in which the United States find themselves, and that will probably not exist any longer so in time of peace. I thought for some time that he had renounced public affairs, but he was secretly preparing all the machinery that he has just put into motion to procure for the States of the East participation in the fisheries on the banks of Acadia, of Newfoundland, et al. After having prompted his State to send its delegates the instructions of which I have had the honor to send you a copy, he has employed all the influence that he can bring to bear on the other delegations to induce them to support the claims of Massachussets. The affair was taken into consideration almost six weeks ago, and debated with a degree of choler proportionate to the measures taken by those who had an interest in making it succeed. The demands of the Massachusetts delegates tended toward having the ultimatum that makes the King master of the negotiations rescinded, save for independence and the treaties of alliance and of commerce, and demanding the admission of the Americans to the fisheries as a condition *sine qua non* of the treaty of peace. The partisans of this system no longer relied, as in the past, on their former possessions as subjects of Great Britain. Mr. Gerard having previously demonstrated the absurdity of their reasonings, they have abandoned them in order to attach themselves to proving that fishing belongs to all men by virtue of the common right, that the very existence of the Eastern States depends upon it, and that it does them an injury to deprive them of the exercise of a right or even of a freedom to which their preservation is connected. Such are the two cardinal points of their arguments, but the debates have begotten a crowd of other reasonings, as much concerning the right in itself as concerning the possiblity of having it recognized at the peace.

The success of the allied Army in Virginia; the taking of St. Eustatius, which we learned of around the same time; the situation of the English, which we believe to be very critical in India; and the conquests of General Greene in the South will furnish arms to that party and those who compose it. It will be concluded from these favorable conjunctures that we may dictate the law as victors, and that the English will be obliged to submit to all the conditions that we may wish to impose on them. It was stated positively that the right in question should extend to all the fishing banks of America, and particular mention was made of three leagues from the coasts, but without claiming to dry fish on shore. It was established as an invariable fact that if the four states of New England did not enjoy this right in the most unlimited manner, they would soon be depopulated and deserted; that the lands there had only a mediocre fertility; that the inhabitants, trained for navigation, are engaged in it all the time; that an infinitely numerous class would fall into poverty and despair if it were deprived of this resource; that the East as well as the other parts of the United States would draw continually from Europe, from Asia, and from the Sugar Islands merchandise that could be regarded as an object of primary necessity, but that having neither mines nor produce of the land that could form a medium of exchange, to deprive them of the fisheries that nature had put in their grasp was clearly to wish to annihilate them at the moment when they were beginning to exist; that the war had furnished employment to a numerous navy that was desolating the commerce of the Enemy; that the Eastern States had at Sea four Privateers for every one that the other States combined could arm; that these brave and useful subjects, after having merited so much from their country, were going to fall into idleness at the moment of peace; that these same States, and particularly that of Massachusetts, could flatter themselves with having had the most considerable part in the revolution; that at this moment even their contingents in the Continental Army were equal to those of the nine other States taken together; that at the peace those nine States would enjoy the benefits of independence so dearly bought; that their wheat, their tobacco, their indigo, their rice, their cotton, and all the produce of their lands carried into all the markets of the Universe would procur for them easy returns and a richness that would continually grow, while the inhabitants of the North, as the prize for all their sacrifices, would find themselves at the peace in a worse condition than before the revolution; that independence would only be disastrous for them alone; and that after having made astonishing efforts to throw off the Britannic yoke, they would find themselves with cause to regret it.

These notions have been continually presented to Congress from the time deliberations commenced on this matter. Mr. Samuel Adams, who at the beginning of this revolution directed in an astonishing manner the movements of the people by forming them into Committees, thought he could adapt this same machinery to the affair of the fisheries. He again convoked the people into committees to deliberate on this subject, and to the reasonings of which I have just rendered you an account he joined others less specious, but equally appropriate to carry along the multitude.

"That the navy was the safeguard of independence; that the only means of maintaining sailors in time of peace was to have abundant fisheries; that it was necessary to profit from the present war to assure themselves of the unlimited right, or that the lost occasion would never recur; that fishing was surely of common right, and that all the Powers enjoyed it, since no vessel crossing the Grand Banks or any other fishing bank had ever been forbidden to cast a line or to take all the fish in its path."

I was informed of several other arguments as vague and as feeble which were used to seduce the people, and which produced only too much effect on the inhabitants of the East, naturally disposed to adopt a system that flattered their inclination and their interests.

Several meetings were employed to expose to Congress the basis of the claims of the State of Massachussets, with which those of Rhode Island and of Connecticut will be combined. Delaware inclined towards the same party. The Delegates of Georgia also let themselves be carried along by the hope that they were given of support for their claims to lands in the West as a form of compensation.

The other Delegates were slower to form their opinion.

Several Delegates have come with full confidence to inform me of these circumstances, and of the discomfort caused them by an affair in which it was a question of producing a violent disgust in the States of the North. They told me that the majority of Congress felt the indecency of the conduct that Mr. Lovell wanted to dictate to that assembly; that even though it was persuaded that the principles advanced by this Delegate from the State of Massachussets had foundation, it would be infinitely loath to diminish anything of the confidence it had shown to the King and to produce new demands immediately after the successes in Virginia; that it seemed more in conformity with the dignity of the United States to keep to its first resolutions and to continue without variation to show His Majesty the most unlimited confidence without changing the System with events. "However," they continued, "we can see ourselves pulled by the very opinion of the people against our own sentiment. It is they who are the authors of the revolution; we must avoid anything that could make it disagreeable to them; it is already insinuated to them that Congress, despite the opposition of some delegates to giving unlimited powers to the King, and that His Majesty himself having an interest in excluding them from the Newfoundland fishing, this has made him the arbiter of his own cause; it is important to our reputation and even to our safety that we should not be accused of having abused the confidence of the people, and if the torrent of public opinion should force us to make the fisheries an ultimatum, we wish to know if His Majesty would consider himself obliged to continue the war in order to keep them for us."

I did not hesitate to respond that there was no reason to suppose it, and I founded my response as much on our treaties with the United States as on the impossiblity of proposing to the Mediators a new and unknown claim, while it is manifest that our obligations are only understood to assure the independence of the United States. The Delegates seemed to me to be expecting my response. Articles 9 and 10 of the treaty of commerce have been scrupulously examined in Congress, and Mr. Lovell claimed to find in the latter a recognition of the right of the inhabitants of the United States to fish on the banks of Newfoundland. I was told that he argued in the following manner: Article 10 of the treaty holds that we will not trouble the French in the exercise of the right to fish on the Newfoundland banks; thus we have the right to fish there as long as we do not trouble them, and the fishing being inexhaustible, the French and American fishermen can attend to it reciprocally without causing themselves the least trouble. I responded to those who communicated this reasoning to me that the consequence would be just, if after having stipulated that the Americans could not trouble us, a parallel clause had been inserted in favor of the Americans stating that we could not trouble them; that this latter not having taken place, it was clear that Article 9 remained in all its force, and that Article 10 should only develop and fortify the sense of it. They insisted, and I was told that if according to my opinion the United States should not participate in the portion of the fisheries that belonged to us, I would at least agree that they had the right to claim the portion belonging to England. I was in fact convinced of it, but I asked the Delegates where their resources and their means to conquer it were. They could not deny that the United States were totally lacking therein, and by a vicious circle they fell again into the discussion of our obligation to conquer the English portion on behalf of the Americans. This reasoning was so false and so contrary to the letter and to the spirit of our treaties that it was easy for me to refute it. We passed then to the examination of the question: if we had an interest in possessing a more considerable portion of the fisheries than that which is necessary to our consumption. Some persons had established that we were not carrying on any foreign commerce in fish caught off Newfoundland. I responded to the question that was put to me in that respect, that the treaty being clear on this matter, I could spare myself from entering into any ulterior explanation, that nevertheless I could assert that the foreign commerce in dried cod in Spain and in Italy had in former times produced for us eight million in clear and net profit, without speaking of the employment and the training of our sailors. I then made use of the arguments that your despatch N°· 2 contains to prove to the Delegates who consulted me how unseemly it was on the part of the United States to wish, despite their weakness, to invade all they believe to be in their grasp, and particularly an object that we had reserved for ourselves in the treaty after having renounced Canada and Nova Scotia, in spite of the advantage that we could obtain from conquering them. There is perhaps some disadvantage to articulating at this moment in a manner so precise the interest that we have in the fisheries, and I am persuaded that many delegates will take alarm from it and will reproach Congress for the confidence that it has placed in His Majesty's friendship. It nevertheless seemed preferable to me to inculcate in them early a truth that they must perceive sooner or later, and not to suffer them to entertain a hope which they will probably be obliged to renounce in the future peace. I can only applaud the effects of this frankness on the sane party and on the majority of Congress. This Senate seems to want to adhere invariably to its first measures, but the better-intentioned are not themselves without anxiety as to the consequences which the dissatisfaction of the peoples of the East could have. As for me, My Lord, I think as they do that this privation will be evident to them, and that it is impossible to obtain for the United States a peace in which all the classes of inhabitants are satisfied. But they need peace. The people appear tired of the war. Congress needs to sustain and to nourish by all sorts of means their disposition to continue it and to oppose a dignity to their penchant for peace. I am therefore persuaded that whoever guarantees the independence of the 13 States and procures for them conditions as advantageous as circumstances will permit as to the boundaries and the confiscated goods and, if possible, to the portion of the fisheries in which participation could not infringe upon our own interests will be received with eagerness by the major part of the population. There will certainly be difficulties to combat, but I do not think they are insurmountable.

I am with respect, My Lord, Your very humble and very obedient servant

Le Chr de la Luzerne

Received 3 March 1782.

FFAA: Pol. Corr., U.S., v. 20, N°. 1 (LC transcription).

David Hartley to Benjamin Franklin

My Dear Friend,   London, January 2, 1782.

I have received the favour of yours of the 15th of December by Mr. Alexander.[1] I most heartily join with you in the wish that we could find some means to stop the spreading flames of this *devilish war*. I will not despair. The communications which he has imparted to me from you have revived my hopes of peace. I laid them before the minister immediately. We are at a suspense for the present upon a very material preliminary. I did not intend writing to you at the present pause, that we might make our ground good as we go on; but an incident which has happened obliges me to do it without delay. For having had a most essential question transmitted to me from Lord North[2] for explanation, when I would have applied to Mr. Alexander I could not hear of him; and now I find that he has left his hotel these four or five days, and his return uncertain, I must apply to you. I will state to you what has passed.

Upon my first interview with Mr. Alexander, he told me that the late events would make no difference in the prospect of peace; that America had no other wish than to see a termination of this war; that no events would make them unreasonable on that subject, which sentiments likewise your letter expresses; and that no formal recognition of independence would be required. I thought this a very fair opening; but the next point which he explained to me seemed to be still more material towards peace, viz. *that America was disposed to enter into a separate treaty with Great Britain, and their allies were disposed to consent to it.* I believe that it has been the unfortunate union of common cause between America and France, which has for the last three years turned aside the wish of the people of England for peace. I verily believe (so deep is the jealousy between England and France) that this country would fight for a straw to the last man, and the last shilling, rather than be dictated to by France. I therefore consider this as the greatest rub out of the way. I have often argued this point with you upon former occasions, having at all times foreseen that it would be the greatest rub in the road to peace; and I have often stated it to you as an act of *justice* due to America from her allies, not to drag her through a war of European resentments and jealousies beyond her original views and engagements; and moreover I think the separation of the causes in the negotiation promises much the shortest road to a general peace.

Upon Mr. Alexander's opening thus much to me, I told him I would apply for the earliest opportunity of laying these matters before the minister. Accordingly, on Friday morning (December 21), I applied through the means of the Earl of Guildford (father to Lord North), a nobleman of a most respectable character, advanced in years, and attached by every possible tie to a son now in a most arduous situation. I therefore requested the favor through his hands, as giving me the most conciliatory access to the minister, to whom I was preparing to make an application for peace. After the appointment was made with Lord North for Friday evening, I returned to Mr. Alexander to consider the specific manner and terms in which I should make my application. It had occurred to me from what Mr. Alexander had stated to me, that the conciliatory bill[3] which I had moved in the last parliament, on June 27, 1780, would still serve as a foundation to proceed upon. I therefore carried it with me. He told me that he and you knew the sense of the bill very well, and that it would be entirely consonant to your sentiments, that I should state it to Lord North, as drawing an outline for negotiation of peace. However, to avoid all errors, I read the bill through to him, and explained the view of each clause, viz. the style of *provinces of North America* – a general phrase to avoid any term denoting dependence or independence. The truce – for an indefinite term. The articles of intercourse for ten years certain – to restore an amicable correspondence, and to abate animosities. The suspension of certain acts of parliament – to avoid every possible question of dependence or independence. And to finish the work by a ratification of each article of intercourse as agreed to, thereby to prevent all possible return of war. I compared the articles of intercourse for a short term, and their ratification into a permanent peace, to a well-known mode of proceeding in the laws of England, by lease and release, from temporary to perpetual amity and peace. Upon these grounds I took my commission from him for Lord North, viz. the question of dependence or independence *sub silentio* – a separate treaty with America, and to state the conciliatory bill of June, 1780, as the outline of negotiation. I saw Lord North in the evening, and stated the foregoing propositions to him, as I have now stated them to you. After having stated the compromise *sub silentio* and the separate treaty, I left with Lord North the copy of the bill of June, 1780, together with a paper intitled Conciliatory Propositions, as explanatory of that bill (both inclosed with this). The next morning (viz. Saturday, December 22), I saw Mr. Alexander and reported to him what I had stated to Lord North, and showed him a copy of the paper intitled Conciliatory Propositions. He told me that I had executed my commission perfectly to his intelligence of the matter. I should tell you, that at the conclusion of my conversation with Lord North, we both settled jointly the result thus: "I recommend to your Lordship the propositions which I have had the honour of stating to you, as *the general grounds of a proposed negotiation leading towards peace, under liberal constructions.*" Lord North said in answer, "So I understand them."

Upon this footing matters rested for some days. On Sunday last (December 30), I received a message from Lord North through the means of Lord Guildford, requesting an explanation of this point, viz. "Who is authorised to treat on the part of America? whether you or Mr. Adams, or both jointly? and whether the propositions above stated would be acknowledged as general grounds of negociation towards peace, by the person or persons authorised to treat, because it was necessary before he could lay a matter of so great importance before the cabinet council, that he should be entitled to say, "These propositions and general outlines come to me from responsible and authorized persons?" The moment I received the request of Lord North I agreed entirely with the necessity of an explanation on that head. I had partly expected such an inquiry, and it gave me satisfaction when it came, as I thought it the first reply towards a parley. If the propositions had not gained some attention, it would have been of very little importance to have inquired whence they came. As to the caution itself, it appears to me not only prudent but indispensable. The forms of caution in such cases are the essentials of caution. I had determined on my own account before this message to have writ to you, that I might have received your sentiments directly from yourself without any other intervention, that we might proceed with caution and certainty in a matter of such infinite importance. This message has only quickened my dispatch. The two points of explanation requested, I take to be these; whether the outlines above recited are properly stated, always considering that they imply no farther than *general grounds of negotiation towards peace, under liberal constructions*; and secondly, by what authorised person or persons any answer on this subject would be accepted; in short, a requisition of credentials preparatory to a formal answer, which is so much the more necessary on the supposition of a favorable reception of the first hint towards negotiation.

When I last saw Mr. Alexander, about four or five days ago, he had met with some desponding impressions, as if the ministry were indisposed to peace, and that things would not do, &c. He did not tell me upon what ground he had formed such apprehensions: however, lest he should have imparted any such by letter to you, I will state that point to you, because it may have infinite ill consequences to be too touchy on such suspicions. A premature jealousy may create the very evil it suspects. The ministry in this country are not every thing. The sense of the people when really expressed and exerted, would be most prevalent. Suppose then it were a proved point that every man in the ministry were in his heart adverse to peace. What then? withhold all overtures? By no means. I should advise the very contrary in the strongest manner. I should say, let the overtures be made so much the more public and explicit, by those who do wish for peace. It is the unfortunate state of things which has hitherto bound the cause of France to any possible treaty with America, and which has thereby thrown a national damp upon any actual public exertions to procure a negotiation for peace with America. I have the strongest opinion that if it were publicly known to the people of England that a negotiation might be opened with America upon the terms above specified, that all the ministry together, if they were ill disposed to a man, would not venture to thwart such a measure. But why should it be supposed that the ministry to a man are ill disposed to a peace? Suppose them to be half and half, and the public wish and voice of the people in favor of negotiation, it is evident on which side the balance would incline. But why should we seek to throw a damp prematurely upon any chance? Why presume even against any individual? I grant that it would be a bitter trial of humility to be brought to a formal recognition of independence at the haughty command of France, and I believe every part of the nation would proceed to every extremity before they would submit to that. But if that touchy point can be provided for *sub silentio*, and if the proposed treaty with America may be carried on free from control by France, let us give the cause of peace a fair trial; at the worst, we should but be where we were if we should fail. But why should we expect to fail when the greatest rub is removed by the liberty of entering separately into a treaty? I think it a most favorable event leading towards peace. Give us a truce with its concomitants, and a little time so given for cooling will have most excellent effects on both sides. Eternal peace and conciliation may then follow. I send this to you by the quickest dispatch, that we may bring this point to a fair issue before the meeting of parliament. God prosper the blessed work of peace. I am ever yours most affectionately,   D. H.

[Conciliatory Bill]

In the title and preamble of the bill the words *provinces of North America* are used as general words, neither implying dependence or independence.

Clause 1. The truce is taken from the conciliatory act of 1778, and is indefinite as to the proposed duration of the truce. Under this clause it might be proposed to negotiate three points, viz. the removal of the British troops from the thirteen provinces of North America, and connectedly with this article a stipulation for the security of the friends of the British government. The third article might be a stipulation that the respective parties during the continuance of the truce should not either directly or indirectly give assistance to the enemies of each other.

Clause 2. Articles of intercourse and pacification. Under this clause some arrangements might be settled for establishing a free and mutual intercourse, civil and commercial, between Great Britain and the aforesaid provinces of North America.

Clause 3. Suspension of certain acts of parliament. By this clause a free communication may be kept open between the two countries, during the negotiation for peace, without stumbling against any claim of rights which might draw into contest the question of dependence or independence.

Clause 4. The ratification by parliament. The object of this clause is to consolidate peace and conciliation step by step, as the negotiation may proceed, and to prevent, as far as possible, any return of war, after the first declaration of a truce. By the operation of this clause a temporary truce may be converted into a perpetual and permanent peace.

Clause 5. A temporary act. This clause creating a temporary act for a specific purpose of negociation in view, is taken from the act of 1778.

P.S. January 8, 1782.

Since writing this letter I have seen Mr. Alexander, and shall see him from time to time to communicate with him. I do not suppose I shall have an answer from Lord North till the preliminary points are so settled as to enable him to give an answer in form. Ministry might undoubtedly give a short negative if they thought proper; but I do not expect that. You may be assured that I have and shall continue to enforce every argument in the most conciliatory manner to induce a negotiation. I am very sorry for Mr. A.'s confinement on his own account, and on that of his friends, and because probably in the future state of his business, his personal exertions may be very serviceable in the cause of peace. Every assistance and every exertion of mine will always be most heartily devoted to that cause. I have nothing farther to add, either upon my own reflections or from my subsequent conversations with Mr. A. to what I have stated in the foregoing letter. If we once make a good beginning upon the plan there stated, I should hope that such a negotiation, founded on such principles, would promise fair to produce every salutary and pacific consequence in the event.   David Hartley

WTF: Franklin Memoirs, v. 4, pp. 45-55.
   [1] Alexander, William, Jr. British secret agent. Scottish trader who owned property in the West Indies. A resident of France, 1776-1781, having allegedly fled to the continent to avoid creditors, he was Franklin's neighbor at Passy. He attempted to promote peace through talks with Franklin, 1777-1778, and with David Hartley, 1781-1782.
   [2] North, Frederick, Lord (1732-1792). British political figure. Lord of the treasury, 1759-1765. Paymaster general, 1766-1767. Chancellor of the exchequer, 1767-1770. Chief minister and first lord of the treasury, 1770-1782. With Charles James Fox, secretary of state under the nominal leadership of the Duke of Portland, April-December 1783. From 1790, Earl of Guilford.
   [3] Conciliatory Bill. A motion put forward in the House of Commons in June 1779 by David Hartley, which would have suspended hostilities with the American colonies for ten years and withdrawn British troops from America. It was voted down after Lord Shelburne pointed out that the terms of the Franco-American treaty of alliance precluded a separate peace. [See enclosure.]

Chevalier de la Luzerne to Comte de Vergennes

[Translation]

Nº 207   Philadelphia, 5 January 1782

My Lord.

   The Delegation from Massachusetts Bay, seeing the fruitlessness of its efforts near Congress to prove its rights to the Fisheries, has had recourse to an extraordinary means to force that assembly to adopt its opinions. Mr. Lovell has shown himself alarmed by the dire consequences which the abandoning of such a precious right might expose; he has announced that all the news that he receives from the East gives him reason to fear deplorable movements among the People; that they were so persuaded of the justice of their claims that he feared that they would reject the peace if it deprived them of that prerogative. It was insinuated in private conversations that the Union might in this circumstance receive strong attacks; that the Ratification of the Treaty of peace would become doubtful; that the discontent of the People might lead to causing Independence to be detested, and that England was so well informed of what was happening in the Midst of the United States as to seize such a favorable occasion and to offer to the inhabitants of the East these same Fisheries that were so dear to them to purchase them perhaps at the price of their liberty, and make their horror for British domination cease. The Delegates who apprised me of these discourses told me that the preservation of the Union was so important a point that they had to expose themselves to everything before placing it in danger of dissolution; that they knew the dispositions of the People of the East, the influence that some substantial leaders have over them; that they thought that it was perhaps a question on this occasion of considering not only what was just, but also what was prudent. I responded to them that the first Point had already been discussed, and that with regard to the second I could not be persuaded that when the People, who lacked neither wisdom nor notions of justice, were instructed on the state of the question, the danger at which Mr. Lovell had shown himself alarmed ought to be feared, and that for an unjust cause they were ready to sacrifice advantages bought so dearly. Many Delegates, full of reason and of moderation, told me that they could not envisage the affair from the same point of view as I; that they knew the People of these States, and the difficulty of stopping them once they were put in motion; that they could not suspect, without the greatest injustice, Mr. Samuel Adams of any view of reconciliation with England, but that his Vehemence and the obstinancy of his character might carry him too far, and that it was necessary to be on guard even against his imprudence and that of his Party. Among the persons who confided to me their uneasiness on these conjectures was Mr. Thomson, an unemotional, sensible man who has constantly fulfilled the functions of Secretary since 1774.

I have, he told me, a long familiarity with this assembly; I am not easily alarmed. I cannot prevent myself, nevertheless, from becoming uneasy at the ardour with which the People of the East pursue their objective. They seem so attached to the Fisheries that I would not be surprised if they return to the arms of England rather than renounce them.

In the middle of these agitations, My Lord, a great Majority of Congress fully rejected the idea of making the least change in the full confidence that it has shown in His Majesty; but I saw that most of the Delegates were equally pained by the necessity of greatly displeasing many of their co-States, and feared the consequences that might result from it....

.   .   .   .   .

I am with Respect My Lord Your most humble and most obedient servant   le chr de la luzerne
Received 3 March.

FFAA: Pol. Corr., U.S., v. 20, f. 10 (LC transcription).

Robert R. Livingston to Benjamin Franklin

No 6   Philadelphia 7 January 1782
Dear Sir

As it does not appear improbable that the humiliation and misfortunes of Great Britain may produce the same sentiments, which a Spirit of Moderation dictates to the other belligerent powers, and lead her to concur With them in their wishes for Peace, It cannot be improper to acquaint you with the objects America most wishes to obtain, and to furnish you with the Arguments, on which they found their Claim to them. For such is their Confidence not only in the justice of his most Christian Majesty, but in his friendship; that they firmly persuade themselves that he will not only preserve for them, their undoubted Rights, but that he will even go so far as to procure for them, those advantages they may reasonably demand on the close of a successful War; and I am perfectly satisfied that the loose hints, that a detail of their Sentiments, may afford to you and our other Commissioners will be strengthened and improved by your lights, in such Manner, as to come before his Majesty in the most advantageous form.

The first point of discussion will be the limmits of the United States, the instructions given to Mr Adams on the   day of   last[1] explain the wishes of Congress on that subject, nor can they admit of many doubts, except so far as they relate to our Southern extent, the bounds between us and Canada, being very well ascertained by grants, Charters, Proclamations and other Acts of Government; and more particularly by the settlements of the people who are engaged in the Same Cause with us, and who have the same rights with the rest of the subjects of the United States. Our Western and Northwestern extent will probably be contested with some warmth, and the reasoning on that subject be deduced from general principles, and from proclamations & Treaties with the Indians. The Subject is undoubtedly intricate and delicate, yet upon candid investigation, I believe it will appear that our extention to the Mississippi is founded in justice, and that our claims are at least such as the events of the War gives us a right to insist upon; your situation furnishing you amply with the various documents, on which Great Britain founded her claim to all the Country east of the Mississippi, previous to the Treaty of Paris, I will not trouble you with references to them, which would at any rate be imperfect from the want which prevails here of Books & papers. Taking it for granted that the King of Great Britain was entitled to that extent of Country (which he at least cannot contravene) it only remains to examine how far he considered it, as within the limits, of some or other of the United States, because he can no more pretend to abridge those Limmits, than claim by any other right of which the United States are in possession. His Idea of these limmits is apparent from Charters granted by the Crown, and from recent grants made by its representatives in several of the States, it appears that they considered their Authority to grant lands to the westward coextensive, with the right of Great Britain, unless they were restricted by their interference with other Governments, upon this principle the Servants of the Crown in New york granted Lands on the Borders of lake Erie, to the westward of Niagara. And Virginia even after the proclamation in 1763, patented considerable tracts upon the Ohio, far beyond the Appalachian Mountains. It is true that several Governments were prohibited at different times from granting lands beyond certain limmits, but these were clearly temporary restrictions, which the policy of maintaining a good understanding with the Natives dictated, and were always broke through after a Short Period, as is evinced by the grants above mentioned made Subsequent to the proclamation in 1763, and indeed the proclamation itself furnishes a Substantial argument of the Opinion of Britain with respect to the right which some or other of the States had to extend to the Westward of the limmits it prescribed, otherwise, it would not have been necessary to prohibit their Governors from granting, as their Patents would in such cases have been invalid, and themselves Subjected to the censure of their Master, upon Whom they were dependent, unless therefore these proclamations absolutely destroyed the right, they must be considered as proofs of its existence at, and after they were issued. The Slightest examination of them show that they did not take away, but restrained an existing right, and the subsequent grants by the Governors, evidence that they were as before asserted mere temporary restrictions. The same reasoning applies to the Treaty at Fort Stanwix, and to other arguments taken from Treaties with the Indians; Strong evidence in our favor, is also found in a map made by the Kings Geographer, in which Virginia and the Carolinas are laid down as extending to the Mississippi shortly after the last War. Arguments may be drawn against us from the Quebec Bill, but as this is one of the Laws, that occassioned the War, to build any thing upon it, would be to urge one wrong in support of another. But this matter may perhaps be seen in a different light, and our pretentions placed upon a more extensive Basis by running to general principles, and asking whence Great Britain derived her right to the waste Land in America. Evidently from the allegiance which a Subject is supposed to carry with him wherever he goes, even though he dislikes his Constitution, and seeks one that pleases him better. Upon this false principle the oppressed Subjects of Great Britain, seeking freedom in the Wilds of America, were supposed to extend to it the Sovereignty of the Kingdom they had left. The rights of the King of Great Britain, then, to America were incident to his right of Sovereignty over those of his Subjects that settled America and explored the Lands he claims: for the Idea of right derived from mere discovery, and the vain Ceremony of taking possession, without planting and continuing that possession, is now fully exploded. If then we admit what is necessary to our independence, that the right of Sovereignty over the people of America is forfeited, it must follow that all rights founded on that Sovereignty are forfeited with it, and that upon our setting up a new Sovereign in America, the rights which the first claimed, as such, devolves upon the Second; upon this principle Great Britain is left without a foot of Land in America, beyond the limmits of those Governments which acknowledge her Jurisdiction.

It is vain to say that the King of Great Britain holds these back lands by a Cession from other powers, since those Cessions were grounded upon a prior Claim, derived through the people of America, and only served to confirm the right which they gave the King of Great Britain while he was their Sovereign, and which he loses with his Sovereignty over them: this mode of reasoning is warranted by the practice Great Britain uniformly held of treating with the Indian Nations, through their American Governors, who having frequently executed with them the most Solemn acts, and sometimes extended the Kings Protection, to the Nations which occupy the waste lands, which are the Subject of our present Claim. The expences of retaining these in friendship, almost always devolved upon the respective States; who till lately, particularly in New York, voted the sum necessary to support Smiths among them, and to procure the presents which were annually made them. From hence then it follows that if the King of Great Britain has any right to the back Lands in America, it must be as the King of the people of America; Ceasing to be King of those people, his right also ceases. If he has no right over the back Lands but merely as protector of the Savage Nations that inhabit them, that connection and duty devolves upon us, since they evidently claimed that protection from him as King of the Colonies, and through the Governors of those Colonies, and not as sovereign of a Country 3000 Miles from them. This country having chosen a new Sovereign, they may rightfully claim its protection.

There is some reason to believe that Great Britain considered their rights, in many instances as extending no farther than their right of preemption and protection, as may be infered from passages in the negotiations for a peace with France, in the year 1761 refered to in the Margin. {Answer of the King to the ultimatum of France received Sept 1761 2nd Sec. of 11th art.}[2] This Suggests a New Idea, which however, I am not warranted by any act of Congress in mentioning, and therefore you will only consider it as the Sentiment of an Individual. If the Mediators should not incline to admit our claim, but determine on restricting our limmits, either by the extent of our Grants, the course of the Mountains, the Sources of the Rivers, or any other of those arbitrary rules, that must be sought for when sollid principles are relinquished, perhaps it would not be difficult to bring them to agree, that the Country beyond those limmits, belongs to the Nations which inhabit it. That it should enjoy its independence under the guaranty of France, Spain, Great Britain and America, and be open to the Trade of those whose lands bordered upon them.

This tho' restrictive of our rights would free us from the well grounded apprehensions, that the vicinity of great Britain, and their Command of the Savages would give us. They already possess Canada and Nova Scotia. Should that immense Territory which lays upon the rear of the States from the Gulph of St Lawrence to the Gulph of Mexico be acknowledged to be vested in great Britain, it will render our Situation truly hazardous. The lands as you know, are infinitely better than those on the Coast, they however open communication with Sea by the Rivers St Lawrence and the Mississippi, and with each other by those extensive inland Seas, with which America abounds, they will settle with the utmost rapidity from Europe, but more particularly from these States. Attachment to the Government, freedom from Taxes, a prospect of bettering their fortunes, and the fertility of the Soil will invite numbers to leave us. This Co-opperating with the Leven of disaffection, which will continue to work here for many years, may produce the most dangerous effects, especially upon the Southern States, which will from the Nature of their Soil and husbandry, be thinly Settled for many years, while the Lands which lay near them beyond the Mountains, will soon be filled with a hardy race of people inimical to them, who to their own Strength will be able to join that of the Savages, Subject to their command.

If it is an object with the maritime powers, to lessen the powers and by that means diminish the dangerous dominion that Great Britain has in Some measure usurped over the Ocean, they must prevent her possessing herself of the Country in question, Since besides the whole furr and Peltry trade that she will thereby engross: the demand of this great Country will give a new Spring to her Manufactures, which tho' the Floridas should be added to Spain, will find their way into it by the River St Lawrence and the numerous Lakes and Rivers which communicate with it; add to this that Settlements are already formed beyond the Apalachian Mountains, by people who acknowledge the United States, which not only give force to our claims, but render a relinquishment of their interest highly impolitic and unjust. Those and a variety of other reasons, which will suggest themselves to you, and the gentlemen joined in the Commission with you, will doubtless be urged in such terms, as to convince the Court of France, that our mutual Interests conspire to keep Britain from any Territory on

this Continent beyond the bounds of Canada. Should the Floridas be ceded
to Spain, she will certainly unite with you on this point, as the Security of
that Cession will depend on its success.

The Fisheries will probably be another source of litigation, not because
our rights are doubtful, but because great Britain has never paid much
attention to rights, which interfere with her views.

The Arguments on which the people of America found their claim to
fish on the Banks of Newfoundland, arise, first, from their having once
formed a part of the British Empire, in which State they always enjoyed as
fully as the people of Britain themselves the right of Fishing on those
Banks; they have shared in all the Wars for the extension of that right, and
Britain could with no more justice have excluded them from the injoyment
of it (even supposing that one Nation could possess it to the exclusion of
another) while they formed a part of that Empire, than they could exclude
the people of London or Bristol – If so, the only inquiry is, how have we
lost this right, if we were Tenants in Common with Great Britain, while
United with her, we still continue So, unless by our own act, we have
relinquished our title. Had we parted with mutual Consent, we should
doubtless have made partition of our Common right by Treaty: but the
oppression of Great Britain forced us to a seperation (which must be
admitted, or we have no right to be independent) it cannot certainly be
contended, that those oppressions abridged our rights, or gave new ones to
Britain, our rights then are not invalidated by this seperation, more
particularly, as we have kept up our claim from the commencement of the
War, and assigned the attempt of great Britain to exclude us from the
Fisheries, as one of the causes of our recurring to Arms.[3]

The second Ground upon which we place our right to fish on the Banks
of Newfoundland, provided we do not come within such distance of the
coasts of other powers as the Laws of Nations allow them to appropriate–
Is the right which nature gives to all Mankind to use its common benifits
so far, as not to exclude others. The Sea Cannot in its nature be
appropriated, no Nation can put its mark upon it. Tho' attempts have some
times been made to set up an Empire over it, they have been considered as
unjust usurpations, and resisted as such, in turn, by every Maritime Nation
in Europe. The Idea of such Empire is now fully exploded by the best
writers.

The Whale Fishing in every Sea and even upon the Coasts of Princes,
who do not exercise it themselves, is considered as a common right, and is
enjoyed by those nations that chuse to pursue it. The Cod Fishery upon the
dogger Bank, and other parts of the European Seas, is claimed exclusively
by no nation. The Herring Fishery is carried on daily by the Dutch on the
Coast of England, and if the Banks of Newfoundland are not equally

common, it is because some nations have relinquished their rights, and others find it impossible to exercise them for want of Harbours to receive their Vessels, or Shores to dry their Fish on – When we say we are willing to exercise it under these inconveniences, there can certainly be no farther dispute about our right, and the only remaining question will be the distance we ought to keep from the Shores possessed by the Enemy, tho' strictly Speaking, from our first principles, we have no common right in them. The subject is treated so much at large by Grotius[4] & Vattel,[5] that I do not think it necessary to detail arguments, which tho' urged by people here from their feelings, you will find much better stated there: give me leave however to urge some that arise from our particular circumstances. All the New England States are much interested in this point: the State of Massachusetts more particularly, it has no staple, it does not raise its own Bread, its principal commerce before the War was in Fish, which it supplyed to the rest of the Continent in exchange for rice Flour &c, and to the West Indies for Rum, Sugar, and Molasses – It Shiped little to Europe 1st. because it could not fish so cheap as the people of England, 2nd because their Fish was not so well cured in general, owing to their Fishing at improper Seasons, and to their using salt which is said to be of a more harsh nature, than what the European Vessels bring out with them. Should this State and New Hampshire which is almost in Similar Circumstances, be excluded from the Fisheries they must be reduced to great distress, it will be impossible for them to pay for the necessaries they must recieve from abroad, they will see with pain, their Sister States, in the full enjoyment of the benifits which will result from their independence, while their own Commerce checked and their State impoverished, they will consider their interests as Sacrificed to the happiness of others, and can hardly forbear to foster that discontent, which may be productive of disunion and the most dangerous divisions.

An Idea has also gone ~~forward~~ forth, and it is fomented by the disafected, that France wishes from Interested views, to monopolize the Fishery, at least to exclude all other competitions but Great Britain. Those who have attended to the disinterested conduct of France during the War, oppose to this sentiment, the honor and good faith of their ally; the Little interest that he can have in excluding a people from a right, which would not interfere with his, since France does little more than supply itself, and the New England Fishery for the most part, only supplies the Continent and Islands of America, they see the care with which France has indeavored to cultivate a good understanding between that Kingdom and these States, and they are persuaded so inconsiderable an object will not be put in Competition, with the harmony which ought to subsist between them, or administer food to those unworthy Jealousies; and so much does this

Sentiment prevail in Congress, that their present prospects have not induced them to alter your instructions, more particularly as they have received through the Minister of France, assurances that His Majesty was pleased with the proofs Congress had given him of their Confidence, and that he would in no event make any Sacrifices of their essential interests which necessity should not compel him to. That he had no reason to apprehend from the events of the War, that such necessity would exist. These events have become so much more formidable, since the date of the Letter which contained those assurances, that Congress persuade themselves his Majesty will not be driven to make sacrifices equally painful to him, and injurious to us; but that as we owe our success in war to his Magnanimity and generosity, we may be equally indebted to his justice and firmness for an honorable Peace.

It is not improbable that Great Britain will indeavor to make some stipulations in favor of their American partizans, who have been banished [from] the Country, or whose property has been forfeited. You will doubtless be sensible of the inconvenience and danger to which their return will Subject us, and the injustice of restoring to them what they have so justly forfeited, while no compensation is made to us for the loss of property, and the calamities they have occasioned

There can be little doubt that every society may rightfully banish from among them those who aim at its subversion, and forfeit the property which they can only be entitled to, by the Laws, and under the protection of the Society, which they attempt to destroy. Without troubling you therefore on the point of Right, I will just mention a few of the Consequences, that would result from a Stipulation in their favor.

1st. It will excite general dissatisfaction & tumults. They are considered here as the Authors of the War. Those who lost relations and Friends by it, those who have been insulted by them while Starving in prisons, and prisons Ships, those who have been robed and plundered, or who have had their houses burned, and their Families ill treated by them, will, in spite of all Laws and Treaties, avenge themselves if the real, or supposed authors of these calamities ever put themselves in their power, nor will the Government be able to prevent what the feelings of the Body of the people will justify

Should they be permitted to reside among us they will neglect no means to injure and Subvert our Constitution and Government, and to Soe divisions among us in order to pave the way for the introduction of the Old System. They will be dangerous partizans of the Enemy, equally unfriendly to France, and to us, and will Show themselves Such upon every Occasion. To restore their property in many States is now become impossible, it has been sold from hand to hand, the Money arising from it has been sunk in depreciation, in the public Treasury, to raise the value by Taxes, or to wrest the lands from the hands of the proprietors are equally unjust and impossible; many of the very people who would demand the restitution, have grown rich by the Spoil and plunder of this Country; many others who were beggars at the beginning of this War owe their present affluence to the same cause. So that at least the account between the two Nations should be liquidated before any claim can be set up by the aggressors. How far it will be possible to obtain a Compensation for the injuries wantonly done by the Enemy you will be best able to judge, be assured it is anxiously desired.

Give me leave to mention to you the necessity of Stipulating for the safe delivery of all records and other papers of public and private Nature which the Enemy possessed themselves, particularly of the Records of New York, which Mr Tryon[6] sent to England, and the private papers of many Gentlemen of the Law in different parts of the Continent, by which the rights of individuals may be materially affected. Thus Sir, I have touched upon the Principal points that America wishes to obtain in the Peace, which must end this Bloody War. Perhaps in so doing I have given both you and myself unnecessary trouble, Since I have urged nothing but what your own knowledge of the Country, and that of the other Gentlemen in the Commission, would have suggested to you. However, conceiving that Circumstances might render it Necessary for you to declare that you spoke nothing more than the prevailing sentiments of your own Court, this Letter will Serve to vouch the assertion

Should the Floridas be ceded to Spain, as there is nothing that Congress have more at heart, than to maintain that Friendly intercourse with them Which this Revolution has happily begun, it will be essential to fix their limmits precisely, for which purpose the instructions to Mr Adams will serve as your directions.

...I have the honor to be dear Sir &c &c &c   Robert R. Livingston

• • • • •

NA: PCC, item 79, v. 1, pp. 350-365 (LBkC); M247, reel 105.

[1] Presumably a reference to the instructions Congress gave John Adams on August 14, 1779, which cover the question of boundaries in some detail.

[2] {Margin Note}

[3] Left margin note reads "Declaration of the reason for taking arms."

[4] Grotius, Hugo (1583-1645). Dutch jurist, sometimes called the father of modern international law. His most influential work was De jure belli ac pacis (On the Law of War and Peace), published in 1625, in which he asserted that nations have certain universal, reasonable, and unchangeable duties and responsibilities in their conduct towards each other. His Mare liberum (Freedom of the Seas), published in 1609, asserted the Dutch right to unrestricted commercial navigation on the basis that no nation has

sovereignty over the high seas.

[5] *Vattel, Emmerich de (1714-1767). Author of* Law of Nations.

[6] *Tryon, William (1725-1788). British colonial official. Appointed lieutenant governor of North Carolina, 1764; governor, 1765-1771, during which time he put down the revolt of the Regulators. Governor of New York, 1771-1778. Commanded loyalist and British military forces in New York and Connecticut, 1777-1780.*

Chevalier de la Luzerne to Comte de Vergennes

[Translation]

N°· 208.   Philadelphia, 11 January 1782

My Lord.

When amidst the troubles without number that are crushing the United States one sees many members of the Confederation obstinately busying themselves with plans of ambition, one cannot help concluding that it is essential for us to put ourselves on guard early against their enterprises and their avidity. The peoples of the East solicit admission to the fisheries with so much ardor, that we can foresee that they will one day be more dangerous rivals for us than the English themselves. They are close to the fisheries, they would have a still greater advantage if, having conquered Acadia or some of the Islands in the Gulf of St. Lawrence, they were to find themselves in a position to dry their fish near the fishing banks without being obliged to take to their own coasts for that operation. Our fishermen on the contrary, obliged to leave France in ballast or with simple cargoes of salt, will incur considerably greater expenses and will eventually be constrained to renounce this commerce if we do not adopt measures capable of redressing the balance early.

I have seen some people so greatly exaggerate the advantages of the Americans over us in this branch of commerce, that they regard the benefits that would procure us the sale of oils and of dried cod and our exports to Spain and to Italy as lost to the Realm. Permit me to submit to you my ideas on this matter, My Lord. It is a question of preserving employment for that great quantity of sailors that the present war has trained, of maintaining during the peace the number of them henceforth necessary to the proportion of our naval forces and to the formidable merchant marine that has just been created, of increasing the value of our salt fish, of favoring the construction and the manufacture of vessels, of preserving for our own Navigators and Merchants an object of consumption important for the Realm, of preventing our rivals from seizing it, of nourishing an important branch of foreign commerce whose benefits are as certain as those that our Colonies procure for the Realm, as clear as those of culture itself. These great subjects excite my zeal, and will perhaps induce you to pardon me for the errors into which my ignorance could plunge me.

I am persuaded that we can by vigorous and just measures recover all the advantages that fishing has procured for us in the past, or at least push back for a great number of years the time when we must lose them. These measures seem to me to have to be prepared before this war is finished, and the peacemaking should secure the duration of it. I think that they would consist principally of our seizing Cape Breton. That island, the advantages, soil, and situation of which are too well known to us for me to need to mention them here, is also convenient for the Eastern States, and if they had a moment to breathe, I am persuaded that they would hasten to seize a possession that would remove the obstacles with respect to their claims to the fisheries. I am assured, although I cannot guarantee the fact, that there are only two hundred forty men to garrison the whole Island; that they are employed in working the mines, and that only a few men defend Spanish Bay, and that the fortifications of Louisbourg have been razed. Given the present state of our navy, it seems that we can well hope to retain it if we are once masters of it. Situated at the entrance to the Gulf of St. Lawrence, it can become the center of considerable smuggling with Canada and Nova Scotia if those two provinces continue to belong to England. It produces masts and other woods that would be a great resource to the vessels that come to these parts. It would procure for our fisheries an extent and a stability they could never have at the rate fixed by the previous boundaries. Commerce with the thirteen states could still invigorate that of Cape Breton. In a word, we would long be in a position to thwart the projects that the ambition of the Eastern States might engage them to form. We must, it is true, expect all the enterprises that number, audacity, and avidity may permit, but I think that we could, after the peacemaking, take with England the proper measures to assure to the King's Subjects the rights that belong to them.

It will certainly be difficult to persuade the Americans to renounce the fisheries expressly. There would be great difficulties in forcing their hand in that respect. It is even desirable that we should obtain some satisfaction for them, such as the right to fish on the banks of Nova Scotia, independently of fishing on their own coasts, which is vested in them without need of sanction, but at the same time France and England could be mutually guaranteed fishing on the other banks by an article of the treaty or by a separate article, either on the basis of the preceding treaties, if we cannot make any conquest in these parts, or in consequence of the changes that the acquisition of Cape Breton or of any other island in the Gulf of St. Lawrence might produce. I perceive, My Lord, the difficulties which this system may bring us, and that I am perhaps preparing for myself in particular. The Americans cannot conceal from themselves that we have adopted it from distrust of them, and it will doubtless follow from it that peace will be less agreeable to them, but I think that in spite of these difficulties, the object of the fisheries is too important not to take while we have arms in hand, all the measures appropriate to assure for us the portion to which we can justly aspire. As for England, she will be sufficiently clairvoyant to judge that her interests and ours are common in this circumstance, and not be put off by stipulations that, while protecting our rights, serve at the same time as a defense of hers.

Some delegates are, on the contrary, of the opinion that this Power will admit Americans there, either to foster prejudice against us, or to regain their affection. I can hardly share their anxieties in this respect, but if they have a basis, this ought to be a new motive for us to acquire an Island, possession of which could surely provide stability and duration to our rights to fish in these parts.

I am with Respect, My Lord, Your very humble and very obedient servant   le chr de la luzerne
Received 3 March.

FFAA: Pol. Corr., U.S., v. 20, f. 14 (LC transcription).

John Adams to the President of Congress

Sir,   Amsterdam Jany. 14th 1782.

Having received the Advice of several Gentlemen, Members of the States, and also the Opinion of the Duc de la Vauguiyon, and the Comte de Vergennes, I went to the Hague on Tuesday the 8th. day of this month, and the next morning at ten waited on the President of their high Mightinesses, M^r. Van den Sandheuvel[1] of Dort, a City of Holland, to whom I made a verbal Requisition in the following words, the French being the Language of the Court.

"The 4th of May last I had the honor of a Conference with the President of Their High Mightinesses, in which I informed him that I had received a Commission from the United States of America, with full powers and instructions to propose and conclude a Treaty of Amity and Commerce between the United States of America and the United Provinces of the Netherlands.

In the same conference I had the honor to request an Audience of Their High Mightinesses, in order to be able to present to them my Letters of Credence and full powers.

The President assured me that he would report everything that I had told him to Their High Mightinesses, so that the matter might be transmitted to the several members of the Sovereignty of these lands, to be submitted to their deliberation and decision.

I have not yet been honored with a response; and for this reason I have the honor of addressing myself to you, Sir, to request from you, as I do request, a categorical response, which I may transmit to my Sovereign." ⊗

The President assured me, that he would not fail to make Report to their high Mightinesses. After this, I sent a Servant to the grand Pensionary Bliswick, to know at what hour I should have the honor of a little Conversation with him. The Answer returned to me, with the Compliments of the Grand Pensionary, was, that he was sick, unable to attend the Assembly of the States, and to receive any Visits at home from anybody: but if my business was of a public Nature, I might communicate it to his Secretary, which would be as well as to himself. Upon this, I requested Mr· Dumas to call upon the Secretary, and communicate my Intentions to him, which he did.

I went next morning at ten to the Secretary of their high Mightinesses, Mr· Fagel, and communicated to him the Step I had taken the day before, who told me that he had already been informed of it, for that the President, according to his promise, had made his Report to their high Mightinesses: that it was true that the Baron de Linden de Hemen had made his Report to their high Mightinesses, on the fourth of last May, of my Proposition to him, and that it had been forthwith taken ad referendum by all Provinces, but that no Member of the Sovereignty had yet returned any Answer at all, either in the affirmative or negative: that my proposition of yesterday had in like manner been taken ad referendum by all the Provinces, and that it was necessary to wait to see what Answer they would give. The Secretary, who is perfectly well with the Court as his Ancestors and Family have been for a long Course of Years, and who is as complaisant to England as any Man in this Country, received me with perfect politeness, and when I took leave insisted upon accompanying me through all the Antichambers and long Entries quite to my Chariot Door in the Street, where he waited until We entered and drove off. After this, I went to the House of Dort, the Pensionary of which City, Mr· Gyselaer,[2] recieved me with Confidence and Affection, told me, that all he could say to me in his public Character was, that he thanked me for the Communication I had made to him, and would communicate it to the Deputation and to the Regency of his City, and that he hoped I should have as friendly an Answer as I desired, for that he personally saw me with great pleasure, and very readily acknowledged my Character and that of my Country.

I went next, at the hour agreed on, to the House of Haerlem, where I was recieved by the whole Deputation, consisting of two Burgomasters, two Schepins and a Pensionary. Here passed a Scene, which really affected my Sensibility and gave me great pleasure. The five Gentlemen were all aged and venerable Magistrates, who recieved me with an Affection and Cordiality, which discovered in their Air and Countenance the Sincerity and Satisfaction they felt in the Words of their Pensionary when he told me, that they were only Deputies; that by the Constitution of the City of Haerlem like all the others in the Republick, the Sovereignty resided in their Constituents the Regency: that they thanked me for the Communication I had made to them, that they would communicate it to the Regency of their City, and that for themselves, they heartily wished it success, for that the United States, as Sufferers for and Defenders of the great Cause of Liberty, might depend upon the Esteem, Affection and Friendship of the City of Haerlem, and that they heartily wished a Connection between the two Republicks, and they congratulated Us on the Capture of Lord Cornwallis, to which We returned to them a Congratulation for the Recapture of St Eustatia, and took our Leave.

At the House of Leyden We were recieved by the Pensionary, who told Us he had the Orders of his Burgomaster to recieve me; to thank me for the Communication, and to promise to communicate it to their Regency.

At the House of Rotterdam We were received by the whole Deputation, consisting of two Burgomasters, two Schepins or Judges and the Pensionary. We recieved thanks for the Communication and a promise to lay it before the Regency. At the House of Gouda and the Brille, the same Reception and the same Answer. At another House, where the Deputies of five small Cities lived together, the same Answer. At the House, where the Deputies of Alhmaar and Enkhuisen reside, we were recieved by the whole Deputations, recieved the same Answers with the addition of professions of Esteem and Wishes, that in time there might be a closer Connection between the two Nations.

Thus I had been introduced to the Ministers of the Republick and to the Deputies of all the Cities of Holland except Amsterdam. In my Messages to the Deputations I had followed the order of the Cities, according to the Rank they held in the Confederation. I had sent to the House of Amsterdam in its Course. The Messenger the first time found only one of the Burgomasters at home, Mr Rendorp,[3] who returned for answer that the Gentlemen were not then together, but that they would send me word at what time they would recieve me, but no Answer came for a day or two. I sent again. The Messenger found only the same Burgomaster, who returned the same Answer. On Friday Morning, having no Answer, I sent a third time. The Answer from the same Burgomaster was, that the Gentlemen were then setting off for Amsterdam, being obliged to return upon business, and could not then see me, but would send me Word. Upon this I concluded to return to Amsterdam too, and to make the Communication there in writing to the Regency: but reflecting that this step would occasion much Speculation and many Reflections upon Amsterdam, I desired Mr· Dumas to wait on Mr· Vischer,[4] the Pensionary, who remained in Town, and consult with him. The Result was, that I made my Visit to the House of Amsterdam, and made the Communication to Mr· Vischer, who recieved me like a worthy Minister of the great City.

It may not be amiss to conclude this Letter by observing, that every City is considered as an independent Republick. The Burgomasters have the Administration of the Executive, like little Kings. There is in the great Council, consisting of the Burgomasters and Councillors, a limited legislative Authority. The Schepins are the Judges. The Deputies are appointed by the Regency, which consists of the Burgomasters, Councillors and Schepins; and in the large Cities, the Deputies consist of two Burgomasters, two Schepins or Councillors and one Pensionary. The Pensionary is the Secretary of State, or the Minister of the City. The Pensionaries are generally the Speakers upon all Occasions, even in the Assembly of the States of the Province.

These Operations at the Hague have been recieved by the Public with great appearance of approbation and pleasure, and the Gazettes and Pamphlets universally cry against the Mediation of Russia, and for an immediate Alliance with France and America. But the Leaders of the Republick, those of them I mean who are well intentioned, wish to have the two Negotiations, that for Peace under the Mediation of Russia, and that for an Alliance with France, Spain, and America, laid before the States and the Public together, not so much with an Expectation of accomplishing speedily an Alliance with Bourbon and America, as with a hope of checking the English Party, and preventing them from accepting a Peace with England, or the Mediation of Russia to that End upon dangerous or dishonorable Terms.

If it was in any other Country, I should conclude from all Appearances, that an Alliance with America and France at least would be finished in a few Weeks: but I have been long enough here to know the Nation better. The Constitution of Government is so complicated and whimsical a thing, and the Temper and Character of the Nation so peculiar, that this is considered everywhere as the most difficult Embassy in Europe. But at present it is more so than ever: the Nation is more divided than usual, and they are afraid of every body – afraid of France, afraid of America, England, Russia and the Northern Powers, and above all of the Emperor who is taking Measures, that will infallibly ruin the Commerce of this Country if they do not soon change their Conduct.

I have the honor to be, with the greatest Respect, Sir, your most obedient and most humble Servant. John Adams

⊗ Quoted material translated from the French language.

NA: PCC, Misc. Papers, Adams Despatches; M332, reel 1, ff. 481-486.
[1] Santheuvel, Bartholomeus van den. Dutch political figure. Delegate from Holland to the States General, 1782. President of the States General, January 1782.
[2] Gijselaar, Cornelis de (1751-1815). Dutch political figure. From 1778, pensionary of Dordrecht. Friend of John Adams. A leader of the Patriot party.
[3] Rendorp, Joachim (1728-1792). Dutch political figure. From 1781, a burgomaster of Amsterdam. A moderate conservative who balanced between the Patriot and Orange parties, eventually earning the distrust of both. An Orange spokesman at the time of the Prussian invasion, 1787.
[4] Visscher, Carel Wouter. Dutch political figure. Pensionary of Amsterdam, 1781-1783.

Benjamin Franklin to David Hartley

Dear Sir, Passy, Jan[y]. 15. 1782

I received a few Days since your Favour of the 2[d.] Instant; in which you tell me, that M[r.] Alexander had informed you, "America was disposed to enter into a separate Treaty with great Britain." I am persuaded, that your strong Desire for Peace has misled you & occasioned your greatly misunderstanding M[r.] Alexander, as I think it scarce possible he should have asserted a Thing so utterly void of Foundation. I remember that you have, as you say, often urged this on former Occasions, and that it always gave me more Disgust than my Friendship for you permitted me to express. But since you have now gone so far as to carry such a Proposition to Lord North as arising from us, it is necessary that I should be explicit with you, & tell you plainly that I never had such an Idea, and I believe there is not a Man in America, a few English Tories excepted, that would not spurn at the Thought of deserting a noble and generous Friend for the sake of a Truce with an unjust and cruel Enemy. I have again read over your conciliatory Bill, with the Manuscript Propositions that accompany it, and am concerned to find that one cannot give Vent to a simple Wish for Peace, a mere Sentiment of Humanity without having it interpreted as a Disposition to submit to any base Conditions that may be offered us rather than continue the War: For on no other Supposition could you propose to us a Truce of ten years, during which we are to engage not to assist France while you continue the War with her! A Truce too wherein nothing is to be mentioned that may weaken your Pretensions to Dominion over us, which you may therefore resume at the End of the Term, or at Pleasure; when we have so covered ourselves with Infamy by our Treachery to our first Friend, as that no other Nation can ever after be disposed to assist us: Believe me, my dear Friend, America has too much understanding and is too sensible of the Value of the World's good Opinion to forfeit it all by such Perfidy: The Congress will never instruct their Commissioners to obtain a Peace on such ignominious Terms; and tho' there can be but few Things in which I should venture to disobey their Orders, yet if it were possible for them to give me such an Order as this, I certainly should refuse to act, I should instantly renounce their Commission, and banish myself for ever from so infamous a Country.

We are a little ambitious too of your Esteem, and as I think we have acquired some Share of it, by our Manner of making War with you, I trust we shall not hazard the Loss of it by consenting meanly to a dishonourable Peace.

Lord North was wise in demanding of you some authorised Acknowledgment of the Proposition from responsible Persons. He justly thought it too improbable to be rely'd on so as to lay it before the Privy Council. You can now inform him that the whole has been a Mistake, & that no such Proposition as that of a separate Peace has been is or is ever likely to be made by me; & I believe by no authorised Person whatever in behalf of America. You may farther, if you please, inform his Lordship, that M^r· Adams, M^r· Laurens, Mr Jay & myself have long since been impowered by a special Commission to treat of Peace, whenever a Negociation shall be opened for that Purpose: But it must always be understood that this is to be in Conjunction with our Allies conformably to the solemn Treaties made with them.

You have, my dear Friend, a strong Desire to promote Peace, and it is most laudable & virtuous Desire. Permit me then to wish that you would in order to succeed as a Mediator, avoid such invidious Expressions as may have an Effect in preventing your Purpose. You tell me that no Stipulation for our Independence must be in the Treaty, because you verily believe (so deep is the Jealousy between England and France) that England "would fight for a Straw to the last Man and the last Shilling rather than be *dictated to* by France." And again, that "the Nation would proceed to every Extremity rather than be brought to a formal Recognition of Independence at the haughty Command of France." My dear Sir, if every Proposition of terms for Peace that may be made by one of the Parties at War is to be called and considered by the other as *Dictating*, and a *haughty Command*, and for that Reason rejected with a Resolution of fighting to the last Man rather than agree to it, you see that in such Case no Treaty of Peace is possible. In Fact we began the War for Independence on your Government which we found tyrannical, & this before France had any thing to do with our Affairs; the article in our Treaty, whereby the "two Parties engage that neither of them shall conclude either Truce or Peace with Great Britain without the formal Consent of the other first obtained; and mutually engage not to lay down his Arms untill the Independence of the United States shall have been formally or *tacitly* assured by the Treaty or Treaties that shall terminate the War" was an Article inserted at our Instance, being in our Favour. And you see by the Article itself, that your great Difficulty may be easily got over, as a formal Acknowledgement of our Independence is not made necessary. But we hope by God's help to enjoy it, and I suppose we shall fight for it as long as we are able. I do not make any Remarks on the other Propositions, because I think that unless they were made by Authority, the Discussion of them is unnecessary & may be inconvenient. The Supposition of our being disposed to make a separate Peace, I could not be silent upon, as it materially affect our Reputation & essential Interests. I have been a little Warm on that offensive Point, reflect on your repeatedly urging it, and endeavour to excuse me. And whatever may be the Fate of our Poor Countries, let you & I, die, as we have lived, in Peace with each other. Assuredly I continue, with great & sincere Esteem, my dear Friend, Your most affectionate   B. Franklin

LC: *Benjamin Franklin Papers, microfilm reel 2 (LBkC).*

Chevalier de la Luzerne to Comte de Vergennes

[Translation]

Nᵒ 210.   Philadelphia, 18 January 1782
My Lord

I carried out at the time the orders contained in the despatch with which you honored me on 7 September last, relative to the preliminary articles proposed by the Mediators and to the responses that His Majesty judged proper to make to them. Mr. Livingston, to whom I announced these circumstances, appeared to me to perceive the full value of the fidelity with which the King fulfills his engagements, and of the zeal with which he attends to the interests of his Allies. I said at the same time to that Minister that if Congress regretted having too much restrained the powers of its plenipotentiaries, it was free to give them more extensive ones. I also made known to him the inconveniences that could result for Congress from any change of this kind, but leaving him free to inform Congress of His Majesty's dispositions. This he did, and Mr. Lovell sought right away to take advantage of this communication in order to engage Congress to insert in the ultimatum the recognition of the right to the fisheries; his efforts and those of his party could not shake the resolution taken by Congress to make no innovations there. Mr. Livingston told me that he had written a very detailed letter on this subject to Mr. Franklin. He is endeavoring to prove in it the rights of the United States to the fisheries and to extend their boundaries up to the Mississippi, and the impossibility of reestablishing the partisans of England in their possessions confiscated and sold. His arguments are nearly the same as those which I have had the honor to report to you. They seemed very weak to me, with the exception of those regarding the confiscations. Full restitution will present infinite difficulties, and whatever may be the Stipulations of the Treaty, I think it will be impossible to reintegrate the Exiles and the proscribed.

· · · · ·

Received 5 March.   le chr de la luzerne

FFAA: Pol. Corr., U.S., v. 20, f. 20 (LC transcription).

Robert R. Livingston's Notes of a Meeting with Chevalier de la Luzerne

Jany 29th. 1782.

The Minister of France informed me that he was desirous of making Some communications from Letters received by the *Sybil.* Ten o'clock this day was appointed to receive them. He accordingly came and read to me passages from a letter of the Count de Vergennes to him dated 17th. Octr. 1781, which contained in substance: That France wished (as was evident from her going into the war on our account) to obtain every advantage for us; that powers at war must often be governed by Circumstances; that if Events would enable her to command them, we might depend on every thing She could obtain.

That his political System depended not only on America, but on the other powers at War. That if France should continue hostilities merely on account of America, after reasonable terms were offered, it was impossible to say what the event might be. That his Majesty was however at all events determined to adhere to the true principles of the alliance, and would further endeavour to obtain for us whatever we demanded, as far as events would justify.

He observed that people in America appear to be greatly deceived with respect to the disposition of the Belligerent and mediating Powers, and to imagine that all were anxious for a peace; that this was so far from being the case, that Great Britain had not yet returned any answer to the overtures of the imperial courts – nor had any reply been made by the latter to the answer given them by France – From which delay it might be easily imagined peace was far distant.

That from the present situation of Spain, there was strong reason to suppose that She could not spare us any money, her own operations requiring all she had. That he hoped France would not be called upon to make up her deficiencies, as they were in no situation to make new grants, besides that in order to rid us of our embarrassments they had already made efforts in our behalf, which they had reason to believe exceeded even our expectations, and that what they had done for America this year, entitled them to an exemption from further demands.

In a letter of the 20th of October 1781 from the count de Vergennes to the Minister of France, it is observed:

That the United Provinces would not, as he had strong reason to believe, embarrass themselves at present by an alliance with us – till after a peace shall been concluded; that in this they will follow the example of Spain; that however it will be prudent to keep an Agent in Holland, and direct him to advise constantly with Dr Franklin, that we may observe Some consistency in our politics.

That he fears America founds hopes on the aid of Russia; that nothing can be more groundless. — That tho' he believes She is not averse to the independence of America, yet that we ought not to expect that She will move a Step in our favour; that She has no particular interest in terminating the war; that as She means to assume the Character of a mediator, she must preserve that of justice & impartiality; — That nothing therefore can extort from her measures favourable to us but a conviction that we cannot be brought back to the dominion of Great Britain; that this should lead us to think (a Sentiment which he desires the minister to inculcate) that our success depends upon our exertions; & upon our relinquishing the inactivity into which the false hopes excited by success do sometimes plunge us.

He repeated that France could lend us no more money; that the ten millions borrowed upon our account in Holland were greatly sunk by advances made in France; That no bills would be paid in France which the minister did not authorize us to draw, that he hoped our Officers would have too much prudence to risk the credit of the United States by drawing.

That the negociations are still inactive, & will remain so till events oblige one or other of the parties to sue for peace; that the success of the expedition against Portsmouth, (that being the supposed post of Cornwallis) might possibly have some effect.

That the great object of England is America; that She will not cede it while she can carry on the war; – That She will certainly make great exertions [in] the ensuing campaign; that equal exertions are therefore necessary on our part.

That Spain & Holland view America as the great obstacle to a peace from which consequences may flow, which people of judgment may easily foresee.   Robt R Livingston

NA: PCC, *item 95, v. 2, pp. 73-78* (DS); M247, *reel 123.*

Francisco Rendón to Robert R. Livingston

Sir: Philadelphia, 30 January 1782

With the greatest pleasure I avail myself of the generous offer you have deigned to make me regarding your willingness to instruct me about all that it may be important to communicate to my court so that by this means it may find itself in condition to be able to judge the advantages it could derive from a close relation with the United States in case its intentions extend to that point; which I have always desired to see accomplished, and as far as the limited positive knowledge I have of my court's manner of thinking permits me to judge, I believe that never has it been so inclined in favor of America as at present.

. . . . .

I have reduced the memorandum of the matters on which I wish to be informed to several simple questions. . . .

. . . . .

I kiss your hand, Your most attentive true faithful servant.

                                          Francisco Rendon[1]

(Enclosures)

Questions proposed to the Most Excellent Sir Mr. Robert R. Livingston, Secretary of the United States in the Department of Foreign Affairs.

1. What will be the complement of the American army at the opening of the next campaign?
2. On what object ought the sum of eight million dollars recently voted by Congress to be apportioned?
3. Is it thought that this sum will be collected totally or if deficient to what amount will it come more or less?
4. What will the resources of Congress possibly be, compared with the ordinary expense of the campaign of next year?
5. If these resources are not sufficient, whence does the Congress hope to

obtain what is lacking?

6. What will possibly be the commercial connection between America and Spain in case that the latter responds to the proposed treaty?

7. Will America cooperate with Spain to impede clandestine commerce of the islands and continental possessions of this power in America with the subjects of the United States?

8. If it agrees to this, what will be the means it will employ to this end?

9. To what point will it be permitted to Spain to build ships of the line in the territories of the United States?

10. In case that Spain succeeds in conquering East Florida, what will possibly be the pretensions of Congress in regard to the southern boundaries of Georgia?

E. *James Ferguson, editor*, The Papers of Robert Morris, 1781-1784 *(Pittsburgh: University of Pittsburgh Press, 1973 —), hereafter cited as Ferguson*, Robert Morris Papers, *v. 4, pp. 589-593.*

¹ *Rendón, Francisco. Spanish government official. Secretary to Juan de Miralles, Spain's unofficial representative in the United States, 1779-1780. Successor to Miralles, 1780-1785. Secretary to Diego de Gardoqui, 1785-1786. Spain's intendant for the Floridas and Louisiana, 1793-1795.*

John Jay to the President of Congress

Sir,   Madrid 6ᵗʰ· February 1782.

. . . . .

There is little prospect of our receiving speedy Aids from this Court, and Doctor Franklin gives me reason to fear that a great number of the Bills drawn upon me, must, after all our Exertions to save them, be finally protested for non-payment. I have from Time to Time given the Doctor a great Deal of Trouble on this Subject, and I ought to acknowledge that I am under many and great Obligations to him for his constant Attention to our affairs here.

. . . . .

Notwithstanding all our Difficulties here, I think we should continue to oppose Obstacles by Perseverance and Patience, and my recall should rather be the Result of cool Policy than of Resentment. I am somewhat inclined to think that it may become politic to suspend it on the Reply of the Court to a Demand of a categorical Answer. Unless the Minister's System should change (for they still give me Hopes) it might perhaps also be proper for me to consult with Doctor Franklin, and Mʳ· Adams on the Subject, and send

Congress the Result. For this Purpose I submit to Congress the Propriety of giving me Permission to go to France or Holland.

Advantages are certainly to be derived from preserving the Appearance of being well here; and such is the general Opinion at present; But I am still much inclined to think it advisable to push this Court by a Demand of a categorical Answer. I doubt their venturing to break with us. The French Ambassador thinks it would be rash, and opposes it – Hence principally arises my Suspense.

I have the Honor to be, &ᶜ   John Jay

NA: PCC, item 110, v. 2, pp. 3-5 (LBkC); M 247, reel 135.

Benjamin Franklin to David Hartley

Dear Sir,   Passy 16. February 1782
                              . . . . .

My dear Friend, the true Pains you are taking to restore Peace, whatever may be the Success, intitle you to the Esteem of all good Men. If your Ministers really desire Peace, methinks they would do well to impower some [person] to make Propositions for that Purpose. One or other of the Parties at War must take the first Step. To do this belong properly to the Wisest. America being a Novice in such Affairs has no Pretence to that Character, and indeed, after the Answer given us by Lord Stormont[1] (When we proposed to him something relative to the mutual Treatment of Prisoners, with humanity) *that the King's Ministers received no Applications from Rebels, unless when they came to implore his Majesty's Clemency*, it cannot be expected that we should hazard the exposing ourselves again to such Insolence. All I can say farther at present is, that in my Opinion your Enemies do not aim at your Destruction, and that if you propose a Treaty, you will find them reasonable and equitable in their Demands, provided that on your Side they meet with the same good Dispositions. But do not dream of dividing us; you will certainly never be able to effect it.

With great Regard & Affection, I am ever, Dear Sir, your &c.

                                          Benjamin Franklin

LC: *Benjamin Franklin Papers, microfilm reel 2 (LBkC).*
    [1] Stormont, David Murray, Lord (1727-1796). *British diplomat and political figure. Envoy extraordinary to the court of Saxony, 1756-1761. Envoy extraordinary to Austria, 1763-1772. Envoy extraordinary to France, 1772-1778. Secretary of state for the southern department, 1779-1782. President of the council, April-December 1783, 1794-1796. From 1793, Lord Mansfield.*

John Adams to Robert R. Livingston

No. 3 Triplicate   Amsterdam Feb^y· 27th· 1782.
Sir,

Friesland has at last taken the Provincial Resolution to acknowledge the Independence, of which United America is in full Possession.

It is thought that several Cities of Holland will soon follow this Example, and some say it will be followed forthwith by the whole Republick. The first Burgomaster of this City has said within a few days past, that in six Weeks at furthest, the Independence of America would be acknowledged by all Seven of the United Provinces: but I have no Expectation of such haste. This Government does nothing with such Celerity.

By what I hear and read of their Speculations, it seems to me that the general Sense is at present not to shackle themselves with any Treaties either with France or Spain, nor to make any Treaty of Alliance with America, nor to make even a Treaty of Commerce with America as yet for a considerable Time; but for the several Members of the Sovereignty one after another, to acknowledge the Independence of America in the manner that Friesland has done; and for the States, the Prince and the Admiralties to exert themselves in preparing a Fleet to command the North Sea, and wash out some of the Stains in their Character, which the English have so unjustly thrown upon it, in their Blood. There is a loud Cry for Vengeance, a stern demand of a Fleet and Battle with the English, and if the Court contrive to elude it, the Stadtholder will run a great Risque of his Power.

Sensible and candid Men tell me, We wait for Spain and We wait for Russia. We wont make any Treaty with You. It is of no great Importance to Us or to You. We see there is a tremendous Power arising in the West. We can't meddle much; but We will at all Events be your good Friends. Whoever quarrels with You, We will not.

In short I expect no Treaty. I don't expect that our Independence will be acknowledged by all the Provinces for a long Time. Nevertheless, it appears to me of indispensable Importance that a Minister should reside constantly here, vested with the same Powers from Congress, with which they have honoured me: for which Reason, having the offer of a large and elegant House in a fine Situation, on a noble Spot of Ground at the Hague, at a very reasonable Rate, I have, in pursuance of the Advice of M^r· Barclay,[1] M^r· Dumas and other Friends, purchased it, and shall remove into it on or before the first of May. In Case I should be recalled, or obliged to go away upon other Services, any Minister that Congress may appoint here in my <****> Room will find an House ready furnished at the Hague ready for him.

The Negotiation for the Purchase was conducted secretly: but when it came to be known, I am informed it gave a great deal of Satisfaction in general.

To pay for it, I have applied all the Money I had of M^r· de Neufvilles Loan, and some Cash of my own which I brought with me from America, and for the Second Payment I must borrow from a Friend, if D^r· Franklin cannot furnish the Money, for which indeed I dont love to ask him, he has so many demands upon him from every Quarter. The House, including Purchase and Charges &^c, will amount to about sixteen thousand Guilders, ten thousand of which I paid yesterday. I have been obliged to take the Title in my own Name, but shall transfer it to the United States as soon as they are acknowledged and the Account settled, provided Congress approves of the Transaction; otherwise I shall take the Risque upon myself and sell it again: I shall live hereafter at a smaller Rent than I ever did before, tho' in an House much Superior.

With great Respect I have the Honour to be, Sir your most obedient and most humble Servant   J. Adams.

NA: PCC, Misc. Papers, Adams Despatches (LS); M332, reel 1, ff 537-539.

¹ Barclay, Thomas (1728-1793). Philadelphia merchant and patriot. Vice-Consul (June-October 1781), then Consul in France. Commissioner to settle the accounts of the United States in Europe, 1782-1786. Agent to negotiate treaty of peace and commerce with Morocco, 1785-1786. Appointed Consul to Morocco in 1791, but died in Lisbon while en route to his post.

Robert R. Livingston to John Adams

No 5.   Philadelphia 5th March 1782.
Dear Sir

. . . . .

...The success of the Allied Arms in America, the recapture of the Dutch Islands and the avowed superiority of the French in the West Indies have so changed the face of affairs, that there is strong reason to beleive Negotiations will be set on foot this winter, whether Britain is yet sufficiently humbled to desire peace is still doubtful, but whether she is, or is not, she will probably negotiate, in which case your presence in Europe will be necessary, so that I beleive you cannot at the most flatter yourself with any thing more than a conditional leave to return.

Your state of the decline of Commerce in the United Provinces agrees exactly with that we have received from other hands, I lament that a Nation which has such important reasons for exertions, and such means in their Power, should want Vigor to call them forth. They must and will however sooner or later be brought to it, a separate peace with England is now impossible without degrading the character of the nation, and exposing it to greater evils, than they are threatened with from England. Besides what advantages are to be derived from such a peace, can Britain restore her Conquests now in the hands of the French? can she give back the plunder of St. Eustatius or the cargoes of the India men now divided among the captors? can she afford them a compensation for the loss of last Year's commerce, or can she draw from her exhausted Purse sufficient sums to defend their Barrier against the Troops of france who would certainly avenge herself for such ingratitude?

The distress of the Nation then must in the end force them to exertions, and however reluctantly they may go into the war, they must still go into it with vigor – But Sir tho' your Letters detail the politicks of the Country, tho' they very ably explain the nature and general principles of the government, they leave us in the dark with respect to more important facts – they have not led us into the dock Yards, or arsenals, they have not told us what Ships are prepared for Sea, what are preparing, what the naval force will be this Spring, or how it is to be applyed. – You have not introduced us to any of the leading Members of the great Council, – you have not repeated your private conversations with them, from which infinitely more is to [be] collected, than from all the Pamphlets scattered about the Streets of Amsterdam. – if they avoid your Company and Conversation it is a more unfavorable symptom than any you have mentioned, and shews clearly that your public Character should have been concealed till your address had paved the way for its being acknowledged. If you have formed connections with any of these People, and I cannot but presume that you have attended to so important a point, it will be very interesting to us to have their most striking features delineated – their sentiments with respect to us and our opponents detailed, and the influence of each in the Assembly of the States, this will best acquaint us with the principles of the Government, and direct our Conduct towards them – Among other things I wish to know in what light they view our cause as just or unjust? – what influence they imagine our Independance will have upon the general system of Europe or their own States. – What expectations they form from our Commerce: whether the apprehension of its being altogether thrown into another Channel; if infused with address would not awaken them into action? what are their Ideas of the comparative power of France and Britain so far as it may affect them? – whether they have entered into any Treaty with France since the war? if they have what are its objects? if they have not, whether any such thing is in contemplation? None of your letters take the least notice of the french Ambassador at the Hague, is there no intercourse between you? if not, to what is it to be attributed? – It appears to me that our Interests in Holland are similar to those of France, they are interested with us in forwarding our Loans, in procureing a public acknowledgement of our Independance, in urging the States to exertion. They have considerable influence on the Government as appears from the success that the Loan opened under their guarantee met with. I must again therefore request you to spend much of your time at the Hague that great center of Politicks, to cultivate the acquaintance and friendship of the french Ambassadour, to confer with him freely and candidly upon the state of our Affairs, and by his means to extend your acquaintance to the other Representatives of Crowned Heads at the Hague. – your having no public Character, together with an avowed Contempt for rank and idle Ceremony will greatly facilitate your intercourse with them and enable you to efface the ill impressions they daily receive of us from our Enemies.– You see Sir, I rely so much upon your good sense as to write with freedom to you, and to mark out that line which I conceive will best tend to render your Mission useful, should I suggest any thing which you may not approve, I should be happy to be informed of it, and the reasons upon which you act, so that I may be able fully to Justify your measures if at any time they should not be entirely approved on this side the water. – ...

.   .   .   .   .

I write nothing to you on the subject of a negotiation, conveyances to Doctor Franklin being more easily obtained as well as more secure, every instruction on that head is sent to him, and will of course be communicated to you by the time you need it. — ...

.   .   .   .   .

I have the honor to be, Dr Sir with great Respect and Esteem Your most Obed$^{t:}$ humble servant   Rob R Livingston

MHS: *The Adams Papers, microfilm reel 356 (LS).*

Robert R. Livingston to Francisco Rendón

Sir,   Philadelphia March 6$^{th.}$ 1782
    I will with pleasure give you such information on the subjects you write upon as I can with propriety mention to a Gentleman of whose attachment I entertain no doubt, but who has nevertheless given me no reason to think that his inquiries have any farther object than his personal satisfaction
    In answer to the first question, I can only inform you that Congress have voted thirty six thousand Infantry which with the Cavalry & Artillery will

amount to about forty thousand men – It is not probable however, that the whole of this number will be raised – I think it would be prudent to make a deduction of about one fourth, But you have been too long in this Country to form any Judgment of the strength of our army from the regular establishment, since it has been and always will be increased (more particularly in the northern States) by large bodies of militia when their apprehensions or the hope of splendid advantages shall call them forth – Of this the events of the year 1777 among others afford the most striking evidence.

2^d It is not expected that in the present situation of the country, the whole sum of eight millions of dollars can be raised in time, what the deficiency will be, must depend upon the motions & strength of our Enemy early the next spring – the success of our Commerce – the remittances that shall be made to this Country by our Allies which being expended here may by frequent taxes be brought into the public Treasury and repeatedly applied to public use.

3^d The resources of the next campaign lay in taxation, in the strictest oeconomy, and in the assistance which we may reasonably hope to receive from the enemies of Great Britain while we are making every exertion in the common cause – We flatter ourselves that those powers who wish for peace & who see America as the great object of Britain in carrying on the War, will not suffer it to be lengthened out beyond the present Year, when by a moderate supply to us they can terminate it in the course of one campaign – We form some expectations from the wisdom & generosity of Spain and as we know she has the means so we cannot suppose she will want the inclination to promote her own interests, insure the esteem & gratitude of a rising nation whose commerce & alliance cannot but be important from the situation of her colonies

The 5th question is answered above, only it may be proper to observe that if in this reasonable expectation America should be disappointed she will still find resources in herself, not indeed to expell the Enemy, but to preclude them from extending their conquests, & to compel them to offer her such terms as are necessary for her security, tho' perhaps short of her wishes.

6. The commercial connection between the United States & Spain, will naturally be very extensive if it meets with the least encouragement – The Spanish Islands will be supplied with provisions from them at such easy rates as must give them great advantages in the cultivation of sugars for which America will afford a considerable market. Fish, Lumber & Iron will also be exported to them if it should be permitted, & salt as well as sugar brought back in return if the duties should be lowered or a drawback allowed on the exportation.

Our trade with Spain will consist chiefly in naval Stores, masts, Iron, furs fish & tobacco in return for which we shall take the produce & manufactures of Spain of almost every kind.

7. It is impossible for the United States to use means to prevent an illicit commerce with the Spanish colonies, without interfering in their internal regulations – all they can do is to consider the regulations made for that purpose as binding upon their subjects, & not to demand satisfaction if they suffer by the penalties which the laws attempted to be infringed may impose.

To this they will not object while the punishment is reasonable & confined to crimes committed within the jurisdiction of the power imposing it. If it is extended further, such further extension must depend upon treaties between the United States & Spain, & will be the subject of discussion whenever such treaty shall be set on foot – To this must also be referred the 8$^{th.}$ question.

9$^{th.}$ Spain will be allowed without the least difficulty, either to purchase Vessels built in America or to appoint Agents of her own for building Vessels of any kind as well as for arming them if she thinks proper from the iron founderies which were lately created here, & which will continue to increase in proportion to the encouragement which shall be given them.

The last question must be referred to a general treaty, & is of such a nature as not to be properly answered here. I am with great regard & esteem Sir, Your most obed^t hum serv$^{t.}$ Robt R. Livingston

NA: PCC, *item 119, p. 81-86 (LBkC); M 247, reel 139.*

David Hartley to John Adams

Dear Sir   London March 11 1782
...I understand that Mr Jay Dr Franklin Mr Laurens and yourself are impowered by a special commission to treat. I hope the powers of that commission will soon be called forth into action and that success may attend. The public proceedings of parliament & the proposed bill to enable the Crown to conclude peace or truce with America are or will certainly be made known to you. The first object will be to procure a meeting of authorized persons and to consult upon the preliminaries of time place & manner, but the requisites, above all others, are mutual good dispositions to conciliate & to accommodate, in the confident hope that, if the work of peace were once well begun it w^d soon become general. Permitt me to ask whether the four gentlemen above specified are empowered to *conclude*

as well as to *treat* and whether jointly so or severally. The bill now depending in Parliament on the part of this Country is to *conclude* as well as to *treat*. As to other provisions of it I cannot speak positively but I understand (from the best authority) that the general scope of it is to remove the parliamentary obstructions now subsisting, w^h ~~may~~ would frustrate the settlements w^h may be made at the termination of the war.– I heartily wish success to the cause of peace.

I am Dear Sir With great respect Your most obed^t Servt

D. Hartley

PS Mr Digges[1] who will deliver this to you will explain many things of great importance on the Subject of peace. I have been witness of the Authority upon w^h they have been delivered to him. When the first application was made to him, he consulted me as knowing that such topics had more than once passed thro my hands. I have recently had many conferences on my own part with the Ministry here relating to the mode of entering into negotiation of peace, & am fully informed of the subject of Mr Digges's commission to you. You may therefore be assured that it comes to you from the highest Authority.

MHS: *The Adams Papers, microfilm reel 356* (ALS).

[1] *Digges, Thomas Attwood (1742-1821). Maryland expatriate who lived in London and Lisbon during the American war. Accused of being a liar, a speculator, a trader with the enemy, and a secret agent for the British. Embezzled charitable funds entrusted to him for the relief of American prisoners, for which he earned the condemnation of Benjamin Franklin.*

François Barbé de Marbois to Comte de Vergennes

[Translation]

N° 225. Quintuplicate.   Philadelphia, 13 March 1782.
My Lord.

· · · · ·

...Mr. Samuel Adams is making every effort to spread the seeds of a violent opposition to peace in the State of Massachusetts, if it does not assure the Eastern States admission to the fisheries and particularly to those of Newfoundland. Mr. Adams takes pleasure in trouble and difficulties; he glories in forming a party of opposition against the Government, although he himself is president of the Senate. His attentions, his constant labors tend to render the minority formidable, and at this very moment he is attacking the constitution of Massachusetts, although it is in large part his work, but it has ceased to be agreeable to him since the people have shown a unanimous attachment to it. It is necessary to expect that with this character, no measure can obtain the approbation of Mr. Samuel Adams, and if the United States were once tranquil on the subject of the fisheries and on his claim to participate therein, all his resources, all his intrigues would be turned towards the conquest of Canada and of Nova Scotia. But he could not employ an instrument more appropriate than the fisheries to put in motion the passions of the peoples of the East. In arousing this negotiation, dormant during the two years that he has been absent from Boston, he has excited the imagination of the inhabitants of Massachusetts to an extraordinary point. The Almanacs, the Gazettes expound the importance of the fisheries. The preferred toast in the East is that the United States forever maintain their rights to the fisheries. *No peace without the fisheries* has frequently been repeated in the deliberations of the general assembly. However clear may be the principles on this matter, it would be useless and even dangerous to try to enlighten the people by means of the public papers, but it seems to me that there are some means of preventing the results of the maneuvers of Mr. Samuel Adams and of his party, and I am taking the liberty of submitting them for your insight and your indulgence. One would be that the King have Congress or Mr. Franklin witness "his surprise that the Newfoundland fisheries have been included in the additional instructions, in which the United States announce their claims without regard for His Majesty's rights, and without considering the impossiblity of their conquering and keeping the portion that belongs to Great Britain. His Majesty could at the same time promise Congress his assistance in procuring admission to other fisheries, but by declaring at the same time that he is not answerable for success and that he is not desirous of anything, given the silence of the Treaty on this article."

This declaration being made before the peace, the intriguers cannot feed the hopes of the people or say one day that we have left them in error on this point. It even seems desirable that this declaration be made while New York, Charlestown, and Penobscot are in the hands of Enemies. Our allies will be less manageable than today on these questions as soon as they have recovered these important posts; there are many sensible persons to whom one can speak of abandoning the fisheries and the Western lands for the love of peace; but there are enthusiasts who utter high cries at this idea, and their number cannot help but grow when, after the expulsion of the English from this Continent, the burden of war will scarcely be felt there. It can already be noted that peace has declared partisans only in the rural areas. The inhabitants of the Towns which Commerce enriches, the artisans there who receive a larger salary than before the war, and five or six times more considerable than in Europe, do not desire peace. Besides, it is fortunate that this apportionment is very nearly equal in Congress and in the States, given that our influence will tilt the Balance either for peace or for war, on whatever side we throw ourselves. Another means of maintaining for France the possession of so important a branch of her commerce and her navigation would be that which M. de la Luzerne has already proposed, My Lord, that is to say, the conquest of Cape Breton. It seems to me, as to this Minister, that this is the sole assured means of keeping at bay, after the peace, those swarms of Smugglers who, without respect for the Treaties, would employ all their activity, their audacity, and their resources towards the fisheries, and whose enterprises Congress will never have the Force and perhaps the will to restrain.

If there is reason to think that the peace that will put an end to the present war will be disagreeable to someone from the United States, it seems to me, My Lord, that a rather sure means of preventing the effects of discontent, of anticipating the protestations of some States and other resources that restless spirits will work up to take advantage of the circumstance, would be that His Majesty have sent to Congress a memoir in which he informs it of the usage that its Ministers have made of the powers that that assembly confided to him and of the causes that may have prevented obtaining complete Satisfaction on all points. This step would certainly be agreeable to Congress, and if it becomes necessary to make this Memoir known to the people, the matter would not be difficult. They would be flattered by it, and they would probably win over Votes and public opinion.

I am submitting these ideas to you early, although peace seems still far away, My Lord, because of the slowness and the difficulty of communications, and because the time of peace will be a moment of crisis in which the partisans of France and England will show themselves openly, and in which that Power will spare no artifice to diminish our influence and reestablish its own. It is true that the independent party will always have a great need for our support; that the jealousies and disquiet that will inspire the memory of former domination will be the safeguard of the Alliance, and the guarantees of the attachment of the Americans for us; but it seems advantageous to hold ourselves ready against all discontent, even if it be only transient.

Some persons observe that England, having abundant fisheries independent of Newfoundland, will herself perhaps work to have the Americans admitted to those of the Grand Bank to acquire their affection or obtain some compensation or establishment, objects of jealousy between them and us, but it seems little probable that she would take a position so contrary to her true interests; and if she must take it, it will still be useful to have early declared with Frankness to the Americans that their claim is not well-founded, and that His Majesty does not intend to support it.

I am with a profound respect, My Lord, Your very humble and very obedient Servant,   Marbois

Received 13 July.

FFAA: Pol. Corr., U.S., v. 20, N° 129 (LC transcription).

Benjamin Franklin to John Jay

Dear Sir,   Passy March 16ᵗʰ· 1782.

...I congratulate you upon the change of Sentiment in the British Nation. It has been intimated to me from thence, that they are willing to make a separate Peace with us exclusive of France, Spain, and Holland, which, so far as relates to France, is impossible: and I believe they will be content that we leave them the other two: But Holland is stepping towards us, and I am not without hopes of a second Loan there. And since Spain does not think our Friendship worth cultivating, I wish you would inform me of the whole Sum we owe her, that we may think of some means of paying if off Speedily.

With sincerest Regard, I am, &c. &c.   B. Franklin

NA: PCC, item 110, v. 2, pp. 106-107 (LBkC); M247, reel 135.

Benjamin Franklin to
Joseph Matthias Gérard de Rayneval

Sir,[1]   Passy, March 22. 1782

With this I have the honour of sending you *all the Letters* I have received from or written to England on the Subject of Peace. M. de Vergennes should have seen them sooner if I had imagined them of any Importance: for I have never had the least Desire of keeping such Correspondence secret. I was, as you will see, accidentally drawn into this; and conceiving it of no Use, I have been backward in continuing it.

· · · · ·

With great Esteem I have the honour to be Sir, Your most obedient and most humble Servant   B. Franklin

FFAA: Pol. Corr., U.S., v. 20, f. 138 (LC transcription).
[1] Rayneval, Joseph-Matthias Gérard de (1736-1812). French diplomat. Undersecretary

of state to the Comte de Vergennes, with rank of minister plenipotentiary. Briefly, Minister to Great Britain, early 1783.

Comte de Vergennes to Chevalier de la Luzerne

[Translation]

N⁰· 30. Triplicate.   Versailles, 23 March 1782

There has just been a revolution in the Parliament of England, Sir, that will surely cause a great sensation in America, and which seems to me to merit a particular attention on our part. The first of this month General Conway presented the motion of which you will find a translation enclosed; it passed by a plurality of votes; the address agreed upon by the House of Commons was presented to the King of England, and His Britannic Majesty made the response which you will also find enclosed. The motion evidently has as its basis the inclination of the English nation toward peace; but the result presented is nothing but a defensive war and inextricable difficulties for the Ministry. The King's response obligates that prince to nothing besides no longer marching his troops uselessly into all parts of America; it does not change the state of the war, it changes only its form. The motion of the Attorney General made on the 5th is more significant; that member of Parliament proposed a bill to provide His Britannic Majesty the means to make a Truce or peace with America; this motion passed unanimously. On the 14th another motion was made by the same member; it passed in the same way. Its purpose is the renovation of all the acts that annoyed the Americans, and which were of a nature to impede a reconciliation.

In examining attentively, Sir, all the facts that I have just indicated, I find, in the last analysis, that England would like to remain in the posts she now occupies on the continent of America; that she will try to establish her cruisers in a manner to intercept all the American commerce, and that at the same time she will set to work among the partisans to dispose their minds to a reconciliation.

The goal of the King of England in adopting the System of Parliament cannot be more apparent. That Prince will endeavor to persuade the Americans that he is sincerely inclined to be repatriated with them, and he will spare nothing to seduce some and corrupt others either to bring about a schism in the interior of America or to draw the Americans into some act of perfidy with regard to France.

To examine only the position of the United States compared with that of England, there should not be the slightest doubt of the impression that the new plan of the Court of London will make on them, and of the resolutions that it will inspire in them: but the propensity of the Americans to inertia; their need and desire for peace; the difficulty of their means to continue the war, the great number of partisans that England still has among them; all the reasons taken together may make them fear that the wish of the people may prevail over the patriotism and the zeal of Congress; and that that Body be forced to give ear to the alleged peace overtures from the Court of London.

You will perceive perfectly, Sir, that such a determination could not but be infinitely disagreeable to us, because it would distort the object and the course of the war; augment the hostile abilities of Great Britain; and make us lose in large part the fruit of the costly efforts that we are making to save America.

It is therefore essentially important to us, Sir, that the United States persist invariably in the principles that they have followed up to now, i.e., that they remain immovable in their alliance with the King and that they imitate the example that His Majesty gives them in refusing to make a separate accord with the Court of London. Honor and interests equally proscribe this conduct to the Americans, and if they deviate from it, they would be branded as a perfidious nation from their debut in the political world, and they would sooner or later suffer the penalty. England would be the first to punish them for it; she would not fear that a people which would not blush at violating the most sacred engagements, engagements which are the basis and the security of her existence, would henceforth find either ally or friend.

But whatever may be our interest, Sir, that the Americans not allow themselves to be shaken by the false caresses of the English Ministry, we should fully refrain from showing the slightest apprehension in that regard; the least Symptom of fear or suspicion would incline them to think that we cannot do without their concurrence; that without them we could only conduct a disadvantageous war; and they would raise their tone and their unreasonable demands towards us by reason of the interest they would suppose us to have in the continuation of their present System.

Thus, Sir, you should, as at present, carefully avoid in your discourses anything that would have the air of fearing a defection on the part of the Americans. You will on the contrary affect the greatest confidence in their principles and their perseverance, and if you are consulted, you will limit yourself to responding that, in your opinion, the new plan of the Court of London is only an enticement to deceive the American nation, and that you do not doubt that the insinuations and offers of that Court will be rejected with a perfect unanimity. If, however, Sir, which we should not presume, you perceive some vacillation in their minds, I think that in that case you would do well to adroitly remind the most substantial members of Congress of the treaties which unite their homeland to France, of the enormous sacrifices which the King has made to maintain American independence; of the dangers which the United States would run in permitting the least infidelity; of the little security with which they would treat with a power embittered because it could not subdue them. This language, considered appropriate especially if it does not seem to have been dictated by fear, may produce a salutary effect; it is left to your prudence to indicate to you the moment in which it is suitable to employ it.

But it will not suffice, Sir, that the Americans remain faithful to France; it is important to the common cause and especially for them that they redouble their efforts to achieve the expulsion of the enemy from the continent of the thirteen States; and it is an established fact that they have never had a better time than now to accomplish their objective: the English armies will not be augmented; those now in America will no longer act offensively; they will be concentrated principally in New-York and Charles-Town: either I am greatly mistaken, or it will be possible to attack these two places with Success. In any case, Sir, if General Washington judges them unassailable, it would be better that he employ his troops in any other manner so as not to leave them in idleness.

The subject of this despatch, Sir, is very important; it interests essentially the King's Service, and I am sure that you will employ all your zeal and all your activity to fulfill His Majesty's desires: I repeat, I cannot persuade myself that the Americans are rendering themselves guilty of a defection that nothing could justify: but there cannot be perfect security with regard to a nation whose ideas are not yet thoroughly mastered and among whom the spirit of party seems to have a great influence. So, Sir, we shall await your news with much impatience; it is important to us to receive it all the more promptly, because if desire for peace or indifference should gain the ascendancy, we could find ourselves in need of making some kind of changes in our general plan of campaign.

If things come to the point that you have reason to suspect the fidelity of the Americans, you will take care, Sir, to inform me by the promptest means; you should not hesitate to send me an aviso and give it orders to land at Cadiz as the Point at which landfall is the easiest. You will address your packages to the King's Consul, recommending to him that he forward them to our ambassador by a Courier.   Vergennes

FFAA: Pol. Corr., U.S., v. 20, f. 142 (LC transcription).

Comte de Vergennes to Chevalier de la Luzerne

[Translation]

N⁰· 31.   Versailles, 23 March 1782

I do not want to leave you unaware, Sir, that the English ministry has just sent here a secret emissary to propose to us a separate peace. The conditions that he has advanced would have satisfied His Majesty if he had no allies: he enumerated among others the *uti possidetis*, the removal of the English commissioner at Dunkerque, and advantages in India. But these offers did not shake the King: His Majesty, knowing no other rule than that which is traced in his engagements, has made reply: that however sincere his wishes for the restoration of peace may be, he could not begin negotiations to this end without the participation of his allies.

The English emissary protested against this response because he understood perfectly that it concerned America as well as Spain. He objected to me that in conceding it, England would recognize the independence of her Colonies, which did not enter into her System. I replied that it formed the basis of that of the King, upon which he asked me if there were no way to avoid negotiating the affairs of America with us. I referred him to our response to the first peace overtures that were communicated to us by the mediators, and which I sent you with my despatch N⁰· 25. I observed, moreover, that whether England discusses American affairs with us or she broaches a direct negotiation with the United States to that effect, she cannot avoid treating with the deputies of Congress, by means of which she will have to recognize the authority of that assembly in one manner or another.

I cannot foresee, Sir, whether the English ministry's step will have any result, or whether it had any other purpose than to throw an apple of discord between us and our allies. But whatever may have been the intention of the English ministers, it results at least in their overture, that it has caused the King himself to give his allies a new proof of his fidelity toward them. I am persuaded, Sir, that you will have no trouble in making the Americans perceive that it is their duty and their interest to imitate the example that His Majesty gives them and that he renders them too much justice to permit himself the slightest doubt in this respect.

It is to be noted, Sir, that the English emissary left London after the motions of the first and fifth of this month, that is to say, after the desire of the English nation for peace was manifested: this reflection should prove to the Americans that they would be grossly mistaken if they were persuaded that the Court of London wants peace exclusively with America, and that its intention is to continue the war with the house of Bourbon; in a word, the conduct of the English ministers clearly proves that in speaking of peace with their former colonies, they wish only to mislead them in order to be able then all the more easily to punish them for their alleged felony. If the Americans lost sight of these verities, the dangers to which they would be exposed would be incalculable. You must, Sir, communicate to Mr. Livingston and to the principal members of Congress the facts that this despatch contains; as for the reflections, you will make use of them as the circumstances seem to require.   Vergennes

FFAA: Pol. Corr., U.S., v. 20, f. 143 (LC transcription).

John Adams to Benjamin Franklin

Sir   The Hague March 26. 1782

One day, last Week, I rec^d at Amsterdam a Card from Diggs, inclosing two Letters to me from Mr David Hartley. The Card desired to see me upon Business of Importance: and the Letters from Mr Hartley contained an Assurance that to his Knowledge the Bearer came from the highest Authority. – I answered the Card, that in the present Situation of Affairs here and elsewhere, it was impossible for me to See any one from England without Witness, but if he was willing to See me in Presence of Mr Thaxter my Secretary and that I should communicate whatever he should Say to me to Dr Franklin and the Comte de Vergennes, I would wait for him at home at ten O Clock, but that I had rather he should go to Paris without Seeing me and communicate what he had to Say to Dr Franklin, whose situation enabled him to consult the Court without Loss of time. at ten, however he came, and told me a long Story about Consultations with Mr Pen,[1] Mr Hartley Lord Beauchamp[2] and at last Lord North, by whom he was finally Sent, to enquire of me, if I, or any other, had Authority, to treat with Great Britain of a Truce. – I answered, that I came to Europe last with full Powers to make Peace, that those Powers had been announced to the public upon my Arrival, and continued in force untill last Summer, when Congress Sent a new Commission, containing the Same Powers to five Persons, whom I named. – That if ~~some~~ the King of England were my father, and I the Heir apparent to his Throne, I would not advise him even to think of a Truce, because it would be but a real War under a simulated appearance of Tranquility, and would ~~finally~~ end in another <***> open and bloody War, without doing any real good to any of the Parties.

He Said, that the Ministry would send, some Person of Consequence over, perhaps General Conway, but they were apprehensive, that he would be ill treated or exposed. – I Said that if they resolved upon such a measure, I had rather they would send immediately to Dr Franklin, because of his Situation near the French Court. – But there was no doubt, if they sent any respectable Personage properly authorised who should come to treat honourably, he would be treated with great Respect. – But that if he came to me, I could give him no opinion upon any thing without consulting my Colleagues, and should reserve a Right of communicating every Thing to my Colleagues, and to our Allies.

He then Said, that his Mission was finished. That the Fact to be ascertained was Simply, that there was a Commission in Europe to treat and conclude, but that there was not one Person in G. Britain who could affirm or prove that there was such a Commission, altho it had been announced in the Gazettes.

I desired him and he promised me not to mention Mr Laurens, to the Ministry without his Consent, and without informing him that it was impossible he should Say any thing in the Business, because he knew nothing of our Instructions, because altho it was possible that his being in such a Commission might induce them to release him, yet it was also possible, it might render them more difficult concerning his Exchange.

The Picture he gives of the situation of Things in England, is gloomy enough for them. The Distresses of the People and the Distractions in Administration and Parliament, are such as may produce any Effect, almost that can be imagined.

The only Use of all this I think is, to Strike decisive strokes at New York and Charlestown. There is no Position so advantageous for Negotiation, as when We have all our Enemies Armies Prisoners. I must beg the favour of you, Sir, to Send me, by one of the C de Vergennes's Couriers to the Duc de la Vauguion, a Copy of in Letters of our Peace Instructions. I have not been able to decypher one Quarter Part of mine. Some Mistake has certainly been made.

Ten or Eleven Cities of Holland, have declared themselves in favour of American Independence, and it is expected that to day or tomorrow, this Province will take the decisive Resolution of Admitting me to an Audience. Perhaps Some of the other Provinces, may delay it for, three or four Weeks. But the Prince had declared that he has no hopes of resisting the Torrent and therefore that he shall not attempt it, The Duc de la Vauguion has acted a very friendly and honourable Part in this Business, without, however doing any ministerial Act, in it.

With great Respect, I have the Honour to be, Sir, your most obedient and most humble servant   J. Adams

MHS: The Adams Papers, microfilm reel 102 (LBkC).
[1] Penn, Richard (1735-1811). Pennsylvania provincial official, British political figure.

Lieutenant governor of Pennsylvania, 1771-1773. Carried Congress' "Olive Branch"
petition to Great Britain, 1775. Member of Parliament, 1784-1811.

² *Beauchamp, Francis Seymour Conway, Lord (1719-1794). British political figure,*
brother of General Henry Seymour Conway. Lord chamberlain, 1766-1782, April-
December 1783.

John Jay to Benjamin Franklin

Dear Sir,   Madrid, 29 March 1782

. . . . .

That Britain should be desirous of a separate Peace with us is very
natural, but as such a Proposal implies an Impeachment of our Integrity I
think it ought to be rejected in such a Manner as to shew that <our
Feelings are hurt by such invidious Suspicions of our Honor>¹ we are not
ignorant of the Respect due to our Feeling on that Head. As long as France
continues Faithful to us I am clear that we ought to continue Hand in
Hand <with them in> to prosecute the War until all their as well as all
our reasonable Objects <are obtained> can be attained by a peace; for I
would rather see America ruined than dishonored. As to Spain and Holland
we have as yet no Engagements with them and therefore are <at present>
not <further> obliged to consult either their Interest or their Inclinations
further than may be convenient to ourselves, or than the Respect due to
our good allies may render proper.

France in granting you six million has acted with Dignity as well as
Generosity. Such gifts, so given, command both gratitude and Esteem, and
I think our Country possesses sufficient Magnanimity to recieve and to
remember such marks of Friendship with <all the> a proper Degree of
Sensibility, <very different has been the Conduct of this Country,
pompous in assurances, niggardly in their grants, daily making promises and
daily breaking them. All high and mighty in words, all mean and little
in>.

I am pleased with your Idea of paying whatever we owe to Spain. Their
pride perhaps <would> might forbid them to recieve <our> the money;
but <my> our Pride has been so hurt by the littleness of their Conduct
that I would in that Case, be for leaving it at the gate of the Palace and
quit the Country. At Present such <Conduct> a Step would not be
expedient, though <I think> the Time <may and> will come when
Prudence <will> instead of re[s]training will urge us to hold no other
Language or conduct to this Court than that of a just, a free, and a brave
People who have nothing to fear from nor to <hope or expect from>
request of them.

With perfect Regard and Esteem I am, Dear Sir, your obliged and affectionate Servant. [John Jay]

Morris, Jay Papers, v. 2, pp. 143-144.
[1] Indicates text deleted in original document.

Benjamin Franklin to Robert R. Livingston

Sir, Passy, March 30[th.] 1782

In mine of the 9[th.] Instant I acknowledged the Receipt of yours of January 7[th.] and I have not since received any of later Date.

The News Papers, which I send you by this Conveyance will acquaint you with what has, since my last, passed in Parliament. You will, there, see a Copy of the Bill brought in by the Attorney Gen[l.1] for impowering the King to make Peace with the Colonies. They still seem to flatter themselves with the Idea of dividing us, and rather than name the Congress, they empower him, generally, to treat with *any Body or Bodies of Men, or any Person or Persons, &c.* They are, here, likewise endeavoring to get us to treat separately from France, at the same Time they are tempting France to treat separately from us, equally without the least Chance of Success. I have been drawn into a Correspondence on this Subject, which you shall have with my next. I send you a Letter of M[r.] Adams's just received which shews, also, that they are weary of the War, and would get out of it, if they knew how. They had not then received the certain News of the Loss of S[t.] Christophers; which will probably render them still more disposed to Peace. I see that a Bill is also passing through the House of Commons for the Exchange of American Prisoners, the Purport of which I do not yet know.

In my last I promised to be more particular with Respect to the Points you mentioned as proper to be insisted on the Treaty of Peace. My Ideas, on those Points, are, I assure you, full as strong as yours. I did intend to have given you my Reasons for some Addition, and if the Treaty were to be held on your Side the Water, I would do it, otherwise, it seems on second Thoughts to be unneccessary, and, if my Letter should be intercepted, may be inconvenient. Be assured, I shall not willingly give up any important Right or Interest of our Country, and unless this Campaign should afford our Enemies some considerable Advantage, I hope more may be obtained than is yet expected.

. . . . .

With great Esteem, &c. B. Franklin.

NA: PCC, item 100, v. 1, pp. 256-258 (LBkC); M247, reel 127.
[1] Sir James Wallace, Attorney-General of England.

Comte de Vergennes to Comte de Montmorin

[Translation]

N° 17.   Versailles, 1 April 1782

. . . . .

Le Courrier de l'Europe of March 22 that you will receive by this post will inform you that the former British Ministry, perceiving that it could no longer resist the discredit into which it had fallen and the frequent attacks daily repeated against it, finally seeing itself at the point of being turned out by a vote of Parliament, has made the decision to announce its resignation. The work was to be consummated on the 25th; the stormy weather that has prevailed for several days rendering access to our Coasts very difficult, we do not yet know what will be the composition of the new ministry, and still less what will be the system that it will want to follow, the opposition not having ceased to blame that of the former ministry even before attacking individuals. It might be thought that in the State of dilapidation in which it finds affairs, its thoughts would turn towards peace. This would be even better, seen from its side, because it would make the reproach of an unequal peace fall upon the bad administration of the preceding ministers; but this option, although the most reasonable one, may very well not be the one that will be adopted and followed. The members of the opposition have always affected to be persuaded that the separation of America resulted less from the love of Independence than from the hatred of the Americans for the ministers: I think their Error is complete in this Regard, but it will take time to convince them of it, and it could well be only when they are disabused of it that they will return to desiring a general peacemaking. Already Mr. Franklin in Paris and Mr. Adams in Holland have been sought and sounded out on a separate peace. The first very certainly by the former ministry, and from appearances, the other by the party that should replace it, which makes me presume that Mr. Adams was offered a Conference with General Conway. Now the latter is a member of the opposition; be that as it may, the two American plenipotentiaries, who are in no way acting together, explained themselves very affirmatively and very fittingly on the positive intention of their constituents not to countenance any treaty of peace or truce without the Intervention and the Concurrence of France. We have great interest, Sir, that this ally persists invariably in this disposition. On its perseverance will depend the approach, more or less near, of peace. We are neglecting nothing from this Side to strengthen it, but it seems to me that the Court of Spain, which shares with us at least an interest in preventing its defection, should give it some evidence of benevolence and encouragement.

. . . . .

I have not heard talk of Mr. Forth[1] since my last Conference with him. He only left Paris on the 24th. The changes that have arisen in his country leave little Hope that he will return even though the new ministers are of a Will to negotiate. He was Lord North's man, that is a reason that he is not his successor's.

. . . . .

Vergennes

FFAA: Pol. Corr., Spain, v. 606, f. 210 (LC transcription).

[1] Forth, Nathaniel Parker. British agent employed intermittently by Lord North as an intermediary with France, 1777-1782.

Benjamin Vaughan to Lord Shelburne

My Lord,[1]   Thursday morning. [April 4, 1782]
     The inclosed is for your lordship's perusal – from M*r* Laurens.

This gentleman will be in town to day; and unless directed otherwise, I shall bring him to Berkeley Square when he arrives & there leave him, whatever be the hour, should he be well enough.

He says, with magnanimity much may be done, and he shall not despair of hearing of a house of England, as well as a house of Bourbon; but if we mean war he shall not like talking, and wishes we would go on with war and let him alone. He thinks it very impolite to lay any blame on the *king*; it must be laid on his ministers, & the king must from the late reform of things, be considered as *deceived*.... He is pleased with being applied to, (unless war is on the carpet, when he will be *very* fretful and unmanageable,) and will probably be very willing to go to consult with his brother on the continent.

Your lordship must by *no* means whatever, consider him as a close man; he professes not to like secrets. He will at times be wordy, and get into repetitions; but at times & generally be very distinct & also sensible. But he is peevish; and he cannot bear any one posture long, nor any hour after 9 or 10 in the evening unless on extraordinary occasions perhaps. – He will also like *plainness*.– This I mention in addition to my *former* hints, and the whole (to save trouble,) by letter. I have the honor to be, my lord, your lordship's ever faithful & respectful serv*t*   Benj*n.* Vaughan

University of Michigan, William L. Clements Library, hereafter cited as Clements Library: Shelburne Papers, v. 72, pp. 261-263 (ALS).

¹ *Shelburne, William Petty, Lord (1737-1805). British political figure. President, Board of Trade and Foreign Plantations, under Bute, 1763. Secretary of state for the southern department (which included the American colonies until January 1768) under Chatham, July 1766-October 1768. Opposed Lord North's American policy, but favored reconciliation with the American colonies rather than recognition of American independence. Secretary of state for home and colonial affairs under Rockingham, March-July 1782. Chief minister and first lord of the treasury, July 1782-February 1783. Created Marquis of Lansdowne, December 1784.*

Benjamin Franklin to David Hartley

My dear Friend,   Passy, April 5. 1782.

I wrote a few Lines to you the 31ˢᵗ· past, and promised to write more fully. On pursuing again your Letters of the 11ᵗʰ· 12ᵗʰ· & 21ˢᵗ· I do not find any Notice taken of one from me dated Febʸ· 16. I therefore now send you a Copy made from it in the Press. The Uncertainly of safe Transmission discourages a free Communication of Sentiments on these important Affairs; but the Inutility of Discussion between Persons, one of whom is not authoris'd but in Conjunction with others, and the other not authoris'd at all, as well as the obvious Inconveniences that may attend such previous handling of Points that are to be considered when we come to treat regularly, are with me a still more effectual Discouragement, and determine me to waive that Part of Correspondence: – As to Digges, I have no Confidence in him, nor in anything he says or may say of his being sent by Ministers. Nor will I have any Communication with him, except in receiving & considering the Justification of himself which he pretends he shall be able to make and intends for his excessive Drafts on me on Account of the Relief I ordered to the Prisoners, and his Embezzlement of the Money. You justly observe, in yours of the 12ᵗʰ· that "the first Object is to procure a Meeting of qualified and authorized Persons" and that you "understand the Ministry will be ready to proceed towards opening a Negociation as soon as the Bill shall pass; and therefore it is necessary to consult of Time and Place, and Manner and Persons on each Side" If the new have the same Intentions, & desire a general Peace, they may easily discharge Mʳ· Laurens from those Engagements that make his acting in the Commission improper; and, except Mʳ· Jefferson, who remains in America, and is not expected here, we the Commissioners of Congress can easily be got together; ready to meet yours at such Pleace as shall be agreed to by all Powers at War, in Order to form the Treaty. God grant that there may be Wisdom enough assembled, to make if possible a Peace that shall be perpetual, and that the Idea of any Nations being natural Enemies to each other may be abolished, for the honour of Human Nature.

With regard to those who may be commissioned from your Government, whatever personal Preferences I may conceive in my own Mind, it cannot become me to express them. I only wish for wise and honest Men. With such a Peace may be speedily concluded. – With contentious Wranglers the Negociation may be drawn into length & finally frustrated.

I am pleased to see in the Votes & parliamentary Speeches, and in your public Papers that in mentioning America, the Word *Reconciliation* is often used. It certainly means more than a mere Peace. It is a sweet Expression. Revolve in your Mind, my dear Friend, the means of bringing about this *Reconciliation*. When you consider the Injustice of your War with us, and the barbarous manner in which it has been carried on, the many suffering Families among us from your Burnings of Towns Scalpings by Savages &c. &c. will it not appear to you, that tho' a Cessation of the War may be a Peace, it may not be a Reconciliation? Will not some voluntary Acts of Justice and even of Kindness on your Part, have excellent Effects towards producing such a Reconciliation? Can you not find means of reparing in some Degree those Injuries? You have in England and Ireland twelve Hundred of our People Prisoners, who have for Years bravely suffered all the Hardships of that Confinement rather than enter into your Service to fight against their Country. Methinks you ought to glory in Descendants of such Virtue. What if you were to begin your Measures of Reconciliation by setting them at Liberty? I know it would procure for you the Liberty of an equal Number of your People, even without a previous Stipulation; and the Confidence in our Equity with the apparent Good Will in the Action would give very good Impressions of your Change of Disposition towards us. Perhaps you have no Knowledge of the Opinions lately conceived of your King and Country in America, the enclos'd Copy of a Letter[1] may make you a little acquainted with them, & convince you how impossible must be every Project of Bringing us again under the Domination of such a Sovereign. With great Esteem, I am, Dear Sir, Your most obedient & most humble Servant   Benjamin Franklin

LC: *Benjamin Franklin Papers, microfilm reel 2 (LBkC).*
[1] *Not further identified.*

Lord Shelburne to Benjamin Franklin

Dear Sir,   London 6[th.] April 1782.
I have been favored with your Letter and am much obliged by your Remembrance. I find myself returned nearly to the same Situation, which you remember me to have occupied nineteen Years ago, and should be very

glad to talk to you as I did then, and afterwards in 1767, upon the means of promoting the Happiness of Mankind, a Subject much more agreeable to my Nature, than the best concerted Plans for spreading Misery and Devastation. I have had a high Opinion of the Compass of your Mind, and of your Foresight. I have often been beholden to both, and shall be glad to be so again, as far as is compatible with your Situation. Your Letter discovering the same Disposition has made me send to you Mr. Oswald.[1] I have had a longer Acquaintance with him, than even I have had the Pleasure to have with you. I believe him an honest Man, and, after consulting some of our common Friends, I have thought him the fittest for the Purpose. He is a pacifical Man, and conversant in those Negotiations, which are most interesting to Mankind – This has made me prefer him to any of our speculative Friends, or to any Person of higher Rank. He is fully apprized of my Mind, and you may give full Credit to every Thing he assures you of. At the same Time, if any other Channel occurs to you, I am ready to embrace it. I wish to retain the same Simplicity and Good faith, which subsisted between us in Transactions of less Importance.

I have the Honor to be, &c.   Shelburne.

NA: PCC, item 100, v. 1, pp. 360-361 (LBkC); M247, reel 127.
  [1] Oswald, Richard (c.1705-1784). British merchant and political figure. Consulted by North Ministry because of his knowledge of American commercial affairs. Friend of Benjamin Franklin and Lord Shelburne. Plenipotentiary to negotiate peace with the American commissioners in Paris, April-November 1782.

Arthur Lee to James Warren

Dear Sir,[1]   Philadelphia April 8th. 1782.

. . . . .

...Dr. Franklin is appointed one of the Commissioners to negociate a peace, because France wills it; & Congress are complaisant enough to say – they trust in his zeal & integrity, God forgive them!

The Fishery, I am afraid, is the object & will be the sacrifice of this appointment. This question will come on in Congress, & I think your ablest members shoud be here. But Instructions from Congress will avail little, if a corrupt Commissioner is entrusted with them, who certainly never meaning to return to this Country, will feel himself very easy about our reproaches, while he is enjoying in France the reward of his treachery. I know from what passd at the treaties we concluded, that to monopolize the Fishery is the object of France, & I am most sure that Dr. Franklin will be the instrument of effecting it.

. . . . .

I am, with the truest esteem, Dear Sir, yr. most Obedt Servt,   A. Lee

Smith, *Letters of Delegates, v. 18, pp. 440-442.*
  [1] *Warren, James (1726-1808). Massachusetts merchant, farmer, and political figure.*
President, Massachusetts Provincial Congress, 1775-1776. Paymaster general, Continental
Army, 1775-1776. Member, Massachusetts House of Representatives, 1776-1778, 1779-
1780, 1787; speaker, 1776, 1787. Member, Navy Board for the Eastern Department,
1776-1781. Consistently a radical; sympathized with followers of Daniel Shays. Member,
Governor's Council, 1792-1794.

Comte de Vergennes to Chevalier de La Luzerne

[Translation]
N°· 33   Versailles, 9 April 1782
    The English Ministry, Sir, has just now fallen, and the principal members
of the opposition compose the new administration: Admiral Keppel[1] is First
Lord of the Admiralty, the Marquess of Rockingham[2] replaces Lord North,
and the ministry of foreign affairs is entrusted to Messrs. Shelburne and
Fox. The former is also charged with the affairs of America.
    This revolution must naturally bring about a new order of things, and it
is more than probable that America will hold the attention of the new
ministers from preference.
    As the wish of the English nation is for peace, and as the opposition has
been its voice and support, it seems evident that the cabinet of St. James
is going to take all possible steps to be reconciled and settle differences with
its former colonies. It will surely make them some very seductive offers, and
perhaps will even bring itself to sacrifice its supremacy, but it will want to
make a separate peace and break the ties that exist between France and the
Americans.
    I do not fear, Sir, that the latter will allow themselves to be drawn into
that System of perfidy, because they are sufficiently enlightened to see that
they would dishonor themselves forever. But if they should hesitate an
instant on the choice to make, two principal reasons, it would seem to me,
should prevent them from yielding to the English Suggestions; the first, that
it is impossible that the Court of London would pardon the United States
for their alleged felony, and that it not maintain the desire to punish them
if ever the the occasion presents itself; the Second, that if the English
ministry appears outwardly calm and pacific, it is because it sees the
impossibility of bringing the Americans back to obedience in the present
state of things, and because it hopes to prepare more favorable

circumstances, by breeding them through the lure of peace, to separate them from their friends and to render them unworthy of finding others: it is evident that in the latter event, the United States would be at the mercy of England and that all Europe would be a tranquil spectator of the vengeance which that angry power would exact from them after having misled and isolated them.

These reflections, Sir, will have escaped neither the members of Congress nor the enlightened part of the American Nation: but will they make the same impression on the people, on the rural inhabitants, who commence to support the burden of the war impatiently and who have long sighed for peace? We should expect to see England multiply her emissaries; rouse into activity all the Tories scattered on the vast surface of America; scatter money; make promises; in a word, employ all the means of Seduction and of corruption to arrive at her ends. It seems to me, Sir, that Congress has only one means, and one sure means, to cut short all the schemes of the English Ministry, and that is to declare frankly to the Court of London that the United States will not make peace without the concurrence of their allies, and that if England has peace overtures to make to them, the American plenipotentiaries who are now in Europe are sufficiently authorized to listen to them and even to treat of peace if they are admissible. This language, peremptorily pronounced, will shelter Congress from the obstacles that the English ministry will not fail to instigate for it, and will protect America from the troubles and factions that will infallibly arise if England is allowed to negotiate there.

To give, Sir, all the more weight to the expedient that I have just indicated to you, and to determine Congress to adopt it all the more easily, you will do very well to observe to it that it cannot consent to treat with England in America without separating itself thereby from the allies of the United States, and in consequence without being negligent of the first of its obligations: Congress would be no less lacking towards the courts of Vienna and of St. Petersburg, to the mediation of which it has agreed.

Moreover, Sir, although we desire that Congress not start any direct negotiation and that it not make a separate peace, we do not intend thereby to hinder that Body from following the System that we ourselves have laid out in the response that we have made to the two mediating courts. We are and always will be disposed to consent that the American plenipotentiaries in Europe treat in conformity with their instructions, directly and without our intervention with those of the Court of London, while we treat in the same way on our side, on condition that the two Negotiations proceed at an equal pace, and that the two treaties be signed at the same time, and not resolve one without the other.

There is, Sir, a new circumstance that should prevent the Americans
from yielding to the Court of London, and from making a fraudulent peace
with it. It is the revolution which is being prepared in Holland, and which
from all appearances will not be long in coming. The provinces of Friesland
and of Holland have unanimously resolved to recognize the independence
of the United States and to admit Mr. Adams in quality of their
plenipotentiary. This important question is now submitted to the
deliberations of the States General, and no one doubts that their resolution
will be for the affirmative. Behold therefore a new friend, a new ally that
the Americans are going to acquire, and a guarantor moreover of their
independence and of their Safety. It seems impossible to me that Congress
would sacrifice this surplus of advantages in the expectation of a chimerical
peace and tranquility. The new system of the United Provinces will profit
America all the more because they have proposed to the King a concert of
operations against the common enemy, and because they have engaged
themselves not to make a separate peace for as long as this concert lasts.
There results therefrom a powerful diversion in favor of America, and the
English will find themselves as little in a position to act vigorously against
America as to maintain their engagements at will, if they succeed in
wresting a separate accommodation from Congress.   Vergennes

FFAA: Pol. Corr., U.S., v. 21, f.11 (LC transcription).

[1] Keppel, Augustus (1725-1786). British admiral and political figure. A leading Whig
Member of Parliament, 1761-1780, he was a political opponent of the Earl of Sandwich,
his civilian superior. He fought an indecisive battle off Ushant, July 27, 1778, after which
he was brought to trial for neglect of duty. His acquittal was considered a defeat for the
North Ministry. First Lord of the Admiralty under Rockingham and Shelburne, 1782-
1783.

[2] Rockingham, Charles Watson-Wentworth, Marquess of (1730-1782). Headed British
ministry that repealed Stamp Act and passed Declaratory Act, 1766. Opposed coercive
measures in America. Advocated recognition of American independence, March 1778.
Opposed war with the Netherlands, January 1781. Headed coalition ministry intent upon
peace with the United States, March-July 1782.

Benjamin Franklin to Henry Laurens

Sir   Passy April 12th. 1782.
   I should sooner have paid my respects to you by Letter if I had not till
lately expected you here, as I understood it to be your intention. Your
enlargement gave me great pleasure; and I hope that the terms exacted by
the late Ministry will now be relaxed; especially when they are informed

that you are one of the Commissioners appointed to treat of Peace. Herewith I send you a copy of the Commission; the purport of which you can communicate to the Ministers if you find it proper. If they are disposed to make Peace with us and our Ally at the same time, I will on notice from you, send to M^r· Jay to prepare for meeting at such time and place as shall be agreed on. As to our treating seperately and quitting our present Alliance, which the late Ministry seemed to desire, it is impossible. Our Treaties, and our Instructions, as well as the honor and interest of our Country forbid it. I will communicate those Instructions to you as soon as I have the pleasure of seeing you. If you have occasion for Money, please to acquaint me with the sum you desire, and I will endeavour to supply you.

   With very great Esteem and Respect, I have the honor to be, Sir Your Most Obedient & Most humble Servant   B. Franklin

Clements Library: Shelburne Papers, v. 72, p. 59 (C).

Benjamin Franklin to John Adams

Sir,   Passy April 13th· 1782.
   Inclosed with this I send to your Excellency the Pacquet of Correspondence between Mr Hartley and me which I promised in my last. You will See we have held nearly the same Language which gives me Pleasure.

   While Mr Hartley was making Propositions to me, with the Approbation or Privity of Lord North, to treat Separately from France, that Minister had an Emissary here, a Mr Forth, formerly a Secretary of Lord Stormonts, making Proposals to induce this Court to treat with us. I understand that several Sacrifices were offer'd to be made, and among the rest Canada to be given up to France. The Substance of the Answer appears in my last Letter to Mr Hartley. But there is a Sentence omitted in that Letter which I much liked viz: "that whenever the two Crowns should come to treat, his most Christian Majesty would shew how much the Engagements he might enter into were to be rely'd on by his exact observance of those he already had with his present Allies."

   If you have received anything in consequence of your Answer by Digges, you will oblige me by communicating it. The Ministers here were much pleased with the Account given them of your Interview, by the Ambassador.

With great Respect, I am, Sir, Your most obedient & most humble
Servant.   B Franklin
{You will be so good as to return me the Papers when you have a good
Opportunity.}

MHS: *The Adams Papers, microfilm reel 356 (LS).*

Benjamin Franklin to David Hartley

Dr Sr Passy Ap 13 1782
    Since mine of the 5th I have thought farther of the Subjects of our late
letters. You were of opinion that the late Ministry desired a reconciliation
with America,$^\circledast$ and with that view a seperate peace with us was proposed.
It happened that at the same time Lord North had an Emissary here to
sound the French Ministers with regard to Peace, and to make them very
advantageous propositions in case they w^d abandon America. You may judge
from hence my Dear friend what opinion I must have formed of the
intentions of your Ministers. To convince you of the truth of this I may
acquaint you that the Emissary was Mr Forth and that the answer given him
to carry back to the English Ministers was, *que le Roi de France desiroit la*
paix – autant que le Roi d'angleterre; qu'il s'y preteroit dès qu'il le pourroit avec
Dignité & Sureté: mais qu'il importoit avant tout a SMTC de savoir si la Cour
de Londres etoit disposée a traiter egallement avec les Alliées de la France,[1] M^r
Forth went off with this Answer for London but probably did not arrive till
after the dismission of the Ministers that sent him. You may make any use
of this information that you judge proper. The new Ministry may see by it
the principles that govern this Court; and it will convince them I hope that
the project of dividing us is as vain as it w^d be to us injurious. I cannot
judge what they will think or do in consequence of the Answer sent by M^r
Forth; (if they have seen it.) If they love peace as they have persuaded the
English Nation and all Europe to believe, they can be under no Difficulty.
France has opened a path wch in my opinion they may use without hurting
the dignity of their Master or the honour of the Nation. If they do not
chuse it they doubtless flatter themselves that war may still produce
successes in favour of England that have hitherto been withheld. The
Crowning or frustrating such hopes belongs to divine providence. May God
send us all more wisdom. I am, ever My Dear friend Yours Most affect^{ly}
                                                              BF
$\circledast$ NB I thought that some part of the late ministry were tired out with an
unsuccesfull, & impracticable war, and therefore that some of them at least
were desirous of Peace.

Clements Library: Shelburne Papers, v. 72, pp. 47,49 (C).

[1] that the King of France is as desirous of peace as the King of England; and that he would accede to it as soon as he could with Dignity and Safety; but it is a matter of the utmost importance for His Most Christian Majesty to know whether the Court of London is disposed to treat on equal terms with the Allies of France.

Comte de Montmorin to Comte de Vergennes

[Translation]

N⁰· 25.   Aranjuez, 15 April 1782
Sir,

. . . . .

There is little likelihood, Sir, as you observe, that Mr. Forth will return near you; the recent revolution in the English Ministry should probably put an end to his mission, but it is very likely that the new Ministry will make every effort to manage to separate the United States from us. M. de Floridablanca perceives, as fully as you, Sir, the necessity of preventing their defection, but I do not know if he is completely free to employ the means that would be the most appropriate. I enclose, Sir, a note which that Minister received from a private individual,[1] and which he very much wanted to communicate to me. He himself does not attach any great importance to it, and as for me, I think the news that it contains entirely destitute of foundation, but I thought I should send it to you inasmuch as M. de Floridablanca communicated it to me.

I have the honor to be with respect, Sir, Your very humble and very obedient Servant

. . . . .

Le cte. de Montmorin.

R. the 27th.

FFAA: Pol. Corr., Spain, v. 606, f. 244 (LC transcription).
[1] Unknown sender to Floridablanca, 13 April 1782 (FFAA: Pol. Corr., Spain, v. 606, f. 243).

Robert R. Livingston to John Jay

Dear Sir,   Philadelphia. 16 April 1782
Returning from an excursion to the State of New York I found your letter of October 3 which on account of my absence had been committed to a

committee of Congress. They have shown me their report. It will try their sentiments on a very interesting point if it goes through, but as they may not suddenly come to a resolution. and I have just heard of a vessel which will sail in two hours for Cadiz, I avail myself of it to inform you that your conduct through the whole of your negotiation has been particularly acceptable to Congress.

The condition you have annexed to the proposed cession is extremely well calculated to hasten the Spanish Ministry and I think ought to be adhered to for unless some important advantage can be gained by it, the claim with the means we have of enforcing it is too valuable to be relinquished. Spain may flatter herself with the hopes of gaining that at a general peace by the favor of the mediators which she is unwilling to purchase of us by the smallest concession. In this, however, I conceive she will find when too late that a partial regard to triffling interests has led her to sacrifice those of a more extensive and important nature. Spain can have no claims to the Mississippi but what are derived from her late conquests. Our claims are valid, those of Britain are at least specious, both will be opposed to her's at a general peace. And as she has made the cession of Gibraltar a preliminary to a peace she can hardly expect that the mediators, if they gratify her in that, will add to it other countrys to which she has no claim, more particularly as the right of Britain is next to ours incontestably the best that can be set up, so that there is little doubt if the negotiation should open when the success of our affairs gives us importance in the eyes of the mediators that they will recognize our right. If, on the other hand, we should meet with any reverse of fortune, those of Britain will become more respectable thereby, and the weak claims which Spain may set up from the conquest of a few inconsiderable posts in a country of such immense extent, already in part conquered and possessed by us, can only serve as arguments of unbounded ambition without establishing a right.

Sound policy then certainly dictates as a sure means of attaining this great object such a vigorous prosecution of the war as will reduce Great Britain to the necessity of making the mortifying cessions which Spain requires, and give more validity to the rights with which we are willing on certain conditions to invest her. Pecuniary aids afforded to us will be the most effectual means of destroying the common enimy and reducing them to accept such terms as Spain may chuse to dictate, while the purchase of our rights will enable her to support them with dignity and to appear at the congress as a sovereign power who has supported a distressed ally without availing herself of that distress to deprive her of rights which she has paid no equivalent for.

America considers her independence as placed beyond all doubt. She begins now to look forward to other important objects. She knows the value of the country which is washed by the Mississippi. It is also well known to the nations of Europe. By the cession of her right to it she is satisfied that she can procure important advantages in commerce from any of the maritime powers in Europe. Some of the northern potentates, who have means of giving validity to our claims, would consider an establishment, under the restrictions with which we have offered it to Spain, as cheaply purchased by an alliance with us, and a much greater advance in money than we have yet thought of asking from Spain, if our present wants should make it expedient to pursue this Idea. Spain has not laid such obligations upon us, notwithstanding our respectful and patient attention to her, as to render us chargeable with the slightest degree of ingratitude in so doing.

You will therefore persist in the line in which you now are, declaring explicitly that the sessions you propose are only dictated by your desire to make early and vigorous efforts against the common enemy; that if they are not accepted so soon and upon such terms as to afford you a prospect of obtaining this desirable end, you will not consider your offers as binding upon you. I am persuaded that in this I speak the sentiments of Congress, and you may deliver them as such.

. . . . .

... I am, Dear Sir, With the greatest respect and esteem, Your Most obedient humble Servant, Robt. R.Livingston

Morris, Jay Papers, v. 2, pp. 148-151; see also NA: PCC, item 79, v. 1, p. 404, and item 118, pp. 136-144, M247, reels 105 and 139 respectively.

John Adams to Benjamin Franklin

Sir Amsterdam April 16. 1782

Yesterday noon, M[r] William Vaughan of London,[1] came to my House, with M[r] Laurens, the son of the President, and brought me a ~~Ligne~~ from the latter, and told me, that the President was at Harlem, and desired to see me. – I went out to Haarlam and found, my old Friend at the golden Lyon.

He told me that he was come partly for his Health and the Pleasure of Seeing me and partly, to converse with me and see if he had at present just Ideas and Views of things, at least to see if We agreed in Sentiment, and having been desired by Several of the new Ministry to do so. –

I asked him if he was at Liberty? he said no, that he was still under Parole but at Liberty to Say what he pleased to me.

I told him that ~~being a P~~ I could not communicate to him, being a Prisoner even his own ~~Commission and~~ Instructions, nor ~~any~~ enter into any

Consultation with him as one of our Colleagues in the Commission for Peace. that all I should Say to him would be as one private Citizen conversing with another. but that upon all such Occasions I Should reserve a right to communicate whatever Should pass to our Colleagues and Allies.

He Said that Lord Shelburne and others of the new Ministers, were anxious to know whether, there was any Authority to treat of a Seperate Peace, and whether there could be an Accommodation, upon any Terms short of Independance, – That he had ever answered them, that nothing short of an express or tacit Acknowledgement of our Independance, in his opinion would ever be accepted, and that no Treaty was would or could be made Seperate from France. He asked me if his answers had been right? I told him I was fully of that opinion. He said that the new Ministers had received Digges Report, but his Character was such that they did not choose to depend upon it. – That a Person, by the Name of Oswald I think ~~was~~ set off for Paris to see you, about the same time, that he came away to see me.

I desired him, between him and me to consider, without Saying any thing of it to the Ministry whether We could ever have a real Peace with Canada or Nova Scotia in the Hands of the English? and whether, We ought not to insist, at least upon a Stipulation that they should keep no standing Army or regular Troops, nor erect any fortifications, upon the frontiers of either. That at present I saw no Motive that We had to be anxious for a Peace, and if the nation was not ripe for it, upon proper terms, We might wait patiently till they should be so. –

I found the old Gentleman, properly sound in his System of Politiques. He has a very poor Opinion both of the Integrity and Abilities of the new Ministry as well as the old. – He thinks they know not what they are about. – that they are Spoiled by the Same Insincerity, Duplicity Falshood, and Corruption, with the former. Ld. Shelburne still flatters the King with Ideas of Conciliation and seperate Peace &c – Yet the Nation and the best Men in it, are for an universal Peace and an express Acknowledgment of American Independance, and many of the best are for giving up Canada and Nova Scotia.

His ~~Mission~~ Design Seemed to be, Solely, to know how far Diggs's Report was true. after an hour or two of Conversation, I returned to Amsterdam and left him to return to London.

These are all but Artifices to raise the Stocks, and if you think of any Method to put a stop to them, I will cheerfully concur with you. – They now know Sufficiently, y^t our Commission is to treat of a general Peace, and with Persons vested with equal Powers – and if you agree to it, I wish never to see another Messenger that is not a Plenipotentiary.

It is expected that the Seventh Province, Guelderland will this day

Acknowledge American Independence. – I think, We are in such a Situation now that We ought not, upon any Consideration to think of a Truce, or any Thing short of an express Acknowledgement of the Sovereignty of the United States. I should be glad however to know your Sentiments upon this Point

    I have the Honour to be   John Adams

MHS: The Adams Papers, microfilm reel 102 (LBkC).
1 Vaughan, William (1752-1850). British merchant. Younger brother of Benjamin Vaughan. Helped to pacify the naval mutiny at the Nore, 1797. An authority on docks.

The Peace Talks Begin

News of British general Lord Charles Cornwallis' surrender at Yorktown reached London on November 25, 1781. Blame was placed on Lord George Germain, the Minister for War, whose mismanagement of military affairs indeed had played a large role in Britain's loss of America. French capture of the Caribbean islands of St. Eustatius, St. Christopher, Nevis, and Montserrat, plus the loss of Minorca to Spain, served to further undermine the position of the North Ministry.

On February 27, 1782, General Henry Conway, a critic of the American war, introduced a resolution in the House of Commons that denounced those who were attempting to conduct "offensive war in America" and authorized an enabling act permitting the king to make peace with the American colonies. Its passage marked the beginning of the end of the North government. Legally barred from actively pursuing the war in America, the ministry now attempted to separate the United States from France for negotiations based on territory possessed, or the concept of uti possidetis.

The North Ministry dispatched the spy Paul Wentworth to the Netherlands to explore such possibilities, but the Dutch Patriot faction demanded he leave the country before anything was accomplished. British agent Nathaniel Parker Forth turned up in Paris to propose peace based on territories in hand, but French Foreign Minister Vergennes refused to negotiate until the British would treat with the United States on equal terms. American expatriate and suspected British agent Thomas Digges visited John Adams in Amsterdam to learn whether the American Commissioners had powers to negotiate a truce. Adams satisfied Digges' curiosity by showing him his commission, and specified that the commissioners preferred to negotiate a peace, but only on terms that would also satisfy France. Digges' report to the North Ministry distorted Adams' reply, a circumstance which would not have surprised Franklin, who had declared Digges an embezzler. Nothing came of these peace probes, because on March 20, Lord North announced his resignation.

The new ministry had Rockingham, serving as First Lord of the Treasury, as the first minister, with Charles James Fox as Secretary of State for Foreign Affairs and Shelburne as Secretary of State for Home, Colonial, and Irish Affairs. George III did not like Rockingham and Fox, who favored American independence, and regarded Shelburne, who hoped to keep the Americans within the empire, as Rockingham's virtual equal. Given this state of affairs, either Fox or Shelburne could have taken charge of the negotiations with the Americans, and both sent envoys to Paris.

On March 21, Franklin received a note from the English nobleman Lord Cholmondeley,[1] who was en route from Nice to London, asking if he might call upon the American statesman the following morning. They spoke of mutual friends, affairs in England, and Conway's resolution. Cholmondeley told Franklin that he knew Lord Shelburne had a great regard for him, that he was sure Shelburne would like to hear from him, and that he would be happy to be the bearer of any missive Franklin might care to send.

Franklin accordingly wrote a note in which he assured Shelburne of his continuing respect, congratulated him on Britain's "returning good Disposition" towards America, and expressed the hope that it would "produce a General Peace." The note closed with a reference to some gooseberry bushes which Shelburne had sent to a mutual acquaintance. Cholmondeley departed, and soon after Paris learned of North's fall and Shelburne's participation in the new ministry.

On April 12, British merchant Richard Oswald arrived at Passy to confer with Franklin. He was the bearer of two letters. One, from Shelburne dated April 6, introduced Oswald, "an Honest Man...pacifical ..., and conversant in those negotiations, which are most Interesting to Mankind....He is fully appriz'd of my Mind, and you may give full credit to every thing he assures you of." The other, from Henry Laurens dated

April 7, vouched for Oswald as "a Gentleman of the strictest candour and integrity," whom Laurens had known for nearly 30 years.

Oswald proceeded to speak of the independence of the United States, saying that if it was accepted by all parties, there was no other point in dispute. However, if France insisted upon peace terms that were too humiliating to England, the war would continue. Franklin replied that the United States would not treat except in concert with France. Since none of the other American Commissioners were in Paris, he could do nothing in this regard. The doctor then offered to present Oswald to Vergennes, which he did on April 17, 1782, having provided the French foreign minister with copies of all the pertinent correspondence beforehand.

[1] *Cholmondeley, George James, Earl of (1749-1827). British nobleman who offered to carry a letter for Benjamin Franklin to Lord Shelburne in March 1782. In that letter, Franklin expressed a desire to work for a general peace.*

Notes of Conversation between Benjamin Franklin and Richard Oswald

[April 18, 1782]

To make a Peace durable, what may give occasion for future Wars, should, if practicable be removed.

The Territory of the United States, and that of Canada, by long extended Frontiers touch each other.

The Settlers on the Frontiers of American Provinces are generally the most disorderly of the People, who being far removed from the Eye & Controll of their respective Governments, are more bold in committing Offences against Neighbours, and are forever occasioning Complaints & furnishing Matter for fresh Differences between their States.

By the late Debates in Parliament, & publick Writings, it appears that Britain desires a *Reconciliation* with the Americans − It is a sweet Word. It means much more than a mere Peace, & what is heartily to be wish'd for. Nations may make a Peace whenever they are both weary of making War − But if one of them has made War upon the other unjustly, & has wantonly & unnecessarily done it great Injuries, & refuses Reparative, tho' there may for the present be Peace, the Resentment of those Injuries will remain, & will break out again in Vengeance, when Occasions offer. These Occasions will be watch'd for by one side; fear'd by the other; & the Peace will never be secure; nor can any Cordiality subsist between them.

Many Houses & Villages have been burnt in America by the English & their Allies the Indians – I do not know that the Americans will insist on Reparation – Perhaps they may. But would it not be better for England to offer it? Nothing could have a greater Tendency to conciliate! And much of the future Commerce of returning Intercourse between the two Countries may depend on the Reconciliation. Would not the advantage of Reconciliation by such means be greater than the Expence?

If then a Way can be proposed which may tend to efface the Memory of Injuries, at the same time that it takes away the Occasions of fresh Quarrel & Mischief, will it not be worth considering, especially if it can be done not only without Expence but be a means of saving –

Britain possesses Canada. Her chief Advantage from that possession consists in the trade for Peltry. Her Expences in governing & defending that Settlement must be considerable. It might be humiliating to her to give it up on the demand of America. Perhaps America will not demand it. Some of her politic Rulers may consider the fear of such a Neighbour as a Means of keeping the 13 states more united among themselves, & more attentive to Military Discipline. But on the Minds of the people in general would it not have an excellent Effect if Britain should voluntarily offer to give up this Province; tho' on these Conditions, that she shall in all times coming have & enjoy the Right of Free Trade thither unincumbered with any Duties whatsoever; & that so much of the vacant Lands there shall be sold, as will raise a sum sufficient to pay for the Houses burnt by the British Troops & their Indians; & also to indemnify the Royalists for the Confiscation of their Estates

This is mere Conversation–matter between M[r.] O. & M[r.] F. as the former is not impower'd to make propositions, & the latter cannot make any without the concurrence of his Colleagues —

Clements Library: Shelburne Papers, v. 87, no. 1, f. 183-184 (C).

Benjamin Franklin to Lord Shelburne

My Lord,   Passy April 18[th.] 1782.

I have received the Letter your Lordship did me the Honor of writing to me the 6[th:] Inst[t.] I congratulate you on your new Appointment to the honorable and important Office you formerly filled, so worthily, an Office which must be so far pleasing to you as it affords you more Opportunities of doing good and of serving your Country essentially in its great Concerns. I have conversed a good deal with M[r.] Oswald, and am much pleased with him. He appears to me a wise and honest Man. I acquainted him, that I was commissionated, with others, to treat of and conclude a Peace: That full Powers were given us for that Purpose, and that the Congress promised in good Faith to ratify, confirm, and cause to be faithfully observed the Treaty we should make but that we would not treat separately from France, and I proposed introducing him to M^r. le Comte de Vergennes, to whom I communicated your Lordship's Letter containing M^r. Oswald's Character, as a Foundation for the Interview. He will acquaint you that the Assurance he gave of his Britannic Majesty's good Dispositions towards Peace, was well received, and Assurances returned of the same good Dispositions in his most Christian Majesty. With Regard to Circumstances relative to a Treaty, M^r. De Vergennes observed, that the King's Engagements were such as that he could not treat without the Concurrence of his Allies; that the Treaty should, therefore, be for a general not a partial Peace; that if the Parties were disposed to finish the War speedily by themselves, it would, perhaps, be best to treat at Paris, as an Embassador from Spain was already there, and the Commissioners from America might easily and soon be assembled there. Or, if they chose to make Use of the proposed Mediation, they might treat at Vienna: but that the King was so truly willing to put a speedy End to the War, that he would agree to any Place the King of England, should think proper. I leave the Rest of the Conversation to be related to your Lordship by M^r. Oswald, and that he might do it more easily and fully than he could by Letter, I was of Opinion with him that it would be best he should return immediately and do it *vivâ voce*.

Being myself but one of the four Persons now in Europe, commissioned by the Congress to treat of Peace, I can make no Proposition of much Importance without them. I can only express my Wish, that, if M^r. Oswald returns hither, he may bring with him the agreement of your Court to treat for a general Peace, and the Proposal of Place and Time, that I may immediately write to Messieurs Adams, Laurens, and Jay. I suppose that in this Case your Lordship will think it proper to have M^r. Laurens discharged from the Engagements he entered into when he was admitted to Bail. – I desire no other Channel of Communication between us than that of M^r. Oswald, which I think your Lordship has chosen with much Judgment. He will be Witness of my acting with all the Simplicity and Good Faith, which you do me the Honor to expect from me, and if he is enabled when he returns hither, to communicate more fully your Lordship's Mind on the principal Points to be settled, I think it may contribute much to the blessed Work our Hearts are engaged in.

. . . . .

With great and sincere Respect, I have the Honor to be, my Lord, &c.

B. Franklin.

NA: PCC, item 100, pp. 366-369 (LBkC); M247, reel 127.

Richard Oswald's Journal.

Paris – Thursday 18th April 1782.

Sunday 7th – We left London at one o'Clock. We were stopt near 2 days at Margate by a contrary Wind, & one day at Ostend for want of post Horses. We arrived at Paris on Sunday the 14th at two o'Clock.

I understood that Doct^r Franklin lived at Passy, about 3 Miles up the River. Mr Whiteford[1] called upon him in the Evening to let [him] know that I should wait of him next Morning. He said he would be glad to See me. I accordingly called upon him on Monday about Eleven. After some Conversation about indifferent matters, I told him that to Save his time, I would put into his hands a Letter I was charged with upon my leaving London. Upon which Mr Whiteford went into another Room. I then delivered my Lord Shelburnes Letter as also a Letter from Mr Laurens to the Doctor.

When he had perused these Letters, he said he supposed I had seen the one from Lord Shelburne. I said I had. However the Doct^r gave it to me to read. He said he had a great Regard for His Lo^p – on the foundation of a long acquaintance in former times, more happy than the present &c^{a.}

The Doct^r told me then, that if I had any Propositions to offer in consequence of this Commission, he would be glad to hear them. I replied that I could not say that I had Viewed any particular Instructions ~~from H~~ to that purpose from His Los^p which I was not Surprised at considering the present Situation of things in various Shapes, which might make it more than usually difficult explicitly to condescend upon particulars. That the extent of my Commission was confined to the delivery of that Letter; & if His Lo^p had anything further in view by sending me hither, he must have so far trusted to my discretion – & I was answerable alone, for anything I should venture to Say on the Subject of publick affairs. The Doctor then said he would be glad to have my opinion of them.

I replied – That although I was Sensible he would be at no loss as to that Situation of affairs in England, yet, with his permission, I would make no Scruple in telling him what I thought of some parts of them particularly Regarding the War. Which was that I believe our Court was desirous of Peace; and we were happy to find that he & other Commissioners of the Colonies were equally well disposed towards that purpose. & I was in hopes they had Powers to treat. That I had heard so in England, but was afraid there might be a mistake in the Report of these Powers being absolute & unlimited. In answer to which the Doctor said, Their Powers were absolute & unlimited; & Such as would So bind the Congress as there would be no objection in America to what Should be concluded by him & the other

Delegates now here. That it had been thought proper to give them Such unlimited Commission, So as to Save time in putting an end to the Miseries of Mankind, which would be lost in going back to America for a Confirmation – I replied, that I was extremely happy to be so informed, & from Such good authority, & it was the more fortunate that England had already gone So far on the way towards Peace by their Resolution which the House of Commons had passed, That all active Hostilities on our part Should cease over the whole of the revolted part of the American Continent, By which the British Troops now there when not attackt, might, for a time, be considered as harmless as the Pallisades of their Trenches. Of which I made no doubt he was fully informed.

As also, I said, he must have been informed That a Bill has lately been brought in Parliam^t, empowering His Majesty (for the Sake of concluding a Truce or Peace with the Said revolted part of the Colonies) had it in his power to dispense with & annul every Act of Parliam^t which he had hitherto Subsisted in relation to them. By which when that Peace was concluded, His Majesty might for ever free the said Colonies of every former Restraint Legislative or Commercial.

Upon that, I put a Copy of the Said Bill into the Doctors hands, which I told him I had received from my Lord Shelburne; & that it had gone So far through the House of Commons that it was Committed, & I was told there was little doubt of its passing into a Law.

. . . . .

In passing over this kind of Conversation, & coming to talk of Peace, I found it became me to be cautious of what I said, having no particular Instructions on that Subject – Yet under ~~the~~ Cover of the Permission that was at first granted me, of Speaking my private Opinion, of which I again reminded the Doctor, I ventured to proceed in Some Such way as follows, & took this latitude the more freely that I made no doubt but the Doctor would Report to the Minister what ever I should Say that might be properly Communicated, & was worth his notice. In doing of which, ~~I did not think~~ I had principally in view the difficulties which might occur in obtaining a Restoration of what we had <*> already Lost, & might be now in the way of losing in the W. Indies, as well as in checking any exorbitant Demands on the part of France in ye East Indies, or to prevent an unreasonable Interposition for an Indemnification to the Hollanders, &c^a–

From these motives I ventured to proceed as follows, Viz That with respect to America, it could not be otherwise but that the People of Engl^d were desirous that there might be a Seperate Peace made with these Colonies. & that a wish of that kind & ~~in~~ even an expectation, still prevailed over the Country, at least in a great many parts of it. The Doctor replied – That was impracticable & that they could not proceed, or conclude any thing but in Communication with the Minister of France. I told the Doctor I made no doubt that was the Case – yet I could not See but it was in the power of the Commissioners of the Colonies, by meeting & Consulting together to Smooth the way to an equitable Settlement of general Negotiation, by framing Some particular points <*> Seperately regarding Great Britain, which might Stand invariably as the basis of a general pacification, & which might govern future proceedings so far, & prevent France from taking too great an advantage of the present Situation of things respecting Great Britain. That they are unfortunate, can be no Secret; yet it appeared that it was in the power of the Deputies of the Colonies previously to draw <****> such with regard to the Interests of G. Britain, as Should Set Some reasonable bounds to the Demands of France. In doing of which they might possibly consult the common Interest of all parties, & prevent much further trouble & bloodshed. Since it could not be Supposed that G. Britain, under all her present & unexpected Difficulties, would Submit to any Conditions that would be dishonourable to her Character, or uniformbly unfavourable to her Interest.

That although it could not be denied that her Funds in the usual way of production, <*> are a good deal Shraitned, yet on Such extraordinary occasion, her People would universally unite in the great passion of Supporting their national Character, & would be reconciled to the Inconvenience of the utmost pressure – In that temper they would be at no loss to find Resources of various kinds among others, I would name one – Such as a partial Sacrifice of a part of the annual Income of all the Inhabitants of Estate over the whole Kingdom. So as a Person having, Such a Sum as £500. a year Should be contented to live upon £400. Upon which the Doctor Said, perhaps it would not be the worse for them. I told him I had no authority for Saying this, or otherwise than as my private opinion, & Such as was most likely to happen in a case of extremity as I had mentioned. In which event, now that I Supposed the expense of the American part of the War was pretty near off our hands, in case the Surplus of our future Levies of Supply Should be thrown into the Sea Service, France might in the end come to be tired of the ~~Conquest~~ Contest; & So as to wish She had been upon this occasion moderately temperate in her demands. That She had now, a quiet time on the Continent of Europe, Which might not be always So. – and there was the more reason to be moderate at the close of the day that ~~France~~ S in abstracting or Seperating So much of the American Continent from England (in case His Majesty Should be encouraged to adopt the Powers granted by the intended Act of Parliam') France would gain all she aimed at by ~~or~~ taking part in the War; And the American Commissioners <*> would have Reason to be Satisfied & not wish that, England Should Sustain any farther loss, as their

Constituents would also be in possession of all the Object they had in view at any time Since the first Commencem^t of the American troubles –

I therefor repeated the just & natural expectation that they Should take the matter into consideration & contribute their good offices in discouraging any Such unreasonable Demands as should prevent England from < * > putting a period to the War. That I was a Stranger to the nature & extent of their Engagements with France & whether they thought Themselves bound, as had been said, to guarantee such Conquests as France might make elsewhere. & therefor must leave that to rest < * > as to particulars for the present – I just mentioned the word Sugar Islands once, but did not chuse in this stage of the business to go farther, least Something Should come out from the Doctor in relation to Grenada & other Islands which fell into our hands at the last Peace, as to which possibly he might have been informed of the Intentions of this Court, & upon which it did not become me to pass any observation. Upon my touching upon the Subject of the Colony Engagements – and guaranteeing < *** > Conquests of – the Doctor Said "They had been much obliged to France" – And that they could do nothing without consulting the Minister, (the Count d'Argennes)^2 That he must lay the Papers I brought before him. These papers were My Ld Shelburnes Letter, & one I received from Mr Laurens; & the two Copies of the Acts of Parliam^t For this purpose, the Doct^r said he would go next day (Tuesday) to Versailles, & would call at my Lodging on Wednesd^y morning, & that I must go with him to the Minister, if I had no objection. I told him I had none. He said the Count was a candid moderate Man, & had a Secretary who could Speak English, and would explain if I could not speak French. I told him that I understood French, though I could not Speak it properly.

In talking farther of our apprehensions of unreasonable Demands the Doctor Said he did not imagine that would happen. & that the French were not anxious or desirous of extending their dominion, & wished only that things should be put on such footing as they might be Safe, – or Something to that purpose. One thing he Said they might perhaps insist on, as a point of honour, & follow our example when we took advantage of Circumstances, as in the Article of Dunkirk – to which I made no Reply. He at Same time Said he did not know but the Dutch would expect Some Indemnification for their Losses. That he understood we had lately made proposals to them for a Cessation of Hostilities, & a Peace to be closed on the footing of the Treaty of 1674 –

Upon the whole, the Doctor Shewed me a good deal of Civility and although Sparing of his words, he Said enough to convince me that he Sincerely wishes the War was at an end. At which period he Said we Should all be good Friends, & would Certainly have a large Share of their

Commerce &c.

I omitted to observe that in the course of our Conversation I entirely avoided Saying anything relative to the Colonies which had not revolted – Canada, Nova Scotia & East Florida, nor of NewfoundLand & the Doct.ʳ took no manner of nottice of them –.

I cannot say that the above is exactly in the Words as they passed between us, but they are as exact as my Memory will Serve me and I am Certain that, as to Substance, there is no mistake.

In the Evening of the 16th I received from the Doctor the Letter herewith Sent.

According to the Appointment, I called on him next morning; & after Breakfast he carried me to Versailles.

We Stopt first at the Office of the Ministers Secretary He spoke a bad English. yet full better than I spoke French. Doct.ʳ Franklin was present. The Secretary Seemed to be informed of the purport of My Lord Shelburnes Letter to the Doctor, & likewise to understand that our Court were inclined to put an end to the War, & entered upon the Subject as if he had been Commissioned to that purpose. He Said their Court were exceedingly pleased to hear that ours ~~had~~ were So disposed; & he could assure me that there was nothing more earnestly desired by that Court; & that they were ready to enter into a Treaty on terms mutually just & equitable without any unnecessary loss of time: of which I would be Satisfied when I had the honour to See the Count de Vergennes. The Secretary touched upon Several points relative to the Subject & was answered by me in a general way. Both of us deploring the unhappy Consequences of a continuance of the War; & he repeating his assurances of its being the earnest desire of their Court to put an end to it. and I on my part, venturing to give my opinion, as before, that upon just & honourable terms the King of England was ready to close with them – as a proof which, Regarding one part of the Subject in question, I quoted the Advances we had made by what had passed in a Parliamᵗ relative to the Colonies; of which no doubt they had been informed.

After about half an hours Conversation in this manner with the Secretary, he Speaking Sometimes in English & Sometimes in French, & I making my Replies in one or the other language in the best manner I could, & Doctʳ Franklin interfering when necessary, We were called to attend the Minister.

The Doctor & I together with the Secretary, went to his Office – He Received me with a Civility corespondent to what Mʳ Franklyn told me I might expect of a Gentleman of his Character. He began by condescending to pay me Some Compliments, as having heared the best accounts of my "*droiture* &cᵃ" – and then askt me if I could Speak French. The Secretary

Said I understood French; & if His Excell^{cy} would Speak Slow I would be at no loss in taking up his meaning.

The Minister then delivered himself, in Relation to the Calamities of War, in much the Same manner as the Secretary had done; & if possible, more Strongly expressing their desire to put an end to them without the least delay; & with the Strongest assurances of their proceeding therein with all the Candour, *franchise* &c^a that could be expected or desired of them. That he Rejoiced exceedingly to find that the King of England was equally well disposed to bring that business to a happy conclusion, &c^a –

The Secretary then informed the Minister of which I had Said to him of our desire of laying the foundation of a general Treaty by a Truce with the Colonies; & Such as Should give time for Settling points of more general Concern; & without leaving the Troops of G. Britain stationed in the Several Garisons of America, in the unpleasant Situation < ****** > they would be reduced to, if continued under the Restraints proposed by the Resolutions of Parliam^{t.} That as an actual Amnesty was by those Resolutions declared on one Side, I told his Excell^{cy}, it was but reasonable that Hostilities Should cease on the other; Which might be done by sending out Expresses from the Commissioners of the Colonies, as I had proposed to Mr. Franklyn. That by that means so much of the Calamities of War, which all Parties were desirous of putting an end to, would remain under Suspensⁿ, untill they were finally ~~brought under~~ controuled by the Restrictions of a general Pacification.

The Minister Said that they could not think of this matter being Settled by an Seperate agreement of Truce or otherwise. That by their Treaty with the Colonies, there was an express Stipulation that there Should be nothing treated of Seperately of either Side. ~~Seperately~~ To which Dr Franklyn assented.

I said, however that might be, I could not think the Proposal unreasonable on the part of my Sovereign. Since His Majesty had gone so far towards a general Peace as to have Shewen a willingness to abate of his Rights over a Country as large as a great part of Europe, in the manner as proposed in Parliam^t, and ~~al~~ thought it hard if G.B. could not be indulged, in this decent method of taking leave of Friends we had been So long acquainted with: & bowing to the Doctor, I said I was extremely Sorry for it.

Upon this the Minister Said it was not in their power to consent to any Such Seperate Truce or Treaty; & he would tell me one of their Reasons for it, Which was an apprehension that, if they did So, we would Reduce these Garrisons to the lowest State, & fall upon their Settlements elsewhere with the Remainder, or Such part as Should be withdrawn.–

The Minister then Said this War could not be closed by a general Treaty,

& in which Spain must be a Party, as they were Strictly bound to them by a particular Treaty; & they must accordingly proceed in Communication with that Court. The Count also mentioned Holland upon this occasion, but I cannot recollect that he Said there was any Treaty with them. Only I am almost positive he said they must be included in the Negotiation.

He also mentioned Mediators, – the Court of Vienna frequently; & once or twice that of Russia.

At this period, the Minister repeated, with an appearance of the most unaffected Candour & Sincerity, what he had before Said of their earnest desire of putting an end to the distresses of War, & with as much dispatch as Circumstances could possibly admit of. And that it was his opinion this might be done quickly, & without much of those Intrigues & formalities that usually attended those Negotiations: for which he Said there was no occasion where a good disposition & good Sense prevailed on both Sides, & where nothing of course would be desired but what was mutually fair & just –

. . . . .

And as a further demonstration of their intentions & Sincerity, he said the Place of Treaty Should depend on the King of Englands pleasure. He owned Paris would be the most convenient as being most Centrical for a Correspondence with Madrid, Holland, & Vienna & other Courts of Mediation, yet there Should be no obstacle as to that matter, & it Should be just as the King of England pleased. To this I made no reply, only that I ventured to Say that in my private opinion there would be no objection to Paris. Upon which the Count added that no retardment ~~Should~~ on account of the Mode & Manner of conducting this important business Should arise on their part – & digressing a little ~~further~~ again on the Calamities of War, Said he Should think himself happy, & thrice happy must all those be who could assist in putting an end to them & Such period too as Should leave no room to apprehend the return of them in any assignable ~~period~~ point of time – by laying the foundations of Peace, *Solidement.* Doct^r Franklin I observed approved of this turn of the Conversation – & if I am not mistaken repeated this last part either in French or English – I don't know which, but I would easily guess at his particular object of Reference being that of giving up forever So much of America to that part of what the Count had been pleased to Say on this of proceeding *quickly* & by the Shortest course to actual Negotiation – to a Solid Conclusion.

And I thought it a good time to propose that the great Outlines of Such Negotiation might be drawn here, & that I should think myself extremely happy to have the honour of carrying them over to England.

Upon this the Count said the propositions could not come from them.

(to which Doct' Franklyn assented) & must come from the King of England. For, that His Majesty being Single in the question had no occasion to consult any other Court. Whereas they being bound to Sundry Allies, particularly to those of Spain, they could not venture to State Propositions however general, without Such Communications as would be attended with great delay &c^a· This the Count Said I might represent in a proper manner to the Minister in England. I replied I should do so if I might obtain a free passage for my Letters; it was answered that I might depend upon it, & had best Send a Courier.

Upon a little reflection, & considering how ill qualified I was to support a Correspondence of this nature, I said I believed if His Excell^cy had no objection, ~~I thought~~ it would be the best way for me to carry home the Answer myself, & turning to the Doct' as if desirous of having his opinion, both the Minister & he entirely approved of that proposal as every way more expedient & considered to expedition.

I then Said, I had come by Ostend, but would wish to return by Calais. The Minister Said I Should have a passport to that purpose; but as it might be Signed by the King, I could not have it before next day about Noon, when it Should certainly be Sent to Doct' Franklyn. I then took my leave, & returned with the Doctor to Passy, with whom I promised to dine next day.

According to that appointment, I went to Passy next day, being Thursday, & received the Passport for Calais. After Dinner the Doct' askt me what time I intended to Sett out. I told him, very early in the Morning. He Said he wished I would wait a little, & that he would breakfast with me, not only to bring me an Answer to My Lord Shelburnes Letter – but likewise to have Some farther Conversation with me. I accordingly waited, & the Doctor came & delivered me his Letter to My Lord Shelburne, & we ~~passed~~ Spent about an hour in a familiar Conservation which passed the more easily on account of Some little acquaintance that arose from these frequent Interviews & I considered, myself in some degree more at liberty from the restraints of my Commission & at the Same time that I thought Something might come out in that way which might be of use in forwarding its purposes – without betraying in any Shape the Confidence the Doctor Seemed to place in the fairness of my Intentions. If upon reflection I can Recollect anything of this nature, I may possibly make a Minute of it to Serve as Supplem^t to this writing, which I have mostly wrote in a hurry at paris, & the rest on my road to Calais & London –

After parting with the Doct' I sett out about Noon & have not lost any time that could be Saved in getting back to London.   Richard Oswald

Whether what has been mentioned in the above papers be of any importance or not, I can promise that no part of them Shall be taken nottice of by me to any Person whatever. Being mostly wrote on the Spott for the Sake of exactness as to the Sense at least, I chuse to deliver these Minutes as they Stand rather than transcribe them hoping to be excused, although wrote in the rough manner

British Public Record Office, hereafter PRO: Journal of Richard Oswald, April 18, 1782 (Journal).

   ¹ Whitefoord, Caleb (1734-1810). British merchant, diplomat, and literary figure. Neighbor and friend of Benjamin Franklin during his residence in London. Secretary of Richard Oswald during peace negotiations, 1782. Contributed humorous political commentaries to London newspapers. Friend of David Garrick, Dr. Samuel Johnson, and Oliver Goldsmith.
   ² Vergennes.

Comte de Vergennes to Comte de Montmorin

[Translation]

Nᵒ· 18.   Versailles, 18 April 1782

M. the Comte de Montmorin.

The King, Sir, not wishing to leave the King His uncle anything to desire of his most intimate confidence and his scrupulous fidelity to fulfill his engagements, orders me to dispatch this Courier to you to inform you of an approach that was made to me yesterday that seems to announce that the new English ministry is no less inclined to peace than the preceding one had shown itself to be when it was seen on the edge of the precipice into which it ended up falling.

Lord Shelburne, who has always been a personal friend of Mr. Franklin and who has shown himself zealous for the American Cause in the opposition party, has sent here his friend Mr. Oswald, the bearer of a letter of credence for Mr. Franklin and of very satisfactory propositions for a peace with America.

The interview took place on the 15th. Mr. Franklin, having rejected every overture that tended to separate the Cause of America from that of France, made the English deputy understand that peace could not be negotiated without our intervention, and he induced him to wish to see me and to converse with me.

Yesterday I saw this Mr. Oswald, who was brought to see me by Mr. Franklin.

He told me that, charged by the English ministry to work toward a peace with America, he perceived that it could only take place in so far as it would be general, and although he did not have formal orders to confer with me, he nevertheless thought that he was entering into the intentions of his principals in seeking to discover and to assure himself of our dispositions to cooperate therein. My response was appropriate; I assured him that the King would always be inclined toward peace when he could accept it with honor and with security.

Mr. Oswald protested to me concerning the sincerity of the English ministry's wishes, and particularly of Lord Shelburne to procure a great good for humanity; he did not conceal from me that the new ministers felt the burdensomeness of the weight which they have taken upon themselves and that, thoroughly convinced of the necessity of yielding on the affairs of America, they were disposed to give the most complete satisfaction on that subject.

As Mr. Oswald insisted greatly on this article and seemed to regard it as the only interesting one for the reestablishment of peace, I observed to him that America was not the King's only ally, that His Majesty had one in the King of Spain, from whom he would not be separated in any case, and that he could and would only agree to a peace negotiation with the consent of and in concert with His Catholic Majesty. I also added that even though we had no engagement with the United Provinces of the Netherlands the King would nevertheless demand that they be admitted to the peace negotiations, His Majesty estimating that the War could be soundly terminated only by extinguishing all the fires that might relight it.

This Language did not seem to frighten Mr. Oswald. He even gave it the most complete approbation. He would very much have liked also to engage me or to expound to me on the proper means to facilitate the negotiation. It was not difficult for me to make him understand that we were not in a position to make propositions and that it was from the English ministry that we would expect them. This deputy being without a mission on the subject, he threw himself into generalities to make me perceive the appropriateness of moderation, and of requiring nothing that would humiliate England, persuaded, he said, that this would be to throw it into despair and to reduce it to the most extreme choices. I strongly assured him that the intention of the King was not to humilate England, but rather to efface all the old humilations, because His Majesty is convinced that peace cannot be solid as long as that exists in any part.

If Mr. Oswald were charged with any proposal for us, he had it for the Americans and he made of it a thing very strange to me. He announced to me that orders had been sent to the English generals on the Continent of America to keep within the posts they occupy and to abstain from committing any hostility, and he proposed to me in some manner to engage the Americans to keep to the same measures vis-à-vis the English. This view was so absurd that I had no need of an effort of imagination to disabuse him that it could be admitted. I told him in the presence of Mr. Franklin, who did not disavow me, that the armistice before the peace ought to be general, and that it could only take place in so far as the solid foundations of a peace were posed by generally accepted preliminaries.

Such is, Sir, the substance of my Conference with Mr. Oswald. He seemed satisfied with the tone of frankness and honesty that I employed here. At first he thought to dispatch a Courier to Lord Shelburne to inform him of this conversation. He turned then to thinking that it would be better if he himself went to England, and he was determined on it, hoping, he told me, that he would not be long in returning. I expedited a passport for him, and to render his voyage less painful I procured for him the facility of crossing at Calais.

I must not forget to note for you, Sir, that in discoursing on the different ways of starting a negotiation, I recalled and insisted on the idea of mediation, but it seemed to me that the wish of England is not to treat by this Channel. We shall see what will happen.

Should you wish, Sir, to relate these details to the Conde de Florida Blanca, I permit neither reflections nor foresight on what could happen. The English ministry has been in place for too little time to judge soundly of its intentions and its views. I see very well that it would doubtless be better to make peace, but even the most enlightened men do not always prefer the best. It is not rare that one goes astray.

As it may nevertheless happen that this first step may have consequences, perhaps it would be desirable that the Conde d'Aranda be authorized at least to listen to the English emissary if he returns. My confederate delicacy would suffer if I had to see him frequently alone; besides, it is good politics to show a disposition towards peace even when one thinks it the least possible.

But the hope of peace ought not to slow the operations of the War. It is more than ever a case of pressing the preparations of the Expedition against Gibraltar if it is to take place, and of bringing about a union of forces that can make the enemy feel his impotence. It will be horrible for the English, who at the moment can only bring together 22 Vessels to control the Channel and the Gulf of Gascony during the summer months.

The state of the Americans appears about decided, and their independence no longer being equivocal, it is time for the Court of Spain to appear to humor them more than it has up to now and to occupy itself with the arrangements that it may have to make with them. The Dutch have jumped at the opportunity; already six provinces have voted for the recognition of Mr. Adams in his representative character and the making of a treaty of Commerce with the United States. The accession of the Gueldres, who have still not deliberated, is not to be doubted.

Mr. Oswald is not a braggart and a charlatan of Mr. Forth's sort. He is a wise man who seems not to have even the idea of intrigues. Rich himself, devoid of ambition, he has yielded to his friendship for Lord Shelburne in coming here, and he does not claim other recompense than the glory of rendering a useful Service to his homeland and to humanity.

I have the honor to be &c.   Vergennes

FFAA: Pol. Corr., Spain, v. 606, f. 252 (LC transcription).

∞ *Dutch Recognition* ∞

On April 19, 1782, John Adams' efforts to secure recognition from the Dutch government proved successful. Their High Mightinesses the States General of the United Povinces resolved to accept Adams as the diplomatic representative of the United States. Following his recognition, Adams turned his efforts towards negotiating a treaty of amity and commerce.

Thomas Barclay to Robert R. Livingston

No. 2 Duplicate   [No earlier than 20 April 1782]
Sir,

I had the honour of Writing to you the 7th. of last Month and of stating to you some Public Events thinking that posibly my letter might give you the first account of them other ways it did not Contain any thing of the least Consequence. Since that time American Affairs here have made a Progress with a Rapidity seldom Known in Holland, and Mr. Adams was the 19th. Instant acknowledged as Minister Plenipotentiary from the United States of America. This was done amidst the greatest Efforts and Intrigues of the Court of England and the new Ministry, Mr. Adams has Exchanged some Propositions of the Treaty of Commerce with the States General, and every thing go's on with unexampled Cordiality. he has been a faithfull labourer in the Vineyard and I am happy that he has reaped the reward of his Industry.

· · · · ·

...Sir, your Most Obedient   Thos. Barclay.

NA: PCC, item 91, v. 1, pp. 5-6 (LS); M247, reel 119.

Benjamin Franklin to John Adams

Sir,   Passy, April 20th. 1782.

...With this I send a fresh Correspondence which I have been drawn into, viz: 1. A Letter I sent to Lord Shelburne before he was Minister. 2. His Ans^r. since he was Minister by Mr Oswald. 3. A Letter from Mr Lawrens. 4. My Letter to M. de Vergennes. 5. My Ans^r to Lord Shelburne. 6. My Answer to Mr Lawrens. 7th Copy of Digges's Report. These Papers will inform you pretty well of what pass'd between me and Mr Oswald, except that in a Conversation at parting I mention'd to him, that I observed they spoke much in England of obtaining a *Reconciliation* with the Colonies; that this was more than a mere *Peace*; that the latter might possibly be obtained without the former; that the cruel Injuries wantonly done us by burning our Towns &c^{a.} had made deep Impressions of Resentment which would long remain; that much of the Advantage to the Commerce of England from a Peace would depend on a *Reconciliation*; that the Peace without a Reconciliation would probably not be durable; that after a Quarrel between Friends, nothing tended so much to *conciliate*, as Offers made by the Aggressor, of Reparation for Injuries done by him in his Passion. And I hinted that if England should make us a *Voluntary Offer* of Canada expressly for that purpose, it might have a good Effect. Mr Oswald liked much the Idea, said they were too much straiten'd for Money to make us pecuniary Reparation, but he should endeavour to persuade their doing it in this Way. He is furnish'd with a Passport to go and return by Calais, and I expect him back in ten or twelve Days. I wish you and Mr Lawrens could be here when he arrives; for I shall much want your Advice, & cannot act without your Concurrence. If the present Crisis of your Affairs prevents your coming, I hope at least Mr Lawrens will be here, and we must communicate with you by Expresses, for your Letters to me p^r Post are generally open'd. I shall write p^{r.} next Post requesting Mr Jay to be here also as soon as possible.

. . . . . .

With great Esteem, I have the honour to be, Sir, Your Excellency's most obedient & most humble Ser^t: B Franklin

If Mr Laurens has left Holland, please to seal his Letter with a Wafer and let it follow him.

I shall be glad to have again all the Papers of this and the former Packet; but you can keep Copies of any you may think worth the Trouble ans^d May 2. rec^d May 1.

MHS: *The Adams Papers, microfilm reel 356 (LS).*

Benjamin Franklin to Henry Laurens

Sir,   Passy, April 20th. 1782.

I received by Mr Oswald the Letter you did me the honour of writing to me the 7th Inst. He brought me also a Letter from Lord Shelburne, which gave him the same good Character that you do, adding "He is fully appriz'd of my Mind, and you may give full Credit to every thing he assures you of." Mr Oswald, however, could give me no other Particulars of his Lordships Mind, but that he was sincerely disposed to Peace. As the Message seem'd therefore rather intended to procure or receive Propositions than to make any, I told Mr Oswald that I could make none but in Concurrence with my Colleagues in the Commission; and that if we were together we should not treat but in Conjunction with France; and I proposed introducing him to M. De Vergennes, which he accepted. He made to that Minister the same Declaration of the Disposition of England, to Peace; who reply'd that France had assuredly the same good Dispositions; that a Treaty might be immediately begun, but it must be for a *general*, not a *particular* Peace: That as to the Place, he thought Paris might be the most convenient, as Spain had here already an Ambassador, and the American Commissioners could easily be assembled here; this upon the Supposition of the Parties treating directly with each other, without the Intervention of Mediators: But if the Mediation was to be used, it might be at Vienna. The King his Master however was so truly disposed to Peace, that he would agree to any Place that the King of England should chuse: and would at the Treaty give Proof of the Confidence that might be placed in any Engagements he should then enter into, by the Fidelity & Exactitude with which he should observe those he already had with his present Allies. Mr Oswald is returned with these general Answers, by the Way of Calais, and expects to be here again in a few Days. I wish it might be convenient for you and Mr Adams to be here at the same time. But if the present critical Situation of Affairs there make his being in Holland necessary just now, I hope you may nevertheless be here, bringing with you his Opinion & Advice. I have proposed to Lord Shelburne to discharge you from the Obligations you enter'd into at the time of your Enlargement, that you may act more freely in the Treaty he desires. I had done myself the Honour of writing to you a few days before the Arrival of Mr Oswald. My Letter went by Mr Young,[1] your Secretary, and inclosed a Copy of our Commission, with an Offer of Money if you had occasion for any. Hoping that you will not return to England before you have been at Paris, I forbear enlarging on the State of our Affairs here and in Spain. M. de Vergennes told me he should be very glad to see you here. I found Mr Oswald to answer perfectly the Character you gave me of him, & was much pleased with him.

I have the honour to be with great Esteem, Sir, Your Excellency's most obedient & most humble Servant   B Franklin

Recd 10th. May [1782]

South Carolina Historical Society: Henry Laurens Papers (LS).
[1] Young, Moses. *Government clerk, secretary. Clerk in Secretary of Congress Charles Thomson's office, 1777. Assistant paymaster to the Board of War, 1778. Secretary to Henry Laurens, October 1779-May 1782.*

Benjamin Franklin to John Adams

Sir,   Passy April 21. 1782.

I have just received the Honour of yours dated the 16th. Instant, acquainting me with the Interview between your Excellency and Mr. Lawrens. I am glad to learn that his political Sentiments coincide with ours; and that there is a Disposition in England to give us up Canada and Nova Scotia.

I like your Idea of seeing no more Messengers that are not Plenipotentiaries; But I cannot refuse seeing again Mr. Oswald, as the Minister here consider'd the Letter to me from Lord Shelburne as a kind of Authentication given that Messenger, and expects his Return with some explicit Propositions. I shall keep you advised of whatever passes.

.   .   .   .   .

With great Respect, I am, Sir, Your Excellency's most obedient and most humble Ser t.   B. Franklin

MHS: The Adams Papers, microfilm reel 356 (LS).

Benjamin Franklin to John Jay

Dear Sir,   Passy, April 22. 1782.

I have undertaken to pay all the Bills of your Acceptance that have come to my knowledge, and I hope in God no more will be drawn upon us, but when Funds are first provided. In that Case your constant Residence at Madrid is no longer so necessary. You may make a Journey either for Health or Pleasure without retarding the Progress of a Negociation not yet begun. Here you are greatly wanted, for Messengers begin to come & go, and there is much talk of a Treaty proposed, but I can neither make or agree to Propositions of Peace without the Assistance of my Colleagues. Mr. Adams

I am afraid cannot just now leave Holland; Mr Jefferson is not in Europe, and Mr Lawrens is a Prisoner, tho' abroad on Parole. I wish therefore that you would resolve upon the Journey, and render yourself here as soon as possible. You would be of infinite Service. Spain has taken four Years to consider whether she should treat with us or not. Give her Forty. And let us in the mean time mind our own Business. I have much to communicate to you but chuse rather to do it *vivâ voce*, than trust it to Letters. — I am ever, my Dear Friend, Yours most affectionately   B Franklin
Rec^d 3 May 1782

Windsor Castle Library: Selected Papers of John Jay, LC microfilm reel 11415 (ALS).

John Adams to Robert R. Livingston

N° 9.   Hague April 23. 1782
Sir,
    On the 23 of April, I had the Honour of a Conference with Mr Van Citters,[1] President of their High Mightinesses, to whom I presented the following Memorial.
                    Hauts & Puissants Seigneurs
Le Soussigné, Ministre Plenipotentiaire des Etats Unis de L'Amerique a L'honneur d'informer Vos Hauts Puissances, qu'il est chargé par les Instructions de Son Souverain, de proposer aux Etats Generaux des Provinces-Unies des Pays-Bas, un Traité d'Amitié et de Commerce entre les deux Republiques, fondé sur le Principe d'un Avantage égal et reciproque, et compatible avec les Engagemens déjà pris par les Etats Unis avec leurs Allies, ainsi qu'avec tels autres Traités qu'ils ont l'Intention de former avec d'autres Puissances. En Consequence, le Soussigné a l'honneur to proposer à Vos Hauts Puissances de nommer quelque Personne ou Personnes, avec Pleins pouvoirs de conferer et traiter avec lui, Sur cet important Sujet.⊛

                              a la Haye 23. Avril 1782
                              Signe John Adams

    Their High Mightinesses, on the Same day, appointed a grand Committee to treat, to whom I was introduced with great Formality by two Noblemen, and before whom I laid a Project of a Treaty, which I had drawn up, conformably to the Instructions of Congress. - I prayed the Gentlemen to examine it, and propose to me their Objections if they should have any, and to propose any further Articles which they should think proper. it has been examined, translated printed and sent to the

Members of the Sovereignty.

The greatest Part of my Time, for several Days has been taken up, in receiving and paying of Visits, from all the Members and Officers of Government, and of the Court, to the Amount of 150 or more.

I have the Honor to be, &c.   J. Adams

⊗ High and Mighty Lords

The underwritten, Minster Plenipotentiary of the United States of America, has the Honor to inform your High Mightinesses, that he is charged by the Instructions of his Sovereign to propose to the States General of the United Provinces of the Netherlands, a Treaty of Amity and Commerce between the two Republics, founded upon the Principle of equal & reciprocal Advantage, & compatible with the Engagements already entered into by the U. States with their allies, as also with such other Treaties, which they design to form with other Powers. The undersigned has therefore the Honor to propose that your H. M. would nominate some Person or Persons with full Powers, to confer & treat with him on this important Subject.

NA: PCC, Misc, Papers, Adams Despatches; M332, reel 1, ff. 563-565. For translation of French passage, see NA: PCC, item 104, v. 4, p. 91 (LBkC); M247, reel 131.

¹ Citters, Willem van. Dutch political figure. President of the States General in April 1782.

John Adams to Robert R. Livingston

Sir   Hague 23ᵈ April 1782

I ought not to omit to inform Congress, that on the 23ᵈ of April the French Ambassador made an Entertainment for the whole Corps Diplomatick, in Honor of the United States, at which he introduced their Minister to all the foreign Ministers at this Court.

There is nothing I suppose in the whole voluminous Ceremonial, nor in the idle Farce of Etiquette, which should hinder a Minister from making a good Dinner in good Company; and therefore I believe they were all present, and I assure you I was myself as happy as I should have been, if I had been publicly acknowledged a Minister by every one of them: and the Duke de la Vauguyon more than compensated for all the Stiffness of some others, by paying more Attention to the new Brother, than to all the old Fraternity.

Etiquette, when it becomes too glaringly Affectation, imposes no longer neither upon the Populace nor upon the Courtiers, but becomes ridiculous to all. This will soon be the Case every where with Respect to American Ministers.

To see a Minister of such a State as blank and blank assume a distant misterious Air towards a Minister of the United States, because his Court has not yet acknowledged their Independence, when his Nation is not half equal to America in any one Attribute of Sovereignty, is a Spectacle of Ridicule to any Man who sees it.

I have had the honor of making & receiving Visits in a private Character from the Spanish Minister[1] here, whose Behaviour has been polite enough. He was pleased to make me some very high Compliments upon our Success here, which he considers as the most important and decisive Stroke which could have been struck in Europe.

I have the Honor to be Sir your most obedient and most humble Servant

J. Adams

NA: PCC, item 84, v. 4, pp. 77-78 (LS); M247, reel 112.

[1] Llano y de la Quadra, Sebastián de, Conde de Sanafé y Vizconde de Llano. Spanish diplomat. Minister to the United Provinces of the Netherlands, 1780-1793.

Robert R. Livingston to John Jay

N°· 7   Philadelphia 27th· Apl· 1782
Dr· Sir,

. . . . .

Acquainted with the expectations of Congress, and the grounds on which they formed them, you will easily believe, that they are equally surprised and concerned, at the little attention hitherto shewn by Spain to their respectful solicitations....I would not have you infer from what has been said, that the favourable sentiments, which the United States have hitherto entertained of the Court of Madrid, has undergone the least alteration. They are satisfied that nothing would be more injurious to both Nations, than to permit the seeds of distrust or jealousy to be sown among them.

But tho' those who are well informed feel no abatement of respect or esteem for the virtue and magnaminity of his Majesty, and do full justice to the integrity and abilities of his Ministers, accepting the apologies you mention and attributing to their true causes, the delays and neglects you have unhappily experienced, yet they are in the utmost pain, lest they should work some change in the sentiments of the people at large in whom with us the sovereignty resides, and from thence diffuse themselves into the Government, and be productive of Measures ruinous to that friendly intercourse, that spirit of amity which it is the wish of those who are acquainted with the true interests of both Countries to promote.

. . . . .

I persuade myself therefore, that Spain will not risk the loss of so important an object, as the exclusive Navigation of the Mississippi by postponing the treaty to a general peace, more particularly as a treaty with us will secure our concurrence in their views at a general Congress, as well as save them the necessity of making demands inconsistent with that character for Moderation, which their great power renders important to them.

Congress flatter themselves that the surmises on this subject are groundless, and that before this reaches you, the treaty will be far advanced. Should they be mistaken, you will take measures to know from Spain, whether she accepts your concession as the price of an alliance, and upon what terms — If they are such as you cannot close with, and the treaty must break off, be persuaded that any steps you have taken or shall take, not inconsistent with the respect due to his Catholic Majesty to prevent the cessions you are impowered to make, from militating against our rights, will be approved by Congress.

· · · · ·

I have the Honor to be &c   Rob⁺ R. Livingston

NA: PCC, *item 79, v. 1, pp 409-416 (LBkC); M247, reel 105.*

Robert R. Livingston to John Jay

Dear Sir,   Philadelphia, 28 April 1782

You will receive with this, a letter dated yesterday. Reasons which need not be explained induce me TO MAKE THIS A SEPARATE DISPATCH.[1] I beleive with you, that the COURT OF MADRID DOES NOT WISH TO enter into engagements with [us] during the war, influenced as I presume not only by the reasons you suggest, which our late success must have weakened, but by another that ALARMS ME MORE. THEY APPEAR TO EXTEND THEIR views TO THE COUNTRY ON THIS SIDE OF THE Mississippi AND TO ENTERTAIN [hopes] OF HOLDING IT IN VIRTURE OF THEIR LATE CONQUEST. THEY PRESUME that the acceptance of OUR CESSION WOULD MILITATE AGAINST THEIR FURTHER CLAIM, and BE CONSIDERED AS AN ACKNOWLEDGMENT OF OUR RIGHT TO ALL WE DO NOT CEDE.

It is not improbable that they are acquainted with the POWER WHICH THE COURT OF FRANCE WILL HAVE OVER THE negotiations FOR PEACE. They may build much upon THEIR FRIENDSHIP, AND EXPECT to obtain through it MORE THAN WE WILL YIELD. Should you believe these apprehensions to [be] well founded, you will doubtless endeavour to shew on every proper occasion THE RIGHT OF THESE STATES TO ALL THE COUNTRY IN QUESTION. You will urge the right, if Conquest can give any, which may be derived from WILLING'S.[2] You will judge how far it may be expedient to ground demands on the right we have to a compensation for our Share of the Burden and expence of the war, if the issue should be as favorable as we have reason to expect. Our Strength is so much underated in Europe that you will find it proper to represent it, as it really is. Our regular Army including the French Troops will consist of about TWENTY THOUSAND men. They are well disciplined, cloathed and fed and having for the most part seen a seven years hard service, I believe they may be counted equal to any Troops in the world. Our Militia are in excellent order and chiefly disciplined by Officers, who have left the regular service. While the Army lies in the middle States it can in ten or fifteen days receive a reinforcement of EIGHT OR TEN THOUSAND men for any particular service. Facts that you can easily call to mind will evince that any deficiency in the regular Corps is amply made up by this supply. These are loose hints by no means directory to you. Congress mean[s] as little as possible to clog you with instructions. They rely upon your judgement and address to reconcile whatever differences may appear to be between the views of Spain, and the interest of these States.

...I have the honor to be Dear Sir, with great respect and esteem your most obedient humble servant,   Rob. R. Livingston

Morris, Jay Papers, v. 2, pp. 163-164; NYHS: John Jay Papers, Box 1.
¹ *Capitalized material encyphered in the original.*
² *James Willing, a captain in the U.S. Navy, raided West Florida in 1778.*

John Jay to Robert R. Livingston

Dear Sir,   Madrid 28th. April 1782.

. . . . .

On the 30th. March I was surprised by the following Note, being the first of the kind which I have received from the Minister since my Arrival.

. . . . .

The Count de Florida Blanca has been to take the Orders of V. S.® for Aranjuez, where he hopes to have the Honor of the Company of V. S. at his Table every Saturday after the 11th. of May next ensuing.

This Invitation is imputable to the late News from England, and the grant of six Millions by France was probably accelerated by it. Both Courts are watching and Jealous of us. We are at Peace with Spain, and she neither will nor indeed can grant us a present Subsidy. Why then should we be anxious for a Treaty with her, or make Sacrifices to purchase it? We cannot now treat with her on terms of equality, Why therefore not postpone it? It would not perhaps be wise to break with her; but delay is in our power, and resentment ought to have no Influence. Time would Secure advantages to us, which we should now be obliged to yield. Time is more friendly to Young, than to Old nations, and the Day will come when our Strength will Insure our Rights: Justice may hold the Balance and decide, but if unarmed Wil for the most part be treated like a Blind Woman. There is no doubt that Spain requires more Cessions than England, unless extremely humbled can consent to. France knows, and fears this. France is ready for a Peace, but not Spain. The King's Eyes are fixed on Gibraltar. The Spanish Finances indeed are extremely mismanaged, and I may say pillaged. If England should offer us peace on the terms of our Treaty with France, the French Court would be very much embarrassed by their Alliance with Spain, and as yet we are under no obligations to persist in the war to gratify this Court. It is not certain what England will do, nor ought we to rely on the present promising appearances there; But can it be wise to instruct your Commissioners to speak only as the French Ministers shall give them utterance? Let whatever I write about the French and their Ambassador here, be by all means kept Secret. – Marbois gleans and details every scrap of news – His Letters are very minute, and detail names and Characters. Sweeden is leaning towards us, and it will not be long before the Dutch become our allies. Under such Circumstances Spain ought not to expect such a Price as the Mississippi for acknowledging our Independence.

. . . . .

You may observe from the Copy of the Count De Florida Blanca's Note, containing an Invitation to his Table at Aranjuez and left at my House by his Servant, that it was not expressly directed to me. This omission raised some Doubt in my Mind of its being intended for me, but on Inquiry I found that the other Ministers had, in the same Manner, received similar ones, and not directed to them by Name. I mentioned my having received it to the Ambassador of France – He told me the Count had not mentioned a Syllable of it to him. I desired him to take an Opportunity of discovering from the Count, whether or no there was any Mistake in the Case, and to inform me of the Result, which he promised to do.

On the 23ᵈ April Instant, the Ambassador being then in Town, I paid him a Visit. He told me, that on mentioning the matter to the Count, he said it must have happened by Mistake, for that he intended only to ask my Orders for Aranjues, but that he was nevertheless glad the Mistake had happened, as it would give him an opportunity, by mentioning it to the King to obtain his Permission for the Purpose, and to that End desired the Ambassador to write him a Note stating the Fact. The Ambassador did so, and the Count afterwards informed him that he had communicated it to the King, who with many Expressions of Regard for our Country, had permitted him to *invite me as a private Gentleman of Distinction belonging to it*. He authorized the Ambassador to communicate this Invitation to me, and also to inform me that I might bring Mr Carmichael with me.

Much Conversation ensued between the Ambassador and myself, consisting of my Objections to accepting this Invitation, and his Answers to them. But as we continued to differ in Sentiment and he was going out, I agreed to think further of the Matter before I gave my final Answer.

For my Part, I doubt there having been any mistake. I think it more probable, that the Minister, afterwards reflecting on the Use that might be made of this Note, wished to render it harmless by imputing it to mistake, and substituting a more cautious Invitation: For it can hardly be supposed, either that his Servant would, for the first Time in two Years, leave such a Note at my House, unless ordered; or that he himself would for the first Time in his Life, and that in Writing, inform me of his having called to take my Orders for Aranjuez, without taking Care that his amanuensis wrote as he dictated. He was probably warmed by the news from England and Holland, and in the Perturbation of Spirits occasioned by it, was more Civil than on cool Reflection he thought was expedient, especially on further considering that the Ambassador might not be well pleased at not having been privy to it.

A few Days afterwards I wrote the Ambassador the following Letter on the Subject.

Sir,   Madrid 27th April 1782.

Be pleased to accept my Thanks for the very friendly Part you have acted relative to the Minister's written Invitation left at my House, and the verbal one since conveyed from him to me by your Excellency. I have deliberately re-examined my former Sentiments respecting the Propriety of accepting it; and as they remain unaltered, my Respect for your Judgment, leads me to refer them, fully explained, to your further Consideration.

As the Minister informed your Excellency that the written Invitation was left at my House by mistake, I think nothing remains to be said relative to it. On the discovery of that mistake, the Minister it seems was so obliging as to apply for, and obtain the Consent of the King, to renew the Invitation, not in general Terms, but in terms expressly declaring that it was given to me as a private Gentleman, and was to be accepted; with the additional Favor nevertheless of being permitted to bring Mr Carmichael with me.

The only Objection which opposes my accepting it, arises from this Question, Viz^t Whether a Minister or Representative of an independent Sovereign, can with the Propriety accept any Invitation, which in the Terms of it, impeaches his Title to that Character? So far as this Question respects the Ministers of independent States and Kingdoms in general, your

Excellency will agree with me in Opinion, that it must be answered in the Negative....

.   .   .   .   .

Reasons similar to those assigned for this Refusal, have induced me ever since my arrival, to decline going to Court where I might also have been presented as a Stranger of Distinction, but as M^r· Carmichael had been presented in that Character previous to my coming to Madrid, I never objected to his making subsequent Visits.

I am, Dear Sir, With great Regard and Esteem, Your most Obedient and Very humble Servant,   John Jay

[⊗] Vuestra Senoria We have no title that exactly corresponds with this.

NA: PCC, item 110, v. 2, pp. 7-132 (LBkC); M247, reel 135.

Congressional Resolution Approving
John Jay's Conduct in Spain

[Philadelphia] Tuesday April 30. 1782.

On a motion of Mr Madison...

Resolved That the minister plenipotentiary of the United States at the court of Madrid be informed that Congress entirely approve of his conduct as detailed in his letter of the 3^d of Oct^r· last: that the limitation affixed by him to the proposed surrender of the navigation of the Mississippi in particular corresponds with the views of Congress: that they observe not without surprize and concern, that a proposition so liberal in itself and which removed the only avowed obstacle to a connection between the United States and his Catholic Majesty, should not have produced greater effects on the counsels of the latter: that the surrender of the navigation of the Mississippi was meant as the price of the advantages promised by an early and intimate alliance with the Spanish Monarchy; and that if this alliance is to be procrastinated till the conclusion of the war, the reason of the sacrifice will no longer exist: that as every day which the proposed treaty is delayed detracts from the obligation and inducement of the United States to adhere to their overture, it is the instruction of Congress that he urge to the Ministers of his Catholic Majesty the obligation it imposes on Spain to make the treaty the more liberal on her part, and that in particular he use his endeavours to obtain in consideration of such delay either an enlargement of her pecuniary aids to the United States, a facilitating of the Use of the Mississippi to the citizens thereof or some peculiar indulgences in the commerce of the Spanish colonies in America.—

NA: PCC, item 4, pp. 145-146 (Journal); M247, reel 18.

Charles James Fox's Draft of Instructions to Thomas Grenville

[No 1]   St. James's April 30. 1782
Mʳ· Grenville[1]
Sir

Although from the conversation we have had together upon the objects of your Journey to Paris, I have no doubt but you are perfectly master of the line of conduct which you are wished to follow there: yet as it may be a satisfaction to you to have some written instructions upon the subject, I am commanded by His Majesty to acquaint you that it is his pleasure that you should proceed in the following manner. When you arrive at Paris you will endeavour to see Mʳ Oswald as soon as possible who will probably have announced your arrival, & from whom you may possibly collect whether the sentiments of Mons de Vergennes & Dʳ Franklin continue to be the same as they appeared to him in the first interview he had with them. You will then go to Mons de Vergennes with whom your conversation will be more or less open, as you find him (either from previous information or otherwise) more or less inclined to entertain sentiments favourable to the object of your Journey. You will first of all assure him of H. M's sincere & ardent wishes for the blessings of a general Peace, and acquaint him that in order to save the effusion of human blood His M. wishes the time & place of treating to be those which are most likely to bring matters to a speedy issue. With this View you will name Paris provided it can be so managed as to give no cause of offence to the courts of Vienna & Petersburgh. With respect to time you will inform him that you are ready to send over hither for plenipotentiary powers whenever matters shall appear to be ripe for such a measure. These things being settled you will naturally propose to him to state to you some general outlines of his ideas upon the subject of general pacification which if he should refuse, as there is too much reason to suppose he will, you will naturally enough be led to throw out yours; but with what degree of authority you are to state them, whether as merely your own, or as those which from your intimacy & confidence with me you know me to share in common with you, or as those of His Majesty & his Ministers, must be left entirely to your discretion, which will of course be guided in a great measure by what you see & hear upon the spot, & by the degree of sincerity which you suppose to be in Mons de Vergennes's pacific professions. As to the manner therefore you are to judge, but the substance must be this: That His Majesty is willing to cede to His Most Christian Majesty and his Allies, the point which they have at various times & upon various occasions declared to be *the subject of the War* & particularly in the last answer from the Court of Versailles to the mediating Courts; that is to say, to accede to the complete Independency of the thirteen American States and in order to make the Peace; if it should take place, solid & durable to cede to the said states the towns of New York & Charlestown together with the Province of Georgia including the town of Savannah, all which are still in His Majesty's Possession, provided that in all other respects such a general & reciprocal restitution shall take place in every quarter of the Globe on the part of the belligerent Powers as shall restore things to the state they were placed in by the treaty of Paris 1763. When this is stated as the Basis of the intended treaty, you will of course understand & explain if necessary that it does not exclude any exchanges of Possessions which may be made to the mutual satisfaction of both the Parties. You will not fail to dwell upon the importance of those places which we should be to restore upon such a treaty taking Place. The acquisitions in the E. Indies, St. Pierre & Miquelon, places so necessary to their fisheries, and above all $S^{te.}$ Lucie must be principally insisted upon. The importance of this last can scarcely be exaggerated beyond the opinion which I have reason to think they entertain upon the subject. After having seen Mons de Vergennes you will go to $D^{r.}$ Franklin, to whom you will hold the same language as to the former, and as far as his Country is concerned there can be no difficulty in shewing him that there is no longer any subject of dispute & that if unhappily this treaty should break off his Countrymen will be engaged in a War in which they can have no interest whatever either immediate or remote. It will be very material that, during your stay at Paris, & in the various opportunities you may have of conversing with this Gentleman, you should endeavour to discover whether, if the treaty should break off or be found impracticable on account of points in which America has no concern, there may not in that case be a prospect of a separate Peace between G. Britain & America, which after such an event must be so evidently for the mutual interests of both Countries, As the *direct* object of your journey at present is rather to fix the time & place of a treaty than to treat, it is not certainly *necessary* that you should communicate with the Count d' Aranda in this stage of the business; but whether it may not be adviseable is a question of some doubt, & perhaps you can not do better than to consult the French Minister upon the subject. This Step will be attended with this advantage at least, that it will take away all suspicion of our attempting any separate peace with Spain, &

shew a degree of confidence which is always useful in business. I need not say that it is H. M.'s wish to have as frequent & exact accounts as may be of any thing material that may pass between you & any of those with whom you are instructed to treat, as well as any interesting intelligence you may be able to procure with respect to the state of the French Cabinet, & the influence that most prevails there. I have nothing further to add but to acquaint you that H. M. relies with the utmost confidence upon your abilities for the dexterous management of a Business upon which the situation of this country may so much depend.

I have the honour to be &.c.   Charles James Fox

P.S. It may not be amiss if your first Introduction to Mons.r de Vergennes should be through D.r Franklin himself, with whom you may have as much previous conversation as you may think adviseable.

British Public Record Office: Foreign Office Files, Foreign Correspondence, France, hereafter cited as PRO: FO 27/2, v. 557, f. 83 (LC transcription).

¹ *Grenville, Thomas (1755-1846). Member of Parliament, 1780-1818, with few interruptions. Initiated European negotiations to end war, 1782. Subsequent diplomatic assignments to Austria, 1794, and Prussia, 1798. First Lord of the Admiralty, 1806-1807.*

Robert R. Livingston to the Governors of the States

Sir   Office of foreign affairs, Philadelphia 2nd of May 1782
    The enclosed resolution of Congress will explain the cause of this Letter – The information it refers to, is an assurance of the [fact] that Britain has absolutely declined any interference of the mediating powers between them & what they call their rebel subjects – They persist on every occasion in representing us as a divided people who anxiously wish to return to our connection with England – In this they have two objects equally important to them – 1st. They encourage England to continue a War which they expect to see terminated by our own weariness & languor and 2dly. They put such a face upon their affairs as will entitle them on a negotiation to make demands at our expence which they would not presume to think of if the Mediators were acquainted with our firm resolution never to return to our obedience to their government. – Besides which, they cast a degree of odium upon the conduct of France, representing it as the support of a discontented faction, rather than as the generous ally of an oppressed nation – There is reason to apprehend that in order the better to secure the advantages of this deceitful Policy to themselves they will make proffers to each of the United States, if any of them should listen to them (which

cannot however be presumed) they will urge that as a proof of their assertions — if they should even decline receiving their proposals, and refer them to Congress, as from the nature of our Union, they undoubtedly must — still as the result of the experiment cannot be known for some time in Europe — they will avail themselves ~~in some measure~~ of it, in part if negotiations should open — This Artifice of the Enemy may be counteracted in two ways, both deserve the serious attention of your Legislature, the first and most important is by making such exertions to procure a respectable Army early in the Season, that the Mediators casting their Eyes upon the muster rolls may there read a full refutation of all that british Artifice can suggest, (I need not observe that this measure must go hand in hand with taxation, since an Army without the means of supporting them would only increase our evils). The second is to anticipate the attempts of Great Britain by such Resolutions as the information contained in this letter suggests — Resolutions which strongly mark a spirited determination in the Legislature of each State to listen to no negotiations except thro' the intervention of Congress, which manifest their Attachment to the Independance of their Country inviolable regard to the faith they have pledged to each other, and to their Allies — These may either prevent the attempt I apprehend, or arrive in time to counteract this effect, which the false expectations built thereon might otherwise have in Europe — I mention this to Your Excellency without any express direction from Congress — it is more than probable that your Judgement, and the Zeal and wisdom of the Legislature may improve these loose hints to the general advantage of the United States — I have the pleasure of assuring your Excellency and the Legislature that the fairest prospects are now before us of terminating the war by a single exertion, tho' I am not at liberty to say that the plan of the ensuing Campaign is absolutely determined on, yet I have great reason to believe, that we shall receive such powerful military Aid, as with becoming exertions on our part will free every State in the Union from the grasp of the Enemy — Here Sir, I might pause and suffer my imagination to dwell upon the animating prospect before us — But reasoning from the past to the future, I dare not indulge the pleasing idea, we have at no period been in a situation to second fully the endeavours of our Ally to serve us — we either neglected to assemble our Army in time, or to provide the means for supporting or moving them — A feather would have turned the ballance last year, notwithstanding the powerful Aid we received from abroad — Providence blinded our Adversary — to their temerity we owe our success — But Sir let me ask, whether any State did then, or has even now done all in its power to enable our Generals to prosecute this victory? or rather let me turn to what is more within my line, by observing that the inferiority of our Army in point of numbers to that of [our] Ally while they acted at

Yorktown, has been considered in Europe as a proof of the assertions of Britain – has been urged as an argument of our weakness, our weariness of the war, or our internal divisions – A Moments reflection will shew the advantages that this Affords our Antagonist in a negotiation. How much it weakens the claims we make, and how many important Benefits may be lost forever by our appearing in Europe to receive our Independance rather as a Gift than to have established it by our exertions – But sir, it is still in our power to repair these errors, let us avail ourselves of this favorable moment for expelling the Enemy, and recovering our diminished credit among the nations of the Earth – I make no appology for the liberty I take. Your Excellency I am persuaded is too sensible of the truth of these observations to think they cou'd be delivered with less earnestness by one who feels their importance, and I am confident that you will bring them before the Legislature of your State in such manner as will best serve to ensure them their attention – I have the honor to be, with the greatest Respect and Esteem Your Excellency's most Obed^t· humble servant

Robt· R Livingston

NA: PCC, item 119, pp. 96-103 (LBkC); M247, reel 139.

John Adams to Benjamin Franklin

Sir, Amsterdam, May 2^d 1782.

. . . . .

M^r· Laurens and M^r· Jay will, I hope, be able to meet at Paris, but when it will be in my Power to go I know not. Your present Negotiation about Peace falls in very well to aid a Proposition which I am instructed to make, as soon as the Court of Versailles shall judge proper, of a triple or quadruple Alliance. This Matter, the Treaty of Commerce, which is now under Deliberation, and the Loan, will render it improper for me to quit this Station, unless in Case of Necessity. If there is a real Disposition to permit Canada to accede to the american Association, I should think there would be no great Difficulty in adjusting all Things between England and America, provided our Allies are contented too. In a former Letter, I hinted that I thought an express acknowledgment of our Independence might now be insisted on: but I did not mean that we should insist upon such an Article in the Treaty. If they make a Treaty of Peace with the United States of america, this is acknowledgment enough for me....

. . . . .

I have the Honor to be, &c. John Adams.

NA: PCC, item 100, v. 1, pp. 387-390 (LBkC); M247, reel 127.

Comte de Vergennes to the Duc de la Vauguyon

[Translation]

N⁰ 7   Versailles, 5 May 1782

M. le D. de la Vauguyon

. . . . .

The recognition of Mr. Adams' character destroys at its Source the System of peacemaking proposed by Mr. Fox, and irrevocably binds the Republic's cause to that of the King; in admitting the contrary supposition, it would be necessary also to admit that the States-General have only recognized the independence of America in order to have the gratuitous shame of disavowing it. This reflection will surely not escape the Empress of Russia, and it will have prepared that Power for the negative resolution that the States-General are on the point of approving on the allegedly pacific office of its two ministers.

If this resolution is such that it has been delayed by the States of Holland, it will leave nothing to desire on the principal question, and we can only applaud it, although it increases our perplexity relative to the proposed entente. If the course to take depended on us alone, the uncertainty of the States-General would soon be dissipated; but we have an ally without which we cannot and should not dispose of the common forces. I await with great impatience the last courier that I sent to Madrid, because I hope that he will report a satisfactory solution. You may, from now on, Sir, assure M. le Stadhouder[1] and Mr. Van der hop[2] that the combined fleet will soon put to sea — that it will certainly be stronger than that of England; that it will establish its cruising ground from the entrance to the Mediterranean up to the Channel, and that it will only withdraw when the Season or some other unforeseen cause forces it to do so. It follows from these facts, Sir, that the English will have only very mediocre forces in the North Sea, and that the Dutch may send their squadron into that sea without difficulty and send their merchant ships into the Baltic. I beseech you, Sir, to make use of these observations; I think them proper to calm M. le Stadhouder, and not to give us time to receive the response from the Court of Madrid. Apply yourself especially, Sir, to making that prince perceive that such is the Station of our squadrons that they will force that of England to remain united and to place itself in the West or even to move towards the South. We shall have at least 40 vessels, and if I am well informed, it is impossible for England to bring together 25. You may appreciate by that the significance of the squadron which that Power might have cruising in the North.

I have reported to the King, Sir, the overture that some Patriots have made to you relative to renewing the commercial ties between France and the United Provinces. His Majesty is not far from yielding to the desires which the United States will make known to him in this regard, and you may, if you judge it fitting, confide this disposition to the persons who have sounded you out; you will observe to them at the same time that the Republic will find in the treaty made with the Americans the principles that will serve as the basis for what may be done with it: justice and reciprocity will be the essential bases of it. In addition, Sir, I think that it will be fitting to fathom the dispositions of the Dutch relative to the treaties both of alliance and of commerce that existed between the Republic and Great Britain: you will perceive for yourself that it would be suitable neither to the King's dignity nor to the interest of his Crown to lavish his favors on the Dutch if they should, at the peace, again take up the yoke of Great Britain.

· · · · ·

Vergennes

FFAA: Pol. Corr., Holland, v. 549, f. 10 (LC transcription).
¹ Willem V, Prince of Orange and Nassau (1748-1806). Stadhouder of the United Provinces of the Netherlands, 1751-1795.
² Hoop (Hope), Joan Cornelis van der. Dutch political figure. Financial counsellor of the College of the Admiralty in Amsterdam.

Benjamin Franklin to John Adams

N° 16.   Passy, May 8ᵗʰ· 1782.
Sir,

Mʳ· Oswald, whom I mentioned in a former Letter, which I find you have received, is returned and brought me another Letter from Lord Shelburne,¹ of which the above is a Copy. It says Mʳ· Oswald is instructed to communicate to me his Lordship's Thoughts. He is, however, very sparing of such Communicaton. All I have got from him, is, that the Ministry have in Contemplation, the allowing Independence to America on Condition of Britain being put again into the State she was left in by the Peace of 1763 "which, I suppose, means being put again in Possession of the Islands France has taken from her." This seems to me a Proposition of selling to us a Thing that is already our own, and making France pay the Price they are pleased to ask for it. Mʳ· Grenville, who is sent by Mʳ· Fox, is expected here daily; Mʳ· Oswald tells me that Mʳ· Laurens will soon be here also.

· · · · ·

With great Respect, I am, Sir, &c.   B. Franklin

NA: PCC item 100, v. 1, pp. 401-402 (LBkC); M 247, reel 127.
    [1] Lord Shelburne to Benjamin Franklin, 6 April 1782 (NA: PCC, item 100, v. 1, pp. 360-361; M247, reel 127).

John Jay to Benjamin Franklin

Dear Sir   Madrid 8[th.] May 1782
    I have rec[d.] your Favors of the 22 & 23 Ult. They have determined me to set out for Paris. I shall leave this Place the latter End of next Week. M[rs.] Jay & my Nephew go with me. Be pleased to take Lodgings for me, and to inform me of them, by a Line to M[r] Delap[1] or M[r] Bondfield[2] at Bordeaux
    The Embassador of France does not dislike this Step, and the Count de Florida Blanca will refer the Instructions intended for ~~the~~ M[r.] Del Campo, to the Count de Aranda at Paris.
    I am Dear Sir with great Regard & Esteem Your obliged & obed[t.] Servant,   John Jay

University of Pennsylvania, Van Pelt Library: Special Collections (ALS).
    [1] *Delap, John Hans. One of the members of the Bourdeaux merchant house of S. & J.H. Delap, which served as U.S. commercial agents. The firm sold one of the prizes taken by John Paul Jones' Ranger.*
    [2] *Bondfield, John (fl. 1775-1790). Montreal merchant who provided supplies to American forces retreating from Canada in early 1776. He resettled at Bordeaux in 1777, and the following year was appointed Amercian commercial agent for Bordeaux and several other French ports. Although he never held a formal diplomatic or consular position, he remained a strong supporter of American interests throughout the 1780s.*

Robert R. Livingston to John Jay

No. 9.   Philad[a.] 9[th.] May 1782
D[r.] Sir,

                    . . . . . .

    Since my last of the 28[th.] of April, we have been informed of the change in the British Administration, have seen the act for enabling the King to make peace, and the new plan has begun to open itself here under the direction of Sir Guy Carleton.[1] You who know your Countrymen will feel little anxiety on this subject, it is proper however, that you should be enabled to calm the apprehensions which those, who know us less, and are interested in our Measures, may entertain. I have the pleasure of assuring you that it has not produced the slightest alteration in our sentiments, that we view a change of Men and measures with the most philosophic indifference – We believe that God has hardened the heart of Pharaoh, so that he cannot let the people go, till the first-born of his land are destroyed, 'till the hosts are overthrown in the midst of the sea, and till poverty and distress like the lice of Egypt shall have covered the land. The general sentiment here seems to be, that new endeavours will be used to detach us from our Ally, that the best answer to such attempts to disgrace us, will be a speedy and *spirited* preparation for the ensuing campaign....I am particular in giving you every information on this head, because I am persuaded, that means will be used by our Enemies to induce a belief that this Country pines after peace, and its ancient connection with England. It is strictly true they are very desirous of peace, but it is also true, that the Calamities of war press lighter upon them every day from the use they are in to bear them, & from the declining strength of the Enemy. They consider themselves as bound, both in honour and interest, to support the Alliance which they formed in the hour of distress, and I am satisfied no man would be found in any public assembly in America sufficiently hardy to hint at a peace upon any terms which should destroy our connection with France.

· · · · ·

In all our transactions in Spain, we are to consider the delicate situation in which they stand with France– the propensity of the former to peace, and the need that the latter has of their assistance. I should conceive it necessary therefore rather to submit with patience to their repeated delays, than give a handle to the British party at Court– for this reason; I conceive that no advantage could result from demanding a categorical answer, and that it might involve us in disagreeable circumstances. The Resolutions enclosed in my last, will either serve as a stimulus to the politics of Spain, or leave us a latitude on the negotiation for a peace, which will be of equal advantage to us, with any of those slight aids which Spain seems willing or able to give us. Congress have found so little advantage from sending Embassies to Courts, who have shewn no disposition to aid them, that they have passed the enclosed Resolution N$^{o.}$ 4 – Every saving is an object of importance with them, and they feel very heavily the expense of their foreign Embassies, which are in some particulars unnecessarily expensive.

· · · · ·

...It must have been long since you heard from me, our ports have been totally shut up for some time, and no less than three vessels with despatches from me to you, have been taken & carried into New-York within two Months.

· · · · ·

I have the honour to be Dr Sir, with great respect and Esteem Yours &c.

Robt R. Livingston

Resolves enclosed on the above letter 10th Augt 1781, May 8th Feby 22^d 1782

NA: PCC, item 79, v. 1, pp. 714-723 (LBkC); M247, reel 105.

[1] *Carleton, Guy (1724-1808). British military officer. Lieutenant governor of Quebec, 1766-1775; governor, 1775-1778. Heavily involved in formulating Quebec Act, 1774. Commander of British troops in Canada, 1775-1777; knighted, 1776, for defense of Quebec. Commander-in-chief in America, 1782-1783. Created Baron Dorchester, 1786. Governor of Quebec, 1786-1796.*

Benjamin Franklin's Peace Journal

Passy May 9th 1782.

As, since the Change of Ministry in England, some serious Professions have been made, of their Disposition to Peace, and of their Readiness to enter into a general Treaty for that Purpose; and, as the Concerns and Claims of five Nations are to be discussed in that Treaty, which must, therefore, be interesting to the present Age, and to Posterity, I am inclined to keep a Journal of the Proceedings, as far as they come to my Knowledge, and, to make it more complete, will first endeavor to recollect what has already past.

．．．．．

I had but just sent away...[a]...Letter, when Mr Oswald came in, bringing with him Mr Grenville, who was just arrived....

．．．．．

I imagined the Gentlemen had been at Versailles, as I supposed M^r G: would first have waited on M^r De Vergennes before he called on me. But, finding, in Conversation, that he had not, and that he expected me to introduce him, I immediately wrote to that Minister, acquainting him that M^r G: was arrived, and desired to know when his Excellency would think fit to receive him, and I sent an Express with my Letter. I then entered into Conversation with him on the Subject of his Mission, Mr Fox having referred me to him as being fully acquainted with his Sentiments. He said that Peace was really wished for by every Body, if it could be obtained on reasonable Terms, and, as the Idea of subjugating America was given up, and both France and America had thereby obtained what they had in View, originally, it was hoped that there now remained no Obstacle to a Pacification. That England was willing to treat of a general Peace with all the Powers at War against her, and that the Treaty should be at Paris. I did not press him much for further Particulars, supposing they were reserved for our Interview with Mr de Vergennes. The Gentlemen did me the Honor of staying Dinner with me, on the Supposition which I urged that my Express might be back before we parted. This gave me an Opportunity of a good deal of general Conversation with Mr Grenville, who appeared to me a sensible, judicious, intelligent, good tempered, and well instructed young Man, answering well the Character Mr Fox had given me of him. They left me, however abt. Six O Clock, and my Messenger did not return till near Nine. He brought me the Answer of M. le Comte de Vergennes, that he was glad to hear of Mr Grenville's Arrival, and would be ready to receive us to Morrow at 1/2 past 10, or 11 O Clock. I immediately inclosed his Note in one to Mr Grenville, requesting him to be with me at Passy by 8, that we might have Time to breakfast, before we set out....

. . . . .

We set out, accordingly, the next Morning in my Coach from Passy, and arrived punctually at Mr de Vergennes's, who received Mr Grenville in the most cordial Manner, on Account of the Acquaintance and Friendship that had formerly subsisted between his Uncle and M. De Vergennes, when they were Embassadors together at Constantinople. After some little agreeable Conversation, Mr Grenville presented his Letters, from Mr Sec^y Fox, and, I think, from the Duke of Richmond.[1] When these were read the Subject of Peace was entered on. What my Memory retains of the Discourse amounts to little more than this, that after mutual Declarations of the good Dispositions of the two Courts, Mr Grenville having intimated that, in Case England gave America Independence, France, it was expected, would restore the Conquests she had made of british Islands, receiving back those of Miquelon & St Pierre. And the original Object of the War being obtained, it was supposed that France would be contented with that. The Minister seemed to smile at the proposed Exchange; and remarked that the Offer of giving Independence to America, amounted to little. America, says he, does not ask it of you; there is Mr Franklin, he will answer you as to that Point. To be sure, I said, we do not consider ourselves as under any Necessity of bargaining for a Thing that is our own, which we have bought at the Expense of much Blood and Treasure, and which we are in Possession of. As to our being satisfied with the original Object of the War, continued he, look back to the Conduct of your Nation in former Wars. In the last War, for Example, what was the Object? It was the disputed Right to some waste Lands, on the Ohio and the Frontiers of Nova Scotia; did you content yourselves with the Recovery of those Lands? No you retained at the Peace all Canada, all Louisiana, all Florida, Granada and other West India Islands, the greatest Part of the northern Fisheries, with all your Conquests in Africa, and the East Indies. Something being mentioned of its not being reasonable that a Nation after making an unprovoked and unsuccessful War upon its Neighbors, should expect to sit down whole, and have every Thing restored which she had lost in such a War, I think M^r· Grenville remarked that the War had been provoked by the Encouragement given by France to the Americans to revolt. On which M. de Vergennes grew a little warm, and declared firmly, that the Breach was made and our Independence declared long before we received the least Encouragement from France, and he defied the World to give the smallest Proof of the Contrary. There sits, says he, M. Franklin, who knows the Fact, and can contradict me if I do not speak the Truth. He repeated to M^r· Grenville what he had before said to M^r· Oswald, respecting the King's Intention of treating fairly and keeping faithfully the Conventions he should enter into, of which Disposition he should give at the Treaty convincing Proofs by the Fidelity and Exactitude with which he should observe his Engagements with his present Allies; and added, that the Points which the King had chiefly in View were *Justice* and *Dignity*; these he could not depart from. He acquainted Mr Grenville that he should immediately write to Spain and Holland, communicate to those Courts what had passed, and request their Answers; that, in the mean Time he hoped Mr Grenville would find Means of amusing himself agreeably, to which he should be glad to contribute; that he would communicate what had passed to the King; and he invited him to come again the next Day.

On our Return Mr G. expressed himself as not quite satisfied with some Part of M^r· De Vergennes's Discourse, and was thoughtful. He told me, that he had brought two State Messengers with him, and, perhaps, after he had had another Interview with the Minister, he might dispatch one of them to London: I then requested Leave to answer, by that Opportunity, the Letters I had received from Lord Shelburne and Mr Fox; and he kindly promised to acquaint me, in Time, of the Messenger's Departure. He did not ask me to go with him the next Day to Versailles, and I did not offer it.

The coming and going of these Gentlemen was observed, and made much Talk at Paris; and the Marquis de la Fayette, having learnt Something of their Business from the Ministers, discoursed with me about it. Agreeable to the Resolutions of Congress, directing me to confer with him and take his Assistance in our Affairs, I communicated to him what had passed. He told me that during the Treaty at Paris for the last Peace, the Duke de Nivernois[2] had been sent to reside in London, that this Court might, through him, state what was from Time to Time transacted in the Light they thought best, to prevent Misrepresentations and Misunderstandings. That such an Employ would be extremely agreeable to him, on many Accounts; that, as he was now an american Citizen; spoke both

Languages, and was well acquainted with our Interests, he believed he might be useful in it; and that, as Peace was likely, from Appearances, to take Place, his Return to America was, perhaps, not so immediately necessary. I liked the Idea and encouraged his proposing it to the Ministry. He then wished I would make him acquainted with Mess⁷ˢ Oswald and Grenville, and, for that End, proposed meeting them at Breakfast with me, which I promised to contrive if I could, and endeavor to engage them for Saturday.

Friday Morning, the 10ᵗʰ· of May, I went to Paris and visited Mʳ Oswald. I found him in the same friendly Dispositions, and very desirous of doing good, and of seeing an End put to this ruinous War. But I got no farther Light as to the Sentiments of Lord S. respecting the Terms. I told him the Marquis de la Fayette would breakfast with me Tomorrow, and, as he, Mʳ Oswald, might have some Curiosity to see a Person who had in this War, rendered himself so remarkable, I proposed his doing me the same Honor. He agreed to it cheerfully. I came home intending to write to Mʳ Grenville, whom I supposed might stay and dine at Versailles, and, therefore, did not call on him....

·   ·   ·   ·   ·

The Gentlemen all met accordingly, had a good deal of Conversation at and after Breakfast, staid till after one OClock and parted much pleased with each other.

The Monday following I called to visit Mʳ· G. I found with him Mʳ Oswald, who told me he was just about returning to London. I was a little surprised at the Suddenness of the Resolution he had taken, it being, as he said, to set out the next Morning early. I conceived the Gentlemen were engaged in Business, so I withdrew, and went to write a few Letters, among which was...[one]...to Lord Shelburne, being really concerned at the Thought of losing so good a Man as Mʳ Oswald.

·   ·   ·   ·   ·

NA: PCC, item 100, v. 1, pp. 357-358, 402-410, and 413-414 (Transcription); M247, reel 127.

¹ Richmond, Charles Lennox, Duke of (1735-1806). British political figure. Vociferous opponent of the North Ministry's American policy and of the American war. Master general of the ordinance in Rockingham and Shelburne cabinets, 1782-1783, and in Pitt's administration, 1784-1795.

² Nivernais, Louis-Jules-Barbon Mancini-Mazarini, Duc de (1716-1798). French diplomat and political figure. Ambassador to Rome, 1748-1752, and Prussia, 1755-1756. Negotiated the Treaty of Paris, 1763, which ended the Seven Years War. Of a liberal opinion, he served as minister of state without portfolio, June 1787-July 1789. Did not emigrate; imprisoned during the Terror.

Substance of the First and Second Peace Conferences with Mr. Grenville, 9–10 May 1782

[Translation]

Mr. Grenville, after having handed the Comte de Vergennes two letters, one from Mr. Fox and the other from the Duke of Richmond, expressed the wish of the King of England for a prompt reconciliation, and declared that His Britannic Majesty had chosen Paris by preference as the site of the negotiation. The Comte de Vergennes responded by expressing, on his part, the King's desire to see peace soon reestablished on a solid and lasting basis, and by announcing that His Majesty would have in view only reciprocal justice and dignity; that moreover His Majesty did not attach any glory to seeing the negotiation established under his eyes, and that he was disposed to choose such other site as might suit the King of England, and even to let the negotiation proceed by way of mediators. Mr. Grenville replied that Paris was the most suitable site in all respects, but he declined the intervention of mediators.

This first point determined, the Comte de Vergennes said that it could not be a question of a partial peace, and asked if the intention of the English ministry was to make a general peace. Mr. Grenville, after having made an affirmative response, said that the English Ministers wished to know if general proposals could be admitted according to which it could be hoped to establish a negotiation with probability of success. The response of the Comte de Vergennes was that the King, having allies, could make neither overture nor proposition, because he knew only their wish for peace and not the conditions on which they were disposed to make it; the Comte de Vergennes observed at the same time that England, having neither ally nor associate to consult, was free in her conduct as in her language, and that she could without inconvenience express her intentions and her views.

This reflection led Mr. Grenville to make the following overture. As the independence of America is the direct object of the present war, this article must essentially be the subjet of the negotiation. The Comte de Vergennes, after having made it understood that this proposal was not exact, nevertheless accepted the first part in observing that it is matters of justice that the King and his allies will have to demand; that the Treaty of Paris, fruit of the abuse that the Court of London made of its prosperity, had need of revision; that moreover the Comte de Vergennes could not explain himself more at present, that he would report Mr. Grenville's overtures to the King, and that he hoped to be able to be more explicit at the next conference, set for tomorrow.

2ⁿᵈ·

The conference continued with M. the Comte d'Aranda present. The same subjects that were discussed the previous day were dealt with anew, and as it were in the same terms, without either side being more forthcoming or having occasion to formulate expedients. The result was that Mr. Grenville would write to London and the Comte d'Aranda to Madrid to procure instructions.[1]

FFAA: Pol. Corr., England, v. 537, f. 27 (LC transcription).

[1] There were seven such meetings relating to the start of the European peace negotiations. For each meeting, French diplomat Joseph-Matthias Gérard de Rayneval produced a memorandum of conversation, to which Vergennes also added material. All seven memorandums appear chronologically in this collection.

Thomas Grenville to Charles James Fox

Sir,   Paris. May 10. 1782.

Having arrived at Paris on the 7ᵗʰ· I accompanied Mʳ· Oswald on the 8ᵗʰ· to Mʳ Franklin at Passy. Mʳ Franklin told me that Mʳ Laurens, Mʳ· Jay, Mʳ Adams & himself had full powers, all or any of them that should be present, to bind Congress by any treaty to which they should subscribe; that Mʳ· Adams was very much busied in forming a treaty with the Dutch, & therefore could not come to Paris, but that he expected Mʳ· Laurens & Mʳ· Jay very soon: that as to the connections of America with France, America was free from every sort of engagement but those which existed in the two publick treaties of commerce & alliance, and that those two treaties were such as any other nation was free to make with America, that America had been greatly obliged to France, & must shew her good faith in the observance of her treaties: I said that the extent of that obligation was what I wished him to consider, & whether in the independance of America if that should be the basis of a treaty, he did not see gratification enough for France; he said it was a great deal, but that Spain might want something, he supposed would want Gibraltar, & that perhaps it would be of little use to us now we had lost Minorca & had less commerce to defend: I told him I hoped Spain would be found to entertain no such idea, that the opinion of the whole nation & those who understood it's interests best was I believed so decided upon that subject, that I hoped it would make no part of any negotiation that looked to a prosperous conclusion, he immediately said it was nothing to America who kept or who had Gibraltar. I trusted therefore, I said, that things foreign to the subject of the quarrel would not be permitted to break off a treaty & lead America on in a war where she could find no interest, particularly as I could not help believing there was still in America a good disposition towards England: he said there were *roots*, that they would want a good deal of management, that knowing much of both countries he believed he could give good Counsel upon the subject; that he wished reconciliation as well as peace, that he thought there were Circumstances in the power of England which might bring it about, that shewing kindness to the American prisoners, particularly those now going home, that enabling those persons whose houses had been wantonly burnt to rebuild them, such things if spontaneously done would he was sure have the greatest effect to a real reconciliation: I could only answer that every *practicable* measure would probably be taken to bring about a reconciliation by those who desired so sincerely to bring about a peace. in this as well as in a subsequent conversation, his language in manner as well as substance expressed a very earnest & unaffected wish for peace, tho' always accompanied with professions of a strict adherence to the treaties America had made.

Yesterday morning I carried your letter Sir to Versailles, & by Mr de Vergennes's desire M$^{r\cdot}$ Franklin went with me. as soon as I had stated to M$^{r\cdot}$ de Vergennes His Majesty's sincere wish & disposition to put an end to the calamities of war, & the concurrence he was pleased to give that Paris should be the place of Treaty, he said he could assure me that the King his Master had the same good dispositions to peace, but that regarding as the first object his good faith to his Allies, H.M.C.M. could do nothing without them, and must previously to anything else send to Madrid and Holland for persons authorised to confer with me.

I answered that he must have been aware in reading Mr Fox's letter, that I had no formal authority whatever, but that I had conceived it could not but be useful previous to the necessary arrangements of a Treaty to have that sort of communication by conversation with him which might shew some general ideas upon which both parties might enough agree to find in them the basis of a treaty.

he said he could make no overtures, nor any answer to mine till after a communication with the King his Master's allies. I told him I was now only looking to those general points which might supply a prospect sufficient to the foundation of a negotiation, & went on to say that one naturally looked towards that which had been the motive of the war, & avowed to be such by France as well as America, and that, was that cause of contest removed, it seemed perfectly just that in every other instance, things should be placed exactly in the same state in which they were before the contest existed; he said he could not allow the independance of America to be the only cause of war, for that France had found & not made America independant; but even supposing that true, I must not forget that tho' the last war began only upon the subject of Nova Scotia, we had not confined ourselves to that at the Peace.

I answered that the comparison did not appear to me just, for that the independance of America would be a point gained more essential to the interests of France in the separation of Thirteen Provinces from England, than any acquisition, we had made by the last peace, had been to us. when I mentioned the important possessions we had to restore, he interrupted me in speaking of S[t.] Pierre & Miquelon by crying out "Oh pour la peche, nous allons arranger cela bien d'une autre maniere"[1] – he said we had checked & constrained the French in all the quarters of the world, that he wished for a treaty of peace more just and durable than the last, & that the two principal objects they should attend to were justice & dignity. I answered that in any treaty to be made, he must not forget, that justice & dignity were as essential objects to one great nation as another.

I did not find it easy to make him advert to St Lucie & to the East Indies, he contenting himself with saying I did not tell him all (he saw) at the first word, & finished the conversation by telling me he would see me the next morning & that the Spanish Ambassador should meet me: and going out of the room said, he did not foresee that what had been now talked of would be the basis of a treaty. When I saw M[r.] de Vergennes again this morning, he told me he had his Master's orders to say, that H.M.C.M. partook very sincerely of those dispositions which His Britannick Majesty felt to put an end to the calamities of war, and would do everything in his power to facilitate that end, but that having indissoluble engagements with his allies, he could not enter into any treaty without their participation, but would in conjunction with them listen to any overtures, as soon as persons empowered by them could be here. he then informed me that the Spanish Ambassador would immediately send for powers to Madrid, & that there would be time for me to send for powers that I might be ready when the others were. the Spanish Ambassador added that H.C.M. had the same good dispositions towards peace with H.M.C.M.

I sayed I would communicate to M[r.] Fox what they had told me; – there was then pretty near the same discussion with that of the day before, the Spanish Ambassador insisting still more strongly that his Master's griefs were totally distinct from the independance of America, & that to make a durable peace, we must begin he said from the point at which we now are. at my suggesting again to day the idea of ceding to H.M.C.M. & his Allies the independance of America, M[r.] de Vergennes with great earnestness said that, the King his Master could not in any treaty consider the independance of America as ceded to him, & that [to] do so would be to hurt the dignity of his Britannick Majesty; which idea I conceive to be thrown out, only to lessen the value of the sacrifice by disclaiming all share in it.

M.ʳ de Vergennes was more explicit than yesterday about the East Indies; he asked why we should not content ourselves with Bengal, said it was a great & rich province, that our arms were grown too long for our body, that the French had experienced from us in India every sort of indignity, and that chiefly owing to the terms of the last peace, that for his part he could not read the last peace without shuddering, (*sans fremir*) & that in making a new treaty they must be relieved from every circumstance in which their dignity had been hurt.

Having thus Sir, endeavoured to state to you the most material parts of the conversations I have had in the three days that I have passed here, you will not I am persuaded expect much comment upon them; perhaps however it may not be unnecessary to add, that M.ʳ de Vergennes's manner expressed a very strong persuasion that England must make infinitely more important & extensive sacrifices to give to a negotiation much prospect of success; the line of the last peace seeming to be that which of all others both he & M.ʳ D'Aranda are most intent upon excluding from the present negotiation.

Permit me Sir, only farther to observe that it did not appear to me that anything could be facilitated by using the latitude which was given to me of making a direct proposition, & therefore confined whatever I said to mere matter of conversation, and of that conversation I have already related to you everything that seemed in the least respect worth leaving to your consideration.

I have the honour to be with great truth & regard – Sir Your very obedient humble Servant   Thomas Grenville.
R. 14.ᵗʰ

PRO: FO 27/2, v. 557, f. 115 (LC *transcription*).
  ¹ "Oh, as to the fishing, we are going to settle that in another manner."

Comte de Vergennes to Comte de Montmorin

[Translation]

Nᵒ 26   Versailles, 11 May 1782
M. le Comte de Montmorin

M. le Comte d'Aranda, Sir, learned before me of the return of Mr. Oswald from England, he reported it to his Court by the shipment that I had the honor of sending you on the 4th of this month. I did not speak to you of it because I was unaware of it, and because that ambassador did not think to inform me of his discovery; my Courier was already very distant when I was informed of it.

Mr. Oswald visited me on the morning of the 6th, accompanied by Mr. Franklin. Sent by Lord Shelburne, he had no Commission for me because, the Secretary of State having in his department only America and Ireland, it is Mr. Fox alone who is charged with the affairs of Europe; but he informed me preliminarily: 1st. that the King of England was disposed to discuss a general peace; 2nd. that he preferred that the negotiation be established in Paris; 3rd. that the Independence of America would no longer be an obstacle to the reestablishment of the Peace; and 4th. finally that I would not be long in seeing the arrival of an Emissary sent by Mr. Fox, who would confirm to me all that he had just set forth. Mr. Oswald being without a mission in my regard, I thanked him for his Communication, and there we remained.

On the evening of the 8th, I received a note from Mr. Franklin, who indicated to me that Mr. Grenville, brother of Lord Temple,[1] had arrived, that he had been sent by Mr. Fox, and that he had charged him to evince to me his eagerness to see me. I responded courteously and gave them an appointment for 10:30 the following morning.

These Gentlemen were on time for the rendezvous. Mr. Grenville began by handing me two Letters, one from Mr. Fox and the other from the Duke of Richmond; the enclosed Copies exempt me from making mention of their Contents. He then spoke to me of the desire of the King of England and his Council for a prompt reconciliation, and of His Britannic Majesty's desire that the negotiation be established at Paris by preference. My response was courteous, I expressed the King's desire for the reestablishment of a secure and lasting peace that would reconcile the justice and the dignity of the belligerent powers; I added that His Majesty attached no price to having the negotiation established under his eyes, that any other place that suited the King of England would be acceptable to him, and that he would see the negotiation proceed by way of the mediators with pleasure. Mr. Grenville, without explaining what concerned them, replied that Paris was in all Respects the most suitable Place to treat.

This first point decided, I said, Sir, that there being no question of a partial peace, it was important to know if the Intention of the English ministry was to make the peace general. Mr. Grenville responded affirmatively that, yes, and it was for that very reason that the English ministers wished to know if general proposals could be agreed upon according to which one could hope to establish a negotiation with a probability of Success.

I observed to Mr. Grenville that, the King having allies without whom he could not and would not treat, His majesty would permit himself neither overture nor proposal, because he only knew their desire for peace and not the conditions on which they might be disposed to make it. I insisted that, England being alone, and only having to take Counsel from her Will and her Interest, she was free in her Conduct as in her Language, and that she could express her Intentions and Her Views without disadvantage. I consequently asked Mr. Grenville whether he was authorized to confer with M. le Comte d'Aranda and with the ambassador of Holland. His response having been that his mission was direct, I declared to him that it was necessary that he be authorized by his Court to enter into Conference with those ministers. I made him understand that he should have less regret at the loss of time which this would occasion than I. I was in a position to write to Spain to report his arrival and the Subject of his mission, and to know the Intentions of the Catholic King, without whose participation the King would not take the least step.

Either Mr. Grenville did not understand me well or some other motive was acting on him. This declaration seemed to pain him. A Silence of sadness followed; I asked him the cause of it, he did not conceal from me that what I had just told him stopped his mouth, because he inferred that I was not disposed to listen to anything. I responded to him by joking that in my place I often had a closed mouth, but that my ears were always open; thus nothing prevented him from making me such overtures as he pleased, and that if there was anything that interested our allies, I would be very exact in reporting it to them.

The Explication having reconciled Mr. Grenville, he told me that the Independence of America being the object of the present war, it should essentially be that of the negotiation, and that England being determined to grant full Satisfaction in that Regard, there was no longer a reason for Disputes, and consequently for the Continuation of the War.

I did not allow this strange assertion to pass, as you may judge; the inference from the facts furnished me the victorious means to demonstrate that the Independence of America was only a very indirect Cause of the War, that it would have been incited even if the ministers then in place had not viewed with eyes of pride the declaration which was made to them of our recognition; I observed to him that even admitting his principle, the necessary Consequence would not be that the negotiation of peace should be limited to that object alone.

I cited for him the Treaty of Paris and the immense sacrifices that it had cost us in all parts of the world, although the Dispute revolved in principle only around some lands along the banks of the Ohio. You cannot, said I to Mr. Grenville, reject this Example, it is the work of your uncle Lord Chatham.[2]

It would be tedious, Sir, to inform you of all that passed in a discussion that was much longer than it was interesting, and to which I only yielded in order not to have the air of guiding the negotiation and the negotiators. As it was necessary to finish, I recapitulated that the King could only broach the matter in Concert and with the consent of his allies; that His Majesty would treat seriously of his Interests only as far as those of these same allies could be satisfied; and finally that I was going to write to Madrid and to The Hague in order to invite those powers to authorize their ambassadors to enter into negotiations with him.

Mr. Grenville in closing the Meeting asked me for a passport to dispatch a Courier to his Court. I pointed out to him that that Action was at least premature since, only having been able to express to him my personal Sentiments, he was not in a position to report anything concerning those of the King. I delivered it to him the following day and summoned him at the same hour with the design of having him meet with M. le Comte d'Aranda and of being able to explain myself in the presence of that ambassador. This precaution seemed good to me to prevent the Ambiguities and distrusts that might result from it. Our second interview, Sir, took place yesterday. M. le Comte d'Aranda was present; I recapitulated all that had passed in that of the day before. Mr. Grenville contradicted nothing, but he did not advance a Line further than he had. He did not draw back from the idea that the Independence of America should hold a place of full Satisfaction for the belligerent powers. The weakness of this reasoning was demonstrated to him, but as he apparently has orders not to abandon it, he brought it forward to us again in all possible forms. Finally he reached something rather ordinary. It is that after having spoken at length, each remained firm in his opinion. It is precisely in that Situation that a conference that lasted a good two hours ended. M. le Comte d'Aranda expressed himself with much Wisdom, reserve, and dignity. Affirmative of the Desire of the King his master for peace, he excused himself by his lack of instructions from explaining himself concerning the conditions on which His Catholic Majesty would concur. The sole point on which we agreed is that each would write respectively to his Court in order to obtain Instructions. I strongly invited Mr. Grenville to do so, so that he is sent what tends more directly toward the Goal than those with which he appears charged. I do not argue against the pacific Intentions of the English Minister because the powers of that Emissary are excessively restrained. His mission up to now has only had for its object entering into negotiations to learn on what bases the allied Courts are disposed to comprehend the reestablishment of a general peace; it is natural that the Court of London is more occupied with penetrating us than with opening itself up. The Wisdom of the Catholic King and of his Ministry will decide to what point it is agreed to advance. I think that this is not a business that should be discussed by merchants, and that if one is disposed to enter into negotiations, it is necessary to begin them with frankness, nobility, and firmness.

Mr. Grenville is very suitable to handle the mission with which he is charged. He is a young man of 30 or more who displays much Spirit, Wisdom, honesty, and modesty. He belongs to an important family which is connected by Interest with the present ministry, and it is not very likely that the latter would intend him for a role so dull and so little analogous to his birth and his condition as that of coming to amuse and delude us. Moreover, the Interest of the present ministry is very certainly to make peace if it can obtain one on reasonable conditions.

I request, Sir, that you communicate this letter to M. le Comte de Florida Blanca, that you even leave him a Copy of it if he desires one. Pledge him, I pray you, to inform us with the least possible delay of the Intentions of the King his master.

I am going to write to Holland to inform that Republic summarily of the overtures which have been made to us and to inform it that it may choose to take part in the negotiation that may begin at Paris.

I have the honor to be &ᵃ.   Vergennes

FFAA: Pol. Corr., Spain, v. 607, f. 50 (LC transcription).

¹ Temple, George Nugent-Temple-Grenville, Lord (1753-1813). British political figure. Son of George Grenville, brother of Thomas Grenville. Member of Parliament, 1774-1779. Lord-lieutenant of Ireland, 1782-1783, 1787-1789.

² Chatham, William Pitt, Lord (1708-1778). British political figure. Prime minister, as Secretary of State for the Southern Department and leader of the House of Commons, 1756-1757. Secretary of State for War and Foreign Affairs, 1757-1761. From 1766, Earl of Chatham. Prime minister, 1766-1768, although largely incapacitated, May 1767-October 1768. Opposed efforts to subdue the American colonies militarily, but favored redress of grievances rather than recognition of American independence.

Richard Oswald to Lord Shelburne

My Lord   London 13ᵗʰ· May 1782

If I understood Your Lordship when I had the honour of attending You the other day, Your desire was that I should State to You the general situation of the sufferers by the American War and how far their Interests might be affected by the different Circumstances which might regulate the Terms of a Settlement, with a view of attending to those Interests upon such an Event. I shall endeavour to give Your Lordship such Information upon this as I am possessed of, and sincerely wish it were more satisfactory, towards answering the humane purposes of Your Enquiries.

With respect to the Merchants who Traded to America before the commencement of the present Troubles, and who have great sums due to them from that Country, the recovery of their Debts must appear extremely precarious, let the matter terminate in any way, if they are to look for Payment only to those with whom they had Dealings. The general diminution of property and the distress occasioned by the War, with the rapid depreciation of the Paper Currency, added to other Causes, must have incapacitated very many of these from a possibility of discharging the Demands against them. The Colonies of Virginia & Maryland have passed Acts confiscating British Property of all Kinds, and I think these are the only Governments who have interfered in that matter, so that in their Case should an equitable settlement take place, the British Merchants will have a responsible object to look to. As to those who have traded to America since the Year 1775, they have no ground of complaint for Losses incurred, as they have acted with their eyes open to the risque and in opposition to the Laws of both Countries.

The American Loyalists who have suffered by this unhappy War are either such as have been obliged to abandon their Country, and take refuge with the British Army, or have still remained at home, but refusing to abjure the King's Supremacy and Swear Allegiance to the New Governments. Each of those have been subjected to peculiar Penalties. The former have, I believe, without exception been attainted and their Estates real and personal forfeited. the latter have generally been excluded from the Privilege of voting at Elections or holding Offices, and have been rated in some Provinces doubly in others trebly to the Public Assessments. The first seem to be at present the particular objects of Your Lordship's attention, tho' it is hoped that the Interests of the last will also be thought deserving of it. For tho' no Compensation can be properly expected for the partial Losses they may have sustained, still they must naturally hope that their situation will not be overlooked in a general Settlement, and that should Government even be induced to acknowledge the Independence of America some Stipulation should be made that the Penalties and Disfranchisement under which they now labour, should be taken off and they be readmitted to the Common Rights of Citizens. Those who are Refugees, have, as has been mentioned, been attainted, either by Act of Assembly in which they have been particularly named or Inquisition taken by the Grand Jury of the respective Counties where their Estates lay. These Estates have been generally sold and in many Instances have already passed thro' different hands. The Debts due to them by Bond, Mortgage or otherwise have been declared forfeited and ordered to be paid into the several Provincial Treasuries, with severe Penalties on the Debtors for non compliance or concealment, and this it cannot be doubted has been done in most Cases as Persons under these Circumstances must have gladly embraced the opportunity of discharging their Debts for a small part of what was really due by making the Payments in a depreciated Currency. From this State of the Case may be foreseen the Difficulties which will arise in securing to the Sufferers a restoration of their Property, or an Indemnification for their Losses. Supposing Government should be disposed to make this a point in any settlement which shall take place much will depend on the future degree of connection to be established between the two Countries. If the authority of the Crown should be solidly restored in America the weight of that support may enable them in some measure to effectuate the Provisions which may be stipulated in their favor, but if the exigence of Affairs shou'd enforce an Agreement which should leave to Government only a Nominal authority, and should admit either a total or partial Independence in America it is doubtful whether that Country would consent to make a Compensation to the Loyalists and much more so that such Agreement would be carried into execution: but admitting this, no Resolution of the Congress or respective Assemblies to repeal the Acts of Forfeiture or make Compensation would in such a situation be adequate. For if it be left to the Sufferers to pursue his Property through the channel of the Courts of Law under the Sanction of such Acts of repeal, it cannot be expected that he will have much chance of Success, when the Juries & Officers of the Court (composed of Persons opposite to him in Principles and warm in their resentments) must look with an evil eye on his Claim, and be disposed to favour every plausible pretext in his Adversary's Defence. Indeed it may be doubtful whether such suits could be prosecuted consistently with personal safety, at least they would be attended with great violence and Animosity. An Agreement on the part of America, for the different Governments generally to make compensation to the Sufferers, would also be equally inadequate, as the measure of such compensation would certainly be the Price for which the forfeited Estates had been Sold. And when it is considered that these Sales have been made whilst the Contest was depending on the precarious issue of which the validity of the Titles rested, it cannot be supposed that any thing like a fair Price could be given. And accordingly we find in the Instances which have come to our knowledge that the Estates have Seldom produced above a fifth or sixth part of their real Value. Under these Circumstances it appears to me that the only mode if such can be attained which promises the Sufferers a prospect of any thing approaching to an Indemnification, would be by stipulating that the different Governments should take upon themselves the burthen of restoring the Party to the possession of his real Estate, which might be done by inserting in the Acts repealing the Forfeiture a Clause Commanding the Sheriffs of the respective Counties, where the Lands lay, to give possession without further process, and that the Purchaser under the Forfeiture should resort to the Public for any Claims he may have for Damages sustained or Monies expended on the Estate. With respect to the personal Chattles which have been Sold as a restoration of them is impossible, all that can be expected will be a Satisfaction to the amount of what they produced at the Sales.

As to the number of Persons under the description of Refugees, I cannot speak with precision, and it is impossible to form any Estimate of the amount of the confiscated Estates. As far as I can collect there have been about three hundred of all Ranks attainted in Pensylvania, and nearly that number in New Jersey and perhaps about the same proportion in most of the Colonies. In the Province of New York upwards of Sixty of the principal Gentlemen in point of rank and fortune have been included in one Act of attainder. I have not as yet been able to succeed in my Search after the different Acts of Assembly relating to this subject, but whenever I do, shall take the liberty of laying them before Your Lordship.

I have the honour to be &c. –   Richard Oswald

Clements Library: Shelburne Papers, v. 70, pp. 7-14 (C).

Thomas Grenville to Charles James Fox

Sir,   Paris. May 14[th.] 1782.

. . . . .

Every thing that I have hitherto seen and heard, leads me to believe, that the demands of France, and Spain, will be found such, as it will be difficult perhaps impossible for England to comply with, as they are at present conceived, that Spain looks to Florida, and Gibraltar; that France looks to very essential alterations in the state of the Newfoundland Fishery, to perhaps more than Grenada in the West Indies, & to very extensive surrenders of commerce and territory in the East Indies. It is from the expectation the courts of Madrid and Versailles entertain of being supported by America in these claims, that they will derive the greatest confidence in making them; and if so, whatever measure could be found practicable to weaken that support, or to give to France and Spain even the apprehension of losing it, would be to take from them the strongest ground of their pretensions in a negotiation, and, could it be effectually done, would put them more within our reach in the prosecution of a war. It is true, that the present state of America's connection with France, and the good faith she professes to observe in it, has given no prospect for proposing to make with her a separate and distinct Treaty; but, whether, by giving in the first instance independance to America, instead of making it a conditional Article of general Treaty, we might not gain the effects tho' not the form of a separate Treaty, whether, more would not so be gained in well-founded expectation than would be lost in substance, whether, America once actually possessed of her great object would not be infinitely less likely to lend herself to other claims, than if that object should remain to be blended with every other and stand part of a common interest, whether, the American commissioners would think themselves warranted after such a measure in adhering to the demands of France and Spain, or whether, supposing that they should, the Thirteen Provinces would consent to the carrying on the war upon such motives, whether too the Treaty now forming with Holland would not so be baffled in it object, & that we should have as it were concluded with America before she had finally, engaged herself with Holland.

All these are questions which seem of immediate and important consideration, and I must say, for my apology in venturing to state them, arise more from the critical situation of things than from any opinion I can presume to form about them. Should I not however add that M$^{r.}$ Franklin's conversation has at different times appeared to me to glance towards these ideas? while he was with me this morning he went so far as to say, that, when we had allowed the independance of America, the treaty she had made with France for gaining it ended, and none remained but that of commerce, which we too might make if we pleased; he repeated that he did not know what France would ask, or would expect to be proposed, but mentioning immediately the article of Dunkirk,[1] I confess that by putting his conversation together, I was distantly led to suppose, that, in case of America's being first satisfied, she might be more likely to save the honour of her good faith, by supporting France in such articles as that of Dunkirk, than in the more essential claims upon the East Indies: he ended by saying that he saw the considerations of so many interests might make the business very tedious, but assured me that whatever influence he had at this Court should be used to accommodate things: he had too once before said, that in forming a Treaty, there should he thought without doubt be a difference in a Treaty between England & America, and one between England and France, that always had been at enmity: in these expressions, as well as in a former one, where he rested much upon the great effect that would be obtained by some things being done spontaneously from England, I think you will perhaps trace something not altogether wide of those ideas which I suppose may have weighed with him. what weight they will have in your better judgement is not for me to consider, I conceived it important to state them, and after that have but to receive your orders upon the subject, repeating only, that as yet there seems little hope of a succesfull negotiation with France, and that America which was the road to the war seems to offer the most practicable mode of getting out of it, perhaps too threatens the greatest danger if she continues to assist the prosecution of it.

I have the honour to be, Sir, your very obedient, humble Servant.

Thomas Grenville.

R. 21ˢᵗ:

PRO: FO, 27/2, v. 557, f. 143 (LC transcription).
¹ Article of Dunkirk. An article in the Treaty of Utrecht, 1713, which forbade France to fortify Dunkirk.

Henry Laurens to Benjamin Franklin

Ostend 17ᵗʰ· May 1782.

Sir,

. . . . .

...I sincerely and heartily thank you, Sir, for the cordial Contents of your last Letter, but, from the most mature Reflection and taking into Consideration my present very infirm State of Health, I have resolved to decline accepting the Honor intended me by Congress in the Commission for treating with great Britain, and I find the less Difficulty in coming to this Determination from a Persuasion in my own Mind that my Assistance is not essential, and that it was not the View or Expectation of our Constituents that every one named in the Commission should act....God prosper your Proceedings in the great Work, you shall be called Blessed by all the grateful of the present Generation and your Name will be celebrated by Posterity. I feel myself happy in reflecting that in the great Outlines for a Treaty, our Opinions exactly coincide, that we shall not want the Countenance and Assistance of our great and good Ally, and that you have so honest a Man as Mʳ Oswald to deal with for Preliminaries; I know him to be superior to all Chicanery, and am sure he will not defile his mind by attempting any dirty Thing.

. . . . .

...with the highest Esteem & Respect, Sir, &c.   Henry Laurens.

NA: PCC, item 100, v. 1, pp. 424-427 (LBkC); M247, reel 127.

Chevalier de la Luzerne to Comte de Vergennes

[Translation]

N° 239   Philadelphia, 19 May 1782
My Lord

. . . . .

I have had frequent conversations with Mr. Livingston since the news received from Europe has given reason to think that England would offer the Delawarians terms of reconciliation. The knowledge that that Minister has of the affairs of his Country and what I think are the dispositions of Congress do not leave me any anxiety on the conduct that this assembly will display; but it appears from M. Carleton's despatches and from the debates of the Parliament of England that it is towards particular assemblies and towards individuals that the efforts of the new Commander in Chief will be directed. It is therefore prudent to hold oneself on guard from that side, although nothing up to the present gives reason to fear a bad effect from these circumstances. In consequence, by order of Congress he has sent to the various Legislatures a letter,[1] the translation of which is enclosed, and he has told me that it might without difficulty be printed in the public papers in Europe in its entirety, or with the Suppressions that will be judged necessary. I do not doubt that most of the Legislative Assemblies, and probably all without exception, will pass the laws recommended to them by this Letter....

The goods confiscated from the royalists, the boundaries, and the fisheries are the principal subjects of conversation at this moment. The confiscated goods especially occasion an extreme anxiety. An infinite number of persons is interested in it, and several have had frequent conversations with me on this matter. I could only repeat what I have had the honor of writing to you previously in that regard; — but I beseech you to permit, My Lord, that I return to the subject of the Fisheries. The New England party is preparing maneuvers of all kinds to involve this point in the peace; it is not doubtful that Mr. John Adams will sustain it with an extreme obstinacy in future negotiations; I have made every effort to destroy the hopes that have been nourished in this regard, and by causing them to fear that the Americans will be excluded from the Grand Bank fisheries by a positive stipulation, I have led the most intractable persons to desire that the Treaty remain silent on this point, and not contain any exclusion. Even this Silence will be regarded as a signal advantage. It is clear from this disposition of minds that the New Englanders would take this opportunity, by virtue of the alleged right communicated, to spread themselves over all the fishing banks; but if we wish to keep them away from those which are

reserved to us, if we wish to render vigor to this important branch of our commerce and of our navigation, it seems to me very essential, My Lord, to put ourselves early in a position to restrain their enterprises in the waters where they will not have the right to establish their Fisheries....
Received 13 July.   Le Che. de la luzerne.

FFAA: Pol. Corr., U.S., v. 21, f. 62 (LC transcription).
[1] *Presumably Robert R. Livingston to the Governors of the States, May 14, 1782 (NA: PCC, item 119, pp. 106-107; M247, reel 139).*

Lord Shelburne to Benjamin Franklin

Sir,   Whitehall 21st May 1782
I am honoured with your Letter of the 10th. Inst and am very glad to find that the Conduct which the King has empowered me to observe towards Mr Laurens and the American Prisoners has given you pleasure.

I have signified to Mr Oswald His Majesty's Pleasure that he shall continue at Paris till he receives Orders from hence to return.

In the present State of this Business, there is nothing left for me to add, but my sincere wishes for a happy Issue, and to repeat my Assurances that nothing shall be wanting on my part that can contribute to it.

I am &c.   Shelburne

Clements Library: Shelburne Papers, v. 70, p. 1 (C).

Instructions to Thomas Grenville from George III, King of England

21 May 1782
Instructions for Our Trusty & Wellbeloved Thomas Grenville Esqre, whom We have appointed Our Minister to Our Good Brother The Most Christian King. Given at Our Court at St. James's the 21st Day of May 1782. In the Twenty Second Year of Our Reign.

Whereas in consequence of Our earnest Desire to put an End to the Calamities of War in which Our Kingdoms are engaged by the Aggression of Our Enemies, We have thought fit to direct You to repair to the Court of France, & have already directed You to be furnished with such Papers and Information as may have enabled You to make Overtures of Peace, &

to explain to the Minister of Our Good Brother the most Christian King, the Basis on which a Negociation for the Purpose of concluding a Peace between Us & our said Good Brother can be entered upon; And You having reported to One of Our Principal Secretaries of State, for Our Information, what passed in your Conferences with the Count de Vergennes, We have now thought proper to give You the following Instructions for Your Conduct in the Execution of the important Trust we have reposed in You.

1. – On the Receipt of these Our Instructions, together with Our Full Power and Credential Letter to The Most Christian King, You are to desire an Audience of the Count of Vergennes Minister & Secretary of State for Foreign Affairs, in which You will inform him that You are furnished with a Credential Letter as Our Minister to His Most Christian Majesty; But You are not to deliver it, (with it's Copy,) to the Count de Vergennes, till You shall receive Our farther Instructions from one of Our Principal Secretaries of State.

2. – You will, in this Audience of the Count de Vergennes, express Our Regard for The Most Christian King, and Our sincere Desire to see a speedy and happy End put to the Evils of a War which has so long subsisted between the two Crowns; And You will likewise acquaint the Count de Vergennes that you have a Full Power from Us, a Copy whereof you will deliver to that Minister, at the same Time declaring that You are ready to produce the Original when desired.

3. – For your letter Guidance & Direction in this important Negociation, We have judged proper to lay down & fix the following essential Points, by which You are to govern Yourself in your future Conferences with the Comte de Vergennes.

4. – You will repeat, in Our Name, the Assurances which you have already given of Our Desire to prevent the farther Effusion of Human Blood, & Our Wishes that the Time and Place of treating may be those which are most likely to bring Matters to a speedy Issue. With this View You will again name Paris, provided it can be so managed as to give no Cause of Offence to the Courts of Vienna & Petersbourg. With respect to the Time, You will inform the French Minister that You are authorized by Us to present Your Letter of Credence whenever Our Good Brother the Most Christian King shall name a Person, on his Part to repair to Our Court in Quality of Minister from the said Most Christian King.

5. – If the Court of France should declare their Intentions of naming such a Person, You will declare that You are ready & desirous to learn any Ideas & Intentions they may have for carrying into Effect, with more Speed & Certainty, Our earnest Wishes to restore Peace & Amity between the Two Crowns.

6. – You will acquaint the Count de Vergennes, that in Order to attain this desirable End, We are willing to declare Our Intentions to cede to His Most Christian Majesty, & His Allies, the Point which they have, at various Times, & upon various Occasions, declared to be the Subject of the War, & particularly in the last Answer from the Court of Versailles to the Mediating Courts: That is to say, to accede to the complete Independency of the Thirteen American States, and in order to make the Peace, if it should take Place, solid & durable, to cede to the said States the Towns of New York and Charlestown, together with the Province of Georgia, including the Town of Savannah, all which are still in His Majesty's Possession, provided, that in all other Respects such a general & reciprocal Restitution shall take Place, in every Quarter of the Globe, on the Part of the Belligerent Powers, as shall restore Things to the State they were placed in by the Treaty of Paris 1763.

7. – This being the Basis of the intended Treaty of Peace, You will explain to the French Minister that it does not exclude any Exchanges of Possessions which may be made to the mutual Satisfaction of both Parties.

8. – You will not fail to dwell upon the Importance of those Places which We should be to restore upon such a Treaty taking Place. The Acquisitions in the East Indies, St Pierre & Miquelon, Places so necessary to their Fisheries: and above all St Lucie, must be principally insisted upon.

9. – In Case Monsr de Vergennes should not consider your Overture as a sufficient Basis to form a Treaty upon, or should reject the Terms offered by You as inadmissible You will acquaint him that We having, on Our Part, made such a Proposal as appeared to us reasonable, We expect on their's either a Concurrence in Our Ideas, or some Proposition of their own; And you will immediately transmit to One of Our Principal Sectaries of State, for Our Information, the French Minister's Answer to this Request. You will observe to him how idle it would be for both Countries that much Time should be spent in this Negociation unless there are some Hopes of Agreement and therefore press for as little Delay as possible in giving an Answer to Your Proposition, declaring that if that Answer should be a Refusal without any Suggestion of Proposals on their Part We cannot avoid considering such a Conduct as a Proof that there is no real Desire in the Court of Versailles to put an End to the War at present.

10. – With regard to any Openings Insinuations, or Ideas which may be thrown out by the Count de Vergennes either relative to the particular Peace of the Two Crowns, or in reference to any Views or Notions France may entertain for conciliating the other Belligerent Powers, Our Will & Pleasure is that you do receive all such Matters *ad referendum* promising to transmit the same faithfully to Your Court, & taking Care to hold such Language as may best avoid giving Room to the Court of France to take

Umbrage or Offence at Your Reserve, & making use of all those Arguments which Your Prudence & Address will suggest.

11. – Notwithstanding You are by Our Full Power authorized to conclude & sign any thing that may be agreed on between the Two Courts, It is our express Will and Pleasure that You do not in Virtue of the said Power, proceed to the Signature of any Act whatever with the Court of France, without first having our Special Orders for that Purpose from One of Our Principal Secretaries of State.

12. – If it shall be agreed between the Two Courts that You and the Person to be nominated by His Most Christian Majesty shall respectively enjoy in France & in England, all the Rights, Prerogatives, Franchises, & Liberties, belonging to your Characters, as if the Two Courts were in full Peace, You are to be duely attentive to maintain Our Dignity in all Things touching the same, & to take Care that You be treated in the same Manner as Ministers of Your Rank from Spain or any other Crowned Head, except as to the Form of not delivering Our Credential Yourself to the Most Christian King in an Audience.

13. – You shall use your particular Endeavours to inform Yourself of the Interior Situation of the Court of France, & of the actual State & Disposition of the French Nation. You will also give a Watchful Attention to the Conduct & Motions of the Spanish & Dutch Ambassadors, and also to those of the Minister or Agents from the American Congress there; And of all Matters which may be of Consequence & worthy of Our Knowledge, You shall constantly give an Account to Us by One of Our Principal Secretaries of State, from whom You will receive such farther Instructions & Directions as We shall think fit to send You, which You are to observe accordingly.

PRO: FO 27/2, v. 557, f. 183 (LC transcription).

Charles James Fox to Thomas Grenville

N.º 2.   St James's 21ˢᵗ May 1782
Sir

. . . . .

His Majesty was pleased to refer it to the consideration of his confidential Servants and in consequence of their advice has thought proper to invest you with the full powers & to give you the instructions which accompany this Dispatch – From the tenour of those instructions, you will I trust easily perceive what line of conduct you are expected to hold with respect to the direct object of your mission, but as it may be of much advantage that you should be acquainted with the general designs & views which have influenced the conduct of the King's Servants upon this occasion in order that you may shape yours accordingly, His Majesty has directed me to explain them to you more fully. Upon reading your letter it was impossible not to perceive that the whole cast & complexion of the French Minster's conversation was very unfavourable to the expectation of any fair or equitable Peace in the present moment & it was therefore the principal concern of the King's Servants what steps should be taken to enable them to turn to account the probable failure of this negotiation.

The two objects which suggested themselves first to their view were 1° – to detach from France if possible some of her present Allies 2° – to gain some for this Country.

To these two might possibly be added a third vizt to draw forth the exertion of this Country & to induce the People to bear their heavy burdens with patience by shewing them that, if the War continues, it is not for want of reasonable endeavours to make Peace on the part of the Crown.

To all these objects the same means seemed applicable, & there appeared nothing for us to do but to convince the world of the sincerity of our wishes for Peace, & our readiness to make reasonable sacrifices, and to contrast these dispositions with the ambitious views of our Enemies which it must be our business as much as possible to unmask. No better method could be thought of for compassing these ends than by authorizing you to make in the King's name the propositions contained in your first Instructions, as a basis for a treaty, & in case of that proposal not being agreed to, to solicit some proposition on their part. If they should make any that wear in any degree the appearance of reason & moderation, you will undoubtedly be instructed to negotiate upon & to enter into a discussion of those points in which may differ from our ideas; I[f] on the contrary they should make one consisting of exorbitant & absurd demands or refuse to make any, it will then surely be in our power to convince the world in general & America & Holland in particular that everything has been done on our part towards reconciliation & that if they still persist in the war, they persist in it without any interest of their own, & for the sole & at last avowed purpose of aggrandizing the House of Bourbon. You will easily perceive how consistent it will be with these views that you should cultivate Dr Franklin & the Dutch minister in a peculiar manner, the former of whom there is all reason to believe very sincere in his wishes for Peace. If in the course of this negotiation a foundation could be laid for a separate one afterwards either with Holland or with America or both, it will have been a most fortunate undertaking.

You will no doubt make all the use possible of the advantageous time in which you are authorized to make these overtures immediately after the most important & decisive Victory that has happened during the War, which though it has undoubtedly given the greatest satisfaction to His Majesty & the most essential turn to his affairs has nevertheless made no alternation in those sentiments of moderation & humanity which incline H.M. to make so many sacrifices for the sake of Peace. The very different face of things from that which they lately wore with respect to the prospect of the West Indian Campain might surely furnish abundant lessons of moderation to those who think of grounding high & unreasonable demands upon the good fortune they have hitherto experienced in War. I need say no more upon this topic as I am sure it would be superfluous to observe that with the more modesty & even delicacy you speak of this great event, the more the weight of it will be felt by those with whom you are to converse upon it.

I send you inclosed the Gazette containing Sir George Rodney's[1] letters & the account of the advantages gained in the East Indies.... I am likewise commanded by H.M. to authorize you to agree to the revival of the intercourse between Dover & Calais by Packet Boats, if such a measure should be (as there is reason to suppose) agreeable to the French Court. I have nothing more to add but to signify to you the King's approbation of the manner in which you have hitherto conducted yourself, and of the very clear and distinct account which you have given of your conversations with the different Ministers.

I have the honour to be &c. —   Charles James Fox

PRO: FO 27/2, v. 557, f. 171 (LC transcription).

[1] Rodney, George Brydges (1719-1792). British admiral. Appointed to command the fleet on the Leeward Islands station, with the additional duty of relieving Gibraltar, he defeated a Spanish squadron off Cape St. Vincent on January 16, 1780, capturing six ships. Knighted, 1780. Fought three indecisive actions against the French fleet under Guichen, April-May 1780. Captured St. Eustatius, early 1781. Because of ill health, resigned command to Sir Samuel Hood, August 1781, and returned to England. Returned to the Caribbean, February 1782. Defeated and captured De Grasse in the Battle of the Saintes, April 1782. Baron Rodney, June 1782.

Charles James Fox to Thomas Grenville

N° 3   St. James's, May 21. 1782.
Sir

Mr Oswald is just arrived with your letter of the 14th Inst: which I shall immediately lay before the King. As I do not see any thing in the contents of it or in the account which Mr Oswald gives of the state of affairs at Paris which makes the sending of the full Powers & Instructions to you less necessary I shall immediately dispatch the Messenger as I had intended, in order that there may be no loss of time in taking the first steps in this business. The only new observation which I think myself at present authorized to make is that it may not be improper for you to mark as distinctly as possible that if Spain & Holland are brought into this negociation, it is not by your desire but by that of the Court of Versailles....

I have the honour to be &c.   Charles James Fox

PRO: FO 27/2, v. 557, f. 203 (LC transcription).

Lord Shelburne to Richard Oswald

Sir,   Whitehall 21ˢᵗ· May 1782.

I have had the honor to lay Your Letter of the 10 insᵗ· before the King, and I have His Majesty's commands to signify to you his approbation of your conduct hitherto.

Mʳ Grenville will I make no doubt acquaint you of the powers sent him by the present Messenger, together with all such other matters, as may be necessary to govern your intercourse with Doctor Franklin and with the other American Commissioners, which you will continue to cultivate by all fair and honorable means, avoiding to give cause of Jealousy to the Court of France. It is His Majesty's pleasure that you shou'd furnish Mʳ· Grenville any Lights which may occur to you in the course of your communication with any of these Gentlemen, which may be useful to him, in his Transactions with the French Ministers, or those of any of the other powers of Europe, who may be to Enter into the proposed Negotiation, and, I must recommend to You to omit no opportunity of letting it be understood that there subsists the strictest Union in His Majesty's Council upon the great subject of Peace and War.

I am sorry to observe that the French Minister gives very little reason to expect that his Court is likely to make good their Professions, which they made thro' so many channels of a desire of Peace upon Terms becoming this Country to accept, upon the strength of which Doctor Franklin invited the present Negotiation. I have that entire Confidence in Doctor Franklin's Integrity and strict honor, that if the Court of France have other views, and that they have been throwing out False Lures to support the appearance of Moderation throughout Europe, and in the hope of misleading, and the chance of Dividing us, I am satisfied, that he must have been himself deceived, and in such a case, I trust that if this shall be proved in the course of the present negotiation, he will consider himself and his Constituents freed from the Ties which will appear to have been founded upon no Ideas of common Interest.

We shall however I hope, speedily ascertain the real purposes of France by their conduct in the future progress of this negotiation, which the King will not suffer to go into any length. In the mean time you will govern your conversation with the American Commissioners with all possible prudence, collecting their Sentiments, and every other Information, which you conceive may hereafter prove useful, and I have his Majestys commands to acquaint you, that it is His pleasure you shou'd continue at Paris, 'till you receive his orders to return, of which you will acquaint Doctor Franklin and Monsr le Comte de Vergennes.

I am &c.   Shelburne.

•   •   •   •   •

PRO: FO 27/2, v. 557, f. 207 (LC transcription).

Charles James Fox to Thomas Grenville

N°. 4   St James's 26th May 1782
Sir

I had the honour of laying your letter of the 14th Inst: before the King. His Majesty was pleased to refer it to the consideration of his confidential Servants and in consequence of their Advice has commanded me to signify to you his pleasure that you should lose no time in making all the advantage possible of the concession which H.M. has from his ardent desire of Peace, been induced to make with respect to the Independancy of the thirteen States. and in order to this end I have it in command from H.M. to authorize you to make the offer of the said Independancy in the first instance instead of making it a conditional article of a general treaty. I need not point out to you the use that may be made of this method of commencing the Business as you seem to have a very just idea of the advantages that may be derived from it. The principal one appears to me to be like this: that the American Agents must clearly perceive, if there should now be any obstacle to the recognition which they have so much at heart, and which after all must be a matter infinitely interesting to them, that the difficulty comes from the Court of Versailles & not from hence, and that it is chiefly owing to the number of Allies with which that Court thinks fit to encumber America in the negotiation for a Peace although she was never benefited by their assistance during the War. When this point shall have been reasoned and understood I can not help flattering myself that it will appear upon the face of the thing unreasonable and intolerable to any honest American, that they having gained the point for which they contested should voluntarily & unnecessarily submit to all the calamities of War without an Object, till all the Powers in Europe shall have settled all the various claims & differences which they may have one with the other, and in which it is not even pretended that America has any interest whatever either near or remote. You will not fail to press Mr· Franklin's own idea, that the object of the treaty of Alliance with France being attained, the treaty determines, to which if that Gentleman should adhere we may fairly consider one of the ends of your mission as attained. As to the good faith which is supposed to be pledged by Congress to France not to make a separate Peace, I think it can only be understood that Congress is bound not to enter into any treaty separately or without the knowledge & consent of France, but surely not that when a general Peace is proposed Congress is bound to support every claim set up by the Court of Versailles & her Allies, which would be a kind of engagement that never was I believe entered into by any State at any time. It has often been stipulated between two allied Powers that one shall not make peace till the other has attained some specific object named in the treaty, but that one country should bind herself to another to make war till her Ally shall be satisfied with respect to all the claims she may think fit to set up, claims undefined & perhaps unthought of at the time of making the engagement, would be a species of treaty as new I believe as it would be monstrous. – If this view of the thing should produce the effects you seem inclined to hope from it, I need not observe to you how greatly all the advantages of a separate Peace would be encreased by the late events in the W. Indies; but I have the satisfaction to assure you that those events have in no degree abated H.M.'s most ardent & sincere desire for a general pacification and I concur with you in your conjecture that the extravagance of the French expectations arises chiefly from the support they expect from America, & consequently will be considerably abated whenever they see reason to fear the loss of that Support; so that if things should take a right turn with respect to the American Agents, the best road may probably be open to a general as well as a separate Peace....

I am commanded by H.M. to direct you to communicate with Mr· Oswald with the greatest freedom & openness upon the concerns of your mission. which are connected more & more every day with the business of America. With respect to Mr· Franklin if he continues in those friendly dispositions which your letter and Mr· Oswald's account seem to indicate the more confidence you shew to him, the better chance there will be of bringing this business either in one way or in the other to a succesful Issue.

I am, Sir, &c.   Charles James Fox

PRO: FO 27/2, v. 557, f. 251 (LC transcription).

Third Peace Conference

[Translation]

26 May 1782

Mr. Grenville opened the conference by informing the Comte de Vergennes that he was formally authorized to renew the assurances that he had already given of the peaceful dispositions of the King of England, and to repeat formally on the part of that Prince the peace overtures that had been made only by means of discourse in the first conferences. To justify his mission Mr. Grenville handed the Comte de Vergennes a copy of the full powers that had just been sent to him.

The Comte de Vergennes, after having assured Mr. Grenville of the perfect reciprocity of the King's sentiments for the prompt reestablishment of peace, had the full powers read, but having observed that they authorized Mr. Grenville to treat of peace only with France, and that there was no mention made of the King's allies, the Comte de Vergennes remarked on it to Mr. Grenville, and he evinced all the more astonishment that from the first conferences he had warned that the King neither wished nor could hear of a separate peace, and that this preliminary question ought to have been the principal subject of the expediting of the courier that Mr. Grenville sent to England, and in consequence, of the responses that he received from his Court. The Comte de Vergennes again declared to the English plenipotentiary that the King would not treat separately from his allies, and particularly from Spain, and that if Mr. Grenville was not furnished with full powers to that effect, the negotiation would be held up at its beginning, and that the Comte de Vergennes no longer had the option of speaking to him.

Mr. Grenville avowed that he had no other powers than those which he had just produced, and on the question whether his instructions did not include anything in that regard, he responded that he was only authorized to receive *ad referendum* the objections that were made to him. M. the Comte de Vergennes repeated what he had already said of the King's resolution not to treat without his allies, adding that he would report to the King all that Mr. Grenville had just said to him, and that he would not delay in informing him of His Majesty's response.

Mr. Grenville then asked whether there was also a question of admitting the Dutch. M. the Comte de Vergennes responded that the United Provinces, having been drawn into the war without cause by Great Britain, had addressed themselves to the King to obtain his support; that His Majesty rendered them services, and that although he was not bound to anything, he thought it in accord with his justice and his generosity not to desert them; that moreover the King desired all the more that Holland take part in the general peacemaking; that, the war continuing between that Republic and England, and given the connections and the political liaisons that exist among all the nations of Europe, it was to be feared that it would be rekindled with all the powers soon after the signing of peace. Mr. Grenville agreed with the accuracy of these reflections, and he avowed that it would be desirable that the peace be general, because this would be the only means to render it lasting, but he was not authorized to make any engagement on that subject. The Comte de Vergennes having again expressed his regret at not being able, given the nature of Mr. Grenville's full powers, to enter into the matter with him, the latter remarked a desire to express nevertheless the proposals that he was authorized to make; and the Comte de Vergennes having responded that although he did not have the option of speaking, he well had that of listening, the English plenipotentiary said to him: that the King of England was disposed to recognize the independence of the United States of North America; and that he would cede even New York, Charlestown, Savannah, and all of Georgia, on condition that for the remainder things would be left, around the Globe, in the state in which they were in virtue of the Treaty of Paris. This proposal gave rise to the observation, already made in the first conference, that in order to make a lasting peace, it was fitting that the parties render reciprocal justice to each other.

The Comte de Vergennes terminated the session by informing Mr. Grenville that he would report everything to the King, and that he would inform the English plenipotentiary of His Majesty's decision.

FFAA: Pol. Corr., England, v. 537, f. 82 (LC transcription).

Robert R. Livingston's Report of a Conversation with Chevalier de la Luzerne

[Philadelphia] 28th. May 1782

The Minister of his M.C.M. has the honor to inform Mr. Livingston of several particulars relative to the negotiation that the court of London appeared disposed to open in Europe. The first steps were taken under the former administration. This remark is essential because it is possible that the new Ministers may take others more decisive or it is equally possible that they may entirely change the system & continue the war still longer.

Emissaries have been sent to Paris and to the Hague to sound on the one hand Mr John Adams & in the hope that his connection with some Independent members might facilitate an accommodation, & on the other side <*> in the hope that very advantageous offers might seduce his majesty & engage him by a separate peace to abandon his allies. The Chevalier De la Luzerne is not informed of the steps that have been taken at Madrid or by the States General.

The proposition made so secretly to France tended to a partial peace it offered France the possession of their conquests in the west Indies the suppression of an English commissary at Dunkerque & advantages in the East Indies. These offers were certainly satisfactory to his majesty & he would have had no reason to reject them if he had had no allies. But his engagements marked out another line of conduct. He replied, that however sincerely soever he was disposed to peace he could commence no negotiation to this end without the participation of his Allies. The Emissary easily comprehended that this answer related as well to the united States as to Spain – And pretended that the condition was inadmissible that England in treating upon this foundation would acknowledge the independance of her colonies which made no part of his system – The Minister of his Majesty replied that their independance was considered by the king as an indispensable point & that it made the basis of his system.

The English agent then demanded if there were no means to avoid treating with us of the affairs of America. The Count De Vergennes replied by refering him to the answer given to the first overtures of pacification made by the mediators & communicated to Mr Livingston.

It should be observed that whether Eng^d treats of the affairs of the United States with the court of Versailles, or whether she opens a direct communication with the United States she can not avoid treating with the American negotiators sent by congress – in either case she will be under the necessity of acknowledging that body.

The conduct of his majesty on this occasion being strictly conformable to justice & his engagements his minister confines him self to a simple communication of it to Mr Livingston – He confides also to him, that M^r Le Cte De Vergennes in declaring to the English agent that his majesty could not listen to any negotiation for a peace if the court of London did not treat at the same time with his allies, added verbally that the king did not attend to ~~object for~~ his own satisfaction till that of his allies was procured.

Besides this the effects of these steps taken by the court of London has been to engage France to pursue with redoubled vigor the measures that have given birth to these appearances of peace but which would certainly not terminate in it if England perceived that her enemies relaxed their efforts in any manner – It is above all things indispensable that the United States should in the course of this campaign be in a situation to cooperate in vigorous enterprizes which may be formed it appears that the design of the court of London pointed out by the debates in parliament is to reduce by a defensive war their operations upon this continent. The Minister of his most Christian majesty has at present no information relative to the plans of the approaching campaign. But whatever they may be it would be useful to be enabled to inform his court that the United States will not adopt an inactivity which would be equivalent to the truce requested. But that their design is to trouble the repositing that the enemy wish to deliver themselves to, and that the operations, whether combined, or separately undertaken by the united States, will be pushed with activity during the ensuing campaign.

As to the place of the negotiations Congress *** *** ****** knew in 1779 when they named a plenipotentiary, & in 81. when they gave him three colleagues that it could only be in Europe & that this was the most effectual means of preventing delays & jealousy & of ~~supporting~~ maintaining the confidence & harmony which has so happily subsisted hitherto between the allies. It would be important that the minister of his Majesty could inform his court – that congress persists in these dispositions & that in case ~~that~~ commissaries offer to treat upon this continent they should be referred to the ministers of the united States who are provided with instructions on this subject in Europe. That the court of London should address itself to them, & that it is impossible that the seat of negotiation should be in America – When these overtures were made to the court of Versailles the agent made no mention of those that were to be made in America or to the American Ministers in Europe. It is obvious that the design of this conduct is to inspire reciprocal distrust. And the Chevalier De La Luzerne conceives it can in no way more effectually be prevented than by a full communication of every circumstance which shall relate to the pacification & to the interests of the alliance which shall come to his knowledge –

Made to congress by the Secretary for foreign affairs.

Robt R. Livingston

NA: PCC, item 79, v. 2, pp. 221-227 (DS); M247, reel 105.

Robert R. Livingston to Benjamin Franklin

Nᵒ· 12   Philadelphia 30ᵗʰ· May 1782
Dʳ· Sir,

                          .   .   .   .   .

I have told you we have nothing to apprehend here from the offers of
Britain – I have had no reason since to change that opinion – The way
however to put it out of doubts is to enable us to expel the Enemy from
this Continent. – The task is not difficult, and the object is sufficiently
important, not to let it depend upon other operations –

                          .   .   .   .   .

You draw an agreeable picture of the French Court, and their favourable
dispositions. They stand very high in the esteem of this Country and tho'
we sometimes entertain the hope of repaying by our Commerce and alliance
the friendship they have shewn us, we are not on that account, the less
sensible of our obligation to them. The distrust and jealousies which secret
Enemies have endeavoured to excite have died away – One successful
exertion in our favour will secure to them for ever the affections of this
Country....

                          .   .   .   .   .

I have the honour to be Sir, with great respect and esteem Your Excellʸ
most obedᵗ &c.
                                              Robᵗ R. Livingston

NA: PCC, item 79, v. 1, pp. 445-450 (LBkC); M247, reel 105.

Thomas Grenville to Charles James Fox

Sir,   Paris May 30, 1782.
I received on the 25ᵗʰ your two letters of the 21ˢᵗ· together with the
instructions & Full Power which accompanied them, and at the same time
the account of the glorious victory obtained by his Majesty's Arms in the
West Indies, & the important acquisitions in the East, upon which great
events I beg leave to offer my most humble but hearty congratulations.
I saw Mʳ de Vergennes on the 26ᵗʰ· and having informed him that I had
a Credential Letter which I should be authorised to deliver, whenever
H.M.C.M. should name a person in quality of Minister on his part, I gave
him at the same time a Copy of the Full Power which I had received; in
reading it, he immediately made the objection I had expected from him,
viz, that the Full Power enabled me only to treat with the French Minister,
whereas H.M.C.M. had already declared, that he could only treat in

conjunction with the other belligerent powers, & that he was connected by the ties of blood to Spain, and by friendship to Holland who had been thrown into this war: I took this opportunity of complying with your instructions by reminding Mr. de Vergennes that to include Spain & Holland in this negotiation had not been the desire of the Court of London, but that of the Court of Versailles; and when he observed, that a general peace was the most essential object, I agreed that it was so, but said that it might perhaps be most easily produced by not complicating those interests, which the more simple they were kept, the more easily they would be discussed; he said he would send for me another day to inform me of the King his Master's answer, but seemed to think this in the first step an insurmountable difficulty: I however went on to tell him that I was authorised by his Majesty to make those propositions as a Basis for a Treaty which I had in a former conversation spoken of as probable to occur; and I did this, notwithstanding his previously declining to answer what I should state, because I conceived it to be your wish that no time should be lost in making a direct proposition, independent of the manner in which it might be received. it was not till this morning that I received Mr. de Vergennes's answer; he told me that H.M.C.M. had found the Full Power sent to me very insufficient, as it did not enable me to treat with the Ministers of the other beligerent powers, without whose concurrence he had already declared he could enter into no treaty. Mr de Vergennes then explained the H.M.C.M. did not require that all the Parties should be included in one Full Power, but that at least I should have sufficient separate authorities to treat with them: he mentioned Spain and America as allies, and speaking of Holland I desired him to explain himself acurately whether or no he considered Holland as an Ally; he said certainly not, but they were in *communautè de guerre*, & that his Master was too noble in his sentiments, to think of treating without giving Holland an opportunity of making peace at the same time, if she chose: I reminded him upon this, that the objection therefore now made, was not matter of obligation on the part of France, but of choice. the business then rests upon this difficulty, and waits your answer to it.

I have not, I own, at these conversations dwelt much upon the late glorious victory; an event so decisive best speaks it own importance, and the propositions I was charged with unaltered by that success, perhaps in being so, most strongly speak the temper and moderation of his Majesty's Councils: indeed, added to this, it has been & still is so sorely felt here that it would not be very easy to allude to it with sufficient delicacy; I wish I could say, that the sensation it creates seemed likely to assists the business of pacification, but the reverse is so much the truth, that publick opinion looks less than ever favourable to it; and this I am persuaded a good deal owing to some publick expressions of the King's which are adopted and repeated with great earnestness: *il faut etre fachè mais non pas consternè; j'ai, perdu* cinq *vaisseaux, Je serai faire quinze a leur place et on ne me trouvera pas pour ceci plus* traitable *à la paix.*[1] it does not seem improbable that this loss may prove fatal to Monsr de Castries's situation, whose influence is now supposed so weak, that Monsr de Chatelet[2] is much talked of to succeed him.

I am to inform you, Sir, with respect to the proposed reestablishment of the passage from Dover to Calais, that this Court is ready to accede to it, provided that there shall be permitted as many French packet-boats as English:....

Mr Franklin's conversation continues to express a strong desire for peace, & constant attention to the idea of establishing a solid Union between England and America but I must add does not lose sight of that part of America's treaty with France, which restrains either party from making peace or truce without the consent of the other: he appears to be intent upon keeping the treaties of peace distinct between the several parties, tho' going on at the same time; & to this idea which seems to correspond in part with your intentions, I give every encouragement I can. I have reason to think that when I see him next in two or three days, he may be something more explicit, but there has been already so much delay in sending this Courier notwithstanding my pressing for a speedy answer, that I will no longer retard him, but reserve for a future occasion what I may learn more from Mr Franklin.

permit one to remind you, Sir, that I shall not perhaps be allowed to send you another Courier till I shall have received your answer from London: & I should add that it is clear from Mr de Vergennes's conversation that the French Court are determined not to consider the independance of America as in any respect ceded to them, and that such will be the principal part of their first answer to your propositions, should the previous difficulty about the Full Power be got over by any alteration made in it.

I have only farther to express how highly sensible I am of the honour done me by His Majesty's approbation of my conduct.

I have the honour to be Sir your very obedient humble Servant

Thomas Grenville.

R 5th June (by Ogg.)

PRO: FO 27/2, v. 557, f. 267 (LC transcription).
[1] *We may be angry but not dismayed; I have lost five vessels, I will build fifteen in their place and will not be more amenable to peace for that reason.*

² *Châtelet-Lomont, Louis-Marie-Florent, Duc de (1727-1793). French military leader and diplomat.*

Fourth Peace Conference

[Translation]

Thursday, 30 May 1782

The Comte de Vergennes declared to Mr. Grenville that he had placed under the King's eyes the full powers of which Mr. Grenville had delivered him a copy; that His Majesty had been surprised to see that these powers made no mention of his allies; that this omission prevented His Majesty from establishing even a Semblance of a negotiation; because he was unalterably resolved not to make peace without his allies.

This ministerial response gave Mr. Grenville cause to ask who the King's allies were; the Comte de Vergennes responded that those allies were the King of Spain and America, and that the Dutch, without being allies of France, should have a part in the negotiation. The observation concerning Spain and America gave no cause for objection on the part of Mr. Grenville; but the statement relative to Holland gave Mr. Grenville cause to ask what connection existed between the King and the United Provinces; whether the latter had engagements with His Majesty that prevented them from treating of their peace separately. To this question, the Comte de Vergennes responded: that no engagement of that nature existed between the King and the Republic; that the Dutch were only in community of war with His Majesty; that the King, when England had drawn them into the war, had rendered them all the Services that depended on him, and that he would continue so to render them; but that those Services had been free and voluntary; that the Dutch have all their liberty, that nothing prevents them from making their peace separately if that suits them; that the King would not encourage them any longer to refuse the offer that the English Ministry makes them in that regard, that he did not provoke them to take up arms: but that if the Dutch judge it in their interest not to separate their cause, and if they are determined not to treat separately with the Court of London, the King thinks that his dignity, his magnanimity, and even the tranquillity of Europe would be interested in his not leaving them in a trap vis-à-vis a power as considerable as Great Britain.

That article thus clarified, Mr. Grenville repeated the proposals that he had made in the conference on the 26th. He said that, America being the object of the war, and the King of England being disposed to give full satisfaction on that article, the war should cease for want of an object. The Comte de Vergennes replied 1$^{st.}$ that the article of America should be treated directly with the United States and not with France, which is not authorized to that effect; 2$^{nd.}$ that while admitting that America is the object of the war relative to France, that object is not the only one; that the great number of our grievances are recorded and in the offices of the English Ministers and in large part in the observations made on the evidentiary memorandum of the Court of London; that when one wishes to treat seriously, one proceeds from the point at which one finds oneself, in order to make justice reciprocally; that in addition, while admitting America as the sole object of the war with France, there remained Spain to satisfy, that power never having had anything in common with the Americans, whose independence she still did not recognize. But Mr. Grenville always returning to his text, and citing in order to justify it a phrase included in the confidential observations dispatched to the two mediating courts; it was observed to him that the Court of London itself was so persuaded that France, as well as Spain, had interests separate from those of America that in a response which it had dispatched to the mediators, it regarded the discussion concerning America as an affair purely national and domestic; it rejected any intervention by any other power, and offered to treat with France and with Spain on subjects that might concern those two powers. Mr. Grenville made no objection against this reasoning; however, he did not speak of desisting from his proposal. Mr. Grenville did not conceal the motive for which the Court of London wishes to discuss the affairs of America directly with the King; it would like to present the independence of the United States as a compensation for the conquests made by His Majesty's arms, and Mr. Grenville fears that in treating with the Americans, that compensation would have no place. The Comte de Vergennes responded that this was still not the moment to take up that object, that it would be necessary beforehand to agree on the preliminary objects that should bring about the establishment of the negotiation.

It was observed to Mr. Grenville that the negotiation to be established directly between England and the Americans was only an affair of form; but he responded that this form would remove the foundation, since if the negotiation relative to America should be unknown to France, it could no longer be a question of compensation, an object nevertheless that would enter into the views of the English Ministry. To this observation it was replied that the response of the Comte de Vergennes, without accepting the principle, did not reject it, and that it was a matter to be examined when one was ready to discuss the foundation.

FFAA: Pol. Corr., England, v. 537, f. 101 (LC transcription).

Congressional Resolution

[Philadelphia] Friday May 31. 1782

On a report of a committee...to whom was referred the foregoing verbal communication of the honorable the Minister plenipotentiary of France to the Secretary for foreign Affairs.

Resolved That the Secretary for foreign Affairs acquaint the Minister Plenipotentiary of France that the signal proofs of inviolable constancy to his engagements given by his most Christian Majesty, in the answer to the attempts of the British Court to seduce him into a separate peace, has been received by Congress with the sentiments with which it ought naturally to inspire faithful and affectionate Allies, and entirely corresponds with the expectations which the magnanimity and good faith of his past conduct had established. That Congress embrace with particular satisfaction this occasion of renewing to his most Christian Majesty the assurances which they have so often and so sincerely repeated of a reciprocal and equal resolution to adhere in every event to the principles of the Alliance and to harken to no propositions for peace which are not perfectly conformable thereto – That the insidious steps which the Court of London is pursuing render it improbable that any propositions conformable to those principles will be made to the United States; but that in case such propositions should be made, Congress will not depart from the measures which they have heretofore taken for preventing delay and for conducting the discussions of them in confidence, and in concert with His Most Christian Majesty – And that as Congress observe with the warmest approbation the purpose of his most Christian Majesty to oppose to the false appearances of peace held out by Great Britain those redoubled efforts which may render her sincerely disposed to it, so his Majesty may be persuaded that they are no less impressed with the necessity of such concurrent exertions on the part of the United States as may frustrate the views of the common enemy in the new system which their policy seems to have adopted on this Continent.

NA: PCC, item 5, pp. 685-687 (Journal); M247, reel 19.

Comte de Vergennes to Comte de Montmorin

[Translation]

Nᵒ 33A   Versailles, 31 May 1782.

M. Le Comte de Montmorin.

. . . . .

The Courier whom I informed you, Sir, that Mr. Grenville had dispatched to England returned on the 23rd. That Emissary informed me of it the same day, and requested an interview with me. I fixed it for the following day. I can no better apprise you of what happened in that Conference than by communicating to you the Minutes of it that I had drawn up by M. de Rayneval, who was present. The method of having a witness appeared necessary to me to prevent misunderstandings.

You will observe in the Minutes, Sir, that although I was very affirmative in barring all Hope of entering into negotiations as long as Mr. Grenville does not have a special power to treat with the King's allies and friends, namely with Spain, I reserved explaining myself definitively until I received His Majesty's orders.

I did so yesterday at a new conference to which I had invited the English Emissary. I declared to him categorically that his Court hoped in vain that the King might be disposed to listen to any peace overture and to admit the least Semblance of negotiations if they were not common to his allies and friends; that the first preliminary to fulfill, which the King would in no Case yield, was that the Court of London give him a special power to treat with the King of Spain and with all His Majesty's allies and friends.

Mr. Grenville showed no resistance in regard to Spain, he seemed to understand the necessity of this preliminary, but he was also quite constant in regard to the States General. He asked me if an alliance existed between the King and that republic, or an Engagement that does not permit them to treat of peace separately from each other: my Response was that nothing of that Kind existed, but that His Majesty's magnanimity would make up for that deficiency. The Dutch, I told him, having been drawn into a Community of war with us that we had neither sought nor provoked, the King cautioned them by all the good offices and all the services that depended on him: The same Sentiments that animated His Majesty in principle still apply in all their force, and he thinks his glory and the interest of humanity engaged not to allow them into the trap of a war too unequal for them if peace is restored among all the other belligerent powers. But, Mr. Grenville returned, cannot the Dutch themselves treat of peace separately? Yes, Monsieur, I replied, they have the most complete Liberty in that Regard; the King, who has hastened to serve them, has not sought to impede them in anything, and even today does not wish to influence their deliberations and their resolutions, but as long as the States General do not declare themselves for a separate peace, the King will not cease to insist that they be admitted to the general peacemaking. His Majesty would think the tranquillity of Europe compromised if in making peace, there remained a Seed of War. I made this Statement less relative to

England, which I have little Interest in enlightening, than in regard to Russia, which continues to put into its offices to establish the negotiation of a *particular* peace between England and the republic an ardour that reconciles itself very imperfectly with the Impartiality from which a mediator should in no event stray. The Court of Petersburg, which isolates subjects instead of seeing them in a great ensemble, has just taken a step so much the more singular vis-à-vis us, for it seems to want us to cooperate in its noble plan to detach Holland from us and reconcile it with England. I reserve, Sir, explaining this step to you and sending you a Copy of the letter of M. le Comte d'Ostermann[1] and M. le Prince Bariatinsky[2] until the King has agreed upon the draft of the response to be made.

There is another point on which it would be interesting for me and for the course of the negotiations, if they should be begun, to explain myself in a precise manner to Mr. Grenville. You will have noted, Sir, in the Minute of the conference of the 26th that he offered me, without being provoked to it, and that he threw at my head, so to speak, the Cession of New York, Charles Town, and Savannah.

In reflecting upon this premature offer, I could only attribute it to two motives. One, which is sufficiently out in the open, is to have us take them as sufficient Compensation for the claims that we can make for the Sacrifices we were disposed to make in America. The other motive, which should be more secret, is doubtless to compromise us with that same America whether we accept or reject the offers made. In the first Case, we will be represented as wanting to hold it in a Kind of tutelage and dependence in order to compromise all its Interests; in the second, they will not be negligent in insinuating to it that we are sacrificing its interests to ours, and that after having made America the Cause of this war, we are prolonging it and delaying its Satisfaction only to bring about our own and to give vent to our ambition. It is to forestall these stratagems and to obviate the Consequences that they may produce that I informed Mr. Grenville peremptorily that, being without the ability and without the power to discuss the affairs of the Americans, it was useless for him to make me offers that he can make to them, that it is with their deputies that he should treat directly, and that in no Case could I take it upon myself to be their agent. I did not conceal from the English Emissary that, given the King's intention of only working toward peace conjointly with his allies, His Majesty could not yield to any step that might give them Anxiety or alter the Confidence that he has merited on their part. I pointed out to him at the same time that if the King's justice were interested in leaving to his friends the Care of settling their Interests, the dignity of the King of England would not be less in that he appeared to cede to the King what he might be disposed to do in favor of the Americans, which would be for him that that new republic should have what His Britannic Majesty could or would accord to him.

It is possible, Sir, that the English ministry, although determined upon the recognition of the Independence of the 13 united provinces, is loath to give a special full power to its Emissary to treat with the American plenipotentiaries on that jealous subject. To recognize them in that quality would be to acknowledge the sovereign and independent State of their Constituents, and consequently to judge the trial before pleading the case; if that sole difficulty is hampering the opening of the negotiations, I would not be reluctant to find Expedients to conciliate it, but we are not at that point. It is necessary to await what the Courier that Mr. Grenville is sending to London will report. If he is not sent a new general power to treat with all the King's allies, or at least a special power to treat with Spain, I think that it will be a Case of putting a stop to an appearance of negotiating, the prolonged illusion of which could also be useful to our Enemies, which could be injurious to us.

I estimate, Sir, that the mediators would view this rupture with great Satisfaction. M. le Comte de Florida Blanca will surely be informed by the most recent Despatches from Vienna of the harm at Court which the decision the English have taken of addressing themselves directly to us has caused M. le Prince de Kaunitz.[3] It is a Kind of guile which he puts in motion to inspire in us early a distrust that I share, but which I will guard myself well from allowing him to perceive, and to impress upon us early that the English are throwing upon us the reproach of frustrating the mediators of the glorious Role which would be bestowed upon them.

M. de Kaunitz has done me the honor of proposing the *uti possidetis*, on which he thinks that the negotiations are being established, although it was only a question of the role of Mr. Forth, who was sent by Lord North; that I disregarded him at the time, and that he has said no more of it since. It is also at my urging that the new English ministers have decided to move the Seat of the negotiations to Versailles. I listen to everything with composure, and I walk my road tranquilly. You reckon well that I do not fly into a passion over such ineptitudes. I content myself with smiling; although on occasions I summon up in a suitable manner for the English Emissary the interests of the Mediators and the Attentions due them, it is not with that force of reason that would change his Conviction. I think there is always gain in handling one's affairs oneself. Moreover, I do not reckon sufficiently on the favor for us and even on the impartiality of the mediators for having more Envy than reason to confide our Interests to their direction.

Setting aside personal prejudices, I think them much more interested in prolonging this war than in ending it. It opens for them sources of riches from which they benefit. This, of course, is not to our Advantage; it is necessary to finish, and the sooner the better, when we can do it with dignity and justice. Those two words are the Gospel which I preach on every occasion to Mr. Grenville.

You would do well, Sir, to communicate this letter and the enclosed writings to M. le Comte de Florida Blanca, even giving him Copies if he requests them. I hope that he will recognize my fidelity to the principles which I established in commencing it.

. . . . .

Vergennes

FFAA: Pol. Corr., Spain, v. 607, f. 135 (LC transcription).
¹ Osterman, Ivan Andreevich, Count (1715-1811). Russian political figure. Vice-Chancellor, 1775-1796.
² Bariatinskii, Ivan Sergeevich (1740-1811). Russian diplomat. Minister to France, 1773-1786.
³ Kaunitz-Rietberg, Wenzel-Anton, Prince von (1711-1794). Austrian political figure and diplomat. Ambassador to France, 1750-1752. Chancellor, 1752-1792.

Benjamin Franklin to John Adams

Sir,   Passy, June 2ᵈ 1782.

Since mine of May 8ᵗʰ I have not had any thing material to communicate to your Excellency. Mʳ Grenville indeed arriv'd just after I had dispatch'd that Letter, and I introduc'd him to M. De Vergennes; but as his Mission seem'd only a Repetition of that by Mʳ Oswald, the same Declarations of the King of England's sincere Desire of Peace, and willingness to treat of a General Pacification with all the Powers at War, and to treat at Paris, which were answer'd by the same Declarations of the good Dispositions of this Court, and that it could not treat without the Concurrence of its Allies, I omitted writing till something should be produc'd from a kind of Agreement that Mʳ Vergennes would acquaint Spain & Holland with that Overture and that Mʳ· Grenville would write for full Powers to treat & make Propositions &cᵃ, nothing of Importance being in the meantime to be transacted.

Mʳ· Grenville accordingly dispatch'd a Messenger for London, who return'd in about 12 Days. Mʳ· G. call'd on me after having been at Versailles and acquainted me that he had received the Power, and had left a Copy of it with M. de Vergennes, & that he was thereby authoris'd to treat with France and her Allies. The next time I went to Versailles, I desired to see that Copy, and was surpris'd to find in it no mention of the Allies of France or any one of them; and on speaking with M. De

Vergennes about it I found he began to look upon the whole as a Piece of Artifice to amuse us & gain Time; since he had uniformly declar'd to every Agent who had appear'd here, viz: to Forth Oswald & Grenville, that the King would not treat without the Concurrence of his Allies, and yet England had given a Power to treat with France only, which shew'd that she did not intend to treat at all, but meant to continue the War. I had not 'till Yesterday an Opportunity of talking with M^r. Grenville on the Subject, and expressing my Wonder, after what he told me, that there should be no mention made of our States in his Commission: He could not explain this to my Satisfaction; but said he believ'd the Omission was occasioned by their Copying an old Commission given to M^r. Stanly[1] at the last Treaty of Peace, for that he was sure the Intention was that he should treat with us, his Instructions being fully to that purpose. I acquainted him that I thought a special Commission was necessary, without which we could not conceive him authoris'd and therefore could not treat with him. – I imagine that there is a Reluctance in their King to take this first Step, as the giving such a Commission would itself be a kind of Acknowledgment of our Independence; their late Success against Count de Grasse may also have given them Hopes that by Delay & more Successes they may make that Acknowledgment & a Peace less necessary.

M^r. Grenville has written to his Court for further Instructions. We shall see what the Return of his Courier will produce. If full Powers to treat with each of the Powers at War against England does not appear, I imagine the Negociation will be broken off. M^r. G. in his Conversations with me insists much on our being under no Engagements not to make Peace without Holland. I have answer'd him that I know not but you may have enter'd into some, and that if there should be none, a general Pacification made at the same time, would be best for us all, & that I believ'd neither Holland nor we could be prevail'd on to abandon our Friends. What happens farther shall be immediately communicated. Be pleased to present my Respects to Mr Lawrens to whom I wrote some Days since. Mr Jay I suppose is on his Way hither. –

With great Respect, I have the honour to be, Sir, Your Excellency's most obedient & most humble Servant,   B Franklin

MHS: The Adams Papers, microfilm reel 357 (ALS).

[1] Stanley, Hans (1720?-1780). British political figure. Member of Parliament, 1743-1747, 1754-1780. A follower of Newcastle and Pitt. A lord of the admiralty, 1757-1765. Chargé d'affaires for peace negotiations with France, May-September 1761. Appointed ambassador extraordinary to Russia, 1766, to negotiate a triple defensive alliance of Great Britain, Russia, and Prussia, but did not serve, owing to Prussian disinterest.

Thomas Grenville to Charles James Fox

Sir,   Paris June 4th 1782.

Mr Oswald arrived here on the 31st,...and I received by him the honour of your letter of the 26th.

You will have seen by my last of the 30th, that Monsr de Vergennes's objections to the Full Power are such, as, while they subsist, preclude any farther discussion of business; I have therefore with regard to him nothing new to inform you of. it cannot however Sir have escaped your notice, that the offer of Independance in the first instance instead of making it a conditional article of general Treaty, necessarily changes part of the propositions I had in charge to make to Monsr de Vergennes. I take it for granted therefore that in any future conversation with the French Minister, it was your intention that I should omitt the mention of Independance, and confine myself simply to the Peace of 1763 as the basis of a treaty: but as I should be very sorry to mis-interpret this or any part of your instructions, I flatter myself that you will have the goodness to direct me upon this subject: the doubt which has arisen from Monsr de Vergennes and Mr Franklin about the Full Power, gives sufficient time for this explanation without any additional delay.

It is I see in the sense I mention that Mr Franklin wishes it, for when I spoke to him of the offer your last letter would authorise, he expressed very great satisfaction at it's being kept out of the treaty with France, adding that the more good England did to America the more America would assist this business: to repeat therefore the same offer as a proposition to France would defeat it's purpose with America.

I hope soon to receive your orders upon this as upon the subject of my last letter, in which I ought to have added that Mr Franklin seemed not a little jealous of there being no powers yet sent to treat with America.

I have the honour to be Sir with great truth, your most obedient, and most humble Servant   Thomas Grenville

R. 8th

PRO: FO 27/2, v. 557, f. 274 (LC transcription).

Benjamin Vaughan to Benjamin Franklin

June 5th: [1782]

—That great effects might be obtained by something < ******* > being done spontaneously from England.

Upon this & other considerations, his majesty has been induced to give a striking proof of his royal magnanimity and disinterested wish for the restoration of peace; by commanding his majesty's ministers to direct Mr Grenville that *the Independence of America should be proposed by him in the first instance, instead of making it the condition of a general peace.*

I have given a confidential information to you of these particulars, that you may take such measures as shall appear to you most adviseable for making a direct communication of the substance of the same either immediately to congress or through the medium of General Washington, or in other manner which you may think most likely to impress the well disposed parts of America with the fairness & liberality of his majesty's proceedings in such great and spontaneous concessions.

The advantages which we may expect from ~~the~~ such concession are – that America once apprized of the king's disposition to acknowledge the independence of the thirteen states, and of the disinclination in the French court to terminate the war must see that it is from this moment to be carried on with a view of negotiating points in which she can have no concern, whether they regard France, or Spain & Holland, at the desire of France; but some of which on the contrary may be in future manifestly injurious to the interests of America herself – That [***] if the negotiation is broke off, it will ~~doubtless~~ undoubtedly be for the sake of those powers, and not America, whose object is accomplished the instant she accepts of an independence, which is not merely held out to her in the way of negotiation by the executive power, but a distinct unconditional offer arising out of the resolutions of parliament, and therefore wanted by the sense of the nation at large.

These facts being made notorious, it is scarce conceivable, that America, composed as it is, will continue efforts under French ~~government~~ direction, and protract the distresses & calamities which it is ~~still~~ well known that war has subjected ~~them~~ her to. It is to be presumed that from that moment she will look with jealousy upon the French troops in that country, who may from allies become dangerous enemies.

If however any particular state or states, men or description of men, should continue, against the general inclinations of the continent, devoted to France, this communication will surely direct their views, expose their motives, and deprive them of their influence in all matters of general concern or exertion – You will however take particular care in your manner of conducting yourselves, not only that there should not be the smallest room for suspicion of our good faith and sincerity; but that we have no view in it of causing dissension among the colonies, or even of separating America from France upon terms inconsistent with her own honor – You must therefore convince them that the great object of this country is, not merely peace, but reconciliation with America on the noblest terms & by the noblest means.

(Verte)

LC: *Benjamin Franklin Papers, microfilm reel 7 (AD)*.

Lord Shelburne to Sir Guy Carleton and Admiral Robert Digby

Secret & Confidential   Whitehall. 5th June 1782.
Gentlemen,[1]

It is essential to the King's Service that I should acquaint you with an Account of what has passed between His Majesty's Ministers and D[r] Franklin, one of the Commissioners of the revolted Colonies now resident at the Court of France, in the first Instance, and afterwards with the Count de Vergennes the French Minister for Foreign Affairs.

This intercourse was opened by a Letter from D[r] Franklin to me soon after my appointment to the Office I now hold, dated 22[d] March, expressive of his Hope that the Resolutions of the House of Commons upon the Subject of the American War might produce a general Peace, to which he would with infinite Pleasure contribute every Thing in his Power.

I answered this Letter on the 6th April, expressing my Readiness to promote it upon Grounds of the utmost Simplicity & Good Faith. I sent this by M[r] Oswald, with Instructions to hear whatever Proposals D[r] Franklin had to offer upon the Part of the thirteen Provinces. Upon this Gentleman's conversing with D[r] Franklin, it appeared that no Proceedings upon that subject could be had without Communication with the French Minister; and M[r] Oswald was accordingly introduced to the Comte de Vergennes, who made strong Professions of the M.C. King's Desire of Peace, and that he was glad to find the same Disposition in His Majesty. He objected however to the Proposal of laying the Foundation for a general Peace by a Truce with the Colonies, because by express Stipulation between France & Them, there was nothing to be treated of *separately* on either Side. He added, that the War could not be closed but by a general Treaty, in which Spain must be a Party, & that Holland also was to be included in the Negotiation. Nor would he be induced to state any Propositions on the Part of his own Court, alledging that the Propositions could not come from France, because being bound to several Allies, particularly to Spain, She could not venture to state Propositions, however general, without such

Communication to Them as would be attended with great Delay: – In regard to the Place of Treaty, the Comte de Vergennes observed that Paris would certainly be the most convenient Place, but that this Point should occasion no Obstacle, and it should be left to the Choice of His Majesty.

M^r. Oswald himself brought back this Answer from Paris, & arrived in London the 22^d. April. He brought at the same Time a Letter from D^r. Franklin to me dated 18th of that Month, in which D^r. Franklin informed me of the Commission which he had with others to treat of & conclude a Peace, which Congress had promised in good Faith to ratify and confirm. He observed however that the Treaty must be for a *general*, not a *partial* Peace, and intimated his Preference of Paris as the Place for the Purpose of more speedily finishing the War, as there was already there an Ambassador from Spain, and the Commissioners from America might easily and soon be assembled in that Capital, with which Intent he would immediately upon the Determination of this Point write to Messrs. Adams, Laurens & Jay.

His Majesty's Ministers on the 23^d. April advised His Majesty that M^r. Oswald should return to Paris, with Authority to name Paris as the Place, and to settle with D^r. Franklin the most convenient Time for setting on foot a Negotiation for a general Peace, and to represent to him *that the principal Points in Contemplation were, the Allowance of Independence to America, upon Great Britain's being restored to the Situation She was placed in by the Treaty of 1763, and that a proper Person should be sent to make a similar Communication to M. de Vergennes.*

M^r. Oswald reached Paris on the 5th. Ult^o., where he was joined by M^r. Grenville on the 7th. — In the Conferences which ensued, D^r. Franklin seemed to discover a very unaffected Desire of Peace, and he declared that as to the Connections of America with France, America was free from every Sort of Engagement but those which existed in the two public Treaties of Commerce & Alliance, and that these were such as any other Nation was free to make with America. – But that They had been greatly obliged, I must not be insensible of their Obligations to France.

The Language of M. de Vergennes, tho' full of Professions of a Desire for Peace, was at the same Time high & presuming with respect to Articles of Concession. He insinuated that the *French King* could not consider the Independence of America as ceded to *Him; that the Fishery at Newfoundland was to be arranged in a different Manner from what it had been: – That a Peace more just & durable than the last must be concluded.* Their Expectations of Concession in the East Indies appeared to be very great; and, in short the French Minister's whole Manner express'd a very strong Persuasion that Great Britain must make infinitely more important & extensive Sacrifices to give a Negotiation much Prospect of Success, the line of the last Peace seeming to be that which of all others both he & the Spanish Minister, Count d'Aranda, were most intent upon excluding from the present Negotiation.

In consequence of these Advices it was resolved, *That Full Powers should be given to M*^{r.} *Grenville to treat at Paris, & also that Propositions should be made by him to the Belligerant Powers upon the Basis of Independence to the thirteen Colonies in North America, and of the Treaty of Paris; and in case of such Proposition not being accepted, That he should call upon M. de Vergennes to make some Proposition on his Part, which M*^{r.} *Grenville might report to His Majesty's Ministers.*

These Resolutions & Instructions were sent to Mr. Grenville on 21st. ult^{o.}, and Letters were at the same Time dispatched to him & to Mr Oswald, directing them to profit by every fair & honorable Opportunity of representing to the American Commissioners & reminding them, that they had of their own Accord declined to treat *separately* with us; and that France would enter into no Negotiation in which Spain was not to be included, & possibly Holland.

That if therefore any unreasonable Demands should be made by these European Powers, which it would be impossible for us to concede, the Commissioners on the Part of America would do well to consider whether they would suffer themselves to be drawn into a Rejection of Offers so very advantageous to their Constituents, merely to gratify the Ambition of France, or the interested Views of those Powers who, tho' Allies of France, were not so of America.

Mr. Oswald however return'd to London on the 22^{d.} ult^{o.} and brought with him a Letter dated 14th. of the same Month from Mr. Grenville, who again as well as Mr. Oswald, represented the Difficulties which arose in the Outset of the Negotiation from the Demands of France & Spain, which he conceived to be such as it would be perhaps impossible for England to comply with, it appearing *that Spain looked to Florida & Gibraltar; That France pretended to make very essential Alterations in the Newfoundland Fishery, & would require perhaps more than Grenada in the West Indies, besides very extensive Surrenders of Commerce & Territory in the East Indies.*

It seemed at the same Time to be not less evident, *that France & Spain formed these Pretensions & relied for their Success on the Expectations of being supported by the American Colonies.*

It naturally therefore and necessarily became a Chief Consideration with His Majesty's Ministers to draw from the Information they were possessed of, some probable Clue by which the real Disposition & Views of the American Deputies might be discovered, in order to form a Judgment how far the Expectations of the House of Bourbon were well founded, & whether if the great Ground of Contention between Great Britain & the revolted Provinces was removed, either America or her Delegates would in such Case be willing, or think themselves bound to risk the full Enjoyment of their favorite Object by adhering to & supporting all the Demands of France & Spain.

The Turn of Dr Franklin's Conversation at several Times both with Mr Grenville & Mr Oswald had encouraged a Beleif entirely negative to these Suppositions, especially when he had expressly said That – *"When we had allowed the Independence of America, the Treaty She had made with France for gaining it ended, & none remained but that of Commerce, which we too might make if we pleased."* – He had also said at another Time, that *"there should, he thought, be a great Difference made in a Treaty between England & America, and one between England & France, which had been always at Enmity;* repeating frequently – That great Effects might be obtained by some things being done *spontaneous* from England.

Upon these & other Considerations, His Majesty has been induced to give a striking Proof of His Royal Magnanimity & disinterested Wish for the Restoration of Peace, by commanding His Minister to direct Mr Grenville, That *the Independency of America should be proposed by him in the first Instance, instead of making it a Condition of a general Treaty.*

Mr Oswald was sent back to Paris on the 26$^{th.}$ ult., with this important Commission, & Mr Grenville is instructed to make all the Advantage possible of the Concession which His Majesty from His ardent Desire of Peace has been induced to make with respect to the Independency of the thirteen States, especially by pressing Dr Franklin's own Idea, *that the Object of the Treaty of Alliance with France being attained, the Treaty determined.*

I have given a Confidential Information to you of these Particulars, that you may take such Measures as shall appear to you most adviseable for making a direct Communication of the Substance of the same either immediately to Congress, or through the Medium of General Washington, or in any other Manner, which you may think most likely to impress the well disposed Part of America with the Fairness and Liberality of His Majesty's Proceedings in such great & spontaneous Concessions.

The Advantages which we may expect from such Communication are: – That America once appriz'd of the King's Disposition to acknowledge the Independance of the thirteen States, and of the Disinclination in the French Court to terminate the War, must see that it is from this Moment to be carried on with a View of negotiating Points in which She can have no Concern, whether they regard France, or Spain & Holland, at the Desire of France; But some of which on the contrary may be in future manifestly injurious to the Interests of America herself – That if the Negotiation is broke off, it will undoubtedly be for the sake of some of those Powers, & not of America, whose Object is accomplish'd the Instant

She accepts of an Independance, which is not merely held out to her in the way of Negotiation by the Executive Power, but a distinct, unconditional Offer arising out of the Resolutions of Parliament, & therefore warranted by the Sense of the Nation at large.

The Facts being made notorious, it is scarcely conceivable that America compos'd as it is, will continue Efforts under French Direction, & protract the Distresses and Calamities which it is well known the War has subjected her to. It is to be presum'd That from that Moment She will look with Jealousy upon the French Troops in Her Country, who may from Allies become dangerous Enemies.

If however, any particular State or States, Man, or Description of Men should continue, against the general Inclinations of the Continent, devoted to France, this Communication will surely detect their Views, expose their Motives, & deprive them of their Influence in all matters of general Council or Exertion – You will however take particular Care in your Manner of conducting yourselves, not only that there shall not be the smallest room for Suspicion of our good Faith & Sincerity; But that we have no View in it of causing Dissension among the Colonies, or even separating America from France upon Terms inconsistent with Her own Honor – You must convince them that the great Object of this Country is, not only Peace, but Reconciliation with America on the noblest Terms & by the noblest Means.

I am further to acquaint you That in the Beginning of this Intercourse with D.^r. Franklin, & before M.^r. Grenville went to Paris, it was resolv'd by His Majesty's Ministers to discharge M.^r. Laurens from those Engagements which he had entered into when he was admitted to Bail. This Measure seemed to give great Satisfaction to D.^r. Franklin, who made very thankful Acknowledgments for the Favor; And M.^r. Laurens himself in return for his being thus enlarged without any Conditions whatsoever, declared of his own Accord that he consider'd L.^d. Cornwallis as freed from his Parole, & that he would get Doctor Franklin to join him in declaring him so.

I returned to M.^r. Laurens immediately after his Enlargement all the Papers which had been taken with him, without having read a single Line of them.

I also inform'd D.^r. Franklin of the Steps we had taken, in regard to the American Prisoners in general, by having actually prepared Transports for the purpose of conveying them to America to be there exchanged, and I assured him, that due Attention had not been wanting to their Accommodation and good Treatment. D.^r. Franklin expressed very great Pleasure at this Proceeding, & pronounced the good Effect which the Return of those People to their own Country under the Impression of our Kindness would have towards lessening the Resentment & conciliating the

Minds of their Friends to us.

It will be needless for me to point out to you the Expediency of giving all the additional Weight you can to the Influence which these Reports may create in our Favour, by taking all occasions of manifesting an humane Attention to the Prisoners, and to expedite their Exchange as much as possible. I am the more anxious that you should make appear your studious Punctuality & Zeal (of which I entertain not the smallest Doubt) in this particular Point, because I venture to carry forward my Hopes to such good Consequences from it, as may tend to the more probable Attainment of an Object which is uppermost in my Mind; I mean the Safety & Security of the Loyalists. I have very earnestly recommended to Mr. Oswald That in his Intercourse with Dr. Franklin & the other Deputies from the Colonies who may assemble at Paris, he should ever bear it in mind and employ his constant Exertions to procure an Establishment for the Loyalists besides taking other Steps in their Favour to influence the several States to agree to a fair Restoration or Compensation for whatever Confiscations have taken Place. I address the same Recommendation in the most pointed Earnestness to You, and I shall therefore add no more to what I have repeatedly said in other of my Letters upon this Subject, trusting entirely that you will warmly co-operate with each other in every Measure which may be conducive to the accomplishment of The King's wishes, & the essential Advancement of His Majesty's Service in all these Particulars. I have therefore real Pleasure in assuring you That His Majesty has the highest Satisfaction in reflecting that He could not have entrusted the Management of such important & delicate Transactions to more able or zealous Servants; and that you will use every earnest Endeavour to effect the great Purpose of Your Delegation, to restore the Blessings of Peace, and as much as possible to reconcile & reunite the Affections & Interests of Great Britain & the Colonies.

I am &c^a   Shelburne.

British Public Record Office: Colonial Office Files, Colonial Correspondence, America, *hereafter cited as PRO: CO 5/178, pp. 437-461 [v. 302, f. 307-321] (LC transcription).*
   [1] *Digby, Robert (1732-1814). British admiral. Commander-in-chief of naval forces in North America, 1781-1783.*

Richard Oswald to Lord Shelburne

My Lord   Paris 9th. June 1782

. . . . .

I have nothing of Business to trouble Your Lordship with. Only that upon one occasion, since my last arrival, the Doctor said they, the Americans, had been totally left out in Mr Grenville's Powers, as they extended only to treating with the Minister of France. I told him the deficiency would, no doubt, be supplied in due time as might be supposed, since in the mean while they had been assured by Mr Grenville that His Majesty had agreed to grant Independence in the first Instance. The Doctor said it was true, and he was glad of it, and supposed that was all that could be done until the Act depending in Parliament was passed.

He then talked of Treaties and said he thought the best way to come at a general Peace was to treat separately with each Party and under distinct Commissions to one and the same, or different Persons. By this Method he said many difficulties which must arise in discussing a variety of Subjects, not strictly relative to each other, under the same Commission and to which all the several Parties are called, would be in a great measure avoided. And then at last there will only remain to consolidate those several Settlements into one general and conclusive Treaty of Pacification, which upon enquiry I found he understood to be the indispensible mode of final Accommodation.

However material that part of the Question might be (regarding the possibility of an equitable coalescence of so many different Propositions and Settlements) there was no explanation offered as to the extent of their relative dependence on each other. And I did not think it proper to ask for it. (He only explained as to the Commissions, that there might be one to treat with France, one for the Colonies, one for Spain, and, he added, one for Holland if it should be thought proper. Mr. Grenville being very well with the Doctor, he has, no doubt, mentioned the same things to him, yet I thought it my duty to communicate to him the substance of this Conversation.)

. . . . .

I have the honor to be My Lord Your Lordships Most obedient humble Servant   Richard Oswald

Clements Library: Shelburne Papers, v. 70, pp. 18-22 (C).

Charles James Fox to Thomas Grenville

N⁰· 5.   S$^{t.}$ James's. 10 June. 1782
Sir

. . . . .

As it is his Majesty's intention that nothing shall be wanting on his part that may be supposed to facilitate the great work of Peace He has been graciously pleased to order further full Powers to be made out by which you will be authorized to treat & conclude not only with H. M. C. M. but with any other of the Enemies of G Britain, and these full Powers I have the honour of sending you herewith inclosed.

With respect to the contents of your last Dispatch, you certainly conceive it rightly, that you are no longer to mention that Independence of America as a cession to France, or as a conditional article of a general treaty: but at the same time you will not fail to observe to the French Ministry that the Independence of America *is* proposed to be acknowledged, and to remark that this being done spontaneously, which they have at different times and particularly in their last answer to the Imperial Courts emphatically called the object of the War, little difficulty ought to remain with regard to other points which may be considered rather as collateral & incidental than as principal in the present dispute.

The War was begun on their part as they profess not for the sake of Conquest but for the purpose of protecting their trade with N. America: All restraint upon that trade being now out of the question and perfect liberty of commerce with N. America being proposed as a basis of a treaty, the cause of the War is gone, and the War ought to cease....

. . . . .

I am Sir, etc   Charles James Fox

PRO: FO 27/2, v. 557, f. 284 (LC *transcription*).

Richard Oswald to Lord Shelburne

My Lord   Paris 12th June 1782
Doct$^{r.}$ Franklin called on me this Morning and returned your Lop' Letter to me in relation to Mr Walpole.[1]...

After discussing this Business, with the Doct$^{r.}$ & talking Of Lord Cornwallis affair & my thanking him for so generously Settling the principles upon which he founded His Lop' release from his Parole

notwithstanding of his having no ~~general~~ Powers of Exchange, conclusive
of Gen[l] Burgoyne,[2] which he declared was the Case – I say after that affair
was over, he told me he had taken a convenient opportunity the other day
to talk to Monsieur de Vergennes. That they seemed to wonder there was
no return of M[r] Grenvilles Courier with more enlarged Powers. But that
upon explaining to him how that depended upon the Enabling Act being
passed, the Count seemed or was perfectly Satisfied as if there was no
alteration apparently in the Sentiments of Our Court with respect to Peace.
That as to that Court there was none, & that the King his Master had
declared that his Sentiments were so fixed as to a final Conclusion on just
and equitable terms, that whatever might be the fate of the War & on
which Side Soever occasional advantages might happen, they would make
no impression on his mind, nor occasion any alteration in his plan of
adjustment – A good deal more to the Same purpose, needless to be
repeated. I could only say that for any thing I knew there was no change
in the Sentiments of His Majesty or his Ministers as to the desire of a
Speedy Peace upon fair terms: as would be seen by the Enlargement of M[r]
Grenville's powers, which might be expected in a few days. Upon which
occasion, as upon all others, I avoided saying a word of our Victory in the
W. Indies, or of what is said here of what has lately happened off Brest.
The Doctor then slipt into the common State of loose Conversation, in
which he was pleased to express himself very kindly with respect to myself.
as I must own he always has done. for which I must consider myself obliged
to him, unless I was to doubt of his Sincerity. Which from anything I have
been able to learn in my Communication with him, or in hearing from
others cannot be justly imputed to him. The Doctor at same time ~~had~~ told
me that Mons[r] de Vergennes had a very good opinion of me &c[a.] This I
liked also to hear, though I should have been more Surprised at it, if I had
not thought that possibly the Doctors good nature & benevolence might
have been so far extended as to give occasion to this prejudice in my
favour. For it could come no other way. I told the Doctor that whatever
might be the case as to Capacity & qualifications for this business, I was
certain of one thing, no Person whatever would be more desirous than I was
to forward the purpose which I knew he had so much at heart, being that
of putting an end to all the distresses of the present War. Which I was
persuaded our Court did not incline to protract into an unreasonable
length, & that they ought to take example of the Court, which never
ceased in its Attempts, & when they had gained a point, by which their
Neighbors had plunged deeper into their difficulties, stopt short to avoid
embarassm[t] & waited patiently for another occasion, & so there was no end
to the miseries of mankind. To which the Doctor assented & said that if
Princes before they went to War were to make an Estimate of their

Expenses they would be found to exceed the value of their Conquests, and therefor a Peace could not be too dearly bought. & he hoped & wished, the present Treaty might be properly begun & go on smoothly and quickly to Conclusion....

. . . . .

My great Concern at present is for what may happen in N. America. If we get safe off from the places we intend to quit, & the Colonies don't push into the others, things may go on the better here. But in the Interim to have any chance of a tolerable Treaty our War at Sea must be pushed with the utmost rigour. I have the honour to be My Lord Your Lop' most obedient humble servant   Richard Oswald

. . . . .

Clements Library: Shelburne Papers, v. 71, pp. 49-53 (ALS).
   [1] *Mr. Walpole is not further identified. His business involved land holdings on the West Indian island of Grenada.*
   [2] *Burgoyne, John (1722-1792). British general. Commanded British invasion force moving south into New York from Canada, 1776-1777. Surrendered at Saratoga, October 17, 1777.*

John Adams to Benjamin Franklin

Sir,   The Hague, 13 June, 1782.

. . . . .

I have not as yet taken any Engagements with the Dutch not to make a Peace without them, but I will take such Engagements, in a moment if the Dutch will take them, and I believe they will chearfully. – I shall not propose it however untill I have the Concurrence of the Duke de la Vauguion who will do nothing without the Instructions of his Court. I would not delay it, a moment from any Expectation that the English, will acknowledge our Independence and make Peace with Us, because I have no such Expectations.– I confess, it would be with infinite Reluctance that I should see a Peace made between England and any of her Ennemies, unless it is made with all.– if France, Spain and America should make Peace with England, and leave Holland alone at War, she would be at Mercy, and she would find the tenderest of it, Cruelty. The permanent and lasting Friendship of the Dutch, may be easily obtained by the United States: that of England never. it is gone with the days before the Flood. – If We ever enjoy the smallest degree of sincere Friendship again from England I am totally incapable of seeing the Character of a Nation or the Connections of Things, which however may be the Case, for what I know. They have brought themselves by their Frenzy into such a Situation. Spain has such Pretensions, Holland has such Pretensions, America has such Pretensions, the Armed Neutrality has such Pretensions, that where is the English Minister, or Member of Parliament that dares to vote for the Concession to them? The Pretensions of France I believe would be so moderate that possibly, they might be acceded to. – But I fear that Spain who deserves the least will demand the most. in Short the Work of Peace appears so impracticable, that I am happy in being restrained to this Country by my Duty and by this means excused from troubling my Head much about it....

The States of Holland and Several other Provinces have taken the Resolution, against the Mediation for a Separate Peace, and this nation seems to be well fixed in its System and in the common Cause.

My best Respects and Affections to my old Friend Mr. Jay, if you please.

John Adams.

MHS: *The Adams Papers, microfilm reel 107 (LBkC).*

Fifth Peace Conference

[Translation]

15 June 1782

Mr. Grenville delivered to the Comte de Vergennes a copy of the new full power that he had asked for. After having read it the Comte de Vergennes, in disclosing that he personally found the full power satisfactory, said that he would hasten to bring it to the King's attention and to make known to Mr. Grenville His Majesty's response, but that Mr. Grenville himself surely perceived that the King could make no response for His allies; that the full power would be communicated to Messrs. D'Aranda, Franklin and de Berkenrode.[1] Mr. Grenville accepted this communication. But he observed that, in his opinion, it ought not to hinder him from following up on the conditions that he should be authorized to make for the achievement of peace. The Comte de Vergennes having shown himself disposed to listen to him, Mr. Grenville said that, the King of England being disposed to recognize directly and of his own accord the independence of America, that subject ought not to be considered as a conditional clause of the general peace; that by means of this disposition of it, Mr. Grenville was charged with renewing his proposition that he had already made previously, to know that the Treaty of Paris would be taken as the basis for the future treaty of peace. The Comte de Vergennes responded that he could not hear the Treaty of Paris mentioned without shuddering; that according to him it was necessary, to make a just and lasting peace, to forget both this treaty and all the preceding treaties, and to settle the interests of all the belligerent parties according to the principles of justice and according to their reciprocal convenience. Mr. Grenville, without discussing or rejecting the idea of the Comte de Vergennes, observed that when he proposed the Treaty of Paris as the basis for the peace, he did not mean to say that that treaty ought to be renewed and confirmed in all its points, that he meant only that the treaty in question should serve as the basis for the negotiation, and that if this proposition was not agreeable to the King, the King of England would invite His Majesty to make another that would suit all parties. The meeting ended with the announcement on the part of the Comte de Vergennes that he would communicate the whole to the King and to the ministers of His allies, and that his speed in transmitting a response to him, would be analogous to the wishes that he personally holds for the prompt reestablishment of peace.

FFAA: Pol. Corr., England, v. 537, f. 171 (LC transcription).

   [1] Lestevenon van Berkenrode, Mattheus. Dutch diplomat. Ambassador to France, 1778-1787.

Comte de Vergennes' Verbal Response
to Thomas Grenville

[Translation]

21 June 1782

The King too much desires the prompt reestablishment of peace not to have learned with the greatest satisfaction:

1st. That the King of England is disposed to treat at the same time with all the Powers implicated in the war.

2nd. That His Britannic Majesty proposes to recognize and to declare directly the independence of the United States of North America, and that this subject will no longer be regarded as a conditional clause of the future general peacemaking.

His Majesty, persuaded that the King of England sincerely wishes the reestablishment of a firm and durable peace, and far from all that could give rise to new discussions between the two nations, does not doubt that his intention is that it be extinguished and that it be respectively anticipated that any stipulation which bears a mark of restraint or humiliation would only serve to revive and perpetuate between the two Nations the hatreds that should be assuaged.

In this confidence, the King, in order to correspond to the dispositions of His Britannic Majesty and to manifest, on his part, his wish to facilitate all that can accelerate the salutary and so desirable work of peace, consents, as to what concerns His Majesty, to adopt, as the King of England proposes, the Treaty of Paris as the basis for the negotiation that is in contemplation; but this acceptance cannot in any manner be regarded as a confirmation, an avowal, and a renewal of all the Stipulations included in the said Treaty. His Majesty expressly reserves it to himself to ask the King of England what concerns him, various exceptions and changes among others:

1ˢᵗ. regarding new arrangements concerning the East Indies

2ⁿᵈ. regarding new stipulations relative to Africa

3ʳᵈ. An equitable and mutually useful rule in relation to the agreed fishing of Newfoundland.

4ᵗʰ. An arrangement of Commerce at the convenience of the two nations in Europe.

The King does not yet explain himself on the matter of restitutions and compensations because it can only be discussed when the negotiation is established, but the King of England can be assured that His Majesty will direct himself in this regard to all others in accordance with the principles of justice and moderation that form the essential basis of his policy.

If these overtures, as the King hopes, enter into the views of the King of England, and if that Prince accepts them, His Majesty will not refuse to explain himself further with as much frankness as precision on the different points included in his counterproposal.

. . . . .

FFAA: Pol. Corr., England, v. 537, f. 195-196vo., 199-200 (LC transcription).

Sixth Peace Conference

[Translation]

Friday, 21 June 1782

The Comte de Vergennes read to Mr. Grenville the King's verbal response, both to the King of England's new full power and to the proposals that must serve as the basis for the negotiation. Mr. Grenville found the account of his proposals exact; he asked only that in the article that concerns the independence of America, one put *disposed* instead of *resolved*, and lower down, that to the word *peacemaking* be added *general*. Mr. Grenville made a copy of the King's response and signed the original.

The Comte d'Aranda having arrived unexpectedly during the conference, both the King's response and Mr. Grenville's new full power were read to him. That ambassador remarked that the full power named the King of France explicitly, and that it named the other powers who must take part in the peacemaking only in general terms; he made it understood that this form was contrary to the dignity of the King of Spain, and that he anticipated that that prince would not subscribe to it. This Comte d'Aranda, to forestall lengthy discussion, proposed to Mr. Grenville to ask for a separate full power for Spain, or a new full power in which no one would be named explicitly, such as was done at Aix-la-Chapelle[1] and at the time of the last Treaty of Paris. Mr. Grenville perceived the justice of these remarks, and promised to report them to his Court. He also took *ad referendum* the King's response; for which purpose he dispatched a courier the same day, June 21.

FFAA: Pol. Corr., England, v. 537, f. 194 (LC transcription).
[1] *The Treaty of Aix-la-Chapelle, 1748, ended the War of the Austrian Succession.*

Thomas Grenville to Charles James Fox

Sir, Paris. June 21. 1782.
    Having received on the 14th the honour of your letter of the 10th, I took a copy of the Full Power which accompanied it, and gave it to Mr de Vergennes on the next day, the 15th; as he did not object to it, tho' he seemed to think it might have been more satisfactory to have named the parties, I lost no time in telling him that I was commissioned formally to propose to him the peace of Paris as the basis of the Treaty, adding more than once the very reasonable expectation the Court of London now entertained that, should the proposition already made by them not be accepted at Versailles, some others would be stated in return by the French Minister; and farther I observed to him, according to your directions, that it is proposed spontaneously to acknowledge the independance of the American States. It was not till this morning that I received Mr de Vergennes's answer, which I send you enclosed, having copied it at Versailles. the object of it appears to me to be the keeping in view the former general expressions of a pacifick disposition, tho' perhaps the articles it includes seem to threaten that extensive and wide scope in their demands which I have always thought I have traced in every conversation about the peace of Paris: a strong expression of Mr. de Vergennes upon this subject lately was, that in any new treaty which should refer to that of 1763, instead of saying that the treaty of Paris should stand good except in certain

specified articles, he would rather express it that the treaty of Paris should be annulled except in certain specified articles no very promising qualifications of what now stands as the proposed basis of the intended negotiations! — but you will see Sir, in the paper which I enclose, that the French Minister does not at present enter into any detail, so that I cannot add more for your information than you will have in reading his answer. I must however observe to you that the Spanish Ambassador is by no means satisfied with the Full Power. he told me that the King his Master tho' an ally of France, had made war on his own account; and that his Court would without doubt object to the French King's being named in the Full Power without any particular mention being equally made of the King of Spain; he said he mentioned this now as much time might be lost if that difficulty was not removed, which might be done in three modes, either by the giving a general power without naming any one of the parties, a power naming both of them that is the Kings of France and Spain, or a power separate and distinct for each; should it therefore be His Majesty's pleasure to proceed farther in this business and to remove this objection, you will excuse me for observing, that if either the second or third of the expedients proposed should be adopted, a similar requisition will probably be made by Holland and America. I have already felt myself under some embarrassment respecting Mr Franklin, not seeing precisely how far the expression of *"Princes & States"* in the Full Power can apply to America till the independance is acknowledged, and knowing that he finds and expresses much doubt about it himself, & some disposition to ask a more explicit description; indeed I have purposely avoided seeing him, till I had got Mr de Vergennes's answer, which it seemed important to your views to transmit immediately, least Mr Franklin might have made a formal objection to me about the Full Power, and perhaps have stood in the way of the answer from Versailles till his objection should have been removed. I have not lately had so much communication with Mr Franklin, or been able to draw from him any satisfactory information; the last time I saw him he contented himself with observing that the sooner the independance was declared, the less would the business be retarded....

.   .   .   .   .

I have the honour to be with great truth & regard Sir you most obedient humble Servant   Thomas Grenville
R. 24th (by Ogg.)

PRO: FO 27/2, v. 557, f. 297 (LC transcription).

John Jay's Diary of the Peacemaking

[June 23-26, 1782]

1782. 23 June. Arrived at Paris about noon. Spent the afternoon at Passy with Doctor Franklin. He informed me of the State of the Negociation, and that he kept an exact Journal of it.

24. Waited upon Mr. De Vergennes with the Doctor. The Count read to us his Answer to the British Minister. Dined with the Doctor, and found Dr. Bancroft[1] there.

25. Wrote to Count Aranda.

26. After Breakfast with the Doctor, met with Mr. Grenville on our Return. Received a Visit from Marquis la Fayette.

· · · · ·

Morris: Jay Papers, v. 2, pp. 446-447.

[1] *Bancroft, Dr. Edward (1744-1821). Spy. Born in Westfield, Massachusetts, he studied medicine in England before the war. There he became acquainted with Benjamin Franklin, for whom he acted as a spy, making frequent trips from London to Paris. He became a double agent, reporting to British spymaster Paul Wentworth, and used his knowledge of secret affairs to manipulate the London Stock Exchange. After the war, Bancroft used his knowledge of chemistry to make important discoveries in dyeing fabrics.*

Comte de Vergennes to the Duc de la Vauguyon

[Translation]

Nº. 14.   Versailles, 23 June 1782
M. le Duc de la Vauguyon

· · · · ·

It seems to me, Sir, that Mr. Adams is putting a great acceleration into his political steps, and I greatly fear that they will end by appearing suspect to the Dutch; this reason causes us to desire that Mr. Adams limit himself for the present to his treaty of commerce: he will have plenty of time to probe minds concerning a treaty of alliance: such is, Sir, the sentiment of the King and of his Council. In addition, you may tell Mr. Adams that we do not in any way intend to impede him in the execution of his orders, that we suppose him too enlightened and too prudent to wish to compromise the interests and the dignity of his homeland, and that we suppose that if he takes some step towards the object in question, he is assured in advance that they will be efficacious. It is important for us, Sir, to put Mr. Adams at ease, because he is naturally very suspicious, and he would think the independence of the United States offended if he suspected us of wanting to be the arbiters of his conduct: we have up to now avoided this suspicion, although it was suggested to Congress; and we find ourselves too far advanced to resolve to change it.   Vergennes

FFAA: Pol. Corr., Holland, v. 549, f. 132 (LC transcription).

John Jay to Robert R. Livingston

Dear Sir,   Paris 25th. June 1782.

My Letters from Madrid, and afterwards a few Lines from Bordeaux, informed you of my being called to this place by a pressing Letter from Doctor Franklin.

The slow manner of travelling in a Carriage through Spain, Mrs. Jay's being taken with a Fever & Ague the Day we left Bordeaux, and the Post Horses at the different Stages having been engaged for the Count du Nord,[1] who had left Paris with a great Retinue, prevented my arriving here until the Day before Yesterday.

After placing my Family in a Hotel, I immediately went out to Passy, and spent the Remainder of the Afternoon in conversing with Doctor Franklin on the Subjects which had induced him to write for me. I found that he had *then* more Reason to think my Presence necessary than *it seems* to be at present.

Yesterday we paid a Visit to Count de Vergennes. He gave me a very friendly Reception, and entered pretty fully with us into the State of the Negotiation. His answer to the british Minister appeared to me ably drawn. It breathes great Moderation, and yet is so general as to leave Room for such Demands as Circumstances, at the Time of the Treaty, may render convenient.

There is Reason to believe that Mr. Fox and Lord Shelburn are not perfectly united, and that Rodney's Success will repress the Ardor of our Enemies, for an immediate Peace. On leaving the Count, he informed us that he was preparing Dispatches for America, and that our Letters, if sent to him Tomorrow Morning, might go by the same opportunity. This short Notice, together with the Interruptions I meet with every moment, oblige me to be less particular than I could wish, but as Doctor Franklin also writes by this Conveyance, you will doubtless receive from him full Intelligence on these Subjects.

My last letters also informed You that the Court of Spain had Commissioned the Count de Yranda, their Ambassador here to continue with me the Negotiation for a Treaty with our Country. I have not yet seen him, and Doctor Franklin concurs with me in Opinion that it is more expedient to open this Business by a Letter than by a Visit....

        · · · · ·

Mr Adams cannot leave Amsterdam at present, and I hear that Mr Laurens thinks of returning soon to America, so that I apprehend Doctor Franklin and myself will be left to manage at least the skirmishing Business, if I may so call it, of our Commission, without the Benefit of their Counsel and Assistance. You know what I think and feel on this Subject, and I wish Things were so circumstanced as to admit of my being indulged.

You may rely on my writing often, very often — My Letters will now have fairer play, and you will find that I have not ceased to consider Amusement and Rest as secondary Objects to those of Business.

I shall endeavor to get Lodgings as near to Doctor Franklin as I can – He is in perfect, good Health, and his Mind appears more vigorous than that of any Man of his Age I have known – He certainly is a valuable Minister, and an Agreeable Companion.

        · · · · ·

I am, Dear Sir, &c.   John Jay.

NA: PCC, item 110, v. 2, pp. 135-139 (LBkC); M247 reel 135.
  ¹ Nord, Comte du. Name used by Paul Petrovich, Tsarevich of Russia, when travelling in France. Paul (Pavel) I (1754-1801), Emperor of Russia, 1796-1801.

Comte de Vergennes to Comte de Montmorin

[Translation]

N.º. 41   Versailles, 26 June 1782
M. le Comte de Montmorin
I do not doubt, Sir, that M. le Comte de Florida Blanca has already informed you of a step that the Courts of Vienna and of Petersburg have determined to take near the belligerent powers in order to endeavor to take up the mediation again, which they naturally would not see escape without regret.

It was yesterday, Sir, that M. le Comte de Mercy¹ and M. le Prince Bariatinsky entrusted to me two Writings, of which I have the honor to send you copies. One is a response from England to our replies of the month of February last that bears the date of 28 April. The other is a verbal insinuation from the mediators who, recapitulating what can be found analogous in our previous Explications and in the statement of the new English ministers, affect ignorance of the steps that the latter have taken near us to begin a direct negotiation, and invite us quite frankly to open one in Vienna.

I had foreseen this order of Things, Sir, and it was to ward off the effects of it, which I do not think can be advantageous to us, that I had thought it was interesting that the King, profiting from the overtures that England was making to him, was pressing to begin the negotiations, taking care, however, to make it approach more or less rapidly to the will of his interests, to those of Spain and of our other allies and friends. Reread, I beseech you, Sir, my despatch of the 22nd of this month. You will observe in it that this foresight has directed the verbal response that we have made to Mr. Grenville's proposals. The Comte d'Aranda confessed to me yesterday that his opinion had totally differed from mine, but that he did not hesitate to recognize that I had seen better and judged better than he.

I would applaud myself, Sir, if the office of the mediators had not forestalled the response that we expect from the English ministry. As it is probable that it would have been communicated to it at the same time as to us, if indeed it was not concerted with it, it would be very interesting, before explaining ourselves, to know the more or less Regard that it is disposed to have for the claim of the mediators. If the Court of London is showing good faith in its desire for Peace, if it is determined thereon from the Sentiment reflected by its Interests, it should understand that the designated mediators may not be the most efficacious fellow-workers for reaching that so salutary end; they find in fact advantages so immense in the Continuation of the War that it would be necessary to suppose them to have a supernatural Virtue to be persuaded that they are in the generous resolution of thereby making a gratuitous Sacrifice to the happiness of humanity.

Not being able to plan with the English ministry the response to make to the mediators, we have two great Stumbling-blocks to avoid. One is not to ensnare ourselves in the mediation, and the other is not to charge ourselves with the reproach of refusing it. I have had up to now, Sir, too few moments to myself to have very fixed ideas, but it seems to me at first glance that we will not compromise ourselves if, in relating the date of 28 April last, the Time of the response sent to the mediators by the English Ministry, we bring together in a concise historical table all the steps that the latter has taken near us and near the Americans in order to open a direct negotiation. As I do not consider that it is in the interest of the belligerent powers to break off that negotiation in order to throw themselves into the arms of the mediators, mention can be made, without indicting or irritating the English ministers, of the attention with which we have reminded them of the officious solicitude of the mediators and the confidence we place therein, as also of our insistence that the peace be a general one, a condition without which no overture of peace can be heard.

This step, equally simple and honest, would authorize us to assert the rights of humanity which, protesting against the effusion of human Blood, could not permit the King and his high allies to refuse the means offered them to make it cease; for the same consideration still opposes itself to the fact that they may be the first to break off the negotiations whose Establishment England proposed, but whatever may be the issue, either that it should lead to a happy conclusion, or that a new negotiation take place, His Majesty declares for what concerns him that he will always be very disposed to profit from the intervention and the general attentions of the mediators to faciliate the Success of it, and that he hopes that they will not refuse the Cooperation of their good offices in whatever place and manner peace can and should be negotiated. This response can be made palatable with some flattering Compliments for the mediators, which may satisfy them regarding the Confidence placed in their Impartiality and their generous dispositions.

This, Sir, is still only a rough idea that I am submitting at this moment to the reflection of the Comte de Florida Blanca, and that I will not delay in submitting to the deliberation of the King's Council. I still have no Assurance that it will be adopted there; but what I have very certainly gained is that we should measure our language so well that we do not shock the mediators and that we may make fall upon the English ministers, without however overtly charging them with the Reproach of having rejected the mediation, the failure of the Attentions due to the mediators. This step is all the more necessary to take, although some members of the new English ministry are sincerely disposed for peace. This Spirit is not unanimous. Discord is already very lively and very strong among them. The Rockingham party, of which Mr. Fox is the mainstay and spokesman, is at daggers drawn with that of Lord Shelburne, supported by Lords Camden[2] and Grafton,[3] in a Conflict in which it is still not known who will have the advantage. There should result from it at least some Delays and Impediments to peace, perhaps even a Cessation of negotiations. Already I see some tergiversations that do not edify me; it was a question of passing a bill to authorize the King of England to treat with the Colonies of America; it had been proposed, and is said to have been postponed until another session....						Vergennes

FFAA: Pol. Corr., Spain, v. 607, f. 214 (LC transcription).

[1] Mercy d'Argenteau, Florimond-Claud, Comte de (1727-1794). Austrian diplomat. Ambassador to France, 1766-1790. Governor general of the Austrian Netherlands, 1790-1794. Ambassador to Great Britain, 1794.

[2] Camden, Charles Pratt, Lord (1714-1794). British political figure. Attorney general, 1757-1762. Chief justice of the court of common pleas, 1762-1766. Lord chancellor, 1766-1770. Opposed Lord North's American policy. President of the council under Rockingham and Shelburne, 1782-1783, and under William Pitt, 1784-1794.

[3] *Grafton, Augustus Henry Fitzroy, Duke of (1735-1811). British political figure. Secretary of State for the Northern Department, July 1765-May 1766, in Rockingham's administration. First Lord of the Treasury under Pitt, July 1766-September 1767. Prime Minister, September 1767-January 1770. Privy seal in Lord North's administration, June 1771-November 1775, resigning in opposition to North's American policies. Lord privy seal under Rockingham and Shelburne, March 1782-April 1783.*

Benjamin Franklin to Richard Oswald

Sir   Passy. June 27th 1782.

The opinion I have of Your Candour Probity, good understanding and good Will to both Countries made me hope that you would have been vested with the Character of Plenipotentiary to treat with those from America. When Mr Grenville produced his first Commission which was only to treat with France, I did imagine that the other to treat with Us was reserved for You, and kept back only till the Enabling Bill should be passed. Mr. Grenville has since received a Second Commission which as he informs me has additional Words empowering him to treat with the Ministers of any other Prince or State whom it may concern and he seems to understand those general Words comprehend the United States of America. There may be no doubt that they comprehend Spain and Holland, but as there exist various Publick Acts by which the Government of Britain denies Us to be States, and none in which they acknowledge Us to be such it seems hardly clear that We could be intended, at the time that Commission was given, the Enabling Act not being then passed. So that tho' I can have no objection to Mr Grenville, nor right to make it if I had any yet as your long residence in America has given you a Knowledge of that Country Its People Circumstances Commerce &c, which added to your experience in Business may be useful to both sides in facilitating and expediting the Negotiation, I cannot but hope that it is still intended to vest you with the Character above mentioned respecting the Treaty with America, either separately or in conjunction with Mr. Grenville as to the wisdom of your Ministers may seem best. Be it as it may, I beg you will accept this Line as a testimony of the sincere esteem and respect with which I have the honor to be Sir &c

                                                    B. Franklin

Clements Library: Shelburne Papers, v. 70, pp. 28-29 (C).

John Jay to Robert R. Livingston

Dear Sir,   Paris 28th. June 1782.
     I had the pleasure of writing to you on the 25th. Instant – As the Express
which is to carry the Letter, will not depart 'till tomorrow Morning, I have
a good Opportunity of making this Addition to my Dispatches.
     Agreeable to the Desire of Congress, as well as my own Wishes, I have
had the Satisfaction of conferring with the Marquis de la Fayette, on several
interesting Subjects. He is as active in serving us in the Cabinet, as he has
been in the Field; and (there being great Reason to believe that his Talents
could be more advantageously employed here, than an inactive Campaign
in America would admit of there) Doctor Franklin and myself, think it
advisable that he should postpone his Return for the present – The marquis
inclines to the same Opinion, and, though anxious to join the Army, will
remain here a little longer.
     The Intentions of the British Ministry, with Respect to us, are by no
Means clear – They are divided upon the Subject. It is said that Mr. Fox
and his Friends incline to meet us on the Terms of Independence, but that
Lord Shelburn and his adherents entertain an Idea of making a Compact
with us, similar to that between Britain and Ireland, and there is Room to
apprehend that Efforts will be made to open a negotiation on these Subjects
at Philadelphia. When it is considered that the Articles of general Peace
cannot be discussed in America, and that propositions for a *separate* one
ought not to be listened to, it is evident to me, that their sending out
Commissioners can be calculated for no other purpose than that of Intrigue.
I should enlarge on this Topic, were I not persuaded that you will see this
matter in the same point of View, and that any Proposition which they may
offer will be referred to the American Commissioners in Europe. – How far
it may be prudent to permit any British Agents to come into our Country
on such an Ostensible Errand, is an easy Question, for where an
unnecessary Measure may be dangerous, it should be avoided – They may
write from New York whatever they may have to propose, and may receive
Answers in the same manner.
     If one may Judge from Appearances, the Ministry are very desirous of
getting some of their Emissaries into our Country, either in an avowed, or
in a private Character and, all things considered, I should think it most safe
not to admit any Englishman, in either Character, within our Lines at this
very critical Juncture. A mild, and yet firm Resolution on the Impropriety
and Inexpediency of any Negotiation for Peace in America would give great
Satisfaction to our Friends and confirm their Confidence in us – We
indeed, who know our Country, would apprehend no Danger from any

Thing that british Agents might say or do to deceive or divide us – But the Opinions of Strangers, who must Judge by appearances, merit Attention; and it is doubtless best not only to be steadfast to our Engagements, but also to avoid giving occasion to the Slightest suspicions of a contrary Disposition.– An Opinion does prevail here, that in the Mass of our People there is a considerable number who, though resolved on Independence, would nevertheless prefer an Alliance with England to one with France, and this opinion will continue to have a certain Degree of Influence during the War. This circumstance renders much Circumspection necessary.

I am, with great Regard & Esteem, Dear Sir, &c.   John Jay

NA: PCC, item 110, v. 2, pp. 139-142 (LBkC); M247, reel 135.

Comte de Vergennes to Chevalier de la Luzerne

[Translation]
Nᵒ· 35.   Versailles, 28 June 1782

. . . . .

I think, Sir, that I should inform you of the turn that our political affairs have taken since my despatches of 9 April; it is all the more important that you have a perfect knowledge of it, for Congress will certainly have need of direction in the important deliberations that are about to occupy it, and the result of which interests us as much as the United States themselves.

The new English Ministry had scarcely entered upon its duties, when it sent an emissary to Mr. Franklin to propose a separate peace to him; the same overture was made at almost the same time to Mr. Adams, and the former ministry had previously taken some oblique paths to make it reach the first of these plenipotentiaries. Mr. Franklin responded to both in the most appropriate manner; and on the communication that he gave me of the mission of Mr. Oswald (that is the name of the most recent English emissary), I charged him with proposing to the latter to see me, if he thought to dare it. Mr. Oswald made no difficulty in presenting himself to me and in repeating to me all that he had orders to say to Mr. Franklin. My response conformed to that of the American plenipotentiary; and as Mr. Oswald let me perceive the desire as well as the need that the Court of London had for peace, I did not hesitate to assure him that the King, on his part, was very disposed to end the war when he could do it with honor and safety. It was necessary that the dispositions that I demonstrated be fairly analogous to those of the Ministry in London, since Mr. Oswald was determined to return to London himself in search of a response. That Emissary did not delay in returning, and he was followed closely by Mr.

Thomas Grenville, the brother of Lord Temple and a personal friend of Mr. Fox. The first was charged with renewing to Mr. Franklin the dispositions of the Cabinet of St. James with regard to America, the second was charged with assuring himself of those of the King, and of declaring that the King of England demanded no more than to treat impartially of peace with His Majesty. This overture could only be very agreeable to us; I responded to Mr. Grenville, at the express order of the King, that His Majesty was ready to negotiate peace, on condition that it be general, and that His Majesty's allies and friends be satisfied. All this, Sir, happened before news reached Europe of the unfortunate day of 12 April; there was reason to fear that the defeat that our arms had just experienced, and information regarding which had just reached us, so to speak, when I was giving my response to Mr. Grenville, might alter the peaceful disposition of the Ministry of London. But my apprehensions in this regard have not been justified: the King of England has had a full power drawn up in form to authorize Mr. Grenville to treat of peace with His Majesty.

In communicating that full power to me, the English emissary declared to me that the King of England, in order to facilitate peace, was disposed to treat of the independence of the United States with His Majesty, on condition that, for the Remainder, things would be restored on the basis of the Treaty of 1763. The King's response to this proposition was: 1$^{st.}$ that the full power of Mr. Grenville was insufficient, because it did not make any mention of His Majesty's allies; 2$^{nd.}$ that His Majesty could not treat of America's interests, because he was without power in that regard; that moreover it was worthy of the dignity of the King of England, as of that of the United States, to establish a direct negotiation between them on that subject; 3$^{rd.}$ that to make a solid and durable peace, it should have as a basis not the Treaty of Paris, but the justice and the dignity of all the contracting parties.

The English Ministry sounded out the force and the justice of these observations, and it did not hesitate to take them into consideration. It has, consequently, just sent Mr. Grenville a new full power that authorizes him to treat with all the powers implicated in the war. In giving me a copy of this act, Mr. Grenville declared to me: that, the King of England being disposed to recognize and to declare directly the independence of America, that subject would no longer be a conditional clause of peace; and as for that which concerns France, the English plenipotentiary proposed to take the Treaty of Paris as the basis not of peace, but of the negotiations that it is a question of establishing. On the 21st of this month I communicated the King's response to Mr. Grenville, and I let him take a copy of it in order to assure the exactitude of his report; you will also find one enclosed.

Such is, Sir, the present state of affairs: I have nothing to add, other than that Holland is admitted to the general peacemaking, and that that Republic, in order to participate therein, is going to decline for the second time the mediation that the Empress of Russia offered it for a separate peace.

I will not examine, Sir, the secret motives that the English Ministry may have for showing so great an eagerness for peace, nor the designs that it may have for appearing so accommodating on the article of America: I content myself with supposing that the British Ministers feel more and more the difficulties of continuing the war, and the impossiblity of reconquering America. The difficulty was without doubt to find a course that could save the King of England at least a part of the humiliation that would result from the forced acknowledgment of the independence of his former Colonies; I imagine that it is with this design that His Britannic Majesty proposes to observe this independence of his own impulse, and without making of it a subject of negotiation: this illusory act of a prostrated sovereignty would appear to the English at least to save appearances, and we have no interest in disabusing them in this regard; the essential point is that independence be recognized, and that nothing be required of us, that we bought it by right of compensation, as it was at first the System of the English Ministry.

I do not doubt, Sir, that that Ministry is hastening to make known these dispositions in America and that it is trying to assert them either to force Congress, by the cry of the people, to a separate peace, or at least, to procure some commercial advantages. We should no longer fear disaffection; for it would be from now on without object, and the Americans would dishonor themselves without utility as without motives. As for the regulations that it may be a question of making relative to commerce, we have neither the right nor the intent to thwart them; the only thing that we have to require and on which we rely, is that Great Britain will not be accorded any sort of preference. Moreover, Sir, as the intrigues of the English emissaries in America will probably be very active, and as it is possible that they will succeed in exciting some ferment, I persist in thinking that the best means of closing the door on them, is that Congress declare peremptorily, that it will not itself begin any negotiations with the Court of London, and that it has given its full powers irrevocably to several of its ministers who are now in Europe. To this declaration it would be appropriate that Congress add another, namely: that not only will the United States not make a separate peace, but also that they will continue to act hostilely against the common enemy in some manner or other, until it has given satisfaction to their allies. This declaration, made with energy, will make known to the English Ministry that it will not get rid of the Americans by acknowledging their independence; and that in withdrawing the English troops from the American continent, it should fear that they not show themselves outside their quarters if it does not give its approval to a general peacemaking; this double declaration should not, in our opinion, suffer the least difficulty since it is founded on the text as on the spirit of our treaties with the United States, treaties that form their safeguard, and the faithful observance of which will force, as much as weapons, the Court of London to listen to an equitable peace.

I foresee, Sir, that there will still be great debates in Congress on the Subject of the fishery and on the subject of the boundaries of some States. If Congress does not let itself be carried away by personal interest and the clamors of the Northern provinces, it will envisage peace as the greatest of benefits that it can desire; it will beware of demanding the least favor, as a right, from a power, an enormous portion of whose domain is about to escape it; that it will limit itself to asking for what the common law assures to Americans, and that it will keep itself from asking for a much greater extension when England proposes commercial arrangements to it. I especially hope, Sir, that the Americans will not claim that the King strengthens himself by procuring for them the extension of the fishing that they covet, and still less that he make the sacrifice of his own fisheries to compensate them for the refusal of Great Britain. His Majesty will consent neither to the one nor to the other: all that he can do will be to accord his good offices according to what the circumstances will permit him: but he is invariably resolved not to sacrifice the reestablishment of peace to a poorly-founded claim. You would do well, Sir, to insinuate these verities when you judge it necessary, and to employ all the means that your prudence and your dexterity will suggest to you to have them adopted. I owe to Mr. Franklin the justice that he has perfectly understood them; and if he were not bound by the will of Congress, I do not doubt that he would take them without difficulty as a rule of his conduct. Moreover, Sir, if Congress does not succeed in obtaining such fishing as it desires, I see nothing that should force it to renounce it explicitly; it could keep silent, and hold itself in readiness to assert its claims when conjectures appear proper to favor them.

As for the regulation of the boundaries of some states, we will not involve ourselves therein; but we desire that the Americans not impede the negotiations by unsustainable claims. Their continent is not too vast for their population, and they will long be without need to extend it; why then would they prefer to peace a contingent future that will cause neither their happiness nor that of their descendants!

. . . . . .

The United States will act all the more wisely, Sir, in not giving an exclusive Confidence to the enticements of the new English ministers, for no obvious fact yet justifies the apparent good will of which they boast for America. The first step that should have been ascertained was the passage of a Bill to authorize the King of England to treat and conclude peace or truce with the United States of America. The bill was announced and proposed and, without the reason for it being known, withdrawn and postponed to the first session of the new parliament that it is said to be a question of forming. This variation augurs little Stability in the Councils and very little accord among the ministers. They are in fact said to be very divided among themselves. Time will enlighten us, while waiting for our American allies, who have nothing better to do than to hold themselves in readiness to resist fraud and force.

· · · · ·

Vergennes

FFAA: Pol.Corr., U.S., v. 21, f. 103 (LC transcription).

Comte de Vergennes to Chevalier de la Luzerne

[Translation]

N⁰· 36.   Versailles, 28 June 1782

According to the news that comes to me from England, Sir, I have reason to judge that the disposition for peace of the new English ministry is something less than unanimous; that discord is already very lively among the different members who compose it; that the Rockingham party, of which Mr. Fox is the support and the voice, and which seems inclined toward peace, is at daggers drawn with that of Lord Shelburne, suppported by Lords Camden and Grafton. From this conflict, the outcome of which is impossible to predict, there must result at least some delays and obstacles to peace; perhaps it will even entail a cessation of the negotiations, the first foundations of which have just been laid. I already see tergiversations that inspire some suspicion in me: it was a question of immediately passing a bill to authorize the King of England to treat with the Colonies of America; it is even claimed that this bill had already been proposed to the two Chambers of Parliament; and I am assured today that it has been sent back to the first session of the new Parliament that is being convoked.

On the other hand, I am instructed that Lord Shelburne has Agents in America authorized to propose to the United States that they adopt the constitution that has just been accorded to Ireland, that is to say, to free them from the Legislature of the British Parliament and to accord them one that would be appropriate for them, reserving the assent of the Crown. This plan, Sir, is certainly a pure dream, and I am persuaded that Lord Shelburne will not delay in convincing himself thereof. But it is no less true that this Minister will inundate all the corners of America with emissaries who will strive to extol the system that I have just indicated to you, and people everywhere are credulous: it is all the more frightening that that of America allows itself to be led astray, that it desires peace, and that it will think it has gained everything in triumphing over the former English ministry, which will be presented to it with affection as the sole author of its sufferings. I am very sure, Sir, that Congress and the enlightened people will not be the dupes of these lying insinuations and that, unvarying in their principles, they will see the health and the happiness of their homeland only in the independence for which they have been fighting for six years: but the people are very powerful in America, and it is possible that in shaking them a fermentation will be excited that will give the greatest hindrances to Congress. In order to prevent this inconvenience, I think that too much care cannot be taken with the means of becoming familiar with the British emissaries and with rendering their secret machinations fruitless. We are of the opinion, Sir, that in order to cut short their perfidious intrigues, the best thing that Congress could do would be to proscribe them, or to invite the various legislatures to take that step. Without this precaution, all that could be done would only be palliatives, and would let Congress come up against all that the most perverse politics could suggest to the British Ministry to seduce and subjugate America.

The King's intention is, Sir, that you allow knowledge of these notions to the members of Congress, upon the discretion and influence of which you think you can rely, and you will omit nothing to make them perceive how important it is that they make use of that which their prudence will suggest to them to break up in advance the measures of the Court of London, and to maintain among the American people the unanimity with which they have defended up to the present the independence that they have acquired at the price of their repose and of their blood.

Vergennes

FFAA: Pol. Corr., U.S., v. 21, f.104 (LC transcription).

Lord Shelburne to Richard Oswald

Sir   Whitehall June 30th 1782

. . . . .

I must own, that I have been disappointed in not receiving any letter from You by two Messengers, who brought dispatches from Mr. Grenville, especially as at this moment it is very essential to have early & regular intelligence. I take it however for granted, that you had nothing of business to communicate, which would indeed be naturally suspended, till the passing of the Act in question enabled me to send the necessary Powers. This was completed the end of last week, and I lost no time in taking the King's commands for directing a Commission to be made out conformable to the Powers given to His Maj^r

I hope to receive early Assurances from You, that my confidence in the sincerity & Good Faith of Mr Franklin has not been misplaced, & that He will concur with you in endeavouring to render effectual the great work, in which our Hearts & Wishes are so equally interested. You will observe, that We have adopted his idea of the best method to come at a General Pacification by treating separately with each Party. I cannot but entertain a firm reliance, that the appointment of the partic^r Commissioners will be no less satisfactory to him; He has very lately warranted me to depend upon that effect in the instance of y^r Nomination, & He will not be surprized at the choice of y^r Collegue Mr Jackson,[1] when he considers, how very conversant Mr Jackson is with the subject of America, & how very sincere a Friend He has uniformly shewn himself to the reestablishment of Peace and Harmony between that Country & this. It cannot have escaped Mr Franklin's memory, that when I was formerly engaged in the same employment, which I have now the honor to hold, & was accustomed with so much satisfaction & advantage to myself to converse freely with him upon all American Subjects, I was at the same time in habits of similar intimacy with Mr Jackson, whose particular acquaintance with these Subjects recommended him to the Office of Council to the Board of Trade. I persuade myself, that you will find him an agreeable Associate to y^r self, & as far as can depend upon the choice of Men, that I shall find your joint Labors usefull to the Public.

It will be altogether unnecessary for me to give you any additional instructions to those accompanying the Commission with Mr Jackson, especially as He will communicate to You the substance of a full & confidential conversation, I have had with him on the Subject.

· · · · ·

Lord Shelburne

PRO: FO 27/2, v. 557, f, 323 (LC transcription).
[1] *Jackson, Richard (d. 1787). British jurist and political figure. Close friend of Lord Shelburne. Member of Parliament, 1762-1784. A lord of the Treasury, July 1782-April 1783.*

Lord Shelburne to General Sir Guy Carleton and Admiral Robert Digby

Secret and Confidential.   Whitehall 8th July 1782
Gentlemen.

Since my last Dispatch to you of the 5th Ultimo, wherein I acquainted you of the State of the Negotiation at Paris, nothing has been wanting on Our Part to advance that important business to some determinate issue. M$^{r.}$ Oswald reached Paris on the 31st May on his return from London with Letters and Instructions to M$^{r.}$ Grenville, in consequence of the resolution which I before mentioned, of proposing the Independence of America in the first instance instead of making it a condition of a general Treaty. Some delay however arose to impede the progress of the Negotiation from an exception taken by the French Minister to the Full Power sent to M$^{r.}$ Grenville, because it did not enable him to treat with the Ministers of the other Belligerent Powers, without whose Concurrence Mons$^{r.}$ de Vergennes had already declared, he cou'd enter into no Treaty.

On the 10th Ultimo fresh Powers were sent to M$^{r.}$ Grenville, under which he received Authority to treat with All the other European Powers engaged in the War; And by a Letter from M$^{r.}$ Fox of the same date, He was more particularly directed no longer to mention the Independence of America as a Cession to France, or as a Conditional Article of a general Treaty, but He was at the same time instructed to observe to the French Ministry, that the Independence of America was proposed to be acknowledged, and to remark, that this, which they had emphatically called the *Object of the War*, being done spontaneously, little difficulty ought to remain with regard to other Points, which might be considered rather as collateral and incidental than as Principle in the present dispute.

M$^{r.}$ Grenville delivered a Copy of His full Power to Mons$^{r.}$ de Vergennes on the 15th Ultimo – It was not 'till the 21$^{st.}$ that the French Minister returned an Answer, which, however full of general expressions of a Pacifick Disposition, and of satisfaction in His Majesty's readiness to Enter into Negotiation with All the Powers at War, and to declare the Unconditional Independence of the United Colonies of America was replete with Views little consonant to that spirit of moderation, on which were to be founded the best hopes of a speedy Pacification.

Adopting the Treaty of Paris for the Basis of the Negotiation the Court of Versailles declared, that such acceptance did not preclude several exceptions and alterations, to which His Majesty's assent would be expected. Among others,

1$^{st.}$ Some new arrangements concerning the East Indies.

2. Some new Stipulations relative to Africa.

3. An equitable regulation of mutual Utility with respect to the Newfoundland Fishery.

4th. A Commercial Arrangement to the satisfaction of the two Nations in Europe, concluding however with an explicit declaration, that He wou'd neither treat or conclude than inasmuch as the Interests of His Allies and Friends shou'd be discussed and regulated at the same time either separately or in conjunction, as the Parties should all Agree.

I need not point out to Your observation the almost indefinite scope of these demands, and of course the unpromising aspect of the Negotiation on the supposition, that the influence of France will be obsolute over the conduct of the American Commissioners.

The death of Lord Rockingham, and the resignation of Mr. Fox, which have caused a temporary delay in the prosecution of this business, will make no change in those principles and intentions upon which His Majesty's Ministers have already made known their wishes to complete the work of Peace. You will be acquainted of the further proceedings of this Negotiation, in which the Chief Object of our concern will naturally be to fix upon that plan and those means, which may make the greatest impression on the Commissioners for the Revolted Provinces by convincing them of Our Good Faith, and setting before them in the strongest light the benefits proposed to their option and contradistinction to the risk and expence of a War, which cou'd no longer be productive of additional advantage to their Constituents.

I have communicated these particulars to You, that You may be fully acquainted with the State of Affairs, by the knowledge of which You are to regulate Your own conduct both as Commanders of His Majesty's Forces by Sea and Land, and more particularly in your Capacity as Commissioners for restoring Peace. I am most earnestly to recommend it to you to make use of the information I send You, to counteract every misrepresentation, which the malice of Our Enemies may strive to diffuse into the minds of Men, who still heated with the spirit of Party may be too ready to imbibe them, and of course to keep at a distance from all explanation and reason. I must therefore upon this plan, and with these views again refer you to the directions contained in my former dispatches, not doubting that you will take care to make known when it will have effect, the fair and honorable designs and wishes of Great Britain to put an end to every subject of dissention, and to seal the terms of Peace and Reconciliation with a lasting impression of mutual Good Faith and Contentment.

I am &ca   Shelburne.

PRO: CO 5/178, pp 463-474 (LC transcription).

Richard Oswald to Lord Shelburne

My Lord.   Paris, Monday 8th. July 1782

I beg leave, under this, Cover to transmit to your Lo^P a Letter directed to myself from Doct^r Franklin, which he Sent to me ten days ago, on the day it is dated; and I will also take nottice of what passed between him & me in consequence of it.

Two days before that Letter was sent to me, the Doctor called upon me, and said that agreeable to the Memorandum I shewed him, he had wrote me a Letter, which I might send to your Lo^P if I thought fit. Upon the perusal of it, I observed he said that I might be appointed Singly for the Colonies, or jointly with Mr Grenville; or included in Mr Grenville's general Commission to treat with all Parties concerned in the War. To this last part I objected for various reasons, needless to be here taken notice of. ...And accordingly on the 27th of last Month he sent me the one inclosed.

I have kept it in my hands untill now, to go by the return of the first Courier that arrives, which Mr. Grenville has been expecting daily. But as none had appeared, & thinking that the Doctor could have no meaning in putting such a Letter into my hands but with a view to its being forwarded to your Lo^P & might perhaps be disappointed or disobliged, if delayed, I thought it right to let him know that it was not sent, & the reason of it's still remaining in my hands. On that account, & wishing to have an opportunity of talking to him on the subject of it, I went out to his House on Saturday the 6th & staid with him about an hour.

After thanking him for his good opinion of me, as expressed in that Letter, & giving the reason for its not being forwarded, I told him that this Interval of delay had given occasion to sundry questions in my own mind as to the Business we should have to treat about in case I should be appointed, & should undertake the Office he was pleased to recommend in that Letter.

With France & the other Parties I was sensible there must, be many points to be settled. But with respect to the Colonies I told him I could not easily conceive how there could arise any variety of subject to treat upon. That as to a final Conclusion, the Treaty with France might make it necessary to wait the event of a Determination as to them, so as both might be included in one Settlement. But until then, I could not see there would be much field for Negotiation between G. Britain & the Commissioners of the Colonies, after their Independence had been granted. And which being in a manner acknowledged, I had been in hopes there remained no Questions of either side that would require much discussion. If he thought it would be otherwise, I told him I would be much obliged to him, to give me a hint of them, as the question could not but be material to me, in considering whether I might venture upon such a Charge. That this I would request of him as a Friend, & I hoped I might also expect of him as a Friend to England, Which I must Still Suppose him to be. And in which I was not singular, believing it was the universal opinion at home, & particularly with regard to your Lo^P who I had reason to be assured, had the greatest confidence in his good Intentions towards our Country. That I did not just then desire, or expect an answer, But if he would name any other day, I should wait of him, in hopes of having his opinion & advice upon the particular subject of this Colony Treaty, & his Sentiments in general upon the whole of these Affairs. Which I was certain would be of service in guiding us how to proceed in the safest & quickest Course to a final Conclusion of this unhappy business.

That I had too just a notion of his Character to expect any Information but such as would not be inconsistent with particular Engagements. But where that did not interfere, his granting the favour I askt might be doing a good office to all Parties concerned. For I could not help thinking that the Commissioners of the Colonies had it much in their power to give dispatch to the general Treaty, & to end it on just & reasonable terms, even notwithstanding their particular Treaty with France. Upon this the Doct^r said, They had no Treaty with France but what was published. I said I was glad it was so, since I saw nothing there, however guarded against a seperate Peace, that should direct or Controul the Conditions of a Treaty between them & G Britain, excepting the provision for the great Article of Independence which was now out of the question.

· · · · · ·

I went on, & said that with respect to France, whatever She might desire beyond the Separation of the Thirteen Colonies, would be more than She had just reason to expect, being abundantly indemnified thereby for the amount of all her Expences in the present War. That hereafter She had nothing to fear from England. But England had now much to fear from France; as would be seen in a few years after the first Peace, since we might then be assured that She would begin again with us wherever She thought we were weakest; and I could have no doubt the E. Indies would be the next Scene of Contest.

And upon the whole, that the Terms of the approaching Settlement were of the most interesting Consequence to our future Safety.

That whatever advice or hints regarding that purpose the Doct^r would be pleased to give me, I would make no indiscreet use of, but would pledge my honour that they should be strictly kept under such directions of Communication as he should think fit to prescribe.

After allowing me to go on in this way, he said there were some things which he wished England to think of, or to agree to (I forget which) & yet he should not like that they were known to have been suggested by him. At last he told me, If I would come out to his House on Wednesday, the 10th, he would show me a Minute of some things which he thought might be deserving of nottice upon the occasion. If we agreed in opinion it was so far well if not, that I should let him know, & he would be glad to have my opinion. And where we agreed, I might make use of his sentiments as my own, to any good purpose I might think proper.

.   .   .   .   .

...I have the honour to be with much respect My Lord Your Lop⁸ obedient humble Servant   Richard Oswald.

.   .   .   .   .

PRO: FO 27/2, v. 557, f. 359 (LC transcription).

Comte de Montmorin to Comte de Vergennes

[Translation]

Nᵒ· 51   St. Ildefonso, 8 July 1782
Sir

I had the honor, in writing to you by M. le Chevalier de Clonard,[1] of helping you understand the manner in which the Spanish Ministry envisages the most recent step of the two Mediating Courts and what its approximate response will be. It is such as I informed you, as you will see by the two enclosed pieces marked B and C. But I should report to you all that has happened in this regard, and on my conversations with M. le Comte de Florida Blanca in accordance with your preceding despatches.

And at first M. Zinoviev[2] spoke only very vaguely to this minister of the step taken with you by the Prince de Bariatinski to inform you of the new solicitations of his court to Holland and to invite you to cooperate in their Success; but in return he insisted rather strongly on the desire of his court to see peace reestablished in Europe through its mediation. M. le Comte d'Ostermann expressed himself in the same tone with the Spanish chargé d'affaires in Petersburg, the latter had reported it to M. de Florida Blanca, who made him a response of which he gave a copy to M. Zinoviev. He also communicated it to me, informing me that he had accompanied it with many general and honest remarks to express to Russia Spain's desire to have peace at its hands. I enclose here under Nᵒ· A a copy of that response. I found that it relied a little too much on our account of the negotiations going on in Paris, and that it allowed too much conjecture that Spain would only pursue them in order not to be separated from us. I remarked on it to M. de Florida Blanca, who responded that in his conversation he had made the Russian Minister understand that, England having taken the first steps to establish this negotiation in Paris, it had been neither decent nor appropriate for us to refuse it. I informed him that I would have desired that his response in writing had also contained the expression of this opinion; but it was done and transmitted; there was no longer a remedy. The following day I received your despatch of 22 June, which was delivered to me by a Spanish courier. I went to M. de Florida Blanca's, and it was not difficult for me to perceive from the first instant that the account that M. d'Aranda rendered of what had happened at Versailles had not made an agreeable impression on the Spanish Minister. He found (and in that he was of the same opinion as the ambassador) that you had been very quick; and his imagination already painted the negotiations for him as very advanced and Spain as forced into a peace that would fulfill only very imperfectly the objects that she had proposed. He recalled to me what he had predicted from the commencement of the war, that peace would be accomplished as soon as the independence of the United States would be assured. He finally terminated his conversation by saying to me that he saw with regret that the manner in which peace was being made would raise a chill between the two crowns, because he was more than ever persuaded that the closest union was useful and even necessary to them at all times. As I saw that the agitation of M. de Florida Blanca was great and that in wishing to calm him I was producing a contrary effect, I limited myself to asking that he reread attentively the end of your response to Mr. Grenville and reflect on what would happen if, by denying ourselves all that could establish a direct negotiation, we left to the two Imperial courts the facility again to bring up the Mediation.

I returned to M. de Florida Blanca the following day and found him calmer. He agreed that by our response we were reserving to Spain all the means of discussing its interests without leaving the Court of London the least hope of seeing us consent to peace before they were settled. He then entered into detail with me and told me that what had angered him at first was that you had pressed M. d'Aranda to explain what Spain could give in exchange for Gibraltar, assuring him that the English would absolutely wish to preserve a foothold in the Mediterranean. He told me then what had passed between you and that ambassador and that, pressed by you, M. d'Aranda had confessed to you that Spain could cede Minorca or Oran; that you had discussed together which one of these two places would inconvenience us least in the hands of the English, and that you had found that this would be Oran, as being more distant from our Mediterranean ports. M. de Florida Blanca is of the same opinion, and thinks moreover that in case of war, that port, being susceptible of being easily blockaded, would become useless to the English; but he was angry that M. d'Aranda had discussed the matter with you, the sacrifice of Oran to obtain or preserve Gibraltar having to be made by Spain only in the most extreme case. He therefore feared that for the purpose of facilitating the establishment of the negotiations, you would open your mind to Mr. Grenville on these dispositions. Although I had indicated nothing in this regard, I did not hesitate, Sir, to reassure M. de Florida Blanca. I pointed out to him that the verbal response which you had given to Mr. Grenville indicated exactly only what concerned France and treated even that matter in a manner so vague and general that it could be assured that in the case wherein you had been sounded out on the dispositions of Spain, your responses would have been still less explicit. Finally, Sir, I succeeded in nearly calming the anxieties of M. de Florida Blanca on the use you had made of M. d'Aranda's confidence; and as he had told me that that Ambassador had spoken to you about preserving neutrality in time of war in the Mediterranean as a means imagined by that Minister of consoling England for not having more of an establishment there, I employed all my efforts to prove to him that it would not be knowledge of Spain's dispositions that would hinder the Court of London from adopting that expedient. I then represented to him how essential it was that M. d'Aranda be authorized to negotiate seriously with Mr. Grenville, at least until the formal establishment of the negotiations; that without this, the alacrity of the mediators could not be guaranteed; that he knew what had been the inclination of M. le Prince de Kaunitz upon being informed by England of the steps that had been taken at Versailles; that, finally, the new office of the Minister of Russia should serve to prove to him at last that the two Imperial Courts had not abandoned the design of taking up the mediation again. We spoke of the danger there would be in what that design would accomplish; and I can assure you that M. le Comte de Florida Blanca would not see with more pleasure than you, Sir, our interests in the hands of those two courts. What can have deluded M. le Comte de Kaunitz, or at least motivated the account that he rendered to his father of the manner in which the Spanish Ministry envisaged this matter, is that when the Imperial ambassador spoke to him of all the anger that the part the Court of London had taken in opening a negotiation at Versailles had caused M. le Prince de Kaunitz, M. de Florida Blanca still took pleasure in exaggerating the injury that the English had done the Court of Vienna and in describing their bad faith with heat. The Spanish Minister recalled to him on that occasion what the King his master had felt on England's part when he was mediator between her and us; and that he had predicted to the Imperial Courts that they would experience the same behavior. Then, comparing the conduct of the Spanish Ministry to that of the English

Ministry, he applied himself to show the complete Frankness of the one and the duplicity of the other. M. le Comte de Kaunitz doubtless attributed the heat with which M. de Florida Blanca expressed himself to ill humor at seeing the negotiations being established in Paris; and moreover he was not perhaps displeased with taking the credit with his father for having led the Court of Madrid to desire to see its interests discussed in Vienna rather than at Versailles.

The very day of my conversation with M. de Florida Blanca, M. le Comte de Kaunitz received the courier who brought him the order to take the same step with the Spanish Ministry that M. de Mercy had taken with you; and the following day in the evening L'Epine[3] delivered to me your despatch of 26 June. I went the following morning to the Spanish Minister's in order to confer with him on the Mediators' new step before he saw their Ministers and to be able to communicate to him your ideas on the response to make to them. I read to him a part of your despatch No. 41. He seemed to me to enter absolutely into your views. We agreed that he would tell the Mediating Ministers that before responding to them, he would consult with me, and that he would give them an appointment for Saturday the 6th. The Princess des Asturies[4] giving birth that very day, the conference was put off until Sunday the 7th; and he delivered to them the response of which you will find the translation enclosed, marked B. You will also find under the letter C that of the response which M. le Comte d'Aranda will be charged to transmit to the Courts of Vienna and of Petersburg, after having communicated it to you and made in it the changes that you think appropriate. I have proposed one, as well as an addition that you will see in the margin. M. de Florida Blanca has adopted both and has had his response edited in consequence.

I should not omit, Sir, that M. de Kaunitz in his conversations with M. de Florida Blanca told him that the Minister of England in Vienna had sought to excuse the establishment of a negotiation at Versailles by pointing out that the Preliminaries could be settled at Versailles, and then pursue the negotiations at a Congress that would be assembled under the mediation of the two Imperial Courts. This would appear to exculpate the English from the bad faith of which they could be suspected, and would reduce the Mediators to a representation that could perhaps be left to them.

I thought, Sir, that I should enter into detail on all that happened in order to put you in position to judge the manner in which the Spanish Ministry envisages the whole negotiation at this moment. Although the suspicions that M. de Florida Blanca had conceived as the result of what Mr. d'Aranda sent him seem to me in part dissipated, I cannot conceal from myself that he is reluctant to see the English Emissaries established in Paris. He understands nevertheless the necessity of maintaining them there, but the role that the Court of London has taken in recognizing purely and simply the independence of the United States worries him. This difficulty, which he regarded as the greatest between England and us, being once removed, he fears that the other subjects will not arrange themselves very easily, given the restitutions that we are in a position to make. He perceives that Spain is not in that situation by a great deal, since, far from having anything to restore, she is not in possession of what she wants to obtain. Even the taking of Gibraltar would not put her in the position in which she would like to be, and would not remove all the difficulties, because then she would want to retain that place without giving anything in exchange. The greatest expenses of this enterprise having already been made, you may well judge, Sir, that before negotiating seriously, one wishes to expect the success of it (which one regards as nearly certain). Here then is what Spain's system is reduced to at this moment: negotiate if it is absolutely impossible to avoid it; and if one is extremely pressed, concede in exchange for Gibraltar one of the places of which M. le Comte d'Aranda spoke to you, but delay as long as one can the moment of explaining oneself in the hope that the outcome at Gibraltar will be favorable, and then not concede any compensation for that place. If things go thus, it seems impossible to me that we would not be forced to undertake the next campaign. Therefore, almost nothing was denied from what was demanded in the Memoir of which M. de Saavedra[5] was the bearer, as you will see in my despatch No. 53. The King of Spain and his Minister have told me more than once that as soon as the siege of Gibraltar is ended, all the Spanish forces will be at the dispositon of the King. In fact, one can scarcely conceal from oneself that, given the state of affairs, it is almost solely for Spain that we continue the war. May this verity not be too perceptible in the eyes of the Americans, who have no reason to be interested in the satisfaction of that Power, and to whom the war would soon become insupportable if it had no more than this object.

M. d'Aranda will doubtless have informed you of the other claims of his Court. He will have been able to do it in two words. They include all that is stipulated in the Convention. It would be desirable that its means be proportionate to it, but unfortunately a great deal is necessary for that....

Recd. by Courier the 16th.   Le c^te De Montmorin.

FFAA: Pol. Corr., Spain, v. 608, f. 15 (LC transcription).

[1] Not further identified.

[2] Zinov'ev, Stepan S. Russian diplomat. Ambassador to Spain.

[3] Not further identified.

[4] *Asturias, Maria Luisa of Parma, Princess of (1751-1819). Crown princess of Spain, 1765-1788; thereafter, queen of Spain.*

[5] *Saavedra, Francisco de (1746-1819). Spanish diplomat, colonial administrator, and political figure. Named secretary of the embassy in Portugal, 1778. Assigned to the Ministry of the Indies, he was captured by the English on his way to America and taken to Jamaica. After his exchange, he was present at the fall of Pensacola. Intendant of Caracas, 1783-1788. Later, minister-secretary of State and of the Treasury.*

Thomas Grenville to Lord Shelburne

My Lord,   Paris July 9 1782

I received last night the honour of your Lordship's letter of the 5th ins[t.], & in obedience to His Majesty's commands, have acquainted the French Minister, the Spanish ambassador, & M[r] Franklin, that no change will be made in the measures of His Maj[ty] government, particularly in His Majesty's ardent desire of peace, upon terms which may be consistent with the dignity of his Crown, & the welfare of his people.

I have had no intercourse with the Ministers of any other foreign powers; from the interference of the court of Russia, in order to bring about a particular peace with Holland, & there having been till a very few days since, no positive declaration of the Dutch being determined to treat only in conjunction with France, it appeared to me, to be most prudent, & most agreable to the spirit of my instructions, to avoid, as long as it was possible, the including Holland in this negotiation; & I have consequently taken every opportunity to remind M de Vergennes, that it had not been our desire to include Holland in this business; I learned however from him to-day, that the Dutch having formally requested of the Court of Versailles to make no peace but in common with them, every assurance of that nature had, by the French King's orders, been given to them. Your Lordship will perhaps have learnt from the official letters, I have at times sent to M[r] Fox, that the French Minister has not gone into any detail as yet; the state of the negotiation is therefore exactly what it was when I had the honour of transmitting the written answer I had copied at Versailles on the 21st ult, which consents to a future explanation, provided the general grounds there stated, should be adopted in England; of that however, I took the liberty of expressing some doubt by my last of the 21[st.], as I observed in them, that very wide extent, which from my first coming here to this moment, I have uniformly considered, as a most unpromising feature in the proposed pacification: it is not easy to weigh the precise sense of general terms, but a new treaty of commerce is always foremost in the conversation of the French Spanish and American Ministers. M. D'Aranda dwells incessantly upon our giving up Gibraltar, notwithstanding the little disposition he finds in me to that discussion, & only varies what he says upon it, by stating that if we give it by treaty, we shall get something for it, whereas if it should be taken, the Court of Madrid can never hear of it's being reclaimed by us. Mr. Franklin the other day, for the first time, gave me to understand that America must be to have her share in the N: Foundland Fishery, & that the limits of Canada would likewise be a subject for arrangement. he seems much dis-inclined to an idea he expects to be stated, of going into an examination, for the mutual compensation of the losses of individuals, insisting, perhaps with reason, upon the endless detail that would be produced by it; nor does he cease to give the most decided discouragement to any possible plan of arrangement with America, short of compleat and distinct independance, in it's fullest sense: when I last saw him, he read to me upon this subject, the resolutions of the 16th of May last, that passed unanimously both houses of assembly in Maryland, against making any peace but in concert with France, and with an admission of independance; resolutions, he said occasioned by Sr. Guy Carleton's supposed commission, and which spoke the determination, he was sure, of all the Thirteen Provinces. Having touched, My Lord, upon those few circumstances, that seem in any way important to this business, I forbear to enlarge upon them, in full trust that I shall be permitted to come incessantly to London, where His Majesty's Ministers will certainly command the little information I can have to give them; it being my fixed purpose; firmly, tho' as humbly & respectfully as it is possible, to decline any farther prosecution of this business.

I have therefore to request of your Lordship, as speedily as may be, to lay before His Majesty, in every expression of duty and humility, my earnest & unalterable prayer, that His Majesty will be graciously pleased to recall from me the commission I am honoured with at Paris. I am highly sensible to the very flattering expression of your Lordship's regard, and have the honour to be, with great truth and respect, My Lord, your Lordship's most obedient, and most humble Servant,   Thomas Grenville.
R. 12th by Ogg.

PRO: FO 27/2, v. 557, f. 367 (LC transcription).

Seventh Peace Conference

[Translation]

9 July 1782

Mr. Grenville betook himself this morning to the Comte de Vergennes and told him in a very afflicted air that he had received the deplorable news of the death of Lord Rockingham; that Lord Shelburne had been named to the place of First Lord of the Treasury, and that Mr. Fox had judged it appropriate to tender his resignation, which had been accepted.

The Courier charged with bearing these details to Mr. Grenville with orders to inform us of them delivered to him no instruction relative to the negotiation of peace; he is only charged with declaring that this change has no effect on the dispositions of the King of England to contribute to the reestablishment of peace, provided that it can be done in a sure and honorable manner.

He is given notice of the immediate Dispatch of another Courier with instructions.

FFAA: Pol. Corr., England, v. 537 f. 324 (LC transcription).

Benjamin Franklin to David Hartley

Dear Sir,   Passy, July 10, 1782.
I do not know why the good work of peace goes on so slowly on your side. Some have imagined that your ministers, since Rodney's success, are desirious of trying fortune a little further before they conclude the war: others, that they have not a good understanding with each other. What I have just heard seems to countenance this opinion. It is said Mr. Fox has resigned. We are ready here on the part of America to enter into treaty with you, in concurrence with our Allies; and are disposed to be very reasonable; but if your *plenipotentiary*, notwithstanding that character, is upon every proposition obliged to send courier and wait an answer, we shall not soon see the happy conclusion. It has been suspected too, that you wait to hear the effect of some overtures sent by General Carleton for a separate peace with America. A vessel just arrived from Maryland, brings us the unanimous resolutions of their assembly for continuing the war at all hazards rather than violate their faith with France. This is a sample of the success to be expected from such a measure, if it has really been taken; which I hardly believe.

.   .   .   .   .

...I am, my dear sir, with great esteem and affection, yours ever,
                                            B. Franklin.

WTF, Franklin Memoirs, v. 4, pp. 226-228.

Richard Oswald to Lord Shelburne

My Lord,   Paris, Wednesday 10th. July 1782.

In consequence of Dr. Franklin's Appointment, as mentioned in my Letter of the 8th under this Cover, I went out to his House this morning & staid near two hours with him, with an view of obtaining the Information & advice I wished for, as to the Terms & Conditions upon which He thought a Treaty between Great Britain & the Commissioners of the Colonies might be carried on, & proceed to a conclusion. Having reminded him of what he in a manner promisd on this head on the 6th. He took out a minute, & from it read a few hints or articles. Some he said as necessary for them to insist on; others which he could not say he had any Orders about, or were not absolutely demanded, & yet such as it would be advisable for England to offer for the sake of Reconciliation, and her future Interest, Viz:

1st. Of the first Class, *necessary* to be granted. Independence full & complete in every sense to the 13 States & all Troops to be withdrawn from thence.

2^{d.} A settlement of the boundaries of *their* Colonies, & the loyal Colonies.

3^{d.} A Confinement of the Boundaries of Canada, at least to what they were, before the last Act of Parliament, I think in 1774, if not to a still more contracted State, on an ancient footing.

4. A freedom of fishing on the Banks of Newfoundland, & elsewhere, as well for Fish as whales. I own I wonder'd he should have thought it necessary to ask for this priviledge. He did not mention the Leave of drying Fish on shore in Newfoundland, & I said nothing of it. I dont remember any more articles which he said they would insist on, or what he calld necessary for them to be granted.

Then as to the *adviseable* Articles, or such as he would as a Friend recommend to be offer'd by England Viz.

1st. To indemnify many People who had been ruind by Towns burnt & destroy'd. The whole might not exceed the Sum of Five or Six hundred thousand pounds. I was struck at this. However the D^{r.} said though it was a large Sum, it would not be ill bestow'd; as it would conciliate the Resentment of a multitude of poor Sufferers, who could have no other Remedy, & who without some Relief, would keep up a Spirit of secret Revenge & Animosity for a long time to come, against Great Britain: whereas a voluntary Offer of such Reparation, would diffuse an universal Calm & Conciliation over the whole Country.

2^{d.} Some Sort of Acknowledgment in some public Act, of Parliament or otherwise, of our Error in distressing those countries so much as We had done. A few words of that kind the D^r said, would do more good than People could imagine.

3^d Colony Ships & Trade to be receiv'd & have the same priviledges in Britain & Ireland, as British ships & Trade. I did not ask any Explanation on that head for the present. British & Irish Ships in the Colonies to be in like manner on the same footing with their own ships.

4. Giving up every part of Canada.

If there were any other Articles of either kind, I can't now recollect them; But I dont think there were any of material Consequence: and I was perhaps the less attentive in the Enumeration, that it had been agreed to give me the whole in writing. But after some Reflection the D^r said, he did not much like to give such writing out of his Hands; and hesitating a good deal about it, ask'd me if I had seen Mr Jay. the other Commissioner, lately come from Madrid. I said I had not. He then told me it woud be proper I should see him and he would fix a time for our meeting. And seemd to think he shou'd want to confer with him himself, before he gave a final Answer. I told him if I had such final Answer, and had leave, I wou'd carry it over to England. He said that wou'd be right: But that as Mr Grenville told him, he expected another courier in 4 or 5 days, I had better wait so long, & he woud write along with me.

Upon the whole the D^r express'd himself in a friendly way towards England & was not without hopes that if We shou'd settle on this occasion in the way he wish'd, England would not only have a beneficial Intercourse with the Colonies, but at last it might end in a foederal Union between them. In the mean time we ought to take Care not to force them into the hands of other people. He shew'd me a Copy of the enabling Bill as it is calld, & said he observ'd the word revolted was left out – and likewise added – that the purpose of it was to dispense with Acts of Parliament which they were indifferent about, and that now they were better prepar'd for war, & more able to carry it on than ever they were. That he had heard we entertaind some Expectation of retaining some sort of Sovereignty over them, as his Majesty had of Ireland: and that if we thought so, We shoud find ourselves much disappointed, for they would yield to nothing of that sort.

. . . . .

From this Conversation, I have some hopes, my Lord, that it is possible to put an End to the American quarrel in a short time, & when that is done, I have a notion that a Treaty with the other powers will go more smoothly on. The Doctor did not in the Course of the above Conversation hesitate as to a Conclusion with them, on account of any Connection with those other states; and in general seem'd to think their American Affair must be ended by a separate Commission. On these occasions I said I suppos'd, in case of such Commission he meant that the power of granting Independence would be therein expressly mention'd. He said, no doubt. I hinted this, thinking it better in the power of treating to include Independence, than to grant Independence separately, & then to treat about other matters, with the Commissioners of such independent States; who by such Grant are on the same footing with the ministers of the other powers By anything the Doctor said I did not perceive, he made any account of this Distinction; and I did not think it proper to say any thing more about it.

I forgot one thing the Doctor said with respect to some Provision or Reparation to those calld the Loyal sufferers. It would be impossible to make any such provision – they were so numerous, & their Cases so various – that he could not see that it could make any part of the Treaty. There might be particular Cases that deserv'd Compassion. These being left to the several States, they might perhaps do something for them; but they, as Commissioners, could do nothing. He then read to me the Orders in Carolina for confiscating & selling of Estates under the Direction of the military, by which so great a number of Families had been ruin'd – and which the people there felt so much, as would stifle their Compassion for the sufferers on the other side.

I remember the Doctor in a former proposal in April hinted that a Cession of the back lands of Canada, wou'd raise a Sum, which would make some Reparation to the Sufferers on both Sides. Now he says, one of the *Necessary* Articles is a Cession of these back Lands, without any Stipulation for the loyal Sufferers.

And as an *advisable* Article, a Gift of 5 or 6 hundred thous.^d Pounds, to indemnify the Sufferers on their side. I shou'd hope he would be perswaded to Alter that part of the Plan.

I have the honour to be My Lord Your Lop' most obedient humble Servant   Richard Oswald

PRO: FO 27/2, v. 557, f. 371 (LC *transcription*).

Benjamin Franklin to Benjamin Vaughan

Dear Sir,   Passy, July 11, 1782.
In mine of yesterday which went by Mr. Young I made no mention of yours of May 11, it not being before me. I have just found it.

You speak of a "proposed dependent State of America, which you

thought Mr. Oswald would begin with." As yet, I have heard nothing of it.
I have all along understood (perhaps I have understood more than was
intended) that the point of dependence was given up, and that we were to
be treated with as a free people. I am not sure that Mr. Oswald has
explicitly said so, but I know that Mr. Grenville has, and that he was to
make that declaration previous to the commencement of the treaty. It is
now intimated to me from several quarters, that Lord Shelburne's plan is
to retain sovereignty for the king, giving us otherwise an independent
parliament, and a government similar to that of late intended for Ireland.
If this be really his project, our negotiation for peace will not go very far;
the thing is impracticable and impossible, being inconsistent with the faith
we have pledged, to say nothing of the general disposition of our people.
Upon the whole I should believe that though Lord S. might formerly have
entertained such an idea, he had probably dropped it before he sent Mr.
Oswald here: your words above cited do however throw a little doubt in my
mind, and have, with the intimations of others, made me less free in
communication with his Lordship, whom I much esteem and honor, than
I should otherwise have been. I wish therefore you would afford me what
you can of *éclaircissement*.

. . . . . .

With sincere esteem, I am ever, my dear friend, yours most affectionately,
                                                            B. Franklin.

WTF, Franklin Memoirs, *v. 4, pp. 229-230.*

Richard Oswald to Lord Shelburne

My Lord   Paris 11th July 1782.
    Referring to my Letter of yesterday date, here inclosed, relative to my
Conversation with Doctr Franklin on the Subject of a Treaty with the
Colonies, I am now to own receipt of your Lop Letter of the 5th...which
came to hand on the 8th.
    I don't know how far such a load of Business will be supportable to your
Lop, but I think I may safely congratulate your Country on your taking up
this last Charge, and sincerely wish your Lop much Satisfaction & Success
in the discharge of it.
    When I went out yesterday to Doctr. Franklin I read to him such parts
of the above Letter as you desired to be communicated to him.
    I thank your Lop for the Caution with respect to Gibralter, or any Affairs
under Mr Grenville's direction. As to the First, it was proposed by the Doctr

in such a way as I understood it to be in express Commission from the French Minister. And having an Opportunity of Major Ross,[1] I put it down in my Letter, as it seemed to shew that this Court would be glad to be excused taking part in the Attempts of recovering the Place in any other way. In answer, it is true I said, Territorial possession was the only proper Equivalent if England chose to part with it, & I happened to mention Porto Rico as what, in such case would be agreeable to many people. That passed as in the way of Conversation, although the proposal I supposed was designedly prompted as above ment.ᵈ I never heared any thing more on the Subject. As to Mʳ Grenvilles business, it would have been quite wrong in me to meddle in it in any Shape. & so cautious I was that I scarce askᵗ him any question as to the progress of his affairs. thinking it sufficient if by an Intercourse with Mʳ Franklin I could help to bring on a Settlement with the Colonies, upon which I alwise believed a Conclusion with the other Parties would in a great measure depend both as to dispatch & Conditions.

Even in this business I had scarce taken any Step since my last coming over in the end of May. It was impossible to do so, as Mʳ Franklin seemed to attend to the expectation & Issue of Mʳ Grenville's Powers & Instructions; which he said were imperfect at first, & not compleated at last to his Satisfaction with respect to them. So that the Doctʳ did not incline to talk of Business to me; and I had nothing to write, even if I had known at times when Mʳ Grenville's Couriers were dispatched. The Situation was not agreeable, but I could not help it. And I believe the Doctʳ was not pleased; although he said little to me on the Subject. However, at last, being I suppose desirous that something should be done in their affairs, he very unexpectedly put his Letter into my hands of the 27ᵗʰ of June which g'os under Cover with this

When I received it, I thought it my duty to take the steps mentioned in my Letter of the 8ᵗʰ, in consequence of it. If after seeing Mʳ Jay, I can procure from those Gentlemen some Sketch in writing of what they demand, I will talk to them on the Subject, and try to bring it into some Form of a Settled Agreement, or rather Propositions, to be submitted to discussion at home as necessary in the like cases.

Upon that foundation a Commission may be granted to carry on the Treaty to a Conclusion For I plainly see the Doctor inclines that their Business should be done under a Seperate Commission. As to any Information I can give in relation to these affairs, which your Loᵖ recommends to me, I beg leave to say that although I had better opportunities of Conversation than I have, there is very little to be got here. I will however not scruple to give my opinion as things occur to me viz. That the more anxious we appear to be for Peace the more backward the People here will be, or the harder in their terms, which is much the same thing. And that having fully satisfied this Court of our desire to put an end to the War, as has been done, the more vigourously our Exertions are pushed in the Interim, we shall come sooner to our purpose & on better terms. With respect to the Commissⁿ of the Colonies, our Conduct towards them, I think ought to be of a Stile somewhat different. They have shewen a desire to Treat, & to end with us on a Seperate footing from the other Powers, & I must say in a more liberal way, or at Least with a greater appearance of feeling for the future Interests & Connections of Great Britain, than I expected. I speak so from the Text of the last Conversation I had with Mr Franklin, as mentioned in my Letter of yesterday. And therefore we ought to deal with them tenderly, & as supposed conciliated Friends, or at least well disposed to a Conciliation. And not as if we had any thing to give them, that we can keep from them, or that they are very anxious to have. Even Dr. Franklin himself, as the subject happened to lead that way, as good as told me yesterday, that they were their own Masters, & seemed to make no account of the Grant of Independence as a favour. I was so much Satisfied beforehand of their Ideas on that head, that I will own to your LoP, I did not read to the Doctr that part of your Letter, wherein you mention that Grant as if it in some shape, challenged a Return on their part. When the Doctor pointed at the object of the Enabling Bill, as singly resting on a Dispensation of Acts of Parliamt they cared not for, I thought it enough for me to say, they had been binding & acknowledged. To which no answer was made. When the Doctr mentioned the Report as if there was an expectation of retaining the Sovereignty, I ventured a little farther, (though with a guarded Caution,) to touch him on the only tender side of their supposed present Emancipation, & said that Such a Report was possibly owing to the Imaginations of people upon hearing of the Rejoicings in America on the Cessation of War, Change of the Ministry, &ᶜ, Which they might conclude would have some effect in dividing the Provinces, & giving a different turn to affairs; as no doubt there was a great proportion of these People, notwithstanding all that had happened, who from Considerations of original affinity, Correspondence, & other Circumstances, were still strongly attatched to England &cᵃ· To this also there was no answer made.

At same time I cannot but say that I was much pleased upon the whole with what passed on the occasion of this Interview. And I really believe the Doctr sincerely wishes for a speedy settlement; & that, after the loss of Dependance, we may lose no more; but on the Contrary, that a Cordial Reconciliation may take place over all that Country

Amongst other things I was pleased at his shewing me a State of the aids they had received from France, as it lookt as if he wanted I should see the amount of their Obligations to their ally; & as if it was the only foundation of the Ties France had over them excepting Gratitude which the Doct^r owned in so many words. But at same time said the Debt would be punctually & easily discharged; France having given to 1788 to pay it. The Doct^r also particularly took nottice of the Discharge of the Interest, to the Term of the Peace, which he said was kind & generous. It is possible I may make a wrong Estimate of the Situation of this American business, & of the Chance of a total or partial Recovery being desperate. In that Case my opinion will have no weight, & so will do no hurt – Yet in my present Sentiments, I cannot help offering it, as thinking that Circumstances are in that situation that I heartily wish we were done with these People, & as quickly as possible, since we have much to fear from them, in case of their taking the pet, & throwing themselves into more close Connection with this Court, & our other Enemies

I make no doubt, My Lord, but you'l find fault with my troubling you with so much writing at a time, Which must come very unseasonably in the midst of so much other business. But we are so imprisoned here in our Correspondence, that we cannot divide it as in other Countries. To write any thing by Post would be to no purpose. So that everything must go by a Messenger on purpose, licensed by a Passport obtained by the formality of an Address to the Minister at Versailles.

I have the honour to be My Lord Your Lo$^{p.}$ most obedient humble Servant   Richard Oswald.

P.S. I beg leave to repeat what was mentioned in a former Letter, that in my late Conversations with Dr Franklin, I could not perceive that He meant that the progress & Conclusion of their Treaty was to have any Connection, or would be influenced by what was doing in the Treaties with the other Powers. But that the Colony Commissioners were Free Agents and Independ^t of these Powers. And Consequently, I suppose they consider themselves restrained by their Alliance with France only in the point of Ratification. Which indeed infers, that untill we agree with France, we can have neither peace or Truce with the Colonies. But then, if we Settle Terms with the Colonies, & France is unreasonable the Colonies may interpose. Or France may not chuse to risk the possibility of such Arbitration. At the same time I am entirely perswaded, that Dr Franklin do's not take the least Step, in their own affairs, even in such as his late Communication with me, but what has been settled between him & the Count de Vergennes, and Consequently if from such Communication it may be presumed that the Doct^r wishes for a Conclusion of their Treaty, it may be supposed that the French are in like manner disposed with respect to theirs. I ask^t Doct^r Franklin as to the Answer Mr Grenville had from this Court to his last Memorial, & he told me, that the proposition from Eng^d

being to take the Treaty of 1763. for the Basis, it was answered, that it should be so, & that the sundry Articles in the said Treaty should be gone over, & Suteable Alterations should be made as a foundation or Conditions of the present Treaty.

Since writing the above I am told by a Friend who had some Conversation with D^r· Franklin this morning that he the D^r· had received a Letter from some person in England, who is no friend to the late Changes, giving, among other things an account as if the new admin^n were not so well disposed to end so quickly & agreeably with the Colonies as those who have left it. &c^a &c^a· This the Gentleman told me led the Doct^r to express himself very Strongly as to his desire of quick despatch, as he wanted much to go home, & have the Chance of a few years repose, having but a short time to live in the World, & had also much private business to do. I should therefor hope it may be possible soon to bring their business near to a final Close, & that they will not be any way stiff as to those articles he calls *adviseable*, or will drop them altogether. Those he calls Necessary will hardly be any Obstacle. I shall be able to make a better guess when I have another meeting with him, jointly with M^r· Jay, Which I hope to have by the time this Courier returns. Allow me my Lord to observe that if I continue here any time I would wish to have a Messenger attending....

PRO: FO 27/2, v. 557, f. 387 (LC transcription).
^1 Not further identified.

Benjamin Franklin to Richard Oswald

Sir   Passy July 12th 1782

I enclose a Letter for Lord Shelburne, to go by your Courier with some others, of which I request his care. They may be put into the Penny Post. I have received a note informing me, that "some opposition given by his Lordship to M^r· Fox's decided *Plan of unequivocally acknowledging American Independency* was one cause of that Gentleman's Resignation" this, from what you have told me, appears improbable. It is further said "that M^r· Grenville thinks M^r· Fox's Resignation will be fatal to the present Negotiation." This perhaps is as groundless as the former. M^r· Grenville's next Courier, will probably clear up Matters, I did understand from him that such an acknowledgment was intended previous to the commencement of the Treaty; and until it is made and the Treaty formally begun Propositions and Discussions seem, on Consideration, to be untimely; nor can I enter into particulars without M^r· Jay who is now ill with the

Influenza. My Letter therefore to his Lordship is merely complimentary on his late Appointment. I wish a continuance of your Health, in that at present sickly city being, with sincere esteem Sir &c.

B. Franklin

P.S. I send you enclosed the late Resolutions of the State of Maryland, by which the general Disposition of the People in America may be guess'd respecting any Treaty to be propos'd by General Carleton, if intended, which I do not believe

LC: Benjamin Franklin Papers, microfilm reel 2 (LBkC).

Richard Oswald to Lord Shelburne

My Lord–   Paris 12 July 1782
                                                  (3 Afternoon)
    The Courier has been in waiting some time for Doct Franklins Letters. They are just come to hand, with one to myself, Which I think proper to Send to your Lo^{P.} with the Maryland paper that was inclosed in it.
    I am glad to See by the Doct^{n} Letter, as if he wishes a Settlement with them may not be stopt. I think that may be presumed from his Sending me this Letter, & the Explanations therein mentioned.
    On the other hand, I cannot but be concerned at this Report, which has been conveyed to him, of a Response intended in the Grant of Independance; being the first time I ever heard of it. At least Mr. Grenville did not tell me that his Signification on that head was accompanied with any Such Reservation. And upon the faith of that, I have in my Letters to your Lo^{P}, & in Conversation with Dr Franklin, alwise Supposed that the Grant was meant to be absolute & unconditional – which last, however, ~~was~~ is a Term I never used, thinking such qualification unnecessary. It's being given out that a difference subsisted & Resignations happened on this account, must naturally occasion this Hesitation in the Commiss^{n} of the Colonies; & So I see by the Doct^{n} Letter to me, he puts a Sort of Stoppage upon the preliminaries of Settlement with them, which had been pretty well Sketched out, and defined in his Conversation with me on the 10th Instant. & untill there is a further Explanation under your Lo^{P.} authority, on the Said head of Independence, I am in a manner forbid ~~or~~, in the Doctor's Letter, to go back upon the plan of that Conference, & to Claim any right to the propositions thereof. Which, if Compleat Independence was meant to be granted, is a little Unlucky; & there is Reason to Regret that any Body Should have been so wicked as to throw this Stumbling

Block in the way. By which not only Peace with the Colonies is obstructed, but the General Treaty is Suspended, which I cannot help Still thinking hangs upon a Settlement w^t the Colonies, And So by this unlucky Interjection, the Peace of the Country at home is disturbed, & the blame thrown upon the New Administration, & upon your Lo^p by name.

. . . . .

I have the honour to be My Lord Your Lo^ps most obedient humble Servant   Richard Oswald

P.S. I shan't be Surprised if the next meeting with the Doct^r should turn out more unfavourably than the former. Your Lo^p will no doubt do what is necessary to prevent it.   Richard Oswald

PRO: FO 27/2, v. 557, f. 403 (ALS).

Commission for Richard Oswald from George III, King of England

[July 25, 1782]

Our Will and Pleasure is and We do hereby authorize and Command You forthwith to prepare a Bill for Our Signature to pass Our great Seal of Great Britain in the Words or to the effect following Viz^t.

George the Third by the Grace of God King of Great Britain, France and Ireland Defender of the Faith &c^a. To Our Trusty and Wellbeloved Richard Oswald of Our City of London Esqr Greeting. Whereas by Virtue of an Act passed in the last Session of Parliament, intituled "An Act to enable His Majesty to conclude a Peace or Truce with certain Colonies in North America therein mentioned it is recited" that it is essential to the Interest, Welfare and Prosperity of Great Britain and the Colonies or Plantations of New Hampshire, Massachusets Bay, Rhode Island, Connecticut, New York, New Jersey, Pensylvania, the three lower Counties on Delaware, Maryland, Virginia, North Carolina, South Carolina and Georgia in North America, that Peace Intercourse, Trade and Commerce should be restored between them. Therefore and for a full Manifestation of Our earnest Wish and Desire and that of our Parliament to put an End to the Calamities of War it is enacted that it should & might be lawful for Us to treat, consult of, agree & conclude with any Commissioner or Commissioners named or to be named by the said Colonies or plantations or with any Body or Bodies, Corporate or Politick or any Assembly or Assemblies or Description of Men or any Person or Persons whatsoever a Peace or a Truce with the said

Colonies or plantations or any of Them, or any part or parts thereof, any Law, Act or Acts of Parliament, Matter or Thing to the contrary in any wise notwithstanding. Now know Ye that We reposing especial Trust in Your Wisdom, Loyalty, Diligence and Circumspection in the Management of the Affairs to be hereby Committed to Your Charge have nominated and appointed constituted and Assigned and by these Presents do nominate and appoint, constitute and Assign You the said Richard Oswald to be Our Commissioner in that behalf to use and exercise all and every the Powers and authorities hereby entrusted and committed to You the said Richard Oswald, and to do, perform and execute all other Matters and Things hereby enjoined and Committed to Your Care during Our Will and Pleasure and no longer according to the Tenor of these our Letters Patent. And it is Our Royal Will and Pleasure and We do hereby authorize empower & require You the said Richard Oswald to treat, consult of and conclude with any Commissioner or Commissioners named or to be named by the said Colonies or Plantations, and any Body or Bodies Corporate or Politick, or any Assembly or Assemblies, or Description of Men, or any Person or Persons whatsoever, a Peace or Truce with the said Colonies or Plantations, or any of them, or any part of parts thereof, any Law, Act or Acts of Parliament, matter or thing to the contrary in any Wise notwithstanding. And it is Our further Will and Pleasure that every Regulation, Provision Matter or Thing which shall have been agreed upon between You the said Richard Oswald and such Commissioner or Commissioners, Body or Bodies Corporate or Politic, Assembly or Assemblies, Description of Men, Person or Persons as aforesaid, with whom you shall have judged meet and Sufficient to enter into such agreement shall be fully and distinctly set forth in writing and authenticated by your Hand and Seal on one side, and by such Seals or other Signatures on the other as the occasion may require, and as may be suitable to the Character and Authority of the Commissioner or Commissioners &c^{a.} as aforesaid so agreeing and such Instrument so authenticated shall be by you transmitted to Us through one of our Principal Secretarys of State. And it is Our further Will and Pleasure, that you the said Richard Oswald, shall promise and engage for Us and in Our Royal Name and Word that every Regulation, Provision Matter or Thing which may be agreed to and concluded by you, Our said Commissioner shall be ratified & confirmed by Us in the fulest measure and extent and that We will not suffer them to be violated or Counteracted either in whole or in part by any person whatsoever. And We do hereby require and Command all Our Officers, Civil & Military and all other Our loving subjects whatsoever to be aiding and assisting unto you the said Richard Oswald in the execution of this our Commission and of the Powers & authorities herein contained, Provided always and We hereby declare and

Ordain, that the several Offices, Powers and Authorities hereby granted shall cease determine and become utterly null and void on the first day of July which shall be in the year of our Lord 1783. although we shall not otherwise in the mean time have revoked and determined the same in Witness &cᵃ· And for so doing this shall be your Warrant. Given at Our Court at Sᵗ· James's the Twenty fifth Day of July 1782 In the Twenty Second Year of Our Reign.

By His Majesty's Command   Thoˢ· Townshend

Clements Library: Shelburne Papers, v. 70, pp. 85-90 (C).

Reflections on Richard Oswald's Commisssion

[Translation]

[c. July 25, 1782]

Reflections

On the act of 25 July 1782, by which the King of England authorizes Mr. Oswald to treat with the Commissioners of Congress.

1ᵒ· This act is styled a *letter patent*

2ᵒ· it is limited to the term of one year

3ᵒ· the United States are named *Colonies* or plantations

4ᵒ· Civil and military officers are required to assist and aid the English Commissioner.

It follows from this that the act in question is a domestic act and not a political instrument.

But it is observable, on the other hand,

1ᵒ· That the King says simply *the Colonies*, and not *our Colonies*, and that he does not style them rebels, as has been the practice up to the present time.

2ᵒ· that it is a question of reestablishing peace, communication and commerce between England and the Colonies. Between princes and their revolted subjects there is amnesty or reconciliation; the word "peace" is not commonly used.

3ᵒ· A legal and political authority is recognized in the United States, since he is prepared to treat with their commissioners.

Thus the act introduced by Mr. Oswald must not be regarded as being a purely domestic act.

In order to prevent any subterfuge and any false interpretation on the part of the English ministry, it seems that Mr. Franklin could explain himself ministerially and in writing in the following manner.

We, the undersigned, Minister plenipotentiary of the United States of North America near His Majesty the King of France, and one of their commissioners plenipotentiary named to treat of peace with His Majesty the King of Great Britain, declare by the presents that, having closely examined the form and the tenor of the act by which His Britannic Majesty authorizes Mr. Richard Oswald to treat of peace with us, the said Commissioners plenipotentiary of the United States, not drawn up in the form used among the independent powers and states; however, to facilitate the opening of peace negotiations, we are inclined to accept the said act produced by Mr. Richard Oswald on condition that the Court of London, on its part, will approve and accept the full power that has been sent to us by the Congress of the United States of North America; it being clearly understood that nothing will later be inferred contrary to the independence of the said United States from the tenor of the said act, which on the contrary will be regarded as null and void in the event that the negotiations to be opened are fruitless.

If Mr. Oswald receives this declaration, the American plenipotentiaries will be safe from any false interpretation and inference; if he refuses it, one could require of him that he give one that could serve as a safeguard for Messrs. Franklin and Jay: if he refuses both, one must be suspicious of the intentions of the English Ministers, and require another power.

The pace of negotiations between the Dutch and Spain could not serve as a guide in the present circumstances: The first political act made between Spain and the United Provinces is the Truce of 1607. It is recorded in a declaration made by the Archdukes themselves, received by the States-General of the United Provinces in quality and as keeping them for the free Countries, provinces and States, of which the Archdukes claim nothing &c.

The ambassadors of France and of England were consulted to learn whether the ratification of the King of Spain would be accepted; their opinion was in the affirmative, although, as President Jannin[1] says, *the said ratification was in the form of a placard, and in the Spanish language,* signed "I" and "King".

It was therefore thought that the form can be yielded when the substance is assured.

It will doubtless be remarked that the Archdukes and the King of Spain explicitly recognized the United Provinces as free countries and states and that there is nothing said of all that either directly or indirectly in Mr. Oswald's Commission. But it must be considered that the intention of the King and of the United States has constantly been to show respect for the dignity and the delicacy of the King of England, that never has it been a question of requiring from that Prince the direct avowal of the independence of America: one would destroy this system, worthy of the wisdom and the moderation of the King, if one wished to take as rule what the King of Spain did in 1607.

Besides, in the very supposition that the King of England is determined to recognize explicitly the independence of his former Colonies, it seems that this recognition can only be recorded in the treaty itself, and that it would be premature in the full power; it should suffice that this full power not be contradictory with the subject of the treaty; and one could only say of Mr. Oswald's that it is completely irregular; and this irregularity would suffice to reject them if one did not wish to treat; but in the contrary case these irregularities can be mitigated without inconvenience.

In presupposing that it is important to establish the negotiation in some manner or other, it can be asked if, in order to prevent any false inference on the part of England, the act of protest expressed above is necessary; or if the pure and simple receipt and acceptance by Mr. Oswald of the full powers of Messrs. Jay and Franklin would not fulfill the same object? It is observable that the King of England in no part of his commission puts forward and names the Colonies as his subjects or vassals; while in the American full powers the Colonies are named the United States of North America. It seems to result from this comparison that the acceptance of Mr. Oswald's commission will not carry with it the avowal of England's supremacy over the Americans, and that the acceptance of the full power of Messrs. Franklin and Jay will carry with it the indirect avowal of the independence of the United States.

FFAA: Pol. Corr., U.S., v. 21, f. 145 (LC transcription).
[1] Not further identified.

Instructions to Alleyne Fitzherbert from George III, King of England

July 27, 1782

Whereas in consequence of Our earnest Desire to put an End to the Calamities of War in which Our Kingdoms are engaged by the Aggression of Our Enemies, We thought fit to direct Our Trusty and Welbeloved Thomas Grenville Esq[r] to repair to the Court of France to make Overtures of Peace, and to explain to the Minister of Our Good Brother The Most Christian King the Basis on which a Negociation for the purpose of concluding a Peace between Us and Our Good Brother could be entered upon. And Whereas the said M[r] Grenville, after having made some

Progress in the Business with which We had charged him, has desired and obtained Our Leave to return to England, We have now thought proper to direct you[1] to repair to the Court of France furnished with such Papers and Information as may enable you to continue the Prosecution of this important Business; and to give you the following Instructions for your Conduct in the Execution of the Trust We have reposed in you.

And Whereas for the more speedy Attainment of the desirable Object of putting and End to the Calamities of War, We have thought fit to give you Full Powers for the purpose of treating of Peace between Great Britain and any of the Powers or States with which She is now at War, and for concluding and signing the same.

We hereby authorise you to make Overtures of Peace to, and to confer and treat on the Subject with, the Ambassadors or Ministers of the said Powers or States.

1. – You are carefully to peruse and attend to the Contents of the various Instructions given from time to time to M[r.] Grenville, as well as by Ourself, as by Our Direction thro' Our Principal Secretary of State. You are to look on what you shall find therein prescribed, as the Rule of Your conduct, and you are to exert yourself in the Execution of the several Points which are thereby recommended and enjoined. And you are principally to direct your Attention to such parts of them as appear to remain hitherto unexecuted. For that purpose you are, on your Arrival at Paris, to desire an Audience of the Count de Vergennes, Minister and Secretary of State for Foreign Affairs in which you will inform him of the Object of Your Mission, and that you are furnished with a Credential Letter as Our Minster to His Most Christian Majesty; But you are not to deliver it (with it's copy,) to the Count de Vergennes, till you shall receive Our farther Instructions from One of Our Principal Secretaries of State.

2. You will in this Audience of the Count de Vergennes repeat the Assurances of Our Regard for the Most Christain King, and Our sincere Desire to see a speedy and happy End put to the Evils of a War which has so long subsisted; And You will likewise acquaint the Count de Vergennes that you have Full Powers from Us for entering into Negociation with the Ambassadors or Ministers of the Belligerant Powers or States, and that, you are ready to produce them when necessary.

3. You will acquaint the Count de Vergennes and the Ambassadors or Ministers of the other Belligerent Powers or States, that in order to attain this desireable End, We are willing to declare Our Intentions to cede to His Most Christian Majesty and His Allies the Point which has been at various times, and upon various occasions, declared to the Subject of the War; That is to say, to accede to the complete Independency of the Thirteen American States; and in order to make the Peace, if it should take place,

more solid and durable, to cede to the said States the Towns of New-York and Charlestown, together with the Province of Georgia, – including the Town of Savannah all which are still in Our Possession; provided that in all other respects such a general and reciprocal Restitution shall take place in every Quarter of the Globe, on the part of the Belligerant Powers, as shall restore Things to the State they were placed in by the Treaty of Paris 1763.

4. You are in like manner to proceed to carry into Execution all such Parts of Our Instruction to Mr. Grenville as are applicable to the State of the Negociation at the time of its being intrusted to you.

5. You will inform the French Minister that you will be authorised by Us to present Our Letter of Credence whenever Our Good Brother the Most Christian King shall name a Person, on His Part, to repair to Our Court in Quality of Minister from the said Most Christain King.

6. As it is extremely material that the Court of France should look upon Your being sent there as a Continuation of the Commission with which Mr. Grenville had been charged, You will be particularly attentive to remove any Impression which his coming away & not returning may have occasioned. It was at his own most particular and pressing Request that he was not longer continued to be employed on this Service, as You will explicitly point out that no Alteration whatever has or can take place in Our Most earnest & sincere Wish to see the Blessings of Peace restored on a solid, permanent and honorable footing.

7. A Paper dated the 21st of June last & delivered to Mr. Grenville, is the last Transaction which passed between him and the French Minister; So that carrying the Answer to it & enforcing it with very possible Argument, will be the first Point of Your Duty.

8. Being furnished with Full Powers to treat with the Ambassadors or Ministers of the Courts of Spain and Holland, You will to them respectively give the fullest Assurances of Our Desire of Peace & communicate to them the Proposition which has been made to France, & which contains such unequivocal Proof of the Sincerity of Our Intentions.

9. As it is more than probable that the Spanish Ambassador will alledge that the Concessions made with regard to America, are not Matters in which The Catholic King is at all concerned, & that the Causes of the War with Spain are different from those of that with France, you will observe to him that the Questions said by Her to be in Dispute shall have the fullest & fairest Discussion, & that as the Principle of adopting the Treaty of Paris as a Basis of Negotiation does not preclude any subsequent Restitutions & Compensations, You are ready to receive any Proposals which the Court of Spain may think fit to make.

10. With regard to Holland you will not fail to express Our earnest Desire to restore the Ancient Harmony which had so long subsisted between the Two Countries. And you will hold out to them that the *Utipossidetis* might be the Basis of an Arrangement with them.

11. Having thought fit to appoint Our Trusty & Well Beloved Richard Oswald of the City of London Esqre. Our Commissioner for treating & concluding a Peace with any Commissioner or Commissioners named or to be named by the Thirteen American States, You will preserve the most constant and intimate Communication from time to time with the said Richard Oswald, for the purpose of aiding and assisting each other in the Objects of your respective Commissions.

12. Notwithstanding You are by Our Full Powers authorised to conclude & sign any thing that may be agreed on between the several Parties with whom you are to treat, It is Our express Will & Pleasure that you do not, in virtue of the said Powers, proceed to the Signature of any Act whatever without first having Our Special Orders for that purpose from One of Our Principal Secretaries of State.

13. If it shall be agreed on between the Courts of Great Britain & France that you & the Person to be nominated by H.M.C.M. shall respectively enjoy in France & in England all the Rights, Prerogatives, Franchises & Liberties, belonging to Your Characters, as if the Two Courts were in full Peace, You are to be duly attentive to maintain Our Dignity in all Things touching the same, & to take care that you be treated in the same manner as Ministers of Your Rank from Spain or any other Crowned Head, except as to the Form of not delivering Our Credential Yourself to The Most Christian King in an Audience.

14. You shall use Your particular Endeavours to inform yourself of the Interior Situation of the Court of France, & of the actual State and Dispositions of the French Nation. You will also give a watchful Attention to the Conduct & Motions of the Spanish & Dutch Ambassadors, & also to those of the Minister or Agents from the American Congress there; And of all Matters which may be of consequence and worthy of Our Knowledge, You shall constantly give an Account to Us by One of Our Principal Secretaries of State, from whom You will receive such further Instructions & Directions as We shall think fit to send you, which You are to observe accordingly.

PRO: FO 27/3, v. 558, f. 49 (LC transcription).

[1] *Fitzherbert, Alleyne (1753-1839). British diplomat. Minister to the Austrian Netherlands, 1777-1782. Plenipotentiary to negotiate peace with France, Spain, and the United Provinces, August 1782-January 1783. Envoy extraordinary near the Empress of Russia, 1783-1787. Chief secretary to the lord lieutenant of Ireland, 1787-1789. Envoy*

extraordinary to the United Provinces, 1789-1790. Ambassador to Spain, 1790-1794. Created Baron St. Helens, 1790. Ambassador to the United Provinces, 1794. Concluded treaty with Russia, 1801.

Lord Shelburne to Richard Oswald

Dear Sir,   Shelburne H$^{o.}$ 27$^{th.}$ July 1782.
    I am to acknowledge the receipt of your several Letters of the 8$^{th.}$ 10$^{th.}$ 11$^{th.}$ & 12$^{th.}$ Inst....They give me the greatest Satisfaction, as they contain in my Apprehension unequivocal Proofs of D$^{r.}$ Franklin's Sincerity and Confidence in those with whom he treats. I am sure it will be the Study of His Majesty's Ministers to return it by every possible Cordiality.
    I cannot say that the Subject of your Letter of the 12$^{th.}$ and of D$^{r.}$ Franklin's to you of the same Date gives me so much Uneasiness as it seems to do you. I know the Correctness of my own Conduct, and that it can stand every Test. A French Minister might not so easily be brought to understand the Conduct of others. But those with whom you have particularly to treat, know too much of the Partys incident to our Constitution, and of the Violence & Inveteracy occasion'd by personal Disappointment, to be easily misled by false Assertions or NewsPaper Comments: I need only appeal to your own knowledge. However, as you may not wish it to rest entirely upon that, I have obtain'd His Majesty's Leave to send you my Dispatch to Sir Guy Carleton & Vice Adm$^{l.}$ Digby dated so long ago as the 5$^{th.}$ June, & M$^{r.}$ Fox's Letter to M$^{r.}$ Simolin[1] of the 28. June; – and you are at liberty to communicate to D$^{r.}$ Franklin such Parts of both, as may be sufficient to satisfy his mind, that there never have been two Opinions since you were sent to Paris, upon *the most unequivocal Acknowledgement of American Independancy* to the full Extent of the Resolutions of the Province of Maryland inclos'd to you by D$^{r.}$ Franklin. But to put this Matter out of all Possibility of Doubt, a Commission will be immediately forwarded to you, containing Full Powers to treat and to conclude, with Instructions from the Minister who has succeeded to the Department which I lately held, to make the Independancy of the Colonies the Basis & Preliminary of the Treaty now depending & so far advanc'd, that hoping, as I do with you, that the Articles call'd *adviseable* will be dropp'd, & those call'd *necessary* alone retain'd as the Ground of Discussion, it may be speedily Concluded.
    I have only to add on this Subject, that these Powers have been prepar'd since the 21$^{st.}$ June, were begun upon within 24 hours of the passing of the Act, and compleatly finish'd in four Days following; and have been since delayed owing to it's being asserted that your Continuance at Paris

prejudic'd everything that was depending, which requir'd that they should be entrusted exclusively to M^r. Grenville. You know best the Truth of this Assertion.

You very well know I have never made a Secret of the deep Concern I feel in the separation of Countries united by Blood, by Principles, Habits, & every Tie short of Territorial Proximity. – But you very well know that I have long since given it up *decidedly* tho' *reluctantly*: and the same motives which made me perhaps the last to give up all Hope of the union, makes me most anxious if it is given up, that it shall be done *decidedly*, so as to avoid all further Risque of Enmity, & lay the Foundation of a new Connection better adapted to the present Temper & Interests of both Countries. In this View, I go further with D^r. Franklin perhaps than he is aware of, & farther perhaps than the profess'd Advocates of Independance are prepar'd to admit.

My private Opinion would lead me to go a great way for Foederal Union: – But is either Country ripe for it? If not, means must be left to advance it.

I am oblig'd to you for your kind Compliments on My succeeding to the Treasury, a Situation to make the most warlike Minister wish for Peace. I am persuaded however you will not be a Loser by the Minister you will have to correspond with. You will find in M^r. Townshend great Habits of Business join'd to the most honorable Principles, and I can venture to assure you of the strongest Prepossessions in favour of your Character. Your Correspondence will of course be with him – I only desire to add that I shall consider myself as pledg'd to the Contents of this Letter – You will find the Ministry united, in full Possession of The King's Confidence, and thoroughly dispos'd to Peace, if it can be obtain'd upon reasonable Terms; If not, determin'd to have recourse to every means of rousing the Kingdom to the most determin'd Efforts. – The liberal Spirit which has taken Place in our Domestick Government, new Plans which are offering every Day for augmenting the Navy, The National Spirit which must result from ill Treatment & oppression, The open & weak Parts of some of our Enemies who have large & distant Dominions as well as ourselves to play for, will I am sure produce greater Effects than our Enemies imagine: — But the Public Expectation will be proportionably rais'd, distant Expeditions relied upon, and Peace render'd more difficult than ever.

Let it be well understood that no Offer on our Part is now wanting to prevent this Series of Calamities by an immediate Reconciliation.

Lord Shelburne

Clements Library: Shelburne Papers, v. 71, pp. 61-70 (C).

  [1] *Simolin, Ivan Matveevich (1720-1799). Russian diplomat. Minister to Great Britain, 1779-1785.*

Instructions to Richard Oswald from
George III, King of England

[St James's 31 July 1782]

Whereas Report has been made to Us by One of Our Principal Secretaries of State of Information which He had received from B. Franklin Esqr of Philadelphia, now residing at or near to Paris to this Effect. – "that He, the said B Franklin was commissioned with Others (whom he named to be Messrs Adams Laurens, and Jay) to treat of and conclude a Peace; That full Powers were given to them for that purpose, and that the Congress promised in good Faith to ratify, confirm and cause to be faithfully observed the Treaty They should make. But that they could not treat separately from France."

And whereas having received Assurances of His most Christian Majesty's sincere Disposition towards Peace; and Paris having been mutually fixed upon, as the most convenient Place, at which all Parties might assemble for the purpose of entering upon Negotiation, We have already sent Our Trusty and Wellbeloved Thomas Grenville Esq to that capital with full Powers to commence a Negotiation with the Court of France and the other belligerent Powers in Europe; Now in consequence of the Overtures above mentioned on the part of Persons thus stating themselves to be deputed by the Assembly of Delegates of the Revolted Colonies, and out of Our earnest desire to put an End to the calamities of a War, which has so long subsisted; and because it has also been reported to Us by One of Our Principal Secretaries of State, that the said Benjamin Franklin Esqr had expressed a strong desire of "keeping the Treaties of Peace distinct between the several Parties, tho' going on at the same time;" – We have taken these premises into Our consideration, and have thought fit by Our Commission under Our Great Seal of Great Britain to constitute You, the said Richard Oswald Our Commissioner for concluding a Peace, and have caused You to be furnished with such Papers and Information as may enable You to interchange Overtures of Peace, giving You at the same time the following Instructions for Your Conduct in the Execution of the important Trust, We have reposed in You.

1st On the Receipt of these Our Instructions together with our Commission You will forthwith enter upon a Conference with the American Commissioners or as many of them as may be assembled, and You will inform them of Our Purpose in granting You Our Commission with full Powers, a Copy whereof You will deliver to them, at the same time declaring that You shall be ready to produce the Original when desired.   You will moreover deliver to them a Copy of the Act of

Parliament, upon which the Powers granted You by Our Commission are founded.

2. You will then express Our Wishes, that the mutual Powers of treating and concluding may be so general and definitive that matters may thereby be brought to a speedy and determinate Issue. With this View You will desire to be informed of, and to see the Nature & Extent of the Authority with which the Commissioners are invested by the Congress; and We hereby authorize You to admit any Persons, with whom You treat, to describe themselves by any Title or Appellation whatever, and to represent their Superiors, from whom they state themselves to derive authority, under any Denomination whatever.

3. These Preliminaries being settled, You will declare, that You are ready and desirous to learn any Ideas and Intentions They (the American Commissioners) may have for carrying into Effect with most speed and certainty Our earnest Wishes to restore Peace and Amity between Our Kingdoms and the said American Colonies.

4 In case you find the American Commissioners are not at liberty to treat on any terms short of Independence, You are to declare to them that You have Our Authority to make that Concession; Our earnest Wish for Peace disposing Us to purchase it at the Price of acceding to the complete Independence of the Thirteen States, namely New Hampshire &c.

5 You are moreover empowered to engage Our Promise in Order to make the Peace, if it should take place, more solid & durable, to cede to the said Colonies the Town and District of New York, and any other Territory Town or Garrison within the Limits of the said Colonies which may be in Our Possession at the time of signing the Treaty.

6 The question of Independence this removed, You will not fail of course to turn Your attention to the consideration of such Proposals, as it is to be hoped, They will think it incumbent upon them to make for the purpose of rendering whatever Terms may be agreed upon, permanent and mutually satisfactory and beneficial; In the Course of this Discussion You will not fail to pay due attention to the Rights and Interests of Individuals, and You will particularly press the Speedy Enlargement of such Persons as may be now imprisoned or confined on Account of their Attachment to the Government of Great Britain. Under this head You are to consider and claim as a Matter of absolute Justice all Debts incurred to the Subjects of Great Britain before 1775, and if, as has been intimated You should find the Commissioners unauthorized to engage for a specifick Redress in this particular, You will insist on the Justice of these Demands, and that they would promise and engage for the sincere interposition of Congress with the several Provinces to procure an ample and full satisfaction.

7 Whereas many of Our Loyal Subjects having valuable Property in the

Colonies in question have nevertheless in these unhappy disputes taken part with Great Britain, & in consequence thereof have been considered as having thereby exposed their Property to Confiscation, Justice as well as Compassion demands, that a Restitution or Indemnification should be required on behalf of such Sufferers. On this head You will propose a Restoration of all Rights as they stood before the Commencement of Hostilities, and a General Amnesty of All offences committed or supposed to be committed in the Course of them.

8. If you should collect from the Answer made to these Representations, that their Consent to the preceding Article cannot be obtained without some further Concession on our Part, and the Cession before proposed of New York &c^a be not sufficient, You may in that Case propose to stipulate for the Annexation of a Portion of Our ungranted Lands to each Province in lieu of what shall be restored to the Refugees and Loyalists, whose Estates They have seized and confiscated.

9. In regard to the question of any national Substitution for the dependent Connection with Great Britain, You must in the first place seek to discover the dispositions and Intentions of the Colonies by the Intimations and Propositions of the Commissioners, and if it shall appear to You to be impossible to form with them any Political League of Union or Amity to the Exclusion of Other European Powers, You will be particularly earnest in your Attention and Arguments to prevent their binding themselves under any Engagement inconsistent with the Plan of *absolute and universal Independence*, which is the indispensible Condition of our acknowledging their Independence on Our Crown and Kingdoms.

10. It were much to be wished, that a foundation for an amicable Connection could be laid in some mutual principle of Benefit & Indulgence. In this View We would direct You to propose as a friendly Token of Reconciliation and of Propensity to those Tyes, which are consonant to Our mutual Relation, Habits, Language and Nature, that in future an unreserved System of Naturalization should be agreed upon between Our Kingdom and the American Colonies.

11. But notwithstanding You are by Our Commission authorized to conclude and sign any thing that may be agreed upon between You and the American Commissioners, it is Our express Will and Pleasure that You do not, in Virtue of the said Power, proceed to the Signature of any Act whatever with the Commissioners for the Colonies, without first having received Our Special orders for that Purpose from One of Our Principal Secretaries of State.

12. Whereas We have at the earnest desire and suggestion of the said Commissioners as above stated actually commenced a Negotiation with the Court of France, which has been extended to other Belligerant Powers, and

entrusted as above our Trusty and Wellbeloved Alleyne Fitzherbert Esq˙
with the necessary Powers for that purpose, Our Will and Pleasure is, that
You preserve the most constant and intimate communication from time to
time with the said Alleyne Fitzherbert, and in case You shall learn from
such Communication, that the Proposals of the Court of France or of the
other Belligerant Powers, without whose Concurrence the Court of
Versailles will not conclude a Treaty, should be such as We cannot
consistently with a due regard to our own Honor, and the Interests of Our
Kingdom accept, and the Design of a general Treaty should be thereby
frustrated; You will in that event point Your whole Attention to dispose the
American Commissioners towards a separate Negotiation, in the hope, that
the concessions You are authorized to make, will appear to them to satisfy
the Interests and the Claims of their Constituents, as in that case They can
have no justifiable motive to persist in a War, which as to them will have
no longer any Object, and it is to be hoped, will not be inclined to lend
themselves to the purposes of french Ambition. At any rate, You will not
fail to inform Yourself accurately what will content them, and report to Us
accordingly through One of Our Principal Secretaries of State, waiting for,
and expecting further Instructions, which shall be sent You with all suitable
expedition.   G.R.

PRO: FO 27/2, v. 557, f. 457 (LC transcription).

Benjamin Vaughan to Lord Shelburne

My Lord,   Paris, July 31. 1782
    I was happy in finding very favorable dispositions subsisting in a certain
quarter at my arrival. What had passed in the House of Lords and what
appeared in a previous letter of mine, left me very little room for remedying
what was evil, though I have had much opportunity of confirming what was
good.
    As I soon recollected that it was not quite proper for me to lodge at
Passy, I have only visited Dr. Franklin every second or third day, as his
engagements permitted; though, by mutual wish, those visits were prolonged
as much as possible. The speedy return I meditated has been deferred,
because Dr. Franklin told me he would think of and write upon paper his
answers to my inquiries, and when I proposed that this letter should follow
me to London, he signified that by waiting I might perfect my business, as
he could not tell yet what he might have to say. In fact, he kept himself
open till a courier should advise the final disposition of the court of

London. As this suited your lordship's own intimations to me, I resolved to remain here some days longer.

In the meantime I have to advise your lordship that Dr. Franklin has not the same zeal in approving Mr. Fox's proceedings or disapproving your lordship's, that some others having take the liberty of expressing and I will guarantee to your lordship at least an equal, and I think a much more confidential footing with Dr. Franklin, than Mr. Fox would have at present; though some anxiety seems to have been used, to reverse this situation between you in his favor. In short, I must add to your lordship, that whatever I have said has been heard with great attention and great *good humor*; and that no inconsiderable portion of it appears to have been duly credited. Though I must not at the same time dissemble that in consequence of the delay in your lordship's despatches, some little ground was lost to us; and suspicions either arose or were confirmed, that the court of London might be waiting for the accounts of the temper of America by which to dictate its own measures at home. But these doubts I trust will soon finally cease.

.   .   .   .   .

...I have to inform your lordship, that when Dr. Franklin was instructing me in the temper of the French minister, he assured me that he had various & many concerns with M. Vergennes during five or six years, in which he never gave a promise or expectation that he did not fulfill; & this minister had said to him that his master wished for peace or fair & reasonable terms. Dr. F - added that the delays and difficulties had been ours and not theirs, & that they had suspected Rodney's victory had altered our designs a little. Dr. F - has given the same ideas to Mr. Jay, who says that peace will be quicker made perhaps than we suspect, and that America in particular has only certain points to gain & nothing in the way of bargain. He has also said to me, that the first French adventures had disgusted America, but the second set had won them back again; & that France herself dealt in the most handsome way giving them a loan lately of six millions without a question, & always throwing in a million or two when closing their accounts. It is some satisfaction to me to say that Mr. Jay is a very pleasant man, who has no unreasonable notions or passions, and that both the commissioners here will treat with great good humor & some consideration. Mr. J. Adams is a man of more vivacity and intrigue, but as he has occupations at the Hague and *personal controversees* with M Vergennes, I hope he will stay in Holland, to the parties in which he much contributes. I think moreover much good may be done by keeping Mr. Walpole in better humor than since his letter to Lord Cambden, and perhaps it were best done by expressions in a letter to me. He has much influence here, & his friend Dr. Bancroft is not without a share. Young Mr. Franklin I have to inform your lordship has intimated hopes to see something done for his father, as he was the only governor that gave to his court plain & wholesome advice before the war.[1] I asked him what he would relish: he replied something in the *corps diplomatique*, he thought. This therefore I think is another important matter to keep in mind. Mr. Oswald more & more pleases me. He is very worthy, very humane, has good experience, a large way of thinking & is very tenacious of his instructions, which he will always mean to pursue. I have told Mr. Oswald what I know of Mr. Fitzherbert, whether personally or by character, and I am putting him well with the Americans. As to Mr. Hartley, young Mr. Franklin so scouted his name [when I told who had been the various people thought of for his grandfather] as an eternal talker and pest; that I have hardly thought it worth while to get Dr. Franklin's opinions over again from himself, relative to this gentleman.

. . . . .

...With respectful compts. to Lady Shelburne, I have the honor to be, My Lord, Your Lordship's ever faithful & respectful servt.

Benjn. Vaughan

. . . . .

APS: *Benjamin Vaughan Papers (Transcription)*.

[1] *Franklin, William (1731-1813). Loyalist, son of Benjamin Franklin. Governor of New Jersey, 1763-1776.*

John Witherspoon to Unknown

Sir   [August ? 1782]

. . . . .

...What Mr Adams had done by which he had incurred the Displeasure of the Ministers of the King of France had been undoubtedly from his Zeal & Attachment to the Interest & honor of the united States. His Ability & his unshaken Fidelity was well known. In such a Case to displace a Minister merely because he had given umbrage to some at the Court where he resided by an excess of well Meant Zeal seemed to be a most pernicious Example & probably would have the worst Effects upon succeeding ministers & therefore ought not to be done. The Writer in this Memorial of Facts in particular was clearly of Opinion that Mr Adams judged wrong in both the Points which he contested in his Correspondence with the D. de Vergennes the Reasons for which need not now be mentioned. Yet he was as clearly of Opinion to sacrifice a Minister of unquestionable Integrity ought not on any Acct to be submitted to merely because he had more Zeal than good Manners & therefore it was proposed that a Clause should be added to the Instructions to this purpose and that he should *do nothing without the Consent & approbation of the Court of France.*

Another Committee was appointed to confer with the Minister & made this Communication. But in Conference this also was in his Opinion insufficient. He repeated the Fears they had of Difficulties with Mr Adams & insisted that by this New Clause he was only bound negatively that he could not indeed do any Thing without the Consent of the Court of France but he might obstruct every Measure & unless he were perfectly satisfied effectually prevent any Thing being done.

When this was repeated to Congress the Matter appeared exceedingly delicate & difficult. It was discussed at great Length. All the Objections against removing Mr Adams remained in their full force. But on the other it appeared humiliating at least if not dangerous to deliver ourselves up entirely to the Court of France. However after full Deliberation it was agreed by the Majority in Congress to add to the Instruction that he should be *ultimately guided by the Opinion & Judgment of the Court of France.*

As This particular Resolution appeared so dubious to several Worthy Members of Congress & there were so many Attempts to reconsider & revoke it and as it will in due Time be the subject of discussion by the Public at large it seems necessary to recollect which Circumstances are fresh in our Minds & to record the Necessity or the Reasons that induced the Plurality to embrace it. It is not intended in this recollecting Memorial to attempt distinguishing between the Opinions of one Mem[ber] & another but just to mention as many as possible of the Sentiments that were proposed & advanced by those who finally voted for it.

It was plain that from the first Rise of the Controversy we had been greatly indebted to the Court of France. They had interposed effectually & Seasonably in our Cause. They had exerted themselves with much Vigor & Free[dom &] put themselves to a very great Expense upon our Acct. At the very Time when this Debate was agitated our most necessary Expenses were supported by them & even the Subsistence & Support of many Delegates in Congress was from Bills drawn upon France. We had accustomed ourselves & many public & Authentic Acts to call the K of France our great & generous Ally. Perhaps there were as humiliating Expressions on many of the public Acts & proceedings of Congress as could be in this Resolution which might well be considered as the effect of grateful & generous Sentiments.   John Witherspoon[1]

Smith, Letters of Delegates, *v. 19, pp. 111-117.*

[1] *Witherspoon, John (1723-1794). Presbyterian clergyman. President of the College of New Jersey (Princeton), 1768-1794. Member, Continental Congress, 1776-1782. Drafted the instructions of June 15, 1781, to the American peace commissioners.*

Arthur Lee to James Warren

Dear Sir,   [August ? 1782]

.   .   .   .   .

By the absolute order of France, Dr. Franklin & Mr Jay were joind in commission with Mr. Adams for negociating a Peace. At this very time Congress had the fullest evidence and conviction that Dr Franklin was both a dishonest & incapable man. Mr. Laurens & Mr. Jefferson were added, but the first was a prisoner, & the latter woud not go. Mr. Jay has with a very becoming spirit desird to be left out of a Commission, which is accompanied with Instructions to obey ultimately the opinion of the french Ministers. This he states as in his apprehension, so humiliating to the Commisioners, so disgraceful & injurious to America that he cannot submit to it. I have movd in vain for a reconsideration of these Instructions. The yoke is riveted upon us, & the man who I am sure sold us in the negociation with France, is the sole adjunct with Mr. Adams, in a negociation on which every thing that is dear & honorable to us depend. He, good man, felt no qualms at such a commission, no sense of dishonor or injury to his Country. On the contrary he expressd the utmost alacrity in accepting it, & I beleive most cordially; since it puts him in the way of receiving money, which is the God of his Idolatry.

The French therefore are to make a peace for us; we have presumed only to desire Independence; but whether it shall be on secure & honorable terms, whether by the stipulations annexd to it we shall participate in the Fishery, in the navigation of the Missisippi, or in the western territory, whether conditions Trenching nearer, & more shamefully on our rights will accompany the naked & nugatory assertion of Independance, is in the soverign arbitration of the french Court. To judge what is for our own interest, to instruct our Plenipotentiaries, for them to think & act for us, are treason against the Alliance, by which we were acknowledgd independent & soveriegn. In short, the most servile display of the most servile principles, is what alone must entitle us to the patronage of our great and generous Protector. This was not the sentiment, or language, that commencd the revolution, & I can plege myself it is not the sentiment or language that will bring it to a happy issue. But there seems to be no public here to appeal to. Sordid pursuits & servile attachments have apparently absorbd all the Faculties of our fellow Citizens. In the last resort, I hope the jealousy of G. Britain & of the other Powers in Europe will prevent France from abusing the power which we have thus basely & imprudently confided to her.

Spain has behavd towards us with very little wisdom, or decency; but it is much to be suspected that the French are at the botton of it; insomuch that a well-informd person on the spot, writes thus "I have many reasons for believing that the french Court does not wish to see us declard independent by other Nations, lest we shoud become less manageable as we become less dependent on her for support." I have endeavord to inculcate this truth into those to whom it woud be useful, & yet they constantly act in opposition to it.

.   .   .   .   .

I beg you will make my best & most respectful wishes acceptable to Mrs. Warren & believe always, with the most perfect esteem, Dear Sir, your most sincere friend   Arthur Lee

Smith, Letters of Delegates, *v. 19, pp. 109-111.*

John Jay to John Adams

Sir   Paris 2ᵈ· Augᵗ· 1782

Your friendly Letter of the 8ᵗʰ· ult. should not have remained so long unanswered, had I not been obliged by Sickness which lasted several Weeks to postpone writing to any of my Correspondents. Mʳˢ· Jay has also been much indisposed – Indeed neither of us have been blessed with much Health since we left America –

Your Negotiations in Holland have been honorable to yourself as well as useful to your Country – I rejoice in both, & regret that your Health has been so severely Taxed by the Business of your Employment – I have also had my share of Perplexities, & some that I ought not to have met with. I congratulate you on the Prospect of your Loan's succeeding, and hope your Expectations on that Subject may be realized – I commend your Prudence however in not relying on appearances – They decieve us sometimes in all Countries –

My Negociations have not been discontinued by my leaving madrid – The Count d'Aranda is authorized to treat with me, and the Disposition of that Court to an Alliance with us seems daily to grow warmer. — I wish we could have a few Hours Conversation <**> on this subject, and others connected with it – as we have no Cypher, I must be reserved. I had flattered myself with the Expectation of seeing you here, and still hope that when your Business at the Hague will admit of a few Weeks absence, you may prevail upon yourself to pay us a Visit. I really think that a free Conference between us might be useful as well as agreable especially as we should thereby have an opportunity of making many Communications to each other that must not be committed to paper.

Mr Oswald is here, and I hear that M$^{r.}$ Fitzherbert is to succeed Mr Grenville. Ld Shelburne continues to profess a Desire of Peace – but his Professions unless supported by Facts can have little Credit with us – he says That our Independence shall be acknowledged – but it is not done, and therefore his Sincerity remains questionable. War must make peace for us – and we shall always find well appointed armies to be our ablest Negociators –

The Intrigues you allude to, I think may be also traced at Madrid, but I believe have very little Influence anywhere except perhaps at London. Petersburgh & Copenhagen in my opinion wish well to England, but are less desirous to share in the War, than in the Proffits of it – perhaps indeed further accessions of Power to the House of Bourbon may excite Jealousy, especially as America as well as Holland is supposed to be very much under the Direction of France –

Did you recieve my Letters of 18 March & 15 Ap.? Think a little of coming this Way –

I am Dear Sir with great Esteem & Regard Your most ob$^{t.}$ & very h'bl Servt　　　　　　　　　　　　　　　　　　　　　John Jay

· · · · ·

MHS: *The Adams Papers, microfilm reel 357* (ALS).

Conde d'Aranda to Conde de Floridablanca: Memorandum on Boundary Discussions

1st session, Paris, 3 August 1782

On Saturday the 3rd of August, Sir John Jay came at ten o'clock in the morning, and on his entering my study, I shewed him a big Map of North America, whose title read :

"*Amérique septentrionale avec les routes, distances en milles, villages et établissements–les 8 feuilles françois et anglois–parle Dr. Mitchel traduit de l'anglois par Le Rouge Ingenieur Geographe du Roi rue des grands Augustins 1753.*"

"*North America so Doctor Mitchel zu London in 1775 den jahr ansgegeben jetzaber in des französische übersetzet.*"[1]

He informed me that there were other partial and provincial maps. I replied that I would show them to him later, because we should first consider the matter in the large and in its totality in order to draw a line of demarcation between the territories that would be kept by Spain and those by the 13 United States; such line, in my opinion, should run from the principal and ineffaceable points without arguing over a hundred leagues more or less; that in any case that dividing line would have to run, in greater part, through the lands of the Indians, whom each of us would have to pacify in order to have peaceful boundaries between both Empires.

This observation having been accepted in general, I asked Jay where he would draw his dividing line. He replied that a separation was already marked out, notably the Mississippi River, and pointed with his finger to its source, tracing it down almost to New Orleans. I asked him then, if his idea was to deprive us of all of Western Florida which, besides having been ours in former times, we had recently reconquered from England.

He replied that inasmuch as the Colonies had claimed for themselves the rights of England, including these acknowledged boundaries, one could not deny them boundaries running from the source of the Mississippi to where the true boundary of Western Florida began. I immediately used his own argument to refute his proposition, pointing out that Spain, having reconquered Florida, which had been the basis for fixing the whole of the Mississippi as the boundary in the treaty of Paris, Spain had claimed for herself, through the reconquest of that province, all rights under that treaty.

He rejoined, arguing that when the Colonies had been settled under the authority of the British Crown, they claimed, according to their charters or titles, an indefinite extension at their backlands, and that that part of the Mississippi which was not the former boundary of Florida, was not included in the Spanish reconquest, but belonged to England and consequently to the Colonies, her representatives.

I told him that such an extension conceived to have been granted by the British Crown to her Colonies, gave equal rights in these imaginary spaces to any other monarch; and even Spain was able to draw her boundaries from Louisiana and the coast of Florida, from both sides, going upwards between parallel lines, to the less known and frozen country of the North, but in this form the lines would overlap, and the maps would be reduced to lineal squares, with equal rights to each party: that it appeared more likely that he who already held the mouth of the Mississippi, and its interior course over a long distance, would have the right to consider it as his perpetually; and finally, that he must abandon his claims based on undefined lines on the English maps, for even the one I showed him, had them, and I had always considered that they did not signify anything; that the territory the Colonies had inhabited and possessed, appeared on the very same map, as well as on the provincial ones that we would consider later; that all the territory, we were looking at, beyond the principal line of the boundaries of the Colonies, was Indian land, to which both parties had equal rights, or equally unjust claims, and that for this reason we should divide it between us by means of clearly defined points, after which each one would dress that naked body according to its resources.

I aired my views about the division, always bearing in mind that the course of the rivers, from a certain point downwards at least, remained with only one proprietor. He asked me to mark it out on the map clearly, and I agreed, offering to send him one map bearing a clear demarcation which he might peruse, reserving for a later occasion his doubts, concerning which in turn I would seek to give satisfaction.

Let me now state my reasons:

As regards that part of the line in controversy, I explicitly picked the end of the Lakes, starting in at *Superior*, following their borders until the end of the Erie or Oswego, in such position that there would be nothing disputable to its rear, and with the idea in mind that Spain would erect forts at certain points, which were in sight of her neighbor, and would be able to permit, or otherwise, trade within her possessions. Then I went down to the junction of the Great Kanawha with the Ohio, tracing it to the largest entry into North Carolina, with the idea of continuing to run the demarcation line through some line of sight, such as a lake, in the land of the Apalachees, or George River, but without reaching it and only marking the end of the line as an indication, and without continuing it when it approached the boundary between Georgia and Florida, until finding out which would be the definitive one.

Mr. Jay asked me why I stopped there, without continuing the line to the lake; I answered him that, since East Florida was still an English possession, we should not draw interior lines therein, to which he agreed.

The point that I had in mind in fixing the principal boundary in that way, was to force the Americans to adopt a more moderate position, and to counteract Mr. Jay's pretension to the whole Mississippi as a boundary line.

．　　．　　．　　．　　．

My first explanation embraces whatever modification, from the Lakes downwards, that is from North to South, which is the territory known to us, and therefore more important to us, than that from the Lakes upwards. To leave the use and navigation of the Lakes, which are interconnected, such as the so-called Superior, Michigan, Huron, Erie or Oswego, and Ontario, to the Americans, shall please them, while to us they are useless because they do not connect with our rivers. To divide them would cause disturbances in that distant wilderness.

This first proposal, which had been formulated early in the day, was meant to demonstrate that we were entering into negotiations, and that we have opened the door to the Americans to set forth all their own views, by which we shall be governed subsequently.

．　　．　　．　　．　　．

Paris, 19-30 August 1782

On Monday the 19th of August when I was leaving the house of M. de Vergennes, Franklin and Jay were getting out of their coach. We greeted each other, and I asked Jay whether he had amused himself with the atlas of the colonies I had given him, and whether he had found it useful. He answered, "Yes. It was very good," adding that he did not know which were better maps, mine or the English ones. I added that whenever he wanted we would talk, and he volunteered that he would arrange for it as soon as possible.

On Wednesday the 21st I returned to Versailles, and M. de Vergennes showed me the big map of Mitchell, which I had loaned to Jay last Monday, with the demarcation of boundaries I proposed.

On seeing this, I expressed my gratification to M. de Vergennes that Jay had taken His Excellency into his confidence, and I told him that we had put off discussions for another day as he seemed busy then.

On Friday the 23d I returned to Versailles with the sole purpose of acquainting myself with M. de Vergennes' ideas, and to instruct him properly about what was advisable. He took the map and I demonstrated to His Excellency how Jay first proposed to draw the boundaries along the entire length of the Mississippi River, which, of course, he [Vergennes] considered unacceptable; I recapitulated several reasons that I had advanced to Jay, which he deemed appropriate, and I explained to him that the reason I had drawn the red line in that form was to seek out known and clearly legible spots as principal points of those boundaries, while at the same time, to persuade Jay to modify his original pretension, by proposing a counter-line of a different color to serve as a basis for further discussion.

M. de Vergennes informed me that Jay had pointed out to him that the colonies already had some outposts far beyond their back-country, and consequently beyond the red line. I replied that I wanted Jay to identify that very spot on the map, that I was ready to acknowledge as many posts as they had already established, but that, until he would point these out, we ought to govern ourselves by the boundaries on the maps; and that, for the express purpose of giving Jay the opportunity to make his nominal claims, I had started drawing such a line. Indeed so far as I could see, considering his poverty of words, compounded by his difficulties in understanding French and Spanish, it was not possible to carry on a long discourse with him. That according to my instructions I could not accept the Mississippi as the boundary line, which for many obvious reasons was not suitable. Apart from this, I would not quibble over some leagues more or less in such a vast extent of territory; and that if His Excellency wanted to take the trouble to mediate, I would appreciate it: but he should begin by requiring Jay to explain himself clearly and concretely.

M. de Vergennes showed himself disposed to do that, and asked me if I had any objection to dealing also with his first deputy, M. de Rayneval, a person well informed on the issue in question, and the only one who was capable of arguing with Jay, because he had had more frequent dealings with him and spoke English. I replied by accepting, and he sent for him.

M. de Rayneval came down . . . and then Rayneval and I repaired to another chamber with the map. I began by explaining the background of my conversations with Jay, and by observing that Jay's claims were rendered all the more extreme when one considers those English possessions as consisting of two parts: The first might be designated the Colonies, with definite limits; the other, the possessions of the Crown conquered from other empires, for instance Canada and both Floridas, whose internal extension was no concern of the Colonies, but also that the same English monarch, who had allowed the Colonies to draw indefinite boundaries from East to West, in distant times and arbitrarily, proved no longer disposed to consenting to these boundaries, but sought to cut the Colonies off by others running from North to South, from Canada to Florida, which two possessions he considered to be a conquered partrimony of the Crown. Moreover, situated in the center were several nations not even as yet brought under control by any one. Yet, despite all these considerations, Jay proposed to extend his line all the way to the Mississippi.

M. de Rayneval told me that my observation was correct while Jay's was excessively optimistic; in support thereof he informed me that, while Louisiana and Canada had belonged to France, she had always considered all the intermediate territory as hers, even the lakes, without stopping to fix a middle line, according to the principle that Canada, or Louisiana, all belonged to the same proprietor. But what could be advanced against Jay even further was the fact that once France had lost Canada, it was then that the issue arose regarding her boundary with respect to Louisiana, which remained French. The English argued that the limits of Canada extended along the entire course of the Ohio and the Mississippi, for so M. de Vaudreuill,[2] the French Governor of Canada, had described them in a provisional protocol that had been entered into between the commanding officers of both nations when the English conquered Canada. In support of this argument, when the treaty of peace was signed, the English continued to bound Canada by the Mississippi, running the length of this river to the sea, on the ground that Florida had been conquered from Spain, as well as the French part of Mobile. On this ground, the Americans could not claim that their territory extended beyond the right bank of the Ohio, for not having taken possession of Canada, it belonged to England. On like grounds, they could not acquire the left bank, because the same British Crown could claim an extent of territory from both Floridas up to the

Ohio, behind Georgia, the Carolinas, and Virginia.

M. de Rayneval sought to find the fort called Toulouse which we located on the Alabama River; and he told me that when France had possession of part of Mobile, on the other side of the Mississippi, between this point and Spanish Florida, she built up that fort as a point of support as well as a limit for the English and the Spaniards, and that the territory from the mouth of the said river upwards had always been called under the generic name of Louisiana, which, as such, was joined at its upper limits with Canada.

Considering M. de Rayneval's ideas as so far removed from Jay's, with due respect to his fund of information about those places, I told him that he could return that map to Jay in order to dissuade him from pursuing his ends and to moderate his pretensions. For a start he could disabuse him of the notion that the settlements were in an advanced state. Having an abundant supply of similar maps, I would transmit one to the Comte de Vergennes for his personal use. Then we could mark the maps with the controversial lines, and once the final boundaries had been fixed, they would be entered separately in other maps similar to that. He appeared satisfied, and even assured me he would prepare a relevant report, for which I expressed my gratitude.

M. de Vergennes came in. We informed him about our discussion. He seemed agreeable, and we concluded our conversation.

On Saturday the 24th I sent the promised map.

Sunday the 25th was Ambassadors' Day, moved up from last Tuesday on the occasion of the celebration of the great festival of St. Louis, which everybody was obliged to attend at Versailles, according to custom. I met M. de Rayneval as he was coming out of the Minister's study, with the map under his arm, and since I recognized it as mine, I started to talk about it. He replied, repeating that he would make all the necessary annotations; and I encouraged him to do so, not only as a service to the Catholic King, but also for the kindly treatment he had accorded me.

In turn, I went in to confer with M. de Vergennes. He asked me if I insisted on the red line. I responded "No," provided that we would keep the colonists a considerable distance away from the Mississippi, and that we could settle upon some clear points. He appeared satisfied with my answer. He told me that if Jay could not understand this argument, there would still be room for an agreement, one which would leave the Indian nations in the intermediate areas neutral and free to trade with both Spaniards and colonists. "No doubt," I replied, but I pointed out the consideration that such an arrangement would in time have to be altered because the colonists were a new and growing nation, which, concerned with restricting or punishing the barbarians, would be pressing to take possession of those much better and more temperate lands than the ones along the coast. It would be always good policy, even in the case of the neutrality of those nations, to set some kind of meridian or clear line across which no one on either side could pass.

His Excellency picked up Jay's map, which he still had. We reexamined it, and he told me that in order to satisfy the Americans it was necessary to concede them more territory at their rear. To accomplish this I could move the line that crossed the junction of the Great Kanawha with the Ohio, to the lower junction of Wabash with the Ohio, pointing out that even with this change considerable distance remains to the Mississippi. I proposed to His Excellency that it would suffice to draw it as running between the two lakes that are located midstream of the aforesaid two rivers, in whose gap is inscribed Etang Castor. He replied that he himself would not oppose it, but because it was the intent of the Americans to trade along the interior rivers, they would resist the loss of the Wabash which, once preserved by his more westerly divisional line, would remain entirely in their hands as far as the Ohio, and thus open up for their use a considerable distance beyond the Colonies, as well as the Great Kanawha, claims which they would have to curb or moderate.

I remarked to M. de Vergennes that France once claimed Canada as extending northwards from the Ohio, and belonging now to the English. It was necessary to remember that while we were treating the boundaries between the Americans and us, the territory could be said still to belong to the English, and that neither one nor the other of us had exercised such control over it as to justify a claim to possession. Bearing this consideration in mind, the agreement should, while substantially the same, provide that if there would be any case in which either nation were to extend beyond its actual boundaries – whether because the territories were uninhabited or because of war with the Indians located in between – and having reached any one of the points designated as the frontier line, assuming it to be fixed now, then neither party would be allowed to go beyond that point, whether by reason of its being vacant or of the presence of the uncivilized Indians. Accordingly, should Jay refused to be reasonable and to renounce claims to the Mississippi, he would have to yield to the objection that Spain would not treat on that subject with the Americans, but instead with the English; and that in any case the divisional line already acknowledged, or preparatory for the future, had always been accepted as being far distant from the Mississippi.

M. de Vergennes said that to draw the line from the fort of Toulouse on the Alabama River could not be opposed by the Americans, because when that part called Mobile belonged to France, that was her boundary. To this I added that, if Fort Toulouse and the Alabama River were the limits of the

French possessions when they adjoined Spanish Florida, now it had been retroceded to Spain not only on the grounds of original ownership but because it was essential to leave the Alabama River as an interior line, and to draw another line which would include Pensacola and adjacent areas already reconquered by Spain.

M. de Rayneval returned. He offered to work to clarify all the details; and in the presence of M. de Vergennes himself I asked him to do what was proper, according to his understanding. With that our conversation was then terminated.

On Monday the 26th Jay came to see me between one and two o'clock in the afternoon. I asked him if he was satisfied with my maps. He answered me that, as regards the atlas, he was very much so, but less so with the big map, because it seemed to him to be inaccurate. I told him that there was a general map in the atlas, too, and that to me it made no difference which was used, but obviously none better was available. Then, in a candid manner, I remarked that no map would be satisfactory to him unless he abandoned his first proposition of the Mississippi as the boundary, because to draw the boundary in that way one needed no maps, but merely a pen to write it down.

He replied that on his departure from the Colonies, he had been so instructed without discretion, and that, therefore, he was not able to alter it.

I had carefully noted that the copy of his powers, which he had given to me and whose transcription I sent to the Court on the 10th of August with the number 2266, did not touch on the issue of adjusting boundaries, but only those of commerce and amicable relations; yet I did not wish to tell him this explicitly for I would have given him a pretext to affirm that he was not so authorized and then to justify his insistence on the Mississippi.

Bearing this in mind, I took the contrary position, and reminded him that instructions were one thing, powers another; that in dealing with the issue of boundaries one always proposed what would be agreeable; yet, considering the fact that there could be no negotiation or practical discussion, unless the ground rules were already agreed upon: first, it would have to be confirmed — *prius et esse, quam operari.*[3] That the Congress was sufficiently intelligent to appreciate the fact that it would be accorded like intent; that it could not have failed to bear in mind that there would be conflicting claims; that to treat with a totally new establishment, a thousand leagues away, concerning a large and indeterminate interior navigation, when it had not sent an attorney with power to make concessions to another's arguments, and to set the matter in such a form that it would satisfy everyone; that a man of the stature of Mr. Jay, who had been its President, who was loved and respected by his countrymen,

and whom all of us considered a plenipotentiary, and that if he himself
claimed to have done the bidding of Congress without any power to agree
to alterations – then all the conferences, geographical maps, and persuasive
arguments were absolutely fruitless.

He repeated that in the matter of the Mississippi Congress had neither
told him anything, nor did he have any powers. I asked him immediately
how he had made out in Madrid when he had had to deal with boundaries.
He replied that only once, when he had entered into a general explanation
of them, had he made a reference to the Mississippi River, to which he was
plainly told *that it was unacceptable*, without giving him a further
explanation; and having left the matter in that status, he had decided not
to budge under any circumstances.

I explained that the reply of my Court had been natural and proper
considering his extraordinary claim, and since he learned that it was
inadmissible at the outset, it was his duty to inquire what Spain was
prepared to offer, and then rebut her notions by advancing the views of
Congress. Although he had lacked sufficient powers to enter into an
agreement, at least he would have made clear the converse pretensions, and
with enough time he would have informed his superiors about the aspect
and state of this issue; in view of which they would have dispatched to him
their final instructions to complete the partial ones; and, as a result, he
would have them to explain to me and to serve as a basis for discussion. He
answered me that since no one in Madrid had raised the issue any further,
he had left the matter as it then stood.

Disagreeing with him, I said that, according to what he had told me, we
would have to remain as we were; because I had denied not only the
Mississippi, but I had drawn a line with more fundamental *right* to support
it than he had on his part to back up his claim of extension to the
Mississippi. He replied that by virtue of my line I was compelling him to
enter into an argument because he now had seen several grounds that
neither the Congress nor he himself had been able to foresee, and that,
now having been enlightened quite differently from his understanding when
he had left his own country, he would be able to explain to the United
States the difficulties he had encountered.

I asked him if under his commission Dr. Franklin was equally authorized
to act. He answered "No," that only he had powers with regard to Spain.

Holding firm to my position that I had considered him in the character
of plenipotentiary, I repeated to him that he ought to peruse his papers
closely, that he should distinguish between instructions and the credentials
of a plenipotentiary. I pointed out that it was not possible, since the fate
of the Colonies was to be dealt with in Europe, that its commissioners were
supposed to ask advice from Philadelphia, as if the business were to be

transacted between Paris and Madrid, for which latter case an answer by safe passage could come in a fortnight while in this case it was a matter of a half year's navigation jeopardized by enemies and storms.

Observing that my argument threw him off guard and unable to respond, I asked him if he would have confidence in placing his case in the hands of the ministry at Versailles and in listening to what it would have to say about this matter. He answered, "Yes," and I persuaded him to do so; but, pointing out by way of concluding, that if he would find upon reviewing his documents that he was not authorized to discuss the boundaries, nor to arrange them, he would let me know in writing; because, having once started to set them down formally, I now found that I would not be able to continue with it; to which he replied that he would inform me after duly reflecting on his position.

In the course of the conversation I considered it appropriate to remind him how much Spain had helped the Colonies with the secret aids as well as with the declaration of war, which had diverted the forces of the enemy. Jay responded very coldly that it was true in regard to some financial assistance, but so far as the war was concerned, he said that Madrid had promised him that they would help the Colonies with the Spanish army, and at most the army had been deployed in the conquest of Florida for itself, and this had not helped them at all in New York or Charleston. In reply, I stated that I did not anticipate, with due respect to his intelligence, such a curious assumption that attacking the enemy in its possessions was not distracting it, that according to basic rules of warfare, any binding ally ought to move on his own course. Therefore, with Spain in possession of Louisiana, and thereby able to draw towards Florida that part of the English army which could have been situated on other fronts, Spain had done what reason dictated.

He replied that he wished we would not have taken Pensacola, because then the British troops were removed to New York, and their strength provided a considerable reinforcement for the English. I answered him that he was offending us by assuming that we had acquiesced in the removal of the English troops from Pensacola to New York; that it had been an interpretation on the part of the English and in bad faith; and the only thing that I was able to say was that the terms of capitulation could have been more specific, pointing out that they must not take up arms again against any one of the belligerents, instead of the allies, or to have demanded explicitly their return to Europe, and although there might have been a certain carelessness in this matter, it should be put down to the official who signed the articles, not to the Court.

He left, stating in his customary few words, that he was looking at the matter in a very different manner from when he had come, and that he wished that his commission could be satisfactorily carried out.

On Friday the 30th I went to Versailles, and at a meeting with M. the Comte de Vergennes and M. de Rayneval, informed them of the visit of Sir John Jay last Monday the 26th, and since they both expressed doubts about the observation I had made to them to the effect that Jay's powers only embraced commerce and amity, without touching the issue of boundaries, I showed them a copy of them, which surprised them both.

They told me that according to the correspondence of the Chevalier de la Luzerne, the Court of Spain had initiated the discussion about boundaries, in the Colonies themselves, through Don Juan de Miralles; to which I replied that that explained why this matter had not been advanced in Madrid

....M. de Vergennes left M. de Rayneval and me to continue the discussion of boundaries.

We reexamined the map, and drew a line from the mark that indicated the beginning of Eastern Florida in the direction of Fort Toulouse, to include Western Florida and attach her to Louisiana.

From the said Fort Toulouse, to reach the Ohio, M. de Rayneval had drawn a line going upwards throughout the Toulouse River, following the Cherokee or Hogohegee River, which flows into the Ohio, but a very short distance from the Mississippi; and after I had made the observation that this would place the Americans too close to the course of the Mississippi, we changed the line to pass across the Cherokee through the confluence of the Pelisipi, going upwards until its source, then to take the Cumberland River, and following it to the Ohio, to move downwards to its junction with the Mississippi. In this form the Americans would be positioned far from the latter. Granted that the English would always be the owners of the territory between the Mississippi and the Ohio northwards, still it was impossible to deny it to them as a part of Canada yielded by France.

M. de Rayneval read to me the report on which he was working, giving information about all those lands, and whether England had considered them to be hers, or to belong to other independent and neutral nations, and after having asked him for a copy of it, he promised me one.

From the discussion that we had in the meantime, I inferred that Jay had indicated how little pleased he had been with the Court of Madrid; yet, he had also begun to realize that his claim to the Mississippi River would be neither as legally based nor as sufficiently supported as he originally had conceived.

· · · · ·

Morris, Jay Papers, v. 2, pp. 270-282. Original document in Archivo Histórico Nacional, Madrid.

[1] *Mitchell's map. The reference is to* A Map of the British and French Dominions in North America With the Roads, Distances, Limits, and Extent of the Settlements, Humbly Inscribed to the Right Honourable The Earl of Halifax, And the Other Right Honourable The Lords Commissioners for Trade & Plantations, By Their Lordships Most Obliged and Very Humble Servant Jno. Mitchell *(London: Andrew Millar, 1755). John Mitchell (d. 1768), a physician, botanist, and cartographer, practiced medicine in Virginia, 1735-1746, thereafter residing in or near London.*

[2] *Vaudreuil-Cavagnal, Pierre de Rigaud, Marquis de (1698-1765). French colonial official. Governor of New France, 1755-1760. Charged with maladministration for surrendering Canada to the British, but acquitted in the subsequent trial.*

[3] *Literally, it must exist before it can be operative.*

Richard Oswald to Thomas Townshend

Sir[1]   Paris 5th August 1782.

.   .   .   .   .

Upon receipt of your Letter, I went out to Doctor Franklin, & read to him that part in which he is mentioned. I ventured to do so, believing it was proper, (as things were Circumstanced) & also that it was intended. But particularly on account of having lately observed, on different occasions, a kind of anxious desire in the Doct[r.] that their Colony business should be sett in motion.

From what passed at that time & since, I was happy to see no reason to apprehend any alteration in his Inclinations & Sentiments, respecting the Plan & Conclusion of their affairs, from what he had signified on a former occasion, as reported by me at the time. At least, if he had adopted any New Ideas on that subject, he did not think proper to give me any hint of them.

Of other Occurrences since M[r.] Grenvilles departure, I don't recollect any thing necessary to be mentioned relative to Colony affairs, Excepting that about a Week past, when I was with the Doctor, & having told him I had waited on M[r.] Jay & happening to say I thought him a good natured Man, the Doctor replied he was so; & also a Man of good sense. That he had been ill, but was now recovering, & at present was busy with the Spanish Ambassador. That while at Madrid he had been trying to conclude a Treaty with Spain; but they had delayed & put him off from time to time; so that he was at last obliged to quit that Place, & repair to Paris to join him. But that now the Court of Spain had sent to their Ambassador here, full Power to conclude.

I askt the Doct[r] what sort of Treaty it was; He said a Treaty of Commerce; & after a short hesitation, added Alliance & at last said, it was just the same kind of Treaty as they had with France. I said I made no doubt it was so; & made no farther observation.

This Intimation came from the Doct[r] in the easy way of Conversation, as any matter of less importance would have passed. Yet I imagine with a view to its being properly markt, & communicated. And most likely also with the same good Intention, as on former occasions, of shewing the expediency of getting on with their business; & also perhaps, the farther danger of attempting to break in upon the plan of Pacification they have sketched out for themselves. I cannot help thinking it was meant so; Since, in case the Conditions which those Commissioners have settled, will not, in their apprehension, admit of an Alteration in material Articles, their giving this early nottice unaskt, of this additional Support, by a closser Union with Spain, shews in my opinion, a desire that the Consequences of a Mistake on our part may be duly attended to, & in that sense, perhaps friendly to England; & in all events evidently tending to promote a Speedy Conclusion of that part of the War.

. . . . .

When Mr. Fitzherbert arrived I informed him of this Intimation respecting the Spanish Treaty.

. . . . .

I have the honour to be Sir Your most obedient humble Servant
R 11th
                                              Richard Oswald

PRO: FO 27/2, v. 557, f. 483 (LC transcription).
  [1] Townshend, Thomas (1733-1800). British political figure. Member of Parliament, 1754-1783; a Whig. A lord of the treasury under Rockingham, 1766, and Grafton, 1766-1767; joint paymaster of the forces under Grafton, 1767-1768. Opposed Lord North's policies. Secretary of State for War in Rockingham's administration, March-July 1782. Secretary of State for Home Affairs under Shelburne, July 1782-April 1783. From March 1783, Baron Sydney. Secretary of State for Home Affairs under Pitt, December 1783-June 1789.

Richard Oswald to Lord Shelburne

My Lord.   Paris 5 August 1782

. . . . .

With respect to the Report of my Continuance here being a prejudice to the depending Treaty, which Your Lo[p] refers to me for an Answer, I can only say that in that Misrepresentation there is a Compliment paid to me which I had no right to: having never been of consequence enough to hurt any Treaty if I had been so inclined. As to M[r] Grenvilles Treaty, I never medled in it in any Shape, excepting twice or thrice when I called to see him; & observing him despondent, & once appearing tired, & wishing it was in any other hands, I took the liberty to encourage him to keep up his Spirits, in hopes of making this Court Speak out, & by so doing to carry on the business a part of the way to a termination. That was all the part I ever took in the affairs of that Treaty. Excepting occasionally hinting to Doct^r Franklin that I apprehended this Court was disposed to use us hardly in that business; & that in Such Case, it would be expected that He & his Collegues would not look on with Indifference. Of that kind, I confess much guilt, but no other. But this, though meant to Smooth the part of the Treaty had not that effect; as appeared by the last Intimation to Mr Grenville. Indeed there never was any bottom laid upon which a Treaty Could properly Stand. So it could not be hurt by me or any body else. If Mr Grenville himself is askt, I am sure he will give a different explanation of the matter than has been reported.

With Respect to the French Minister Monsr de Vergennes he had no objection to my remaining here, because when I anounced Mr Grenvilles appointm^t, he told me himself, that notwithstandin^g thereof, he wished I might stay, & it is not above a month since Mr Franklin made a Report from him of a Complim^t to much the same purpose.

.   .   .   .   .

I have the honour to be My Lord Your Lo^{ps} most obedient humble Servant,   Richard Oswald

Clements Library: Shelburne Papers, v. 71, pp. 73-75 (C).

Arthur Lee to Samuel Adams

Dear friend,   Philadelphia Augt. 6th. 1782

.   .   .   .   .

Every thing from England seems to announce a real disposition to peace. But it is very surprising that by six or seven opportunities from France, we have not receivd a line from our Minister. Not even by Major Franks, who came as a special Messenger. And what is yet more astonishing, we have not a word from Mr. Adams relative to the late important proceedings in Holland. I am apprehensive, his Dispatches were sent, thro France; & were stopt there. This profound silence on subjects so very interesting together with the perilous & humiliating situation we are in touching the negociation for Peace, I own alarm me. I am very much inclind to think that France will be for protracting the war, or for turning the cheif advantages of it to herself & to Spain. Mr Jay's last Letter suggest strong suspicions of that Court, & we have put ourselves shamefully & entirely inher power as to the conditions of Peace.

Spain appears to have been acting a part as silly as it is selfish; & to be covering the weakness of her Councils, by the insincerity of her conduct. Some spirited measures will be taken respecting that Court; merely because bravado in one instance, is some consolation for servility in another. For our interests seem out of the question in that quarter, She being no ways desirous of treating with us.

. . . . .

...My respects to Mrs. Adams & remembrances to...all our friends.
Farewell.   Arthur Lee

NYPL: Rare Books and Manuscripts Division, Samuel Adams Papers.

Congressional Resolutions

[Philadelphia] August 7th. 1782
On motion of Mr. Rutledge[1] seconded by Mr. Telfair[2]

Resolved That the Minister Plenipotentiary at the Court of Spain be instructed to forbear making any overtures to that Court or entering into any stipulations in consequence of overtures which he has made –

Ordered That the instructions passed yesterday be redrawn so as to comprehend the above which is to be inserted immediately before in case as follows

Resolved That the Minister Plenipotentiary of the United States at the Court of Spain be instructed to forbear making any overtures to that Court or entering into any stipulations in consequence of overtures which he has made, and in case any propositions be made to him by the said Court for a treaty with the United States to decline acceding to them until he shall have transmitted them to Congress for their approbation, unless the treaty proposed be of such a tenor as to render his accession thereto necessary to the fulfilment of the stipulation, on the part of the United States, contained in the separate and secret Article of their treaty with His Most Christian Majesty –

Resolved That Mr. Jay be at liberty to leave Spain and go into any other part of Europe whenever the state of his health may require it –

NA: PCC, item 5, pp. 695-696 (Journal); M247, reel 19.
[1] *Rutledge, John (1739-1800). South Carolina political figure, jurist. Member, Continental Congress, 1774-1775, 1782-1783. President and commander-in-chief of South Carolina, 1776-1778; governor, 1779-1782. Member, Constitutional Convention, 1787.*

Associate Justice, U.S. Supreme Court, 1789-1791. Chief justice of South Carolina, 1790-1795. Nominated chief justice, U.S. Supreme Court, 1795, but not confirmed.
² Telfair, Edward (1735-1807). Merchant, Georgia political figure. Member, Continental Congress, 1778, 1780-1782. Governor of Georgia, 1786, 1790-1793.

Richard Oswald's Minutes of Conversations with Benjamin Franklin and John Jay

Paris Wednesday 7ᵗʰ August 1782

Yesterday Evening at 7 o'Clock, the Courier...arrived and brought my Commission for treating with the Commissioners of the Colonies and the King's Instructions &cᵃ·

This afternoon I went to Passy, and carried a Copy of the Commission to Doctor Franklin.

After perusal he said he was glad it was come That he had been at Versailles yesterday, And Monsʳ de Vergennes had ask'd about it; and upon the Doctor telling him it was not come, he said he could do nothing with Mʳ Fitzherbert till it arrived; as both Treaties must go on together hand in hand.

I shewed him Mʳ Townshend's Letter accounting for a copy being only sent, as the Chancellor and Attorney General were at a distance in the Country. The Doctor seemed to be satisfied, and said, as on a former occasion, He hoped We should agree and not be long about it. There were no particulars touched upon. And after sitting about a quarter of an hour, I proposed calling on Mʳ Jay, the only other Commissioner at Paris. The Doctor said it was right, and returned me the Copy of the Commission to be left with Mʳ Jay, which he would bring back to the Doctor as he was to Dine at Passy.

I accordingly returned to Paris, and called on Mʳ Jay. He is a Man of good sense; of frank, easy and polite Manners: he read over the Copy of the Commission and Mʳ· Townshend's Letter accounting for its not being under Seal and then said, by the quotation from the Act of Parliament in the Commission, He supposed it was meant that Independence was to be treated upon, and was to be granted perhaps as the Price of Peace. That it ought to be no part of a Treaty. It ought to have been expressly granted by Act of Parliament, and an Order for all Troops to be withdrawn, previous to any Proposal for Treaty. As that was not done, the King, he said, ought to do it now by Proclamation, and order all Garrisons to be evacuated; And then close the American War by a Treaty. He said many things of a retrospective kind; such as the happy effects a Declaration of that Nature at earlier periods would have produced; if Great Britain had handsomely and nobly made this Grant before such deep Wounds had been given to that Bias & attachment which till then subsisted all over that Country in favor of G.B. even in Spite of their Petitions being repeatedly rejected. That in such case, they would undoubtedly have concerted such Plan of Treaty, as would have not only restored Peace, but would have laid a Solid Bottom of amity and conciliation, and such as would have obliterated from their Memory in a short time all Remembrance of preceeding Acts of Distress and Violence....

. . . . .

...He returned to the Subject of Independence, as not being satisfied with its being left as a Matter of Treaty. I wished much to get him of it; and for that purpose said that the method proposed was much the same as what he meant, and perhaps such as the nature of the British Constitution made necessary.

Independence on Great Britain in the most complete sense would be granted without any reserve; allways supposing that their States should be equally Independent of other Nations. And so the Treaty might proceed in the Course which was thus markt out for it, until it ended in Peace. He said Peace was very desirable and the sooner the better. But the great point was to make such a Peace as should be lasting....

. . . . .

...the Peace he meant was such, or so to be settled that it should not be in the *Interest* of either Party to violate it. This he said was the only security that could be proposed to prevent those frequent Returns of War, by which the World was kept in perpetual Disturbance.

I could guess what he meant by the present Parties being bound by Motives of Interest to be quiet, and askt for no Explanation.

As I happened to mention the last Treaty of Paris, Mr Jay said, We had taken great advantage of the French in that Treaty. I did not ask him as to the Articles he objected to. But further to try his Sentiments on these Subjects, I said I woundered that he, being of America, should complain of that Treaty, as if the French had not been tenderly enough dealt with in it; since that long and expensive War, to which it put a period, was entered into entirely on account of America; and to save them from the Consequences of that constant Course of Hostility which the French were avowedly carrying on against them on their Western Frontiers, in the times of profound Peace in every other Quarter of the World, and to which they were Solemnly bound by the Treaty of Aix la Chappelle.

. . . . .

At one or other of the Periods of this Conversation, he said, you seem to think that France ought to consider the Independence of our States, as a Sufficient Indemnification for all Her Expences in the War (this however

I had never said to him, although I had often said so to Doctor Franklin) but continued Mr Jay that ought not to be admitted, as it in the first place puts Us under a greater obligation to France than We incline to: as if to Her alone We are indebted for our Independence. And in the next place (I have forgot the precise terms, but it was to this purpose) that in course of the War France had made Conquests, and They, the Americans, had a Treaty with them, by which they were bound not to give Us Peace, but in concurrence with our settlement with them....After enlarging on these obligations, and the gratitude they owed to France; He proceeded to Spain and Holland and talked also, though in a more general way, of their Alliances with them; and their great obligations to them for advance of Money; and as if by the Conditions of Treaty, they could not conclude or have Peace with Great Britain separately from those two Powers, I did not think it right to be over inquisitive as to their intentions regarding them, but it appeared to me as if he considered those two Courts as much under their Protection as that of France; and as if they the Commissioners of the Colonies, would agree or refuse to close with Us according as they should consider the Terms which those two Powers shall insist on, to be reasonable or unreasonable.

. . . . . .

Paris Sunday 11th & 13th Augt 1782
Conversation with Doctor Franklin &c^a.

I went out this forenoon to Doctor Franklin, to know whether he was inclined to enter upon Business. He told me he had carried the Copy of the Commission I gave him to Versailles, the Day before, and had some Conversation on the Subject with Monsr· de Vergennes; who was of Opinion with him, that it would be better to wait untill a real Commission arrived this being neither signed nor Sealed, and could be supposed as only a draft or order, in which there might be alterations; as in the Preamble it said only "to the Effect following &c." To this objection I had nothing to say, as I did not incline to shew them the Instructions, though signed and Sealed.

Finding no alteration in the Doctor's manner, from the usual good natured and friendly way in which he had formerly behaved to me (as I had reason to apprehend from what had lately passed with his Colleague) and having a quiet and convenient opportunity, I was anxious to learn whether the Doctor entertained those Ideas, which in the preceeding Papers, I suspected Mr Jay had in view, regarding the *means* of preventing future Wars, by settling the Peace in such manner as it should not be the Interest of the Parties to break it.

. . . . . .

The Doctor replied, the method was very plain and easy. Which was to settle the Terms in the first projection on an equal just and reasonable footing; and so as neither Party should have cause to complain, being the Plan which Monsr de Vergennes had in view, and had always recommended in his conversations with him on the Subject of Peace. And the Doctor said it was a good Plan, and the only one that could make the Peace lasting....

. . . . .

The second thing the Doctor touched upon was Independence. He said by the Quotations of Acts of Parliament, he saw it was included in the Commission. But that Mr Grenville had orders to grant it in the first instance. I replied it was true; And that though supposed to be granted under this Commission, and in the course of the Treaty, I hoped it would make no difference with Gentlemen who were so well disposed to put an end to this unhappy Business as I knew him to be.

He then askt if I had Instructions. I said I had, and that they were under His Majesty's hand and Seal; and that by them it appeared Independence, unconditional in every sense, would be granted, and that I saw no reason why it should not make the first Article of the Settlement or Treaty....

I then said after that was done, I hoped there would not be many things to settle. And that the Articles called Necessary, which he specified on the 10$^{th.}$ of July, would pretty nearly end the Business. And that those called Adviseable, which, as a Friend to Britain and to Reconciliation he had then recommended would be dropt, or modified in a proper manner. That I had fairly stated the Case at home, and could not but confess that I had this Answer from one of his Friends. To this I cannot say I had any reply.

I then told the Doctor there was a particular circumstance, which, of myself, I wished to submit to his consideration, as a Friend to returning Peace. England has ceased all Hostilities against America by Land. At Sea it was otherwise, and however disposed We might be to stop these proceedings there also, I could not see how it could be done until the People of America adopted the same Plan. At the same time I was sensible, that by the strict Letter of their Treaty with France, the Americans could not well alter their Conduct before We came to a final Settlement with that Nation. That this was an unfortunate Dilemma for both of Us; That We should be taking each others Ships, when perhaps We might, in other respects, be at perfect Peace; and that notwithstanding thereof We must continue in this Course, waiting for a Conclusion with France and other Nations, perhaps at a distant period. That although I had no orders on this head, yet as a Continuance in this Species of Hostility seemed to be so repugnant to the Motives and Principles, which had determined a Cessation on the part of England by Land, and was certainly a bar to that cordial

Reconciliation which he so much wished for, I could not avoid Submitting the Case to his Consideration, to see whether he could find some Remedy for it. The Doctor replied he could not see how it could be done. It would be a difficult thing. However at last he said he would think of it.

I next touched upon the Subject of the Loyalists, but could not flatter myself with the hopes of its answering any good purpose; the Doctor having from the beginning assured me they could take no part in that Business, as it was exclusively retained under the Jurisdiction of the respective States upon whom the Several Claimants had any demands; And there having been no Power delegated to the Congress on that head, they as Commissioners, could do nothing in it....

Upon the whole of this Matter the Doctor said nothing, but that he was advised that the Board of Loyalists at New York was Dissolved by General Carleton, which he was glad of.

The Doctor at last touched upon Canada, as he generally does upon the like occasions, and said there could be no dependence on Peace and good Neighborhood: while that Country continued under a different Government, as it touched their States in so great a Stretch of Frontier. I told him I was sensible of that Inconveniency. But having no Orders, the consideration of that Matter might possibly be taken up at some future time. At my coming away, the Doctor said that although the proper Commission was not come over, yet he said Mr Jay would call on me with a Copy of their Credentials. This being Sunday, he said the Copy would be made out on Monday. On Tuesday he must go to Versailles, being the Levee Day. But on Wednesday they would call with their Papers. So that tomorrow I shall probably have the honour of seeing those Gentlemen, and of course may have something still to add to these tedious Writings.

Paris 15th August 1782.

Observations

In the conclusion of the Papers of the 13th inst I said that Doctor Franklin and Mr Jay were to call on me as yesterday to exchange Credentials. But they did not call, I went out therefore this Morning to the Doctor to inform him that the Commission had come to hand; of which I told him I would have informed him sooner, if I had not expected him yesterday. He excused himself on account of Company coming in, which made it too late for coming into Paris that forenoon. But that tomorrow he and Mr Jay would certainly call. He said he was glad the Sealed Commission was come. There was nothing material said on the Subject of Business. I returned to Paris and called on Mr Jay to inform him in like manner of the Commission being arrived. At meeting with this Gentleman, I own I was under some concern on account of our former Conversation.

But I was agreeably disappointed having found him in the best humour and disposed to enter into a friendly discussion on the Business I came about.

. . . . .

...he delivered his Sentiments in a manner the most expressive of a sincere & friendly intention towards Great Britain. I should not do him Justice if I said less. And I am the more inclined to be particular in this part of the Report that I was so free in my Remarks on his former Conversation; especially in my suspicions of an actual, or premeditated Connection with Foreign States, on account of his particular Idea of guarding against the violation of Treaties, as mentioned in the preceeding Papers; but which although I could perceive was present to his mind on this occasion also, yet I am now convinced had gone no farther than Speculation; And as he said himself: and which I really believe he would be heartily sorry they should have recourse to.

At proper times I said what occurred to me as necessary to bring this Question to some sort of desireable period; & in particular wished to have Mr Jay's Idea of such way of declaring this unconnected ascertainment of Independence as would satisfy them.

His former proposal of doing it by Proclamation he gave up, as liable to sundry objections, needless to be here repeated. He then proposed it should be done by a particular & Separate Deed, or Patent under the Great Seal, in which my Commission for a Treaty might also be narrated: and that such Patent should be put into the possession of the Commissioners, to be by them sent over to Congress; and accordingly M^r· Jay brought me a Draft of the Patents. As I could see no other way of satisfying those Gentlemen, and it appearing highly necessary that some beginning should be made with them, since until that was done the Foreign Treaty could not proceed in its course, I agreed to send the Draft over to His Majesty's Secretary of State by a Courier express for that purpose with my own Opinion rather in favor of the Proposal than otherwise. And so it was settled with the Commissioners....

. . . . .

I have now to add, in relation to my last Conversation with M^r· Jay that after having quitted the Subject of their particular affairs and thinking myself at liberty to enter into a greater freedom on Conversation, I wished to take the opportunity of saying something relative to Foreign Affairs to a Man of good Sense and Temper; who in his present and future Situation may have it in his power, here and elsewhere, to exemplify by his good Offices, those favourable Inclinations respecting Great Britain which he so freely and warmly expressed on the present occasion. Accordingly at proper periods, I made no Scruple in throwing out the following Observations. That after settling with them, which I hoped would end to the Satisfaction of both Parties Our next concern regarded a Settlement with France and other Foreign Nations. That as yet I understood We could make no guess at what France aimed at. They kept themselves on the reserve perhaps partly with a view of being in some measure governed in their proposals by the manner in which Our Settlement of American Affairs may proceed.

That in the course of the American War, they had taken the Opportunity of making Separate Conquests for themselves; And encouraged by this late alteration in Our System, it may be supposed they were projecting some hard terms of Settlement for Us by their delay in coming to particulars. Excepting only their declaration of having no Interest, or concern in the Article of American Independence; and consequently that in every view of equivalent, it is to have no place in abatement of their Claims of Retention or farther Requisition.

That having taken the Spanish and Dutch concerns also under their Cover, and so as not to treat but jointly, or in concurrence with them, the prospect of a speedy and favorable Settlement for Great Britain became still the more unpromising; unless they, the Commissioners of the Colonies should interfere to check the Exorbitancy of the Terms which thus might be expected to be insisted on by such Combination of Foreign States.

And this prospect I said was still the worse that I understood he himself (Mr Jay) had concluded, or was about to conclude a Treaty with Spain on the same footing with that which the Congress had settled with France. That the restraining Clause in those Treaties, regarding Truce or final Peace between England and America, until there was also a final Settlement with those Foreign States, was a most unlucky circumstance, and therefore the more of those Treaties the Commissioners entered into, so much the worse for England.

. . . . .

In answer Mr Jay replied to the following purpose. That We had only to cut this Knot of Independence to get rid of many of those Apprehensions – That if We lookt better to our Conduct for the future We might be sure of recovering and preserving a solid and beneficial Friendship with the Americans. That for the last Twenty Years he could not say much for Us yet he said more particularly regarding the fairness and sincerity of our professions than I chuse to repeat. He continued by saying that England under a wise Administration was capable of great things. Such a Country, Such a People and blessed with Such a Constitution had nothing to fear and in Thirty years would forget all her present Difficulties &c &c &c:

That as to the Spanish Treaty he had not proceeded far in it and unless We forced them into those Engagements he did not see that the People of America had any business to fetter themselves with them. And in the mean time he assured me, he would Stop as to this of Spain, which I was very glad to hear of.

He said he supposed the Terms of France would be moderate. And in that Case he would give his advice that when they came to light; that the Court of England would consider them with temper; and after making a deliberate Estimate of the Price they can afford to give for Peace, to strike at once without hagling about it. That if their Independence was once settled, he hoped that next Winter would put an End to the War in general. That it was true there was a look here towards another Campaign, and what might be the possible consequences of the Operations in the Interim, and touched upon the East Indies, as if great Expectations from thence were entertained at this Court &c. Amongst other things I omitted when We were talking of Independence, that I mentioned by the by, as if it was understood, that when America was Independent of England, they would be so, also of all other Nations. Mr Jay smiled, and said that they would take care of that, and seemed in his Countenance to express such disapprobation of any Question being put on that head, as would make one cautious as to the manner in which any Stipulations on that Subject should be proposed to those Gentlemen.

Paris 17 $^{th.}$ Augt. 1782
Richard Oswald

Clements Library: Shelburne Papers, v. 70, pp. 113-174 (C).

Charles Thomson's Notes of Debates

August 8th. [1782]

. . . . .

M^r. Lee arose and reminded the house that there was a business before them of the greatest importance; that the interest, the honor and the safety of these States were so much concerned that he could not be easy nor stand justified to himself or his constituents until he had done everything in his power to bring it to determination. He therefore moved

"That the instructions given on the 15 June 1781 to the ministers plenipotentiary for negotiating a peace be reconsidered." This was seconded by Mr Bland & some other members. But Mr Root[1] rising and expressing a desire that the motion might be expressed in such terms as to avoid all debates concerning the effects of a reconsideration, he moved "That a Com^{tt} be appointed to revise and consider the instructions given to our ministers for negotiating a peace with Great Britain, and report what alterations ought to be made therein."

Mr Lee said he wished only for a fair discussion of the subject and to avoid every difficulty and debate arising from forms and therefore withdrew his motion and seconded that of Mr Root.

Mr Rutledge is resolved to adhere strictly to the principles of the alliance with France, and to shew her all the respect and confidence which one nation would shew another. He had full confidence in her magnanimity, but is doubtful whether Congress had power to surrender themselves into her hands. The case is delicate; he does not wish to give an opinion; he may upon mature deliberation. The Com^{tt} think it proper not to alter the instruction. It deserves consideration. He is therefore for appointing a Committee; if upon the most mature deliberation the Com^{tt} shall be of opinion that any alterations should be made they will report what they think proper; if they are of a contrary opinion they will say nothing about them. He found by looking over the journals that instructions had been given respecting a treaty of commerce and that afterwards these were withdrawn & repealed and nothing farther done on the subject. He thought the Com^{tt} to be appointed should be instructed to take this matter into consideration & report what was proper to be done.

Mr Williamson[2] said he had listened with the greatest attention to the arguments offered He had examined the instructions given. He did not think them of so dangerous a nature as was represented. The independence of the States and the principles of the alliance and treaty of commerce were fully secured. These were made ultimate, and not to be given up on any account. The matters in which the ministers were ultimately to be governed by the opinion of France were only what respected disputed boundaries, the fisheries and other matters which might come into discussion at the treaty.

Mr Rutledge. The boundaries were everything; what are the States? They must have boundaries. Is France to say what those boundaries shall be and must we submit?

Mr Lee differs in opinion with the gentleman from North Carolina. It is not sufficient that the independence of these States is secured. But he doubts whether even that is secured by the instructions. He is afraid of the accompaniment. That we shall be so circumscribed in our boundaries that our independence will be a nugatory independence. France in making a treaty will be governed by her own interest and from her long and close connection with Spain and prefer it to ours. Is it wise, is it proper to give a nation the absolute disposal of our affairs that is under the influence of two interests which she is bound to consult in preference to that of these States? This unlimited confidence will render us despicable in the eyes of France and make her less attentive to our rights. We have been informed by a minister of France that Spain has large claims on the lands beyond the mountains. Her conduct shews that she means to support her claim to that Country. She wishes to confine us to the lands lying below the heads of the waters falling into the Atlantic. We are told that she thinks she has a right to possess herself of all to the westward. And shall we submit it to France, her old friend and ally, whether her claims shall be confirmed & we be excluded from the possession of that Country? Besides the power and instructions we have given will be dangerous to France and render her suspected by the other nations of Europe. Her language to the other powers of Europe has been that she entered into the war to support our independence; that we were left at liberty to grant the same indulgence and privileges to other nations that were granted to her. What will the other nations of Europe think when at the treaty of peace they find her entrusted with the whole, the absolute disposal of our affairs? Will they not become jealous? Will they not think she has deceived or means to deceive them? The instructions are also dangerous to the United States. It is essentially giving up the independence of these States and becoming dependents on the minister of France. For notwithstanding what is said in the former part of the instructions respecting independence & adherence to the principles of the treaties, as the clause comes afterwards by which our ministers are bound to govern themselves ultimately by the advice and opinion of France he is strong in the opinion and thinks he will be warranted by the rules of construction & the judgment of all men that this supersedes the former: and shall this be suffered to come in doubt? He is for binding the minister to pay the utmost respect and place the utmost confidence in France, to take no steps without consulting her. Thus everything will be done that can and ought to be done. Can any friend of France desire more? Can any gentleman in this house wish to continue to her a power that will be ruinous to our independence, dangerous to herself, expose us to the contempt and scorn of all the nations of Europe, and bring upon both her and us their jealousy & perhaps their resentment?

Mʳ Madison grants that the instructions given are a sacrifice of national dignity. But it was a sacrifice of dignity to policy. The situation of affairs and circumstances at the time rendered this sacrifice necessary. Nothing essential is given up, nor did it render our situation less precarious than it was before; nay he was persuaded that this mark of confidence gave an additional security to our interests as the Court of France must be sensible that the odium of unequal or hard conditions will now rest wholly on her.

At least he was sure that the instructions given did not weaken that security. Our interests are as safe in her hands now as they were before or as if the ministers were left wholly to their discretion. Our ministers may still, notwithstanding the instructions given, state & assert our claims and contend with the utmost earnestness for our rights, and it is only in the last extremity when all their pleas, all their reasoning and all their most earnest endeavours prove ineffectual that they are ultimately to govern themselves by the advice and opinion of the Court of France; and must not this have been the case if the instructions had never been given?

France has voluntarily bound herself by the treaties she has entered into with us to secure and guarantee our independence & sovereignty absolute and unlimited as well in matters of government as commerce. What indication has she given of any alteration of sentiment or conduct towards us? It is her interest as well as policy to secure the affections of the people of these States and forever separate us from G. Britain. She can never think us formidable to her while we continue absolutely independent, nor will she ever object to our enlarging our boundaries or increasing our commerce & naval power unless we give her reason to suspect a want of confidence in her and a disposition to reunite ourselves with her ancient enemy. In that case interest and policy will both unite and induce her to keep us as weak as possible. Whether withdrawing our confidence at this critical moment will not give just grounds of suspicion and jealousy he leaves gentlemen to determine. There was a passage in Mr Jay's letter lately read which made a strong impression on him; he did not know whether it made the same on others. He meant that passage which mentioned the fears and suspicions occasioned by the late change in the British administration, lest the men now in office who had always professed themselves friends to America and had is such severe terms condemned the war might influence the councils and conduct of the Americans. The withdrawing the instructions given on the 15th June, 1781, added to what has passed with regard to Spain, will increase that jealousy.

Let us consider how it will operate on Great Britain. Tired with the war and disappointed in all her attempts to separate us from France, there is reason to think there are serious thoughts of peace, but flushed with her late success and flattered with the hopes of rising dissentions & jealousies between us & the other belligerent, will she not be encouraged to prosecute the war with new vigour & try by redoubled efforts to reduce us to her power?

But it is said our dignity is stained, and that we must revoke the instructions in order to wipe off that stain and restore its lustre. But will this do? Will it repair our loss of dignity in the eyes of the nations of Europe to convince them we are a people unstable in our councils & measures, governed wholly by circumstances, *abject & profuse* of promises when in distress and difficulties, but who veer about on a change of circumstances & on whose promises and professions no reliance can be placed? In a word, continued he, I am persuaded that a change in the instructions will not add to our security. I am persuaded that it will give umbrage to our ally, and by a seeming act of ingratitude or of diffidence awaken her suspicions and jealousies, and abate her zeal in our favour. I am persuaded that the umbrage and jealousy which this measure will excite will be prejudicial to us and will give encouragement to our enemy to prosecute the war. I am persuaded it is now too late to alter, and that withdrawing our confidence will not cure the wound given to our national dignity. For all these reasons I shall be against touching the instructions given. But if any member thinks that anything farther can be done to secure to the United States the several objects claimed by them, I shall have no objections to that, it being well understood that no encroachment is to be made on the instructions given, but they are to remain in their full force. I shall therefore move that the motion before the house be postponed, and if that is carried I shall then move –

That a Com^{tt} be appointed to take into consideration and report to Congress the most advisable means of securing to the United States the several objects claimed by them and not included in their ultimatum for peace of the 15th day of June 1781.

I now move that the consideration of the motion before the house be postponed.

Mr Witherspoon seconded the motion. Said that if he had been agst the instructions at the time they passed, he would now from circumstances be against altering them. But he would remind gentlemen that the passing the instructions of the 15 June 1781, against which exceptions were now taken, was only the least of two evils which Congress were reduced to a choice of. A difference in sentiment had arisen between the Count de Vergennes & Mr Adams respecting the use the latter thought he ought to make of the discretionary powers with wch he was intrusted. This dispute was maintained by Mr Adams with a pertinacity that gave just offence more especially as it must be allowed & Congress were sensible he was wrong. Besides this Mr Adams entered into another dispute with Count de Vergennes on a subject which had no immediate connection with his mission. These disputes had given such offence that Congress were under the necessity either of recalling him or passing the instructions. They chose the latter as the least injurious to their national dignity. He was satisfied at the time & is still satisfied that it did not lessen our security. The Court of France by her treaties with us was bound only to maintain our independence absolute and unlimited as well in matters of government as commerce. These being secured she had a right to judge whether she would continue the war for other objects claimed by us, in the same manner as we had to judge whether we would continue the war on her account for objects not contained in the treaty. Our ministers were not restrained from urging everything they thought proper to obtain what we wished or desired. They could contend to the last and if obliged to submit they could enter their protest. Could they have done more if left quite at liberty? Congress adopted the only thing in their power to secure the rights of all the States. They added more members to Mr Adams and those from different parts of the continent. This removed every suspicion or fear that the interest of one part would be sacrificed to secure that of another. He then touched upon the jealousy which a change in our instructions w^d excite, the opinion that would be formed of our instability & possibly of our ambition. G. B. had taken great pains to impress the Courts in Europe with an opinion that we aim at conquest. France had even imbibed some suspicion of that sort & therefore her former minister had in a free conference with Congress urged the necessity of moderation. He concluded with observing that as the confidence placed in France was a mere compliment and not a giving up any real security, he should be against withdrawing it and should therefor vote for postponing.

Mr Rutledge said it was true France was bound to maintain the independence of the States but he wanted to know what were the States. He did not enter into the war for himself or for those inhabiting the lands on the waters falling into the Atlantic, but for posterity; for those who would hereafter inhabit the country beyond the mountains to the extent formerly claimed by the crown of Great Britain as belonging to these thirteen States. He would continue the war forever rather than be circumscribed in narrower bounds. He should therefore be against postponing.

The question being put passed in the affirmative.

Mr Madison then proposed his resolution and was seconded by Mr Witherspoon.

Mr Rutledge resumed the debate; he was against the motion as explained. It is absolutely to ascertain our boundaries & define our other claims. He understood that the minister of France in a conference with the Com^tt who brought in the instructions of June 1780 had pressed them to fix the claims of the U.S. They ought to have done it; as they did not then do it it ought to be done now. They had no business to suppose we had disputed boundaries. There were other matters that might come on the carpet in a negotiation for peace. We had withdrawn the instructions and powers formerly given respecting a treaty of commerce with G.B.; we should say something on that matter.

He therefore would propose to postpone the present motion & if that was carried he would move –

That a Com^tt be appointed to revise the instructions to the ministers plenipotentiary of the U.S. for negotiating and concluding a treaty of peace with G. B. & to consider & report if any and what instructions should be given them respecting such treaty & for negotiating a treaty of commerce with G. B. The motion for postponing being seconded by Mr Dyer.[3]

Mr Witherspoon seemed to admit that the minister had desired the Com^{tt} to fix their boundaries; that it could not be done so as to make it an ultimatum to the satisfaction to all the States. He observed that the happiness of the people on this side of the Alleghany Mountains was a sufficient object to induce them to enter into the war; that some of the States had their boundaries fixed and determined; that the State he had the honor to represent was one of them; that it had not entered into the war nor would it he believed be willing to continue it for the sake of boundless claims of wild uncultivated country; more especially as it was a matter of dispute & will undoubtedly occasion much contention among the States to whom that country if ceded will of right belong that what relates to a treaty of commerce will come within the objects of the present motion; he is therefore against postponing it.

Mr Jackson[4] wished to have an exposition of our rights made out and laid before the King of France, & that he should be informed nothing less will satisfy the people of this Country.

Mr Telfair. For his part he thinks it no matter who gives up our rights if they must be given up, whether the King of France or our ministers; he is for fixing our boundaries to the Mississippi. As to our claims beyond that to the South Sea he would leave them to discretion. Something more was said but rather in the way of conversation.

The question for postponing being passed in the negative. On the question for agreeing to Mr Madison's motion, the yeas and nays being required by Mr. Telfair –

. . . . .

The Com^{tt} was appointed consisting of Mr Madison, Mr Rutledge, Mr Witherspoon, Mr Jackson and Mr Duane.[5]

Smith, Letters of Delegates, v. 19, pp. 40-47.

[1] Root, Jesse (1736-1822). Connecticut jurist and political figure. Continental Army officer. Member, Continental Congress, 1778-1782. State's attorney, 1785-1789. Judge, state superior court, 1789-1796; chief justice, 1796-1807.

[2] Williamson, Hugh (1735-1819). Physician, scientist, North Carolina merchant and political figure. Obtained the Hutchinson-Oliver letters from Massachusetts which Benjamin Franklin made public. Member, Continental Congress, 1782-1785, 1788. Member, Constitutional Convention, 1787. Member, U.S. House of Representatives, 1790-1793.

[3] Dyer, Eliphalet (1721-1807). Connecticut jurist and political figure. Prominent in the affairs of the Susquehanna Company, 1753-1783. Member, Connecticut general assembly, 1756-1784. Member, Continental Congress, 1774-1779, 1782-1783. Judge of superior court, 1766-1793; chief justice, 1789-1793.

[4] Jackson, Jonathan (1743-1810). Massachusetts merchant and political figure. Member, Continental Congress, 1782. U.S. marshal, district of Massachusetts, 1789-1791. Treasurer, Commonwealth of Massachusetts, 1802-1806.

⁵ Duane, James (1733-1797). New York jurist and political figure. Member, Continental Congress, 1774-1783. Mayor of New York City, 1784-1789. U.S. district judge for the district of New York, 1789-1794.

Robert R. Livingston to John Jay

Dear Sir,   [Philadelphia, 8 August 1782]
                                                         Quadruplicate

Your Letter of the 28th April was received by Major Franks, WHEN THE CONTENTS WERE COMMUNICATED TO CONGRESS. THE REPEATED SLIGHTS AND NEGLECTS YOU HAVE EXPERIENCED EXCITED THEIR WARMEST RESENTMENT. SEVERAL MEMBERS[1] feeling that our Obligations to SPAIN WERE EXTREAMLY SMALL; THAT OUR AFFAIRS HERE AND IN EUROPE GAVE US A RIGHT TO THINK AS AN independent People WERE FOR ENTERING INTO RESOLUTIONS which might perhaps have presented a more lively Picture of their own SENSATIONS THAN GOOD POLICY COULD JUSTIFY. After much Deliberation they came to the inclosed Resolution in which they have in some Measure entered into your Sentiments. THEY EXPECTED SOME EQUIVALENT FOR THE CESSIONS THEY HAVE OFFERED. If in this Expectation they are deceived, they see no Reason why they should STAND OPEN AGAINST THEM. THE COMMERCE BETWEEN THIS COUNTRY AND SPAIN IS A VERY important object to AMERICA. THE TRADE THAT AN Industrious PEOPLE CARRY ON WITH THOSE WHO DO NOT manufacture FOR THEMSELVES IS ALWAYS valuable, and perhaps TREATIES OF COMMERCE WITH ANY OTHER NATIONS MAY BE CONSIDERED AS DISADVANTAGEOUS. I could therefore have wished to see his CATHOLIC MAJESTY'S MINISTERS SENTIMENTS ON THAT POINT. From the Conversation you relate in your Letter of the 3d October to have passed between you and the Count de Florida Blanca on that Subject, I am led to think he expected WE WOULD ASK PECULIAR PRIVILEDGES. How far it might be possible to OBTAIN A COMMERCIAL CONNECTION WITH THEIR COLONIES IT IS difficult TO SAY, BUT ANY INTERCOURSE WOULD BY THE INGENUITY OF OUR MERCHANTS BE TURNED TO ADVANTAGE.

What the Sentiments of Congress on the Subject OF THE PROPOSED GUARANTEE OF EACH OTHER'S TERRITORIES IN AMERICA, I know not, but I most heartily wish that we could avoid ENTERING INTO IT WITH SPAIN. IT MAY ONE DAY COMPEL US TO WHAT NEITHER OUR INTEREST OR consciences will justify, nor can it in any SENSE BE CONSIDERED AS EQUAL, SINCE THE GUARANTEE OF SPAIN WILL BE OF LITTLE Moment to us AFTER THE WAR. I need not remind you of the caution that will be necessary on your part to prevent this GUARANTEE FROM EXTENDING TO THEIR

CONQUESTS ON THE MISSISSIPPI.

. . . . .

I have the honour to be with the greatest Respect and Esteem Your Excellency's most obedient and humble Servant

Robt. R. Livingston

. . . . .

Morris, Jay Papers, v. 2, pp. 312-315.

¹ Words in capital letters are encyphered in original document.

Alleyne Fitzherbert to Thomas Townshend

Private   Paris August 8ᵗʰ 1782.

My Dear Sir,

. . . . .

...I have seen here Dʳ Franklin & Mʳ Jay, but nothing remarkable passed in my conversation, excepting only that in the course of it Mʳ Jay dropped an expression which I thought had a tendency towards a cavil against that part of Mʳ Oswald's full Power which relates to the independancy of America, but the expression was a very faint one and I could not succeed in my endeavours to make him explain himself farther. I take it for granted however that in case it shall be agreed upon between Monʳ de Vergennes & the American Plenipotentiaries to cavil against that or any other part of the above mentioned paper, we shall hear of it in sum in a day or two, and in that case Mʳ Oswald will of course dispatch...immediately with a state of their objections. Upon this subject I can not help mentioning to you, my Dear Sir, in the confidence of friendship, that notwithstanding all I have found in my predecessor's letters respecting the unfeigned desire which Dʳ Franklin has expressed of a cordial reconciliation with England, notwithstanding all that Mʳ Oswald has said to me upon the same subject, & notwithstanding the extreme diffidence and unwillingness with which I beg myself to differ in opinion from either of those Gentlemen, but particularly the latter, I am very much inclined to doubt of the American Minister's sincerity in these expressions – as on the one hand I have been assured by an intimate friend of mine here who is in a situation to see & know what is going forward, and who I am certain would not willingly deceive me, that nothing can equal the close connection & unreserved confidence in which Dʳ Franklin lives with Mʳ de Vergennes, ("we own it (my friend said) "that you may be morally certain that the latter was not only <**> informed of, but that he often concerted before hand the Doctor's conversations both with Mʳ Oswald & Mʳ Grenville, and that the same will be the case as to his conversations with you") and as on the other hand we all of us know that the French are too good Politicians, and too well acquainted with the advantages they have drawn from America during this war, not to use their utmost efforts to keep up the same connection with them after the Peace & to exclude us from any sort of share in it. – Every body must allow that there was something extremely disingenuous (not to use a stronger expression) in Dr Franklin's saying, or at least giving to Understand, both to Mr Oswald & Mr Grenville, that though his committ[m]ents were engaged to enter into no peace or truce with G.B. but by ye consent of France, yet that when the independancy of America should be acknowledged by us, they should consider that engagement as an *encumbrance* which they should get rid of as soon as they honourably might; at his holding I say this language, and being at the same time busied in erecting to them two more voluntary *encumbrances* of a like nature by the treaties with Spain & Holland, & that too when he was moreover morally certain that we should consent to acknowledge the independancy of America – now after this instance of duplicity, it seems to me that it is not carrying suspicion to any unwarrantable length to be tempted to suspect that he & the other American commissioner, Mr Jay, have thoughts of prolonging these *engagements of theirs not only with France, but with Spain & Holland, till after the peace*, by which means they will in fact receive to themselves that solid and lasting ~~friendship with~~ England which is so constantly in their mouths; i.e. by imposing upon us dishonourable conditions at present, and, by the dread of so formidable a combination, preventing our ever daring to resent in future any insults either from them or any other of the powers united in alliance. – I do not purpose mentioning this idea in any of my publick letters till I shall have found some better grounds for it than my own opinion, or till the latter shall be corroborated by Mr Oswalds – with regard to whom by the way I can not help observing that he grows daily more & more distrustful of the good faith & good intentions of the American Commissioners. Yesterday in particular he had I understand a violent altercation with Mr Jay, wherein the latter let fall some very indecent expressions of animosity against G. Britain, & though nothing of that sort ever escapes Dr Franklin, it is impossible that living together as they do in the closest intimacy (independantly of their joint commission) their sentiments upon that head can be entirely at variance. – for the rest I think it necessary upon every account, again to request of you my Dr Sir that the whole of the foregoing political dissertation may remain <******>.

. . . . .

...Believe me ever with the truest and most unalterable Respect and Attachment, My Dear Sir, Your most faithful and most devoted Servant
Alleyne Fitz-Herbert

Clements Library: Shelburne Papers, v. 87, no. 1, f. 185-189 (ALS).

Robert R. Livingston to Benjamin Franklin

Nᵒ· 15   Philadelphia, 9ᵗʰ August 1782
Dear Sir

Having written to Mʳ Jay, who I presume is with you, I do not think it necessary to repeat what I have mentioned to him – We have not heard from you Since March, a very long period, considering the interesting events that have taken place between that time & this – many vessels have arrived without bringing us a line from you – I am apprehensive that Mʳ Barclay does not communicate to you the frequent opportunities that offer of writing – I shall write to him upon the Subject – Sir Guy Carleton and Admiral Digby have informed the general that a negotiation for a general peace is now on foot & that the King his master has agreed to yield the independence of America, without making it conditional – I shall enclose a copy of his Letter at large, which refers to another object – the exchange of Prisoners – This great point once yielded, I see nothing that will obstruct your negotiations, except three points of discussion which I have before written to you about – I wish it had been possible to obtain the estimates I mention, as they might have been rendered useful to you upon one of them – But the negligence of the Governors or Legislatures of the several States have rendered all my endeavours hitherto unsuccessful Notwithstanding repeated promises to give this Subject their earliest attention – the restoration of confiscated property has become utterly impossible, & the attempt would throw the Country into the utmost confusion – The Fisheries are too important an object for you to lose sight of, & as to the back lands, I do not conceive that England can Seriously expect to derive any benefit from them that will be equivalent to the Jealousy that the possession of them would awaken & keep alive between her and this Country — ...

I just now learn that Carlton has published his & Digby's Letter to the General the design of this must either be to see whether the people of this Country will catch so eagerly at the proposition for a peace which yields them their independence, as to be careless about the Alliance – or to impress ~~them~~ with an Idea that we are indebted for our freedom to the generosity of Great Britain rather than to the attention of France to our interests in the general treaty – It is not to be doubted that the good sense & the gratitude of this Country will defeat both these objects

I have the honor to be Sir with the highest respect & esteem Your Excellency's Most obedient humble Servant   Robt R Livingston.

.   .   .   .   .

University of Pennsylvania, Van Pelt Library: Special Collections (LS).

John Jay's Draft of a British Declaration of American Independence

Draft proposed by Mr Jay 10th Augt 1782
But now dispensed with as unnecessary

George the Third &c. To Richard Oswald Esqr &c. Greeting. Whereas by a certain Act &c. (here insert enabling Act). And Whereas in pursuance of the true intent and meaning of the said Act, and to remove all doubts and Jealousies which might otherwise retard the Execution of the same. We did on the   Day of   last instruct Sir Guy Carleton &c Our General &c. to make known to the People of the said Colonies in Congress Assembled, Our Royal disposition and intention to recognize the said Colonies as Independent States, and as such to enter with them into such Treaties of Peace, Amity and Commerce as might be honorable and convenient to both Countries. And Whereas further in pursuance of the said Act We did on the   Day of   authorize and Commission you the said Richard Oswald (here insert Commission). Now therefore that an end may be put to the Calamities of War, and Peace Commerce and mutual Intercourse may be the more speedily restored, We do hereby agreeable to Our Royal Word for Ourselves and Our Successors, recognize the said Thirteen Colonies as free and independent States. And it is Our Will and Pleasure that you do forthwith proceed to treat with the Commissioner or Commissioners already appointed or to be appointed for that purpose by the Congress of the said States, (and with him or them only, of and concerning the object of your said Commission, which We do hereby confirm; and that this Declaration be considered by You as a preliminary Article to the proposed Treaty, and be in Substance or on the whole inserted therein or incorporated therewith. And it is Our further Will and Pleasure that on receiving these Letters which we have caused to be made Patent, and Our Great Seal to be herewith affixed You do deliver the same to the said

Commissioner or Commissioners to be by him or them transmitted to the Congress of the United States of America as an Earnest of the Friendship and Good Will which We are disposed to extend to them. –

Witness &c.

Clements Library: Shelburne Papers, v. 70, pp. 174-176 (C).

Comte de Vergennes to Chevalier de la Luzerne

[Translation]

Nᵒ 37. 1ˢᵗ·   Versailles, 12 August 1782

You will have seen, Sir, by my despatches Nᵒˢ 35 and 36 the nature and the state of the negotiations established here by Messrs. Oswald and Grenville. They have been held up for an instant by the unexpected retirement of Mr. Fox, and by the departure of Mr. Grenville: but they have just been taken up again by Mr. Fitz-Herbert; and I think I should make you aware of the present position of things.

You have seen by my preceding despatches, Sir, that, according to him who had been announced to us ministerially, the King of England, authorized by Parliament, was disposed to recognize directly the independence of America, and that this subject would no longer be a conditional clause of peace. We supposed that in order to fulfill this object, the King of England would have a declaratory act adopted by the Parliament of England; and we were confirmed in this opinion by Mr. Grenville's language. But the act in question has never appeared, and we were waiting for it, to no purpose, when we learned of Mr. Fox's retirement. You will have seen in the public papers, Sir, the quarrel that was established between that Secretary of State and Lord Shelburne on the motives that have determined him to withdraw from the council: if we judged by the subsequent facts, we are authorized to think either that Lord Shelburne wanted to abuse Mr. Fox's good faith, or that he varied in the principles that he had manifested in returning to the Ministry. What seems constant is that Mr. Fox frankly and loyally wanted the general peace with the independence of America, and that Lord Shelburne had no other goal than to deceive everyone, and especially to inspire acts of perfidy in the Americans. We know that at the very moment in which it was a question of establishing the negotiation here, that is to say, at the beginning of the month of June last, M. Shelburne ordered M. Carleton to propose peace in America, and to announce the best dispositions of the King of England with regard to independence, on condition that the United States would put down their arms and leave to France the trouble of settling its particular quarrel with Great Britain. Lord Shelburne followed this oblique and conspicuous course, I can say, to the edge of complete dishonesty, while Mr. Grenville negotiated with us on the basis that I transmitted to you in my despatch N$^{o.}$ 35.

The removal of Mr. Fox has necessarily suspended the negotiations; the existing ministry has limited itself to having assured us that the change of ministers would not bring about any change in the principles of the King of England, nor even in the proposals made up until now. We were awaiting the proof and the effects of this declaration when we were warned that a commission was going to be expedited to authorize Mr. Oswald to treat with the plenipotentiaries of Congress, and another to authorize Mr. Fitz-Herbert to take up again the vagaries of the negotiation begun by Mr. Grenville. Mr. Fitz-Herbert in fact presented himself to me on the 4th of this month and produced for me the necessary powers to treat with us, with Spain, and with the United Provinces. As for Mr. Oswald, he has as yet received only an authenticated copy of his commission, the absence of the Chancellor having prevented it from being sealed. The former has delivered to me a signed response to the counterproposal of which I sent you a copy, and this document includes the complete proof of the variation of which Lord Shelburne has been accused; the independence of America is no longer presented as a separate subject in it and as not having any longer to be a condition of peace; on the contrary, it is put forward as having to be the price of peace, and it is asked in consequence that all things be placed on the footing on which they were by virtue of the Treaty of 1763. You will judge for yourself, Sir, that after this thesis, astonishment was shown at the 4 points included in our counterproposal, and that admitting them would be guarded against. However, they have not been entirely rejected; we have been asked for an explanation. Such is the present state of affairs as it concerns us. As for Mr. Oswald, he presented himself to Messrs. Franklin and Jay with his commission; but those two plenipotentiaries deferred from accepting it or rejecting it until they knew our sentiment on the form and on the tenor of that document. Our opinion in this regard is not yet settled, and I think that it will be only after the conference that I will have tomorrow on this subject with the two American pleni-potentiaries: in that case I will inform you of it by a postscript. All I can tell you while waiting is that Mr. Oswald's commission is in the form of letters patent: that it is conceived like all the domestic acts of the English government; but that the Colonies were presented neither as rebels nor as subjects of the British crown. I have, Sir, few reflections to add to the details into which I have just entered; I shall limit myself to observing that it is with the greatest repugnance that the English ministry, especttially Lord

Shelburne, countenances a general peace, and that it will only negotiate seriously and in good faith when it has decidedly lost hope of dividing the allies, and of being able to treat separately with each. The English ministers are very convinced that we, as well as Spain, are unshakeable in the resolution of not countenancing any Schism; and we are persuaded on our side that the United States will not change the principles that they have announced in that regard: but it is presumable that the British Ministry will continue to be under an illusion concerning their perseverance, and that it will not cease to make attempts to mislead Congress or the American people until peace is signed. What you send us of the dispositions of both rids us of every kind of distrust, and our security will be perfect when all the States have imitated the example of those of Maryland, Virginia, and New Jersey. What Congress has done leaves us nothing to desire, and the King charges you with assuring that Body that His Majesty has applauded it very sincerely. But it is not everything, Sir, to show patriotism and fidelity towards the allies; one must still place oneself in position to dominate one's enemies; and that unfortunately is what the Americans do not do, and concerning which, in consequence, you could not preach to them too much.

Before leaving this matter, Sir, I think I should speak to you of the mediators.

While the English ministry was preparing the means to establish a direct negotiation in Paris, the two Imperial courts renewed their entreaties to that of London to engage it in putting their mediation into effect; this step gave rise to a response by which the British ministry, keeping silent on the direct negotiation, declared that it was ready to receive all the peace overtures that would be made to it through the channel of the mediators, and even to admit the Americans and the Dutch to the negotiations. This response is from 29 April; and at that time Mr. Oswald was already in France: the English ministers did not continue less to pursue direct negotiation, and they sent Mr. Grenville powers and letters of credence dated 21 May:

The English ministry did not hide its steps from the two mediating courts; but they presented us as having sought it.

This false accusation, and especially the fear of seeing the mediation evaporate, persuaded the two mediators to communicate to us as well as to Spain the last writing of the court of London, and to exhort us at once to establish the negotiation under their auspices. It was easy for us, Sir, to exculpate ourselves from the unjust and maladroit accusation of the English ministry; and I think that we have done it with success. In regard to the heart of the new office of the mediators, we have made the response of which you will find the copy enclosed: you will see therein that, without refusing the good offices of the two mediating courts, we are resolved to follow the direct negotiation as long as that is agreeable to the Court of London. As for the response of that court, we are still ignorant of it: but it should be little satisfying to the cabinets of Vienna and St. Petersburg, since it has not prevented the sending of Mr. Fitz-Herbert and the commission of Mr. Oswald.

We neither know nor foresee, Sir, what part His Catholic Majesty will take in consequence of our negative responses, what is certain is that our conduct has always been frank, uniform, and consistent, and that we will willingly entrust our interests to the mediators, according to the bases established heretofore, as soon as it pleases the Court of London to break off the direct negotiation that it has called forth, and that it persists in pursuing: the King does not doubt that Congress shares his dispositions in that regard, and His Majesty will not hesitate, if circumstances require it, to give assurance of it to the two mediating Courts.

Vergennes

P.S. The day before yesterday I saw Messrs. Franklin and Jay; we discussed the form and the essence of Mr. Oswald's commission; we have agreed that they will deliver a copy of their full power to that English Commissioner, and that despite his entreaties, they would defer entering into matters with him until he had produced the actual original of his commission....

FFAA: Pol. Corr., U.S., v. 22, f. 16 (LC transcription).

John Adams to John Jay

Dear Sir,   The Hague August 13, 1782.

. . . . .

...It is my duty to be explicit with you, and to tell you Sincerely My sentiments, I think we ought not to treat at all untill, we see a minister authorized to treat with the *United States of America*, or with their ministers. Our country will feel the miserable consequence of a different conduct. If we are betrayed into negociations, in or out of a congress, before this point is settled, if Gold & Diamonds, & every insidious Intrigue & wicked falshood, can induce any Body to embarrass us, and betray us into Truce & bad conditions, we may depend upon having them played off against us. We are and can be no match for them at this Game. We shall have nothing to negociate with but Integrity, perspicuity and Firmness.

There is but one way to negociate with Englishmen that is, clearly & decidedly. Their Fears only govern them – If we entertain an Idea of their Generosity, or Benevolence towards us, we are undone. They hate us, universally from the Throne to the Footstool, and would annihilate us, if in their power, before they would treat with us in any way. We must let them Know, that we are not to be moved from our purpose; or all is undone. – The pride & vanity of that nation is a Disease; it is a Delirium. It has been flattered & enflamed so long by themselves, & by others, that it perverts every thing. – The moment you depart one iota from y[r] character, and the distinct Line of Sovereignty, they interpret it to spring from fear or Love of them, & to a desire to go back.

Fox saw we were aware of this, and calculated his system accordingly. We must finally come to that Idea, and so must G[t] Britain. – The latter will soon come to it; if we don't flinch, if we discover the least weakness or wavering, the Blood and Treasures of our countrymen will Suffer for it in a great Degree.

Firmness, firmness & patience for a few Months, will carry us triumphantly to that point where it is the Interest of our allies, of neutral nations, nay even of our Enemies, that we should arrive: I mean a Sovereignty, universally acknowledged by all the world. Whereas the least oscillation will in my opinion leave us in dispute with the world, & with one another, these fifty years.

With great respect & regard I have the honour to be   J. A.

NA: PCC, *item* 101, v. 2, pp. 274-276 (C); M247, *reel* 127.

Charles Thomson's Notes of Debates

Thursday, August 15th. [1782]

The Com[tt] appointed on the 8th to take into consideration and report the most advisable means of securing to the United States the several objects claimed by them, and not included in their ultimatum for peace of 15 June, 1781, reported as their opinion: "That the Com[tt] to whom was referred the report of a previous Com[tt] relative to the said claims, be instructed to deliver over to the Sec[ry] for Foreign Affairs the materials which they may have collected in support thereof, and that the said Sec[ry] perfect & transmit the same to the Ministers Plen[ry] for negotiating peace, for their information & use; provided that nothing which shall be done by virtue of this resolution shall be construed to affect any dispute which now does, or may hereafter exist between individual States, or between the United States & individual States. That the Min. Plen. for negotiating peace be instructed to communicate to his M. C. M. so much of the facts & observations so transmitted, & in such form as they shall judge fit, representing to his M[r] that Congress have caused the same to be compiled & laid before him, under a persuasion that he will find therein such clear proofs, both of the validity and importance of all their claims, as will silence any pretensions by which they may be opposed. This representation of the grounds of the said claims was rendered the more essential on the part of Congress by the extreme solicitude of their Constituents, with regard to those objects, and by the ardent desire of Congress, not only that this just solicitude should be eventually satisfied, but that it may be found that every useful precaution had been taken to that end; that the favourable circumstances under which a negotiation is likely to be carried on, afford additional confidence that the issue will not disappoint the expectations of the U. S., nor the zeal with which his Ma[jest]y has assured them he shall support their interests; but, on the contrary, that the magnanimity and wisdom which led his Ma[jest]y into the war in their behalf, and which have marked his conduct through the course of it, will appear with fresh lustre in the act by which it is to be terminated, and that the alliance and amity which have been cemented by the mingled blood of the two nations, will derive still further stability from the final attainment of the just demands of both of them."

. . . . .

Mʳ Madison said it was the design of the Comᵗᵗ that Congress should give no opinion or judgment in the matter. That the papers should go to our Ministers merely as information, not as instructions; that this would not be the case if Congress decided thereon, or even if the Secretary for Foreign Affairs laid before Congress what he proposed to transmit. For by the instruction of the office for foreign affairs papers going in that way from the Secʳʸ for Foreign Affairs to our Ministers abroad were to be considered as acts of Congress & binding on the ministers, whereas the letters and papers from him to them which were not submitted to the view or consideration of Congress were only to be regarded as mere private opinion and information, by which the conduct of the Ministers would be influenced no farther than their judgement directed.

Smith, Letters of Delegates, *v. 19, pp. 68-69.*

Richard Oswald to Thomas Townshend

Sir   Paris 17ᵗʰ August 1782.
    Referring to my Letters of the 5ᵗʰ to 6ᵗʰ...I am now to acknowledge the honour of your Letter of the 10ᵗʰ by Gurnell,[1] together with my

Commission under the Great Seal. Which I have Shewen to the American Commissioners, & they are entirely satisfied therewith.

. . . . .

By the Packet of this date, you'l please to observe that the American Business is now brought to that point that Independence must be absolutely & unconditionally granted otherways all farther Corespondence with the Commissioners must cease, as well as Mʳˑ Fitz Herberts Negotiation in the foreign Treaties. I was so well convinced of that being the event of a delay & the disagreeable Consequences thereof, that I have promised to the Commissioners that I would dispatch this Courier Express on that Subject, with my Opinion of the necessity of complying with their Demand, having given them at Same time such Assurance as I can venture upon that they will not meet with either delay or refusal.

By the third page of the packet of this date, you will please to observe that the Commissioners have given up their demand of a Certification of the Grant by a Seperate Deed or Patent under the Great Seal, & will be satisfied with its being included in the Treaty, & standing as an Article thereof. Only that it must, upon being inserted there, be ratified or declared as absolutely & irrevocably acknowledged, & as not depending upon the event of other or Subsequent Articles. It will be easily settled in that manner, to the satisfaction of those Gentlemen, for which I shall only want your permission to make the Declaration. If the Commissⁿ should desire an Extract of that Article, I can Certify it, & they will be satisfied, as Mʳ Jay assured me. If it is His Majesty's pleasure that the Grant should be made, the sooner I have a return to this the better, there having been of late an anxiety & appearance of diffidence in those Gentlemen as to this matter which I presume to think it would be proper to put an end to, if only to have the chance of proceeding more agreeably & a[d]vantageously through the rest of the Treaty.

When they called together on the 15ᵗʰ I expected they would have left a Copy of their Powers with me as Doctʳ Franklin proposed some days before, but they said nothing of them Which shewed that they are determined not to treat untill their Independence is acknowledged either seperately, or in the preliminary Article of the Treaty. Knowing this was the case I did not ask for their Papers.

. . . . .

I have the honor to be Sir Your most obedient humble Servant

Richard Oswald

R. 21ˢᵗˑ

PRO: FO 27/2, v. 557, f. 495 (LC transcription).
¹ Not further identified.

Alleyne Fitzherbert to Lord Grantham

No 52.   Paris August 17th 1782.
My Lord,[1]

. . . . .

The last time I saw M[r] de Vergennes, which was on Wednesday the 14th he told me that he had been exceedingly busy for several days before, & in particular during three hours that very morning, in preparing, agreeably to what he had mentioned in our former conversations, a circumstantial and specifick state of the terms of peace which this Court would be willing to accede to, and that he hoped to be able to finish it very shortly. On hearing this, as it struck me that it might be of use to learn from him beforehand what the substance of those terms would be, and that he, on his part, might possibly have no objection to communicating them to me in the way of general conversation, I thought it right, without urging him directly to the point, to say what would be sufficient to lead him to such a communication were he otherwise disposed to it, but he declined the subject for the present, giving me however to understand at the same time that he might possibly enter into it with me at a future day, previously to his putting the finishing hand to the paper in question. – should this happen, I hope it is needless for me to assure Your Lordship that I shall be careful, in the whole course of our conference, to confine myself strictly to the letter of the Treaty of Paris, and in case the French Minister deviates from it, (as he probably will in many particulars) to take whatever he shall say or propose merely *ad referendum*.

Having been frustrated in this attempt to procure immediately a correct state of the demands of the French Court, I can only transmit to Your Lordship for the present such particulars concerning them as I have been able to collect from other sources of intelligence, and the general result of which is as follows.

1[o]· In regard to the Newfoundland Fishery, I understand that the French will expect, amongst other concessions, that we shall cede to them the full and entire Sovereignty of that part of the said Island which they have hitherto been permitted to frequent in the fishing season for the purpose of drying their Fish, marking out by a precise boundary the limits of that district, and leaving them the entire and exclusive enjoyment of the Fishery upon the Coasts of it.

2[o]· As to the African Trade, I have not heard anything positive respecting Senegal, but I am very credibly assured that in regard to the Gold Coast, they will insist upon being admitted not only to trade but to erect Forts and other Establishments upon every part of that Shore which is not actually occupied and settled by us.

3ᵒˑ In the East Indies, that they will demand the restitution of Chandernagore with an acknowledgement of their right to fortify that settlement as they shall think fit, and of Pondicherry, with a considerable addition to it's Territory, as also, both in Bengal and the Carnatick, such new arrangements in regard to Trade, as shall put the two nations in that respect upon a footing of the most perfect equality.

4ᵒˑ That France (with a view to the ingratiating herself with the Court of Russia) will include in the list of her demands a requisition to us to subscribe to the doctrines of the Armed Neutrality, admitting them as lasting and fundamental Principles of the Law of Nations.

5ᵒˑ That we shall renounce our right of preventing the erection of any fortifications about the Town & Port of Dunkirk and

6ᵒˑ That in consideration of these cessions and restitutions France shall restore to us all her conquests in the West Indies; – though upon this last head many persons are of opinion that either Dominica, or Grenada, or both, will be attempted to be kept back, at least for the present. To all these articles a concluding one will of course be super-added, importing that though they should be agreed upon by us no treaty can be concluded till we shall likewise have satisfied (besides the demands of America) the demands of Spain and the States General: in regard to the former of which it is well known that she expects the cession of Minorca, and (whatever may be the issue of the impending attack upon that fortress) of Gibraltar likewise, together with a renunciation of our right to cut Log-Wood in the Bay of Honduras; and in regard to Holland, that she looks to the gratuitous restitution of all the settlements which she has lost since the commencement of the War. If this outline of the claims of our enemies be, as I have the greatest reason to believe it is, a tolerably exact one, I fancy I shall run no risque of being deemed too presumptuous, if I venture to pronounce beforehand that they will appear to Your Lordship totally unreasonable and consequently inadmissible; – however whether it will therefore be advisable to reject them in the first instance, or else to wait, in the hope of having them essentially modified hereafter by means of the successful progress of the negotiation with the American Commissioners, is a most important question, the decision of which must depend entirely on the judgement which Your Lordship and the rest of His Majesty's Ministers shall form of this last-mentioned business, as stated in Mʳˑ Oswald's letter of this day to Mʳˑ Secretary Townshend. In the meantime I can only observe in regard to it, that should it appear to you to hold out a reasonable basis for such a hope, it will behove Mʳˑ Oswald and myself to be, on our parts, extremely attentive to two points, the one to omit no means of discovering the sentiments which the American Commissioners entertain respecting the reasonableness of the demands of our enemies; (and which it may perhaps be not very difficult to obtain an intimation of through M^r· Jay whose disposition seems to be in general much more open & unreserved than that of his colleague, D^r· Franklin;) the other, to be particularly careful that the object we have in view be kept an intire secret from the Count de Vergennes; as there can be no sort of doubt but that should he suspect, and be really apprehensive of our making use of the conciliation with America as a means of setting France down, at the end of the war, upon less advantageous ground than that which he has been marking out for her ever since the commencement of it, he will employ all those resources of artifice and intrigue which he is so abundantly possessed of in order to defeat our purpose by breaking off the Negotiation altogether. I mention this the rather as he has displayed of late manifest symptoms of his desire to create new mistrusts and jealousies between Great-Britain and America, amongst which may be mentioned particularly the various cavils and objections which he suggested to Messrs. Franklin & Jay upon the subject of M^r· Oswald's Full Powers, and which the latter will of course have stated at large in his letter to M^r· Townshend one of them more especially (I mean his dissuading the American Commissioners from entering upon business, before the original of the Full Powers should arrive under the pretence that it might possibly be found to vary from it's copy before transmitted) is so injurious to the King's honour, that it is impossible to think of it without feeling the liveliest indignation, however it will be so far useful as it will teach me what idea I am to entertain of the liberality of this Minster's Sentiments, and of the real extent of that candour and frankness which he never fails to assure me I shall find in him in the course of our negotiation.

I have seen a great deal of the Spanish Ambassadour since my arrival here, and have the greatest reason to be satisfied with His personal civilities, but we have had little discourse upon business, excepting in a general way, though he seems to hint that he only defers entering upon it more particularly, till the arrival of his Full-Powers which he says he expects about the end of next Week. With regard to the Dutch Ambassadour I have met with him very rarely, as he goes out but little; however I fancy that if I had had more opportunities of cultivating his acquaintance, scarcely any advantage could have been made of them, as I understand that he has little credit at home and that he is moreover personally at the devotion of this Court. – Perhaps something more and better may be expected from his future colleague, who I am told is a M^r· de Brantzen,)[2] though as he will be named of course by the Faction which now governs the Dutch Republick there is reason to fear that he will be found to be no less decidedly a partisan of the French Interests. In General, whatever may be the result of these overtures towards a peace, I think it right to acquaint Your Lordship that the Ministers of this Court do not relax in the smallest degree the various preparations which will be necessary for another Campaign, – the plan of that Campaign I mentioned to Your Lordship in my last, as far as it relates to the West Indies, and I now understand that they purpose sending out early in December to the East Indies, a squadron of six or seven Sail of the Line, which is to be composed principally out of the Ships of War which are lately come home from the West Indies, and are now refitting with all possible expedition at Brest. I am likewise told that in regard to America, the French are not without hopes of concerting with the Commissioners here a plan for a vigorous attack upon His Majesty's garrisons on that continent, and that the Marquis de la Fayette, who is still at Paris, is detained in order to carry over the said Plan, and assist in the execution of it....

.   .   .   .

I have the honour to be with the greatest Respect, My Lord, Your Lordship's most obedient and most humble Servant

Alleyne Fitz-Herbert.

R. 21ˢᵗ·

PRO: FO 27/3, v. 558, f. 127 (LC transcription).

¹ Grantham, Thomas Robinson, Lord (1738-1786). British diplomat and political figure. Ambassador to Spain, 1771-1779. First commissioner of the board of trade and foreign plantations, 1780-1782. Secretary of state for the foreign department, July 1782-April 1783, under Shelburne.

² Brantsen, Gerard (1734-1809). Dutch peace commissioner, 1782-1784. Subsequently, Dutch ambassador to France.

Richard Oswald to Lord Shelburne

My Lord,   Paris Sunday 18ᵗʰ Augᵗ 1782

I am just now, jointly with Mʳ Fitzherbert, Sending off a Courier on the Subject of this American business, with So great a Volume of writing, that I would be ashamed to touch upon it Seperately, & think it unnecessary; as I make no doubt Your Loᵖ will desire to see some parts of it, which I very much wish for – on different accounts. & amongst others that I may know Your Loᵖˢ Sentiments, & have your directions, & also Corrections where you think necessary. – In these Papers Your Loᵖ will see that that the Amer[n] Commissioners will not move a Step untill the Independance is acknowledged. And all I have been able to gain upon them, is to take it into the body of a Treaty, but there as a preliminary Article to be Signed & Sealed as a ratified Deed, come of the Subsequent Articles, what may. I hope however in that way we may get on provided Orders are Sent me to make the Acknowledgem[t] in the final form as abovementioned. If that is granted the sooner the Order comes the better. Untill the Americans are contented M[r] Fitzherbert cannot proceed. I cannot pretend to advise any thing, & therefor must leave the Issue to Such Conclusions as can be inferred from the Facts in the papers I now send over, which I answer for.

. . . . .

I have the honour to be with Sincere regard and esteem My Lord Your Lo[ps] most obedient humble Servant   Richard Oswald

Clements Library: Shelbourne Papers, v. 71, p. 81 (ALS).

Richard Oswald to Thomas Townshend

Sir.   Paris Sunday 18th Aug[t] 1782.
Before the Courier setts out, I find myself under a necessity of troubling you with this Addition to my Letter of yesterdays date, So as I may have your particular Instructions on the Subject thereof. It relates to the Garrisons of New York, & other Stations, if any are still remaining in our hands within the Districts of the Thirteen States.

The Commissioners here insist on their Independence, and Consequently on a Cession of the whole Territory, And the Misfortune is that their Demand must be complied with in order to avoid the worst Consequences, either respecting them in particular, or the object of general Pacification with the foreign States, as to which nothing can be done untill the American Independence is settled.

Allow me then, Sir, to suppose that you give me permission to declare this Independence, as the first Article of the Treaty, & to Certify the same as so much absolutely finished in the process; & which thereby becomes a ratified Act, let what will happen afterwards in the Subsequent Demands of either side in the course of the Treaty, Which is I believe what the Commiss[rs] will insist on, or will not treat at all.

Our Garrisons, if still remaining, are then at their Mercy, unless saved here by an Exception in the general Cession. Which won't be liked, & would be difficult to settle. Or by a Second Article or Stipulation on the part of the Commiss^{rs} solemnly ratified in the same manner as was that of the preceeding one of Independence.

This I think would be the smoothest way, & which I would fain hope they would agree to. And yet I did not think it prudent to state any Questions to those Commiss^{rs} on the Subject, fearing I should not receive such agreeable Answer as I could wish, untill they are Satisfied that I have authority to settle the point of Independence, & are thereby in humour to take Subordinate things into reasonable consideration.

Now supposing that those Garrisons are left to be taken care of & covered by such reciprocal Article of Engagement on the part of the Commissioners, I would beg the favour to be instructed as to the manner in which that Article ought to be digested, as to Time & Circumstances.

We have at New York, & other Places, a number of brave Troops, whose honour in the mode of Removal must be attended to. There are many Loyalists, whose personal Safety is in danger There are besides no doubt large quantities of Merchandize not disposed of. In the Magazines there must be great Assortments of Government Stores of all sorts. And on the Ramparts great quantities of valueable & costly Artillery, particularly at New York.

It is possible, & I hope it is true, that the Time & Manner of the Evacuation of those places, has been already fixed by Government, & may be accordingly at this time in the train of Execution. If so, the above Questions are unnecessary; and yet I am induced to state them upon observing that by the 5th Article of my Instructions, I am allowed to plead upon the Score of surrendring those Districts of New York, &c^a at the time of Signing the Treaty.

In case of a previous Evacuation of those Garrisons, under a Capitulation with the Congress or Gener^l Washington, the Conditions would be properly Settled in America. Or if ordered without Capitulation, and by way of Surprise, no doubt the most safe & proper Measures have been or will be taken that Circumstances would admit of.

But if in neither of those ways, & that the Evacuation is to proceed in consequence of an Agreement with the Commissioners here, I beg leave to say as beforementioned that it will be proper that I have particular Instructions on the head, both as to Time & Manner. In which case I will do the best I can to get the matter settled on a safe & honourable footing; & so as the American General & People may in this particular be put under the Controul of a Sutiable Concert with the said Commiss^{rs.} In this Case, I suppose it will be a sort of serious Question at this Court as to the Place of Retreat of those Troops.

And upon the whole, supposing that those Evacuations are not to be brought under Consideration at all here; it may however be of Service to me in other parts of the Treaty to be informed as to what has been done, or is intended to be done in this matter, openly or privately by Orders from home; as I should then consider our burthen here so much the lighter, & would in proportion proceed with more freedom & Courage in other Articles.

.   .   .   .   .

I have the honour to be Sir Your most obedient humble Servant
                                                     Richard Oswald

.   .   .   .   .

R. 21ˢᵗ·

PRO: FO 27/2, v. 557, f. 541 (LC transcription).

Richard Oswald to Thomas Townshend

Sir   Paris, Wednesday, 21ˣ August 1782

.   .   .   .   .

...I have the pleasure to think that this Court are inclined to put their business forward, from what Mʳ Fitzherbert told me last night of his Conference yesterday with Monsieur de Vergennes; in which there was a pretty full discussion of the material point of the Newfoundland Fishery; & which proceeded in a temper of good humour, & an appearance of Moderation, respecting the first Sketch of the Conditions.

As before observed, I beg leave, Sir, to say, that this looks as if they do not incline to put off the time in the Settlement of their affairs, once the great Line of American Independence is fairly drawn.

For it is to be observed that on the day before I received the Unsealed Copy of my Commission, Doctʳ· Frankling being at Versailles, Monsieur de Vergennes askt him if any such Commission was arrived, & upon the Doctʳ telling him there was none, the Minister replied, Then they could do nothing with Mʳ Fitzherbert, since both Treaties must go together hand in hand. And next day, the Copy having arrived, & being delivered by me to the Doctor, & by him carried to Versailles, Monsieur de Vergennes told him it would not do & that it would be proper to wait untill a real Commission was Sent.

At last the said Commission being come to hand, & nottice thereof being given by me to the Commissioners on Thursday the 15ᵗʰ, & having also on Saturday satisfied them, in the manner as advised in my Letters, that I actually had Powers in my Instructions, to declare their Independence, & if the same was Confirmed, was determined to do it. It may be supposed that Information thereof was immediately Communicated at Versailles.

In consequence of which, Monsieur de Vergennes having on Monday the 19th, desired a Conference with Mr Fitzherbert for yesterday; & the same having passed in the way abovementioned, I think may be considered, as far as appearances can go, as a happy omen that this Court is not inclined to delay a Settlement of the conditions of Peace in relation to their own affairs. Even although it has been said that they had an eye to the Operations of another Campaign, as also, that in case there had been any farther hesitation about the American Independence, which it was thought they were Still suspicious of, they were determined to begin a new game in N. America this ensuing Winter; & possibly for that purpose, kept the Marquis de Fayette here, waiting the event of a final determination on that head.

.   .   .   .   .

I have the honour to be Sir Your most obedient humble Servant
R. 25   Richard Oswald

PRO: FO 27/2, v. 557, f. 545 (LC transcription).

Richard Oswald to Lord Shelburne

My Lord   Paris 21ˢᵗ August 1782
Before this comes to hand, your LoP· will probably have received my Letter of the 18th, advising that I was obliged to inform the American Commissioners that I had orders to declare their Independence, upon finding that, one at least, of them entertained a Suspicion of its not being intended to be granted through the Channel of their Commission; but on the Contrary that Orders had been given to Sir Guy Carleton to open a Treaty in America.

It also appeared to me that while this doubt remained on their mind, although I knew it was without foundation, their Correspondence & mine must cease, or answer no good purpose, & therefore I found it necessary on my own account, to convince them of their Mistake by shewing them that Article of my Instructions. With which they were entirely satisfied. And there is now such Confidence restored between us will remove every Impediment to the progress of the Business I am charged with.

The Intimation of this Grant being actually intended having been Carried to Versailles, has had another good effect, in opening the Treaty between the French Court & Mr· Fitzherbert, which had remained in suspense on account of those Suspicions. But which being removed as above mentioned, M.͏ʳ Fitzherbert was invited to a Conference two days ago, & made a beginning yesterday with Monsieur de Vergennes; of which he writes by this Courier, whom he sends Express for that purpose.

I was happy to find by the Strain of that Conference, as told me last night by M.͏ʳ Fitzherbert, that there is some reason to think the French do not intend to put off the time in coming to a Conclusion; & that the Conditions they will insist on may possibly not be so hard, after Independence is fully settled, as might have been expected.

I have wrote a short Letter to M.͏ʳ Townshend to much the same purpose. I shall be proud to have Your Lo.͏ᵖˢ Commands as occasions offer,

I have the honour to be My Lord Your Lo.͏ᵖˢ most obedient humble Servant   Richard Oswald

PRO: FO 27/2, v. 557, f. 549 (LC transcription).

Comte de Vergennes to Comte de Montmorin

[Translation]

N.͏ᵒ 64   Versailles, 22 August 1782

M Le C.͏ᵗᵉ de montmorin

I see with pleasure, Sir, by letter No. 58 which you have done me the honor of writing me, that M. le Comte de Florida Blanca shares the opinion that I had indicated to you concerning the necessity of engaging direct negotiation with England before the mediators can take it up again.

. . . . .

We demonstrate clearly to M. le Prince de Kaunitz that the Establishment of the direct negotiation is the act of England, that it is England that called it forth and continued it without regard to the repeated mention we made of the mediation and of the Respect due to the powers that offered it; nothing made an impression on M. le Chancellor of the Court. He is even compelled to acknowledge that the British Court is late in responding to the mediators' most recent office, despite which it is our fault if the mediation does not have its full activity. To listen to him, it would be better to keep fighting the War forever than to make peace without the Intervention of the mediators. All these reasons being excellent to convince us of the necessity of our doing without it, I have taken the King's orders to open the Conferences with the English plenipotentiary. I would have wished to wait for the response of the Spanish Court before resorting to this step. Circumstances made it my duty to forestall it; I did so only for a few hours, and I have the satisfaction of not being mistaken in the opinion that I had conceived that it would be affirmative.

It was on the morning of the day before yesterday that I saw Mr. Fitz Herbert. I opened the meeting by telling him that although I was not yet in a position formally to treat with him, the full powers of the Court of Spain and of Holland not having yet arrived, I had thought nevertheless that we could begin in a consultative manner and commence to prepare the grounds. I warned him that we would treat in this first conference only of the fishing of Newfoundland. I will not give you the details of a conversation that was longer than it was substantial. After an appropriate Exposition of the State of affairs, I asked, 1st, either that we be reestablished in our fishing and drying rights on the Coasts of Newfoundland which were assigned to us by the Peace of Utrecht, or that if the totality of the same Coasts could not be returned to us, we be furnished the Equivalent of them, and that this Equivalent be calculated not only on the basis of the Extent of the ground, but also on the basis of the value of the fishing that we had given up. 2nd, that the fishing in the places that would be assigned to us be exclusively for the French without the English being able to interfere there for whatever reason there may be. 3rd, the cession of some island outside of the Gulf of St. Lawrence but within range of Newfoundland, which the King would possess in full Sovereignty with the right to fortify it as he sees fit.

These proposals did not appear to alarm him; in fact, they are not of an alarming nature, for they do not include anything, if the will of the English ministers is for peace and for a solid and lasting peace that reconciles their Convenience as much as ours. Their sovereignty over the island is not impaired, and some Cessions of greater or lesser extent to dry fish on the Shores of Newfoundland should seem very immaterial to them; they keep those that are most full of fish, and where consequently the fishing is more abundant and easier. They have, besides the Gulf of St. Lawrence, the islands that it includes and the Coasts of Acadia, where the fishing is good. There is assuredly enough to place and to occupy all their fishermen usefully, of whatever number they be. To wish that they also share the more sterile Coasts that will be given up to us would be to give rise to quarrels between the two nations and to revive the distrusts that one desires to extinguish. As for the Sovereignty of the islands of St. Pierre and Miquelon, or of any other island more to our Convenience that we may be ceded, if any such exists, it cannot inconvenience England in any manner, because it is not possible that at any time we would make it an entrepot menacing to their possessions.

Mr. Fitz Herbert took note of these subjects in order to report on them to his Court. The return of his Courier and the tone of the discussion that will be prescribed to him will enlighten us on the Confidence that we should place in the dispositions that the English ministry announces for the general peacemaking.

You will observe, Sir, that I have modelled myself a little on the nature of the points of view proper to bring about the reconciliation that I addressed to you with my letter No. 60. I am not taking up again here that subject, which should sleep until the arrival of your response, which I hope will not be delayed in Regard to the importance of the subject. While waiting, M. le Comte de Grasse has written in compliance with what I had the honor of sending to you by my letter of the 18th of this month. I have delivered his to Mr. Fitz Herbert, who sent it by the Courier whom he had to dispatch yesterday to his Court.

I have not been in a Position, Sir, to discuss with Mr. Fitz Herbert what concerns the Americans. He is not charged with that task, which is reserved for Mr. Oswald. The latter has received the power that had been promised him; the American plenipotentiaries have made observations thereon and have shown some difficulty in accepting it, because although nothing qualifies the dependence of the provinces that compose the United States of America and that are designated under the name of plantations and colonies, nothing also states their independence, of which they would explicity like to have recognition. That is called putting the effect before the cause. This is the observation that I made to Messrs. Franklin and Jay; Mr. Oswald was not advised of it, he confided to them on the contrary that he was permitted by his instructions to give them a declaration of it in writing if it was required, but as the same instructions obliged him not to sign any act without having previously communicated the draft of it, he dispatched a Courier to his Court to obtain the power that he lacks; if the English ministry countenances giving the declaration that regards the United States and wants to treat with them on the basis of Independence, it will be necessary to believe that it sincerely wants peace. There is reason to think, Sir, that neither Lord Shelburne nor any of his Colleagues any longer hope to engage America in a defection from our alliance; the resolutions of Congress, that of several provinces, are so formal as not to be lacking in the gratitude and the fidelity which they owe us, and their intentions and the Conduct of their plenipotentiaries seem so loyal that we should, by a sentiment of justice, believe them safe from the seduction of the British ministry and of its agents.

. . . . . .

Vergennes

FFAA: Pol. Corr., Spain, v. 608, f. 151 (LC transcription).

Benjamin Vaughan to Lord Shelburne

My Lord,   Paris, August 24, 1782.

. . . . .

On monday last, the 19th the American ministers went to communicate their late conferences with Mr. Oswald, & the news of his having proposed independence to his court, as a measure to be by them adopted. They went as if to say a thing that was to prove acceptable. M. Vergennes however, professed not to understand the good sense of their measures, & thought that independence should be a subject of general treaty. Much conversation passed, but he did not *choose to understand* their reason for the *measure* they had taken. In the course of what had passed M. Vergennes told them that he should send to or see Mr. Fitzherbert (I cannot find which were the exact words) on the Tuesday, which was the 20th. I understand Mr. Fitzherbert did see England [Oswald], by whom I did not write, having no notice of it. The quarter however whence I have this intelligence adds that M. Vergennes seemed to wear the appearance of being not a little embarrassed by the supposed approach of the acknowledgement of independence.

I have also to mention to your lordship, that Mr. Jay said to me one day, when alone in his carriage, "why will not your court cut the cord that ties us to France; and why can they suppose we can be quiet (while the very end of the treaty is independence) till independence is guaranteed." He also suffered me to understand that while on the one hand little was to be got by *bargaining* with America, that much would be done by conceding this one point to her, & that the best way England's making a good bargain with *France* was by making a good agreement with America; (evidently because France could make better terms having America in *her* own interests that [than] when America became in England's interests;) he said if this thing was not guaranteed that was written for, there was end to all confidence; and he would rather the war should go on to his grandson than independence be given up. Much conversation of this sort passed in which he was wholly without reserve. Fearing however the most, I endeavored to state & prepare reasons, that I said *might* induce the English ministry to postpone their declaration, notwithstanding the best intentions and grounds of confidence still subsisting in their favor. But I cannot say that these arguments had entire weight. Such, my Lord, is the specimen of the many things I hear in this place. I am more of a doubting politician than your lordship suspects, but nevertheless I cannot but give weight to evidence, supported by the knowledge both of the *interests* & *temper* of the particular parties, when I find them combined in favor of the same general point.

. . . . .

I have the honor to be My Lord, Your Lordship's faithful & respectful
servt.   Benjan. Vaughan

. . . . .

Henry Laurens to John Adams

Dear Sir.   Nantes 27ᵗʰ· August 1782

. . . . .

...If the British Ministers sit down with, they acknowledge you to be a
State Interested or whom it doth concern & the late Act of Parliment for
enabling the King to make Peace &cᵃ· lame as it is, affords a sanction. But
remember I plead ignorance; And in that Case you may rest tranquil,
regardless of Lord Shelburne's "mind". But I still see it possible, that a
General Peace may be agreed upon, by a Treaty or Treaties, which shall
terminate the War, Independence tacitly or formally assured to the United
States France & America at Liberty to lay down their Arms & you
Gentlemen Commissioners not called upon to sit down about the business
except by the Court of France for your formal consent. This I know was not
the meaning of our Ally in 1778. and I have already said, tis inconsistent
with the honor & the Interest of the Court of France to subject the United
States to such an affront, wherefore I am not apprehensive on that score,
there is nevertheless a possibility. If the formal Consent is refused, what
then? I have given the answer. Congress in that Year or the next bound
themselves by a declaratory & explanatory ~~clause~~ Resolve, which only
proves that on their side there were doubts, our Ally was pleased by that
Act But I know of no mutual obligation. Be this as it may, unless Great
Britain has a deep design, first to make a general Peace, submiting to the
Letter of our 8ᵗʰ· Article, then to pick a quarrel with us & renew hostilities,
she must come to us, in the general Treaty, or seperately, but hand in hand
with the other – France will look at this with a jealo[u]s Eye, & we have
enough in reserve, but the United States should be on their guard & not
too suddenly, "*lay down their Arms.*" I have spoken of possibilities, of what
may happen, founded on a certain ground of suspicion that the King of
Great Britain Aims at effecting a general Peace, without a direct
participation by his revolted subjects. Thence the apparent ambiguity of the
words you have quoted; I have said, the Court of France will not, or will

not suddenly, gratify his humor, there is another Court to whom we are not yet known as an Independent Nation; You will receive light from the first serios Convention. I repeat that I would not so freely Commit myself to every Man.

"Don't you wish yourself one of the Peace Makers"? I have long since given a possitive answer, & have only to add, the business is in very good hands, Three, especialy at this time, is a more convenient & safe number than four, the fourth might prove an incumbrance But could add no weight of abilities. Proceed quietly, do not be embarrassed by appearances, make a good Peace & you shall partake of the blessing you have pronounced.

God bless you & give you success.   Henry Laurens.

MHS: The Adams Papers, microfilm reel 357 (ALS).

John Jay to John Adams

Dʳ· Sir   Paris 1 Septʳ 1782

I am this Moment informed of a safe opportunity of conveying you a Letter, and as such another may not soon offer, I must not omit it.

my opinion coincides with yours as to the Impropriety of treating with our Enemies on any other than an equal footing. We have told Mʳ Oswald so, & he has sent an Express to London to communicate it, and to require further Instructions. He has not yet recᵈ an answer. herewith enclosed is a Copy of his Commission. Mʳ Vaughan has no public Character. Mʳ Fitzherbert is employed to talk about Preliminaries with this Court. Nothing I think will be done until the Return of Mʳ Oswalds Express – We shall then be enabled to form some Judgment of the british Ministry's real Intentions.

Adieu. I have only time to add that I am with great Esteem Sir your most obᵗ Servᵗ   John Jay

MHS: The Adams Papers, microfilm reel 358 (ALS).

Thomas Townshend to Richard Oswald

Sir   Whitehall 1ˢᵗ Sepʳ· 1782.

I have received and laid before the King your Letters of the 17ᵗʰ· 18ᵗʰ & 21ᵏ inst together with the three Packets of Papers containing conversations with Doctor Franklin and Mʳ Jay and your Observations thereupon enclosed in your Letter of the 17ᵗʰ And I am commanded to signify to you His Majesty's approbation of your conduct in communicating to the American Commissioners the 4ᵗʰ· Article of your Instructions, which could not but convince them, that the Negotiations for Peace, and the Cession of Independence to the Thirteen United Colonies, were intended to be carried on and concluded with the Commissioners in Europe. Those Gentlemen having expressed their Satisfaction concerning that Article it is hoped they will not entertain a doubt of His Majesty's determination to exercise, in the fullest extent, the Powers with which the Act of Parliament hath invested Him; by granting to America full, compleat and unconditional Independence in the most explicit manner as an Article of Treaty. But you are at the same time to represent to them, if necessary that the King is not enabled by that Act to cede Independence unconnected with a Truce or Treaty of Peace and that therefore the Cession of Independence cannot stand as a single, separate Article to be ratified by itself, but may be (and His Majesty is willing shall be) the first Article of the Treaty, unconditionally of any compensation or Equivalent to be thereafter required in the said Treaty. You will observe that the very Article of your Instructions referred to, is conformable to this Idea as it is expressly mentioned to be offered by His Majesty as the price of Peace; and that Independence, declared and ratified absolutely & irrevocably, and not depending upon the Event of concluding an entire Treaty, might in the end prove a Treaty, for the purpose of Independence alone and not for a Peace or Truce; to which objects all the Powers of the Act refer.

· · · · ·

If the American Commissioners are, as His Majesty is, sincerely disposed to a speedy termination of the Calamities of War, it is not to be conceived that they will be inclined to delay, and to embarrass the Negotiation by refusing to accept the Independence as an Article of the Treaty, which by that means may be to them secured finally & completely, so as to leave no possible ground of Jealousy or Suspicion. But in order to give the most unequivocal proof of the Kings earnest wish to remove every impediment, I am commanded to signify to you His Majesty's Disposition to agree to the Plan of Pacification proposed by Doctor Franklin himself, including as it does the great point in question as part of the first Article.

The Articles as specified by Doctor Franklin to you, and recited in your Letter to the Earl of Shelburne of the 10th. July last are as follows vizt.

1st Of the first Class *necessary* to be granted Independence full and complete in every sense to the Thirteen States, and all the Troops to be withdrawn from thence.

2nd A Settlement of the Boundaries of *their* Colonies, and the Loyal Colonies.

3^d A confinement of the Boundaries of Canada, at least to what they were before the last Act of Parliament, you think in 1774 if not to a still more contracted State, on an ancient footing.

4th a Freedom of Fishing on the Banks of Newfoundland, and else where as well for Fish as Whales.

These Articles were stated by you as all that Doctor Franklin thought necessary; and His Majesty trusting that they were suggested with perfect sincerity and good Faith, has authorized you to go to the full extent of them. The 3^d Article, however, must be understood and expressed to be confined to the limits of Canada, as before the Act of 1774. As to the 4th *The liberty of Fishing.* The priviledge of *drying* not being included in Doctor Franklin's demand it is taken for granted that it is not meant to be inserted in the Treaty. His Majesty is also pleased for the Salutary purposes of precluding all future delay and embarrassment of Negotiation, to wave any Stipulation by the Treaty for the undoubted Rights of the Merchants whose Debts accrued before the year 1775, and also for the Claims of the Refugees for compensation for their Loses as Dr. Franklin declares himself unauthorized to conclude upon that Subject, yet His Majesty is well founded it is hoped, in his expectation, that the several Colonies will unite *in an equitable determination of Points* upon which the future Opinion of the World, with respect to their Justice and humanity, will so obviously depend. But, if after having pressed this Plan of Treaty to the utmost, you should find the American Commissioners determined not to proceed unless the Independence be irrevocably acknowledged, without reference to the final Settlement of the rest of the Treaty you are to endeavor to obtain from them a Declaration, that if this point of Independence were settled they would be satisfied as far as relates to America with such farther concessions as are contained in the four Articles as above Stated. You are then but in the very last resort, to inform them, on manifestation of the King's most earnest desire to remove every Impediment to Peace, that His Majesty is willing, without waiting for the other branches of the Negotiation, to recommend to His Parliament to enable him forthwith to acknowledge the Independence of the Thirteen united Colonies, absolutely and irrevocably and not depending upon the Event of any other part of a Treaty.

But upon the whole, it is His Majesty's express Command that you do exert your greatest address to the purpose of prevailing upon the American Commissioners to proceed in the Treaty, and to admit the Article of Independence as a part, or as one only of the other Articles which you are hereby empowered to conclude.

I am Sir &c^a   T Townshend

Clements Library: Shelburne Papers, v. 70, pp. 188-195 (C).

Lord Shelburne to Richard Oswald

Private.   Shelburne House 3 Septr 1782.
Dear Sir,

 .   .   .   .   .

I communicated your Letter of the 18th· to Mr Townshend, thinking it the best way of Suggesting the Caution you recommended in regard to his Office. I had less Difficulty in doing so because if your Suspicion arose from D^r· Franklin's Reference to Sir Guy Carletons Instructions, the fault if it lies any where is probably due to my own misjudgment and to no one's Carelessness whatever.

 .   .   .   .   .

M^r· Vaughan on the other hand brought me a Letter from D^r· Franklin to him which I have still in my Possession; from which the following is a Extract: —

"You speak of a 'propos'd dependant State of America, which you thought Mr Oswald would begin with.'

"As yet I have heard nothing of it. I have all along understood (perhaps I have understood more than was intended) that the Point of Dependance was given up, & that we were to be treated with as a Free People. I am not sure that Mr Oswald has explicitly said so, but I know that Mr Grenville has, & that he was to make that Declaration previous to the Commencement of the Treaty. It is now intimated to me from several Quarters That Lord Shelburne's Plan is to retain Sovereignty for The King, giving us otherwise an independent Parliament, and a Government similar to that of late intended for Ireland. If this be really his Project, our Negotiation for Peace will not go very far; the Thing is impracticable & impossible, being inconsistent with the Faith we have pledg'd, to say nothing of the general Disposition of our People. Upon the whole, I should believe that tho' Lord S. might formerly have entertain'd such an Idea, he had probably dropt it before he sent M^r. Oswald here. Your words above cited do however throw a little Doubt into my Mind, & have with the Intimations of others, made me less free in Communication with his Lordship, whom I much esteem & honour, than I should otherwise have been. I wish therefore you would afford me what you can of *Ecclaircissement*.

"By the return of the Courier, you may much oblige me by communicating what is fairly communicable of the History of M^r. Fox's and Lord J. Cavandish's[1] Resignation with any other Changes made or likely to be made."

Giving full Credit, as I have done throughout this Negotiation to Dr Franklin's Sincerity, I explain'd to M^r. Vaughan how little Foundation there was for such Suspicion, and upon his offering to go to Paris instead of writing for the single Purpose of satisfying D^r. Franklin's mind upon the matter of Fact, I allow'd him to copy in shorthand the particular Passages which I afterwards marked to you, as fit to be communicated for his private Instruction. His Instruction was to return in two Days. He has staid at the earnest Desire of D^r. Franklin. I have had several Letters from him – They contain no Return of Confidence from D^r. Franklin whatever, nor any Account how far his Communication went, but Anecdotes of the Day which I hope were pick'd up rather from the Conversation of D^r. Franklin's Family than his own, as they were more calculated to intimidate than to grace. I have never written to him, as you will perceive by the Terms of a Letter which I now enclose under a flying Seal for your Inspection.

I did not think it necessary to trouble you with these Particulars, as I flatter'd myself they would have explain'd themselves to you in the Course of the Negotiation, having been calculated to remove Distrust, and facilitate every Communication.

In this View however I think it highly material that you should not let Dr Franklin conceive you ignorant of what was never intended to be conceal'd from you....

     •   •   •   •   •

Lord Shelburne

Clements Library: Shelburne Papers, v. 71, pp. 111-121 (C).

[1] *Cavendish, Lord John (1732-1796). British political figure. Member of Parliament, 1754-1790, 1794-1796. A lord of the treasury in Rockingham's first ministry, 1765-1766. Chancellor of the Exchequer, March-July 1782 and April-December 1783. On February 22, 1783, he proposed the resolution censuring the terms of peace that brought about Shelburne's resignation.*

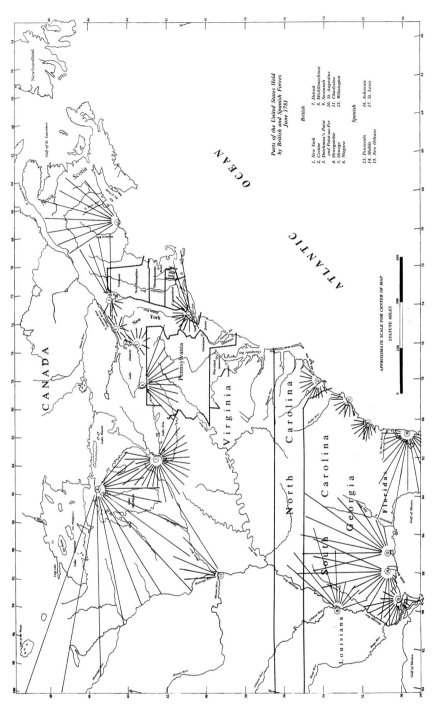

Parts of the United States held by British and Spanish forces, June 1781.

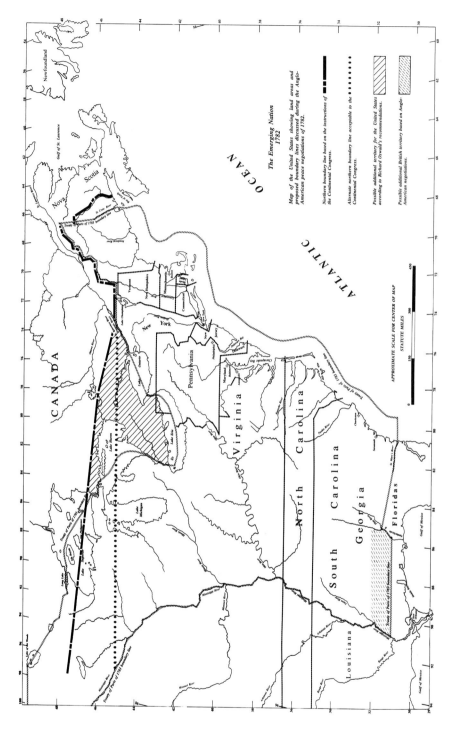

Land areas and proposed boundary lines discussed during the Anglo-American peace negotiations of 1782.

The Emerging Nation
1782

Map of the United States showing land areas and proposed boundary lines discussed during the Anglo-American peace negotiations of 1782.

▬ ▬ ▬ Northern boundary line based on the instructions of the Continental Congress.

● ● ● ● ● Alternate northern boundary line acceptable to the Continental Congress.

▨ Possible additional territory for the United States according to Richard Oswald's recommendations.

▨ Possible additional British territory based on Anglo-American negotiations.

APPROXIMATE SCALE FOR CENTER OF MAP
STATUTE MILES
0   150   300   450

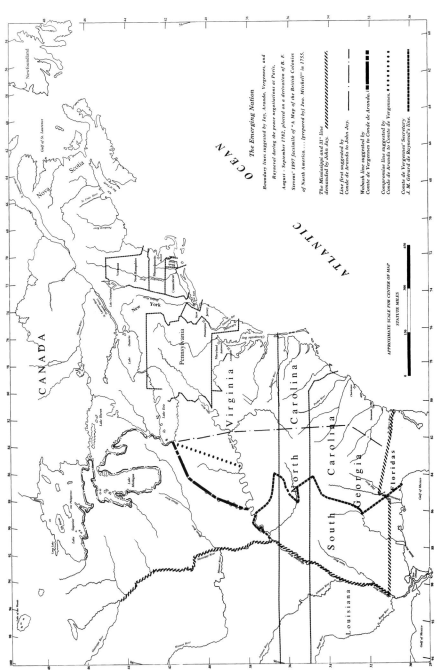

Boundary lines suggested by Jay, Aranda, Vergennes, and Rayneval during the peace negotiations at Paris, August–September, 1782.

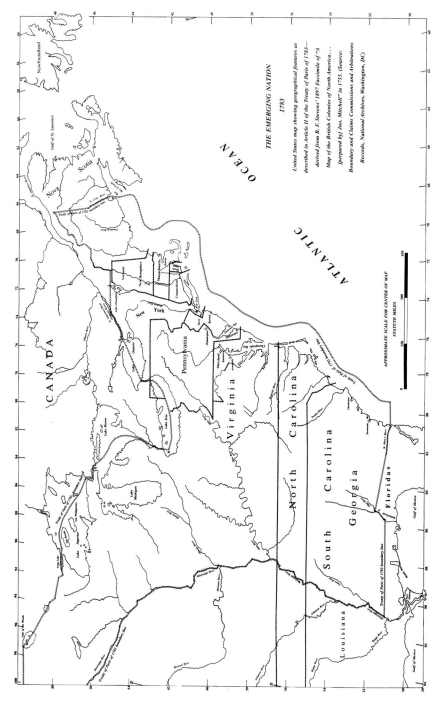

The Emerging Nation, 1783.

Surrender of the Army of Cornwallis designed by Berbier and engraved by Godefroy. Courtesy of the Library of Congress.

John Adams by John Singleton Copley. Courtesy of Harvard University.

Benjamin Franklin by Joseph Siffred Duplessis. Courtesy of Independence
National Historical Park.

John Jay engraved by B.B.E., published by R. Wilkinson, 1783. Courtesy of the Library of Congress.

Charles Gravier, Comte de Vergennes, engraved by Vangelisti. Courtesy of the Library of Congress.

Henry Laurens by John Singleton Copley. Courtesy of the National Portrait Gallery, Smithsonian Institution.

David Hartley, M.P., 1783 by George Romney. Courtesy of Columbia University in the City of New York.

Richard Oswald and Benjamin Franklin Discussing the Treaty of Peace at Paris, drawn by Howard Pyle. Courtesy of the Library of Congress.

The Treaty of Paris by Benjamin West. Courtesy of the Winterthur Museum.

George III by Allan Ramsay. Courtesy of the Colonial Williamsburg Foundation.

Louis XVI by C. C. Bervic. Courtesy of the National Portrait Gallery, Smithsonian Institution.

Chevalier de la Luzerne by Charles Willson Peale. Courtesy of Independence National Historical Park.

Robert R. Livingston by Charles Willson Peale. Courtesy of Independence National Historical Park.

Lord Grantham to Alleyne Fitzherbert

N°. 4.   St. James's 3^{d.} Sepr. 1782.
Sir,

. . . . .

Your Observation upon M. de Vergennes's objecting to the Belligerant Powers treating separately was judicious & wellfounded, for besides the Conveniency of adjusting in that manner a variety of different Claims, from so many quarters, it is further to be said; that Spain has ever set forth the Causes of her War with G. Britain as quite distinct from those which France alledged as the foundation of her Conduct & that Holland can have no pretence to make a common Cause with France, in any respect whatever.

It is exceedingly to be lamented indeed, that the Combination of His Majesty's Enemies, & the Events of War have given any of them an Opportunity of holding high Language & drawing Comparisons between their Situation & ours; I should hope that in the Course of Negotiation, this would not often be urged, & am sure that Your Address will prevent it's being carried too far, as the Object of all Parties in the Work of Reconciliation ought to be the Establishment of a permanent Peace, upon solid & reasonable Grounds. & not to impede it either by ye Mode of treating upon it, or the Terms to be arranged by it.

I observe that M. de Vergennes asked you if you had any particular Instructions on the Subject of the Mediation. I can on this head only instruct you to continue the proper Language, which you have hitherto used, & to employ it so discreetly, and respectfully towards the Mediators, that France shall have no Pretence to make more Mischief than has already been attempted with great Success I doubt at Vienna. For that Court has with Avidity imbibed the Suggestions of France & spares no pains to influence the Empress of Russia, I trust hitherto without much Effect.

The Ministers of the mediating Courts, have, as you know, pressed us by an *Insinuation Verbale* to open a Congress & omit no Opportunity of expressing their Impatience for fresh Assurances of our Adherence to that System. They are anxious especially to know with Certainty, when and at what Period of the Negotiation at Paris, it may be transferred to the Mediation. You will readily judge how impossible it is to give them any precise Answer to such an Expectation, while our principal Business is fairly & plainly to proceed in discovering the Extent of the Pretensions of our Enemies, by a direct Negotiation with them.

I should see with much great Concern, the several Instances of Disingenuousness, which the French Minister has betrayed in treating with you, if I did not at the same time mark the Acuteness with which you do not suffer them to excape you. Further Examples of this will probably break out, chiefly on Points which concern the Interests of France singly; But if you discover any which tend particularly to affect the Concerns of America, you will of course point them out to Mr Oswald in order that a proper Use may be made of them. Indeed I have reason to think that even the Independency of America, however ultimately advantageous to France, would not if accepted now by the Commissioners, be a Measure agreable to her, as the Bond between them would thereby be losened before the Conclusion of a Peace. It will therefore be highly material for you to watch the Impression which such an Offer proposed to them as amply as it can be, will make on Mr Vergennes, & Mr Oswald will undoubtedly endeavour to counteract the Discouragement which that Minister may throw in the way of their accepting it. A Discovery of their Opinion of the French Proposals at such a moment would be highly usefull.

I have heard the Abilities of M. Brantzen much commended; He is represented as an Ambitious Man much attached at present to the Grand Pensionary of Holland, but likely to think & act for himself. Of this you will be the best Judge upon a closer Acquaintance.

. . . .

After what passed between you & M. de Vergennes in your second Conversation with him, in which he said that if he learnt positively from Dr Franklin that he was satisfyed with the full Powers, he would on his part reduce into a Set of specific Demands the four Proposals contained in the Counter proposition of ye 21^t of June, to which he would even add a fifth – I say after that Conversation, there was every Reason to expect that he would fairly have entered upon some Explanation of them all, instead of producing a Single Article to be discussed; And I must add that after making his Progress in the Business, depend upon the American Commissioners, opening their Negotiation, he shifts his Ground exceedin[g]ly in pretending that he cannot go on, till the Spanish and Dutch full Powers shall arrive. This Objection however is surely removed by this time as M Aranda's full powers have doubtless reached him, & M Brantzen will probably have brought his with him from Holland. This Change in M. Vergennes Mode of proceeding is I agree with you, to be accounted for, by his Desire to Secure a Portion of the Coast of Newfoundland, before any American Claims may be set forward; There is no Doubt of great Jealousy between them on that Score of which the enclosed Extract & Copies are an abundant Proof. A Circumstance this, which it is highly necessary for you to be informed of, I therefore send them merely for your own Use & Guidance.

Mr de Vergennes's Conduct is further to be accounted for, from an Intention in him to create Delay himself, but to throw upon us the Blame of it. For He is too enlightened a Minister to suppose that any Decision can be formed upon an Article started in so unconnected a Shape; He must well know that it is unprecedented & feel that it is far from Candid. A Refusal from us to comply with the first single Proposal might afford him a Pretence for not proceeding, & on the other hand, Our Acceptance of it, might engage us into granting the whole Extent of Concession on one Point before others could be at all investigated.

This is too obvious to be dwelt upon.

I have it therefore in Command from the King to instruct you to declare, that His Majesty has no Wish more sincere & more ardent than the Return of Peace upon a fair & permanent footing. That as the Operations & Events of the War have been extended to every quarter of the World, he is ready to enter into any reasonable Adjustment of the Interests of both Kingdoms, wherever they are concerned, & for this purpose, still wishes to know the Terms upon which a Pacification may be expected & to see them proposed with the Candour which the Court of France professes. In order that being apprized of their Extent, he may weigh them all together tho' the Separate Articles must of course be considered & settled separately.

This being the Case, it is impossible to give any precise Answer upon any one Proposition till they are all brought forward together. At the same Time you are authorized to say, that declining in this Stage of the Negotiation to comply with the Expectation entertained on this head, does in no Respect preclude the Arrangement of the respective Relations of G. Britain & France upon the Fisheries, becoming a point of Discussion; whenever it shall come forward accompanied with the Specification of the other Articles, which I must repeat that you are entitled to receive from Mr Vergennes, upon his own Declaration.

I am &^{c} Grantham.

PRO: FO 27/3, v. 558, f. 179 (LC transcription).

Benjamin Franklin to John Jay

Dear Sir,   Passy, Sept. 4, 1782.

Mr. Oswald's courier being returned, with directions to him to make the independence of America the first article in the treaty, I would wait on you, if I could, to discourse on the subject: but as I cannot, I wish to see you here this evening, if not inconvenient to you. With great esteem, I have the honor to be, dear Sir, your most obedient and most humble servant,

B. Franklin

WTF, Franklin Memoirs, v. 4, p. 238.

John Adams to Robert R. Livingston

Sir,   The Hague Septr 6th 1782.

In your Letter of 5th March, You ask "whether this Power has entered into any Treaty with France since the War, and whether any such thing is in Contemplation?" They have made no Treaty, but a Convention concerning Re-captures, which You must have seen in the Papers. The East India Company have concerted Operations with France in the East Indies, and the Prince, by the Resolution of the States, has concerted Operations in these European Seas for this Campaign, and the City of Amsterdam has lately proposed in the States of Holland, to renew the Concert for next Year, and to revive an old Treaty of Commerce with France. In my Letter of the 18th August, I have sent you a Copy of the Instructions to their Ministers for Peace, "not to make Peace, Truce, or Armistice, but with the Simultaneous Concurrence of all the belligerent Powers," among whom the United States of America are certainly one in the Sense and Meaning of their High Mightinesses.

You observe, Sir, "that France is interested with Us, in procuring a public Acknowledgment of our Independence." You desire me to write freely, and my own Disposition inclines me to do so: This is a delicate Subject, and requires to be cautiously handled. Political Jealousy is very different from a suspicious Temper....there is a Party in France that blame the Ministry for putting themselves into the Chains "Fers" of Congress, and for not keeping Us dependent enough upon them. Is it not natural for them to wish to keep Us dependent upon them, that We might be obliged to accept such Terms of Peace, as they should think would do for Us? If the House of Bourbon should be suspected by any neutral Power to grow too fast in Wealth and Force, and be disposed to form a League against it, is it not natural for it to wish, that We may be kept from any Connections with such Powers, and wholly connected with it, so as to be obliged to engage with it in all its Wars. It is impossible for me to prove, that the delay of Spain to acknowledge our Independence has been concerted between the French and Spanish Ministry: but I candidly ask any Man, who has attended to the Circumstances of this War, if he has not seen Cause to suspect it? For my own part I have no doubt of it, and I don't know that We can justly censure it....

Now I avow myself of a totally opposite System, and think it our indispensible Duty, as it is our undoubted Right, to send Ministers to other Courts, and endeavour to extend our Acquaintance, Commerce and political Connections with all the World, and have pursued this System, which I took to be also the Wish of Congress and the Sense of America, with Patience and Perseverance, against all Dangers, Reproaches, Misrepresentations and Oppositions, until, I thank God, he has enabled me to plant the Standard of the United States at the Hague, where it will wave forever. I am now satisfied, and dread nothing. The Connection with Holland is a sure Stay. Connected with Holland and the House of Bourbon, We have nothing to fear. I have entered into this detail, in Answer to your Inquiry, and the only use of it I would wish to make is this – to insist upon seeing with our own Eyes, using our own Judgment, and acting an independent part; and it is of the last Importance We should do it now thus early; otherwise We should find it very difficult to do it hereafter. I hope I have given You my Sentiments, as You desired, with Freedom, and that Freedom I hope will give no offense either in America or France, for certainly none is intended.

.   .   .   .   .

Some Weeks ago, I agreed with the Duke de la Vauguyon to draw up a Project of a Memorial to their High Mightinesses, proposing a triple or quadruple Alliance, according to my Instructions to that purpose. The Duke, in his private Capacity, has declared to me often, that he is of opinion, that it would be adviseable to make this Proposition, as soon as the Treaty of Commerce is signed; but could not give me any ministerial Advice, without consulting the Comte de Vergennes. We agreed, that he should transmit the Project to the Comte. Two days ago the Duke called upon me, and informed me, that he had the Comte's Answer, which was, that he did not think this the time, because it would tend to throw Obscurity upon the Instructions lately given by the States General to M. Brantzen, not to make any Treaty or Armistice, but simultaneously with all the belligerent Powers.

.   .   .   .   .

There is but one Alternative. Either Congress should recall all their Ministers from Europe, and leave all Negotiations to the French Ministry, or they must support their Ministers against all Insinuations. If Congress will see with their own Eyes, I can assure them, without fear of being contradicted, that neither the Colour, Figure or Magnitude of Objects will always appear to them exactly as they do to their Allies. To send Ministers to Europe, who are supposed by the People of America to see for themselves, while in effect they see or pretend to see nothing but what appears thro' the Glass of a French Minister, is to betray the just Expectations of that People.

I have the honor to be, Sir, with the great Consideration and Esteem Your most obedient & most humble Servant   John Adams

NA: PCC, item 84, v. 4, pp. 149-154 (LS); M247, reel 112.

∞ The Rayneval-Shelburne Talks ∞

On August 10, 1782, the Comte de Grasse, the French admiral captured by the British in the Battle of the Saintes that spring, made a courtesy call upon Lord Shelburne, the head of the British Ministry. Within the week, de Grasse returned to France, where he informed French Foreign Minister Vergennes of a conversation he had had with Shelburne regarding peace terms. According to de Grasse, Shelburne was ready to acknowledge the complete independence of the United States, to return certain Caribbean islands to France, to give Spain her choice of Gibraltar or Minorca, and to accede to various other arrangements that would make a very satisfactory settlement from the French point of view.

Vergennes was providing tacit support for Spain's position in the negotiations between John Jay and the Conde d'Aranda, Spain's ambassador to France, regarding the western boundary of the United States. In accordance with his instructions, Jay never wavered from the Mississippi as the western boundary. Joseph-Matthias Gérard de Rayneval, Vergennes' first secretary, was serving as the interpreter in these talks, and had prepared memorandums on territorial claims along the Ohio and the Mississippi during and after the Seven Years War which were used to support various Franco-Spanish proposals that Jay found unacceptable. By early September, Jay was preparing to break off the talks with Aranda because the latter lacked the powers to conclude an agreement.

On September 5, Rayneval informed Jay that he would be away "for some days." After providing Aranda with another memorandum in which he denied any American claims to the area northwest of the Ohio derived from the activities of George Rogers Clark in 1779, Rayneval set out for

London on September 7 to confer with Shelburne. Vergennes had informed certain members of the diplomatic corps of Rayneval's trip, but not the American commissioners. Nevertheless, Jay learned of Rayneval's trip on September 9.

The next day a member of the British peace commission handed Jay a copy of an intercepted despatch which François Barbé de Marbois, the Secretary of the French Legation in the United States, had written to Vergennes on March 13. In it the French diplomat had denounced the New Englanders for insisting on a share of the fisheries off the Grand Bank. The Americans should have been informed at the outset that France would not support such claims, complained Marbois; now the British might support them in an effort to separate France and the United States. The March 13 despatch accurately reflected the French position on the fisheries. Rayneval, when involved in talks with British peace commissioner Alleyne Fitzherbert, had implied to that envoy a willingness to join the British in excluding the Americans from any involvement in the fisheries. Furthermore, Vergennes had instructed the Chevalier de la Luzerne, France's minister to the United States, that he should oppose any American attempt to conquer Canada. Luzerne was to keep France's position a secret, so as not to affect the talks between Jay and Aranda.

Jay's reaction to news of Rayneval's trip and to the Marbois despatch was predictable: he immediately broke off the talks with Aranda. Jay's concern was justified. Rayneval had his first meeting with Shelburne on September 13. Vergennes' instructions were that should Shelburne disavow what de Grasse had told Vergennes, Rayneval was to leave England. Shelburne in fact insisted that the admiral had misunderstood him, but in such a conciliatory manner that Rayneval decided to continue the talks. Although the Rayneval-Shelburne conversations chiefly revolved around peace terms for the European powers, the two did discuss the Anglo-American negotiations. Rayneval told Shelburne that France did not want the Americans to share in the fisheries, and left Shelburne with the impression that France would not support the American position on western boundaries.

Alarmed by what he perceived as French perfidy, Jay determined to safeguard that mainspring of the negotiations, independence. Convinced that Vergennes was also deliberately working to delay British recognition of independence, Jay resolved to send his own messenger to Shelburne to insist upon its unconditional acknowledgement. Without informing either Franklin or Vergennes, he chose British agent Benjamin Vaughan for the mission. British acceptance of the arrangement would be manifested in the wording of a revised commission for Oswald. Vaughan left Paris on September 11. A week later the British Cabinet met to consider the matter, and on September 19 the new commission was sent to Paris. Jay had scored a major diplomatic victory.

British acknowledgement of American independence meant that the United States had achieved one of its two stated war aims. Satisfaction of the other, recognition of the Mississippi as the new country's western boundary, as well as obtaining a share in the Newfoundland fisheries, would require patient negotiations by the American commissioners.

Joseph Matthias Gérard de Rayneval to John Jay

Versailles, 6 September 1782

I am honored Sir, to send you as you wished, my personal ideas concerning the manner of ending your boundary dispute with Spain. I trust that they seem to you worthy of being taken into consideration.

I have reflected, Sir, on what you told me yesterday concerning the lack of powers of the Spanish ambassador. I do not believe that you should use this ground to forgo dealing with this ambassador without offending him and impeding the preliminary steps that you have taken with him. This thought leads me to advise you, Sir, to meet with M. le Comte d'Aranda again, and to make him a proposal on the aforementioned subject; the one which is covered in my memorandum seems the best one to effect a reasonable conciliation, but it is for you to judge if I am mistaken, because you alone have knowledge of the titles on which the United States lays claim to their territories at the expense of the nations whose independence England herself recognized.

. . . . .

RAYNEVAL: SUGGESTION CONCERNING THE MANNER OF DETERMINING AND DISCUSSING BOUNDARIES BETWEEN SPAIN AND THE UNITED STATES FROM THE BANKS OF THE OHIO TOWARDS THE MISSISSIPPI

[Versailles, 6 September 1782]

There is a discussion between Spain and the United States of North America concerning the setting of respective boundaries towards the Ohio and the Mississippi. The Americans argue that their territory extends to the Mississippi, and Spain maintains the contrary.

Obviously the Americans can only borrow from England the right the latter claims to extend as far as the Mississippi. Therefore to determine this right, it is necessary to examine what the court in London has thought and done on this subject.

We know that prior to the Treaty of Paris, France owned Louisiana and Canada and that she considered the Indians living East of the Mississippi as either independent or as under her protection.

This claim has caused no dispute. England has only sought to raise the issue as regards the lands situated towards the source of the Ohio River, in the part where England named the river the Allegheny.

There ensued at this time a discussion about boundaries between the Courts of Versailles and London. But it would be useless to pursue these details; we can merely note that in 1755 England proposed the following boundary:

It started from the point where the River de Boeuf flows into the Ohio at the place called Venango. It extended up that river towards Lake Erie for a distance of twenty leagues, and starting again at Venango. England drew a straight line to the last mountains of Virginia which slope towards the ocean.

As for the Indians living between the aforesaid line and the Mississippi, the English Minister considered them independent.

As a result of these propositions of the London court, almost the whole course of the Ohio belonged to France, and the countries to the west of the mountains were considered as having nothing in common with the colonies.

When peace was negotiated in 1761, France ceded Canada to England. The setting of the boundaries of this colony and those of Louisiana was in question. France claimed that almost the entire Ohio River was part of Louisiana, and the Court of London, to prove that this river belonged to Canada, produced several authentic documents, among others the map that M. de Vaudreuil turned over to the English commander in surrendering Canada. The English Ministry maintained at the same time that part of the Indians living West of the Mississippi were independent, another part under its protection, and that England had purchased a part from the five Iroquois nations. France's troubles cut short the discussion. The Treaty of Paris fixed the Mississippi as a boundary between the possessions of France and those of Great Britain.

Let us look at the dispositions which the Court of London made as a result of the Treaty of Paris:

If she had considered the vast territories east of the Mississippi as part of her original colonies, she would have so stipulated and would have made the dispositions accordingly. Far from doing that, the King of England, in a proclamation of October 1763, made known in a precise and positive manner that these same territories are situated between the Mississippi *and the original English colonies.* Thus it is clearly evident that the English court itself when it was still sovereign over the Thirteen Colonies, did not consider the abovementioned lands as being part of these colonies. Hence, it clearly follows that at the present day they have no right to these lands. To maintain the contrary, it would be necessary to subvert every principle of the laws of nature and nations.

The principles now established are as applicable to Spain as to the United States. This nation cannot extend its territories beyond the bounds of its conquests. She cannot pass beyond the fort of Natchez situated near the 31st degree of latitude. Therefore her rights are limited to this degree of latitude; that which is beyond is either independent or belongs to England. Neither Spain nor the Americans have any claims to it; only the future peace treaty can settle the respective claims.

The consequence of all that has been said is that neither Spain nor the United States has any rights of sovereignty over the Indians in question, and that any such negotiations over this territory would serve no purpose.

But the future could well bring forth new circumstances, and this reflection persuades me that it would be useful for the Courts in Madrid and the United States to reach an eventual agreement.

This agreement could be drawn from the eastern angle of the Gulf of Mexico which separates the two Floridas to Fort Toulouse situated in the country of the Alabamas; thence that it would ascend the river Locushatchee from the mouth of which a right angle should be drawn to the fort or factory Quanessee; from this last place, we would follow the course of the River Euphasee until it joins the Cherokee. We would follow the course of this last river until it meets the Pelisipi, and then follow this to its source, from whence a straight line is to be drawn to the Cumberland River whose course is to be followed until it falls into the Ohio.

The Indians west of the line described should be free, under the protection of Spain; those to the eastward should be free, and under the protection of the United States, or rather, the Americans may make such arrangement with them as they find most convenient. Trade should be free to both parties.

Glancing at the map, we can see that Spain would lose almost the whole course of the Ohio River and that the American establishments on this river would remain untouched, and that even a very extensive space remains to form new towns.

As to the course and navigation of the Mississippi, they would follow with the property, and would belong, therefore, to the nation to which both banks belonged. If, then, by the future peace treaty, Spain keeps western Florida, she alone will be the sole owner of the course of the Mississippi from the 31st degree of latitude to the mouth of this river.

Whatever the fate of that part which is north of this point, the United States cannot claim it, not being master of either bank of this river.

As regards the lands situated northward of the Ohio, there is reason to presume that Spain will lay no claims thereto. Their fate must be decided by the Court of London.

Morris, Jay Papers, v. 2, pp. 329-332.

Comte de Vergennes to Chevalier de la Luzerne

[Translation]

N⁰ 39.   Versailles, 7 September 1782

I have received, Sir, the despatches that you have done me the honor to write me up to N⁰ 252, together with the various documents enclosed therein.

You have seen in a postscript to my last despatch the terms of the two American plenipotentiaries vis-à-vis that of the Court of London; their negotiation has made no progress since that time: Messrs. Franklin and Jay have made some objections concerning the form and the basis of Mr. Oswald's Commission, and the latter awaits the solution thereof: they are not of a nature to cause difficulties, and if the Court of London does not take them into consideration, they may without inconvenience be regarded as null. The American plenipotentiaries ask that the King of England explain himself concerning the article of independence previous to any negotiation, and that he treat with the United States as equal to equal. I would not anticipate from what viewpoint the English ministry will envisage that request: if it accepts it, as Mr. Oswald would have us hope, all will be agreed; if it rejects it, because it does not think it should begin with what it expects to end, I think that the negotiation should nonetheless be begun: one may judge the intentions of the Court of London by its first proposal: if it has independence as its basis, it will go on; in the contrary case it will be broken off. Such are, Sir, the observations that I made to Messrs. Franklin and Jay; I shall renew them if circumstances require, and in that case I shall neglect nothing to have them adopt them; it is necessary, in politics, to know to yield on the form when one has reason to be satisfied with the substance.

The negotiations of Mr. Adams at The Hague have had the most complete success; the draft of the treaty of commerce proposed by that plenipotentiary has been accepted with some minor modifications, and it will soon be signed. Mr. Adams intends to propose to the States General an alliance for the duration of the war according to the instructions of Congress, of which you sent me a copy at the time. That minister has had to consult us concerning this new plan through the channel of M. le Duc de la Vauguyon, and we have had to respond to him that his step would be without purpose, since the States General are determined not to separate their cause from ours, and in consequence from that of the Americans. I am persuaded that Mr. Adams will have respect for this consideration, and that it will determine him to renounce his plan, at least for the present.

· · · · ·

Vergennes

FFAA: Pol. Corr., U.S., v. 22, f. 60 (LC transcription).

Congressional Resolutions

[Philadelphia] September 10th. 1782

On motion of Mr. Madison seconded by Mr. Lee

Resolved That the Secretary for Foreign Affairs be and he is hereby directed to obtain as speedily as possible authentic returns of the Slaves and other property which have been carried off or destroyed in the course of this War by the Enemy and to transmit the same to the Ministers Plenipotentiary for negotiating a Peace.

On the question to agree to this the yeas & nays being required....So it was resolved in the affirmative –

Resolved That in the mean time the Secretary for Foreign Affairs inform the said ministers that many thousands of Slaves and other property to a very great amount have been carried off or destroyed by the Enemy; and that in the opinion of Congress the great loss of property which the Citizens of the United States have sustained by the Enemy will be considered by the several States as an insuperable bar to their making restitution or indemnification to the former Owners of property which has been or may be forfeited to or confiscated by any of the States –.

NA: PCC, item 5, pp. 740-742 (Journal); M247, reel 19.

John Jay to Richard Oswald

[10 September 1782]
D$^{t.}$ of a proposed Letter to Mr Oswald

Sir

It is with Regret that we find ourselves obliged by our Duty to our Country to object to entering with you into negociations for Peace on the plan proposed – one Nation can treat with another Nation only on terms of Equality, and it cannot be expected that we should be the first and only Servants of Congress who would admit Doubts of their Independence.

The Tenor of your Commission affords Matter for a Variety of Objections which your good Sense will save us the Necessity of enumerating. The Journals of Congress present to you unequivocal and uniform Evidence of the Sentiments and Resolutions of Congress on the Subject, and their positive Instructions to us speake the same Language –

The Manner of removing these Obstacles is obvious, and in our Opinion no less consistent with the Dignity than the Interest of G. Britain – If the Parliament meant to enable the King to conclude a Peace with us on Terms of Independence, they necessarily meant to enable him to do it in a Manner compatible with his Dignity, and consequently that he should previously regard us in a point of View that would render it proper for him to negociate with us – What this point of View is, you need not be informed –

. . . . .

As to referring an acknowledgm$^{t.}$ of our Independence to the first article of a Treaty, permit us to remark, that this implies that we are not to be considered in that Light until after the Conclusion of ~~it~~ the Treaty, and our ~~agreeing to it~~ acquiescing, would be to admit the Propriety of our being considered in another Light during that Interval – Had this Circumstance been attended to, we presume that the Court of Great Britain would not have pressed a Measure which certainly is not delicate, and which cannot be reconciled with the rec^d Ideas of national Honor.

You may rest assured Sir of our Disposition to peace on reasonable Terms, and of our Readiness to enter Seriously into Negociations for it, as soon as we shall have an Opportunity of doing it in the only Manner in which it is possible for one Nation to treat with another Vi$^t.$ on an equal footing. Had your Commission been *in the usual form*, we might have proceeded, and as we can percieve no legal or other Objection to this, or some other such like Expedient, it is to be wished that his Majesty will not permit an Obstacle so very unimportant to Great Britain, but so essential & insuperable with Respect to us, to delay the Reestablishm$^{t.}$ of peace, especially as in Case the Business could be but once begun, the Confidence we ~~repose~~ have in your Candor and Integrity would probably render the settling all our Articles, only the Work of a few Hours —

John Jay

Clements Library: Shelburne Papers, v. 71, pp. 91-92 (AD).

John Jay's Proposed Alteration to Richard Oswald's Commission, with Comment by Richard Oswald

. . . . .

10th Sepr. 1782[1]

A Commission (in the usual form) to Richard Oswald Esq· to treat of Peace or Truce with Commissioners or Persons vested with equal Powers by and on the part of the Thirteen United States of America would remove the objection to which his present Commission is liable, and thereby render it proper for the American Commissioners to proceed to treat with him on the Subject of Preliminaries.

11th August. In case the proposed alteration in the commission should be agreed on, I humbly submit whether it will not be proper in the description of the American Parties to be treated with to leave out a great part or all that variety of Denominations of Colonies, Bodies Corporate, Persons &c. as they now stand in the Commission, and to confine the description to just what is necessary as in the Sketch above mentioned, or with such further addition only as may not give Offence to the Commissioners. I have not said any thing to Mr Jay respecting the Words of the abovementioned Memorandum having forgot to do so, but I think the Words or Commissioners would stand properly after or before the Word Persons in the above Minute. —

Clements Library: Shelburne Papers, v. 70, pp. 220-221 (C).
[1] *Sent to Lord Shelburne by Richard Oswald on September 11, 1782.*

John Jay to Conde d'Aranda

Sir.   Paris, 10 September 1782.

Agreable to your Excellency's *Request* I have now the Honor of repeating in writing, that I am not authorized by Congress to make any Cessions of any Countries belonging to the United States, and that I can do nothing more respecting the Line <and Propositions proposed >[1] mentioned by your Excellency than to <request> wait for, and to follow such Instructions as Congress on recieving that Information may think <expedient> proper to give me on the subject.

Permit me nevertheless to remind your Excellency that I have full Power "to confer, treat, agree, and conclude with the Embassador or plenipotentiary of his Catholic Majesty, vested with equal powers; of and concerning a Treaty of Amity and Commerce and of Alliance," on principles of Equality Reciprocity and mutual Advantage.

I can only regret <the Reasons> that my <Propositions> overtures to his Excellency the Count de Florida Blanca, who was ex officio authorized to confer with me on such Subjects, <were never answered> have been fruitless. It would give me Pleasure to see this Business begun, and I cannot omit This opportunity of assuring your Excellency of my wish and Desire to <commence the necessary Conference> enter upon it as soon as your Excellency shall be pleased to inform me that you are authorized and find it convenient to proceed.

I have the Honor to be with great Respect and Esteem Your Excellency's most obedient and most Humble Servant.   John Jay

Morris, Jay Papers, *v. 2, pp. 362-363.*
[1] *Deleted text in original document.*

Richard Oswald to Thomas Townshend

Sir   Paris 10th September 1782

By the Courier...who arrived here on the 3d, I had the honour of your Letter of the 1st Instant. Upon receipt of it, I went out to Doctr Franklin, He askt me whether I had any directions relative to the point upon which the last Courier had been dispatched to England, regarding a previous Declaration of their Independence before a commencement of Treaty. I told him I had got Instructions upon that head, which although they empowered me only to make such Declaration as in the first Article of the Treaty yet I hoped upon a due Consideration of the matter, they would appear to be fully satisfying.

He said, if there was no particular objection, he could wish to have a Copy of that Instruction. I told him it should be sent to him. He was ill at the time; and as he could not come to Town, he gave me a Letter to Mr Jay, desiring him to come out to him in the Evening.

I called on that Gentleman, When, informing him of the manner in which I was authorised to treat, He said they could not proceed unless their Independence was previously so acknowledged, as to be entirely distinct and unconnected with Treaty. In the course of this Conversation, and the day thereafter, a good deal was said of the same nature with what had passed on former occasions relative to this Subject, as advised in my Letters of last Month.

Two days ago, Doct^r Franklin sent to me, desiring a Copy of the Instruction, which I had promised, as above mentioned. I copied out the first part of your Letter of the 1st Instant, leaving out some immaterial words, & sent it inclosed in a Letter from myself. Of both of which papers there is a Duplicate under this cover.

Since then, I have seen Mr Jay frequently, and have used every Argument in my power to get him over his Objections to Treating, without a seperate and absolute acknowledgement of Independence. And for that purpose, I found it necessary, (although unwillingly) yet as of my own private opinion, to tell him, that there might be a doubt whether the Powers in the Act of Parliament, went so far, as to allow of making that Grant, otherwise than as in the course of a Treaty for Peace, which, as you are pleased to observe, was the Sole object of the Act.

I said moreover, That if they persisted in this Demand, there could be nothing done untill the meeting of Parliament, & perhaps for some considerable time thereafter; That certain Articles had been already agreed upon; and if we went on and Settled the Treaty on that footing, with Independence Standing as the First Article of it, we might give opportunity to the foreign Treaties to be going on at the same time; So as, for a Conclusion of General Peace, there might be nothing wanting at the meeting of Parliament, but a Confirmation of the said first Article, incase it should be then thought necessary; which I imagined would not be the case.

In answer to this, Mr Jay said, there could be no judgement formed as to when the foreign Treaties would end: and that untill that with France was concluded, they of the Colonies could not give us either Peace or Truce. Nor could they presume, so much as to give an Opinion of the Demands of France, whatever they might be; Since untill their Independence was acknowledged, absolutely, and unconnected with Treaty, they were as no body; and as no People. And France could tell them so, if they were to pretend to interfere; having failed in acquiring that Character, for which they had jointly contended. And therefor, they must go on with France, untill England gave them satisfaction on the point in question. That to this they were bound by Treaty; which their Constituents were determined honestly and faithfully to fulfill.

That being the case, it could not be expected that they, as Servants, could take it upon them to dispense with the said Acknowledgement.

That by looking over the sundry Resolves of their Congress, I might see that that Assembly did not mean to seek for their Character in an Article of any Treaty. And for that purpose, Mr Jay recommended to me the perusal of sundry parts of their proceedings, as they stood in the Journals of the Congress, which he would mark out for me; And if I would extract, & send them to England, they would serve, at least as an Excuse, for them as Commissioners, in thinking themselves bound to abide by their demand. M^r· Jay accordingly gave me Four Volumes of their Journals, with sundry Passages markt out as above....[Copies from these] are enclosed.

Mr Jay was kind enough also to read to me an Article of their Instructions to the same purpose, and likeways certain paragraphs of two late Letters from his Colleague, M^r· John Adams in Holland, expressly declaring, that they ought not to proceed in a Treaty with England, untill their Independence is acknowledged.

In the course of these Conversations it may be Supposed this Gentleman took frequent Opportunities to refer to the offer by M^r· Grenville, to acknowledge their Independence in the first instance. Which they always considered to be absolute, & unconnected in every shape with the process of a Treaty; and could not conceive the reason why that which we were willing to give them in May, should be refused in August. If it proceeded from there being less Confidence on our side, on this occasion, the Change ought to make them still more cautious than usual on their part. Mr Jay also insisted on that Offer of Mr Grenville, as a proof, that the same thing being denied now, could not proceed from any Supposition of restraint in the Enabling Act.

To avoid being tedious, I forbear repeating a great many more things to the same purpose which passed in those Conversations with M^r· Jay.

D^r· Franklin being so much out of order, I could not think of disturbing him by frequent Visits to Passy, and therefor continued taking proper Opportunities of talking to M^r· Jay; & the more readily that by any Judgem^t that I could form of his real Intentions, I could not possibly doubt of their pointing directly at a Speedy conclusion of the War; & also leaning as favourably to the side of England, as might be consistent with the duties of the Trust he has undertaken.

To convince me that nothing less than this stood in the way of agreeing to my request of accommodating this Difficulty in some shape or other, he told me at last that if Doct^r· Franklin would consent, he was willing, in place of an express & previous Acknowledgement of Independence, to accept of a constructive Denomination of Character, to be introduced in the preamble of the Treaty, by only describing their Constituents as the

Thirteen United States of America. Upon my appearing to listen to this, and to consent to the Substitution, He said, but you have no authority in your Commission to Treat with us under that denomination. For the sundry Descriptions of the Parties to be treated with, as they stand in that Commission, will not bear such application to the Character we are directed to claim & abide by, as to support and authenticate any Act of your Subscription to that purpose, & particularly to the Substitution now proposed. There are such a variety of Denominations in that Commission, that it may be applied to the People you see walking the Streets, as well as to us.

When, in reply, I imputed that Variety to the official stile of such like Papers, M^r· Jay said it might be so, but they must not rest a Question of that Importance, upon any such explanation. And since they were willing to accept of this, in place of an express Declaration of Independence, the least they could expect was, that it should appear to be Warranted by an Explicit Authority in the commission.

I then ask^t, if, instead of States, it would not do to say Provinces; or States or Provinces. M^r· Jay said neither of these would answer.

I then begged the favour of him, to give me in writing some Sketch of the Alteration he would have to be made in the Commission. He readily did so, in a Minute which is inclosed;[1] to be more largely explained, if necessary when the Commission comes to be made out. He also said, that this new Commission must be under the Great Seal, as the other was.

Before I quitted this Subject I tried one other expedient for saving time, & avoiding the necessity of a New Commission; by reading to M^r· Jay the Second Article of my Instructions, which empowers me to treat with them, as commissioned by Constituents of any denomination whatever. And told him that although this Power meant only to apply to Character as assumed by them & not to an admission by me without exception; yet in the present described Character of States, I would not only admit their assuming that Appellation, in the preamble of the Treaty, but I would venture to repeat it, so as it should appear to be an Acknowledgement on my part. In doing so I could not suppose any hazard of objection at home, considering what had passed on a former occasion as abovementioned; together with the said power in my Instructions. But M^r· Jay said they could admit of no Authority but what was explicitly conveyed to me by a Commission in the usual form. And therefor, to put an end to this difficulty, there was an absolute necessity of a new Commission.

He at the same time told me, That to satisfy His Majestys Ministers of the propriety of their conduct, as Persons under trust, he had sketched out a Letter to me, which I might send home if I pleased. He read the scroll of it to me, & promised to write it out fair, & give it me before the departure of a Courier.

So the Affair rested yesterday the 9th When I received a Letter from Doct^r Franklin desiring a Copy of the 4th Article of my Instructions, which I had shewen to Mr Jay, as formerly advised. Inclosed there is a Copy of the Doctor's Letter.

Doubting as to the propriety of giving such things in writing, I thought it best to go out to the Doctor, carrying the Instructions along with me, to see whether a Reading of that Article would satisfy him. But after reading it, as he still expressed a desire of having a Copy, I told him, that although I had no orders to that purpose, yet at any hazard whatsoever, since he desired it, I would not scruple to trust it in his hands. And then sat down & wrote out a Copy & signed it. Which after comparing with the Original, he laid by, saying very kindly, that the only use he proposed to make of it, was, that, in case they took any liberties, for the sake of removing difficulties, not expressly specified in their Instructions, he might have this paper in his hands to shew, in justification of their Confidence. Or some words to that purpose; for I cant exactly quote them. The Doct^r then desired, I would tell Mr Jay that he wished to see him in the Evening. He did go out that night, and again this morning. No doubt with a view of agreeing upon an expedient for removing those Obstacles to their proceeding, as hinted at in the Doctor's Letter to me.

At Noon and since writing the above, Mr Jay called, & told me, that upon farther consultation & consideration of the matter, it was thought adviseable not to press upon His Majestys Ministers those Arguments which he proposed to make use of in the Letter he intended to write me, (& which it was understood I might send home) as considering it somewhat more than indelicate for them to pretend to see more clearly than the Kings Ministers might do, the expediency, if not the necessity, at this critical time, to decide with precision and dispatch, upon every measure that can be reasonably taken, for extricating Great Britain from out of the present embarrassing Situation in which her Affairs must continue to be involved, while there remains any Hesitation in coming to an Agreement with the States of America.

I liked the Scroll of the Letter so much when it was read to me yesterday, that I was Sorry it was witheld, I even pressed to be entrusted with it, in gratification of my own private wish that the Writer of it might receive from good Men, that share of applause that is due to those who wish well to the peace of Mankind in general, and who seem not to be desirous of expunging altogether from their breast the Impressions which had been fixed there by those habits & natural feelings by which Individuals are tied in attachment to particular combinations of Society and Country. But I could not prevail, and was obliged to be contented with a Recommendation to say what I thought proper in my own way.

Finding it so. There remained for me only to ask a Single and final Question of M^r· Jay. Whether in this his last conference with Dr Franklin, this morning (for he was just then come in from him) it was Settled between them, That upon my receiving from His Majesty a new Commission, under the Great Seal, such as the Last, with an Alteration only as beforementioned, of my being empowered to Treat with them as Commissioners of the Thirteen United States of America, naming the said States by their several provincial distinctions, as usual I said Whether in that case, they would be satisfied to go on with the Treaty, and without any other Declaration of Independence, than as standing as an Article of that Treaty. M^r· Jay's answer was, That with this they would be satisfied, and that immediately upon such Commission coming over, they would proceed in the Treaty. And more than that, said, they would not be long about it; and perhaps would not be over hard upon us in the Conditions.

Having stated those Conversations and other Circumstances as they actually passed to the best of my remembrance, it would not become me to go further, by giving any Opinion as to the Measures proper to be taken in consequence thereof. Yet, Sir, I hope you will excuse me, & I think it my duty to say this much, that, by what I have been able to learn of the Sentiments of the American Commissioners, in case the Compromise now proposed (which with great difficulty they have been perswaded to agree to) is refused, there will be an end to all farther Confidence and Communication with them. The Consequences of which I will not presume to touch upon, either as regarding American or Foreign Affairs. On the other hand, if the Expedient of a New Commission is adopted, I beg leave to say that no time ought to be lost in dispatching it.

. . . . .

I have the honour to be Sir Your most obedient & most humble Servant

Richard Oswald.

Rec^d· 14th Sept^r· at half past Two p.m.

PRO: FO 27/2, v. 557, f. 579 (LC transcription).
^{1} See above for copy.

Richard Oswald to Thomas Townshend

Sir   Paris 11th Sepr 1782

Not being certain of an opportunity of another Courier for perhaps some considerable time, I shall take the liberty of putting up in this Packet some Papers relative to a Settlement with the American Commissioners, which

I made for my own Government about a forthnight past. I dont suppose them of any material consequence, as I doubt there will be little room for Us to come and go upon, from any Plan that those Gentlemen may think fit to dictate on that Subject. And by the good disposition they seem to be now in, as you'll observe by my other letter of yesterday's date; I scarcely think it will be adviseable to be over tenacious with them small Affairs. However I beg leave to trouble you with the Papers, so as in case you should think proper to give me Instructions upon any part of them, I may receive the same in good time, supposing a Treaty takes place. I should in particular be glad to be informed as to the limits of the Colony of West Florida and Georgia; and if there was any change by Proclamation, as I have heard it said, in these Southern Provinces so as the West Florida Colony may be carried pretty well up on the Missisippi without interfering with the English Charter of Georgia.

I have the honor to be &c.   Richard Oswald

I have mentioned to Mr Jay a wish that the limits of West Florida could be stretched farther to the Northward, even though it should be at the expence of Georgia. He did not say it would be impossible. He thinks that some time after last Peace there was some change of Boundaries in these Colonies by Proclamation. If so I should be glad to be informed of the particulars. I have only to add that there is another Packet to the same address as this.   R.O.

Minutes regarding the intended Treaty with the Commissioners of the Colonies, and what is required of me by His Majesty's Instructions on that head. 29 Augt 1782.

Indepence I presume must be granted; and confirmed by the same being signed and Sealed as a Preliminary.

If admitted into the Treaty as the first Article thereof, I suppose it will be understood that the same is only for form's sake; and most likely a separate acknowledgement will be demanded, under all the formality of Ratification.

The Treaty being thus begun, and Independence granted, I shall then ask the Commrs whether that is sufficient to satisfy them, so as an end may be put to the War between Great Britain and the Thirteen States of America and shall wait their Answer.

Supposing they make further Demands, and they are the same as proposed by Doctor Franklin on the 10th July last, and divided into two Classes as on that occasion, Necessary or indispenseable, and adviseable.

As to the Class of adviseable Articles I may reply, that however benevolent the object of them may be, as tending to promote a cordial

Reconciliation between the two Countries, yet on various accounts it will be proper to leave those Propositions out of the Treaty altogether; and to Settle such as are of more immediate concern, being those upon which a Restoration of Peace is to depend; and by which a friendly intercourse and Correspondence being renewed between Great Britain and those States; it is to be hoped that in the course thereof each country will soon perceive the advantage of a more firm and intimate connection and will accordingly concert every means that are most likely to answer that purpose. In which it may be expected that Great Britain will not fail on Her part; although no particular Stipulations on that head should be demanded of Her on the present occasion.

In some such manner it may be tried to get over the difficulty of those adviseable Articles; And which is the more to be hoped for, that Dr Franklin did not possitively insist on them, and owned he had not any express directions on that Subject; and proposed them out of a friendly regard to Great Britain.

In that case I shall only have to consider of the other Class, being the Articles said to be necessary or indispensable.

Necessary 1$^{st.}$ Independence. Supposed to be granted as a Preliminary.

Article 2. A Settlement of Boundaries between the Thirteen States, and the King's Colonies of Canada, Nova Scotia, St John's Island, Cape Breton, Newfoundland, East Florida, & West Florida. As to this Article; I beg leave to refer to a Separate Paper, in which there are some Queries on this Subject, on which I would wish to have some Instructions; and they will be the more necessary, as the Commissioners had sent over to London for a complete Set of the best and largest Maps of north America. –

Article 3^d A Cession to the Thirteen States, or to the Congress, of that part of Canada that was added to it by Act of Parliament in the year 1774. said to be necessary and indispensable. –

The Question is, whether the King will consent to it. If not granted, there would be a good deal of difficulty in settling the Boundaries between that Colony and Sundry of the Thirteen States, especially on their Western Frontier, as the said addition sweeps round behind them; and I make no doubt a Refusal would occasion a particular grudge as a deprivation of an extent of valuable Territory the several Provinces had always counted upon as their own, and only waited to be settled, and taken into their respective Governments, according as their Population increased, and encouraged a farther extension Westward.

I shall therefore suppose this Demand will be granted upon certain conditions; or at least that certain conditions will be proposed to be annexed to the Grant: as will hereafter be taken Notice of. –

Article 4$^{th.}$ A Freedom of Fishery on the Banks of Newfoundland and elsewhere: said to be another indispensable Article

This was proposed and read out of the Minute by Doctor Franklin on the 10th July under this general description. I did not then think it proper to ask for an Explanation; nor whether he included a priviledge of drying Fish on the Island of Newfoundland.

As to fishing on the great Bank or any other Bank, I own I did not think it material to ask any Questions; as I supposed the priviledge would not be denied them: or if denied, I doubted whether their Exclusion could be maintained but by continuing in a State of perpetual Quarrel with the People of the New England Governments. An Explanation was still the less necessary, that a Question on the same subject would come under consideration in our Treaty with France. In the determination of this last Point, perhaps it may be no loss to Great Britain that the Americans are (with respect to the fishing part) admitted to an equal Priviledge with the French.

These four Articles were to the best of my remembrance all that were said by the Doctor on the 10th July, as indispensable in a Settlement of any kind. –

The others, and what he called adviseable, and proper to reconcile the Americans to a cordial and friendly correspondence with Great Britain and which indeed he thought were necessary to erase those Impressions of Resentment for past Injuries, which otherwise must remain on the minds of the Inhabitants of those Colonies, for ages to come vizt.

Advisable 1[st.] a Sum of Five or 600,000 £ to be granted by Great Britain as an Indemnification to the Sufferers of the Thirteen States, by the burning and destroying their Towns, Houses & other Property.

Article 2[d.] Some sort of an acknowledgement, in some Public Act of Parliament or otherwise, of our concern for those Misfortunes &c.

Article 3[d.] American Ships and Trade to be on the same footing in England, and Ireland, as Our own Ships and Trade. The like Priviledges in America in favor of English and Irish Ships.

This Proposal (to judge of the expediency of it with regard to Great Britain) would require an Explanation. But I did not in the then situation of things think it proper to ask for any. –

Article 4[th.] A surrendry to the Congress, of every part, or the remainder of Canada after the said Reduction to the limits preceeding 1774 beforementioned, reserving to Great Britain a full Freedom to Fishing and of importing and exporting in general, free of all charge of Impost or other Duties. –

These were the adviseable Articles, which at Opening the Treaty I shall, as I have said, endeavor to persuade the Commissioners to pass over; and to confine their Demands to the others, said to be Necessary and indispensable. Possibly when it comes to a Treaty, there may be some addition to these last mentioned. until then, the above is all that could have been learnt of those Gentlemen's Intentions.

In obedience to my Instructions I shall endeavour to procure the best Terms I can, on the other Points as aforementioned viz.ᵗ·

5ᵗʰ Article of Instructions

The cession of the Town and District of New York. I beg leave to refer to my Letter on that head of 18ᵗʰ· Inst:

6ᵗʰ Article of Instructions

The Enlargement of Persons imprisoned or under Confinement.

Will be demanded.

Payment of Debts due to Subjects of Great Britain before 1775.

In case the Commissioners continued to say as they always have done "that they have no Power" I shall press them to engage to recommend this matter to Congress; and to request their Interposition with the Sundry Provinces in favor of the British Creditors. Doctor Franklin & Mʳ Laurens have always said, that they thought all private Debts bona fide contracted, ought to be paid. At same time I own, I have but a very indifferent Opinion of the Chance of those Creditors. –

7ᵗʰ· Article. A Restoration of the Property of the Loyalists, as it stood before the commencement of Hostilities which had been confiscated or is detained in the hands of the Provinces. or an Equivalent in the way of Indemnification. Will be proposed. And in Case the same answer is made as formerly "That the Commissioners have no authority" they will be requested, as in the former Article, to recommend those claims to Congress, for their Interposition with the Provinces in favour of the sufferers.

A general Amnesty for all Offences committed, or supposed to be committed. Will be requested.

8 Article The offer of resigning to the Sundry Provinces, the ungranted Lands, in lieu of so much of the Estates of the Loyalists and Refugees which had been seized or confiscated.

On this Subject I may venture to set this Concession as so much in Balance against the Restoration of the Property of the Loyalists; as being a distinct Right of the Crown, unconnected in every relative Sense, with what is surrendered under the head of Independence, which includes only Sovereignty, Legislation and Government. And therefore the claim of Property ought to be admitted. Especially as it will be appropriated to the Benefit of the Inhabitants of those Countries.

On the subject of the Canada Lands, which were added to that Colony in 1774. In case His Majesty should consent to resign them to the Congress, there is still more to be said than as above for the unpatented Lands in the several Provinces; since in granting the Sovereignty to

Congress His Majesty may except and specially reserve the Property, to his own Disposal

In April when I first came over Doctor Franklin mentioned this Resignation only as a thing very desireable, for the sake of preventing Disturbances and Quarrels between the Inhabitants, living under different Governments; and proposed, in case the grant was made, that the Lands should be sold and the value applied for Relief of Sufferers on both sides the Question; as expressly specified in a Writing which he put into my hands, with a liberty of perusal when necessary. Since then and particularly in July last he proposed that these back lands of Canada should be given up, and no allowance made out of that Fund, for the Sufferers of either side. But on the contrary, That a Sum of Money should be granted by Great Britain for the Sufferers in the American Cause. I am affraid it will not be possible to bring him back to the Proposition made in April. although I shall try it. Mean time I can plead that by resigning the Sovereignty into the hands of Congress, the purpose for which he wished to have these additional Lands given up (being that of preventing Quarrels amongst the Inhabitants) will not be disappointed since the Congress may settle them in any manner they may think proper, which ever way the value or Price of the Land is disposed of.

As to the 9th & 10th Articles of my Instructions, and the first part of the 6th Article, I am humbly of Opinion it will not be of any Service, but may be attended with Inconvenience to touch upon the Subjects mentioned in them at this Time and Place; and while there is any Treaty in dependance. I even presume to think that the object of the 10th Article would not be attended to on the part of the Americans, or if carried would rather be to the prejudice of Great Britain, than to its advantage. I forbear giving any reasons for saying so, lest I should be troublesome. However if desired I will send them.

Article 12th. According to the temper in which this Negotiation with the Commissioners may proceed, and the prospect of success in its final Termination, a due regard is to be had to what is ordered in this Article; And if it should happen that the Commissioners are so far satisfied, as to what particularly concerns themselves, as to be sensible of the Incumbrance of their foreign Engagements, on account of unreasonable Terms being insisted on by France, I say in that case it may be tried whether they will so far listen to our desire of Peace with America, as to conclude their Treaty on a Separate footing. At same time I must speake my Sentiments freely on this Subject; That this is what I believe will hardly ever come into Question. Since nothing could give any countenance to such a Proposition, but an evident Presumption that the French Minister was under such mistake, as to the importance of the adherence and Support of the

Americans as to insist on Great Britain submitting to Terms which the colony Commissioners did not approve of an Event not likely to happen from any thing I could ever learn of the mode of Communication and Correspondence which subsists between those Parties.

Paris 29th. August 1782.

Boundaries &c. of the Sundry Colonies 29th. August 1782

With respect to the Article of Boundaries between the Thirteen States and His Majesty's Colonies, to settle which the Commissioners have sent to London for Maps.

Canada
If the additions of 1774 are given up, there will be no difficulty; as no doubt the ancient Boundary is well known. –

St John's Island.
There can be no Question about its limits, although I am uncertain whether it is now a separate Government, or a part of Canada or Nova Scotia

Cape Breton.
The same Question. A Possession which ought not to be parted with.

Nova Scotia.
Marches with Massachusets. The Boundaries I suppose, are properly ascertained.

E^{t.} Florida.
Marches with Georgia to the North, and with West Florida to the West.–

W^{t.} Florida
Marches on the East with Georgia, and part of South Carolina; at least it is so said in a French Map now before me, also on the North with South Carolina, and goes beyond the Latitude of 34°. In another Map it goes only to the Latitude of 31° which I doubt is the true Line. –

Newfoundland.
There can be no dispute about it or the Islands adjoining to it.

NB West Florida, though in hands of Spain, I hope it will be recovered. The situation is important, at least may come to be so, on some future occasion. after passing the Sandy land on the edge of the Gulph, the Soil is excellent, and more productive than any part of British America. It appears to be a Square of about 300 Miles each way,[1] and the Mississipi running along one side of it, makes it still the more valuable. The Events of the present times are not encouraging to schemes of planting these American Woods, at the expence of our own Population, either of Britain, or Ireland. Yet while we make account of holding Settlements to the Northward, in less productive and less Hospitable Climates, Our Rights to the possession of that happy Country, I am humbly of Opinion ought not to be slighted or easily parted with. especially as I think its Settlement and population might be quickly completed at a very small Expence to Government, and without the extraction of any of the Inhabitants from Great Britain or Ireland; which in all future times ought to be guarded against, and in this case would require only an order to the Governour not to allow the priviledges of Settlement and even of Residence to any Persons whatever (Seafaring Men only *excepted*) without having his permission by Passports under his own hand, or the hands of his Deputies; and he at the same in his Instructions being forbid to grant such Passports to any Natives of Great Britain or Ireland, who had emigrated from thence later than 1781 or 1782. An encouraging and well regulated Plan of Settlement for the distribution of the Lands, which would not be difficult to adjust, would bring People enough from the other Colonies, and from Europe. Who not being allowed to Scatter themselves to great distances, but on the contrary to proceed in closer order than is common in those Countries, according as the Population encreased, and the goodness of the Land, in the next vicinity, invited an extension, there would soon be formed such a compacted strength of Militia as would bid defiance to any attempts from Spain, as that by which this Colony was lately taken out of Our hands.–

A small Body of regular Troops having charge of the principal Seaport, and with such additional strength of Fortification as might be fit occasionally to receive an aid of Militia would secure the Colony from any such Surprize: And settling an amicable plan of Alliance and Incorporation, with the Indian Nations in the Neighbourhood, We might, in the Field, be equally formidable and safe against any force the Spaniards might venture to Land around our Garrisons. If West Florida is not recovered, East Florida will not be worth the keeping, on account of the Expence of securing it against the Spaniards. Indeed, though it was a more tempting Country than it really is, no Body of any consequence would chuse to settle there, while West Florida remains under the Dominion of Spain.

NB This Paper was wrote about 14 days ago before I had such good hopes of an agreement with the Commissioners of the Colonies.–

I have only for the present to take Notice that I believe the Charter of

Georgia carries it quite on to the Missisippi, in which case it leaves West Florida only as a Slip along shore of the Gulph, and consequently of little Importance. Yet in that Case I would gladly try to get the Commissioners to agree to give it more depth Northwards, although at the expence of Georgia, by some accommodation on account of the back Lands of Canada I should therefore wish to know whether Georgia going so far Westward is ascertained by their original Charter.— or what that Charter really is as to their limits.

I think there was some Proclamation regarding the British Lands of these Colonies since the last Peace. — If so, it might be worth while to have the particulars.

Clements Library: Shelburne Papers, v. 70, pp. 221-239 (C).
   [1] *Margin note reads: I believe a mistake Since it goes only to latitude 31.*

Richard Oswald to Lord Shelburne

My Lord   Paris 11ᵗʰ Sepʳ· 1782

. . . . .

I have wrote Mʳ Townshend by this Courier, that I have now Settled with the American Commissⁿ, that they will not insist on a previous & absolute Acknowledgement of their Independence, provided the Commission for Treating with them shall give them the Denomination of the Thirteen United States of America. And then they will be contented with their Independence Standing only as an Article of Treaty. With great difficulty they have yielded to this mode of Compromise. I hope His Majesty will grant it. If it is refused Mʳ Fitzherbert as well as me, may go home. And in my opinion it will not be an easy matter for any others to take up the same Clue for extricating the Nation out of its difficulties which I think is within our reach. Both the Commissⁿ I really think are well disposed, much better than I expected some time ago. Mʳ· Jay seems to be particularly anxious, that as they have agreed to go even beyond the limits of their Instructions, His Majesty's Ministers may not balk their good Intentions either by refusal or delay. To prevent this he Scrolled out a Letter to be directed to me, Shewing the necessity of our attention and Compliance, with a view to my Sending it home, But upon consulting farther about it, he was advised by his Friend to drop it. & would not give me the Letter. I have mentioned this in my Letter to day to Mʳ Townshend. However I afterwards with much Intreaty I got him to give me the Scroll, upon condition of my making only a ~~particular~~ Such use of it, as it should not appear in any publick way, and So as it Should not be heard of either here or elsewhere, not even by Some of his own Friends. I take the liberty to Send that Paper inclosed. When Mr Townshend Sees it, to which I can have no objection, I dare say he will excuse my not Sending it to him, Since I was not certain but that in Such Case it must be laid for Inspection with other papers in the Course of the Negotiation. It is a clear proof of this Commiss$^{r.}$ being particularly desirous of Smoothing the path of this awkward business. If the proposal abovement^d be agreed to by His Majesty, Which is only treating with them as States instead of Colonies, I should think your Lo^p may have the pleasure of meeting Parliam^t with a Peace in hand. At least there would be a kind of certainty, as far as appearances can be relied on, to have So far Satisfied America, as that she will not only Control but Spur on the other parties. This would calm the Disturbances at home, by disappointing those who may wish to inflame them. I was once afraid that if Mr Grenvilles proposition could not be regranted or repealed that all the Treaties must wait to have the Seal of Parliam^t to that Grant for laying the first foundation of any of the Negotiations. Now all that is required is to say States instead of Colonies, & the whole Machine is put into Motion & will go its course. I will not allow myself to doubt of there being any hesitation on the Subject. The only Inconvenience is that there must necessarily be a New Commission. If that is agreed on, I hope there will not be an hour lost in despatching it.

By what I can understand the French Court, of all things, wish the Colonies may not be Satisfied, but rather that they should go on Treating without any Acknowledgement of Independence, & have actually told them they were Seeking for the effect without the Cause, Since it could only with propriety arise out of the Treaty. And so wishing that they should continue unfixed & unsatisfied untill their affairs & those of their Allies were satisfied, & there might be then no fear of Checks but rather help from the American Quarter – The Marquis de la Fayette is always going about the Comm^m, anxious to know how they are like to proceed On which head one of those Gentlemen has had Sundry Applications & he makes no Scruple to give me these hints –

Monsr de Vergennes who keeps these Agents in motion it is said is to send his Secretary Monsr Gerard etc^a over to London upon some particular Negotiation it's thought in favour of Spain – That Court wishes to have the whole of the Country from W. Florida, of a Certain Width, quite up to Canada so as to have both Banks of the Missisippi clear. & would wish to have such Cession from Eng^d before a Cession to the Colonies takes place. If that Gentleman go's over, there can be no difficulty in amusing him. The Span^{ds} have the French Title & would gladly compleat one to the whole of that District by patches from the English pretensions Which they could not hope for once we have agreed with the Colonies. –

.   .   .   .   .

...I have the honour to be with Sincere regard & esteem My Lord – Your Lo^p most obedient humble Servant.   Richard Oswald

Clements Library: Shelburne Papers, v. 71, pp. 85-89 (ALS).

Benjamin Vaughan to Lord Shelburne

My Lord,   Paris, Septr. 11. 1782.

.   .   .   .   .

...I think it necessary to inform your lordship, that the French court have given out that Mr. Rayneval's journey has for its object the bringing your lordship to some immediate decision; that they are dissatisfied with late transactions at particular coasts, and are determined not to be made *dupes to settle negotiations themselves.* Other objects for this journey are suspected. Some think an underhand bargain is intended to be proposed in favor of Spain, in which Britain is to be made to assist, by ceding some of her rights to Spain: but I cannot think England will hazard a measure which will be followed by the most unhappy circumstances. Others think that a fund of intelligence is meant to be established in London; & particularly that *the disposition of the North American troops* is meant to be an object of enquiry of the first consequence; which I myself think not improbable, as they have not been able to learn the fact here with any precision.

Be these things as they may, I have to suggest to your lordship on the footing of ancient indulgence and present danger, that this is a crisis of the first consequence, and that to procure delay is of the utmost moment in treating with M. Rayneval. If France could have favorable hopes for a moment she would be contented to wait perhaps your lordship's pleasure *in referring your answer to the medium of Mr. Fitzherbert*; but I dread her thinking she has nothing to hope but from war; for in this case M de Vergennes [it is probable] would state conditions impossible to be received in order to break up all negotiations instantly, *before* America can adjust her pretentions. Perhaps your lordship is not yet informed of a private article, which forbids America to *treat* without the consent of France. We all know the public article about the *conclusion* of a treaty, but this relates to the very act of treating.

At the same time, my lord, that I speak of smoothness and delay to France, I must beg permission to suggest the most *instantaneous* dispatch for the parties in America. My Lord, does your lordship consider the critical situation of the commissioners here after the precedents [of which Mr. Jay sends a catalogue by this courier] & the orders, of congress? History, private honor, and even *life*, are perhaps all in question for the consideration of these commissioners upon this occasion. Under this commission I see *they will not act*. But I believe, if your lordship instantly endeavored to procure an *equivocal* commission, which made no specific recital of the act of parliament and called the colonies the "territories" of New Hampshire & so on, and the people here "commissioners on the part of the representatives of the people & inhabitants of the said territories"; and if at the same time that the commission was equivocal, the instructions were definite and explicit for acknowledging these commissioners for acting on the part of the "United States of America"; I say, my lord, I think I have solid grounds for knowing that if this etiquette were thus settled, the formal deed of independence might with pleasure be reserved for the court of England to satisfy its own mind with, in the *course* of the treaty. But America *must have a character*, to use the words of Mr. Adams; & in America the British officers have allowed it.

. . . . .

I have the honor to be, as ever, My Lord, Your Lordship's faithful & respectful servt.   Benjn. Vaughan

. . . . .

APS: Benjamin Vaughan Papers (Transcription).

Comte de Vergennes to Comte de Montmorin

[Translation]

Nᵒ. 70.   Versailles, 14 September 1782

M. Le Cᵗᵉ· de Montmorin

The Courier, Sir, that Mr. Fitzherbert sent to London returned on the 7th of this month. The following day I saw that Emissary, who did not give me great clarifications concerning that which had formed the subject of his despatch. According to what he told me, his Court neither rejects nor accepts our Explications concerning the fishing and the drying on the Island of Newfoundland, but before making up its mind, it would wish to have the whole of our propositions in order to be able to pronounce at one time on what it is possible to agree. This Exigency possibly being a trap, I responded to Mr. Fitzherbert so as to leave him in great uncertainty about what we might do. The path to take in this regard depends in a high degree on what M. de Rayneval's trip to London will produce. He should have arrived during the day on the 9th. His return will clear up for us the dispositions of the English ministry for peace; with this information, it will be easier for us to take a decisive position, be it to continue or to break off a negotiation which for us will become too disadvantageous if it does not bring about the reestablishment of peace.

The Copy of Lord Shelburne's response to M. le Comte de Grasse which I have the honor to enclose, Sir, can be regarded as the Confirmation of the overtures which that general officer told us had been made to him, but it is not explicit enough to assure us that he did not exceed in his report the conditions on which the British Ministry would consent to treat for peace.

Mr. de Brantzen, deputy to the ambassador of Holland in the quality of minister plenipotentiary, has arrived. I saw him yesterday. His Instructions are such as we might desire for the Establishment of a Concert among all the belligerent powers which binds them not to be able to conclude independently from each other. M. le Comte d'Aranda having been authorized to act here, that part of our negotiation will not be difficult to put in order. I would very much wish that the rest would be as easy, but I do not dare to hope for it.

I have the honor to be with a sincere and inviolable attachment, Sir.

Vergennes

FFAA: Pol. Corr., Spain, v. 608, f. 218 (LC transcription).

Robert R. Livingston to Henry Laurens

N° 1   Philadelphia 17th. Septr 1782.
Sir,

Having learned by your Letter to Congress of your enlargement from the long and severe confinement, it becomes my duty to inform you that Congress were pleased to appoint me their Secretary to the United States for the department of foreign Affairs, and to direct that all communications with them from their Ministers should be thro' me – In this view Sir, I have the honor to open this correspondence forwarding the anexed Resolutions by the first of them[1] marked N°. 1 you will learn that they are unwilling to deprive themselves of your Assistance in the great Business of the negotiations for a general peace, which tho' languid at present, cannot fail to be quickened by the first turn of fortune in favor of the Allied Powers, since the King and Ministry of England are evidently trusting to the weak hope that some brilliant stroke will turn the popular tide in favour of the prosecution of the war, should she, as she probably will be disappointed in this, She will be compelled to fly to peace for refuge against impending ruin – The second Resolution needs no comment – We have no intelligence here, but what I have written to some of the Gentlemen in Commission with you, or what may be found in the papers I do myself the honor to transmit you.

. . . . .

I have the honor to be Sir with great Respect your most obedient humble serv^t

Robt R Livingston

Received 18$^{th.}$ Novem.
Answ^d 14$^{th.}$ Decem.

South Carolina Historical Society: Henry Laurens Papers (LS).
[1] *Congressional Resolution of September 17, 1782, instructing American peace commissioners to "punctually attend and assist in the negotiations for peace...."*

John Jay to Robert R. Livingston

Dear Sir,   Paris 18$^{th.}$ September 1782.

I send you herewith enclosed a Copy of a Translation of an important Letter.[1] The Original in French I have not seen, and at present is not accessible to me, though I shall endeavor to get a Copy of it, in Order the better to decide on the Correctness of the Translation. I am not at Liberty to mention the Manner in which this Paper came to my Hands. To me it appears of Importance that it should, for the present, be kept a profound Secret, though I do not see how that is to be done, if communicated to the Congress *at large*, among whom there always have been, and always will be, some unguarded Members. I think, however, as I thought before, that your Commissioners here should be left at Liberty to pursue the Sentiments of their Country, and such of their own as may correspond with those of their Country.

I am persuaded (and you shall know my Reasons for it) that this Court chuses to postpone an Acknowledgment of our Independence by Britain, to the Conclusion of a general Peace, in order to keep us under their Direction until not only their and our Objects are attained, but also until Spain shall be gratified in her Demands to exclude every body from the Gulph, &c. We ought not to let France know that we have such Ideas; while they think us free from Suspicion they will be more open, and we

should make no other use of this Discovery than to put us on our Guard.
Count de Vergennes would have us treat with M^r· Oswald, though his
Commission calls us Colonies and authorizes him to treat with any
Description of Men &c. In my Opinion we can only treat as an
independent Nation, and on an equal Footing. – I am at present engaged
in preparing a State of Objections in a Letter to him, so that I have not
Time to write very particularly to you. The Spanish Embassador presses me
to proceed, but keeps back his Powers. I tell him that an Exchange of
Copies of our Commissions, is a necessary, and usual previous Step – This
Court, as well as Spain, will dispute our Extension to the Mississippi. You
see how necessary Prudence and entire Circumspection will be on your
Side, and if possible Secrecy. I ought to add that Doctor Franklin does not
see the Conduct of this Court in the Light I do, & that he believes they
mean nothing in their Proceedings but what is friendly, fair and honorable.
– Facts and future Events must determine which of us is mistaken. As soon
as I can possibly have Time and Health to give you Details, you shall have
them. – Let us be honest and grateful to *France*, but let us think for
ourselves. With great Regard & Esteem, I am, &c.   John Jay.

NA: PCC, *item 110, v. 2, pp. 163-165 (LBkC)*; M 247, *reel 135*.
  [1] *See Marbois to Vergennes, March 13, 1782.*

Richard Oswald's Revised Commission

[19 September 1782]

Our Will and Pleasure is, and We do hereby authorize and Command
you forthwith to prepare a Bill for Our signiture to pass Our Great Seal of
Great Britain in the Words or to the effect following vizt·

George the Third, by the Grace of God, King of Great Britain, France
and Ireland, Defender of the Faith &c^a·: To Our Trusty and Wellbeloved
Richard Oswald of the City of London Esquire, Greeting. Whereas by
Virtue of an Act passed in the last Session of Parliament intituled "An Act
to enable His Majesty to conclude a Peace or Truce, with certain Colonies
in North America therein mentioned," it is recited, "that it is essential to
the Interest, Wellfare and Prosperity of Great Britain and the Colonies or
Plantations of New Hampshire, Massachusets Bay, Rhode Island,
Connecticut, New-York New Jersey, Pensylvania, the lower Counties on
Delaware, Maryland, Virginia, North Carolina, South Carolina, and
Georgia in North America, that Peace, Intercourse, Trade and Commerce
should be restored between them." Therefore, and for a full manifestation
of Our earnest Wish and Desire and of that of Our Parliament, to put an

End to the Calamities of War, it is enacted, that it might and should be lawfull for Us to treat, consult of, agree and conclude with any Commissioner or Commissioners named or to be named by the said Colonies or Plantations, or any of them respectively, or with any Body or Bodies, Corporate or Politic, or any Assembly or Assemblies, or description of Men or any Person or Persons whatsoever, a Peace or a Truce with the said Colonies or Plantations, or any of them or any part or parts thereof, any Law, Act or Acts of Parliament, matter or thing to the contrary in any wise notwithstanding.

Now know ye that We reposing a Special Trust in your Loyalty, Wisdom, Diligence & Circumspection in the management of the Affairs to be hereby committed to your charge, have nominated and appointed, constituted and assigned, and by these Presents do nominate, and appoint, constitute and Assign, you the said Richard Oswald to be Our Commissioner in that behalf, to use and exercise all and every the Powers and authorities hereby entrusted and committed to you the said Richard Oswald, and to do perform and execute all other matters and Things hereby enjoined and committed to your care during Our Will and Pleasure and no longer according to the Tenor of these Our Letters Patent; And it is Our Royal Will and Pleasure and We do hereby authorize empower and require you the said Richard Oswald, to treat consult of and conclude with any Commissioners or Persons vested with equal Powers by and on the part of the Thirteen United States of America viz⁺ New Hampshire, Massachusets Bay, Rhode Island, Connecticut, New York, New Jersey, Pensylvania, the three lower Counties on Delaware, Maryland, Virginia, North Carolina, South Carolina, and Georgia in North America, a Peace or a Truce with the said United States, any Law, Act or Acts of Parliament, matter or thing to the Contrary in any wise notwithstanding. –

And its Our further Will and Pleasure that every regulation, Provision, Matter or Thing, which shall have been agreed upon between you, the said Richard Oswald, and such Commissioners or Persons as aforesaid, with whom you shall have judged meet and sufficient to enter into such agreement, shall be fully and distinctly set forth in Writing and authenticated by your Hand and Seal on one side, and by the Hands and Seals of such Commissioners or Persons on the other, and such Instrument so authenticated shall be by you transmitted to Us, through one of our principal Secretaries of State.

And it is Our further Will and Pleasure, that you the said Richard Oswald shall promise and engage for Us, and in Our Royal Name and Word that every Regulation, Provision, Matter or Thing which may be agreed to or concluded by you Our said Commissioner shall be ratified and confirmed by Us, in the fullest manner and Extent, and that We will not suffer them to be violated or counteracted, either in whole or in part by any person whatsoever.

And We do hereby require and Command all our Officers, Civil and Military, and all other Our loving Subjects whatsoever, to be aiding and assisting unto you the said Richard Oswald in the Execution of this Our Commission, and of the Powers and Authorities herein contained. Provided always and We do hereby declare and ordain that the several Officers, Powers and Authorities hereby granted shall cease, determine and become utterly Null and Void on the first day of July, which shall be in the year of Our Lord 1783, although We shall not otherwise, in the mean time, have revoked and determined the same.

And Whereas in and by Our Commission and Letter Patent under our Great Seal of Great Britain bearing date the seventh Day of August last, We nominated and appointed, constituted and assigned him the said Richard Oswald to be our Commissioner to treat, consult of, agree and conclude with any Commissioner or Commissioners named or to be named by certain Colonies or Plantations in America, therein Specified a Peace or Truce with the said Colonies or Plantations, Our Will and Pleasure is, that you insert a Clause in the said Bill revoking and determining Our said Commission and Letters Patent and all and every Power, Article and Thing therein contained: And for so doing this shall be your Warrant. Given at Our Court of St James's the 19th day of September 1782; in the 22nd year of Our Reign.

By His Majesty's Command   T Townshend
To Our Attorney or Solicitor General

Clements Library: Shelburne Papers, v. 70, pp. 294-299 (C).

Richard Oswald to Lord Shelburne

My Lord.   Paris. 19th Septem^r 1782

When anything occurs which may help to Smooth the way to a Reconciliation with the Americans, I cannot resist the occasion; although sometimes I may thereby incur the charge of officiousness. That may possibly be the case at present, in my presuming once more to trouble your Lo^P on the Subject of Mr Laurens. He is now going over to America, I believe not ill disposed towards England. By his Capacity, & great activity, he is capable of doing good. yet being perhaps Sowered with prejudices of resentment, it were to be wished, however unjust, that they could be softned by any means of Nottice & Civility that may tend to quiet those

Irritations of temper, which too often interfere with the operation of the
Soundest & most benevolent principles.

. . . . .

In doing so, I beg leave to submit to your Lo^P whether it may not be
proper to take some nottice of this Gentleman upon his arrival in England,
particularly in ordering it to be told him, that he may have from
Government, any passage passport or Protection that will convey him Safe
to America without any hazard of Stoppage or Interruption by our Cruisers.

. . . . .

At Same time, I think it proper to inform Your Lordship, that, excepting
the Gratification of such Civility as I have mentioned, which he must
naturally feel, I imagine he will not be desirous of being thought to have
been much attended to while on this Side the Atlantic, on account of that
Consistency of Character which Gentlemen, in his way may wish to carry
back to their Country. Whether owing to a peculiarity in the State of his
Connections, or that, by avoiding Suspicions of preengagement and
partiality, he may be more able to contribute to the general good I cannot
Say: but I have observed a Caution of this kind often attended to.–

Mr Laurens has some particular reason, unknown to me, for declining to
act in his Commission at this Place.

...I remain with much respect and esteem My Lord Your Lo^P^s most
obedient humble Servant   Richard Oswald

Clements Library: Shelburne Papers, v. 71, pp. 97-99 (ALS).

Thomas Townshend to Richard Oswald

Sir   Whitehall 20th September 1782
I received on Saturday last your Packets of the 10th & 11th. of this
Month.

A Meeting of the King's confidential Servants was held as soon as
possible to consider the contents of them; and it was at once agreed to
make the alteration in the Commission proposed to you by Mr Jay, I trust
that the Readiness with which this proposal was accepted, will be
considered as an ample Testimony of the Openness and sincerity with
which the Government of this Country is disposed to treat with the
Americans.

The Commission is passing with as much dispatch as the Forms of Office
will allow, but I thought it material that no delay should happen in giving
you Notice of the determination of His Majesty's Council upon this
Subject.

I am &c.   T. Townshend

Clements Library: Shelburne Papers, v. 70, p. 291 (C).

Comte de Montmorin to Comte de Vergennes

[Translation]

Nº 72   San Ildefonso, 20 September 1782

Sir

I could not respond the day before yesterday to your despatch N°. 68, with which you honored me on the 7th. of this month. I also lack the time today, and I shall limit myself to informing you of the state of things relative to Spain's views on peace. You understand, Sir, that the event on which I had the honor to report to you the day before yesterday must have brought some change; would that it does not cause one in those of the English ministry!

M. le Comte d'Aranda is ordered by the courier dispatched to him today to limit himself to making the three principal points that Spain proposes in the Preliminaries: the preservation of conquests in the Gulf of Mexico, the expulsion of the English from the Gulf of Honduras, and the return of Gibraltar as well as the retention of Minorca. In exchange for these latter objects, M. d'Aranda is authorized to offer Oran and Mazalquivir, as he was before, with the difference that the same offer holds good whatever the fate of Gibraltar: for which he was not authorized in his first instructions. If the English Minister does not accept the offer of Oran and Mazalquivir and insists on the retention of Gibraltar or Minorca, M. d'Aranda should disclose that the King his master might decide to return Minorca, but he must not take a definitive position on this latter object before having new orders from his court which authorize it with regard to Spain's other claims. If the admission suffers the least difficulties, he must postpone them to the negotiation that will follow the Preliminaries.

M. d'Aranda will surely render you a very detailed account of his new instructions. As for me, time does not permit me to enlarge any further. M. de Florida Blanca awaits my letters in order to send off his courier, and has given me only two hours to send them to him.

I have the honor to be with respect Sir Your very humble and very obedient servant.   Le cᵗᵉ· De Montmorin.

Recd by Courier the 25th.

FFAA: Pol. Corr., Spain, v. 608, f. 244 (LC transcription).

John Adams to Robert R. Livingston

Triplicate   The Hague. Septem[r] 23[d] 1782.
Sir,

  As this is a moment of great Expectation, news of the greatest Importance, from the West Indies, the East Indies and North America, from Gibraltar, from Lord Howe's[1] fleet, and the combined fleet, being hourly looked for, I took this opportunity to return to the Spanish Minister, a visit which I owed him.

  He told me, that he trembled for the news we should have from Gibraltar. I asked him if he thought there would be a battle at Sea. He answered Yes, He believed the combined fleet would meet Lord Howe & give him battle. I said, that in this Case it would probably be but a running fight. His Lordships object was to protect his Convoy and get into the Port, and he would not stop to fight more than should be unavoidable. D. Llano however said, that he believed the Fate of Gibraltar would be decided before Howe could arrive, either the Place taken or the Assault given over. By his Advices, the Attack was to begin the 4[th.] or 5[th.] of Septem[r]. Howe sailed the 12[th.], and would probably be 20 days, at least, on his way, which would leave a space of 27. or 28. days for the Attack, which would decide it one way or another.

  I did not think it proper to tell him my own apprehensions, and I wish I may be mistaken, but I have no expectation at all, in my own mind, that the combined fleet will meet them; that there will be any naval Engagement. or that Gibraltar will surrender....The earnest Zeal of Spain to obtain that impenetrable Rock, what has it not cost the House of Bourbon, this war? And what is the Importance of it? A mere point of Honour! a trophy of Insolence to England and of Humiliation to Spain! – It is of no Utility, unless as an Assylum for Privateers, in time of War: for it is not to be supposed that the Powers of Europe, now that the freedom of Commerce is so much esteemed, will permit either England or Spain, to make use of this fortress and assylum, as an Instrument, to exclude any Nation from the Navigation of the Mediterranean.

  From the Hotel d' Espagne, I went to that of France, and the Duke de la Vauguyon informed me, that he had a letter for the Comte de Vergennes, informing him, that he had received, in an indirect manner, a set of Preliminary Propositions, as from the British Ministry, which they were said to be ready to sign: That, he had sent M. de Rayneval to London, to know with certainty, whether those Preliminaries came from proper Authority or not.

Thus we see, that two Ministers from England and another from Holland, are at Paris to make Peace. The Comte d'Aranda is said too, to have powers to treat on the part of Spain. M^r· Franklin & M^r· Jay are present on the part of the United States, and M. Gerard de Rayneval is at London. Yet with all this, the British Ministry have never yet given any proof of their Sincerity, nor any authority to any one to treat with the United States. I believe the British Ministry, even my Lord Shelburne would give such powers, if they dared. But they dare not. They are afraid of the King, of the old Ministry, and a great party in the Nation, irritated every moment by the Refugees, who spare no pains, and hesitate at no impostures, to revive offensive hostilities in America. If Gibraltar should be relieved, and their fleets should arrive from the West Indies & the Baltick, and they should not have very bad news from the East Indies, the nation will recover from its fright, occasioned by the Loss of Cornwallis, Minorca and St Kitts, and the Ministry will not yet dare to acknowledge American Independence. In this case, M^r· Fox & M^r· Burke will lay their foundation of Opposition, and the State of the Finances will give them great weight. But the Ministry will find means to provide for another Campaign.

But to return to the Duke de la Vauguyon, who informed me further that he had received Instructions, to propose to the Prince of Orange, a new plan of Concert of Operations, viz. That the Dutch fleet, or, at least, a detachment of it, should now in the absence of Lord Howe, sail from the Texel to Brest, and join the French Ships there, in a Cruise, to intercept the British West India fleet. The Prince does not appear pleased with this plan. He has not yet accepted it. The grand Pensionary appears to approve it, and support it with warmth. There is now a fine opportunity for the Dutch fleet to strike a blow, either alone upon the Baltick Fleet. or in conjunction with the French, or even alone upon the West India fleet – But the main Spring of the Machine is broken or unbent. There is neither Capacity, nor good will, among those who direct the Navy –

. . . . .

I have the honor to be, Sir, Your humble servant,   J. Adams

NA: PCC, Misc. Papers, Adams Despatches (LS); M332, reel 1, ff. 680-683.
¹ Howe, Richard, Lord (1726-1799). British admiral. Brother of General Sir William Howe. Appointed naval commander-in-chief in North America, February 1776. With his brother, commissioned to treat with the American rebels and to attempt a conciliation with the American colonies, May 6, 1776; Congress refused to treat on these terms. Provided naval support for British army maneuvers, 1776-1778. Fought indecisive engagement with French squadron off Newport, August 1778; returned to England, October 1778, and

resigned his command. Commander-in-chief in the Channel, April-July 1782. Commanded British fleet that relieved Gibraltar, October 1782. First Lord of the Admiralty, 1783-1788. Commanded British fleet in its victory over the French on the Glorious First of June, 1794.

Lord Shelburne to Richard Oswald

Dear Sir   Shelburne House 23ᵈ Septʳ 1782

Having said & done every thing, which has been desired, there is nothing left for me to trouble you with except to add, that we have put the greatest Confidence, I believe was ever placed, in Men, in the American Commissioners. It is now to be seen, how far They or America are to be depended upon. I will not detain you with enumerating the difficulties, which have occurred. There never was greater risk run. I hope the Publick will be the Gainer. Else our Heads must answer for it, & deservedly.

Lord Shelburne

Clements Library: Shelburne Papers, v. 71, p. 123.

Thomas Townshend to Richard Oswald

Sir   Whitehall 24ᵗʰ· September1782.

I now send you the Commission, which has met with no delay more than was absolutely necessary for the forms through which it was to pass.

I hope that the frankness with which We deal will meet with a suitable return.

I have ordered the Office to be searched for all Papers which can give any Information concerning the Boundaries which you mention in your Letter of the 11ᵗʰ of this Month; but it has not been in my power to have so exact a state of that Matter, made out, as may be necessary for your direction in your Negotiation.

· · · · ·

I am &c.   T Townshend

· · · · ·

Clements Library: Shelburne Papers, v. 70, pp. 292-293 (C).

Robert Morris to Benjamin Franklin

1st. (By C[ipher] Nr. 4)

Sir,   Philadelphia 28th. Sept. 1782

In my Letter of yesterday, I have dwelt on the resolutions of Congress, in the manner requir'd by my duty as their Servant.[1] I will now add a few hints, as Your friend. Your Enemys industriously publish, that your age and indolence have unabled you for your station, that a Sense of obligation to France seals your lips when you should ask their aid, and that (whatever your friends may say to the contrary) both your connections and influence at Court are extremely feeble. I need not tell you that messieurs Lee and company are among the foremost who make these assertions, and many others not worthe mention. I should not have given you the pain of reading even these but that (as you will see from the resolution of the twenty third instant)[2] Congress have believed your grateful sensibilities might render you unwilling to apply with all that warmth which the sense of their necessities convinces them is necessary. In addition to the general reflection how envy has pursued superior merit in all ages, You will draw a farther consolation from this, that many who censure you are well disposed to cast like censure on France, and would fain describe her as acting only the part of self interest, without a wishe to render us effectual aid. You will I am sure attribute what I now say to a friendly desire of apprizing you of things useful for you to know, and you will so act, as to convince every man that your exertions are what I verily believe them to be. I am Sir, your most obedient Servant   Robt Morris

Ferguson, Robert Morris Papers, v. 6, p. 455.

[1] *See Worthington Chauncey Ford et. al., eds., Journals of the Continental Congress, 1774-1789, 34 vols. (Washington, DC: United States Government Printing Office, 1904-1939), v. 23, pp. 594-595, hereafter cited as JCC.*

[2] *Ibid., v. 23, pp. 595-596. Congressional resolution directed Franklin to "use his utmost endeavors to effect the loan...."*

John Jay to Robert R. Livingston

Dear Sir,   Paris 28th September 1782.

I have only Time to inform you that our objections to Mr· Oswald's first Commission have produced a second, which arrived Yesterday. It empowers him to treat with the Commissioners of the *thirteen United States of America*.

I am preparing a longer Letter on this Subject, but as this Intelligence is interesting, I take the earliest Opportunity of communicating it.

With great Regard and Esteem, I am, &c. John Jay.

NA: PCC, item 110, v. 2, p. 142 (LBkC); M 247, reel 135.

Comte de Vergennes to Comte de Montmorin

[Translation]

N$^{o.}$ 78. Versailles, 28 September 1782

M. le C$^{te.}$ de Montmorin.

I have too little time to myself, Sir, and my Spirit has not sufficiently recovered from the strong shock the unfortunate event that took place at Gibraltar has given it to discuss that which could relate to peace.

M. de Rayneval is back from London. I am not displeased with what he has reported to us; M. de Grasse would be greatly displeased if he knew that he had been almost entirely disavowed by Lord Shelburne, who had not made or charged him to make any overture. According to the report which M. de Rayneval made to us of his various conferences with Lords Shelburne and Grantham together and separately, the dispositions of the British ministry for peace are sincere; it will consent to some Sacrifices to obtain it, but I cannot conceal from you, Sir, the fact that it showed the greatest aversion to the cession of Gibraltar. It did not say that it could not take place, but if it can be brought about, we need not flatter ourselves it will regard the cession of Oran and Mazalquivir as a sufficient indemnity and be content. It will demand an indemnity more extensive and more to the liking of its nation. M. de Rayneval is working to summarize in a journal all that passed between him and the English ministers concerning Spain. This extract will be given to M. le Comte d'Aranda, who will forward it to his Court in order to receive the orders that it will judge necessary to give him in Consequence. While waiting, I deem that we ought no longer to defer making our formal proposal. In accordance with my opinion, the preliminaries for the peace ought to be either settled or very close to agreed upon before the 15th of November, or the negotiation entirely broken off. M. le Comte d'Aranda must dispatch a courier next week. I shall profit thereby to write to you in more detail on all that relates to the peace, as well as on all that passes between Mr. Fitzherbert and me. I expect him today.

It does not appear that the English will force our hand for the mediation; their way of thinking could not be further removed from it, and they would willingly act in accord with us if we wish to elude it.

I have the honor to be &cᵃ·   Vergennes

FFAA: Pol. Corr., Spain, v. 608, f. 267 (LC transcription).

Chevalier de la Luzerne to Comte de Vergennes

[Translation]

Nᵒ· 275. 1ˢᵗ·   Philadelphia, 28 September 1782
My Lord

.   .   .   .

I am persuaded that you are entirely reassured concerning the possibility of a defection, overt or disguised, general or particuliar, on the part of the United States. Congress and the people are perfectly on guard against the artifices of the Enemy, and I think I can respond to you fully about them. Congress was most satisfied with the details that I communicated to it concerning the negotiation commenced by Messrs. Grenville and Oswald.

...The article relative to the fisheries has occasioned some observation, but I am very comfortable with the early information that an equitable and mutually useful regulation of the future peace should assure even better our rights to the fishing off Newfoundland. That is one of the points that prepares the most difficulties for us, but if, as I have had the honor of informing you, the treaty is silent concerning the Americans and does not exclude them from it formally, the complaints of the Eastern merchants will make little impression on the mass of the people. I have long prepared Congress and even the Eastern delegates for the verities that you charge me to make known to them, and although the claims at first were and still are truly excessive, one nevertheless expects today only what you announce that His Majesty is disposed to do. Our policy with regard to this point and to that of the boundaries is now sufficiently known by Congress, so that we ought not to fear any inopportune movement when the United States are apprised of the principles that His Majesty has followed in the course of the negotiation. There will be malcontents, but according to the knowledge that you resolve to give me of the plan that His Majesty proposes to follow with regard to America in the peacemaking, I hope to succeed in disconcerting their measures....The English, My Lord, as you had foreseen, have put all their efforts into having their Emissaries penetrate the United States; but Congress at first impeded them by refusing Mr. Morgan, secretary of Sir Guy Carleton, permission to come to Philadelphia. There is not, to my knowledge, any man as suspect as Mr. Temple.[1] Congress has spared nothing to have him banished, and even in this circumstance it has compromised its authority; as he is the son-in-law of a very accredited man in Massachusetts, those who have taken his defense were almost as numerous as those who have attacked him, and he has remained in Boston, where he continues to be watched, but without much fruit. I do not fear his maneuvers, and they are still less feared in Massachusetts than they would be in any other State. I have nonetheless contributed to excite public surveillance against him, persuaded that even if it is without success, that jealousy and that attention concerning the first Emissary who shows himself would discourage those who might be tempted to follow him. I therefore think, My Lord, that we can be, at least for some time, at rest from that side. You will see in the paper packet that the extract is continued of a Pamphlet[2] that was done in Boston with the intention of alarming the Americans concerning our influence and persuading them that it is not less to be feared than that of Great Britain....

le chr de la luzerne

Received 26 November.

FFAA: Pol. Corr., U.S., v. 22, f. 89 (LC transcription).

[1] *Temple, Sir John (1731-1798). British colonial and consular official. Surveyor of customs at Boston before 1771, when he emigrated to England. Fought duel with Thomas Whately, recipient of the Hutchinson-Oliver letters, 1774. Loyalist, married to a daughter of James Bowdoin. Returned to America with Dr. John Berkenhout, a British secret agent acting in support of the Carlisle peace commission, 1778. Returned to England, 1780. After obtaining weak letter of recommendation from John Adams, returned to America, 1781. British consul general at New York, 1785-1798.*

[2] *Not further identified.*

Richard Oswald to Thomas Townshend

Sir. Paris 2ᵈ Octʳ· 1782

I had the honor of your Letters of the 20th· and 24th of September. the last accompanying His Majesty's New Commission, altered as desired. Upon receipt, I produced it to the American Commissioners, and they were entirely satisfied therewith. I have also to advise that Yesterday I delivered to them a Copy of said Commission after its being compared with the original and certified by me; and in exchange received from them a Copy of their Commission, which being in like manner compared with the original was certified by Mʳ· Jay one of the Commissioners, a Duplicate of said Copy you have enclosed.

Doctor Franklin being still but in an indifferent state of Health, he could not come to Town, and left this first part of the Business to Mr Jay. From any thing that passed on this occasion, I have no reason to think worse of the farther progress of it, than as mentioned in my last Advices. In a few days I hope we shall agree upon the principal Articles of which the Treaty is to consist. When that is done, I shall transmit the same so as to have your Instructions thereon. We have as yet only talked of them in a loose way viz$^{t.}$

First Independence.

2nd Settling the Lines of separation or Boundaries between those of the Thirteen States and the British Colonies.

3^d Giving up the additional Lands of Canada.

4$^{th.}$ Freedom of fishing to the Thirteen States for Fish and Whales.

These, I say, are all that have as yet been mentioned between Mr Jay and me, whether any other will be proposed, or insisted on by them I cannot say; but I hope there will not. Mean while, as there will probably be time for a Return of a Courier, before We proceed much farther, I would beg to have an Explanation as to some of the particulars in my Letter of the 11$^{th.}$ Ult^o, respecting the Articles of Boundaries of Canada, Nova Scotia and Georgia, East Florida, and particularly West Florida, how its Boundaries are to be determined with regard to Georgia. That must depend upon the Charter of Georgia, by Grant or Proclamation. I have nothing here to go by, but Maps; and they are no authority even though they agreed, which these do not: By the former Courier I wrote Sundry Things about this Colony of West Florida, rather in some haste, as the Messenger was just then upon setting off. I have given Mr Jay an account of it; and he greatly approved of the Proposal. He is indeed anxious that Great Britain should regain possession of that Colony, on the same footing it stood before the War, since he said their States would not by any means like that the Key of that part of the Gulph should be in the hands of the Spaniards, as the whole, or the greatest part of the Trade and produce of that great back Country, would most naturally and beneficially issue there and which he says would soon be very considerable and would ultimately fall into the hands of the English on the Mobile and Missisippi; both in the supply of English Merchandize, & Importation of American Commodities in return. Rather than leave it in the hands of the Spaniards, he said it would be worth while to embark some of the Troops from New York and Charles Town, and retake it. I mention this only to shew how desirous they are that that Colony should not remain with the Spaniards; and in confirmation of the Opinion I took the liberty to give on the subject in my former Letters.

In order to make it a Kings Government of some consequence, I again tried Mr Jay, whether without regard to what might be the Chartered limits of Georgia, We might not settle it so in the Treaty, that West Florida should be extended to about the Latitude of 34. To which he answered that although he could wish to give every Encouragement to that Settlement, yet it would not be in their Power as Commissioners, to dismember any of the States: But that it was a matter of little Consequence whether that upper part, which I aimed at, was under British Government, or theirs: The People would agree very well, having one common Interest in the Settlement and Prosperity of that great and fertile Country, and in which their People would in a manner be dependent on Great Britain, as having the Command of Navigation into the Gulph of Mexico, through which the bulk of that Trade must pass, He added that their Traders from the Northern Colonies have lately crossed the Missisippi into the Spanish Territories, and will continue to do so to a still greater extent after the War is over, and they begin to Stretch further back in their Settlements; which will occasion an additional Demand for British Merchandize, as those which are laid down near the spot by Importation from the Gulph through the English Settlements, will have the preference on account of the saving of the Land Carriage from the Atlantic Side. consequently he thinks, as I do that the Ports of West Florida may be of great advantage to England, as this would become the Mart or Center of a great part of the Trade of America to the Southward, as would Quebec be to the Northern parts; By which means, upon the whole, England, having those two Keys in its hand, may still enjoy an exclusive Monopoly of a large share of North American Commerce: and consequently may not happen to be, in point of Trade, so great a loser by the change, as is generally imagined.

In the course of this last conversation with Mr Jay, he repeated his Wish that the Spaniards might be dislodged from West Florida and said "what are you doing with 20,000 Men (he called them so many) lying idle spending of Money in New York and Charles Town, and keeping up a Jealousy and animosity between you and Us at a time when We are here endeavoring to bring about a Restoration of friendship and good Will. Why not employ some of those Troops to recover that Colony."

Upon another occasion, he said your Ministry ought to take the first opportunity to write to Sir Guy Carleton an account of Our being likely to come soon to an amicable and final agreement here, on the footing of an unconditional Independence; and to desire that he would immediately publish that Intelligence and at same time give orders to discountenance all those Murderous attempts by scouting Parties of what you call Loyalists, or Indians in the Remote parts of the Country &c."...

I have the honor to be Sir &c.ᵃ·   Richard Oswald

PS. since writing the above, I have had some farther conversation with Mr Jay, about the conditions of the Treaty. I hope to get clear of the adviseable Articles. But as to some of those in my Instructions I doubt I shall not succeed. For the present I only touched upon the following vizt·

Ungranted Lands within the United States. He said all must go with the States.

Pardon to the Loyalists. The Congress cannot meddle in it. The States being Sovereigns, and the Parties in fault answerable to them, and them only. Besides he said, it is his opinion, that many of them could not be protected by their Governments, and therefore ought to depart with the Troops.

Drying fish in Newfoundland, I find is to be claimed as a priviledge in common, We being allowed the same on their Shores; I did not think it proper to say much on this Subject at present, and wish that granting this freedom may be found to be of no material loss to England, being afraid if refused it may be a great loss in other things. Mr Jay came again upon the Subject of West Florida, and expects and insists for the Common Good, Our own as well as theirs, that it may not be left in the hands of the Spaniards. And thinks we ought to prepare immediately for the Expedition, to execute it this Winter. At same time he earnestly begs it may not be known that he advised it. And wishes I had mentioned it as of myself. As I approved of the thing, I thought the Proposal should be strengthened by his opinion, and to speak the truth I could not suppress the Credit due to him for attending to it.

I am to Dine with Doctor Franklin to morrow, when it is likely We shall talk farther of the Conditions of the Treaty, and I am in hopes that the next Courier may carry a Sketch of them. When agreed on, they must remain without Effect or Operation until We have closed with France, so they positively say. I *really believe the Commissioners are sorry they are so tied up.* But they say there is no remedy.

Clements Library: Shelburne Papers, v. 70, pp. 253-267 (C).

Congressional Committee Report

[Philadelphia] Oct. 3. 1782

The com^tt·...to whom were referred the notes of the Communication made by the Minister of France to a com^tt of Congress on the 24 Sept brought in a report which was agreed to as follows

. . . . .

That his Most Christian Majesty's declaration to the British Minister at Paris that he will neither treat nor terminate any Negotiation unless the interests of his Allies & Friends shall be considered and determined, is entirely correspondent to the part which these United States are resolved to take in any Negotiation for peace.

. . . . .

That Congress place the utmost confidence in his Majesty's assurances that he will readily employ his good offices in support of the United States in all points relative to their prosperity, and considering the territorial claims of these states as heretofore made, their participation of the fisheries and of the free Navigation of the Mississippi not only as their indubitablerights, but as essential to their prosperity, they trust that his Majesty's efforts will be successfully employed to obtain a sufficient provision and security for those rights. Nor can they refrain from making known to his Majesty, that any claim of restitution or compensation for property, confiscated in the several States will meet with insuperable obstacles, not only on account of the Sovereignty of the Individual States by which such Confiscations have been made, but of the wanton devastations which the Citizens of these States have experienced from the Enemy and in many instances from the very persons in whose favour such claims may be urged. That Congress trust that the circumstances of the Allies at the Negotiation for peace will be so prosperous as to render these expectations consistent with the spirit of moderation recommended by His Majesty.

. . . . .

NA: PCC, item 5, pp. 770-776 (Journal); M 247, reel 19.

Preliminary Articles of Peace: First Draft Treaty

Paris, [5-8] October 1782

Articles agreed upon by and between Richard Oswald Esqr., the Commissioner of His Britannic Majesty for treating of Peace with the Commissioners of the United States of America on the behalf of His said Majesty on the one part. And Benjamin Franklin, John Jay of the Commissioners of the said States for treating of Peace with the Commissioner of His said Majesty on their behalf, on the other part. To be inserted in, and to Constitute the Treaty of Peace proposed to be Concluded between the Crown of Great Britain, and the said United States. But which Treaty is not to be Concluded untill His Britannic Majesty shall have agreed to the Terms of a Peace between France and Britain, proposed or Accepted by His Most Christian Majesty; and shall be ready to conclude with him Such Treaty accordingly. It being the Duty and Intention of the United States not to desert their Ally, <nor to conduct any Separate Peace or Truce, >[1] but faithfully, and in all things, to abide by and fulfill their Engagements with His most Christian Majesty.

Whereas reciprocal advantages and mutual Convenience are found by Experience to form the only permanent foundation of Peace and Friendship between States, It is agreed to frame the Articles of the proposed Treaty on Such principles of liberal Equality and Reciprocity, as that partial advantages (those Seeds of discord) being excluded, Such a beneficial and Satisfactory Intercourse between the two Countries may be established, as to promise and Secure to both, the blessings of perpetual Peace and Harmony.

I His Britannic Majesty acknowledges the Said United States, Viz. New Hampshire, Massachusetts Bay, Rhode Island and Providence Plantations, Connecticut, New York, New Jersey, Pennsylvania, Delaware, Maryland, Virginia, North Carolina, South Carolina and Georgia, to be free, Sovereign, and Independent States; That he treats with them as Such; and for himself, his Heirs and Successors, relinquishes all Claims to the Government, Propriety, and territorial Rights of the same and every part thereof. And that all disputes which might arise in future on the Subject of the Boundaries of the Said United States may be prevented, It is hereby agreed and declared, that the following are, and Shall Remain to be, their Boundaries Viz.

The Said States are bounded North by a Line to be drawn from the North west angle of Nova Scotia along the High Lands which divide those Rivers which empty themselves into the River St. Lawrence from those which fall into the Atlantic Ocean, to the Northermost [sic] head of Connecticut River; thence down along the midle of that River to the forty fifth degree of North Latitude, and thence due West in the Latitude forty five degrees North from the Equator, to the Northwestermost Side of the River St. Laurence or Cadaraquii, thence Streight to the South end of the Lake Nipissing and then Streight to the Source of the River Missisippi; West, by a Line <by a str[aight][2]> to be drawn along the midle of the River Missisippi from its Source to where the Said Line Shall intersect the Thirty first degree of North Latitude. South by a Line to be drawn due East from the termination of the Line last mentioned in the Latitude of thirty one degrees North of the Equator to the midle of the River Appalachicola or Catahouchi, thence along the midle thereof to its junction with the Flint River, thence Strait to the head of St. Marys River; and thence down along the <head> midle of St. Marys River to the Atlantic Ocean. And East (alteration as Undernoted) by a Line to be drawn along the midle of St. Johns River, from its Source to its Mouth in the Bay of Fundy

Comprehending all Islands within Seventy Leagues of any part of the Shores of the United States, and lying between Lines to be drawn due East from the points where the aforesaid Boundaries between Nova Scotia on the one part, and East Florida on the other, shall respectively touch the Bay of Fundy and the Atlantic Ocean.

2 From and immediately after the Conclusion of the proposed Treaty, there Shall be a firm and perpetual Peace between His Britannic Majesty and the Said States, and between the Subjects of the one and the Citizens of the other. Wherefor all hostilities, both by Sea and Land, shall then immediately Cease, All Prisoners on both Sides Shall be Sett at liberty; And His Brittanic Majesty Shall forthwith, and without causing any destruction, withdraw all his Armies, Garrisons and Fleets, from the Said United States, and from every Port, Place and Harbour within the Same; leaving in all Fortifications the American Artillery that may be therein, And Shall also order and [cause all Archives, Records, Deeds and Papers belonging to either of] the said States or their Citizens, which in the Course of the War may have fallen into the hands of his Officers, to be forthwith restored and delivered to the proper States and persons to whom they belong.

3 That the Subjects of His Britannic Majesty and People of the Said United States Shall continue to enjoy unmolested the Right to take Fish of every kind on the Banks of Newfoundland and other places where the Inhabitants of both Countries used formerly, Viz. before the last War between France and Britain, to fish; And also to dry and Cure the Same at the acustomed Places, whether belonging to His Said Majesty or to the United States. And His Britannic Majesty and the Said United States will extend equal Priviledges and Hospitality to each others Fishermen as to their own.

4 That the Navigation of the River Missisippi from its Source to the Ocean Shall for ever remain free and open, And that both there and in all Rivers, Harbors, Lakes, Ports and Places, belonging to His Britannic Majesty or to the United States in any part of the World, the Merchants and Merchant Ships of the one and the other Shall be received, treated and protected like the Merchants and Merchant Ships of the Sovereign of the Country. That is to say the British Merchants and Merchant Ships on the one hand Shall enjoy in the united States, and in all places belonging to them, the Same Protection and Commercial priviledges, and be liable only to the Same Charges and Duties as their own Merchants and Merchant Ships. And on the other hand, the Merchants and Merchant Ships of the United States Shall enjoy in all places belonging to His Britannic Majesty the Same protection and Commercial priviledges, and be liable only to the Same Charges and Duties as British Merchants and Merchant Ships Saving

always to the Chartered Trading Companys of Great Britain, Such exclusive Use and Trade, and their respective Posts and Establishments, as neither the other Subjects of Great Britain, nor any the most favoured Nations participate in.

A true Copy of what has been agreed on between the American Commissioners and me, to be Submitted to His Majestys Consideration.

RICHARD OSWALD

Alteration to be made in the enclosed Treaty, respecting the Boundaries of Nova Scotia, Viz. at the Word East, the true Line shall be Settled by Commissioners as Soon as conveniently may be after the War.

Morris, Jay Papers, v. 2, pp. 389-392.

[1] *Deleted material in original document indicated by angle brackets.*

[2] *Text provided indicated by square brackets.*

Marquis de Lafayette to John Adams

My dear Sir   Paris October the 6th 1782

. . . . .

I am Happy to Hear you have Walked on with our Dutch friends to the wished for Conclusion of the treaty of Commerce – Amidst the Wonders You Have Performed in that Country, I Greatly Rejoice at Your Having Succeeded in Monney Matters – the More so, as I Apprehend Our financier Needs Much An European Assistance, and the Great Expenses they Have Made in this Country Give me But little Hope to Obtain a further Supply than the Six Millions, and the Ballance of Accounts which Have Been determined upon since the time I Arrived from America.

M. Jay Advances But Slowly with the Spaniards – in fact, He does not Advance at All, and tho' Count d'Aranda has Got Powers, tho' He Has with a Pencil drawn an Extravagant Line this Side of the Mississippi, Yet Untill Powers Are Exchanged Upon an Equal footing, and Untill the Spanish Pencil is transported Three Hundred Miles Westward, there is No doing Any thing towards settling a treaty with that Nation.

As to the Great Affair of Peace, there are Reasons to Believe it will take Place. Many Attempts Have Been Made to treat upon an Unequal footing, Which By the Bye was a Very impertinent Proposal – But We stood firm, deaf, and dumb, and As france Refused to Enter into Business Untill we were Made to Hear and to Speack, at last, With Much Reluctance, And Great pains, His Britannic Majesty and Council were Safely delivered of A Commission to treat with Plenipotentiaries from the United States of America.

. . . . .

...and Have the Honor to Be with the Highest Regard My dear Sir your
obedient hm^be Servant   Lafayette

MHS: The Adams Papers, microfilm reel 358 (ALS).

Comte de Vergennes to Comte de Montmorin

[Translation]

N° 81.   Versailles, October 6, 1782

M. le Cte de Montmorin.

The Extract, Sir, that I have the honor to address to you of part of the
report that M. de Rayneval made to us on his Conferences with Lord
Shelburne and Lord Grantham, the duplicate of which has been sent to M.
the Comte d'Aranda, spares me from entering into the details that you will
find recorded in this writing.

You will observe therein, Sir, that these English Ministers are anything
but disposed to cede Gibraltar, and to make them amenable, it would
require Equivalents of a completely different price and of a greater renown
than Oran and Mazalquivir. I do not permit myself, Sir, to prejudge the
value that one may give to an idea that escaped Lord Shelburne when,
discoursing with M. de Rayneval on the Satisfaction claimed by the Court
of Spain, he let it be known that the Cession of the Floridas with a district
in the environs of New Orleans joined to the vast lands that are situated
between the Mississippi, the Lakes, and the western frontiers of the United
States of America would form an equivalent sufficient to flatter and to
satisfy the English nation, and that would not expose the Minister who
would consent to such an arrangement to paying for it with his head.

I consider, Sir, that prudence counsels us at this moment to indulge
Spain on the merit that it will please her to attach to this overture (if this
should be one). If we were to permit ourselves to recommend it, it would
be inferred from it that we are in accord with the English, and one would
not be negligent in protesting that we wish to deprive Spain of the most
legitimate and the most important of the satisfactions that it demands.
Florida, consigned to nullity if it stays in the hands of the Spanish, would
acquire the highest importance from then on.

This Consideration invites me to implore and recommend to you, Sir,
that you not reveal yourself with the Comte de Florida Blanca to be
instructed by the Communication that I am making to you, and wait in
silence for him to seek you out in order to expose your ideas and reflections
to him.

There is one, Sir, that I am borrowing, from the fashion of thinking known from the Court of Spain, and of which it may be useful that you be warned in any Event.

Since the English Colonies have been separated from their metropolis, Spain has seemed much more to fear their proximity than that of the English, and this apprehension has directed all her Conduct, which has not been able to win for her the affection of the United States.

As this apprehension without doubt bears upon the solid motives that in Consequence are still in all their force, Spain may find an Interest in distancing from her frontiers a people whose rapid growth will render it always very enterprising to procure for itself new lands. Spain has an Indication of its views in the claims that Mr. Jay makes in advance in the settlement to make of the frontiers of Florida.

If the English recovered this province, placed betweeen Spain and the United States along the Mississippi, Spain would have nothing to fear from Invasions of the latter, and there is reason to think that two nations equally avid and ambitious, placed next to each other in this region, would live in a state of defiance, of Disquiet, and even of hostilities that would contribute to the tranquility of Spain's frontiers. As for Contraband, its seat cannot be in Florida. It is in Jamaica.

M. the Count d'Aranda has communicated to me the memoir that he proposes to send to Mr. Fitzherbert. All the pretentions of Spain are very exactly articulated therein. I doubt that the English ministers hasten to subscribe to it.

I have avoided up until now, Sir, the Epidemic known as Grippe, but I find myself so very indisposed that I am obliged to lay down my pen. I am going to hand it to M. de Rayneval, who will summarily inform you of the dispositions that he has remarked in England in our Regard.

I have the honor to be &c.   Vergennes

FFAA: Pol. Corr., Spain, v. 609, f. 22 (LC transcription).

John Adams to John Jay

Dear Sir   The Hague Oct 7. 1782

Your favour of the 28 Ult. was brought me last night, on Fryday last I was notified, by the Messenger of their H.M. that the Treaties would be ready for Signature on Monday (this day). I am accordingly at Noon, to go to the Assembly and finish the Business. But when this is done, Sometime will be indispensable, to prepare my Dispatches for Congress and look out for the most favourable Conveyances, for them.– I must also Sign another

Thousand of Obligations at least, that ~~my~~ the Loan may not Stand Still. All this Shall be dispatched with all the Diligence, in my Power, but it will necessarily take up Some time, and my health is so far from being robust, that it will be impossible for me to ride, with as much rapidity, as I could formerly, although never remarkable for a quick Traveller. If any Thing in the mean time Should be in agitation, concerning Peace, in which there Should be any difference of Opinion between you, and your Colleague, you have a right to insist upon informing me, by Express, or waiting till I can come.

8. The Signature was put off yesterday, till to day, by the Princes being in Conference with their H. M. and laying his orders to the Navy before them.

With entire Esteem, your most obt.   J. Adams

Columbia University Libraries, John Jay Papers (ALS).

Richard Oswald to Thomas Townshend

Sir   Paris 7th Octr 1782

Referring to my Letters of the 2^d & 3^d, by the Courier...and to one of the 5th, which go[e]s under this Cover, I have the honour to send you inclosed the plan or Articles of a final Treaty proposed between Great Britain and the Thirteen States of America; Which being settled, was deliver'd to me by Mr Jay on the 5th in his own hand writing, after it had been approved of by Doct^{r.} Franklin, as he at same time informed me.

And which, by any Conversation I previously had with those Gentlemen, or Since I received it, may be considered as including the whole of their Demands, Necessary, or Advisable, and, if agreed to on our part, as a Compleat and finished Treaty; with an Exception only of the usual formalities of reference to Commissions &c^{a.} Also that, as to the point of Ratification, so as to establish Peace, it must wait for our Conclusion with France; as you will please to observe is declared in the preamble.

After considering the Terms, as they stand in the Treaty, I thought there was no reason to object to the Boundary Lines of the Thirteen States, excepting that there is a part of Nova Scotia cutt off on the Bay of Fundy. I called on Mr Jay this morning, and found him willing to sett that matter to rights, so as the Masachusetts Governm^t shall have no more of that Coast than they had before the War. He took his directions from Maps, and they are not distinct, nor do they agree in this matter. This is in the mean time referred, to be afterwards properly adjusted.

I next talkt to him about the Claim of Drying Fish on the Island of Newfoundland; as not having been mentioned, or included in Dr Franklins Necessary Articles, Mr Jay said he put them into the Treaty to avoid an Appearance of unneighborly distinctions, and considering it as not material to us, there being room enough for both of us, as well as for the French. But if we thought otherways, he would not say but they might give it up, rather than we should be dissatisfied about it, believing their People would not much value the Priviledge; and would in general chuse to bring their Fish to their own Coasts, as they used to do. On this Subject if I might Speak my Opinion, it is a question whether we ought to insist on their Exclusion, while the French enjoy that Conveniency: and on that account, altho' the Americans had not desired a Similar privilege whether there would have been any harm in offering it to them; Since their Exclusion would be always attended with a grudge.

In my last Letters I advised that the value of the Ungranted Lands in the Several Colonies could not be Saved, as a Fund at His Majesty's disposal, as the Commissioners insisted that every property belonging to the Crown must go with other Rights within the Thirteen States. In case Sir, you should think it proper that I should press this matter farther, you will be pleased to let me know. At same time I must confess that considering the little chance of success, and that I look upon the Treaty as now closed, I doubt whether it would be proper to open it on this account. In any other Case, one would not say so. But where there is no Controul on one Side & Circumstances press for decision perhaps it may be proper, if other things are right, not to insist on a provision of this kind Standing part of the Treaty. At same time as a great Sum may be raised out of this Property, as well as out of what is cutt of from Canada, it would not be taken amiss by the Commissioners, if it was submitted to their Consideration & equity in a Seperate way A Seperate Letter on that Subject, laying Claim to their Justice & good Sense, in distinguishing a Resignation of property, no way connected with those of Legislation and Government, & intended for the relief of unfortunate Sufferers, may have some weight with the Several provinces in softening their resentment against some of those People, and extending their Indulgence to them accordingly in the way of Restitution or Indemnification. But, as I have said, If the Treaty is otherways approved of, I offer it as my humble opinion, that an Expectation of this kind had best be suggested independently, and sent me in a Seperate Letter, to be laid before the Commissioners.

I touched also upon the Debts due to British Subjects, and my apprehensions of Loss by Confiscations. Mr Jay replied that he had heared of no such Confiscations but in the province of Maryland; which he seemed not to approve of. However, as I had before been satisfied that they, as

Commissioners, could do nothing in the matter, I did not insist farther upon it.

Before we parted, this Gentleman came again upon the subject of West Florida, and pled in favour of the future Commerce of England, as if he had been of her Council, & wishing to make some reparation for her Loss. Amongst other things, he repeated, that there is Water Carriage by Rivers or Lakes all the way within Land from Canada to the Mouth of the Missisippi, excepting a few Short stoppages of Portage; So that, for Outward Merchandize, we might engross the whole of their Supplies, for a Stretch of Country between two and three thousand Miles. And in like manner (chiefly by means of the Missisippi) receive their Country Commodities in return and particularly should embrace the whole of the Fur Trade. In all which I am satisfied he is well founded.

At last he said he wished much to be informed recovering that Colony, so as he might know how to shape his conduct with respect to Spain; and desired to be at a Certainty before he had any farther Conference with their Ambassador to which he is much sollicited with a view to entering into a Treaty with them; in which he understands they want, amongst other things, that we shall be entirely shutt out of any part of the Gulph of Mexico from Cape Florida to Cape Catoche.

In answer I told Mr Jay that I should write immediately, and should inform him of any Commands I had on the Subject. But told him, there would be a difficulty, as I had mentioned before, regarding the Evacuation of those Garrisons, without the necessary Letters from them to make it safe and easy.

To which he replied. The best way will be this. "Do you now send over this Treaty to your Ministry. If they approve of it, You and We will sign a Copy of it when it is sent back; and the same being returned to England it may be sent over to Sir Guy Carleton, with Orders to publish it as a finished business: and he may at same time upon the foundation of it, Settle a Convention With Gener^l Washington for the evacuation of the Garrisons; and We shall also write him what is necessary; which may be sent from England along with the Treaty: adding at same time that Count Rochambau is under Gener^l Washingtons Orders, and can do nothing Seperately.

If this should be approved of he said Your Court may keep a Frigate ready to go at a moments warning with these papers, and any orders that may be necessary for Convoy, Transports &c^a.

He at the same time called for the inclosed Copy I had made of the Treaty, and Scored the Words which you see Struck out, being That "*they neither should*["] He also interlined the two words in the preamble, "*or accepted.*["] and Sett out for Dr Franklins Quarters to have his opinion as to their writing Letters to General Washington on the Subject of the Evacuation of the Garrisons, and also respecting the Boundaries of Nova Scotia. When he returns I shall make a Report of his Answer in a Seperate Letter.

In the meantime I have called on Mr Fitzherbert and have shewen him this Sketch of the Treaty, and have informed him of any thing which I think may be of use in his Business. And he has informed me of the Count de Vergennes Propositions, and has shewen me the Memorial of the Count d'Aranda. If the West Florida Scheme were to take place, I think it would settle some of the points in that Memorial, as well in the recovery of that Colony, as of all the Bahama Islands we have lost. Untill Mr Jays return, I have not farther to add, but that I am Sir Your most obedient humble Servant   Richard Oswald.
R. 11$^{th.}$

PRO: FO 27/2, v. 557, f. 665 (LC transcription).

Richard Oswald to Thomas Townshend

Sir   Paris 8th Oct$^{r.}$ 1782
Mr Jay, upon his return last night from Passy, told me that Doct$^{r.}$ Franklin could not determine as to the Boundary Line between Nova Scotia and Massachusetts Bay, and thought it was best to leave it to be Settled by an express Commission for that purpose, after the War; and accordingly added a Minute of that Clause to the inclosed Treaty, to stand as a part of it when Signed.

He also told me that with respect to their writing Letters to Gener^l Washington on the Subject of the Evacuation of the Garrisons. the Doctor thought it would not be proper for them to appear in it, in that way, on account of particular Connections, And that it was unnecessary, Since upon Sight of the Treaty, Signed by them, Gener^l Washington would readily settle a Convention with Sir Guy Carleton that would make every thing easy in the evacuation of the Garrisons. They wish much to have an Answer from you as soon as possible, so as the Treaty may be finally closed.

After that is done, I will, agreeable to my Instructions, bespeak their attention to the Sundry Articles not included therein, but recommended to the justice and humanity of the Commissioners. And shall not forget that one in particular, respecting a closer Union hereafter. I have no great hopes of such a thing, yet what Doct^r Franklin once said, That they might possibly at last enter into a Confederacy with us, will give me a fair pretence to touch upon the Subject. Mr Jay also said something like it, the other day But I did not seem to attend to it, And think it best to defer touching upon things of that kind untill their Treaty is signed, and they are entirely free, as they have always appeared so jealous of its being thought that the Merits of their Claim of Independence were to rest on Assurances of any other Conditions than what ought to constitute an Agreement between States treating on an equal footing.

With a view to a Smooth & quick Conclusion with those Gentlemen, I would beg leave to suggest that if the Inclosed Draft is found to be right in the main, & exceptionable only in immaterial Articles, that I may have Orders to Sign the Treaty, with the necessary Amendments respecting those Articles, if they can be Carried, but Leaving it to my best endeavours to obtain a Consent to those Amendments, if they are not so indispensible as not to be left under that uncertainty.

Under such discretionary permission I shall do the best I can; and if I find I cannot Succeed, I shall avail myself of such general power, & sign the Treaty, and so put an end to all Differences with America, in the way Mr Jay said to me last night – "Once we have signed this Treaty, We shall have no more to do but to look on and see what the People here are about. They will not like to find that we are so far advanced; and have for some time appeared anxious & inquisitive as to our plan of Settlement; upon which Subject I was lately tried by a certain Marquis, but I gave him no Satisfaction and wish that for some time as little may be said about it as possible," Upon the whole respecting the foreign Treaties, I am apt to think, if the Demands are unreasonable, even on the part of France, they will not be Countenanced by those Commissioners. Mr Jay having Scored out the words, relative to *peace or Truce*, I thought was done under an Impression of that nature. And with respect to Spain, I believe they think themselves very little Concerned.

Mr Fitzherbert being anxious to dispatch this Messenger immediately, I am obliged to write these Letters in some hurry, & hope you'll be so good to excuse the Inacuracies which I have not time to alter or correct.

We have only one Courier remaining here, but hope soon another will be sent over – In case Georgia had no Chartered right to go back to the Missisippi, I can still get W. Florida carried higher up than the Latitude of 31. at least I hope so. And I beg leave to add that if the Line between Nova Scotia & Masachusets could be determined with certainty, by Charter or otherways, it would be very desireable, Since I own I do not like opening a Commission with the New Eng^d Men, after all our other Differences are settled by Treaty. I tried to avoid it, but could not. If a Line of Seperation is quoted, I should wish that the time or period of Ascertainm^t and proofs or signs of acquiescence on the part of Masachusets, was also mentioned. My Friend Mr Richd Jackson I believe could get those two points Settled.

I have the honour to be Sir Your most obedient humble Servant
R. 11th.   Richard Oswald.

PRO: FO 27/2, v. 557, f. 705 (LC transcription).

Sundry Articles Recommended in Richard Oswald's Instructions but not Included in the Treaty

Paris 11th. Octr 1782

Minutes of Sundry Articles recommended in my Instructions, not included in the Treaty.

1   provision for Debts due to British Subjects

2   Restitutions to Loyalists & Refugees.

          Dispensed with in a posterior Article, and yet may be touched upon by me on a proper occasion if included in the Observations

3   pardon of supposed Crimes. I was answered, they were under provincial Jurisdiction. the Congress having no power in that respect.

4   Immediate Release of prisoners. In the Treaty this is referred to a general peace, yet I should think an Order may be obtained for a release of all prisoners of War immediately on the Execution of the Treaty. Or if any difficulty, it will be only to wait on Exchange. in case of Captures at Sea in the Interim

5   Drying Fish in Newfoundland, Excepted in the Instruct^ns but demanded in the Treaty. Quere. if material. Supposed not so. When the priviledge of Fishing was ask^t by Dr F. in August, this was not mentioned particularly, and I did not think it proper to appear so attentive & tenacious of such like Indulgences, so as to ask any questions about it. And when lately demanded, although I objected, yet did not insist, for the same reason. And now although M^r. Jay seems not positively to say that the Priviledge is indispensible, yet I own I wish much that it may not be considered in Eng^d as a matter of such Consequence as to occasion a Claim of Exception. For to tell the truth, When D^r. Franklin stated the priviledge of Fishing I suspected Drying was included, though not mentioned. Otherways I should have wondered at his asking our leave for Americans catching Fish in the open seas, so near their own Coasts, and wrote so in my Letters at the time.

6th   Foederal Union. I thought it best not to touch upon the Subject, as inferring a Right to a return of Favour the sense of which those

Gentlemen had always disclaimed. And which if demanded at
Paris, would undoubtedly be known to this Court and would be
either Opposed: or a Similar Compact in their favour expected and
insisted on. Once indeed Dᶠ Franklin mentioned these Words
without being askt, as a thing that might perhaps happen And
that may plead my excuse in mentioning the thing again –
although I own without any hopes of Success.

7   Value of Ungranted Lands in the several States
If Observations are sent over, it may be proper to State the
Importance of this Resignation. Being a Fund including the Back
Lands of Canada, of immense amount.

Since according as the population increases, & the People go
Settling backward, these Lands will be sold for high prices for the
benefit of the respective provinces. Which can be easily managed
under the direction of a Land Officer in each of them. So that
they will be annually receiving an Increase of Revenue. And if
they should, for any particular purpose want to borrow Money, &
incline to Anticipate they can be at no loss; Since I should
consider a Mortgage on that Revenue, in proportion to the amount
of its actual or estimated production, as good Security as any in
Europe, or any other part of the World.

The Back Countries of Virginia, North Carolina, South Carolina
and Georgia, will be particularly fortunate in this respect, as they
go all the way to the Mississippi through the most fertile
Countries, and Singularly happy in the convenience of Inland
Navigation, and the Climate the best in the World. So that they
will be continually drawing Inhabitants from the New Engᵈ &
other Northern Colonies and nothing will prevent their making
Great Drafts upon Europe but the danger and expence of a long
Sea passage.

As these things cannot be disputed by the Commissʳˢ themselves,
I think this is a good time for its being taken nottice of, in the
Observations on the Treaty, in hopes, by *shewing them that we are
apprised of the Importance of the Concession*, they will consider it as
a farther proof of His Majestys willingness to Satisfy the
Inhabitants of those New Countries in thus resigning into their
hands a property of the Crown of such immense value, and which,
in no just sense whatever, can be Supposed to stand in any
relation or Connection with the publick Rights for which they had
been contending.

Upon the merits of which I think we may plead in favour of
Loyal Sufferers. Or in some other respects ought to make some

impression on good natured and Sensible Men, and who abstracting from Mistakes as to Motives of publick Conduct, appear in the view of private life highly deserving of Confidence and Consideration.

What makes me insist so much on an Expectation that a State of this matter offered to those Gentlemen would have a good effect, is the Conversation I had with Dr F. in April, when he Sett such value on the Chance of gaining the additional Lands of Canada. as advised in my Letters at the time. &^{c}. If taken nottice of: I will endeavour to do justice to the Subject.

8   Independence of all other Nations, as of England.

I did not propose it, being certain it would be to no purpose and would have been ill received if not resented by the Commissioners considering the present situation of things. Besides, if anything can be promised upon regarding those Communities or States – this is an Event I could venture to say will never happen. Since taking them Conjunctively they will soon grow out of the reach of Comparison as to Consequence with almost any Nation in Europe. And at this time could have no motive for bending to any of them.

However there is one thing Which might not be improper to get included as a Clause in the Treaty, if it can be carried easily. Viz. That none of the States shall alienate to any Power in Europe, any Island, Harbour. Post or Territory by Lease or temporary Assignment. Since that might be done both to the Northward & Southward so as to be hurtful to G. Britain both in Peace & War. For it is to be considered that as each of these States are Independent within themselves, as to their Territories and particular affairs, they might enter into such Compact with France or Spain without any violation of the general Confederacy, unless restrained on this occasion and there is no saying but Grants of this nature might be carried in their Assemblies by Factious people under the temptation of lucrative compensations. I have mentioned this to Mr Jay Since the Treaty was sent off, and he has promised to take it into consideration.

Richard Oswald

PRO: FO 27/2, v. 557, f. 719 (LC transcription).

Richard Oswald to Thomas Townshend

Sir   Paris 11th Octr 1782.

By the Courier...who went from hence on the 8th, I did myself the honour of writing you of that date, inclosing a Copy of final Propositions of Peace, between Great Britain and the American Colonies. To which their Commissioners had assented; and agreed, that, if approved of by His Majesty, they would immediatly Sign it; So as there should be nothing further wanting to put an end to all Differences between the two Countries, but a Termination of the War with France.

As there are Sundry Articles not included in Said Treaty which are recommended in my Instructions, it is proper I should give my reasons for not insisting on them; or for appearing to approve of the Plan without their being Submitted to further discussion.

I wished to do this by the last Courier; but Mr Fitzherbert was so pressing to get him dispatched that I could not overtake him in time. However having met with a Private Hand, just going over, who may possibly arrive before an Answer is returned to said propositions, I take the Opportunity of sending the inclosed Minute of the said Articles; with some other general Remarks relative to the business; the whole Submitted to your private Consideration; and to be taken nottice of, in a different way, more or less, as to you may Seem proper.

I shall however, in general, take the liberty here to say. That I thought it of importance to bring on the business so far, knowing of what material Consequence a prospect of such Agreement must, even of itself, be to the Nation; and how much besides it might influence the foreign Treaties to our advantage. And therefor did not think it adviseable to throw in any Impediments in the way of a Conclusion, by Demands which I apprehended would not have been attended to – And if offer'd and not admitted, and sent home in that way, would have left every thing so open upon the return of an Answer, that the Commissioners here might think themselves entitled to make an addition of new Demands, to ballance those disputed Articles. And so we might be no further on towards a Conclusion, than we had been for some Months past.

Besides, I knew that it hath always been the wish of the Minister of this Court, that the Americans should go no faster in their Treaty than they do themselves. And indeed, that the main Question regarding America should not be quickly determined. Or rather the Grant to be postponed, so as to close with the final determination of both. For this I had the best authority, by a quotation of the Ministers expressions on the Subject. Viz Why they should not seek for the Effect before the Cause; meaning the progress of the Treaty &^{c}

On this account, I thought it best, to assent as far as depended on me, to the propositions as offered, in this general way; and to rest the Issue upon the broad bottom of a Mutual disposition to a renewal of former Corespondence & friendship, without Seeming to attend to a variety of Subordinate Stipulations, which might betray a want of Confidence in the declared professions of good will; and for the Contravention of which, were it to happen, there never would in any future time, be any Remedy in our power.

. . . . .

...I have the honour to be Sir Your most obedient humble Servant

Richard Oswald

. . . . .

R. 18th.

PRO: FO 27/2, v. 557, f. 713 (LC transcription).

John Jay to Robert R. Livingston

Dear Sir,   Paris 13th. October 1782.

I hope my Letter to you of the 18th September, of which I also sent a Duplicate, has come safe to hand, for it contained important Matter – namely a Copy of a Letter from Marbois to Vergennes against our sharing in the Fishery.

This Court advised and persuaded us to treat with Oswald under his first Commission, I positively refused.

C. Aranda will not or cannot exchange Powers with me, and yet wants me to treat with him. This Court would have me do it but I decline it.

I would give you Details but must not until I have an American to carry my Letters from hence.

Oswald is well disposed. You shall never see my Name to a bad Peace, nor to one that does not secure the Fishery.

I have received many long Letters from you, which I am as busy in decyphering as my Health will permit.

M. Fayette is very desirous to give us his aid – but as we have a competent Number of Commissioners it would not be necessary to give him that Trouble.

I am, Dear Sir, With great Esteem and Regard, Your most obedient Servant,   John Jay.

. . . . .

NA: PCC, item 110, v. 2, pp. 271-272 (LBkC); M247, reel 135.

John Jay to Gouverneur Morris

Dear Morris   Paris 13 Octr. 1782

I have received your festina lente Letter, but wish it had been, at least partly, in Cypher; you need not be informed of my Reasons for the wish, as by this Time you must know that Seals are, on this Side of the water, rather matters of Decoration, than of use. It gave me nevertheless great Pleasure to recieve that Letter, it being the first from you that had reached me the Lord knows when, except indeed a few Lines covering your Correspondence with a Don.[1] I find you are industrious, and of Consequence useful – so much the better for yourself, for the public, and for our friend Morris, whom I consider as the Pillar of american Credit.

The King of Great Britain by Letters patent under the Great Seal, has authorized Mr Oswald to treat with the Commissioners of the United States of America. His first Commission litterally pursued the enabling act, and the authority it gave him was expressed in the very Terms of that Act vizt. to treat with the Colonies, and with any or either of them, and any part of them, and with any Description of Men in them, and with any Person whatsoever, of and concerning peace, &ca.

Had I not violated the Instructions of Congress their Dignity would have been in the Dust for the french Minister even took Pains not only to perswade us to treat under that Commission but to prevent the second, by telling Fitzherbert that the first was sufficient. I told the Minister that we neither could nor would treat with any nation in the World on any other than on an equal footing.

We may, and we may not have a peace this Winter. Act as if the War would certainly continue, keep proper Garrisons in your strong posts, and preserve your army sufficiently numerous, and well appointed until every Idea of Hostility and Surprize shall have compleatly vanished.

I could write you a volume, but my Health admits only of short Intervals of application.

Present my best wishes to Mr and Mrs. Morris,...and such other of our Friends as may ask how we do. I am dear Morris, very much Yours

John Jay

Ferguson, Robert Morris Papers, *v. 6, p. 579.*
[1] *Not further identified.*

Benjamin Franklin to Robert R. Livingston

Sir,   Passy, Oct. 14. 1782.

I have but just received Information of this Opportunity, and have only time allow'd to write a few Lines.

In my last of the 26th past I mentioned that the Negociation for Peace had been obstructed by the Want of due Form in the English Commissions appointing their Plenipotentiaries. In that for treating with us, the Mentioning our States by their public Name had been avoided, which we objecting to, another is come of which I send a Copy inclosed. We have now made several preliminary Propositions, which the English Minister, M^r· Oswald, has approved & sent to his Court. He thinks they will be approved there; but I have some Doubts. In a few Days however the answer expected will determine. By the first of these articles the King of Great Britain renounces for himself and Successors all Claim and Pretension to Dominion or Territory within the thirteen United States; and the Boundaries are described as in our Instructions; except that the Line between Nova Scotia & New-England is to be settled by Commissioners after the Peace. By another Article the Fishery in the American Seas is to be freely exercis'd by the Americans wherever they might formerly exercise it while united with Great Britain. By another, the Citizens and Subjects of each Nation are to enjoy the same Protection & Privileges in each others Ports and Countries, respecting Commerce, Duties &c. that are enjoy'd by native Subjects. The Articles are drawn up very fully by M^r· Jay; who I suppose sends you a Copy. If not it will go by the next Opportunity. If these Articles are agreed to, I apprehend little Difficulty in the rest. Something has been mention'd about the Refugees and English Debts; but not insisted on, as we declar'd at once that whatever Confiscation had been made in America, being in Virtue of the Laws of particular States, the Congress had no Authority to repeal those Laws, and therefore could give us none to stipulate for such Repeal.

. . . . . .

The different Accounts given of Lord Shelbourne's Character with respect to Sincerity, induced the Ministry here to send over M. de Rayneval, Secretary of the Council, to converse with him, and endeavour to form by that Means a more perfect Judgment of what was to be expected from the Negociation. He was five or Six Days in England, saw all the Ministers, and return'd quite satisfy'd that they are sincerely desirous of Peace; so that the Negociations now go on, with some Prospect of Success. But the Court & People of England are very changeable. A little Turn of Fortune in their Favour some times turns their Heads; and I shall not think a speedy Peace to be depended on till I see the Treaties signed.

I am obliged to finish. With great Esteem I have the honour to be, Sir, Your most obedient and most humble Servant

B. Franklin

NA: PCC, item 82, v. 2 pp. 281-284 (LS); M247, reel 108.

Comte de Vergennes to Chevalier de la Luzerne

[Translation]

Nᵒ 40   Versailles, 14 October 1782

I have received, Sir, the despatches that you have done me the honor of writing me from Nᵒ. 253 to Nᵒ. 263 inclusively, as well as all the papers with which they were accompanied.

You have done very well, Sir, to hold firm vis-à-vis Mr. Morris on the article of subsidies. As the King has not contracted any obligation to furnish them, he wants to be the master of acting in this regard according to his good pleasure; and the more unreasonableness the Americans show, the less facilities they will find. Up to now the King has given Congress proofs of the greatest generosity, and I do not doubt that if circumstances require it, next year His Majesty will make a new effort to assist the United States. But if we are so happy as to arrive at peace, it is sensible that the King must cease to pay the American army, which would then become as useless as it is habitually inactive, but it would be dangerous, I think, in the present state of affairs, to make this announcement to Congress. Therefore, if someone speaks to you of help for next year, you will limit yourself to responding that you are still unaware of the King's intentions in this regard. However, you will not conceal from Mr. Morris that we are astonished at the demands that do not cease to be made on us, while the Americans obstinately refuse the payment of taxes; that it seems to us infinitely more natural to raise from them, rather than from the King's subjects, the funds that the defense of their cause requires. As for the payment of interest, you may declare peremptorily that the King will not take it upon himself, and that the discontent that might result from this determination will serve only to estimate at their just value the gratitude and the attachment of the Americans for France. I do not have, Sir, any new reflection to transmit to you on the sums that Congress owes His Majesty. This affair is as a rule in return for the contract that I have signed with Mr. Franklin, a copy of which I addressed to you with my despatch Nᵒ 38.

As this year's campaign is entirely finished, Sir, it would be superfluous to undertake an examination of the different plans that you have proposed. As for what is the destination of our troops, that has been indicated to M. de Rochambeau, and I presume that that general will not have left you unaware of the dispositions that he will have made in consequence of His Majesty's orders.

I myself am very much relieved, Sir, that the plan regarding Canada has not been placed in execution. It would have cost us, in pure loss, a great deal of time, money, and men. You know our system with regard to

Canada. It is invariable, in the same way that all that hinders the conquest of that country will enter essentially into our views. But you will yourself perceive, Sir, that this fashion of thinking ought to be an impenetrable secret from the Americans. It would be a crime for which they would never pardon us. It is therefore appropriate to leave them in the illusion, to make all the demonstrations necessary for them to think that we share it, and to oppose without affectation the endeavors to which it might draw them, if we are required to cooperate therein. We think like the Americans, Sir, on the importance of the establishment of the English at Oswego; this station, at the same time that it overawes the Savages, places the English in position to trouble the rear of the province of New York. But Congress should have made these reflections sooner, and have taken measures in consequence. Moreover, I do not see on what grounds the Americans would form claims to the lands that border Lake Ontario. Either these lands belong to the Savages, or they are a dependency of Canada. In either case the United States have no right to them. But I know, Sir, all the extravagance of the Americans' claims and views. According to Congress the Charters that emanated from the British Crown extend the domains of America from the ocean to the South Sea. Such is the system proposed by Mr. Jay as the basis for his negotiations with Spain. A parallel delirium does not merit being seriously refuted; however, a confidential note has been sent to Mr. Jay by which it is pretty much demonstrated that the boundaries of the United States south of the Ohio are limited to the mountains in following the watershed, and that what is to the north of that river, namely the lakes, has earlier been part of Canada. For the rest, Sir, these notions are for you alone. You will take care not to show yourself informed thereon, because we wish so much the less to intervene, at least for the present, in the discussion subsisting between M. the Comte d'Aranda and Mr. Jay, that the two parties demand countries to which neither of them has acquired rights, and which it will be very nearly impossible to accord them.

According to the letters of M. de Verac, Mr. Dana conducts himself rather well in Petersburg, and directs his steps exactly according to the counsels of the King's Minister. It is true that the latter has prevented the American agent from displaying his character, and he has thereby rendered an essential service to Congress, because Mr. Dana would have inevitably compromised it. If we were to recognize in Russia a tendency to appreciate and to treat the Americans as independent, it is natural to suppose that we would concur in it with zeal, since we have been making war for five years to support their independence. If Mr. Dana had made this reflection, he would, I think, be wary of accusing M. the Marquis de Verac of indifference. But the American agents are not conspicuous for healthy views adapted to the political situation of Europe. They have all the presumption of ignorance, but there is reason to think that experience will not delay in enlightening and correcting them.

You are of the opinion, Sir, that Mr. Adams has proposed to the Dutch an article relative to the commerce of the Islands. I have absolutely no knowledge of such a proposition, and if it has been made without our knowledge I have reason to think that it has not been accepted. Whatever may be the case, St. Eustatius and the other Dutch Colonies are not in a state to fill America's needs for products of the Islands. I say the same of the Danes. However, Sir, your reflections on this matter, an abstraction made from the conduct of the Dutch, have long held the attention of the King and of his council, and I am persuaded that it will be seriously deliberated when peace provides us the tranquility necessary for objects of this nature. You are right to think, Sir, that it would be useful if the United States had some sort of navy, and the King has approved the insinuations that you have made to have them adopt this system, but it is impossible for us to support it. We ourselves have an urgent need of our naval stores as well as of our workers, and we cannot give up either one. That is what you may reply if you are asked for our good offices on the objects in question.

I have informed you by my despatch N° 39, Sir, of the situation in which Messrs. Franklin and Jay have found themselves vis-à-vis Mr. Oswald. The objections that they have proposed against the form of the full power of this English agent, joined to the observations that I myself have made to Mr. Fitzherbert, have been taken into consideration by the Council of St. James. A new full power has been drawn up in which the Colonies are named the United States. This full power has been exchanged for that of the American plenipotentiaries; thus this article is perfectly in order according to the desire and the satisfaction of Congress. I have been assured that substantive negotiations are underway, and that the English plenipotentiary was rather accommodating, but I am beyond the state of telling you anything positive in this regard, Messrs. Jay and Franklin holding themselves in the most absolute reserve in my regard. They have not yet even given me a copy of Mr. Oswald's full power. I think, Sir, that it would be useful for you to relate this particular circumstance to Mr. Livingston, so that he can, if he judges it appropriate, remind the two American plenipotentiaries of the tenor of their instructions. But you will take the greatest care not to present what I tell you as a complaint, and you will pray Mr. Livingston not to make any reproach to Messrs. Franklin and Jay, because that would give them dissatisfaction, which must be avoided. It will suffice that this minister prompts them to show us the confidence that is prescribed for them and which is analogous to the liaisons that subsist between the King and the United States.

The negotiations have just been linked by formal proposals with France, Spain, and Holland, and we are awaiting responses from the Court of London. It would be difficult for us to anticipate it. All we know is that the dispositions of the King of England and of his council are as sincere as our own. We are as certain of it as it is possible to be from the conversations that M. de Rayneval, whom the King recently sent to England, had with the British ministers. This mission had no other object than that of acquiring information on the overtures that he had made for us by an indirect route. The first object of M. de Rayneval's conferences was the independence of America, and the dispatching of Mr. Oswald's new power places us in a position of appreciating the language he has pursued on this subject. I enter into this detail, Sir, because M. de Rayneval's trip to England will later become known in America from the newspapers, and it is possible that some ill-disposed persons would seek to give a false color to our action.

I am sending you herewith, Sir, the most recent account of the siege of Gibraltar. You will observe there the destruction of the floating batteries. I do not know yet whether the siege will be raised or continued, but what I can assure you is that the event in question will not influence the plan of the King and of the King of Spain, and that Their Majesties are resolved to continue the war unless they succeed in making peace on equitable conditions.   Vergennes

FFAA: Pol. Corr., U.S., v. 22, f. 115 (LC transcription).

John Jay's Diary of the Peacemaking

[October 18, 1782]
18. Dined with spanish Embassador, a large Company,...etc., etc., etc. I took occasion to mention to the Embassador <with>[1] Mr. Oswalds *new* Com[missio]n[2] and my Regret that Spain should be later than Britain in acknow[ledgin]g our Independence. He said he had powers to treat with me *tres bellement* whenever I should be authorized to settle our Limits, which must be done previous to our Engagements. He asked whether I had mentioned that Matter to the Congress. I told him I had. He said that when my further Instructions should [arrive] we might proceed etc.

· · · · · ·

Morris, Jay Papers, v. 2, p. 447.
  [1] Deleted material in original document in angle brackets.
  [2] Text provided in square brackets.

John Jay's Diary of the Peacemaking

[October 20-21, 1782]

[20]...Count de Vergennes speaking of the british Com[missione]rs here said, that unless they decided within ten Days or a Fortnight, they should not be permitted to stay here to keep up their Stocks and intrigue.

21 October 1782. Visited Mr. Oswald. He told me that he expected the Answer of his Court to the Articles, within a few Days, and as he had recommended them warmly, did not doubt of their being agreed to....

. . . . .

Morris, Jay Papers, v. 2, p. 448.

Lord Shelburne's Notes of Verbal Instructions for Henry Strachey for the Peace Negotiations

[Oct. 20. 1782.][1]

Urge our Right to all the Backlands, the Claims of the Provinces having been Bounded by the Proclamation of 1763, and acquiesced in.

Urge the Right of the King to *the soil*, under the Charters however understood –

Urge the French Boundery of Canada.

Urge the Boundary Established by the Quebec Act, which was acquiesced in.

Urge all this with a view to obtain some Compensation for the Refugees, either by a direct Cession of Territory in their favour, or by engaging the Half, or some Proportion of what the back Lands may produce when Sold, or a Sum Mortgaged on those Lands, or at least a favorable Boundary of Nova Scotia, extending it, if possible, so as to include the Province of Main; If that can't be, the Province of Sagadahock, or at the very least to include Penobscott.

Urge the Just Boundarys of West Florida.

But it is understood that if nothing of this can be obtained after the fairest and most strenuous Trials, it may be left to Commissaries to Settle, and the American Propositions accepted, leaving out the Right of Drying Fish on the Island of Newfoundland, and Confining them to what hitherto they have used, as a *Drift Fishery* and expunging all the last Article except what regards the Missisippi, administration having no Power as to the Act of Navigation.

It must appear authentically § that every instance has been used in favor, both of the Refugees, and of the Debts prior & Subsequent to 1775, and the most favorable terms obtained, if possible, in the way of Absolute and positive Engagement: if not, in the way of Recognition   to return as soon as possible.

The Refugees are of great importance, but if the Province of Main be left to Nova Scotia and the Americans can be brought to join Us in regard to West Florida, there are Resources which may satisfy them; But the Debts require the Most Serious attention. – that *honest* Debts may be *honestly* paid in *honest* Money. –

No Congress Money.

Some Security as to the American Courts of Justice, in lieu of their right of Appeal which subsisted when the Debts were Contracted.

§ that is a Signed answer.

LC: *Miscellaneous Manuscripts Collection, Sir Henry Strachey Papers (AD).*

[1] *Strachey, Henry (1736-1810). British political figure. Appointed private secretary to Lord Clive during his last visit to India, 1764. Member of Parliament, 1768-1778, 1780-1807. Secretary to the Carlisle Commission for restoring peace in America, 1778. Assisted Richard Oswald in negotiations with the American peace commissioners, 1782.*

Lord Shelburne to Richard Oswald

Private.   Shelburne House. 21. Octr 1782.
Dear Sir,

I am to acknowledge your Letters of the 19$^{th.}$ Sept^r & 11$^{th.}$ of Octr upon the Subject of Mr Laurens. Though the Business was finish'd exactly in the Manner recommended in your Letter, previous to the receipt of it, It may be expedient however to apprize you how little this Gentleman is to be depended on....But it is right for me further to apprize you that Mr Lauren's Conduct has been fraught with the most active Malignity, which seems to have been pointed in Preference to every Person in Proportion to his Obligation to them, confining his real Confidence to the most exceptionable Characters with whom he had to do. It would be wasting Time to go into further Particulars of his Ingratitude, Insincerity, & total Want of Principle.

I trust & hope you are better grounded in your Judgement of the American Commissioners now at Paris. I am dispos'd to expect every Thing from Dr Franklin's comprehensive Understanding and Character. And, as I know nothing to the contrary, I am open to every good Impression you give us of Mr Jay. But as you desire to be assisted by my Advice, I should act with great Insincerity, if I did not convey to you that I find it difficult if not impossible to enter into the Policy of all that you recommend upon the Subject both of the Fishery and the Boundaries, and of the Principle which you seem to have adopted of going before the Comm^{rs} in every Point of Favour or Confidence. The Maxim is not only new in all Negotiations; but I consider it as no way adapted to our present Circumstances, but as diametrically opposite to our Interests in the present moment. Supposing the Colonies to return to the State they were in in 1763, I consider it as of the utmost Importance to keep the Fishery as distinct as possible, to avoid the numberless Disputes which occurred perpetually before the present War: But the Seperation on the point of taking place makes it ~~But in case of Sepas the~~ indispensible for the Wellfare of both Countries to prevent future contortion.

In regard to Refugees, I speak of the Mass of them, avoiding to enter into particular odious Cases which may always occur in such great Concussions, – Can there in nature be any thing more reasonable than to insist on the Justice due to them? Nor can a single argument be offer'd against it except what you urge of the particular Situation of the Commiss^{n} acting under Thirteen Provinces with different Interests, and in fact no Common Centre. To remedy this, the Matter of the Boundaries & Back Lands naturally presents itself. Independantly of all the nonsense of Charters, I mean when they talk of extending as far as the Sunsets, the Soil is, & has always been acknowledg'd to be The King's. For the Good of America, whatever the Government may be, new Provinces must be erected on those back Lands & down the Mississippi; and supposing them to be sold, what can be so reasonable as, That Part of the Produce, where The King's Property alone is in question, should be applied in part to furnish Subsistence to those, whom for the sake of Peace he can never consistent with his Honor entirely abandon. The Debts due to our Merchants previous to 1775 cannot be lightly pass'd over – They ~~are~~ regard some of our most considerable Merchants, who are full of apprehensions, & are making daily applications to Government. *Honest* Debts must be *honestly* paid and in *Honest* Money and To prove them Honest Some Security is expected in lieu of the Right of Appeal which existed when they were contracted. These are Considerations dictated by Honour & Justice, which can never be sufficiently dwelt & insisted on.

I beg ~~at the same Time~~ to recommend the Question of Policy to your most serious Reflection. If we are to look to regain the Affections of America, to Reunion in any Shape or even to Commerce & Friendship, is it not ~~to~~ the last Degree of consequence to retain every means possible to gratify America at a future, I hope not very distant Day, when the Negotiation will not be carried on at a Foreign Capital, not under the Eye, if not Controul of inveterate Enemies, nor under the reputed Impulse of absolute Necessity. This is to me such an obvious Line of Policy, that I cannot believe it possible for it to escape your Attention, and indeed am very clearly of opinion that your whole Endeavour should be pointed to it, and if there is the Disposition you mention in the Commissioners towards Great Britain, and it is stated to them with Address, I should think they might be brought to enter into it, as they must ~~and is~~ feel it perfectly consistent with the Language hitherto held to them, It ~~being~~ is at the same time certainly of Importance to preserve their confidence & Good Will, when it can be done with out Sacrifices which ~~no private Mom Spee~~ mere Speculation can ~~not~~ never warrant.

I have nothing else to add, except the particular Satisfaction which it gives me to find that what has pass'd hitherto in the American or French Negotiation has given rise to no Speculation in the Funds. I need not tell you the numbers which are upon the Watch, and of how much Importance it is to the Reputation of every Person concern'd to avoid the Possibility of it, which can only be done by the most determin'd Reserve on every Particular where Communication can by any Labour or Pains be avoided.

Lord Shelburne

Clements Library: Shelburne Papers, v. 71, pp. 151-159 (AD).

Thomas Townshend to Benjamin Franklin

Sir   Whitehall 23ᵈ Octʳ 1782.

As Mʳ Strachey is going from hence to Paris with some particulars with Mʳ Oswald, which were not to be easily explained in Writing, I take the liberty of Introducing him to your acquaintance, tho' I am not sure that he is not already a little known to you.

The confidential situation in which he stands with me, makes me particularly desirous of presenting him to you.

I believe Sir, I am enough known to you for you to believe me when I say, that there has not been from the beginning a single Person more averse to the unhappy War, or who wishes more earnestly than I do, for a return of Peace and mutual Amity between Great Britain and America.

I am with great Regard Sir &c.   T. Townshend.

Clements Library: Shelburne Papers, v. 70, p. 318 (C).

Lord Shelburne to Richard Oswald

Private   Shelburne House 23ᵈ Oct 82.

Dear Sir

On my return from Streatham this morning I find Mʳ Strachey has deferred his Journey for the sake of some papers which were to be Copied. This gives me an opportunity of writing to You a few Lines, as it may be agreeable to You to know something more of him, than his being the Confidential Secretary of Mʳ Townshend, He is a most amiable well instructed Man, and as it was judged proper that some person shou'd be sent to explain the Boundary's and the authentic Documents, which were only to be found here, I thought it very lucky for Your sake, and for that of the great object we have all in view, that Mʳ Townshend's Choice fell upon him.

⋯ ⋯ ⋯ ⋯ ⋯ ⋯

… I am very truly Yours   Shelburne

PRO: FO 27/2, v. 557, f. 749 (LC transcription).

John Jay's Diary of the Peacemaking

[October 24, 1782]

24 October. Mr. Oswald told me he had recieved a Courier last night. That our articles were under Consideration, and that Mr. Strachey, < Ld. > Mr. Townsend's Sec[retar]y,[1] was on the way here to confer with us about them.

Mr. Oswald declined informing me of the particular Objections, but it was easy to perceive from his Conversation that they related to the back Lands, and he further said "he believed this Court had found means to put a Spoke in our Wheel": he told me that Fitzherbert had received an answer to the french Propositions, that the answer inadvertently gave away the Gum Trade, and that he had *in vain* desired him to postpone the Delivery of the Answer till he should apprize his Court of the Mistake, and give them an opportunity of correcting it. He consulted me on the possibility of keeping Mr. Stracheys coming a Secret. I told him it was not possible, and that it would be best to declare the Truth about it. vizt. that he was coming with Books and Papers relative to our Boundaries.

⋯ ⋯ ⋯ ⋯ ⋯

Dined with Dr. Franklin. I found Mr. De Raynevalle there. Just < before > after Dinner, the Doctor informed me that Raynevalle had sent him word that he would dine with him to Day and would be glad to meet me there. I told the Doctor what I had heard from Oswald about Strachey, and that I thought it best not to say more to Rayneval than that we met with Difficulties, and that Oswald expected to recieve Instructions in a few Days.

We retired with Rayneval. He asked how Matters stood between us and Oswald. We told him that we could not agree about all our Boundaries. We mentioned the one between us and Nova Scotia. He asked what we demanded to the north. We answered that Canada should be reduced to its ancient Bounds. He then contested our Right to these back Lands, etc., etc.

He asked what we expected as to the Fisheries, we said the same Right we had formerly enjoyed. He contested the propriety of that Demand, adding some Strictures on the ambitious and Restless views of Mr. Adams, and intiminated that we might be content with the Coast Fishery.

Morris, Jay Papers, v. 2, pp. 449-450.
[1] Deleted text in original document in angle brackets; provided text in square brackets.

Richard Oswald to Lord Shelburne

My Lord   Paris 24 Octr 1782.

About two hours ago I had the honour of your Lo^p Letter of the 21st. I should have been sorry to have given So much trouble about the Person mentioned in one of my former Letters,[1] if I had not apprehended that in a certain temper, and in a different Situation, he might have been prompted to act the part it would appear he has actually taken on this Side the Water. I have no other motive, So I hope to be excused on account of former favourable prejudices. & that it is impossible absolutely to determine as to peoples Sentiments, where there are no Certain facts to go by.

I am much pleased that Mr Streachy is Coming over, He may be assured of every Assistance I can give him, in the way he may chuse or advise. And I cannot but own that the Objects mentioned in Your Lo^p Letter are of Such Consequence as to be deserving of farther Investigation, & to be taken up afresh. I say nothing in Apology for myself, if I have gone too fast, or have given too much way to Speculation; Since in matters of this Importance, where anything is to be gained for the Public, all private or personal Considerations are not worth thinking of. And I am extremely happy to find that our Affairs are in that Situation, respecting the general State of things, that there is So little Scruple in risking an immediate refusal of the propositions of the American Commissioners. Which I could not help thinking very hard, and limited to too narrow a line of Accommodation –

But in all the time I have been here, as my chief business has been applied to the Sounding this Channel to a general pacification, and Seeing at last no prospect of doing better, I received the propositions as offered, after having upon repeated trials, as to Certain Articles not provided for, received the Answer of the Commiss[r], of their want of Authority to enter upon them and generally attended with Insinuations, easily understood, regarding the Consequences of a Refusal. And to the period, of which there was generally so little time assigned, as could not fail to make an Impression, when there appeared So little effect to be expect[d] from a Dissent. Upon those occasions it was often thrown out, on the Subject of Lands or Boundaries, "We give you Nova Scotia &c[a.] – We shan't medle with them.["] And I have been Since told. "If you want more Land, by persisting you may get less." And when the last Commission came over – One of those Commiss[r], taking the Copy in his hand, and Still objecting to the quotation of Acts of Parliamen[t], Said – "Well this may do – & we are Satisfied and it is well it is done – For let me tell you, Your people have here escaped a very unpleasant piece of business, and at a very critical time." These kind of things had naturally Some effect in reconciling me the better to the plan of the Treaty sent over – About the Drying of Fish, it would appear I have made a great Mistake in thinking it of less importance than it really is. & therefor forbore insisting on the Exceptions for the reasons as mentioned in my Letters. But I hope it be rectified; & possibly a better Accommodation obtained in other Articles, in which my Care & best offices Shall not be wanting. I have a Letter from M[r] Strachey, and have wrote him by the present Messenger to Calais, that I have provided Quarters for him, in the Hotel where I lodge, where there are Apartments to spare in the Lodging's I have taken – As this Courier from M[r] Fitzherbert is just upon his departure, I am obliged to write this in Some haste – which I hope your Lop will excuse. I have the honour to be My Lord Your Lo[p] most obedient humble Servant

Richard Oswald

Clements Library: Shelburne Papers, v. 71, pp. 163-165 (ALS).
[1] *Presumably a reference to John Jay.*

Thomas Townshend to Richard Oswald

Sir   Whitehall. 26th Octr 1782

. . . . .

There was one part of your Letter which referred to a Proposal of Mr Jay's which seems to have been frequently and eagerly urged by him. I mean that of an Expedition against West Florida. I do not think he went so far as to guarantee a quiet Evacuation of New York. This is a matter of great delicacy, and though in some points of view the Proposal appears to be one, with which We might be tempted to close, yet We might put ourselves too much in the power of Friends very newly reconciled to Us, as well as of those who might remain our Enemies, by carrying a large Force to the Southward of all our West India possessions. To be sure We are not disinclined to prefer an attack upon the Spaniards to one upon the French, provided We could by that means bring off Our Army Artillery and Stores without difficulty or insult, and that We should not run a chance of meeting the whole force of France and Spain in defence of the Possessions of the Latter, when the former were apprized of our being tied up from attacking them, or of having that of France employed in the mean time against our Islands.

The Colony of West Florida, is certainly an object of our attention and We should be extremely glad to adopt such measures as might ensure to Us the repossession of it.

If you have any Opportunity of Sounding the Commissioners on this head, or if Mr Jay should return to the Charge, it seems adviseable to see how far he thinks himself enabled to Engage for the Evacuation, and then We shall be better able to judge, in what manner the rest of the Scheme might be put in Execution. I am Sir &c^{a.}   T. Townshend

. . . . .

Clements Library: Shelburne Papers, v. 70, pp. 320-321 (C).

Comte de Vergennes to Comte de Montmorin

[Translation]

N°. 87.   Versailles, 27 October 1782
M. le Cte. de Montmorin

I have received, Sir, the two despatches that you have done me the honor of writing me the 17th of this month under N°s. 83 and 84.

The event that was to take place in the Mediterranean could not fail to have important consequences for whichever side victory has fallen, and you will easily understand the impatience with which we await news of it. I speak to you of neither our fears nor our hopes on the outcome of the fighting, because all I say would be perfectly useless.

But I have apprehensions of another kind, Sir, which torment me greatly. I foresee that if we do not have the worst of it, the Court of Madrid will raise its tone and its pretentions, and it will thereby increase the obstacles its present demands place on peace. I am judging thus from the conduct which M. le Comte de Florida Blanca has followed with you, by the mournful silence which M. d'Aranda has pursued with me on the contents of his last instructions, and most of all by the manner in which he has spoken of the hopes which the presence of the two fleets gives him. I dispense, Sir, with entering into details today in this regard; I will discuss this matter in depth when I know the reply of M. le Comte D'Aranda to the response which the Court of London has made to his first overtures.

This reply, Sir, was to be communicated yesterday; it is only verbal, because the English ministry is so little satisfied with the excess of the Spanish pretentions and the form in which they are presented, by which it could prevent breaking off the negotiations outright. It therefore preferred a verbal response, in the hope that M. D'Aranda, better advised, will make propositions that can be taken into consideration. I am awaiting the issue of the conference, and if M. D'Aranda, making a truce in his misplaced reserve, communicates to me his ulterior determination, I shall not let slip the occasion thoroughly to impress upon him our position, the need we have for peace, and the necessity of undertaking the negotiations promptly and especially in good faith. If I do not succeed in converting this ambassador, or if his instructions tie his hands, I shall not hesitate to address myself directly to the Ministry in Madrid; we owe each other truth as much as we owe each other assistance, and these are circumstances in which dissimulation is unpardonable.

Mr. Fitzherbert yesterday gave me, Sir, the ministerial response of his Court to our propositions. I cannot yet give you the details, because I have not yet reported thereon to the King. All I can say is that it is in general sufficiently satisfactory, although it seems to me at first glance to require some modifications on our part. Moreover, the manner in which it is conceived and the language with which Mr. Fitzherbert has accompanied it more than ever warrant thinking that the English ministry sincerely desires peace, and above all, if it must be done, that it will be prompt. We share its wish in this regard, for if we delay only a little, it will be necessary to prepare for the next campaign whether we want to or not. That reflection merits the most serious attention on our part and on that of Spain, and you must not neglect an occasion to impart this to M. the

Comte de Florida B.

I hope that it will not induce that minister to regard it as a symptom of the defection of which he has the misfortune to suspect us. If we want peace, it is necessary that the groundwork be laid before the 26th of November, the day of the return of the Parliament of England. If we miss that date, the English ministry will no longer be the master of its resolutions, and God knows when the negotiations could be renewed. I say nothing of the consequences which new events may have, nor of the anxieties which the Antilles give me.   Vergennes

FFAA: Pol. Corr., Spain, v. 609, N° 71 (LC transcription).

John Jay's Diary of the Peacemaking

[October 28-29, 1782]

October 28, Monday. Mr. Adams was with me 3 Hours this morning. I mentioned to him the Progress and present State of our Negociation with Britain, my Conjectures as to the Views of France and Spain, and the Part which it appeared to me adviseable for me to act. He concurred with me in Sentiment on all these Points. He recounted the affairs of his Negociation in Holland and the Advice given him by the french Emb[assador] there. He spoke freely what he thought of Dr. Franklin....

29. Mr. Oswald informed me that Mr. Strachey arrived Yesterday. He spoke of limiting our western Extent by a longitudinal Line on the East of the Mississippi. I told him if that was insisted upon it was needless to talk of Peace, for that we never would Yield that point. He proposed to bring Mr. Strachey to see me. He did so.

Mr. Strachey came, and soon after Mr. Adams. Some loose conversation ensued about the Refugees, English Debts, Drying Fish, etc. We are to meet him Tomorrow at 11 oClock at Mr. Oswalds.

Oswald told me in confidence that his court had not yet given an answer to the Spanish Propositions, and that they had offered to give Trinidad for Gibralter.

Morris, Jay Papers, v. 2, pp. 450-51.

Richard Oswald to Lord Shelburne

My Lord.   Paris 29th Octr 1782.

Mr. Strachy arrived here yesterday at noon. & delivered me the Letter Your L^p did me the honour to write me of the 23^{d.} for which I am much obliged to Your Lo^{p.} The Objects therein mentioned are of great importance. And the Alternatives proposed in Your Lo^{ps} Note to Mr Strachy are Certainly very proper. Both he and I will do all we can to make the most of them. Last night we were employed on the Maps and Charters. This Forenoon I introduced Mr Strachy to Mr Jay. When we run over the Several Exceptions to their plan of Treaty. and were joined by Mr Adams, who is come from Holland to take up his Place in this Commission

We then went out to Doct^r Franklin, when the same Subjects, in the way of Conversation, under went another discussion. I cannot say with what Success. Only that I think there is an appearance as that Some things may be gained. To morrow at Eleven o'Clock the Three Commiss^{rs} have agreed to meet at my Quarters, to examine Maps & papers. and thereafter all to dine together at Mr Jays. We are now, at night again employed in that way So as to be the better prepared for them, at least as well as can be done from Materials of Such indefinite construction – .... I have the honour to be with the most Sincere respect My Lord Your Lo^{ps} most obed^t h^l Servt

Richard Oswald

PS It seems to be agreed by all the Comm^{rs}, that *the Debts before the War Should be paid*, if the Debtors are in Circumstances. and that the several provinces Should be liable for Such of them as their Assemblies have levied & taken into their Treasury.

Clements Library: Shelburne Papers, v. 71, pp. 167-169 (ALS).

Henry Strachey to Thomas Townshend

Sir   Paris 29th October 1782

I arrived Yesterday Noon, and passed the remainder of the Day in discussing the several Points with Mr. Oswald. This Morning, we saw Mr Jay, and also Mr Adams (who came hither a few days ago from Holland) and afterwards went to Dr. Franklin at Passy. It is impossible, from the general Conversation, held with each of those Gentlemen, to judge what will be the Result: and hitherto I can only venture to say, that it appears as if we shall be able to gain some Ground.

To morrow Morning we are all to meet, and to go through the different Topics together. My Object will be, to act fully up to Your Intentions, in every Particular; and to expedite the Business without a Moments Delay. But I fear it will be several (I hope not many) Days, before Matters come to a Conclusion. I have the honor to be with the greatest Respect Sir Your most faithful and obedient Servant

H. Strachey.

R 3^d Nov$^{r.}$

PRO: FO 27/2, v. 557, f. 775 (LC transcription).

John Adams to Robert R. Livingston

Sir   Paris October 31 1782.

Having executed the Treaty of Commerce, at the Hague and dispatched four Copies of it, by four different Vessells bound to America from the Texel, and having signed a sufficient Number of Obligations to leave in the Hands of Messr$^{s.}$ Willinks, Vanstaphorsts, and De La Lande and Fynje,[1] and having received Information from Mr Jay, that M$^{r.}$ Oswald had rec^d a Commission from the King his Master under the Great Seal of Great Britain, to treat with the Commissioners of the United States of America I set off, for Paris, where I arrived, on Saturday the Twenty Sixth of this Month, after a tedious Journey, the Roads being on account of long continued Rains, in the worst Condition, I ever knew them.

I waited, forthwith, on M$^{r.}$ Jay, and from him learned the ~~present~~ State of the Conferences. – It is not possible at present to enter into Details. All I can say is in General, that I had the Utmost Satisfaction in finding that he had been all along acting here upon the same Principles upon which I had ventured to Act in Holland, and that we were perfectly agreed in our Sentiments and Systems. – I cannot express it better than in his own Words "To be honest and gratefull to our Allies, but to think for our selves." – I find a Construction put upon one Article of our Instructions by some Persons, which I confess I never put upon it myself. it is represented by some, as Subjecting Us to the french Ministry, as taking away from us, all right of Judging for ourselves, and obliging Us to agree to whatever the french Ministers shall advise Us too, and to [do] nothing without their Consent. – I never Supposed this to be the Intention of Congress. if I had, I never would have accepted the Commission, and if I now thought it their Intention, I could not continue in it. I cannot think it possible to be the Design of Congress. if it is, I hereby resign my Place in the Commission and request that another Person may be immediately appointed in my Stead.

Yesterday, We met Mr Oswald, at his Lodgings, Mr Jay Mr Franklin and myself, <our> on one Side and Mr Oswald assisted by Mr Stretchey, a Gentleman whom I had the Honour to meet in Company with Lord Howe upon Staten Island, in the year 1776 and assisted also by a Mr Roberts, a Clerk in some of the public Offices, with Books, Maps, and Papers, relative to the Boundaries. We have to search, the Boundaries of Grenada the two Floridas, ancient Canada according to the Claims of the French, Proclamation Canada, Act of Parliament Canada &c and the Bounds of Nova Scotia and of most if not all the thirteen States.–

I arrived in a lucky moment, for the Boundary of the Massachusetts because I brought with me, all the essential Documents relative to that object, which are this day to be laid before ~~the Gentlemen~~ my Colleagues in Conference at my House, and afterwards, before ~~that Brit~~ Mr. Oswald.

It is now apparent at least to Mr. Jay and myself, that in order to obtain the Western Lands, the Navigation of the Missisipi, and the Fishery or any of them We must act with Firmness and Independence as well as Prudence and Delicacy. With these there is little doubt We may obtain them all.

Yesterday I visited Mr Brantzen the Dutch Minister, and was by him very frankly and candidly informed of the whole Progress of the Negotiation on their Part. – it is very shortly told. They have exchanged full Powers with Mr Fitzherbert, and communicated to him, their Preliminaries, according to their Instructions, which I have heretofore transmitted to Congress. – Mr. Fitzherbert has sent them to London and rec^d an Answer, but has communicated to them no more of this answer, than this, that those Preliminaries are not relished at S^t· James's.– He excused his not having seen them for 6 or 7 days, by pretence of Indisposition, but they are informed that he has made frequent Visits to Versailles during those days, and sent off and received several Couriers.–

How the Negotiation advances, between Mr Fitzherbert and the C. de Vergennes <****> and the C. De Aranda, We know not.–

The object of Mr D. Raynevals journey to London, is not yet discovered by ~~either of my Colleagues or by me~~ any of Us.– It is given out, that he was sent to see, whether, the British Ministry were in Earnest. But this is too general, it is suspected that he went to insinuate something relative to the Fishery and the Boundaries, but it is probable he did not succeed respecting the former, and perhaps not entirely with respect to the latter.–

With Great Respect &c   John Adams

MHS: The Adams Papers, microfilm reel 108 (LBkC).
[1] Willinks, Vanstaphorsts, de la Lande, and Fynje. The quartet of Amsterdam banking

houses that handled the Dutch loans contracted by the United States. The firms were those of: (1) Wilhem and Jan Willink, (2) Nicolaas and Jacob van Staphorst, (3) Jacobus de la Lande, and (4) Hendrik Fynje.

From John Adams' Journal

Sunday Novr 3^d

In my first Conversation with Franklin on Tuesday last, he told me of M^r· Oswald's Demand of the payment of debts & compensation to the Tories – he said their Answer had been, that we had not Power, nor had Congress. I told him, I had no Notion of cheating any body. The Question of paying Debts, and that of compensating Tories were two. I had made the same Observation that forenoon to M^r· Oswald and M^r· Strachey, in Company with M^r· Jay at his House – I saw it struck M^r· Strachey with peculiar pleasure – I saw it instantly smiling in every Line of his Face – M^r· O. was apparently pleased with it too.

In a subsequent Conversation with my Colleagues I proposed to them that we should agree that Congress should recommend it to the States to open their Courts of Justice for the Recovery of all just debts. They gradually fell into this Opinion, and we all expressed these Sentiments to the English Gentlemen, who were much pleased with it, and with Reason; because it silences the Clamors of all the British Creditors against the Peace, & prevents them from making common Cause with the Refugees.

M^r· J came in & spent two hours in Conversation upon our Affairs, & we attempted an Answer to M^r· Oswald's Letter. He is perfectly of my Opinion, or I am of his, respecting M^r· Dana's true Line of Conduct, as well as his with Spain, & ours with France, Spain & England.

V. has endeavoured to persuade him to treat with d'Aranda, without exchanging Powers – He refuses. V. also pronounced Oswald's first Commission sufficient, & was for making the Acknowledgment of American Independence the first Article of the Treaty – J. would not treat. The consequence was, a complete Acknowledgment of our Independence by Oswald's new Commission under the great Seal of G.B. to treat with the Commissioners of the United States of America. Thus a temperate firmness has succeeded every where, but the base System no where.

... How far are we bound to favor the Spaniards? Our Treaty with France must & should be sacredly fulfilled, & we must admit Spain to accede when She will: but until She does our Treaty does not bind us to France to assist Spain.

The present Conduct of England & America resembles that of the Eagle

& Cat. An Eagle, scaling over a Farmer's Yard, espied a Creature, that She thought an Hare – He pounced upon & took him up in the Air – the Cat seized him by the Neck with her Teeth, & round the Body with her fore & hind Claws. The Eagle, finding himself scratched and pressed, bids the Cat let go & fall down – No says the Cat, I wont let go & fall – you shall stoop & set me down.

NA: PCC, *item 84, v. 4, pp. 242-244; M247, reel 112.*

Richard Oswald to the American Peace Commissioners

Gentlemen,   Paris, 4th. Novem^r 1782.

You may remember that, fm. the very first beginning of our Negotiation for settling a Peace between Great Britain and America, I insisted that you should positively Stipulate for the restoration of the Property of all those Persons, under the denomination of Loyalist or Refugees, who have taken part with Great Britain in the present war; Or, if the Property had been resold & passed into such variety of persons, as to render the restoration impracticable, (which you asserted to be the Case in many instances,) you should stipulate for a Compensation or indemnification to those persons, adequate to their Losses. To these Propositions you said you could not accede – Mr. Strachey, since his arrival at Paris, has most strenuously joined me in insisting upon the said Restitution, Compensation or Indemnification, and in laying before you every argument in favour of those demands, founded upon national honor, and upon the true Principles of Justice –

These demands you must have understood as extend, not only to all persons, of the abovementioned description, who have fled to Europe, but likewise to all those, who may be now in any parts of North-America, dwelling under the protection of his Majesty's arms or otherwise.

We have also insisted upon a mutual stipulation for a general Amnesty on both sides, comprehending thereby an enlargement of all persons, who, on account of offences, committed or supposed to be committed, since the commencement of hostilities, may be now in Confinement; and for an immediate repossession of their Properties, and peaceable enjoyment thereof under the Government of the United States – To this you have not hitherto given a particular or direct answer –

It is, however, incumbent upon me, as Commissioner of the King of Great Britain, to repeat those several demands; and without going over those arguments upon paper, (which we have so often urged in Conversation,) to press your immediate attention to these subjects; and to urge you to enter into proper stipulations for the restitution, compensation and Amnesty abovementioned, before we proceed further in this negotiation –

I have the honor to be, &^{ct} Rich$^{d.}$ Oswald

NA: PCC, *item 85, pp. 274-276(C)*; M247, *reel 114.*

Preliminary Articles of Peace: Second Draft Treaty

[4-7 November 1782]

Articles agreed upon by and between Richard Oswald Esquire the Commissioner of his Britannic Majesty for treating of Peace with the Commissioners of the United States of America, on behalf of his said Majesty on the one part; and Benjamin Franklin, John Jay and John Adams, three of the Commissioners of the said States, for treating of Peace with the Commissioner of his said Majesty, on their behalf on the other part. To be inserted in, and to constitute the Treaty of Peace proposed to be concluded between the Crown of Great Britain, and the said United States. But which Treaty is not to be concluded untill his Britannic Majesty shall have agreed to the Terms of a Peace between France and Britain, proposed or accepted of by his most Christian Majesty; and shall be ready to conclude with him, such Treaty accordingly; it being the Duty and Intention of the United States not to desert their Ally, but faithfully and in all things, to abide by and fulfill their Engagements with his most Christian Majesty.

Whereas reciprocal advantages, and mutual Convenience are found by Experience to form the only permanent Foundation of Peace and Friendship between States, It is agreed to form the Articles of the proposed Treaty, on such Principles of liberal Equality, and Reciprocity as that partiall Advantages (those seeds of Discord) being excluded, such a beneficial and satisfactory intercourse between the two Countries may be established as to promise and secure to both perpetual Peace and Harmony.

His Britannic Majesty acknowledges the said United States Viz. New Hampshire, Massachusetts Bay, Rhode Island & Providence Plantations, Connecticut, New York, New Jersey, Pennsylvania, Delaware, Maryland, Virginia, North Carolina, South Carolina and Georgia, to be free Sovereign and independent States. That he treats with them as such, and for himself, his Heirs and Successors relinquishes all Claims to the Government Propriety and territorial Rights of the same, and every part thereof; and that all Disputes which might arise in future on the subject of the Boundaries of the said United States may be prevented, It is hereby agreed and declared that the following are, and shall be their Boundaries Viz:

From the north west Angle of Nova Scotia, being that Angle which is formed by a Line drawn due north, from the source of St. Croix River to the Highlands which divide the Rivers that empty themselves into the River St. Laurence, from those which fall into the Atlantic Ocean, and along the said High Lands, to the northwestern head of Connecticut River, thence down along the middle of that River to the forty fifth Degree of north Latitude, following the said Latitude, untill it strikes the River Missisippi. Thence by a Line to be drawn along the middle of said River Missisippi, untill it shall intersect the northernmost part of the Thirty first Degree of Latitude, north of the Equator. South, by a Line to be drawn due East from the determination of the Line last mentioned in the Latitude of Thirty one Degrees to the middle of the River, Apalatchicola or Catahouche; thence along the middle thereof, to its junction with the Flint River; thence straight to the head of St. Mary's River; and thence down along the middle of St. Mary's River to the Atlantic Ocean. East by a Line from the mouth of said St. Mary's River to the mouth of the River St. Croix in the Bay of Fundy and by a Line drawn through the middle of said River to its Source; and from its Source directly north, to the aforesaid High Lands which divide the Rivers that fall into the Atlantic Ocean, from those which empty themselves into the River St. Laurence, comprehending all Islands within twenty Leagues of any part of the Shores of the United States, and laying between Lines to be drawn due East from the points where the aforesaid Boundaries of St. Croix River, and St. Mary's River shall respectively touch the Bay of Fundy, and the Atlantic Ocean; excepting allways such Islands as now are, or heretofore have belonged to the Colony of Nova Scotia, or have been within the Limits thereof.

Upon a farther Consideration of the just Limits and Boundaries of the Province of West Florida it is agreed that its northern Boundary shall extend from the said thirty first Degree of Latitude to a Line to be drawn due East from the place where the River Yassous falls into the River Missisippi, and along the said Line due East to the River Apalachicola.

It is agreed that all such Loyalists or Refugees, as well as all such British Merchants or other Subjects, as may be resident in any of the United States at the Time of the Evacuation thereof by the Arms and Garrisons of his Britannic Majesty, shall be allowed six months thereafter to remove to any part of the World; and also at their Election to dispose of, within the said Term, or to carry with them their Goods and Effects. And it is understood that the said States shall extend such farther Favour to the said Merchants; and such Amnesty and Clemency to the said Refugees, as their respective Circumstances, and the Dictates of Justice and Humanity may render <fit> just and reasonable and particularly that Amnesty and Indemnity be granted to all such of the said Refugees as may be unaffected by Acts, Judgments, or Prosecutions actually passed or commenced a month previous to such Evacuation.

That the Subjects of his Britannic Majesty, and the People of the said United States shall continue to enjoy unmolested the Right to take Fish of every kind, on all the Banks of Newfoundland; also in the Gulph of St. Laurence, and all other places where the Inhabitants of both Countries used at any time heretofore to fish; and also to dry and cure their Fish on the Shores of the Isle of Sables, Cape Sables, and the Shores of any of the unsettled Bays, Harbours or Creeks of Nova Scotia, and of the Magdalene Islands. And his Britannic Majesty, and the said United States will extend equal Priviledges and Hospitality to each others Fishermen as to <his> their own.

Whereas certain of the United States excited thereto by the unnecessary Destruction of private Property, have confiscated all Debts due from their Citizens to British Subjects; and also in certain Instances Lands belonging to the latter;

And whereas it is just that private Contracts made between Individuals of the two Countries before the War, should be faithfully executed; and as the Confiscation of the said Lands may have a Latitude not justifiable by the Law of Nations, It is agreed that British Creditors shall notwithstanding meet with no lawful Impediment to recovering the full Value or Sterling Amount of such Bona fide Debts as were contracted before the year 1775. And also that Congress will recommend to the said States so to correct (if necessary) their said Acts, respecting the Confiscation of Lands in America belonging to real British Subjects, as to render the said Acts consistent with perfect Justice and Equity.

As to the Cession made of certain Lands in Georgia by a number of Indians there, on the first June 1773, for the purpose of paying the Debts due from them to a number of Traders. The American Commissioners say that the State of Georgia is alone competent to consider and decide on the same; for that it being a matter of internal police, with which neither Congress nor their Commissioners are authorized to interfere, it must of necessity be referred to the Discretion and Justice of that State, who without Doubt will be disposed to do, what may be just and reasonable on the Subject.

. . . . .

From and immediately after the Conclusion of the proposed Treaty there shall be a firm and perpetual Peace between his Majesty and the said States; and between the Subjects of the one, and the Citizens of the other: Wherefore all Hostilities, both by Sea and Land, shall then immediately cease: All Prisoners on both sides shall be set at Liberty and his Britannic Majesty shall forthwith, and without causing any Destruction, withdraw all his Armies Garrisons and Fleets from the said United States, and from every Port Place and Harbour within the same; leaving in all Fortifications the American Artillery that may be therein. And shall also order and cause all Archives, Records, Deeds and Papers belonging to < either > any of the said States, or their Citizens, which in the Course of the War may have fallen into the hands of his Officers, to be forthwith restored and delivered to the proper States and Persons to whom they belong.

That the navigation of the River Missisippi from its Source to the Ocean shall forever remain free and open.

Separate Article

It is hereby understood and agreed, that in case Great Britain, at the Conclusion of the present War, shall recover, or be put in possession of, West Florida, the Line of north Boundary between the said Province and the United States, shall be a Line drawn from the mouth of the River Yassous where it unites with the Mississippi, due East to the River Appalachicola.

Morris, Jay Papers, v. 2, pp. 400-404.

Henry Strachey to the American Peace Commissioners

Gentlemen   Paris 5ᵗʰ Novʳ 1782

Knowing the Expectation of the Kings Ministers, that a full Indemnity shall be provided for the whole Body of Refugees, either by a Restitution of their Property; or by some stipulated Compensation for their Losses, and being confident, as I have repeatedly assured you, that your Refusal upon this Point will be the great Obstacle to a conclusion & Ratification of that Peace, which is meant as a solid, perfect, permanent Reconciliation & Re-Union between Great Britain and America, I am unwilling to leave Paris, without on[c]e more Submitting the Matter to Your Consideration. It affects equally, in my Opinion, the Honour and the Humanity of Your Country, and of Ours. How far you will be justified in risking every favorite Object of America, by contending against those Principles, is for you to determine. Independence, and a more than reasonable Possession of

Territory; seem to be within your reach. Will You suffer them to be outweighed by the Gratification of Resentment against Individuals? I venture to assert that such a Conduct has no parallel in the History of Civilized Nations.

I am under the necessity of setting out by Two o'Clock today. If the time is too short for your Reconsideration, and final Determination, of this important Point, I shall hope that you will enable Mr Oswald to dispatch a Messenger after me, who may be with me before morning at Chantilly, where I propose Sleeping to Night, or who may overtake me before I arrive in London, with a Satisfactory answer to this Letter. I have the honor to be Gentlemen &c   H. Strachey

Clements Library: Shelburne Papers, v. 70, pp. 372-373 (C).

Richard Oswald to Lord Shelburne

My Lord   Paris 5 Novem^r 1782
By a Messenger who was dispatched from hence soon after Mr Stracheys arrival, I did myself the honour of acknowledging the Receipt of Your Lordships Letter of the 23^d of last Month; And, have now to repeat my opinion of the propriety of Sending over that Gentleman at this critical time. He has done all that was in his power with these Commissioners. after eight days hard work Some material points are gained; although as to Refugees, far Short of what was wanted: And a provision for the Debts is taken into the new plan of Treaty, in the most express terms we could obtain; instead of resting upon the faith & event of a Seperate Declaration as before proposed and promised.

. . . . .

By Mr Adams coming here, the French Interest I think seems not to have gained any thing, if one may judge from what he says on that head, as well as from his expressions of a Strong desire of a Solid and lasting friendship with England. As to the younger Commissioner, he makes no Secret of his Suspicions of the Intentions of this Court, and the necessity of Caution on their part, after a punctual Compliance with what they are Strictly bound to. I have the honour to be My Lord Your Lo^p most obedient humble Servant   Richard Oswald

Clements Library: Shelburne Papers, v. 71, pp. 175-176 (ALS).

John Adams to Robert R. Livingston

Triplicate   Paris 6th. Novem^r 1782.
Sir.

. . . . .

I was unconditionally rec^{d.} in Holland & promised upon record, Conferences and Audiences whenever I sh^{d.} demand them, before I entered into any Treaty; and without this I sh^{d.} never have entered into any: And full Powers were given to the Committee for foreign affairs, before I entered into any Conference with them. I have ventured to act upon the same principle in the affairs of Peace, & uniformly refused to come to Paris untill our Independence was unconditionally acknowledged by the K. of G.B. Mr Jay has acted on the same principle with Spain & with G. Britain. The dignity of the united States, being thus supported, has prevailed in Holland & G. Britain; not indeed as yet in Spain; but we are in a better Situation, in relation to her, than we sh^{d.} have been if the principle had been departed from – The advice of the C. de Vergennes has been contrary; but, however great a Minister he may be in his own department, his knowledge is insufficient & his judgement too often erroneous in our affairs to be an American Minister.

. . . . .

If it were in my power to do any thing for the honor of the department, or Minister of foreign Affairs, I would cheerfully do it, because I am a friend to both; and to this end you will, I am sure, not take it amiss, if I say, that it is indispensably necessary for the service of Congress & the honor of the office, that it be kept impenetrably secret fm. the French Minister in many things. The Office will be an engine for the ruin of the reputation of your Ministers abroad, & for injuring our Cause in material points, the Fishery, the Western Lands & the Mississippi &^{ct} if it is not.

. . . . .

As so the Negotiations for Peace, we have been, night & day, employed in them, ever since my arrival on the 26th. October. Dr Franklin, without saying any thing to me, obtained of Mr Jay a promise of his vote for Mr W.T. Franklin to be Secr^{y.} to the Commission for Peace, and as the D^{r.} & his Secr^{y.} are in the same house, & there are other Clerks eno: I suppose he will transmit to Congress details of the Negotiations. I shall be ready to lend them any assistance in my power; and I will endeavor, as soon as I can, to transmit them myself. But, after spending forenoon, afternoon & evening in discussions, it is impossible to transmit all the particulars. No man's Constitution is equal to it.

The English have sent Mr. Oswald, who is a wise & good man, & if, untrammeled, would soon settle all – & M^r· Strachy, who is a keen & subtle one, altho' not deeply versed in such things – and a Mr Roberts[1] who is a Clerk in the Board of Trade – and Mr Whithead,[2] who is private Secr^y· to M^r· Oswald – These Gentlemen are very profuse in their professions of national friendship; of earnest desires to obliterate the remembrance of all unkindnesses, & so restore Peace, Harmony & Friendship, and make them perpetual, by removing every seed of discord. All this, on the part of Mr Oswald personally, is very sincere – on the part of the nation it may be so, in some sense, at present; but I have my doubt whether it is a national disposition, upon w^{ch}· we can have much dependence, and still more, whether it is the sincere intention of the Earl of Shelburne. He has been compelled to acknowledge American Independence, because the Rockingham Administration had resolved upon it, &, by Carleton & Digby's letter[3] to Gen. Washington, had make known that resolution to the world – because the nation demanded that Negotiations sh^d· be opened with the American Ministers, & they refused to speak or hear, untill their Independence was acknowledged, unequivocally & without Conditions – because Messrs· Fox & Burke had resigned their Offices, pointedly on account of the refusal of the K. & my Ld Shelburne to make such an acknowledgement & these eloquent Senators were waiting only for the Session of Parliament to attack his Ld.ship on this point – it was therefore inevitable to acknowledge our Independence & no Minister co^d have stood his ground without it –

But still I doubt whether his L^{d}ship means to make a general Peace. To express myself more clearly, I fully believe he intends to try another Campaign, & that he [will] finally refuse to come to any definitive agreement with us upon articles to be inserted in the general Peace.

We have gone the utmost lengths in our power to favor the Negotiations. We have at last agreed to Boundaries with the greatest moderation. We have offered 'em the choice of a line thro' the middle of all the great lakes, or the line 45°. of N. lattitude, the Missisippi, with a free navigation of it, at one end, & the River S^t· Croix, at the other. We have agreed that the Courts of Justice be open for the recovery of British Debts, due before the war – To a general amnesty for all the Royalists, agst· w^m· there is no judgement rendered, or prosecution commenced. We have agreed that all Royalists, w^h· may remain at the evacuation of the States shall have 6. m^o. to sell their Effects & to remove with them. These are such immense advantages to the Minister, that one w^d think he c^d· not refuse them. The agreement to pay British debts, will silence the Clamors of all the Body of Creditors & seperate them fm. the Tories, with w^m· they have hitherto made common Cause. The amnesty & the term of 6. m^o. will silence all the Tories, except those who have been condemned, banished & confiscated

– Yet I do not believe they will be accepted – I fear they will insist a little longer upon a compleat Indemnification to all of y^e· Refugees; a point, w^h· without express instructions fm. all the States, neither we, nor Congress can give up, & how the States can ever agree to it, I know not, as it seems an implicit Concession of all the religion & morality of the war. They will also insist upon Penobscot as the Eastern boundary. I am not sure that the Tories, the Ministry & the nation are not secretly stimulated by french Emissaries, to insist upon Penobscot, & a full Indemnification to the Tories. It is easy to see that the french Minister, the Spanish & Dutch Ministers w^d not be very fond of having it known thro' the world, that all points for a general Peace were settled betw^n· G.B. & America, before all parties were ready. It is easy to comprehend how French, Spanish & Dutch Emissaries in London & in Paris & Versailles may insinuate, that the support of the Tories is a point of national & royal honor, and propagate so many popular arguments in fav^r· of it, as to embarrass y^e· British Minister. It is easy to see that the French may naturally revive their old assertions, that Penobscot or Kennebec are the Boundary of Nova-Scotia, altho' against the whole stream of British Authorities & the most authentic Acts of the Governors Shirley,[4] Pownal, Bernard[5] & Hutchinson. M^r· Fitzherbert, who is constantly at Versailles is very sanguine for the Refugees. Nevertheless, if my Ld Shelburne sh^d not agree with us, these will be only ostensible points – he cares little for either. It will be to avoid giving any certain weapons against himself to the friends of Ld North & the old Ministry.

The Negotiations at Versailles, betw^n· the C. de Vergennes & M^r: Fitzherbert, are kept secret, not only fm. us, but fm: the Dutch Ministers & we hear nothing ab^t· Spain. In general I learn that the French insist upon a great many fish. I dined yesterday with Mr Berkenrode, the Dutch Ambassador, & Mr Brantzen, his Colleague. They were both very frank & familiar, and confessed to me, that nothing had been said to them, & that they co^d learn nothing as yet of the progress of the Negotiation. Berkenrode told me, as an honest man, that he had no faith in the sincerity of the English for peace as yet; on the contrary, he tho't that a part of Ld Howe's fleet was gone to America & that there was something meditated against the French West India Islands. I doubt this however; but we shall soon know, *** where my Ld Howe is. That something is meditating against the French & Spaniards, & that they think of evacuating N. York for that end, I believe. Berkenrode seemed to fear the English & said, like a good man, that, in case any severe stroke sh^d be struck against France, it wo^d be necessary for Holland & America to discover a firmness. This observation had my heart on its side. But, without an evacuation of N York, they can strike no blow at all, nor any great one with it –

Mr Oswald has made very striking overtures to us – To agree to the evacuation of N York – to write a letter to Gen. Washington & another to Congress, advising them to permit this evacuation – to agree that neither the people, nor the army sh.ᵈ oppose this evacuation, or molest the British army in attempting it – nay further, that we sh.ᵈ agree that the Americans sh.ᵈ afford them all sorts of aid & even supplies of Provisions – These propositions he made to us, in obedience to an Instruction fm. the Ministers – and he told us their army were going ag.ˢᵗ W. Florida, to reconquer that fm. the Spaniards. Our answer was, that we co.ᵈ agree to no such things; that Gen. Washington co.ᵈ enter into a Convention with them, for the terms, upon w.ʰⁱ they sh.ᵈ surrender the City of N York, & all its dependencies, as Long Island & Staten Island &.ᶜᵃⁱ to the arms of the U:S: – All we co.ᵈ agree to was, that the Effects & Persons of those, who sh.ᵈ stay behind, sh.ᵈ have 6. m°. to go off, nor co.ᵈ we agree to this, unless as an article to be inserted in the general Peace –

With great respect I have the honor to be, Sir, Your hum.ᵇˡᵉⁱ Servant.

J. Adams.

NA: PCC, item 84, v. 4, pp. 234-237 (LS): M247, reel 112.

¹ Not further identified.

² Caleb Whitefoord.

³ Dated August 2, 1782. NA: PCC, item 152, v. 10, pp. 669-672 (C); M247, reel 171.

⁴ Shirley, William (1694-1771). British colonial official. Governor of Massachusetts, 1741-1757. Heavily involved in military actions again the French in Canada. Captured Louisburg, 1745. Commander-in-chief of British forces in America, 1755-1756.

⁵ Bernard, Sir Francis (1711?-1779). British colonial official. Governor of New Jersey, 1758-1760. Governor of Massachusetts, 1760-1771; recalled, 1769.

Richard Oswald to Thomas Townshend

Sir.   Paris 6ᵗʰ Novemʳ 1782

Referring to the Letter I had the honour of writing by Mʳ Strachey, who left this Place yesterday afternoon, I beg leave to inform you that I called on Mʳ Jay this Morning for an Answer to a Letter from me to the American Commissioners, delivered to him some days past, in relation to the Refugees and Loyalists, and also to one Sent to him from Mʳ Strachey yesterday, on the Same Subject. To this, Mʳ Jay told me that he intended this day to call on Mʳ Franklin and Mʳ Adams on that business, and to take their Sentiments thereon; and that whatever Should be agreed between them, should be stated in a Letter to me, to Serve as an Answer to both Mʳ Stracheys Letter and mine; which he hoped would be in my hands tomorrow, to be sent to England, if I thought proper.

This Interview gave occasion to the subject of the Refugees being again taken up in the way of Conversation, When Mr Jay went over much the same Arguments against a Restitution of their Estates, as he and Doctor Franklin had done on many former occasions; and particularly in their Conversation with Mr Strachey; with an addition of sundry other Observations, relative to the American business, Viz

That there were certain of those Refugees they never would forgive, for reasons that would be recited in their Letter to me. That they would not suffer them to live in their neighborhood, although we had Lands to sett them down upon, nor would those persons be Sure of their lives there.

That, however, they were not of any great number; and as to the Others, less obnoxious, the Clause of Amnesty in the Plan of New Treaty, would make all such of them as were not under Judgement, or prosecution, perfectly easy in their Several Stations, and he made no doubt but after a Peace the several states would treat them with as much lenity as their Case would admit of. And the bulk of these being besides of law rank, they would successively fall into the sundry Occupations of the Country; and so Government would be saved the Expence of transporting and subsisting them.

That with respect to those above-mentioned, under Exception, Since, failing of a Restoration of their Estates, we pressed to have a Fund for Compensation allotted to us, they had given us Land; at a proper distance, which they might occupy, and if not occupied, it might be sold. That Money might be raised upon that Land. If not enough, the Difference might be supplied without their assistance. That such Difference would be a small matter in Comparison of the Expence of going on with the War another year. Which he said would be the certain Consequence of refusing to close with them on the present occasion: And that according as we should determine, they would be guided in their Reports and Advices to the Congress; and their Attention, more or less, to this Court.

That they had just now received fresh Advices from the Congress dated in the end of Septem^r. By which he found the People of that Country were universally suspicious of the Intentions of Great Britain towards them. That their printed publications were brim full of these Insinuations, and they were preparing themselves accordingly for the Consequences.

That they the Commissioners were, however, perrfectly satisfied that England was sincere, and meant to give them their Independence, and to put an end to the War. And as they equally, and most ardently longed to see their Country settled in peace, Mr Jay said he hoped we would not let this Opportunity slip, but resolve speedily to wynd up this long Dispute, so as we might be again as one People.

That they had hitherto acted in this Negotiation under Instructions of the year 1779, when their Affairs were not in quite so good a Situation as at present, and had gone to the full stretch of them, and farther.

But if we broke up now, we might be assured of their receiving new Instructions, and of a very different kind from the present. In which, among other things, he made no doubt they would be directed to state all the Depredation, plunder and unnecessary Destruction of Property over all their Country, in Charge against the British Demands of bona fide Creditors, for which in the body of the Treaty, they have now established an Independent Security.

That by the last Advices in Septem^r they understood, the State of pensylvania had begun upon these Estimates; and there was a Committee actually sitting at Philadelphia for making up an Acco^t of all those Damages not occasioned by the direct and necessary Operations of War. Which, when collected from the Reports of the several states and brought to a head, would leave no room for any Claims in behalf of the said British Creditors. That now was the time for G. Britain to take the benefit of the Security offered to those Creditors; and wisely to avoid the Consequences of former Mistakes. For Mr Jay was pleased to say, & which I think myself bound to repeat, That in every stage of the War our offers and Acceptances had always come too late, and we had consequently worse Terms in the next propositions.

That with respect to those British Debts, he had at all times jointly with his Collegues declared that all that were contracted before the War must be duely paid; Yet if their States, by our refusal of Accommodation, should be continued under their present expensive Establishments, he would not answer for the same favourable determination hereafter. The Time he said was precious. as they would soon be under a necessity of writing to their Congress in answer to their late Letters – Mr Jay after repeating his wishes that G. Britain might determine in a manner suitable to the present situation of things said That in case we meant to close with them on this occasion, he would take the liberty to request, that His Majesty would order his Ambassadors at the Neutral Courts to give so much Countenance to the peace with America, as formally to Intimate its being in the Train of Negotiation; and when signed, that the same should also be notified. The Advice of this, he said, would soon reach America, and would produce the happiest effects there, as well to our benefit as theirs; even although the final Conclusion must wait a Settlement with France. That even that Conclusion would also feel the benefit of those Notifications.

Soon after, Mr Adams, the other Commissioner called upon me, and expressed himself equally anxious that there might be an end to all our Differences

In the meantime he delivered me the inclosed Packet from their Congress to Mr Laurens, with a request that I would send it by the first Courier, and to recommend it so as it might get safe to his hands. Which I promised to do, and hope it will be taken care of. Mr Adams also signified in like manner as Mr Jay had done a Wish that the above-mentioned Intimation might be made at the Neutral Courts. He seemed so earnest about it, that I could not avoid asking him as to the object of Such Intimation. He answered that among other things, it would make them more Independent, or Indifferent about this Court. Which they wished exceedingly might be brought about. That neither he nor Mr Jay had any particular Instructions relative to this Court, nor had any Corespondence with it, farther than as they were bound by the Letter of their Treaty with them. Farther than that, he said as much, as if they gave themselves no concern about them.

That in a Case of a particular Commission, long Residence, and habits of Corespondence, it was natural to suppose a corespondent Complaisance would be created, even under the guidance of the most upright Intentions and Conduct upon the whole; but as to them Two, this Gentleman said, they were not even under those kind of biasses.

. . . . .

I have the honour to be Sir Your most obedient humble Servant
R 12th   Richard Oswald

PRO: FO 27/2, v. 557, f. 787 (LC transcription).

The American Peace Commissioners to Richard Oswald

Sir,   Paris 7th. November 1782
In answer to the letter you did us the honor to write on the 4th. ins^{t.} we beg leave to repeat what we often said in Conversation, viz. that the Restoration of such of the Estates of Refugees, as have been confiscated, is impracticable; because they were confiscated by Laws of particular States, &, in many instances, have passed by legal titles through several hands – Besides, Sir, as this is a matter evidently appertaining to the internal Polity of the separate States, the Congress, by the nature of our Constitution, have no authority to interfere with it –

As to your demand of Compensation to these Persons, we forbear enumerating our Reasons for thinking it ill-founded. In the moment of conciliatory Overtures, it would not be proper to call certain Scenes into view, over which, a variety of Considerations should induce both Parties, at present to draw a veil. Permit us therefore only to repeat, that we cannot stipulate for such Compensation, unless, on your part, it be agreed to make retribution to our Citizens for the heavy Losses they have sustained by the *unnecessary* Destruction of their private Property –

We have already agreed to an Amnesty, more extensive than Justice required; and full as extensive as Humanity could demand – We can therefore only repeat, that it cannot be extended further–

We should be sorry if the absolute Impossibility of our complying further with your Propositions on this head, should induce Great Britain to continue the War for the sake of those, who caused & prolonged it; but, if that should be the Case, we hope that the utmost Latitude will not be again given to its rigours–

Whatever may be the Issue of this Negotiation, be assured Sir, that we shall always acknowledge the liberal, manly, and candid manner, in which you have conducted it; and that We shall remain, with the warmest Sentiments of Esteem and Regard, Your Most Obed^{t} hum$^{ble.}$ Servants,

John Adams
B. Franklin
John Jay

PRO: CO 5/8-3, p. 319 *microfilm reel 5 (LS).*

Comte de Montmorin to Comte de Vergennes

[Translation]

No. 91   Escorial, 7 November 1782
Sir,

. . . . .

I can add nothing, Sir, to what I had the honor to send you in my preceding despatches relative to the negotiations for peace. M. le Comte de Florida Blanca assured me very positively that he had sent to M. le Comte d'Aranda instructions and powers with which he could finish, but he did not make known to me the nature of these instructions, and it is impossible for me to give you any light on this subject. I do not doubt that M. le Comte d'Aranda has been open with you and that you now know what to believe. That Ambassador should have received a courier the day before yesterday, through whom he is ordered to finish in one way or another in the course of this month, which follows your views completely. It is certain that if the bases for peace are not established before the Parliament of England returns, all negotiations will henceforth be at least unavailing. M. de Florida Blanca is too knowledgeable not to appreciate at their true value the means of France and Spain to continue the war, and I am fully convinced that he keenly desires peace. He doubtless thinks that we can still undertake this campaign, and even hope for success, but if it does not go as we might wish, it is certain that it would be almost impossible for us to undertake another one, and that then we would be far from able to expect to obtain conditions as advantageous as at this moment. All these reflections have certainly not escaped M. de Florida Blanca.

As to the reserve he places on being open with me, and M. d'Aranda with you, regarding the conditions on which Spain will consent to peace, he doubtless has some special reasons on which it does not behoove me to question him.

. . . . .

Received the 20th.   Le Cte. de Montmorin

FFAA: Pol. Corr., Spain, v. 609, Nª 90 (LC transcription).

John Adams to Jonathan Jackson

Sir[1]   Paris November 8. 1782.

. . . . .

...If Mr Jay and I, had yielded the Punctilio of Rank and taken the Advice of C. de Vergennes and Dr. F. by treating with the English or Spaniards, before We were put upon the equal Footing that our Rank demanded, We should have Sunk in the Minds of the English French Spaniards Dutch and all the Neutral Powers. The C: de Vergennes certainly knows this. if he does not, he is not even an European Statesman. if he knows it, what Inference can We draw but that he means to keep us down if he can. − to keep his Hand under our Chin, to prevent Us, from drowning, but not to lift our Heads out of Water.

The Injunctions upon Us to communicate, <***> and to follow the Advice that is given Us, Seem to be too strong, and too universal.− understood with reasonable Limitations and Restrictions they may do, very well.

... When the French Ministers in America or Europe communicate every Thing to Us, We may venture to be equally communicative with them, But when every Thing is concealed from Us more cautiously I believe than it is from England, We shall do ourselves Injustice if We are not upon our guard.−

If We conduct ourselves with Caution, Prudence, Moderation and

Firmness We shall Succeed in every great Point, but if < *** > Congress, or their Ministers abroad Suffer themselves to be intimidated, by Threats, Slanders or Insinuations, We shall be duped out of the Fishery the Missisippi ~~the~~ much of the Western Lands, Compensation to the Tories and Penobscot at least if not Kennebeck.– This is my Solemn Opinion, and I will never be answerable to my Country Posterity or my own Mind, for the Consequences that might happen from concealing it.

. . . . .

With great Respect and Esteem I have the Honour to be Sir your most obedient & humble Servant   J. Adams

MHS: *Miscellaneous Bound Collection (ALS).*
    [1] *This letter was originally intended for Robert R. Livingston, but Adams evidently decided to mail it to Jonathan Jackson, a Massachusetts delegate to Congress.*

Benjamin Franklin to Comte de Vergennes

Sir,   Passy, Nov.ʳ 8ᵗʰ 1782.

The Congress disregarding the Proposals made by Sir Guy Carleton, and determined to continue the War with Vigour, 'till a Peace can be obtained, satisfactory as well to the King as to themselves; (as will appear by their Resolves hereto annex'd) but being disabled by the great Deficiency in their Taxes arising from various temporary Causes, have found it absolutely necessary to borrow another Sum in Europe, which they have accordingly directed me to endeavour by all means possible. The Necessity of this Measure is so clearly express'd, in the Letter of Mʳ· Morris their Financier, and Mʳ Livingston their Secretary, which are subjoined, that there is little Occasion for any Remarks of mine; I shall therefore only observe, that from what pass'd in some of the last Conferences we had with the English Negotiators here, I apprehend Peace to be still at a Distance, and that another Campaign can scarcely be avoided; our Enemies being well informed of our present Distresses for want of Money & conceiving great Hopes that we shall no where find a Supply. The Congress on this important Occasion have therefore sent a Packet Boat express with their Orders to me to implore the Aid of his Majesty, our Friend & Father, which I hereby do most earnestly from a full Conviction that unless the Loan is obtain'd, our Army can neither be kept up nor safely disbanded.

With the greatest Respect, I am, Sir, Your Excellency's most obedient & most humble Servant,   B Franklin

FFAA: *Pol. Corr., U.S., v. 22, f. 433-434, microfilm reel 13 (ALS).*

Richard Oswald to Henry Strachey

Private.   Paris Friday 8 Nov.ʳ 1782
Dear Sir

. . . . .

M.ʳ Jay sent to me yesterday for a Copy of the proposed Treaty. I compared it with him, he kept one Copy. He was singularly attentive to all the particulars and did not admit of the least alteration from the words of his own plan.

He scored out of the Treaty the seperate Article respecting W. Florida. But admitted it, in addition at the bottom as a seperate Article. In so far you was right, & I was wrong in putting it into the Treaty.

In this Article, he also insisted that his own words should be replaced. Viz He had said that in case G. B at the conclusion of the present War shall *be*, or be put in possession, We said, shall *recover* or be put in possession He scored out the Word *recover* and put in the word *be* as above.

This seperate Article must therefore stand, as it was added only to the foot of your Copy, and without the preamble as in the body of the Treaty of *Upon a further consideration of the just Limits &c.*

M.ʳ Jay also struck out of the Treaty the Exception as to the Nova Scotia Islands, which I was surprized at saying that if saved by the general principle of Sea Boundaries, there was no occasion for an Exception.

I did not think it worth while to dwell upon that matter since if any of those Islands are within 20 Leagues of the Mouth of S.ᵗ Croix River, he will surely not scruple to except them as pertinents of the Colony of Nova Scotia. Meantime the Exception must be left out of any Copy you send over.

And I would also beg leave to add that from this Gentlemans precision & attention to the Identity of these Copies in comparison with the Original Drafts, I would advise that there should not be the least Alteration, not a single Word, different from those Drafts.

. . . . .

Being in a hurry to dispatch the Messenger I have only to add that I am with Sincere regard Dear Sir Your most obed.ᵗ hum.ˡ Servant

Richard Oswald.

. . . . .

R.ᵈ by Staley the Messenger 12.ᵗʰ Nov.ʳ

PRO: FO 27/2, v. 557, f. 799 (LC transcription).

Henry Strachey to Thomas Townshend

Sir,   Calais, 8 November 1782

The Moment I arrive at Dover, I shall dispatch a Messenger with the enclosed new Terms of Treaty, as a Paper which You will be most anxious to see. It is accompanied with a Map, upon which are drawn the Boundary Line originally sent to You by Mr. Oswald, and Two other Lines proposed by the American Commissioners after my Arrival at Paris. Either of these, You are to chuse. They are both better than the original Line, as well in respect to Canada as to Nova Scotia, though neither of them equal to Your hopes. The Boundaries, according to the first-proposed of these Two new Lines, are described in an enclosed Paper, No. 2. Those according to the second-proposed, are described in the Treaty, merely because they are contained in a lesser Compass of Writing.

It is unnecessary at present to trouble You with the Arguments urged by us, to enlarge the Circle of Canada and to extend Nova Scotia to Kennebeck, or even to Penobscot. The Limitation of this Province to the River St. Croix (which is the Boundary by the King's Commission to the Governor) being inadmissable under the Instructions Lord Shelburne gave me, could not be acquiesced in, and the American Commissioners would not recede from their Extention of the Massachusetts to that River. Nor would they agree to the Appointment of Commissaries, unless it were to settle where the River St. Croix really is, for it is not laid down in the same place in all the Maps.

No. 3 is what I contended for, as the proper Article concerning the Fishery, which I take to be precisely consonant with your Intention. After a little Dispute, they gave up the Point of drying Fish on Newfoundland, but they insisted upon a Right to fish in the Gulph of St. Lawrence, and in all other Places where they and we used formerly to Fish; and also to dry on the Shores of the Isle of Sables, Cape Sables, the Magdalene Islands (which are said to be uninhabited) and on the Shores of any unsettled Bay in Nova Scotia. Mr. Oswald is satisfied with the Article, so expressed, and I enclose (No. 4) his Observations upon the Subject.

The Recovery of the Property of the Refugees, and of the Debts due to British Subjects before and since the War, are Points which have been obstinately fought for. You will see by the Treaty all that could be obtained. The Debts prior to 1775 appear to be safe. Those since that period were alledged to have been illegal, and therefore not recoverable but under the Honor of those who contracted them.

With regard to the Refugees, You will observe that something is done in favor of those now under the Protection of the British Army. But with regard to all others of that Description, I see nothing for them, except what You have in Canada, and the little Piece now added to Nova Scotia, between the original Boundary sent to You by Mr. Oswald, and that now obtained. The written Remonstrance, by a Letter from Mr. Oswald to the American Commissioners (No. 5) was made in the view of having an authentic Proof that every Effort had been used, agreeably to my Instructions from Lord Shelburne, upon a Point wherein the National Honor is so deeply concerned. No. 6 is the rough Draft of a Letter which I also wrote upon the same Subject. Neither of these Letters had been answered when I left Paris. But Mr. Oswald had seen the intended Answer to his Letter, which was that the Refugees should have Compensation, provided Great Britain would compensate for all the Towns, Houses, Barns etc. destroyed during the War!

Upon the Return of a Messenger to Paris, with Your definitive Answer, if not very repugnant to the Terms now sent, the American Commissioners will, I doubt not, immediately sign the Treaty, so that You may have it in London before the Meeting of Parliament.

They would not stipulate for the quiet Evacuation of New York, on Account of their Treaty with France, which provides that America shall not make a separate Peace, or Truce, and they pretend to fear that their writing upon such a Point would be construed into a Proposition for a Truce. But they express themselves to be confident that Washington, upon Sight of this provisional Treaty, signed by them, will not obstruct the Evacuation.

I have the Honor to be, with the greatest Respect, Sir, Your most obedient and most humble Servant.

H. Strachey

[Enclosure]

First Proposition: Alternative Boundaries
Proposed by the American Peace Commissioners

[7 November 1782]

From the North west angle of Nova Scotia vizt. That angle which is formed by a Line drawn due North from the Source of St. Croix River to the High Lands, along the said High Lands which divide those Rivers that empty themselves into the River St. Lawrence from those which fall into the Atlantic Ocean to the Northwesternmost head of Connecticut River; thence down along the middle of that River to the 45th Degree of North Latitude, from thence by a Line due West on said Latitude until it strikes the River Iroquois or Cataroquy, thence along the middle of said River into Lake Ontario through the middle of said Lake until it strikes the communication by water between that Lake and Lake Erie, thence along the middle of said communication into Lake Erie through the middle of said Lake until it arrives at the water communication between that Lake and Lake Huron, thence along the middle of said water communication into Lake Huron, thence through the middle of said Lake to the water communication between that Lake and Lake Superior, thence through Lake Superior Northward of the Isles Royal and Philipeaux to the Long Lake, thence through the middle of said Long Lake and the water communication between it and the Lake of the Woods, to the said Lake of the Woods, thence through the said Lake to the most northwestern point thereof, and from thence on a due western Course to the River Mississippi, thence by a Line to be drawn along the middle of the said River Mississippi until it shall intersect the northernmost part of the 31st Degree of North Latitude; South by a Line to be drawn due East from the determination of the Line lastmentioned in the Latitude of 31 Degrees North of the Equator to the middle of the River Apalachicola, or Catahouche, thence along the middle thereof to its junction with the Flint River, thence strait to the head of St. Mary's River, and thence down along the middle of St. Mary's River to the Atlantic Ocean; East by a Line to be drawn along the middle of the River St. Croix from it's mouth in the Bay of Fundy to it's Source, and from it's Source directly North to the aforesaid High Lands which divide the Rivers that fall into the Atlantic Ocean from those which fall into the River St. Lawrence; comprehending all Islands within twenty Leagues of any part of the Shores of the United States, and lying between Lines to be drawn due East from the points where the aforesaid Boundaries between Nova Scotia on the one part and East Florida on the other shall respectively touch the Bay of Fundy and the Atlantic Ocean, excepting such Islands as now are, or heretofore have been, within the Limits of the said Province of Nova Scotia.

[Enclosure]
Henry Strachey:
Observation on the Article of the Fishery

[7 November 1782]

3. That the People of the said United States shall continue to enjoy unmolested the Right of fishing <unmolested> on the Banks of Newfoundland, in the manner they have hitherto used, without Anchorage, but by drift.

[Enclosure]
Richard Oswald: Observations on the Article
of the Fishery

[7 November 1782]

Since Mr Adams Came here, the Commissioners, have taken more nottice of the <pro[posal]>[1] refusal of admitting their having the priviledge of Drying in Newfoundland than I expected from what they told me at Settling the Plan of Treaty which was sent to England. But at last after a great deal of Conversation at different times on that Subject, It was agreed to be left out, upon Condition of their being allowed to dry upon any of the Unsettled parts of the Coast of Nova Scotia, when they happened to be so far from home as that their fish might run some risk of being Spoilt before they reached their own Shores.

Doctor Franklin said he believed it would be only on Such occasions that they would use <even> that priviledge, and even then it would be then only for a partial drying and Salting, so as to prevent the Fish Spoiling before they went home and delivered them to their Wives & Children to compleat and finish the Drying.

Also said. I observe as to *Catching Fish.* You mention only the Banks of Newfoundland. Why not all other places, and amongst others the Gulph of St. Lawrence? Are you afraid there is not Fish enough, Or that We should Catch too many; at the Same time that you know that we shall bring the greatest part of the Money we get for that Fish, to Great Britain to pay for your Manufactures? He agreed it might be proper not to have a mixture of their people with ours for Drying on Newfoundland, <He> But Supposed there would be no Inconveniency in throwing onshore their Fish for a few days on an Unsettled Beach, Bay or Harbour, on the Coast of Nova Scotia.

I am Sorry that I should have given occasion to so much trouble on this head by trusting to what was said by the Comm[issione]rs, as not being so positive in the matter but what they would give up the point, if objected to at home, and have now only to Submit it to Consideration, Whether it will not be proper to allow of Drying in Nova Scotia And also to let the Clause regarding the Catching of Fish be so expressed as <that> not to appear as if we're afraid of the Americans extending that branch of Commerce as far as they incline to pursue it, Since I really believe they will not like it, and that it will not be an easy matter to restrain them, if we should incline to do so.   R.O.

Morris, Jay Papers, v. 2, pp. 413-417.

[1] Deleted material in original document indicated by angle brackets; added text indicated by square brackets.

Henry Strachey to Thomas Townshend

Calais, 8 November 1782
Sir,   Private

Considering the Anxiety of my mind and the Fatigues I have gone through, having travelled 16 and 18 hours a day, in very bad Roads, and with miserable Horses, you will not expect that I should have been perfectly clear in the Dispatch accompanying this. But I thought it necessary to send You some Account of the Business and the Messenger will certainly reach You several hours before I can. On my arrival here this Morning, I found that the Wind had been adverse for seven days past, and that there were at least Sixty English in one House waiting for a Passage.

The Treaty must be written in London in a regular Form, which we had not time to do at Paris; and several of the expressions being too loose, should be tightened; for these Americans are the greatest Quibblers I ever knew. The paragraph about the Indian lands in Georgia (a Subject which I thought it right to take up, though I had no particular Instruction concerning it) seems to be too indecisive to be inserted at all in the Treaty. It was put in amongst the Articles that You might have everything before You.

From an accurate Attention to Words which fell from Jay and Adams in the course of our conversations, I venture to tell You, that I am inclined to think, if You make the Restitution or Indemnification to the Refugees, a sine quâ non, the American Commissioners will accede, rather than Break off the Treaty upon such a point; more especially if a Mode not too odious, could be devised of admitting exceptions of some few People, against whom they are particularly irritated. Mr. Oswald is not however of my opinion. The matter is too serious, either way, to be hastily determined. You are in some degree relieved from the inundation of Refugees that might have been expected from America; but still those at home will be a heavy load.

I am sorry that I have been able to do no more than I have done, but as my Journey has not been quite fruitless, I hope not to meet with your Disapprobation. I must add that not a moment of Time has been lost. We have been in Conference from Eleven o'clock every Morning, though Franklin lives at Passey, and dined all together Four times in order to pursue Our Business in the Evening. They are apparently jealous of the French, and I believe wish to conclude with England.

The sudden Arrival of Dispatches from America prevented their answering Mr. Oswald's Letter, and mine....

I am most truly Sir Your faithful and obedient Servant,

H. Strachey

Morris, Jay Papers, v. 2, pp. 411-412.

John Adams to Robert R. Livingston

N⁰. 8.   Paris Novem͏ʳ 11ᵗʰ· 1782.

Sir,

On my first arrival at Paris I found my Colleagues engaged in Conferences with Mͬ Oswald. They had been before chiefly conducted by Mͬ Jay, Mͬ Franklin having been mostly confined for 3. mᵒ· by a long & painful illness: At this time, however, he was so much better, altho' still weak & lame, as to join us in most of our subsequent Conferences; and we were so constantly engaged, forenoon, afternoon & evening, that I had not been out to Versailles, nor any where else. On Saturday last the Marqᵗ· de la Fayette called upon me, & told me he had been to Versailles, & the C. de Vergennes had sᵈ to him, that he had been informed, by the returns of the Police, that I was in Paris, but not officially, & he shᵈ take it well if I woᵈ come to see him. I went to dine with Mͬ Franklin the same day, who had just returned fm. delivering his memorial & repeated to me the same message. I sᵈ to both, I wᵈ go the next morning, & accordingly on Sunday, 9ᵗʰ· I went to make my Court to his Excellency. He recᵈ me politely & asked me questions abᵗ· our progress. I answᵈ him, that the English Minister appeared to me to divide with us upon ostensible points; that I still doubted of his intentions to make an universal Peace; that yᵉ cry of the Nation was, for something to be done or sᵈ with the American Ministers, & to satisfy this, the K. of G.B. had been advised to be the 3ᵈ Power in Europe to acknowledge our Independence. As this was a Royal act, under yᶠ· great Seal of his Kingdom, it coᵈ never be denied, or revoked; but still it did not render the nation unanimous, & to avoid finally disgusting any great party, the Minister wᵈ still pursue his usual studied obscurity of Policy: Points must be conceded to the Americans before a compleat agreement coᵈ be made with them, even on terms to be inserted in the universal peace, wʰ· wᵈ open the full cry of a powerfull party upon him, among wʰ· were the Refugees. It coᵈ not be supposed that yᵉ Refugees & Penobscot were such points with the nation, or Minister that they wᵈ continue yᵉ· war for them only, if they were ready to strike with France, Spain & Holland.

The C. then asked me some questions respecting Sagadahoc, wʰ I answᵈ by showing him the records, wʰ I had in my pocket, particularly that of Govͬ· Pownal's solemn act of possession in 1759; the Grants & settlements of Mount Desert, Machias & all the other townships East of Penobscot River: the orig. Grant, of James I[st.1] to Sir W[m.] Alexander,[2] of Nova Scotia, in w[h.] it is bounded on S[t.] Croix River; (This grant I had in Latin, French & English;) the dissertations of Gov[rs.] Shirley & Hutchinson, & the Authority of Gov[r.] Bernard, all shew[ed.] the Right of Mass[tts] to this tract to be incontestible. I added, that I did not think any British Minister w[d.] ever put his hand to a written Claim of that tract of land, their own national Acts were so numerous & so clear against them. The C. said, M[r] Fitzherbert had told him that it was for the Masts that a point was made of that tract; but the C. said Canada was an immense resource for masts. I said there were so few masts there, that this co[d.] not be the motive; that the Refugees were still at the bottom of this. Several of them had pretensions to lands in Sagadahoc, & the rest hoped for Grants there.

The C. said, it was not at all surprizing that the B. Ministry sh[d.] insist upon Compensation to the Tories, for that all the Precedents were in their favor: in the case of the united-Provinces with Spain, all were restored to their possessions; & that there never had been an example of such an affair, terminated by treaty, but all were restored. He said, it was a point well-settled by Precedents. I begged his Excell[ys.] pardon for this, & that there was no precedent in point – a restitution of an Estate, *not alienated*, altho' confiscated to a Crown, or State, co[d.] not be a precedent in point, because, in our case, these estates had not only been confiscated, but alienated by the State, so that it was no longer in the power of the State to restore them. And when you come to the Question of Compensation, there is every argument of national honor, dignity of the State, public & private Justice & Humanity, for us to insist upon a Compensation for all the Plate, Negroes, Rice, Tobacco stole, and Houses & Substance consumed, as there is for them to demand Compensation to the Tories; and this was so much the stronger in our favor, as our Sufferers were innocent people, and theirs guilty ones.

M[r] Rayneval, who was present, said something about the K. & Nation being bound to support their Adherents. I answ[d] that I co[d] not comprehend this doctrine. Here was a set of People, whose bad faith & misrepresentations had deceived the K. & deluded the nation to follow their all-devouring ambition untill they had totally failed of their object; had bro't an indelible reproach on the British name & almost irretrievable ruin on the nation, and yet that nation is bound to support their deceivers and ruiners: If the national honor was bound at all, it was bound still to follow their ambition, to conquer America, & to plant the Refugees there in pomp & power; and, in such Case, we all know whose estates w[d] be confiscated, and what Compensation would be obtained. All this M[r] Rayneval said was very true –

The Compte asked me to dine, which I accepted, and was treated with more attention & Complaisance than ever, both by him and the Comtess.

. . . . .

America has been long enough involved in the Wars of Europe. She has been a football between contending Nations from the Beginning, and it is easy to foresee, that France & England both will endeavor to involve us in their future wars. It is our Interest and Duty to avoid them as much as possible, and to be compleatly independent, and have nothing to do with either of them but in Commerce – My poor tho'ts & feeble efforts have been, from the beginning, constantly employed to arrange all our European Connections to this end, and will continue to be so employed, whether they succeed or not. My hopes of Success are stronger now than ever, they have been, because I find M.r Jay precisely in the same sentiments, after all the Observations & Reflections he has made in Europe, and M.r Franklin at last, appears to coincide with us.

We are all three perfectly united in the affair of the Tories, and of Sagadahoc, the only points, in which the British Minister pretends to differ from us –

. . . . .

If Congress should wish to know my conjecture, it is, that the Ministry will still insist upon Compensations to the Tories, and thus involve the nation, every month of the war, in an expence, sufficient to make a full Compensation to all the Tories in Question. They would not do this, however, if they were ready with France & Spain.

With great respect I have the honor to be, Sir, Your most Obed.t hum.l Servant,   J. Adams

NA: PCC, item 84, v. 4, pp. 238-241 (LS); M247, reel 112.
   ¹ James I (1566-1625). As James VI, King of Scotand, 1567-1625. King of England, 1603-1625.
   ² Alexander, Sir William (1567?-1640). British statesman and poet. Appointed master of requests, 1614. Received the grant of Nova Scotia, 1621. Appointed secretary of state for Scotland, 1626. Named Viscount Stirling, 1630; Earl of Stirling, 1633; Earl of Devon, 1639.

Richard Oswald to Thomas Townshend

Sir   Paris 15.th Novem.r 1782.
   As M.r Fitz Herbert informs me he intends to dispatch a Messenger to night, I take the Opportunity of referring to the Letter which I had the

honour of writing you on the 7th by the Courier...who sett out on the 8th, at three in the afternoon.

In that Letter I made a full Report of my last Conversation with the American Commissioners as near to their own words as I could recollect them; which I thought it my duty to do, however unpleasant they might appear to be. They principally turned on the question regarding the Refugees & Loyalists both as to Restitution and Compensation.

Since that time I had not seen any of those Gentlemen, untill this Morning; when I called on Mr Jay and Mr Adams; Seperately and sat with them a considerable time; trying to persuade them to take that matter again into consideration. But to no purpose. I had the same Answers as I have always had from each of them on that Subject, from the beginning of my Cor[r]espondence with them. Viz That it should never be said that they had agreed to any Measures for the gratification of those who had been so instrumental in encouraging this War, and had so cruelly assisted in the prosecution of it; with many other Reflections relative to their opinion of their principles, Motives, and Conduct, as unpleasant as unnecessary to be here repeated. Adding, as they alwise have done, that if Peace with Great Britain, was not to be had on any other terms, than their agreeing to those Provisions, the War must go on, although it should be for these seven years to come. And that neither they nor their Congress had any power in this matter, notwithstanding what they had ventured to do for the personal safety, and the Effects of those Loyalists remaining with the Garrison of New York; And upon the whole, that things of the consequence proposed rests entirely with the States.

At same time those two Commissioners owned that they were extremely desirous of Peace; and that the Treaty sent over may be agreed to. But if refused they said they must wait for New Instructions from their Congress. That upon their report of such refusal to that Assembly, they would refer the question in dispute to the States. It might take six Months severally to have them assembled; & perhaps Six Months, or longer, to have Instructions on their Resolutions, from the Congress. Before which time, as the several Provinces will have made some progress in the liquidation of the unnecessary Destruction of private Property, they might expect to receive positive Orders to insist on reparation thereof in their next Instructions.

Both of those Gentlemen told me to day, that this Court had thought fit to take up the Question regarding the Loyalists, and become Advocates for them; and Mr. Adams said he had been sent for last Week to Versailles, and that Monsr de Vergennes had talkt to him strongly in their favour. But that he paid no regard to his Opinion or recommendation on the Subject; and could guess at his motive for interfering, as intending to prevent a speedy agreement with G. Britain so as in the Interim they might bring forward their own Treaty and those of their Allies, to a more favourable Conclusion. The other Gentleman took nottice also of this Circumstance and gave the same account of his opinion of the object of it. How far they are right, I dont pretend to say.

I at last proposed to those Gentlemen, that since they would not positively undertake for a Restitution or Compensation to the Refugees & Loyalists, that they would add a Clause, to the Treaty, of Recommendation to the Congress in their favour in general, leaving it to them to discriminate, according to Circumstances. Or that they, the Congress, should upon such Recommendation, make one general sweep of Acquittance reserving the right of certain Exceptions to themselves. This Expedient was proposed on account of a few particular Names which I had been often accustomed to hear at making Applications on this Subject. But all to no purpose. At same time those Gentlemen owned that they had an esteem and good will towards many of those Parties and would be glad to serve them as Opportunities offered. But in either of those ways they could be of no use to them.

I then talkt of the Evacuation of New York. Mr. Adams admitted that, without a due precaution, there might be some cross accident in accomplishing it. However, he thought Gener^l Washington could have no objection to receiving a surrendry of the Place by Capitulation; to which their Treaty with France could not furnish any objection; since, by that Treaty, each Nation was at liberty to prosecute the War in their own way. And so their General could do in that matter as he thought fit, and without consulting the General of the French Troops, who was under his command. Mr Adams said, that by last Letters, they had now a well disciplined Army of near 20 Thousand Men, including the French, who were about 4000 partly with Genl Washington, the rest in different places.

He also said, and so did Mr Jay, that their last Advices from the Congress complained of our mode of evacuating the Garison of Savannah, as if we had carried off, in the way of booty. (they used that word) a number of Negros to be sold in the W. Indies. I said it must have been Negros belonging to Loyalists who retired with the Troops. And I was perswaded the Congress was misinformed. I hope it will prove so.

However it would appear that these Reports have so far gained ground amongst those People that they are alarmed in Carolina, being apprehensive of something of that kind at the Evacuation of Charlestown. Which, although surely without any just reason, yet it is certain that by Letters from Carolina just now received at Paris, the People there are apprehensive about some part of this kind of Property, which happens to be in the hands of our Garrison. However unjust those Imputations may be, I think myself bound to intimate the Reports, since they come to me in a way which do's not admit of my suppressing them. If New York is evacuated by Capitulation, every pretence to Charges of this malicious kind will of course be prevented.

I have the honour to be Sir Your most obed^t humble Servant

Richard Oswald.

R 20

PRO: FO 27/2, v. 557, f. 841 (LC transcription).

Richard Oswald to Lord Shelburne

My Lord   Paris. Saturday 16th Novemb^r 1782

I wrote yesterday by Mr Fitzherberts Courier to the Secretary of State, and having the Opportunity...I venture to Scrawl these few Lines to Your Lop. on the Subject of the Refugees & other Loyalists. I am Sensible of the Strait the Kings Ministers must be in on their account. And therefor have been doing every thing in my power with the Commiss^{rs} here, Since Mr Strachey Sett out, to get an Alteration in their favour, but hitherto without Success: I tried Mr Jay again this Morning, and had a full and free Conversation with him on the Subject. He gave me Such Assurance of the determination of their Congress on that head, ~~which~~ as was I think enough to shew that the point is not to be carried here. And also that if insisted on as a preliminary of a Peace, We may expect to have a Continuance of the War with that Continent, Which he said the Americans would, of themselves, carry on without any Regard to our making a Settlem^t with France. That they were aware of what France was about; as well as foresaw what would be the issue of a partial Settlement with them: Which they could not conclude, & leave the Americans out; And then England has them both to contend with, to get peace of any sort; & a peace, from them, much worse than they have now offered. That even if France was to leave them, or to be against them, they were not uneasy, America would Carry on the War with Eng^d for 50 years rather than Subscribe to such evidence of their own iniquity as by making a provision for Such Cutthroats &c^a – That if we rejected the present Treaty we would never have Such another, And if the late Letters from their Congress of the last of Sep^r & 1st of Octr had come a few days Sooner, they durst not have agreed to it – and if ever another was opened they would positively insist on a Reparation of their private & unnecessary losses, and to which Account they would Sacrifice ye British Debts –

He asked me, as Mr Adams did yesterday, whether I did not think that Mr F. would have a just appeal to the people of Eng^d for the reasonableness of their being kept under the distress of an American War, on account of obtaining a Compensation for those who gave occasion to stay and whom he had reprobated on all occasions – That the Nation would bear a disappointm^t of a Conclusion with France & Spain but not with America. That one Month's Expence of an American War & its Consequences would indemnify all those people that were worth public nottice &c^a &c^a –

I tried to persuade Mr Jay to go over privately to London, tomorrow Morning, to lay this Case before Your Lop. He offered objections. But the Chief one was his being assured of one of his Colleagues not assenting, or insisting on a Communication & Consent of this Court, which he was Sure would not be obtained although Mr Reinval was Sent over without their knowledge. I offered to go out and ask this Consent – Mr Jay said the first question would be whether *you have talkt to me*: And I would not chuse that Should be answered in ye affirmative – If I may form a guess from what these Gentlemen say, they will make very little account of France making a Settlement for herself in the meantime. They have of late frequently made that Declaration I mean Jay & Adams – and have positively Said We ~~Shall~~ Should not on that account find ourselves one jot further advanced in our Conclusion with them. That France wants to play a trick to them as well as to England, and would consider it as an Impeachment of their address, if they concluded otherwise with any Nation whatever. That if after Such preliminary Conclusion, & France joined them, a good part of their present Army would ship themselves off for the W. Indies, rather than return to the planting of Turnips and jointly together they would soon decide the question in that part of the World – That if they were to provide for the Loyalists, the Treaty would be rejected by the Congress. That some of their States, particularly those to the Northward, would not in point of Conscience think themselves justified in pardoning and providing for those who had burnt their Towns, & murthered their Women and Children – & So a Treaty Signed here would be of no Service. The Bearer having got his pass – & being just upon departure, I am obliged to sett these things down in this irregular way, which I hope Your Lop will excuse – I have the honour to be My Lord Your Lops most obed^t humble Servant   Richard Oswald

Clements Library: Richard Oswald Papers (ALS).

John Jay to Robert R. Livingston

Dear Sir,   Paris, 17th. November 1782.

Although it is uncertain when I shall have an opportunity either of finishing or transmitting the long particular Letter which I am now undertaking to write, I think the matter it will contain is too interesting to rest only in my Memory, or in short Notes, which no body but myself can well unfold the meaning of. I shall therefore write on as my health will permit, and when finished shall convey this Letter, by the first prudent American, that may go from hence, to Nantes or L'Orient.

My reception here was as friendly, as an American Minister might expect from this polite and politic Court; for I think they deceive themselves, who suppose that these kinds of Attentions are equally paid to their private, as to their public Characters.

Soon after the enabling Act was passed, I was shewn a Copy of it, and I confess it abated the Expectations I had formed of the intention of the British Ministry to treat in a manly Manner, with the United States, on the footing of an unconditional acknowledgment of their Independence. The act appeared to me to be cautiously framed to elude such an acknowledgment, and therefore it would depend on future Contingencies, and on the terms and nature of the bargain they might be able to make with us.

Mr. Grenville indeed told the Count de Vergennes, that His Majesty would acknowledge our Independence unconditionally; but, on being desired to commit that Information to writing, he wrote that his Majesty was *disposed* to acknowledge it.– This had the appearance of Finesse.

. . . . .

On the 25th. of July 1782, the King of Great Britain issued a Warrant, or order directed to his Attorney, or Solicitor, General....[1]

. . . . .

A Copy of this Warrant was sent by Express to Mr. Oswald with an Assurance that the Commission should be completed and sent him in a few Days – He communicated this Paper to Doctor Franklin, who, after shewing it to me, sent it the Count de Vergennes....

. . . . .

On the 10th. August we waited upon Count de Vergennes, and a Conference between him and us, on the Subject of Mr. Oswald's Commission, ensued.

The Count declared his opinion, that we might proceed to treat with Mr. Oswald under it, as soon as the original should arrive. He said it was such an one as we might have expected it would be; but that we must take care to insert proper Articles in the Treaty, to secure our Independence and our limits against all future Claims.

I observed to the Count that it would be descending from the Ground of Independence to treat under the description of Colonies. He replied, that names signified little; that the King of Great Britain's stiling himself King of France, was no obstacle to the King of France's treating with him; That an acknowledgment of our Independence, instead of preceding, must in the natural Course of Things be the Effect of the Treaty, and that it would not be reasonable to expect the Effect before the Cause. He added, that we must be mindful to exchange Powers, with M^r. Oswald, for that his acceptance of our Powers, in which we were stiled Commissioners from the United States of America, would be a tacit admittance of our Independence. I made but little reply to all this singular reasoning. The Count turned to Doctor Franklin and asked him what he thought of the matter. The Doctor said he believed the Commission would do – He next asked my opinion – I told him that I did not like it, and that it was best to proceed cautiously –

On returning, I could not forbear observing to Doctor Franklin, that it was evident the Count did not wish to see our Independence acknowledged by Britain, until they had made all their uses of us. It was easy for them to foresee difficulties in bringing Spain into a Peace on moderate Terms, and that if we once found ourselves standing on our own legs, our Independence acknowledged, and all our other Terms ready to be granted, we might not think it our Duty to continue in the War for the attainment of Spanish objects: But, on the contrary, as we were bound by Treaty to continue the war 'till our Independence should be attained, it was the Interest of France to postpone that event until their own views and those of Spain could be gratified by a Peace – and that I could no otherwise account for the Minister's advising us to act in a manner inconsistent with our dignity, and for reasons, which he himself had too much understanding not to see the fallacy of.

The Doctor imputed this Conduct to the moderation of the Minister, and to his desire of removing every obstacle to speedy negotiations for Peace. He observed that this Court had hitherto treated us very fairly and that Suspicions to their disadvantage should not be readily entertained. He also mentioned our Instructions, as further reasons for our acquiescence in the advice and Opinion of the Minister. – A Day or two afterwards I paid a visit to M^r. Oswald, and had a long Conversation with him, respecting his Commission....

. . . . .

... I reminded him, that the judgment and Opinion of America, respecting the disposition and views of Britain towards her must be determined by

Facts and not by professions. That the enabling Act, and the Commission granted to him in pursuance of it, by no means harmonized with the language of these Instructions to Sir Guy Carleton: That, unless the offers and promises, contained in the latter, were realized by an immediate declaration of our Independence, America would naturally consider them as specious appearances of magnanimity, calculated to deceive and disunite them, and, instead of conciliating, would tend to irritate the States. I also urged, in the strongest terms, the great impropriety and consequently the utter impossibility of our ever treating with Great Britain on any other than an equal footing, and told him plainly, that I would have no concern in any negotiation, in which we were not considered as an independent people.

M^r· Oswald upon this, as upon every other occasion, behaved in a candid and proper Manner, He saw, and confessed the propriety of these remarks; He wished his Commission had been otherwise; but was at a loss how to reconcile it with the King's dignity, to make *such* a declaration, immediately after having issued *such* a Commission. I pointed out the manner in which I conceived it might be done: He liked the thought, and desired me to reduce it to writing.... M^r· Oswald approved of the draft and said he would recommend the measure to the Minister. The next Day, however, he told me that he had an Instruction which he thought enabled him to make the declaration; but that it would be necessary to obtain the previous Consent of the Minister for that purpose – He then read to me the 4th· Article of his Instructions, of which the following is a Copy – Viz^t·

"In Case you find the American Commissioners are not at liberty to treat on any terms short of Independence, you are to declare to them, that you have our Authority to make that Cession, our ardent wish for Peace disposing us to purchase it at the Price of acceding to the complete Independence of the thirteen Colonies...."

31st· July 1782. He said he would immediately dispatch a Courier to London, and would press the Ministry for permission to acknowledge our Independence without further delay, which he accordingly did.

At this Time the Commission, under the great Seal, had arrived, and Doctor Franklin and myself went to Versailles to communicate that Circumstance to the Count de Vergennes, and, (agreeable to our Instructions) to inform him of what had passed between M^r· Oswald and us.

The Count and myself again discussed the propriety of insisting that our Independence should be acknowledged previous to a Treaty. He repeated, that it was expecting the Effect, before the Cause, and many other similar remarks, which did not appear to me to be well founded. I told the Count, that a declaration of our Independence was, in my opinion, a matter of very little Consequence; that I did not consider our Independence as requiring any aid or validity from British Acts, and provided that nation treated us, as she treated other Nations, vizt. on a footing of equality, it was all that I desired. He differed with me also in this Opinion. He thought an explicit acknowledgment of our Independence in the Treaty, very necessary, in order to prevent our being exposed to further Claims. I told him we should always have Arms in our hands to answer those Claims, that I considered mere Paper fortifications as of but little consequence; and that we should take care to insert an article in the Treaty whereby the King of Great Britain should renounce all claims of every kind to the Countries within our limits.

The Count informed us, he had delayed doing business with M[r.] Fitzherbert, until we should be ready to proceed with M[r.] Oswald, and that he expected to see him the next Day or the Day after.

M[r.] Fitzherbert went the next Day to Versailles, and immediately despatched a Courier to London.

The answer of the British Ministry to M[r.] Oswald is contained in the following Extract of a Letter to him from M[r.] Townshend, dated Whitehall, 1[st.] September 1782:

"Sir,
I have received and laid before the King your Letters of the 17[th.] 18 & 21[st.] Ult:...and I am commanded to signify to you His Majesty's approbation of your Conduct, in communicating to the American Commissioners the 4[th.] Article of your Instructions; which could not but convince them that the negotiation for Peace and the Cession of Independence to the 13 United Colonies, were intended to be carried on and concluded with the Commissioners in Europe.

Those Gentlemen, having expressed their satisfaction concerning that Article, it is hoped they will not entertain a doubt of his Majestys determination to exercise, in the fullest extent the Powers with which the Act of Parliament hath invested him, by granting to America, full, complete, and unconditional Independence, in the most explicit manner, as an Article of Treaty."

When M[r.] Oswald communicated this Letter to me, I did not hesitate to tell him that his Court was misled by this, for that the language of M[r.] Townshend corresponded so exactly with that of the Count de Vergennes, and was, at the same time, so contrary to that of the Instructions to Sir Guy Carleton, as to be inexplicable on any other principle. I also told him, I suspected that the Courier dispatched by M[r.] Fitzherbert on his return from Versailles had been the means of infusing these Ideas. He smiled, and after a little pause said, "Why Count de Vergennes told M[r.] Fitzherbert that my Commission was come and that he thought it would do, and therefore they might now go on, and accordingly they did go on to discuss certain points, and particularly that of Newfoundland."

Mr. Oswald did not deny or contradict the Inference I drew from this, vizt. That Mr. Fitzherbert, struck by this Conduct of Count de Vergennes, and finding that the Commission given to Mr. Oswald was deemed sufficient by him, thought it his Duty directly to inform his Court of it, and thereby prevent their being embarrassed by our Scruples and Demands on a point, on which there was so much reason to think that our Allies were very moderate.

For my own part I was not only persuaded that this was the Case, but also that the ill-success of Mr. Oswald's Application was owing to it.

These Considerations induced me to explain to him what I supposed to be the natural Policy of this Court on the Subject, and to shew him that it was the Interest of Britain to render us as Independent on France as we were resolved to be on her. He soon adopted the same Opinion, but was at a loss to see in what manner Great Britain considering what had just passed, could consistently take further Steps at present. I told him that nothing was more easy, for that the issuing of another Commission would do it. He asked me if he might write that to the Ministry – I told him he might – He then desired, in order to avoid mistakes, that I would give it to him in writing, which I did as follows vizt.

"A Commission (in the usual Form) to Richard Oswald Esquire to treat of Peace or Truce with Commissioners vested with equal Powers by and on the part of the United States of America, would remove the Objections to which his present one is liable, and render it proper for the American Commissioners to proceed to treat with him on the Subject of Preliminaries."

.   .   .   .   .

Being convinced that the Objections to our following the Advice of Count de Vergennes were unanswerable, I proposed to Doctor Franklin that we should state them in a Letter to him; and request his Answer in Writing, because as we were instructed to ask and to follow his Advice on these Occasions, we ought always to be able to shew what his advice was.

The Doctor approved of the Measure, and I undertook to prepare a Draft of such a Letter.

.   .   .   .   .

On the 9.th. September I received certain Information that on the 7.th. Mr. Rayneval had left Versailles and was gone to England; That it was pretended he was gone into the Country, and that several precautions had been taken to keep his real destination a Secret.

.   .   .   .   .

I also learned from good Authority, that, on the Morning of M.^{r.}

Rayneval's departure, the C. d'Yranda had, (contrary to his usual practice) gone with Post Horses to Versailles, and was two or three Hours in Conference with the Count de Vergennes and M^r· Rayneval, before the latter set out.

All these Facts, taken together, led me to conjecture, that M^r· Rayneval was sent to England for the following purposes –

1$^{st.}$ To let Lord Shelburne know, that the demands of America, to be treated by Britain as independent, previous to a Treaty, were not approved or countenanced by this Court; and that the offer of Britain, to make that acknowledgment, in an Article of the proposed Treaty, was, in the Count's Opinion, sufficient.

2$^d.$ To sound Lord Shelburne on the Subject of the Fishery, and to discover whether Britain would agree to divide it, with France, to the exclusion of all others.

3$^d.$ To impress Lord Shelburne with the determination of Spain to possess the exclusive navigation of the Gulph of Mexico, and of their desire to keep us from the Mississippi; and also, to hint the propriety of such a Line, as on the one Hand, would satisfy Spain, and, on the other, leave to Britain all the Country, North of the Ohio.

4$^{th.}$ To make such other verbal overtures to Lord Shelburne, as it might not be advisable to reduce to writing; And to judge from the general tenor of his Lordship's answers and Conversation, whether it was probable that a general Peace, on terms agreeable to France; could be effected; in order that, if that was not the Case, an immediate Stop might be put to the Negotiation.

Having, after much Consideration, become persuaded that these were M^r· Rayneval's objects, I mentioned his journey to M^r· Oswald, and, after stating to him the first three of these Objects, I said every thing, respecting them, that appeared to me necessary; but at the same Time, with a greater degree of Caution than I could have wished, because I well knew it would become the Subject of a long Letter to the Ministry. On reflecting, however how necessary it was that Lord Shelburne should know our Sentiments and Resolutions, respecting these matters, & how much better they could be conveyed in Conversation than by Letter; and knowing also, that M^r· Vaughan was in confidential Correspondence with him, and he was, and always had been strongly attached to the American Cause, I concluded it would be prudent to prevail upon him to go immediately to England.

I accordingly had an interview with M^r· Vaughan and he immediately dispatched a few Lines to Lord Shelburne, desiring that he would delay taking any measures with M^r· Rayneval, until he should either see, or hear further from him.

M^r· Vaughan agreed to go to England, and we had much previous Conversation on the points in Question; the substance of which was.

That Britain, by a Peace with us, certainly expected other advantages than a mere suspension of hostilities, and that she doubtless looked forward to Cordiality, Confidence and Commerce.

That the manner, as well as the matter of the proposed Treaty, was therefore of importance, and that if the late assurances, respecting our Independence were not realized by an unconditional Acknowledgment, neither Confidence nor Peace could reasonably be expected: That this measure was considered by America as the touchstone of British Sincerity, and that nothing could abate the Suspicions and doubts of her good faith, which prevailed there.

That the Interest of Great Britain, as well as that of the Minister would be advanced by it, for as every Idea of Conquest had become absurd, nothing remained for Britain to do, but to make friends of those whom they could not subdue: That the way to do this, was by leaving us nothing to complain of either in the negotiation, or in the Treaty of Peace, and by liberally yielding every point, essential to the Interest and Happiness of America, – the first of which points was, that of treating with us on an equal footing.

That, if the Minister really meant to make Peace with us, it was his Interest to make us believe so, and thereby inspire us with a certain degree of Confidence, which could no otherwise be obtained: That his Enemies charged him with insincerity on this very point, and that it must be useful to him to convince all the World that such a charge was groundless.

That it would be vain to amuse themselves with expectations from the affected moderation of France on this Head, for that America never would treat on any but an equal footing and therefore, although such expectations might cause delay, they would ultimately be fruitless.

That a little reflection must convince him, that it was the Interest and consequently the policy of France to postpone, if possible, the acknowledgment of our Independence to the very conclusion of a general Peace, and, by keeping it suspended until after the War, *oblige us, by the terms of our Treaty and, by regard to our safety, to continue in it to the End.*

That it hence appeared to be the obvious interest of Britain immediately to cut the Cords, which tied us to France; for that, though we were determined faithfully to fulfil our Treaty and Engagements with this Court, *yet it was a different thing to be guided by their or our Construction of it.*

That among other things we were bound not to make a separate Peace or Truce, and that the assurance of our Independence was avowed to be the Object of our Treaty. While therefore Great Britain refused to yield this Object, we were bound, as well as resolved, to go on with the War, although perhaps the greatest obstacles to a Peace arose neither from the demands of France or America – Whereas, that Object being conceded, we should be at liberty to make Peace, the moment that Great Britain should be ready to accede to the terms of France and America, without our being restrained by the demands of Spain, with whose views we had no concerns.

That it would not be wise in Great Britain to think of dividing the Fishery with France and exclude us; because we could not make Peace at such an expense and because such an attempt would irritate America still more, would perpetuate her Resentments, and induce her to use every possible means of Retaliation by withholding Supplies in future to the Fishery, and by imposing the most rigid restraints on a Commerce with Britain.

That it would not be less impolitic to oppose us on the point of Boundary and the Navigation of the Mississippi.

1$^{st.}$ Because our Right to extend to the Mississippi was proved by our Charters and other Acts of Government; and our Right to its Navigation was deducible from the Laws of Nature, and the Consequences of Revolution which vested in us every British territorial Right. It was...easy therefore to foresee what opinions and sensations, the mere attempt to dispossess us of these Rights, would diffuse throughout America.

2$^{dly.}$ Because the profits of an extensive and lucrative Commerce, and not the possession of vast Tracts of Wilderness, were the true Objects of a commercial European Nation.

That by our extending to the Mississippi, to the West and to the Proclamation bounds of Canada, to the North, and by consenting to the mutual free Navigation of our several Lakes and Rivers, there would be an inland Navigation from the Gulph of S$^{t.}$ Lawrence to that of Mexico, by means of which the Inhabitants, West and North of the Mountains, might, with more ease, be supplied with foreign Commodities, than from the Ports on the Atlantic, and that this immense and growing Trade would be in a manner, monopolized by Great Britain, as we should not insist that she should admit other Nations to navigate the Waters that belonged to her. That therefore the Navigation of the Mississippi would in future be no less important to her than to us, it being the only convenient outlet, through which they could transport the productions of the Western Country, which they would receive in payment for Merchandize vended there.

That as to retaining any part of that Country, or insisting to extend Canada, so as to comprehend the Lands in Question, it would be impolitic for these further Reasons. Because it would not be in their power, either to settle or Govern that Country, that we should refuse to yield them any Aid; and that the utmost exertions of Congress could not prevent our People from taking gradual possession of it, by making establishments in different parts of it. That it certainly could not be wise in Britain, whatever it might be in other Nations, thus to sow the Seeds of future War in the very treaty of Peace, or to lay in it the foundation of such distrusts and Jealousies as, on the one hand, would forever prevent Confidence and real friendship, and, on the other, naturally lead us to strengthen our Security by intimate and permanent Alliances with other Nations.

I desired Mr. Vaughan to communicate these remarks to Lord Shelburne, and to impress him with the necessity and policy of taking a decided and manly part respecting America.

Mr. Vaughan set off the Evening of the 11th. of September – It would have relieved me from much anxiety and uneasiness to have concerted all these Steps with Doctor Franklin; but, on conversing with him, about Mr. Rayneval's Journey, he did not concur with me in Sentiment, respecting the Objects of it; but appeared to me to have a great degree of Confidence in this Court, and to be much embarrassed and constrained by our Instructions.

Nothing now remained to be done, but to complete the Letter we had agreed to write to the Count de Vergennes, stating our Objections to treat with Mr. Oswald under his present Commission....

. . . . .

I think it was on the 24th. September that I was informed of the Intention of the British Court to give Mr. Oswald such a New Commission as had been recommended.

On the 26th. of September I went to pay a Visit to the Count de Vergennes at Versailles. I found the Marquis de la Fayette in the Anti Chamber, and the Ambassador of Spain shortly after entered. After some common Conversation the Ambassador asked me, when we should proceed to do Business. I told him as soon as he should do me the Honor of communicating his Powers to treat: He asked whether the Count de Florida Blanca had not informed me of his being authorized – I admitted that he had, but observed that the usual mode of doing business rendered it proper that we should exchange Certified Copies of our respective Commissions. He said that could not be expected in our Case; for that Spain had not yet acknowledged our Independence. I replied, that we had declared it, and that France, Holland and Britain had acknowledged it. Here the Marquis de la Fayette took up the Subject, and it continued between him and the Ambassador, 'till the Count de Vergennes came in. The Marquis told the Ambassador among other things, that it would not be consistent with the Dignity of France for her Ally to treat otherwise than as independent. This Remark appeared to me to pique the Count d'Yranda not a little.

The Count de Vergennes, on coming in, finding the Conversation earnest, inquired whether we could not agree – The Ambassador stated my Objections. The Count said I certainly ought to treat with the *Ambassador*, and that it was proper we should make a Treaty with Spain in the same manner that we had done with France. I told him, I desired nothing more, and that the Commission to M$^{r.}$ Gerard and the Reason assigned by this Court to the King of Great Britain for entering into Alliance with us, pointed out both the manner and the principles, which were observed and admitted on that Occasion. The Count did not seem pleased with my allusion to the Communication made of our Alliance to England. He observed, that Spain did not deny our Independence, and he could perceive no good Reason for my declining to confer with the Ambassador about a Treaty, without saying any thing about our Independence, an acknowledgment of which would naturally be the Effect of the Treaty proposed to be formed. I told the Count that being Independent, we should always insist on being treated as such, and therefore it was not sufficient for Spain to forbear denying our Independence, while she declined to admit it, and that notwithstanding my Respect for the Ambassador and my Desire of a Treaty with Spain, both the Terms of my Commission and the Dignity of America forbid my treating on any other than an equal footing.

The Count carried the Ambassador into his Cabinet, and when he retired, I was admitted.

The Count commenced the Conversation by explaining the Reason of sending M$^{r.}$ Rayneval to England, which he said was, that by conversing with Lord Shelburne about Peace and matters connected with it, he might be able to judge whether a pacific Disposition really prevailed in the British Court, and therefore whether any Dependence might be placed in his Lordship's Professions on that Head – that he was satisfied with M$^{r.}$ Rayneval's Report, and that he believed that Lord Shelburne was sincerely desirous of Peace.

A few words then passed about M$^{r.}$ Oswald's new Commission; the Count observing in general Terms, that as it removed our former Objections, we might now go on to prepare our preliminaries.

The Conversation next turned to our negotiation with Spain, and to her Claims East of the Mississippi. Nothing new passed on the first Topic; as to the latter, the Count made only some very general Remarks, such as that he hoped we should on confering further about the matter, approach nearer to each other; that those Limits ought to be settled, and while they remained in Contest a Treaty with Spain could not reasonably be expected – That as soon as we should agree upon those points, Count d'Yranda would have a further or more formal Commission to conclude the Treaty, &c.

I remarked that these Claims of Spain were of recent date, for that on my first arriving in Spain, the Count de Florida Blanca told me, that the Success of my Mission would probably turn upon one single point, vizt. the Cession of our Right to the Navigation of the River Mississippi; from which as well as from their subsequent and Uniform Demands on that head it was evident, that they then considered that River as our Boundary; for it would have been very strange indeed, that they should insist on our forbearing to Navigate a River whose waters washed no part of our Country, and to which we could not of consequence have any pretence of Claim.

The Count smiled, but avoided making any direct Reply; he hoped we should nevertheless agree, and that we must endeavor to approach and meet each other. I told him I could not flatter myself with such expectations while Spain continued her Claims to those Countries, for that we should be content with no Boundary short of the Mississippi.

I went from the Count's to Mʳ· Rayneval's Chamber, for I had not seen him since his return from England. He gave me the same Reason for his Journey which I had just received from the Count. We then talked of his Memoir and the Spanish Negotiation. He said much in favor of the *conciliatory Line* he had proposed, and of the Advantages of placing the Indian Nations on the *West* side, under the *Protection* of Spain, and those on the *East*, under that of the United States: That the Rights of those Nations would be thereby secured, and future Disputes between us and Spain avoided. I replied that so far as our Claims might affect those Indian Nations, it was a matter solely between us and them; and that admitting them to be independent, they certainly had a Right to choose their own Protectors; and therefore that we could have no right, without their Knowledge or Consent, to choose for them. I also made the same Remark to him respecting the recency of these Spanish Claims, which I had just before done to Count de Vergennes. He said it was a Subject which Count de Florida Blanca had not understood, and imputed their former Ideas of our extending to the Mississippi, to their Ignorance respecting those matters. Hence it became evident from whom they had borrowed their present Ideas.

On the 27ᵗʰ September Mʳ· Vaughan returned here from England with the Courier that brought Mʳ· Oswald's new Commission, and very happy were we to see it. Copies of it have already been sent to you, so that I will not lengthen this Letter by inserting it here: Nor will I add any thing further on this Head at present than to assure you that Mʳ· Vaughan greatly merits our Acknowledgments.

The next thing to be done was to prepare and draw up the proposed Articles. They were soon completed and settled between us and Mʳ· Oswald, by whom they were sent to his Court with Letters declaring his Opinion that they ought to be accepted and agreed to – but they differed with him in Opinion.

.   .   .   .   .

These Articles, for very obvious Reasons were not communicated to the Count de Vergennes.

M͏ͬ· Oswald did not receive any opinion from his Court relating to our Articles until the 23͏ͩ· October, when Letters from the Minister informed him that the Extent of our Boundaries, and the Situation of the Tories &c. caused some objections, and that the Minister's Secretary was on the way here to confer with us on those Subjects.

On the 24͏ͭͪ· October I dined at Passy with Doctor Franklin, where I found M͏ͬ· Rayneval. After dinner, we were in private with him a considerable Time. He desired to know the state of our Negotiation with M͏ͬ· Oswald. We told him that difficulties had arisen about our Boundaries, and that one of the Minister's Secretary's was coming here with Papers and Documents on that Subject. He asked us what Boundaries we claimed. We told him the River S͏ͭ· John to the East, and ancient Canada as described in the Proclamation to the North. He contested our Right to such an Extent to the North, and entered into several Arguments to shew our Claim to be ill founded. These arguments were chiefly drawn from the Ancient French Claims, and from a Clause in the Proclamation restraining Governors from making Grants in the Indian Country &c.

He inquired what we demanded, as to the Fisheries. We answered that we insisted on enjoying a Right in common to them with Great Britain. He intimated that our views should not extend further than a Coast Fishery, and insinuated that Pains had lately been taken in the Eastern States to excite their Apprehensions and increase their Demands on that Head. We told him that such a Right was essential to us, and that our People would not be content to make Peace without it; and Doctor Franklin explained, very fully, their great Importance to the Eastern States in particular. He then softened his manner, and observed, that it was natural for France to wish better to us than to England, but as the Fisheries were a great Nursery for Seamen, we might suppose that England would be disinclined to admit others to share in it, and that for his part he wished there might be as few obstacles to a Peace as possible. He reminded us also that M͏ͬ· Oswald's new Commission had been issued posterior to his arrival at London.

On the 26͏ͭͪ· October M͏ͬ· Adams arrived here, and in him I have found a very able and agreeable Coadjutor.

.   .   .   .   .

I am sensible of the impression which this Letter will make upon you, and upon Congress, and how it will affect the Confidence they have in this Court. These are critical Times, and great necessity there is for Prudence and Secrecy.

So far and in such matters as this Court may think it their Interest to support us, they certainly will; but no farther, in my opinion.

They are interested in separating us from Great Britain, and, on that point, we may, I believe, depend upon them; but it is not their Interest that we should become a great, and formidable People, and therefore they will not help us to become so.

It is not their Interest that such a Treaty should be formed between us and Britain, as would produce Cordiality and mutual Confidence. They will therefore endeavour to plant such Seeds of Jealousy, Discontent, and Discord in it, as may naturally and perpetually keep our Eyes fixed on France for Security. This Consideration must induce them to wish to render Britain formidable in our Neighbourhood, and to leave us as few resources of wealth and power as possible.

It is their Interest to keep some point or other in contest between us and Britain to the end of the War, to prevent the possibility of our sooner agreeing, and thereby keep us employed in the War, and dependent on them for Supplies. Hence they *have* favored, and will continue to favor, the British Demands, as to matters of Boundary and the Tories.

The same views will render them desirous to continue the War in our Country as long as possible, nor do I believe they will take any measures for our repossession of New York, unless the Certainty of its evacuation should render such an attempt advisable. The Count de Vergennes lately said that there could be no great use in Expeditions to take places which *must* be given up to us at a Peace.

Such being our Situation it appears to me advisable to keep up our Army to the end of the War, even if the Enemy should evacuate our Country; nor does it appear to me prudent to listen to any overtures for carrying a part of it to the West Indies, in case of such an Event.

I think we have no rational dependence except on God and ourselves, nor can I yet be persuaded that Great Britain has either Wisdom, Virtue or Magnanimity enough to adopt a perfect and liberal System of Conciliation. If they again thought they could conquer us they would again attempt it.

We are, nevertheless, thank God, in a better situation than we have been. As our Independence is acknowledged by Britain, every obstacle to our forming Treaties with Neutral Powers, and receiving their Merchant Ships, is at an end – so that we may carry on the War with greater advantage than before, in case our Negotiations for Peace should be fruitless.

It is not my meaning, and therefore I hope shall not be understood to mean, that we should deviate in the least from our Treaty with France; our Honor and our Interest is concerned in inviolably adhering to it. I mean only to say that, if we lean on her love of liberty, her affection for America, or her disinterested Magnanimity, we shall lean on a broken reed, that will sooner or later pierce our Hands, and Geneva as well as Corsica justifies this Observation.

I have written many disagreeable things in this Letter; but I thought it my duty. I have also deviated from my Instructions, which, though not to be justified, will I hope be excused on account of the singular and unforeseen Circumstances which occasioned it.

Let me again recommend Secrecy, and believe me to be Dear Sir, &c.
John Jay.

*   *   *   *   *

NA: PCC, item 110, v. 2, pp. 142-247 (LBkC); M247, reel 135.
[1] See Commission for Richard Oswald from George III, King of England, above.

Francis Dana to Robert R. Livingston

[18 November 1782]
Sir   St. Petersbourg Nov.r 7th. 1782 O.S.[1]
When I was informed by M.r Adams that M.r Jay had written to him from Paris, that the British Commissioner there, had received full powers "to treat of a peace with the Commissioners of the United States" I waited upon the French Minister to consult him on this special occasion upon the expediency of communicating my Powers to this Court. It would be imprudent, thro' this channel, to go into the reasons he assigned against it. It may be sufficient to say I found him strong in the opinion that all attempts made prior to a peace, would be fruitless. As his opinion is the rule by which I am to be governed in this case, nothing can be attempted till the period arrives when we shall not feel ourselves under strong obligations to any Sovereign in the world who shou'd even make advances to form political connections with us, or acquire much eclat from any such connections. I thought the opportunity favourable when the only Power which had any pretence of right to contest our Independance, had consented by so formal an act to treat with us upon the footing of a sovereign and independent State. The consideration we shou'd acquire by a political connection with the illustrious Sovereign of this Empire during the war, and the advantages we might reasonably expect to derive from it in our negotiation for a peace (for I have never considered independance as our only object) have ever made me desirous, if possible, to effect it during the war. Scarce any political measure of great importance can be

undertaken with "an absolute certainty of success." If therefore upon mature deliberation, the state of things is found to be such that success is not improbable, and the benefits of it great and permanent, while the disadvantages of a failure, comparatively speaking, are small & of a transient nature, in such a case it wou'd seem that the measure shou'd be hazarded. Tho' I do not believe this to be the very moment in which Her Imperial Majesty wou'd wish to form any political connection with the United States, but, on the contrary, that She wou'd wish to postpone it till the conclusion of the War, and be well pleased that no advances shou'd be made on our part till then because this wou'd afford her opportunity to claim much merit of the Court of London, in having withheld any encouragement to us, when at the same time not only any offence to the United States wou'd be avoided, but she might allege without a possibility of contradiction, that if an earlier application had been made by them, she Wou'd have been happy to have had an occasion to manifest her respect for them and the early interest she took in their concerns.

Nevertheless there is room to suppose that if our propositions were communicated while the British King is in fact treating with the United States as with an Independant Sovereign Power, that they wou'd not be rejected. And if they were received, this circumstance might be productive of great benefit to our permanent Interests. It wou'd in all probability bring on a declaration of our Independance by some other very considerable Powers of Europe, particularly Sweden and Prussia. The Neutral Maritime Powers wou'd extend the protection of their commerce and navigation to America, and no longer suffer their flags to be insulted on our Coasts. The Court of London wou'd treat of Peace with more zeal and good faith. They wou'd the more readily give up certain claims and pretensions which they will doubtless make upon the United States: and wou'd be exceedingly cautious how they broke off any negotiations which they had opened. In a word we shou'd stand on a more advantageous and independant ground of Treaty. For the attainment of objects like these, had any discretionary powers been left to me, I shou'd have thought it as clearly my duty to have made the attempt here in this moment, as I now consider it to be my duty to wait for the conclusion of the War, the period which is pointed out to me as the only proper one, and when most certainly nothing will remain to be hazarded.

.   .   .   .   .

I have the honour to be Sir with great respect Your most obedient humble Servant   Fra Dana

NA: PCC, item 89, v. 2, pp. 663-665 (LS); M247, reel 117.
[1] Old Style, i.e., Julian calendar.

John Adams to Robert R. Livingston

Sir   Paris November 18. 1782

The Instruction from Congress, which directs Us to pay So Strict an Attention to the French Ministry, and to follow their Advice is conceived in Terms so universall and unlimited, as to give a great deal of Anxiety to My Mind.

There is no Man more impressed with the Obligation of Obedience to Instructions. But in ordinary Cases, the Principal is so near the Deputy, as to be able to attend to the whole Progress of the Business, and to be informed of every new Fact and of every Sudden Thought. Ambassadors in Europe can send Expresses to their Courts, and give and receive Intelligence, in a few days, with the Utmost Certainty. In such Cases, there is no Room for Mistake, Misunderstanding or Surprise. But in our Case, it is very different. We are at an immense distance.– Dispatches are lyable to foul Play; and Vessells are subject to Accidents. – New Scenes open, the Time presses, various Nations are in Suspence and, Necessity forces Us to act.

What can We do? If a french Minister advises Us, to cede to the Spaniards, the whole River of the Missisippi, and five hundred miles of Territory to the Eastward of it are We bound by our Instruction to put our Signature to the Cession, when the English themselves are willing We should extend to the River, and enjoy our natural Right to its Navigation? If We should be councilled to relinquish our Right to the Fishery, on the grand Bank of Newfoundland, when the British Ministry are ready by Treaty to acknowledge our Right to it, are We obliged to relinquish it? If We are advised to restore and compensate the Tories, are We to comply? – If We know or have Reason to believe that Things which will have Weight upon The Minds of the British Ministry, against Us upon some Points, will be communicated to them in some Way or other Secret or open, if We communicate it to this Court, are We bound to do it?

I can not think, that a Construction so litteral and Severe was ever intended to be put upon it, and therefore I see no way, of doing my Duty to Congress but to interpret the Instruction, <****> as We do all general, Precepts and Maxims, by such Restrictions and Limitations as Reason, Necessity and the Nature of Things demand.

. . . . .

...Congress cannot do too much to give Weight to their own Ministers, for they may depend upon it great and unjustifiable Pains are taken to prevent them from acquiring Reputation, and even to prevent an Idea taking root in any Part of Europe, that any Thing has been or can be done by them.– and there is nothing that humbles and depresses, nothing that shackles and confines, in short nothing that renders totally useless all your Ministers in Europe, so much as these Positive Injunctions to consult, and communicate, with French Ministers upon all occasions, and to follow their Advice.– And I really think it would be better, to constitute the Count de Vergennes our Sole Minister, and give him full Powers to make Peace and treat with all Europe, than to continue any of Us in the Service under the Instructions in being– if they are to be understood in that unlimited Sense which Some Persons contend for.

· · · · ·

With great Respect and Esteem I have &c.   John Adams

MHS: *The Adams Papers, microfilm reel 108 (LBkC).*

Thomas Townshend to Richard Oswald

Most Secret and Confidential.   Whitehall 19ᵗʰ· Novʳ· 1782.
Sir,

The good Correspondence which subsisted between you and Mʳ· Strachey, when he was lately at Paris, and the great advantage likely to be derived in the present Negotiation from your Communication with a Person who has so lately conversed with most of the King's Ministers upon that subject, determined me to send him over to You again, as he is in possession of the Sentiments of the whole Council. By him we send such a Treaty as we can sign. You will find in it full satisfaction given to the Americans in the principal points of the Controversy, and what any impartial Man must imagine the only ones worth their dispute.

These consist of the Independence in the first place; the Boundaries, the Surrender of New York and Charles Town, with all the Artillery in them that shall have been taken in the War from the Americans.

The Alterations we have made in their Project are such as I am sure they must find upon reflexion what they may assent to consistently with what they have agreed to already, and as are indispensibly necessary to the honor and Interest of this Country.

I must therefore assure You that it is the Unanimous Resolution of the Cabinet to adhere to the Treaty now proposed, and I do not chuse to prognosticate the danger of the effects of the Refusal of the Commissioners or that Spirit of Conciliation, which has now for some time prevailed in this Country, if it prevents the Treaty being Signed before the Meeting of Parliament.

As Mr Strachey is, as I said before, fully acquainted with the Opinion of the King's Servants upon this head, I shall refer you to him for all further particulars, and Arguments.

You are by the 6th Article of Your Instructions directed not to proceed to the Signature of any Act whatever with the Commissioners of the Colonies, without having received the King's Special Order for that purpose, I am now therefore to signify to You that it is His Majesty's Pleasure that in the present State of this business with regard to every Article of the Treaty, and any possible Alteration or Modification, which may yet be wished by the American Commissioners you should consult most Confidentially with Mr Strachey and Mr Fitzherbert. The recent personal Intercourse of the former with His Majesty's Ministers has put him in full possession of their Sentiments, and the minute acquaintance of the latter with the State of the Foreign Negotiation will render his Assistance of the greatest Advantage to You. Mr Fitzherbert has from the beginning been instructed to communicate with you on every Point in which the two Treaties may affect each other. He has now particular Instructions to furnish You with every Assistance towards the Success of Your Negotiation, which may be drawn from the present dispositions of the Court of France to conclude a General Peace. And if either the American Commissioners shou'd as there is great reason to expect, agree to the Articles of the Treaty in the Shape they are now Transmitted from Hence, or if you and Mr Fitzherbert and Mr Strachey shou'd on your joint Consideration be of Opinion that such Alterations or Modifications as they may propose are admissable, I am to signify to you the King's Special Commands, that you should in that Case forthwith sign the Articles so agreed upon between You and the American Commissioners without waiting for any further Instructions or directions from hence.

In a matter however of this extreme delicacy and Importance, I can not omit recommending to You for the same reasons which I have already stated to You, that You should have the precaution previous to Your Signing to receive from Mr Strachey and Mr Fitzherbert their Opinions under their hands signifying their concurrence in the measure.

I am &c.   Thos Townshend

PRO: FO 27/2, v. 557, f. 855 (LC transcription).

Lord Shelburne's Private Notes

[19 November 1782]

To send a Copy of the Preliminarys, as settled last night for the Americans to Take or Leave.

To send *general* Instructions to Mr Oswald referring him for every particular to Mr Strachey

To give Mr Strachey *private* Instructions relative to the last Article, stating the different classes of Loyalists, and which of them are to be finally Insisted on and which only contended for.

These Instructions not to be communicated but to assist Mr Strachey's memory, and govern his and Mr Fitzherbert's Judgement as to finally agreeing.

To order Mr Oswald to sign whenever Mr Fitzherbert Mr Strachey & himself agree in thinking it expedient.

Care must be taken to refer to Mr Oswald's original Instructions that there may be no doubt as to powers.

To empower Mr Fitzherbert to avail himself of France so far as he may Judge prudent from circumstance.

Mr Fitzherbert's Interposition will be usefull, if it be for no other purpose than to let the Americans see the *possibility* of an appeal to France on our part.

Private exceptions are always understood to be admissible.

Clements Library: Shelburne Papers, v. 87, no. 2, f. 203-204 (AN).

Robert R. Livingston to Benjamin Franklin

N°. 21.

Sir   Philadelphia 21st: Novr. 1782

Congress a few days since passed the enclosed Resolution N°. 1 by which they have added M^r. Jefferson to the Commission for concluding a peace;[1] the established character of this Gentleman gives me reason to hope, that his appointment will be very acceptable to you, and the other Gentlemen in the Commission, I have not yet learned, whether he will take the task upon him, but I have reason to beleive he will, the death of his Wife having lessened in the opinion of his friends the reluctance which he has hitherto manifested to going abroad – I think it would be proper to make a formal anunciation of this Resolution to the Court of France you will naturally give such a representation of M^r. Jefferson's character as will

secure to him there, that esteem and confidence which he justly merits –
....

I am, Sir, with great Respect and Esteem your most obed^t humble
Servant   Robt R Livingston.

. . . . .

University of Pennsylvania, Van Pelt Library: Special Collections (LS).
[1] *Congressional Resolution of November 12, 1782. See JCC, v. 23, pp. 720-721.*

Robert R. Livingston to John Jay

Dear Sir,   Philadelphia, 23 November 1782

I have before me your letters of the 25th and 28th June. I congratuate
you on your safe arrival at Paris, where I venture to hope your residence
will on many accounts be more agreable than it was at Madrid....You need
be under no apprehensions that Commissioners from the Court of Great
Britain will be allowed to negotiate with Congress, their sentiments on this
subject are sufficiently manifested in the resolutions that are sent to you
and Doctor Franklin with this....

That in the mass of our people there are a great number, who though
resolved on independence prefer an alliance with England to one with
France must be a mere speculative opinion which can be reduced to no
kind of certainty. If we form our Judgement from acts of government we
would suppose that no such sentiment prevailed. They all speak a different
language, if from the declarations of individuals we must entertain the same
opinion, since independence and the alliance with France connect
themselves so closely together that we never speak of them separately. The
mass of the People here are not so ignorant of the common principles of
policy as to prefer an alliance with a nation whose recent pretentions and
whose vicinity renders them natural Enemy's to that of a prince who has
no claims upon them and no territory in their Neighbourhood; at least till
the principles of his Government shall be changed and he gives evident
proof of his Justice and moderation. I see but one source from which
differences between us and France can ever arise. IF SPAIN SHOULD PERSIST
IN HER WILD PRETENTIONS TO BOUNDLESS TERRITORY IN THIS COUNTRY
AND BE SUPPORTED IN THOSE PRETENTIONS BY THE OTHER BRANCH OF
THE HOUSE OF BOURBON SHE WILL SHARE IN THE RESENTMENTS AND
JEALOUSIES THAT SUCH PRETENTIONS EXCITE. I LEARN FROM MR.
Carmichael THAT THE COUNT D'ARANDA'A PAWERS ARE NOT YET
EXPEDITED SO THAT AS FAR AS I CAN SEE THE FARCE OF NEGOTIATION
IS THE SAME THOUGH THE SCENE AND THE PLAYERS ARE ALTERED.[1]

. . . . .

I am Dear Sir with great Regard and Esteem your most obedient humble servant,   Robert R. Livingston

Morris, Jay Papers, v. 2, pp. 425-427.
  [1] Capitalized text encyphered in original document.

Lord Shelburne to Richard Oswald

Private.   Shelburne House. 23ᵈ Novʳ· 1782
Dear Sir,

I flatter myself that the American Commⁿˢ· will consider the Step we have taken in regard to Parliament, the City &ᶜ in it's due Light.

In regard to the Fishery, we wish nothing but to keep distinctly to the Principle so much dwelt upon by Dʳ· Franklin in the Commencement of the Negotiation, Vizᵗⁱ the necessity of laying the Foundation of permanent Peace, and that no occasion, much less Temptation be left for future Dissention. I need not tell you that the Bickerings of Fishermen, if not guarded against, may easily revive all that honest men of both sides are endeavouring to bury.

The same Principle extends to the Refugees. It is no Idea of Interest actuates us in regard to them, 'Tis a higher Principle – This Country is not reduc'd to Terms of *Humiliation*, and certainly will not suffer them from America. If Ministers through Timidity or Indolence could be induc'd to give way; I am persuaded the Nation would rise to do itself Justice, & to recover it's wounded Honor. If the Commissioners reflect a moment with that Coolness which ought to accompany their Employment, I cannot conceive they will think it the Interest of America to leave any Root of animosity behind, much less to lodge it with Posterity in the Heart of the Treaty.

'Tis a very inferior consideration, and what you will do me the Justice to acknowledge that I never leant to, what affects the Ministers of the Day. Our uniform Conduct ought to speak for itself, and it must lie with the Americans what Return they chuse to make.

If the American Commissioners think that they will gain by the whole coming before Parliament, I do not imagine the Refugees will have any Objection.

I am &c.   Lord Shelburne

Clements Library: Shelburne Papers, v. 71, pp. 179-182 (C).

Comte de Vergennes to Chevalier de la Luzerne

[Translation]

N⁰· 43.   Versailles, 23 November 1782

. . . . .

The speech which the Duke of Richmond made to the American prisoners set at liberty proves nothing but the very great desire of the English ministry to regain the affection of a people whom it courts only because it could not subjugate them and whom it would soon consign to the cruelest Extremities if it had a force sufficient to subject them to its obedience. Moreover, we ought not to complain, Sir, of the imputation of ambition which the Lord made of us so gratuitously, since it gave occasion for the majority of the delegates to explain themselves in a decent and suitable manner concerning their attachment to the alliance and their fidelity to fulfilling its Conditions. The King will not be less exact in keeping to them on his part, but there is nothing in our treaties that obliges him to prolong the War in order to sustain the ambitious claims which the United States may form either with regard to the fishing or to the Extent of its Boundaries.

I had no knowledge, Sir, that there was still a question between the English plenipotentiary and the American commissioners on the article of the Fishing. What has occupied them for a very long time is the article of the boundaries, it is not exempt from difficulties. Both parties would like to reserve to themselves the Penobscot river, doubtless a very interesting object to both Powers. The difficulties will not diminish when one proceeds to the boundaries in the Interior of the country. The Americans are no less practiced than the English in the art of drawing indefinite Lines and in pretending to a title and a right therefrom. They think they show off their moderation if they are willing to content themselves with the left bank of the Mississippi for an extreme term of demarcation. Such is, Sir, nearly the State of the negotiation, at least I should suppose it, according to what the American Commissioners wish to tell me. The only useful thing they have obtained is the reformation of the English plenipotentiary's power, in which the thirteen provinces are styled the United States.

If the American Commissioners are exact in the Accounts which they render to their Constituents, they will not complain that we seek to influence and to impede them in their negotiation. I receive what they want to tell me, they know that if possible I shall render them the good offices that are in my power, but I do not apply myself to learn more than they may be disposed to tell me; I shall always be in time to come to their aid, for I foresee that they will have more than one difficulty to vanquish, and even very great ones, if they persist in their first claims. Despite all the Cajoleries which the English Ministers squander on the Americans, I do not promise myself that they will show themselves compliant either on the fishing or on the boundaries as the Commissioners of the United States understand them. The latter object can be arranged by sacrifices and mutual Compensations; but with regard to the former, in order to be able to establish an opinion on the probable outcome, it would be necessary to know what the Americans mean by fishing. If it is deep-sea fishing, that which is done on banks far from the Coasts, it seems to me a natural right, but if they claim it such that they exercise it by right of English subjects, can they in good justice wish to retain the rights attached to a quality which they renounce? What would the Americans say if the English claimed to practice fishing on their Coasts? The difficulties relative to the boundaries and to the fishing are not the only ones to vanquish; there exists one, Sir, perhaps more intricate than the two others. That is the fate of the loyalists. The American commissioners, doubtless in accordance with their instructions, appeared resolved to listen to nothing and to countenance no facility in that regard. But can the English decently, and would they wish to, abandon to scorn and misery people who have sacrificed themselves by their attachment to them?

It is a practice generally accepted by all civilized nations to stipulate in their treaties of Peace amnesty and restitution of confiscated goods for those of their subjects who are separated from their homeland and have followed the Cause of the power that made War on it. The American Commissioners oppose to that practice: 1st. The impossibility on their part of effecting a restitution of goods even if they were to stipulate it, considering that the former were confiscated by the individual legislatures, which have disposed of them, and that Congress is without authority over them to engage them and to oblige them to yield, and 2nd. The little safety which the so-called Loyalists will enjoy if they return to the United States; the resentment which the people retain of their cruelties being deeply engraved in all Hearts. These reasons are doubtless good ones, but they do not save the dignity of England, which cannot entirely abandon people who today are in Trouble because they have remained faithful. It is therefore very essential, if one wants peace, to seek and find Expedients that remove this difficulty. The Commissioners of the United States who find themselves here do not seem very eager to work on it. The continuation of the War does not alarm them. I confess that it alarms me more, especially when I reflect that the United States, without their own means and without the Energy to procure them by themselves, constantly fall back on us to obtain them.

If the negotiation for peace, Sir, were more advanced in any way, I would employ the influence which Congress did well to give the King to render the American plenipotentiaries more conciliatory, but as the Conclusion of peace does not depend solely more or less on the facility which they bring to bear on it, it would be premature to press them, because the mistrust which they would conceive of our efforts would render them more recalcitrant. I therefore limit myself, on the few occasions on which I see them, to inspiring them and recommending to them the Spirit of moderation and justice, of which we seek always to give them an Example. It would be good, Sir, if on your part you would make analogous Insinuations to those of the delegates of Congress with whom you can explain yourself more confidently, without ever resorting to ministerial office. It can only be useful to prepare their Minds for the necessity of peace and to lead them to think that it can never be obtained without respective sacrifices.

I say nothing to you, Sir, of the State of our own negotiation. There is reason to think that it would not be delayed if that of the other belligerent parties were more advanced. I can only think, Sir, that the American Commissioners are not exact in informing their Constituents of the State of their negotiation with England, but the occasions to write are rare and often unsafe; I strongly fear that they will become infinitely more so if the Embarkation of our troops at the orders of M. le Comte de Rochambeau for the islands takes place, as we have anticipated from the letters of that general from the beginning of October.

The King has approved, Sir, the gratuity that you gave to the Writer[1] whom you employed to forewarn the people against the impressions that the English are working to give them and against the artifices which they employ to detach them from our alliance.

· · · · ·

Vergennes

FFAA: Pol. Corr., U.S., v. 22, f. 160 (LC transcription).

[1] Probably Thomas Paine (1737-1809), author of the pamphlet Common Sense and of a series of articles subsequently brought together as The Crisis, both published in 1776. Secretary to the Committee for Foreign Affairs, 1777-1779, then clerk of the Pennsylvania Assembly, Paine is known to have accepted money from Luzerne for writing pro-French newspaper articles.

Henry Strachey's Remarks
to the American Peace Commissioners

[Paris] 25th. Novr. 1782

Since I was here last, I have seen, and conversed with, almost every one of the King's Council. They are unanimous in the desire of concluding the Peace. But they are also unanimous in declaring that they think You unreasonable in refusing a general Amnesty and Restoration of Property, to the Refugees. They are unanimous in declaring that those Two Points must be insisted upon, and that every Thing ought to be risqued, rather than submit to Terms highly dishonorable to the British Government. And I must add that those of His Majesty's Ministers, who have been the most zealous Advocates for the Independence of America, are the most forward (if there is the least difference) in condemning America for making a moment's hesitation upon these Points, which seem to affect equally the Honor, the Justice, and even the Policy of America, as of Great Britain.

The Article of the Fishery is another Point. They were determined to resist the Proposition I carried over. They are apprehensive of future Quarels – To obviate which as much as possible, they have expunged that part of the Article, which proposed the Privilege of drying on Cape Sables, and upon the Shores of Nova Scotia, but have left to You what is conceived will be amply sufficient for Your Accommodation.

Objections were made to almost the whole of the Paper I carried from hence, as deficient in point of Form and Precision. The King's Ministers have therefore drawn out the Articles as they wish them to stand, and in Form similar to all other Treaties – They have left out several Preambles, as unnecessary, and unusual. The Point regarding the Debts, though somewhat altered in the Forms of Expression, is exactly as You put it, in respect to Substance. The Article of Independence, is adopted precisely in the Words dictated by Yourselves. The Boundaries, they are not satisfied with; and they hope upon a little more Consideration of the real Rights of the Crown, You will have no Objection to admit of the Extention of Nova Scotia to Penobscot – That is left open for amicable Discussion. But I will acknowledge, (depending upon your not taking Advantage of what I say) that they are not disposed to break off the Treaty absolutely, upon that Article.

The Restitution of the Property of the Loyalists, is the grand Point upon which a final Settlement depends – If the Treaty breaks off now, the whole Business must go loose, and take it's Chance in Parliament, where I am confident the warmest Friends of American Independence, will not support the Idea of the Confiscation of private Property.

Here is the Treaty in such shape as Mr. Oswald can immediately sign –
and the War is for ever I hope, at an end – By this Treaty, You have your
Independence confirmed, and in Your own identical mode of Expression.
By this Treaty You acquire that vast Extent of Territory You have claimed
– New York, with all Your Artillery there, is ceded to You – You will
consider well whether You will reject these great Objects for which You
have so long and bravely fought, merely upon the Non-admission of a
Demand the most humiliating and degrading to Great Britain, and clearly
repugnant to the Honor, the Justice, and even the good Policy of America
herself.

It is necessary I should apprise You, that in the Article of Restitution,
the Words *Rights and Properties* are added to the Word *Estates*, in the view
of securing the Proprietary Interests, derived from ancient and solemn
Charters –

As much as I could recollect of my opening to the Commiss™ at Paris –

NYPL, *Rare Books and Manuscripts Division: Bancroft Collection No. 35-37, American
Papers, 1700-1800.*

Comte de Vergennes to Comte de Montmorin

[Translation]

Versailles, 26 November 1782 7 p.m.

I received at this moment, Monsieur le Comte, a second courier from M.
de Rayneval. He reports on our private negotiation, which is in some
respects still a subject of discussion and difficulties. I would hope, however,
to smooth away the latter if nothing more is left to settle, but the affairs of
Spain excite my solicitude the more, for without sufficient information to
negotiate, I cannot respond to the impatience of a Ministry that requires
a peace to sustain itself. The opening of Parliament, which should have
taken place today, has just been postponed until 5 December. This
resolution met with a most vigorous opposition in the British Council,
where Lord Shelburne and Lord Grantham would have been worsted had
not the King, of whose trust the former seems assured, declared himself for
that party. The successes of this campaign have restored the courage of the
nation and of a party of Ministers who want, at all costs, the continuation
of the war. I am not taken in, being well acquainted with English elation.
The Navy is in a better state than it has ever been, and the means of
funding have been found.

My trouble is that they press for a categorical response and that it is not
possible for us to receive any from Madrid in enough time that it be
delivered to England before 5 December. What course to take? There is the

difficulty. We have shown enough deference to Spain that she does not accuse us of wishing to violate her resolutions; but we shall let slip an opportunity that we shall not find again, perhaps for a long time, to make a suitable Peace, and one which is no less necessary to Spain than to ourselves. If that crown wanted to renounce Gibraltar, the two Floridas would be at her feet, but if she received that place in consideration for the equivalent which we would provide with regard to the promised compensation, do you think, Sir, that she would be dissatisfied if she kept Florida, returned Minorca, and if the articles concerning Honduras, Campeche, and Commerce were postponed to the general peace?

I confess that, as jealous of Spain's glory and interests as M. le Comte de Florida Blanca may be, I would think the step good and advantageous, and I would be much tempted to propose it. I am writing you in haste in the manner of a man who sails without a compass and without a pilot. The King has not yet seen M. de Rayneval's despatch; consequently, I cannot know what he thinks and what he might order me to do. Moreover, before settling anything, I shall see M. d'Aranda, and if I cannot excite his trust, I shall at least leave him nothing to desire from mine.

I request you, Sir, to return to me a copy of this letter, of which I have no time to have a minute made, and to accept the assurance of my tender and faithful attachment. D. V.

FFAA: Pol. Corr., Spain, v. 609, Nᵃ 137 (LC transcription).

Benjamin Franklin to Comte de Vergennes

Sir, Passy, Nov. 29. 1782

I have the honour to acquaint your Excellency, that the Commissioners of the United States, have agreed with Mʳ Oswald on the Preliminary Articles of the Peace between those States & Great Britain. To-morrow I hope we shall be able to communicate to your Excellency a Copy of them. With great Respect I have the honour to be, Sir, Your Excellency's most obedient and most humble Servant B. Franklin

FFAA: Pol. Corr., U.S., v. 22, f. 165 (ALS); LC microfilm reel 13.

Henry Strachey to Thomas Townshend

Private   Paris 29ᵗʰ· Novʳ: 1782.

Dear Sir

Your private Letter...deserves my warmest acknowledgements, and I am now only anxious to find at my Return that you continue Satisfied with my best endeavors. – We consider the Article of the Refugees, as now Settled, much more advantageous than any of the modifications you sent. The Article of Exceptions, would surely have been humiliating. The American Commissʳˢ continued to assert that they had not the Power of Stipulation in that Point, but that the Recommendation of the Congress would have all the Effect We proposed. – We had determined this morning to send home, before we would admit the Article of the Fishery, but when some alterations were made and we saw every thing would otherwise be afloat, We agreed.

I need not tell you that Mʳ Fitzherbert's Abilities and Conduct have been of infinite Use. Indeed you would have had no Treaty without him. I must defer entering into a detail of the whole Business, till I have the pleasure of seeing you, which I think will be before Thursday.

I am with the truest esteem Dear Sir &c.   H. Strachey

Clements Library: Shelburne Papers, v. 70, pp. 398-399 (C).

Henry Strachey to Evan Nepean

private   Paris 29ᵗʰ Novʳ 1782.

Dear Nepean[1]

I thank you for your Letter....Your Report of Lord Shelburnes expressions concerning me was well meant. The anxiety and Mortification I have undergone in the Business here (exclusive of what I shall always think inferior Considerations whilst matters of great public concern are at Stake) required a little sweetening. But I can assure you I did not want any thing to be said, merely to keep me in good humour. When I undertake a Business, I think of nothing but the Business, and persevere in doing my best – What is now accomplished must give Satisfaction, as it is much much beyond the most Sanguine Expectations.

The best way to prevent Stock Jobbing, will be to publish in all the News Papers, immediately some account of the Truth.

You will observe that the Modification of the Refugee Article, is more favorable than any thing sent from home. at least so We three have thought: The Supplemental Article is also added. And there is no Secret Article of a List of Exceptions, which certainly would have been humiliating, however cloaked. The Article of general Amnesty is altered in Words, but we have agreed to it, as the same in substance. The Fishery we have been obliged to alter considerably, but there could be no Treaty at all without it, and as some motive to our acquiescence, the Article relating to Debts, instead of providing for those incurred before 1775 which was all you originally hoped, and as much as you now expect, is framed for the equal Security of *all* Debts. This will relieve Mr. Townshend from another Sett of Sollicitors. The Words *Rights & Properties* are added to *Estates*, as was wished, on account of the Proprietary Interest....Now are We to be hanged, or applauded for thus rescuing you from the American War? I hope to arrive by the meeting of Parliament, tho' that is not material as you will have the Treaty itself. I hope tomorrow.

. . . . . .

I am half dead with perpetual anxiety, and shall not be at ease till I see how the great Men receive me – If this is not as good a Peace as was expected, I am confident it is the best that could have been made – adieu for a few Days.

Yours ever   H. Strachey

Clements Library: Shelburne Papers, v. 70, pp. 399-401 (C).

¹ *Nepean, Evan (1751-1822). British government official. After an early career as clerk or purser in the navy, appointed secretary to the port admiral at Plymouth, 1782. Undersecretary of state in the Shelburne ministry, 1782-1783. Appointed a commissioner of the privy seal, 1784. Undersecretary for war, 1794-1795. Secretary of the Admiralty, 1795-1804. From 1802, baronet. Chief secretary for Ireland, January-September 1804. One of the lords commissioners of the admiralty, 1804-1806. Governor of Bombay, 1812-1819.*

Henry Strachey to Thomas Townshend

Sir   Paris 29th. Novr. 1782. Eleven at Night

A very few hours ago we thought it impossible that any Treaty could be made. We have at last however brought Matters so near to a Conclusion that we have agreed upon Articles, and are to meet tomorrow for the purpose of signing.

Enclosed are such of the Articles as are altered, and an additional one which we mean as a Security in case it be true that Bermuda is taken.

The Article of the Fishery has been particularly difficult to settle, as we thought the Instructions were rather limited. It is however beyond a Doubt, that there could have been no Treaty at all, if we, had not adopted the Article as it now stands. Mr. Fitzherbert was satisfied that it would not interfere with the French Negociation and we all Three concurred in Opinion that this Article, and all the others, as in the inclosed Paper, should be concluded upon.

The 4th Article, which was intended for the Security of Creditors before the War, is now extended to *all Creditors*.

The 5th regarding the Refugees, is different from any of the Modifications which You left to our choice – But we think it will meet with Your Approbation in several Respects, especially as it is not attended with any secret Article of Exceptions. The Words, Rights and Properties, are added to the Word Estates, agreeably to Your Wish; and the supplemental Article, relating to Debts, & Marriage Settlements (with the addition of *or otherwise*) is also inserted.

The 6th. Article, of general Amnesty, after much Debate, and all agreeing that our Meanings were the same, was altered in Words, but remains in Substance, as it stood before:

We attempted to have the 9th. Article in more explicit Terms, but could not contend farther than as it now stands, without raising a Suspicion of what we really meant, and it was evident that the American Commissioners had yet received no Advices concerning Bermuda.

That the Treaty may be safely transmitted to America, it is proposed that You should send to Mr. Oswald a Pass for the American Packet, the *Washington*, Capt. Barney,[1] and that the Commissioners here should furnish You with an American Pass for one of our Packets.

As soon as the Treaty is signed tomorrow, Mr Oswald will dispatch a Messenger with it, and I shall follow as expeditiously as my indifferent State of Health will permit. I have the honor to be with the greatest Respect Sir Your most obedient and most humble Servant   H. Strachey.

R 3^d December

PRO: FO 27/2, v. 557, f. 915 (LC transcription).

[1] *Barney, Joshua (1759-1818). Maryland seafarer, naval officer, privateersman. Served as courier bearing official despatches to Benjamin Franklin in Paris, 1782. Served as captain and chief of division in French navy, 1796-1802. Commanded naval contingent in Battle of Bladensburg, 1814.*

From John Adams' Journal

[Paris] Saturday November 30^(th·)[1782] S^(t·) Andrews Day
We met first at M^(r·) Jay's, then at M^(r·) Oswald's, examined & compared
the Treaties. M^(r·) Strachey had left out the limitation of Time, the 12.
Months, that the Refugees were allowed to reside in America, in order to
recover their Estates if they could. D^(r·) Franklin said this was a surprise upon
us. M^(r·) Jay said so too. We never had consented to leave it out, and they
insisted upon putting it in, which was done.

M^(r·) Laurens said, there ought to be a Stipulation, that the British Troops
should carry off no Negroes or other American Property. We all agreed. M^(r·)
Oswald consented.

Then the Treaties were signed, sealed & delivered, & we all went out to
Passy to dine with D^(r·) Franklin – Thus has proceeded this great affair. The
unravelling of the Plot has been to me, the most affecting & astonishing
Part of the whole Piece.

As soon as I arrived in Paris, I waited on M^(r·) Jay, & learned from him
the rise & progress of the Negotiations. Nothing that has happened since
the beginning of the Controversy in 1761 has ever struck me more forcibly
or affected me more intimately, than that entire Coincidence of Principles
& Opinions between him & me. In about 3. days I went out to Passy, &
spent the Evening with D^(r·) Franklin, & entered largely into Conversation
with him upon the Course & present State of our foreign Affairs. I told
him without Reserve my Opinion of the Policy of this Court, & of the
Principles, Wisdom and Firmness, with which M^(r·) Jay had conducted the
Negotiation in his sickness & my Absence, & that I was determined to
support M^(r·) Jay to the utmost of my Power in the pursuit of the same
System. The D^(r·) heard me patiently, but said nothing.

The first Conference We had afterwards with M^(r·) Oswald, in considering
one point & another, D^(r·) Franklin turned to M^(r·) Jay & said, I am of your
Opinion & will go on with these Gentlemen in the business without
consulting this Court. He accordingly met with Us in most of our
Conferences, & has gone with Us, in entire Harmony & Unanimity,
throughout, & has been able & useful, both by his Sagacity & his
Reputation in the whole Negotiation

I was very happy, that M^(r·) Laurens came in, altho' it was the last day of
the Conferences, and wish he could have been sooner. His Apprehension,
notwithstanding his deplorable Affliction under the recent loss of so
excellent a Son, is as quick; his Judgment as sound, & his Heart as firm as
ever. He had an opportunity of examining the whole, and judging &
approving, and the Article, which he caused to be inserted at the very last,
that no Property should be carried off, which would most probably in the

Multiplicity & hurry of Affairs have escaped Us, was worth a longer Journey, if that had been all. But his Name & Weight is added, which is of much greater Consequence.

. . . . .

From first to last, I ever insisted upon it with the English Gentlemen, that the Fisheries and the Mississippi, if America was not satisfied in those Points, would be the sure & certain sources of a future War – shewed them the indispensible Necessity of both to our affairs, & that no Treaty we could make, which should be unsatisfactory to our People upon those points, could be observed. That the Population near the Mississippi would be so rapid & the Necessities of the People for its Navigation so < ** > pressing, that nothing could restrain them from going down, and if the Force of Arms should be necessary, it would not be wanting: that the Fishery entered into our Distilleries, our coasting Trade, our Trade with the Southern States, with the West India Islands, with the Coast of Africa, & with every part of Europe in such a Manner, and especially with England, that it could not be taken from Us, or granted Us stingily, without tearing & rending – that the other States had Staples – We had none but Fish – no other means of remittances to London, or paying those very Debts they had insisted upon so seriously: that if We were forced off, at 3. leagues distance, we should smuggle eternally, that their men of War might have the Glory of sinking now & then a fishing Schooner – but this would not prevent a Repetition of the Crime – it would only inflame & irritate and enkindle a new War – that in 7. years We should break thro' all Restraints & conquer from them the Island of Newfoundland itself & Nova Scotia too.

M^r. Fitzherbert always smiled, & said, it was very extraordinary, that the British Ministry & We should see it in so different a light. That they meant the Restriction, in order to prevent disputes & kill the seeds of War, & We should think it so certain a Source of Disputes & so strong a Seed of War: but that our Reasons were such, that he thought the probability of our side.

I have not time to minute the Conversations about the Sea Cow Fishery, the Whale Fishery, the Magdalene Islands, the Labradore Coasts & the Coasts of Nova Scotia – It is sufficient to say, they were explained to the utmost of our Knowledge, & finally conceded.

I should have noted before the various deliberations between the English Gentlemen & us, relative to the words indefinite & exclusive Right, which the C. de Vergennes & M^r. Gerard had the precaution to insert in our Treaty with France. I observed often to the English Gentlemen, that, aiming at excluding us from fishing upon the North side of Newfoundland, it was natural for them to wish that the English would exclude us from the South side. This would be making both alike, & take away an odious distinction. French Statesmen must see the tendency of our Fishermen, being treated kindly & hospitably, like friends, by the English, on their side of the Island, and unkindly, inhospitably & like Enemies on the french side – I added further, that, it was my opinion, neither our Treaty with the French, nor any Treaty or Clause to the same purpose, which the English could make, would be punctually observed. Fishermen, both from England and America, would smuggle, especially the Americans, in the early part of the Spring, before the Europeans could arrive. This therefore must be connived by the French, or odious measures must be recurred to, by them or us, to suppress it, & in either Case it was easy to see what w^d be the effect upon the American mind. They, no doubt therefore, wished the English to put themselves upon as odious a footing, at least as they had done – .

Dr Franklin said that there was great weight in this observation, and the Englishmen shewed plainly enough that they felt it –

I have not attempted, in these notes, to do justice to the arguments of my Colleagues; all of whom were, thrôout the whole business, when they attended, very attentive & very able – especially Mr Jay's, to whom, the French, if they knew as much of his negotiations as they do of mine, would very justly give the title, with which they have inconsiderately decorated me, that of "Le Washington de la Negotiation" – a very flattering Compliment indeed, to which I have not a right; but sincerely think it belongs to Mr Jay –

NA: PCC, item 84, v. 4, pp. 278-284 (Journal); M247, reel 112.

Alleyne Fitzherbert to Thomas Townshend

Private   Paris 30 Novr 1782
Dear Sir

I cannot suffer our Friend Mr Strachey to leave Paris without writing you a line by him just to say in regard to the weighty Business of the signature of the American Treaty, that though it gave me great pain (as it did likewise to Mr Strachey) to be obliged to concur therein, I took that step under the fullest conviction that it was a necessary one, and that I should not be any how justifiable in acting otherwise.

For the rest, as Mr Strachey will of course explain to you very fully every thing that relates to that whole Business, it is needless that I should trouble you here with a repetition of any part of the same detail. There is only one particular which his narrative to you will probably be defective in, and which it therefore behoves me to mention. – I mean that at the several conferences with the American Commissioners which I was present at, nothing could exceed the uncommon Vigilance and dexterity which he shewed in seizing upon and turning to the best advantage every opportunity that offered of inserting the Stipulations we wished for, nor the indefatigable perseverance with which he disputed inch by inch those parts of the ground which we were finally obliged to recede from.

I have the honor to be with the most unalterable attachment and Respect Dear Sir &c   Alleyne Fitzherbert

Clements Library: Shelburne Papers, v. 70, pp. 402-403 (C).

Richard Oswald to Thomas Townshend

Sir   Paris 30th Novr. 1782

I have the honor to enclose the Articles of Treaty, signed and sealed, We have been under the necessity of admitting into the 5th Article a limitation of Time (Twelve Months) for those Refugees who may go to America for the purpose of endeavoring to obtain Restitution of their Property.

We have also admitted in the 7th Article, after the Words, "without causing any Destruction", the Words, *or carrying away any Negros, or other Property of the American Inhabitants.*

The 9th Article as settled yesterday, we judged barely sufficient with a view to Bermuda, and therefore have got it altered so as effectually to secure that object.

I have the honor to be with the greatest respect Sir &c

                                                    Richard Oswald

Clements Library: Shelburne Papers, v. 70, p. 404 (C).

Richard Oswald to Thomas Townshend

Sir   Paris 30th Novr 1782.

I take this opportunity of Mr Strachey to acknowledge the honor of your Letters of the 19th & 22^d & 23^d Inst. and to advise that we have at last come to an agreement with the American Commiss^{rs} as to the Terms of the Treaty. They are not exactly what were proposed by the Draft which Mr Strachey brought over with him, but are the best we could possibly obtain of them.

If We had not given way in the Article of the Fishery, We should have had no Treaty at all. Mr Adams having declared that he would never put his hand to any Treaty, if the restraints regarding the 3 Leagues and 15

Leagues were not dispensed with, as well as that of denying his Countrymen the Privilege of Drying Fish on the unsettled parts of Nova Scotia.

M^r· Fitz-Herbert and Mr Strachey finding this, and there being a discretionary Power in Mr Strachey's Instructions, regarding the whole of this Article, as well in extent as manner, they thought it adviseable to avail themselves of it rather than send again to London on this critical occasion, for farther Instructions, which although in the most certain prospect of obtaining assent to such Dispensation might have been of bad consequence, not only in the loss of so much time, but in leaving the Commissioners in such humour, as in the interim, to have suggested some new Demands under the head of one or more of the other Articles, which might have been of worse consequence, than that of giving up these Restraints of Fishery. One Specimen of which We had yesterday, while sitting with them and under hesitation on this Subject, when one of those Gentlemen, pulling a Paper out of his Pocket, proposed that His Majesty should recommend to His Parliament, to make Provision for the payment of certain Effects which had been seized by order of His Generals and entirely out of the Line of the consequences of Military Irregularitys, and such as they could bring undoubted proofs of. And which he said ought to be paid upon the same principles of Justice, as was urged in favour of the recovery of Debts. On these and other accounts, and being in a manner certain that without an Indulgence in this Article of Fishery, there would have been no Treaty with America. The above mentioned Gentlemen thought it best to close with the Commissioners by admitting this Article in the way they proposed. In which they not only had my concurrence, but I own I used the freedom to encourage and press them to give their consent; being of Opinion that I would be under no difficulty in shewing that the Grant was not of that Importance as to be put in comparison with the consequences of splitting with America at this time. Among other things it occurred to me that if our caution in this particular regarded our Marine, and an apprehension of its being abridged by this Interference of the Americans to a greater extent in this Trade, we might come to suffer much more by what the Commissioners insinuated and indeed threatened in case of a Refusal, which was to pass an Act of Navigation, by which, after a certain time all the Ports of America should be shut against English Ships, in so far as the Exportation of their produce should be concerned. – And in the other view of the Profits of the Fishing Trade, and our being deprived of such part of it as the Americans would gain by this admission, I was of Opinion that in leaving the Fishing Sea Ports in the West of England, I would not have far to go Inland, to be satisfied that the Loss by continuing the Dispute some time longer with the Americans, or even laying the foundation of a National Grudge, would, ten times over, counterbalance the amount of the said Loss; even supposing that the Conditions of those Restraints could be enforced; by keeping the Americans to their proper distances, which I am of opinion would be difficult if not doubtfull. Or if attempted by our Men of War on that Station, might be the means of bringing on Quarrels of States, instead of being useful in preventing Quarrels of Fishermen, as one of the Motives insisted on in justification of this Refusal.

Sometime after our giving up this Article one of those Gentlemen came over to our lodging, and told Us that if in this particular we had made any stretch beyond the limits of our Instructions, they would, in return do the same by theirs; And instead of confining the Payment of Debts to what preceded the Year 1775. They would make all recoverable since that period.

...So that I have only to Subscribe myself Sir &c.

Richard Oswald

. . . . . .

Clements Library: Shelburne Papers, v. 70, pp. 416-421 (C).

Preliminary Articles of Peace between the United States and Great Britain

Paris. November 30 1782

Articles agreed upon, by & between Richard Oswald Esquire, the Commissioner of his Britannic Majesty for treating of Peace with the Commissioners of the United States of America, in behalf of his said Majesty, on the one part, and John Adams, Benjamin Franklin, John Jay and Henry Laurens, four of the Commissioners of the said States for treating of Peace with the Commissioner of his said Majesty, on their behalf, on the other part: To be inserted in, and to constitute the Treaty of Peace, proposed to be concluded between the Crown of Great Britain, and the said United States; but which Treaty is not to be concluded, untill Terms of a Peace shall be agreed upon, between Great Britain & France, and his Britannic Majesty shall be ready to conclude such Treaty accordingly.

Whereas, reciprocal Advantages & mutual Convenience are found, by experience, to form the only permanent foundation of Peace & Friendship between States, it is agreed, to form the Articles of the proposed Treaty on such Principles of liberal equity & reciprocity, as that partial advantages, (those seeds of discord.) being excluded, such a beneficial and satisfactory Intercourse, between the two Countries, may be established, as to promise & secure, to both perpetual Peace & Harmony.

Article. 1$^{st.}$–

His Britannic Majesty acknowledges the said United States viz$^{t.}$ New Hampshire, Massachusetts Bay, Rhode Island & Providence Plantations, Connecticutt, New-York, New-Jersey, Pennsylvania, Delaware, Maryland, Virginia, North Carolina, South Carolina & Georgia, to be free, sovreign & independent States; that he treats with them as such; & for himself, his Heirs & Successors, relinquishes all Claims to the Government, Propriety & Territorial Rights of the same, and every part thereof; and, that all disputes, which might arise in future on the the Subject of the Boundaries of the said United States, may be prevented, it is hereby agreed & declared that the following are & shall be their Boundaries, viz$^{t.}$

Article. 2$^{d.}$–

From the North-west angle of Nova-Scotia, viz$^{t.}$: that Angle which is formed by a line, drawn due north from the source of S$^{t.}$ Croix River to the Highlands – along the said Highlands, which divide those Rivers, that empty themselves into the River S$^{t.}$ Lawrence, from those which fall into the Atlantic Ocean, to the North-westernmost head of Connecticut River – thence, down along the middle of that River to the 45°. of North Latitude, from thence by a line due West on said Latitude, untill it strikes the River Iroquois or Cataraquy, thence along the middle of said River into Lake Ontario, through the middle of said Lake untill it strikes the Communication by Water between that Lake and Lake Erie, thence along the middle of said Communication into Lake Erie through the middle of said Lake untill it arrives at the Water-Communication between that Lake & Lake-Huron, thence along the middle of said water-Communication into the Lake-Huron, thence through the middle of said Lake to the water-Communication between that Lake & Lake Superior, thence through Lake Superior, Northward of the Isles Royal & Philipeaux to: the Long Lake, thence through the middle of said Long Lake, & the water Communication between it, & the Lake of the Woods, to the said Lake of the Woods – thence through the said Lake to the most North-western point thereof, and from thence, on a due West Course, to the River Mississippi, thence, by a line to be drawn along the middle of the said River Mississippi untill it shall intersect the northernmost part of the 31°. of North-Latitude.

South, by a line to be drawn due East from the Termination of the line, last mentioned, in the Latitude of 31°. North of the Equator, to the middle of the River Appalachicola or Catahouche, thence, along the middle thereof, to its junction with the Flynt-River, thence strait to the head of S$^{t.}$ Mary's River, and thence down along the middle of S$^{t.}$ Mary's river, to the Atlantic Ocean. *East*, by a line to be drawn along the middle of the River S$^{t.}$ Croix, from its mouth in the Bay of Fundy; to its Source, and from its

Source directly North to the afores^d. Highlands, which divide the Rivers, that fall into the Atlantic-Ocean, from those which fall into the River S^t. Lawrence; comprehending all Islands, within 20. leagues of any part of the Shores of the United-States, and lying between Lines to be drawn due East from the points where the aforesaid Boundaries between Nova-Scotia, on the one part, and East-Florida, on the other, shall respectively touch the Bay of Fundy & the Atlantic Ocean, excepting such Islands as now are, or heretofore have been within the limits of the Said Province of Nova-Scotia.

Article. 3^d.

It is agreed, that the People of the United-States shall continue to injoy, unmolested, the Right to take Fish, of every kind, on the grand Bank, & on all the other Banks of Newfoundland, also, in the Gulph of S^t. Lawrence, & at all other Places, in the Sea, where the Inhabitants of both Countries used, at any time heretofore to fish: And also, that the Inhabitants of the United-States shall have liberty to take Fish, of every kind, on such part of the Coast of Newfoundland, as British Fishermen shall use – (but not to dry or cure the same on that Island – :) And also, on the Coasts, Bays, & Creeks of all other of his Britannic Majesty's Dominions in America; and that the American Fishermen shall have liberty to dry & cure Fish in any of the unsettled Bays, Harbours & Creeks of Nova-Scotia, Magdalene-Islands, & Labradore, so long as the same shall remain unsettled; but, so soon as the same, or either of them shall be settled, it shall not be lawfull for the said Fishermen to dry or cure Fish at such Settlement, without a previous agreement for that purpose with the Inhabitants, Proprietors, or Possessors of the Grounds.

Article. 4th. –

It is agreed, that Creditors, on either side, shall meet with no lawful Impediment to the recovery of the full value in sterling money, of all bonâ fide Debts, heretofore contracted.

Article. 5th. –

It is agreed, that the Congress shall earnestly recommend it to the Legislatures of the respective States to provide for the restitution of all Estates, Rights & Properties, which have been confiscated, belonging to real British Subjects; and also, of the Estates, Rights & Properties of Persons, resident in districts, in the possession of his Majesty's Arms, and who have not borne arms against the said United-States; and that Persons of any other description shall have free liberty to go to any Part or Parts of any of the thirteen United-States, and therein to remain twelve months, unmolested in their endeavors to obtain the Restitution of such of their Estates, Rights & Properties, as may have been confiscated; and that Congress shall also earnestly recommend, to the several States, a

Re-consideration & Re-vision of all Acts or Laws regarding the Premises, so as to render the said Laws or Acts perfectly consistent, not only with Justice & Equity, but with that Spirit of Conciliation, which, on the return of the blessings of Peace, should universally prevail: And that Congress should also earnestly recommend to the several States, that the Estates Rights & Properties, of such last mentioned Persons, shall be restored to them, they refunding to any Persons, who may be now in possession, the bonâ fide price (where any has been given) which such Persons may have paid on purchasing any of the said Lands, Rights, or Properties since the Confiscation.

And it is agreed, that all Persons, who have any Interest in confiscated Lands, either by debts, marriage-settlements, or otherwise, shall meet with no lawfull impediment in the prosecution of their just Rights.

Article. 6th.-

That there shall be no future Confiscations made, nor any Prosecutions commenced against any Person or Persons, for or by reason of the part which he or they may have taken in the present war, and that no person shall, on that account, suffer any future Loss or Damage, either in his Person, Liberty or Property, and that those, who may be now in Confinement on such Charges at the time of the Ratification of the Treaty in America shall be immediately set at Liberty, and the Prosecution so commenced, be discontinued.

Article. 7th.-

There shall be a firm and perpetual Peace, between his Britannic Majesty and the said States, and between the Subjects of the one, and the Citizens of the other; Wherefore, all hostilities, both by Sea & Land shall then immediately cease; all Prisoners, on both sides, shall be set at liberty, and his Britannic Majesty shall, with all convenient speed, & without causing any destruction or carrying away any Negroes, or other Property of the American Inhabitants, withdraw all his Armies, Garrisons, and Fleets from the said United-States; and from every Port, Place & Harbor, within the same; leaving in all Fortifications the american Artillery that may be therein: and shall also order & cause all Archives, Records, Deeds & Papers, belonging to any of the said States, or their Citizens, which, in the course of the war, may have fallen into the hands of his Officers, to be forthwith restored and delivered to the proper States and Persons to whom they belong.

Article. 8th.-

The Navigation of the River Mississippi, from its source to the Ocean, shall forever remain free & open to the Subjects of Great-Britain, and the Citizens of the United-States.

Article. 9th.

In case it should so happen, that any Place or Territory, belonging to Great-Britain or to the United-States, should be conquered, by the arms of either, from the other, before the arrival of these Articles in America, it is agreed, that the same shall be restored, without difficulty, and without requiring any Compensation.

Done at Paris. November. 30th. 1782

John Jay (L.S.)	Richard Oswald (L.S.)
Henry Laurens (L.S.)	John Adams (L.S.)
	Benjn Franklin (LS.)

Witness.

    Caleb Whiteford, Secreyʳ to the British Commission
    W. T. Franklin, Secreyʳ to the American Commission

Seperate Article—

It is hereby understood & agreed, that, in case Great-Britain, at the Conclusion of the present war, shall recover or be put in possession of West-Florida, the Line of North Boundary, between the said Province, and the United-States, shall be a Line drawn from the mouth of the River Yassous, where it unites with the Mississippi, due East to the River Appalachicola.

Done at Paris the thirtieth day of November, one thousand, seven hundred & eighty two.

Richard Oswald (L.S.)
John Adams (L.S.)
Benjn Franklin (L.S.)
John Jay (L.S.)
Henry Laurens (L.S.)

Attest.   Caleb Whiteford, Secreyⁿ to the British Commission.
Attest.   W. T. Franklin, Secreyʳ to the American Commission.

NA: PCC, item 85, pp. 262-270 (C); M247, reel 114.

Robert R. Livingston to the President of Congress

Sir   Philadelphia 2d Decʳ 1782.

Having lately learned that the business of the court of Chancery in the State of New York has encreased so much as to demand more of my attention than is consistant with the duties of the place I have the honor to hold under the United States, I must pray your Excellency to lay before

Congress my request to be permitted to resign the latter, & to assure them at the same time of the grateful sense which I shall always retain not only of the honor done me by the appointment, but of those distinguished marks of confidence which I have experienced repeatedly, as well from Congress at large as from its respective members.

That the business of this office may sustain no injury by my resignation, I will, if Congress approve, continue to perform its duties till they shall be pleased to appoint a Gen^t to succeed me, or to direct some other mode for carrying it on, in confidence, that they will make their arrangements as early as is consistant with the deliberation they may conceive them to require –

.   .   .   .   .

As it is probable Sir that Congress in making a new appointment would wish to adapt the salary to the necessary expence of the department of which they have heretofore had no means to be fully informed, I owe it as well to them, as to my successor, to assure them that with the utmost oeconomy which my situation would admit of, I have been compelled to expend something more than three thousand dollars beyond the allowance of Congress – exclusive of Carriages, horses, & household furniture, all of which I brought with me – As I have now no personal interest in mentioning this circumstance, Congress will, I am persuaded, attribute the liberty I have taken to my desire of seeing a department in which I have had the honor to preside, supported with dignity – Be pleased Sir to receive my sincere acknowledgments for your personal attentions, & believe me to be with the most respectful attachment your Excellency's Most Ob^t hum: Servt Robt R. Livingston

NA: PCC, item 79, v. 2, pp. 395-398 (ALS); M247, reel 105.

Benjamin Franklin to Robert R. Livingston

Sir,   Passy, Decr 4. 1782.

We detain the *Washington* a little longer expecting an English Pass port for her in a few Days; and as possibly some Vessel bound for North America may sail before her. I write this Line to inform you that the French Preliminaries with England are not yet signed, tho' we hope they may be very soon. Of ours I enclose a Copy. The Dutch & Spain have yet made but little Progress, and as no definitive Treaty will be signed till all are agreed, there may be Time for Congress to give us farther Instructions if they think proper. We hope the Terms we have obtained will be satisfactory, tho' to secure our main Points we may have yielded too much in favor of the Royalists. The Quantity of Aid to be afforded us remains undecided. I suppose some thing depends on the Event of the Treaty. – By the *Washington* you will be fully informed of every Thing.

With great Regard, I have the honour to be: Sir, Your most obedient & most humble Servant   B. Franklin

NA: PCC, *item 82, v. 2, p. 289 (LS); M247, reel 108.*

Richard Oswald to Lord Shelburne

My Lord   Paris 4th Decem[r] 1782
I had the honour of writing Your Lo[p] by M[r] Strachey, and have by this Opportunity Sent to the Secretary of State, two certified Copies of the American Treaty.

At same time I have sent to M[r] Strachey a Paper relative to West Florida. I wrote it before he came over the last time, when I was convinced that the Commissioners would not yield in agreeing to a Restitution of the Estates of the Refugees and Loyalists, and consequently supposed that all of them must be left on the hands of Government, to be reestablished, Compensated or Indemnified in a Suteable manner according to the merit of their respective Claims, Necessity of their Condition, and other Circumstances, to be considered of by Government, and provided for accordingly in Such discretionary manner as Should not disappoint those unfortunate People of the relief they were entitled to; but Still under Such Latitude of Administration as should leave it in the power of Government to make proper distinctions in the application, and so as to accommodate the same as much as possible to publick Oeconomie & Conveniency.

In that view I sketched out those Florida papers, as supposing that a great, or the greatest part of those Confiscated people might there find a proper Compensation for Their Losses, without any material Expence to the public.

But M[r] Stracheys last Instructions having directed that a particular mode of Compensation for these People should be introduced into the Treaty, these Florida papers are of less Consequence. Yet still I think it may be worth while to look into them, so as in case that Colony should remain with us at the Peace, it may be considered whether Governm[t] may not Still find it expedient to assign, to some of those people, proper Settlements there, rather than be obliged to repurchase the Identical Estates of a multitude of people at prices which might possibly be run up to exorbitant rates by fraud Collusion & Impositions of various kinds.

. . . . .

I will however further observe that with respect to the Number of confiscated Loyalists, and an Idea of the Amount of their forfeited Property, I am, and always have been an entire Stranger, having never had an opportunity of being informed of either of those particulars. Nor could I, in spite of all Trials, ever gain any Information from the Commissioners here. So that, whether they be only Tens, Twentys, or may run up to Hundreds, I really cannot say. If there are only a few, and their Estates of no very great Importance, all these proposals of Caution may be Unnecessary and Impertinent. I could only make some guess by what dropt from one of the Commissioners, when I was trying him on the Subject – That they thought it not good policy in England to mar the Treaty by being so tenacious on account of these people, since by taking them altogether on their own hands, and leaving them out of the Treaty, the Expence of 3 Months continuance of the War would pay for all the Damage in the way of Compensation. One of those Gentlemen said at last that he did not know but the Expence of One Month might do the whole business.

. . . . .

...Begging Your Lo^p^ pardon for all the freedom I remain with Sincere esteem & respect; Your Lordships most obedient & most humble Servant

Richard Oswald

Clements Library: Shelburne Papers, v. 71, pp. 189-192 (ALS).

Alleyne Fitzherbert to Lord Shelburne

Private   Paris December 4th 1782.
My Lord,

Your Lordship will have seen before this letter reaches you the signed copy of our conditional preliminary articles with America, and you will likewise have received from Mr Strachey an ample detail of all the references upon that convention and of the prating which inclined that Gentleman and myself to concur in opinion with Mr Oswald as to the expediency of signing it without waiting for further instructions. I can truly assure Your Lordship that in regard to the Fishery, no pains or instances were spared in order to settle that article according to the ideas of the British Cabinet 1st. by restraining the Americans to the Fishery upon the Great Bank, 2^d^ by restraining them, (agreeable to the hint thrown out in Your Lordship's letter of the 24th) merely to the Cod Fishery, 3^d^ by preventing them from drying their fish on the shores of N. Scotia, and lastly by having the article so worded as that the Fishery on the Great Bank should be stipulated for, not as a matter of right, not as a matter of Grace and Favour, but upon all these articles the Commissioners in General &

particularly the sliest of them, Mr Adams, (who Your Lordship knows is from N. England) were absolutely inflexible, – We however obtained, and I can assure your Lordship that it was not without difficulty, the exclusion of the American Fishermen from drying upon Newfoundland, and from fishing any part of that Coast, excepting what we ourselves use, a clause, by which all complaints from this Court of having been unfairly dealt with are effectually precluded. Upon the whole with regard to this American Treaty I must take the Liberty to deliver it to your Lordship as my opinion, that *all* the articles in it were, *as matters then stood,* the most honourable that could possibly have been obtained. I say, *as matters then stood,* because, had the negotiation been managed differently at the first setting into, it is not improbable that the Commissioners might have been inclined to pay some consideration for what we call *our grant of*, and they *our acquiescence in* American Independancy. – But I likewise apprehend that this consideration would have consisted partly in a more favourable boundary to the Province of Canada, and partly in some more indulgence to the unfortunate Loyalists, and not in any relaxation < *** > with regard to the Fishery, Mr Adams having declared throughout that it was absolutely impossible for him both on account of his positive instructions, and on account of the ideas which he knew were entertained in his province, to consent to that article under any other form but that which it at present wears. – I cannot help saying one word more upon the last subject which is that upon our urging amongst other arguments for excluding America from the Coast-Fishery, that if she were admitted to it, it would prove an endless source of disputes to the two nations, they held on the contrary that it would become a most powerful bond of connexion to unite us, and supported this doctrine by many plausible inductions of reasoning.

I need not tell your Lordship how anxious we are here to know the result of Monsr de Rayneval's last journey to England, and whether or no the terms he has held out from the Spanish Ambassador will be deemed admissible. – the latter has been for some time past, and particularly since M. de Rayneval's last journeys to England wonderfully closed and reserved with me upon all the points of the negotiation, which I imagine proceeds from his having found me formerly much more so in regard to the Article of Gibraltar, than he perhaps now thinks that I had any reason to be. – However your Lordship knows very well how little my instructions warranted at that time my treating in any shape what ever upon that delicate and important object.

·   ·   ·   ·   ·

...I have the honour to be with the greatest Respect and Attachment, My Lord, Your Lordship's, most obedient and most humble servant

Alleyne Fitz-Herbert

Clements Library: Shelburne Papers, v. 71, pp. 313-319 (ALS).

Comte de Vergennes to Joseph Matthias Gérard de Rayneval

[Translation]

Versailles, 4 December 1782

You did not doubt, Sir, when you left here that the negotiation of the Americans was at the point of its Conclusion. The morning of the following day, I received a note from Mr. Franklin which informed me that all was agreed and was on the point of being signed, in fact, the preliminary articles were signed the same day, by Mr. Oswald on one side, and by the four American plenipotentiaries on the other.

The translation of these same preliminaries, which I enclose, Sir, excuses me from entering into any detail concerning their content. You will remark that the English are purchasing the peace rather than making it. Their concessions in fact, as much for the Boundaries as for the fisheries and the Loyalists, exceed all that I had thought possible; what the motive is that could occasion a readiness that could be interpreted as a Kind of abandonment, you are more in a Position than I to discover. But what I cannot restrain myself from remarking, and what I have observed to Mr. Franklin, is that despite the reservation that the aforesaid preliminary articles will only have their effect when the terms of a peace are settled between France and England, the Signing is no less premature.

If the love of peace has wrung from the English ministers the sacrifices which they make so generously to America, I should think, Sir, that, the sentiment extending to all the objects of the War, the conditions of which you have been the bearer will have been received favorably. You should be able to confirm this to us at once. The news will be better received here than in Madrid, where, according to all my notions, the Cession of Minorca will be extremely displeasing.

Starting from the most satisfying hypothesis, that in which a certain Hope will commence to dawn, we have, Sir, various points to concert with the English ministers: in the 1st place, the ministerial declaration which they should give us. The reading of the preliminaries of the Americans will make you understand the full importance, of which there is an Example of ambiguity in regard to the exclusive Exercise of our right of fishing. The Americans acquiring that of fishing everywhere concurrently with the

English fishermen, it is not expedient to allow them opportunity or pretext to trouble us. A 2nd object no less important will be to concert and to agree on the language and the Conduct to employ with the two mediating Courts. Would it not be appropriate to make them a direct part of the Business of the negotiation and to invite them to furnish their respective ministers with full powers to confirm the preliminary treaties by their mediation?

These things settled and the great difficulties overcome, the form to give to the definitive treaties not requiring a solemn parade, is it the intention of the British Ministry that the negotiation continue where and as it commenced, or does it desire the convocation and holding of a Congress in a suitable neutral place? The King will lend himself willingly to whatever is acceptable in that regard to the King of Great Britain; there is, however, Sir, one consideration which appears to me of some consequence. If we assemble a Congress, we cannot prevent the Gathering of some powers that would like to interfere in it, and who pretend to treat there of affairs that could be foreign to us and perhaps injurious to our own interests. In addition, the King will deem it good and lend himself with pleasure if it suits England to admit the Powers of the North and to sanction that which concerns the principles that have served as the basis of the association that comprises the armed Neutrality.

Do not leave England either, Sir, without having agreed upon the means to be taken, if there are any, in order to make the respective nations enjoy the blessings of peace more promptly, and to shorten the term of depredations and rapine. You would also do well to sound out the English ministers on disarmament. I think that, the preliminaries signed and peace consequently assured, it should suit them and all the belligerent powers to relieve themselves of the oppressive burden of the expense of the strong armies that we have in readiness. An understanding could be reached concerning the times and the proportion of a disarmament. Report to me, please, the ideas on this subject of the Court where you are. If the cession of Guadeloupe takes place, I hope, Sir, that there will be no difficulty in regard to the preservation of the Catholic religion on the footing in which it is established in that island, and to giving the propertied inhabitants a term of at least three years to decide concerning the course it will suit them to take, to sell or to stay. The last difficulty to arise is in regard to the Dutch, whose apathy is much superior to all my activity. I doubt that their plenipotentiaries have yet made their proposal; but I anticipate that it will comprise three objects. The 1st, the most complete and independent Freedom of navigation. The 2nd, the restitution of all the Conquests that have been or may be made respecting them. The 3rd, the indemnity of losses which their Commerce has suffered by the unforeseen declaration of

War. The first two matters do not seem susceptible to difficulties. The third, which would be very costly, seems able to be postponed to the definitive treaty. We have just given a good example of disinterestedness by the assurance of restoring to the republic without any Condition those of its possessions that we have recovered from England.

I have the honor to be most perfectly, Sir,   Vergennes

FFAA: Pol. Corr., England, v. 539, f. 158 (LC transcription).

Benjamin Franklin to Robert R. Livingston

Sir,   Passy, Dec.ʳ 5.ᵗʰ 1782.

· · · · ·

The Arrival of Mʳ Jay, Mʳ Adams and Mʳ Lawrens has relieved me from much Anxiety, which must have continued if I had been left to finish the Treaty alone; and it has given me the more Satisfaction, as I am sure the Business has profited by their Assistance.

Much of the Summer was taken up in objecting to the Powers given by G. Britain, and in removing those Objections. The using any Expressions that might imply an Acknowledgement of our Independence seem'd at first industriously to be avoided. But our refusing otherwise to treat, at length induced them to get over that Difficulty; and then we came to the Point of making Propositions. Those made by Mʳ Jay and me before the Arrival of the other Gentlemen, you will find in the Paper Nᵒ· 1. which was sent by the British Plenipotentiary to London for the Kings Consideration.[1] After some Weeks, an under Secretary, Mʳ· Strachey, arriv'd with whom we had much Contestation about the Boundaries and other Articles which he proposed; we settled some which he carried to London, and returned with the Propositions, some adopted, others omitted or alter'd, and new Ones added; which you will see in Paper Nᵒ· 2.[2] We spent many Days in disputing, and at length agreed on and signed the Preliminaries, which you will receive by this Conveyance. The British Ministers struggled hard for two Points, that the Favours granted to the Royalists should be extended, & our Fishery contracted. We silenc'd them on the first, by threatning to produce an Account of the Mischiefs done by those People; and as to the second, when they told us they could not possibly agree to it as we required it, and must refer it to the Ministry in London, we produced a new Article to be referr'd at the same time, with a Note of Facts in support of it, which you have Nᵒ· 3.[3] Aparently it seem'd that to avoid the Discussion of this they suddenly changed their Minds, dropt the Design of recurring to London, and agreed to allow the Fishery as demanded.

You will find in the Preliminaries some Inaccurate and Ambiguous Expressions that want Explanation, and which may be explained in the definitive Treaty. And as the British Ministry excluded our Proposition relating to Commerce; and the American Prohibition of that with England, may not be understood to cease merely by our concluding a Treaty of Peace, perhaps we may then, if the Congress shall think fit to direct it, obtain some Compensation for the Injuries done us, as a Condition of our opening again the Trade. Every one of the present British Ministry has while in the Minority declared the War against us unjust, and nothing is clearer in Reason than that those who injure others by an unjust War, should make full Reparation. They have stipulated too in these Preliminaries, that in Evacuating our Towns they shall carry off no Plunder; which is a kind of Acknowledgement, that they ought not to have done it before.

The Reason given us for dropping the Article relating to Commerce, was that some Statutes were in the Way, which must be repealed before a Treaty of that kind could well be formed; and that this was a Matter to be consider'd in Parliament.

They wanted to bring their Boundary down to the Ohio, and to settle their Loyalists in the Ilinois Country. We did not chuse such Neighbours.

We communicated all the Articles as soon as they were signed, to M^r le Count de Vergennes, (except the Separate one) who thinks we have manag'd well, and told me that we had settled what was most apprehended as a Difficulty in the Work of a General Peace, by obtaining the Declaration of our Independency.

Decr 14$^{th.}$ I have this Day learnt, that the Principal Preliminaries between France and England, are agreed on, viz:

1. France is to enjoy the Right of fishing and drying on all the West Coast of Newfoundland, down to Cape Ray. Miquelon and S$^t.$ Pierre to be restored and may be fortified.

2. Senegal remains to France, & Goree to be restored. The River Gambia entirely to England.

3. All the Places taken from France in the East Indies to be restored, with a certain Quantity of Territory round them.

4. In the West Indies, Grenada and the Grenadines, S$^t.$ Christophers, Nevis & Monserat to be restored to England; St Lucia to France; Dominique to remain with France, and St Vincent's to be neutraliz'd.

5. No Commissioner at Dunkirk.

The Points not yet quite settled, are, the Territory round the Places in the Indies, and the Neutralization of S$^t.$ Vincents. Apparently these will not create much Difficulty.

Holland has yet hardly done anything in her Negotiation.

Spain offers for Gibraltar to restore W. Florida and the Bahamas. An Addition is talked of, the Island of Guadaloupe which France will cede to Spain in exchange for the other half of Hispaniola, and Spain to England: but England it is said chuses rather Porto Rico. Nothing yet concluded.

. . . . .

I am now entering my 78[th.] Year. Public Business has engross'd fifty of them. I wish now to be, for the little time I have left, my own Master. If I live to see this Peace concluded, I shall beg leave to remind the Congress of their Promise then to dismiss me, I shall be happy to sing with Old Simeon, *Now lettest thou thy Servant Depart in Peace, for mine Eyes have seen thy Salvation.*

With great Esteem, I have the honor to be, Sir, Your most obedient & most humble Servant.   B. Franklin

NA: PCC, item 82, v. 2, pp. 305-316 (LS); M247, reel 108.

[1] See Preliminary Articles of Peace: First Draft Treaty, [5-8] October 1782, above.

[2] See Preliminary Articles of Peace: Second Draft Treaty, [4-7 November 1782], above.

[3] See Henry Strachey: Observations on the Article of the Fishery, [7 November 1782], and Richard Oswald's Observations on the Article of the Fishery, [7 November 1782], both above.

John Adams to Francis Dana

Dear Sir   Paris Decr 6. 1782

You may easily guess from your own Feelings, what mine may be in communicating to you, the Intelligence that the Preliminary Treaty, to be inserted in the diffinitive Treaty was signed the 30 Decr.[1] by the Plenipotentiaries on each Side. – We have tolerable Satisfaction in the Missisippi the Boundaries, & the Fisheries and I hope not much to regret with regard to the Tories or anything else.

M[r] Franklin, M[r] Jay, M[r] Laurens as well as my Self are of Opinion, that this is the proper Time for you to communicate to the Ministry where you are, your Mission. But I believe we shall write you a joint Letter upon this Subject.

Meantime, I have the Honour to be with great Esteem & Affection, as well as Respect, dear Sir, your most humble and most obedient Servant

John Adams.

Pierpont Morgan Library: Adams Papers (ALS).

[1] Marginal correction: Nov[r].

Comte de Montmorin to Comte de Vergennes

[Translation]

N°· 97.   Madrid, 7 December 1782

Sir

At the moment when I was about to have my despatch copied which responds to yours of 26 November and to the private letter of the same date, I received your despatch of the 29th, and in order to show more diligence, I cancelled that despatch, which was not yet copied. I was reporting to you, Sir, on the manner in which the King of Spain and his Minister have envisioned the picture you have made of the present state of affairs, and I ended by telling you that I eagerly wished that you had taken it upon yourself to make the proposition that you were tempted to make, in full certainty that you would be entirely approved and avowed by this court. His Catholic Majesty would wish only to keep the part of the Island of Minorca which borders the Spanish coasts and which serves as the haunt of Algerian corsairs; but he added that if the peace depended only upon the entire restitution of the Island of Minorca, he would consent to it. This morning I have had this definitive response from M. de Florida Blanca, who yesterday evening had received the orders of the King his master, and I was finishing the despatch in which I reported to you when that Minister sent me your despatch of the 29th. I visited him and saw with the utmost satisfaction that M. le Comte d'Aranda's action was entirely approved. I had thought, Sir, that I could not better describe the situation in which you found yourself than by communicating your private letter of the 26th to M. de Florida Blanca. I even left it with him so that he could show it to the King his master. It has made the greatest impression on that Prince, and this morning in giving me the response of the King his master, M. de Florida Blanca very nearly said to me that he wished you had taken it upon yourself to make the proposition for Spain as you expressed it. After that, Sir, you will easily judge that the part M. d'Aranda has taken was entirely approved. It is with much joy and eagerness that I dispatch this courier to you. I would like to give him wings. I foresee the great work of peace as probable and near, and it is assuredly a great success in every respect....

Le c^te De Montmorin

. . . . .

FFAA: Pol.Corr., Spain, v. 609, f. 150 (LC transcription).

Henry Strachey to Alleyne Fitzherbert

Sir,   Whitehall 10th. December 1782

I arrived, with all my anxieties, early on Thursday Morning. You know I had not the smallest apprehension of our being disavowed by Mr. Townshend; and indeed I had soon the pleasure of being assured that our Conduct had given him perfect satisfaction. Nor did I remain long in doubt with respect to Lord Shelburne. I was received by his Lordship with great Cordiality, and with Expressions of acknowlegdement, little short of obligation, the Sincerity of which I have hitherto had no reason to doubt. As the whole Responsibility would not, in any Event, have fallen upon me, I had no Right to more than my small Proportion of such Merit as might be attributed to the Execution of the Trust reposed in us; & therefore you will do me the justice to believe that I did not fail to represent the ingenious and effective Part you had taken in the Negociation – It was essentially necessary that the Business should be concluded; and I am clear, that without your Assistance, we should not have had any Treaty at all.

Lord Grantham and Mr Pitt[1] have also expressed their Satisfaction – These Four are the only Ministers I have yet seen.

But you desired me to communicate to you the whole Truth, and therefore I venture to tell you that I understand the Duke of Richmond, & Lord Keppel (there may be others, but I have not heard of them) are highly displeased at the two great articles, the Refugees, and the Fishery. – What the Objections are, or how founded, I yet know not. But I am particularly surprized at the Versatility of the Duke, because he was present at the drawing up of the different modifications of the 5th. Article, not one of which was nearly so advantageous as that which we obtained. With regard to the Fishery, I do not rest upon the extent of our discretionary Power, but I insist, that if we had not admitted that Article, as it stands, the American Commissioners would not have signed the Treaty, which I am sure would have been a great disappointment to most of our Ministers. It is difficult to say what might have been the consequence of our breaking off; but I am much mistaken if those who now complain, would not have been amongst the foremost to censure our diffidence; especially when they should have seen, as I am confident they soon would, that a Renewal of the Negociation was embarrassed with Demands of Compensation for Damages suffered by Americans, and perhaps with Exceptions of Individuals from a general Amnesty, pointed out by the Congress itself, as well as with other Articles too humiliating for any Ministry to adopt.– and the Moment our Troops had been withdrawn from New York, I should be glad to know, what Power would have remained to contend against Demands however exorbitant?

You will see by the Debates, which I inclose, all that has as yet been said in Parliament. – I suppose the Treaty itself will soon be brought forward, and you shall then be furnished with the Observations that arise upon the different Articles. It cannot be supposed that every Individual will be satisfied; but I am inclined to think that the sober sense of both Houses, reconciled as it is to the Dismemberment of the Empire by the Grant of Independance, will feel and acknowledge, the advantages of a final Close of the ruinous Contest, even upon the Terms we have settled.

I shall trouble you with another Letter when I have any thing worth saying. For the present I have given you enough of Politics, & shall only detain you now till I repeat what I hesitated not to assure you of at Paris, that you are possessed of M$^{r.}$ Townshend's sincere Regard and Attachment. Allow me to add that I am &^{c}. &^{c}.   H. Strachey

NYPL: *Rare Books and Manuscripts Division: Bancroft American Collection, v. 356, Henry Strachey Letters, 1776-1784.*

^{1} *Pitt, William (1759-1806). British statesman. Second son of William Pitt, Earl of Chatham (1708-1778). Member of Parliament, 1781-1782; a supporter of Lord Shelburne. Chancellor of the Exchequer in Shelburne's cabinet, July 1782-March 1783; viewed recognition of American independence as implicit and irrevocable from the outset of peace negotiations. Prime minister, as First Lord of the Treasury and Chancellor of the Exchequer, December 1783-March 1801, and May 1804-January 1806.*

Comte de Montmorin to Comte de Vergennes

[Translation]

N°. 98   Madrid, 10 December 1782
Sir

The courier whom M. de Florida Blanca dispatched today to M. d'Aranda has no other object but to give him instructions on the various subjects of the present negotiations, especially the cession which Spain will make to us of the Spanish part of St. Domingue. I had the honor to send you word the day before yesterday that the arrangement you proposed relative to that cession would not suffer any difficulty. The exchange of which you speak will be made willingly, so that Spain in turn can cede Guadeloupe and Dominica to England.

. . . . .

If we conclude peace on the conditions you have proposed, everyone will be content, and it will not be a small satisfaction to you, Sir, to see end through your attentions, to everyone's liking, so important and so necessary a work.

. . . . .

Received by Courier the 18th.   Le Cte· de Montmorin

FFAA: Pol. Corr., Spain, v. 609, N^a. 159 (LC transcription).

John Jay to Robert R. Livingston

Dear Sir,   Paris 12th December 1782.

. . . . .

Before I left Spain, and by Letters since my arrival here, I desired M^r· Carmichael to make out and transmit the public Accounts. Our negotiations with that Court are at a Stand. The Count Yranda, either has not, or does not choose to shew me, a Commission to treat. He is exceedingly civil, and frequent Visits pass between us.–

It gives me pleasure to inform you that perfect Unanimity has hitherto prevailed among your Commissioners here, and I do not recollect that, since we began to Negotiate with M^r· Oswald, there has been the least Division or opposition between us. M^r· Adams was particularly useful respecting the Eastern Boundary, and Doctor Franklin's Firmness and Exertions on the Subject of the Tories did us much Service. I enclose herewith a Copy of a Letter he wrote about that Matter to M^r· Oswald. It had much Weight, and is written with a Degree of acuteness and Spirit seldom to be met with in Persons of his Age. I have the Honor to be, with great Regard and Esteem, Dear Sir, &c.   John Jay

NA: PCC, item 110, v. 2, pp. 262-263 (LBkC); M247, reel 135.

Joseph Matthias Gérard de Rayneval to Comte de Vergennes

[Translation]

Private Letter   London, 12 December 1782
My Lord

I cannot judge by myself the effect which my despatch of the third produced on you. I can express to you neither the harm which it has done me nor the efforts which I have employed to render Mr. Shelburne more conciliatory. I have been able to obtain nothing, because that minister was too shocked by all that was happening in the Council: it is necessary to be on the spot in order to judge the ferment that reigns in this country. I do not seek to penetrate into the secret places of Mr. Shelburne's heart, I only answer for his integrity in consequence of results: but what I think I see clearly are the difficulties of all kinds which encircle that minister, and the absolute necessity of his justifying his conduct by all the advantages which it is possible for him to obtain. Lord North has a party in the Parliament called the *party of neutrals*; if it decides against the Court, the ministerial majority will be extremely uncertain, and all our labor will fall to nothing. Mr. Shelburne sees that position perfectly, and you understand, My Lord, that it must make him both difficult and circumspect. He will have Subsidies without difficulty, and they were due to vote 110,000 sailors yesterday evening: the two circumstances prove the Nation's dispositions, and should encourage the ministry. In addition, I think that our preparations force him to it, and I think that we would do well to have circulated the news of how it may affect the English enthusiasts for war.

To return to pacific work, would you not think, My Lord, that it would be well to scrutinize on occasion the question of the equivalent for Gibraltar while awaiting the King of Spain's response? If you are of this opinion, I beseech you to furnish me the materials, explaining to me the form in which I should employ them. I dare to think that in the end it will not be a question of equivalency; for it seems to me that Spain has been offered satisfactory conditions: she will have Minorca, the Floridas; she will purge the English from Campeche; she will probably obtain some new arrangement of commerce. What more can she desire? If she does not make peace on such conditions, she cannot justify her conduct, and if she involves us in a continuation of the war, what part will the Americans take? I confess to you, My Lord, that I did not expect such terms on the part of England; in my opinion, they demonstrate its desire for peace and to keep Gibraltar: "If we are fortunate enough to keep that place," Mr. Grantham said to me, "we will be invincible to the opposition, and you will gain as much as we do."

I pressed that Minister on the business of India; I asserted the King's sentiment with warmth. I think I can assure you, My Lord, that Mr. Grantham is sincerely disposed to please His Majesty and to convince you of the fairness of his character: you may believe in it. I have reason to suppose that this matter will be discussed in a few days, as well as the Rest of our articles, and I foresee that I shall be in a position to dispatch a courier to you in order to transmit to you the results of our labor.

You may wish, My Lord, that I had not encouraged Mr. Shelburne to let stand the article in the King's speech concerning expectations of peace: but I ask you to put yourself in my position: the alternative was to excite the nation to peace or to war: I thought I should prefer the former. I ask you to consider besides that the King of England, having given expectations for peace, is obliged to sustain them, and in consequence to be less inflexible on the conditions: such is in fact the position of the English Ministry; and Mr. Shelburne has not concealed it from me. In addition, My Lord, I regard the observation that you made to me as a particular mark of kindness, and I dare to ask you to indicate to me the very slightest nuance that strikes you in my conduct and in my language. My desire to fulfill the King's and your expectation is extreme: but I may be mistaken in my abilities: it is up to you to direct me in a labor as delicate as it is laborious.

You will perceive, My Lord, in the summary that I sent to Mr. Grantham an equivocation concerning the cession of St. Lucia and Martinique. I thought I should make use of it so as to reserve to you the ability to lay stress upon the Sacrifice of the first of these Islands and on that of the second, and to increase the equivalent. You will still have time to yield if that becomes absolutely necessary. Mr. Grantham made no objection concerning that article.

The treaty with America seems to me a dream. I am persuaded that the English ministers, in countenancing it, possibly had the defection of the Americans in mind. However, I am rather inclined to believe that this ministry has gotten into a fix, if I may so express myself, and that it will think twice before exposing itself, by breaking off with us, to seeing itself frustrated by America. The King of England, by pronouncing the word independence, has done it with the Sound of a constrained voice that has astonished the whole world. Moreover, the prince has spoken with much dignity.

I am with the most respectful devotion, My Lord, Your very humble and very obedient servant.   de Rayneval

I enclose a letter for Mr. Fitzherbert.

Received the 15th at 3:30 p.m.

FFAA: Pol. Corr., England, v. 539, f. 220 (LC transcription).

American Peace Commissioners
to Robert R. Livingston

Sir,   Paris, Decr. 14. 1782.

We have the honour to congratulate Congress on the Signature of the Preliminaries of a Peace between the Crown of Great Britain & the United States of America, to be inserted in a definitive Treaty so soon as the Terms between the Crowns of France & Great Britain shall be agreed on. A Copy of the Articles is here inclosed, and we cannot but flatter ourselves, that they will appear to Congress as they do to all of us, to be consistent with the honour and Interest of the United States, and we are persuaded Congress would be ~~ever~~ more fully of that Opinion if they were apprized of all the Circumstances and Reasons which have influenced the Negotiation. Although it is impossible for us to go into that Detail, we think it necessary nevertheless to make a few Remarks on such of the Articles, as appear most to require Elucidation.

Remarks on Article 2ᵈ relative to Boundaries.

The Court of Great Britain, insisted on maintaining all the Territories comprehended within the Province of Quebec, by the Act of Parliament respecting it. They contended that Nova Scotia should extend to the River Kennebeck; and they claimed not only all the Lands in the Western Country, and on the Missisippi, which were not expressly included in our Charters and Governments, but also all such Lands within them as remained ungranted by the King of Great Britain: It would be endless to enumerate all the Discussions and Arguments, on the Subject. We knew this Court and Spain to be against our Claims to the Western Country, and having no Reason to think that Lines more favourable could ever have been obtained, we finally agreed to those described in this Article: indeed they appear to leave us little to complain of, and not much to desire. Congress will observe that although our Northern Line, is in a certain Part below the Latitude of Forty five, yet in others it extends above it, divides the Lake Superior, and gives us Access to its Western & Southern Waters, from which a line in that Latitude would have excluded us.

Remarks on Article 4ᵗʰ· respecting Creditors.

We had been informed that some of the States, had confiscated British Debts, but although each State has a Right to bind its own Citizens, yet in our Opinion, it appertains solely to Congress, in whom exclusively are vested the Rights of making War and Peace, to pass Acts against the Subjects of a Power with which the Confederacy may be at War. It therefore only remained for us to consider, whether this Article is founded in Justice & good Policy.

In our Opinion no Acts of Government could dissolve the Obligations of Good Faith, resulting from lawfull Contracts between Individuals of the two Countries, prior to the War. We knew that some of the British Creditors were making common Cause with the Refugees, and other Adversaries of our Independence; besides, sacrificing private Justice to Reasons of State and political Convenience, is always an odious Measure, and the Purity of our Reputation in this Respect in all foreign Commercial Countries, is of infinitely more Importance to us, than all the Sums in question. It may also be remarked, that American and British Creditors, are placed on an equal footing.

Remarks on Articles 5 & 6: respecting Refugees.

These Articles were among the first discussed, and the last agreed to. And had not the Conclusion of their Business, at the Time of its Date, been particularly important to the British Administration, the Respect, which both in London and Versailles, is supposed to be due to the honour, Dignity and Interests of Royalty, would probably have forever prevented our bringing this Article so near to the Views of Congress and the sovereign Rights of the States, as it now stands. When it is consider'd, that it was utterly impossible to render this Article perfectly consistent, both with American and British Ideas of Honour, we presume that the middle Line adopted by this Article, is as little unfavourable to the former, as any that could in Reason be expected.

As to the Separate Article, We beg leave to observe, that it was our Policy to render the Navigation of the River Missisippi so important to Britain, as that their Views might correspond with ours on that Subject. Their possessing the Country on the River, North of the Line from the Lake of the Woods, affords a Foundation for their claiming such Navigation: and as the Importance of West Florida to Britain was for the same Reason rather to be strengthened than otherwise, we thought it adviseable to allow them the Extent contained in the Separate Article, especially as before the War it had been annex'd by Britain to W. Florida, and would operate as an additional Inducement to their joining with us in agreeing, that the Navigation of the River should forever remain open to both. The Map used in the Course of our Negotiations, was Mitchells.

As we had reason to imagine that the Articles respecting the Boundaries, the Refugees & Fisheries, did not correspond with the Policy of this Court, we did not Communicate the Preliminaries to the Minister, until after they were signed; and not even then the *Separate Article*. We hope that these Considerations will excuse our having so far deviated from the Spirit of our Instructions. The Count de Vergennes, on perusing the Articles appear'd surprized, but not displeased, at their being so favourable to us.

We beg leave to add our Advice that Copies be sent us of the Accounts directed to be taken by the different States, of the unnecessary Devastations and Sufferings sustained by them from the Enemy in the Course of the War; – should they arrive before the Signature of the definitive Treaty they might possibly answer very good purposes.

With great Respect, We have the honour to be, Sir, Your most obedient, & most humble Servants.

John Adams
B Franklin
John Jay
Henry Laurens.

Enter'd on the Minutes
W.T. Franklin Sec.

NA: PCC, *item 85*, pp. 254-259 (LS); M247, reel 114.

John Jay to Robert R. Livingston

priv   Paris 14 Dec' 1782

Dear Sir

From our Preliminaries and the Kings Speech the *present* Disposition and System of the british Court may in my opinion be collected. Altho' particular Circumstances constrained them to yield no more than perhaps they wished, I still think they meant to make (what they thought would really be) a satisfactory peace with us. In the Continuance of this Disposition & System too much Confidence ought not to be placed, for disappointed Violence and mortified Ambition are certainly dangerous Foundations to build implicit Confidence upon: but I cannot forbear thinking that we ought not, in the common phrase, to throw cold water upon it, by improper Exultation, extravagant Demands, or illiberal publications – Should such a Temper appear it would be wise to discountenance it. It is our policy to be independent in the most extensive Sense, and to observe a proper Distance towards all Nations, minding our own Business, and not interfering with or being influenced by the Views of any, further than they may respect us.

Some of my Colleagues flatter themselves with the Probability of obtaining Compensation for Damages. I have no Objection to the Tryal, but I confess I doubt its Success, for Britain has no money to spare, and will think the Confiscations should settle that account; for they do not expect that Retribution will be made to all.

Our affairs have a very promising Aspect, and a little prudence will secure us all that we can reasonably wish [or] expect. The Boundaries between the States should be immediately settled, and all Causes of Discord between them removed. It would be imprudent to disband the army while a foreign one remains in the Country; and it would be equally unwise to permit americans to spill the Blood of our Friends in the Islands, for in all of them there are many who wish us well. (The sale of the *continental* Lands would if properly regulated and appropriated to that purpose, form a Fund on which we might borrow Money – especially if Foreigners could see good Reason to rely on our good Faith which, by being in certain Instances violated, has lost much of its Credit – I allude particularly to the Interest on Loan Office Certificates and the publications in our papers on that Subject, which do us Harm in Europe–)

Adieu I am D'' Rob'' your friend   John Jay

NYHS: *Robert R. Livingston Papers, microfilm reel 2* (ALS).

Comte de Vergennes to Benjamin Franklin

[Translation]

Versailles, 15 December 1782

I cannot but be surprised, Sir, after the explication that I had with you and the promise you gave me, that you would not press to obtain an English Passport for the dispatch of the Packet *Washington*, that you inform me that you have received such a passport, and that at ten o'clock tomorrow morning your courier will set out to carry your Despatches. I am rather at a loss, Sir, to explain your conduct and that of your colleagues on our account. You have concluded your preliminary articles without informing us, although the instructions of Congress stipulate that you do nothing without the participation of the King. You are going to hold out a certain Hope of peace to America without even informing yourself of the State of our negotiation. You are wise and discreet, Sir; you understand the proprieties; you have fulfilled your duties all your life. Do you think you are satisfying those that connect you to the King? I do not wish to carry these reflections further; I commit them to your integrity. When you have been so good as to satisfy my doubts, I will entreat the King to enable me to respond to your requests.

I have the honor to be with true Consideration, Sir, &ᵃ· Vergennes

FFAA: Pol. Corr., U.S., v. 22, f. 180 (Draft); LC microfilm reel 13.

Robert R. Livingston to the President of Congress

Sir   Office for Foreign Affairs Philadelphia 16ᵗʰ· Decʳ 1782

I have the honor to enclose for the inspection of Congress a short letter from Mʳ Jay which contains important information & explains some passages in Docʳ Franklins Letters – Unless the commission given to Mʳ· Fitzherbert on the 24ᵗʰ of July is revoked, it will be difficult to account for Mʳ· *Oswalds* being appointed to treat with the "13 United States of America" – unless we suppose either that his powers are more limited or that the British administration may design to treat under the mediation of neutral powers upon the plan proposed by the imperial courts – so as that the negotiations with the United States may be considered as distinct from those with the other belligerent powers – Just as I was closing this a private Letter was delivered me from Mʳ Jay of the 4ᵗʰ· of Sepʳ· — which contains the following remarkable passage — "I am preparing a map to shew you the

line which C^t· D'Aranda proposes for our western boundary it will not be
finished in time for this conveyance, I am persuaded it is best for us to take
time, my further reasons shall be explained at large in a future letter which
I shall begin as soon as my health will permit": He adds, "that Spain has
issued more bills & that the depreciation is encreased."

I delay reporting on the passage in Doc^r· Franklins letter relative to the
demands of Spain, as there is no immediate opportunity of writing to
Europe & as I am in hourly expectation of receiving something more
particular on this subject. I have the honor to be sir with the most perfect
respect & esteem Your Excellencys Most obt. hum. Servt·

                                                              R R Livingston

Rec'd same day
Secret

NA: PCC, item 79, v. 2, pp. 423-425 (ALS); M247, reel 105.

Benjamin Franklin to Comte de Vergennes

Sir   Passy, Dec^r· 17. 1782
I received the Letter your Excellency did me the Honour of writing to me
on the 15th· Instant. The Proposal of having a Passport from England was
agreed to by me the more willingly, as I at that time had Hopes of
obtaining some Money to send in the *Washington*, and the Passport would
have made its Transportation safer, with that of our Dispatches, and of
yours also if you had thought fit to make use of the Occasion. Your
Excellency objected, as I understood it, that the English Ministers by their
Letters sent in the same Ship might create inconvenient Expectations in
America. It was therefore I propos'd not to press for the Passport till your
Preliminaries were also agreed to. They have sent the Passport without
being press'd to do it; and they have sent no Letters to go under it; and
ours will prevent the Inconvenience apprehended. In a subsequent
Conversation, your Excellency mention'd your Intention of sending some
of the King's Cutters; from whence I imagin'd that Detaining the
Washington was no longer necessary; And it was certainly very incumbent
on us to give Congress as early an Account as possible of our Proceedings,
who must think it extremely strange to hear of them by other means
without a Line from us. I acquainted your Excellency however with our
Intention of dispatching that Ship, supposing you might possibly have
something to send by her.

Nothing has been agreed in the Preliminaries contrary to the Interests of France; and no Peace is to take Place between us and England till you have concluded yours. Your Observation is however apparently just, that in not consulting you before they were signed, we have been guilty of neglecting a Point of *Bienséance*. But as this was not from Want of Respect for the King, whom we all love and honour, we hope it may be excused; and that the great Work which has hitherto been so happily conducted; is so nearly brought to Perfection, and is so glorious to his Reign, will not be ruined by a single Indiscretion of ours. And certainly the whole Edifice falls to the ground immediately, if you refuse on that Account to give us any farther Assistance. I have not yet dispatch'd the Ship, and shall beg leave to wait upon you on Friday for your final Answer. –

It is not possible for any one to be more sensible than I am, of what I, and every American, owe to the King, for the many & great Benefits & Favours he has bestow'd upon us. All my Letters to America are Proofs of this; all tending to make the same Impressions on the Minds of my Countrymen, that I felt in my own. And I believe that no Prince was ever more belov'd and respected by his own Subjects, than the King is by the People of the United States. The English, I just now learn, flatter themselves they have already divided us. I hope this little Misunderstanding will therefore be kept a perfect Secret; and that they will find themselves totally mistaken.

With great and sincere Respect, I am, Sir, Your Excellency's most obedient and most humble Servant   B Franklin

FFAA: Pol. Corr., U.S., v. 22, f. 183-184 (ALS); LC microfilm reel 13.

Alleyne Fitzherbert to Lord Grantham

N° 78)   Paris December 18ᵗʰ· 1782.
My Lord,

I have received the honour of Your Lordship's dispatches Numbers 26,27, 28, 29 & 30 with their Inclosures.

I beg leave to return Your Lordship my warmest thanks for having been pleased to take so early an opportunity of transmitting to me the King's Speech, together with the agreeable intelligence that the addresses upon it had passed the two Houses without a dissentient Voice: – a circumstance which as it proves fully the eminent degree of cordiality and confidence which subsist between His Majesty and His Parliament produced of course a great effect upon the minds of people here. – With regard to the Speech itself it would be presumptuous in me were I speak [to] my sentiments concerning it, but I cannot help saying that all the Principal Ministers of His Court, such of the Foreign Ministers as I have intercourse with, the American Commissioners, and a variety of other intelligent persons in this Capital have agreed in testifying to me in the strongest terms their warm admiration of it. I did not fail to send a copy of it to Monsieur de Vergennes the moment I receive it.

In regard to Your Lordship's dispatches N°s 28 & 29 I can at present only express my best acknowledgements to you for the full and confidential Communication which you have been so good as to make to me of every thing that has passed between Yourself & M. de Rayneval in regard to the Negotiation. I understood Yesterday, to my great satisfaction from the Spanish Ambassadour, that he had ventured of himself to accept of the proposition transmitted by Your Lordship on the 11th Instant to Mr de Rayneval, and as he at the same time informed me that a Courier had been dispatched from Versailles to London on the 16th with that important intelligence, Your Lordship will of course have received it long before this reaches you. – M. d'Aranda mentioned to me at the same time that he was going to dispatch his Secretary of Embassy, M. de la Herredia,[1] to London as [of] this morning, in order to settle the only point which remained to be settled between the two Courts, viz the Logwood Trade at the Bay of Honduras, and he requested that I would furnish him with letters of introduction to Your Lordship and Lord Shelburne, which desire I of course complied with. I must add that in speaking of this commission of M. de la Herredia's he gave me to understand that he would be authorized to settle the Commerce of the Logwood upon our own terms, provided we should consent to take it from the Spanish settlers, but he seemed to wish to convince me that he had no powers to consent to any stipulations which should entitle us (in any shape or under any restriction whatsoever) to cut the logwood ourselves.

I shall make it my business to attend as closely as possible to the several points, which Your Lordship has directed me to observe; – At present I can only speak to the first of them, viz the Temper of the American Commissioners, in regard to which I understand that three of their Number, viz, Messrs Adams Jay & Laurens have little or no communication with Versailles, and not only distrust, but are strongly distrusted by that Court; but the fourth, Dr Franklin, keeps up (though perhaps in a less degree than formerly) his connections with the French Minister, and on that account, and on account of the private animosity and resentment which he still entertains against England, he prevents his colleagues, on whom (though they rather fear than are attached to him) he has great influence, from inserting in their joint letters to the American Congress such representations of matters on this side as would lead the latter to abandon the close and intimate connexion which they have formed with the Court of Versailles and place a due degree of confidence in Great Britain – In regard to the three other Commissioners, I know but little of Mess^r Adams & Laurens, but I must say in Justice to Mr Jay that he has always appeared to me to judge with much candour and consistency of the true interests and policy of his Country as considered in relation to the Powers of Europe being convinced that the assistance afforded to America by such of them as are leagued against England, had originated not from any motive of good-will towards the former Country, but from enmity to us, & that therefore she was under no obligation to support them at present, (her own peace being settled) in the prosecution of their quarrels, any otherwise, that is to say, than as she is strictly bound by the letter of her Treaty with France – Though from the difference of the views and opinions of some of his colleagues Mr Jay has not had in his power to enforce these sentiments in the publick letters which he has written conjointly with them, on the present occasion of the signature of the provisional Treaty, to their Committents in America, I have great reason to think that he has stated them very strongly in his individual capacity to several of the leading Members of the Congress.

Nothing whatsoever has transpired here respecting the differences that prevail between the two Imperial Courts and the Porte, but from the frequent dispatch of Couriers between this place and Vienna it should seem that something important must be in agitation – In regard to the mediation of the two above mentioned Courts. I shall make it my business the next time I see M. de Vergennes to bring that subject upon the tapis, & shall be careful to observe whether the language he may hold to me in regard to it shall deviate in any material respect from his former declarations; however I cannot but be persuaded from what fell from him on that head in our last conversation concerning it (which took place about two months ago) that what Your Lordship intimated to M. de Rayneval respecting the dispositions of this Court in regard to the mediation was perfectly consonant to their present sentiments, & consequently that the steps that Minister alluded to must have been taken at a much earlier period.

. . . . . .

I have the honour to be with the greatest Respect, My Lord, Your Lordship's most obedient and most humble Servant, Alleyne Fitz Herbert R 22^d

PRO: FO 27/3, v. 558, f. 913 (LC transcription).
^{1} *Heredia, Ignacio, Conde de la. Spanish diplomat. Secretary of the embassy in France, 1782-1783.*

Alleyne Fitzherbert to Henry Strachey

My dear Sir,   Paris December 19th. 1782

I am sure I need not tell you how truly and inexpressibly I feel myself obliged to you for your letter of the 10th., which has given me so full and satisfactory an account of the sentiments of the principal members of Cabinet in regard to the terms of the American Treaty, and to our conduct in consenting that it should be signed. – Lord Grantham had before hinted to me that some of the Ministers (but he did not at all specify who) had been dissatisfied with the Fishery & Refugee Articles. however he added that they were *all* glad that the business was finished, & indeed everything that has happened since seems to prove sufficiently that the judgement which we had formed of the *situation of things at home*, and which you know alone determined us to conclude at that critical moment without waiting for farther instructions, was in all respects perfectly well founded. – I find likewise from Lord Grantham's letters how infinitely I am indebted, my Dr. Sir, to you, for your kind and *partial* representation of my conduct in the whole business. – I say *partial*, because, without any false affectation of modesty, I am really convinced that my interference in it was, as things turned out, of little or no use. – *Possibly* it might have been of *some* as to the Fishery Business had I been allowed Fair Play, but you must recollect that our colleague, instead of co-operating with us in our efforts as to that point, openly counterworked them, and that too in a manner which rendered our pursuing the argument any farther not only useless but in a manner ridiculous; since as the Commissioners could not but infer from his language that we were authorised to make in the end, the sacrifice in question, it stood to reason that they must become from that moment (even if they were not so before) immutably fixed in their determination to insist upon it – the fact is that Mr. Oswald has never from the very first, sufficiently understood, though I have spared no pains to impress him with the idea, that a person in a situation, like his & mine, of delegated trust, is in fact the *hand* merely, & not the head, and is bound to consider what his instructions *are*, and not what he thinks *they ought to be*; – however I say this of course merely in the utmost confidence between us two, as I should upon every account, both publick and private, be extremely sorry to injure him in the opinion of his superior.

I take it for granted that Lord Shelburne will have shewn you (more especially as it is strictly speaking *your* property) Bancroft's letter of Yesterday, and that you will have made your reflexions upon it. Before I had received the Doctor's intimation of Mr. Laurens's schemes my mind had misgiven me that something of that sort might possibly be in the wind, from an expression which Dr Franklin had dropped in presence of Mr. Oswald, importing "that he & his brethren were to meet soon in order to consider of such farther clauses as might be necessary to *complete the definitive Treaty*;" and accordingly, upon M.^{r.} O's repeating to me this expression I directly suggested the necessity of our drawing either from that Commissioner or his Colleagues some explanation of it; but I afterwards waved the idea, Mr. Oswald having heard the bare mention of it with a sort of terror, (saying that such a step on our part would alienate the Commissioners and their Country forever) and having assured me that he had every reason to be persuaded that what Franklin had said alluded merely to some commercial stipulations which we should have full liberty to accept or reject. – at present however that my supicions have been confirmed, and more than confirmed, by Mr. Bancroft's information, I shall think it my duty to take the first opportunity of asking one or other of the commissioners the meaning of the abovementioned expression of Dr. Franklin's, & though I do not expect anything like a direct or satisfactory answer, what I shall say will serve at least to remind them that nothing can be farther from our thoughts than to submit tamely to so scandalous & unwarrantable a proceeding as the foisting in any fresh articles (much less such very obnoxious ones) into our treaty. – the truth is that the medical maxim of the "principiis obsta" is in all things the safest that can be followed, but more especially in our dealings with such grasping & interested people as these Commissioners. – In regard to the other great point in Mr. Bancroft's letter, viz. the storm of indignation which Mr. de Vergennes has at last given vent to on account of the signature of the American treaty, and the retort courteous made to it by the commissioners, I have only to say that it must completely re-assure such persons in England as were apprehensive that the hostilities committed against America by G.^{r.} Br.^{n.} and the friendship & protection she met with at the same time from France would rivet her for ever in an inveterate animosity against the former Kingdom, and a firm alliance and union with the latter, since it is manifest that even now, when the war cannot be said to be finished, we stand to the full as well with them, as their allies here. For the rest, you know I always said that nothing was farther from Mr. de Vergennes's expectations than that the Commissioners should take upon them to *sign* the provisional Treaty, and indeed, acquainted as I am with his habits of dissimulation I cannot easily conceive how he contrived to stifle at his first interview with the Commissioners after that event the surprize and indignation which the news of it must have given him. – I have only one word more to say about Mr. Bancroft which is that I have strongly recommended to Lord Shelburne to advance to him immediately the arrears of his stipend, as he has richly deserved, and is I believe in great want of it. – the truth is that he is at this moment an invaluable treasure to us, and though the double game he has been playing with P. Wentworth[1] is certainly against him, yet it should seem from his eagerness to get out of that Gentleman's hands, that it must now be at an end, unless his game in testifying that eagerness be a very refined one indeed.

．．．．．

Adieu, my D^r· Sir...Your most faithful & obliged humble Servant
                                                    Alleyne Fitz Herbert

．．．．．

Recd 30th·

NYPL, *Rare Books and Manuscripts Division: Bancroft American Collection no. 356, Henry Strachey Letters, 1776-1784.*
  [1] *Wentworth, Paul (d. 1793). British spy. Stock market speculator who owned a plantation in Surinam. Possibly related to Governor John Wentworth of New Hampshire. Recruited Edward Bancroft as a double agent. Made great efforts to halt Franco-American treaty negotiations, 1777-1778. Member of Parliament, 1780.*

Comte de Vergennes to Chevalier de la Luzerne

[Translation]
N^o· 45   Versailles, 19 December 1782

I have the honor to send you, Sir, the translation of the preliminary articles that the American plenipotentiaries have settled, approved, and signed with that of Great Britain, to be drafted into treaties when the terms of Peace are stipulated between France and England.

You will surely applaud, Sir, as do I, the very extensive advantages which our allies the Americans will reap from the peace, but you will certainly be no less surprised than I have been at the conduct of the deputies. In following the instructions of Congress, they should have done nothing without our participation. I had apprised you, Sir, that the King would seek to influence the negotiations only so far as his offices should be necessary to his friends. The American deputies will not say that I have sought to intervene, still less that I have wearied them with my Curiosity. They have carefully kept themselves distant from me. One of them, Mr. Adams, come from Holland, where he had been graciously received and attended by our ambassador, was almost three weeks in Paris without fancying that he owed me a mark of attention, and probably I would still not have seen him if I had not contacted him. When I have had occasion to see one of them and to question them succinctly on the progress of the negotiations, they have always confined themselves to generalities, seeking to make me think that it was not advancing and that they had no confidence in the English ministers' sincerity.

Consider my surprise, Sir, when Mr. Franklin informed me on the 30th of November that the Articles had been signed. The reserve they have shown in our Regard does not pardon the breaking of the promise we had made each other only to sign conjointly. I owe Mr. Franklin the justice to say that the next day he sent me a copy of those same articles. He certainly will not complain that I did not receive it with demonstrations of sensibility. It was only a few days later that, the minister having come to see me, I allowed myself to make him understand that his conduct in hastening that Signing had been not very obliging to the King. He seemed to understand that, and made the best excuses he could for himself and his colleagues. Our Conversation passed amiably. Mr. Franklin spoke to me of his desire to send the articles to Congress, and that to that end, he and his colleagues had agreed to an Exchange of passports with the English minister for the safety of the ships that will be sent. I observed to him that this usage appeared dangerous to me, since the articles were only provisional and subject to the result of our still very uncertain negotiations. I thought that this appearance of collusion with England, following the signing of the articles, might make the people of America think that peace had been consummated and embarrass Congress, of whose loyalty I was quite confident. I added several other arguments, of which Mr. Franklin and Mr. Laurens, who accompanied him, seemed to feel the force. They spared nothing to convince me of the Confidence we should have in the fidelity of the United States, and they left me with assurances that they would lend themselves to what I desired.

Consider my surprise, Sir, when on the evening of the 15th, I received from Mr. Franklin the note of which you will find a Copy enclosed. The tone of it seemed to me so singular that I thought I should make him the reply which I likewise transmit to you. I am unaware of the effect it has produced; I have not heard anything since from the American Commissioners. Their Courier has not come to pick up my despatches, and I have no knowledge whether they are indeed being sent out. It would be singular, after the rebuke I administered to them, that they would not have had the Curiosity to inform themselves of the Status of our negotiation in order to apprise their masters. It is still not so advanced as it concerns us, Sir, as is that of the United States. This is not to say that His Majesty, if he had shown no more delicacy in his conduct than the American delegates, could not have signed articles with England long before them; there is no very essential difficulty today between France and England, but the King wishes all his allies to be fully satisfied, and has quite determined to continue the war, despite any particular advantage that might be offered him, if Great Britain wishes to wrong anyone.

It still remains to conciliate the interests of Spain and those of Holland. I have reason to hope that we shall soon have agreement with regard to the first; the fundamental bases have been laid down, and it is only a question of agreeing on the forms. I think that the United States would do well to reflect upon Spain and treat her with respect. She will have them for neighbors. As for Holland, I fear that its affairs will cause us delays and embarrassments. The dispositions of the English ministry toward that republic seem to me something less than favorable.

So, Sir, that is the present State of things. I hope it improves, and soon, but no matter what may transpire, I think that it is appropriate that the most influential members of Congress be informed of the irregular Conduct of their delegates in our Regard. You will restrain yourself in speaking of it, not attaching to your words the Character of a complaint. I do not accuse anyone, I do not even blame Mr. Franklin. Perhaps he yields too easily to the impulses of his Colleagues, who pretend to know nothing of any Regard. All their attentions are for the English whom they meet in Paris. If we may judge the future from what is now passing before our eyes, we shall be ill-paid for what we have done for the United States of America and for assuring them their rights.

I say nothing to you, Sir, concerning the requests for money that are made to us. You may well understand that the present conduct does not encourage us to show ourselves forthcoming.

I have the honor to be   Vergennes

FFAA: Pol. Corr., U.S., v. 22, f. 185 (LC transcription).

Comte de Vergennes to Chevalier de la Luzerne

[Translation]

Nᵒ· 46.   Versailles, 20 December 1782

. . . . .

The boundaries between the United States and the English possessions are clearly stated in the provisional accord that has just been signed; I think, Sir, that there will be no difficulties on that subject, but in the West the Americans will have need of much wisdom in order not to bring upon themselves a war with the Savages, which would retard the progress of their population and throw them into expenses at a time when they have need to busy themselves with the reestablishment of their finances. It would be very good to moderate, as much as you can, the avidity of the inhabitants of the frontiers from that part who would like to expand at the expense of the Savages without calculating the risks they would run by irritating them.

We should expect, Sir, to see the new Republic disturbed by factions the more active for no longer being distracted by external affairs. I can only prescribe for you in that regard the same discretion you practiced at the time when the clash of parties bore on the subjects which directly interested us. If to all the benefits which the King has poured out upon this people His Majesty can join that of inspiring in it a constant inclination for concord, he will assure its happiness, but perhaps it will have need of some unfortunate lessons to establish its habitual manner of being, and I much fear that the germs of division now existing will produce much evil before the Republic acquires stability.

It is strongly to be desired, Sir, that means be found to restore at least one portion of England's partisans to their respective states, so that the horde which has just settled in Acadia is not too numerous, and that the hatred that will exist between it and the subjects of the United States may not give rise to blows that could have consequences. I hope that, once assured of independence, the people will no longer be so embittered against those who were opposed to its establishment. The attention of Congress should be disposed to favor the return of these people, if not to their former homes, at least to some parts of the United States.

I do not conceal from myself, Sir, that Spain's conduct with regard to the United States establishes a system of antipathy between the two nations of which the consequences could be troublesome. But it has been impossible for us to prevent this evil, and it is probable that their proximity, which is going to extend much more than one at first thought, would have produced it anyway. Although that may be so, the Court of Madrid has much to work out in order to establish a good system of conduct with regard to the United States. It should reap a great part of the activity and the future riches of that nation, but this will not be without difficulty. I foresee that we will be asked to act as arbitrators or at least conciliators of all the differences that will arise between the two nations, and that the King's Minister in the United States will be occupied almost as much with these affairs as with our own. It will be necessary, Sir, to set rules for you in that respect, but I am postponing that labor to another time.

· · · · ·

Vergennes

FFAA: Pol. Corr., U.S., v. 22, f. 188 bis (LC transcription).

Comte de Vergennes to Chevalier de la Luzerne

[Translation]

Nᵒ· 47.   Versailles, 21 December 1782.

My letter Nᵒ· 45, Sir, was already enciphered when Mr. Franklin, perceiving the irregularity of the conduct for which I had reproached him, wrote to me to vindicate himself and asked me for an interview, which took place yesterday. It passed very amiably for both of us. He assured me that the Intention of his principals was not to take the least action at any time that might detract from the fidelity which they owed to their Engagements and which, in spite of the necessity and the Expediency of peace, they would renounce rather than neglect the obligations they have to the King and the gratitude they owe him. Mr. Franklin added that he and his Colleagues did not think differently and that they would be inconsolable if their Conduct should have displeased the King and cooled his affection for the United States. Mr. Franklin justified as best as he could the attempted precipitate Dispatch of the packet *Washington*, the departure of which was delayed, and concluded by entreating me to consign the misunderstanding to silence and oblivion.

As I so promised him, you would do well, Sir, not to make use of my letter Nᵒ· 45, inasmuch as the American plenipotentiaries will have informed Congress of that to which it relates.

You are aware, Sir, of Congress' requests to the King for pecuniary assistance. They amount to no less than making them a loan of 20 million of our Livres. That Sum far exceeds all the proportions under consideration; however, His Majesty, wishing to give the United States a new proof of his friendship and of the interest which he takes in their Welfare, accords then for the year 1783 a loan of six million of our Livres, 600,000 of which will be immediately advanced to Mr. Franklin to be sent by the *Washington* to Mr. Morris. I would not conceal from you, Sir, that this effort is a burden after five years of a war, the expenses of which have been and still are enormous, and which we are not assured of seeing ended so soon.

You will take care, Sir, to display this new mark of interest to Congress, but you would do well at the same time not to allow any Hope that the King might be disposed to give it more scope, either through new advances or by standing security. The United States do not show themselves sufficiently disposed to establish the means of meeting their debts themselves for one to reasonably think of acquiring Credits for them. This will certainly be the last.

I can tell you nothing affirmative, Sir, concerning the peace. It will only be toward the end of next week that we will perhaps be able to judge with precision what we have reason to hope for. If the *Washington* packet has not yet sailed, I will be punctual in informing you of the true State of things.

I have the honor to be.   Vergennes

FFAA: Pol. Corr., U.S., v. 22, f. 189 (LC transcription).

James Madison's Notes of Debates

Teusday 24 Decr. [1782]

The letter from Mr. Jay inclosing copy of the intercepted letter from [Marbois] was laid before Congress.[1] The tenor of it with the comments of Mr. J affected deeply the sentiments of Congress with regard to {France}.[2] The policy in particular manifested by {France} of keeping us tractable by leaving the British in possession of posts in this country awakened strong jealousies, corroborated the charges on that subject, and with concomitant circumstances may engender the opposite extreme of the gratitude & cordiality towards {France}; as the closest friends on a rupture are apt to become the bitterest foes. Much will depend however on the course pursued by Britain. The liberal one [Oswald] seems to be pursuing will much promote an alienation of temper in A[merica]. from {France}. It is not improbable that the intercepted letter from Marbois came thro' his hands. If G.B. therefore yields the Fitsheries & the back territory, A. will feel the obligation to her not to {France} who appears to be illiberal as to the 1st & favorable to Spain as to the 2nd object; and consequently has forfeited the confidence of the States interested in either of them. Candor will suggest however that the situation of {France} is & has been extremely perplexing. The object of her blood & money was not only the independence, but the commerce and gratitude of America; the commerce to render Independence the more useful, the gratitude to render that Commerce the more permanent. It was necessary therefore she supposed that America should be exposed to the cruelities of her Enemies, and be made sensible of her own weakness in order to be grateful to the hand which relieved her. This policy if discovered tended, on the other hand to spoil the whole. Experience shews that her truest policy would have been to relieve A. by the most direct & generous means, & to have mingled with them no artifice whatever. With respect to Spain also the situation of {France} has been & is peculiarly delicate. The claims & views of Spn & A. interfere. The former attemps of B. to seduce Sp. to a separate peace, & the ties of {France} with the latter required of her to favor Spain, at least to a certain degree, at the expence of A. Of this G.B. is taking advantage.

If {France} adheres to Sp., G.B. espouses the views of A.; & endeavours to draw her off from {France}. If {France} sd. adhere to A. in her claims, B. might espouse those of Sp & produce a breach between her {France}, and in either case B. wd. divide her enemies. If {France} acts wisely she will prefer the friendship of A. to that of Spain. If A. acts wisely she will see that she is with respect to her great interests, more in danger of being seduced by B. than sacrificed by {France}.

> . . . . .

Smith, Letters of Delegates, v. 19, pp. 501-502.

[1] See François Barbé de Marbois to Comte de Vergennes, 13 March 1782.

[2] Text in brackets indicates encyphered material in original document.

Comte de Vergennes to Chevalier de la Luzerne

[Translation]

Versailles, 24 December 1782

Mr. Franklin, Sir, wishing to dispatch his Courier in order to inform Congress of his Transactions with England, I do not think I should persuade him to detain him still, although it is painful to me to see the announcement of the peace precede its Certainty in America. Our Negotiation with England still allows uncertainties and doubts, and I cannot say when and how they will be resolved. It is therefore very important, Sir, that you warn the Members of Congress of the true State of things, so that, seduced by the apparent Hope of peace, they do not allow themselves to yield to demonstrations that might cause one to suspect a plan of defection that I think entirely opposed to the principles and the intentions of that Body. The King has done too much in favor of the United States up to now for them to doubt that His Majesty sincerely wishes to procure for them the most prompt enjoyment of peace. It is a benefit whose sweetness he will share with them, and which he is very concerned to procure for his people. But his will alone cannot do everything. The Cooperation of the King of England is necessary. But by wanting peace at least in appearance, he makes difficulties arise that may delay it, if not make it miscarry. As soon as the Negotiation takes a decided turn, I will hasten to inform you of it by the quickest route. Perhaps the Negotiation would have proceeded more rapidly if the plenipotentiaries of the United States, by reflecting more on the Consequences, had been less hasty to sign their provisional articles.

I have the honor to be with a sincere attachment, Sir,   Vergennes

FFAA: Pol. Corr., U.S., v. 22, Nᵒ 192 (LC transcription).

Comte de Vergennes to Benjamin Franklin

Sir   Versailles. 25[th.] Decem. 1782

I have the honor of sending you Sir my dispatches for the Chev[r.] de la Luzerne. The packet is large but it *incloses* several duplicates.

I should have been happy could I have informed him that our Negociation is advanced as far as *Yours*, but it is far distant as yet. I cannot even foretell what will be the issue of it; for even difficulties < ******** > proceed from the *facility* with which we have listened to their proposals. It will be well for you to advise Congress to be on their guard against any thing that may happen. I do not despair, ~~but~~ I rather hope, but every thing is as yet uncertain.

I have the honor to be with perfect respect   De Vergennes

Faithfully translated from the Original by John Pintard.[1]

NA: PCC, *item 82, v. 2, pp. 337 (translation); M247, reel 108.*
[1] *Pintard, John (1759-1844). New York merchant. Served as French-language interpreter for the Department of Foreign Affairs, 1785-1790.*

Joseph Matthias Gérard de Rayneval to Comte de Vergennes

[Translation]

My Lord,   London, 25 December 1782

I did not think I should express in my official letter any of the ill-humor which the politeness of the request concerning the cutting of logwood gave My Lord Shelburne; but I think I should tell you in confidence that it was extreme, and that that Minister did not hesitate to tell me that matters were only brought nearer as yet and by no means united, and he much desires that Spain's conduct, which he has sharply censured, not cause a rupture at the moment when everything seems disposed for a prompt and sincere reconciliation. I sought to vindicate Spain, on the basis of her having committed herself to her form of proceeding; but I gained nothing; and My Lord Shelburne, in order to show me with what facility the conduct of that Power could still cause a revolution, confided to me, under the seal of secrecy and for you only, My Lord, the assault he endured during a lengthy Council in which St. Lucia was demanded. Five members wished absolutely to profit from the signing of the treaty with the Americans to break off negotiations with us entirely; and it was only by incredible efforts, and by the preponderance which his position gives him, that he brought everyone back to his opinion; that at this moment the same members are still for war, and that the Remainder of the Council, composed of 11 persons, would be easy to win over to the same side. This confidence gave me cause to speak to Lord Shelburne of the precipitous course which has been pursued with the Americans, and I do not conceal from you, My Lord, that my language held a little reproach. My Lord Shelburne observed to me that this was a very delicate business, as much in regard to the Council, as in regard to the American Commissioners, in giving me an answer; however, he did tell me of the desire, on their part, to finish with the Americans before the return of Parliament, as they wish to finish with us, because they want to prevent parliamentary questions and interference; that, moreover, he, My Lord Shelburne, was unaware until the report made to the Council that matters were so far advanced, and that such facilities had been given to the Americans, and that inwardly he disapproved of them. I wished to seize this occasion to make some remarks on the difficulty the article which accords the Americans navigation of the Mississippi would give to Spain; but My Lord Shelburne responded to me with spirit that this was immaterial to him; that all that might concern Spain was of little import to him; that that Power only merited attentions because it is allied with His Majesty, but that he would take no step in her favor. I would have attempted in vain to insist upon my object: I will await a calmer moment to take it up again.

My Lord Shelburne begs you with urgency, My Lord, to guard for him the secret of the events which he has confided to me, because he wishes to avoid vexations; and he told me without evasion that if something gets out about them, I would lose his confidence: you judge rightly that I hastened to reassure him. That Minister is not unaware of all the suspicions there have been and probably still are in France concerning his probity, and he is so much the more affected because he believes he does not merit them. I venture to be of his opinion, My Lord. Seeing things up close, and having daily experience with My Lord Shelburne, I think myself ready to understand him up to a certain point. If I do not deceive myself, that Minister has an heroic soul and a bold and decisive character, together with most engaging manners; he sees things on a broad scale and detests the minutiae; he is not obstinate in discussions: but he must be convinced, and Sentiment operates more on his soul than reasonings; I have more than one proof of this last verity. I will add that M. Shelburne has for friends, that he has around him, men the choice of whom does him honor; not an intriguer, not an equivocal man: an individual of this cast is commonly neither false nor cunning, and I think I can say that My Lord Shelburne is neither one nor the other, although certain individuals say it who think they know him and who do not know him at all. You will ask me perhaps, My Lord, how it is possible to combine with what I have just said the conduct of My Lord Shelburne relative to the equivalents? I have given you above and in my several dispatches the key to that conduct. That of the American plenipotentiaries has contributed essentially to it, and My Lord Grantham, like My Lord Shelburne, has foreseen the effects of it. The unhappy news of the signing, which they did without our knowledge, has given cause for the extension of the equivalents demanded for Gibraltar. If My Lord Shelburne had refused the request, the Council, in all probability, would have decided on the rupture of the negotiation.

Lack of time forces me to finish. I cannot, however, refrain from pointing out to you, My Lord, that the English ministers often compare the treaty they are about to make with that of Paris, and that in examining the situation of the belligerent parties, they speak with ill-humor of the sacrifices to which they have been led: the affair of India has more than once given cause for this reflection: it must be confessed, My Lord, that neither France nor Spain has anything to complain of.

I am with the most respectful devotion, My Lord, Your very humble and very obedient servant   de Rayvenal

. . . . .

Received the 29th.

FFAA: Pol. Corr., England, v. 539, f. 314 (LC transcription).

Benjamin Franklin to Dr. Samuel Cooper

My dear Friend,[1]   Passy, Dec$^{r.}$ 26. 1782.

. . . . .

We have taken some good Steps here towards a Peace. Our Independence is acknowledged, our Boundaries as good & extensive as we demanded; and our Fishery more so than the Congress expected. I hope the whole Preliminaries will be approv'd, and with the Definitive Treaty, when made, give entire Satisfaction to our Country. But there are so many Interests to be considered between Five Nations; & so many Claims to adjust, that I can hardly flatter myself to see the Peace soon concluded, tho' I wish and pray for it, and use my best Endeavours to promote it.

I am extreamly sorry to hear Langage from Americans on this side the Water, and to hear of such Language from your Side, as tends to hurt the good Understanding that has hitherto so happily subsisted between this Court and ours. There seems to be a Party with you that wish to destroy it. If they could succeed, they will do us irreparable Injury. It is our firm Connection with France that gives us Weight with England, and Respect throughout Europe. If we were to break our Faith with this Nation *on whatever Pretence*; England would again trample on us, and every other Nation despise us. We cannot therefore be too much on our guard how we permit the private Resentments of particular Persons to enter into our public Counsels. You will hear much of an interrupted Letter communicated to us by the British Ministry. The Channel ought to be suspected. It may have received Additions and Alterations. But supposing it all genuine, the forward mistaken zeal of an Undersecretary, should not be imputed to the King who has in so many ways provided himself our faithful and firm Friend and ally. –

I long to see you and my Country once more before I die, being ever, my dear Friend, Yours most affectionately.   B. Franklin

FFAA: Pol. Corr., U.S., v. 22, f. 193-194 (LC transcription).
    [1] Cooper, Samuel (1725-1783). Boston clergyman and patriot. French agent, 1779-1783.

James Madison's Notes of Debates

[December 30, 1782]
From Teusday 24 Decr. the journals suffice untill Monday 30 Decr.

A motion was made...to revise the instructions relative to negociations for peace, with a view to exempt the american Plenipotentaries from the obligation to conform to the advice of France. This motion was the effect of impressions left by Mr. Jay's letters & the intercepted one from Marbois. This evidence of separate views in our ally, and the inconsistency of that instruction with our national dignity, were urged in support of the motion. In opposing the motion many considerations were suggested, and the original expediency of submitting the commission for peace to the counsels of France discanted upon. The reasons assigned for this expediency were that at the juncture when that measure took place, the American affairs were in the most deplorable situation, the Southern States being over run

& exhausted by the enemy, & the others more inclined to repose after their own fatigues than to exert their resources for the relief of those which were the seat of the war; that the old paper currency had failed, & wth. it public credit itself to such a degree that no new currency could be substituted; & that there was then no prospect of introducing specie for the purpose, our trade being in the most ruinous condition, & the intercourse with the Havannah in particular unopened. In the midst of these distresses, the mediation of the two Imperial Courts was announced. The general idea was that the two most respectable powers of Europe would not interpose without a serious desire of peace, and without the energy requisite to effect it. The hope of peace was therefore mingled with an apprehension that considerable concessions might be exacted from America by the Mediators, as a compensation for the essential one which Britain was to submit to. Congress on a trial found it impossible from the diversity of opinions & interests to define any other claims than those of independence & the alliance. A discretionary power therefore was to be delegated with regard to all other claims. Mr. Adams was the sole minister for peace, he was personally at variance wth. the French Ministry; his judgment had not the confidence of some, and his impartiality in case of an interference of claims espoused by different quarters of the U.S. the confidence of others; a motion to associate with him two colleagues, to wit, Mr. F[ranklin] & Mr. Jay had been disagreed to by Congress; The former of these being interested [as one of the Land Companies][1] in territorial claims which had less chance of being made good in any other way, than by a repossession of the vacant country by the British Crown; the latter belonging to a State interested in such arrangements as would deprive the U.S. of the navigation of the Mississippi & turn the wartime trade thro' N.Y.; and neither of them being connected with the So. States. The idea of having five Ministers taken from the whole union, was not suggested until the measure had been adopted, and communicated to the Chevr. de Luzerne to be forwarded to France, when it was too late to revoke it. It was supposed also that Mr. Laurens then in the tower wd not be out, & Mr. Jefferson wd. not go &. that the greater the no. of Ministers, the greater the danger of discords & indiscretions, add that as it was expected that nothing would be yielded by G.B. which was not extorted by the address of France in managing the Mediators, and that it was the intention of Congress that their minister should not from the sentiments of France oppose a peace recommended by the latter & approved by the former it was thought good policy to make the declaration to France, & by such a mark of confidence to render her friendship the more responsible for the issue. At the worst it could only be considered as a sacrifice of our pride to our interest.

These considerations still justified the original measure in the view of the members who were present & voted for it. All the new members who had not participated in the impressions which dictated it and viewed the subject only under circumstances of an opposite nature disapproved it. In general however the latter joined with the former in opposing the motion arguing with them that supposing the instruction to be wrong, it was less dishonorable, than the instability tht wd. be denoted by rescinding it; that if G.B. was disposed to give us what we claimed, France could not prevent it; that if G.B. struggled agst. those claims our only chance of getting them was thro' the aid of France; that to withdraw our confidence would lessen the chance & degree of this aid; that if we were in a prosperous or safe condition compared with that in which we adopted the expedient in question, this change had been effected by the friendly succours of our ally, & that to take advantage of it to loosen the tie, would not only bring on us the reproach of ingratitude but induce France to believe that she had no hold on our affections but only in our necessities; that in all possible situations we sd. be more in danger of being seduced by G.B. than of being sacrificed by France; the interests of the latter in the main necessarily coinciding with ours; those of the former being diametrically opposed to them. That as to the intercepted letter, there were many reasons which indicated that it came through the hands of the Enemy to Mr. J. that it ought therefore to be regarded even if genuine, as communicated for insidious purposes; but that there was strong reason to suspect that it had been adulterated if not forged; and that on the worst supposition, it did not appear that the doctrines maintained or the measures recommended in it had been adopted by the French Ministry and consequently that they ought not to be held responsible for them.

Upon these considerations it was proposed...that the motion...should be postponed, which took place without a vote. Mr. M[adison] added that the letter from Docr. Franklin of the 14 Oct. 1782 shd. be referred to a Committee with a view of bringing into consideration the preliminary article proposing that British subjects & American Citizens sd. reciprocally have in matters of commerce the privileges of natives of the other party; and of giving to the American Ministers the instruction which ensued on that subject. This motion succeeded and the Committee appointed...

. . . . .

Smith, Letters of Delegates, v. 19, pp. 518-521.
[1] *Text inserted later by Madison.*

Robert R. Livingston to John Jay

No. 16   Philadelphia 30th Dec$^{r.}$ 1782.
Dr Sir

. . . . .

It is so important to us to be able to judge rightly of the designs of a court wth whom we have lodged such extensive powers, that I most earnestly wish you had enlarged upon the reasons which have induced you to form the opinion you intimate – an opinion which must if well founded render your negotiations extreamly painful, & the issue of them very uncertain. If on the other hand it should have been taken up too hastily, it is to be feared notwithstanding that prudence & self-possession by which you are happily distinguished, that it will sometimes discover itself in a reserve & want of confidence which may afford hopes to our artful antagonists of sowing jealousies between us & our friends. My wishes lead me to hope that you carry your suspicions too far, & the more so as Doc^r Franklin to whom I dare say you have communicated them freely does not (as you say) agree in sentiment with you. But not having the advantage of seeing from the same ground I pretend not to judge. Perhaps facts which I have collected here, & with which you are not acquainted may serve to throw light upon this subject. The policy you suppose to influence France can only be founded in a distrust which I persuade myself she can hardly entertain of those who have put their most important interests in her hands. She is too well informed of the state of this country to believe, there is room to imagine that we entertain the most distant Idea of a separate peace. If such distrust realy existed it w^d not in my opinion manifest itself in the way you seem to suppose, policy would dictate to France to obtain an explicit acknowledgment of our independence in the first instance rather than render it an object of negotiations when satisfied on that point & having nothing to apprehend on our own account we will more patiently attend to those objects which our allies wish to obtain. Whereas should it be witheld & made the price of concessions on the part of our allies which they may be unwilling to grant, they dissatisfy & may incline us to listen to separate proposals. France appears to have conformed to this principle in the answers she has hitherto given as well to the propositions of Great Britain as to those made by the imperial courts....

. . . . .

Whatever the sentiments of the count de < *** > Vergennes may be with respect to the claims of Spain, in a Letter which I have seen he treats them, as well as ours, as chimerical, & declares that he does not mean to interfere in them – You can judge of the sincerity of this declaration if otherwise I am at a loss to determine why he treats them so lightly in his letters or why those letters were communicated to me – For my part I believe their situation with respect to Spain is very delicate & that they are embarrased by her demands. I mention these matters that you may judge how far the language held here & with you agrees –

As to the Letter of 566,-166-143- [Marbois?] I am by no means surprized at it; he always endeavoured to persuade us that our claim to the Fisheries was inadmissable. Yet it is remarkable, & I think evinces the design of France to serve us even on that point. The advice (had the contrary been their object) is certainly judicious, yet we find that no steps have been taken in consequence of it – On the contrary we have been told in a formal communication that the King will obtain every thing for us that circumstances will admitt & that nothing but sad necessity shall induce him to relinquish any of those objects which we have at heart & that he does not imagine from the then view of his affairs that such necessity will exist This communication was made on the 23^d of Novr 1781. and has been renewed informaly at different periods, this fact may be of use, you have a right to avail yourself of this engagem^t if necessary, since Congress relying upon it have made no alteration in their instruction – notwithstanding their success in Virginia. This letter of 566-166-143- and the conduct of the Court markes the distinction between a great politician & a shortsighted one. France can by prohibiting the importation of Fish supply herself, she can not navigate so cheaply as to do more. Our exclusion would only be a benefit to England And the ill will it would create the disputes it would give birth to w^d in the course of a few years obliterate the memory of the favors we have rec^d England by sacrificing a part of her fisheries & protecting us in the enjoyment of them would render herself necessary to us, our friendship would be transfered to her & France would in the end be considered as a natural enemy – She has I hope sufficient wisdom to see this object in its true light – I know not how far the 583-485-6-388-497[1] may merit y^r confidence you are the best judge of his conduct I ought however in justice to him to mention that he has steadily in his letters recommended an adherence to our western claims & to the fisheries, assuring us that they were both attainable if we were firm.

You see Sir that I have leaned to the opinion which is most opposed to yours, not because I think you wrong, but because you may possibly be so. The slightest jealousies may occasion such evils that I would wish you to examine yours very carefully. I dread least the last hope of Britain that of sowing distrusts among her enemies should succeed.

. . . . .

I do not find that the C^t DeVergennes gives any account of your propositions to the Minister here tho' his letters are a day later than those I have from you – I should, conclude from that circumstance that they had not been communicated, if I was not persuaded that acting under the instructions you do, you would not withold them except for the most weighty reasons, & that if such reasons existed you would have assigned them in your Letters – presuming therefore that you had communicated them I have made no secret of them to the Minister who appeared much pleased with them tho' a little surprized at the Latitude of the Last article which may not perhaps be agreeable to them in all its extent as it will occasion a revolution in their system of commerce if they would share ours – I am extremely pleased that in freeing ourselves, we have a prospect of unfettering the consciences, & the commerce of the world.

I am far from regretting that the Marquis D'Aranda has no powers to treat We think with you that it is time to adopt the Spanish system, & to retort upon them all the delays we can interpose, without descending to the contemptable shifts they have put in practize. Any time will be better than the present. But the instructions you have already rec^d are full on this head....

. . . . .

I am Dr Sir with great respect & esteem your &c.

R R Livingston

NA: PCC, item 118, pp. 384-397; M247, reel 139.

¹ Text not decyphered.

William Carmichael to Robert R. Livingston

No. 18 Quadruplicate   Madrid 30th Decr 1782
Sir

On the 10th Inst I had the honor to Inform you that I had seen a French Translation of a Conditional Treaty Concluded between the Commissioners of the United States at Paris and Mr Oswald on the Part of G. Britain the 30th Ult^o I have since received a Letter from Docter Franklin enclosing a Copy of it. I hope it will prove satisfactory to Congress and the People at large – Various are the reflections to which this Event has given rise here – I am persuaded that this Court was far from expecting that G. Britain would make the Concessions, which it has made to the States – The surprize and even the Chagrin of several of the Ministry & their Adherents was apparent & from the inst^t They received the Intelligence, I am convinced that their whole attention has been turned to Peace. – It has been suggested that our Commissioners signed this Treaty without the privity of the Court of France. This suggestion was made with a view to pacify this Court & to Calm the resentment which at Versailles it was supposed might be conceived here on this Acc^t The means employed prove that the French Ministry apprehended this resentment but were in no manner sufficient to Answer the purpose they were intended to serve. The C^t de Florida Blanca speaking of France on this Occasion said to a Friend of mine with Some emotion The French *Ministry* was too precipitate in beginning the war & is equally so in their Endeavours to conclude it. Mr Musquir, the Minister of Finance, and Mr Del Campo have expressed the same Sentiments & have insinuated to some that France Concerted this Measure with our Commissioners to Force Spain to a Peace – To others they have expressed their Apprehensions that Ld Shelburne had duped the French Cabinet. They fear the Duplicity of the latter Minister and this fear joined to their present Situation has probably rendered them more reasonable in their Demands and Concessions. They will now style this Conduct Moderation – I conjecture this, because the C^{t.} de F.B. speaking to the Russian Minister on the Subject of the Peace, told him, that were the propositions on the Part of Spain towards an Accommodation known All Europe would be convinced of the Moderation of his Catholic Majesty & that for his part he should have no Objection to make them Public. On the 28th Ins^t a courier was dispatched to Paris with further Instructions to the C^{t.} de Aranda On the 18th one was sent to the Same Minister with propositions which were then Regarded as their Ultimata. It is now rumored in the Palace that Spain has consented to Leave Gibraltar in the Possession of England. Since the Departure of this Courier the C^{t.} de F.B has spoken of the Peace as certain, if the British Ministry are candid –

. . . . .

...I have the honor to be Sir Your Most Obed^{t.} & Humble Ser^{t.}

Wm. Carmichael

NA: PCC, *item 88, v. 2, pp. 332-336 (ALS); M247, reel 116.*

James Madison's Notes of Debates

Tuesday Decr. 31. 1782.

The report of the Committee made in consequence of Mr. M's motion yesterday instructing the ministers plenipo. on the article of commerce, passed unanimously as follows: "Resolved that the Ministers Plenipy for negociating peace be instructed, in any commercial stipulations with G.B which may be comprehended in a Treaty of peace, to endeavor to obtain for the Citizens and inhabitants of the U.S a direct Commerce to all parts of the British Dominions & possessions, in like manner as all parts of the U.S. may be opened to a direct Commerce of British subjects; or at least that such direct Commerce be extended to all parts of the British

Dominions & possessions in Europe & the West Indies; and the said ministers are informed that this stipulation will be particulary expected by Congress, in case the Citizens & subjects of each party are to be admitted to an equality in matters of commerce with natives of the other party."

Smith, Letters of Delegates, *v. 19, pp. 523-524.*

Chevalier de la Luzerne to Comte de Vergennes

[Translation]

Nº. 298   Philadelphia, 2 January 1783

My Lord,

I had the honor of informing you last summer of Mr. Livingston's disposition to tender his resignation in the course of this winter. The state of his private affairs, the impossibility of meeting the expenses which living in Philadelphia requires with the salary which he receives from Congress, and the necessity of choosing between the post of Secretary of Congress for foreign Affairs and that of Chancellor of the State of New York determined him to renounce the former. Congress, to which he wrote to tender his resignation, named a Committee, according to the report of which the 19th of last month was designated for proceeding with the election of his Successor.

Mr. Livingston, a man estimable for his talents and his character, has had no occasion to display much competency during the term of his Ministry; I have been nothing but pleased with his confidence, and I am vexed that, circumstances having forced him to this course, from which I have in vain attempted to deter him, his vanity did not permit him to live here without fame, and his dependence on *Congress* completed making his functions disagreeable.

By the terms of his instructions, which he drew up at the time in concert with me, and which I have the honor to send you, he is obliged to resolve nothing in essential affairs without the consent of Congress. However, this indispensable form of the constitution of that assembly involves delays and vexations of which Mr. Livinston is weary, and which have contributed to make him desire his discharge; Congress has viewed it with sorrow, and the Committee charged with this affair has evinced to him that it is desired that he take the time necessary to reflect on the course he proposes to take. He has persisted therein, and they are occupied with the choice of his successor; but it has not been easy to find someone as suitable as Mr. Livingston for this position, and two persons of merit which public opinion named have already testified that they could not accept it without disturbing their affairs and losing a revenue certain and considerable which their practice as Attornies procures them.

Mr. Lee has been spoken of, but very weakly, and after some irresolutions, it was agreed that Mr. Livingston would remain in place until the month of May next, and that his successor will be named then.

. . . . .

Le ch^r de la Luzerne

Received 16 October 1783.

FFAA: Pol. Corr., U.S., v. 23, f. 12/29-32 (LC transcription).

Robert R. Livingston to Benjamin Franklin

N° 25.   Philadelphia 6th January 1783.
Sir

. . . . .

...I do not pretend to justify the negligence of the States in not providing greater supplies – some of them might do more than they have done – none of them all that is required – It is my duty to confide to you that if the war is continued in this Country it must be in a great measure at the expence of France, if peace is made a loan will be absolutely necessary to enable us to discharge an Army, that will not easily separate without pay– ...I wish the concession made of our trade may be *on condition* of similar priviledges on the part of Great Britain. You will see that without this precaution every Ally we have that is to be treated as the most favoured Nation may be entitled to the same priviledges, even tho' they do not purchase them by a reciprocal grant.

As to confiscated property it is at present in such a State, that the restoration of it is become impossible – English Debts have not that I know of been forfeited unless it be in one State, and I should be extremely sorry to see so little integrity in my Countrymen as to render the Idea of withholding them a general one – however it would be well to say nothing about them if it can conveniently be done.

I am more and more convinced that every means in your power must be used to secure the Fisheries – they are essential to some States – and we cannot but hate the Nation that keeps us from using this common favor of Providence – It was one of the direct objects for carrying on the war – While I am upon this subject – I cannot but express my hope that every means will be used to guard against any distrusts or jealousies between you and France the United States having shewn their confidence in her by their instructions – She has repeatedly promised to procure for us *all we ask*, as far as it lies in her power – Let our conduct leave her without appollogy if she acts otherwise which I am far from suspecting –

. . . . .

As to the designs of Spain they are pretty well known, and Mr. Jay and Congress concur so exactly in sentiment with respect to them, that I hope we have now nothing to fear from that quarter –

. . . . .

I have the honor to be– Sir with great Respect and Esteem your most obed^{t.} humble Servant   Robt R Livingston

. . . . .

University of Pennsylvania, Van Pelt Library: Special Collections (LS).

Richard Oswald to Henry Strachey

Dr Sir   Paris 8th January 1783 –
    Agreeable to my promise, I lookt out for the paper I wrote about the Newfoundland Fishery when you was here. But I have it not, and must have thrown it into the fire along with other useless papers, after it was settled with the American Commissioners. However I recollect the Contents, and Since you desire it, you have them as under, Viz.
    There are two Seasons of Cod Fishery on the American Coasts – an Early and a Late one.
    The Early Fishery begins in the *Month* of *Febry*, when the *Codfish go inshore* into the Bays, Harbours, and even into the Mouths of the Rivers, seeking the Small Fish along Shore, and then continue *untill* the *summer* Comes on. When its said they retire *into deeper Water* – from Bank to Bank, and at last settle in abundance on the Great Bank – in the Months of May and June.
    I don't pretend to say but there may be an Inshore Fishery even in Summer. But it is in that Season only when Ships can safely pursue it on the Banks out at Sea, Where I believe the Fish are of a *better* Sort, and in *greater abundance* than *along shore*. This is called the Late Fishery, and continues to the Autumn, or as long as the ships chuse to pursue it –
    From thence there arises this Distinction in the prosecution of these Fisheries – Viz.
    The Americans by their Vicinity, and accustomed practice, are in a condition to proceed upon the Early Fishery ~~in the~~ as soon as the Winter breaks up, in the Month of Febry, and pursue it along the Shore in Safety

under the Shelter of the Bays and Harbours which are frequent on that Coast.

The Europeans, *English* and *French*, by their *remote distance, can't get out* in time to overtake this Fishery and are therefor obliged to content themselves with that of the Later Season, which I think begins in May & June. When the Americans join them, and also pursue that Fishery to the end of the season.

By the Americans being allowed the priviledge of this Early Fishery, in which the Europeans have no Share, these last feel it in the Sale of their late Fish when they come to the Markets of portugal Spain and Italy, in the Autumn and Winter. And consequently, in a Mercantile view, it is natural for them to complain of the Market being so far overstockt by the Americans – & to wish that they might not be allowed the priviledge of this Early Fishery along shore; but that they should be kept off to a distance of 3 Leagues in the open Sea.

To the English, the said reduction of Price is an evident Discouragement to the Extension of the business – The French feel it less as they have a great Sale in their own Country, and don't admit the Fish of Foreign Nations –

This is a Simple state of the Case of this Fishery, as mentioned in the former Papers, to the best of my remembrance.

I will next add what was then stated, and as to what passed with the American Commissioners, particularly Mr Adams, the New England Member, when we came to treat of this Article, and to propose keeping off the Americans to a Distance from the Shore in the prosecution of their Fishery; as well as in Drying the Fish on the Coasts of Newfoundland.

I had Sundry Conversations with this Gentleman on the Subject, before you came over the last time. When his Language was as follows –

That the *Fishery* was *their all* – their *Bread.* That other states had *Staples* of *production*; they had *none* but what they raised out of the Sea; they had enjoyed ~~the~~ a *freedom* of *Fishery time out* of *mind*, and their people would never part with it. That in depriving them of the priviledge in question, we should Strike a deeper Stroke into their Vitals than any perhaps they had suffered since the War Commenced. That our Refusal was *unfriendly, ungenerous, Invidious.* Since we could not say that the question turned upon Fish that belonged to us, as *we Could not come out* in time to overtake them; And when we did Come, we did *not miss* them, there being Fish enough for all Nations, during the whole time we chose to Seek for them. But that we grudged that they should avail themselves of the natural Conveniency of their Situation – only to prevent our getting Somewhat less for that part which it was convenient for us to overtake. That we made *no difficulty* in accommodating the *French* in this matter – Which of itself

would make their people more sensibly feel the effect of the Exclusion –
That his Constituents were alarmed, and particularly attentive to this
question; and sent him *Instructions* that would *by no means allow* of his
signing any Treaty in which this Priviledge should be excepted. That he
never would sign any such Treaty. That if he was to do so, he should
consider it as Signing a ~~perpetual~~ *Declaration of perpetual War* between
England and America. That if things were to come to the worst their States
would support that War of themselves without the help of France or any
other Nation – That if we lost somewhat in the sales of our Fish by their
interfering with us, it would in part be made up in the sale of our
Manufactures, since the more Money they got for their Fish, the more they
would buy of those Manufactures.

These Observations ~~I had~~ passed, as I have said, at different times in
Conversation with him, some part of which he also mentioned in your
hearing

And you'l remember, the other Commissioners were equally Stiff in
refusing to proceed in the Treaty while we proposed to deprive their People
of the Coast or Inshore Fishery.

And also that one of those Gentlemen said that if we insisted on keeping
their People at a distance of 3 Leagues from our Shores, we could not
complain if they also forbad our Ships from coming within the like distance
of the Coasts of the Thirteen States.

With respect to drying their Fish, the same Gentleman said, he thought,
if we would not allow of their landing upon the unsettled parts of our
Shores at a certain Season in the year, they would justly deny us the same
priviledge in all parts of their Country.

Another of those Commissioners who had all along expressed himself
with great resentment at their People being thus unfavourably distinguished
from the French, declared that it was a matter of indifference to them as
to what prohibitions we should put their People under, since they could
easily make *Reprisals* in another way to their advantage, by *an Act of
Navigation* that should exclude English ships forever from any participation
in the American Trade, either Inwards or Outwards.

In answer to all these Arguments, some of which, as I have said, passed
in your hearing, you will remember we had not much to Oppose – We did
not think it proper to insist on the right of the Sovereignty of the Coast –
Nor to say anything as to how such Grant would affect the Treaty with
France – And upon the whole were confined to the single object of
preventing Quarrels among the Fishermen, as the supposed Consequence of
allowing the Americans to come within 3 Leagues of the shore of
NewfoundLand and other places.

In answer to which Mr Adams said that he made little account of *Squables* among *Fishermen* which were *soon made up* But that *Quarrels* between *States* were *not so easily* settled. And which were most likely to happen; since when we came to sett our Men of War to watch in those Seas, so as to keep their Ships to the precise distance of 3 Leagues (and which Stations they must take in the earliest season in the spring) *Disputes* might *arise,* and *Men* would be *killed* and *Redress* could be had only by Appeals to Government of either Side; And ~~upon~~ in the end would be attended with such unpleasant Consequences that he should be sorry it should ever happen. And would therefor advise that we should overlook the loss we apprehended by their Interference in this Early part of the Fishery, and end the matter so as ~~that~~ their People should not be put in mind upon all these occasions that they were not Englishmen –

The above is the Substance of what the American Commissioners said at different times upon the unpleasant subject of this intended Exclusion, and as near their Words as I can remember. I had put them in writing from time to time as they occurred in my Conversation with the Commissioners – and when you came over & shewed me the altered plan of the Treaty, and how this Article was guarded in all the Instructions & Letters – I owned I despaired of any Settlement with America before the meeting of Parliament; But there being happily a discretionary power, as well regarding the Extent as the manner of dispensing with this Article in your Instructions, I used the freedom of pointing it out, and insisting on it – and you very properly as well as M$^{r.}$ Fitzherbert took the benefit of it & so gave your Consent to my Signing the Treaty. To which if there is still any exception, I must take my share of the blame, as I took the Liberty to mention to the Secretary of State in the Letter which I troubled you with upon your return to London. If your asking for this Paper is to answer some purpose in Parliam^t, in case of a Challenge on this head, you can judge what parts will be suteable to be brought under public review – perhaps not many. The best general one is; that without giving way in this particular there would have been no provisional Articles. That is very Certain. I am Dear Sir Your most obed^t hum^l Servant   Richard Oswald

PS 13th January – Mr Adams shewed me his Instructions the day before yesterday wherein the Massachusets Governm^t Charge him not to sign any Treaty with England in which a perfect Freedom of Fishery is not allowed – And tell him besides that the Several States of the Union had bound themselves to each other never to agree to any Peace where there was an Exception of this nature –

Clements Library: Richard Oswald Papers (ALS).

Benjamin Franklin to Richard Oswald

Sir,   Passy, Jan.ʸ 14. 1783.

I am much oblig'd by your Information of your intended Trip to England. I heartily wish you a good Journey, and a Speedy Return....

I enclose two Papers that were read at different times by me to the Commissioners; they may serve to show if you should have Occasion, what was urg'd on the Part of America on certain Points; or they may help to refresh your Memory. I send you also another Paper which I once read to you separately. It contains a Proposition for improving the Law of Nations, by prohibiting the Plundering of unarm'd & usefully employ'd People. I rather wish than expect that it will be adopted. But I think it may be offer'd with a better Grace by a Country that is likely to suffer least & gain most by continuing the ancient Practice, which is our Case, as the American Ships laden only with the Gross Productions of the Earth, cannot be so valuable as yours fill'd with Sugars or with Manufactures. – It has not yet been considered by my Colleagues; but if you should think or find that it might be acceptable on your side, I would try to get it inserted in the General Treaty. I think it will do honour to the Nations that establish it–

With great & sincere Esteem, I am, Sir, Your most obedient & most humble Servant   B. Franklin

Clements Library: Shelburne Papers, v. 71, pp. 233-234 (ALS).

[Enclosure]
Propositions relative to privateering, &c.
communicated to Mr. Oswald.

It is for the interest of humanity in general, that the occasions of war, and the inducements to it should be diminished.

If rapine is abolished, one of the encouragements to war is taken away, and peace therefore more likely to continue and be lasting.

The practice of robbing merchants on the high seas, a remnant of the ancient piracy, though it may be accidentally beneficial to particular persons, is far from being profitable to all engaged in it, or to the nation that authorises it. In the beginning of a war some rich ships not upon their guard are surprised and taken. This encourages the first adventurers to fit out more armed vessels, and many others to do the same. But the enemy at the same time become more careful, arm their merchant ships better; and render them not so easy to be taken; they go also more under protection of convoys; thus while the privateers to take them are multiplied, the vessels subject to be taken and the chances of profit are diminished, so that many cruizes are made wherein the expenses overgo the gains; and as is the case in other lotteries, though particulars have got prizes, the mass of adventurers are losers, the whole expense of fitting out all the privateers during a war, being much greater than the whole amount of goods taken. Then there is the national loss of all the labor of so many men during the time they have been employed in robbing; who besides spend what they get in riot, drunkenness, and debauchery, lose their habits of industry, are rarely fit for any sober business after a peace, and serve only to increase the number of highwaymen and housebreakers. Even the undertakers who have been fortunate, are by sudden wealth led into expensive living, the habit of which continues when the means of supporting it ceases, and finally ruins them. A just punishment for their having wantonly and unfeelingly ruined many honest innocent traders and their families, whose subsistence was employed in serving the common interests of mankind.

Should it be agreed and become a part of the law of nations, that the cultivators of the earth are not to be molested or interrupted in their peaceable and useful employment, the inhabitants of the sugar islands would perhaps come under the protection of such a regulation, which would be a great advantage to the nations who at present hold those islands, since the cost of sugar to the consumer in those nations, consists not merely in the price he pays for it by the pound, but in the accumulated charge of all the taxes he pays in every war, to fit out fleets and maintain troops for the defence of the islands that raise the sugar, and the ships that bring it home. But the expense of treasure is not all. A celebrated philosophical writer remarks, that when he considered the wars made in Africa for prisoners to raise sugars in America, the numbers slain in those wars, the numbers that being crowded in ships perish in the transportation, and the numbers that die under the severities of slavery, he could scarce look on a morsel of sugar without conceiving it spotted with human blood. If he had considered also the blood of one another which the white nations shed in fighting for those islands, he would have imagined his sugar not as spotted only, but as thoroughly died red. On these accounts I am persuaded that the subjects of the Emperor of Germany, and the empress of Russia, who have no sugar islands, consume sugar cheaper at Vienna and Moscow, with all the charge of transporting it after its arrival in Europe, than the citizens of London or of Paris. And I sincerely believe, that if France and England were to decide by throwing dice which should have the whole of their sugar islands, the loser in the throw would be the gainer. The future expense of defending them would be saved: the sugars would be bought cheaper by all Europe if the inhabitants might make it without interruption, and whoever imported the sugar, the same revenue might be raised by duties at the custom-houses of the nation that consumed it. And on the whole I conceive it would be better for the nations now possessing sugar colonies to give up their claim to them, let them govern themselves, and put them under the protection of all the powers of Europe as neutral countries, open to the commerce of all, the profits of the present monopolies being by no means equivalent to the expense of maintaining them.

ARTICLE

If war should hereafter arise between Great Britain and the United States, which God forbid, the merchants of either country then residing in the other shall be allowed to remain nine months to collect their debts, and settle their affairs, and may depart freely, carrying off all their effects without molestation or hindrance. And all fishermen, all cultivators of the earth, and all artisans or manufacturers unarmed, and inhabiting unfortified towns, villages or places, who labor for the common subsistence and benefit of mankind, and peaceably follow their respective employments, shall be allowed to continue the same, and shall not be molested by the armed force of the enemy, in whose power by the events of the war they may happen to fall; but if any thing is necessary to be taken from them, for the use of such armed force, the same shall be paid for at a reasonable price. And all merchants or traders with their unarmed vessels, employed in commerce, exchanging the products of different places, and thereby rendering the necessaries, conveniences, and comforts of human life more easy to obtain, and more general, shall be allowed to pass freely unmolested. And neither of the powers, parties to this treaty, shall grant or issue any commission to any private armed vessels empowering them to take or destroy such trading ships, or interrupt such commerce.

WTF, Franklin Memoirs, v. 4, pp. 287-291.

Alleyne Fitzherbert to Lord Shelburne

Private   Paris January 15th 1783.
My Lord,

...Having been employed during the whole day in preparing an official letter to go by Mr Oswald who is impatient to set out, I have only time by this opportunity to thank Your Lordship for the very obliging as well as instructive letter which you honoured me with by the last Messenger. − I found M. de Vergennes prepossessed with an opinion how derived I can not pretend to say, that when that Messenger came away, Yr Lordship & the rest of the King's Ministers were persuaded that this Court had laid aside all thoughts of Peace, however I used my utmost endeavours (and I believe succeeded in them) to prove that he was mistaken. – I say nothing of the paper from Dr Franklin which Mr Oswald carries over excepting that (though the expedient would be a disagreeable one) I am persuaded that this Court would, if urged to it, join us in representing to the American commissioners the monstrous injustice of introducing fresh articles into the treaty. However I mention this only as a *pis aller* being still unwilling to believe that Mr Franklin will insist seriously upon the new articles or if he does that his colleagues will join him in it. I have the honour to be with the most unalterable Attachment, My Lord, Your Lordship's most obedient and most obliged humble Servant

Alleyne Fitz-Herbert

Clements Library: Shelburne Papers, v. 71, pp. 385-387 (ALS).

Comte de Vergennes to
Joseph Matthias Gérard de Rayneval

[Translation]

Versailles, 20 January 1783

It is with the sweetest satisfaction, Sir, that I inform you that the preliminary articles of peace were signed this morning by France, Spain, and England. The Dutch Plenipotentiaries not having been able to cooperate therein, Mr. Fitzherbert gave M. le Comte d'Aranda and me a declaration that includes the republic of the United Provinces in the armistice, our Courts engaging themselves to procure the acceptance of the States General.

The provisional articles settled and signed between Great Britain and the United States of America not having provided for the suspension of arms, and Mr. Oswald being in England, the American plenipotentiaries, whom I had invited to the Signing of our Preliminaries, exchanged with Mr. Fitzherbert respective declarations which establish that suspension of arms between Great Britain and the United States of America with the same clauses and the same times as we had allowed. I am not sending you copies of these documents because there is not enough time for me to have them transcribed, and besides I calculate that Lord Grantham will not refuse to communicate them to you.

The King wishing to indicate to the King of England all the satisfaction which the first fruits of the happy reconciliation give him and wishing to give you a proof of his satisfaction with your Services, His Majesty has ordered me to send you the letter of Credence which I enclose here together with a Copy.

We are only giving you the title of Minister there because that of which Mr. Fitzherbert is bearer does not comprise a greater scope; but as that omission will not hinder his being treated as a Minister plenipotentiary, I hope that through reciprocity you will be allowed to enjoy the same amenities in London. I do not mark out for you the language which you will employ with His Britannic Majesty. You know what fits the circumstance, but you may make assurances that the war never altered the King's esteem for the qualities of that Monarch and his sincere friendship for his person.

I expect to write to the two Ministers, but that will be in haste. Make up, Sir, for what I may not say by your knowledge of my sentiments for Lord Shelburne and for Lord Grantham, assure them that they have in me an Admirer and a zealous partisan.

I hope, Sir, that you will be willing to take the necessary measures so that my son has the honor of being presented to the King and the royal family of England; I hope that he will be allowed to share in the esteem that you have shown for me.

Your mission will be short; I expect to have M. le Comte de Moustier[1] set out at the beginning of next week, you would do well to install him and then return; my health is indeed hard-pressed, you have told me, Sir, of charging my son to carry the ratification. I have not fully understood that proposal; if it is an agreeable commission, I consent to it willingly, but it is up to you to arrange the thing and guide me.

I think, Sir, that the severity of the British Ministers for Holland is owing to their excessive complaisance for the Empress of Russia, who perhaps sees with jealousy that the Republic owes to us the benefit of peace; if this were the only difficulty in that regard, we would cheerfully see that Sovereign procure them better conditions than those I wrested from M. Fitzherbert. You are on the spot, and can judge the intentions and the possibilities better than I. I also suspect that the British Ministers would be more ready for the renewal of the Treaty of 1674 if the Dutch would countenance renewing that of 1678. The passage from open war to alliance will be very precipitate.

The American Commissioners have evinced to me some concern that Parliament would contest the commission which the King of Great Britain issued to treat with them and in that way render void the articles agreed upon with them and revoke the recognition of their independence. It is possible that some hotheads have conceived that plan, but I am fully assured that the Ministry will make it fail; it is by virtue of an act of Parliament that the King of England issued his powers, it will be less the Americans who would be attacked than the royal prerogative; moreover, it would be to reverse a peace made and signed. I have calmed the American plenipotentiaries as much as possible.

· · · · ·

Vergennes

FFAA: Pol. Corr., England, v. 540, f. 236 (LC transcription).
¹ Moustier, Eléonore François Elie, Comte de. French diplomat. Envoy to Great Britain, January-April 1783. Minister to the United States, February 1788-October 1789.

Principal Articles of the Preliminaries
of the Peace Made by Great Britain, France, and Spain

[January 20, 1783]

France preserves Tobago and Senegal. France restores to England the Grenades, S^{tt} Vincent, Dominica, and S^{tt} Christophers, and delivers S^{tt} Eustatia, Demerara, Issequibo, Berbice to Holland. England restores to France, Gorée, S^{tt} Lucia, S^{tt} Pierre, and Miquelon.

The Fishery of France and England, on the Coast of Newfoundland shall remain on the Footing of the Treaty of 1763, excepting that Part of the Coast from Cape Bonavista to Cape St. John, which shall be ceded to the English.

France shall be re-established in India, as well in Bengal, as on the East and West Coasts of the Peninsula, agreeable to the Regulation of the Treaty of 1763.

The Article of the preceding Treaties, concerning the Demolition of Dunkirk to be suppressed.

Spain preserves Minorca and West Florida.

England cedes to Spain East Florida.

An Arrangement shall be made between Spain and England, respecting cutting Wood in the Bay of Campeachy.

England keeps the Dutch Settlement of Negapatnam.

England restores to Holland Trincomalé, if it is not retaken, S^{tt} Eustatia, Demerara, Berbice, and Issequibo, returned by the French.

England acknowledges the Independence of the thirteen United States of North America.

The Limits of the thirteen United States, acknowledged by England, shall be formed by the River St. Croix, from its Mouth in the Bay of Fonda to its Source, along the Highlands from this Source until the 45th. Degree, by this Parallel of 45 Degrees until the River of   by a Line which strikes through the Middle of the Lakes Ontario, Erie, Huron, and Lake Superior, to the Northward of the Islands Pontchartrain, Phillippeaux, and Royal, by a Line continued from Lake Superior through Long Lake, until the Lake of the Woods, by a Line tending towards the South and connecting this Lake with the River Missisippi, following the Course of the River until the 32$^{d.}$ Degree, by this Parallel of 32 Degrees, from the River Missisippi until the Source of the River S$^{t.}$ Mary, and along this River to its Mouth.

The Americans shall fish in Conjunction, on the Coasts of Newfoundland before assigned to the English, as well as all the Islands and Coasts of the River S$^{t.}$ Lawrence. But they shall not establish Places to dry their Fish on any Part of these Coasts and Islands. They may only dry and prepare their Fish, in the unsettled Harbors, Bays, and Creeks of Nova Scotia, Magdalen Islands, and Labrador.

NA: PCC, item 100, v. 2, pp. 313-315 (LBkC) ; M247, reel 127.

British Declaration of Armistice with the United States

[January 20, 1783]

As the preliminary Articles concluded & signed this day between His Majesty the King of G. Britain & His Majesty the most Christian King on the one part, & also between His said Britannic Majesty & His Catholic majesty on the other part, include the stipulation for the cessation of Hostilities between those three powers, which is to commence after the exchange of the ratifications of the said preliminary articles; And as, by the provisional Treaty signed the thirtieth of November last, between His Britannic Majesty & the U$^{d.}$ States of North America it has been stipulated that this treaty sh^{d} take effect as soon as the peace between the said Crowns should be established, The undersigned His Britannic Majestys Minister plenipotentiary, declares, in the name & by express order of the King his Master, that the said U^{d} States of N$^{o.}$ America their subjects & their possessions shall be comprehended in the aforementioned suspension of Arms & that they shall in consequence enjoy the same benefit from the cessation of hostilities, at the same time, & in the same manner as the three aforesaid Crowns, their subjects & their respective possessions, the whole on condition, that on the part & in the name of the said U$^{d.}$ States of N$^{o.}$ America, a similar declaration be delivered which proves their assent to the present suspension of Arms & includes the assurance of the most perfect reciprocity on their part.

In faith whereof, we His Britannic Majestys Minister Plenipotentiary, have signed the present declaration & have thereto affixed the seal of our Arms.

At Versailles 20$^{th.}$ January 1783
Alleyne Fitz Herbert.

We the undersigned Ministers Plenipotentiaries from the U^d States of N°
America having received on the part of M. Fitz Herbert His Britannic
Majesty's Minister plenipotiary, a declaration relative to a suspension of
arms to be established between His said Majesty & the said States, in terms
as follows < ******** >

Have in the name of the said ~~States of the~~ U^d States of N° America &
by virtue of powers with which We are furnished accepted the aforesaid
declaration, we do accept of it by these presents, without exception or
reserve, & we do reciprocally declare that the said States shall cause all
hostilities to cease against His Britannic Majesty his subjects & his
possessions, at the terms, & the periods agreed on between his said Majesty
the King of G. Britain, his Majesty the King of France & his Majesty the
King of Spain, in the same manner as has been agreed on between these
three & to answer the same purpose.

In faith whereof We the Ministers Plenipotentiaries of the U^d States of
North America have signed the present declaration & have thereto affixed
the seal of our arms

At Versailles 20th. January 1783
John Adams
B Franklin

Faithfully translated from the Original by John Pintard.

NA: PCC, item 84, v. 4, pp. 329-330 (translation); M247, reel 112.

Declaration of the American Plenipotentiaries
[Translation]

January 20, 1783

We, the undersigned Ministers Plenipotentiary of the United States &^ca.

Declare that by agreeing and consenting to sign the articles which have
been discussed between us and Mr. Oswald, who has been furnished with
full powers for this purpose by His Majesty the King of Great Britain, to be
inserted into the future Treaty of Peace, we have had as our purpose only
to facilitate and confirm the negotiation in which the interests of our
Sovereigns have been previously discussed. While the preamble of these
articles expressly stipulates that they will only take effect in the event that
a Treaty of Peace is concluded between H. M. C. M. [His Most Christian
Majesty] and His Britannic Majesty, we believe that we should most
especially manifest the intentions of our sovereigns in this regard because
we perceive that the title of *Preliminary Treaty* which is given to these
articles both in England and in the public papers of Europe could give rise

to an error regarding the nature of the document which we signed the 30th of last month.

The United States of North America, desirous of making known their fidelity to discharge their engagements and their gratitude toward H. M. C. M., regard their cause as inseparably linked to that of His Majesty. This is the basis of the instructions they have given us, and none of our proceedings can deviate from that principle. We therefore discharge one of our most important duties in declaring that the articles agreed upon and signed between us and the plenipotentiary of His Britannic Majesty will change nothing in the position of the United States towards England so long as the peace between H. M. C. M. and His Britannic Majesty is not concluded, and that we reject any interpretation of the said articles which is contrary to this assertion. We hope that these well-known verities will dissipate all the suspicions which anyone may seek to propagate concerning the sentiments of a naissant Republic, whose honor and interests equally demand that it establish itself in the general opinion as placing above all else the fidelity and constancy of its engagements.

Done at Passy this 20th of January 1783.

FFAA: Pol. Corr., U.S., v. 23, f. 27/70-71 (LC transcription).

John Adams to Robert R. Livingston

Sir,   Paris Jan.ᵞ· 22ᵈ 1783.

Upon a sudden notification from the Comte de Vergennes, Mʳ· Franklin and myself, in the Absence of Mʳ Jay and Mʳ· Laurens, went to Versailles, and arrived at the Comte's Office at 10. °Clock on Monday, the twentieth of this Month At Eleven arrived the Comte d' Aranda & Mʳ· Fitzherbert. The Ministers of the three Crowns signed & sealed the Preliminaries of Peace, and an Armistice, in presence of Mʳ· Franklin and myself, who also signed & sealed a Declaration of an Armistice, between the Crown of Great Britain and the United States of America, and recieved a Counter-Declaration from Mʳ· Fitzherbert – Copies of these Declarations are inclosed. The King of Great Britain has made a Declaration concerning the Terms that he will allow to the Dutch, but they are not such as will give Satisfaction to that unfortunate Nation, for whom on Account of their Friendship for Us, and the important Benefits We have received from it, I feel very sensibly and sincerely. Yesterday we went to Versailles again to make our Court to the King and Royal Family, and received the Compliments of the foreign Ministers.

The Comte D'Aranda invited me to dine with him on Sunday next, and said he hoped, that the Affair of Spain and the United States would be soon adjusted *à l'amiable* – I answered, that I wished it with all my Heart. The two Floridas and Minorca are more than a *quantum meruit* for what this Power has done, and the Dutch unfortunately are to suffer for it.

It is not in my Power to say, when the definitive Treaty will be signed. I hope not before the Dutch are ready. – In Six Weeks or two Months at farthest, I Suppose.

It is no longer necessary for Congress to appoint another Person in my Place in the Commission for Peace, because it will be executed before this reaches America — But I beg Leave to renew my Resignation of the Credence to the States General and the Commission for borrowing Money in Holland, and to request that no Time may be lost in transmitting the Acceptance of this Resignation, and another Person to take that Station, that I may be able to go home in the Spring Ships.

I have the honor to be, with great Respect, Sir, your most obedient & most humble Servant.   John Adams.

NA: PCC, *item 84, v. 4, pp. 321-327 (LS); M247, reel 112.*

Alleyne Fitzherbert to Lord Grantham

N° 11   Paris, 25 Jan.ʸ 1783.
My Lord

I have the honour to enclose to your Lordship herewith a duplicate in English of the declaration of the American Commissioners, which I forwarded to your Lordship in my letter N° 9. I have delivered to those gentlemen a copy of my full-power to treat with France, which, in virtue of the words "*aliorum principum et statnum*" made use of in it, they have consented to accept of, as a full-power to treat with them likewise, as well in regard to the aforesaid business of our reciprocal accessions to the suspension of arms, as in case any other pressing business should arise, which it might be necessary to dispatch before Mr Oswald's return.

Dr Franklin mentioned to me yesterday a circumstance, which seems to come eminently under that description, I mean the conclusion of a mutual agreement to repeal all such laws as are now in force in both countries for preventing all reciprocal intercourse between them whether by commerce or otherwise; as unless some such precaution shall be immediately taken, there is too much reason to fear that before the English Merchants shall obtain liberty to send a supply of European commodities to the American markets, they will be forestalled and glutted from other quarters. Dr Franklin added that an article for that purpose had been inserted in the project of preliminaries transmitted by himself and his colleagues, but that it had been left out in that which was brought back from England by Mr Strachey: to which I replied that I conceived that must have been owing to the wide scope which that article had comprehended, as it seemed to extend itself not only to our particular acts respecting America but to every other of our trade laws, and especially to the Navigation Act, which, he knew, could not be meddled with, Without the most serious and mature deliberation; – and I therefore told him, that I thought it would be better to confine the article he spoke of, if agreed to now, merely to such acts as had been passed on both sides on account of the war. To this He seemed to assent, but added that it would of course be expected, that all such parts of our Trade & Navigation acts as spoke of or considered America as a dependency of Great Britain, must become, ipso facto, null & void.

Having mentioned this, Dr Franklin went on to speak of what he called *the settlement* of the *definitive treaty* between Great Britain and America, saying that it would perhaps be necessary to insert in it some articles (of what nature he did not specify) in addition to those already agreed to. To this I replied, with much seeming surprise at his last words, that it had always appeared to me, that the only step that was necessary for converting the treaty of the 30th of Novr into the definitive treaty, was to annull the expressions which rendered it only provisional, by a declaration signed by the Plenipotentiaries on both sides, setting forth, that from the day of the exchange of the ratifications of the Preliminary treaty between Great Britain and France, it was to have its full force and effect. In answer to this, he shewed a disposition to cavil upon some expressions used in the preamble to the treaty of the 30th of Novr which, he said, set forth that the articles of that treaty were to *make part* of the definitive treaty; but I replied that on the contrary the preamble in question expressly said that those articles were to constitute the said treaty, and that besides he knew as well as myself, that when they were signed, it was perfectly well understood, that no fresh matter was to be introduced on either side. To this He made no other reply, than that he conceived this could not preclude the two countries from entering into such fresh stipulations as should be mutually agreeable – a position which I did not controvert, but observed that the articles He spoke of must necessarily turn upon matters of no great moment, all the important points having already been definitively settled.

Though my share in this conversation was directed entirely to the fresh propositions which Dr Franklin had sent over by Mr Oswald, I cannot possibly affirm that he saw the drift of it, nor indeed did I wish to bring on an immediate discussion of that subject, but I thought it right to hold this sort of preparatory language, under the idea, that from the obnoxious nature of these propositions, they could not fail of being judged by His Majesty's ministers to be utterly inadmissible.

I have the honour to be with the greatest Respect, My Lord, Your Lordship's most obedient and most, humble Servant

Alleyne Fitz-Herbert.

R. 2ᵈ Febry by Pearson.

PRO: FO 27/5, v. 560, f. 479 (LC transcription).

John Adams to the President of Congress

Sir,   Paris. Febʸ· 5ᵗʰ 1783.

. . . . .

If there are in Congress any of those Gentlemen, with whom I had the honor to serve in the years 1775 and 1776, they may possibly remember, that in arguing in favor of sending Ministers to Versailles to propose a Connection with that Court, I laid it down as a first principle, that We should calculate all our Measures and foreign Negociations in such a manner, as to avoid a too great dependence upon any one Power of Europe – to avoid all Obligations and Temptations to take any part in future European Wars – That the business of America with Europe was Commerce, not Politicks nor War – And that above all, it never could be our Interest to ruin Great Britain, or injure or weaken her any farther, than should be necessary to support our Independence and our Alliances – And that as soon as Great Britain should be brought to a Temper to acknowledge our Sovereignty and our Alliances, and consent that We should maintain the one and fulfil the others, it would be our Interest and Duty to be her Friends, as well as the Friends of all the other Powers of Europe, & Enemies to none.– We are now happily arrived, through many tremendous Tempests, at that period – Great Britain respects Us as Sovereign States; and respects all our political Engagements with foreign Nations; and as long as She continues in this Temper of Wisdom, it is our Duty to respect her. – We have accordingly made a Treaty with her, and mutually sworn to be Friends. – Through the whole period of our Warfare and Negociations, I confess I have never lost Sight of the Principles and the System, with which I set out, which appeared to me too to be the Sentiments of Congress with great Unanimity, and I have no Reason to suppose that any Change of Opinion has taken place; if there has not, every one will agree with me, that no Measure We can pursue will have such a Tendency to preserve the Government and People of England in the right System for their own and our Interest, and the Interest of our Allies too, well understood, as sending a Minister to reside at the Court of London.

In the next place, the Court of London is the best Station to collect Intelligence from every part; and, by means of the Freedom of the Press, to communicate Information for the benefit of our Country to every part of the World. – In time of Peace, there is so frequent travelling between Paris, London and the Hague, that the Correspondence of our Ministers at those Courts may be carried on by private Hands, without hazarding any thing from the Infidelity of the Posts, and Congress may reasonably expect Advantages from this Circumstance.

In the third place, a Treaty of Commerce with Great Britain is an Affair of great Importance to both Countries. – Upon this Occasion I hope I shall be excused, if I venture to advise, that Congress should instruct their Minister not to conclude such a Treaty, without sending the Project to them for their Observations and fresh Instructions – And I should think it would not be improper upon this Occasion to imitate the Dutch Method, take the Project *ad referendum*, and transmit it to the Legislatures of all the States for their Remarks, before Congress finally resolve. – Their Minister may be authorized and instructed in the mean time, to enter into a temporary Convention for regulating the present Trade for a limited period of Months or Years, or until the Treaty of Commerce shall be compleated.

In the fourth place, it is our part to be the first to send a Minister to Great Britain, which is the older, and as yet the Superior State. It becomes Us to send a Minister first, and I doubt not the King of Great Britain will very soon return the Compliment – Whereas if We do not begin, I believe there will be many Delicacies at S.t James's about being the first to send. – I confess, I wish a British Minister at Philadelphia and think We should derive many benefits from his Residence. While we have any foreign Ministers among Us, I wish to have them from all the great Powers, with whom We are much connected.– The Corps Diplomatick at every Court is, or ought to be, a System representing at least that part of the System of Europe, with which that Court is most conversant. In the same manner, or at least for similar Reasons, as long as We have any one Minister abroad at any European Court, I think We ought to have one at every one, to which We are most essentially related, whether in Commerce or Policy, and therefore while We have any Minsters at Versailles, the Hague, or London, I *think* it clear We ought to have one at each. Tho' I confess I have sometimes thought, that, after a very few Years, it will be the best thing We can do to recall every Minister from Europe, and send Embassies only on special Occasions.

If, however, any Members of Congress should have any Delicacies, least an American Minister should not be recieved with a Dignity becoming his Rank and Character, at London, they may send a Commission, to make a Treaty of Commerce with Great Britain, to their Minister at Madrid, or Versailles, or the Hague, or St. Petersbourg, and instruct him to carry on the Negociation from the Court where he may be, until he shall be invited to London, – or a Letter of Credence may be sent to one of these with Instructions to go to London, as soon as the King shall appoint a Minister to go to Philadelphia. – After all however, my own Opinion is, that none of these Manoeuvres are necessary, but that the best way will be, to send a Minister directly to St. James's, with a Letter of Credence to the King, as a Minister Plenipotentiary, and a Commission to treat of a Treaty of Commerce; but with Instructions not to come to any irrevocable Conclusion, until Congress and all the States have an Opportunity to consider of the Project, and suggest their Amendments.

There is one more Argument in favor of sending a Minister forthwith – It is this – While this Mission lies open, it will be a Source of Jealousy among present Ministers, and such as are or may be Candidates to be foreign Ministers – a Source of Intrigue and Faction among their Partizans and Adherents, and a Source of Animosity and Division among the People of the States.–...

. . . . . .

Your most obedient and most humble Servant,   John Adams
Read April 28. 1783

NA: PCC, *item 84, v. 4, pp. 339-350 (LS); M247, reel 112.*

Joseph Matthias Gérard de Rayneval to Comte de Vergennes

[Translation]

Nᵒ· 24   London, 6 February 1783

My Lord,

My Lord Grantham communicated to me yesterday the draft of the orders that should be sent to India for the execution of the preliminary articles relative to that part of the world, that draft will be communicated to you by Mr. Fitzherbert, and My Lord Grantham hopes that you will also communicate hither the orders which the King will send to the French commandants in India. Mr. Fitzherbert will explain to you, My Lord, the object of the epoch of 1776, which is mentioned in the English draft in interpretation of the term *former possessions*; he will also tell you the reasons why the return of the territories which should be procured by us will be dependent upon whether circumstances require the pacification of the Indian princes. My Lord Grantham assures me that this clause is one of pure precaution, and that it will be regarded as void if, upon the arrival of news of peace in India, Hyder Ali no longer occupies, or abandons after 4 months, the lands which should revert to us. I made no objection because it seems to me that England is not mistress of giving up to us lands possessed by her enemies, I also did not discuss the epoch of 1776 for want of having had sufficient ideas; moreover, I judged, My Lord, that you would arrange that article at a glance with Mr. Fitzherbert.

I spoke to My Lord Grantham of our exclusive fishing. That minister indicated to me the greatest desire to leave the terms, at this moment, without change, because of the next debates of Parliament: If the article of the fishing, after having been discussed, causes no very lively sensation, My Lord Grantham will himself propose to voice our exclusive right in the treaty itself; in the contrary case, that Minister takes it upon himself to have the most precise orders expedited so that our exclusive right is well established: I have no doubt, My Lord, of Mr. Grantham's exactitude in discharging the engagement he is undertaking.

The 3rd article which I discussed with that minister concerns the inhabitants of the Islands that we are returning. He promised me in the most solemn manner that those among the inhabitants who have shown some predilection for France will not be harassed, and that he would issue the most positive orders in that regard.

I have had the honor to inform you, My Lord, that I would be drawing up a draft of the definitive treaty. I enclose a copy herewith. I have communicated it to My Lord Grantham; he told me that he found nothing therein to change; that he was going to submit it to the Council, and that he would then transmit to Mr. Fitzherbert the order to confer on it with you:

News of the exchange of ratifications is awaited here with much impatience: it is supposed that you will not wait for those of Spain; it is the more important that this formality be promptly discharged, for letters of marque, which are granted by virtue of an act of Parliament, will not be revoked beforehand.

Mr. Franklin ought to have made several proposals to Mr. Fitzherbert; but I excuse myself from transmitting them to you because I do not doubt that they have been communicated to you.

It is claimed, My Lord, that the debates on the peace will be very lively, and that principally the excessively advantageous conditions accorded to the Americans will be attacked. My Lord Grantham has greatly regretted not having given us his full confidence when we dealt with him: he is persuaded that the conditions that were accorded them would have been better accepted; he is certain that it is difficult to conceive the reason why they have been treated with a generosity that it is probable they did not themselves expect.

I have had the honor to inform you, My Lord, of the arrival of M. le Comte de Moustier. This morning I presented him to the King as a simple foreigner; tomorrow I shall present him also to the Queen. Similarly, on Friday I will send in M. le Vicomte de Vergennes[1] with my letters of recall, and M. de Moustier will send in his letters of credence, and M. le Vicomte and I will set out on Monday at the latest. Mr. Grantham would have wanted me to defer my departure until close to the debates of Parliament, but I am too eager to perform my duty to remain here for any reason after having fulfilled all the obligations that my character thrusts upon me.

I am with a profound respect, Your very humble and very obedient servant.   Gerard de Rayneval

. . . . .

FFAA: Pol. Corr., England, v. 540, f. 371 (LC transcription).
[1] Vergennes, Constantin Gravier, Vicomte de (1761-1832). Son of the Comte de Vergennes.

Alleyne Fitzherbert to Lord Grantham

(Private.)   Paris, February 9th. 1783.
My Lord,

Dr. Franklin chicaned to the very last upon the business of the Passports, and finally moved for the inserting in them this odious & ungracious Clause "that they should not be considered as Protections for *any Ships bound to Ports in North America.*" This Motion was founded upon the Prohibitory Acts passed by Great Britain which he affects to consider as still in force, but he was overruled in it by his Colleagues without any Instance from me. I have felt the Pulse of the latter upon the subject of the Definitive Treaty, and find that the only fresh Articles which they wish to introduce into it, are "An Article about Prisoners, similar to that in our Preliminaries with France," and "An Article or Clause to define and ascertain the Situation and Property of those Islands in the Bay of Fundy which lie off the St. Croix & Penobscot Rivers;" But that they have little or no Intention of supporting Dr. Franklin in his unfair & unreasonable Demand of a Compensation from Great Britain for Damages sustained by America from the Depredations of the British Armies. This Circumstance makes me anxious to see the Definitive Treaty concluded before Mr. Laurens, who, tho' he is otherwise no Friend of Dr. Franklin's, thinks with him upon this Point, should return.

Dr Franklin seems anxious to return to America, which I am sorry for, being persuaded that he will do his utmost, when there, to prevent all Revival of Goodwill & Cordiality with the Mother Country, his Rancour & Inveteracy against which are as violent as ever. I could mention to Your Lordship Instances of this which would be almost ludicrous, if any thing can deserve that Name which is likely to produce such serious Consequences. He has entirely finished & signed the Treaty between America & Sweden.

I understand that Count d'Adhemar's[1] Nomination to the Embassy to England was made publick at Versailles today. I need not say that that of Lord Carmarthen,[2] who is well known here, both personally and by Reputation, has given the most universal Satisfaction.

Alleyne Fitz Herbert

Clements Library: Shelburne Papers, v. 71, pp. 399-400 (C).

[1] Adhémar, Jean Balthazar d'Azémar de Montfalcon, Comte d'. French diplomat. Ambassador to Great Britain, 1783-1787.

[2] Carmarthen, Francis Osborne, Marquess of (1751-1799). British political figure. Opponent of Lord North's Ministry. Appointed ambassador to Paris, February 1783, but did not serve, resigning upon the fall of Shelburne's administration. Secretary of State for the Foreign Department in Pitt's Ministry, 1783-1791. From March 1789, Duke of Leeds.

Chevalier de la Luzerne to Comte de Vergennes

[Translation]

N° 308   Philadelphia, 9 February 1783

My Lord

I have the honor of sending you a copy of an advertisement which is in the New York papers. This writing and private reports concur in representing St. John's Island in the Gulf of St. Lawrence as fertile and of a moderate enough temperature in regard to its situation. Some families propose to leave New York at once to go and settle there. These successive and numerous emigrations permit no doubt that the intention of the English government is to prepare in good time the means to evacuate that place either because the Peace makes this measure necessary soon or because it enters into the plan of military operations which that power has in view.

. . . . .

The Americans well understand that none of the belligerent nations has so great an interest as they in the outcome of this war. No class of Citizens here can be indifferent to that great event. For them all, it is a question of securing their rights, their liberties, their existence as a nation; one general inclination draws them towards peace. The former partisans of England themselves, fatigued from a struggle of 6 years, want the end of the war and independence. Mr. Penn, after a long seclusion, returns to Society, without distinction of party.

Necessity and boredom have made even him one of the apostles of independence. The Merchants, who have almost all suffered for two years, sigh after a time in which their operations may be more regular and more certain. Some among them who have goods stored see, it is true, their value diminish by half, and they want the war not to end until after they have consummated their sales, but they dare not oppose the general inclination, and not one voice is heard for the continuation of the war. True or false articles have come through the Islands, the news has been printed in Haste; it is read with avidity in the Circles, the taverns, and the public places. The articles are discussed; they are examined from all sides, and as all individuals without exception take part in public affairs and are naturally talkative or inquisitive, I have not seen a man in three days who has not asked my opinion of the peace, and who has not given me his; amidst this agitation, a small number of delegates already show themselves anxious with regard to the boundaries and the fisheries, and they continue to maintain the most extravagant Theses on these two Points.

. . . . .

le che de la luzerne.

Received 18 May.

FFAA: Pol. Corr., U.S., v.23, f. 51/151-155 (LC transcription).

Robert R. Livingston to John Adams

N⁰· 15.   Philadelphia 13th· February 1783.
Sir

...I congratulate you most sincerely upon having surmounted all the obstacles, that opposed themselves to the completion of our important Connection with the United States[1] – It has I think given the last blow to the pride of Britain, its power so far as it could endanger us was past recovery before, except as it derived force from its pride, which like the last Struggles of a dying Man, gave an appearance of vigor to the Body which it was about to destroy.

This covers a ratification of the Treaty, the first Copy sent by Mr· Jefferson has not been signed by me, owing to my absence – that

Gentleman has not yet sailed from Baltimore, having been delayed by a number of the Enemy's Cruisers which infest the Bay –

. . . . .

I am Sir with very great Respect and Esteem your most obed^t humble Servant   Robt R Livingston
rec^d 28 May

MHS: *The Adams Papers*, microfilm reel 360 (LS).
^{1} Presumably a reference to the United Provinces of the Netherlands.

George III's Proclamation of a Cessation of Arms

[London, February 14, 1783]
By the King.
A Proclamation

Declaring the Cessation of Arms, as well by Sea as Land, agreed upon between his Majesty, The most Christian King, The King of *Spain*, The States General of the *United Provinces*, and the United States of *America*, and enjoining the Observance thereof.
George R.

Whereas Provisional Articles were signed at *Paris*, on the thirtieth day of *November last*, between our Commissioners for treating of Peace with the Commissioners of the United States of America, and the Commissioners of the said States, to be inserted in and to constitute the Treaty of Peace proposed to be concluded between us and the said United States, when the Terms of Peace should be agreed upon between us and his most Christian Majesty. – And Whereas Preliminaries for restoring Peace between us and his most Christian Majesty, were signed at *Versailles* on the twentieth day of January last, between the Ministers of Us and the most Christian King. – And Whereas Preliminaries for restoring Peace between Us and the King of Spain were also signed at Versailles, on the twentieth day of January last, between the Ministers of Us and the King of Spain; – And Whereas, for putting an End to the Calamity of War as soon, and as far, as may be possible, it hath been agreed between Us, His most Christian Majesty, The King of *Spain*, The States General of the *United Provinces*, and the United States of *America*, as follows, that is to say, that such Vessels and Effects as should be taken in the Channel and in the North Seas, after the Space of twelve Days, to be computed from the Ratification of the said Preliminary Articles, should be ordered on all Sides: – That the Term should be one Month from the *Channel* and the *North Seas* as far as the *Canary Islands* inclusively, whether in the Ocean or in the *Mediterranean*; Two Months from the said *Canary Islands* as far as the Equinoxial Line or Equator; And lastly, Five Months in all other Parts of the World, without any Exception, or any other more particular Description of Time or Place.

And Whereas the Ratifications of the said Preliminary Articles between Us and the most Christian King, in due Form, were exchanged by Ministers of Us and of the most Christian King, on the third Day of this Instant *February*; And the Ratifications of the said Preliminary Articles *between* us and the King of *Spain*, were exchanged between the Ministers of Us and of the King of *Spain*, on the Ninth Day of this Instant *February*; From which days, respectively, the several Terms above mentioned, of Twelve Days, of One Month, of Two Months and of Five Months, are to be computed. And Whereas it is our Royal Will and Pleasure that the Cessation of Hostilities between Us and the States General of the *United Provinces*, and the United States of *America*, should be agreeable to the Epochs fixed between Us and the most Christian King:

We have thought fit, by and with the Advice of our Privy Council, to notify the same to all our loving Subjects; And We do declare, That our Royal Will and Pleasure is, and We do hereby strictly Charge and Command all our Officers, both at Sea and land, and all other Our Subjects whatsoever, to forbear all Acts of Hostility, either by Sea or Land, against his most Christian Majesty, The King of *Spain*, The States General of the *United Provinces*, and the United States of *America*, Their Vessels, or Subjects, from and after the respective Times above mentioned, and under the Penalty of incurring our highest Displeasure.

Given at our Court at St. *James's the Fourteenth Day of February, in the Twenty Third Year of our Reign, and in the Year of our Lord One Thousand Seven hundred and Eighty Three.*

God save the King

NA: PCC, *item 52, pp. 87-90, M247, reel 66.*

United States Declaration of the Cessation of Arms

Paris, 20 February 1783

By the Ministers Plenipotentiary of the United States of America

for making Peace with Great Britain.
A Declaration of the Cessation of Arms, as well by Sea, as Land,
agreed upon between His Majesty the King of Great Britain
and the United States of America.

Whereas Preliminary Articles were signed, at Paris, on the thirtieth Day of November last between the Plenipotentiaries of his said Majesty the King of Great Britain, and of the said States, to be inserted in, and to constitute the Treaty of Peace, to be concluded between his said Majesty and the said United States, when Terms of Peace should be agreed upon between his said Majesty and his most Christian Majesty: And Whereas, Preliminaries for restoring Peace, between his said Majesty the King of Great Britain, and his most Christian Majesty, were signed at Versailles, on the twentyeth Day of January last, by the respective Ministers of their said Majestys: And whereas Preliminaries for restoring Peace, between his said Majesty the King of Great Britain, & his Majesty the King of Spain, were also signed at Versailles, on the Twentieth Day of January last, by their respective Ministers, and whereas, for putting an End to the Calamity of War, as soon and as far as possible, it hath been agreed, between, the King of Great Britain, his most Christian Majesty, the King of Spain, the States General of the United Provinces, and the United States of America as follows, that is to say

That such Vessels and Effects as should be taken in the Channell & in the North Seas, after the Space of twelve Days, to be computed, from the Ratification of the said Preliminary Articles, should be restored on all Sides; that the Term should be one Month from the Channell and North Seas, as far as the Canary Islands inclusively, whether the Ocean or the Mediterranean; Two Months from the said Canary Islands, as far as the equinoctial Line or Equator, and lastly Five Months, in all other Parts of the World, without any Exception, or any other more particular Description of Time or Place.

And Whereas the Ratifications of the said Preliminary Articles between his said Majesty the King of Great Britain, and his most Christian Majesty in due Form were exchanged by their Ministers, on the Third Day of this instant February, from which Day the several terms abovementioned, of twelve Days, of one Month, of two Months and of five Months are to be computed, relative to all British and American Vessels and Effects.

Now therefore, We, the Ministers Plenipotentiary, from the United States of America, for making Peace with Great Britain, do notify to the People and Citizens of the said United States of America, that Hostilities on their Part against his Britannic Majesty, both by Sea and Land, are to cease, at the Expiration of the Terms herein before specified therefor, and which Terms are to be computed from the third Day of February instant. And We do, in the Name and by the Authority of the said United States, accordingly warn and enjoin all their officers and Citizens to forbear all Acts of Hostility, whatever, either by Land or by Sea against his said Majesty the King of Great Britain, or his Subjects under the Penalty of incurring the highest Displeasure of the said United States.

Given at Paris the Twentieth Day of February, in the Year of our Lord one Thousand seven hundred and Eighty Three, under our Hands and Seals

John Adams
B. Franklin.
John Jay.

MHS: *The Adams Papers, microfilm reel 103(C).*

Conde de Floridablanca to Marquis de Lafayette

Sir,   Pardo, 22^d feb^y· 1783

I cannot comply better with your desire than by asking your leave to give you here my Answer – You have perfectly well understood whatever I have had the honor to communicate to you with respect to our dispositions towards the United States – I shall only add that altho' it is his Majesty's intentions to abide for the present by the limits established by the Treaty of the 30th· of November 1782, between the English & the Americans, the King intends to inform himself particularly whether it can be in any ways Inconvenient or prejudicial to settle that affair amicably with the United States –

I have the Honor &c.   Florida Blanca

NA: PCC, *item 156, pp. 330-331 (translation); M247, reel 176.*

Benjamin Vaughan to John Adams

Dear sir,   London, Feb^r 25th·, 1783.

. . . . .

...The event of the peace, & the reception it meets in parliament, will tell you who were America's best friends. They were those who made least profession and had most understanding. It is unnecessary to hint more to you. — All ranks are satisfied with peace, but the *great* are not satisfied with a minister who had so few of *them* in his train: They therefore say we might have had a better peace. You are one of those that know, and I ask your opinion about the fact of a better peace being easy without more war, or even with it.

. . . . .

...I have the honor to be, with much respect, Dear sir, Your most obedient & most humble servant,   Benj[n] Vaughan

MHS: *The Adams Papers, microfilm reel 360* (ALS).

Comte de Vergennes to Chevalier de la Luzerne

[Translation]

N[o.] 49.   Versailles, 27 February 1783

I have received, Sir, the despatches that you have done me the honor of writing me from N[o.] 292 to N[o.] 298 inclusively. I informed you by my N[o.] 48 of the Signing of the preliminaries among France, Spain, and England. The exchange of the respective Ratifications took place the 3rd and the 9th of this month, and the Parliament of England, although disapproving of the conditions of peace, has promised His Britannic Majesty full support in enforcing it religiously; thus we can regard this important and salutary work as consummated. You will find two copies of our treaty enclosed.

We are in expectation, Sir, of the part which the Dutch will take, and we see only one, i.e., to acquiesce in the conditions that have been proposed to them; they are very tolerable with regard to the losses that the Republic has suffered in all parts. We will know at the end of this Week the final resolution of the States-General.

We are going to occupy ourselves with the definitive treaties, and this work does not present any difficulty; it is only retarded by the invitation that we have made to the two mediating Courts to take part in it. We await their response.

Peace establishes a new order of things in America; the Americans, henceforth acknowledged by all the Powers of Europe, will doubtless occupy themselves with fixing the principles that should serve as the basis for relations as much political as mercantile, which they will seek to establish everywhere, and principally with their former metropolis.

You will yourself perceive, Sir, that it is important to the King to be enlightened in this regard with the greatest promptitude, because his future conduct should be modelled on the system that the United States will develop. Although we did not count at all on the gratitude of the Americans, we nevertheless regard our alliance as unalterable. As for commerce, we shall never claim exclusive advantages there: but we hope that no other nation will obtain any to our prejudice: such are, Sir, in a few words our principles and our expectation with regard to the United States.

I have informed you, Sir, that the King was willing to advance them this year a sum of 6 million; you may inform Mr. Morris that it will be acquitted exactly; but you will deprive that Superintendant of any hope of obtaining the slightest augmentation for this year, and of any aid for the next: the state of our finances would not permit it; besides, an entire year of the enjoyment of peace after an inactive campaign will place Mr. Morris in a condition to meet the expenses with which he is charged.

I understand, as do you, Sir, the necessity of promptly concluding the convention relative to Consuls, and I count on being occupied with it immediately. I have already sent you the reasons that lead me to terminate this labor here. They prevent me from satisfying a desire, and I truly regret it.   Vergennes

FFAA: Pol. Corr., U.S.,v. 23, f. 64/188-189 (LC transcription).

Lord Shelburne's Precis of Measures Taken in Consequence of the Exchange of the Provisional and Preliminary Articles of Peace

[December 3, 1782 - February 28, 1783]

1782. Decr. 3.

Mr Strachey arrived from Paris with Provisional Articles of Peace, which had been agreed upon by the King's Commissioner and the Commissioners of the United States of America, signed the 30th. November.

. . . . .

Decr. 31.

Wrote to the King's Commissioners in North America, and transmitted an attested Copy of the Provisional Articles of Peace to be sent immediately to Congress.

1783.
Jany. 23

A Messenger arrived from Paris with the Preliminary Articles of Peace with France and Spain, signed at Versailles the 20th. and an Account that a Suspension of Hostilities had been agreed upon with Holland, with a Declaration signed by the American Commissioners to accede to the General Cessation of Hostilities.

. . . . .

27.   Laid before the House of Commons the Preliminary and Provisional Articles.

. . . . .

February 2.   Received from Lord Grantham a Copy of the French King's Letter to the Marquis de Vaudreuil, Commander in Chief of His Most Christian Majesty's Forces in America and the West Indies, directing him to abstain from all Acts of Hostility.

February 2.   Wrote to the Admiralty, directing their Lordships to order the Commanders in Chief in America and the West Indies, to abstain from all Acts of Hostility against the French.

5.   D^o· to extend the Cessation of Hostilities to Spain and the United States of America, on the Coast of *America and the West Indies*.

               Sent to the Attorney Genl· The Preliminary and Provisional Articles &c^a· and directed him to prepare the Draft of a Proclamation for a general Cessation of Hostilities.

February 8.   The Preliminary Articles ratified with France, arrived.

. . . . .

February 13.   A Messenger arrived with the Ratification of the Preliminary Articles with the Court of Spain, and an Instrument of Accession to the Cessation of Hostilities with Holland.

. . . . .

[15.]   To the Admiralty to order a General Cessation of Hostilities to take place at Sea.

February 16.   To Sir Guy Carleton, not to commence the Evacuation of New York till the King's further Pleasure is known, except that of embarking the heavy Artillery and Stores, which are to be kept in readiness to be transported, either to Halifax, or the West Indies.

               To endeavour by all means to establish Harmony and Union between the Two Countries, and to use every conciliatory Effort to obtain for the Loyalists the full

               effect of the 5th· Article of the Preliminaries with regard to the Restitution of Property.

. . . . .

Marquis de Lafayette to Robert R. Livingston

Dear Sir   Bordeaux March the Second 1783

. . . . .

The Reasons of My Going from Cadiz to Madrid Being known to You, I Shall only inform You that upon My Arrival there I Waited upon the King and paid a Visit to Conde de Florida Blanca....

In the Course of our Conversation I Could See that American Independence Gives Some Umbrage to the Spanish Ministry – they fear the Loss of their Colonies and the Success of our Revolution Appear to Be An Encouragement. Upon this their King Has pretty odd Notions as He Has indeed Upon Every thing – the Reception of Mr. Carmichael they Wanted to procrastinate and Yet they knew it Must Be done – in offering My opinion to Conde de florida Blanca I did it in a Pressing and a Very free Manner. I Rejected Every idea of delay and Was the Happier in My Moral and physical description of America and of Each of the States, as Conde de florida Blanca Appeared to me to know Very little Upon these Matters. While I Abated their fear from our Quarter, I Endeavored to Awaken them Upon other Accounts – It is Usless to Mention the Particulars of this Conversation Which lasted Very long and Which He promised to lay Before the King — two days After He Said He Would Pay me a Visit at Madrid

Agreeable to the Appointment, I Waited for Conde de florida Blanca and there in presence of the french Ambassador He told me that the King Had determined immediately to Receive the Envoy from the United States – our Conversation Was Also Very long, and I owe to compte Montmorin the Credit to say that not only at that Moment But in Every Instance When He Should take Advantage of Conde de florida Blanca in our favor He threw in all the Weight of the french influence.

. . . . .

...I took the liberty to say that on Saturday I must set out and it Was at last fixed that on friday Mr Carmichael Should deliver His Credentials and on Saturday Would Be invited to the dinner of the Foreign Minister.

As to More Important Matters I Conversed upon the Affair of limits Upon the Navigation of the Missisipy to the Sea of Which Point I found Him Very Repugnant. I spoke Upon the Cod fish duties. I wanted to Have a Preference Engaged for in writing Upon all Bargains Respecting tobacco and Naval Stores in a Word I did My Best and Should Have Been More Particular on points of Monney, Had not the Minister's Answer put it out of My Power to do it in Any other Way But Such as Was inconsistent With the dignity of the United States.

. . . . .

...I Have not Neglected Speaking Upon the Same Subject With the other Ministers. Mr de Galvez in whose department the Indies Are, Appears Much Averse to the English Limits. He Has for the present Sent orders to the Spanish Governors to Abide By the Limits and an Official Copy of this Order Has Been Promised to Me – But Mr de Galvez Was of Opinion that those Limits Would not do. I Have therefore thought it proper Officially By Writing and Before Witnesses to Especially to Bind them that the Affair of Limits Cannot Now But Be Settled on this Side independent of their Hand writing france through Her Ambassador is a Witness to the engagements and yet Being in a private capacity I took Care Not to Engage America to Any thing

Never Was a Man further from a partiality to Spain than I am – But I think I Now Have Left there in a Sincere and a Steady Intention to Cultivate the friendship of America the french party at that Court Will Be for it and Both ideas Will be joined together. They Labor under fits of territorial Madness. They have an ill Understood and as ill Conducted Pride it is disagreeable to treat with them and their own interest does not persuade them out of their prejudices But tho they had Rather there was no such a thing as North America, they are truly and Earnestly desirous to Maintain a Good Harmony and live in friendship and Good Neighborly Union With the United States — Mississippy is the Great Affair and the Mention of it in My Letter is the Most favorable Communication I Could Snatch in our Conversations – it is I think, the interest of America to be Well With Spain – at least for Many Years – and particularly on Account of the french Alliance so that I Very Much Wish Success to Mr Jay's Negociations. I Have Advised Mr Carmichael to Continue His Conferences and I think they will Be of Service.

. . . . .

...I Have the Honor to be With the Most Affectionate Regard Dear Sir Your obedient Humble Servant   Lafayette

NA: PCC, item 156, pp. 344-350 (ALS); M247, reel 176..

Benjamin Franklin to Benjamin Vaughan

Dear Sir,   Passy, March [5], 1784 [1783]
    You mention that I may now see verified all you said about binding down England to so hard a peace. I suppose you do not mean by the American

treaty; for we were exceeding favourable in not insisting on the reparations so justly due for the wanton burnings of our fine towns and devastations of our plantations in a war now universally allowed to have been originally unjust. I may add that you will also see verified all I said about the article respecting the royalists, that it will occasion more mischief than it was intended to remedy, and that it would have been better to have omitted all mention of them. England might have rewarded them according to their merits at no very great expence. After the harms they had done to us, it was imprudent to insist on our doing them good.

I am sorry for the overturn you mention of those beneficial systems of commerce that would have been exemplary to mankind. The making England entirely a free port would have been the wisest step ever taken for its advantage.

. . . . .

I know not what foundation there can be for saying that I abuse England as much as before the peace. I am not apt, I think, to be abusive: of the two I had rather be abused.

Inclosed are the letters you desire. I wish to hear from you more frequently, and to have through you such new pamphlets as you may think worth my reading. I am ever, my dear friend, yours most affectionately,

B. Franklin.

WTF, Franklin Memoirs, v. 4, pp. 227-228.

Henry Laurens to Benjamin Franklin

Sir,   London 6ᵗʰ· March 1783.

. . . . .

Mʳ· Oswald said to me yesterday, he was going to the proper place for learning whether he should be soon, or when required to attend upon the business of a Definitive Treaty & promised to acquaint me with the result of his enquiry. I have not since heard from him. While I am here I find employment. I have upon proper occasions offered my sentiments upon the Lamentations over the good people called Loyalists & if appearances are to be trusted I have afforded consolation to some folks.

An active M P. said to me this Morning, he had thoughts of impeaching Lord Shelburne for Sins of omission & was proceeding to make special enquiries, which I took the Liberty of interrupting by an observation that these were things out of our Line. – he went on, "do you know that Lord Shelburne declared to the House of Lords, the Provisional Treaty was obtained from the American Ministers without the concurrence or

participation of the Court of France, that the Court was not pleased &
consequently would not hereafter be so friendly to the United States, I am
afraid added our friend of ill consequences, I suspect every thing & shall
suspect till the Troops are entirely withdrawn from your Country." I replied
do not be anxious Sir, You talk'd just now of an impeachment, admit the
Case to be as Lord Shelburne has stated, which I do not admit, say to Lord
Shelburne & from me if you please, that John Adams, Benjn Franklin, John
Jay & poor Henry Laurens, may be impeached & hanged for aught I know
but the United States will not be hurt nor the friendship of the Court of
France shaken by the infidelity of those fellows. for my own part I am no
more afraid of being hanged than I was in your Tower of London. Our
friend was pleased with the explanation & I presume Lord S. will hear of
it. With respect to your Troops at New York, I appeal to you Sir, If there
was a Serjeant's Guard in your House, would you proceed on business 'till
they were effectually removed? No.

I send by the hands of Mr Storer[1] for the use of the Commissioners at
Paris, The Bill for the Provisional Establishment of Commerce between
Great Britain & the United States. My opinion has been often asked; I say,
it may very well suit the purpose of one party, that there ought to be two
to a bargain. But are we not very liberal in opening the Trade upon such
terms? Undoubtedly – you want to purchase Rice & other Provisions for
home consumpt & for the West Indies, you are desiros of selling your
Woolen & Iron Wares – you are liberal. but we cannot profit of your
bounty, while the Serjeant's Guard is in the House. – Don't be uneasy the
Troops will be removed as speedily as possible – suspend then your
beneficent Acts until they are removed. possibly America may ask, When
you were accustomed to send Troops to <***> that Country, were you
puzzled to find Transport Ships for the purpose?

. . . . .

I beg my Compliments to your Grandson & that you will be assured I am
with the most sincere & affectionate Regard Sir Your Obliged & Obedient
Servant   Henry Laurens

. . . . .

LC: *Benjamin Franklin Papers, microfilm reel 7 (ALS).*
[1] *Not further identified.*

Benjamin Franklin to Robert R. Livingston

Sir,   Passy, March 7. 1783.

I but this moment hear of this Opportunity, by which I can only send you a Line to acquaint you, that I have concluded the Treaty with Sweden, which was signed on Wednesday last. You will have a Copy by the first good Opportunity. It differs very little from the Plan sent me, in nothing material. – The English Court is in Confusion by another Change of Ministry; Lord Shelburne & his Friends having resigned; but it is not yet certainly known who will succeed; tho' Lord North & M[r.] Fox are talk'd of as two, they being reconcil'd!! I cannot add but that I am, with great Esteem Sir, Your most obedient humble Serv[t.]

B. Franklin

PS The Change in the Ministry is not suppos'd of any Importance respecting our Definitive Treaty, which must conform to the Preliminaries: But we shall see!
Read July 16, 1783

NA: PCC, item 82, v. 2, pp. 361-364 (ALS); M247, reel 108.

James Madison's Notes of Debates

Wednesday 12, Th. 13, F. 14, S. 15 of March [1783].

These days were employed in reading the despatches brought on Wednesday morning by Capt. Barney commanding the *Washington* Packet. They were dated from Decr. 4 to 24 from the Ministers Plenipo. for peace, with journals of preceding transactions, and were accompanied by the Preliminary articles signed on the 30th of Novr. between the said Ministers & Mr. Oswald the British Minister.

The terms granted to America appeared to Congs. on the whole extremely liberal. It was observed by several however that the stipulation obliging Congs. to recommend to the States a restitution of confiscated property, altho it could scarcely be understood that the States would comply, had the appearance of sacrificing the dignity of Congs. to the pride of the British King.

The separate and secret manner in which our Ministers had proceded with respect to France & the confidential manner with respect to the British Ministers affected different members of Congs. very differently. Many of the most judicious members thought they had all been in some measure ensnared by the dexterity of the British Minister, and particularly disapproved of the conduct of Mr. Jay in submitting to the Enemy his jealousy of the French without even the knowledge of Dr. Franklin, and of the unguarded manner in which he, Mr. A. & Dr. F. had given in writing sentiments unfriendly to our Ally, and serving as weapons for the insidious policy of the Enemy.

The separate article was most offensive, being considered as obtained by G.B. not for the sake of the territory ceded to her, but as a means of disuniting the U.S. & France, as inconsistent with the spirit of the Alliance, and a dishonorable departure from the candor, rectitude & plain dealing professed by Congs. The dilemma in wch Congs. were placed was sorely felt. If they sd communicate to the F. Minister every thing, they exposed their own Ministers, destroyed all confidence in them on the part of France, & might engage them in dangerous factions agst Congs. which was the more to be apprehended, as the terms obtained by their management were popular in their nature. If Congs. sd. conceal everything, & the F. Court sd. either from the Enemy or otherwise come to the knowledge of it all confidence wd. be at an end between the allies; the enemy might be encouraged by it to make fresh experiments, & the public safety as well as the national honor be endangered. Upon the whole it was thought & observed by many that our Ministers particularly Mr. Jay, instead of making allowances for & affording facilities to France in her delicate situation between Spain & the U.S. had joined with the enemy in taking advantage of it to increase her perplexity; & that they had made the safety of their Country depend on the sincerity of Ld. Shelburne, who was suspected by all the world besides, and even by most of themselves. See Mr. L———'s letter Dcr. 24.[1]

The displeasure of the French Court at the neglect of our Ministers to maintain a confidential intercourse & particularly to communicate the preliminary articles before they were signed, was not only signified to the Secty. of F.A. but to sundry members by the Chevr. de la Luzerne. To the former he shewed a letter from Ct. de Vergennes directing him to remonstrate to Congs. agst. the conduct of the Amr. Ministers; which a subsequent letter countermanded alledging that Docr. F. had given some explanations that had been admitted; & told Mr. L. that the American Ministers had deceived him (de Vergennes) by telling him a few days before the preliminary articles were signed, that the agreement on them was at a distance; that when he carried the articles signed into Council, the King expressed great indignation, & asked if the Americans served him thus before peace was made, & whilst they were begging for aids, what was to be expected after peace &c. To several Members he mentioned that the King had been surprized & displeased & that he said he did not think he had such allies to deal with.

To one of them who asked whether the Ct. of F. meant to complain of them to Congs. Mr. Marbois answered that Great powers never *complained* but that they *felt & remembered*. It did not appear from any circumstances that the separate article was known to the Court of F. or to the Chevr. de la Luzerne.

The publication of the preliminary articles excepting the separate article in the Newspapers was not a deliberate act of Congs. A hasty question for enjoining secresy on certain parts of the despathes which included these articles, was lost; and copies havg. been taken by members & some of them handed to the Delegates of the Pena. one of them reached the printer. When the publication appeared Congs. in general regretted it, not only as tending too much to lull the States, but as leading France into suspicions that Congs. favored the premature signature of the articles and were at least willing to remove in the minds of people the blame of delaying peace from G.B. to France.

Smith, Letters of Delegates, *v. 20, pp. 15-17.*
   [1]   *See Henry Laurens to Robert R. Livingston, December 24, 1782 (NA: PCC, item 89, pp. 245-247; M247, reel 117).*

John Adams to Henry Laurens

Dear Sir,   Paris March 12 1783

. . . . .

Appearances, on the Side where you are, dont please me more than you. But I hope the Weather will soon clear up, and that We shall Soon have the Pleasure of Seeing you and M[r.] Oswald here, to put the last hand to the Peace.

It is not worth while for any Noble lord to "boast of his Art" in obtaining the Provisional Treaty, without the Knowlege of our great and good Ally. – It was not owing to "his Art." – But how does he know what Knowledge was communicated to our Ally? As to getting "John Adams and C[o.] hanged," this would be no more than a Hillsborough,[1] Germain, or Sandwich[2] would have done if y could. This would be no Feat for a Whig Minister to boast of.

This same "Hanging" is however a grave Business, and perhaps the aforesaid C[o.] may have reflected upon the Nature of it more seriously than his Lordship, unless it has struck him lately – But I cannot think our Country will hang her Ministers merely for their Simplicity in being cheated into Independence, the Fisheries and half the great Lakes. Our

Countrymen love Buck Skins, Beaver skins, Tom Cod & Pine Trees too well, to hang their Ministers for accepting them, or even for purchasing them by a little too much "Reciprocity" to the Tories.

Be it as it may, if a French Minister and an English Minister should form a Coalition as curious as that of the Fox and the Geese, to [get] J. A. hanged, he is pretty well prepared for this, or to be recalled, censured or flattered or Slandered, just as they please.

I wish I could See more Serious Preparations for evacuating New York and Penobscot. – our People will not feel like freemen in friendship with G. Britain till this is done. – if any one Thinks that keeping Poss^n of N. York will help the Refugees, he deceives himself. G. Britain's Misfortunes have arisen, from the Ignorance ~~of~~ in her Rulers of the American Character. – if Ministers are incapable of learning it, they never will Succeed in addressing themselves to it. – if They think that Fear will work for the Refugees, they will find it operates against them.

But Why is the definitive Treaty delayed? Congress will not take the Preliminaries into Consideration, till they have the definitive Treaty. There can be no Ratification, untill Congress have that, and in my Opinion the States, after the Ratification and Recommendations will take none of them into Consideration, untill they are evacuated by the Troops. in this I may be mistaken.

My Respects to your good Family, and believe me with great Esteem and Respect, Sir your most obedient and most humble sert   J. Adams.
Recd. 25th·

Kendall Whaling Museum, Sharon, MA: Kendall Collection (ALS).

[1] *Hillsborough, Wills Hill, Earl of (1718-1793). British political figure. Secretary of state for colonies, 1768-1772, and for the northern department, 1779-1782. Opposed conciliatory policies toward America.*

[2] *Sandwich, John Montagu, Lord (1718-1792). British political figure. Originally a Bedford Whig; served as a lord commissioner of the admiralty, 1744-1748. Plenipotentiary for conferences at Breda, 1746, and for the peace talks, 1747-1748, that resulted in the Treaty of Aix-la-Chapelle. First Lord of the Admiralty, 1748-1751. Secretary of State, 1763-1765. Postmaster General, 1768-1770. Secretary of State, 1770-1771. First Lord of the Admiralty, 1771-1782.*

John Adams to Benjamin Vaughan

Dear Sir,   Paris March 12th 1783.
M^r· Storer arrived yesterday with your favor of 25th ult^o· I thank You for the Pamphlets, which are an Amusement in this place, how little soever

there is in them of Sense or Candor.

The Refugees however seem to judge right in their own Affair – Sensible that they have no Claim at all upon America for Compensation, they demand it of Great Britain, upon whom the pretensions of some of them may be very just.

But why has no Man dared to mention tens of thousands of Sufferers in America, as innocent, as meritorious at least, as any of the Refugees? Who is to make Restitution and Compensation to these?

.   .   .   .   .

Those who say you might have had a better Peace, speak from Conjecture, not from Knowledge – They reason from a false Comparison of the Forces of the belligerent Powers – Their Imaginations magnify the Finances and military Power of Great Britain, and diminish those of France, Spain, Holland & America, & then they reason from this delusive Comparison, that the Peace is inadequate to the relative Situations – I am afraid that the Vote to this purpose, will be [an] unhappy one for Great Britain – Will it not nourish a continual discontent in your Nation, & a continual Jealousy in all the Powers that have been at War with You?

I will answer You with great Sincerity, I do not believe you could possibly have obtained a better Treaty with America – On the contrary, the least delay would have lost You some Advantages which you now have.

What Conditions might have been obtained from France and Spain, I know not. – France appears in the Treaty with great Moderation in the Eyes of Europe, and her Aversion to continue the War could arise from no other Motive. Spain appears to have conquered her predeliction for Gibraltar – If therefore instead of wasting the Force of 40 or 50 Ships to guard that Rock, She had acted with France in the West Indies or against New York or both with 25. 20 or even only 15. Dutch Ships in the North Seas or the Channel, where would have been your Hopes? Surely only in the defensive – Admitting what is very extravagantly improbable, that you could have defended all another year at an expence of 20. Millions, would you have been then able to demand better Terms, or your Adversaries disposed to grant them? I know not – On the contrary, their Courage & Pretensions would have advanced.

America did you a very kind Turn you may depend upon it, when She rapidly hastened on the Signature of the Provisional Treaty – Think of it as you will, you would have had no Peace at this hour, but for this able Seizure of the Moment of the Tide in the Affairs of Man, for which you are indebted to M^r· Oswald & his Principals – Without this, the Negotiations would have dreamed on, until D'Estaing had sailed from Cadiz, and then *voilà! une autre Campaigne.*

I should be very glad to see the better sort of Pamphlets you mention, &

particulary some to shew the Policy & the Necessity of an immediate Evacuation of New York & Penobscot.

I have the honor to be very respectfully, Sir &c

John Adams

MHS: *The Adams Papers, microfilm reel 108 (LBkC).*

Alleyne Fitzherbert to Lord Grantham

N$^{o.}$ 31)   Paris March 13$^{th.}$ 1783.

My Lord

I took the earliest Opportunity of communicating to the American Commissioners, the printed Bill contained in your Lordship's Letter N$^{o.}$ 32. They all of them expressed to me in very warm terms, the Satisfaction they felt from its contents, and from the liberal spirit that prevails in every part of it; saying further that it could not fail of proving a most powerful means of restoring not only the commercial Intercourse, but the Harmony and good will which formerly subsisted between the two Countries. They have likewise authorized me to acquaint your Lordship, that they conceive themselves to be impowered, & are ready to secure reciprocally to the Commerce of Great Britain, the same advantages which are granted by this Bill to the Commerce of America, and they will take this step forthwith, in the shape, either of a Declaration from themselves to the proposed effect, or of a separate & additional Article in the definitive Treaty. They however rather prefer the latter of these forms, principally from the Idea that by that means, a commercial Intercourse with Ireland, (which Kingdom is not comprehended in the aforesaid Bill,) may possibly be secured to them likewise: but as this is a most delicate point, I could not venture to speak to it, without special Instructions.

As this matter seems to press for a speedy conclusion, it may not be amiss to repeat to your Lordship, that in case M$^{r.}$ Oswald should not be able to return forthwith, the American Commissioners would make no Difficulty of signing such an Article as that I have mentioned above, jointly with myself, upon the Strength of the general Expressions used in the several full powers I am intrusted with.

I have the honour to be with the greatest Respect, My Lord, Your Lordship's most obedient and most humble Servant

Alleyne Fitz-Herbert

R. 17$^{th:}$

PRO: *FO 27/6, v. 561, f. 141 (LC transcription).*

Chevalier de la Luzerne to Comte de Vergennes

[Translation]

N° 314   Philadelphia, 15 March 1783

My Lord,

The Packet-boat dispatched by Mr. Franklin and his Colleagues to bring here the draft of the Treaty between England and America arrived the day before yesterday....

I have still not been able to make to Congress and to receive from it the communications which the circumstance requires; up to this moment I have been no more able to judge with any degree of certainty the impression which the news will make upon thinking; but as an American ship is sailing this morning for L'Orient, I thought I should send you a quick sketch of public dispositions, instead of a more exact account in a few days. It seems that some individuals, either from ignorance or from ill will, from the outset have regarded the treaty as definitive in the event that Congress wished to ratify it, and there is talk of sending the *General Washington* back immediately to carry that ratification. Congress has judged more soundly. It does not think that the communication of the act of 30 November requires any public step on its part at present; it considers it as a very suitable basis to serve as the foundation of a definitive treaty, and is generally satisfied with conditions; some individuals have dared to raise their voices against the weak stipulations in favor of the Loyalists, but the almost universal satisfaction imposes silence on them; however, it is thought that Congress will make some representations concerning that article. It was at first proposed to publish that act under the authority of Congress; but I requested Mr. Livingston to have that publication deferred until it could be determined whether it was prudent to do so; in consequence, it limited itself to giving the public an extract of the articles and abstained from investing it with Congress' seal of authority. On my part, I am having placed in the gazettes of neighboring States some paragraphs which inform the people of this possible act, present it in its true point of view, and clearly establish that the war has not ended. I have written in confidence and in a detailed manner to General Washington, in order to explain to him the necessity of not supporting the views of England by giving even tacit consent to a truce, consent which would be equivalent, ipso facto, to a signed truce, which cannot take place without our concurrence; various circumstances give me cause to think that the English Plenipotentiaries in Paris have proposed to those of Congress an arrangement for the evacuation of New York.

I foresee that it will be difficult to engage the Americans to place obstacles there themselves; however, I invite General Washington not to suffer the provisions that will be necessary to accomplish that evacuation to be imported into that place, and to invest the enemy as closely as possible, and I propose that that General confer with M. le Duc de Lauzun, on his return from Boston, concerning the use to make of the French legion, as soon as the season will permit that it set out; this Corps is very suitable for impeding communications along the lines, and commerce in provisions with New York will take place with less liberty under the eyes of a French division than if it remains distant from the American army.

. . . . .

le chr de la luzerne

Received 18 May.

FFAA: Pol. Corr., U.S., v. 23, f. 112/315-320 (LC transcription).

Francis Dana to John Adams

Sir   March 16ᵗʰ 1783 St Petersbourg

. . . .

As to the extract of WLs letter and your answer upon it as well as your advice to me to communicate my mission to the Minister of the Emperor, and the Ministers of all the other Courts which have acceded to the Armed Neutrality, I think at present it is not advisable to make this communication on that occasion. for first I have no authority to make any *commercial* Treaty with the Emperor. and as to that part of my commission which respects the Armed Neutrality or Neutral Confederation, I have long since upon consideration, giving it to Congress as my opinion, that America cou'd not become a party in it, or accede formally to the marine convention so long as she continued a belligerent Power: and also, that that Convention from its terms and nature, was limited to the duration of the War. But if I shou'd be mistaken in this last point, I think it is not worth while for America *at this time,* to pay near five thousand pounds sterling to the Ministers of this Court for the liberty of acceeding to the Marine Convention: and if it was, I have not the money to at my disposal. The communication you are sensible must be general to all the parties to that Confederation, and of course to this Court. To make the communication which wou'd amount to a proposition on my part to acceede to the Convention, and not to be able to do it for want of what I know is essential to the end, wou'd be only to expose the honour of the United Staes without the prospect of any advantage. It is quite enô to pay Five thousand pounds sterl^g for a Treaty of Commerce with this Empire, I think it my duty therefore to keep the Marine Convention out of sight as long as possible, and to confine myself to the Treaty of Commerce, into which I have adopted the leading principles of the Marine Convention and shall endeavour to conclude both points in one Treaty. If I fail in this I must fail in both, and shall immediately quit this Court. I must exercise my discretion in some things, and as you have done, submit my conduct to the judgment of those whose right it is to decide upon it. If they furnish me not with the means they must not expect the accomplishment of my Mission. – I pray you to give me your advice upon these matters with the utmost freedom, and as soon as possible. Thô I have ventured not to follow it in this particular case, yet I give you my reasons for not doing it, that you might judge upon them, and am not the less obliged to you for your advice.

I have not received an answer in form to my letter communicating my Mission to the Vice-Chancellor, but only a verbal message in excuse of the delay for a time entirely past. I do not like this delay – The *immediate* assurances mentioned in my letter in which I informed you of this Communication, came from a Member of her Majesty's private Cabinet, who sought an interview with me for that occasion. But I refer you to a passage in my last letter "I am sick" &c God send me speedily a happy deliverance from them. Adieu my dear Sir, Yours &c,

[Francis Dana]

. . . . .

ans^d 1. May 1783.

MHS: *The Adams Papers, microfilm reel 360 (AL).*

Henry Laurens to Benjamin Franklin

Sir,   London 17th March 1783.

I beg leave to refer to my letter of the 6th Instant by the hands of Mr Storer – to speak in the current stile, Government is still a float. In the moment when it was thought an Administration would be formed, the prospects of the Coalition have been dashed – The K. it seems has been the stipulator, insisted upon keeping the Lord Chancellor and introducing Lord Stormont and His M. immediately went out of Town. The Duke of Portland[1] will not submit to recieve materials into the foundation which may endanger the Fabric. On one side Chagrin on the other Sneering, is visible, on our part We keep Lent, I cannot hide from myself the mortification which I suffer. Not a step taken towards a Definitive Treaty and establishing the important "*Then*" — The Bill of which I sent my Colleagues a Copy by M⁺ Storer is annihilated and another, called an Amendment, introduced. A Copy of this for their uses, You will recieve under the present Cover, You will read my idea of its merit in three words interlined in the Title. I am persuaded it will be torn to pieces to day – I hold the language steadily. "Make what Acts you please for opening Commerce, however suitable to the purposes of Great Britain or speciously conducive to the mutual interests of Great Britain and the United States, I think there cannot be, I hope there will not be, an intercourse permitted on our part until a Definitive Treaty is concluded and the British troops completely withdrawn from our Territories."

I lately saw in a Morning Chronicle a Publication of M⁺ Adams's first Commission for making a Treaty of Commerce with Great Britain and of the revocation of that Commission, I know but of one Man in this Kingdom capable of giving such intelligence, I wish he may not be possessed of more important Documents. Shall I request you Sir to inform me if it be not improper, whether there is at this time a subsisting Commission for entering into such a Treaty.

...Sir Your obliged & Most Obedient Servant   Henry Laurens.

•   •   •   •   •

LC: *Benjamin Franklin Papers, microfilm reel 7 (LS).*
   ¹ Portland, *William Henry Cavendish Bentinck, Duke of (1738-1809). British political figure. A Rockingham Whig, he remained in opposition throughout Lord North's ministry. Lord lieutenant of Ireland, April-July 1782. Chief minister in the Fox-North coalition ministry, April-December 1783. Secretary of State for Home Affairs, 1794-1801. Prime Minister, 1807-1809.*

Benjamin Franklin to Jonathan Shipley, Lord Bishop of St. Asaph

[Sir,]¹   Passy, March 17ᵗʰ 1783

I received with great pleasure my dear & respected Friend's letter of the 5ᵗʰ Instant, as it informed me of the Welfare of a Family I so much esteem & love.

The Clamour against the Peace in your Parliament would alarm me for its duration, if I were not of opinion with you, that the Attack is rather against the Minister. I am confident none of the Opposition would have made a better Peace of England if they had been in his Place; at least I am sure that Lord Stormont who seems loudest in Railing at it, is not the Man that could have mended it. My Reasons I will give you when I have what I hope to have, the great happiness of seeing you once more, and conversing with you. They talk much of there being no Reciprocity in our Treaty: They think nothing then of our passing over in silence the Atrocities committed by their Troops and demanding no satisfaction for their wanton Burnings and Devastations of our fair Towns and Countries. They have heretofore confest the War to be unjust, & nothing is plainer in Reasoning than that the Mischiefs done in an unjust War should be repaired. Can Englishmen be so partial to themselves, as to imagine they have a right to Plunder and destroy as much as they please, and then without satisfying for the Injuries they have done, to have Peace on equal Terms? We were favorable, and, did not demand what Justice entitled us to. We shall probably be blamed for it by our Constituents: And I still think it would be the Interest of England voluntarily to offer Reparation of those Injuries, and effect it as much as may be in her power. But this is an Interest she will never see.

Let us now forgive and forget. Let each Country seek its Advancement in its own internal Advantages of Arts and Agriculture, not in retarding or preventing the Prosperity of the other. America will, with God's blessing, become a great and happy Country; and England, if she has at length gained Wisdom, will have gained something more valuable, and more essential to her Prosperity, than all she has lost; and will still be a great and respectable Nation. Her great Disease at present is the number and enormous Salaries and Emoluments of Office. Avarice and Ambition are strong Passions, and separately act with great Force on the human Mind; but when both are united and may be gratified in the same Object, their violence is almost irresistable, and they hurry Men headlong into Factions and Contentions destructive of all good Government. As long therefore as these great Emoluments subsist, your Parliament will be a stormy Sea, and your Public Counsels confounded by private Interests. But it requires much Public Spirit and Virtue to abolish them; more perhaps than can now be found in a Nation so long corrupted.   B.F.

LC: Benjamin Franklin Papers, microfilm reel 7 (LBkC).

[1] Shipley, Jonathan (1714-1788). British clergyman. Bishop of St. Asaph, 1769. Friend of Benjamin Franklin. As a member of the House of Lords, consistently opposed repressive measures in America and prosecution of the American war.

Robert R. Livingston to the President of Congress

Sir   Philadelphia March 18th. 1783.

The important matter contained in the dispatches lately recd renders me unwilling to reply to them without being well satisfied of the sentiments of Congress. But, as the subjects on which I wish to be informed are of too delicate a nature to be rendered formal acts, I shall submit to them the draft of my reply to the joint Letter of our Ministers now at Paris – Previous to this it will be necessary that Congress come to some express determination upon some points which arise out of the treaty, & which if they see in the same light that I do they will consider as the most embarrassing, as well as the most important that can claim their attention. Congress have hitherto in every one of their acts, both of a public, & private nature, manifested the utmost confidence in the court of France In answer to every communication, they have reiterated their resolutions on that subject, and so lately as the 4th. of Octr. last, resolved unanimously "That they will not enter into the discussion of any overtures for pacification, but in *confidence* & in *concert* with his most christian majesty" – And directed that a copy of the above resolution should not only be furnished to the Minister of france – but be sent to all the Ministers of the United States in Europe, & published to the world. Yet sir, it has unfortunately so happened, that the Ministers of these States have imagined they had sufficient grounds to suspect the sincerity of the court of France And have not only thought it prudent to agree upon & sign the preliminaries with great Britain without communicating them till after the signature to the Ministers of his most Christian majesty, but, have permitted a separate article to be inserted in their treaty, which they still conceal from the court of France –

This reduces Congress to the disagreeable necessity, either of making themselves parties to this concealment, & thereby to contradict all their former professions of confidence in their ally, made not only to that ally, but to their own citizens, and to every court at which they had a minister – or of revealing it at the expence of the confidence they would wish to maintain between their ministers & the court of France. And that too when those Ministers have obtained such terms from the Court of London, as does great honor to them & at least equals our highest expectations.

I feel the more pain on this subject, because as well from the manner in which this Treaty is drawn, as well as from the article itself, I am inclined to believe that England had no other view in its insertion but to be enabled to produce it as a mark of the confidence we reposed in them, & to detach us from our ally, if the nation could be brought to continue the war –

The preamble, drawn by our ministers, contained professions of attachment to the alliance & declared that the treaty should not be obligatory till his britanic Majesty shall have agreed to accept the terms of a peace between France & Britain proposed or accepted by his most Christian majesty, & shall be ready to conclude *with him* such treaty. The preamble agreed to & as there is reason to conclude, framed in England, is so expressed as to render it very doubtful whether our treaty does not take place the moment France & England have agreed on the terms of their treaty, tho' france should refuse to sign till her allies were satisfied – This construction is strongly supported in the house of commons by administration.

The separate article is in itself an object of no moment, the territory it cedes is of little importance, & if as our ministers assert it made a part of West Florida previous to the war, it will on the peace be annexed to the nation that shall retain that colony, But it is extremely well calculated to sow the seeds of distrust & jealousy between the United States & their Allies – It demonstrates a marked preference for the English over the present possessors, And seems to invite Britain to reconquer it – Tho' this may promote particular interest, it never can consist with our honor to prefer an open enemy to a nation engaged in the same cause with us & closely connected to our ally. This article would in my opinion if avowed by the United States fully justify Spain in making a separate peace without the least regard to our interests – But this Sir is an inconsiderable evil, compared to those which may result from its having been concealed from the Court of Versailles. Mr Lawrence informs Congress (& that too from Letters of a late date from London) "That the people of England still retain the Idea of our *late colonies* & of *reconciliation. that Government gives every possible encouragement to this humour* – That it has been their incessant endeavour to detach < **** > us from our ally, And that it is given out in London that by *signing the late preliminaries they have out manoeuvred the court of France,* That every engine had been set at work, But every degree of craft under the mask of returning affection will be practized for creating jealousies between the States, & their good & great ally." Mr Adams's letters of Novr speak the same lauguage – If Sir we suppose these Gen^t to have been well informed, how much reason have we to apprehend that this secret article will prove in the hands of Britain a most dangerous engine – They may reveal to the court of France the jealousies our ministers entertain, the confidence they repose in them with such falshoods and additions as will best serve their purposes, and by producing this secret article gain credit for all they advance – This line they certainly have pursued with respect to France, revealing all that they learnt from the C^t De Vergenues relative to his opinion of the first commission nor is there room to doubt, that Marbois Letter was rec^d thro' the same channel – And there is no reason to believe if (as our Ministers suppose) the C^t of france had put themselves more in their power, that they would neglect such promising means of increasing the suspicions ~~they~~ our plenipotentiaries already entertained –

Add to this, that this article may be used in parliament, & with the British nation at large as a most powerful argument for continuing the war, aducing from the resentment it discovers to Spain, & the distrusts it manifests of France, that the quadruple knot is untied –

But suppose, what may possibly be the case, that the British administration are sincere, how is the honor & good faith of the United States to be justified to their allies, & to the world, if by any of those causes which daily operate, this secret which is now known to sixty or seventy people should be discovered – to tell the world that we suspected France will not suffice, unless we can shew probable grounds for such suspicion – Our Ministers inform us that when they communicated the articles of the treaty to the C^t De Vergennes "he appeared surprized but *not displeased* at their being so favourable to us" – Mr Lawrance declares expresly "That he sees no cause for entertaining more particular jealousy than ought to be kept up against every negotiating court in the world, & not half so much as should at this moment be upon the watch against every motion arising from our new half friends"

I confess Sir (tho' my sentiments are of little moment) that I am fully of this opinion, and that I tremble, least we should be at this hour on the edge of a precipice the more dangerous as we have fixed our Eyes on the flattering prospect which lies beyond it – I am persuaded that the old maxim "Honesty is the best policy" applies with as much force to States as to individuals. In that persuasion I venture humbly to recommend, that such measures be adopted as to manifest that ~~the~~ repeated professions of fidelity to their engagements, & confidence in their ally, may not appear to have been made by Congress to mask deceit. The caution which negotiations require, & the light in which objects have appeared to our ministers may justify them, & perhaps intitle them to credit for attempting to serve us at every personal hazard.

But Sir it certainly can not consist with the honor of these States, upon such slight grounds, to contradict their own resolutions, & forfeit the confidence of an ally it has been so much indebted to, & whose aid it is at this moment supplicating for the means of carrying on another campaign. Under these impressions I humbly submit these resolutions –

That the Secretary for foreign affairs be directed to communicate the separate article in the provisional preliminary treaty with G. B. to the Minister of his most christian majesty, in such manner as will best tend to remove any unfavourable impression it may make on the court of France of the sincerity of these States or their Ministers.

That the Ministers for negotiating peace be informed of this communication, and of the reasons which influenced Congress to make it. That they be instructed to agree that in whatsoever hands west Florida may remain at the conclusion of the war, the United States will be satisfied that the line of North boundary be as described in the said separate article –

That it is the sense of the United States in Congress, that the articles agreed upon between the Ministers of these States, & those of his britanic Majesty, are not to take place until a peace shall have been actualy signed between their most Christian, & britanic majesties.

Congress will easily believe that I offer these sentiments with the utmost diffidence. That I see many & powerful arguments that militate against them, that I feel extreme pain in advising a measure which may hurt the feelings of ~~our~~ Ministers to whom we are indebted for their continued zeal, & assiduity – all of whom I respect, & with one of whom I have had the closest & most intimate friendship – from our earliest youth – But Sir it is a duty that my office requires, and I am happy in reflecting that, that duty is discharged when I < ** > have proposed what I think right & that the better judgment of Congress is to determine.

I have the honor to be Sir with great respect Your Excellencys Most Ob^t Hum: Serv$^{t.}$

R R Livingston

NA: PCC, item 79, v. 3, pp. 41-54 (ALS): M247, reel 105.

James Madison's Notes of Debates

Wednesday March 19 [1783].

A letter was read from the Superintendt. of Finance inclosing letters from Docr. Franklin accompd. with extracts from the Ct. de Vergennes relative to money-affairs, the Supt. thereupon declaring roundly that our credit was at an end & that no further pecuniary aids were to be expected from Europe. Mr. Rutlidge denied these assertions & expressed some indignation at them. Mr. Bland said that as the Supt. was of this opinion it would be absurd for him to be Minister of Finance and moved that the come. on his motion for arranging the department might be instructed to report without loss of time. This motion was negatived as censuring the Come. but it was understood to be the sense of Congs. that they sd. report.

The order of the day viz the letter form the Secretary of F. A. was taken up.

Mr. Wolcot[1] conceived it unnecessary to waste time on the subject as he presumed Congs. would never so far censure the Ministers who had obtained such terms for this Country, as to disavow their conduct.

Mr. Clarke[2] was decided agst. communicating the separate article, which wd. be sacrificing meritorious Ministers, & wd. rather injure than relieve our national honour. He admitted that the separate article put an advantage into the hands of the Enemy, but did not on the whole deem it of any very great consequence. He thought Congress ought to go no farther than to inform the Ministers that they were sorry for the necessity which had led them into the part they had taken, & to leave them to get rid of the embarrassmt. as to the separate article in such way as they sd. judge best. This expedient would save Congress & spare our Ministers who might have been governed by reasons not known to Congress.

Mr. Mercer[3] said that not meaning to give offence any where, he should speak his sentiments freely. He gave it as his clear & decided opinion that the Ministers had insulted Congress by sending them assertions without proof as reasons for violating their instructions, & throwing themselves into the confidence of G. B. He observed that France in order to make herself equal to the Enemy had been obliged to call for aid & had drawn Spain agst. her interest into the war: that it was not improbable that She had entered into some specific engagements for that purpose; that hence might be deduced the perplexity of her situation, of which advantage had been taken by G. B. – an advantage in which our Ministers had concurred for sowing jealousies between F. & U. S. & of which further advantage wd. be taken to alienate the minds of the people of this Country from their ally by presenting him as the obstacle to peace. The British Court he said havg gained this point may easily frustrate the negociation & renew the war agst. divided enemies. He approved of the conduct of the Count de Vergennes in promoting a treaty under the 1st Commission to Oswald as preferring the substance to the shadow & proceeding from a desire of peace. The conduct of our Ministers throughout, particularly in giving in writing every thing called for by British Ministers expressive of distrust of France was a mixture of follies which had no example, was a tragedy to America & a comedy to all the world beside. He felt inexpressible indignation at their meanly stooping as it were to lick the dust from the feet of a nation whose hands were still died with the blood of their fellow-citizens. He reprobated the chicane & low cunning wch. marked the journals transmitted to congress, and contrasted them with the honesty & good faith which became all nations & particularly an infant republic. They proved that America had at once all the follies of youth and all the vices of old age: thinks it wd. [be] necessary to recall our Ministers: fears that France may be already acquainted with all the transactions of our Ministers, even with the separate article, & may be only awaiting the reception given to it by Congs. to see how far her hopes of cutting off the right arm of G. B. by supporting our revolution may have been well founded: and in case of our basely disappointing her, may league with our Enemy for our destruction and for a division of the spoils. He was aware of the risks to which such a league wd. expose F. of finally losing her share, but supposed that the British Islands might be made hostages for her security. He said America was too prone to depreciate political merit, & to suspect where there was no danger: that the honor of the King of F. was dear to him, that he never wd. betray or injure us unless he sd. be provoked & justified by treachery on our part. For the present he acquiesced in the proposition of the Secy. of F. A. But when the question sd. come to be put, he sd. be for a much more decisive resolution.

Mr. Rutlidge said he hoped the character of our ministers wd. not be affected, much less their recall produced by declamations agst. them: and that facts would be ascertained & stated before any decision sd. be passed: that the Ct. de Vergennes had expressly declared to our Ministers his desire that they might treat apart, alluded to & animadverted upon the instruction which sumbmitted them to French Councils; was of opinion that the separate article did not concern France & therefore there was no necessity for communicating it to her; & that as to Spain she deserved nothing at our hands, she had treated us in a manner that forfeited all claim to our good offices or our confidence, she had not as had been supposed entered into the present war as an ally to our ally and for our support; but as she herself had declared, as a principal & on her own account. He sd. he was for adhering religiously to the Spirit & letter of the treaty with France, that our Ministers had done so; & if recalled or censured for the part they had acted, he was sure no man of spirit would take their place. He concluded with moving that the letter from the Secy. for F. A. might be referred to a special comme. who might enquire into all the facts relative to the subject of it. Mr. Holten[4] 2ded the motion.

Mr. Williamson was opposed to harsh treatment of Ministers who had shewn great ability. He said they had not infringed the Treaty, and as they had recd. the concurrence of the Ct. de Vergennes for treating apart, they had not in that respect violated their instruction. He proposed that Congress sd. express to the Ministers their concern at the separate article & leave them to get over the embarrassment as they shd. find best.

Mr. Mercer in answer to Mr. Rutlidge said that his language with respect to the Ministers was justified by their refusal to obey instructions, censured wth. great warmth the servile confidence of Mr. Jay in particular in the British Ministers. He said the separate article was a reproach to our character, and that if Congress wd. not themselves disclose it he himself would disclose it to his Constituents who would disdain to be United with those who patronize such dishonorable proceedings. He was called to order by the Presidt. who said that the article in question was under an injunction of secresy & he cd. not permit the orders of the House to be trampled upon.

Mr. Lee took notice that obligations in national affairs as well as others ought to be reciprocal & he did not know that France had ever bound herself to like engagements as to concert of negociation with those into which America had at different times been drawn. He thought it highly improper to censure Ministers who had negociated well, said that it was agreeable to practice & necessary to the end proposed, for Ministers in particular emergences to swerve from strict instructions. France he said wanted to sacrifice our interests to her own or to those of Spain, that the French answer to the British Memorial contained a passage which deserved attention on this subject. She answer'd the reproaches of perfidy contained in that Memorial by observing that obligations being reciprocal, a breach on one side absolved the other. The Ct. de Vergennes he was sure was too much a master of negociation not to approve the management of our Ministers instead of condemning it. No man lamented more than he did any diminution of the confidence between this country & France, but if the misfortune should ensue it could not be denied that it originated with France, who has endeavoured to sacrifice our territorial rights, those very rights which by the Treaty she had guarantied to us. He wished the preliminary articles had not been signed without the knowledge of France but was persuaded that in whatever light she might view it, she was too sensible of the necessity of our Independence to her safety ever to abandon it. But let no censure fall on our Ministers who had upon the whole done what was best. He introduced the instruction of June 15, 1781, proclaimed it to be the greatest opprobrium and stain to this Country which it had ever exposed itself to, & that it was in his judgment the true cause of that distrust & coldness which prevailed between our Ministers & the French Court, inasmuch as it could not be viewed by the former without irritation & disgust. He was not surprized that those who considered France as the Patron rather than the ally of this Country should be disposed to be obsequious to her, but he was not of that number.

Mr. Hamilton urged the propriety of proceeding with coolness and circumspection. He thought it proper in order to form a right judgment of the conduct of our Ministers, that the views of the French & British Courts should be examined. He admitted it as not improbable that it had been the policy of France to procrastinate the definitive acknowledgmt. of our Independence on the part of G. B. in order to keep us more knit to herself & untill her own interests could be negociated. The arguments however urged by our Ministers on this subject, although strong, were not conclusive; as it was not certain, that this policy & not a desire of excluding obstacles to peace, had produced the opposition of the French Court to our demands. Caution & vigilance he thought were justified by the appearance & these alone. But compare this policy with that of G. B. survey the past cruelty & present duplicity of her councils, behold her watching every occasion & trying every project for dissolving the honorable ties which bind the U. S. to their ally, & then say on which side our resentments & jealousies ought to lie. With respect to the instruction submitting our Ministers to the advice of France, he had disapproved it uniformly since it had come to his knowledge, but he had always judged it improper to repeal it. He disapproved also highly of the conduct of our Ministers in not shewing the preliminary articles to our Ally before they signed them, and still more so of their agreeing to the separate article. This conduct gave an advantage to the Enemy which they would not fail to improve for the purpose of inspiring France with indignation & distrust of the U. S. He did not apprehend (with Mr. Mercer) any danger of a coalition between F. & G. B. against America, but foresaw the destruction of mutual Confidence between F. & U. S. which wd. be likely to ensue, & the danger which would result from it in case the war should be continued. He observed that Spain was an unwise nation, her policy narrow & jealous, her King old, her Court divided & the heir apparent notoriously attached to G. B. From these circumstances he inferred an apprehension that when Spain sd. come to know the part taken by America with respect to her, a separate treaty of peace might be resorted to. He thought a middle course best with respect to our Ministers; that they ought to be commended in general, but that the communication of the separate article to take place. He observed that our Ministers were divided as to the policy of the Ct. of France, but that they all were agreed in the necessity of being on the watch against G. B. He apprehended that if the ministers were to be recalled or reprehended, that they would be disgusted & head & foment parties in this Country. He observed particularly with respect to Mr. Jay that altho' he was a man of profound sagacity & pure integrity, yet he was of a suspicious temper, & that this trait might explain the extraordinary jealousies which he professed. He finally proposed that the Ministers sd. be commended & the separate articles communicated. This motion was 2ded by Mr. Osgood,[5] as compared however with the proposition of the Secy. for F. A. and so far only as to be referred to a Committee.

Mr. Peters[6] favored a moderate course as most advisable. He thought it necessary that the separate art. sd. be communicated, but that it wd. be less painful to the feelings of the Ministers if the doing it was left to themselves; and was also in favor of giving the territory annexed by the separate art. to W[est] F[lorida] to such power as might be invested with that Colony in the Treaty of peace.

Mr. Bland said he was glad that every one seemed at length to be struck with the impropriety of the instruction submitting our Ministers to the advice of the French Court. He represented it as the cause of all our difficulties & moved that it might be referred to the come. with the several propositions which had been made. Mr. Lee 2ded the motion.

Mr. Wilson[7] objected to Mr. Blands motion as not being in order. When moved in order perhaps he might not oppose the substance of it. He said he had never seen nor heard of the instruction it referred to untill this morning; and that it had really astonished him; that this Country ought to maintain an upright posture between all nations. But however objectionable this step might have been in Congs. the magninimity of our Ally in declining to obtrude his advice on our Ministers ought to have been a fresh motive, to their confidence and respect. Altho they deserve commendation in general for their services; in this respect they do not. He was [of the] opinion that the spirit of the treaty with France forbade the signing of the preliminary articles without her previous consent; and that the separate article ought to be disclosed; but as the merits of our Ministers entitled them to the mildest & most delicate mode in which it cd. be done, he wished the communication to be left to themselves as they wd. be the best judges of the explanation which ought to be made for the concealment; & their feelings wd. be less wounded than if it were made without their intervention. He observed that the separate article was not important in itself & became so only by the mysterious silence in which it was wrapt up. A candid and open declaration from our Ministers of the circumstances under which they acted & the necessity produced by them of pursuing the course marked out by the interest of their Country, wd. have been satisfactory to our ally, wd. have saved their own honor, and would have not endangered the objects for which they were negociating.

Mr. Higginson[8] contended that the facts stated by our Ministers justified the part they had taken.

Mr.[Madison] expressed his surprise at the attempts made to fix the blame of all our embarrassments on the instruction of June 15, 1781, when it appeared that no use had been made of the power given by it to the Ct. of France, that our Ministers had construed it in such a way as to leave them at full liberty; and that no one in Congs. pretended to blame them on that acct. For himself he was persuaded that their construction was just; the advice of France having been made a guide to them only in cases where the question respected the concessions of the U. S. to G. B. necessary & proper for obtaining peace & an acknowledgt. of Indepe.; not where it respected concessions to other powers & for other purposes. He reminded Congress of the change which had taken place in our affairs since that instruction was passed, and remarked the probability that many who were now perhaps loudest in disclaiming, would under the circumstances of that period have been the foremost to adopt it. He admitted that the change of circumstances had rendered it inapplicable, but thought an express repeal of it might at this crisis at least have a bad effect. The instructions he observed for disregarding which our Ministers had been blamed, and which if obeyed would have prevented the dilemma now felt, were those which required them to act in concert & in confidence with our ally: & these instructions he said had been repeatedly confirmed in every stage of the revolution by unanimous votes of Congress; Several of the gentlemen present who now justified our Ministers having concurred in them, and one of them, having penned two of the Acts, in one of which Congs. went farther than they had done in any preceding act; by declaring that they would not make peace untill the interests of our allies & friends as well as of the U. S. sd. be provided for.

As to the propriety of communicating to our Ally the separate article, he thought it resulted clearly from considerations both of national honor & national security. He said that Congress having repeatedly assured their ally that they would take no step in a negociation but in concert & in confidence with him, and havg. even published to the world solemn declarations to the same effect, would if they abetted this concealment of their Ministers be considered by all nations as devoid of all constancy & good faith; unless a breach of these assurances & declarations cd. be justified by an absolute necessity or some perfidy on the part of France; that it was manifest no such necessity could be pleaded, & as to perfidy on the part of France, nothing but suspicious & equivocal circumstances had been quoted in evidence of it & even in these it appeared that our Ministers were divided; that the embarrassmt. in which France was placed by the interfering claims of Spain & the U. S. must have been foreseen by our Ministers, and that the impartial public would expect that instead of co-operating with G. B. in taking advantage of this embarrassment, they ought to have made every allowance & given every facility to it consistent with a regard to the rights of their Constituents; that admitting every fact alledged by our Ministers to be true, it could by no means be inferred that the opposition made by France to our claims, was the effect of any hostile or ambitious designs agst. them, or of any other design than that of reconciling them with those of Spain; that the hostile aspect wch. the separate art. as well as the concealment of it bore to Spain, would be regarded by the impartial world as a dishonorable alliance with our enemies against the interests of our friends; that notwithstanding the disappoint-ments & even indignities which the U S. had recd from Spain it could neither be denied nor concealed that the former had derived many substantial advantages, from her taking part in the war & had even obtained some pecuniary aids; that the U. S. had made professions corresponding with these obligations; that they had testified the important light in which they considered the support resulting to their cause from the arms of Spain by the importunity with which they had courted her alliance, by the concessions with which they had offered to purchase it, and by the anxiety which they expressed at every appearance of her separate negotiations for a peace with the common Enemy.

That our national safety would be endangered by Congress making themselves a party to the concealment of the separate article, he thought could be questioned by no one. No definitive treaty of peace he observed had as yet taken place, the important articles between some of the belligerent parties had not even been adjusted, our insidious enemy was evidently labouring to sow dissensions among them, the incaution of our Ministers had but too much facilitated them between the U. S. and, France; a renewal of the war therefore in some form or other was still to be apprehended, & what would be our situation if France & Spain had no confidence in us: and what confidence could they have if we did not disclaim the policy which had been followed by our Minsters.

He took notice of the intimation given by the British Minister to Mr. Adams of an intended expedition from N. York agst. W. Florida, as a proof of the illicit confidence into which our Ministers had been drawn, & urged the indispensable duty of Congs. to communicate it to those concerned in it. He hoped that if a Come. sd. be appd. for wch. however he saw no necessity that this wd. be included in their report & that their report wd. be made with as little delay as possible.

In the event the Lettr. from Secy of F. A. with all the despatches & the several propositions which had been made, were committed to Mr. Wilson, Mr. Ghorum,[9] Mr. Rutlidge, Mr. Clarke, & Mr. Hamilton.

Smith, Letters of Delegates, v. 20, pp. 56-63.

[1] Wolcott, Oliver (1726-1797). Connecticut lawyer and political figure. Member, state council, 1774-1786. Member, Continental Congress, 1776-1778, 1780-1783. Militia general. Lieutenant governor, 1786-1796; governor, 1796-1797.

[2] Clark, Abraham (1726-1794). New Jersey political figure. Member, Continental Congress, 1776-1778, 1780-1783, and 1786-1788. Member, U.S. House of Representatives, 1791-1794.

[3] Mercer, John Francis (1759-1821). Jurist, soldier, political figure. Member, Continental Congress, 1783-1784, from Virginia. Member, Constitutional Convention, 1787, from Maryland. Member, U.S. House of Representatives, 1791-1794, from Maryland. Governor of Maryland, 1801-1803.

[4] Holten, Samuel (1738-1816). Massachusetts physician and political figure. Member, Continental Congress, 1778-1780, 1783-1785, and 1787. Opposed ratification of Federal Constitution. Member, U.S. House of Representatives, 1793-1795.

⁵ Osgood, Samuel (1748-1813). Massachusetts political figure. Member, Continental Congress, 1781-1784. Postmaster General of the United States, 1789-1791.

⁶ Peters, Richard, Jr. (1744-1828). Military officer, jurist. Secretary of the Continental Board of War, June 1776-June 1781. Member, Continental Congress, 1782-1783. Pennsylvania political figure. Judge, U.S. district court of Pennsylvania, 1792-1828.

⁷ Wilson, James (1742-1798). Pennsylvania jurist and political figure. Member, Continental Congress, 1775-1777, 1783, 1785-1786. Member, Constitutional Convention, 1787. Associate justice of the U.S. Supreme Court, 1789-1798.

⁸ Higginson, Stephen (1743-1828). Massachusetts merchant and seafarer. Member, Continental Congress, 1783. Prominent in putting down Shays' Rebellion.

⁹ Gorham, Nathaniel (1738-1796). Massachusetts merchant and land speculator. Member, Continental Congress in 1782-1783, 1786-1787 and 1789; president, June 1786 to February 1787. Member, Constitutional Convention, 1787.

Chevalier de la Luzerne to Comte de Vergennes

[Translation]

N⁰· 315   Philadelphia, 19 March 1783

My Lord

Congress has been occupied until today with the reading of the post it has received from Europe; the conditional Articles have been read with the most scrupulous attention, and Congress having expressed no opinion on the content of that Act, some delegates, and even some private citizens of this town, give it the interpretation that pleases them; moreover, public curiosity makes conjecture of articles and stipulations that do not exist; to forestall this trouble, Congress ordered that the Articles be communicated to the various legislatures; they were forthwith sent to the representatives of Pennsylvania, and the same day the gazettes made them known to the public. Some ill-disposed people and all those who belong to the pacific Sects that people Pennsylvania will not be negligent in saying that they are definitive and should be executed at once....

...Mr. Livingston has been ordered to send the various legislatures a copy of the definitive articles and at the same time to write them in a manner to forewarn the People against the impression that that act could make on them; I am persuaded that that Minister will carry out this task in the most proper manner. Although one is generally satisfied with the provisional articles, one is nevertheless surprised by the extreme negligence with which they were drawn up and by the equivocal judgment which some present. The preamble seems to allow the King of England the liberty of concluding a Treaty conforming to these articles, while the same liberty is not reserved to the United States. They seem to have availed themselves chiefly of a journal printed by a Traveller, for in fixing the boundaries from Lake

Superior to the sources of the Mississippi, one has no hope of obtaining a boundary so extensive in that area; One thinks that the Plenipotentiaries, by extending their possessions to the Lake of the Woods inclusively, are preparing for their posterity, in times still very distant, a communication with the Pacific Ocean. It is the opinion of many of the travellers that some rivers that have their mouths on the Sea have their source in the Vicinity of the *Lake of the Woods*. This boundary places the Americans in possession of a vast Commerce with the Savages and makes Forts *Oswego, Niagara, Detroit, and Michilimackinac* fall to their lot; four barriers that they were not able to force during this war, and which were the object of most of the expeditions undertaken in the earlier ones. This presumed acquisition of an immense territory has already had an influence on the Value of those lands that are closer to the Coasts; they have declined in price. A great number of French Establishments, hardly known but very flourishing, although without regular government, are going to be part of the United States. The Vermont country is comprised therein in its entirety. The Article what assigns the left bank of the Mississippi and the navigation of that river to the Americans has been considered as prejudging the question so long agitated between the Court of Madrid and them.

I have responded that the English could only cede their claims, and not a positive and present right, since they themselves do not have possession. The acquirers of confiscated goods are already deploying their batteries to impede the effect of the recommendations which Congress may make with regard to the refugees, and I think that it will not be difficult for them to render them nearly null; even the debts contracted before the war by the Americans towards the English will not easily be recovered by the latter.

The debtors object to payments that the war has ruined them, that their vessels and cargoes have been captured; that their plantations have been ravaged; and that it is unjust that the authors of these ravages and this damage are going to reclaim the debts without interruption, having placed their debtors beyond the condition of paying them.

All the New-York News, My Lord, indicates the Departure of various irregular Corps, which will greatly facilitate the final evacuation, if it is decided. There are five or six months for preparing to send into deserted parts of Nova Scotia the proscribed inhabitants who are without hope of remaining in this Continent after the peace. One responds that the German Troops who cannot be made to serve in the Islands by the terms of the Conventions are destined to reconquer East Florida or to lay siege to New Orleans. As for the English Troops, it appears that they will be sent to Jamaica. I cannot hope to get the Americans to raise obstacles to the evacuation of New York; I shall limit myself to asking them to prevent, as efficaciously as possible, the importation of Subsistence into the Place; this is an indirect means of delaying the evacuation; and the lack of Subsistence, when the English leave there, may cause them trouble in their subsequent operations. As for attacks being made on the Lakes, on Penobscot, or in any other country contiguous to the United States, the boundary decreed in the articles renders any enterprise of this nature fruitless from now on; the point towards which I shall direct my efforts will be the exclusion of English merchandise from this Continent, for England seems to wish to recover all the benefit of that Commerce. This exclusion is an indirect means of making them want peace. The abandonment which it has shown itself disposed to make of all its claims on the United States, the cessation of hostilities, and the evacuation of New-York will give the Court of London the disposition of considerable funds deposited in that place; but it flatters itself that this measure will help it recover the affection of its former subjects, and I hope I can raise obstacles to the renewal of those ties until the time of a general peace....

                                                 le chr de la luzerne

Received 18 May.

FFAA: Pol. Corr., U.S., v. 23, f. 119/330-344 (LC transcription).

Robert R. Livingston's Notes of a Meeting with Chevalier de la Luzerne

[Philadelphia] Office for foreign affairs, 22^d March 1783–
The Minister of France, waiting upon Mr Livingston at twelve o'clock, agreeable to appointment communicated to him a Letter from the Count de Vergennes dated the 19th of November.

This was wholly confined to matters of finance, & contained in substance nothing more than Congress have already seen in the Letter written by the Minister of France to Mr Morris – He then read to Mr Livingston a Letter of 25th November which related to the satisfaction the King his master had received in the testimony the United States had given of their friendship, in presenting the America. The substance of this Letter is contained in the note sent to Congress on the 20th instant.

The Minister also read to Mr Livingston a Letter of the 19th of December from the Count de Vergennes in which he informs him – that their treaty was not so forward as that of the Americans, Tho' if his Majesty had wished it, he could have Signed before the American plenipotentiaries as no essential difference existed between France & Great Britain. But that the king's delicacy induced him to wish that all his allies were first satisfied, & had accordingly resolved to continue the war whatever advantages might be offered him – If Great Britain should bear hard upon any of them That it still remained to reconcile the interests of Spain & those of Holland; That he had reason to believe with relation to the first that they would Soon be fully Settled – That the foundation was already laid, & that nothing now remained but to settle forms – That he was of opinion that it was for the interest of the United States to facilitate a connection with this power, which will be their neighbour – That it would become the wisdom of Congress to discover moderation with respect to them – That he is persuaded England will see with pleasure divisions introduced between the United States & the Court of Madrid, and that it is probable that they will even endeavour to animate them one against the other – That British Emissaries have been employed to inspire Spain with apprehensions as to the ambitious views of America – That they will now avail themselves of their intimacy with the American Ministers to render them suspicious of Spain, & even to excite their resentments against her Congress will defeat this design by removing the difficulties which now oppose themselves to a union with his Catholic Majesty – That the King wishes so much to see his allies enjoy a solid & durable peace, that in exciting the Americans on one side to discover a more conciliating spirit, he will spare nothing on the other to remove the difficulties which may be raised by the Court of Spain

That he apprehends delays and embarrassments from Holland – That the British Administration appear very unfavourable to them.

The Minister of France then read to Mr. Livingston another Letter from the Count de Vergennes, dated Dec^r· y^e 20$^{th·}$ 1782 which contained in substance: That peace was not yet concluded tho' it was anxiously desired by the King – That his Majesty's obligations to his allies had not yet permitted him to pronounce with certainty as to the termination of the war–

That expecting peace, prudence required that the allies should act as if the war was to continue – That Congress will judge of the manner in which they can most effectually contribute to distress the common enemy – That in the present state of things, it would not be prudent to invite the Americans to form any direct enterprise against the common enemy – That the provisional Articles would when executed at the general peace put into the hands of the Americans New York &c – That Congress could judge better than they could what part it would be expedient for them to take in the then state of things – That proposing nothing, they have every thing to their discretion That the Minister should however inform them that he could not yet determine whether they were at the eve of a peace, or if another campaign must be opened – That in the latter case those were two essential objects on which the Minister of France should impart to Congress the opinion of his Court & the desires of His Majesty.

That tho', if their Towns were evacuated the Americans could not take an active part, yet they can compel the enemy to wish for peace by excluding them from all connection with them, & prohibiting under very severe penalties the consumption or importation of British manufactures – That a considerable party among the British wish to form commercial connections with the United States – That when they shall be convinced that they can reap no benefit therefrom but by a solid definitive peace conformable to the Treaty agreed upon, they will become more tractable & conclude the definitive Treaty which will give force & vigor to the provisional Articles, & set the seal to the independence of America That it would also be proper to State to Congress the necessity of providing means to prevent the Sending provisions into New York, by which the British armaments are amply supplied with fresh provisions of every kind – That the King persuades himself that the Legislatures of the respective states will concur in measures for this salutary purpose, when they shall be informed of the injury occasioned to their Ally by the want of necessary precautions on this subject That these precautions will not be unnecessary if the Enemy are about to abandon New York, without which the Enemy will carry with them the means of Supplying the places to which they transport their Troops.

That he persuaded himself that Congress will perceive that they are indebted to the harmony that has subsisted between the king & them for the present happy state of their affairs, but that nothing being yet concluded, the present moment is precisely that in which it is of most importance to pursue the same System.

                                                      R R Livingston

25th March. 1783

NA: PCC, *item 79, v. 3, pp. 85-91 (DS); M247, reel 105.*

Benjamin Franklin to David Hartley

Dear Sir,   Passy, March 23, 1783

The general proclamations you wished for, suspending or rather putting an end to hostilities, are now published; so that your "heart is at rest," and mine with it. You may depend on my joining my hearty endeavors with yours, in "cultivating conciliatory principles between our two countries," and I may venture to assure you, that if your bill for a provisional establishment of the commerce had passed as at first proposed, a stipulation on our part in the definitive treaty to allow reciprocal and equal advantages and privileges to your subjects, would have been readily agreed to. With great and sincere esteem, I am ever, &c.   B. Franklin

WTF, *Franklin Memoirs, v. 4, p. 292.*

Robert R. Livingston to the American Peace Commissioners

No. 1 2plicate   Philadelphia 25ᵗʰ· March 1783
Gentlemen,

I am now to acknowledge the favor of your joint Letter by the *Washington,* together with a Copy of the preliminary Articles – Both were laid before Congress – The Articles have met with their warmest approbation, and have been generally seen by the People in the most favorable point of view.

The steadiness manifested in not treating without an express acknowledgment of your Independence previous to a Treaty, is approved; and it is not doubted but it accelerated that declaration. The Boundaries are as extensive as we have a right to expect, and we have nothing to complain of with respect to the Fisheries – My Sentiments as to English Debts you have in a former Letter, no honest Man could wish to withhold them. A little forbearance in British Creditors till People have recovered in part the losses sustained by the war will be necessary to render this Article palatable, and indeed to secure more effectually the Debt. The Article relative to the Loyalists is not quite so accurately expressed as I could wish it to have been. What, for instance, is intended by *real British subjects?* It is clear to me that it will operate nothing in their favor in any State in the Union; but as you made no secret of this to the British Commissioners, they will have nothing to charge you with, and indeed the whole Clause seems rather to have been inserted to appease the clamours of these poor Wretches, than to satisfy their wants. Britain would have discovered more candour & magnanimity in paying to them three months expence of the war establishment which would have been an ample compensation for all their losses, and left no germ of dissatisfaction to bud and blow, and ripen into discontents here – another Administration may think the non-compliance of the Legislatures with the Recommendations of Congress on this subject a sufficient cause for giving themselves and us new trouble – You however were perfectly right in agreeing to the Article – the folly was theirs, who did not either insist upon more, or give up this.

But, Gentlemen, tho' the issue of your Treaty has been successful, tho'

I am satisfied that we are much indebted to your firmness and perseverance, to your accurate knowledge of our situation, and of our wants for this success; yet I feel no little pain at the distrust manifested in the management of it, particularly in signing the Treaty without communicating it to the Court of Versailles till after the Signature, and in concealing the seperate Article from it even when signed. I have examined with the most minute attention all the reasons assigned in your several Letters to justify these Suspicions. I confess they do not appear to strike me so forcibly as they have done you, and it gives me pain that the Character of Candour and Fidelity to its Engagements, which should always characterize a great People should have been impeached by them thereby. The concealment was in my opinion absolutely unnecessary. For had the Court of France disapproved the terms you had made after they had been agreed upon, they could not have acted so absurdly as to counteract you at that late day, and thereby have put themselves in the power of an Enemy, who would certainly betray them, and perhaps justify you in making terms for yourselves.

The secret Article is no otherwise important than as it carries in it the Seeds of Enmity to the Court of Spain, and shews a marked preference for an open Enemy.

It would in my opinion have been much better to have fixed on the same Boundaries for West Florida into whatever hands it fell without shewing any preference, or rendering concealment necessary – since all the Arguments in favor of the Cession to England would then have operated with equal force, and nothing have been lost by it, for there can be no doubt, that whether Florida shall at the close of the War be ceded to England or to Spain, it will be ceded as *it was held* by Britain. The seperate Article is not I suppose by this time a Secret in Europe, it can hardly be considered as such in America. The Treaty was sent out to the General with this Article annexed by Sir Guy Carleton, without the smallest injunction of Secrecy – so that I dare say it has been pretty generally read at Head Quarters. Congress still conceal it here. I feel for the Embarrassment explanations on this subject must subject you to, when this Secret is known to your Allies.

...I make no Apology for the part I have taken in this business. I am satisfied you will readily acquit me for having discharged what I concieved my duty upon such a view of things as you presented to me. In declaring my Sentiments freely, I invite you to treat me with equal Candour in your Letters; and in sending original papers I guard against misrepresentations that might give you pain. Upon the whole I have the pleasure of assuring you, that the Services you have rendered your Country in bringing the business to a happy issue are very gratefully recieved by them, however we may differ in Sentiment about the mode of it doing it. I am sorry that the extreme negligence of the different States has prevented, and will probably long prevent my being able to send you a State of the injury done to real property, and the Number of Slaves destroyed and carried off by the British Troops and their Allies – Tho' no pains have been or shall be wanting on my part to urge them to it.

I have the honor to be, Gentlemen, with great Respect & Esteem, your most obedient hble Servant.   Robt. R. Livingston

MHS: *The Adams Papers, microfilm reel 360 (C)*.

James Madison's Notes of Debates

Wednesday March 26.[1783]

Communication was made thro' the Secy of F.A. by the Minister of France, as to the late negociation, from letters recd. by him from Ct. de Vergennes dated in Decr. last, & brought by the *Washington* packet. This communication shewed though delicately that France was displeased with our Ministers for signing prely. arts. separately; that she had laboured by recommending mutual concessions to compromise disputes between Spain & the U.S., and that she was apprehensive that G.B. would hereafter, as they already had, endeavor to sow discords between them. It signified that the "intimacy between our Ministers & those of G.B." furnished a handle for this purpose.

Besides the public communication to Congress other parts of Letters from the Ct. de Vergennes were privately communicated to the Presidt. of Congs. & to sundry members, expressing more particularly the dissatisfaction of the Ct. of F. at the conduct of our Ministers; and urging the necessity of establishing permanent revenues for paying our debts & supporting a national character. The substance of these private communications as taken on the 23 instant by the President is as follows: Finance.   "That the Ct. de Vergennes was alarmed at the extravagant demands of Docr. F. in behalf of the U.S.; that he was surprised at the same time that the inhabitants paid so little attention to doing something for themselves: If they could not be brought to give adequate funds for their defence during a dangerous war, it was not likely that so desireable an end could be accomplished when their fears were allayed by a general peace, that this reasoning affected the credit of the U. S. and no one could be found who would risque their money under such circumstances; that the King would be glad to know what funds were provided for the security and payment of the 10 Million borrowed by him in Holland; that the Count de Vergennes hardly dared to report in favor of the U. S. to the King & Council, as money was so scarce that it would be with the greatest difficulty that even a small part of the requisition could be complied with....

. . . . .

Negociations   "He complains of being treated with great
                    indelicacy by the American Commissrs. they
having signed the Treaty without any confidential communication — that had France treated America with the same indelicacy she might have signed her Treaty first as every thing between France & England was settled, but the King chose to keep faith with his allies, and therefore always refused to do any thing definitively, till all his allies were ready; that this conduct had delayed the definitive Treaty, England having considered herself as greatly strengthened by America; that Docr. Franklin waited on Ct. de Vergennes & acknowledged the indelicacy of their behavior & had prevailed on him to bury it in oblivion: that the English were endeavoring all in their power to sow seeds of discords between our Commissrs. & the Court of Spain, representing our claims to the Westward as extravagant and inadmissible — that it became Congress to be attentive to this business, & to prevent the ill effects that it might be attended with — that the King had informed the Court of Spain, that tho' he heartily wished that the U. S. might enjoy a cordial coalition with his Cat. Majesty, yet he should leave the whole affair entirely to the two States and not interfere otherwise than as by his counsel & advice when asked — that altho' the U. S. had not been so well treated by Spain as might have been expected, yet that his Majesty wished that America might reap the advantage of a beneficial Treaty with Spain — That as the peace was not yet certain, it became all the powers at war, to be ready for a vigorous campaign, and hoped Congs. would exert themselves to aid the common cause by some offensive operations against the Enemy — but if the British should evacuate the U. S. the King earnestly hoped Congs. would take the most decided measures to prevent any intercourse with the British, and particularly in the way of merchandize or supplying them with provisions, wch. would prove of the most dangerous tendency to the campaign in the W. Indies — that the British now had hopes of opening an extensive trade with America, tho' the war should continue, which if they should be disappointed in, might hasten the definitive Treaty, as it would raise a clamor among the people of England."

. . . . .

Smith, Letters of Delegates, *v. 20, pp. 112-113.*

Robert R. Livingston to Benjamin Franklin

N°· 26   Philadelphia 26ᵗʰ March 1783
Sir

I need hardly tell you that the intelligence brought by the *Washington* diffused general pleasure here – We had long been in suspense with respect to the negotiations, & had received no other lights on that subject than those the speech of his Britannic Majesty, & Mʳ Townshend's Letters threw upon it – These were by no means Sufficient to dissipate all our apprehensions – The terms you have obtained for us comprize most of the objects we wish for – I am sorry however that you found it necessary to act with reserve & to conceal your measures from the Court of France. I am fearful that you will not be able to produce such facts as will justify this Conduct to the world, or free us from the charge of ingratitude to a friend who has treated us not only justly but generously – But this is a disagreeable subject, & I refer you for my Sentiments and those of Congress to my Letter in answer to the joint Letters from our Ministers – I am sorry that the commercial Article is struck out – it would have been very important to us to have got footing at least in the British West Indies, as a means of compelling France to pursue her true interest & ours by opening her ports also to us.

We have just learned by a Vessel from Cadiz that the preliminary Articles for a general peace were signed the 20ᵗʰ The abstract of the Treaty sent me by the Marquis de la Fayette does the highest honor to the moderation & wisdom of France – Never has she terminated a war with more glory; & in gaining nothing but that trophy of victory Tobago, she has established a character which confirms her friends, disarms her enemies, & obtains a reputation that is of more value than any territorial acquisition she could make – ...

.   .   .   .   .

I have the honor to be Sir with great respect and esteem Your most obedient and most humble Servant   Robᵗ R Livingston

University of Pennsylvania, Van Pelt Library: Special Collections (LS).

Henry Laurens to John Adams

Dear Sir,   London 26ᵗʰ March 1783.

.   .   .   .   .

...If the proper Ministry shall succeed I have every reason to expect an honest and liberal proceeding with respect to us will immediately ensue. My opinion is founded upon the most explicit assurances from the very best hands – The Tories nicknamed Loyalists, are execrated by the Circle in which I sometimes move and yet they say they must "make some Provision for some of the poor Devils for National honor's sake" – I reply, make what provision you will, it would be impertinent in me to interfere in that Business, but you must not attempt to cram them down our throats, 'tis time you should know that America will not be taxed without her own consent. I have uniformly discouraged all attempts to trade with the United States until the Definitive Treaty shall be concluded, and the British Forces by Land & Sea effectually withdrawn. The Reasonings which I have urged particulary personating the State of New-York have been acknowledged invincible, but some of the Merchants are nevertheless mad, and will send their Ships – let them be mad. I trust the United States will be wise.

...your obedient and most humble servant,   Henry Laurens.

. . . . .

rec^d 9. of April at night.

MHS: *The Adams Papers, microfilm reel 360 (LS).*

Chevalier de la Luzerne to Comte de Vergennes

[Translation]

N° 317   Philadelphia, 26 March 1783
My Lord

. . . . .

The merchants have dispatched expresses in all directions: the various operations of Commerce establish it on a footing of peace. The Shock is violent for Merchants who had considerable Stores and whose merchandise was suddenly reduced to very moderate prices. They do not conceal the fact that Peace keenly distresses them; but the mass of good citizens has shown the greatest joy in it. There will be neither public nor private demonstrations until this event has been communicated in form to Congress and by it to the various Legislatures.

The former partisans of England appear to have replaced their attachment by the most violent hatred. They express themselves without discretion with regard to that Power and to His Britannic Majesty. Only a summary of the articles is available, but such as it is, it has given rise to the most well-founded elogies of His Majesty's Wisdom and moderation. This summary indicates that the line at which the thirty-second degree joins the thirty-third will form the boundary of the United States to the South. This boundary differs in consequence from that which was stipulated by the provisional articles, and causes the Americans to lose a degree from the Mississippi to the Apalachicola river; but this difference will not occasion the slightest murmur. The delegates from the South rejoice even in that, the two Floridas being ceded to Spain, they will no longer have the English as neighbors. The whole Congress evinced to me the most sincere joy at such a happy outcome of this great revolution, and I hear around me only expressions of gratitude for the benefactions which the United States have received from His Majesty. One single circumstance seemed to me to cause extreme pain to most of the members of that assembly, that is the signing of the provisional articles without your participation, My Lord. I should render Congress the justice of saying that it was then occupied with the manner of showing its displeasure to its Plenipotentiraries when the news of peace arrived. A Committee was to make its report the same day, and it intended to reprimand them severely concerning this neglect of their instructions; I was also told that Congress' discontent was so great that, for fear that I might lodge complaints on this subject, the Plenipotentiaries ran the risk of being recalled. The President told me that His Majesty's Silence only made more sensible to Congress the fault of its ministers, that it spread over the United States an appearance of bad faith and of ingratitude of which they were not culpable, that they had gloried in guarding the alliance from every stain and in presenting themselves to Europe through a complete confidence in their Ally and a strict observation of their engagements, and that the precipitancy of their ministers had robbed them of these advantages. When the Committee made its report, My Lord, it was discussed whether it was appropriate to make public resolutions; thus it was proposed to condemn the precipitancy of the American ministers, but it was observed that the news of peace having arrived before these resolutions were passed, they would have the air of being done after the event, they would be without any really useful purpose, and would only serve to give publicity to a fact that is not known. Some resolution will nevertheless be passed on this subject.

· · · · ·

Received 18 May.   le chr de la luzerne

FFAA: Pol. Corr., U.S., v. 23, f. 137/376-381 (LC transcription).

John Jay to Benjamin Vaughan

Dear Sir   Paris 28 March 1783
   Whence came the Idea that the moment a Minister loses a Question in

Parliament, he must be displaced? That Kings should adopt such a maxim is not very unnatural, but that a free Parliam^t should think an influential Dictator over *them* necessary to the Governm^t of the kingdom seems rather a new opinion. perhaps it arose gradually from the Practices of the Court, and the Decay of public Virtue during the last hundred Years.

So far as the Peace respects France and America, I am persuaded that it was wise in Britain to conclude it. The Cessions to France are not in my opinion extravagant, and the Termes settled with America by removing all Causes of future Variance, certainly lead to Conciliation and Friendship.

It appears to me that the Discussion of this Subject might have been more ample and Satisfactory. Why was not Parliament told of our offers as to Commerce and the mutual Navigation of the american Waters? The word *Reciprocity* would not then have been deemed so nugatory.

We have rec^d particular Instructions on the Business of Commerce, and Mr Fitzherbert has been informed of our Readiness to add to the provisional Treaty an article for opening and regulating the Trade between us on Principles as liberal and reciprocal as you please. What more can be said or done? Mr Pit's Bill[1] was a good one, a wise one, and one that will forever do Honor to the Extent and Policy of his Views, and to those of the administration under whose auspices it was formed. For my own part however I think that America need not be exceedingly anxious about the Matter; for it will be in our power to derive from a navigation act of our own, full as many advantages as we should lose by the Restrictions of your Laws.

The Objections drawn from your Treaties with Russia &c. appear to me weak, and have been answered – but why not give them similar Terms, on similar Conditions – They furnish you with raw materials chiefly, and you them with manufactures only – the Gain therefore must be yours – with Respect to Carriage and navigation, they stand in a very different Predicament from us.

As to the Tories who have rec^d Damage from us, why so much noise about *them* and so little said or thought of Whigs who have suffered ten times as much from those same Tories, not to mention the Desolations of an unjust and licentious War – We forget our sufferers ~~sufferings,~~ and even agree to recommend to favor a set of Men of whom very few would consider the having ~~of~~ their Deserts, in the light of a Blessing – How does Reciprocity stand in this account?

Some it seems think that New York should be retained as a Rod to drive us on in this business of the Tories – strange that the Idea of driving us should still be entertained. I pledge myself to you that should such a Design be adopted and become apparent the Refugees will get Nothing, and the progress of Reconciliation will be as slow as the warmest Gallican could wish.

I hear there is to be a Congress here – that is, that Britain and France have requested the two imperial Courts to send mediatorial Embassadors here for the Purpose of being Witnesses to the Execution of the definitive Treaties – a very important Errand no Doubt, and very complimentary to those Sovereigns. Is it probable that a Congress should be called for that poor, single simple purpose? Why your Court agreed to it, is hard to concieve –

I have written to my Countrymen that L. Shelburne's System respecting them appeared to me to be liberal and conciliatory, but that his Hesitations about *avowing* the Acknowledgm^t of our Independence discouraged extensive Confidence without further Facts – I always think it best to be candid and explicit – I hope we shall soon be in the full Possession of our Country and of Peace, and as we expect to have no further Cause of Quarrel with G. Britain, we can have no Inducement to wish or to do her ~~an~~ Injury. on the Contrary, we may become as sensible to her future good offices as we have been to her former evil ones. a little good natured wisdom often does more ~~good~~ in politics than much slippery Craft. by the former the French acquired the Esteem and Gratitude of America and by the latter their Minister is impairing it –

．．．．．

...Dear Sir Your sincere and aff^t Friend   John Jay

Columbia University Libraries: John Jay Papers (C).
^{1} *Not further identified.*

Henry Laurens to Benjamin Franklin

Sir,   London 4th April 1783.

．．．．．

Mr Pitt told the House of Commons, the Commissioners at Paris were well pleased with the outlines of the Provisional Bill, the one in London smiled at the Report, and said he could trust his Colleagues; it was pretty notorious that he had been on the reserve save now and then dropping a cautionary Hint to beware of the old Error of legislating for the United States. My Opinion had been often asked, but for the most obvious Reasons I declined an interference, At length I framed an American Bill for regulating Commerce with great Britain, and held it up to the proper

Characters as a Mirror, from that time, the 22^d March their own Bill which was to have been finished on the 23^d has slept with very little interruption. You will recieve a Copy of the American Bill enclosed which I presented as coming by an expeditious Courier in five Days.

Government as 'tis called is again restored to Great Britain an administration is formed – An Administration which presents me a prospect of doing Business with us immediately & effectually. I shall know more of this Matter before I Seal, meaning presently to pay Compliments of Congratulation.

The acquiescence of Spain in the Boundary lines is excellent, tho I believe very mortifying to some folks here, who I have every reason to believe harboured intentions of renewing the Quarrel.

I am as much at a loss as you are, to know what Employment can be found for Mediators, probably tis only "Talk," but if they come, we must meet them; our Ground is fair.

. . . . .

I have the Honor to be With the most affectionate Esteem & Regard Sir, your obedient and very humble Servant,

Henry Laurens.

PS. I have had a Conference with Mr Fox – reserving neither to Commit nor pledge myself for any opinion I might give Mr Fox discovered a disposition to proceed to business with us with Liberality & effect, I urged the necessity of concluding the definitive Treaty & withdrawing the British Forces from the United States without delay – In answer to supposed difficulties in obtaining Transport Ships, I proposed the Troops to be removed to Long or Staten Island – & added, that we might not insist upon Hostages for their peaceable behavior & final removal, tho' some powers would. that the State of New York ought immediately to be put in possession of the City & Port – Upon the whole the Secretary of State asked if he might Report, "that I believed there was a disposition & powers on the part of the American Commissioners to open an intercourse & Commerce of terms of reciprocity without delay – I assented as my belief & opinion – I hope for the honor of saluting you within ten days. – be pleased Sir to communicate this PS. to Mr Adams & Mr Jay. – HL

LC: *Benjamin Franklin Papers, microfilm reel 7* (ALS).

John Jay to Robert R. Livingston

Dup.   Paris 7 Ap^r· 1783
Dr Sir

After the Preliminaries had been settled and ratified, the spanish Embassador informed me that his Court was ready to receive me not only in Form but "*tres honnêtement.*" He *then* expected full Instructions relative to the proposed Treaty.

The Marq^t· de la Fayette in his Journey thro' Madrid manifested great Zeal to serve us there. A Copy of a Letter from him to the Minister will be sent you by another opportunity. Tho' I imagine he has already forwarded it.

On the 29 Ult. the spanish Embassador communicated to me the Desire of his Court that I would return to Madrid, and there compleat the Treaty; for that in their opinion it ought to be concluded either at *Madrid* or at *Philadelphia.* You will have this Communication at large in another Letter.

. . . . .

...Be assured of my Esteem & Regard. I am Dr Sir Your most ob^t· & h'ble Servt
                                                        John Jay

NA: PCC, *item 89, v. 2, p. 456 (ALS); M247, reel 117.*

Henry Laurens to Robert R. Livingston

No. 12   London 10th April 1783.
Sir,

I beg leave to refer you to the enclosed Duplicate of my last under the 5th· Instant. the "Bill for a provisional Establishment and Regulation of trade" &c seems to be dead indeed. M^r· Fox yesterday moved for reading the titles of the Act commonly called the prohibitory Act and the Act for granting Letters of Marque, which being read he moved for leave to bring in a Bill for repealing so much of the said Acts as prohibit Trade and intercourse with the United States of America, which was ordered accordingly.

My anxiety to see the final turn of this Business, has detained me in London three or four days longer than I had intended. I shall call upon M^r· Fox presently and if any thing new occurs, it shall be noticed in a Postcript. Immediately after sealing this Packet I shall begin my Journey to Paris. M^r· Hartley tells me he will follow upon the 15th· Inst.

I shall enclose a Copy of the Amendment called the third Bill for the information of Congress.

. . . . .

I have the honor to be, With great Regard & Esteem, Sir, your obedient and most humble servant,   Henry Laurens

PS. to April 10th. I have conversed with the right honorable Charles Fox Esqr from whom the body of Merchants by deputation had just retired. their Errand as I learned was on the Business of opening the Communication between Great Britain & the United States. there is a general & pressing eagerness to that Point. I repeated the propriety & necessity of withdrawing the Troops, & of restoring to the Citizens of New York their City & Port. Mr. Fox in return gave the strongest assurances that this should be done with the utmost dispatch, & promised to send to the Ministers at Paris a Copy of the orders to be given for that Purpose. he further informed me that he intended to introduce into the New Bill the Clause on page 4 in the Bill No 2. here enclosed to which I made only a general reply, that when their Plan was compleated, the American Ministers at Paris would give it due consideration & that on our part every Facility would also be given to reasonable Propositions, consistent with our Instructions. that in the present Moment I could not speak in positive terms to particular Points—

16th. April
Just arrived at Paris Mr. Hartley expected the 19th. from the latest words with that Gentleman which happened subsequently to closing the above I entertain apprehensions that his principal errand will be to open a Trade between the two Countries with assurances that the Troops shall be removed as speedily as possible & to take up the Definitive Treaty at more Leisure. I afforded him no encouragement to hope for success in the former point singly.

NA: PCC, Misc. Papers, Laurens Despatches (LS); M332, reel 2, ff. 97-99.

Charles James Fox to David Hartley

N° 4   St James's April 10th 1783
Sir
    As it is possible a Subject may be mentioned in the Course of your negotiation, altho it has, strictly speaking, no Connection with it, I mean the removal of the King's army from New York, I have it in Command from his Majesty to authorize you to give the strongest Assurances, that it

is his Majesty's royal intention to give orders that the said removal shall be effected with as much dispatch as the nature of so great & difficult a business will admitt. Indeed it w^d be as weak as it w^d be unjust in the American Commissioners to doubt the sincerity of Great Britain upon this occasion as she can have no possible interest in continuing the enormous expence attending the present Situation of his Majesty's Army

I am &c   C J Fox

Clements Library: Hartley Papers, v. 1, p. 10 (HC).

John Jay to Robert R. Livingston

Dear Sir   Paris 11 Ap. 1783

I wrote you a short Letter on the 7$^{th.}$ Inst. certain Intelligence has since arrived from England, that the Duke of Portland is first Lord of the Treasury, Mr Fox and L. North Secretaries of State, and Ld John Cavendish Chancellor of the Exchequer. It is also said that Lord Stormont is Presid$^{t.}$ of the Council and the Duke of Manchester Embassador to Versailles.[1] I hear that M$^{r.}$ David Hartley is appointed to conclude a definitive treaty with us.

The Emperor and Russia have been requested in their mediatorial Capacity, to send Plenipotentiaries to assist at the definitive Treaties. The true motives to this measure can as yet, be only conjectured: the ostensible one is, a mark of Respect to their offered but not accepted Mediation. The Proposition originated here. Their answer is expected daily. it is whispered that Russia consents.

Safe opportunities of sending important Letters from Hence to Madrid are so very rare, that I think your's for that Place had better be always conveyed directly to Cadiz or other ports in Spain, where some American of Confidence may be settled.

Numberless applications for Consulships continue to be made, & some will probably reach you. In my opinion Americans only should be employed to serve America. I early entertained this Opinion, & it has been almost daily gathering Strength since my arrival in Europe.

I have the honor to be Sir with great Esteem & Regard Your most ob$^{t.}$ & very hble Servt John Jay

NA: PCC, *item 89, v. 2, p. 460 (ALS); M247, reel 117.*
[1] *Manchester, George Montagu, Duke of (1737-1788). British political figure. Opposed*

Lord North's American policies and the American war. Lord chamberlain and privy councillor under Rockingham and Shelburne, April 1782-April 1783. Ambassador to France, April-December 1783.

James Madison's Notes of Debates

. . . . .

Saturday Apl. 12. [1783]

Mr. Rutlidge observed that as the instructions to Foreign Ministers now stood it was conceived they had no powers for commercial stipulations other than such as might be comprehended in a definitive Treaty of Peace with G. B. He said he did not pretend to commercial knowledge but thought it wd. be well for the U. S. to enter into commercial Treaties with all nations & particularly with G. B. He moved therefore that the Come. sd. be instructed to prepare a general report for that purpose.

. . . . .

Smith, Letters of Delegates, v. 20, pp. 177-178.

Francisco Rendón to Don José de Gálvez

No. 75   Philadelphia, 12 April 1783
Sir:

. . . . .

The Congress and every good American recognize joyfully how advantageous the present peace is to them, but nonetheless there have not been lacking in that body some disgruntled and malcontent spirits who are displeased by certain Articles of the Preliminaries, especially the Fifth, the content of which has aroused different discussions, and gives room for doubt that what is claimed in it in favour of British subjects will be put into effect, no matter how much the Congress recommends it to the several states, as that body has no other power than to recommend what is stipulated in the cited Article, and the states can refuse its recommendation without compromising the honour of the nation. That is undoubtedly what will happen, and therefore, in my opinion, no Royalist should expect to recover the assets he possessed on this continent before the war, and he can base his hopes only on the possibility that the King will indemnify him, in consideration of his having chosen the party which has led him to ruin only because of loyalty and love for King and Country.

One part of the cited Article stipulates that all debts contracted before the war between Americans and British subjects must be paid by American debtors, a point equally displeasing to the public, because a great many merchants who had contracted considerable debts to English merchants have been ruined, and certainly, if their creditors expect to recover their capital, it will be necessary for them not to try to do so by violent means or quickly, but to give time for public indignation on that point, which is intolerable to the merchants, to diminish, for only forbearance can enable them to recover those sums, which amount to four million pounds sterling, one-fourth of which the state of Virginia owes.

The Second Article of the provisional treaty, which fixes the boundaries of the United States, exceeded the hopes entertained by the Americans and the Congress. Having extended the confines of the new republic, Great Britain has tried to prevent wars which could be occasioned in the future by territorial disputes. My opinion, and that of many able persons of this city, is that certainly Florida has been ceded to Spain with the design of drawing Spanish boundaries close to those of the United States so that in the future they will be the origin of dissensions, which the English will undoubtedly find a way to foment between the two nations, so as to benefit from them. Most of the members of the Congress firmly believe that Great Britain's plan is to incite such disputes, and at the first favourable juncture, to take possession of His Catholic Majesty's islands or of other possessions in New Spain, to take out of this land reinforcements of men and provisions enough to put the English on a formidable footing and in a condition to make very profitable propositions to the Congress, such as that of putting it into possession of the Floridas or Louisiana, or able to take those provinces for themselves, permitting to the Americans free trade in them, which more than any other incentive might induce the Americans to accept.

The freedom of navigation on the Mississippi River which is granted to them by the cited treaty seems to be agreed upon with the same insidious designs, and there is not the slightest doubt that the English strategy is to sever the union of Spain and the United States, particularly recognizing how displeased these inhabitants have been during the war by the conduct of His Majesty in not having declared them independent as did France. Ignorant of the powerful motives that Sovereign had for not doing so, they have believed that he was treating them with disdain and indifference, because even though the services which His Majesty has rendered to these United States, directly and indirectly, have filled with due gratitude the wise and well-disposed hearts of those who have [been] in a position to know about them, those are not the individuals who make up the general public, who would have preferred that showy mark of friendship even though it would have been of no use to America.

I protest to Your Excellency that I have lost no opportune occasion to make the people comprehend that His Majesty has been and will constantly be a sincere, unfailing, and protective friend of the United States, with which I have had the satisfaction of convincing of this truth different persons of this government whose influence among the people is great, but with the sorrow of seeing that it is impossible to destroy a resentment which on many occasions appears to be universal and that only time can eradicate.

The Chevalier de la Luzerne also has at every opportunity constantly supported the same cause in favour of the interests of His Majesty with the same zeal as for his Sovereign, and Your Excellency can believe that recently he has employed all his influence to dispose the Congress toward proceeding with a moderated conduct toward the King, and toward calming that resentment among these people.

. . . . .

I believe it would not be amiss to give Your Excellency an idea of the springs which move the politics of the United States. I shall begin by saying that when the French Minister arrived on this continent he found America governed by a party which although in favour of independence was linked to England, and looked upon Spain and France with suspicious eyes as Powers inimical to all freedom, at the head of that party being the Adamses, the Lees, all the respected citizens of the four states of New England, Mr. Reed,[1] former governor of Pennsylvania, and several others whom I need not name. Mr. Arthur Lee, now chief of this party and a member of Congress, an extremely shrewd and reckless man, was the first to become suspicious of France in the negotiations of 1777 and 1778, and at this time those same individuals hope to link themselves more closely with Great Britain, Arthur Lee being the one who has always opposed the wise means which the Congress has thought of adopting for reestablishing their finances, and who recently has caused the annulment of the plan to levy an import tax of five percent on articles imported from abroad.

The members of the diplomatic corps designate these individuals by the name "the English party", and because their sinister views are known by the French Minister and his friends, the latter have succeeded in humiliating them by forming in the Congress a majority party favourable to the House of Bourbon, at whose head are found the most respected persons in America, such as General Washington, Doctor Franklin, Mr. Morris, Mr. Livingston, etc., and although the influence of the former has been diminished, they still prevail in the New England states, in Virginia, and in South Carolina....

. . . . .

The lack of stability of the present constitution of the United States does not constitute any basis for founding a public opinion. The most influential party is making an effort to affirm and augment the authority of Congress, but the opposing party is constantly defended; nonetheless it is believed that necessity will force the Americans to form a more secure and solid constitution, for on the other hand the nation will never possess the slightest credit. The principal objective would be to persuade the states to give the Congress power to impose the taxes which each one must pay, but every measure designed to accomplish that has been ineffectual.

・　・　・　・　・

LC: *Aileen Moore Topping Collection, 1783, pp. 36-43 (Typescript translation).*
  [1] *Reed, Joseph (1741-1785). Military officer, Pennsylvania political figure. Military secretary to General Washington, July 1775-June 1776. Adjutant general of the Continental Army, June 1776-January 1777. Member, Continental Congress, 1778, but did not attend, spending his time with the army. President, Supreme Executive Council of Pennsylvania, 1778-1781.*

John Adams to Robert R. Livingston

Sir,   Paris April 14th 1783.
    You may easily imagine our Anxiety to hear from America, when You know that We have no News to this Hour, either of your Reception of the News of Peace, nor of that of the Treaty with Holland, four Copies of which I put on board four different Vessels at Amsterdam in October.
    We have been in equal Uncertainty about the Turn, which Affairs might take in England – But by Letters from M[r.] Laurens We expect him every day, and M[r.] David Hartley with him, in order to compleat the definitive Treaty. It would have been more agreable to have finished with M[r] Oswald – But the present Ministry are so dissatisfied with what is past, as they say, though nobody believes them, that they chuse to change Hands.
    It will be proposed, I believe, to make a temporary Arrangement of commercial Matters, as our Powers are not competent to a durable one, if to any. Congress will no doubt soon send a Minister with full Powers, as the Treaty of Commerce with Great Britain is of great Importance, and our Affairs in that Country require an Overseer.
    It is confidently asserted in Letters from Holland, that M[r.] Markow,[1] the Minister Plenipotentiary from the Empress of Russia, has received from his Mistress a full Power to come to Paris to the Assistance of the Prince Baratinski at a Congress for a general Pacificiation. There is as yet no Answer recieved from the Emperor. If the two Imperial Courts accept of the Mediation, there will be a Congress – But I suppose it will relate chiefly to the Affairs of Holland, which are not yet arranged, and to the Liberty of

Neutral Navigation, which is their principal Point. I wish Success to that Republick in this Negociation, which will help to compose their interiour Disorders, which are alarming. I know not whether it will be insisted or expected, that We should join in the Congress, nor do I know what we have to do in it, unless it should be to settle that Point as far as it relates to Us. There is nothing in difference between Us and Great Britain, which We cannot adjust ourselves, without any Mediation.

A Spring Passage to America is so great an Object, that I should be very sorry to have the Negociations spun out to such a Length, as to oblige me to lose it, and I take it for granted I shall now recieve the Acceptance of my Resignation by the first Ships.

I have the honor to be, Sir, your most obedient & most humble Servant.

John Adams.

NA: PCC, item 84, v. 4, pp. 355-357 (LS); M247, reel 112.

¹ Morkov, Arkadii Ivanovich (1747-1827). Russian diplomat. Special envoy at The Hague, 1782-1783.

Congress' Ratification of the Preliminary Articles of Peace

[April 15, 1783]

The United States in Congress Assembled
To all who shall see these Presents Greeting

Whereas in and by our Commission dated at Philadelphia the fifteenth day of June in the Year of our Lord one thousand seven hundred and eighty one the Honorable John Adams, Benjamin Franklin, John Jay, Henry Laurens and Thomas Jefferson or a majority of them or of such of them as might assemble, or in case of the death, absence, indisposition or other impediment of the others any one of them were constituted & appointed our Ministers with full power and authority general special to confer, treat, agree and conclude with the Ambassadors, Commissioners and Plenipotentiaries of the Princes and States whom it might concern vested with equal powers relating to the establishment of Peace and whatsoever should be agreed and concluded for us and in our name to sign and thereupon make a Treaty or Treaties and to transact every thing that might be necessary for compleating, securing & strengthening the great work of pacification in as ample form and with the same effect as if we were personally present and acted therein, We promising at the same time in good faith that we would accept, ratify, fulfil and execute what should be agreed, concluded and signed by our said Ministers Plenipotentiary or a majority of them or of such of them as might assemble or in case of the death, absence, indisposition or other impediment of the others by any one of them. And whereas John Adams, Benjamin Franklin, John Jay and Henry Laurens four of our said Commissioners in pursuance of the powers aforesaid on the thirtieth day of November in the Year of Our Lord one thousand seven hundred and eighty two with Richard Oswald Esquire Commissioner of his Britannic Majesty for treating of Peace with the Commissioners of the United States of America in virtue of powers to him granted by his said Britannic Majesty, did conclude and sign on the part of the United States of America and the Crown of Great Britain Articles in the words following.–

(Here insert the Articles)

Now Know Ye that We the United States in Congress Assembled have ratified and confirmed and by these presents do ratify and confirm the said Articles and every part, article and clause thereof on our part concluded and signed as aforesaid.

In Testimony whereof, we have caused our Seal to be hereunto affixed – Witness His Excellency Elias Boudinot President, this fifteenth day of April one thousand seven hundred and eighty three, and of our Sovereignty and Independence the Seventh.

NA: PCC, item 25, v. 2, pp. 275-277 (LBkC); M247, reel 32.

Benjamin Franklin to Robert R. Livingston

Sir,   Passy, April 15 1783.
    You complain sometimes of not hearing from us. It is now near three Months since any of us have heard from America. I think our last Letters came with General de Rochambeau. There is now a Project under Consideration for establishing Monthly Packet Boats between France & New York, which I hope will be carried into Execution: Our Correspondence may then be more regular & frequent.
    I send herewith another Copy of the Treaty concluded with Sweden. I hope however that you will have received the former and that the Ratification is forwarded. The King, as the Ambassador informs me, is now employed in examining the Duties, payable in his Ports, with a View of lowering them in favour of America, and thereby encouraging and facilitating our mutual Commerce.
    M. De Walterstorff,[1] Chambellan du Roi de Dannemark, formerly Chief Justice of the Danish West India Islands, was last Year at Paris, where I had

some Acquaintance with him, and he is now returned hither. The News Papers have mentioned him as intended to be sent Minister from his Court to Congress, but he tells me no such Appointment has yet been made. He assures me however that the King has a strong Desire to have a Treaty of Friendship and Commerce with the United States; and he has communicated to me a Letter, which he received from M. Rosencrone[2] the Minister for Foreign Affairs, expressing that Disposition. I enclose a Copy of the Letter, and if the Congress shall approve of entering into such a Treaty with the King of Denmark, of which I have told M. de Walterstorff. I made no doubt, they will send to me or to whom else they shall think proper the necessary Powers and Instructions for that purpose. In the meantime to keep the Business in Train, I have sent to that Minister, for his Consideration, a Translation of the Plan (*mutatis mutandis*) which I received from Congress for a Treaty with Sweden, accompanied by a Letter, of which I likewise enclose a Copy. I think it would be well to make it one of the Instructions to whoever is commissioned for the Treaty, that he previously procure Satisfaction for the Prizes mentioned in my Letter.

The Definitive Treatys have met with great Delays, partly by the Tardiness of the Dutch, but principally by the Distractions in the Court of England, where for six or seven Weeks there was properly no Ministry nor any Business effected. – They have at last settled a Ministry, but of such a Composition as does not promise to be lasting. The Papers will inform you who they are. It is now said that M[r.] Oswald, who signed the Preliminaries, is not to return here, but that M[r.] David Hartley comes in his staid, to settle the Definitive. A Congress is also talked of, and that some Use is therein to be made of the Mediation formerly proposed of the Imperial Courts. M[r.] Hartley is an old Friend of mine and a strong Lover of Peace, so that I hope we shall not have much difficult Discussion with him; but I could have been content to have finished with M[r.] Oswald, whom we always found very reasonable. M[r.] Laurens having left Bath, mended in his Health, is daily expected at Paris, where Mess[rs] Jay & Adams still continue. M[r.] Jefferson is not yet arrived, nor the *Romulus* in which Ship I am told he was to have taken his Passage. I have been the more impatient of this Delay, from the Expectation given me of full Letters by him. It is extraordinary that we should be so long without any Arrivals from America in any Part of Europe. We have as yet heard nothing of the Reception of the Preliminary Articles in America, tho' it is now near five Months since they were signed. Barney, indeed did not get away from hence before the Middle of January, but Copies went by other Ships long before him: He waited some time for the Money he carried, and afterwards was detained by violent contrary Winds. He had a Passport from England and, I hope arrived safe; tho' we have been in some Pain for him, on account of a

Storm soon after he sail'd.

The English Merchants have shewn great Eagerness to reassume their Commerce with America: but apprehending that our Laws prohibiting that Commerce would not be repealed till England had set the Example by repealing theirs, the Number of Vessels they had loaded with Goods have been detained in Port while the Parliament have been debating on the Repealing Bill, which has been altered two or three times, and is not yet agreed upon. It was at first proposed to give us equal Privileges in Trade with their own Subjects, repealing thereby, with respect to us, so much of their Navigation Act as regards Foreign Nations. But that Plan seems to be laid aside; and what will finally be done in the Affair is yet uncertain.

There is not a Port in France, and few in Europe, from which I have not received several Applications of Persons desiring to be appointed Consuls for America. They generally offer to execute the Office for the honour of it, without Salary. I suppose the Congress will wait to see what Course the Commerce will take, and in what Places it will fix itself, in order to find where Consuls will be necessary, before any Appointments are made, and perhaps it will then be thought best to send some of our own People. If they are not allow'd to Trade there must be a great Expence for Salaries. If they may trade and are Americans, the Fortunes they make will mostly settle at last in our own Country. The Agreement I was to make here respecting Consuls, has not yet been concluded. The Article of Trading is important. I think it would be well to reconsider it.

. . . . .

There is a great Contest among the Ports which of them shall be of those to be declared *Free* for the American Trade. Many Applications are made to me to interest myself in the Behalf of all of them: But having no Instructions on that Head and thinking it a Matter more properly belonging to the Consul, I have done nothing in it.

. . . . .

With great Esteem, I have the honour to be, Sir, Your most obedient & most humble Servant.   B. Franklin

. . . . .

NA: PCC, item 82, v. 2, pp. 365-374 (ALS); M247, reel 108.

[1] *Walterstorff, Ernst Frederick, Baron. Danish diplomat. Minister to France, 1783-1785. Thereafter, assigned to the West Indies.*

[2] *Rosencrone, Marcus Gerhard, Baron. Danish Minister of Foreign Affairs.*

Alleyne Fitzherbert to Charles James Fox

N° 43)   Paris April 18th 1783.

Sir,

In my conference of Yesterday with M. de Vergennes I did not fail to acquaint him with Your Excellency's intentions of transmitting to me forthwith a draught of a definitive treaty, and with your earnest desire that that business might be concluded as speedily as possible. He expressed great satisfaction at this intelligence and told me that he conceived the Spanish Ambassadour would likewise have in readiness in a few days a project of a definitive treaty between G. Britain and his court, as he had applied to him (M de Vergennes) for a draught of the French project in order to model his own conformably to it in the articles which are to be the same in both.

Amongst the other reasons which M. de Vergennes assigned to me for his wishing to forward this business of the definitive Treaties, he mentioned the peculiar expediency of their being entirely arranged previously to the arrival of the Full Powers from the mediating Courts; which might otherwise, notwithstanding the firm determination of all the contracting powers not to suffer them to meddle in any respect whatsoever in the putting together the said treaties, and much less to introduce into them any fresh matter, make attempts towards such an interference, the eluding which might prove difficult and embarrassing. M. de Vergennes founds this suspicion upon some accounts he has received from Russia, and what seems to confirm it almost past a doubt is the appointment of M. Markoff, the Russian Minister at the Hague to repair to Paris in order to act as an adjoint to Prince Bariatinski in this particular transaction; for, however moderate the abilities of the latter may be, they are certainly fully equal to the discharging without the assistance of a colleague, the functions which will be assigned him upon this occasion, and which, according to our ideas, are to amount to nothing more than the going through the accustomed formalities, jointly with the Imperial Ambassadour, on the day of the signature of the definitive Treaties, On the other hand as M. de Markoff is a person of a very busy intriguing character, his appointment authorizes, as I have said, a strong suspicion that the Empress means to make something more of the mediation than a matter of mere form however it is after all not impossible but that M. de Markoff's friends, two of whom are it seems in high Office and Credit at St Petersburgh, may have procured him this commission as a mark of distinction, and as entitling him to a share in the presents usually distributed upon such occasions by the belligerent Powers.

Your Excellency will of course have seen in the correspondence that there are two Ministerial declarations agreed to be made on our part at the signature of the definitive Treaty, the one, for rendering *exclusive* the French Fishery on their share of the coast of Newfoundland; and the other, for the security of the Carib Inhabitants of S^t. Vincent's, and for confirming such grants of unsettled lands in that Island as were made whilst it was in the possession of France. On the other hand this Court is to give in a declaration which shall confirm in like manner such grants as may have been made at Sta Lucia whilst in the possession of G^t Britain. I likewise had it in instruction from Lord Grantham to deliver in a memorial to the French Court stating the ideas of ours as to several other points mentioned in the Treaty, a draught of which memorial his Lordship sent me, but with a power to new model it as, after sounding M. de Vergennes upon those parts, I might think most advisable. I have accordingly prepared such a paper, and take the Liberty of transmitting it herewith to Your Excellency for your consideration. If presented it will of course be answered by this Court, & I have reason to think that that answer will be in the main satisfactory.

In my conversations with M. de Vergennes upon the Definitive Treaty, I have always appeared to consider the conclusion of it as entirely independent of the conclusion of that with America, and I have seen no reason for supposing that his ideas upon that subject differed from mine. I learn't however with infinite satisfaction from Your Excellency's letter N° 47, that this last mentioned treaty as well as the re-establishment of a commercial intercourse with the United States were in a fair way of being speedily terminated having observed that our delays as to those points had begun to create much uneasiness and dissatisfaction in the minds of the Commissioners here. I must mention upon this subject that the French Ministers are on their parts indefatigable in their endeavours to draw to this Kingdom as large a share as possible of the American Commerce, and with that view they have set on foot a variety of enquiries as to the measures which it will be necessary for them to adopt to that end, either by erecting new manufactures of goods proper for the American market, or by altering those already subsisting, or finally by modifying their commercial laws, and their duties of export and import; and in all these researches I understand that they have received the most intire assistance from Dr Franklin. With regard to the other two American Commissioners whom I have had intercourse with, Messrs. Adams and Jay, they appear to the best of my discernment to feel a strong bias in favour of a close connection of commerce and Friendship with G. Britain in preference to one with France, and I am persuaded that Mr Hartley will meet with proofs of this disposition in the course of his dealings with them.

I have the honour to be with the greatest Respect, Sir, Your Excellency's most obedient and most humble Servant

                                                    Alleyne Fitz Herbert

R. 24$^{th:}$

PRO: FO 27/6, v. 561, f. 275 (LC transcription).

Charles James Fox to Benjamin Franklin

Sir,   St James's, April 19,1783.

Although it is unnecessary for me to introduce to your acquaintance a gentleman so well know to you as Mr. Hartley, who will have the honour of delivering to you this letter, yet it may be proper for me to inform you, that he has the full and entire confidence of his majesty's ministers upon the subject of his mission.

Permit me, sir, to take this opportunity of assuring you, how happy I should esteem myself, if it were to prove my lot to be the instrument of completing a real and substantial reconciliation between two countries, formed by nature to be in a state of friendship one with the other, and thereby to put the finishing hand to a building, in laying the first stone of which I may fairly boast that I had some share.

                                                    C. J. Fox

William Temple Franklin et. al., editors, Memoirs of Benjamin Franklin (New York: H. W. Derby, 1861), v. 1., p. 527.

Chevalier de la Luzerne to Comte de Vergennes

[Translation]

N$^{o.}$ 323   Philadelphia, 19 April 1783

My Lord

Congress has long hesitated to ratify the conditional articles, not that they have not completely satisfied that assembly, but because there has not been any mention of this ratification by the plenipotentiaries, and because Congress feared doing a superfluous thing; but they have considered that it could be useful, and that in no case could it be prejudicial, and in consequence it will be sent to the Plenipotentiaries for them to make use of or to suppress, according to the circumstances. It was resolved at the same time that this act will remain a secret....Yesterday a Committee was chosen to consider the powers it would be proper to give to a grand committee of the thirteen United States in the event that Congress thinks it appropriate to adjourn after the final conclusion of the peace. It is thought, in fact, that as soon as the definitive treaty arrives here and is ratified, that adjournment will take place, and during the recess there will be, according to the Articles of Confederation, a grand committee composed of one delegate from each State, the powers of which are indicated by those Articles, but not clearly defined. We must expect that this administration will be even more feeble than was that of Congress; Mr. Morris, and also Mr. Livingston, seem still of a mind to submit their resignations immediately.[1]

. . . . .

The Governor of the State of New York has sent to New York one of the members of the legislature to sound out General Carleton upon various points important to the inhabitants of that State, and among others the date of the evacuation. The English General has said nothing concerning that article; but nothing indicates an imminent evacuation, and everything on the contrary augurs that it will take place only after the definitive Treaty and its ratification. The banished refugees &c. are setting in motion all means imaginable to excite the pity of the Americans, but that sentiment will not go so far as to extract from them the restitution of what they believe legitimately belongs to them, and I do not suppose that these unfortunates are saving any remains of the fortunes they formerly enjoyed.

Whereas His Majesty follows, with regard to the Americans, a System of moderation and generosity, it appears that the Court of London occupies itself with the means of creating there a party against us, of promoting its influence there at our expense, and of alarming the Eastern States concerning our views with regard to the Fisheries. Some of the Plenipotentiaries have sent word of divers circumstances which are kept extremely secret, but according to which they know from the English Ministers or Commissioners that we were formally opposed to having the Americans admitted to the fisheries in so extensive a manner as they were by the provisional Articles. It is insinuated that Mr. Franklin secretly favored our opposition, and that the advantageous terms which the Americans have obtained are due to the firmness of two of the Negotiators and to the generosity of England, resolved to regain, by every kind of means, the affection of the United States, despite all the efforts we make to prevent it.

. . . . .

I do not know what system the Minister that England will send here will adopt in respect to us, but it was well demonstrated that, at the time of the negotiations, the Court of London's design was to create itself a party in America by dint of intrigues and by plotting against us.

If the thing becomes necessary, nothing will be easier than to raise another party capable of counterbalancing the English cabals, but perhaps it will seem more advantageous to you to maintain ourselves here only by the natural and pressing interest which the United States have in remaining attached to His Majesty. Our policy is of a nature to be acknowledged, and I think we can no better make the secret maneuvers of the English miscarry, and perhaps recall them to a System more noble and more conformable to the present State of peace, than by following the very course which your instructions have prescribed for me up to this day.

I am with respect, My Lord, Your very humble and very obedient servant le chr de la Luzerne
Received 15 June.

FFAA: Pol. Corr., U.S., v. 24, f. 60/111-117 (LC transcription).

[1] Article IX of the Articles of Confederation specified that a Committee of the States be appointed to transact the business of the United States while Congress was in recess. By an Act of May 29, 1784, Congress defined the powers of this Committee (see JCC, v. 27, pp. 474-477). Eleven members, one from each State present when the above Act was passed, made up the first such Committee, which sat in Annapolis from June 4 to August 13, 1784, with Virginia delegate Samuel Hardy as chairman.

John Jay to Robert R. Livingston

Dear Sir Paris 22 Apr. 1783

. . . . .

Mr Hartley is not yet arrived, but is daily expected. I am told (by Mr Laurens) he will propose that the <**> People of the two Countries shall have all the Rights of Citizens in each. The Instruction of Congress on this important Point is much to be desired – for my Part I think a temporary Stipulation of that Sort might be expedient. They mean to Court us, and in my opinion we should avoid being either too forward or too coy – I have no faith in any court in Europe, but it would be improper to discover that Sentiment. There are circumstances which induce me to believe that Spain is turning her Eyes to England for a more intimate Connection – They are the only two European Powers which have continental possessions on our side of the water; and Spain I think wishes for a League between them for mutual Security against us. Perhaps this Consideration should lead us to regard the present Fervour of british Advances with the less Indifference.

On looking over one of my former Letters, containing my Propositions to Spain, I find that I had omitted to explain the Reason of the one for a

Guarantee of our Possessions in North America. That we should *so*
Guarantee the Spanish Possessions as to *fight* for them, was as distant from
my Design, as it could be from that of Congress. A common Guarantee
means nothing more than a *Quit Claim*, to which we certainly could have
no objection. When more is intended provisional and express Stipulations
become necessary to any such I never would have consented. A Confidant
of the Minister (and I believe by his Direction) had assured me, that unless
a Guarantee was offered any other Propositions would not induce the
Minister to negociate for a Treaty – to meet that objection I made the
offer in the general Terms you have seen. I had no Doubt but that the
Minister was acquainted with my Instructions, and I considered this
Objection as a Pretext for Delay. My opinion as to a certain proposed
Cession was known, and uses not advantageous to us or to me had been
made of it. It appeared to me adviseable that the Intention of Spain with
Respect to us should have a full Tryal, and such an one as would convince
Congress that I was entirely guided by their Views and Wishes – I therefore
endeavoured so to frame those Propositions as that they should not afford
the Minister any Pretence for refusing to commence the negociation. The
Issue you are acquainted with –

I hope nothing will be done by the States for the Tories, until the british
Forces shall be withdrawn, and then I confess it would in my opinion be for
our Honor to forgive all except the perfidious and the cruel.

. . . . .

I am Dear Sir with great Esteem & Regard Your most ob.ᵗ Serv.ᵗᵗ

. . . . .   John Jay

NA: PCC, *item 89, v. 2, pp. 464-466 (ALS); M247, reel 117.*

Francis Dana to Robert R. Livingston

(N.ᵒ 25)   St. Petersbourg April 14ᵗʰ 1783. O.S. [April 25, 1783]
Sir

In consequence of my second Letter to the Vice Chancellor[1] of the 10ᵗʰ·
Inst. he sent me a verbal message with his compliments on the 12ᵗʰ· in the
morning, and desired to see me at 4°. Clock in the afternoon. I waited
upon him accordingly, and had a conference with him upon the Subject of
my Mission. He began it by saying that he had received the Letters I had
done him the honour to write him. That Her Majesty[2] had been invited by
the Courts of Versailles, Madrid, & London, to mediate in conjunction
with the Emperor, at the conclusion of the Definitive Treaty of Peace
between them; that till those affairs were arranged and the Definitive

Treaty signed, Her Majesty cou'd not consistent with Her character of
Mediator, receive a Minister from America without the consent of those
Powers. That the Treaty of America was provisional only and depended
upon those arrangements, and tho' there was no doubt but they would take
place, and that the Definitive Treaty wou'd be concluded, yet till that was
done Her Majesty cou'd not consider me in my character as the Minister
of America – Here he made a long pause as waiting for an answer but
knowing that the whole had not yet come out, I make no attempts to reply
– He then added, That he supposed my Letter of Credence bore date
before the acknowledgment of the Independence of America by the King
of Great Britain, and asked me if that was not the fact. I told him it must
necessarily be so, as a sufficient time had not since elapsed to receive one
from America. He then said, That when the above arrangements shou'd be
completed, if I shou'd produce new Letters of Credence bearing date since
the King of Great Britain had acknowledged the Independence of America,
Her Majesty wou'd be very willing to receive me as the Minister of America, but that it wou'd be incompatible with that exact Neutrality which Her
Majesty had hitherto observed to do it before – That it wou'd be irregular
also for Her Majesty to admit a Minister from a Power whose Letter of
Credence bore date before She had acknowledged the Independence of that
Power – That besides no Minister had been received from America at the
Court of Great Britain yet, and that I must be sensible it wou'd not be
consistent for Her Majesty to receive one from America before the King of
Great Britain had done it – Here he stopped again, & knowing that he had
gone through his whole subject, which comprises these simple matters only,
viz.

1$^{st.}$ That Her Majesty cou'd not consistent with the character of a
Mediator as above receive a Minister from the United States till the
conclusion of the Definitive Treaty between France Spain & Great Britain.

2$^{dly.}$ That She cou'd not do it even then consistent with the Laws of
Neutrality while his Letter of Credence bore date prior to the acknowledgment of their Independence by the King of Great Britain.

3$^{dly.}$ That She cou'd not do it regularly while his Letter of Credence bore
date before She Herself had acknowledged their Independence.

4$^{thly.}$ That She cou'd not do it consistently before a Minister had been
received from the United States in Great Britain.

I desired him to favour me with a Note containing the substance of this
answer, as it was of great Importance, and much in affairs of this sort
depended upon the very expressions, that with the fairest intentions I might
misrepresent some parts of it through forgetfulness; and that I wou'd deliver
him my observations upon it in writing for consideration when the exact
state of the matter wou'd be known. Finding as I had expected that he

declined this, I began my reply with a preface of this sort – The answer which your Excellency has given me on the part of her Imp. Majesty is wholly unexpected not only to myself but to the United States. I cannot take upon me therefore to say any thing upon it from Instructions. I beg you wou'd be pleased to consider whatever I may say as my private sentiments; whether they will accord with those of my Sovereign, I am not certain. At this great distance I must use my best discretion in all such extraordinary cases. I have no design to oppose myself to Her Majesty's pleasure whatever that may be, but only to make some observations upon the Answer that if they are of any weight they may be taken into Consideration, as I have no doubt they will be. I wou'd beg to improve this occasion to express the high respect which the United States entertain for Her Imperial Majesty, and their sincere desire to cultivate her friendship, that they considered Her as one of the first Sovereigns of the World; and in a manner the great Legislator of Nations by her System of Neutrality w$^{ch.}$ they had early highly applauded, and had made the principles of it the invariable rules of their conduct during the War. That animated with sentiments of this kind, they wished to give some strong proofs of a distinguished attention and consideration for Her Majesty's Person and Government. With this view they had early named a Minister to reside near Her as a compliment to the Sovereign who presided over the Neutral Confederation with so much glory, that he might improve the earliest occasion to display his Character which the Course of Events shou'd afford. From these dispositions they were naturally led to expect as they had intended that Her Imp Majesty wou'd be the first of the Neutral Powers which shou'd receive a Minister from them – That as to the objections which had been made to my present reception I begged leave to observe that the present Mediation differed from the former one which had been tendered by their Imperial Majesties in two essential respects, that that was tendered during the continuance of Hostilities, and that there was a proposition in it which materially concerned the United States, but in this there was no question relative to them, that their negotiations with Great Britain had been conducted apart from those of the other belligerent Powers and were brought to a happy conclusion. I here took up all the facts stated in my second Letter to him of the 10$^{th.}$ inst. and enlarged upon them. I added to them the Bill pending before the House of Commons in the beginning of March for regulating a commercial intercourse between Great Britain &c., and America as between States in fact and absolutely Independent, that the Bill itself recited that the King had < ***** > concluded a peace with them and expressly declared the Vessels of their Citizens shou'd be admitted into all the ports of Great Britain as the < *** > Vessels of other Independent States – that all were agreed to consider them as such. From these matters I drew the same conclusion as is mentioned in that letter. This closed my observations upon the 1ˢᵗ article. As to the second I went over the reasons contained in my Letter of the 11ᵗʰ inst. to you urging strongly the four first and passing gently over the rest. Upon the third it was to be observed – That < ****** > the mode of expression before Her Majesty had acknowledged the Independence of America, seemed to lead beside the matter. That there was no question in < *** > the acknowledgment of that Independence. The only question was whether Her Majesty wou'd receive a Minister from the United States who now presents himself. The United States do not ask the acknowledgment of their Independence, nor have they a wish or do they claim a right to impose their Minister upon any Sovereign. Every Sovereign will judge whether it is for the Interest of his Empire to receive the Minister of another, and may do this without deciding upon the perfect Rights of that other. This is rather what I wou'd have said, than what I did say upon that point. I cou'd not get the Idea wholly in as he several times prevented me by returning upon the matter he had before spoken upon, as if he saw what I intended to say and wished to avoid it. The fourth & last point was chiefly answered by the arguments used upon the first. I did not forget however the distance of the Countries as the only probable cause of that delay – Thus Sir, I have given you as clear an idea of a conference which rests wholly upon my memory, and which had continued an hour wanting a few minutes as I am able to do. Other arguments occurred to me in the Time which might have been urged but I was apprehensive of obtruding too much upon the patience of the Vice Chancellor, whose view it must be considered was rather to communicate the answer than to discuss the points of it. An important question arises out of this state of things. [What] remains to be done on the part of the United States? It belongs to me only to answer what I propose to do further myself, which is to draw up a Memorial containing this answer with such observations upon it as shall occur to me tending to shew the futility of the objections which have been made to my immediate reception, and to send it to the Vice Chancellor. To such a measure I am advised on a good part. If this answer should be persisted in, I believe it may be truly said that the honour of the United States will not suffer by it in the estimation of any other Sovereign of the World. It is so different from the line of conduct which some of the Powers who are Members of the Neutral Confederation have already adopted respecting the United States, as for Example Portugal, Denmark & Sweden, and that which it has been intimated the Emperor was ready to adopt: (Of which Mʳ· Adams received an account through Mʳ· Wᵐ· Lee, and which he immediately transmitted to me, and probably to Congress also) that if I mistake not the effect of it < ***** > ~~It will be seen to be~~ subversive of the very principles upon which it is pretended to be established, and so revolting in its nature that it is utterly impossible the United States cou'd ever comply with it. I plainly told the Vice Chancellor that for myself I cou'd never make the proposition respecting my letters of Credence: and that if I shou'd, I had no expectation they wou'd ever adopt it, and therefore my waiting here the Length of time which would be necessary for me to learn the pleasure of Congress upon it, seemed to be useless. I cannot in any case quit this Country till towards the end of May because there is no getting out of it before by Land or Water – I still hope it will not be thought I have precipitated the measure at a time when, if ever it cou'd be, the Course of events had prepared the way for it: and when it shall be considered too that the first objection arises from a matter which took place since. As to the others they are of so strange a nature that they cou'd not have been expected by anyone, and which no time can do away. I am under a necessity of closing this letter without adding any thing which may attempt to account of this very unexpected Conduct on the part of Her Imperial Majesty otherwise I shall lose the post of the Day.

I have the honour to be with much respect & esteem Sir Your most obedient humble Servant   Fra Dana
Read Aug. 6: 1783

NA: PCC, item 89, v. 2, pp. 739-742 (LS); M247, reel 117.
  ¹ Osterman, Ivan Andreevich, Count (1715-1811). Russian political figure. Vice-Chancellor, 1775-1796.
  ² Catherine II, The Empress of Russia.

David Hartley to Charles James Fox

N° 1   Paris April 27. 1783.
Sir

I have the honour to inform you that I arrived on the 24ᵗʰ instant and that on the 25ᵗʰ I had seperate conferences with all the Ministers of the united States of America who all expressed to me the utmost readiness not only to enter into some convention for the purpose of opening the ports of Great Britain and those of the united states for mutual intercourse of trade and Commerce but likewise to conclude the definitive treaty of peace with all possible dispatch.

On the day following (viz the 26ᵗʰ) I thought it would be proper to wait upon the Minister for foreign affairs at Versailles to inform him of my having had the honour of being appointed his Britannick Majesty's Minister Plenipotentiary to treat with the Ministers Plenipotentiary of the united states of America residing at Paris. Accordingly I waited upon Monsʳ Le

Comte de Vergennes accompanied by Dr Franklin. After the first civilities of introduction upon my being announced to him in a public character he said addressing himself to Dr Franklin *Il faut que nous finissions tous ensemble.*[1] He seemed to me to be immediately sensible that the expression was too hasty. He then added that it would doubtless be proper that we should all of us arrange discuss and prepare our seperate concerns seperately but that we must all conclude together. The remainder of our interview was very short and only upon matters of civility such as inviting me to be presented at Court and so forth.

.　.　.　.　.

As far as I can judge of the disposition of the American Ministers at the first view, they seem to me to be well disposed to concur with any fair and equitable propositions, which may be for the reciprocal of their own country, and of Great Britain, & consistent with their engagements.

I am the more confirmed in this opinion by the very quick expression of Jealousy wch broke from Mons$^{r\cdot}$ de Vergennes upon the first moment of my entering his apartment accompanied by D$^{r\cdot}$ Franklin. Mons$^{r\cdot}$ de Vergennes knows very well that the American Ministers do no think themelves bound to withhold their signatures to the definitive treaty with Great Britain until France may give any formal consent to such a measure on their part. However the American Ministers may very probably be induced to comply with any honorable ceremonial required by the Court of France; provided that such compliance shall not at any time hereafter prevent their entering into the immediate enjoyment of the substantial advantages of peace whenever they shall have arranged the remaining substantial points of negotiation with Great Britain.

I shall probably have the honour of writing to you again soon.

I am Sir with the greatest respect and consideration Your most obedient humble Servant　　　　　　　　　　　　　　　　　　　D Hartley
R 4th May

PRO: FO 4/2, v. 1, f. 41 (LC transcription).
[1] It is necessary that we all finish together.

Charles James Fox to the Duke of Manchester

N° 51　　　　　　　　　　　　　　　St James's, 30$^{th\cdot}$ April 1783
My Lord

I am commanded by his Majesty to transmit to your Grace a copy of Mr Fitz-herbert's dispatch N° 43 together with a copy of a Project of a Memorial inclosed therein.

The reasons which Mons.ʳ de Vergennes assigns for hastening the signature of the definitive treaty are very cogent, and there is but too much reason to think that his apprehensions of the mediating Powers intending to embarrass the treaty with new & foreign matter are well founded. Mons.ʳ de Marcoff's appointment was certainly made with this View, & I have reason to think that it will be proposed to introduce the new maritime Code into the Body of the Treaty. I really think that it is no more the interest of your Court than it is of this to admit such an embarrassment into a treaty to which they wish a speedy Conclusion; and I cannot help flattering myself that the french Ministry will act in concert with your Grace for the purpose of evading if possible, but at all events warding off such a Proposition. The unreasonableness of introducing into a treaty of Peace matters entirely foreign, at the instance of two Powers who have been no wise instrumental in bringing about the Peace in question is so glaring that it needs no comment nor can your Grace want topics of argument to resist it. Your only difficulty will consist in doing it in such a manner as not to displease or to displease as little as possible the two Imperial Courts, and particularly that of Petersburgh. It may be proper to take this opportunity of apprizing your Grace that Mons.ʳ· de Marcoff, though charged in this instance, as we suspect, with a commission of no friendly nature, has yet the character of being a very fair Man, and much disposed to G. Britain. If our accounts do not deceive us, Her I.M. has no subject who is more convinced than this Minister of the true interest of Russia lying in a close & intimate connection with this country. The ideas of his Colleague at Paris are said to be very different. You will therefore naturally converse with Mons.ʳ de Marcoff as confidentially as the nature of your business will allow, and if your Grace upon further acquaintance should find his dispositions to be such as I have represented them, you will undoubtedly cultivate & improve them to the utmost. An intimate connection, or if possible a strict alliance with the Northern maritime Powers of Europe is the obvious and rational system for this country, and more especially as long as the Bourbon Family Compact continues to be in force.

With respect to the two ministerial declarations alluded to in Mʳ Fitzherbert's Dispatch, as his Majesty's Royal word was in some degree pledged to them at the time of signing the Preliminaries they must undoubtedly be renewed at present if the Court of Versailles think such a renewal necessary, and I shall accordingly transmit to your Grace herewith inclosed two declarations to the effect desired. I confess with regard to that relating to the Fishery the words do not go to my understanding so far as Mʳ Fitzherbert seems to think, or as the word *exclusive* which he uses, and which is not in the declaration, seems to intimate.

In regard to the Project of a Memorial transmitted to me by Mr Fitzherbert I am commanded by H. M. to signify to your Grace and to Mr Fitzherbert his entire approbation of it, and it is H. M's pleasure that it should be presented with such alterations only as the difference between the definitive Treaty and the Preliminaries with respect to the articles attended to, may make necessary: It may not be amiss to take this opportunity of acquainting your Grace that it is the Kings wish in general (and the projects for the definitive Treaties have been drawn up in that spirit) that as many points as possible should be cleared up in the treaty itself, and that as little as possible should be left to be explained by declarations or memorials or loose papers of any kind. Your Grace will therefore keep this rule in your mind and adhere to it in every case where it can be applied without risquing much delay or other inconvenience.

If either the French Ministry or the American Commissioners should seem to have it at heart that the treaties should be signed at the same time; Mr Hartley is so fully informed of His Majesty's sentiments upon this subject that no delay is likely to arise from this circumstance.

If the commercial agreement with the United States should be more difficult than I am inclined to hope it is, there is no reason why the definitive treaty should not nevertheless be signed. The commercial Arrangement may be just as well considered after the signature of the treaty as before.

I am, my Lord, &c.

Charles J. Fox

PRO: FO 27/6, v. 561, f. 331 (LC transcription).

Observations on the Principles of Conduct to Maintain towards the Americans

[Translation]

[Paris] 30 April 1783

1$^{st.}$ The stability of Treaties between nations under absolute Monarchs depends ultimately on the will of those Monarchs or on that of their respective Ministers. The people are nothing. Influence can only be procured in such a Nation through the Channel of a Minister or of persons who are connected with him.

2$^{nd.}$ The stability or duration of a Treaty with a Republican State, in which the persons endowed with the supreme authority are frequently changed, and in which the power derived from the People passes, ascending progressivly, through many hands before residing in the supreme Authority,

will depend on the justness of the measures taken to *influence* the People —
by this means the Magistrates and all the persons in place will be elected
under this influence.

3rd. When there are differences in language, manners, Religion, and
Government between these Nations, it is very necessary to devote all one's
attention to this influence on the People in the Republic; but when that
People maintains its old prejudices against the other Nation, it becomes of
the greatest importance, especially when another Nation of the same
language, the same manners, Religion, and Government &c. endeavors to
break the connection between that Republic and its Allies, and when this
Nation has an infinity of friends and of partisans in all parts of the
Republic.

4th. The antipathy of the Americans for the French before the war is well
known. The war has dissipated it among the Whigs, but it has heightened
it among the Tories. On the other hand, although the Whigs may have
shaken it off, their natural prejudices for all that is English, except the
Government, always remain. Now prejudices of this sort continually exert
an imperceptible influence on the spirit of even solid and thinking men,
and dominate the mass of the People everywhere these prejudices prevail
and are carefully fed by a rival Nation. It will not be difficult to excite a
Republic to measures not only injurious to its Allies, but even contrary to
its own interests.

5th. In order to understand this last article better, it will be appropriate to
pay attention to several principal circumstances in America — In order to
prevent at the outset any confusion of ideas, I mean by Loyalists, the
Americans who joined the King's troops; by Tories, all persons devoted to
England, but who from prudence stayed in America — I will then observe
that there are in each state a number of Tories — Half the People in
Pennsylvania are *Quakers*, and almost all the *Quakers* are Tories — There
are several very rich men among the Tories. It is they who did not want
continental money, by which the Whigs have suffered so much — Influence
goes with riches — One can therefore regard the Tories as a powerful and
numerous Body in favor of England. Aroused by their *disappointments*,
which they attribute to France, and impelled by their prejudices and their
attachment to England, they will henceforth be Enemies of France, and as
in a political matter interested Enemies are generally more active than
disinterested Friends, they can be regarded as an active troop of English
Emissaries constantly working to cause old prejudices to revive, to propagate
sentiments and support measures destructive of the connection between
France and America, not in the chimerical intention of restoring America
to English domination, but in the view of uniting it with England by a
social Contract, on equal terms and for mutual advantage.

6th. Emigration from England to America will probably be more considerable than that from any other Kingdom of Europe. But whatever cause brings these Emigrants to America, they will also bring there their attachment to their Customs, their Religion &c and their prejudices against France. These Peoples, possessing the same language as the Americans, will be in a position to support and propagate political opinions, and should be regarded with reason as continual reinforcements of the English cause.

I will say nothing at this moment of the influence of Commerce, but I will do so afterwards. I am limiting myself today to political considerations.

7th. Let us now see what interest France will have naturally in this country. For the superiority of the political interest of both Nations will depend on the Superiority of the Wisdom and of the activity of its Councils – It is thought that France will have for herself in America the Whig party, that the People that she has aided will support the connection and the Treaties existing between the two Countries, and that having the power in its hands, it will take care to guard it – Has she some other *natural* interest; I do not recall any.

8th. That France has laid a noble and sure foundation in the spirit of the Whigs in order to maintain an influence in America is certainly true; provided, however, that she take appropriate measures to increase and support that influence. If she does not take such measures in time, a little reflection on the history of Nations and on the nature of humanity will indicate easily what will ensue. The gratitude of a Nation rarely lasts longer than the moment in which it receives a benefit. But is it to be supposed that the Tories and the other partisans of England will not propagate the opinion that France, in assisting America, serves herself, and consequently that America has no obligation to her? Is it not possible that some Whigs have thought the same thing, and may for this reason think themselves released from all obligation and gratitude, however happy they may otherwise be in *the connection?*

9th. During the war, the Whigs in general neglected their private interest in order to occupy themselves with the public interest. They have suffered greatly through the continental money, and are generally much impoverished. Their influence, which was supported by the violence of the times and encountered no opposition on the part of the disguised friends of England, will diminish. The rich will again resume their weight and influence. Moreover, the Whigs in general, who have not suffered at all from the Enemy, now that peace and independence are established, will gradually recant from their prejudices against the English. As for those who have really been pillaged or otherwise injured by the English, they will doubtless moderate their enmity; these last, moreover, if we consider the movements of the English Troops, should be in very small number relative to those who have not suffered at all.

10$^{th.}$ In admitting the people into the legislatures, the Councils, and the other public places, is it to be supposed that a year or two from now, the bulk of the Whigs will inquire or even think of inquiring, before voting, whether the candidate is attached to the Alliance with France or if he is disposed in favor of England, provided that he be otherwise an honest man? However, is it to be supposed on the other hand that the English Emissaries and the Tories will be so indifferent and so inactive? Is it not rather to be thought that they will bend all their efforts to put in all the public places persons of their own principles and views, in order to be able to obtain a decided influence in the Councils of America, for the purpose of detaching her from France in order to attach her to England?

11$^{th.}$ It seems thereby that England's natural Interest in America will always be increasing, while that of France will always be diminishing, if appropriate measures are not taken to sustain it.

Before proceding to the Suggestion of the political measures necessary to sustain the true spirit of the Alliance between France and America, it will not be useless to make some observations on Commerce, for both that which is conducted today between France and America and that which was conducted in times past between England and America affects the natural interest of both Nations in this Country.

N$^{o.}$ 12. In speaking of Commerce, it is a maxim that a merchant will buy where he can buy at the best price and will sell where he can sell more dear. This maxim is without doubt very true; however, by taking it in a too limited sense, it has led to great errors in subjects of Commerce.

13$^{th.}$ A merchant will not be *influenced* by the simple consideration of buying cheaply and selling dear. For it is certain that he can buy dear in one place and yet gain more there than if he had bought cheaply in another. In determining to which of two places to send a Cargo and to take another from in return, between the cheapness or the dearness of the purchase and of the sale, he will consider all the other circumstances that can definitively affect the profits of his speculation, such as a prompt expedition or a long detention of the Ship; the advances on the Cargo, the credit on the merchandise purchased, the Port duties, the facility, the advantages and disadvantages of making remittances, &c. &c.

14– The American who wants to trade in France only finds subjects of discouragment in the difficulty of forming connections in a Country where he is unknown, of establishing or of obtaining credit, and of doing business with people whose language he does not understand. Supposing that these difficulties are removed, Commerce itself feels the discomfort that all commerce that is not reduced to a regular System must feel. For, that existing, some time must pass before Commerce between France and

America becomes considerable and extensive.

15– Commerce between Great Britain and America before the War had been reduced to a regular System. I do not mean the System of the Government's Regulations, but the System that prevailed among the Traders. The extended connections of Commerce have already existed for a long time among Great Britain, Ireland, and America; and although they may have been suspended and, in many circumstances, even ruptured by the War, by the destruction of the Tory-American Merchants, new Correspondents will take their place, and the connections will revive.

16[th.] There is therefore reason to think that Commerce between France and America will not make, if it remains on the present basis, great progress in a short time, while Commerce among Great Britain, Ireland, and America will revive promptly and will become widespread and considerable.

17[th.] But connections of Commerce in a free Country where all the Magistrates and the other interested persons in the Administration of public affairs are elective, have a great influence on public proceedings. A Merchant in place who has connections of Commerce with England is naturally inclined by interest, by the force of habit, and the connection to be indulgent for it in things that do not affect the happiness of America. A Merchant in place who has connections of Commerce with France will be opposed naturally, by the same reasons, to anything accorded to England that may be incompatible with the Alliance between France and America.

18[th.] These intimate and extensive connections of Commerce between England and America will tend to destroy the animosity that the war has occasioned, and to encourage the natural dispositions and prejudices of the people in favor of all that is English. For is it not reasonable to think that the Whigs, who have suffered by the devastations of the English, would sacrifice their animosity to their interest if they found more facilities and advantages in entering into Commerce with England?

19[th.] Another consequence, but of a greater importance, will result from connections of Commerce betweeen England and America. The Sailors of the two Countries, having the same manners, the same habits, and the same language, will mix, will blend together, and will form only one People. In case of a future war between England and the House of Bourbon, the consequence to fear from this circumstance and from the position of these sailors under the influence of Merchants who would be linked with England does not need to be mentioned in order to have it given the most serious attention.

20[th.] It seems that it is not only the Sentiment of the Court of London, but also that of the English Nation to do everything to regain the affections of America, to facilitate Commerce, to encourage connections, and finally to attach America to England by good offices and a common interest. If they persist in this System, they will increase and accelerate indubitably all the circumstances of which mention was made in favor of English interest and influence in America.

FFAA: Pol. Corr., U.S., v. 24, f. 79/143-148 (LC transcription).

Robert R. Livingston to Francis Dana

N° 9   Philadelphia 1ˢᵗ· May 1783
Sir,

...This is principally designed to cover the enclosed Resolution directing your return unless you should have commenced a Treaty of Commerce – But upon examining your instructions, you will find that the embarrassment you speak of with respect to the money to be paid upon signing the Treaty cannot exist under your present Powers – With respect to the neutral Confederacy it is a Treaty which is now of little consequence to us, and since we were not admitted to it during the War – we ought not to pay for admission upon a peace, besides that it can no more be considered as a Treaty with her Imperial Majesty, than it is a Treaty with all the other Neutral Powers, whose Ministers may with equal propriety demand the perquisites you speak of – Therefore let it be understood, that as the United States or their Servants are above receiving Perquisites or Presents, so they have not the presumption to assume such a superiority over those with whom they treat as to offer them. –

With respect to a Commercial Treaty none can be signed by you, your powers only extend to "communicate with her Imperial Majesty's Ministers on the subject of a Treaty" &c but not to sign it, so that you will find no difficulty upon the subject you speak of, if you should, I am persuaded that it is the wish of Congress rather to postpone any Treaty with Russia, than to buy one at this day.

. . . . .

I am Sir, with Respect your most obedᵗ· humble Servᵗ

Robᵗ· R Livingston

NA: PCC, item 118, pp. 418-420 (LBkC); M247, reel 139.

John Adams to Francis Dana

Sir   Paris May 1. 1783

. . . . .

M^n Hartley is to finish with Us, & We are making Preparations but cannot Say how much Time will be necessary. They talk of a Congress and Mediation and Mr Markoff is coming, but there is no need of either on our Affairs, yet We may be invited to join it, and who would not be ambitious of Sitting in Such a Council of the Caelestials? or rather who would not be curious to "know by what Sort of Men this World is governed!"

With great Esteem I have the Honour to be &c.

J. Adams

MHS: *Dana Family Papers (ALS).*

David Hartley to the Duke of Portland

Private   Paris May 1 1783
My Dear Duke

Everything goes on as well as possible, better & better every day. There is now confidence & the fruit of it. At first they were a little timorous & jealous – we will trust to your friends the D of P and C F in any thing but are you sure that the enemy will not outnumber you and return? I say I am. < ************ > As long as you see me here, you are safe, and according to your own arguments, if you fear any return, you sh^d make use of the time present. They were alarmed at my Commission not being actually made out. – They c^d not treat till they saw it. – and was I sure that some secret ill intention had not unknown to the D of P & C F delayed it, under false pretexts. We had a good battle about this. I told them, that they were very unreasonable, and that the[y] were taking, or rather suborning, every possible chance against their own objects. And before our College broke up, I softened down some apprehensions, & raised others, & they agreed to think matters over in the interim of my waiting for my commission. After our formal conference we talked matters over as we met convivially & in a friendly manner, and they considered the whole amongst themselves, & the very next day they told me that they w^d make me a proposition, wch I might transmitt at the time of writing for my commission.

When D F and I waited upon the Minister he came out to us to bring us into his interior cabinet. I saw instantly a scowl on the brow. The first ceremonies of politeness were scarcely over before he turned shortly to D F and said *Mais Monsr· Il faut que nous finissions tous ensemble.*[1] I will not positively swear to the words *Mais Mons'*: tho I am reasonably sure of them & absolutely sure of the spirit of them. We have conned these words over & over, to no bad effect for *us*. Confidence being come & the troops *being actually* under orders for withdrawing, the Amer^n Ministers are in no mood to be dictated to by France. Amnesty conciliation & the union of *common interests* with their old friends are their topics. The war being at an end and all remnants of Jealousy removed with the troops, each particular man feels the importance to himself of being the instrument of public good in future between two great nations. They seem studious to express that they have no more remains of animosity to a certain personage than to any of their late fellow subjects. The whole is to be laid aside alltogether. They were much pleased when I told them that C F had actually made the proposal to the King for the exchange of Ministers, & that it was consented to. And probably some of them at least look forward to partake personally in those situations. A very conciliatory as well as honorable ambition if (as I suppose) they entertain it. They wish to do their business effectually without alarming the french court needlessly. They will break no obligation nor will they be dictated to. I have hinted this to C F. Support me explicitly in the orders for removing the troops. *Finis corona bit opus.*[2]

Yours ever most sincerely   D H

Clements Library: Hartley Papers, v. 1, pp. 33-34 (HC).

[1] *It is necessary that we all finish together.*

[2] *Literally, the end crowns the work.*

Robert R. Livingston to the President of Congress

Sir   Philadelphia 5th May 1783

On the 7th. of August last Congress were pleased to instruct M^r. Jay to forbear making any overtures to the court of Spain, or to enter into any stipulations in consequence of such overtures as he had already made, & in case any propositions had been made to him by the court of Madrid to decline acceeding to them till he should have transmitted them to Congress &^c As these instructions were dictated by the affected delays of the court of Spain, by their want of attention to M^r. Jay, & above all by their boundless & unreasonable claims, perhaps Congress may deem it proper upon the present apparent change in their system to remove the obstructions to a treaty which the above directions impose and to leave M^r. Jay to the free exercise of the powers he first rec^d.

I mention this matter without giving any opinion thereon, merely upon the presumption that Congress may not advert to the resolution I mention

– I have the honor to be Sir with great respect Your Excellencys Most Obd^t Hum: Servt·   R R Livingston Read same day.

NA: PCC, item 79, v. 3, pp. 203-205 (ALS); M247, reel 105.

Dr. Samuel Cooper to Benjamin Franklin

[Extract]

Boston May 5th· 1782 [1783]

– There is a party among us disposed to avail themselves of every Incident, and of all personal Resentments to weaken and divide our public Counsels, and injure the Alliance. Regard to the general Good, as well as private, and the most constant Friendship oblige me to state Things as they are. It is then confidently whispered among us that Letters have been received from Paris, both in this State and at Philadelphia, which mention, that the Court of France was at Bottom against our obtaining the Fishery and Territory in that great Extent in which both are secured to us by the Treaty. That our Minister at that Court favoured, or did not oppose this Design against us; and that it was entirely owing to the Firmness, Sagacity & Disinterestedness of M. Adams, with whom M^r· Jay united, that we have obtained those important advantages. I have not Seen any of these Letters, and am considered I suppose as too much attach'd to the Alliance with France, and that American Minister who so happily negociated it, to be trusted with such a Communication: they are said, however to come from some of our Plenipotentiaries at Paris, and particularly from M^r· Adams, a Gentleman against whom I never was prejudiced, having had a long Friendship and Respect for him. It is certain some of his particular Friends here have believed and propagated these Reports, as they say, upon the best Authority. It has also been Said from the same Quarter that the Court of France secretly traversed M. A.'^{s} Views in Holland, for obtaining of the United Provinces an acknowledgment of our Independence; and that the Same Part has been acted in Spain and Russia. All these Things are incredible to me, and tho' they make some Impression at present, Truth is great and will prevail. Care I hope will be taken both at Congress and in Europe, as far as public Prudence will permit, to State, as soon as may be, these Matters in a Just Light, and to prevent the public Mischiefs as well as private Injuries that may arise from Misrepresentations in Matters of such Moment. For myself, I stand and Speak and act upon my old Ground, our Independence supported and deffended by the Friendship of France; and they who take the fairest and most effectual Measures to cultivate this

Friendship, are most my Friends as being friendly to my Country. If through Ingratitude, Folly, Personal Piques, or Treachery, we loose so generous, so powerful, so faithful, and in our present Situation so natural a Friend as the King of France, we fall, and deservedly, into Contempt and Ruin. But I am presuaded there is good Sense and Virtue enough in the Government and People of America to prevent so shameful a Fall.

M^r. Adams wrote to Congress on Decr 3. resigning his Employments in Europe; but has intimated in a Subsequent Letter his Readiness to continue them, should he be appointed Minister to the Court of London: Congress has not fill'd the Department that we have heard. –

FFAA: Pol. Corr., U.S., v. 24, f. 105/183-184 (C), microfilm reel 14.

Memorandum of a Conference between George Washington and Sir Guy Carleton

N°. 4.   [May 6, 1783]

The Substance of the Conference between General Washington & Sir Guy Carleton at an Interview at Orange-Town. 6th May 1783.

General Washington opened the Conference by observing that he heretofore had transmitted to Sir Guy Carleton the Resolutions of Congress of the 15th. Ult°, that he conceived a personal Conference would be the most speedy and satisfactory mode of discussing and settling the Business; and that therefore he had requested the Interview. That the Resolutions of Congress related to three distinct matters, namely, the setting at Liberty the Prisoners; the receiving Possession of the Posts occuped by the British Troops, and the obtaining the Delivery of all Negroes and other Property of the Inhabitants of these States in the Possession of the Forces or Subjects of, or Adherents to his Britannic Majesty. That with respect to the Liberation of the Prisoners, he had as far as the Business rested with him, put it in Train by meeting & conferring with the secretary at War, and concerting with him the proper measures for collecting the Prisoners and forwarding them to New York. And that it was to be optional with Sir Guy, whether the Prisoners should march by Land, or whether he would send Transports to convey them by Water. And that the Secretary at War, was to communicate with Sir Guy Carleton on the Subject and obtain his Determination. With respect to the other two matters which were the object of the Resolutions, General Washington requested the Sentiments of General Carleton

Sir Guy then observed, that his Expectations of a Peace had been such as that he had anticipated the Event by very early commencing his Preparations to withdraw the British Troops from this Country. And that every Preparation which his Situation & Circumstances would permit was still continued. That an additional Number of Transports, and which were expected, were necessary to remove the Troops and Stores. And as it was impossible to ascertain the Time when the Transports would arrive, their Passages depending on the Casualties of the Seas, he was therefore unable to fix a determinate Period within which the British Forces would be withdrawn from the City of New York. But that it was his Desire to exceed even our own Wishes in this Respect, and that he was using every Measure in his Power to effect with all possible Dispatch an Evacuation of that and every other Post within the United States, occupied by the British Troops under his Direction. That he considered as included in the Preparations for the final Departure of the British Troops, the previously sending away those Persons, who supposed that, from the Part they had taken in the present War, it would be most eligible for them to leave the Country. And that upwards of 6,000 Persons of this Character had embarked and sailed – and that in this Embarkation a Number of Negroes were comprised.

General Washington thereupon expressed his Surprize, that after what appeared to him an express Stipulation to the contrary in the Treaty, Negroes the Property of the Inhabitants of these States, should be sent off. To which Sir Guy Carleton replied, that he wished to be considered as giving no construction of the Treaty, That by *Property* in the Treaty might only be intended Property at the Time, the Negroes were sent off. That there was a difference in the mode of Expression in the Treaty – Archives, Papers &c. were to be *restored*, Negroes and other Property were only not to be destroyed or *carried away*. But he principally insisted that he conceived it could not have been the Intention of the British Government by the Treaty of Peace, to reduce themselves to the Necessity of violating their Faith to the Negroes, who came into the British Lines under the Proclamation of his Predecessors in Command. That he forbore to express his Sentiments on the Propriety of those Proclamations, but that delivering up the Negroes to their former Masters would be delivering them up some possibly to Execution, and others to severe Punishments, which in his Opinion would be a dishonorable Violation of the public Faith, pledged to the Negroes in the Proclamation. That if the sending off the Negroes should hereafter be declared an Infraction of the Treaty, Compensation must be made by the Crown of Great Britain to the owners. That he had taken Measures to provide for this, by directing a Register to be kept of all the Negroes who were sent off, specifying the Name, Age & occupation of the Person, and the Name & Place of Residence of his former master. General Washington again observed, that he conceived this Conduct on the part of general Carleton, a Departure from both the Letter and the Spirit of the articles of Peace, and particularly mentioned a Difficulty that would arise in compensating the Proprietors of Negroes admitting this Infraction of the Treaty could be satisfied by such Compensation, as Sir Guy Carleton had alluded to, as it was impossible to ascertain the Value of the Slaves from any Fact or Circumstance which may appear in the Register. The Value of a Slave consisting chiefly in his Industry & Sobriety. And General Washington mentioned a further Difficulty which would attend Identifying the Slave, supposing him to have changed his own Name or to have given in a wrong Name of his Master. In answer to which Sir Guy Carleton said, that as the Negroe was free and secured against his Master, he would have no Inducement to conceal either his own true Name or that of his Master. Sir Guy Carleton then observed that by the Treaty he was not held to deliver up any Property, but was only restricted from carrying it away – And therefore admitting the Interpretation of the Treaty as given by General Washington to be just, he was notwithstanding pursuing a Measure which would operate most for the Security of the Proprietors. For if the Negroes were left to themselves without Care or Control from him, Numbers of them would very probably go off, and not return to the Parts of the Country from whence they came, or clandestinely get on board the Transports in such Manner as would not be in his power to prevent in either of which Cases an inevitable Loss would ensue to the Proprietors. But as the Business was now conducted they had at least a Chance for Compensation. Sir Guy concluded the Conversation on this Subject by saying that he imagined, that the Mode of compensating, as well as the Accounts and other Points, with respect to which there was no Provision made in the Treaty, must be adjusted by Commissioners to be hereafter appointed by the two Nations.

The Subject of withdrawing the British Troops from the Territories of the United States was again resumed, and Sir Guy Carleton declared his willingness, at a short Day to be agreed on between him and General Washington, to evacuate all his Posts in West Chester County, and to issue his orders that the British Troops should not on any Pretence, pass the River which separates that County from the Island of New York. but with Respect to a Relinguishment of any part of long Island, he was apprehensive it would be attended with Difficulties & Inconveniences, particularly he was fearful it would tend to favour Desertions from the British Army, and therefore he would give no determinate Answer, but he was disposed immediately to abandon Penobscot if General Washington should choose it, 'tho he said that would necessarily retard the Evacuation of New York, as there were not a competent Number of Transports to convey the Troops and Stores from both Places at the same time.

The Conference lasted some Hours, but as much passed which both generals expressed their Wishes might be considered as desultory Conversation, it is not recapitulated in the above Narrative, which contains only the Substance of the Conference as far as it related to the Points intended to be discussed and settled at the Interview.

We having been present at the Conference do certify the above to be true.   George Clinton[1]

Jn⁰ M Scott.[2]

Egbert Benson[3]

Jon⁴ Trumbull Junr.[4]

PRO: FO 4/2, v. 1, f. 286 (LC transcription).

[1] Clinton, George (1739-1812). New york political figure, military officer. Member, Continental Congress, 1775-1776. Appointed brigadier general of militia, 1776, and of Continental Army, 1777. Governor of New York, 1777-1795, 1801-1804. Vice President of the United States, 1805-1812.

[2] Scott, John Morin (1730-1784). New York lawyer and political figure. Member, Continental Congress, 1780, 1782. New York secretary of state, 1778-1784.

[3] Benson, Egbert (1746-1833). New York lawyer, political figure and jurist. Member, Continental Congress, 1781-1784. Member, Embarkation Commission, 1783. Delegate, Annapolis Convention, 1786.

[4] Trumbull, Jonathan, Jr. (1740-1809). Connecticut political figure. Paymaster, New York department, Continental Army, 1775-1778. Comptroller of the U.S. Treasury, 1778-1779. Secretary and aide-de-camp to General George Washington, 1781-1783. Member, United States House of Representatives, 1789-1794; Speaker, 1791-1792. Member, United States Senate, 1795-1796. Lieutenant Governor of Connecticut, 1796-1797; Governor, 1797-1809.

George Washington to Sir Guy Carleton

Sir   Orange Town 6th. May 1783

In my Letter of the 21st April, I enclosed to your Excellency a Copy of a Resolution of Congress of the 15th instructing me in three Points which appeared necessary for carrying into Effect the Terms of the Treaty between Great Britain and the United States of America, and informed you that such Part as rested on my Decision and which regarded the Release of Prisoners, had been determined, and was then ordered to be carried into Execution. Upon the other two Points, as they respected the receiving Possession of the Posts in Occupation of the british Troops, and the carrying away any Negroes or other Property of the american Inhabitants, and both being within your Controul, I had the Honor to propose a personal Interview with your Excellency, that the Subjects might be freely discussed, and that Measures might be agreed upon for carrying into Execution those Points of the 7th Article of Treaty agreeable to their true Intent and Spirit. –

Having been favored this Day with a personal Conference, – I have now, to prevent misapprehension or misconstruction and that I may be enabled to fulfil my Instructions with Fidelity and with Candor, the Honor to propose, agreeable to our Conversation, that your Excellency will be pleased to give me in writing, Information of what Means are adopting on your Part for carrying into Execution, that Point of the Treaty which regards the Evacuation of the Posts now in Possession of the british Troops, and under your Excellency's Command; and also at what Time it is probable those Posts or any of them may be relinquished, and the Fleets and Armies of his britannic Majesty withdrawn.

Respecting the other Point of Discussion, in Addition to what I mentioned in my Communication of the 21st Ult., I took Occasion in our Conference to inform your Excellency, that in Consequence of your Letter of the 14th of April to R. R. Livingston Esqr, Congress had been pleased to make a further Reference to me of that Letter, and had directed me to take such Measures as should be found necessary for carrying into Effect, the several Matters mentioned by you therein: In the Course of our Conversation on this Point, I was surprized to hear you mention, that an Embarkation had already taken Place, in which a large Number of Negroes had been carried away. Whether this Conduct is consonant to, or how far it may be deemed an Infraction of the Treaty is not for me to decide; I cannot however conceal from your Excellency, that my private Opinion is, that the Measure is totally different from the Letter and Spirit of the Treaty. But waving the Discussion of the Point, and leaving its Decision to our respective Sovereigns, I find it my Duty to signify my Readiness, in Conjunction with your Excellency, to enter into any Agreement, or take any Measures which may be deemed Expedient to prevent the future carrying away any Negroes or other Property of the american Inhabitants.

I beg the Favor of your Execllency's Reply, and have the Honor to be with much Consideration and Respect Sir Yours &ca.

G Washington

NA: PCC, item 121, pp. 47-50 (C); M61, reel 1.

Robert R. Livingston to William Carmichael

No. 6   Philadelphia 7th. May 1783.
Sir

I congratulate you upon the turn our Affairs are like to take with you, and to prospect your Letters open of a speedy Connection between us and the Court of Madrid. Her cold and distant conduct (which I must lament) has somewhat damped the ardor of this Country to render that connection as intimate as possible – No People in the world are more governed by their feelings than the Americans of which the late war was a striking proof, and those feelings have been long sported with in Spain – Yet Men of reflection see the propriety of overlooking the past, and forming in future a durable Connection, we are necessary to Each, and our mutual Friendship must conduce to the happiness of both – Should Spain have the magnanimity to reject partial Considerations, and offer such a Treaty of Commerce as her own true interest and ours require, we shall now lay the foundation of a Friendship that endure for Ages – But should she contend with us for the free Navigation of the Missisippi – which is now ours by the Titles – should she deny us the priviledge of cutting wood in the Bays of Campeache and Honduras – while She grants it to the English – She will without serving herself injure us, and open the Wounds which her kindness should close.

I have no particular directions to give you with respect to your mission – your conduct is perfectly agreable to Congress, and I doubt not that you will continue to pursue such a line as will render you most acceptable to the Court of Madrid – We have now no particular favours to ask, and the ground on which we stand, will I hope preserve us from future neglect and enable you to obtain the justice you have been so long soliciting in those matters of a private Nature which you mention.

· · · · ·

...I am Sir With Esteem your most obed[t] humble serv[t]

Rob[t.] R Livingston

NA: PCC, *item 118, pp. 420-424 (C); M247, reel 139.*

Benjamin Franklin to David Hartley

Dear Friend,   Passy, May 8[th.] 1783

I send you inclosed the Copies you desired of the Papers I read to you yesterday. I should be happy if I could see before I die the proposed Improvement of the Law of Nations established The Miseries of Mankind would be diminished & the Happiness of Millions secured and promoted – If the Practise of Privateering could be profitable to any civilized Nation it might be so to us Americans since we are so situated on the Globe as that the Rich Commerce of Europe with the West Indies consisting of Manufactures, Sugars &c[a.] is obliged to pass before our doors which enables us to make short and Cheap Cruises, while our Commerce is in such bulky low-prized Articles as that ten of our Ships taken by you are not equal in Value to one of yours; and you must come far from Home at a great Expence to look for them. I hope therefore that this Proposition if made by us will appear in its true light as having Humanity only for its Motive. I do not wish to see a *New Barbary* rising in America, and our long-extended Coast occupyed by Piratical States. I fear lest our Privateering Success in the two last Wars should already have given our People too strong a Relish for that most mischievous kind of Gaming mixt with Blood: And that if a Stop is not now put to the Practice, Mankind may hereafter be more plagued with American Corsairs than they have been and are with the Turkish. Try, my Friend, what you can do, in procuring for your Nation the Glory of being, tho' the greatest Naval Power the first who voluntarily relinquished the Advantage that Power seems to give them; of plundering others and thereby impeding the mutual Communication among Men of the Gifts of God and rendring miserable Multitudes of Merchants and their Families Artisans, & Cultivators of the Earth, the most useful, peaceable and innocent Part of the human Species.

    With great Esteem and Affection, I am ever my dear Friend Yours most sincerely   B Franklin

LC: Benjamin Franklin Papers, microfilm reel 2 (LBkC).

Robert R. Livingston to Benjamin Franklin

N⁰· 27.   Philadelphia 9ᵗʰ· May 1783
Sir,

    We have yet had no information from you subsequent to the signature of the Preliminary Articles by France, Spain and Britain, tho' we have seen a declaration for the cessation of Hostilities signed by you, Mʳ· Adams, and Mʳ Jay – We grow every day more anxious for the definitive Treaty, since we have as yet discovered no inclination in the Enemy to evacuate their Posts – and in sending off the Slaves they have directly infringed the provisional Treaty, tho' we on our part have paid the strictest regard to it – This will be more fully explained by the enclosed Copy of a Letter from General Washington containing a relation of what passed between him and General Carleton at a late interview[1] – let me again intreat that no doubt may be left in the Treaty relative to the time and manner of evacuating their Posts here – Without more precision and accuracy in this, than we find in the provisional Articles, we shall soon be involved in new disputes with Great Britain –

Our Finances are still greatly embarrassed – you may in part see our distress, and the means Congress are using to relieve themselves from them, by the enclosed Pamplet,[2] which I wish you and your Colleagues to read but not to publish –

The enclosed Resolution imposes a new task upon you, I hope you will find no great difficulty in procuring the small augmentation to the Loan, which it requires – be assured that it is extremely necessary to sett us down in Peace –

None of the States tho' frequently called upon have sent me the Estimates of their losses by the Ravages of the British, except Connecticut and Rhode Island, and their Accounts are extremely imperfect, such as they are I enclose them; For my own part I have no great expectation, that any compensation for these losses will be procured, however if possible it should be attempted – Commissioners might be appointed to ascertain them here – great part of the Prisoners are on their way to New York, and the whole will be sent in a few days – they will amount to about six thousand Men – Our Ports begin to be crowded with Vessels, there is reason to fear that a superabundance, of foreign Articles will in the end produce as much distress as the want of them has heretofore occasioned –

I have the honor to be Sir, with great Respect and Esteem your most obed[t] humble servant,   R R Livingston

University of Pennsylvania, Van Pelt Library: Special Collections (LS).
[1] See GW to Sir Guy Carleton, 6 May 1783.
[2] Not further identified.

Sir Guy Carleton to George Washington

Sir,   New York May 12th 1783

I can have no objection to the giving of your Excellency, in writing, full information of the measures taken for the evacuation of this place, nor should I have had any to the noting of the whole of our conversation and preserving it in minutes: mistakes or misconstruction might thereby be prevented.

Very soon after the orders for a cessation of hostilities were received here, Letters were written both to Europe and the West Indies, to require that all the shipping which could be procured, might be sent to assist in the evacuation of this place. About the same time all the prisoners of war in our hands were released.

An embarkation was in much forwardness previous to the official information of peace: – soon after, I wrote to the Minister for foreign affairs, to request that Congress would be pleased to empower any person or persons, on behalf of the United States, to be present at New York and to assist such persons as shou'd be appointed by me, to inspect and superintend all embarkations, which the evacuation of this place might require, and that they would represent to me every infraction of the letter or spirit of the treaty, that redress might be immediately ordered; in the mean time, to prevent abuse or delay, and until I could learn the determination of Congress, I requested of Daniel Parker Esq[r.1] one of the Contractors for supplying your army with provisions, and of Major Hopkins,[2] late Deputy Commissary of prisoners, that they would undertake the business, with other persons whom I appointed, which they did accordingly and executed with much diligence. This fleet sailed about the 27th of April, for different parts of Nova Scotia, and including the troops, carried about seven thousand persons with all their effects, also some artillery and public stores, so that you will perceive the evacuation began sooner and was in greater forwardness than could have been expected. Your Excellency will also perceive, from what I have already said, that at present it is impossible to tell when the evacuation of this City can be completed; in truth I cannot guess the quantity of shipping that will be sent me, nor the number of persons that will be forced to abandon this place. The evacuation of Penobscot will require considerably less tonnage, and I should think may soon be effected; if it is most eligible to you that I shou'd give a preference to this object, I shall immediately give orders for its being carried into the most speedy execution.

I enclose a copy of an order which I have given out to prevent the carry-ing away any negroes, or other property of the american Inhabitants. I understand from the Gentlemen therein named, that they visited the fleet bound to Nova Scotia, and ordered on shore whatever came clearly under the above description: There appeared to be but little difference of opinion, except in case of negroes who had been declared free previous to my arrival: as I had no right to deprive them of that liberty I found them possessed of, an accurate register was taken of every circumstance respecting them, so as to serve as a record of the name of the original proprietor of the negro, and as a rule by which to judge of his value: by this open method of conducting the business I hoped to prevent all fraud, and whatever might admit of different constructions is left open for future explanation or compensation. Had these negroes been denied permission to embark, they would, in spite of every means to prevent it, have found various methods of quitting this place, so that the former owner would no longer have been able to trace them, and of course would have lost, in every way, all chance of compen-sation.

The business carried on in this public manner, and the orders nominating persons to superintend embarkations published in the gazette, I had no reason to think either the embarkation or any circumstance attending it, could have been matter of surprise to your Excellency on the 6th of may: I then however learned with concern, that the embarkation which had already taken place, and in which a large number of negroes had been conveyed away, appeared to your Excellency as a measure totally different from the letter and spirit of the treaty.

The negroes in question, I have already said, I found free when I arrived at New York, I had therefore no right, as I thought, to prevent their going to any part of the world they thought proper.

I must confess that the mere supposition, that the King's Minister could deliberately stipulate in a treaty, an engagement to be guilty of a notorious breach of the public faith towards people of any complection seems to denote a less friendly disposition than I could wish, and I think less friendly than we might expect; after all I only give my own opinion. Every negroe's name is registered, the master he formerly belonged to, with such other circumstances as served to denote his value, that it may be adjusted by compensation, if that was really the intention and meaning of the treaty: Restoration, where inseparable from a breach of public faith, is, as all the world I think must allow, utterly impracticable. I know of no better method of preventing abuse, and the carrying away negroes, or other American property, than that I proposed to the Minister of foreign affairs, in my Letter of the 14th of April, the naming Commissioners to assist those appointed by me to inspect all embarkations, and I am pleased to find your Excellency has approved of this method and appointed Egbert Benson Esqr· Lieut· Coll· Smith,³ and Daniel Parker Esqr one of the Contractors for supplying your Army with provisions, Commissioners on your part for this purpose.

I am, Sir, Your Excellency's most obedient and most humble Servant
Guy Carleton

LC: *George Washington Papers,* microfilm reel 91 (ALS).

¹ *Parker, Daniel. Massachusetts merchant and speculator. With John Holker (former French Consul General) and William Duer (Assistant Secretary of the Treasury, 1789-1790), partner in providing supplies to the French expeditionary force and the Continental Army, 1781-1783. Member, Embarkation Commission, April-November 1783. With Robert Morris, financed the voyage of the Empress of China, the first American ship sent to China. Fled to Europe to escape his creditors, 1784. In Europe, speculated in American domestic securities in partnership with Robert Morris, Gouverneur Morris, and the Dutch and French bankers who handled U.S. accounts. Attempted to purchase U.S. debt to France, 1788-1789.*

² *Hopkins, David. (d. 1824). Military officer. Served in Arnold's Canadian expedition, 1775-1776. Served with a Maryland infantry regiment, 1776-1777. Captain, 4th Regiment*

of Light Dragoons, 1777. Major, 1st Regiment of Light Dragoons, 1781. Deputy Commissary of Prisoners, New York, 1783.

³ Smith, William Stephens (1755-1816). Military officer, diplomat, and political figure. Continental Army officer, 1776-1783, with service under John Sullivan, Israel Putnam, and the Marquis de Lafayette. Appointed aide to Washington, July 1781. Supervised British evacuation of New York, 1783. Secretary of legation in Great Britain, 1785-1788. Son-in-law of John Adams. Federal marshal, supervisor of the revenue, and surveyor of the port of New York. Prosecuted, but acquitted, for helping Francisco de Miranda with his filibustering expedition to South America, 1806. Member, U.S. House of Representatives, 1813-1816.

David Hartley to Charles James Fox

Private   Paris May 13 1783
Sir

I have met with a piece of information upon which I can with certainty depend; wch is that a person of very high rank in this Country, either has transmitted or is empowered from the french Ministry to transmitt a proposition to the American Ministers to this effect viz stating that the negotiation between Great Britain & France is now in train of being carried on under the mediation of the Courts of Petersbourg and Vienna, & requesting of them whether they chuse that the American negotiation with Great Britain sh^d be carried on under the same mediation, & if they sh^d so chuse, that they sh^d apply soon. Something to this effect is the proposition. As far as I can venture upon an opinion, I sh^d not think it probable that the American ministers sh^d accept it; because the apparent intention of imposing the mediation of the Court of Petersburgh seems specifically levelled against a proposition to wch they have agreed on their own parts, & to wch they are much attached. If I sh^d hear farther of this matter you shall hear again from me upon it. In the mean time I beg of you to keep this most perfectly secret, least the channel to me sh^d be suspected.

I Am Sir Yours &c   D Hartley

Postscript   May 22 1783
I have heard that the answer given to the foregoing application has been on the part of the American Ministers to the following effect; viz, That they were not sensible of their wanting any mediation – That it appeared a matter of surprize to them that they sh^d be expected to apply for the mediation of the two powers named, as neither of them had as yet acknowledged the Independance of America – To this it was rejoined –

But that is the way to obtain from them an acknowledgement of your Independance.

Clements Library: Hartley Papers, v. 1, pp. 43-44 (HC).

Robert R. Livingston to the American Peace Commissioners

N⁰· 4.   Philadelphia. 31ˢᵗ· May. '83.

Gentlemen,

Congress were yesterday pleased to pass the enclosed Resolutions[1] on the subject of the payment of British Debts – The language they speak requires no Comment –

. . . . .

The 5ᵗʰ· & 6ᵗʰ· Articles of the Provisional Treaty excite much ferment here, for, tho' the most dissatisfied Spirits acknowledge the whole Treaty taken together to answer their highest expectations, yet they wish to take only what they like; & leave out what they disapprove, and such is the relaxation of Governmᵗ so great the disorders & licentiousness introduced by the war, that it will be found very difficult to bridle the just resentments of some, and the unfounded apprehensions that others entertain of re-imbursements, that may affect their particular Interests. –

I have the honor to be, Gentlemen, with the greatest esteem & respect, Yʳ Most Obedᵗ· humˡ· Servᵗ·   Robᵗ R. Livingston –

MHS: The Adams Papers, microfilm reel 360 (C).

[1] *See JCC, v. 24, pp. 369-372. One resolution required the states to remove all obstacles to the execution of Articles IV and VI of the peace treaty and to give serious considertion to their compliance with Article V. A second resolution instructed the commissioners to oppose payment of interest for the wartime period.*

John Jay to Robert R. Livingston

Dear Sir   Paris 1 June 1783

...Business here goes on heavily. The dutch & English are not yet agreed, and some points remain still to be adjusted between the latter and the french and Spaniards. Mʳ· Hartley has an ample and proper Commission to conclude with us. We are discussing the Terms of a temporary commercial Regulation, but as he is waiting for more full Instructions, it may be a

Week or a fortnight before we shall be able to inform you of the real Intentions of Britain on that Subject.

. . . . .

I have the Honor to be with great Esteem & Regard, Dear Sir, your most obᵗ· Servᵗ·   John Jay

NA: PCC, *item* 89, *v. 2, pp.* 472-473 (ALS); M247, *reel* 117.

David Hartley to Charles James Fox

Private   Paris June 5 1783
Dear Sir
I have nothing to say to you in any public letter, until farther business may occur, upon the arrival of a dispatch from you, which I expect every hour, I should rather say, which *we* expect, for the American Ministers express great impatience on this subject, and indeed some degree of discontent, as if their business was neglected in England, or that there were rubs & difficulties. I have talked over the subject of my memorial June 1 1783 in private conversations, and have read it over to them together with some parts of my last public letter to you which I had considered of beforehand, as the best way of conveying sentiments sideways. For instance to say that Great Britain is a formidable American power, with Canada, Nova Scotia, Louisbourg hanging over the States, & a great marine force from Europe, if said directly, would be an offensive threat. To say to you, that I conclude they will do so or so, as being a duty on their part, would if said directly, be instructing or demanding, and so of other things. They feel the whole force of the case. Canada has always been in their thoughts. I can shew you letters from Dʳ Franklin to me upon this subject before the French Treaty. Lord North may perhaps remember my having read such to him in January 1778, hinting that they would bargain for Canada. I believe the 2ᵈ article of the Treaty of commerce with France has a secret respect to this point, viz "who shall enjoy the same favour freely, if the concession was freely made, or allowing the same compensation, if the concession was conditional." They would give any thing to acquire the remaining part of America, now in the British possession, to make their own situation complete, and after that, common reason assumes, that for their own security, they must desire the alliance & friendship of the only power who can in any degree be a terror or restraint to them. They know well enough that neither France nor any other European power would interfere in any continental dispute or war between the British-American Power & the United States. Common reason tells them this. And as I wish to use every

argument of persuasion with them to become accomodating in negotiation, I have explained their case to them, to shew them, what we are aware of, as argument on our side. *Scire tuum nihil est, visi te sure hoc, sciat alter.*[1] I hope this may produce good effects. I am anxious to let you know, that I urge every argument in favour of my country, in the most forcible maner that I can, and that I watch according to the best of my judgement the fittest times and opportunities of so doing.

I am my Dear Sir very sincerely yours   D Hartley

Clements Library: Hartley Papers, v. 1, pp. 95-96 (C).
[1] *You know nothing unless you know your own ignorance.*

James Madison to Thomas Jefferson

My dear Sir   Philada. 10 June 1783
    Congress have recd. two letters from Mr. {Laurens}[1] dated {London}, one the {fiveteenth of March} the {other fiveth of April}. In the former he {persists in} the {jealousy} expressed in {his letter of} the {thirtieth of December of} the {British Councils. He says} that {Shelburne} had {boasted of his success} in {gaining the provisional treaty without the concurrence of France and of the good effects he expected to draw from that advantage}. Mr. {Ls remark was} that {admitting} the {fact which he did not} altho' it {might disgrace} and even {prove fatal to the American Ministers}, it {could have no such effects on the United States}. His {second letter} expresses more {confidence in the D. of Portland and Mr. Fox}. These {ministers} have withdrawn the subject of commerce with the U.S. from Parliamt. and mean to open negociations for a Treaty with their ministers in Europe. Mr. Fox asked Mr. L. whether these had powers for that purpose: his answer was that he believed so, that he had seen a revocation of Mr. Adams' commission noticed in the Gazettes but that he considered the paragraph as spurious. From this it would seem that {Mr A had never communicated this} diminution of {his powers to his colleagues}. These letters leave us in the suspence in which they found us as to the definitive Treaty. Mr. L. thinks that no such event could have been relied on under Shelburnes administration. He was on the 5th of Apl. setting out for Paris with Mr. David Hartley, successor to Mr. Oswald, from whence he sd. proceed to America unless a definitive Treaty was near being concluded. Notwithstanding the daily arrivals from every quarter we get not a line on the subject from our Ministers at Versailles.

· · · · ·

Congress have lately sent instructions to the Ministers in Europe to {contend} in {the final treaty for such} amendment of the {article relating to British debts} as will {suspend payment for three years after the war and expressly exclude interest during the war}.

Mr. Livingston has taken his final leave of the department of Foreign affairs. He wd. have remained if such an augmentation of his Salary had been made as wd. have secured him agst. future expence. But besides the disinclination of several members to augment salaries, there was no prospect of a competent number of States for an appropriation of money until he must have lost the option of the Chancellorship of N.Y. No successor has been yet nominated, altho' the delay for a choice has passed. I am utterly at a loss to guess on whom the choice will ultimate[ly] fall. {A L} will be {started} if the {defection of a} respectable {competitor} shd. be {likely to force votes upon him}. No such has yet {been made a subject of conversation in my presence}

The general arrangement of the foreign System has been suspended by the thinness of Congs. in part, and partly by the desire of further information from Europe. I fear much the delay will be exceedingly protracted. Nothing but final resignation of the Ministers abroad & the arrival of Foreign Ministers here, will effectually stimulate Congs. into activity & decision on the subject....

The Treaty of Commerce with G.B. is another business suspended by the same cause. The Assembly have instructed us to reserve to Congs. a revisal after it shall have been settled in Europe. This will give force to the doctrine of caution hitherto maintained by us....

I am Dear Sir your sincere friend,   J. Madison Jr.

Smith, Letters of Delegates, *v. 20, pp. 321-323.*
[1] *Brackets enclose material encyphered in text.*

John Adams to Robert R. Livingston

Sir,   Paris June 16[th.] 1783.

· · · · ·

I am well aware, that a variety of questions may be started upon the Provisional Articles. The great Points of Sovereignty, Limits and Fisheries are sufficiently clear – But there are too many other things in much Obscurity. No one of us alone would ever have put his Hand to such a writing. Yet there is no one to blame. – It must be confessed that it was done in haste; but that haste was inevitable. The Peace depended absolutely upon the critical Moment, when that Treaty was signed. The Meeting of

Parliament was so near, and the State of the Ministry so critical, that if that Opportunity had been lost, there would have been at least another Campaign. There were never less than three of us, and there were finally no less than three to be consulted on the other side. These Inaccuracies are much to be lamented, but they were quite unavoidable. We shall endeavor to explain them in the definitive Treaty, but I fear without Success.

. . . . .

We are happy to learn the Congress have ratified the Treaty imperfect as it is, and that each Side have released their Prisoners. Mr Hartley communicated to us officially two days ago, that Orders were gone to New York to evacuate the United States.

. . . . .

...I do not think it consistent with the Honor of the United States, any more than with my own, for me to stay in Holland, after the Appointment of any other Minister whatsoever to a Mission upon which I came to Europe, and which has been taken from me, without assigning any Reasons – Congress are the sovereign Judges for themselves and the Public of the Persons proper for all Services, excepting that every Citizen is a sovereign Judge for himself. I have never adopted the Principle, that it is a Citizen's Duty to accept of any Trust that is pointed out to him, unless he approves it. On the contrary, I think it a Right and Duty, that no Law of Society can take away, for every Man to judge for himself whether he can serve consistently with his own Honor, and the Honor and Interest of the Public. When the Existence of our Country and her essential Interests were at stake, it was a Duty to run all Risques, to stifle every feeling, to sacrifice every Interest, and this Duty I have discharged with Patience and Perseverance, & with a Success that can be attributed only to Providence. But in time of Peace, the Public in less Danger abroad than at home, knowing I can do more good at home, I should do a very wrong thing to remove my Family to stay in Holland, merely for the sake of holding an honorable Commission, making and receiving Bows & Compliments, & eating splendid Suppers at Court.

. . . . .

With great Respect and Esteem, I have the honor to be, Sir, your most obedient & most humble Servant.   John Adams.
Read Oct 4. 1783

NA: PCC, *item 84, v. 4, pp. 403-410 (LS); M247, reel 112.*

David Hartley's Memorandums for the Definitive Peace Treaty

[Paris, June 19, 1783]

1. That Lands belonging to Persons of any Description which have not actually been sold shall be restored to the old Possessors without Price

2. That an equal and free Participation of the different carrying Places; and the Navigation of all the Lakes and Rivers of that Country thro' which the Water Line of Division passes between Canada and the United States shall be enjoyed fully and uninterruptedly by both Parties.

3. That in any such Places within the Boundaries assign'd generally to the American States as are adjoining to the Water Line of Division, and which are not specifically under the Dominion of any one State, all Persons at present resident, or having Possessions or Occupations as Merchants or otherwise may remain in peaceable Enjoyment of all civil Rights and in pursuit of their respective Occupations.

4. That in any such Places adjoining to the Water Line of Division as may be under the specific Dominion of any particular State, all Persons at present resident or having Possessions or Occupations untill they shall receive Notice of removal from the State to which any such Place may appertain; and that upon any such Notice of Removal a Term of three Years shall be allowed for selling or withdrawing their valuable Effects, and for settling their affairs.

5. That his Britannic Majesty's Forces not exceeding in Number may continue in the Posts now occupied by them contiguous to the Water Line for the Term of three years, for the Purpose of securing the Lives, Property and Peace of any Persons settled in that Country, against the Invasion or Ravages of the Neighbouring Indian Nations who may be suspected of retaining Resentments in consequence of the late War.

6. That no Tax or Impost whatsoever shall be laid on any Articles of Commerce passing or repassing thro' the Country, but that the Trade may be left entirely open for the Benefit of all Parties interested therein.

NA: PCC, item 85, pp. 322-323 (AD); M247, reel 114.

John Adams to Robert R. Livingston

2plicate.   Paris 27th. June 1783.

Sir,

Yesterday Dr. Franklin, Mr. Jay & myself met to prepare the definitive Treaty, & made so much progress in it, that tomorrow we shall be ready to communicate to Mr. Hartley the result – But I have small. hopes of obtaining any thing more by the definitive Treaty.

The Duke of Manchester & the Comte d'Aranda have arranged every thing between England and Spain, & are ready to finish for their two Courts. France, I presume, waits only for Holland, or perhaps for some other Negotiation with the Imperial Courts. If all the other Parties were now to declare themselves ready, We should be puzzled. In such a Case however, I am determined, (and I believe, but don't know, that my Colleagues would join me) to declare myself ready to sign the Provisional Treaty, *totidem verbis*, for a definitive Treaty. From all I can learn, I am persuaded we shall gain nothing by any further Negotiation. If we obtain any thing, by way of addition or explanation, we shall be obliged to give more for it than it is worth. If the British Minister refuses to agree to such Changes as we may think reasonable, & refuses to sign the Provisional Articles as definitive ones, I take it for granted France will not sign till we do. If they should, We are still safe, for the Provisional Articles are to *constitute* the Treaty, as soon as France has made Peace – And I should rather leave it on that footing, than make any material Alteration.

I have put these several Cases, because I should be surprized at nothing from the present British Ministry. If they have any Plan at all, it is a much less generous one towards America, than that of their immediate Predecessors. If Shelburne, Townshend, Pitt, &^{ca}, had continued, We should have had every thing settled long ago, to our entire Satisfaction, & to the infinite Advantage of Great Britain and America – in such a manner, as would have restored good Humor & Affection, as far as in the Nature of things they can now be restored. After the great Point of Acknowledgment of our Independence was got over, by issuing Mr. Oswald's last Commission, the Shelburne Administration conducted towards Us, like Men of Sense and Honour. The present Administration have neither discovered Understanding nor Sincerity.

The present British Administration is unpopular; and it is in itself so heterogeneous a Composition, that it seems impossible it should last long. Their present design seems to be not to commit themselves by agreeing to any thing. As soon as any thing is done, somebody will clamour. While nothing is done, it is not known what to clamour about.

If there should be a Change in favor of the Ministry that made the Peace, & a dissolution of this profligate League, which they call the Coalition, it would be much for the good of all who speak the English Language. If Fame says true, the Coalition was formed at Gambling Tables, and is conducted as it was formed, upon no other than gambling Principles. Such is the Fate of a Nation, which stands tottering on the Brink of a Precipice, with a Debt of two hundred and fifty five Millions sterling on its Shoulders: the Interest of which, added to the Peace Establishment only, exceeds, by above a Million annually, all their Revenues, enormously and intolerably as they are already taxed.

The only Chance they have for Salvation is in a Reform, & in recovering the Affection of America. The last Ministry were sensible of this, & acted accordingly. The present Ministry are so far from being sensible of it, or caring about it, that they seem to me to be throwing the last Dice for the Destruction of their Country.

With great Respect & Esteem, I have the honor to be, Sir, your most obedient & most humble Servant.   John Adams

NA: PCC, *item 84, v. 4, pp. 428-430 (LS); M247, reel 112.*

David Hartley to Charles James Fox

N° 12   Paris July 1 1783
Sir
     I have the honour of transmitting to you the answers which I have received from the American Ministers to the six Propositions which I made to them for the definitive Treaty, and of which I sent you Copies in my last dispatch N° 11. I beg to receive your instructions relative to these answers – Permit me to make one remark, which is, that mention is twice made of a Negotiation of a Treaty of Commerce. This is not much in itself, but added to other things I think it is constructive. The points referred in these answers to a future Negotiation might easily be decided now. Therefore I conclude that the American Ministers are not at all unwilling that occasions of Negotiation with Great Britain should continue, probably with a view to some future common union of interests with Great Britain. This is a very delicate point for them to conduct, especially in the present conjuncture of their affairs between France and Great Britain. They have been called upon very explicitly by the Memorial of June 1 1783, to look forward to the possibility of some future alliance with Great Britain as a fundamental point, and so to conduct the Preliminaries of the present negotiation as not to foreclose any possible arrangements which may lead

hereafter to the consolidation of common interests with Great Britain. And therefore I may say that that point is explicitly before us. However we must not expect to proceed towards that point as our final object without rubs & jealousies in the way on both sides. We are speaking of nations, who, after very bitter civil Contests, have scarcely had time as yet to return to a state of Complacency towards each other. I am not surprized at many tokens which I see in the American Ministers of jealousy & discontent, when I consider the delicacy of their situation as placed between France & Great Britain. Even listening to Propositions on the part of Great Britain may destroy their present situation without securing to them the certainty of another & better situation. This is a state of great anxiety to the individual Ministers of a Nation which has not as yet acquired any established rank & place. When I argue with them on the part of my own Country, I state that they have no foundation for discontent. The change of extremes from a bitter civil war to alliance (or the prospect of it) must come by degrees. Your expression (in N° 9) concerning the *natural* alliance between the two Countries ought to be satisfactory; viz. when Intercourse is once begun every thing will go on in its *natural* road. Time must bring the rest to maturity.

You will receive Sir enclosed with this, another Paper from the American Ministers entitled "Propositions made to Mr Hartley for the definitive Treaty;" together with some explanatory Papers from Dr Franklin upon the subject of the 4th. Article. I have been a long while aware that such a Proposition would be made by the American Ministers. It seems to me to amount to a Proposition of perpetual alliance, and that such an alliance would be the fittest Basis for it to stand upon. The Conduct of such a measure requires great consideration & management, and it is for this reason that I am earnest in my desire to have some personal Conferences with you. The natural order of things seems to be 1st a temporary Convention of Intercourse, 2dly the definitive Treaty – and 3dly Treaties of Commerce and perpetual alliance. The 6th Proposition made by the American Ministers is a modification of the 10th article of the proposed supplemental Treaty which I brought over with me originally from England, & if approved is certainly within the Scope of the definitive Treaty, but the 4th article seems to me to go beyond the scope of a Treaty, which by its name declares its proposed extent, viz as definitive to the late war. I presume that this construction may be the most commodious to you respecting the 4th article. As that Article is novel in Negotiations and leading to very deep and important consequences, I presume that you may not chuse either to give an immediate negative to it, or to delay the definitive Treaty until so novel & extensive a Proposition with all its concomitant consequences & circumstances can be mutually discussed &

settled – You will observe Sir that all the Propositions from the American Ministers, from that which was inclosed in my dispatch N° 2, to the Articles now inclosed, proceed upon one principle viz that of presupposing perpetual peace & alliance between Great Britain & the American States. When the hour of transitory Contention shall be past and cool reflection shall return, this must appear to be the mutual interest of both parties. This is a most material point for me to be fully instructed upon, and to act thoroughly in concert from you. Therefore as soon as I shall have settled the terms of the preliminary Convention which I am now waiting for from you I shall follow these Propositions for the definitive Treaty to receive your instructions in person and to explain many sentiments to you which cannot be fully expressed in Letters.

I confine myself in this Letter to the mention of the 4th & 6th Articles only, because respecting the others I shall receive your answers as to ordinary & customary propositions in negotiations. When the total account of the past transactions of the war shall be closed between Great Britain & America (which will at the same time ascertain the connexion between France & America to some precise point) all other ulterior propositions tending to alliance may be discussed explicitly & without reserve. As for instance; in the preliminaries to any system of alliance, Great Britain would expect very explicit satisfaction, that, in case of a rupture between Great Britain and France, America should not be at liberty to take part against Great Britain: The discussion of such a point before the conclusion of the definitive Treaty might be very embarrassing to America, although most indispensable to Great Britain

There are many other points besides which require preparation & arrangement on the part of Great Britain such as the claims of several foreign Countries by treaty to the rights of the most favoured nation, in which the mode as well as the matter is essential. No foreign Nation has any right to dictate to what extent the independance of America shall operate upon points not originally contested in the war, such as the 6th Proposition of the American Ministers, viz taking & holding real estates without letters of Naturalization – and so of similar cases respecting favoured nations. If the parties themselves should be of accord that all Harbours, Rivers, Lakes &c. should be mutually navigated as before the war, upon the principle of that point emerging after the war, untouched by the war, what foreign Nation can object or pretend to any similar claim, any more than in the case just mentioned of holding estates without Letters of Naturalization? The parties themselves are sole & competent to decide that point. The case is totally novel & singular, neither was there any idea or presumption of its possible existence at the time of concluding any treaty giving the claim of a favoured nation. No equivalents have ever been conceived in any commercial treaty for any such possible case, & therefore no such right can have been acquired. Great Britain or the American States may either of them say to the other party You shall be aliens, henceforward *in toto et in omnibus*. But no foreign Nation can claim the right to decide any such points either actually or by implication of treaty. The rights of any foreign favoured nations cannot extend farther than the case existing and in contemplation at the time of making the treaty; viz than the claim of any favours then or at any time afterwards granted to any of the then existing foreign States: The letter of the Treaty certainly gives no more: Nor can any claim of equity be set up without the proof of some equivalent having been provided in the original bargain, which certainly was never thought of nor can in the least degree be pretended.

Besides if the right of Construction upon a Case totally novel & unprecedented could admit of any doubt as a general proposition, Yet in the present case what European Nation can set up any such claim? Certainly none of those nations which have taken part in the late war. And full as little right can any of those nations claim who have been confederates in the Northern armed Neutrality. A confederacy, on the part of favoured Nations of premeditated hostility against the maritime power of Great Britain, and such as no motives in the world could have suggested but envy & opportunity. In such a circle of nations I am sure it is necessary that Great Britain should exert & maintain her own rights as the arbitress & protectress of her own most essential concerns. As there is no nation in Europe which has not either directly or indirectly been lying in wait to supplant the naval Power of Great Britain, None can have any right to complain if Great Britain should exert all her rights & powers to repel the effects of their invidious machinations.

The first object of our European rivals at the commencement of the American war was to effect the separation of dominion between Great Britain and America. Their evident object *now* is to prevent their reunion as allies. This principle marks out the line of conduct for Great Britain, viz to keep herself open for every degree of reunion & reconnexion which time & prudence may bring. America foreseeing her final & permanent interest keeps herself entirely open. You have likewise Sir given me your sanction to the principles of the Memorial which I presented to the American Ministers on the subject of the *natural* alliance which ought to subsist between our two Countries. This alliance is not only *natural* but *exclusively* so. From circumstances of vicinity & situation Great Britain & the United States must always be inseparable either as Friends or Foes. Therefore reason dictates the principle of amicable alliance as the only *natural* event of things. It is *exclusively* so; because if any other nation should enter into a special guarantee with the American States, suppose of 20 Sail of the

Line in case of attack, it would be a declaration of perpetual war against Great Britain, for which America could not give any equivalent in price. Whereas the special guarantee being supposed on the part of G^t Britain all danger would be prevented to the United States, the cost would be nothing to Great Britain, and all the alternate conditions would be clear gain to Great Britain.

I have been led Sir into this course of reasoning in consequence of considering the propositions which I have now the honour to transmit to you from the American Ministers, because it seems to me that all the propositions of emphatical distinction which they have made to Great Britain point to the presupposed basis of some future eventual system of amity & alliance. Their situation is that of uncertainty between France & Great Britain; between the contentions of opposite parties & principles. They may be too jealous. They may be difficult in the uncertainty of Expectations, but their Conduct in fundamentals will admit of no consistent Construction but this, viz that they consider the alliance with France as transitory in itself, from its original views & conditions, but that they look to Great Britain as the nation (from her situation in America as well as in Europe) whose alliance is the only natural & necessary alliance to them – The Conduct of the American Ministers would be perfectly unintelligible unless these were their sentiments, and if they are so, I think in common prudence they cannot be more explicit. My Duty is according to the best of my Judgement to state these things to you –

I am Sir with the greatest respect and Consideration Your most Obed^t
Servt D. Hartley

Clements Library: Hartley Papers, v. 2, pp. 41-50 (C).

American Peace Commissioners' Answers to David Hartley's Memorandums for the Definitive Treaty

[Paris ca. July 1, 1783]
Answers to Mr. Hartley's Six Propositions for the definitive Treaty.

To the 1$^{st.}$ This Matter has been already regulated in the 5 & 6$^{th.}$ Articles of the Provisional Treaty to the utmost extent of our Powers: The Rest must be left to the several States.

2^d All the Lakes, Rivers, and Waters, divided by the Boundary Line or

Lines between the United States and his Britannic Majesty's Territories, shall be freely used and navigated by both Parties during the whole extent of such Division. Regulations concerning Roads, Carrying Places and any Land Communications between said Waters, whether within the Line of the United States or that of his Majesty, together with the Navigation of all Waters and Rivers in America belonging to either Party, may be made in a Negotiation of a Treaty of Commerce.

3^d & 4$^{th.}$ That in all Places belonging to the United States in the Country adjoining to the Water Line of Division, and which during the War were in his Majesty's Possession, all Persons at present resident, or having Possessions or Occupations, as Merchants or otherwise, may remain in the peaceable Enjoyments of all civil Rights, and in pursuit of their Occupations until they shall receive Notice of Removal from Congress, or the State to which any such Place may appertain, and that upon any such Notice of Removal, a Term of two Years shall be allowed for selling or withdrawing their Effects, and for settling their Affairs.

5$^{th.}$ That his Britannic Majesty's Forces not exceeding   in Number, may continue in the Posts now occupied by them, contiguous to the Water Line, untill Congress shall give them Notice to evacuate the said Posts; and Garrisons of their own shall arrive at said Posts for the Purpose of securing the Lives, Property and Peace of any Persons settled in that Country, against the Invasion or Ravages of the Neighbouring Indian Nations, who may be suspected of retaining Resentments in consequence of the late War.

6$^{th.}$ The Consideration of this Proposition may be left to the Treaty of Commerce.

NA: PCC, item 85, pp. 324-325 (AD); M247, reel 114.

American Peace Commissioners' Propositions for the Definitive Treaty

[Paris ca. July 1, 1783]

Propositions made to Mr Hartley for the Definitive Treaty.

1$^{st.}$ To omit in the Definitive Treaty, the Exception at the End of the 2^d Article of the Provisional Treaty: Viz: these Words, "Excepting such Islands as now are, or heretofore have been within the Limits of the said Province of Nova Scotia." —

Article

2$^{dly.}$ The Prisoners made respectively by the Arms of his Britannic Majesty & the United States, by Land & by Sea, not already set at Liberty, shall be restor'd reciprocally & bona fide immediately after the Ratification of the definitive Treaty, without Ransom, and on paying the Debts they may have contracted during their Captivity; and each Party shall respectively reimburse the Sums which shall have been advanced for the Subsistence and maintenance of the Prisoners, by the sovereign of the Country where they shall have been detained, according to the Receipts and attested Accounts, and other authentic Titles which shall be produced on each side.

Article

3$^{dly.}$ His Britannic Majesty shall employ his good Offices and Interpositions with the King or Emperor of Morocco or Fez, the Regencies of Algier, Tunis & Tripoli, or with any of them, and also with every other Prince, State or Power of the Coast of Barbary in Africa, and the Subjects of the Said King, Emperor, States, & Powers & each of them, in order to provide as fully & efficaciously as possible for the Benefit, Conveniency and Safety of the said United States, and each of them, their Subjects, People and Inhabitants, and their Vessels and Effects, against all Violence, Insult, Attacks, or Depredations on the Part of the said Princes & States of Barbary, or their Subjects.

Article

4^{thly} If War should hereafter arise between Great Britain and the United States, which God forbid, the Merchants of either Country then residing in the other, shall be allowed to remain Nine Months, to collect their Debts & settle their Affairs, and may depart freely carrying off all their Effects without molestation or Hindrance. And all Fishermen, all Cultivators of the Earth, and all Artisans & Manufacturers unarmed & inhabiting unfortified Towns, Villages, or Places, who labour for the Common Subsistence & Benefit of Mankind, and peaceably follow their respective Employments, shall be allowed to continue the same, and shall not be molested by the armed force of the Enemy, in whose Power by the Event of the War they may happen to fall; but if any thing is necessary to be taken from them for the use of such armed force, the same shall be paid for at a reasonable Price. And all Merchants or Traders with their unarmed Vessels employed in Commerce, exchanging the Products of different Places and thereby rendering the Necessaries, Conveniences and Comforts of Human Life more easy to obtain and more general, shall be allowed to pass freely unmolested. And neither of the Powers, Parties to this Treaty, shall grant or issue any Commission to any private armed Vessels empowering them to take or destroy such trading Ships, or interrupt such Commerce.

Article

5thly. And in Case either of the contracting Parties shall happen to be engaged in War with any other Nation, it is farther agreed in order to prevent all the Difficulties and misunderstandings that usually arise, respecting the Merchandize heretofore called Contraband, such as Arms, Ammunition, & Military Stores of all Kinds, that no such Articles carrying by the Ships or Subjects of one of the Parties to the Enemies of the other, shall on any Acc^t be deemed Contraband, so as to induce Confiscation and a Loss of Property to Individuals. Nevertheless it shall be lawful to stop such Ships & detain them for such length of Time as the Captors may think necessary to prevent the Inconvenience or Damage that might ensue from their proceeding on their Voyage, paying however a reasonable Compensation for the Loss such Arrest shall occasion to the Proprietors. And it shall farther be allowed to use in the Service of the Captors, the whole or any Part of the Military Stores so detained, paying to the Owners the full Value of the same.

Article

6thly. The Citizens and Inhabitants of the said United States or any of them, may take and hold real Estates in Great Britain, Ireland, or any other of his Majesty's Dominions, and dispose by Testament, Donation or otherwise; of their Property real or Personal, in favour of such Persons as to them shall seem fit; and their Heirs, Citizens of the said United States or any of them, residing in the British Dominions or elsewhere, may succeed them *Ab intestato*, without being obliged to obtain Letters of Naturalization.

The Subjects of his Britannic Majesty, shall enjoy on their Part, in all the Dominions of the said United States, an entire & perfect Reciprocity, relative to the Stipulations contained in the present Article.——

Article

7thly. The Ratifications of the Definitive Treaty shall be expedited in good & due Form, and exchanged in the Space of Five Months, (or sooner if it can be done) to be computed from the Day of the Signature.

8thly

Query. Whether the King of Great Britain will admit the Citizens of the United States to cut Log-Wood on the District allotted to his Majesty by Spain, and on what Terms? –

NA: PCC, *item 85, pp. 330-337 (C); M247, reel 114.*

Charles James Fox to David Hartley

Private　　　　　　　　　　　　　　　　　St James' July 2 1783
Dear Sir
　　...In regard to the definitive Treaty, I like your memoranda very much, and see no reason why you should not proceed with expedition in that business. At least I hope the American Commissioners will not put any obstacle in the way of our signing with France, when we are ready....
Yours ever
　　　　　　　　　　　　　　　　　　　　　　　　　　C J Fox

Clements Library: Hartley Papers, v. 2, pp. 39-40 (C).

John Adams to Robert R. Livingston

Sir,　　　　　　　　　　　　　　　　　　Paris. 7ᵗʰ July. 1783
　　We cannot as yet obtain from Mr Hartley or his Principals an explicit consent to any one proposition whatever: Yet England & France, & England & Spain are probably agreed, and Holland I suppose must comply. Our last resource must be to say we are ready to sign the Provisional Treaty, *totidem verbis*, as the Definitive Treaty. I think it is plain that the British Ministry do not intend to sign any Treaty till Parliament rises. There are such dissensions in the Cabinet, that they apprehend a Treaty laid before Parliament, if it did not obtain advantages, of which they have no hopes, would furnish materials to overthrow them. A new Administration is talked of under Lord Temple. –

　　　　　　　　. . . . .

　　With great respect, I have the honor to be, Sir, Your most Obedient, hum^l Serv^{tt}
　　　　　　　　　　　　　　　　　　　　　　　　John Adams.

NA: PCC, item 84, v. 4, pp. 444-447 (LS); M247, reel 112.

John Adams to Robert R. Livingston

Sir　　　　　　　　　　　　　　　　　　Paris 9ᵗʰ July. 1783
　　　　　　　　. . . . .
　　Your late Dispatches, Sir, are not well adapted to give spirits to a melancholy man, or to cure one sick of a fever. It is not possible for me at present to enter into a long detail in answer to them. You will be answer^d I suppose by all the Gentlemen, jointly – In the mean time I beg leave to

say to you a few words upon two Points.

1$^{st.}$ The Seperate Article never appeared to me of any Consequence to conceal from this Court. It was an agreement we had a right to make; it contained no injury to France or Spain: Indeed I know not what France has, or ever had, to do with it. If it had been communicated to this Court it w$^{d.}$ probably have been, by them, communicated to Spain, and she might have tho't more about it, than it was worth. But how you can conceive it possible for us to treat at all with the English upon supposition that we had communicated every, the minutest, thing to this Court, when this Court were neither obliged, nor thought proper to communicate any thing whatever to us, I know not. We were bound by Treaty no more than they to communicate. The Instructions were found to be absolutely impracticable. – That they were too suddenly published is very true. –

2$^{dly.}$ A Communication of the Treaty to this Court, after it was agreed upon, & before it was signed, w$^{d.}$ infallibly have prevented the whole Peace. In the first place, it was very doubtfull, or rather, on the contrary, it is certain the English Minister never w$^{d.}$ have consented that we should communicate it. We might, it is true, have done without his Consent or Knowledge, – but what would have been the Consequence? The French Minister would have said the Terms were very good for us, but we must not sign 'till they signed: & this would have been a Continuance of the war for another year at least – It was not so much from an apprehension that the French w$^{d.}$ have exerted themselves to get away from us terms that were agreed on, that they were withheld. It was then too late, & we have reason to apprehend that all of the kind had been done which could be done. We knew they were often insinuating to the British Ministers things against us, respecting the Fisheries, Tories &$^{ca.}$ during the negotiation – and M$^{r.}$ Fitzherbert told me the C. de Vergennes had "fifty times reproached him for ceding the Fisheries, and said it was ruining the English & French Commerce both" – It was not suspicion – it was certain knowledge, that they were against us upon the points of the Tories, Fisheries, Mississippi, & the Western Country. All this Knowledge, however, did not influence us to conceal the Treaty – We did not, in fact, conceal it. D$^{r.}$ Franklin communicated the Substance of it to the Comte & M. Rayneval. So did I. In a long Conversation with the Comte & M. Rayneval together I told them the substance of what was agreed, and what we further insisted on & the English then disputed –

But the signing before them is the point. This we could not have done, if we had shewn the Treaty & told them we were ready. The Comte would certainly ~~would~~ have said to us, you must not sign till we sign. To have signed after this would have been more disagreeable to him & to us too: Yet we must have signed or lost the Peace. The Peace depended on a day.

Parliament had been waiting long & once prorogued. The Minister was so pressed he could not have met Parliament & kept his place, without an agreement upon terms, at least with America – If we had not signed the Ministry would have been changed and the Coalition come in – and the whole world knows the Coalition would not have made Peace upon the present terms & consequently not at all this year. The Iron was struck in the few critical moments when it was of a proper heat, & has been moulded into an handsome vessel. If it had been suffered to cool, it w^d have flown in Pieces like Glass. – Our Countrymen have great reason to rejoice that they obtained so good a Peace, when & as they did. With the present threat'ning appearances of a Northern war, which will draw in France, if our Peace was still to be made, we might find cause to tremble for many great advantages that are now secured. I believe the Comte himself, if he were now to speak his real Sentiments, w^d say he is very glad we signed when we did, & that without asking his Consent. The Duc de la Vauguyon told me & Mr Brantzen, together, last Saturday, "if you had not signed when you did, we should not have signed when we did" – If they had not signed when they did, D'Estaing would have sailed from Cadiz, and in that case nobody w^d have signed to this day. – It is not possible for men to be in more disagreeable Circumstances than we were. We are none of us men of principles or dispositions to take pleasure in going against your Sentiments, Sir, much less those of Congress. But, in this case, if we had not done it, our Country would have lost Advantages beyond Computation.–

. . . . .

With great respect & Esteem, I have the honor to be, Sir, Your most Obed^t hum$^{le:}$ Serv$^{t:}$ John Adams.

NA: PCC, item 84, v. 4, pp. 448-451 (LS); M247, reel 112.

John Adams to Robert R. Livingston

Sir,   Paris July 10th 1783
    In the present violent heat of the Weather, and feverish state of my own health, I cannot pretend to sit long at my Pen, and must pray you to accept of a few short hints only.
    To talk, in a general stile, of Confidence in the French Court, &$^{ca.}$, is to use a general language, which may mean almost any thing, or almost nothing. – To a certain degree, and as far as the Treaties and Engagements extend, I have as much Confidence in the French Court, as Congress has, or even as you, Sir, appear to have.

But if by Confidence in the French Court is meant, an Opinion that the French Office of foreign Affairs would be Advocates with the English for our rights to the Fishery, or the Mississippi River, or our Western Territory, or Advocates to persuade the British Ministers to give up the Cause of the Refugees, and make a parliamentary provision for them, I own I have no such Confidence, and never had. Seeing and hearing what I have seen and heard, I must have been an Idiot to have entertained such Confidence – And having no such Confidence, I should be more of a Machevilian, or a Jesuit, than I ever was, or will be, to counterfeit it to you or to Congress.

M$^{r.}$ Marbois Letter is to me full proof of the principles of the C. de Vergennes. Why? Because I know, (for it was personally communicated to me upon my passage home by M$^{r.}$ Marbois himself) the Intimacy and the Confidence there is between those two. And I know farther, that that Letter contains Sentiments concerning the Fisheries diametrically opposite to those, which M$^{r.}$ Marbois repeatedly expressed to me upon the Passage, viz$^{t.}$ "That the Newfoundland Fishery was our right, and we ought to maintain it." From whence I conclude that M$^{r.}$ Marbois Sentiments have been changed by the Instructions of the Minister. To what purpose is it, where this Letter came from? Is it less genuine, whether it came from Philadelphia, Versailles, or London? What if it came thro' English Hands? Is there less weight, less evidence in it, for that? Are the Sentiments more just, or more friendly to Us, for that?

M$^{r.}$ Raynevals Correspondence too with M$^{r.}$ Jay. M$^{r.}$ Rayneval is a Chef du Bureau. But we must be very ignorant of all Courts, not to know, that an Under Secretary of State dares not carry on such a Correspondence without the Knowledge, Consent and Orders of the Principal.

There is another point now in agitation, in which the French will never give Us one good word. On the contrary, they will say every thing they can think of to persuade the English to deprive Us of the Trade of their West India Islands. They have already, with their Emissaries, been the chief Cause of the Change of Sentiments in London on this head against Us.

In general, they see with pain every appearance of returning real & cordial Friendship, such as may be permanent between Us and Great Britain. On the contrary they see with pleasure every Seed of Contention between Us. The Tories are an excellent Engine of Mischief between Us, and therefore very precious. – Exclusion ~~of~~ from the West India Islands, will be another.

I hold it to be the indispensible duty of my Station not to conceal from Congress these Truths. Dont let Us be Dupes, under the Idea of being grateful. Innumerable Anecdotes happen daily to shew that these Sentiments are general.

In Conversation a few Weeks ago with the Duke de la Vauguyon, upon the subject of the West India Trade, I endeavoured to convince him, that France & England both ought to admit us freely to their Islands. He entered into a long Argument, to prove that both ought to exclude Us. At last I said, "The English were a parcel of Sots to exclude Us – for the consequence of it would be, that in 15 or 20 Years we should have another War with them." "Tant mieux! tant mieux! Tant mieux! Je vous en felicite,"[1] cried the Duke, with great pleasure. "Tant mieux pour nous,"[2] says I, because we shall conquer from the English in that Case all their Islands, the Inhabitants of which would now declare for Us, if they dared – But it will be not the better for the English. They will be the Sots and Dupes, if they lay a foundation for it. – "Oui Monsieur," says the Duke, "je crois que vous aurez une autre guerre contre les Anglois."[3] And in this wish he expressed the feelings and the Vows of every Frenchman upon the face of the Earth.

If therefore We have it in Contemplation to avoid a future War with the English, dont let Us have too much Confidence in the French, that they will favor Us in this View.

I have the honor to be, with great Respect and Esteem, Sir, your most obedient & most humble Servant.   John Adams.

NA: PCC, item 84, v. 4, pp. 452-454 (LS); M247, reel 112.
    [1] "All the better! All the better! All the better! I congratulate you upon it,"
    [2] "All the better for us"
    [3] "Yes, Sir, I think that you will have another war against the English."

John Adams to Robert R. Livingston

Sir,   Paris July 11th· 1783.

As there are certain particulars, in which it has appeared to me that the friendship of a French Minister has been problematical at least, or rather not to exist at all, I have freely mentioned them to Congress; because I hold it to be the first duty of a public Minister in my Situation, to conceal no important Truth of this kind from his Masters.

But Ingratitude is an odious Vice, & ought to be held in detestation by every American Citizen. We ought to distinguish therefore between those points, for which We are not obliged to our Allies, from those in which We are.

I think then We are under no particular Obligations of Gratitude to them for the Fisheries, the Boundaries, Exemption from the Tories, or for the progress of our Negotiations in Europe.

We are under Obligations of Gratitude for making the Treaty with Us when they did; for those Sums of Money which they have generously given Us, and for those even which they have lent Us, which I hope We shall punctually pay, and be thankful still for the Loan; for the Fleet & Army they sent to America, & for all the important Services they did. By other mutual Exertions a dangerous Rival to them, and I may almost be warranted in saying, an imperious Master both to them and Us, has been brought to Reason, and put out of the Power to do Harm to either. In this respect, however, our Allies are more secure than we. The House of Bourbon has acquiered a great Accession of Strength: while their hereditary Enemy has been weakened one half, and incurably crippled.

The French are besides a good natured and humane Nation, very respectable in Arts, Letters, Arms and Commerce – and therefore Motives of Interest, Honour, & Convenience join themselves to those of friendship and gratitude to induce Us to wish for the Continuance of their friendship & Alliance. The Provinces of Canada & Nova Scotia, in the hands of the English, are a constant warning to Us to have a Care of ourselves, & therefore a Continuance of the friendship and Alliance of France is of Importance to our Tranquility & even to our Safety. There is nothing will have a greater effect to overawe the English, and induce them to respect Us and our Rights, than the Reputation of a good Understanding with the French. My Voice and Advice will therefore always be for discharging, with the utmost Fidelity, Gratitude & Exactness, every Obligation We are under to France, & for cultivating her friendship and Alliance by all sorts of good Offices – But I am sure that to do this effectually, We must reason with them at times, enter into particulars and be sure that We understand one another. We must act a manly, honest independent, as well as a sensible part.

With great Respect, I have the honor to be, Sir, your most obedient & most humble Servant.   John Adams.

NA: PCC, *item 84, v. 4, pp. 456-457 (LS); M247, reel 112.*

Comte de Vergennes to Comte d'Adhémar

[Translation]

N°· 11   Versailles, 12 July 1783

I have received the Letter N°· 15 which you did me the honor to write me the 16th of this month. Yesterday I had another Conference with M. le Duke of Manchester, in which we succeeded in settling all the articles of our definitive treaty. No more difficulty exists for what concerns us, but

I hope that Mr. Fox, having obtained all that excited his solicitude, will not bring up more; but things are not as advanced on the part of Spain. Although they had been terminated in the conference of 20 June last, the English ministry today claims that the considerable Establishment that Spain grants on the Coast of Honduras for the Cutting of Campeche wood does not entail the Exclusion of the clandestine Establishments on the Mosquito Coast, which is diametrically contrary to all the Elements of the negotiation in question. I have done all that depends on me to dissuade M. le Duke of Manchester from putting forward a claim so fitted to revolt Spain. I think in fact that England had everything to gain by leaving it in a salutary obscurity. Up to now she has disavowed all the attempts which her subjects have made to establish themselves on that Coast, particularly in 1774 or 1775, when a certain English doctor armed some Vessels to go to set up an establishment on that very Coast. If Mr. Fox would take the trouble to search the Archives of his department, he would find proof that England has never raised any claim of that nature. The very silence of the Peace of Paris, in which that Crown laid down the law, is another Demonstration. I very much fear, if this English minister holds to his idea, that the Conclusion of our definitive treaty will be set back more than ever.

I do not know how to reconcile, Sir, Mr. Fox's professed desire to finish with the obstacles which he seems to have raised to the Conclusion. I do not speak of what relates to Holland; her Conduct has been uniform in this regard, but the negotiation with the Americans makes no progress. Mr. Hartley, charged to treat with them, is even without instructions; he has been told that they have not arrived. Mr. Fox's system may very well be to fatigue our patience, and to engage us to sign independently of that ally, but I hope to convince him, ipso facto, that ours is inexhaustible. We certainly have not taken advantage of the omission of the American Commissioners, in signing their provisional articles independent of us, to do the same to them. If we have signed the preliminaries without the Dutch, no Engagement binds us to them; we are still in the same Condition, we owe them discretion, we shall act in accord with them, but we are not held toward them to any sacrifice of our interest.

.　.　.　.　.

Vergennes

FFAA: Pol. Corr., England, v. 543, f. 74 (LC transcription).

American Peace Commissioners to David Hartley

Sir,   Passy, July 17. 1783.

We have the honor to inform you, that we have just received from Congress their Ratification in due Form, of the Provisional Articles of the 30th. Novr. 1782, and we are ready to exchange Ratifications with his Britannic Majesty's Ministers as soon as may be.

By the same Articles it is stipulated, that his Britannic Majesty shall with all convenient Speed, and without causing any Destruction or carrying away any Negroes or other Property of the American Inhabitants, withdraw all his Armies, Garrisons and Fleets from the United States, and from every Port, Place and Harbour within the same. But by Intelligence lately received from America, and by the inclosed Copies of Letters and Conferences between General Washington and Sir Guy Carleton, it appears that a considerable Number of Negroes belonging to the Citizens of the United States, have been carried off from New-York contrary to the express Stipulation contained in the said Article. We have receiv'd from Congress their Instructions to represent this Matter to you, and to request that speedy and effectual Measures be taken to render that Justice to the Parties interested which the true Intent and Meaning of the Article in question plainly dictates.

We are also instructed to represent to you, that many of the British Debtors in America have in the Course of the War sustained such considerable & heavy Losses by the Operation of the British Arms in that Country, that a great Number of them have been rendered incapable of immediately satisfying those Debts; We refer it to the Justice and Equity of Great Britain, so far to amend the Article on that Subject, as that no Execution shall be issued on a Judgement to be obtained in any such Case but after the Expiration of three Years from the Date of the definitive Treaty of Peace. Congress also think it reasonable that such Part of the Interest which may have accrued on such Debts during the War shall not be payable, because all Intercourse between the two Countries, had, during that Period, become impracticable as well as improper; it does not appear just that Individuals in America should pay for Delays in Payment which were occasioned by the civil & military Measures of Great Britain. In our Opinion the Interest of the Creditors as well as the Debtors, requires that some Tenderness be shewn to the Latter, and that they should be allowed a little Time to acquire the means of discharging Debts, which in many Instances, exceed the whole Amount of their Property.

As it is necessary to ascertain an Epocha for the Restitutions and Evacuations to be made, we propose that it be agreed, that his Britannic

Majesty, shall cause to be evacuated the Posts of New York, Penobscot and their Dependencies, with all other Posts and Places in Possession of his Majesty's Arms, within the United States, in the Space of three Months after the Signature of the definitive Treaty, or sooner if possible, excepting those Posts contiguous to the Water Line, mentioned in the 4th. Proposition, and those shall be evacuated, when Congress shall give the Notice therein mentioned.

We do ourselves the honour of making these Communications to you, Sir, that you may transmit them and the Papers accompanying them to your Court, and inform us of their Answer.

We have the honour to be, Sir, Your most obedient & most humble Servants   John Adams
                                                    B. Franklin.
                                                    John Jay.

NA: PCC, item 85, pp. 364-366 (LBkC); M247, reel 114.

American Peace Commissioners
to Robert R. Livingston

Sir,   Passy, 18th. July 1783
We have had the honour of receiving by Capt. Barney your two Letters of the 25th of March & 21st of April, with the Papers referred to in them.

We are happy to find that the Provisional Articles have been approved & ratified by Congress, and we regret that the Manner in which that Business was conducted, does not coincide with your Ideas of Propriety. We are persuaded however that this is principally owing to your being necessarily unacquainted with a Number of Circumstances, known to us who were on the Spot, and which will be particularly explained to you hereafter, and, we trust, to your Satisfaction & that of the Congress.

Your Doubts respecting the Separate Article we think are capable of being removed, but as a full State of the Reasons and Circumstances which prompted that Measure would be very prolix, we shall content ourselves with giving you the general Outlines.

Mr Oswald was desirous to cover as much of the Eastern Shores of the Missisippi with British Claims as possible and for this purpose we were told a great deal about the ancient Bounds of Canada & Louisiana &ca &ca &ca The British Court who had probably not yet adopted the Idea of relinquishing the Floridas, seemed desirous of anexing as much Territory to them as possible, even up to the Mouth of the Ohio – M[r.] Oswald adhered strongly to that Object as well to render the British Countries there of sufficient Extent to be, (as he express'd it) worth keeping & protecting; as to afford a convenient Retreat to the Tories, for whom it would be difficult otherwise to provide; and among other Arguments he finally urged his being willing to yield to our Demands to the East, North and West, as a further Reason for our gratifying him on the Point in Question. He also produced the Commission of Gov[r.] Johnson[1] extending the Bounds of his Government of W. Florida up to the River Yassous and contended for that Extent as a Matter of Right upon various Principles which however we did not admit.

We were of Opinion that the Country in Contest was of great Value both on Account of its natural Fertility, and of its Position; it being in our Opinion the Interest of America to extend as far down towards the Mouth of the Missisippi as we possibly could. We also thought it adviseable to impress Britain with a strong Sense of the Importance of the Navigation of that River, to their future Commerce on the interior Waters from the Mouth of the River S[t] Lawrens to that of the Missisippi, and thereby render that Court averse to any Stipulations with Spain to relinquish it. These two objects militated against each other; because to inhance the Value of the Navigation was also to inhance the Value of the Countries contiguous to it, and thereby disincline Britain to the Dereliction of them. We thought therefore that the surest Way to reconcile & obtain both Objects would be by a Composition beneficial to both Parties. We therefore proposed that Britain should withdraw her Pretensions to all the Country above the Yassous, and that we would cede all below it to her in Case she should have the Floridas at the End of the War, and at all Events that she should have a Right to navigate the River throughout its whole Extent. This Proposition was accepted, and we agreed to insert the contingent Part of it in a separate Article for the express purpose of keeping it secret for the present. That Article ought not therefore to be consider'd as a mere Matter of Favour to Britain, but as the Result of a Bargain, in which that Article was a "quid pro quo." It was in our Opinion both necessary & justifiable to keep this Article secret. The Negotiations between Spain France & Britain were then in full Vigour, and embarrass'd by a Variety of clashing Demands. The Publication of this Article would have irritated Spain, and retarded if not have prevented her coming to an Agreement with Britain. – Had we mentioned it to the French Minister, he must have not only informed Spain of it, but also been obliged to act a Part respecting it that would probably have been disagreable to America, and he certainly has reason to rejoice that our Silence saved him that delicate and disagreable Task. – This was an Article in which France had not the smallest Interest, nor is there any thing in her Treaty with us, that restrains us from making what Bargain we pleased with Britain about those or any other Lands, without rendering Account of such Transaction to her or any other Power whatever. The same Observation applies with still greater Force to Spain, and neither Justice or Honour forbid us to dispose as we pleased of our own Lands, without her Knowledge or Consent. Spain at that very time extended her Pretensions and Claim of Dominion not only over the Tract in Question, but over the Vast Region lying between the Floridas and Lake Superior; and this Court was also at that very Time soothing & nursing of those Pretensions by a proposed conciliatory Line for splitting the Difference. Suppose therefore we had offer'd this Tract to Spain in Case She retained the Floridas, should we even have had Thanks for it? or would it have abated the Chagrin she experienc'd from being disappointed in her extravagant and improper Designs on that whole Country? we think not.–

We perfectly concur with you in Sentiment, Sir, *"That Honesty is the best Policy"* but untill it be shewn that we have trespass'd on the Rights of any Man or Body of men, you must excuse our thinking that this Remark as applied to our Proceedings was unnecessary.

Should any Explanations either with France or Spain become necessary on this Subject, we hope & expect to meet with no Embarrassments. We shall neither amuse them nor perplex ourselves with ostensible and flimsy Excuses, but tell them plainly that as it was not our Duty to give them the Information, we consider'd ourselves at Liberty to withhold it, and we shall remind the French Minister that he has more Reason to be pleased than displeased with our Silence. Since we have assumed a Place in the Political System of the World let us move like a Primary & not like a Secondary Planet.

We are persuaded, Sir, that your Remarks on these Subjects resulted from real Opinion, and were made with all Candour and Sincerity. The Best Men will view Objects of this Kind in different Lights even when standing on the same Ground: and it is not to be wonder'd at that we who are on the Spot and have the whole Transaction under our Eyes should see many Parts of it in a stronger Point of Light than Persons at a Distance, who can only view it through the dull Medium of Representation.

It would give us great Pain if any thing we have written, or now write respecting this Court, should be construed to impeach the Friendship of the King & Nation for us. We also believe that the Minister is so far our Friend, and is disposed so far to do us Good Offices, as may correspond with, and be dictated by his System of Policy for Promoting the Power, Riches and Glory of France. God forbid that we should ever sacrifice our Faith, our Gratitude, or our Honour, to any Consideration of Convenience; and may he also forbid that we should ever be unmindful of the Dignity and independant Spirit which should always characterize a free and generous People. –

We shall immediately propose an Article to be inserted in the Definitive Treaty for postponing the Payment of British Debts for the Time mentioned by Congress.

There are, no doubt, certain Ambiguities in our Articles, but it is not to be wonder'd at when it is consider'd how exceedingly averse Britain was to Expressions which explicitly wounded the Tories: and how disinclined we were to use any that should amount to absolute Stipulations in their Favour.

The Words for restoring the Property of *Real British Subjects* were well understood and explained between us not to mean or comprehend American Refugees. Mr. Oswald and Mr. Fitz-Herbert know this to have been the Case, and will readily confess and admit it. This mode of Expression was preferr'd by them as a more delicate Mode of excluding those Refugees, and of making a proper Distinction between them and the Subjects of Britain whose only *particular* Interest in America consisted in holding Lands or Property there.

The 6th. Article vizt. where it declares that no future Confiscations shall be made &c^a ought to have fixed the Time with greater Accuracy: We think the most fair and true Construction is, that it relates to the Date of the Cessation of Hostilities. That is the Time when Peace in Fact took Place, in consequence of Prior informal tho' binding Contracts to terminate the War. We consider the Definitive Treaties as only giving the Dress of Form to those Contracts, and not as constituting the Obligation of them. Had the Cessation of Hostilities been the Effect of a Truce, & consequently nothing more than a temporary Suspension of War, another Construction would have been the true one.

We are Officially assured by Mr. Hartley that positive Orders for the Evacuation of New-York have been dispatched; and that no avoidable Delay will retard that Event. Had we proposed to fix a Time for it, the British Court would have contended that it should be a Time posterior to the Date of the definitive Treaty and that would have been probably more disadvantageous to us than as that Article now stands.

We are surprized to hear that any Doubts have arisen in America respecting the Time when the Cessation of Hostilities took Place there. It most certainly took Place at the Expiration of one Month after the Date of that Declaration in all Parts of the World, whether Land or Sea that lay North of the Latitude of the Canaries. The Ships afterwards taken from us in the more Northerly Latitudes ought to be reclaimed and given up: We shall apply to Mr. Hartley on this Subject, and also on that of the

Transportation of Negroes from New York contrary to the Words and Intention of the Provisional Articles. –

With great Esteem, we have the honour to be, Sir, Your most obedient & most humble Servants.   John Adams.
B. Franklin
John Jay.

NA: PCC, *item 85, pp. 300-312 (LS); M247, reel 114.*

¹ *Johnstone, George (1730-1787). British naval officer, colonial official, and political figure. After an early naval career, Governor of West Florida, 1763-1767. Member of Parliament, 1768-1779, 1781-1787. Member, Carlisle Commission, 1778. Commodore commanding naval squadron on the coast of Portugal, 1779-1781. Commanded expedition against Cape of Good Hope, 1781.*

John Jay to Robert R. Livingston

Dear Rob^(t·)   Passy 19 July 1783

our Dispatches by Barney must be ready the Day after Tomorrow. The many Letters I have written, and have still to write, together with Conferences, Company &^(c·) keep me fully employed. You will therefore excuse my not descending so much to particulars, as both of us indeed might wish –

As little that passes in Congress is kept entirely secret, we think it prudent at least to postpone giving you a more minute Detail than you have already rec^d, of the Reasons which induced Us to sign the provisional Articles without previously communicating them to the french Minister. for your private Satisfaction however I will make a few Remarks on that Subject.

Your Doubts respecting the Propriety of our Conduct in that Instance appear to have arisen from the following Considerations

1 –   That we ~~were~~ entertained and were influenced by Distrusts and Suspicions which do not seem to You to have been altogether well founded –

2.   That we signed the Articles without previously communicating them to this Court.

With Respect to the *first.* In our Negociation with the british Commissionor it was essential to insist on, and if possible obtain his Consent to four important Concessions –

(1)   That Britain should treat with us as being what we were, vi*z·* an independent People.

The french Minister thought this Demand premature, & that it ought to arise from, and not precede the Treaty –

(2) That Britain should agree to the *Extent* of Boundary we claimed –
The french Minister thought our Demands on that head, extravagant in themselves, and as militating against certain Views of Spain which he was disposed to favor.

(3) That Britain should admit our Right in common to the Fishery.
The french Minister thought this Demand too extensive–

(4) That Britain should not insist on our re-instating the Tories
The french Minister argued that they ought to be reinstated

Was it unnatural for us to conclude from these Facts that the french Minister was opposed to our succeeding on these four Points in the Extent we wished? It appeared evident that his plan of a Treaty for America, was far from being such as America would have preferred; and as we disapproved of his Model, we thought it imprudent to give him an opportunity of moulding our Treaty by it–

Whether the Minister was influenced by what he really thought best for us, or by what he really thought best for France, is a Question which however easy or difficult to decide, is not very important to the Point under Consideration – Whatever his Motives may have been, certain it is that they were such as opposed our System; and as in private Life it is deemed imprudent to admit opponents to full Confidence, especially respecting the very Matters in Competition, so in public affairs the like Caution seems equally proper.

Secondly – But admitting the Force of this Reasoning, Why, when the articles were compleated, did we not communicate them to the french Minister, *before* we proceeded to sign them? for the following Reasons –

The Expectations excited in England by Lord Shelbourn's Friends, that he would put a speedy Period to the war, made it necessary for him either to realize those Expectations, or prepare to quit his Place. The Parliament being to meet before his Negociations with us were concluded, he found it expedient to adjourn it for a short Term, in Hopes of then meeting it with all the advantage that might be expected from a favorable Issue of the Negociation. Hence it was his Interest to draw it to a Close before that Adjournment should expire; and to obtain that End both he and his Commissionor became less tenacious on certain Points than they would otherwise have been. Nay we have, & then had, good Reason to believe that the Latitude allowed by the british Cabinet for the Exercise of Discretion was exceeded on that occasion–

I must now remind you that the King of G. Britain had pledged himself, in M.ʳ Oswald's Commission, to confirm and ratify *not* what M.ʳ Oswald should *verbally* agree to, but what he should *formally sign his name and affix his Seal to.*

Had we communicated the Articles when ready for signing to the french Minister, he doubtless would have complimented us on the Terms of them; but at the same Time he would have insisted on our postponing the Signature until the Articles then preparing between France Spain & Britain should also be ready for signing, he having often intimated to us that we should all sign at the same Time and Place. This would have exposed us to a disagreable Dilemma.

Had we agreed to postpone signing the Articles, the british Cabinet might & probably would have taken Advantage of it. They might (if better prospects had offered) have insisted that the Articles were still *Res infecta*. – That M^r. Oswald had exceeded the Limits of his Instructions, and for both these Reasons that they concieved themselves still at Liberty to dissent from his Opinions, & to forbid his executing a Set of Articles they could not approve of. It is true that this might not have happened, but it is equally true that it might, and therefore it was a Risque of too great Importance to run. The whole Business would in that Case have been set afloat again, and the Minister of France would have had an opportunity at least of approving the Objections of the british Court, and of advising us to recede from Demands which in his opinion were immoderate, and too inconsistant with the Claims of Spain to meet with his Concurrence.

If on the other Hand, we had contrary to his Advice and Request, refused to postpone the signing, it is natural to suppose that such Refusal would have given more offence to the french Minister, than our doing it without consulting him at all about the Matter –

Our withholding from him the Knowledge of these Articles until after they were signed, was no Violation of our Treaty with France, and therefore she has no Room for Complaint, on that Principle, against the United States –

Congress had indeed made and published a Resolution not to make peace but in Confidence and in Concurrence with France. So far as this Resolution declares against a *separate* peace, it has been incontestably observed – and admitting that the Words in Confidence and in Concurrence with France, mean that we should mention to the french Minister and consult with him about every Step of our Proceedings, yet it is most certain that it was founded on a mutual Understanding that France would patronize our Demands and assist us in obtaining the Objects of them – France therefore by discouraging our Claims ceased to be entitled to the Degree of Confidence respecting them, which was specified in the Resolution. It may be said that France must admit the Reasonableness of our Claims, before we could properly expect that she should promote them. She knew what were our Claims before Negociation commenced, tho she could only conjecture what Reception they would meet with from Britain. If she thought our Claims extravagant, she may be excusable for not countenancing them in their full Extent; but then we ought also to be excused for not giving her the full Confidence on those Subjects which was promised on the implied Condition of her supporting them –

But Congress positively instructed us to do nothing without the Advice & Consent of the french Minister, and we have departed from that Line of Conduct – this is also true – but there I apprehend that Congress marked out the Line of Conduct for their own Sake, and not for the Sake of France. The Object of that Instruction was the supposed Interest of America, and not of France; and we were directed to ask the advice of the french Minister, because it was thought advantageous to our Country that we should recieve and be governed by it. Congress *only* therefore have a Right to complain of our Departure from the Line of that Instruction.

If it be urged that Confidence ought to subsist between Allies, I have only to remark that as the french Minister did not consult us about his Articles, nor make us any Communication about them, our giving him as little Trouble about our's did not violate any Principle of Reciprocity.

．　．　．　．　．　．

I am D.ʳ· Rob.ᵗ· Your aff.ᵗ· Friend   John Jay

NYHS: *Robert R. Livingston Papers, microfilm reel 3* (ALS).

Comte de Vergennes to Chevalier de la Luzerne

[Translation]

N.ᵒ· 50   Versailles, 21 July 1783

I have received successively, Sir, the despatches which you have done me the honor of writing me from N°. 299 through N°. 331 inclusively.

The representations which you have made to Mr. Morris to hinder him from asking us for additional funds have been to no purpose; this Super-Intendent of Finance, taking advantage of the easy terms that he has met with up until now on our part, has so multiplied his bills that they exceed by nearly 2,000,000 the six which the King has granted for the current year. Messrs. Franklin and Jay have sent me a communication requesting 1,900,000 livres on account from the 3 million stated in the resolution of Congress; I have submitted this request to the King; but His Majesty has found it absolutely impossible to take into consideration; and it is to apprise Mr. Franklin and Mr. Jay of this that I have sent them the two letters of which you will find copies enclosed. It would certainly have been very agreeable to the King to assist with additional aid the finances of the United States: but His Majesty would only have aggravated the weight of the expenses which burden the people on behalf of a nation which rejects with unexampled obstinacy all the measures which have been proposed up to now for putting an end to its distress; besides, the war which has just ended has cost France enormous Sums; the current year is more costly than a year of war, because it is necessary to disarm and to settle all the accounts, and it is unhappily only too evident that all this can only be done by means of loans. You have, Sir, very luminously explained the verities to Mr. Morris, and that Superintendent will know from experience that you have not deceived him. There will probably be grumbling in America, the partisans of England will endeavor to discredit us: but this is an evil which we will delight in remedying; moreover, we have never based our policy with regard to the United States upon their gratitude: this sentiment is infinitely rare between sovereigns, and republics do not understand it at all.

In this manner, Sir, all that we have done with regard to the Americans, is, as you have so well observed, to allow things to follow their natural course; not to depart from the noble, sincere, and disinterested course which we have held up to now with regard to the Americans; to point out the good in all their proceedings, and, if we cannot steer them according to the grand principles which have served as the basis of our alliance with them, to take in time the measures necessary not to be the dupes of their ingratitude and of their false policy.

The future existence of Congress, Sir, presents important questions to discuss, and I foresee that some time will pass before they are decided. I think, like you, that the preservation of Congress would suit us; but what suits us perhaps more is that the United States do not take the political consistency to which they are susceptible, because everything persuades me that their views and their attachments are very versatile, and that we shall not at all be able to count upon them if ever new discussions with England happen unexpectedly. Besides, Sir, what I have just said is only my personal judgment: I have the less examined the matter, which is such as could be the result of the most mature reflections. I judge that even though we would wish it, we are without means to influence the domestic arrangements of the United States, and that in any case we could only be a quiet spectator of the commotions with which their constitution and their internal relations may meet.

The boundaries, Sir, to which England has consented with regard to the Mississippi must have caused some astonishment in America; for it was surely not expected that the English Ministry would go beyond the watersheds of the chain of mountains which border the United States, that is to say, from Ohio to Georgia. However, there is an advantage that results from that, for the American Republic is more ideal than real; in fact, the greater part of the Indian peoples situated between the United States and the Mississippi are independent savages, upon whom the Court of London has only very illusory or at least very equivocal claims; in addition to which England, in yielding the navigation of the Mississippi, has granted that which no longer belongs to them: it is the principle that the rivers belong to those to whom belong the banks; now Spain was, as of 30 November, mistress of the banks of the Mississippi at least from Natchez as far as its mouth in the Gulf of Mexico, and His Catholic Majesty has been maintained incommutably in this ownership by the preliminaries signed the 20th of January. It follows, Sir, that England has ceded to the Americans a rationale or rather a source of quarrels with Spain, and that they cannot, in spite of their treaty, navigate the lower parts of the Mississippi without the consent of the Court of Madrid.

I do not know, Sir, how it could be imagined that the boundaries accorded to the Americans in the West were given us in ill-temper, and that we have tried to persuade the British Ministry to limit them. What is very certain is that I was continually unaware of the state of the negotiation between the English and American commissioners; that in a conversation that I had with Mr. Adams, if I do not delude myself, at the beginning of November, that plenipotentiary told me only the vaguest things about the boundaries in the North without making mention of those in the West, and that I have only been informed by reading the provisional articles.

It is true that Mr. Jay, having begun a negotiation with the Comte d'Aranda relative to the borders of the United States at the Mississippi, and not being able to reach an accord with that ambassador, invited M. de Rayneval to smooth away the difficulties that he encountered, and that he sent him, at the moment of his departure for England, a memoir which demonstrated that neither the Americans nor the Spanish have rights to the tribes which live between the Appalachians and the Mississippi; but this writing expressed only the personal opinion of M. de Rayneval, as he had informed Mr. Jay, and thus could only be considered as non-existent relative to the King's ministry. I enter into this detail, Sir, because I have reason to regard Mr. Jay as the author of the insinuations which must have been made to Congress to render us suspect, and because I judge it my duty, at all events, to put you in a position to destroy them: in order to furnish you all the weapons you may need to accomplish this task, I am sending you a copy of M. de Rayneval's memoir, as well as of the letter with which he accompanied it in sending it to Mr. Jay.

As for the article of the fisheries, we have always voiced our sentiment with the utmost freedom: you may, Sir, convince yourself of this if you would be so good as to return to the correspondence of M. Grand. There will be a difference between establishing principles and expressing wishes: our wishes have always been with the Americans, but our principles have condemned their pretensions; besides, at what time have we manifested them? It was when we saw the State of Massachusetts disposed to make peace and independence the price of the right to fish on the coasts of Newfoundland; but our opinion could not influence the negotiations, seeing that we knew nothing of the details, and that they were terminated in a manner most brusque, most unexpected and, I may say, most extraordinary.

This last circumstance, Sir, obliged us to move quickly, because it was a breach of procedure and of respect of which there exist few examples, and we have never doubted that Congress would share our opinion in this regard. That assembly's intention of dealing severely with its representatives seemed to the King's most complete satisfaction, and His Majesty, content with this demonstration, strongly approved the pains that you have taken to prevent their complaints from having troublesome consequences for the American plenipotentiaries: one must think that the admonition which they have received will make them perceive the necessity of devoting henceforth more propriety and respect to their proceedings. I can also tell you that I have for some time had reason to be satisfied with their conduct. But I am in grave doubt about the principles of Messrs. Adams and Jay; I am told, in their regard, of notions which confirm what you have written me of the content of their despatches. Their jealousy of Mr. Franklin is their principal motivation; it irritates them and blinds them to the point that they do not blush at denouncing that minister as sold to France and at rendering our policy suspect. But I have too much good opinion of the shrewdness and wisdom of Congress to suppose that, despite the ostracism that reigns there, it will not support the man who has rendered the most important Services to his Homeland, and that it will not reject with scorn the insinuations that may be made to it against His Majesty's principles and sentiments. I understand that Mr. Franklin has asked for his recall, but that Congress has not yet acted on his request. I desire that it reject it, at least for the present, because it will be impossible to give Mr. Franklin a Successor as wise and also conciliatory as he; moreover, I fear that we will be left with Mr. Jay, and he is the man with whom I would least like to treat of affairs: he is egotistical, and too accessible to prejudices and ill-humor. In addition, Sir, all these details are for you alone; you will not have any use to make of them, because in wishing to serve Mr. Franklin, we run the risk of harming him by giving a glimmer of probability to the untrue insinuations of his Colleagues; however, the reserve that I recommend to you ought not to prevent you from rendering justice to his loyalty and to the constant Wisdom of his conduct when the occasion presents itself naturally.

I am astonished, Sir, that Congress has called into question the necessity of ratifying the provisional treaty made with the Court of London: this act alone can corroborate the Signing by the plenipotentiaries and give the treaty executory force. I am unaware if they have received it: their silence makes me presume that it has not yet arrived.

They are busy with their definitive treaty; but the negotiation is, by the act of the English plenipotentiary, in a state of languor which is constantly on the point of causing us much embarrassment; in fact, we, as well as Spain, are in accord upon all our business, in such manner that we are in a proper condition to sign: the Dutch are just on the point of being in the same position; and we are being held up solely by the American treaty. If that circumstance occurs, we shall consider means to guard against this inconvenience, the King persisting in wishing to finish only conjointly with his friends.

The American Plenipotentiaries have consulted me relative to the mediation of the two Imperial Courts; I have observed to them that, the two Courts having never offered their mediation to Congress, it could either claim it or decline it. I still do not know at what point it will consider it appropriate to leave off. In my opinion, the simplest course would be to treat without any foreign intervention.

You are inclined to think, Sir, that it is the Court of London which has prepared the rapprochement that just took place between that of Lisbon and the United States, but I have no proper notion to support your opinion in this regard, and I am persuaded that circumstances alone have determined the Portuguese Ministry to court the Americans.

We are very busy, Sir, with all that is relative to our commerce with America, and we perceive more than ever the necessity of according them encouragements and favors. The King has just ordered a reduction of duties on the Salts of Marenne, and I have reason to think that the same operation will take place with regard to brandies. On the other hand, His Majesty has declared L'Orient a free port: it is a place that the Americans have always desired in preference to all others. The point most difficult to fix are the longterm credits of which the American merchants have need: the administration can do nothing there: confidence alone can cause our merchants to entrust themselves to those of America.

Vergennes

FFAA: Pol. Corr., U.S., v. 25, f. 40/63-71 (LC transcription).

Benjamin Franklin to Robert R. Livingston

Sir,   Passy July 22$^{d.}$ 1783

. . . . .

We, the Commissioners, have in our joint Capacity written a Letter to you, which you will receive with this. I shall now answer yours of March 26. May 9 & May 31$^{st.}$ It gave me great Pleasure to learn by the first, that the News of the Peace diffused general Satisfaction. I will not now take upon me to justify the apparent Reserve respecting this Court at the Signature, which you disapprove. We have touch'd upon it in our general Letter. I do not see, however, that they have much Reason to complain of that Transaction. Nothing was stipulated to their Prejudice, and none of the Stipulations were to have force, but by a subsequent Act of their own. I suppose indeed that they have not complained of it, or you would have sent us a Copy of the Complaint, that we might have answer'd it. I long since satisfy'd Count de V. about it here. We did what appear'd to all of us best at the time, and if we have done Wrong, the Congress will do right, after hearing us, to censure us. Their nomination of five Persons to the Service, seems to mark that they had some Dependence on our joint Judgment, since one alone could have made a Treaty by Direction of the French Ministry, as well as twenty. I will only add, that with respect to myself; neither the Letter from M. Marbois handed to us thro' the British Negociators, (a suspicious Channel) nor the Conversations respecting the Fishery, the Boundaries, the Royalists &c^a recommending Moderation in our Demands, are of Weight sufficient in my Mind to fix an Opinion that this Court wished to restrain us in obtaining any Degree of Advantage we could prevail on our Enemies to accord; since those Discourses are fairly resolvable, by supposing a very natural Apprehension, that we, relying too much on the Ability of France to continue the War in our Favour, & supply us constantly with Money, might insist on more Advantages than the English would be willing to grant, and thereby lose the Opportunity of making Peace so necessary to all our Friends.

I ought not however to conceal from you that one of my Colleagues is of a very different Opinion from me in these Matters. He thinks the French Minister one of the greatest Enemies of our Country, that he would have straitned our Boundaries to prevent the Growth of our People, contracted our Fishery to obstruct the Increase of our Seamen, & retained the Royalists among us to keep us divided; that he privately opposes all our Negociations with foreign Courts, and afforded us during the War the Assistance we received, only to keep it alive, that we might be so much the more weaken'd by it: That to think of Gratitude to France is the greatest of Follies, and that to be influence'd by it, would ruin us. He makes no Secret of his having these Opinions, expresses them publickly, sometimes in presence of the English Ministers, and speaks of hundreds of Instances which he could produce in Proof of them, none however have yet appear'd to me, unless the Conversation & Letter abovementioned are reckoned such. If I were not convinced of the real Inability of this Court to furnish the further Supply's we asked, I should suspect these Discourses of a Person in his Station, might have influenced the Refusal; but I think they have gone no further than to occasion a Suspicion, that we have a considerable Party of Antigallicans in America, who are not Tories, and consequently to produce some Doubts of the continuance of our Friendship. As such Doubts may hereafter have a bad Effect, I think we cannot take too much Care to remove them; and it is therefore I write this to put you on your guard, (believing it my Duty; tho' I know that I hazzard by it a mortal Enmity) and to caution you < *** > respecting the Insinuations of this Gentleman against this Court, & the Instances he supposes of their Ill-Will to us, which I take to be as imaginary as I know his Fancies to be, that Count de V. and myself are continually plotting against him & employing the News Writers of Europe to depreciate his Character, &c^a but as Shakespear says, "Trifles light as Air, &c." I am persuaded however, that he means well for his Country, is always an honest Man, often a Wise One, but sometimes and in some things, absolutely out of his Senses.

When the Commercial Article mentioned in yours of the 26th was struck out of our proposed Preliminaries by the British Ministry, the Reason given was that sundry Acts of Parliament still in force were against it, and must be first repealed, which I believe was really their Intention; and sundry Bills were accordingly brought in for that purpose: But new Ministers with different Principles succeeding, a Commercial Proclamation totally different from those Bills has lately appear'd. I send inclosed a Copy of it. We shall try what can be done in the definitive Treaty towards setting aside that Proclamation: But if it should be persisted in, it will then be a Matter worthy the attentive Discussion of Congress, whether it will be most prudent to retort with a similar Regulation in order to force its Repeal; (which may possibly tend to bring on another Quarrel) or to let it pass without Notice, and leave it to its own Inconvenience, or rather Impracticability, in the Execution, and to the Complaints of the West India Planters, who must all pay much dearer for our Produce under those Restrictions. I am not enough Master of the Course of our Commerce to give an Opinion on this particular Question; and it does not behove me to do it; yet I have seen so much Embarrassment and so little Advantage in all the restraining & Compulsive Systems, that I feel myself strongly inclined to believe that a State which leaves all her Ports open to all the

World upon equal Terms, will by that means have foreign Commodities cheaper, sell its own Productions dearer, and be on the whole the most prosperous. I have heard some Merchants say, that there is ten per C$^{t.}$ difference between *Will you buy?* and *Will you sell?* When Foreigners bring us their Goods, they want to part with them speedily, that they may purchase their Cargoes & dispatch their Ships, which are at constant Charges in our Ports; we have then the Advantage of their *Will you buy?* and when they demand our Produce we have the Advantage of their *Will you sell?* and the concurring Demand of a Number also contribute to raise our Prices. Thus both these Questions are in our Favour at home, against us abroad. – The employing however of our own Ships and raising a Breed of Seamen among us, tho' it should not be a matter of so much private Profit as some imagine, is nevertheless of political Importance & must have Weight in considering this Subject.

The Judgment you make of the Conduct of France in the Peace, and the greater Glory acquired by her Moderation than even by her Arms, appears to me perfectly just. – The Character of this Court and Nation seems of late Years to be considerably changed. The Ideas of Aggrandisement by Conquest, are out of Fashion, & those of Commerce are more enlightened, and more generous than heretofore. We shall soon I believe, feel something of this, in our being admitted to a greater Freedom of Trade with their Islands, The Wise here think France great enough, and its Ambition at present seems to be only that of Justice and Magnanimity towards other Nations, Fidelity & Utility to its Allies.

.   .   .   .   .

Be pleased to present my dutiful Respects to the Congress, assure them of my most faithful Services, and believe me to be, with great & sincere Esteem, Sir, Your most obedient & most humble Servant.

                                                      B. Franklin

NA: PCC, *item 82, v. 2, pp. 389-412 (LS); M247, reel 108.*

Arthur Lee to Lord Shelburne

My Lord,   Philadelphia, July 23d, 1783.
    Among the blessings of peace I number that of being able to renew my correspondence with a nobleman I so much respect and esteem. For that peace, honourable to America, and as much so in my judgment for England as the actual situation of things could give any colour of reason to expect, your country and America are indebted to your lordship's wisdom and firmness.

Upon my word, my lord, did I not know so much of the politics of St. James' and St. Stephens', I should be lost in wonder at the vote in the house of commons and the treatment your lordship has received. But I shall never forget Lord Chatham's expression, 'I was duped and deceived.' The outrageous wickedness of visiting upon your conclusion of the war, the evils which the folly of its commencement, and the rapacity, cruelity and profusion of the conduct of it produced, sprung from the same source with the deception practised upon Lord Chatham, which he so emphatically detailed in the house of peers.

I always judged that the author of those measures, who cannot be said to cover himself with the *majesty of darkness*, though he meant the subjugation of America, would in fact conduct her to independence. I judged, too, that he would in the end, bring himself to ruin. Nothing, surely, can more accelerate this event, than introducing again into high office the ostensible minister of those pernicious measures. For as to his whig colleagues, their reign is short; and their fall will assuredly be unpitied.

Of the people of England, on whom in fact the salvation of their country depends, it may be said, that "*aliquando redit in praecordia virtus.*"[1] They have given some proofs of this; and perhaps the last one will bring due punishment upon the author of their near approach to humiliation and ruin; an humiliation and ruin which, had not your lordship interposed, would at this moment have been consummated.

I have flattered myself that your lordship has felt some anxiety about my situation, under the various attacks that have been made upon me. They all originated with the minister, whose politics so much overshot themselves in the late negotiation for peace, and who was determined on my removal, as one who could not be bent to his purposes. He found, however, my successor stubborn; and this country owes immortal gratitude to that gentleman's firmness, spirit and integrity. Yet an attempt was made to sacrifice him, for this very service; and I had the pleasure of defending him against those men, with whom he cooperated in effecting my removal. I am now elected into congress, for the third and last year I am capable of sitting there, by the confederation. I shall then retire into private life, with the satisfaction of dwelling under that constitution which I have laboured to assist in rearing to liberty, virtue and public happiness.

But I am afraid politicians have been too sanguine in their expectations from systems of government. Corruption and intrigue seem inseparable from them all; and these are promoted or restrained more by the genius of the people, than by forms of government, or the operation of laws. Indeed it does not seem so *unwise now*, as it *once* did, in Mr. Pope,[2] to say,

"For forms of government let fools contest;
That which is best adminster'd, is best."

Nor would I promise that a little more experience will not make me a convert to his opinions.

You used to say, my lord, that you would send Lord Fitzmaurice[3] to make the tour of America. Such a tour, I conceive, would be both interesting and instructive. Nature has displayed her powers in the *sublime* and *beautiful* far more in America than in Europe, and the progress of art, considering the time it has had to operate, is astonishing. I shall next year be at liberty to accompany Lord Fitzmaurice in such a tour, and should take a vast deal of pleasure in doing it.

I have the honour to be, with profound respect and regard, your obedient servant,   Arthur Lee.

Smith, Letters of Delegates, v. 2, pp. 442-443.
    [1] *Literally, at last virtue is returning to their breasts.*
    [2] *Pope, Alexander (1688-1744). British poet. The quotation is from* An Essay on Man *(London, 1758), Epistle III, 30.*
    [3] *Son of Lord Shelburne.*

Alexander Hamilton to John Jay

Dear Sir   Philadelphia July 25. 1783
    Though I have not performed my promise of writing to you, which I made when you left this country, yet I have not the less interest myself in your welfare and success. I have been witness with pleasure to every event which has had a tendency to advance you in the esteem of your country; and I may assure you with sincerity that it is as high as you could possibly wish. All have united in the warmest approbation of your conduct. I cannot forbear telling you this, because my situation has given me access to the truth, and I gratify my friendship for you in communicating what cannot fail to gratify your sensibility.

    The peace which exceeds in the goodness of its terms, the expectations of the most sanguine does the highest honor to those who made it. It is the more agreeable, as the time was come, when thinking men began to be seriously alarmed at the internal embarrassments and exhausted state of this country. The New England people talk of making you an annual *fish-offering* as an acknowlegement of your exertions for the participation of the fisheries.

    We have now happily concluded the great work of independence, but much remains to be done to reap the fruits of it. Our prospects are not flattering. Every day proves the inefficacy of the present confederation, yet the common danger being removed we are receding instead of advancing in a disposition to amend its defects. The road to popularity in each state is to inspire jealousies of the power of Congress, though nothing can be more apparent than that they have no power; and that for the want of it, the resources of the country during the war could not be drawn out, and we at this moment experience all the mischiefs of a bankrupt and ruined credit. It is to be hoped that when prejudice and folly have run themselves out of breath we may return to reason and correct our errors.

After having served in the field during the war, I have been making a short apprenticeship in Congress; but the evacuation of New York approaching, I am preparing to take leave of pubic life to enter into the practice of the law. Your country will continue to demand your services abroad.

...I beg you to present me most respectfully to M$^{rs.}$ Jay and to be assured of the affection and esteem of Dr Sir Your Obedient servant,

Alex^r· Hamilton

Windsor Castle Library: Selected Papers of John Jay, LC microfilm reel 11415 (ALS).

American Peace Commissioners to Robert R. Livingston

Sir,   Passy, July 27. 1783.

The Definitive Treaties between the late belligerent Powers are none of them yet compleated. Ours has gone on slowly, owing partly to the Necessity Mr Hartley (Successor of Mr Oswald) thinks himself under of sending every Proposition, either his own or ours, to his Court for their Approbation; and their Delay in answering, thro' Negligence perhaps since they have heard our Ports are open, or thro' Indecision occasioned by Ignorance of the Subject, or thro' want of Union among their Ministers. We send you herewith Copies of several Papers that have pass'd between us. He has for sometime assured us that he is in Hourly Expectation of Answers but they do not arrive. The British Proclamation respecting the Commerce appears to vex him a good deal. We enclose a Copy. And we are of Opinion that finally we shall find it best to drop all Commercial Articles in our Definitive Treaty; and leave every thing of that kind to a future Special Treaty to be made either in America or in Europe as Congress shall think fit to Order. Perhaps it may be best to give Powers for that Purpose to the Minister that probably will be sent to London. The Opinion here is, that it will be becoming in us to take the first Step towards the mutual Exchange of Ministers; and we have been assured by the English Minister who treats with us here, that ours will be well received.

The Dutch Preliminaries are not yet agreed on, and it seems to be settled, that we are to sign all together, in the Presence of the Ministers of the two Imperial Courts who are to be complimented with the Opportunity of signing as Mediators, tho' they have not yet, and perhaps will not be consulted in the Negociations. M⁻ Adams is gone to Holland, for three Weeks, but will return sooner if wanted. The Propositions you mention as made to us from that State, we suppose he has given you an Account of. Nothing was or is likely to be done upon them here, and therefore it was less necessary to say any thing concerning them. A Minister from thence has been gone some time to Congress, and if he has those Propositions in Charge, they will best be consider'd there.

With great Esteem, we have the Honour to be, Sir, Your most obedient & most humble Ser^ts: B. Franklin
                                                           John Jay
                                                           Henry Laurens.

NA: PCC, item 85, pp. 316-318 (LS); M247, reel 114.

Francis Dana to Robert R. Livingston

(N° 36.)   St. Petersbourg July 16ᵗʰ 1783. O.S. [July 27, 1783]
Sir

I have this day been honoured with the Duplicate of your Letter N° 9 of the 2ᵈ of last May, enclosing the Resolution of Congress of the first of April approving of my intention of returning to America, provided I shou'd not be engaged in a negotiation with this Court at the time I shou'd receive that Resolution; but that if I shou'd be, it is the desire of Congress that I shou'd finish such Negotiation before I return. This Letter has come very opportunely to hand, as we are in expectation every moment of receiving the account of the conclusion of the Definitive Treaty of Peace, when I shou'd have immediately had my Audience of Her Imp: Majesty. I shall now think it expedient to decline that honour: for it wou'd be a very useless Ceremony to take an Audience of Reception one day, when the next I must ask one of Departure. For as according to your Letter it not only seems that Congress decline being at the customary expence of concluding a Treaty with Her Imperial Majesty, but you say also "With respect to a commercial Treaty (the only one I had any intention of concluding) none cou'd be signed by me as my powers only extend to communicate with Her Imperial Majesty's Ministers on the subject of a Treaty, &c &c but not to sign it." I confess I had put a very different Construction upon the passage of my Instructions alluded to, which is "You shall assure Her Imp. Majesty and her Ministers of the sincere disposition of the United States to enter into a Treaty of Friendship and Commerce with Her, on Terms of the most perfect equality &c. And you are authorised to communicate with Her Imp: Majesty's Ministers on the form and terms of such Treaty, and transmit the same to Congress for their Ratification." Especially when taken in conjunction with the following paragraph of my Commission "And he is further authorised in Our name and on behalf of the United States to propose a Treaty of Amity and Commerce between these United States and Her said Imperial Majesty, and to confer and treat thereon with her Ministers vested with equal powers, so as the same shall be founded on principles of equality &c. transmitting such Treaty for Our final Ratification. And We declare in good Faith that We will confirm whatsoever shall by him be transacted in the Premises." But it is useless to spend a moments consideration upon the extent of my Powers, when you say "You are persuaded that it is the wish of Congress rather to postpone any Treaty with Russia than to buy one at this day," as I am persuaded no Treaty is to be obtained, or cou'd be honourably proposed without conforming, as other Nations have done, to the usage of this Court in that respect. And that it wou'd be for the Interest of the United States immediately to conclude a Commercial Treaty with Her Imp: Majesty, such a one as I flatter myself I cou'd obtain, I have not the least doubt upon my Mind. As to the Neutral Confederation I have the honour to agree in opinion with you, that it is now of little consequence to us. for this reason I had determined to have nothing to do with it, even if I cou'd not obtain a commercial Treaty without acceding to it, as was the Case with Portugal.

I pray you to be pleased to acquaint Congress that I shall improve the earliest opportunity to leave this Country and to return to America. Happily I shall have a very good one in three Weeks or a Month in the Yatcht of the Duchess of Kingston, which will sail from hence for Boston where I hope to arrive in all November. I have not received the Letter from Mr Morris which you mention, or the original of your N° 9.

I have the honour to be with much Respect Sir Your most obedient & most hble: Servant   Fra Dana

NA: PCC, item 89, v. 2, pp. 801-804 (LS); M247, reel 117.

David Hartley to Charles James Fox

N° 16   Paris July 31ˢᵗ 1783
Sir
    You will be informed by this Courier that Monsieur de Vergennes has
declared to the Duke of Manchester that he will not sign the definitive
Treaty with Great Britain until the signature of the definitive Treaty
between Great Britain & the American States. I shall not enter into all the
vague surmizes which this circumstance might suggest, but only say that I
see no reason why he should not have given that notice to the Duke of
Manchester a month or six weeks ago, viz from the time that the French
& Spanish negotiations apparently verged to a conclusion – However this
is the case now before us. I am not aware of any articles which need draw
into any length of consideration or discussion but the 4ᵗʰ Proposition of the
American Ministers. And the consideration of that article may be referred
to any future treaty of Commerce & Alliance, if the two nations should
proceed to that desirable end alliance – No jealousies on the account of
the Acts of Navigation, or the carrying trade, or of principles of Commerce
can have the least tendency to impede a Treaty definitive to the late War.
You may be sure of the concurrence of America, for on the day of the
signature of the definitive Treaty, she will take possession of her great
object, actual & recognized independance – I think it very possible that
the declaration of Monsieur de Vergennes may have been produced by some
application on the part of the American Ministers, since the revival of their
jealousies, since the American Pamphlet which I have spoken of, and the
Order of Council of 2ᵈ July, because everything that turns them away from
confidence in the good will of Great Britain drives them more closely to
France. The day before Mʳ de Vergennes's declaration to the Duke of
Manchester, one of the American Ministers said to me, speaking of the
forward state of the French negotiations, " I can assure you that France will
not sign the definitive Treaty until the American Treaty shall be finished,
whatever your Ministry may think, don't let them flatter themselves with
that." – You may perceive Sir by this that all their jealousies are revived.
I think it very possible that they may have returned to Monsʳ de Vergennes
his own words. *Mais Monsieur il faut que nous finissions tous ensemble*[1] –

                    .   .   .   .   .

    I am Sir with the greatest respect & consideration Your most obedient
Servant   D Hartley

Clements Library: Hartley Papers, v. 2, pp. 97-100 (C).
    [1] *But Sir we must all finish together –*

Charles James Fox to David Hartley

N° 11   St. James's August 4th 1783

Sir,

I have received your Dispatch N° 13 by the Duke of Richmond, and N° 16 by Lauzun the Messenger, and have laid them both before the King.

As I explained myself so fully to you in my last Dispatch upon the Subject of the Proclamation which has caused so much illfounded alarm, I flatter myself it will be unnecessary to dwell any longer upon that Business in the present Dispatch. One Observation however I think it proper to make, which is that I have never considered any of these Commercial questions as having any Reference to, or any Connection with, the Signature of the definitive Treaty; the Delay of which, it seems, is now brought forward as another Object of Jealousy. I own I did imagine this to be a matter that was no way pressing on either Side, and so far from considering it as the Epoch of their enjoying recognized Independency I had always imagined that the Provisional Articles were to take complete and full Effect upon the Signature of a Treaty between Great Britain and France. The Words are full & strong to that Effect, nor do I even see any Expressions that can look forward to such an Act as a definitive Treaty at all, much less refer to it (as our Preliminary Articles with France & Spain do) for the Execution of any material parts of the Agreement. However if a speedy Conclusion of a definitive Treaty be an Object with them, it appears to me to be one attended with very little difficulty. The fourth Article in their Proposal is, in my Judgement highly exceptionable in this state of the Business, & indeed in general, I should think it desirable to admit as little new matter as possible. I do not desire to detain this Messenger until I have a Project drawn out in form, but I will send you one in a very few days. You understand that I mean for a definitive Treaty only, as that for a Convention will require rather more Time. The Project for the Treaty will certainly be in Substance conformable to the Provisional Articles. I am led to hope from your former Dispatches that some Time will be allowed us for our Garrisons to remain in the Forts without our Boundary. If so it will be a very acceptable thing here.

As this Treaty is now intended to be signed with the French Treaty, and to make a Part as it were of the general Business of Pacification, it would be exceedingly improper, even if we were ready, to insert any commercial agreement into it, or any thing relative to any particular reciprocal advantages to the Subjects of the two States, as these are matters that ought not to come under the Eyes of the French Minister, much less to make Part of a Treaty, the Completion of which he insists upon previous to his signing his own, and which consequently he may, in some degree be said to take under his Protection. If this should appear an unreasonable Jealousy, I am sure it is not so much so as those which are conceived of us, without the least foundation whatever. No Pains have been spared, as well by immediate Orders for the Evacuation of New York, as by various Orders of Council, for opening in various ways, the Intercourse betwen the two Countries, to evince the Sincerity of his Majestys inclination to be upon the most cordial Terms with the United States. That inclination rests upon the foundation of the interests of his Subjects and can not therefore be liable to change. One short reasoning ought at once to convince the Ministers of the United States which way only any rational Jealousy can be pointed; it is the interest of this Country to keep well with them but not embroil them with other Powers, to whom from their distance they can not be very formidable Enemies. It is the interest of France not only to be well with them Herself, but to be continually stirring up Disputes & Jealousies between them & us, to whom, from their Vicinity they are capable of being very troublesome; however I am perfectly aware of the difficulty, if not impossibility of allaying Jealousy by Professions or Reasonings. We trust to our Conduct & to Time to satisfy America, that we see where our Interest lies, and mean to pursue that Interest steadily & uniformly

I am with great Truth and Regard Sir Your most obedient humble Servant

C J Fox

P.S. Since writing the above I have received your dispatch N° 15 by Mr Laurens, whom I have appointed tomorrow. I have but just had time to look at the Papers inclosed but do not think fit to detain this Messenger.

Clements Library: Hartley Papers, v. 3, pp. 36-38 (C).

Ratification of the Provisional Articles of Peace by George III, King of England

[St. James's, 6 August 1783]

George the Third, by the Grace of God, King of Great Britain, France and Ireland, Defender of the Faith, Duke of Brunswick and Lunenburgh, Arch Treasurer and Prince Elector of the Holy Roman Empire &c^a.

Whereas Provisional Articles between us and our good Friends the United States of America, Viz^t. New Hampshire, Massachusetts Bay, Rhode

Island and Providence Plantations, Connecticut, New-York, New-Jersey, Pennsylvania, Delaware, Maryland, Virginia, North Carolina, South Carolina & Georgia, were concluded and signed at Paris, on the thirtieth Day of November, One thousand seven hundred & eighty two, by the Commissioners of US and our said good Friends, duly and respectively authorized for that Purpose; which Provisional Articles are in the Form and Words following.

(Here insert them.)

We having seen and consider'd the Provisional Articles aforesaid, have approved, ratified, accepted and confirmed the same, in all and every one of their Clauses, & Provisos, as we do by these Presents, approve, ratify, accept and confirm them, for ourself, our Heirs and Successors; engaging & promising upon our Royal Word, that we will sincerely and faithfully perform and observe, all and singular the Things which are contained in the aforesaid Provisional Articles, and that we will never suffer them to be violated by any one, or transgress'd in any manner, as far as it lies in our Power. For the greater Testimony and Validity of all which, we have caused Our Great Seal of Great Britain to be affixed to these Presents, which we have signed with our Royal Hand.

Given at our Court at St James's the Sixth Day of August, One Thousand seven hundred and Eighty three, in the Twenty third Year of our Reign. –

George R:

(L.S)

I certify the foregoing to be a faithful Copy of the Original Ratification of the Provisional Articles –   W. T. Franklin

NA: PCC, item 85, pp. 426-428 (C); M247, reel 114.

David Hartley to Charles James Fox

N° 18   Paris August 6 1783
Sir
    I did not receive the Project of the definitive Treaty from the American Ministers till this morning, and have been employed the whole day in transcribing and making some remarks upon it. I now transmit it to you without a moments delay. I think there is not much substantial difference

in this Project, from the separate propositions from the American Ministers, which I have transmitted to you in former letters; only that these Propositions are now reduced into the specific shape of Articles; with a great deal of preambulary recital, which was drawn up by M⁻ Adams a long while ago. You will be so good as to inform me how much of that preambulary recital you think necessary. I beg of you to send a specific draught of the preambulary & formal recitals, and parts of the Treaty, as well as of the essentials, viz the Articles, that our work may be executed in a becoming & proper manner. I have marked the Articles with the letters of the Alphabet, for the purpose of keeping them distinct from the Numeros of the provisional Treaty, and our subsequent Propositions and answers to Propositions &c &c which would otherwise have created Confusion – I beg of you to send me specifically such articles as I may sign that we may not suffer any needless loss of time

I am desired by the American Ministers to say that they consider every Proposition which is additional or supplemental to the Provisional Treaty, to be optional to either Party; that they consider themselves as bound to sign the provisional Articles in *statu quo* as a definitive Treaty of Peace, if called upon by Great Britain so to do. I presume this offer is meant to avoid delay, at the option of Great Britain. I have nothing farther to add at present.

I am Sir with the greatest respect and consideration Your most obed⁻ Serv⁻　　　　　　　　　　　　　　　　　　　　　　　　　D Hartley

Clements Library: Hartley Papers, v.2, pp. 104-105 (C).

Draft Definitive Treaty of Peace between the United States and Great Britain

Nᵒ 4　　　　　　　　　　　　　　　　　　　　　[ca. 6 August 1783]

(Project for) the Definitive Treaty of Peace & Friendship, between his Britannic Majesty, and the United States of America, concluded at　the Day of　　1783.

In the Name of the most Holy Trinity, Father, Son & Holy Ghost. So be it.—

Be it known to all those, to whom it shall or may in any Manner belong.

It has pleased the most High to diffuse the Spirit of Union & Concord among the Nations, whose Divisions had spread Troubles in the four Parts of the World, & to inspire them with the Inclination to cause the Comforts of Peace to succeed to the Misfortunes of a long and bloody War, which having arisen between Great Britain & the United States of America, its Progress communicated itself to France, Spain, and the United Netherlands.

Consequently the United States of America did on the fifth Day of June, in the Year of our Lord, one thousand, seven hundred and Eighty one, name and appoint their Ministers Plenipotentiary, and resolve, ordain & grant their Commission in the following Words, Viz⁺·

(Here insert it)

And his Majesty the King of Great Britain, did on the twenty first Day of September, in the twenty second Year of his Reign, issue his commission under the Great Seal of Great Britain to Richard Oswald Esqʳ· in the Words following Viz⁺·

(Here insert it)

And his said Britannic Majesty on the one Part, and the said United States of America on the other, did lay the Foundations of Peace in the Preliminaries, signed at Paris the thirtieth of November last, by the said Richard Oswald Esqʳ· on the Part of his said Majesty, and by the said John Adams, Benjᵐ· Franklin, John Jay & Henry Laurens Esquires, on the part of the said United States, in Virtue of their respective full Powers aforesaid, and after having mutually shewn to each other their said full Powers in good Form & eventually exchanged authenticated Copies of the same.

And his said Britannic Majesty did, on the twenty fourth day of July in the Year of our Lord one thousand seven hundred and eighty two, and in the twenty second Year of his Reign, issue his Commission signed with his Royal Hand and under the great Seal of G. Britain to Alleyne Fitzherbert Esqʳ· in the following Words, Viz⁺·

(Here insert it)

And the said Alleyne Fitz Herbert on the Part of his said Britannic Majesty, & John Adams & Benjᵐ· Franklin, in the necessary absence of the said John Jay & Henry Laurens, on the part of the said United States, did at Versailles on the twentieth Day of January last, communicate to each other their full Powers aforesaid in good Form, & agree upon an Armistice in the Words following.

(Here insert it)

And his Britannic Majesty did on the   Day of   in the year of our Lord one Thousand Seven hundred and Eighty three, and in the twenty third Year of his Reign, issue his Commission signed with his Royal Hand, and under the great Seal of Great Britain to David Hartley Esquire, in the following Words, Viz⁺·

(Here insert it)

And now the said David Hartley, Minister Plenipotentiary of his said Britannic Majesty, in behalf of his said Majesty on the one Part, and John

Adams, Benjn. Franklin & John Jay Ministers Plenipotentiary of the said United States of America; in behalf of the said States, on the other, having communicated to each other their aforesaid full Powers in good Form, and mutually exchanged authenticated Copies of the same, have by Virtue thereof agreed, and do hereby conclude upon the Articles, the Tenor of which is as follows, Viz^{t.}

Whereas reciprocal Advantages and mutual Convenience are found by Experience to form the only permanent Foundation of Peace and Friendship, between States; it agreed to form the Articles of this Treaty on such Principles of liberal Equity & Reciprocity, as that partial Advantages, those seeds of discord, being excluded, such a beneficial and Satisfactory Intercourse between the two Countries may be established, as to promise and secure to both perpetual Peace & Harmony.

Article, 1^{st:}

The same as art. 1. of the Prel^y – Treaty, but finishing "*at every Part thereof.*"

Art. 2^d   The same as Art. 2^{d.} of the Prel^{y.} Treaty, but commencing with the remaining Part of Art. 1st. "*and that all Disputes*" &c & ending with the Words, "& *the atlantic Ocean*".

Art. 3^d   The same as Art. 3^d of the Prelim^{y.} Treaty.

Article 4th.

It is agreed that Creditors on either Side shall meet with no lawful Impediment to the Recovery of the full Value in sterling Money of all *bonâ fide* Debts heretofore contracted, excepting that the respective Governments on both Sides, may, if they think proper, pass Acts directing that in Consideration of the Distresses & Disabilities brought on by the War and by the Interruption of Commerce, no Execution shall be issued on a Judgment to be obtained in any such Case, until after the Expiration of three Years from the Date of this Definitive Treaty; nor shall such Judgments include any Allowance of Interest for the Time that passed during the War, and until the signing hereof. –

Article 5th.

And whereas Doubts have arisen concerning the true Construction of the 5th. Article of the provisional Treaty, and Great Difficulties are likely to arise in its Execution, it is hereby agreed that the same shall be declared, void and omitted in this definitive Treaty.

And instead thereof it is agreed, that as exact an Account as may be, shall be taken by Commissioners to be appointed for that Purpose on each Part, of all Seizurs, Confiscations or Destruction of Property, belonging to the Adherents of the Crown of Great Britain in America, (exclusive of

Prizes made at Sea and Debts mentioned in the preceding Article). And also an Account of all Seizures, Confiscations or Destruction of Property belonging to the Adherents of the United States, residing either therein or in Canada; and the said Property being duly appraized and Valued; the Accounts thereof shall be compared & the Ballance shall be paid in Money by the Party which had suffered least, within one Year after such adjustment of the said Accounts. And it is further agreed, that all Persons who have any Interest in confiscated Lands, either by Debts or Marriage Settlements or otherwise, shall meet with no lawful Impediment in the Prosecution of their just Rights.

Art. 6th. The same as Art. 6th. of the Preliminary Treaty.

Article 7th.

There shall be a firm and perpetual Peace between his Britannic Majesty and the said States and between the Subjects of the one and the Citizens of the other, and his Britannic Majesty shall with all convenient speed, and without causing any Destructions or carrying away any Negroes or other Property of the american Inhabitants, withdraw all his Armies, Garrisons & fleets from the said United States, and from every Port, Place, and Harbour, within the same, leaving in all Fortifications, the American Artillery that may be therein. And shall also order and cause all Archives, Records, Deeds and Papers belonging to any of the said States, or their Citizens, which in the Course of the War, may have fallen into the Hands of his Officers, to be forthwith restored and delivered to the proper States & Persons to whom they belong. And all Destruction of Property, or carrying away of Negroes or other Property belonging to the American Inhabitants, contrary to the above Stipulation, shall be duly estimated and compensated to the owners. –

Article 8th.

The Navigation of the Rivers Mississippi, & St. Laurence, from their Sources to the Ocean, shall for ever remain free and open to the Subjects of Great Britain, & the Citizens of the United States.

Article 9th.

The Prisoners made respectively by the Arms of his Britannic Majesty and the United States, by Land & by Sea, not already set at Liberty shall be restored reciprocally and *bonâ fide* immediately after the Ratification of the Definitive Treaty, without Ransom, and on paying the Debts they may have contracted during their Captivity: and each Party shall respectively reimburse the sums which shall have been advanced for the subsistence & Maintenance of their Prisoners, by the Sovereign of the Country where they shall have been detained according to the Receipts & attested Accts and other authentic Titles which shall be produced on each Side to

Commissioners who shall be mutually appointed for the purpose of settling the same.

Article 10th.

His Britannic Majesty shall employ his good offices and Interposition with the King or Emperor of Moroco or Fez the Regences of Algier, Tunis & Tripoly, or with any of them, and also with every other Prince, State, or Power of the Coast of Barbary in Africa, & the Subjects of the said King, Emperor, States and Powers and each of them, in order to provide as fully & efficaciously as possible for the Benefit, Conveniency and Safety of the said United States and each of them, their Subjects, People & Inhabitants and their Vessels and Effects, against all Violence, – Insults, Attacks or Depredations on the Part of the s^d Provinces & States of Barbary or their Subjects.

Article 11th.

If War, should hereafter arise between Great Britain & the United States; which God forbid; the Merchants of either Country then residing in the other, shall be allowed to remain 9 Months to collect their Debts and settle their Affairs, and may depart freely carrying off all their Effects without Molestation or Hindrance. And all Fishermen, all Cultivators of the Earth, and all Artisans or Manufacturers, unarmed and inhabiting unfortified Towns, Villages or Places, who labour for the same Subsistence and Benefit of Mankind, and peaceably follow their respective Employment, shall be allowed to continue the same, and shall not be molested by the armed Force of the Enemy in whose Power by the Events of War they may happen to fall; but if any thing is necessary to be taken from them for the use of such armed Force, the same shall be paid for at a reasonable Price. And all Merchants or Traders with their unarmed Vessels employed in Commerce, exchanging the Products of different Places and thereby rendering the Necessaries, Conveniences & Comforts of Human Life more easy to obtain, and more general, shall be allowed to pass freely unmolested. And neither of the Powers, Parties to this Treaty, shall grant or issue any Commission to any private Armed Vessel, impowering them to take or destroy such trading Ships or interrupt such Commerce.

Article 12.

And in case either of the contracting Parties shall happen to be engaged in War with any other Nation, it is farther agreed, in order to prevent all the Difficulties & Misunderstandings that usually arise, respecting the Merchandize heretofore called Contraband, such as Arms, Ammunition and military Stores of all Kinds, that no such Articles carrying by the Ships or Subjects of one of the Parties to the Enemies of the other, shall on any

Account be deemed Contraband, so as to induce Confiscation and a Loss of Property to Individuals; Nevertheless it shall be lawful to stop such Ships and detain them for such Length of time as the Captors may think necessary to prevent the Inconvenience or Damage, that might ensue from their proceeding on their Voyage, praying however a reasonable Compensation for the Loss such arrest shall occasion to the Proprietors. And it shall farther be allowed to use in the Service of the Captor the whole or any Part of the military Stores so detained, paying the owners the full Value of the same, to be ascertained by the current Price at the Place of its Destination.

Article 13th

The Citizens and Inhabitants of the said United States or any of them, may take and hold real Estates in Great Britain, Ireland, or any other of his Majesty's Dominions, and dispose by testament; Donation or otherwise of their Property real or Personal, in favour of such Persons as to them shall seem fit; and their Heirs, Citizens of the said United States or any of them, residing in the British Dominions or elsewhere, may succeed them *ab intestato* without being obliged to obtain Letters of Naturalization.

The Subjects of his Britannic Majesty shall enjoy on their Part, in all the Dominions of the said United States, an entire and perfect Reciprocity, relative to the Stipulations contained in the present Article.

Article 14.

His Britannic Majesty consents that the Citizens of the United States may cut Logwood as heretofore, in the district allotted to his Subjects by the Treaty with Spain, on Condition that they bring or send the said Logwood to great Britain or Ireland, and to no other Part of Europe. –

Article 15.

All the Lakes Rivers, and Waters divided by the Boundary Line or Lines between his Britannic Majesty's Territories and those of the United States, as well as the Rivers mentioned in Art: shall be freely used and navigated by the Subjects & Citizens of his said Majesty and of the said States, in common over the whole Extent or Breadth of the said Lakes Rivers and Waters. And all the Carrying Places on which side soever situated of the said dividing Waters or between the said Rivers and the Water or Territories of either of the Parties, may and shall be freely used by the Traders of both, without any Restraint, Demand of Duties, or Tax, or any Imposition whatsoever, except such as the Inhabitants of the Country may be subject to.

Article 16.

That in all Places belonging to the United States or either of them, in the Country adjoining to the Water Line of Division, and which during the War were in his Majesty's Possession, all Persons at present resident, or having Possessions or Occupations as Merchants or otherwise, may remain in the peaceable Enjoyment of all civil Rights in pursuit of their Occupations, unless they shall within seven Years from the Date hereof receive Notice from Congress or the State to which any such Place may appertain to remove, and that upon any such Notice of Removal a Term of two Years shall be allowed for selling or withdrawing their Effects; and for settling their Affairs.

Article 17.

That his Britannic Majesty's Forces not exceeding   in Number, may continue in the Posts now occupied by them contiguous to the Water Line, until Congress shall give them Notice to evacuate the s$^{d.}$ Posts, and American Garrisons shall arrive at said Posts for the Purpose of securing the Lives, Property and Peace of any Persons settled in that Country against the Invasion or Ravages of the neighbouring Indian Nations, who may be suspected of retaining Resentments in Consequence of the late War.

Article 18.

It is farther agreed, that his Britannic Majesty shall cause to be evacuated the Ports of New-York, Penobscot & their Dependences with all other Posts and Places in Possession of his Majesty's Arms within the United States, in three Months after the signing of this Treaty, or sooner if possible, excepting those Posts contiguous to the Water Line above mentioned, which are to be evacuated on Notice as specified in Art:

Article 19.

It is agreed that all vessels which shall have been taken by either Party from the other, after the Term of twelve Days within the Channel or the North Seas, or after the Term of one Month any where to the Northward of the Latitude of the Canaries inclusively, or after the Term of two Months between the Latitude of the Canaries and the equinoxial Line, or after the Term of five Months in any other Part of the World, all which s$^{d.}$ Terms are to be computed from the 3$^{d.}$ Day of Feb$^{y.}$ last, shall be restored.

His sacred Britannic Majesty and the said United States, promise to observe sincerely and *bonâ Fide*, all the Articles contained and settled in the present Treaty; and they will not suffer the same to be infringed directly or indirectly, by their respective Subjects & Citizens.

The Solemn Ratifications of the present Treaty, expedited in good and due form, shall be exchanged in the City of London or Philadelphia, between the contracting Parties, in the Space of   Months or sooner if Possible, to be computed from the Day of the Signature of the present Treaty.

In Witness whereof, We the Under written, their Ministers Plenipotentiary, have signed with our Hands in their Name, and in Virtue of our full Powers, the present definitive Treaty & have caused the Seal of our arms to be put thereto.

Done at   the   Day of   1783.

NA: PCC, item 85, pp. 398-411 (Draft); M247, reel 114.

Henry Laurens to the American Peace Commissioners at Paris

Gentlemen,   London 9th. August 1783.

. . . . .

I arrived in London late in the night of the 3^{d.} on the 5th. had a conference with the Right Honorable C. J. Fox Esqr. which I committed to writing as soon as it had ended. I shall give it in short Dialogue as the best Way, not pretending to accuracy in every Word, but fully preserving the Sense & Substance. –

Mr. Fox. I Suppose Mr. L., you wish to forward the Ratification of the provisional Articles.

L. I could wish that was done Sir, but tis not the particular Business which I have in charge.

F. I understood from Mr. Hartley's Letter which you sent me it was, but he does not speak positively.

L. No Sir, the only Business I have in charge, is to enquire whether a Minister from the United States of America, would be properly recieved at this Court.

F. Most undoubtedly Sir, I could wish there was one here at present I think We have lost much time from a want of a Minister from your side.

L. Then Sir, will you be so good as to ask his Majesty the Question, and inform me.

F. I'll take the King's pleasure to morrow, & you shall hear from me, I suppose there is already a conditional appointment of some person now in Europe.

L. Not that I know of, tho' I don't know the contrary, but I have an excellent opportunity for writing to Congress & I have no doubt an appointment will be immediately made.

F. That's unlucky; there must be two crossings the Ocean then, If a Minister from Congress had been here, We might have done our Business in half the time We have already spent, but I shall certainly inform you to morrow, this is the very time a Minister from your People is most necessary.

L. Tho' I have nothing particularly in charge except the Business already mentioned, I regret the delay of both the commercial & Definitive Treaty. We had flattered ourselves with hopes in March & April that both would have been finished in a few days.

F. Why as to a Definitive Treaty I don't see any necessity for one or not immediately. The Provisional Articles are to be inserted in and to constitute a Treaty – A Ratification of those I apprehend, will answer all purposes of a Definitive Treaty, they may be made Definitive. The case with respect to France & Spain differs widely, several Articles in our Preliminaries with them, refer to a Definitive Treaty.

L. I agree with you Sir, the Provisional Articles mutually ratified, may, by the consent of the Parties be made Definitive, but there may be additional Articles suggested & agreed to for mutual Benefit.

F. That's true but I don't see any at present, I very much regret the want of a Minister from America.

L. Permit me Sir to ask you, is it intended by the Proclamation of the 2$^{d.}$ July to exclude American Ships from the West India trade between the United States and the British Islands.

F. Yes certainly it was so intended, in order that We might have something to treat for and this will be a Subject for Commercial Treaty.

On the 6$^{th.}$ I waited upon his Grace the Duke of Portland. His Grace was equally clear & positive as M$^{r.}$ Fox had declared himself, that a Minister from the United States of America would be well received at this court, & also regretted that an appointment had not earlier taken place. – I touched upon the Commercial & Definitive Treaty, referred to conversations & assurances in March and April, intimated my apprehensions of pernicious Effects which might arise from excluding American Ships from a freedom of trade between the United States and the British West India Islands adding what I had learned from Doctor Franklin of the commerce intended by the Court of France to be permitted between our America and the French Islands. I can only say the Duke seemed to wish that every thing had been settled to mutual Satisfaction, & hoped that every thing would soon be settled.

Yesterday by desire of M$^{r.}$ Fox, I called upon him again, he said he had not seen the King, but that he had transmitted an Account to His Majesty of my application, that We might be perfectly satisfied however a Minister from Congress would be well recieved, that the appointment of one was much wished for here. That he must take blame to himself in some degree for the long Delay of a commercial Regulation, but that Business would now be soon finished, he had no objection himself to opening the West India Trade to the Americans, but there were many Parties to please & you know added M^r· Fox, the people of this Country very well. Yes Sir, I know something of them and I find not only the West India Planters but some of the most Judicious Merchants anxious for opening the Trade, I have been told by some of them they should be ruined without it – I believe all this said M^r· Fox, but there are other People of a different Opinion. As to the Definitive Treaty there may be as you observed new Articles necessary for mutual advantage & We may either add such to the Provisional Articles & make the whole Definitive or make a New Treaty but I understand it is expected this should be done under the Eye of, or in concert with the Court of France, which for my own part, I don't like and can't consent to.

I replied, in my opinion a New Treaty Definitive would be best, as well for incorporating additional Articles as for clearing away some of the Rubbish in the Provisional, which contained if not Nonsense, more than a little Ambiguity, that tho' I did not see the necessity for it now, yet I had been told it was expected our Definitive Treaty should be finished in communication with the French Court, but as I had formerly observed I had recieved no charge on this head, & spoke only the Sentiments of M^r· Laurens to M^r· Fox, not to a Minister of Great Britain.

· · · · ·

With every good wish, and with very great Respect & Esteem, I have the honor to be, Gentlemen, Your faithful and obedient Servant,

Henry Laurens.

NA: PCC, *item* 89, *v. 1, pp. 325-328 (C); M247, reel 117.*

Charles James Fox to David Hartley

N° 12   St James's 9th· Augt 1783
Sir

I am commanded by his Majesty to transmit to you the Ratification of the Provisional Articles, accompanying this Dispatch, which you will of Course exchange with the Ministers of the United States against the Ratification of the Congress. I should have been able to have transmitted to you this Instrument sooner, if the Great Seal had not been in the hands of the two Commissioners, who are on the Circuit. After this Exchange of Ratifications, which will undoubtedly take place immediately, one would imagine the Provisional Articles were sufficiently secured to be no longer any impediment to our concluding our definitive Treaties with France & Spain; but lest a contrary opinion should prevail, His Majesty has commanded me to transmit to you herewith a Project for the definitive Treaty with the United States, which, if agreed to by the American Ministers, you are authorized to sign without further Instructions. You will observe that it is purposely made out exactly & nearly literally conformable to the Provisional Articles, and indeed there are many Reasons for abiding by this Mode; the principal one is that, which I touched upon in my last Dispatch; that this Treaty being concluded under the Eye of France, and the provisonal Articles, upon which it is founded, depending for their Validity upon the Contingency of the Courts of London & Versailles signing a Treaty, it would be highly improper to let into this Treaty any Matter that might contain any mutual advantages to the Subjects of the two Countries, much more any thing that might lead to Alliance or future Connection – If such Points are to be brought forward (and Nobody is more desirous of them than I am) they ought to make Part of a separate Treaty; with this view I therefore still think it most eligible to rest upon the exchange of Ratifications and upon that Ground to sign with France. This once done we remain on each side independent of and unconnected with, the French Negotiation, which is surely desireable for both of us. Peace being once secured, I say, I think this Mode the most eligible, but have no Objection to transforming the Provisional Articles into a definitive Treaty; if that measure gives any satisfaction. We will immediately afterwards proceed to the discussion of other Points.

Mr Laurens's direct object in coming hither was, to know whether a Minister from the United States would be received at this Court, to which, by his Majestys command, I answered in the affirmative, and have no doubt but Mr Laurens has transmitted this Answer to his Colleagues at Paris.

With respect to the complaints made in the Letter from the American Commissioners to you and in the Papers contained in that Letter, I cannot make full answer till I am further informed upon some Points into which I am now enquiring; but you may depend upon my answer very shortly; in the mean time I can not help being of opinion that Sir Guy Carleton's arguments, as related in the Minute of the conversation between him and General Washington, seem to be solid & founded in Equity. To have restored Negroes, whom we had invited, *seduced* if you will, under a Promise of Liberty, to the tyranny and possibly to the Vengeance of their former masters, would have been such an Act as scarcely any Orders from his Employers (and no such Orders exist) could have induced a Man of Honour to execute; but upon all this I shall write more fully when I am better informed. I should hope there can be now no difficulty remaining of a

Nature to delay the Conclusion of the French Treaty, since it is left entirely to the option of the American Ministers, whether they will have the very unnecessary *form* of a definitive Treaty or not – If it should be objected that there is no term fixed for the complete evacuation of New York, you will urge that when they see us taking every step for completing this business with the utmost expedition, and when they know that the Dispatch with which it can be done must depend upon many Contingencies uncertain in their nature, Arrival of Transports &c; such a Stipulation would be unreasonable & absurd to the last degree. We are using all the expediton we can for our own sakes as well as for theirs. I am with great Truth & Regard Sir your most obedient humble Servant

C. J. Fox

Clements Library: Hartley Papers, v. 3, pp. 52-54 (C).

John Adams to Robert R. Livingston

Sir   Paris August 13 1783

Yesterday, I went to Court with D.ʳ Franklin, and presented to the Comte de Vergennes, our Project of a definitive Treaty, who told us he would examine it, and give us his sentiments upon it. It was Ambassadors day, and I had Conversation with a Number of Ministers, of which it is proper I should give you an Account.

The Dutch Ambassador Berkenrode, told me, that last Saturday the Comte de Vergennes, went to Paris, and dined with the Imperial Ambassador the Comte de Merci in Company with the Duke of Manchester, the Comte d'Aranda, the Prince Baratinskoy and M.ʳ Markoff, with their Secretaries. That after Dinner the Secretaries, in the Presence of all the Ministers, read over, compared & corrected the Definitive Treaties between France, and Great Britain; and between Spain and Great Britain, and finally agreed upon both So that they are now ready for Signature, by the Ministers of Great Britain, France and Spain as Principals and by those of the two Imperial Courts, as Mediators.

The Duke of Manchester told me, that M.ʳ Hartley's Courier who carried our Project of a Treaty, arrived in London last Saturday, and might be expected here, on next Saturday, on his return.

In the Evening, on my Return from Versailles, M.ʳ· Hartley called upon me, at my house, and informed me, that he had just Receiv'd a Courier from Westminster, who had brought him the Ratification of our Provisional Treaty under the Kings own hand and under the Great Seal of the Kingdom inclosed in a Silver Box, ornamented with golden Tassells, as usual, which he was ready to exchange tomorrow morning. He informed me further that he had receiv'd very satisfactory Letters from the Duke of Portland, and Mr Fox, and the strongest assurances that the dispositions of his Court were very good to finish immediately, and to arrange all things upon the best Footing. That he had farther receiv'd, plenary Authority to sign the Definitive Treaty, tomorrow, or to Night if we pleased, that he had receiv'd a Draught, already formed, which he would shew us. – We agreed, to go together to morrow Morning, to my Colleagues, and this morning we went out in M^r· Hartley's Carriage, exchanged the Ratifications, and he produced to us, his Project of a definitive Treaty. It is the Provisional Treaty, in so many Words, without Addition or Diminution. it is only preceded with a preamble, which makes it a definitive Treaty. And he proposed to us, that all Matters of Discussion respecting Commerce, or other Things should be left to be discussed by Ministers to be mutually appointed to reside in London & Philadelphia. We told him that it had been proposed to us that the Ministers of the two Imperial Courts, should sign the Treaty as Mediators, and that we had answered, that we had no Objection to it. He said he had unanswerable ones. 1st· he had no Authority and could not obtain any certainly under 10 days, nor probably ever, for. 2. it would he thought give great Offence to his Court, and they never would agree to it, that any Nation should interfere between them and America. 3. for his Part he was fully against it and should write his opinion to his Court. if he was about to marry his Daughter, or set up a Son in the World, after he was of age, he would never admit any of his Neighbours to intervene, and sign any Contract he might make, as Mediators. There was no need of it.

We told him there was no need of warmth upon the Occasion, or any pretence for his Court to take Offence. That it had been proposed to us that the Imperial Ministers should sign as Mediators. our answer had been that we had no Objection: that we were willing and ready to consent to it or even to request it. His Court had a right to Consent or Dissent as it thought proper. To be sure, the Mediation could not take place without their Consent. That he might write to his Court the proposition and if he receiv'd orders to Consent or Dissent, it would be equally well in the meantime we were ready to sign the definitive Treaty either with, or without the Mediation whenever the other Parties were ready to sign, according to his Project just receiv'd from his Court, that is simply a repetition of the definitive Treaty.

We have agreed to this because it is plain that all Propositions for alterations in the provisional Articles will be an endless discussion, and that we must give more than we can hope to receive. The critical state of Things in England and at the Court of Versailles, and in all the rest of Europe, are pressing Motives to get this Business finished.

Mr Hartley told us from his Court, that they had expected an American Minister at St James's these three Months, and that all further Matters might be there discussed....

I lament very much that we cannot obtain an Explanation, of the Article respecting the Refugees, and that respecting Debts: but it is plain we must give more than they are worth for such Explanations: And what is of more decisive Importance, we must make a long Delay and put infinitely greater Things at Hazard by this Means, even to purchase an Alteration at a dear Rate.

With great Regard, I have the Honour to be, Sir, your most obedient and most humble Servant   John Adams

NA: PCC, *item 84, v. 5, pp. 149-152 (LS); M247, reel 113.*

David Hartley to Charles James Fox

N° 22   Paris Aug: 13 1783
Sir

I have the honour to inform you that I have this morning exchanged with the American Ministers the ratifications of the Provisional Articles. I hope and trust that this Act will prove the foundation of great satisfaction to all parties, and of that perfect confidence from America, which is so justly due to his Majesty for his gracious condescension, and to the confidential advisers of his Counsels – You say to me Sir in your dispatch N° 11 "I am perfectly aware of the difficulty, if not impossibility of allaying jealousies by professions or reasonings. We trust to our conduct and to time to satisfy America." That time is I trust now come. The act which you have enabled me to perform has removed every possible foundation of Jealousy; you have given me firm ground and I have asserted it. I have challenged the total & absolute renunciation of every radical principle of suspicion and jealousy. They have received that challenge in silent content, and have made no reserve of any future right of Jealousy. Our conference was not long. The subject of it was unexpected to the American Ministers. I hope it will prove (as I think it ought) perfectly satisfactory. They are ready to sign the definitive Treaty as you have sent it to me, when France signs, and they desire so to do. I stated all the arguments of your Letter, which therefore I need not repeat to you. They are willing to refer ulterior points to future negotiations. – I informed the Duke of Manchester of all this, who has upon every occasion asserted the King's honour and done justice to his Country. His Grace has made his immediate claim upon the French Minister to sign. This is our state now. I have nothing farther to add at present but that I have agreed with the American Ministers concerning the form of our definitive Treaty; and that our Copies shall be prepared for the earliest day of signature, which may be appointed with other powers: whenever it shall be signed, I shall avail myself of his Majestys permission and bring it over to England in person –

I am Sir with the greatest respect and consideration Your most obed^t Servt D Hartley

PS I have the honour of transmitting to you the ratification of the Provisional Articles which I have received in exchange from the American Ministers –

Clements Library: Hartley Papers, v. 3, pp. 67-68 (C).

John Adams to Robert R. Livingston

(2plicate)   Paris August 15$^{th.}$ 1783
Sir,
    France England Spain and America are all agreed, but Mr Hartley is Sanguine that the Treaty will not be signed, because he says the Comte de Vergennes dont mean to sign it. His Reasons for his opinion I know not and I think he is mistaken. It is very certain however, that the French Minister is embarass'd and would not perhaps be sorry to find good Reasons for postponing the Signature for some time. – Congress may judge in some degree, of the situation of things, by the following Conversation, which I had this morning with Mr Brantzen, the Ambassador Extraordinary from the States General, to whom I returned the Visit he made me Yesterday when I was abroad.
    He told me, he was as far, and indeed farther, than ever from an Agreement with the Duke of Manchester. He had given up he said, all Pretensions to a Compensation for the unjust Damages of the War, and he had in a manner waived his Claim of the restitution of Negapatnam. But the Duke of Manchester now insisted peremptorily upon, not only all the ancient salutations from the Dutch Flagg to the English, but upon an unlimited Liberty of Navigation in all the Seas of the East Indies. He had dispatch'd an Express to the Hague the Day before yesterday who would arrive to Day, but the grand Pensionary was Sick, and the States of Holland not sitting, so that there must be some time before he could have an Answer, concerning the Salutes to the Flagg, there would be different Opinions, but they wou'd be all of a Mind against the liberty of Navigation in the Indies. He could not, therefore expect from their High Mightinesses

Permission to sign, and the Comte de Vergennes would be embarassed, all the other Powers were ready, and to make them wait would raise a cry. To sign without Holland, would raise a terrible Storm in Holland against the Comte, and no small one in France. And even if the States should authorize him to sign a shameful Peace, this would raise no less Clamour in Holland and France against the Comte. He will therefore not know what to do and will seek to postpone, for the Parties of the Marquis de Castries and of M^r: de Breteuil[1] will take Advantage of every Clamour against the Comte as these Parties wish Mr Breteuil in his Place. I am persuaded therefore that the Comte himself looks upon his own Situation as very hazardous. it has been so a long time....

· · · · ·

...Mr de Rayneval however affirmed positively to Mr Hartley that nothing but Death could remove the Comte.

All these Things shew the critical and uncertain Constitution of this Court, and the uncertainty when the definitive Treaty will be signed notwithstanding that four Powers are agreed, and therefore I can give Congress no clear Information upon that head. This is a great Chagrin to me, both on Account of the publick and myself, because I am as uncertain about my own destiny, as that of the Publick

With great Respect I have the honour to be Sir, your most obedient, and most humble Servant.   John Adams.

NA: PCC, *item 84, v. 5, pp. 173-176 (LS); M247, reel 113.*

   [1] *Breteuil, Louis-Charles-Auguste le Tonnelier, Baron de (1730-1807). French ambassador to Austria, 1778-1783. Minister of State, 1783-1787. Strong supporter of the royal prerogative, opponent of fiscal reforms proposed by first Charles Alexandre de Calonne and then Jacques Necker. Chief minister at the time of the storming of the Bastille, 14 July 1789, he resigned, emigrated, and subsequently withdrew from politics.*

Benjamin Franklin to Comte de Vergennes

Sir,   Passy, Augt 16. 1783

I have the honour to inform your Excellency, that the English Ministry do not agree to any of the Propositions that have been made either by us, or by their Minister here; and they have sent over a Plan for the definitive Treaty, which consists merely of the Preliminaries formerly signed; with a short Introductory Paragraph, & another at the Conclusion; confirming and establishing the said preliminary Articles. My Colleagues seem enclin'd to sign this with Mr Hartley, and so to finish the Affair. I am, with Respect, Sir, Your Excellency's most obedient & most humble Servant

B. Franklin

FFAA: Pol. Corr., U.S., v. 25, f. 107/187 (ALS); LC microfilm reel 15.

David Hartley to Charles James Fox

N° 23   Paris August 20 1783
Sir

The Duke of Manchester has told me that in his Letter to you he has alluded to a circumstance which had happened between the American Minister and me, and which I did not mention to you myself in my last letter. I only mentioned it conversationally to his Grace, and should have scarcely thought it worth while to trouble you with – The Day before I proposed the exchange of Ratifications, I received a hint that there was some thoughts of proposing a mediation between Great Britain & the American States, which I beleive arose just at that time from the discontent then subsisting: However before I proceeded to the exchange of Ratifications I requested an explanation of this point fundamentally, as without such an explanation I could not proceed to that exchange. I expressed that in my judgement it could not possibly be admitted to take place or even the proposition be considered in any other light than as extremely offensive, and that I could not possibly proceed in any negotiation until that point was cleared up. The American Ministers did not make any stand upon it, they declared against any intention of giving offence, and so the matter ended. As the Ratifications were then lying upon the table, we proceeded immediately to the exchange. For that exchange and the proposed signature of the definitive Treaty had dispelled ill humour. – I should have considered the introduction of mediators of the two Imperial Courts as a great affront. And this is the meaning of some words in my last letter, that having now firm ground to stand upon I had asserted it.

As to the memorials which I had the honour of transmitting to you from the American Ministers respecting the Negroes, I agree with you entirely upon that subject, that General Carleton's arguments & Conduct were those of a man of solid sense and honour. I expressed the same sentiments to the American Ministers, when they transmitted to me their memorials in conformity to their instructions from America. I did no more than simply transmit them to you in a very short letter. I now attend your Orders; as the American Ministers are very well informed of my sentiments, they will not expect me to be very assiduous or pressing with you in the business.

There is another point in which I hope you do me the justice to beleive that I do most entirely concur with you viz, that no negotiation of any points of reciprocal advantages, or intercourse, or participation, between Great Britain & America should be conducted under the eye of a French Minister. I have given you my pledge that I should be your most zealous minister upon that head. Having resisted the mediation of neutral Courts, you may be well assured that I shall never become an advocate for admitting the guarantee of an enemy without the least degree of right or pretext. And therefore the point of time which you have marked out for settling all points of reciprocal advantage, communication, commerce, connexion, alliance &c &c is unquestionably the only fit & suitable period....

...After the signature of the definitive Treaty we shall have a clear field before us. The sentiments of the nation must decide upon great national and commercial concerns. His Majesty's Ministers will then have ground to act upon with safety and honour.

I am Sir with the greatest respect and consideration Your most obed.ᵗ Serv.ᵗ   D Hartley

Clements Library: Hartley Papers, v. 3, pp. 69-72 (C).

Charles James Fox to David Hartley

N° 13   Sᵗ James's 21ˢᵗ August 1783
Sir

.   .   .   .   .

As the Definitive Treaty is proposed to be in the same words with the Provisional Articles, I do not conceive that you can want any instructions upon that head. One thing only I must remind you of, in point of form. When a treaty is signed between two Crowned heads, in order to prevent disputes about precedency, the name of the one stands first in one instrument, & that of the other in the other, but when the treaty is between a crowned head & a republick, the Name of the Monarch is mentioned first in each instrument. I believe if you will enquire upon this Subject among the *Corps Diplomatique*, you will find this to have been the constant practice. I am &c   C J Fox

Clements Library: Hartley Papers, v. 3, pp. 77 (C).

American Peace Commissioners at Paris
to Henry Laurens

[Paris, ca. 24 August 1783]

. . . . .

We have perused the notes of your Conversation with Mr. Fox, and although in general we approve it, yet candor obliges us to remark, that you seem to have somewhat mistaken our Sentiments on your Proposal to speak to Mr. Fox about the Reception of an American minister by the British Court.

Britain having acknowledged the sovereignty of the United States, and treated with us as with an independent nation, it followed as a natural consequence that they would recieve our minister. Mr. Hartley's official Communication to us on that subject, was in the most explicit Terms. No Doubts could remain on that Head. In conversing with us on this Subject, and about this communication, you observed that there was a wide Difference between a Ministers being ceremoniously and formally recieved, and his being received and treated in a cordial friendly manner, that we were not as yet accurately informed of the Intention of the British Cabinet on the latter point, and that you thought it would be expedient to ascertain it in a Conversation with Mr. Fox. With this Sentiment we coincided; and you promised to inform us of the Result.

The British Court prefer forming a definitive Treaty of the provisional articles, without any alterations or additions. We wish with you that certain matters in them could have been more accurately adjusted, but as at the Time of signing them, you made no Objections to any of the articles or Expressions, we presume you then thought as we did, that they were in the best State that, all things considered, it was in our power to put them.

Morris, Jay Papers, v. 2, pp. 574-575.

David Hartley to the American
Peace Commissioners

Gentlemen   Paris August 29 1783

As the day is now fixed for the signatures of the Definitive treaties between Great Britain France and Spain I beg leave to inform you that I am ready to sign the Definitive treaty between Great Britain & the United States of America whenever it shall be convenient to you. I beg the favour therefore of you to fix the day. My Instructions confine me to Paris as the place appointed to me for the exercise of my functions and therefore whatever day you may fix upon for the signature, I shall hope to receive the honour of your Company at the Hotel de York.

I am Gentlemen with great Respect and Consideration Your most obed$^{t \cdot}$ Serv$^{t \cdot}$ D Hartley

Clements Library: Hartley Papers, v. 3, p. 78 (LS).

American Peace Commissioners to David Hartley

Passy 30th Augt 1783

The American Ministers Plenipotentiary for making Peace with Great Britain present their Compliments to Mr Hartley. They regret that Mr Hartleys Instructions will not permit him to sign the definitive Treaty of Peace with America at the Place appointed for the Signature of the others. They will nevertheless have the Honor of waiting on Mr Hartley at his Lodgings at Paris, for the Purpose of signing the Treaty in Question, on Wednesday Morning at Eight o Clock.

Clements Library: Hartley Papers, v. 3, p. 79 (C).

William Carmichael to Robert R. Livingston

Sir,   S$^{n \cdot}$ Ildefonso 30$^{th \cdot}$ Aug$^{t \cdot}$ 1783.

...On the 5$^{th \cdot}$ Instant I followed the Court to this place where it has been since the 24$^{th \cdot}$ of the last month. – I took the earliest opportunity of waiting on his Excellency the Count de Florida Blanca to remind him of his promise to present me to the King and Royal Family, and of other affairs interesting to Individuals mentioned in former letters for which I had been obliged to apply to him. He gave me the strongest assurances of his desire to terminate to the satisfaction of the parties interested the affairs in question, imputing to other departments the delays I had experienced in their adjustment. – On the subject of my presentation he seemed much embarrassed; stating the difficulties he should be exposed to in procuring that honor for me which his Majesty refused to others vested with the same character, mentioning the case of the Chargé d' affaires of Denmark, a copy of whose letter to this minister on the subject of his presentation, I had the honor to inclose you the 25$^{th.}$ of June – He observed that the Russian and Swedish Ministers, were about to leave the Court and would if I was presented insist on the presentation of their Secretaries also. I begged leave in reply to assure his Excellency of the concern it gave me to expose him to the least inconvenience upon that account, But that he would be pleased to recollect the promise he had made to the Marquis de la Fayette and myself in writing on this subject – That copies of the letter which the Marquis de la Fayette had written to him and of his Excellency's answer had been transmitted to Congress. – That that body, from the confidences which they had in his Catholic Majesty's amicable disposition of which his Excellency had been so often the interpreter undoubtedly expected that I had long ago been presented – That in consequence of his Excellency's assurances to me at various times since the transmission of the copies of the letters before-mentioned I had confirmed my constituents in this belief; – That this being the case, it would be improper for me to go to Court, until I should receive their instructions on the subject; I added that I hoped his Excellency knew me too well to suppose that I was influenced by any personal considerations in this affair – He interrupted me with assurances of his belief to the contrary and that he would do every thing in his power to give me satisfaction, telling me to call upon him in a few days when he would acquaint me with the result of his endeavours – Thus ended our first conference. –

Not to appear too urgent I avoided speaking to him on the subject until ten days ago, altho' I had occasion to see him several times – But hearing that the British minister was on the way to Madrid, I thought it proper to bring this matter to a decision before his arrival and presentation, for which purpose I again waited on the Minister – I soon discovered that he was in ill humour, however as he immediately commenced the conversation by telling me that he had not yet found an opportunity of speaking to the King, I prayed his Excellency to recollect the time which had elapsed since he had been pleased to tell me that I should be presented & recapitulated the reasons before-mentioned. He interrupted me several times, telling me how much he had been persecuted by M$^{r.}$ Elfried[1] and the Russian minister who espoused the interests of that Chargé D'Affaires – adding with warmth that Gentleman will never be presented unless to take leave and receive his present – I replied that his Excellency would do me the Justice to own that I had been by no means importunate. That it was not my intention to be so, and that nothing but my duty joined to my particular desire to cultivate a good understanding between our two Countries made me now press him for an explicit answer – He told me that he was convinced that I did not wish to embarrass him, but observed with some peevishness [blank space in text] as M$^{r.}$ Elfried is by the Russian – He cites precedent and you have none – I answered that I flattered myself his Excellency had too good an opinion of me to suppose that I needed a prompter when either the honour or interests of my Country were in question. That as for precedent, part of my business with his Excellency was to establish one for such of my countrymen as the United States might hereafter send to Spain in the same character in which I had the honor to be employed, – Adding that I had more confidence in His Excellency's word than in all the precedents the book of etiquette of the Court could furnish me; and that to give him a further proof of my unwillingness to embarrass him, I did not insist on my presentation, but on an explicit answer from his Excellency of which I might immediately send copies to Congress not only for my own Justi-fication, but also to enable that body to decide the manner in which Chargé d'Affaires from the Court of Spain should be treated by the United States – He seemed pleased with the reliance placed on his word; for he instantly told me that he would speedily give me an explicit answer, and that I should see that he was a man of his word – That he wished from respect to the States and personal regard for myself to procure me an advantage which was denied to others, but that he was afraid his Majesty was (to make use of his own expression) *trop enteté*[2] on this point – He then asked me for a copy of the translation of the letter from Congress to the King – I had it with me – This is the third copy which I have given to his Excellency. We left his apartments as he was then going to the King. In the antechamber he again repeated aloud in Spanish to me before thirty or forty persons who were waiting to pay him their Court, that I should find him a man of his word, and that I should have an explicit answer; – I took my leave, assuring him that it was all I desired –

I presume that he took his Majesty's orders thereon the same day, for the next he sent me a polite message desiring me to come to his house – Having waited on him agreeable to his request, on my entry he took me by the hand and told me that he hoped I would now be satisfied, for that on conferring with the King his Majesty had been pleased to fix a day for my presentation, that no one felt more sensibly than himself the happy conclusion of this affair, as well on account of his desire to shew every possible respect to the United States as from his esteem for me – That the King, (contrary to his expectations) had consented to change the Etiquette with respect to me on this subject *por acto extraordinario de real benevolencia, an extraordinary act of Royal good will, and that he hoped that his conduct on this occasion would convince Congress of his Majesty's intentions to cultivate in a particular manner their amity. I expressed in reply, the sense which I knew my Constituents would have of this proof of the King's amicable disposition and of my gratitude to his Excellency for the obliging interest which he took in what regarded me personally, assuring him that I would take the earliest opportunity of*

transmitting to Congress this additional proof of his Majesty's desire to cultivate
their friendship and of his Excellency's manner of fulfilling his sovereign intentions
– I then asked him on what day the King chose to receive me, he answered the
day after to-morrow (the 23ᵈ Instant) I expressed some concern that the
Embassador of France then at Madrid would not return before the time
appointed for my reception – He replied that the King having named the
day, no alteration could take place – To this I was obliged to acquiesce,
His Excellency then made me many professions of personal regard which it
is unnecessary to repeat and which perhaps I should not even hint, if the
French Embassador the Marquis de la Fayette and others had not been
witnesses on former occasions to similar assurances. I proceed to mention
to his Excellency the different objects on which I had heretofore addressed
him & prayed him to give me an opportunity at the same time that I
informed Congress of my presentation, to advise them also of the happy
termination of these. He begged me to pass him offices again on these
points, and assured me that I should receive such answers as would be
agreeable and satisfactory to the States. He continued to speak to me in an
open and friendly manner of the obstacles which a well intentioned
minister had to encounter in the Execution of his measures in this Country
– I paid him indirect compliments on what I know to be his favorite
projects, Viz^t the improvement of the roads, the protection and encouragement of manufactures &c, and the changes which he meditates in the
System of finance & Commerce, and after continuing with him some time
longer was about to take my leave – He asked me whom I had left in the
Antichamber, on mentioning the names of the persons, he requested me to
remain with him, observing that he should be plagued by these Gentlemen.
During my stay the conversation rolled on different subjects, in which I
received every proof of candour and politeness. The same evening I
informed the Embassador of France by Letter that the King had consented
to my being presented a circumstance on which he had always entertained
doubts altho' he has ever done every thing in his power that could be
expected from his public and private character to contribute to the success
of our negotiation, perhaps some expressions on the part of Congress,
testifying their sense of the zeal which this Nobleman has manifested to
farther their interests may be ultimately productive of good effects at the
Court of Versailles if not here.

On the day appointed for my presentation, I waited on his Excellency the
Count de Florida Blanca and from his House accompanied by his servant
whom he had the politeness to send with my own, I paid my visits to the
principal officers and ladies of the Palace. This ceremony finished I went
to the King's apartments where the minister appointed me to meet him.
When his Majesty arose from table, His Excellency presented me as Chargé

D'Affaires of the United States – As I had been informed that the King doth not love long harangues, I contented myself with expressing to his Majesty my happiness in being the first of my Countrymen who had the good fortune to assure him of their desire to cultivate his Amity, he answered me in a gracious manner and with a smiling Countenance saying that he hoped I should have frequent occasions of making him the same assurances. He then passed into the audience chamber for the Embassadors & Ministers, where, as several of them have informed me, he was pleased to speak favourably of me – The royal family dining at the same hour and seperately, and the same etiquette being observed, Viz^t the presentation after dinner, it required some days to finish this business. The C^t de Florida Blanca accompanying me more than three quarter's of an hour each day with a politeness and good-nature rarely found in men who have so many important occupations on their hands. The Prince of Asturias spoke of me during the dinner as of a person he had long known and when I was presented he told me so. The Princess who was present spoke to me six or seven minutes in French and Spanish, and among other things said to me that I ought to like Spain, because she had been told that I was much esteemed by the Spaniards; – I replied that the only title I had to their esteem was my well known regard for the nation. The other branches of the Royal family rec^d me equally well. It perhaps may be thought that I have dwelt too long on these minute details but I hope I shall be excused when it is considered that this is the first presentation of a Servt of the States at this Court and that it has already made some noise among the Corps Diplomatic who think themselves entitled to the same privilege which I have obtained; – As soon as the Chargé d'Affaires of Denmark was advised of my presentation, he came hither, the inclosed note to the Minister of which I found means to obtain a copy, will serve to show you in what light his Court regards this preference.

The ceremonial of my presentation being finished, I waited on his Excellency the Count de Florida Blanca to thank him for his obliging attentions in the course of it, and took that opportunity of insinuating to him the propriety of his Catholic Majesty's immediately naming a minister to the United States, I had touched on this subject formerly. He told me that he would speak to his Majesty and inform me of his intentions – He has since acquainted me that the King has made choice of the Chevalier Musquir^3 Son of the C^t de Gousa^4 minister of finance. He is not more than 24 years old, now in London to perfect himself   William Carmichael

NA: PCC, item 108, pp. 314-326 (LBkC); M247, reel 134.
^{1} Elfried, a Danish diplomat, served as chargé d'affaires in Spain, 1783.
^{2} too stubborn

Benjamin Franklin to the President of Congress

Sir,   Passy, Aug⁺ 31. 1783.

After a continued Course of Treating for 9 Months, the English Ministry have at length come to a Resolution to lay aside for the present all the new Propositions that have been made & agreed to, their own as well as ours; and they offer to sign again as a Definitive Treaty the Articles of Nov' 30ᵗʰ· 1782, the Ratifications of which have already been exchang'd. We have agreed to this, and on Wednesday next, the 3ᵈ· Sept· it will be Signed with all the other Definitive Treaties, establishing a General Peace, which may God long continue.

I am with great Respect Sir, Your Excellency's most obedient and most humble Servant

B. Franklin

NA: PCC, *item 82, v. 3, p. 73 (ALS)*; M247, *reel 109*.

David Hartley to Charles James Fox

N° 24   Paris Sept' 1 1783
Sir,

In the present situation of things I have very little to communicate to you. The Treaties are drawn out for signature as you have expressed it, viz, giving Precedence to the Crowned Head. The American Ministers never had a thought of disputing the priority or equality of rank, and therefore I have had no occasion to mention the Subject.

It occurred to me a few days ago that a question might possibly be suggested for signing the American Treaty at Versailles. Therefore to be beforehand with any such proposition I informed the American Ministers that (saving all proper respect to the Court of France & personal respect to the minister) I could not possibly think of signing the treaty anywhere but at Paris, to which place the functions of my Office are confined by my instructions. We have settled that the American Ministers are to sign with me at my Apartments on the morning of the general signature at Versailles. After that we are to proceed to Versailles in consequence of an invitation from Mons' de Vergennes who gives an entertainment this day to all the foreign Ministers. The American Ministers are to dine with me the day after the signature, and in two or three days after that I shall set out for England with the definitive Treaty to receive your farther Instructions

I am Sir, with the greatest respect & consideration Your most obed^t Servt

D Hartley

Clements Library: Hartley Papers, v. 3, pp. 80-81 (C).

David Hartley to the American Peace Commissioners

Gentlemen,   Paris Sept$^{r.}$ 4. 1783.

It is with the sincerest Pleasure that I congratulate you on the happy Event which took Place yesterday, viz, the Signature of the Definitive Treaty between our two Countries. I consider it as the auspicious Presage of returning Confidence, and of the future Intercourse of all good offices between us; I doubt not that our two Countries will entertain the same Sentiments, and that they will behold with Satisfaction the Period which terminates the Memory of their late unhappy Dissensions, and which leads to the renewal of all the Antienties of Amity & Peace. I can assure you that his Britannic Majesty, and his confidential Servants, entertain the strongest Desire of a cordial good understanding with the United States of America. And that nothing may be wanting on our Parts to perfect the great Work of Pacification, I shall propose to you in a very short time, to renew the Discussion of those Points of Amity and Intercourse, which have been lately suspended, to make way for the Signature of the Treaties, between all the late belligerent Powers which took Place Yesterday. We have now the fairest Prospects before us, and an unembarrassed Field for the Exercise of every beneficient Disposition, and for the Accomplishment of every object of reciprocal Advantage between us. Let us then join our hearts and hands together in one common cause, for the reunion of all our antient affections, and common Interests. I am Gentlemen, With the greatest Respect and consideration Your most obed$^{t.}$ Serv$^{t.}$

D. Hartley

NA: PCC, item 85, pp. 416-417 (LBkC); M247, reel 114.

John Adams to the President of Congress

Sir,   Paris Septr 5th 1783.

On Wednesday the third day of this Month, the American Ministers met the British Minister at his Lodgings at the Hotel de York, and signed, sealed and delivered the Definitive Treaty of Peace between the United States of America and the King of Great Britain. Altho' it is but a Confirmation or Repetition of the Provisional Articles, I have the honor to congratulate Congress upon it, as it is a Completion of the work of Peace, and the best we could obtain. Nothing remains now to be done but a Treaty of Commerce. But this in my opinion cannot be negociated without a new Commission from Congress to some one or more Persons. Time, it is easy to foresee, will not be likely to render the British Nation more disposed to a Regulation of Commerce favorable to Us, & therefore my Advice is, to issue a Commission as soon as may be.

.   .   .   .   .

With great Respect, I have the honor to be, Sir, your most obedient & most humble Servant.   John Adams.

NA: PCC, item 84, v. 5, pp. 181-185 (LS); M247, reel 113.

American Peace Commissioners to David Hartley

Sir,   Passy 5 Septr 1783

We have received the Letter which you did us the honour to write yesterday.

Your friendly Congratulations on the signature of the definitive Treaty, meet with cordial Returns on our Part; and we sincerely rejoice with you in that event, by which the ruler of nations has been graciously pleased to give Peace to our two Countries.

We are no less ready to join our Endeavours than our Wishes with yours, to concert such measures for regulating the future Intercourse between Great Britain & the United States, as by being consistent with the honour and interest of both may tend to increase & perpetuate mutual confidence & good will – We ought nevertheless to apprize you that as no Construction of our Commission could at any period extend it, unless by Implication, to several of the proposed Stipulations; and as our Instructions respecting Commercial Provisions however explicit, suppose their being incorporated in the definitive Treaty, a Recurrence to Congress, previous to the signature of them will be necessary, unless obviated by the dispatches we may sooner receive from them.

We shall immediately write to them on the Subject and we are persuaded that the same Disposition to Confidence and Friendship, which has induced them already to give unrestrained Course to British Commerce and unconditionally to liberate all Prisoners; at a time when more Caution would not have appeared singular, will also urge their attention to the Objects in question, & lead them to every proper measure for promoting a liberal & satisfactory Intercourse between the two Countries.

We have communicated to Congress the repeated friendly assurances with which you have officially honoured us on those subjects, and we are persuaded that the Period of their being realized, will have an auspicious & conciliating influence on all the parties in the late unhappy dissensions.

We have the Honour to be Sir, with great Respect & Esteem Your most obed^t & humble Servants   John Adams
                                                                           B. Franklin
                                                                           John Jay

Clements Library: Hartley Papers, v. 3, pp. 87-88 (C).

Benjamin Franklin to David Hartley

My Dear Friend,   Passy Septr 6 1783
    Inclosed is my Letter to Mr Fox. I beg you would assure him, that my Expressions of Esteem for him are not mere Professions. I really think him a *Great* man, and I could not think so, if I did not believe he was at bottom, and would prove himself, a *good* one – Guard him against mistaken notions of the American People. You have deceived yourselves too long with vain expectations of reaping advantage from our little Discontents. We are more thoroughly an enlightened People, with respect to our Political Interests than perhaps any other under Heaven. Every man among us reads, and is so easy in his Circumstances as to have Leisure for Conversations of Improvement, and for acquiring Information. Our Domestic Misunderstandings, when we have them, are of small Extent, tho' monstrously magnified by your microscopic Newspapers. He who judges from them, that we are on the Point of falling into Anarchy, or returning to the Obedience of Britain, is like one who being shewn some Spots on the Sun, should fancy that the whole Disk would soon be overspread by them, and that there would be an End of daylight. The great Body of Intelligence among our People surrounds and overpowers our Petty Dissensions, as the Sun's great Mass of Fire diminishes and destroys his Spots. Do not therefore any longer delay the Evacuation of New York, in the vain Hopes of a new Revolution in your Favour, if such a Hope has

indeed had any effect in causing that delay. It is now nine months since that evacuation was promised. You expect with reason that the People of New York should do your Merchants Justice in the Payment of their old Debts; consider the injustice you do them in keeping them so long out of their Habitations, & out of their Business, by which they might have been enabled to make Payment.

There is no Truth more clear to me than this, that the great Interest of our two Countries is a thorough Reconciliation. Restraints on the freedom of Commerce & Intercourse between us can afford no advantage equivalent to the mischief they will do by keeping up ill humour, and promoting a total alienation. Let you and I, my dear Friend, do our best towards securing & advancing that reconciliation. We can do nothing that in a dying hour will afford us more solid satisfaction.

I wish you a prosperous journey, & a happy sight of your friends, believe me ever, with sincere & great Esteem Yours affectionately   B Franklin.

Present my best respects to your good Br⁸ and Sr⁴˙

Clements Library: Hartley Papers, v. 3, pp. 89-90 (C).

Comte de Vergennes to Chevalier de la Luzerne

[Translation]

Nᵒ 52.
                                         Versailles, 7 September 1783

. . . . .

I see with pleasure, Monsieur, that despite the fermentation which reigns in America, the sentiments owed to France are not weakened. I know, however, that there are some people who endeavor to destroy them, and these people are in France; Mr. John Adams is at their head. I am informed, in a sufficiently positive manner, that the latter has sent word to America that we have sought to thwart them in England relative to the boundaries of the United States and to the fisheries; that we have also sought to create obstacles for him in Holland; that we have hindered Mr. Dana from succeeding in St. Petersburg; and finally that we are the cause of the bad reception that Mr. Jay has continually received at the Court of Madrid. Imputations of this nature are so absurd that they destroy themselves; however, as I have reasons to think that they have some adherents in America, and as Mr. Adams should return there at once, I think I should at all events place you in a position to refute them.

I have nothing to add to that of which I have already informed you concerning the article on the boundaries and concerning that on the fisheries: I should only caution you in this last regard, Sir, that the English ministry thought it should, in the course of last year, communicate to the American Plenipotentiaries a letter from M. de Marbois of the month of March 1782, N°. 225, and that it tried to make us suspect concerning the article on the fisheries by giving a forced interpretation of the reflections which that same dispatch contains on this matter: but there is a peremptory observation to make in this regard: it is that the opinion of M. de Marbois is not that of the King and his Council; anyway, Congress knows perfectly well that the steps indicated in the despatch in question have not been taken; thus, there is no inference to draw from it against the principles that the King may have adopted concerning the fisheries.

As for the obstacles that Mr. Adams should have encountered in Holland through our action, they have only existed in that plenipotentiary's imagination. It is true that in defiance of the circumstances in which the Dutch and the first elements of policy found themselves, he wanted to dispose the States General to treat with him. I pointed out to him then that the Solicitations would be fruitless because prudence would still not permit Their High Mightinesses to listen to them. But as soon as I was in position to judge that the Dutch could no longer spare themselves from taking part in the war, not only did I counsel Mr. Adams to go ahead, but I also endeavored to support his steps through the King's ambassador; and I do not fear being mistaken in saying that our intervention was more efficacious than all the proposals of the American plenipotentiary. I recall that Mr. Adams had the design of linking a treaty of alliance with the treaty of commerce, and that I found his views premature: Congress thought like me, for it authorized its plenipotentiary to conclude an alliance only for the duration of the war.

Concerning Mr. Dana, I remember perfectly well that when proposing to go to St. Petersburg, he consulted me on the conduct it would be appropriate for him to pursue at that Court; I told him with the greatest frankness that, since he could not expect to be received as a representative of the United States, prudence would demand that he not deploy any public character for fear he would compromise the dignity of the Congress, and that he would be limited to presenting himself as a private individual. Mr. Dana went to Holland; he conferred with Mr. Adams; the latter changed his Colleague's mind and caused him to make his way to St. Petersburg. I no longer had any part to take other than that of recommending him to My Lord the Marquis de Verac, and of prescribing to that minister to do what he could to prevent Mr. Dana from delivering his letters of credence. My Lord de Verac's exhortations have succeeded; Mr. Dana has not up to now revealed his character.

There remains Mr. Jay. I appeal to the probity of that minister with regard to the services that M. le Comte de Montmorin has tried to render him: it doubtless will not be claimed in America that the King has had a falling out with his uncle the King for love of the Americans. His Majesty had only the means of representation, and having exhausted it, prudence demanded that he swear himself to Silence.

Such are, Sir, the facts that Mr. Adams and his adherents misrepresent to render us suspect to their compatriots. I do not know if the former acts out of spitefulness; but in pardoning him in this regard, I cannot conceal that he acts at least in a spirit of vengeance: you will no doubt remember, Sir, the complaints that I was forced to make to Congress concerning his principles and his proceedings; you will also remember that it is at my request that he was given two associates: Mr. Adams has never forgiven me; and that is the principle of his insidious relations and of the efforts he is making to render France suspect and odious: such a character is, in my opinion, incapable of serving his homeland well, and I confess to you that I will take much pleasure in seeing him go back across the sea: he will intrigue, he will cabal, he will slander us; but I presume that the facts will be stronger than him, and that his attempts will only result in destroying the confidence that Congress may have placed in his insights and in his probity. In addition, Sir, I pray you to make a discreet use of the details into which I have just entered. You will use them only in case Mr. Adams forces you to do so; and if he holds his tongue, or if his prejudices have not preceded him, you will guard the most absolute silence on your side.

· · · · ·

Vergennes

FFAA: Pol. Corr., U.S., v. 25, f. 144/261-265 (LC transcription).

American Peace Commissioners
to the President of Congress

Sir,   Passy, 10th Septr. 1783.

On the third Instant, Definitive Treaties were concluded between all the late belligerent Powers, except the Dutch, who the Day before settled and signed Preliminary Articles of Peace with Britain.

We most sincerely & cordially congratulate Congress and our Country in general, on this happy Event, and we hope that the same kind Providence which has led us thro' a vigorous War, to an honorable Peace, will enable us to make a wise & moderate Use of that inestimable Blessing.

· · · · ·

Whether the British Court meant to avoid a Definitive Treaty with us, thro' a vain Hope from the exagerated Accounts of Divisions among our People, and Want of Authority in Congress, that some Revolution might soon happen in their Favour, or whether their dilatory Conduct was caused by the Strife of the two opposite and nearly equal Parties in the Cabinet, is hard to decide.

Your Excellency will observe, that the Treaty was signed at Paris, & not at Versailles. Mr Hartley's Letter N°. 5, & our Answer N°. 6. will explain this. His Objections, and indeed our Proceedings in general, were communicated to the French Minister, who was content that we should acquiesce, but desired that we would appoint the signing early in the Morning, and give him an Account of it at Versailles by Express, for that he would not proceed to sign on the Part of France, 'till he was sure that our Business was done.

. . . . .

In whatever Light the Article respecting the Tories may be view'd in America, it is consider'd in Europe as very humiliating to Britain, and therefore as being one which we ought in Honour to perform and fulfil with the most scrupulous Regard to good Faith, & in a manner least Offensive to the Feelings of the King & Court of G. Britain, who upon that Point are extremely tender.

The unseasonable and unnecessary Resolves of various Towns on this Subject, the actual Expulsion of Tories from some Places, and the avow'd Implacability of almost all who have published their Sentiments about the Matter, are Circumstances which are construed, not only to the Prejudice of our national Magnanimity and good-Faith, but also to the Prejudice of our Government.

Popular Committees are consider'd here as with us, in the Light of Substitutes to Constitutional Government, and as being only necessary in the Interval Between the Removal of the former and the Establishment of the present.

The Constitutions of the different States have been translated & published, & Pains have been taken to lead Europe to believe, that the American States not only made their own Laws, but obey'd them. But the continuance of popular Assemblies conven'd expressly to deliberate on Matters proper only for the Cognizance of the different Legislatures & Officers of Government, and their proceeding not only to ordain, but to enforce their Resolutions, has exceedingly lessen'd the Dignity of the States in the Eyes of these Nations.

To this we may also add, that the Situation of the Army, the Reluctance of the People to pay Taxes, and the Circumstances under which Congress removed from Philadelphia, have diminish'd the Admiration in which the

People of America were held among the Nations of Europe, & somewhat abated their Ardor for forming Connections with us, before our Affairs acquire a greater Degree of order & Consistance.

Permit us to observe, that in our Opinion the Recommendation of Congress, promised in the 5th Article, should immediately be made in the Terms of it and published; and that the States should be requested to take it into Consideration as soon as the Evacuation by the Enemy shall be compleated. "It is also much to be wished that the Legislatures may not involve all the Tories in Banishment and Ruin, but that such Discriminations may be made, as to entitle the Decisions to the Approbation of disinterested Men, and dispassionate Posterity."

On the 7th Inst. we received your Excellency's Letter of the 16th June. last, covering a Resolution of Congress of the 1st May directing a Commission to us for making a Treaty of Commerce &c with G. Britain. This Intelligence arrived very opportunely to prevent the Anti-American Party from ascribing any Delays on our Part to Motives of Resentment in England to that Country. Great Britain will send a Minister to Congress as soon as Congress shall send a Minister to Britain, & we think much Good might result from that Measure.

. . . . .

Much we think will depend on the Success of our Negociations with England. If she should be prevailed upon to agree to a liberal System of Commerce, France & perhaps some other Nations, will follow her Example; but if she should prefer an exclusive monopolizing Plan, it is probable that her Neighbours will continue to adhere to their favorite Restrictions.

Were it certain that the United States, could be brought to act as a Nation, and would jointly and fairly conduct their Commerce on Principles of exact Reciprocity with all Nations, we think it probable that Britain would make extensive Concessions. – but on the Contrary, while the Prospect of Disunion in our Councils, or want of Power and Energy in our Executive Departments exist, they will not be apprehensive of Retaliation, and consequently lose their principal Motive to Liberality. Unless with respect to all foreign Nations and Transactions, we uniformly act as an entire united Nation, faithfully executing and obeying the Constitutional Acts of Congress on those Subjects, we shall soon find ourselves in the Situation in which all Europe wishes to see us, viz. as unimportant Consumers of her Manufactures & Productions, and as useful Labourers to furnish her with raw Materials.

We beg leave to assure Congress that we shall apply our best Endeavours to execute this new Commission to their Satisfaction, & shall punctually obey such Instructions as they may be pleased to give us relative to it....

. . . . .

With great Respect, We have the honor to be, Sir, Your Excellency's most obedient & most humble Ser.ᵗˢ

John Adams.
B Franklin
John Jay

NA: PCC, *item 85, pp. 370-385 (LS); M247, reel 114.*

Benjamin Franklin to John Jay

Sir,   Passy, 10 September 1783

I have received a letter from a very respectable person in America containing the following words, vizt.

"It is confidently reported, propagated and believed by some among us, that the Court of France was at bottom against our obtaining the Fishery and Territory in that great Extent in which both are secured to us by the Treaty; that our Ministers at that Court favoured, or did not oppose this Design against us, and that it was entirely owing to the Firmness, Sagacity and Disinterestedness of Mr. Adams, with whom Mr. Jay united, that we have obtained these important Advantages."

It is not my Purpose to dispute any Share of the Honour of that Treaty which the Friends of my Colleagues may be disposed to give them; but having now spent Fifty Years of my Life in public Offices and Trusts, and having still one Ambition left, that of carrying the Character of Fidelity at least, to the Grave with me, I cannot allow that I was behind any of them in Zeal and Faithfulness. I therefore think that I ought not to suffer an Accusation, which falls little short of Treason to my Country, to pass without notice, when the means of effectual Vindicaton are at hand. You, Sir was a Witness of my Conduct in that Affair. To you and my other Colleagues I appeal by sending to each a similar Letter with this, and I have no doubt of your Readiness to do a Brother Commissioner Justice, by Certificates that will entirely destroy the Effect of that Accusation.

I have the honour to be, with much esteem, Sir, Your Most Obedient and Most humble Servant.

B. Franklin

Morris, Jay Papers, *v. 2, p. 584.*

John Jay to Benjamin Franklin

Sir   Passy, 11 Sept.ʳ 1783
   I have been favored with your Letter of Yesterday, & will answer it
explicitly.
   I ~~have never been witness to any action or Conversation of yours which
indicated a Reluctance~~ have no Reason whatever to believe that you was
averse to our obtaining the full Extent of Boundary & Fishery secured to us
by the Treaty. Your Conduct respecting them throughout the Negociation
indicated a strong & ~~evident~~ steady attachment to both those objects, in
my opinion and promoted the attainment of them
   I remember that in a Conversation which M.ʳ de Rayneval, the first
Secretary of Count De Vergennes, had with you and me, in the Summer
of 1782, you contended for our full Right to the Fishery, and argued it on
various Principles.
   Your Letters to me when in Spain, considered our Territory as extending
to the Missisippi, and expressed your opinion against ceding the Navigation
of that River, in very strong and pointed Terms.
   In short Sir: I do not recollect the least Difference in Sentiment between
us respecting the Boundaries or Fisheries. On the contrary, we were
unanimous and united in adhering to, and insisting on them. nor did I ever
percieve the least Disposition in either of us, to recede from our Claims, or
be satisfied with less than we obtained.
   I have the Honor to be with great Respect & Esteem Sir Your most
obedient and very h'ble Serv.ᵗ   [John Jay]

Columbia University Libraries: John Jay Papers (Draft).

John Jay to Robert Morris

D.ʳ Sir   Passy 12.ᵗʰ Sept.ʳ 1783.
   The Definitive Treaty is concluded, and we are now thank God in the
full Possession of Peace & Independance – if we are not a happy People
now it will be our own Fault.
   We daily expect the Commission for a Treaty of Commerce. I wish that
the Sentiments of our Country on that important Subject may be fully
stated in the Instructions w.ʰ will accompany it. I think all our Treaties of
Commerce should be temporary – The Circumstances of our Country may
be greatly changed in twenty or Thirty Years, and what may now be

advantageous may possibly be then inconvenient. Besides as we increase in wealth and Power, we shall find it less difficult to mould Treaties to our minds. In my opinion we should Constantly look forward to a Commercial Intercourse with all the Ports and Places on the american Continent and american Islands to whomsoever belonging. – perpetual Treaties of commerce now made, would probably exclude us from that Prospect.

In a Late Letter to G. Morris I enclos'd him an account of the Invention of Globes where with men may literally soar above the Clouds – There with send you two Prints containing Representations of the Rise and Descent of one of them –

. . . . .

...Be pleased to assure M$^{rs.}$ Morris of our constant regard, and beleive [me] to be Dear Sir Your aff Friend   John Jay

Columbia University Libraries: John Jay Papers (C).

Congressional Committee Report

[Princeton, 18 September 1783]

The Committee...appointed to receive Communications from the honorable the Minister plenipotentiary of France agreeably to his Request: Report that your Committee having appointed the Congress Chamber at six °Clock to receive the Communications of the said Minister, they were accordingly attended by him. That the substance of the said Communications is as follows –

That as he is informed by his Court$^{⊗}$ that it is difficult to determine when a definitive Treaty will be concluded. That France agrees perfectly with England on every point respecting their Treaty: – That the same may be said of Spain – But that that Power as well as France, attached to the true principles by which negociations of such Importance ought to be regulated, will not sign but in Concert: That Holland had not yet settled her Arrangements; but it will be soon done – They have also determined not to sign but in Concert. That therefore the Negociations are retarded by nothing but the American Treaty which —— seems to be in a State of Languor: and occasioned as the Court has Reason to think, —— by the English plenipotentiary – That it seems that the Americans by admitting too precipitably English Vessells in their ports have deprived themselves of a powerful weapon to induce England to a Conclusion of the Treaty – By a Continuation of the former prohibitory Laws untill the final Settlement Of peace it is probable that they wou'd have furnished the most pungent Arms to the party who sincerely wishes that the Treaty with America might be concluded – However the Court is disposed to believe that it will not be much delayed. That Congress may be assured that the definitive Treaty will not be signed but in Conjunction with America's. That the American plenipo⁺ had asked the Advice of Count de Vergennes respecting the mediation of the two imperial Courts: That he had observed to them that these Courts having never offered their mediation to Congress, they were ~~equally entitled~~ at liberty either to claim or to decline it: That he did not know then which part they would take. In his Opinion the easiest would be for them to negociate without the Interference of any foreign Power – That the Court had in View the Commerce of the United States: and had ordered a Diminution of the Duty ~~put upon~~ on the Salt, and that the same Regulation would take place with respect to Brandy. That his Majesty had declared L'Orient a free Port because it is the Port which the Americans have preferred to any other –

The above is the Substance of the Communications made to the Committee the 18ᵗʰ· Septembʳ· 1783.   Jaˢ· Duane Chʳ·
Delivered Sept. 19. 1783.

⊛ 21 July 1783. Count de Vergennes dispatches to Chevʳ· de la Luzerne Minister of France.

NA: PCC, *item 25, v. 2, pp. 295-298; M247, reel 32.*

Chevalier de la Luzerne to Comte de Vergennes

[Translation]

Nᵒ· 345   Philadelphia, 26 September 1783
My Lord,

· · · · ·

His Majesty's refusal to grant the United States a supplement to this year's subsidies was known to Congress at the same time that the despatch to which I have the honor to respond reached me. I went to Princeton and, without waiting to be spoken to, I myself informed several Delegates of the circumstances in which our own finances find themselves and which do not permit us to make new sacrifices; there are reasons so substantial to give to this subject that in no way had I any difficulty in convincing fair minds. As for the others, the impression of dissatisfaction that our refusals may make on them is a passing one, and our kindnesses would not have made a more lasting one. I assure you, My Lord, that this refusal, although painful to announce, will not have a bad effect. The Superintendent is not a man to become discouraged; however, I would not be surprised if he makes new efforts to persuade Congress to repeat its requests, but I do not think that this Assembly favors it, and if Mr. Franklin brings you news thereof, it will probably be to ease his own troubles and without further instructions. If, after this refusal, he succeeded in his solicitations, the Ministers of Congress would take it as a license to renew their importunities without end. It seems to me, My Lord, so much the less useful to yield henceforth, for I foresee in the future a glimmer of amelioration in affairs of Finance, but distress and troubles still continue, and if I should render you a favorable account of it, the time is not at hand.

I have not heard any complaint from Congress concerning this refusal. The Majority of that Assembly does not make its attachment to the Alliance depend on such circumstances, and its gratitude to the King has lost none of its strength. As for England, Congress and the Legislatures of the various States are still little disposed to a cordial rapprochement, the only class of the People that seems disposed to want it is that of the merchants, but the exclusion from commerce with its sugar Islands to which Great Britain seems to want them to submit occasions a strong fermentation, and the genius of that People will raise obstacles to a sincere and complete reconciliation. If England places so important a restriction on her commerce with them, that exclusion in addition will only be perceived in all its force when the Americans have themselves formed their own peacetime shipping. It is above all while they suffer impatiently that their import and export trade with the Islands is conducted by Foreigners. Until now, they have been patient, because the war deprived them of ships suitable for this Commerce, but their stocks are covered with Ships under construction.

I think, as do you, My Lord, that in the future we shall be without means to influence the domestic measures of the United States. As for their national measures relative to their external Policy, the constant justice of the King's conduct bears the stamp of his disinterestedness and of his generosity, which are known even to those who have no part in the management of public Affairs; and our own adhesion to the same principles of equity gives us more strength than the Court of London could acquire through all the resources of intrigue.

The vast extent of the boundaries to which England has consented in fact has caused much Surprise and Satisfaction, My Lord; a large part of these Territories, as you point out, will form a real accession of States only when the Savage tribes that inhabit them today are replaced by civilized people, but every day settlements are formed beyond the mountains; new colonists are constantly pushing the Savages back toward the West. The budding Colonies touch the Mississippi, and I think that in 40 years there will be no more Savage Society on this side of that river, and the only natives left will be those who have agreed to join the Societies that the newcomers may found.

I have read the writing drawn up by M. de Rayneval entitled *"Idea on the manner of determining and fixing the boundaries between Spain and the United States."* The principles established therein are so consistent with equity and with natural and international law, therein prevails an impartiality so exact with regard to Spain and the United States, that it is inconceivable that Mr. Jay could take umbrage at it. But that Plenipotentiary has always exaggerated the rights of the United States, and his reports to Congress have displayed his prejudices in that regard. It is very true that some members of that assembly share his opinions, but the greater number consider our conduct under its true point of view, and have understood that when we endeavored to inspire moderation in the Americans and to confine their claims within just boundaries, it was to keep them prepared for any emergency and to remove in advance the difficulties that could result from the counterclaims of the Court of London. I also think, My Lord, that that court has employed some kind of maneuver which I cannot penetrate and which is not well known here, to inspire distrust and suspicion in the American plenipotentiaries, but this intrigue has made no impression on Congress. I am very much inclined to believe that your suspicions concerning Mr. John Adams are well founded, that that Minister has much ill will toward us, and that the attentions accorded Mr. Franklin and the good reputation which he justly enjoys dishearten his Colleague. I also know that he is working hard to have his compatriots adopt these Sentiments, but he will not succeed. As to Mr. Jay, I think I can, with the utmost confidence, reassure you on his sentiments; I do not think that he has any gratitude to us, but he is incapable of preferring England to us; he prides himself on being independent, and his desire to show his attachment to his Country renders him sometimes unjust, but we should not fear from him any premeditated act capable of being prejudicial to the alliance. I also know for a fact that he writes to Congress and to his friends in the manner most appropriate to inspire confidence and respect for Mr. Franklin in them. He has also written some letters full of Praise of that Plenipotentiary's grandson, and he sincerely does everything in his power to persuade Congress to give that young man a place of confidence in the diplomatic service. Mr. Franklin would also like to obtain a leave, during which his grandson would perform the functions of charge d'affaires, but I do not think that Congress will ever decide to give a place of confidence to this young man, whose Father has shown a violent attachment to England, and that attachment casts a stain upon the son that he will have trouble effacing. I should also, My Lord, render justice to Mr. Jay and to Mr. Adams himself by saying that in their despatches they frequently express their veneration of your virtues and their confidence in your wisdom. Congress is favorably disposed toward Mr. Franklin, and it is with regret that one sees that Minister insist on the recall that he has requested. He is thought extremely attached to France, but it seems to me that no one does him the injury of thinking that he has sold himself to us.

．　．　．　．　．

le ch de la luzerne

Received 10 December

FFAA: Pol. Corr., U.S., v. 25, f. 171/317-326 (LC transcription).

Robert Morris to Benjamin Franklin

Sir,   Office of Finance 30 Septem: 1783.
I am to acknowlege the receipt of your Favors of the seventh of March and twenty seventh of July. For both of them accept my Thanks. You express an Apprehension lest the Union between France and America should be diminished by Accounts from your Side of the Water. This Apprehension does you equal Honor as a Statesman and as a Man. Every Principle which ought to actuate the Councils of a Nation requires from us an affectionate Conduct towards France and I very sincerely lament those Misap-prehensions which have indisposed some worthy Men towards that Nation whose Treasure and Blood have been so freely expended for us. I believe the Truth with respect to some to be this. A warm Attachment to America has prevented them from making due Allowances in those Cases where there Country was concerned. Under certain Prepossession it was natural for them to think that the french Ministry might do more for us, and it was quite as natural for the Ministers to think that we ought to have done more for ourselves The Moment of Treaty with England was of Course the Moment of Profession with english Ministers. I fear that the Impressions made by these were for a little while rather more deep than was quite necessary. But the same Love of America which had raised such strong Irritability where her Interests were concerned, will of Course stimulate it to an equal Degree when those Interests are assailed from another Quarter. I think I may venture to assure you that the Esteem of this Country for France is not diminished and that the late Representations have not been so unfavorable as you fear.

Our Commerce is flowing very fast towards Great Britain and that from Causes which must for ever influence the commercial Part of Society. Some Articles are furnished by Britain cheaper many as cheap and all on a long

Credit. Her Merchants are attentive and punctual. In her Ports our Vessels always meet with Dispatch. I say Nothing of Language and Manners because I do not think they influence so strongly on Commerce as many People suppose but what is of no little Importance is that the English having formed our Taste are more in a Capacity to gratify that Taste by the Nature and fashion of their Manufactures. There is another Circumstance also which must not be forgotten. The great Demand for french Manufactures during the War increased the Price of many and some Time will be required before it can by a fair Competition be discovered which of the two Countries france or England can supply us cheapest. The Delays in the public Bills is a further Circumstance which militates (a momentary Obstacle) against the Trade with France. I must therefore mention to you also a Matter which is of great Effect. Until we can navigate the Mediteranean in Safety we cannot trade in our own Bottoms with the Ports of france or Spain which are on that Sea. And we certainly will not Trade there in foreign Bottoms because we do not find the same Convenience and Advantage in so doing as in our own Vessels – Unless indeed it be on Board of English Ships. This may be a disagreable Fact but it is not the less a Fact. – I beleive that Informations are transmitted from hence to the Court which they ought not to rely on. Their Servants doubtless do their Duty in transmitting such Informations but I am perswaded that they are themselves not well informed. Indeed it is quite natural that Men should mistake when they examine and treat of a Subject with which they are unacquainted. And it cannot well be supposed that political Characters are competent to decide on the Advantages and Disadvantages of allowing to or witholding from us a share in the carrying Trade – On this Subject I will make a further Observation and you may rely on it that I speak to you with Candor and Sincerity not with a View to making any Impressions on the Court. You may communicate or withold what I say and they may or may not apply it to their own Purposes. If any thing will totally ruin the Commerce of England with this Country it is her blind Attachment to her Navigation Act. This Act which never was the real Foundation of her naval Superiority may and perhaps will be the Cause of its Destruction. If france possesses commercial Wisdom she will take Care not to imitate the Conduct of her Rival! The West India Islands can be supplied twenty per Cent cheaper in american than in french or british Bottoms I will not trouble you with the Reasons but you may rely on the Fact. The Price of the Produce of any Country must materially depend on the Cheapness of Subsistence. The Price at which that Produce can be vended abroad must depend on the Facility of Conveyance. Now admitting for a Moment (which by the bye is not true) that France might by Something like a british Navigation Act, increase her Ships and her Seamen these Things would necessarily follow. 1ˢᵗ· Her Islands would be less wealthy and therefore less able to consume and pay for her Manufactures. 2ˡʸ· The Produce of those Islands would be less cheap and therefore less able to sustain the weight of Duties and support a Competition in foreign Markets. 3ˡʸ· The Commerce with this Country would be greatly lessened because that every American Ship which finds herself in a french or english or other Port will naturally seek a freight there rather than go elswhere to look for it because in many Commodities the Difference of Price in different Parts will not compensate the Time and Cost of going from Place to Place to look after them. To these Principal Reasons might be added many others of lesser Weight tho not of little Influence such as the probable Increase of commercial Intercourse by increasing the Connections and Acquaintances of Individuals. To this and to every Thing else which can be said on the Subject by an American I know there is one short Answer always ready viz: That we seek to increase our own Wealth. So far from denying that this is among my Motives I place it as the foremost and [(] setting aside that Gratitude which I feel for France) I do not scruple to declare that a Regard to the Interests of America is with Respect to all Nations of the World my political Compass. But the different Nations of Europe should consider that in Proportion to the Wealth of this Country will be her Ability to pay for those Commodities which all of them are pressing us to buy.

The People of this Country still continue as remiss as ever in the Payment of Taxes. Much of this (as you justly observe) arises from the Difficulties of Collection. But those Difficulties are much owing to an ignorance of proper Modes and an Unwillingness to adopt them. In short tho all are content to acknowlege that there is a certain Burthen of Taxation which ought to be borne Yet each is desirous of Shifting it off of his own Shoulders on those of his Neighbors. Time will I hope produce a Remedy to the Evils under which we labor but it may also increase them.

Your Applications to the Court for Aid are certainly well calculated to obtain it, but I am not much surprized at your ill Success indeed I should have been much surprized if you had been more fortunate. Of all Men I was placed in the Situation to take a deep Concern in the Event but I cannot disapprove of the Refusal for we certainly ought to do more for ourselves before we ask the Aid of others – Copies of your Letters to the Court were laid before Congress and also the Copy of the new Contract. I will enclose with this a further Copy of the Ratification of the old if I can obtain it in Season from Princeton where the Congress now are.

I have written also on the Subject of the Debt due to the farmer's general and should Congress give me any Orders about it I shall attend carefully to the Execution. The Conduct they have maintained with regard to us has been generous and will demand a Return of Gratitude as well as of Justice. This I hope my Countrymen will always be disposed to Pay. I shall take some proper Opportunity of writing to the farmer's General but will wait a while to know what may be the Determination of Congress on their Affairs.

It gives me much Pleasure to find that by the proposed Establishment of Packetts we shall shortly be in Condition to maintain more regular and connected Correspondence for altho I shall not myself be much longer in public Office I feel for those who are or will be charged with the Affairs of our Country both at Home and abroad. – It will naturally occur however that a good Cypher must be made use of not unfrequently when Dispatches are trusted to foreigners. They have no Regard either to Propriety or even Decency where Letters are concerned.

With very sincere Esteem and Respect I am Sir your Excellency's most obedient and humble Servant   RM

LC: *Robert Morris Papers, microfilm reel 8 (LBkC).*

David Hartley to Benjamin Franklin

My Dear Friend,   Bath, Oct. 4, 1783.

I only write one line to you to let you know that I am not forgetful of you, or of our common concerns. I have not heard any thing from the ministry yet: I believe it is a kind of vacation with them before the meeting of parliament. I have told you of a proposition which I have had some thoughts to make as a kind of co-partnership in commerce. I send you a purposed temporary convention, which I have drawn up. You are to consider it only as one I recommend. The words underlined are grafted upon the proposition of my memorial, dated May 21, 1783. You will see the principle which I have in my thoughts to extend for the purpose of restoring our ancient co-partnership generally. I cannot tell you what event things may take, but my thoughts are always employed in endeavoring to arrange that system upon which the *china vase*, lately shattered, may be cemented together, upon principles of compact and connexion, instead of dependence. I have met with a sentiment in this country which gives some alarm, viz. lest the unity of government in America should be uncertain, and the states reject the authority of Congress. Some passages in General Washington's letter have given weight to these doubts. I don't hear of any tendency to this opinion; *that the American States will break to pieces, and then we may still conquer them.* I believe all that folly is extinguished. But many serious and well-disposed persons are alarmed lest *this should be the ill-*

fated moment for relaxing the powers of the union, and annihilating the cement of confederation, (vide Washington's letter,) and that Great Britain should thereby lose her best and wisest hope of being re-connected with the American States *unitedly.* I should, for one, think it the greatest misfortune. Pray give me some opinion upon this. You see there is likewise another turn which may be given to this sentiment by intemperate and disappointed people, who may indulge a passionate revenge for their own disappointments, by endeavoring to excite general distrust, discord, and disunion. I wish to be prepared and guarded at all points. I beg my best compliments to your colleagues; be so good as to show this letter to them. I beg particularly my condolence (and I hope congratulation) to Mr. Adams; I hear that he has been very dangerously ill, but that he is again recovered. I hope the latter part is true, and that we shall all survive to set our hands to some future compacts of common interest, and common affection, between our two countries. Your ever affectionate

D. Hartley.

WTF, Franklin Memoirs, *v. 4, pp. 347-349.*

David Hartley to Charles James Fox

N° 27.   October 9^{th:} 1783.

Sir

Permitt me to suggest a proposition to you respecting the ratification of the definitive treaty lately signed with the united states of America, which is, that the British ratification might be made out without loss of time, and that I might be authorized to inform the American Ministers that our ratification is signed, and that we are ready for the Exchange whenever their ratification shall arrive. I hope there will not be any objection to this step. The provisional Articles were ratified by Congress some months before they were ratified by the British Court, It seems therefore our turn now to be in advance. – But certainly Sir this [is] not the only motive which has induced me to suggest the proposition to you. There is another circumstance which I apprehend (altho' inconsequential in itself) may possibly excite some secret thoughts of jealousy to the American Ministers. I mean the late proclamation of the peace with France & Spain without any notice of the peace with America. The reason in point of form is obvious viz the ratifications not being yet exchanged. Nevertheless it may perhaps carry an equivocal appearance to them in another light as if we quitted the War with reluctance. It may augment the discontent which I know the[y] very strongly entertain from the delay of the long promised evacuation of New York.

I shall not trouble you Sir with any farther argument upon this Subject. A short word is sufficient to you to convey the whole scope of the proposal which I take the liberty to suggest not only for the purpose of avoiding secret jealousies, but as an occasion of acquiring Confidence by Advancing with readiness to the ratification. I think such a voluntary step on the part of the british Court wou'd have a very good effect.

I am Sir with the greatest respect Your most Obed^t Serv$^{t.}$

D Hartley

Clements Library: Hartley Papers, v. 3, pp. 101-102 (C).

Congressional Committee Report

[Princeton, October 21, 1783]

The Committee, to whom was referred the Letters and Communications from the Ministers of the United States for negociating Peace, and the Letter of the 19th inst. from the Secretary for foreign Affairs, together with three Motions thereon, report to Congress the following Resolutions –

Resolved

That Congress entertain a high Sense of the Services of their Commissioners in the Negociation of the provisional Articles agreed to by them and the Commissioner of his Britannic Majesty; and of the Zeal and Firmness, which they have shewn with so much success for the Dignity ~~and thus~~ the Rights and the interests of the United States.

Resolved

That the said Commissioners be instructed to make; to the Court of France, a < *** > Communication of the separate Article entered into with the British Commissioner; to endeavour to have that Article excluded from the Treaty with Great Britain: but, if this cannot be accomplished without inconvenience ~~done~~, then to agree that, to whatever Power West Florida shall remain or be ceded at the Conclusion of the War, its northern Boundary shall be as it is described in the said separate Article.

Resolved

That the Secretary for foreign Affairs be directed to inform the said Commissioners, that it is the ~~Sense~~ Wish of Congress, that the Articles agreed to with the Commissioner of his Britannic Majesty ~~ought to~~ had been communicated to the Court of France before they were signed.

NA: PCC, item 25, v. 2, pp. 281-282; M247, reel 32.

Benjamin Franklin to David Hartley

Passy, Oct. 22, 1783.

I received my dear friend's kind letter of the 4th instant from Bath, with your proposed temporary convention, which you desire me to show to my colleagues. They are both by this time in London, where you will undoubtedly see and converse with them on the subject. The apprehension you mention that the cement of the confederation may be annihilated, &c. has not I think any foundation. There is sense enough in America to take care of their own *china vase*. I see much in your papers about our divisions and distractions, but I hear little of them from America; and I know that most of the letters said to come from there with such accounts are mere London fictions. I will consider attentively the proposition above mentioned against the return of my colleagues, when I hope our commission will be arrived....   B. Franklin.

WTF, Franklin Memoirs, v. 4, p. 350.

The President of Congress to the American Peace Commissioners

Gentlemen,   Princeton 1. Nov. 1783

. . . . .[1]

Yesterday we received from Colo. Ogden[1] the news of the signature of the definitive Treaty on the 3ᵈ of September, and that Mʳ Thaxter was on the way with the official news. We long for his arrival tho' we have no doubt of the fact, which is also announced by the Post this day from Boston.

I do most sincerely congratulate you, Gentlemen, on this most important and happy event, which has diffused the sincerest Joy throughout these States, and the terms of which must necessarily hand down the names of its American Negociators to Posterity with the highest possible honor. May the Gratitude of your Country ever be the fair reward of all your labours.

New-York is not yet evacuated, but Sir Guy Carleton has informed our Commander in Chief, that he shall get clear of it in all this month, tho' I think they will not dare to stay much beyond the 15[th.] instant.

Your &c.   E B

NA: PCC, item 16, pp. 261-262 (LBkC); M247, reel 24.
    [1]Ogden, Matthias (d. 1791). Military officer. Took part in the expedition to Canada, 1775-1776. Lieutenant colonel, 1776, and colonel, 1777, of the 1st New Jersey, a line regiment. Granted leave to visit Europe, April 1783

The President of Congress to John Adams

Private   Princeton 1st November 1783
Sir,

                    .   .   .   .   .

Congress have not come to any further determination on your last letters, relative to your resignation; on account of the peace arrangement not being yet settled.

Perhaps there will be but very few Ministers employed in Europe, and these in the Character of Residents or simply Ministers.

The conduct of Great Britain does not appear yet very conciliating, and her measures on this side the water have rather tended to irritate than otherwise.

Congress will not be in a hurry to send a Minister to the Court of London, till they see how the definitive Treaty will end. We have an account this day from Col. Ogden that it was signed on the 3[d.] of September, and that M[r.] Thaxter is on his way with it, whom we long to see.

Your letters on the subject of our credit abroad and the strengthening and cementing the union at home, came at a happy moment, and have had a very good effect. Your Countrymen were running wild on this subject, but your observations & opinion have helped to check them, and the Legislature of Massachusetts have passed the 5 p Cent. Impost recommended by Congress.

                    .   .   .   .   .

I have the honor to be, with sentiments of high respect and esteem, Sir, Your most obed[t.] & very humb. Serv[t.]   Elias Boudinot

MHS: The Adams Papers, microfilm reel 361 (ALS).

Chevalier de la Luzerne to the President of Congress

Sir,   Philadelphia 2 November 1783

I have received the letter which your Excellency did me the honor to write the 27 of last month with the resolutions of Congress accompanying the same, wherein Congress express their sentiments with regard to the dispositions of his Majesty & the other belligerent powers not to sign the definitive treaty but in concert with the United States. It appears by the last dispatches we have received that this conduct has produced the desired effect and that it has at last been followed by a general peace.

The United States may be assured that the King will with pleasure adopt every arrangement of Commerce which will be advantageous to them & not injurious to his own subjects. I know that it is his Majesty's intention, that the United States should enjoy in the ports of his realm not only all the advantages they had before their Independence but also some favours which till that period had never been granted to them. I am, with respect S^r your Excellency's most obed^t & most humble Servt

Le chev de la Luzerne

NA: PCC, *item 95, v. 2, p. 256 (translation); M247, reel 123.*

John Adams to the President of Congress

Sir   London November 13. 1783.

If any one should ask me what is the System of the present administration? I should answer, "to keep their places" – Every Thing they say or do appears evidently calculated to that End, and no Ideas of public Good no national Object is suffered to interfere with it.

In order to drive out Shelburne, they condemned his Peace which all the Whig Part of them, would have been very glad to have made and have gloried in the Advantages of it. in order to avail themselves of the old Habits and Prejudices of the Nation, they now pretend to cherish the Principles of the Navigation act, and the King has been advised to recommend this in his Speech, & the Lords have echoed it, in very strong terms.

. . . . .

The United States of America, are another Object of Debate, if an Opposition should be formed, and concerted, I presume, that one fundamental of it, will be a Liberal Conduct towards us. They will be very profuse in Professions of Respect and esteem and affection for Us. Will pretend to wish for Measures which may throw a veil over the past and restore, as much as possible the ancient good will. They will be advocates for some freedom of Communication with the West Indies, and for our having an equitable share of that carrying Trade &c.

Administration on the other hand I am confident will with great difficulty be persuaded to abandon the mean contemptible Policy which their Proclamations exhibit.

In my humble Opinion the only suitable Place for us to negotiate the Treaty in is London – Here with the most perfect politeness to the Ministry, we may keep them in awe, a Visit to a distinguished Member of Opposition, even if nothing should be said at it, would have more Weight with Ministers than all our Arguments – Mr Jay is I believe, of the same opinion. But we shall not conduct the Negotiation here, unless Dr Franklin should come over: indeed if Congress should join us in a Commission to treat with other Powers, in my opinion, we might conduct the Business better here than at Paris – I shall however chearfully conform to the sentiments of my Colleagues.

The Delay of the Commission is to me a great embarrassment, I know not whether to stay here return to Paris or the Hague. I hope every moment to receive advices from Congress which will resolve me.

I receiv'd yesterday a Letter from Mr Hartley, with the Compliments of Mr Fox and that he should be glad to see me, proposing the hour of Eleven to day which I agreed to. Mr Jay saw him, one day this Week. Mr Jay made him and the Duke of Portland a Visit on his first Arrival they were not at home But he never heard from them untill my arrival, ten days or a fortnight after informed of this, I concluded not to visit them and did not. But after a very long time, and indeed after Mr Hartley's return from Bath, Messages have been sent to Mr Jay & me that Mr Fox would be glad to see us. it is merely for Form, and to prevent a Cry against him in Parliament for not having seen us, for not one Word was said to Mr Jay of publick affairs, nor will a word be said to me.

The real Friendship of America seems to me the only Thing which can redeem this Country from total Destruction: there are a few who think so, here, and but a few, and the present Ministers are not among them: or at least, if they are of this Opinion, they conceal it, and behave as if they thought America of small Importance. The Consequence will be, that little Jealousies and Rivalries, & Resentments will be indulged, which will do essential injury to this Country as they happen, and they will end in another War, in which will be torn from this Island all her Possessions in Canada, Nova Scotia, and the East and west Indies.

With great Respect I have the honour to be, Sir, your most obedient, and most humble Servant   John Adams

Read Jany 21. 1784

NA: PCC, item 84, v. 5, pp. 219-222 (LS); M247, reel 113.

Robert Morris to John Jay

My Dear Sir,   Philadelphia, 27 November 1783

I Congratulate you on the signing of the Definitive Treaty and on the evacuation of New York which took place on Tuesday. Our Friend Gouverneur Morris is there. He has been gone about 18 Days and I expect him back very soon. He will then give you the Detail and inform you of such things as you may wish to know respecting any of your particular Friends.

I agree with the Sentiments expressed in your letter of the 12th September. Treaties of Commerce are dangerous rather than other wise, and if all Governments were to agree that Commerce should be as free as Air I believe they would then place it on the most advantageous footing for every Country and for all mankind. The restrictions which Great Britain is aiming at will in the end work for our Good, if we can work good out of any thing, which in the present State of things seems doubtful. If Great Britain persists in refusing admittance to our Ships in their Islands, they will probably have great cause to repent for I shall not be surprized to see a general Prohibition to the admittance of theirs into our Ports, and if such a measure is once adopted they may find it very difficult to obtain any alteration and in that Case, the advantages of carrying will be much against them. Should the court of France pursue the same Policy we shall fall in with the Dutch and probably have more Connections in Commerce with them than with any other People.

. . . . .

...I am Dear Sir, Your Affectionate Friend and Humble Servant,

Robt. Morris

Morris, Jay Papers, *v. 2, pp. 650-651.*

Chevalier de la Luzerne to Comte de Vergennes

[Translation]

Nº. 359   Philadelphia, 13 December 1783

My Lord,

The Ministers of Congress have sent it the definitive Treaty between Great Britain and the United States; it was stipulated in it that the ratifications will be exchanged in six months from its date, that is to say, at the latest the third of March next. I doubt that this stipulation can be carried out. The ratification will not experience any difficulty when the States have assembled, but that will not be before next month.

. . . . .

...Mr. Hartley told them [the American plenipotentiaries] by order of his Court that for three months it had been expecting to see an American Minister arrive at St. James, where all further affairs and those of a Treaty of Commerce could be discussed and arranged. That nomination will be a matter for many debates in Congress.

New York was entirely evacuated at the end of last month. It came off very coldly. General Carleton could see from his Vessels the fireworks discharged on the occasion of the peace and the evacuation. General Washington had invited him to attend, but he did not consider it appropriate to do so. Many disorders were feared; the sagacity of the English and American commanders prevented them....

le chr de la luzerne

Recd. 19 February.

FFAA: Pol. Corr., U.S., v. 26, f. 84/195-198 (LC transcription).

Congressional Committee Report on the Definitive Treaty of Peace

[16 December 1783]

The committee to whom were referred the Definitive treaty of peace between the United states of America and his Britannic majesty, and the joint letter from mr. Adams, mr. Franklin and mr. Jay, have agreed to the following report.

Resolved that it is the opinion of this committee that the said Definitive treaty ought to be ratified by the United states in Congress assembled.

That a Proclam Proclamation should be immediately issued notifying the said definitive treaty & ratification to the several states of the Union, & requiring their observance thereof.[1]

That Congress should immediately & earnestly recommend to the legislatures of the respective states, to provide for the restitution of all estates, rights & properties, which have been confiscated, belonging to real British subjects; and also of the estates, rights & properties of persons resident in districts which were in the possession of his Britannic majesty's arms at any time between the 30th. day of November 1782. and the 14th day of December 1783 and who have not borne arms against the said United states and that persons of any other description shall have free liberty to go to any part or parts of any of the thirteen United states, & therein to remain twelve months unmolested in their endeavors to obtain the restitution of such of their estates, rights & properties as may have been confiscated; and that Congress should also immediately & earnestly recommend to the several states a reconsideration & revision of all acts or laws regarding the premises, so as to render the said laws or acts perfectly consistent not only with justice & equity, but with that spirit of conciliation, which, on the return of the blessings of peace, should universally prevail: and that Congress should also immediately & earnestly recommend to the several states, that the estates, rights & properties of such last mentioned persons, should be restored to them, they refunding to any persons, who may be now in possession, the *bonâ fide* price (where any has been given) which such persons may have paid on purchasing any of the said lands, rights or properties since the confiscation.

NA: PCC, *item 29, pp. 315-316 (Draft); M247, reel 36.*
   [1] *The word "Agreed" appears in the left margin next to this paragraph.*

Comte de Vergennes to Chevalier de la Luzerne

[Translation]

N°· 53.   Versailles, 24 December 1783

. . . . .

We could only learn with sorrow of the displacement of Congress and the provisional arrangements it has made for its residence: if these arrangements take place, the Members of Congress will employ all their time in travel, and it will be impossible for them to be equal to their work and, above all, to the expense which their continual journeys will exact. As we have only a few political subjects to treat with Congress, the King thinks that the cost of your transplantation from Trenton to Annapolis and from Annapolis to Trenton will be exceedingly needless;[1] accordingly, His Majesty's intention is that you remain in Philadelphia until further orders: this determination presents so many fewer inconveniences that there is every good reason to suppose that Congress will not be long in seeing what will result from its comings and goings, and that it will hasten to determine a place for a permanent Residence.

You have done very well, Sir, to caution the president of Congress concerning the King's granting of new subsidies: the Request which was made for them has the more displeased His Majesty, as Mr. Morris attempted it in defiance of all the remonstrances which you have made to that Superintendent; moreover, our expenses during five years of War have been excessive, and we have need of all our resources to meet our arrears and to re-establish the state of our finances. If these verities do not touch

Mr. Morris, and if he hazards a new request, he will meet with a new refusal; and Mr.Franklin is so convinced of this, that I am prone to think that he will not hazard new solicitations in spite of the orders of Congress: that Minister knows our needs as he knows our good will, and I owe him the justice that he has continually put the greatest circumspection and the most proper measure in the repeated requests which the inconsiderate Drafts of Mr. Morris have forced him to make of us.

We had been persuaded beforehand, Sir, that the Regulation of the Court of London relative to American Commerce would excite some dissatisfaction in America; and you may judge therefrom that this same Regulation did not cause us displeasure at all. It remains to be seen if the Britannic Ministry, enlightened by experience, will take more politic measures, and if, to bring the Americans into agreement, it will make the Sacrifice of the Commerce of the Islands. I am scarcely able to persuade myself of this because, on the one hand, the navigation of the Islands contributes to the livelihood of sailors and, on the other, because the English Colonies scarcely contribute to the consumption of the Metropolis. It is easy to conceive the influence which the direct and unlimited Commerce of the United States with the English Colonies might have on these two subjects. It is true, Sir, that the intermediate Commerce of the Danish and Dutch Islands will make up the deficiency to a certain point: but between two evils one must choose the lesser, and that is probably what the Ministry of London will do.

We are extremely glad, Sir, that Congress defers granting to Mr. Franklin the leave of absence which he has requested, because the presence of that Minister here seems necessary to us until the situation of America vis-à-vis Great Britain has acquired some consistency: it is not that I have distrust with regard to the principles of his Colleagues; but they have too little affection for France, and I think them too much cosmopolites, so that they make us enter into their plans, if they can glimpse advantages on the Court of London's Side.

. . . . .

Although it has been irrevocably decided that L'Orient will be a free port, the King's Edict has not yet been issued, because it is a question of giving this Establishment all the extension possible without essentially harming our own commerce and the revenues of the State.

As for the privileges of Dunkirk and Marseilles, they give the Americans an entire liberty of frequenting these two Ports with all the products of their soil, and of re-exporting them if they judge it suitable.

. . . . .

I have read with much attention, Sir, the reflections which your Despatch N°. 247 included on American Commerce; I found them very interesting, and I think they merit being taken into consideration. Moreover, Sir, our mercantile relations with America can only be established in succession and in proportion as our merchants perceive the merchandise that will suit the different regions of that vast continent and those which they can receive from it with advantage: it is upon this double subject that I desire, Sir, that you send me detailed ideas: this will be the only means of getting the Administration ready to make up for the ignorance of the Merchants, and of encouraging their speculations.

. . . . .

Vergennes

FFAA: Pol. Corr., U.S., v. 26, f. 102/224-229 (LC transcription).

[1] On October 11, 1783, Congress passed a resolution to adjourn at Trenton on October 22, to meet again at Annapolis on October 31, there to sit until June 1784, when it would return to Trenton (see JCC, v. 25, pp. 669-671).

Benjamin Franklin to the President of Congress

Sir,   Passy, Dec. 25th. 1783.

. . . . .

It was certainly disagreable to the English Ministers that all their Treaties for Peace were carried on under the Eye of the French Court. This began to appear towards the Conclusion, when Mr. Hartley refused going to Versailles to sign there with the other Powers our Definitive Treaty, and insisted on its being done at Paris, which we in good Humour complied with, but at an earlier Hour, that we might have time to acquaint le Comte de Vergennes before he was to sign with the Duke of Manchester....

With respect to the British Court, we should I think be constantly upon our guard, and impress strongly upon our Minds, that tho' it has made Peace with us, it is not in Truth reconciled either to us or to its Loss of us; but still flatters itself with Hopes that some Change in the Affairs of Europe or some Disunion among ourselves, may afford them an Opportunity of Recovering their Dominion, punishing those who have most offended, and securing our future Dependance. It is easy to see by the general Turn of the Ministerial News-Papers; (light Things indeed as Straws and Feathers, but like them they show which way the Wind blows), and by the malignant Improvement their Ministers make in all the Foreign Courts, of every little Accident or Dissension among us, the Riot of a few Soldiers at Philadelphia, the Resolves of some Town Meetings, the Reluctance to pay Taxes &ca &ca all which are exaggerated to represent our Governments as so many Anarchies, of which the People themselves are weary the Congress as having lost its Influence being no longer respected: I say it is easy to see from this Conduct that they bear us no Good Will, and that they wish the Reality of what they are pleased to imagine. They have too a numerous Royal Progeny to provide for, some of whom are educated in the Military Line. In those Circumstances we cannot be too careful to preserve the Friendships we have acquired abroad, and the Union we have establish'd at Home, to secure our Credit by a punctual Discharge of our Obligations of every kind, and our Reputation by the Wisdom of our Councils: Since we know not how soon we may have a fresh Occasion for Friends, for Credit, and for Reputation.

. . . . .

With great Esteem & Regard, I have the honour to be, Sir, Your Excellency's most obedient & most humble Servant.   B. Franklin
Read 5 March 1784.

NA: PCC, item 82, v. 3, pp. 227-238 (ALS); M247, reel 109.

David Hartley to Benjamin Franklin

My Dear friend   X^mas Day 1783 London
    Before you receive this you will have heard of a total change of the British Administration. It is not as yet many hours since this event has taken place. The Cabinet is as follows viz

Mr Pitt first Lord of the treasury
Ld Thurlow[1] chancellor   Marquis of Carmarthen   Secretaries
Ld Gower[2] President of Council Lord Sidney[3]   of State
D of Portland Privy Seal   Ld Howe first L^d of the Admiralty

    It is impossible for me to expect as yet any instructions in my department. In the mean time I beg of you to send me the earliest notice whenever the ratification of our definitive treaty of peace shall arrive from America, that we may loose no time in bringing that blessed event to a complete termination. I am my Dear friend Ever yours most affect^ely
                                                        D Hartley

Clements Library: Hartley Papers, v. 4, p. 65 (C).
    [1] Thurlow, Lord Edward (1731-1806). British political figure and barrister. Member of Parliament, 1765-1778. Solicitor General, 1770-1771. Attorney General, 1771-1778. Strong supporter of Parliament's right to tax the American colonies. Lord Chancellor, 1778-April 1783, December 1783-1792.

[2] *Gower, Granville Leveson-Gower, Lord (1721-1803). British political figure. Member of Parliament, 1744-1755; a Bedford Whig. Lord privy seal, 1755-1757. President of the council, 1767-1779. Initially favored suppressing the American rebellion, but resigned office after coming to doubt the wisdom of continuing the American war. President of the council, 1783-1784. Lord privy seal, 1784-1794. From 1786, Marquis of Stafford.*

[3] *Thomas Townshend*

Congress' Resolution Opposing Ratification of the Definitive Treaty by Fewer Than Nine States

[27 December 1783]

Resolved that however earnestly and anxiously Congress wish to proceed to the ratification of the Definitive Treaty, yet < *Resolved that Congress* >[1] consisting at present of seven states only they ought not to undertake <*the*> that ratification <*of the Definitive treaty*> without proper explanations.

< *1. Because the 9th. article of Confederation takes from them the power, by declaring that Congress shall not 'enter into any treaty unless nine states assent to the same.'* >

1. Because by the usage of modern nations it is now established that the ratification of a treaty by the sovereign power is the essential act which gives it validity; the signature of the ministers, notwithstanding their plenipotentiary commission, being understood as placing it, according to the phrase of the writers on this subject, sub spe rati, only, and as leaving to each sovereign an acknoleged right of rejection.

< *2. Because it would be a precedent replete with danger to these states as under that on future occasions seven states in opposition to six may ratify treaties entered into by ministers in direct opposition to their instructions though such instructions should have had the concurrence of nine states.* >

2. Because ratification being an act of so much energy and substance, the authority to perform it is reserved to nine states by those words in the ninth article of Confederation which declare that Congress 'shall not enter into any treaty, unless nine states assent to the same.'

3. Because by the terms 'enter into a treaty' the Confederation must have intended that the assent of nine states should be necessary to <*the*> it's completion as well as to <*the*> it's commencement <*of a treaty*>; <*it's*> the object having been to guard the rights of the Union in all those important cases wherein it has required the assent of nine states <*is required*>: whereas by admitting the contrary construction, seven states containing less than one third of the citizens of the Union in opposition to six containing more than two thirds may fasten on them a treaty, commenced indeed under <*the instr*> commission and instructions from

nine states, but concluded <*by the ministers*> in express contradiction to such instructions and in direct sacrifice of the<*ir*> interests of so great a majority.

4. Because if 7. states be incompetent generally to the ratification of a treaty they are not made competent in this particular instance by the circumstances of the ratification of the provisional articles by nine states <*and ins*>, the instructions to our ministers to form a definitive one by them and their actual agreement in substance: for either these circumstances are in themselves a ratification, or are not: if they are, nothing further is requisite than to give attested copies of them in exchange for the British ratification; if they are not, then <*seven states have no authority to assume any circumstances where they are themselves*> we remain where we are, without a ratification by 9. states and incompetent to ratify ourselves.

5. Because the seven states now present in Congress saw this question in the same point of view only 4 days ago when by their unanimous resolution they declared that the assent of nine states was requisite to ratify this treaty and urged this as a reason to hasten forward the absent states.

6. Because such a ratification would be rejected by the other contracting party as null and unauthorized, or, if attested to them by the seal of the states without apprising them that it has been expedited by order of seven states only, it will be a breach of faith in us, a prostitution of our seal, and a future ground, when that circumstance shall become known, of denying the validity of a ratification into which they shall have been so surprised.

7. Because there being still 67. days before the exchange of ratifications is requisite, <*we may yet hope the presence of 9. states in time*> and two states only wanting to render us competent, we have the strongest presumptions that the measures taken by Congress will bring them forward in time for ratification and for it's passage across the Atlantic.

And 8 because should we be disappointed in this hope, the ratification will yet be placed on more honourable and defensible ground if made by 9. states as soon as so many shall be present, and then sent for exchange, urging in it's support the small importance of an exchange of ratifications, a few days sooner or later, the actual impossibility of an earlier compliance, and that failures produced by circumstances not under the controul of the parties, <*and*> either in points so immaterial <*can never affect the validity of a treaty*>, as to call for no compensation, or in those which are material and admit of compensation, can never affect the validity of the treaty itself.

Julian P. Boyd, *editor*, The Papers of Thomas Jefferson (*Princeton: Princeton University Press, 1950-), hereafter cited as Boyd, Jefferson Papers, v. 6, pp. 424-425.*
[1] *Text in angle brackets deleted from the manuscript but restored here.*

Congressional Ratification of
the Definitive Treaty of Peace

[14 Jan. 1784]

The United States in Congress Assembled,

To all persons to whom these presents shall come greeting:

Whereas definitive articles of peace and friendship between the United States of America and his Britannic majesty, were concluded and signed at Paris on the 3d day of September, 1783, by the plenipotentiaries of the said United States, and his said Britannic Majesty, duly and respectively authorized for that purpose; which definitive articles are in the words following:

In the name of the most holy and undivided Trinity.

It having pleased the Divine Providence to dispose the hearts of the most serene and most potent prince, George, the third, by the grace of God, king of Great Britain, France and Ireland, defender of the faith, duke of Brunswick and Lunenburg, arch-treasurer and prince elector of the holy Roman empire, &c. and of the United States of America, to forget all past misunderstandings and differences that have unhappily interrupted the good correspondence and friendship which they mutually wish to restore, and to establish such a beneficial and satisfactory intercourse between the two countries, upon the ground of reciprocal advantages and mutual convenience, as may promote and secure to both perpetual peace and harmony; and having for this desirable end, already laid the foundation of peace and reconciliation, by the provisional articles, signed at Paris on the 30th of November, 1782, by the commissioners empowered on each part, which articles were agreed to be inserted in and to constitute the treaty of peace proposed to be concluded between the crown of Great Britain and the said United States, but which treaty was not to be concluded until terms of peace should be agreed upon between Great Britain and France, and his Britannic majesty should be ready to conclude such treaty accordingly; and the treaty between Great Britain and France having since been concluded, his Britannic majesty and the United States of America, in order to carry into full effect the provisional articles above mentioned, according to the tenor thereof, have constituted and appointed, that is to say, his Britannic majesty on his part, David Hartley, Esquire, member of the parliament of Great Britain; and the said United States on their part, John Adams, Esquire, late a commissioner of the United States of America, at the court of Versailles, late delegate in Congress from the state of Massachusetts, and chief justice of the said state, and minister plenipotentiary of the said United States to their high mightinesses the states general of the United Netherlands; Benjamin Franklin, Esquire, late delegate in Congress from the state of Pensylvania, president of the convention of the said state, and minister plenipotentiary from the United States of America at the court of Versailles; John Jay, Esquire, late president of Congress, and chief justice of the state of New York, and minister plenipotentiary from the said United States, at the court of Madrid, to be the plenipotentiaries for the concluding and signing the present definitive treaty: who, after having reciprocally communicated their respective full powers, have agreed upon and confirmed the following articles:

Article 1st. His Britannic majesty acknowledges the said United States, viz. New-Hampshire, Massachusetts-Bay, Rhode-Island and Providence Plantations, Connecticut, New-York, New-Jersey, Pensylvania, Delaware, Maryland, Virginia, North-Carolina, South-Carolina and Georgia, to be free, sovereign and independent states: that he treats with them as such, and for himself, his heirs and successors, relinquishes all claims to the government, propriety and territorial rights of the same, and every part thereof.

Article 2d. And that all disputes which might arise in future on the subject of the boundaries of the said United States may be prevented, it is hereby agreed and declared, that the following are and shall be their boundaries, viz. from the north-west angle of Nova Scotia, viz. that angle which is formed by a line drawn due north from the source of Saint Croix river to the Highlands; along the said Highlands which divide those rivers that empty themselves into the river Saint Lawrence from those which fall into the Atlantic Ocean, to the north-westernmost head of Connecticut river, thence down along the middle of that river to the forty fifth degree of north latitude; from thence by a line due west on said latitude, until it strikes the river Iroquois or Cataraquy, thence along the middle of said river into lake Ontario, through the middle of said lake until it strikes the communication by water between that lake and lake Erie; thence along the middle of said communication into lake Erie, through the middle of said [lake,] until it arrives at the water communication between that lake and lake Huron; thence along the middle of said water communication into the lake Huron, thence through the middle of said lake to the water communication between that lake and lake Superior; thence through lake Superior northward of the isles Royal and Philipeaux, to the long lake; thence through the middle of said long lake and the water communication between it and the lake of the Woods, to the said lake of the Woods, thence through the said lake to the most north-western point thereof, and from thence on a due west course to the river Mississippi, thence by a line to be drawn along the middle of the said river Mississippi, until it shall intersect the northernmost part of the thirty first degree of north latitude. South by a line to be drawn due east from the determination of the line last mentioned, in the latitude of thirty one degrees north of the equator, to the middle of the river Apalachiola or Catahouche; thence along the middle thereof to its junction with the Flint river; thence straight to the head of Saint Mary's river, and thence down along the middle of Saint Mary's river to the Atlantic ocean. East by a line to be drawn along the middle of the river Saint Croix, from its mouth in the bay of Fundy to its source, and from its source directly north to the aforesaid Highlands which divide the rivers that fall into the Atlantic ocean from those which fall into the river Saint Lawrence: comprehending all islands within twenty leagues of any part of the shores of the United States, and lying between lines to be drawn due east from the points where the aforesaid boundaries between Nova-Scotia on the one part, and East Florida on the other, shall respectively touch the Bay of Fundy and the Atlantic ocean, excepting such islands as now are or heretofore have been within the limits of the said province of Nova-Scotia.

Article 3d. It is agreed, that the people of the United States shall continue to enjoy unmolested the right to take fish of every kind on the Grand Bank and on all the other banks of Newfoundland; also in gulph of Saint Lawrence, and at all other places in the sea, where the inhabitants of both countries used at any time heretofore to fish; and also, that the inhabitants of the United States shall have liberty to take fish of every kind on such part of the coast of Newfoundland as British fishermen shall use, (but not to dry or cure the same on that island) and also on the coasts, bays and creeks of all other of his Britannic majesty's dominions in America; and that the American fishermen shall have liberty to dry and cure fish in any of the unsettled bays, harbours and creeks of Nova Scotia, Magdalen islands, and Labradore, so long as the same shall remain unsettled, but so soon as the same or either of them shall be settled, it shall not be lawful for the said fishermen to dry or cure fish at such settlement, without a previous agreement for that purpose with the inhabitants, proprietors or possessors of the ground.

Article 4th. It is agreed that creditors on either side shall meet with no lawful impediment to the recovery of the full value in sterling money, of all bona fide debts heretofore contracted.

Article 5th. It is agreed that the Congress shall earnestly recommend it to the legislatures of the respective states, to provide for the restitution of all estates, rights and properties, which have been confiscated, belonging to real British subjects, and also of the estates, rights and properties of persons resident in districts in the possession of his majesty's arms, and who have not borne arms against the said United States. And that persons of any other description shall have free liberty to go to any part or parts of any of the thirteen United States, and therein to remain twelve months unmolested in their endeavours to obtain the restitution of such of their estates, rights and properties, as may have been confiscated; and that Congress shall also earnestly recommend to the several states a reconsideration and revision of all acts or laws regarding the premises, so as to render the said laws or acts perfectly consistent, not only with justice and equity, but with that spirit of conciliation, which on the return of the blessings of peace should universally prevail. And that Congress shall also earnestly recommend to the several states, that the estates, rights and properties of such last mentioned persons shall be restored to them, they refunding to any persons who may be now in possession of the bona fide price (where any has been given) which such persons may have paid on purchasing any of the said lands, rights or properties since the confiscation. And it is agreed that all persons who have any interest in confiscated lands, either by debts, marriage settlements, or otherwise, shall meet with no lawful impediment in the prosecution of their just rights.

Article 6th. That there shall be no future confiscations made, nor any prosecutions commenced against any person or persons for or by reason of the part which he or they may have taken in the present war; and that no person shall on that account, suffer any future loss or damage, either in his person, liberty or property, and that those who may be in confinement on such charges, at the time of the ratification of the treaty in America, shall be immediately set at liberty, and the prosecutions so commenced be discontinued.

Article 7th. There shall be a firm and perpetual peace between his Britannic majesty and the said states, and between the subjects of the one, and the citizens of the other, wherefore all hostilities both by sea and land, shall from henceforth cease; all prisoners on both sides shall be set at liberty, and his Britannic majesty shall with all convenient speed, and without causing any destruction, or carrying away any negroes or other property of the American inhabitants, withdraw all his armies, garrisons and fleets from the said United States, and from every post, place and harbour within the same; leaving in all fortifications the American artillery that may be therein, and shall also order and cause all archives, records, deeds and papers, belonging to any of the said states, or their citizens, which in the course of the war may have fallen into the hands of his officers, to be forthwith restored and delivered to the proper states and persons to whom they belong.

Article 8th. The navigation of the river Mississippi, from its source to the ocean, shall forever remain free and open to the subjects of Great Britain, and the citizens of the United States.

Article 9th. In case it should happen, that any place or territory belonging to Great Britain or to the United States, should have been conquered by the arms of either from the other, before the arrival of the said provisional articles in America, it is agreed, that the same shall be restored without difficulty, and without requiring any compensation.

Article 10th. The solemn ratification of the present treaty, expedited in good and due form, shall be exchanged between the contracting parties in the space of six months, or sooner if possible, to be computed from the day of the signature of the present treaty. In witness whereof, we, the undersigned their ministers plenipotentiary, have in their name, and in virtue of full powers, signed with our hands the present definitive treaty, and caused the seals of our arms to be affixed thereto.

Done at Paris, this third day of September, in the year of our Lord, one thousand seven hundred and eighty-three.

(L.S.) D. Hartley,

(L.S.) John Adams,
(L.S.) B. Franklin,
(L.S.) John Jay.

Now know ye that we the United States in Congress assembled having seen and considered the definitive articles aforesaid have approved, ratified and confirmed and by these presents do approve, ratify and confirm the said articles and every part and clause thereof, engaging and promising, that we will sincerely and faithfully perform and observe the same, and never suffer them to be violated by any one or transgressed in any manner, as far as lies in our power.

In testimony whereof, we have caused the seal of the United States to be hereunto affixed.

Witness his Excellency Thomas Mifflin,[1] president, this fourteenth day of January in the year of our Lord one thousand seven hundred and eighty four and in the eighth year of the sovereignty and independence of the United States of America.

Boyd: Jefferson Papers, v. 6, pp. 456-461.

[1] *Mifflin, Thomas (1744-1800). Pennsylvania merchant, military leader, political figure. Quartermaster General of the Continental Army, August 1775-March 1778. Member, Continental Congress, 1774-1775, 1782-1784; president, December 1783-June 1784. Member, Constitutional Convention, 1787. Governor of Pennsylvania, 1790-1799.*

Congressional Proclamation of the
Definitive Treaty of Peace

[January 14, 1784]
By the United states in Congress assembled.
A Proclamation.

Whereas Definitive articles of peace and friendship between the United states of America and his Britannic Majesty were concluded and signed at Paris on the third day of September 1783. by the plenipotentiaries of the said United states and of his said Britannic majesty duly and respectively authorized for that purpose which definitive articles are in the words following [here insert them.]

And we the United states in Congress assembled having seen and duly considered the definitive articles aforesaid did by a certain act under the seal of the United states bearing date this 14 day of Jany 1784 approve, ratify and confirm the same and every part and clause thereof, engaging and promising that we would sincerely and faithfully perform and observe the same, and never suffer them to be violated by any one, or transgressed in any manner, as far as should be in our power.

And being sincerely disposed to carry the said articles into execution truly, honestly and with good faith according to the intent and meaning thereof we have thought proper by these presents to notify the premises to all the good citizens of these states, hereby requiring and enjoining all bodies of magistracy Legislative Executive and Judiciary, all persons bearing office civil or military of whatever rank, degree, or powers and all others the good citizens of these states of every vocation and condition that reverencing those stipulations entered into on their behalf under the authority of that federal bond by which their existence as an independant people is bound up together, and is known and acknowleged by the nations of the world; and with that good faith which is every man's surest guide, within their several offices, jurisdictions and vocations, they carry into effect the said Definitive articles and every clause and sentence thereof sincerely, strictly and completely. Given under the seal of the United states. Witness his Excellency Thomas Mifflin our President at Annapolis this 14 day of Jany 1784 and of the sovereignty and independance of the United states of America the eighth.

Boyd, Jefferson Papers, v. 6, pp. 462-463.

The President of Congress to the American Peace Commissioners

Annapolis Jany 14th 1784

Gentlemen,

This Day nine States being represented. Viz. Massachusets, Rhode Island, Connecticut, Pennsylvania, Delaware, Maryland, Virginia, North Carolina and South Carolina, together with One Member from New Hampshire and One member from New Jersey – The Treaty of Peace was ratified by the unanimous vote of the Members – This being done, Congress by an unanimous vote, ordered a Proclamation to be issued, enjoining the strict and faithful Observance thereof and published an earnest Recommendation to the several States in the very words of the fifth Article – They have likewise resolved that the ratification of the Treaty of Peace shall be sent by a proper person to our Commissioners at Paris to be exchanged, and have appointed Colonel Josiah Harmar[1] to that service. he will have the honor of delivering to you the ratification together with copies of the Proclamation of Congress and of their Recommendation to the States conformably to the 5th Article –

I take the liberty of recommending Colonel Harmar as a brave and deserving Officer and am with the highest respect and esteem – Gentlemen Your most Obedient and humble Servant   Thomas Mifflin

NA: PCC, item 16, pp. 281-282 (LBkC); M247, reel 24.

[1] Harmar, Josiah (1753-1813). Military officer. Served as major or lieutenant-colonel of various Pennsylvania regiments, 1776-1783. Colonel, September 1783. Carried ratification of definitive treaty of peace to Paris, 1784. As commander of the army, 1784-1791, engaged in Indian warfare on the Ohio frontier. Adjutant general of Pennsylvania, 1793-1799.

David Hartley to Benjamin Franklin

Dear Sir   London March 26 1784

I have received yours of the 11th instant. I am to inform you in answer that it is not thought necessary on the part of Great Britain to enter into any formal convention for the prolongation of the term in wch the ratifications were to be exchanged as the delay in America appears to have arisen merely in consequence of the inclemency of the season. There will be no delay on our part in exchanging the ratifications of the definitive treaty with the united States as soon as that on their part shall arrive. — I shall be very happy when you send me notice of that arrival, for the pleasing opportunity that it will afford me of seeing you again. I beg my best Comp^{ts} to Mr Adams if at Paris and to Mr Jay & all friends. I am with the greatest affection & Esteem ever Yours   D Hartley

LC: Benjamin Franklin Papers, microfilm reel 8 (ALS).

Benjamin Franklin to John Jay

Dear Sir,   Passy, 30 March 1784
    Yesterday late in the Evening arrived here an Express from Congress with the Definitive Treaty ratified, which I enclose with the Resolutions, Proclamation, and the President's Letter. The Congress anxious that the Ratification should arrive within the Term stipulated, dispatched it seems three Expresses, by different Vessels, with authenticated Copies. This came by the French Pacquet Boat: Major Franks sailed before, with another, in a Ship for London. As the Term is long since expired, and I have already sent to Mr. Hartley the Excuses for the Delay, and as Major Franks may probably be arrived in London, and have delivered his Copy to Mr. Laurens and the Post going on Thursday, I hardly think it necessary to send an Express on the Occasion to London, but shall be glad of your Advice, and to consult with you on the Steps to be taken for the Exchange, in Case Mr. Laurens has not already made it, which I wish he may, as it will save Trouble.
    All the News I learnt from Col. Harmar who brought the Dispatch, is that the Winter has been uncommonly severe in America, that the Pacquet Boat was long detained in New York by the Ice, and that one which sailed from hence in October, was lost on Long Island going in, some of the People and Passengers saved though much frozen, others froze to death. With great Esteem, I am, Your most obedient humble Servant,

                                                B. FRANKLIN

    The Post has the Mail with all the common Letters and the Dispatches for the Court. Our Express is a Day before him. I have received no private Letters from any of my Friends.

Morris, Jay Papers, *v. 2, p. 706.*

David Hartley to Benjamin Franklin and John Jay

Gentlemen   London April 9 1784

I have received the honour of your letter dated March 31 1784, with the enclosures, wch I have communicated to his Majestys Ministers. I have the pleasure to inform you that the ratifications on our part are now making out, and that I have received orders to prepare for the exchange at Paris, with all convenient Speed. Before my departure I shall propose such general sentiments for the Consideration of his Majesty's ministers as have occurred to me in our former negotiations; my utmost wish at all times being to give every possible assistance in my power to effect a cordial and conciliatory intercourse and connexion between our two Countries. I have the honour to be Gentlemen Your Excellencies most obed^t Humble Servt.   D Hartley

Clements Library: Hartley Papers, v. 4, p. 85 (LS).

Benjamin Franklin to the President of Congress

Sir,   Passy, May 12th. 1784.

In my last I acquainted your Excellency that Mr Hartley was soon expected here to exchange Ratifications of the Definitive Treaty. He is now arrived, and proposes to make the Exchange this Afternoon: I shall then be enabled to send a Copy.

Enclosed is the new British Proclamation, respecting our Trade with their Colonies.[1] It is said to be a temporary Provision till Parliament can assemble and make some proper regulating Law, or till a commercial Treaty shall be framed and agreed to. Mr Hartley expects Instructions for planning with us such a Treaty. The Ministry are supposed to have been too busy with the new Elections when he left London, to think of those Matters.

This Court has not completed its intended new System for the Trade of their Colonies, so that I cannot yet give a certain Account of the Advantages that will in Fine be allowed us. At present it is said we are to have two Free Ports, Tobago, & the Mole, and that we may carry Lumber, and all Sorts of Provisions to the Rest, except Flour, which is reserved in Favor of Bourdeaux, and that we shall be permitted to export Coffee, Rum, Molasses, and some Sugar for our own Consumption.

We have had under Consideration a Commercial Treaty proposed to us by the King of Prussia, and have sent it back with our Remarks to M^r

Adams, who will, I suppose, transmit it immediately to Congress. Those planned with Denmark and Portugal wait its Determination.

Be pleased to present my dutiful Respects to the Congress, and believe me to be, with sincere and great Esteem, Sir, &c.

B. Franklin

May 13th: I now inclose a Copy of the Ratification of the Definitive Treaty, on the Part of his Britanic Majesty.

NA: PCC, item 100, v. 2, pp. 212-213 (LBkC); M247, reel 127.

[1] Presumably a reference to the Order in Council of December 26, 1783, which summed up the various pronouncements made regarding Anglo-American trade in 1783.

Lord Carmarthen to David Hartley

Sir   St James's May 28th 1784

I received this morning by Lauzun,[1] your Dispatch N° 5, and private letter of the 24th Instant, together with the Ratification of the Treaty between Great Britain & the United States of America; and I own it was with the greatest surprize that I perceived so essential a want of Form as appears in the very first Paragraph of that Instrument, where the United States are mentioned before his Majesty contrary to the established custom observed in every Treaty, in which a crowned Head and a Republic are the contracting parties.

The Conclusion appears likewise extremely deficient, as it is neither signed by the President, nor is it dated, and consequently is wanting in some of the most essential points of Form necessary towards authenticating the Validity of the Instrument.

I should think the American Ministers could make no objection to correcting these defects in the Ratification, which might very easily be done, either by signing a Declaration in the name of Congress, for preventing the particular mode of Expression, so far as relates to Precedency, in the first Paragraph, being considered as a Precedent to be adopted on any future occasion, or else by having a new Copy made out in America, in which these Mistakes should be corrected, and which might be done without any prejudice arising to either of the Parties from the Delay.

I am with great Truth & Regard Sir, Your most obedient humble Servant   Carmarthen

· · · · ·

Clements Library: Hartley Papers, v. 4, pp. 99-100 (C).

[1] A messenger.

David Hartley to Benjamin Franklin

Sir,   Paris June 1 1784

I have the honour to inform you that I have transmitted to London the Ratification on the Part of Congress of the Definitive Treaty of Peace between Great Britain and the United States of America. I am ordered to represent to you that a Want of Form appears in the first Paragraph of that Instrument, wherein the United States are mentioned before his Majesty, contrary to the established Custom in every Treaty in which a Crowned Head and a Republic are Parties – It is likewise to be observed that the Term Definitive Articles is used instead of Definitive Treaty.

The Conclusion likewise appears deficient as it is neither signed by the President, nor is it dated, and consequently is wanting in some of the most essential Points of Form necessary towards authenticating the Validity of the Instrument.

I am ordered to propose to you Sir that these Defects in the Ratification should be corrected, which might very easily be done either by signing a Declaration in the Name of Congress for preventing the particular Mode of Expression so far as relates to Precedency in the first Paragraph being considered as a Precedent to be adopted on any future occasion, or else by having a new Copy made out in America, in which these Mistakes should be corrected, and which might be done without any prejudice arising to either of the Parties by Delay.

I am Sir with great Respect and Consideration Your most obedient humble Servant   D Hartley

Clements Library: Hartley Papers, v. 5, pp. 9-10 (C).

Benjamin Franklin to David Hartley

Sir,   Passy June 8 1784

I have considered the Observations you did me the honour of communicating to me, concerning certain Inaccuracies of Expression and suppos'd Defects of Formality in the Instrument of Ratification, some of which are said to be of such a Nature as to affect "the Validity of the Instrument." The first is that the United States are named before his Majesty, contrary to the established Custom observed "in every Treaty in which a Crowned Head and a Republic are the contracting Parties." With respect to this, it seems to me we should distinguish between that Act in which both join, to wit, the *Treaty*, and that which is the Act of each separately, the

Ratification. It is necessary that all the Modes of Expression in the joint Act should be agreed to by both Parties; tho' in their separate Acts each Party is Master of, and alone accountable for its own Mode. And on inspecting the Treaty it will be found that his Majesty is always regularly named before the United States. Thus the established "Custom in Treaties between Crowned Heads and Republics," contended for on your Part, is strictly observed; And the Ratification following the Treaty contains these Words; "Now Know ye, that we the United States in Congress assembled, having seen and duly considered the Definitive Articles aforesaid, have *approved, ratified* and *confirmed,* and by these Presents do *approve, ratify,* and *confirm* the said Articles, and *every* Part and Clause thereof," &c Thereby all those Articles, Parts and Clauses wherein the King is named before the United States, *are approved, ratified and confirmed,* and this solemnly under the Signature of Congress, with the public Seal affixed by their Order, and countersigned by their Secretary. No Declaration on the Subject more determinate or more authentic can possibly be made or given, which, when considered, may probably induce his Majesty's Ministers to waive the Proposition of our signing a similar Declaration, or of sending back the Ratification to be corrected in this Point, neither appearing to be really necessary. I will however, if it be still desired, transmit to Congress the Observation and the Difficulty occasion'd by it, and request their Orders upon it. In the mean time I may venture to say, that I am confident there was no intention of affronting his Majesty by this Order of Nomination, but that it resulted merely from that Sort of Complaisance which every Nation seems to have for itself, and of that Respect for its own Government customarily so expressed in its own Acts, of which the English among the rest afford an Instance, when in the Title of the King they always name Great Britain before France

The second Objection is that the Term Definitive Articles is used instead of Definitive Treaty;" If the Words *Definitive Treaty* had been used in the Ratification instead of Definitive Articles, it might have been more correct, tho' the Difference seems not great, nor of much Importance, as in the Treaty itself it is called the present *Definitive Treaty.*

The other Objections are, "that the Conclusion likewise appears deficient, as it is neither signed by the President, nor is it dated, and consequently is wanting in some of the most essential Points of Form necessary towards authenticating the Validity of the Instrument." The Situation of Seals and Signatures in public Instruments differs in different Countries, tho' all equally valid; for when all the Parts of an Instrument are connected by a Ribband, whose Ends are secured under the Impression of the Seal, the Signature and Seal wherever plac'd, are understood as relating to and authenticating the whole. Our usage is to place them both together in the broad Margin near the Beginning of the Piece; and so they stand in the present Ratification, the concluding Words of which declare the Intention of such Signing and Sealing to be the giving Authenticity to the whole Instrument; viz. "*In Testimony* whereof, *we have caused* the Seal of the United States to be herewith affixed, Witness his Excellency Thomas Mifflin Esq[r] President;" and the Date suppos'd to be omitted, (perhaps from its not appearing in Figures) is nevertheless to be found written in Words at length, viz "this fourteenth Day of January in the Year of our Lord one thousand seven hundred and eighty four;" which made the Figures unnecessary –

With great Esteem and Respect I have the honor to be Your Excellency's most obedient & most humble Servant   B Franklin

Clements Library: Hartley Papers, v. 5, pp. 11-14 (C).

David Hartley to the Marquess of Carmarthen

N° 7   Paris June 9 1784

My Lord

In my last I had the honour to inform your Lordship that I had represented to D[r] Franklin the informalities of the american ratification of the Definitive treaty. I now enclose a copy of the letter w[ch] I writ to him upon the subject together with a Copy of his answer w[ch] I have received this day. I must now refer myself to your Lordship whether the answer is satisfactory or whether any farther proceedings may be necessary on the subject.

I will likewise beg leave to add a few remarks to those in D[r] Franklin's letter to me. In the first place D[r] Franklin only speaks in his letter as to the date of time and not of place and I presume the latter was the defect in the ratification to w[ch] your Lordship alluded. I have made this remark to D[r.] Franklin since the receipt of his letter to w[ch] he made me this reply viz whether the term United States *in Congress* assembled, may be accepted as a date of place. There is no other date of place to the American ratification of the provisional treaty w[ch] I received from the American Ministers last year & w[ch] I transmitted to M[r] Fox then Secretary of State. That Ratification & the present are likewise similar in other respects. In the preliminary recital of the American ratification the ministers plenipotentiary on their part are mentioned before his Majesty's Minister. The signs of the president and of the Secretary are in the margin of the first page with this only difference that the Ratification of last year was countersigned by the Secretary for foreign Affairs M[r.] Livingston, whereas at the time of ratifying the Definitive treaty M[r] Livingston had resigned his office and no successor had been appointed. D[r] Franklin has shewn me an original duplicate of the American ratification of the last year. He has likewise shewn me a ratification of a treaty with the Crown of Sweden in w[ch] all things similar viz his own name recited in the preamble before the name of the Swedish Minister altho the King of Swedens name throughout the treaty takes head of the American States – The attestations in the margins of the first page – tho no other date of place but such as arises constructively from the terms united states in *Congress* assembled. An uniformity appears in these instruments. I have some copies of other instruments from the American congress such as the Commission to their ministers for treating of peace &c which is specially dated as to place as well as to time viz done at Philadelphia &c – The proclamation in America respecting this very definitive treaty dated upon the 14th of January 1784, (the same day as the ratification) is dated as to place as well as time; viz done at Annapolis &c altho the date of place is omitted in the ratification itself. The reason of this difference is not obvious, probably it may have been caused from the want of customary precedents.

If his Majesty has any farther commands for me upon this or any other subject I will endeavour to execute them to the best of my power. I beg the favour of your Lordship to inform me whether I am to expect any farther instructions of business at present, or whether I am to follow the directions of your Lordships letter of the 25th of May (immediately preceeding your last) and return to England. I have the honour to be My Lord with the greatest respect and Consideration Your Lordships most obedient humble Servant   D Hartley

Clements Library: Hartley Papers, v. 5, pp. 6-8 (LS).

Index

ISBN 0-16-048498-7

90000

9 780160 484988

CANADA

Long Lake

Isle Royale

Treaty of Paris of 1783 boundary line

Lake   Superior

Isle Philippeaux

Lake Huron

Lake Michigan

Lake   Ontario

Lake Erie

Pennsylvania

Illinois River

Illinois River

Missouri River

Missouri River

Mississippi River

Ohio River

Ohio River

Ohio River

Virginia

Philadelphia

Maryland

Baltimore

Annapolis

Chesapeake Bay

Roanoke River

North   Carolina

Arkansas River

Mississippi River

Pee Dee River

South   Carolina

Yazoo River

Georgia

Charleston

Flint River

Treaty of Paris of 1783 boundary line

Savannah

Treaty of Paris of 1783 boundary line

na

Mississippi River

Treaty of Paris of 1783 boundary line

Apalachicola R.

St. Mary's River

Floridas

APPROXIMATE S

ST

New Orleans

Mobile Bay

0   150

Gulf of Mexico